The Routledge Handbook of Forensic Linguistics

The Routledge Handbook of Forensic Linguistics provides a unique work of reference to the leading ideas, debates, topics, approaches and methodologies in Forensic Linguistics.

Forensic Linguistics is the study of language and the law, covering topics from legal language and courtroom discourse to plagiarism. It also concerns the applied (forensic) linguist who is involved in providing evidence, as an expert, for the defence and prosecution, in areas as diverse as blackmail, trademarks and warning labels.

The Routledge Handbook of Forensic Linguistics includes a comprehensive introduction to the field written by the editors and a collection of thirty-seven original chapters written by the world's leading academics and professionals, both established and up-and-coming, designed to equip a new generation of students and researchers to carry out forensic linguistic research and analysis.

The Routledge Handbook of Forensic Linguistics is the ideal resource for undergraduates or postgraduates new to the area.

Malcolm Coulthard is Professor of Forensic Linguistics at Aston University, UK. He is author of numerous publications, the most recent being *An Introduction to Forensic Linguistics* (co-authored with Alison Johnson, Routledge, 2007).

Alison Johnson is Lecturer in Modern English Language at the University of Leeds, UK. Previous publications include *An Introduction to Forensic Linguistics* (co-authored with Malcolm Coulthard, Routledge, 2007).

Contributors: Janet Ainsworth, Michelle Aldridge, Dawn Archer, Kelly Benneworth, Vijay K. Bhatia, Ronald R. Butters, Deborah Cao, Malcolm Coulthard, Paul Drew, Bethany K. Dumas, Diana Eades, Derek Edwards, Susan Ehrlich, Fiona English, Laura Felton Rosulek, Edward Finegan, Tim Grant, Peter R.A. Gray, Gillian Grebler, Mel Greenlee, Sandra Hale, Kate Haworth, Chris Heffer, Elizabeth Holt, Michael Jessen, Alison Johnson, Krzysztof Kredens, Gerald R. McMenamin, Gregory M. Matoesian, Ruth Morris, Frances Rock, Nancy Schweda Nicholson, Roger W. Shuy, Lawrence M. Solan, Elizabeth Stokoe, Gail Stygall, Peter Tiersma, Tatiana Tkačuková, Traci Walker, David Woolls.

Routledge Handbooks in Applied Linguistics

Routledge Handbooks in Applied Linguistics provide comprehensive overviews of the key topics in applied linguistics. All entries for the handbooks are specially commissioned and written by leading scholars in the field. Clear, accessible and carefully edited *Routledge Handbooks in Applied Linguistics* are the ideal resource for both advanced undergraduates and postgraduate students.

The Routledge Handbook of Corpus Linguistics
Edited by Anne O'Keeffe and Mike McCarthy

The Routledge Handbook of Forensic Linguistics
Edited by Malcolm Coulthard and Alison Johnson

Forthcoming

2010

The Routledge Handbook of World Englishes
Edited by Andy Kirkpatrick

The Routledge Handbook of Multilingualism
Edited by Marilyn Martin-Jones, Adrian Blackledge and Angela Creese

2011

The Routledge Handbook of Applied Linguistics
Edited by James Simpson

The Routledge Handbook of Second Language Acquisition
Edited by Susan Gass and Alison Mackey

The Routledge Handbook of Discourse Analysis
Edited by James Paul Gee and Michael Handford

2012

The Routledge Handbook of Translation Studies
Edited by Carmen Millan Varela and Francesca Bartrina

The Routledge Handbook of Language Testing
Edited by Glenn Fulcher and Fred Davidson

The Routledge Handbook of Intercultural Communication
Edited by Jane Jackson

The Routledge Handbook of Forensic Linguistics

Edited by Malcolm Coulthard
and Alison Johnson

Routledge
Taylor & Francis Group

LONDON AND NEW YORK

First edition published 2010
by Routledge
2 Park Square, Milton Park, Abingdon, OX14 4RN

Simultaneously published in the USA and Canada
by Routledge
270 Madison Ave, New York, NY 10016

Routledge is an imprint of the Taylor & Francis Group, an informa business

© 2010 Malcolm Coulthard and Alison Johnson

Typeset in Bembo by Taylor & Francis Books
Printed and bound in Great Britain by
CPI Antony Rowe, Chippenham, Wiltshire

All rights reserved. No part of this book may be reprinted or reproduced or utilised in any form or by any electronic, mechanical, or other means, now known or hereafter invented, including photocopying and recording, or in any information storage or retrieval system, without permission in writing from the publishers.

British Library Cataloguing in Publication Data
A catalogue record for this book is available from the British Library

Library of Congress Cataloging in Publication Data
The Routledge handbook of forensic linguistics / edited by Malcolm Coulthard
and Alison Johnson. – 1st ed.
   p. cm. – (Routledge handbooks in applied linguistics)
Includes bibliographical references and index.
1. Forensic linguistics.   I. Coulthard, Malcolm.   II. Johnson, Alison, 1959–
   HV8073.5.R68 2010
   363.25 – dc22
            2009037930#

ISBN 13: 978-0-415-46309-6 (hbk)
ISBN 13: 978-0-203-85560-7 (ebk)

This book is dedicated to all the students past and present who studied with us at the Universities of Aston, Birmingham, Leeds and Huddersfield.

Contents

2.2 Multilingualism in legal contexts

2.3 Authorship and opinion

Section III
New debates and new directions   **539**

Note

The chapters marked with * are supplemented by additional material on an accompanying website at: http://www.forensiclinguistics.net/

Illustrations

Tables

Figures

Conventions used

Figures and tables are numbered first according to the chapter number and then sequentially in the chapter, for example: 34.1.

Data extracts and examples are numbered in each chapter and referred to by number, as (1), (2), etc., beginning at (1) for each chapter.

We have used the following abbreviations for participants in data extracts in the majority of the chapters:

Abbreviation Participant(s)

A   Adult speaker (or Answer(er) where data is from official court transcripts)
AA   Appropriate Adult
CT   Call Taker
Ca   Caller
CP   Convicted Person
D   Defence barrister/attorney
IE   Interviewee
IR   Police Interviewer
J   Judge
Pr   Prosecuting barrister/attorney
Q   Question(er) (for Barrister in official court transcripts)
S   Solicitor/Attorney
W   Witness in court

The following transcription conventions have been used (based on Jefferson 2004):

Symbol   Meaning

(.)   short pause
(2.6)   timed pause
( )   empty brackets for transcriber uncertainty
((cough))   double brackets for other sounds or descriptions of events ((telephone rings))

[	left bracket for overlap onset
]	right bracket where overlapped utterances end
=	latched utterance
> <	speech within is speeded up relative to surronding talk
< >	speech within is slowed down relative to surrounding talk
>	rush through into the next sound
↑	rise in intonation
↓	fall in intonation
.hhh	inbreath
hhh	outbreath
°word°	softer sounding than surrounding talk
<u>word</u>	underlining for emphasis
WORD	upper case for louder than surrounding talk
lo:::ng	colon for extended syllable
abil-	cut off utterance

List of contributors and affiliations

Professor Janet Ainsworth, School of Law, Seattle University, Washington, USA

Dr Michelle Aldridge, School of English, Communication and Philosophy, Cardiff University, UK

Dr Dawn Archer, Department of Humanities, University of Central Lancashire, UK

Dr Kelly Benneworth, Department of Sociology, University of York, UK

Dr Vijay K. Bhatia, Department of English and Communication, City University of Hong Kong

Professor Ronald Butters, Emeritus Professor of English and Cultural Anthropology, Duke University, North Carolina, USA

Dr Deborah Cao, Griffith University, Queensland, Australia

Professor Malcolm Coulthard, School of Languages and Social Sciences, Aston University, UK

Professor Paul Drew, Department of Sociology, University of York, UK

Professor Bethany K. Dumas, Department of English, University of Tennessee, USA

Dr Diana Eades, Honorary Research Fellow, University of New England, Armidale, NSW, Australia

Professor Derek Edwards, Department of Social Sciences, Loughborough University, UK

Professor Susan Ehrlich, Department of Languages, Literatures and Linguistics, York University, Canada

Dr Fiona English, Department of Humanities, Arts and Languages, London Metropolitan University, UK

Dr Laura Felton Rosulek, Department of Anthropology, University of Montana, USA

Professor Edward Finegan, Gould School of Law, University of Southern California, USA

Dr Tim Grant, School of Languages and Social Sciences, Aston University, UK

Justice Peter R.A. Gray, Federal Court of Australia, Melbourne, Australia

Miss Gillian Grebler, Freelance consultant and teacher at Santa Monica College, California, USA

Dr Mel Greenlee, Staff Attorney, California Appellate Project, USA

Dr Sandra Hale, School of Humanities and Languages, University of Western Sydney, Australia

Dr Kate Haworth, School of Languages and Social Sciences, Aston University, UK

Dr Chris Heffer, School of English, Communication and Philosophy, Cardiff University, UK

Dr Elizabeth Holt, School of Music, Humanities and Media, University of Huddersfield, UK

Dr Michael Jessen, Bundeskriminalamt Sprecher-Erkennung und Tonträgeranalyse, Wiesbaden, Germany

Dr Alison Johnson, School of English, University of Leeds, UK

Dr Krzysztof Kredens, School of Languages and Social Sciences, Aston University, UK

Professor Gerald R. McMenamin, Department of Linguistics, California State University, USA

Professor Gregory M. Matoesian, Department of Criminology, Law and Justice, University of Illinois at Chicago, USA

Dr Ruth Morris, Freelance Interpreter and Translator, Israel

Dr Frances Rock, School of English, Communication and Philosophy, Cardiff University, UK

Dr Nancy Schweda Nicholson, University of Delaware, USA

Professor Roger W. Shuy, Emeritus Professor, Georgetown University, Washington, DC, USA

Professor Lawrence M. Solan, Brooklyn Law School, New York, USA

Dr Elizabeth Stokoe, Department of Social Sciences, Loughborough University, UK

Professor Gail Stygall, Department of English, University of Washington, Seattle, USA

Professor Peter Tiersma, Loyola Law School, Los Angeles, USA

Ms Tatiana Tkačuková, Department of English, Masaryk University, Brno, Czech Republic

Dr Traci Walker, Department of Language and Linguistic Science, University of York, UK

Mr David Woolls, CEO of CFL Software Limited and Honorary Visiting Fellow, Aston University, UK

Notes on editors and contributors

Janet Ainsworth is the John D. Eshelman Professor of Law at Seattle University. Before joining the law faculty, she practiced law as a public defender. Her scholarship explores the application of linguistics research to legal issues and the analysis of language ideology in law. She is the author of numerous book chapters and articles in social science journals and law reviews.

Michelle Aldridge is a senior lecturer in the Centre for Language and Communication at Cardiff University. Her research interests include child language acquisition, communication disorders and forensic linguistics. Her particular expertise is in the linguistic experiences of vulnerable witnesses in the police interview and court context as well as in the training of professionals within the legal setting.

Dawn Archer is a reader in corpus linguistics at the University of Central Lancashire. Her forensic/legal interests primarily relate to the historical courtroom: she has written one monograph – *Historical Sociopragmatics: Questions and Answers in the English Courtroom (1640–1760)* – and is currently planning a second, which will explore the nineteenth-century courtroom.

Kelly Benneworth is a lecturer in Social Psychology in the Department of Sociology at the University of York. She has a long-standing interest in applying discourse analysis and conversation analysis to interactions in forensic settings and her current work examines how police and suspects describe adult–child sexual relationships in the investigative interview. She has contributed to the edited book *The Language of Sexual Crime* (Palgrave).

Vijay K. Bhatia has been in the teaching profession for 44 years, most recently at the City University since 1993 and at the National University of Singapore (1983–93). In his recent research projects, 'Analyzing Genre-bending in Corporate Disclosure Documents,' and 'International Arbitration Practice: A Discourse Analytical Study,' he has led research teams from more than 20 countries. His research interests are: genre analysis of academic and professional discourses, including, legal, business, newspaper and advertising genres; ESP and professional communication; simplification of legal and other public documents; and cross-cultural and cross-disciplinary variations in professional genres. Amongst his more than a hundred publications, two of his books, *Analysing Genre: Language Use in Professional Settings* and *Worlds of Written Discourse: A Genre-based View*, are widely used in genre theory and practice.

Ronald R. Butters (http://trademarklinguistics.com/) is Emeritus Professor of English and Cultural Anthropology and former chair of the Linguistics Program at Duke University, where he began teaching in 1967. He is president of the International Association of Forensic Linguists (2009–11) and one of the present co-editors of *The International Journal of Speech, Language, and the Law*. He maintains an active presence in American forensic linguistic consulting; his practical and scholarly interests include (1) ethical issues in forensic linguistic consulting, (2) statutes and contracts, (3) death-penalty appeals, (4) copyrights, (5) discourse analysis of linguistic evidence, and (6) semiotic and linguistic issues in trademark litigation.

Deborah Cao is an Associate Professor at Griffith University (Australia). Her books include *Chinese Law: A Language Perspective* and *Translating Law*. She is the editor of the *International Journal for the Semiotics of Law* and Chinese editor of the *Journal of Specialised Translation*.

Malcolm Coulthard is Professor of Forensic Linguistics and Foundation Director of the Centre for Forensic Linguistics at Aston University, which, since 2006, has hosted the annual International Summer School in Forensic Linguistic Analysis. He was the Chair of the Founding Committee of the International Association of Forensic Linguists and its first President and the founding co-editor of *The International Journal of Speech Language and the Law*. Over the past 20 years, he has written reports in some 200 cases. His latest court appearance was at the trial of David Hodgson for the murder of Jenny Nicholl in February 2008. He is co-author with Alison Johnson of *An Introduction to Forensic Linguistics: Language in Evidence* (2007).

Paul Drew conducts research on conversation and interaction, including repair, topic and how social actions (such as offering, requesting and complaining) are managed in interaction. He also works extensively on institutional and workplace interactions, notably questioning in courtroom examination, and medical (especially doctor–patient) interactions. He is author and editor (with John Heritage) of *Talk at Work: Interaction in Institutional Settings* (Cambridge University Press, 1992).

Bethany K. Dumas, J.D., PhD (Professor of English, University of Tennessee) publishes on language variation, discourse analysis, and language and law, especially jury instructions and product warnings. Courses include Language and Law, Rhetoric of Legal Discourse, Lawyers in Literature, American English Dialects, Discourse Analysis, and Talkin' Trash. She has testified in court cases since 1984.

Diana Eades is a Research Fellow at the University of New England, Australia. She has worked in forensic linguistics for more than two decades. Her work addresses assumptions about how the language works and how sociolinguistic and legal processes interact, including a critical linguistic approach to language in legal processes. Her most recent publication is *Courtroom Talk and Neocolonial Control* (Mouton de Gruyter, 2008) and 'Sociolinguistics and the Legal Process' (*Multilingual Matters*, 2010).

Derek Edwards is Professor of Psychology in the Department of Social Sciences, Loughborough University, England. His interests are in the analysis of language and social interaction in everyday and institutional settings. He specializes in discursive psychology, in which relations between psychological states and the external world are studied as discourse categories and practices. Current work focuses on subject–object relations, person descriptions and intentionality in mundane conversation, neighbor dispute mediation, and police interrogations. His books include *Common Knowledge*, with Neil Mercer (Routledge, 1987), *Ideological Dilemmas*, with Michael Billig and others (Sage, 1988), *Discursive Psychology*, with Jonathan Potter (Sage, 1992), and *Discourse and Cognition* (Sage, 1997).

Susan Ehrlich is Professor of Linguistics at York University in Toronto. She does research in the areas of discourse analysis, language and gender, and language and the law. Her books include *Point of View: A Linguistic Analysis of Literary Style* (Routledge, 1990), *Representing Rape* (Routledge, 2001), the edited collection, *Language and Gender: Major Themes in English Studies* (Routledge, 2008) and the forthcoming '*Why Do You Ask?': The Function of Questions in Institutional Discourse* (Oxford), co-edited with Alice Freed.

Fiona English is a Senior Lecturer in TESOL and Applied Linguistics at London Metropolitan University where she works on the Masters programs for English language teachers from all over the world. Her research interests include genres and academic knowledge, pedagogy across cultures and the analysis of verbal texts. Her involvement in forensic linguistics, which concerns assessing detainees' English language performance, began several years ago and she continues to refine her methodology in response to the different experiences that each case brings.

Laura Felton Rosulek is currently an adjunct Professor at the University of Montana. Her PhD dissertation, from the University of Illinois at Urbana-Champaign, was entitled *The Sociolinguistic Construction of Reality in Closing Arguments in Criminal Trials*. Her interests include forensic linguistics, critical discourse analysis, and systemic-functional linguistics.

Edward Finegan is Professor of Linguistics and Law at the University of Southern California. He teaches discourse analysis in the Linguistics department and Law School and has served for over three decades as a consultant and expert in forensic linguistics. He is author of numerous books and articles, including: *Language: Its Structure and Use* (2008); *The Longman Grammar of Spoken and Written English* (with others 1999); and *Sociolinguistic Perspectives on Register* (edited with Douglas Biber 1994).

Tim Grant is Deputy Director of the Centre for Forensic Linguistics at Aston University. His consultancy primarily involves authorship analysis and he has worked in many different contexts including investigations into sexual assault, murder and terrorist offences. His research into text messaging analysis was awarded the 2008 Joseph Lister Prize by the British Science Association.

Peter R. A. Gray is a judge of the Federal Court of Australia.

Gillian Grebler (DPhil cand. Oxon) is a linguistic anthropologist based in Santa Monica, California. She teaches at Santa Monica College and works as an ethnographer and as a consultant on legal cases where spoken language is at issue. Her special interest is in police interrogation and false confessions and resulting miscarriages of justice. Grebler worked in London during the 1980s, carrying out research on police interrogation and false confessions and participating in the BBC's *Rough Justice*.

Mel Greenlee received her PhD in Linguistics and J.D. from the University of California-Berkeley. She is a criminal defense attorney specializing in capital appeals and habeas corpus matters in California. In her academic career, she conducted research on language acquisition, bilingualism and other sociolinguistic topics; she continues to investigate the interface between language and law in her legal career.

Sandra Hale is the leader of the Interpreting and Translation Research Node at the University of Western Sydney. She is an experienced Spanish interpreter, educator and researcher. She was the chair of the Critical Link 5 Congress held in Sydney in April 2007.

Kate Haworth is currently a lecturer at the Centre for Forensic Linguistics at Aston University. She is also a barrister (non-practicing). Her research interests include all aspects of language and the law, especially language as evidence.

Chris Heffer is Senior Lecturer and Director of the MA in Forensic Linguistics at the Centre for Language and Communication Research at Cardiff University. He is the author of *The Language of Jury Trial* (Palgrave 2005) and *Forensic Discourse* (Continuum 2010) and has published articles in linguistic and legal journals on various aspects of the trial process.

Elizabeth Holt is a lecturer in English Language at the University of Huddersfield. She is editor and author (with Rebecca Clift), of *Voicing: Reported Speech and Footing in Conversation* (Cambridge University Press, 2007). She has had papers published in the journals *Language and Society*, *Research on Language and Social Interaction*, *Social Problems* and *Text*.

Michael Jessen (MA Linguistics Universität Bielefeld; PhD Linguistics Cornell University) was lecturer for linguistics and phonetics in the Department of Computational Linguistics and Phonetics at Universität Stuttgart for eight years. Since 2001, he has worked as a forensic expert and research associate at the Speaker Identification and Audio Analysis Department of the Federal Forensics Laboratory of Bundeskriminalamt, Germany. His research interests lie in forensic speaker identification and the interaction between phonetics and phonology.

Alison Johnson is a lecturer in English language and linguistics at the University of Leeds. Her doctoral research was on the pragmatics of questions in police interviews and her research interests in Forensic Linguistics are in the pragmatics of legal talk, narrative and evaluation, children in the legal system, historical forensic linguistics and plagiarism. She is author (with Malcolm Coulthard) of *Language in Evidence: An Introduction to Forensic Linguistics*.

Krzysztof Kredens received his MA in English Studies and PhD in English Linguistics from the University of Lodz, Poland. He is a Lecturer in Applied Linguistics in the School of Languages and Social Sciences at Aston University, UK. His academic interests include corpus linguistics, translation studies and social applications of linguistics. His main research interest lies with language and the law, and particularly the linguistics of the individual speaker and its implications for forensic authorship analysis. He is a practicing public service interpreter.

Gerald R. McMenamin is Professor Emeritus of Linguistics at California State University, Fresno, where he has taught since 1980, after teaching assignments at the Universidad Autónoma de Guadalajara, University of Delaware, and UCLA. His research specialties include Spanish linguistics, second language acquisition, stylistics, linguistic variation, and forensic linguistics. He received his MA (Linguistics) from California State University, Fresno and Doctorado en Lingüística Hispánica from El Colegio de México. He is the author of several books, including *Forensic Linguistics: Advances in Forensic Stylistics*, 2002, and many articles on language acquisition, linguistic variation, and forensic linguistics. He presently works as a consultant and expert witness in forensic linguistics.

Gregory M. Matoesian is Professor in the Department of Criminology, Law and Justice at the University of Illinois at Chicago. He studies verbal and visual conduct in the constitution of legal identity and is author of *Reproducing Rape: Domination through Talk in the Courtroom* (U. of Chicago Press, 1993) and *Law and the Language of Identity* (Oxford U. Press, 2001), as well as numerous articles in linguistic journals.

Ruth Morris is a former Brussels-based European Union staff interpreter. In the early 1980s, she became a freelance interpreter and translator in Israel, where she also gives a research seminar on interpreting in the legal system at Bar-Ilan University's master's program in translation studies. Her first casework sparked an enduring and passionate research interest in the area of interpreting in the legal system, including observations at the multilingual Demjanjuk trial, as well as historical and contemporary views of the interpreter in various English-speaking legal systems.

Frances Rock is a lecturer in Language and Communication at Cardiff University. Her research interests are in discourse analysis, interactional sociolinguistics and literacies. She is currently working on applications of language study to policing and other professional and legal settings. She is author of *Communicating Rights* (Palgrave, 2007).

Nancy Schweda Nicholson has a PhD from Georgetown University and is Professor of Linguistics and Cognitive Science with a Joint Appointment in the Legal Studies Program at the University of Delaware (USA). In addition to her work on allocutions, Dr. Nicholson's research interests include: language planning and policy development for court interpreter services; interpreting at international criminal tribunals; and European Union law.

Roger W. Shuy is Emeritus Professor of Linguistics at Georgetown University following 30 years' service that continues through his company, Roger W. Shuy, Inc., incorporated in 1982. Over the past 40 years he has consulted on some 500 cases and has testified as an expert witness 54 times in criminal and civil trials (in 26 states), as well as before the US Senate and US House of Representatives. He is author of numerous books and articles, including: *Fighting over Words* (2007), *Linguistics in the Courtroom: A Practical Guide* (2006), *Creating Language Crimes: How Law Enforcement Uses (and Misuses) Language* (2005) and *Linguistic Battles in Trademark Disputes* (2002).

Lawrence M. Solan is the Don Forchelli Professor of Law and Director of the Center for the Study of Law, Language and Cognition at Brooklyn Law School. He holds a PhD in Linguistics from the University of Massachusetts and a J.D. from Harvard Law School. His writings address such issues as legal interpretation, the attribution of responsibility and blame, and the role of the expert in the courts. His books include *The Language of Judges, Speaking of Crime* (with Peter Tiersma), and his forthcoming book, *Under the Law: Statutes and their Interpretation*, all published by the University of Chicago Press.

Elizabeth Stokoe is Reader in Social Interaction at Loughborough University. Her research interests are in conversation analysis and social interaction in various ordinary and institutional settings, including neighbor mediation, police interrogation, speed dating and talk between friends. She is the author of *Discourse and Identity* (with Bethan Benwell, Edinburgh University Press, 2006) and is currently writing *Talking Relationships: Analyzing Speed-Dating Interactions* for Cambridge University Press.

Gail Stygall is Professor of English at the University of Washington, Seattle, WA, US, where she teaches English language courses and writes about legal discourse and forensic issues. She has consulted on a variety of cases and is especially interested in cases involving lay understanding of complex documents. She is author of *Trial Language: Differential Discourse Processing and Discursive Formation* (Benjamins, 1994).

Peter Tiersma teaches at Loyola Law School in Los Angeles, where he holds the Judge William Matthew Byrne chair. He has a PhD in Linguistics from the University of California, San Diego, and a juris doctor degree from the University of California, Berkeley. His books include *Legal Language* and *Speaking of Crime: The Language of Criminal Justice* (with Lawrence Solan).

Tatiana Tkačuková is currently affiliated with the Department of English, Faculty of Education, Masaryk University in Brno, Czech Republic. Her research interests lie mainly in the study of spoken courtroom discourse and the interaction between legal professionals and lay people.

Traci Walker's work is grounded in an interest in discovering the order and structure of language in everyday use. Her research combines the methods of Conversation

Analysis with more traditional means of linguistic analysis, and her recent publications show how principled variation in syntactic or phonetic structure is used to achieve different interactional outcomes.

David Woolls is the CEO and founder of CFL Software Limited and an Honorary Visiting Fellow at the Centre for Forensic Linguistics at Aston University. He has designed and built computer programs to assist forensic linguists since 1994, with recent development work in real-time, large-scale, automated applications of such tools.

Acknowledgements

Parts of this handbook have been written in Brazil, England, Holland, Poland, Sicily and several parts of the USA (Chicago, Ithaca and Manhattan) – and that's just the editors – and those locations have provided us with inspiration and wonderful places for writing and editing. We would like to acknowledge the support and hard work of all our contributors and also our grateful thanks for invaluable editorial assistance from Francisco Alberto Gomez Moya (student of the University of Leeds, UK and Universidad de Murcia, Spain) and Robert Coulthard (doctoral student at the Universidade Federal de Santa Catarina, Brazil).

Introduction

Current debates in forensic linguistics

Alison Johnson and Malcolm Coulthard

'Language is as it is because of what it has to do'.

Halliday (1973: 34)

Introduction

When Halliday wrote 'language is as it is because of what it has to do' a functional theory of language was born, giving us a perspective of meaning-making that is grounded in social practice and in the many varied and complex contexts in which we find ourselves. Context is dynamic and socially constructed through and by discourse – both in its linguistic and non-linguistic semiotic modes – and we know that the legal world is context-rich. It is peopled by a hierarchical mini-nation of judges, lawyers, police and law-enforcement officers and then the common man and woman, who walk, like Adam and Eve, unknowing, through this strange world. Its texts are also richly layered with meaning; its language has evolved over many centuries and its peculiar form is a result of this history and specialised use. What legal people do with lay people through legal language, legal texts and legal interaction is the focus of this *Handbook*. Leading scholars from the disciplines of linguistics, law, criminology and sociology examine the ways that language has and is being used, who is using it, how they are writing, where they are speaking, why they are interacting in that way and what is being accomplished through that interaction.

Forensic Linguistics has now come of age as a discipline. It has its own professional association, The International Association of Forensic Linguists, founded in 1993; its own journal, *International Journal of Speech, Language and the Law*, founded in 1994; and a biennial international conference. There are three major introductory textbooks – Coulthard and Johnson (2007), Gibbons (2003) and Olsson (2nd ed. 2008a) – and a growing number of specialist monographs: Cotterill (2003), Eades (2008b), Heffer (2005) Heydon (2005) and Rock (2007), to mention just a few. Modules in forensic linguistics and/or language and the law are taught to undergraduate and Masters level students in a rapidly increasing number of universities worldwide and, at the time of writing, there are three specialist Masters degrees at the universities of Aston, Pompeu Fabra (Barcelona) and Cardiff, and an annual international summer school at Aston training the next generation of forensic linguists.

Aim, contents and organisation

The aim of this *Handbook* is to provide a unique work of reference to the leading ideas, debates, topics, approaches and methodologies in Forensic Linguistics, with chapters written by the world's finest academics, both established and up-and-coming. Our intended audience is advanced undergraduates, graduates and research students as well as established researchers in other disciplines who are new to forensic linguistics. This is a handbook, not a textbook (as we noted above there are already several textbooks, including our own, Coulthard and Johnson 2007), and as such it is a comprehensive advanced introduction to core issues and topics in contemporary forensic linguistics. All the contributions include a richness of examples and case studies to enable the reader to see forensic linguistics applied and in action. Contributors come from Australia, Canada, the Czech Republic, Germany, Hong Kong SAR, Israel, Poland, the UK and the USA and cross several professional and academic areas. The professions represented are numerous too: academic, attorney, computer scientist, forensic speaker identification and audio analyst, freelance consultant, interpreter, judge and translator, and some of the contributors have former professional experience as lawyer and police officer. The academics, as the list of contributors shows (p. xvi), are based in a wide range of departments and span a number of disciplines: anthropology, communication, criminology, English, humanities, law, linguistics, modern languages, philosophy, social science, sociology and translation studies. As a group, we are truly inter- and cross-disciplinary in composition and often in approach.

After this introductory chapter, the almost encyclopaedic range of topics covered in the remaining 38 chapters is organised into three major sections:

Section I: The language of the law and the legal process
Section II: The linguist as expert in legal processes
Section III: New debates and new directions.

Within each of these sections the reader will find small collections of between four and six chapters, which are arranged according to broad topics, but there are, in fact, as many connections across groups as there are between the chapters in a particular group. For example, the common denominator across the six chapters in the section called 'Participants in police investigations, interviewing and interrogation' is a focus on *who* is talking, but in a sense that link is arbitrary, as the contributors themselves didn't identify that theme. Instead, it was the editors who made the connection for the benefit of you, the reader, and we now invite you to see the many other connections that can be made. Such is the nature of reading and research; the intellectual activity that enables us to perceive connections between ideas creates new areas of scholarship and, as each of you reads chapters in the multiple combinations that are possible with such an extensive collection, we anticipate a blossoming research landscape in our next and successive springs. We do make many connections for readers between chapters, though, by saying, for example – Archer (this volume) – to help readers locate relevant material as they read. We hope you will go on a journey of discovery and that soon your own work will join the already extensive library of books, chapters, papers, corpora and software in this field.

Section I – The language of the law and the legal process

The *Handbook* begins with five chapters on legal language in Section 1.1. Though much of the research on legal language focuses on written texts, Holt and Johnson's chapter takes speech as its subject and puts talk ahead of writing as the primary mode of communication, though talk is intertextually linked and contextualised by a whole array of written texts: statutes, the police Caution and other written texts.

1.1 Legal language

Holt and Johnson's chapter is one of several in the volume that examines questions. This most characteristic of legal interactional forms accomplishes important institutional work and the chapter, in focusing on formulations, repeating questions and reported speech (both in questions and responses), explores the socio-pragmatic uses of questions in police interviews and trials. Formulation, or 'saying what has already been said' in prior talk is an important part of institutional evidence construction, which 'fixes facts' for consumption and decision-making by juries. While Holt and Johnson deal with spoken interaction, the chapters by Bhatia, Stygall, Finegan and Cao deal with written legal texts: Bhatia on *specification*, Stygall on *complexity* and Finegan on *attitude* and *emphasis*. Stygall deals with the real-world problems that readers encounter when they try and fail to understand the implications of pension documents. Her chapter also crosses into the area of linguistic expertise in action, as she reports on how her analysis of complexity reveals some of the comprehension and comprehensibility issues that impact on citizens. Bhatia deals with the other side of the argument: when legislation is simplified or made plainer it can, paradoxically, create perhaps unintended difficulties, since it transfers matters of interpretation to the judiciary rather than the legislature (which represents the people). Finegan focuses on a so far little researched area of the legal register, written opinions or decisions of the Supreme Court of the United States, and in particular adverbial expressions of judicial attitude and emphasis in the state of California. Though legal drafters are warned in textbooks against using intensifiers, emphatic adverbs are abundant in Finegan's COSCO corpus (Corpus of Supreme Court Opinions, consisting of nearly 1 million words) and so he examines this 'gap', demonstrating how empirical corpus analysis of judges' opinions can reveal 'justice with attitude'. And Cao deals with the practical challenges for translators of private legal documents, domestic statutes and multilateral legal instruments and she illustrates some of the issues arising from complexities in translating laws in bilingual jurisdictions, with examples from Canada (English–French) and Hong Kong SAR (English–Chinese).

1.2 Participants in police investigations, interviewing and interrogation

Section 1.2's six chapters are concerned with participants in police investigations. In our List of the Conventions used in this *Handbook* (p.xiv) we list all the participants referred to in the course of this book (e.g. *caller, call taker, convicted person, defence lawyer, prosecuting lawyer, interviewee, interviewer, testee, tester, witness*) and it therefore seemed appropriate to have a section specifically devoted to participants (in fact we have two, as section 1.4 is devoted solely to lay participants). Drew and Walker focus on the citizen and their telephone interactions with police call handlers as they request assistance in emergency and non-emergency situations, showing how in their use of questions call takers assess whether there is an urgent need (or not) for dispatch of officers to the incident. They show how particular request forms 'reflect a speaker's assessment of their entitlement to have a request granted' and how 'different forms may be used to display speakers' knowledge of the contingencies surrounding the granting of a request' (p. 100). Ainsworth, Rock, Benneworth, Stokoe and Edwards and Haworth all deal with police interviews and interrogations. 'Interview' seems the preferred term in the UK with 'interrogation' more usual in the US, though Stokoe and Edwards use the term 'interrogation'. The different nomenclature partially reflects the different investigative styles used by the police in the two countries, as readers will see, and in attitudes to interviewees, which are revealed in Ainsworth's disturbing chapter. Ainsworth deals with problems of access to and an effective denial of rights for suspects in the US, while Stokoe and Edwards show how rights are negotiated by suspects and on their behalf, through the support of a lawyer, in interviews where lawyers are successfully accessed and present. Their chapter examines 'lawyer–initiated actions, responses and interjections including objections to police questioning, advice to clients (both spontaneous and in response to requests), various "repair" operations on officers' questions, and actions such as questioning clients, and helping them formulate their evidence' (p. 167) and they show the advantages and disadvantages for the suspect of the varying forms of intervention. Rock's chapter focuses not only on the suspect but also on witnesses. Like Drew and Walker, she recognises the role of witnesses in the investigative process and focuses in particular on the importance of reading and writing. Though she acknowledges the importance of talk, she establishes the central role of reading and writing practices in the interview 'showing how these activities figure, how they are oriented to and how influential they are on the structures, practices and outcomes of police interviews' (p. 126). Benneworth focuses on a particular kind of suspect – paedophiles – and also on the interview itself as an object of study. Her chapter reports on her research, which found that open and closed interviewing styles exist and these produce different evidential effects. Haworth also sees the interview as an evidential object in the judicial process as she explores the different and sometimes competing investigative and evidential functions of the interview and looks at how evidence constructed discursively can be 'contaminated' in the process, and this clearly has implications for the suspect. The chapters in this section use conversation analysis, discourse analysis and critical discourse analysis approaches.

1.3 Courtroom genres

Section 1.3 moves from the interview room to the courtroom and begins with a historical approach to the courtroom genre by Archer, who maps a changing landscape over the seventeenth, eighteenth and nineteenth centuries. The early period is characterised by interactivity between judges and defendants, but Archer shows that 'a decline in the *inter*activity of defendants and judges is mirrored by an increase in lawyers' *inter*activity' and there is 'a move towards adversarialism in its modern form' (p. 185). The other three chapters grouped under the heading of 'Courtroom genres' include Heffer's focus on *narrative* throughout the many phases of the trial; Felton Rosulek's specific look at *closing speeches* and the creation of contrasting prosecution and defence arguments through a range of linguistic techniques; and Nicholson's emphasis on the persuasive power of the *allocution* – the plea for leniency, made to the jury by a convicted murderer in the US system.

1.4 Lay participants in the judicial process

Section 1.4 remains in the courtroom, but this section focuses on the challenges faced by a range of lay participants: jurors (Tiersma), rape victims (Ehrlich), youths and suspected gang members (Greenlee), false confessors (Grebler), vulnerable witnesses such as children and the physically and intellectually impaired (Aldridge) and people who choose to represent themselves in court, rather than engage an advocate (Tkačuková). All of these chapters examine the power of language to complicate meaning-making and make outcomes for lay participants at best difficult and at worst result in 'distorted perceptions' that place severe restrictions on civil liberties.

Section II – The linguist as expert in the legal process

As we move from looking at what legal language does to what the linguistic expert does, we see how linguists can make an important contribution to the presentation of evidence. An expert's opinion is called on in cases where linguistic knowledge – semantic, syntactic, pragmatic, discoursal, phonetic, lexicographic and corpus linguistic – can assist the judge and jury in a particular case.

2.1 Expert and process

Butters, Dumas, Jessen and Solan each offer a different perspective: Butters on trademarks – that particular language that companies try to own; Dumas on consumer product warnings – for example, the way that the language of warnings on tobacco products warns or fails to warn consumers of the dangers; and Jessen on phonetics – the ways that speakers are identified by their voices through technical and descriptive methods. All these encapsulate a struggle between the expert, a client and the legal system. Solan also takes up this theme in his chapter that deals with the linguist's encounter with the adversarial system. Testing of opinions and struggling for the 'truth' involve argument that is based on inquiry and Solan warns against naivety and makes the point that academic research tolerates uncertainty to a higher degree than the legal system. He presents a stark picture of a legal system on the one hand that exploits uncertainty in experts and, on the other, experts who are susceptible to cognitive bias in the pursuit of confirming results.

2.2 Multilingualism in legal contexts

The multilingual legal context is no less fraught for the expert, and Eades, English, Hale and Kredens and Morris have some hard-won lessons to share with readers. The message they all share is one of what Eades calls 'awareness raising'. Linguistic experts have a responsibility to draw attention to potential for serious injustice in the judicial process. For Eades injustice may arise from the misuse of language analysis by governments and immigration departments, for English because assessments of non-native speakers' proficiency may be more complex than is understood, and for Hale and Kredens and Morris, because of ignorance and inadequate interpreting practice that requires a wise allocation of resources – the use of qualified interpreters – both in and outside the courts.

2.3 Authorship and opinion

Experts on authorship have a difficult task – ownership of text is easy to dispute, but difficult to settle, because individual style is difficult to pin down and, as we have said, the legal profession relies on certainties or at the very least being sure. Juries have to base decisions on being sure beyond 'reasonable doubt' and it is the expert's job to give an opinion that is neither inflated nor wavering or indecisive – Coulthard shows how difficult it can be to express an opinion in the first place and then to convert it into jury-friendly language. Grant problematises the notion of idiolect in authorship identification in relation to text messaging data by suggesting that authorship style can instead be determined on the basis of 'observation and description of consistency and distinctiveness'. He then uses 'pair-wise contrasts between text messages by two authors' (p. 521) to take a step towards presenting opinions statistically. McMenamin's theory of idiolect is one that encompasses 'style markers', that is markers that 'are the observable result of the habitual and usually unconscious choices an author makes in the process of writing' (p. 488) and Grant, too, argues for stylometry. McMenamin distinguishes two general types of style marker: one, where the writer makes a *choice* from available optional forms (and this might be 'consistent', to use Grant's term) and second where a writer *deviates from a norm*. Both Grant and McMenamin call for further research to strengthen the science, but what is presented here is the state of the current art.

In Coulthard, Johnson, Kredens and Woolls's chapter on plagiarism prevention and detection we examine some of the claims made by writers and the responses of forensic linguists to allegations of plagiarism. We identify lexical features for establishing similarity and difference and describe how writers usually say the same things uniquely, and so, when writers use the same or similar words and phrases, they are probably not writing independently.

Section III – New debates and new directions

As this is a forward-looking section, it is the shortest; we cannot predict the future, but we offer four chapters that present new debates and new directions for research. In Matoesian's chapter, we see how research in multimodality might be extended to forensic and legal contexts, though this is not without its challenges, given the difficulty of access and permission to videotape interviews, interrogations and judicial proceedings at all levels: lower and higher courts and coroners', military and civil courts, etc. Matoesian demonstrates what a detailed micro-conversation analysis can tell us about the power of talk. In his assertion, future researchers are provided with a challenge:

> Focusing on just words neglects the role of multimodal activities in legal proceedings – how both language and embodied conduct mutually contextualize one another in a reciprocal dialectic – and leaves the study of forensic linguistics with an incomplete understanding of legal discourse.
>
> (p. 541)

Shuy's challenge is as much to the legal community as to the forensic linguistic community in his chapter on terrorism cases. How might law-enforcers and the courts protect the public from terrorism whilst protecting citizens' civil rights? There are worrying trends of potential over-protection of the one at the expense of the other, not only revealed in Shuy's chapter, but also in those by Ainsworth, Grebler, Greenlee and Haworth, which all point future research in a particular direction: towards reassessing and prioritising the suspect's rights.

Woolls's chapter shows the power of computational approaches to forensic linguistics, particularly in commercial and business settings and there is at present a need to attract more computational linguists into collaboration and research in forensic linguistics. Programming and linguistic skills rarely come together, and adding a forensic dimension makes the multi-disciplinarity even rarer, but there is plenty of work to be done. The creation and analysis of large-scale corpora (see also Finegan's chapter – Chapter 5) allows the researcher to say much more about texts and practices and in a post-Daubert era, where forensic linguistic expertise must be quantitatively accountable and measurable. It is one of the ways forward.

Gray's chapter (Chapter 38) reflects on some of the preceding chapters from the perspective of a judge. He argues for a greater cross-disciplinary discussion and exchange of ideas, since, as he says, lawyers, including judges, are woefully unaware of the existence of forensic linguists, linguistics and our expertise. He challenges linguists to start the conversation. Finally, our 'Concluding remarks', Chapter 39, look to the future.

What is forensic linguistics?

Our recent book, *An Introduction to Forensic Linguistics: Language in Evidence* (Routledge, 2007), organised material into two sections: the language of the legal process and language as evidence. In other words, we made a distinction between the description of the language of the law (both written and spoken) and the work of the expert linguist, which, of course, involves both the production of written reports and the presentation of oral evidence in court. This binary distinction blurred the boundary between written and spoken language and there are several good reasons for now sub-dividing the field into three areas:

i)   the study of the written language of the law;
ii) the study of interaction in the legal process, which in criminal cases includes everything from an initial call to the emergency services to the sentencing of someone who has been found guilty; and
iii) the description of the work of the forensic linguist when acting as an expert witness.

This more satisfying tri-partite division must, however, not allow us to forget that

a)   some fixed-form written texts, like the police caution, the Miranda Warnings and Pattern Jury Instructions, are 'performed' or perhaps better 'verbalised' as part of what are otherwise real-time now-encoding spoken interactions;
b)   in some jurisdictions, police investigative interviews are standardly audio- or video-recorded and these recordings are then transcribed into written form using ordinary orthography;
c)   these written transcripts are often reconverted into speech in the courtroom with a lawyer, usually the prosecutor, performing the part of the accused; and
d)   expert forensic linguists typically provide their evidence in both written and spoken modes.

In the previous section, we outlined the contents of the chapters in this *Handbook*, but in the next three sub-sections we will discuss in more detail the three major topic areas outlined above in order to put the chapters in this volume in context. We refer both to research reported in chapters in this volume and to the wider research context.

The language of the law

We begin with the wider topic of legal language, which has been discussed and defined in a range of scholarly works. Cao (this volume) makes a distinction between the language **of** the law, language **about** the law and the language used **in** legal communication. We make a distinction between just two of these; the language **of** the law (written laws, statutes and contracts) and the language used **in** legal communication. This is simply a convention; legal communication can clearly include the written as well as the spoken mode, since lawyers communicate to their clients in letters and there are many other instances of written communication in legal contexts. Here, though, we deal with written law and spoken interaction, and, in relation to the latter (in the next section), we chiefly consider two interactive contexts: the police interview and the criminal trial. We look first at legal writing, because 'talking like a lawyer' (Tiersma 1999: 51) involves using legalese as a professional code, although as Tiersma (1999: 145) says, while we can observe many of the characteristics found in legal writing in the spoken language of the courtroom, 'when lawyers are sufficiently motivated, they quickly abandon legalese'.

The language of written statutes and contracts and many other legal documents has been described in terms of its complexity (see Bhatia; Stygall this volume), and legal talk can also be remarkably complex in terms of syntax and structure. However, legal language is more remarkable for what it does; it has specialised institutional functions and pragmatic effects, or as Tiersma (1999: 145) says the courtroom gives us 'legal language in its most dramatic setting'. Holt and Johnson (this volume) explore the 'dramaturgical quality of [direct reported speech]' in legal talk and its uses not simply 'to replay an interaction but also to enable the speaker to simultaneously convey his or her attitude towards the reported utterance' (Clift and Holt 2007: 7) and Finegan (this volume) also examines attitudes – those of judges in appeal decisions – which are revealed through his corpus linguistic analysis of adverbs and adverbials.

The written language of the law

Legal writing has been traced over a considerable span of history and has been widely characterised by linguists across a range of legal text types, including:

- contracts (Trosborg 1995),
- judgments (e.g. Bhatia 1987; Maley 1985),
- jury instructions (Charrow and Charrow 1979; Tiersma, this volume),
- notices to people in custody (Rock 2007),
- product warnings (Dumas, this volume; Heaps and Henley 1999; Shuy 1990b; Tiersma 2002),
- the police caution (Cotterill 2000; Rock 2007 and this volume) and the Miranda warning (Ainsworth, this volume; Berk-Seligson 2002; Leo 1998, 2001; Shuy 1997),
- statutes (e.g. Bhatia 1994; Gunnarsson 1984; Foyle 2002; Wagner 2002),
- temporary restraining orders (Stratman and Dahl 1996),
- trademarks (Butters 2008c; Shuy 2002),

- and wills (Danet and Bogoch 1994).

These researchers have focused on a wide range of linguistic features – of expression, including lexis, syntax, semantics and pragmatics, and also of reception: comprehensibility, complexity and readability. When we consider the language of legal talk, we have to also examine turn-taking rules and speech acts.

Tiersma (1999: 1) observes that 'Our law is a law of words' and he traces its history from its roots in ancient Britain, through the multilingual Latin and French period to the present day. He notes that:

> there is no single, easy answer to the question of how legal language came to be what it is. Much of the explanation lies in a series of historical developments, each of which left its mark on the language of the law.
>
> (Tiersma 1999: 47)

The extensive range of research on legal language, its history and its distinctive text types exemplifies what Maley (1994: 13) calls the 'great efflorescence of interest in the language of the law'. As she notes, much of this research and writing, in addition to being descriptive, is critical. And Tiersma (1999: 69) argues that reform of legal language may be necessary to protect lawyers from public criticism and rejection, since one perception is that legalese is unnecessarily exclusive and that preserving stylistic features, such as lengthy and complex sentences with a high degree of subordination and embedding, wordiness, conjoined phrases and impersonal constructions, 'excludes those who do not belong'. However, Bhatia (this volume) counter-argues that, in legislative writing, processes of simplification (carried out under a reformist project) can lead to under-specification and this has implications for power and control. If the legislature goes for simplicity, it paradoxically gives power to the judiciary to interpret the law and takes it away from the people, which the legislature represents. Even so, the changes stimulated by the Plain English campaign are interesting and Tiersma's chapter on the simplification of the California Pattern Jury Instructions is instructive.

Rock (2007) also combines descriptive and critical approaches to the analysis of two texts, The Anglo-Welsh caution and Notice to Detained Persons, whose use in a series of police stations she studied in depth. She notes that these two legal texts are capable of creating issues in relation to: *difficulty, multifunctionality, performativity, politics, literacy* and *difference* (Rock 2007: 8–12). Rock's treatment highlights a number of important aspects which are true of most legal texts. Like Danet and Bogoch (1994) she emphasises their performative aspect and the productive and receptive challenges these texts provide for users. Police officers demonstrate a range of attitudes to institutionality in their explanations of the caution, and suspects display a range of understanding and misunderstanding of their rights. Like Bhatia, Rock partially rejects the simplification argument, pointing out that, in rewriting the Notice to Detained Persons to maximise understanding, simplicity can obscure intent. In her analysis of the revisions of the Notice, Rock (2007: 68–70) shows that there is a tension between simplification and comprehensiveness. A badly simplified text can be heard as patronising, and also simplification risks 'register shift, thus changing the *Notice's* character'. Even worse, simplification may create misunderstanding or even transmit an erroneous message.

Linguistic features of legal writing

We have already mentioned some of the linguistic features that have been described and criticised in the plethora of research to date. A range of these features is summarised in Table 1.1, along with examples. For ease of reference the features have been organised alphabetically rather than by linguistic sub-domain, such as syntax or semantics.

Table 1.1 Some of the researched linguistic features of legal language

Linguistic domain	Research	Examples
Binominal expressions and listing	Gustafsson 1975, 1984 Mellinkoff 1963	*by and with* *write, edit, print or publish* *act or omission*
Cohesion	Bhatia 1994	See 'textual mapping' in Bhatia 1994
Complex prepositions prep+noun+prep	Gustafsson 1975 Mellinkoff 1963 Swales and Bhatia 1983	*in respect of* *for the purpose of* *by virtue of*
Generic/cognitive structuring	Bhatia 1994 Swales and Bhatia 1983	Two-part move structure of [provision] and (qualification): *[The Chief Land Registrar shall] (if so requested by the Secretary of State) [supply him](on payment of the appropriate fee) [with an office copy of any document required]*
Impersonal noun phrase constructions – lack of pronoun use in repeated references	Tiersma 1999 Lundquist 1995 Maley 1994	*The sex offender shall register* *The plaintiff alleges* *The lessor shall*
Legal archaisms	Gibbons 2003 Hager 1959 O'Barr 1982 Tiersma 1999	Archaic deictic: *hereunder* Modal verb: *shall* *Be it enacted* – the subjunctive enactment formula in Statutes.
Modality	Foyle 2002 Wagner 2002	*may, shall* and *must* as frequent modal verbs. Ambiguity of *may*: epistemic and deontic.
Negation	Tiersma 1999	*innocent misrecollection is <u>not uncommon</u>* (California jury instruction)
Nominalisation representing processes	Maley 1994 Bhatia 1994 Tiersma 1999	*On the <u>prosecution</u> of a person for bigamy…* *The girl's <u>injury</u> happened at*
Passive constructions	Tiersma 1999 Trosborg 1995	*one hour is allotted for oral argument* *This agreement shall be interpreted*
Sentence length and complexity – subordination, qualification and embedding	Austin 1984 Bhatia 1994 Gustafsson 1975 Hiltunen 1984 Hill and King 2004	See example (1) and 'generic and cognitive structuring' (this table)
Specialised, distinctive and technical legal lexis	Trosborg 1997 Tiersma 1999 Gibbons 2003 Coulthard and Johnson 2007	Frequency of *any* Impersonal nouns: *the parties, any person* Legal lexis: de*fendant*, mens rea, *recognisance, testator*

Example (1) below, which is extracted from a Singaporean Act (Bhatia 1994: 142), shows virtually all of the features listed in Table 1.1 in a single punctuated sentence. You may like to tick them off for yourself.

(1)
No obliteration, interlineation or other alteration made in any will after the execution thereof shall be valid or have effect except so far as the words or effect of the will before such alteration shall not be apparent, unless such alteration shall be executed in like manner as hereinbefore is required for the execution of the will; but the will, with such alteration as part thereof, shall be deemed to be duly exe- cuted if the signature of the testator and the subscription of the witnesses be made in the margin or on some other part of the will opposite or near to such alteration or at the foot or end of or opposite to a memorandum referring to such alteration and written at the end or some other part of the will.

(Section 16 of the Wills Act, 1970, Republic of Singapore)

The example is particularly rich in nominalisations, for example, 'No obliteration, interlineation or other alteration', but the phrase also exemplifies two other of the listed features: negation and listing with 'or'. Pretty much any short extract from a legal statute or contract will be characterised by the generic and register features shown in Table 1.1 and in example (1).

One side of the critical argument in the discussion of the complexity of legal language is that it is deliberately so and its purpose is to distance the layperson and obfuscate; the other side of the critical argument is that legalese is the way it is because of what it is doing. Although we can say that the primary function of statutes and laws is to try to regulate human behaviour through communicative acts that place obligations and prohibitions on members of society (it also sometimes gives permissions), there are paradoxical (Flückiger 2008) and competing tensions in legal writing: vagueness and precision, ambiguity and clarity, flexibility and certainty, simplicity and inclusivity. Long sentences with subordination and embedding, for example, can be accounted for in terms of avoiding uncertainty and attempting to achieve all-inclusiveness (see Bhatia, this volume), but, in terms of speech (consider English's example (this volume) of a police officer speaking 'like a statute' to a non-native speaker: 'I require you to provide two specimens of breath for analysis by means of an approved device'), their primary purpose seems to be to exploit complexity.

But can we really use different arguments to explain the same phenomenon? Is not complexity always obfuscation? Perhaps not; complex prepositions are semantically more precise than simple ones and therefore avoid vagueness. They are found in legal speech as well as in writing, though probably not as densely, although as yet there is no systematic comparative study of their use (or many other lexical features) across both modes and in large corpora (but consider Finegan, this volume, on adverbs and adverbials in his COSCO corpus). Impersonal terms are vague, but inclusive and flexible in statutes and contracts and, as Trosborg (1997: 103) says, the impersonal and decontextualised third person point of view, created, for example, by the selection of the noun phrase 'any person' rather than use of the personal pronoun 'you', 'reduces the immediacy of the illocution, but adds to the generality of the message' and creates a necessary 'social distance between sender and receiver'. Rock (2007), in her discussion of revisions of the Notice to Detained Persons, supports this view in both reference to other research – Solomon

(1996: 289) found that simplification can create 'friendly' texts 'as if this kind of relationship can be assumed' – and with her ethnographic work. Some of her informants liked the informality of one of the revisions, but others felt 'that simplification can be overdone', saying:

> it comes across as being 'we're here to help'
> these guys shouldn't be friendly to me they should be scowling at me and saying 'you're a naughty boy aren't you' [Novice detainee 25]
>
> (Rock 2007: 70)

Flexibility of meaning and interpretation is also desirable when putting the law to its regulatory and punitive uses (but see Bhatia, this volume). By selecting a specialised legal word such as 'reasonable' legislators can, for example, give judges flexibility and discretion in dealing with offences. In the Criminal Justice and Immigration Act 2008 (OPSI 2008), for instance, there are 27 occurrences of the word 'reasonable'. One of these is: 'A person who without reasonable excuse fails to comply with a condition imposed under this section commits an offence' (133, 5). In this Act and others, 'reasonable' collocates with: 'action', 'belief', 'cause', 'enquiries', 'excuse', 'force', 'grounds', 'mistake', 'person', 'precautions' and 'steps'. Looking at the collocates of the word tells us more about the kinds of meanings entailed by 'reasonable', but not what it actually means. This kind of flexibility in drafting practice, according to Maley (1994: 28), 'contrast[s] with the other, and more typical, drafting devices ... those employing technical terms, repetition, single sentence sections with involved syntactic structures, which are intended to achieve certainty in the legal rule'. The regulatory voice of legal writing gains authority through its power to be flexible, while at the same time being precise.

Interaction in the legal process

We illustrate the nature and context of legal interaction with just three research themes that are important in any analysis of interaction in the legal process: asymmetry, audience and context. These issues interact, as we shall see.

Asymmetry

Asymmetry in dialogue is defined by Linell and Luckmann (1991: 4) in terms of 'inequivalences' rather than inequalities, since they say they 'prefer to use that term for various background ... conditions for dialogue, such as (differences in the distribution of) knowledge and social positions'. Asymmetry includes both global patterns of dominance and local properties such as 'the allocation of speaker versus listener roles'. According to Linell and Luckmann (1991: 9) asymmetries are multidimensional and can contain four types of dominance:

> *Quantitative* dominance concerns the relation between the parties in terms of amount of talk ... (words spoken).
>   *Interactional* dominance has to do with the distribution of 'strong' versus 'weak' interactional moves ... .

Semantic dominance [relates to who determines] topics sustained in the discourse, and impos[es] the interpretive perspectives on things talked about.

Strategic dominance involve[s who] contribut[es] the strategically most important interventions.

(Linell and Luckmann 1991: 9)

In thinking about asymmetries it helps to consider what symmetrical discourse is like in order to consider where the balance of roles is different. Symmetrical discourse presupposes conditions such as:

- *commonality* (or sharedness) of knowledge (etc.) between people;
- *mutuality* (of knowledge and assumptions) of common ground;
- *reciprocity* in the circumstances, so that in the co-presence of others, any act by one actor is an act with respect to the other and with the expectation that the other will do something in return.

(adapted from Linell and Luckmann 1991: 2–3)

These aspects vary in strength, moving the discourse from symmetrical to asymmetrical as the variables of commonality, mutuality and reciprocity are weakened by the global context of role, genre and situation (who? what? and where?).

Audience

Who is speaking and to whom is important in relation to the symmetrical/asymmetrical balance; Linell and Luckmann (1991: 9) talk of 'roles tied to professions' and the power such roles give to institutional speakers (e.g. police interviewers and prosecuting barristers), but even greater power is derived from their knowledge and orientation to the conduct and design of their talk for the future audience. Heritage (2003: 57), examining news interviews, says that 'skill in question design is at the heart of the interviewer's (IRs) craft' and questions 'can be primarily geared to the concerns and preoccupations of either the questioner, the answerer, the overhearing audience, or all three of these to varying degrees' (Heritage 2003: 61). Although he is writing about the television viewing audience, there are direct implications for looking at audience design in questions in legal interaction. Audiences for police interviews are future courtroom juries and judges, and records are made for that future audience: either in note form or as audio- or video-recordings. As in news interviews, 'the IR [interviewer] can manage questioning so that particular presuppositions are incorporated in the design of questions and at varying levels of embeddedness' and

the IR can manage questions so that particular audience expectations for the IE's response are mobilised: expectations that the IE may need to resist, and where such resistance may incur an additional burden of explanation than might otherwise be the case.

(Heritage 2003: 86)

But the difference for us with our legal focus is that the IE in a police interview is much less aware of the future co-present audience than is the television IE. This adds to the asymmetrical power of the police interviewer and the dominance of the legal context.

Context

Asymmetries are contextualised in the 'endogenous and exogenous conditions' of talk (Linell and Luckmann 1991: 10), that is in ever widening circles, first within the dialogue, then outside the talk itself in the institutional context and then further out in the wider social context (see Fairclough 1989). Thus, meaning works at multiple levels in the micro-detail of sound, semantics, syntax and non-linguistic semiotics (gesture and gaze) and in the macro-systems of activity type (Levinson 1992), identity and institutionality. Finegan has shown us, in his chapter, the polysemantic nature of adverbs and he demonstrates how an empirical micro-analysis combined with a corpus linguistic approach can uncover the rich semantic detail of attitudinal stance and emphasis that is below the level of notice for the judges who use them. Stygall, in her chapter, which focuses on Pension Plan documents and credit-card disclosures, shows the importance of the 'context of reception', not just of the 'context of production' (Fairclough 1989). She shows that text producers fail to take account of the literacy levels of citizens, lay readers who need to process these highly complex hybrid legal/financial documents.

Lay individuals are always disadvantaged in institutional contexts because they lack an institutional perspective and lack knowledge of the hybrid institutional registers they encounter, as Linell and Jönsson (1991: 96) also point out: lay interviewees are seen to have a personal perspective with regard to their own stories and this generally conflicts with the more 'anonymizing case-type' institutional perspective. The pragmatic resources that are mobilised by institutional speakers mean that blame is assigned in 'institutionalised communicative acts' (Linell, Alemyr and Jönsson 1993), which assume collaboration with the communicative project of interviews or cross-examination: the admission of responsibility. Therefore, as Scollon and Scollon (2003: 1) point out, one of the jobs of discourse analysis in the twenty-first century is to explain meanings made 'in place', what they term *geosemiotics*: 'the study of the social meanings of the material placement of signs and discourses and of our actions in the material world' (Scollon and Scollon 2003: 2). In such a view of meaning-in-context, the abstract meanings made by text producers only gain meaning when we act on them in our daily lives and there may be a semantic gap between one and the other, which it is incumbent on us to explain.

The work of the forensic linguist as expert

Linguistics has a long tradition of describing written and spoken texts and so the description of legal texts and of interactions in a legal context, as exemplified, for example, in Mellinkoff (1963), Solan (1993), Tiersma (1999) and Heffer (2005), could quite easily be regarded as a sub-branch of descriptive linguistics. So, what essentially distinguishes forensic linguistics as a separate sub-discipline is its engagement with the socio-legal consequences of the written and spoken texts it describes. Since the early days when, with the exception of Svartvik (1968), most experts were working in the US – Dumas (1990), Levi (1993), Prince (1984) and Shuy (1993b), for example – this engagement has been almost exclusively reactive, with linguists acting occasionally as expert witnesses, when invited to do so. The range of topics covered and the number of different methodologies used are now enormous – see many of the chapters in section II of this *Handbook*, as well as Coulthard and Johnson (2007), particularly chapter 6 for examples – and linguists have now had a major effect on the outcome of a large number of trials (see Coulthard, this volume).

More recently, we have seen linguists becoming pro-active and setting out, where they feel it is necessary to do so, to change and improve what they have described. Drawing on Caldas-Coulthard, who observed that

> discourse is a major instrument of power and control and Critical Discourse Analysts … feel that it is part of their professional role to investigate, reveal and clarify how power and discriminatory value are inscribed in and mediated through the linguistic system. Critical discourse analysis is essentially political in intent with its practitioners acting on the world in order to transform it.
>
> (Caldas-Coulthard and Coulthard 1996: xi)

We can see them as contributing to a new sub-discipline of Critical Forensic Linguistics (CFL). Examples of CFL in the *Handbook* are (amongst others) the work of Tiersma in improving the comprehensibility of the California Pattern Jury Instructions; the work of Eades, along with fellow linguists, to provide guidelines for the categorisation of asylum seekers by means of language tests (see the website accompanying the *Handbook* for this document); and the work of Haworth towards increasing the efficiency and effectiveness of investigative interviewing and provision of professional development for police officers by the Aston Centre for Forensic Linguistics. Readers will recognise critical and evaluative stances taken in other chapters too, and, like critical linguists, we see part of our role as clarifying and revealing power and discriminatory values in texts through an analysis of micro- and macro-linguistic features.

Concluding observation

We are delighted to have been able to assemble such an exciting collection of contributions which cover all the significant areas of forensic linguistics. Whatever your interests, we are sure that you will find things to inform and inspire you in this *Handbook*. We ourselves have learned a great deal in putting the collection together. Each chapter ends with suggestions for further reading, in case you want to pursue a particular topic in greater depth and there is a wealth of further reading to explore in the very wide scholarship referred to by contributors and contained in the references. Forensic linguistics has not just come of age; we believe this *Handbook* will launch the next generation of researchers into an exciting new world.

There is a website that accompanies this *Handbook*, which can be found on Aston University's website for the Centre for Forensic Linguistics at: http://www.forensiclingu istics.net/

There are documents and powerpoint shows to support chapters by the following authors: Eades (Chapter 27), Jessen (Chapter 25), Kredens and Morris (Chapter 30), Matoesian (Chapter 35), Tkačuková (Chapter 22) and Woolls (Chapter 37).

Section I

The language of the law and the legal process

1.1
Legal language

2

Legal talk

Socio-pragmatic aspects of legal talk: police interviews and trial discourse

Elizabeth Holt and Alison Johnson

Introduction

Probably the most distinctive and most widespread linguistic feature of legal talk is the question – in both interrogative and declarative form and across a range of forensic settings: emergency calls to the police (Drew and Walker, this volume), police interviews (Aldridge; Benneworth; Haworth; this volume), lawyer and client interactions (Kozin 2008) and examination and cross-examination in court (Ehrlich; Felton Rosulek; Heffer; this volume). Lay interactants are largely controlled by and at the mercy of questions from professionals in dyadic legal encounters: a caller to a 999 or 911 number; an interviewee in a police interview; a witness in a trial. Any examination of legal talk must therefore involve an analysis of what is accomplished interactionally through the use of questions, including accounting for the effects of forensic questioning on the lay interactant.

Syntactic and formal features of questioning are important aspects of any linguistic analysis. However, our focus in this chapter is not merely on form, but on the pragmatic effects of legal talk in two important interactional contexts: police interviews and criminal trials. Pragmatic, social and inferential meaning-making is significant for both the institutional and the lay speaker, and what is done through questions and answers is particularly clear in cross-examination, as our first example (1) from Brennan (1994) illustrates. This syntactically complex cross-examination question is directed to a child; embedded clauses are shown by the use of square brackets (our addition).

(1) A cross-examination question to a 15-year-old
Q: Would it be incorrect [to suggest [that it was not so much a tripping] [but [because of the state of inebriation of yourself], that you fell over]]?
(Brennan 1994: 216)

Brennan (1994: 212–16) outlines a whole range of linguistic features of cross-examination questions, including: use of negative; juxtaposition of topics that are not overtly related;

nominalisations; multifaceted questions; unclear questions; embedding and much more. Several of these features are demonstrated in extract (1). It contains a negative: 'would it be incorrect to suggest', rather than positive polarity, which adds to the complexity created by the embedding. It employs the dummy 'it', the subjunctive, and a non-finite verb, rather than the more direct subject pronoun and finite verb form: 'I suggest' and these distance the speaker from the accusation contained in the non-finite subordinate clause 'to suggest'. The negative polarity of the question 'would it be incorrect?' makes it more difficult to deny, because denial would have to be in the affirmative ('yes') and denial is more congruent with 'no' than 'yes'. And it contains nominalisation ('a tripping') which is also negated: 'not so much a tripping'. The double negation provided by the negative question and then the negated noun makes denial even more difficult by making an implied comparison. The questioner uses 'not so much a tripping but you fell over', where the pattern, not so much X but more Y, is upgraded by changing the noun to a verb: 'a tripping' and then 'you fell over'. 'You fell over' is absolute, by contrast with the nominalisation of 'a tripping', and the indefinite article 'a' is replaced by the accusatory 'you'. But, as Brennan notes, the complexity and power of cross-examination questions is not in their syntax alone. It is their pragmatic force that makes them powerful. Complex syntax does mean that the listener has to work extremely hard to answer, but these linguistically tactical questions draw their effect from the fact that the talk is designed to 'make a witness acquiescent' and make material significant for the hearer (a jury) in terms of 'display[ing] evidence' (Brennan 1994: 209–10).

The arrangement and sequencing of clauses produces a powerful effect too, performing what Winter (1994) calls a denial–correction sequence. This does the work of denying the prosecution version of the facts (the witness tripped) and substitutes a more powerful defence version (the witness fell over while drunk).

DENIAL	CORRECTION
it was not so much a tripping	BUT ... that you fell over

And, through the complex syntax, juxtaposition of clauses and embedding, all of the following meanings are possible:

> I suggest: because you were drunk you didn't trip but you fell over.
> you fell over rather than tripping (as you say) and you did that because you were drunk and out of control.
> you are an out-of-control reckless youth.

What the defence does in suggesting that the witness is a reckless drinker is to place him in a particular social category for the jury. As Levinson (1992: 72) says, the 'activity' of cross-examination has

> a corresponding set of inferential schemata [and] these schemata are tied to (derived from, if one likes) the structural properties of the activity in question. ... [Furthermore, in] activities where questions have a focal role [such as cross-examination, they function] to extract from the witness answers that build up to form a 'natural' argument for the jury.
>
> (Levinson 1992: 80 and 84)

Our analysis of the question in (1) shows how the jury is led to construct an argument that is derived from the schema of the anti-social problem-drinker youth. This sort of person is much less credible as a witness, adding to the 'credibility gap' which has already been 'partially created by a language mismatch between the lawyer and the child witness' (Brennan 1994: 216). Brennan (1994: 216) describes this kind of pragmatic work as 'abusing again' the child, by (ab)using the goals of cross-examination: to undermine the prosecution case and prioritise a defence view of the facts for the jury.

Rather than simply seeing language as an abstract grammatical system, then, a socio-pragmatic view of language is concerned with users of language and the uses to which they put it (Mey 2001: 29). Socio-pragmatic aspects of legal interaction form a rich area of study and much is yet to be empirically explored. Here we focus on a small range of interactional patterns and devices that are used in the construction of questions, including formulations, repeats of prior testimony, reported speech and evaluative contrasts.

Legal language

'Talking like a lawyer' (Tiersma 1999: 51) involves using legalese as a professional code, but, as Tiersma (1999: 145) says, 'when lawyers are sufficiently motivated, they quickly abandon legalese' in courtrooms. In police interviews, too, officers move strategically between formal institutional modes of talk and more familiar ones, changing their footing as Johnson (2006) shows.

The language of written statutes and contracts and many other legal documents has been described in terms of its complexity (see Bhatia; Stygall; this volume), and legal talk is also remarkably complex in terms of syntax and structure (as we have seen). However, it is more remarkable for what it does; it has specialised institutional functions and pragmatic effects, or as Tiersma (1999: 145) says the courtroom gives us 'legal language in it most dramatic setting'. In our examination of legal talk, we explore the 'dramaturgical quality of DRS [direct reported speech]' and its uses in questions not simply 'to replay an interaction but also to enable the speaker to simultaneously convey his or her attitude towards the reported utterance' (Clift and Holt 2007: 7).

Legal talk – Questions in court trials and police interviews

Central to the nature of legal talk is the system of turn-taking that participants adopt. Thus, for example, fundamental to the character of court trials is that, at certain points during the proceedings, the judge and lawyers have long turns where no one else contributes (e.g. during opening and closing speeches and in summing up), whereas the examination of witnesses proceeds through a series of question and answer exchanges. Although there can be a considerable number of people present, there are rules concerning who can talk and when (Atkinson and Drew 1979). The same may be said of police interviews where there are rules that dictate that a police officer should begin and end the proceedings, and will invite the suspect to give his version of events and then ask a series of questions which the interviewee may or may not answer (Heydon 2005; Benneworth; Haworth; this volume). There are particular rules for any lawyer present and Stokoe and Edwards (this volume) deal with what is accomplished by these lawyer turns in police interviews.

Maley puts her finger on a central difference between legal writing and legal talk when she says:

> Despite popular belief about the esoteric nature of legal language, courtroom discourse may not be – except in specialised areas like tax or property law – technical at all. But the unique and to most newcomers most inaccessible aspect of what goes on in court lies in its discourse rules. The central business of the court, the examination of witnesses, is conducted in sequences of question and answer.
>
> (Maley 2000: 247)

The almost insurmountable challenge for lay interactants in spoken legal interaction is therefore to transcend the powerful institutional discourse rules and to recognise that courtroom or interview room talk is essentially fairly ordinary language being put to special use. Institutional participants are expert users, whereas the lay participants – suspects, witnesses (even expert witnesses) and defendants – are not and, since the key resource is the highly controlling institutional exploitation of the interrogative turn or question, institutional users are equipped to exploit the special pragmatic uses that language can be put to, making legal talk a potent source of institutional control.

In legal settings and other institutional settings (unlike ordinary conversation), turns are 'preallocated' (Greatbatch 1988). Not only is the pattern of who can contribute fixed in advance, the kind of activity they do in their turns is predetermined. Extract (2) is from a police interview from our data and we can see that the police interviewer's role is to question and manage the interaction and the interviewee's to respond, with little opportunity to alter the topic or ask questions.

```
(2)
 1  IR:  And then you mention this bloke. Do you just want to describe his
 2       actions to me? What-what happened?
 3  IE:  Well, he-he were stood at the bar for ages and he were like staring
 4       over and he kept like look-doing like dirty looks so, I thought oh
 5       I didn't think a lot of it-oh no that's w- and then he went-he sat down
 6       and I were looking and he were saying …
 7  IR:  So this is the same bloke who's been assaulted?
 8  IE:  Yeah
 9  IR:  Right so first of all you said that you saw him-you noticed stood
10       at the bar?
11  IE:  Yeah.
12  IR:  And he were looking over towards your group?
13  IE:  Yeah uh hah
14  IR:  Making comments about you?
15  IE:  Yeah.
16  IR:  And then he sat down?
17  IE:  He was-I think he were with a woman, maybe his wife I don't know,
18       and she were telling him to shut up.
```

Question and answer pairs, though central to talk in many institutional settings (such as news interviews, classroom talk, calls to call centres) have specific roles in police interviews and a number of distinctive features. For example in (2) we note that several of the questions begin with 'and' or 'so' (lines 1, 7, 9, 12 and 16) and we will consider the function of these questions in the next section.

Extract (2) demonstrates some of the different forms and purposes of questions. They may take the form of interrogatives, for example, *what*, *where* and *why* questions (e.g. 'what happened?' line 2); they may involve a statement plus a tag question (e.g. 'This was February the fourteenth wasn't it'); or a declarative which functions as a question, sometimes with questioning intonation (i.e. a rise at the end) (e.g. line 7, 9, 12, 14 and 16). Researchers exploring legal talk (and other institutional environments such as news interviews) have noticed patterns in the design of questions that are associated with particular actions in these environments: *and*- and *so*-prefaced questions (Johnson 2002), formulations (Heritage and Watson 1979; Heritage 1985) and reported speech (Philips 1986; Matoesian 2000; Galatolo 2007). These devices, recurrently employed in questions (and sometimes in other parts of trial discourse such as the use of reported speech in summing up), are often central to one of the main aims of legal discourse: to establish the culpability of one or more parties involved. They are also central to the asymmetry that exists between the participants in these environments (Heydon 2005; Drew 1992).

Gibbons (2003: 95) points out that questions in legal settings have two objectives: 1. eliciting information and 2. obtaining confirmation of a version of events that the questioner has in mind. Many of the devices considered in the subsequent sections appear to be mainly concerned with the latter objective.

And- and so-prefaced questions

Johnson (2002) investigated *so*-prefaced and *and*-prefaced questions in police interviews. She found that *so*-prefaced questions are used to construct evidential discourse and to evaluate and label (Francis 1994) previous utterances produced by the interviewee. Adults who are suspected of being involved in serious criminal offences are largely able, but unwilling, to produce an extensive account of something that may incriminate; for this reason *so*-prefaced questions perform a key role for interviewers. They allow them to repeat previous interviewee discourse, and in the process evaluate and label it, signalling its significance in the developing narrative and producing weighted evidence (lines 17 and 18 in extract (3)). In addition, we can see that these questions can be used by the interviewer to challenge IE to say more (lines 3–4) and to get the interviewee to reformulate an earlier position (lines 25–26).

(3) Interview with rape suspect

1 IR: What did he say?
2 IE: Nothing.
3 IR: So what <u>other</u> conversation was there about T [the rape complainant]
4   then?
5 IE: That was about it.
6 IR: What he-him suggesting that you and K had sex with her in her r-
7 IE: Mm.
8 IR: A- and with or with<u>out</u> her consent?
9 IE: No. <u>With</u> her consent.

. . .
10   IR:Did T tell you to go in there and uhh speak to her?
11   IE: Yeah
12   IR:And did K tell you to go in there and <u>shag</u> her? You're nodding your
13   head.
14   IE: Yes.
15   IR:And did D tell you to go in there and <u>shag</u> her as well?
16   IE: Yeah.
17   IR:So you were a bit under <u>pressure</u> really to go in there and – have <u>sex</u>
18   with her weren't you?
19   IE: Mm.

. . .
20   IR:-at that stage she was obviously saying to you she didn't <u>want</u> you to
21   have sex with her otherwise you wouldn't have said those words <u>would</u> you?
22   IE: No.
23   IR:D'you <u>see</u>? You're nodding your head.
24   IE: Yes.
25   IR:So is it fair to say then that <u>before</u> you had sex with her she was
26   <u>certainly</u> saying to you she didn't want to have sex with you?
27   IE: She says she don't know I think.
28   IR:You <u>think</u>?
29   IE: As far as I can re<u>member</u>.

So-prefaced questions therefore have an important function in evaluatory summary and are effective in challenging and transforming the interviewee's account, to such an extent that they may be forced to reformulate it in a way that is evidentially more significant (see also Johnson 2008a, 2008b; Kozin 2008; on transformation of ongoing discourse in legal processes). And, as we see in lines 25–26 in (3), indirect reported speech is also used within the *so*-prefaced question to summarise. (We return to reported speech later in the chapter.)

Also, countering the powerless asymmetry analysis in the literature, Johnson (2002) argues that these questions have a vital function in interviews with child witnesses. Here the goal for the interviewer is to elicit and represent evidence as fully as possible, using the child's words and as much relevant narrative as possible. Since children may be unwilling and/or unable to produce large stretches of spontaneous narrative, *so*- and *and*-prefaced questions have an important positive role. In this setting power is used supportively, since the questions construct, 'scaffold', support, arrange and rearrange the discourse into a narrative that empowers the child, though this depends on the skill of the interviewers. Aldridge (this volume) gives some examples of the difficulties and challenges faced by interviewers of young children and gives some instances of miscommunication and unproductive interviewing.

Johnson (2002) also notes that in interviews with child witnesses, *so*-prefaced questions have topic opening, developing and sequencing functions, though Heydon (2005: 141) notes their use as 'disjunctive topic shift' markers in interviews with adult suspects. In extract (4) from the first 60 interviewer turns from an interview with a child we see how *so*-prefacing marks topic development.

(4)   *So*-prefacing at the start of an interview with a child.

21 IR:Right so are D and G your brothers?
36 IR:Three. Right. So can you tell me who sleeps in what bedroom then?
52 IR:Ah. Right. So does he work away from home a lot?
53 IR:Oh. Right. So was he at your birthday?

The effect of *so* in questions with suspects also signals topic development, but is additionally used to signal the status of the talk and often marks challenges to the suspect in relation to the evidential value of the talk, as in extract (5) from an interview with a suspect.

(5) Challenging *so*

1 IR:And how many drinks did you have in the Indian restaurant?
2 IE: One.
3 IR:So are you saying that all evening you had four pints?
4 IE: Mm.

IE's responsibility to agree or disagree, is also signalled, with a preference for agreement, because part of the challenge is that they have said it. In extract (5) preferred agreement also seeks to get the IE to accept that his own account is not believed, through the evaluative 'all evening'. Together with *and*-prefaced questions (see also Heritage and Sorjonen 1994; Matsumoto 1999), they help to construct narrative sequence through interviewer turns. In this way, it is often the interviewer who tells the story, as we see in the brief sequence in extract (5).

And-prefaced questions are also very common in trial interaction to do storytelling, as we see in extract (6) from the trial of Harold Shipman (www.the-shipman-inquiry. org.uk).

(6) Examination of Shipman by defence barrister, Shipman Trial, Day 27

Q: By September 1997 you took up your position at the Donneybrook House practice. You were there with a number of other doctors?
A: I was.
Q: How many?
A: 6.
Q: And after one year in practise ?(sic) did you become a partner at that practice?
A: I did.

Coulthard and Johnson (2007: 102) found that of the first 19 questions put to Shipman by his friendly counsel 15 required only confirmation and *and*-prefaced questions accounted for 6 of these (including the one in extract (6)), allowing the lawyer to animate the witness's story and develop an extended narrative on behalf of the witness with only minimal responses and interruptions from him. This enables co-production of authoritative evidence with minimum effort.

Formulations

Garfinkel and Sacks observed that participants in interaction may sometimes *formulate* what it is they are saying:

A member may treat some part of the conversation as an occasion to describe that conversation, to explain it, or characterize it, or explicate, or translate, or summarize, or furnish the gist of it, or take note of its accordance with the rules, or remark on its departure from the rules. That is to say, a member may use some part of the conversation as an occasion to *formulate* the conversation.

(Garfinkel and Sacks 1970: 350)

Heritage and Watson noticed that formulations are a recurrent feature of questions in news interviews. They focused on a subclass of formulations, where they 'characterize states of affairs already described or negotiated … in the preceding talk' (Heritage and Watson 1979: 126). Heritage and Watson describe formulations as manifesting three central properties:

(1) the preservation of some (selected) aspects of the sense and reference of the news materials delivered in the content of the formulating utterance
(2) the transformation of the syntactic and semantic framework within which the news was originally delivered
(3) the deletion of some aspect or aspects of the news delivered.

(Heritage and Watson 1977: 2–3)

Extract (7) is from their collection:

(7)
    IE: The inescapable facts are these, er in nineteen thirty two when he was er aged twenty three mister Harvey was er committed to Rampton hospital under something called the mental deficiency act nineteen thirteen which of course is a statute that was swept away years ago and er he was committed as far as I can er find out on an order by a single magistrate er sitting I think in private.
    IR:How long did he spend in Rampton
    IE: Well he was in er Rampton and Mosside hospitals er alternatively Er until nineteen sixty one
 → IR:That's the best part of thirty years
    IE: That's right. Now in nineteen sixty one …

(Heritage and Watson 1979: 130)

In the (arrowed) formulation the interviewer *preserves* some information, the length of time spent in hospital, *deletes* other information, such as the hospitals; and *transforms* the information, by, for example, referring to the number of years spent there rather than the numerical names of the years (Heritage and Watson 1979: 130; see also Heritage and Watson 1980).

According to Drew (2003) formulations are a generic device in interaction, but the forms they take are associated with the activities managed through formulating in specific settings, and formulations have different interactional functions in different settings. He focuses on those formulations

in which a speaker offers his or her interpretation of what the other meant – an activity which generally takes the form *(So) what you mean/are saying is …* , or something resembling that.

(Drew 2003: 296)

Heydon (2005) considers formulations in police interviews. Extract (8) is from her collection and concerns, in part, alleged criminal damage to the door of a shop.

(8)

IR: uh you <u>saw</u> the glass shatter to the ground

IE: (0.4) I jest kept <u>walking</u>↓

(0.2) I just got in the <u>car</u> =

And <u>Rob</u> (0.6) me <u>friend</u> said what the hell's going <u>on</u>

(0.4) whaddcha <u>do</u>

→ IR: (1.2) so you didn't bother <u>saying</u> anything to them↓

→   that the <u>glass</u> was <u>broken</u> or↓

(Heydon 2005: 123, Extract 4–26 INT1)

IR formulates IE's turns about walking to the car as suggesting that he 'didn't bother <u>saying</u> anything to them↓' (Heydon 2005: 137). According to Heydon, formulations are a powerful tool in constructing the police version of events because they appear to be a summary, for the sake of achieving understanding, of prior talk. But, in instances analysed by Heydon, changes made to the suspect's version 'systematically introduce terms of violence and intentionality that were not present in the original utterances' (Heydon 2005: 141). Komter (1998, 2003, 2006) also examined formulations in police interviews and found that they are an important resource in stating 'the record-thus-far' (Komter 2006: 201).

Holt and Johnson (2006) analysed a device similar to formulations in police interview data. 'Repeating questions' were found to have a similarly formulating function, but in these questions, police interviewers specifically attempt to preserve the interviewee's words or phrases sometimes through the use of reported speech. Direct repetition of IE's previous words does the work of drawing attention to a prosecution point for the record, but these repetitions are arguably even more powerful ways of recording prosecution arguments for future audiences than formulations which change the words of the suspect.

Repeating questions

Extract (9) is a repeating question from a police interview involving an assault charge.

(9)
```
1    IR: How-I mean what did th-what impression did he give, what was
2        he going to do with the stool?
3    IE: He were going to hit him he had it above his head and he were like
4        going for him.
5    IR: What did your brother do?
6    IE: He like he'd stopped and were going to grab it going up like that
7        but I had already hit him so he fell down before he had a chance
8        to hit him.
9  → IR: So you thought that he were going to hit your brother with a stool?
10   IE: Yeah
```

The question in line 9 repeats elements of the suspect's story mentioned earlier in the interview. In lines 3 and 4, IE has already said, in answer to the preceding question, that he believed the victim was going to hit his brother with a stool. In line 5, IR asks a related question about the suspect's brother's actions. Then in line 9, IR does a repeat of IE's earlier answer: he repeats 'he were going to hit' (him/your brother) and adds 'you thought', transforming it, not in the words attributed to IE, but in the comment clause which adds the interviewer's viewpoint.

Holt and Johnson (2006) note four recurrent features of the design of these questions: 1. they are often *so*-prefaced; 2. grammatically they are not built as questions; 3. they repeat elements of the interviewee's testimony, often bringing several elements together; 4. they invite confirmation. Extract (10) illustrates all these features.

(10)
1	IE:	Now then, what did he say? I've g-he said I've come to talk
2		to you I said you want to go talk to the police not bloody me.
3		((cough)) And he swung at me. I pushed him back with my foot
4		he had hold of me foot and my slipper came off with him and I got
5		the kettle which I had on a shelf at the side with acid in and I tossed
6		it on him but unfortunately as he was coming towards me I brought
7		the kettle back and got the bloody acid on myself.
8	IR:	Right

...

23	→ IR:	Right. Just bringing it back to tonight though [First Name] erm so
24	→	he came to your house and you say he took a swing at you?
25	IE:	He took a swing at me

The repeating question in lines 23 and 24 begins with 'so'; it is not built as an interrogative; it repeats elements of the interviewee's testimony – that the person in question came to his house (referred to earlier in the interview) and that he 'swung' at him; and it invites confirmation by the interviewee which it gets in the form of a repeat of the last part. These questions often, but not always, have a 'you say' or other reporting clause, emphasising the repetition of IE's own prior talk.

Holt and Johnson (2006) also found that these repeating questions play an important role in the overall organisation of the interview. They can be used as summaries by linking back across prior turns to bring together several matters mentioned previously (as in extract (10)). In so doing they can initiate a series of questions or bring a section of the interview to a close. An initial *so*-prefaced question can begin a series of *and*-prefaced questions or end a series of *and*-prefaced questions that all serve to confirm aspects of the interviewee's testimony (as in extract (3) lines 10–19 above). Thus, they are part of a freeze-frame effect in the interview where the IE's narrative is frozen and, in that moment of productive paralysis, it is examined by IR, reformulated and then the narrative is restarted. These are moments where evidence is examined and created or 'fixed' for the record (see also Kozin 2008: 221, 226, 235, 236 for 'fixing' of items in talk-to-talk transformations). Kozin (2008) discusses the dangers associated with such fixing, as it settles facts that may not be settled and this has consequences as the facts travel across the legal process, taking on further significance.

The reporting of speech

There are two main ways of reporting speech: directly (sentence (a)) and indirectly (b).

(a) Direct reporting: I said, 'I'd really love to come for dinner, and I was really looking forward to it, but I'm too busy'.

(b) Indirect reporting: I explained that I was just far too busy to go round to eat.

As Toolan (2001: 124) points out, neither is a verbatim report, but 'direct speech pretends to be a faithful verbatim report of a person's actual words'. However in indirect speech, the speech of the reported speaker is not simply reproduced, but 'instead, the narrator's words and deictic orientation' are foregrounded as the reported speech becomes subordinate to the main reporting clause (Toolan 2001: 124). So, if we compare sentence (a) with sentence (b), we can see that in (b) the speech is summarised and summary brings with it the capacity for the speech to be 'fairly remote from [its] hypothesized speech source' (Toolan 2001: 124). An even more remotely reported version is shown in (c).

(c) I politely excused myself from dinner on account of my hectic schedule.

In (c) the reporting verb 'excused' transforms the act of saying or explaining something into a speech act of excusing and the adverb 'politely' represents the manner of the excuse. The noun phrase 'my hectic schedule' tells the listener more than the direct speech 'I'm far too busy' and indirect speech therefore has the power to do pragmatic and inferential work. In legal contexts of evidence giving, it is important for witnesses to report as accurately as possible what was said, and 'the hearsay rule' means that witnesses may only report their own words or what they have direct knowledge of, that is they must have been present when someone said something, but clearly cross-examiners can question witnesses about the accuracy of their attempted report. The remote reporting of (c) would attract even more probing questioning to get closer to the actual words and, if a witness makes a report based on what someone else said they heard, that would be rejected as hearsay. Witnesses therefore have a legal need to report faithfully, but, as we have seen, police interviewers (extract (3) above) and lawyers use a range of direct, indirect and more remote ways of reporting what might have been said with different effects. In the interview with an IE suspected of rape in extract (3) the interviewer uses a range of ways to get at what was said by the victim. In lines 21–22 (extract (3)) IR says:

IR:She was obviously saying to you she didn't want you to have sex with her.

This turn uses the summarising power of indirect reported speech (IRS) to persuade the suspect to accept a version of events, and in another exchange between IR and IE we see that IE uses direct reported speech (DRS) to counter the IRS of IR:

IR:She says that she definitely said no. (Pause) She did say no didn't she at that stage?
IE: She said, 'I don't know'.

So far we have been focusing on systematic patterns identified within questioning turns in court trials and police interviews, but reported speech occurs in both questions and answers during legal talk, as we have just seen, and in monologue (see Felton Rosulek, this volume, for an analysis of its use in trials in closing speeches). One of the central features of reported speech is its evidential function: that is, not only does it purport to portray words (and also thoughts) that occurred previously, but in reproducing them, evidence (both in the lay and legal sense) of their occurrence is simultaneously provided. In this respect, DRS, where the speaker claims to offer a verbatim rendition, is seen as more powerful as witness evidence than IRS (though police officers and lawyers can do powerful things with IRS). Philips (1986, 1992) conducted an analysis of American courtroom trials and found that lawyers exploited the fact that DRS is seen as more reliable than IRS. Further, in court trials lawyers and judges can elect to have sections of police interviews 'reproduced' by playing recordings, distributing transcripts, or even having sections enacted for the benefit of the jury. Matoesian, in an analysis of the Kennedy Smith rape trial analysed a sequence where the defense attorney plays a section of the recording of a police interview of the witness during cross-examination. He showed how, although the

> tape appears to speak for itself and although its meaning appears transparent, it only obtains such a quality because the defense attorney possesses the power to con-textualize it, instruct the jury of its significance, and suggest how it should be interpreted and evaluated.
>
> (Matoesian 2000: 897)

Galatolo (2007) found that witnesses in an Italian court trial recurrently made use of reported speech in their answers. She found that answers often consisted of two parts: a direct answer to the question (e.g. 'yes' or 'no') followed by an expansion. Reported speech recurrently occurs in the expansion. Extract (11) is from her collection (here we have only reproduced the English translation of the talk). The trial concerned the murder of a university student who was shot as she walked through the campus. Two students from the Philosophy and Law department were charged. However, the role of the director of the department, Professor Romano, was also questioned. The witness in the extract was a researcher in the department and she is under direct and therefore friendly examination.

(11)
```
     PM: excuse me but did it happen often that Professor Romano in the evening
            called you at home to ask [how you were↑
     L:                              [it had never-
          (.) it had never happened.hhh e: hm he said (2.0) pt.h did you see
          anything (0.5) or hear anything↑
                         (Galatolo 2007: 204, Extract 3) (PM: Prosecutor, L: witness)
```

In the denial 'it never happened' the witness rejects both the prosecutor's 'did it happen' and what is inferred in IRS 'how you were', that is: 'Was your professor in the habit of ringing you up to pass the time of day?'. This is followed by an expansion that corrects the prosecutor, giving an 'animation' of the other person's words (Galatolo 2007: 204) in DRS. We can see that DRS is a useful device whereby witnesses can try to show that they have first-hand knowledge of events by quoting words, phrases or entire conversations and this gives witnesses credibility, as their 'ability to recall the exact proffered words is generally interpreted as being evidence of having directly and effectively heard those words [and this] is commonly associated with having had a direct experience with those events' (Galatolo 2007: 207). In direct examination, there-fore, correcting the lawyer by replacing IRS with DRS, produces positive effects, as the witness is able to give evidence of what she presents as verbatim memory and experience. However, at the same time, if this were done in cross-examination, the effect would be different, since disagreement in cross-examination is risky as it can negatively affect the jury's opinion of the witness. We deal with this below in terms of contrast.

Galatolo also found that reported speech can be used to convey moral judgments implicitly. Her example is shown in (12) when another witness is examined.

(12)

> PM: e:h later when you the next morning (.) went with your
> daughter to speak with Professor Romano (.) was this decision
> to go-to accompany-(.) your daughter-was it your decision
> or was it your daughter tha: [t
> NL: [NO NO my daughter told me
> that she didn't want to go she used this expression
> because I don't trust him.
>   (Galatolo, 2007: 215, Extract 8) (PM: Prosecutor, NL: witness)

Galatolo draws our attention to the technical form of the reporting expression 'she used this expression' rather than the plainer reporting form 'she said', which 'emphasises the claim of just reproducing what was said, limiting itself to the level of the linguistic (re) production, without any claim about what was meant' (Galatolo 2007: 216). Emphasis is also added through the use of the proximal deictic 'this' making the DRS immediate and present in the courtroom. And then we have the evaluation in the DRS: 'because I don't trust him'. The implicit nature of the moral evaluation of the Professor by the father, as well as the daughter, 'encourages the jury to treat those ele-ments as indirectly proving that Romano's behaviour was effectively blameworthy' (Galatolo 2007: 216). We see then, as Galatolo (2007: 219) points out, that implicit moral work can be accomplished through the use of reported speech, particularly the apportioning of blame. The shift from IRS to DRS between question and answer, in (11) also does pragmatic work in terms of increasing the authenticity of the evidence, and, as Clift and Holt (2007: 8) point out, shifts of footing from IRS and non-reported speech into DRS are worthy of greater study (see also Holt 2009). In our brief look at reported speech, we have seen that there are three central areas of focus, as Clift and Holt (2007: 3) observe: 'form' (whether it is IRS or DRS), 'authenticity' (plausible, probable and improbable quotations) and 'what is done' (blame allocation, moral evaluation, etc.).

Contrasting versions in cross-examination

Pragmatic work is also done across questions and answers through drawing contrasts, as we saw in the contrast in (11) between 'often' and 'never' and IRS and DRS. This works well for friendly examination, but for witnesses in cross-examination there are risks to this kind of work. In a study of cross-examination in a rape trial, Drew (1992) explored both features of witnesses' answers and lawyers' questions. He notes that, when disputing a version of events proposed in the attorney's questions, witnesses can use contrast to avoid overt correction preceded by 'No'. By offering an alternative version, they mitigate the risks associated with disagreement. Extracts (13) and (14) are from Drew (1992).

(13)
A: An' you went to a: uh (0.9) ah you went to a ba:r? in ((city))
   (0.6) is that correct?
   (1.0)
W: It's a clu:b.
                    (Drew 1992: 489, Extract 11) (A: Attorney, W: Witness)

(14)
A: An during that eve:ning (0.6) uh: didn't Mistuh ((name))
   Come over tuh sit with you
   (0.8)
W: Sat at our table.
                    (Drew 1992: 489, Extract 13)

In (13) and (14) the attorney's questions are designed to elicit 'yes'/'no' confirmatory answers, but the witness declines to answer in this way and instead offers descriptions that implicitly disconfirm his version by offering a contrasting version (i.e. describing it as a 'club' instead of a 'bar'; and saying he 'sat at our table' rather than sitting with her on her own). They do not intrinsically exclude hisversion but are 'qualified, guarded versions of what the attorney suggests' (Drew 1992: 490) and they reject the implied meanings in the questions concerning the start of a disputed encounter between victim and alleged rapist. Extract (15) is also from Drew's collection and in this we can see a contrast device that the attorney uses in response.

(15)
A: Well you kne:w at that ti:me that the defendant was. in:terested
   (.) in you (.) didn'n you?
   (1.3)
W: He: asked me how I'(d) bi:n en
   (1.1)
W: J-just stuff like that
A: Just asked yuh how (0.5) yud bi:n (0.3) but he kissed yuh
   goodnight. (0.5) izzat righ:t =
W: = Yeah = he asked me if he could?
                    (Drew 1992: 479, Extract 3 (fragment))

In answer to the attorney's question that she knew he was 'interested in her', the witness offers a contrasting version which suggests that the most that happened between them was that he asked her how she'd been, thus suggesting a much less intimate relationship than the version conveyed in his question. In response, the attorney brings together two pieces of evidence to which the witness has already attested, forming a contrast: the claimed non-intimacy of their greeting, and the intimacy of their parting, thus creating a puzzle. According to Drew,

The contrast works, then to challenge not her characterization of the greeting itself, but the credibility of that as an adequate representation of everything else that happened, of all the scene's other essential particulars and how they are to be glossed.

(Drew 1992: 509)

Drew points out that the preallocation of speaker roles and the types of turns they can take in court trials means that it is only the attorney who is able to put together 'facts' from the prior testimony in order to create a contrast that can be seen as damaging to the cross-examination witness's testimony. He points out that contrasts are summary devices and it is only the attorney who uses 'the power of summary'. Such summaries can end a line of questioning, thus leaving the jury to draw out the implicit, damaging implications alluded to in the question.

Conclusion

Reporting, contrasting, formulating and repeating are at the heart of the process of formulating the facts of the legal story in trials and police interviews. Their use produces important fact-making moments that distil and encode a version of reality, which play an important part in the legal case: an authorised-authoritative version. Repeating questions, reported speech and other formulating devices are part of the 'local accomplishment' of police authority in the interview; it is in these moments that interviewers exert their institutional authority to 'say what is being said' for confirmation by the interviewee, thereby 'fixing' the talk and transferring it from the private to the public, institutional plane of discourse. Reported speech is used in interviews and trial accounts to produce authoritative evidence and to do moral evaluation while contrast is used by cross-examiners to put together contradictory versions that produce damaging accounts and, as Buttny and Cohen (2007) show, 'drawing on the words of others' is a way of creating powerful evidence. All of these devices in some way use repetition or imply summary and the power of summary is one of the most important pragmatic devices used by institutional participants in legal talk. It settles on certain facts and makes the ongoing talk evidentially relevant (see Haworth, this volume for more on evidence).

In the space available here, we can do little more than draw together some observations on research we and others have carried out. There remains much to be said about the use, distribution and significance of reporting forms. Saying what has been and is being said in prior texts, in present texts and across texts and contexts is key work done by institutional speakers across the judicial process and is a central part of evidence construction. Talk about talk – metatalk and metadiscursivity – is at the heart of processes of legitimating and rejecting evidence in the many contexts where the police officers, lawyers and judges formulate the facts of legal stories.

Further reading

Drew, P. (2003) 'Comparative analysis of talk-in-interaction in different institutional settings: a sketch, in P.J. Glenn, C.D. leBaron, J. Mandelbaum and R. Hopper (eds) *Studies on Language in Social Interaction*, Mahwah, NJ: Lawrence Erlbaum Associates, 293–308.

Galatolo, R. (2007) 'Active voicing in court', in E. Holt and R. Clift (eds) *Reporting Talk: Reported Speech in Interaction. Studies in Sociolinguistics 24*, Cambridge: Cambridge University Press, 195–220.

Holt, E. (2009) 'Reported speech', in S. D'Hondt, J.O. Östman and J. Verschueren (eds) *The Pragmatics of Interaction: Handbook of Pragmatics Highlights 4*, Amsterdam: John Benjamins, 190–205.

Johnson, A.J. (2008) '"From where we're sat … ": Negotiating narrative transformation through interaction in police interviews with suspects', Special issue of *Text & Talk*, 28(3): 327–49.

Matoesian, G. (2000) 'Intertextual authority in reported speech: Production media in the Kennedy Smith rape trial', *Journal of Pragmatics*, 32, 879–914.

Tannen, D. (2007) *Talking Voices: Repetition, Dialogue and Imagery in Conversational Discourse. Studies in Interactional Sociolinguistics 6* (2nd edition), Cambridge: Cambridge University Press.

3

Legal writing: specificity

Specification in legislative writing: accessibility, transparency, power and control[1]

Vijay K. Bhatia

Introduction

Legal discourse is different from most other professional discourses, in that the nature of its interpretation process, whether spoken or written, is very much dependant on the context in which it is likely to be applicable. In most professional and disciplinary contexts interpretation of discourse is largely hearer- or reader-based, in that there is some freedom for variable interpretation, of course, with some relevance to the context in which it has been used, but interpretation of legal discourse is most often based on its relevance and hence application to critical moments in specific 'sites of engagement' (Scollon 1998), and is often irrespective of the participants involved, and every effort is made to ensure consistency of interpretation. It is particularly so in the case of legislative writing, which is drafted to correct a specific social 'mischief' and hence invariably interpreted in the context of relevant descriptions of such instances of 'mischief', often treated as the material facts of the case to which a specific legislative statement is applied. Seidman, Seidman and Abeyesekere point out that the 'mischief rule' holds that

> in construing a statute, a court should first examine the social problem at which the statute aims (the 'mischief'), determine the means that the statute ordains to address that mischief, and then construe the statute to further those objectives … Of all the general principles of interpretation, the mischief rule seems best adapted to ensuring that courts construe statutes to carry out the legislative purpose.
>
> (Seidman *et al.* 2001: 293)

In a court of law, particularly in an adversarial system of justice, maximum effort is made to establish the material facts of the case and this is invariably done in the light of the applicable law, including the precedents established through relevant earlier judgements. It is therefore crucial for the negotiation of justice that precedents as well as legislative statements are clearly, precisely, unambiguously and adequately specified (Bhatia 1982, 1983, 1993).

Clarity, precision, unambiguity and inclusiveness

Legislative rules, as far as possible, should have clarity of expression, in that the legislative intentions are clearly textualised without any vagueness. Vague expressions, though not very uncommon in this writing, are often strategically used for specific reasons, some of which, we will take up later in the chapter. One important resource for clarity is the use of terminological explanation, as indicated in example (1) from the UNCITRAL Model Law Article 2:

(1)
For the purposes of this Law:

>   (a) 'arbitration' means any arbitration whether or not administered by a permanent arbitral institution;
>   (b) 'arbitral tribunal' means a sole arbitrator or a panel of arbitrators;
>   (c) 'court' means a body or organ of the judicial system of a State.

>   (Gotti 2005)

Another device used for clarity is complex-prepositional phrases, such as *in accordance with* or *in pursuance of*, instead of simple prepositions.

The second quality of this genre is precision, which requires the use of as few words as possible, which is often achieved through the use of nominalised expressions (e.g. *No will shall be revoked by any presumption of an intention on the grounds of an alteration in circumstances, s.14 of the Wills Act, Republic of Singapore* (Quoted in Bhatia 1993: 107)) to make sentences shorter and keep clause proliferations under control.

The third desirable characteristic of legislative sentences is unambiguity, which means certainty of legal interpretation and application, which is often achieved by inserting relevant qualifications at specific syntactic positions, as in example (2) from s.1 of the Housing Act, 1980, UK:

(2)
A secure tenant has the right—

>   (a) If the dwelling-house is a house, to acquire the freehold of the dwelling-house;
>   (b) If the dwelling-house is a flat, to be granted a long lease of the dwelling-house.

>   (quoted in Bhatia 1993: 112)

The final and perhaps the most controversial characteristic is what I have called 'all-inclusiveness', which deals with adequacy of specification of legal scope. This requirement of adequate specification further leads to the identification of other important issues of accessibility (comprehensibility and interpretability) and transparency, which have important implications for the interpretation of legal discourse. In this chapter, I would like to argue that whereas over-specification in legislative expression creates problems of comprehension, especially for the uninitiated readership, under-specification, on the other hand, creates an even more serious issue of transparency in the construction and interpretation of legislative intent. Specification of scope in legislative statements also has interesting implications for power and control in different socio-political and legal systems. However, before I take up the issue of specification, I would like to discuss, though briefly, the related notion of ambiguity, which is crucial for this chapter.

Ambiguity

Ambiguity is an inherent property of language; it may stem from a text-internal linguistic source, e.g. lack of semantic clarity in the use of a particular lexico-grammatical feature, or from a text-external resource, such as features of context in which the discourse is interpreted or to which it is considered applicable. This is particularly so in the case of legislative discourse, where interpretation is almost entirely dependent on the context in which it is interpreted and to which it is applied. Ambiguity resulting from text-internal factors can be viewed as vagueness and indeterminacy, which have considerable overlap. Without making any detailed attempt in this chapter to identify and differentiate these notions, I would like to suggest that both of the terms have potential for the negotiation of meaning based on the use of a word or expression in a legislative provision, and hence have been effectively and somewhat creatively used by legal draftsmen in legislative discourse. Engberg and Heller (2008) illustrate vagueness resulting from text-internal use of a particular lexico-grammatical feature in example (3) from the Arbitration Act of England 1996.

(3)
If without showing *sufficient* cause a party fails to comply with any order or directions of the tribunal, the tribunal may make a peremptory order to the same effect, prescribing such time for compliance with it as the tribunal considers appropriate.

> (Arbitration Act of England 1996, section 41, 5; emphasis added)

'This sentence', they claim,

> is inherently vague in that a reader, on the basis of the statute's wording, will be unable to decide or describe what amount of justification will be adequate in concrete cases. This difficulty is due to the use of the word *sufficient*. Being one of the key words in the sentence, it leaves it up to the recipient (here the tribunal) to decide whether in a concrete case the cause is sufficient or not; there is no single answer to be found, without knowledge about the case in question or subjective interpretation of the utterance through knowledge of previous uses of the expression.

> (Engberg and Heller 2008: 148)

Legislative discourse can also be ambiguous because of lack of specification or of clarification of semantic information in specific expressions, in which case we encounter vagueness, or it may be because of the unpredictability of the scope or the force of legislative expressions. If it stems from a linguistic source, it is often referred to as **vagueness** or **indeterminacy** (see Engberg and Heller 2008 for a detailed discussion of these aspects); however, when it stems from the fact that law is inherently contestable and hence ambiguous, as it is invariably interpreted in the context of specific descriptions of cases, which are almost impossible to predict, it will be viewed as **ambiguity** (Bhatia 1982, 1993; White 1982). One of the main advantages of vagueness and indeterminacy in language as well as ambiguity in legal interpretation is that all of them allow the legal draftsman to bring in often necessary elements of flexibility and discretion by using vagueness, and precision through the use of qualifications inserted at various points in the syntactic structure of legislative provisions (Bhatia 1982, 1993; Maley 1987, 1994; Channell 1994; Engberg and Heller 2008).

Legislative provisions describe legal action and the cases to which this legal action applies, which typically state what should be done under what circumstances. However, it is rare that such a proposition can be captured simply in terms of an 'if X, then Y' kind of syntactic structure; there are often additional qualifying or explanatory conditions imposed on the doing of such an action (Coode 1845; Crystal and Davy 1969; Bhatia 1982, 1993). There is always a possibility that ambiguity and vagueness will occur in all the three aspects of the legislative sentence (i.e. the legal subject as well as the legal provision), case description, or qualifications (Bhatia 1982) and make it difficult to interpret or execute a certain kind of legal action. Let me now turn to the main topic of this chapter, which is, the source of ambiguity that results from inadequate specification of legal scope in legislative discourse.

Specification of legal scope

As mentioned earlier, legislative expressions are required not only to be clear, precise and unambiguous, but all-inclusive too. Although it appears to be a contradiction in terms, a close analysis will reveal that a clever balance between the two is the essence of the craftsmanship of legislative intent. Before taking up a detailed illustration of this tension between precision and all-inclusiveness, I would like to give a brief contextual analysis of the constraints on legislative construction and interpretation. Draftsmen have always been conscious of the institutional conflicts involved in the specification of legislative intentions as well as the legislative authority, especially in parliamentary democracies. In parliamentary democracies, legislative authority is invested in the legislature as it represents the people who elect them, and they zealously guard this right (Renton 1975) and would not like to hand over this role either to the judiciary or the executive. This creates the possibility of a three-way institutional conflict.

The first dimension of this potential conflict is between the legislature (the parliamentary institution responsible for making socio-political and economic policies) and the executive (the government bureaucratic institution responsible for executing policies discussed and framed in the legislature) especially in parliamentary democracies. The essence of this conflict is the tension between political power that is invested in the legislature by virtue of the fact that they are elected by the people, and the bureaucratic privilege that is often available to the members of the government, who have a duty to implement the socio-political and economic policies of the government and who often believe that they have the privilege to interpret legislative intent in the context of the implementation of policies. Since members of the executive are not present in the legislature when government policies are discussed and formed, there is always a danger of conflict between the interpretations viewed as authoritative by the two institutional players.

The second dimension of this potential conflict is between the legislature and the judiciary. The basis for such a conflict stems from the question, 'Who has the ultimate power to give the most authoritative interpretation of legislative intent?' In parliamentary democracies, the courts at various levels seem to have wide-ranging freedom to authorise final interpretations of the legislative intent, but on the part of the legislature, one often finds maximum control over the way legislative intentions are expressed. A senior parliamentary counsel frames it nicely when he points out that no effort is spared 'to box the judge firmly into a corner' (Edward Caldwell, quoted in Bhatia 1982) from which he cannot escape.

> There's always the problem that at the end of the day there's a system of courts and judges who interpret what the draftsman has done. It is very difficult to box the judge firmly into a corner from which he cannot escape … given enough time and given enough length and complexity you can end up with precision but in practice there comes a point when you can't go on cramming detail after detail into a bin.
>
> (Reported in Bhatia 1982: 25)

The third dimension of this potential conflict, therefore, is often between the judiciary and the executive, which allows absolute freedom to interpret legislative intentions to the system of courts, and at the same time gives unlimited power to the legislature to give voice to peoples' socio-political rights and privileges, on the one hand, and obligations on the other.

Within and across these institutional conflicts, it is the job of the legal draftsman to guard against any possible misinterpretation or misapplication of legislative provisions not only by any of the institutional players, but also by other citizens in conflict who often are prone to extend their rights and privileges and shrink their obligations to unexpected limits. It is almost an impossible task to find an appropriate degree of balance by giving expression to legislative intentions in a way to minimise any chance of such misadventures. Another factor that makes their task even more difficult is that they also need to construct their legislative provisions in such a way as to avoid any potential conflict with any preceded or preceding legislation. Caldwell points out,

> Very rarely is a new legislative provision entirely free-standing … it is part of a jigsaw puzzle … in passing a new provision you are merely bringing one more piece and so you have to acknowledge that what you are about to do may affect some other bit of the massive statute book.
>
> (Quoted in Bhatia 1982)

To make matters more complex, these draftsmen are almost universally criticised for making their provisions inaccessible to ordinary citizens, often questioning their loyalty to their so-called 'real readers'. In fact, one may, with some justification perhaps, claim that legal discourse, especially in common law jurisdictions, is an instance of conspiracy theory, according to which legislative provisions are purposely written in a complex and convoluted manner, so as to keep ordinary readers out of accessible range and to perpetuate dependence on the specialist legal community. Danet (1980b) points out:

> Critics claim that the professions use language in ways that mystify the public or at least stultify critical thinking … Critics argue that the language of the professions is

both a symbol and a tool of power, creating dependence and ignorance on the part of the public. In Gusfield's view, it creates the illusion of authority.

(Danet 1980b: 452)

However, legal discourse written in civil law jurisdictions, which may appear to be simple and plain as compared with similar discourse in common law jurisdictions, presents a different kind of accessibility issue, which is the other side of the coin (Bhatia 2005).

It is necessary to recognise that civil and common law systems have developed from different sources. The civil law system relied almost entirely on legislation, whereas the common law system relies on legal precedents as well as legislation. Most of the European community nations and the People's Republic of China follow some version of the civil law system, whereas most of the countries of the Commonwealth, primarily because of historical reasons, have adopted the British common law system. Let me take two instances of legislative provisions from these two systems to illustrate the differences in drafting styles. First take example (4) from the People's Republic of China's Arbitration Law:

(4)

An arbitration agreement refers to an arbitration clause provided in the contract or other written agreements requesting arbitration concluded prior or subsequent to the occurrence of disputes.

An arbitration agreement shall have the following contents:

(1) an expressed intent to request arbitration;
(2) items for arbitration; and
(3) the choice of arbitration commission.

Compare this to a similar clause (5) from a Commonwealth jurisdiction, that is, India.

(5)

(1) In this Part, 'arbitration agreement' means an agreement by the parties to submit to arbitration all or certain disputes which have arisen or which may arise between them in respect of a defined legal relationship, whether contractual or not.
(2) An arbitration agreement may be in the form of an arbitration clause in a contract or in the form of a separate agreement.
(3) An arbitration agreement shall be in writing.
(4) An arbitration agreement is in writing if it is contained in–
a. a document signed by the parties;
b. an exchange of letters, telex, telegrams, or other means of telecommunication which provide a record of the agreement; or
c. an exchange of statements of claim and defence in which the existence of the agreement is alleged by one party and not denied by the other.
(5) The reference in a contract to a document containing an arbitration clause constitutes an arbitration agreement if the contract is in writing and the reference is such as to make that arbitration clause part of the contract.

The crucial issue here is whether there is a conspiracy of the other kind in civil law jurisdictions, by which simple enactments are used as instruments of socio-political control. Relevant to our discussion here is also the current debate about the use of plain language in legislative contexts, which, on the one hand, makes legal discourse more accessible to ordinary readers, but, on the other hand, has a tendency to reduce transparency. Transparency is reduced by removing the detailed specification of legal scope in the expression of legislative intentions, and thus gives unlimited power of interpretation to either the judiciary or the government at the cost of the legislature and, by implication, of ordinary citizens.

Specification, easification, simplification and plain English

Let me now give substance to this argument by taking examples from legislative discourse from different legal jurisdictions to examine the extent to which the under-specification of information leads to greater accessibility of legal information and to what extent the detailed specification of legal scope leads to greater transparency in legal contexts. I will then discuss the issue of power and control in such interpretations when legal information is either under- or over-specified. Who gets the power and control? Are these members of the judiciary, who make court decisions everyday, or the decision makers in the government, who otherwise are only responsible for carrying out the decisions of the judiciary, or the ordinary people, who constitute the 'real' readership for these legislative provisions? Let me take a simple example (6) of legislative provision to illustrate this issue.

(6) Registration of Clubs (Ireland) Act, 1904 (Original Version)

If any excisable liquor is sold or supplied in a registered club for consumption outside the premises of the club, except as provided in section four, paragraph (h), every person supplying or selling such liquor, every person who shall pay for such liquor and every person authorising the sale or supply of such liquor shall be liable severally, on summary conviction, to a fine not exceeding for a first offence seven pounds, for a second offence fifteen pounds and for a third or subsequent offence thirty pounds, unless he proves to the satisfaction of the court that such liquor was so sold or supplied without his knowledge or against his consent, and, where it is proved that such liquor has been received, delivered or distributed within the premises of the club and taken outside the premises, it shall, failing proof to the contrary, be deemed to have been so taken for consumption outside the premises.

Although this provision was enacted more than a century ago, it is still somewhat typical of much of the legislative writing practised within common law jurisdictions, in which it is still considered advantageous to condense all the necessary information in a single sentence. No doubt, it has the advantage of not allowing the user to interpret any part of the provision out of context, but, at the same time, it tends to carry too much of an information load and hence adds to the problem of lack of accessibility for its intended readers. Much of this is a function of syntactic complexity, which makes cognitive processing almost beyond uninitiated non-specialist readers. Bhatia (1982, 1993, 2004) suggests a number of 'easification' devices (Bhatia 1983, 1987b, 1993), one of which clarifies cognitive structuring by simplifying syntactic complexity. Let me present another version of the same provision using one such device.

43

(7) Registration of Clubs (Ireland) Act, 1904 (Easified Version by Bhatia)
If any excisable liquor is sold or supplied in a registered club for consumption outside the premises of the club, except as provided in section four, paragraph (h), then
every person supplying or selling such liquor, every person who shall pay for such liquor and every person authorising the sale or supply of such liquor shall be liable severally, on summary conviction, to a fine not exceeding

(a) seven pounds, for a first offence,
(b) fifteen pounds, for a second offence and
(c) thirty pounds, for a third or subsequent offence,

unless he proves to the satisfaction of the court that such liquor was so sold or supplied without his knowledge or against his consent,
and,
where it is proved that such liquor has been received, delivered or distributed within the premises of the club and taken outside the premises,
it shall, failing proof to the contrary, be deemed to have been so taken for consumption outside the premises.

This easified version does not compromise on the degree of specification of legal scope in any way; it is as detailed and all-inclusive as the original, yet it displays syntactic complexity in a way that can be processed in chunks favourable to easy accessibility. The use of this and other similar linguistic devices is becoming increasingly common in modern-day legislative drafting, although this is not the main concern of this paper. What is significant here, though, is the fact that this device maintains an adequate level of specification of legal information within a single sentence and yet makes it relatively more accessible to all the stakeholders and wider readership, both within and outside the legal profession.

  Let me now turn to the issue of the specification of legal information, and identify the kind of information that is often sacrificed in an attempt to make the provision simpler, and the implications of such a move. To illustrate what I have in mind, let me take a simplified version of the same provision (8), which is conceptually different from the earlier easified version.

(8) Registration of Clubs (Ireland) Act, 1904 (Simplified Version by Bhatia)
If any excisable liquor is sold for consumption outside the club, then every person who either pays for or authorises the sale of such liquor shall be liable to a maximum fine of

(a) seven pounds, for the first offence,
(b) fifteen pounds, for a second offence,
(c) thirty pounds, for a third or subsequent offence.

The most notable aspect of this simplification process is that it makes the provision more accessible to its intended readership by reducing the level of specification of complicating legal qualifications (Bhatia 1982, 1993), particularly of three different kinds. First of all, the possibility of a potential conflict between this provision and another one in the same Act has not been specified, and hence it is left for the interpreter or the authorised user of the

Act to resolve, if the occasion demands. Secondly, there could be exceptional circumstances such that someone might have sold excisable liquor without the consent or knowledge of the person who holds the license to sell it. Once again, the exceptional circumstances are left for the authorised interpreter to make a decision to figure out, if such an exceptional behaviour should be taken into account in the process of negotiation of justice in a court of law. Finally, this simplified version is also silent on yet another foreseeable case scenario where a person receives liquor within the premises of the club and then takes it out for consumption. The interesting question is whether this act is covered by the provision. The original and the easified versions clearly state that in a case like this, it will be 'deemed to have been so taken for consumption outside the premises' and hence it is covered by the provision. In the simplified version, however, such an exceptional case is not mentioned at all, and it is left to the judiciary to draw its own conclusion. Let me now move to yet another version of the same provision in plain English to make it accessible to ordinary readers.

(9) Registration of Clubs (Ireland) Act, 1904 (Plain Version by Bhatia)
It is unlawful to sell or buy excisable liquor for consumption outside a club and is punishable by fine to a maximum of thirty pounds.

In this case, although the main provision is drafted in simple plain English, clearly accessible to an ordinary readership, it is far from all-inclusive. It leaves a number of qualifications necessary for a precise and unambiguous interpretation in specific sites of application in which the provision is likely to be applicable. Much of this kind of accurate interpretation in real life contexts will require the use of additional specification of legal content, primarily the descriptions of cases to which the provision is likely or not likely to apply. Finally, this plain version also leaves the amount of fine to the judgment of the judiciary. Edward Caldwell, the very experienced and well-established parliamentary counsel already referred to above, underlines the value of this aspect of specification in the drafting process, when he says:

> If you extract the bare bones ... what you end up with is a proposition which is so untrue because the qualifications actually negative [sic] it all ... it's so far from the truth ... it's like saying that all red-headed people are to be executed on Monday, but when you actually read all the qualifications, you find that only one per cent of them are.
>
> (Reported in Bhatia 1982: 51)

I have purposely taken four rather different versions of the same provision, ranging from 1904 to what we might find in modern-day drafting, to illustrate not simply the varying degrees of specification of legal scope in legislative provisions, but also to give some indication of the development of legislative drafting over the years. I would now like to move to the socio-political and jurisdictional implications of different styles of drafting, and identify different aspects of transparency and their implications for those who are empowered by such specification or rather lack of it.

Implications of different drafting styles: power and control

There seem to be different perspectives on this issue. The view from within the drafting community is in stark contrast to the view expressed by some members of the reformist lobby, who claim that legal content can and must be expressed in everyday language accessible to ordinary people who are the real 'recipients' of such legal provisions. The truth, however, seems to lie somewhere in between the two extremes.

Proponents of the plain English movement, in particular Joseph Kimble in his monograph on *Answering the Critics of Plain Language*, claim that traditional legal writing displays 'centuries of inflation and obscurity'. Mellinkoff (1963: 24) describes it as 'wordy, unclear, pompous, and dull'. Friedman (1993: 5) seems to agree with this view when he says: 'The fact is that legal writing is overblown yet timid, homogeneous, and swaddled in obscurity. The legal academy is positively inimical to spare, decent writing.' Similarly, Lindsey (1990: 2) views legal writing as 'the largest body of poorly written literature ever created by the human race'. Thornton, in his well-known book on drafting, also points out:

> The purposes of legislation are most likely to be expressed and communicated successfully by the drafter who is ardently concerned to write clearly and to be intelligible. The obligation to be intelligible, to convey the intended meaning so that it is comprehensible and easily understood, … requires the unremitting pursuit of clarity by drafters. Clarity … requires simplicity and precision … The blind pursuit of precision will inevitably lead to complexity; and complexity is a definite step along the way to obscurity.
>
> (Thornton 1996: 52–53)

Of course, there are many sources of obscurity, such as those resulting from vagueness, wordiness, complexity of syntax, archaic expressions, etc. all contributing positively or otherwise to the requirements of clarity, precision and unambiguity, as discussed earlier. However, the most important source relevant to our discussion here is the one that concerns the extent to which it is necessary to specify the scope of application of legal action, considering specifically the nature and function of qualifications considered essential for the implementation of the provision to a myriad of real life cases.

Any discussion of the nature and function of detailed specification, or lack of it, has to be discussed in the wider context of the legal jurisdiction as well as the wider socio-political context in which the provision is written and interpreted. In parliamentary democracies, particularly in common law jurisdictions, as discussed in the earlier sections, the real authority for legal construction rests with the legislative institution, and not with the judiciary, even though they are given the ultimate power of authoritative interpretation of what the legislative institution drafts. Similarly, the executive arms of the government have no power to construct or even interpret legislative provisions but certainly have the mandate to execute the decisions of the courts. This three-part division of power ensures that no institution can become autocratic in their use or abuse of power. Thus it is one of the major responsibilities assigned to the members of the legislative community to give voice to the people of the country they represent through the legal construction and not to give too much freedom of interpretation to other institutional players, such as the executive or the judiciary, whose job is simply to interpret and apply what the legislature constructs through the parliamentary draftsmen. If this argument is sustainable, and I believe it is, then the first concern for the drafting community is to give an honest expression to the intentions of the legislative institution as comprehensively as the linguistic resources permit. All other concerns, such as the accessibility and ease of comprehension for ordinary users of language, resulting from the complexity of syntax, the over-specification of qualifications, etc., though important, become secondary when compared to their loyalty to legislative intentions.

Another important factor in present-day contexts is that although law has traditionally been considered jurisdictional in nature, because of the recent globalisation of trade, commerce and industrial practices, it is increasingly being constructed, interpreted, used and exploited in settings across jurisdictional boundaries. Sometimes it is done because of other socio-political developments, such as the return of the sovereignty of Hong Kong to the People's Republic of China, and the subsequent establishment of the Hong Kong Special Administrative Region (HKSAR) within the PRC. A similar phenomenon in some respects is seen in Europe as a result of the establishment of the European Union. Similarly, the perception that legislative discourse is impersonal and highly formal, and that differences in linguistic, socio-political, economic and cultural factors across national and ideological boundaries will have no significant influence on its construction and interpretation no longer seems to be entirely valid. Moreover, with the increasing dismantling of international trade barriers as a result of international trade agreements and treaties, laws are often being written and interpreted across geographical and socio-political borders in different ways, such that general assumptions about meanings cannot be taken for granted in these contexts.

There is some evidence of such phenomena from the studies of arbitration laws reported in Bhatia *et al.* (2008). In this chapter, I would like to take a different example focusing on the construction and interpretation of the Basic Law of Hong Kong SAR, which was drafted within the frameworks of the *Sino-British Joint Declaration 1984* and the People's Republic of China's civil law system, but was meant to be interpreted in Hong Kong within the common law system.

A case from Hong Kong

Popularly known in the HKSAR media as the 'right of abode' case, this was one of the most controversial cases involving the interpretation of the Basic Law. The case was decided on 29 January 1999; it brought into focus the unanimous decision of the Court of Final Appeal, which interpreted Article 24 of the Basic Law to allow all those 'persons of Chinese nationality born outside Hong Kong of those residents', who were permanent residents in Hong Kong, irrespective of the fact whether they acquired the status before or after the birth of the child. The Basic Law did not specify whether it was necessary for any of the parents to have had this status of permanent residence at the time of the birth of the child. The Court of Final Appeal took the generous view. According to the Government of HKSAR, this landmark decision opened up the floodgates for millions of mainland people to acquire the right of abode in Hong Kong.

It so happened that a large number of people from Hong Kong had moved to Mainland China prior to the transfer of power on 1 July 1997. They had children born in the Mainland who had no right of abode in Hong Kong under the immigration laws prior to the handover. Many of these children had already entered Hong Kong illegally and thus presented themselves to immigration authorities and claimed their right of abode under Article 24(2)(3). The controversy went to the courts and after a long drawn out battle, the Court of Final Appeal, the highest court in Hong Kong SAR, decided in its 1999 judgment that according to Article 24 of the Basic Law, the Chinese nationals may acquire the right of abode in Hong Kong by one of three ways:

1. if they were born in Hong Kong before or after the transfer of sovereignty (Article 24(2) (1));
2. if they have resided in Hong Kong for a continuous period of not less than seven years before or after the transfer of sovereignty (Article 24(2) (2)); or
3. if they were born outside Hong Kong to persons covered by the above two categories (Article 24(2) (3)).

The Court of Final Appeal affirmed some fundamental constitutional principles in reaching its decision, that is, the Basic Law was a living document, like any other constitution, and hence should be interpreted broadly. The Court ruled that Article 24(2)(3) of the Basic Law gives the right of abode to children born of a Hong Kong permanent resident, 'regardless of whether that parent became a permanent resident before or after the birth of the child'. It became a landmark decision by the highest court in Hong Kong and became the battleground for the contested interpretations of the Article 24 of the Basic Law on the part of the judiciary, the government and the legislating authority based in Beijing, which was responsible for the construction of the Basic Law within the Civil Law system. The Government estimated that the additional eligible persons in Mainland China who could obtain the right of abode within ten years would reach 1.6 million, and would result in very severe social and economic problems, which prompted the Hong Kong Government to ask the Standing Committee of the National People's Congress to reinterpret Articles 22(4) and 24(2)(3) of Hong Kong's Basic Law, which effectively overturned the court decision. This move prompted large protests and debate over whether or not Hong Kong's judiciary remained independent from that of the Mainland. The interpretation offered by the Standing Committee of the National People's Congress was helpful to the Government in appealing against the earlier decision of the Court of Final Appeal, which subsequently ruled that the interpretation of the National People's Congress of Article 24 of the Basic Law was constitutional, thereby subsequently denying the right of abode to all those who were given it in the earlier decision. This scenario presents a very interesting illustration of the lack of specificity in legislative construction which led to this serious contestation among the three institutional perspectives in the process of negotiation of justice, which raised issues of power and politics based on the use of inadequate levels of specificity. This case clearly established that the power of interpretation of legislative provisions, which in the common law system rests with the court of final appeal, was seriously compromised by the overriding power of the legislature, which in the PRC civil law system is invested in the Standing Committee of the National People's Congress. If the Government is likely to get more power in the interpretation and execution of legislative outcomes, then most autocratic institutions would prefer to leave legislative provisions vague, indeterminate, and hence ambiguous as a function of the lack of necessary specification of scope in legal drafting.

One of the main issues brought into focus in this controversy was the question of who should have the final authority to interpret the Basic Law: the highest Court of Final Appeal within the common law system in force in Hong Kong, or the National People's Congress, which operates within a very different civil law system? Although the Basic Law empowers the NPC as the final interpreter of the mini constitution of Hong Kong under the 'one country two systems' framework, the real issue at stake is that a number of such unpleasant controversies and decisions could have been avoided, or at least minimised, by drafting the Basic Law in a legislative style that did not conflict with the normal expectations of the legal system within which it was likely to be interpreted and used. By incorporating, as far as foreseeable, the necessary constraints and qualifications operating on such provisions, one would have made the law more transparent and less controversial. Ghai, a prominent specialist on constitutional law, rightly identifies this lack of specificity in drafting as one of the main reasons for contentious interpretations.

> The two broad areas on which there was considerable contention were the relations between the Central Authorities and the HKSAR and the political structure of the HKSAR. China had fought off the British during the negotiations for the Joint Declaration on these issues, and an appearance of consensus was purchased at the expense of ambiguity and obfuscation.
>
> (Ghai 1997: 61)

The other interesting issue the case brings into focus is that social action in the courtroom often depends not simply on semantically or logically accurate interpretations (Allen 1957), but also on pragmatically appropriate interpretations, keeping in mind the socio-political, economical and cultural constraints, which are often preferred by institutions who hold executive powers. The institutions with executive responsibilities would like to exercise maximum control and power to implement administrative and social policies, and would like to have under their control a measure of flexibility in interpretation, which is often lost through detailed specification in legislative instruments. It is hardly surprising that a high degree of transparency in legislative intention is often negatively viewed by autocratic executive organisations and institutions.

Conclusion

In conclusion, I would like to reiterate that although clarity, precision, unambiguity and all-inclusiveness are the four key aspects of the construction and interpretation of legislative intentions, particularly in the context of common law jurisdictions, all-inclusiveness plays the most significant role in the specification of legal scope, which in turn has implications for accessibility and transparency in the expression of legislative intentions. I also make an attempt to demonstrate that transparency, or rather lack of it, is strategically used in different legal systems in different ways to assign power and control to different institutions which have different roles in the construction and interpretation of legislative intentions. Depending on the institutional roles and the privileges available to institutional players, for instance, the legislature, the judiciary, or the bureaucracy, invariably show preference or dispreference for greater transparency in legislative expressions.

Note

1 This chapter draws on the international projects funded by the RGC-CERG (HKSAR) grant (9041191: CityU 1501/06H) entitled: *International Commercial Arbitration Practice: A Discourse Analytical Study*.

Further reading

Bhatia, Vijay K. (1983) 'Simplification v. easification: The case of legal texts', *Applied Linguistics*, 4(1): 42–54.

——(1987) 'Textual-mapping in British legislative writing', *World Englishes*, 6(1): 1–10.

Bhatia, Vijay K., Engberg, Jan, Gotti, Maurizio and Heller, Dorothee (2005) *Vagueness in Normative Texts*, Bern: Peter Lang.

Danet, Brenda (1980) 'Language in the legal process', *Law and Society Review*, 14(3): 445–564.

Gibbons, John (ed.) (1994) *Language and the Law*, London: Longman.

Maley, Y. (1987) 'The language of legislation', in *Language and Society*, 16: 25–48.

4

Legal writing: complexity

Complex documents/average and not-so-average readers

Gail Stygall

Introduction

In this chapter, I examine two types of complex document: notices required by US retirement law when there are decreases in future benefits for pension plan participants; and the disclosures required in credit card solicitations, contracts and other financial accounts. By complex documents, I mean those dense, intricate, often confusing hybrid documents, typically composed of a combination of legal and financial languages and discourse. These difficult, complex documents often contain critical information that lay readers need to understand in order to make important financial decisions.

The first type of document I discuss here is a notice/warning to participants in a pension plan that their retirement benefits are going to decrease because the pension plan administrators made a change in the way the plan operates. This notice is required by US law. The reason that pension plan participants need the information is to make necessary changes in their retirement plans because one source of their retirement income is going to decrease. With the recent financial crisis, many pension plan administrators have changed their plan, sometimes eliminating it altogether, other times changing the company's contribution to the retirement plan. Sometimes the person with the pension plan might receive a letter or flyer extolling the "new" plan, without any focus on, or perhaps no mention at all, of the negative piece of information. The person might also receive a brief letter, filled with financial and legal terms, such as "freeze," "benefit accrual," and "plan amendment" and little other text.

The second type of documents I discuss here are those associated with credit cards: the letters that we receive asking us to apply for a credit card, the terms of the credit card, and the credit card notices often enclosed with bills from the credit card company. These documents have some terms highlighted, as required by US law, but often contain much fine print that presents excellent examples of legal language unintelligible to most people. These documents are filled with lengthy, complex, and embedded sentences, organization that is difficult to discern, and terms that have legal and financial meanings. These documents include sentences such as

> The 0% introductory Annual Percentage Rate (APR) on Balance Transfers and Convenience Checks is applicable for the first 9 billing cycles after the account is opened and requires that timely payments are received.
>
> (Travelocity 2009)

The long interruptive elements in the first noun phrase are followed, after the verb ('is'), by two more clauses. This information is presented in a tiny type (6 point, 200+ characters per line). How long the introductory rate applies is important information for a consumer and it is likely to be missed because of the way that it is presented both syntactically and graphologically.

Recently, linguists and language scholars have been consulted about the likelihood that average pension plan participants would understand the notices sent to them by their pension plans. Credit card disclosure is an area of possible future consultation with linguists because the Federal Reserve Board and the US Congress have made changes in what information is required for consumers. Although the new regulations are not yet in effect, it seems likely that there will be litigation to test whether these disclosure requirements have been met. My purpose in this chapter is to outline the issues, the standards and the information for a linguist to conduct an analysis of these complex documents. I begin by describing the two types, I follow that with a discussion of literacy issues in the US and I close with a section on additional research that may play a role in understanding how people read these documents. For additional examples of documents, I invite readers to consult similar documents they have received themselves. Any credit card application will include the kinds of features I am discussing here.

Types of documents

Pension plan documents

Over the past two decades in the United States, a number of companies that offered their employees a pension plan have faced litigation from their employees or former employees for violations of the Employee Retirement Income Security Act of 1974 (ERISA). ERISA does not require that employers provide pensions, but when they do, they are required to follow the ERISA statutes and regulations, some of which require plan administrators to communicate with their employees and former employees about specific aspects of their retirement benefits. There are two types of document commonly involved with litigation over ERISA-required communication with "plan participants" (current or former employees): a "204(h) notice" and a summary plan description.

A "204(h) notice" is required to inform pension plan participants who will or are likely to experience a "significant reduction in the rate of future benefit accruals" through an amendment to the pension plan (Consolidated Omnibus Budget Reconciliation Act of 1985, Pub. L. No. 99–272 § 11006, 100 Stat 82, 243 (1986)). This section of the ERISA statute has been amended several times, each time requiring more specific guidelines for the notices. The pension plan administrators are also required to provide a summary plan description (SPD) to each employee and then resend it at least once every five years, though many companies provide the SPD annually. The SPD must include all important benefits and limitations, as well as any amendments and changes. These documents are required to "be written in a manner calculated to be understood by the average plan participant" (For 204(h) notices see 60 Fed. Reg. 64,320 to 64,324, 1995 and 63 Fed. Reg. 68,678, 68,678, 1998). Since 2001, the notices must "provide sufficient information … to allow applicable individuals to understand the effect of the plan amendment" (Economic Growth and Tax Relief Reconciliation Act of 2001, Pub. L. No. 107–16, § 659, 115 Stat. 38, 140 [2001]). These then are the basic parameters with which the linguist conducts an analysis of the documents.

Much of the litigation arose as corporations changed their pension plans from those that offered employees a retirement benefit based on the average salary of the final five years of employment to what is called a "cash-balance" plan. This plan presents an employee with a hypothetical or notional account that is made up of two parts: an annual percentage based on the employee's years of service and an additional interest payment usually based on a financial market indicator, such as the rate for US Treasury bills. The cash-balance plan "increases" each year, at least according to a statement given to employees annually. For some employees, usually older ones, the change from a traditional pension to a cash-balance plan means that their notional account increases, but their actual account does not. Actual account means the money that is paid to an employee at retirement. Although there isn't a separately kept account for each employee, the amount due at retirement for each employee is supposed to increase over time. The cash-balance plan appears to work better for younger employees, while older employees, who have less time to accumulate benefits, do worse (Oppel 1999). Moreover, the way the accrued benefits are calculated at the moment of change from one plan to another means that some plan participants may spend some years without earning any additional pension. This process is called wear away. These "hybrid" cash-balance plans continue to make news, as in Barclays' recent decision to fund only its cash-balance plan and stop contributing to the final average salary plan (Slater and Valente 2009).

Litigation over the duty to inform has had mixed results. In many cases, the most prominent cause of action was age discrimination, with the duty to inform of significant reductions in the rate of benefit accruals sometimes an afterthought, though still a cause of action under ERISA. The age discrimination cause has been resisted by some courts. One of the most important cases involving the issue of 204(h) notices is *Amara v. CIGNA* (Case No. 3:01CV2361(MRK)), tried in the Federal District of Connecticut, now on appeal in the Court of Appeals, Second Circuit. I am participating now as an expert in five cases, none of which has yet come to trial, although depositions are complete in two of them. I am under a confidentiality order in these cases, so I will be drawing on Judge Kravitz's decision in Amara for some of my examples. Congress amended ERISA in 2006 in ways that changed how cash-balance plans are understood. The recent economic climate has meant that most current notices are 204(h) notices of complete freezes of both final average salary plans and cash-balance plans, where no further benefits will be available to any plan participants. Ultimately, this duty to inform is a curious one: it only involves informing plan participants of a negative piece of information—a significant reduction in the rate of future benefit accruals. The negative character of the information transforms the speech act of informing to that of warning.

Pension plan 204(h) notices can take several forms. One prominent means of purportedly notifying pension plan participants of reductions in the rate of future benefit accruals for retirement was to embed "notice" or "news" of a different plan in a "new" benefits promotion document. Judge Kravitz in *Amara v. CIGNA* describes one such document as follows:

> In an inset box on the 1997 Newsletter's cover, a "Message from CEO Bill Taylor" states: "I am **pleased** to announce that, on January 1, 1998, CIGNA will **significantly enhance** its retirement program … These **enhancements** will make our retirement program **highly competitive** [citation omitted]. The 1997 Newsletter tells employees that "the new plan is designed to **work well** for *both* longer- and shorter-service employees," it provides "**steadier benefit growth** throughout [the employee's] career and it "**build[s] benefits faster**" than the old plan [citation omitted].
>
> (Kravitz 22) (bolding added)

The newsletter did not tell employees that some of them were about to undergo a significant reduction in their retirement benefits. Instead, the newsletter extols the new plan. The CEO is "pleased"; the corporation will "significantly enhance" the plan; the new plan is "highly competitive," "works well" with both short- and long-term employees and the plan "builds benefits faster." Judge Kravitz noted, "The 1997 Newsletter did not discuss or even mention wear away" (Kravitz 22). It would be difficult for a reader to know that they were being told about something negative happening to their pension plan. Thus, plan participants in *Amara v. CIGNA* were neither informed nor warned of the consequences of the plan amendment making the changes.

Another strategy for "informing" plan participants of the coming negative consequence is to use a short letter telling plan participants that their pension plan is to be "frozen." I offer a hypothetical "notice" in example (1).

(1) NOTICE
To: Participants in the First Global Megacorporation Retirement Plan
From: Plan Administration Committee of the First Global
           Megacorporation Retirement Plan
Re: Freeze of Plan

  The First Global Megacorporation Retirement Plan has been amended to cease accruals as of December 31, 1998. This amendment freezes the First Global Megacorporation Retirement Plan as of December 31, 1998.

  Beginning January 1, 1999, employees who have at least one year of service will be eligible to participate in the First Global Megacorporation Cash-Balance Retirement Plan.

There is considerable knowledge needed by readers to make sense of this brief hypothetical example of the 204(h) notice. Although it calls itself a notice, this version does not call itself a 204(h) notice; it's simply a notice of something, not required by anyone or anybody. But it certainly has the language of a legal document. Notice that the plan names, First Global Megacorporation Retirement Plan and First Global Megacorporation Cash-Balance Retirement Plan, are the formal, legal names of these pension plans. Additionally, there is language—freeze, amend/amendment, cease, accruals—that is likely to be unfamiliar to plan participants. Those plan participants who didn't understand the terms here would also be faced with a notice that tells them that one plan stops on one day and another plan starts the next day. It would be fair for readers to conclude that there really is no change for them as employees. Unfortunately, the freezing of the first plan will mean for some part of the participant population that their final retirement benefits will be reduced. The "freeze" notice doesn't actually say anything about reductions. There are a variety of other strategies including presentations of pension plan amendments in very technical language or providing question and answer sheets about the "changes" in the pension plan among others. So, as the linguist will find, the analysis of these notices and other pension plan documents will allow him or her to identify many places where understanding begins to dissolve.

Credit card disclosures

If informing/warning is the speech act in pension plan litigation, disclosing is the speech act in making credit card solicitations, card agreements, notifications of changes in card agreements and information included on periodic statements. Governed by the Truth in Lending Act (TILA), 15 U.S.C. § 1601 et seq, Regulations AA (Unfair Acts or Practices) and Z (TILA) of the Federal Reserve, and the corresponding regulations, 12 C.F.R. § 226.5 through 226.16, issuers of credit cards (or, as they call it here, open end credit) must disclose a number of elements of credit card costs. The original idea for the Truth in Lending Act, in 1969, was to allow more consumers to make better, more informed choices from the options that various creditors made available to them. TILA was amended in 1988 through the Fair Credit and Charge Card Disclosure Act, providing more specific disclosure and requiring that the disclosure begin with the moment of solicitation. Even these additional disclosure requirements eventually proved to be inadequate in getting important information to consumers. Recent actions by creditors—changing interest rates at will after offering a promotional low rate, adding little understood fees, reducing grace periods, separating credit card purchases from rules and interest rates on convenience checks—seem to indicate that consumers are surprised and angry when they become aware of these actions.

Concerned consumers and their advocates complained vigorously to Congress and to the Federal Reserve Board. The Federal Reserve Board responded first and conducted extensive consumer testing on current disclosure requirements and made recommendations for change. Macro International conducted the design and testing of various documents that a consumer might receive: a solicitation letter, a periodic statement, and convenience checks (Macro, 16 May 2007; Macro, 15 December 2008). The studies did not take up the comprehension issues of card agreements, which often appear as tiny (3.25 × 7) inserts mailed to consumers. As far as I could ascertain, the research also did not involve making organizational or syntactic changes. For the solicitation letters and enclosures, it may have been difficult to change the organization as the graphic boxes, (named Schumer boxes after the Senator who sponsored the 1988 Fair Credit Act), have certain, quite specific current requirements, such as the 18 point size on the Annual Percentage Rate (APR).

These studies were conducted in various cities in the United States and used focus groups, interviews and "cognitive interviews" to develop their recommendations. Their work was tested on a variety of documents and the interviewers asked participants about their understanding in careful ways. This is, in essence, usability testing, by asking actual consumers to examine and use the documents and to identify where and how there were problems in understanding. Although better labeling, movement of key phrases, changes of vocabulary and the creation of tables could improve participants' understanding somewhat, there were at least three areas with deeper problems: the calculation of interest charges, fees versus interest rates, and balances on different types of transactions (Macro, May 16, 2007: 52–53). They conclude that

> fundamental gaps, such as [the three] listed above are difficult to address through disclosures. Effectively explaining the difference between a 5% fee on balance transfer and a 5% APR on balance transfers, for example, would require a great deal of text—so much, in fact, that the consumer for whom it was intended would be unlikely to read it.
>
> (Macro, May 16, 2007: 53)

They conclude this report by referring to a Federal Reserve Board proposal to use its website for consumer education. But they acknowledge that web-based consumer education would not solve the problem. Consequently, they follow this first conclusion with a second: "expand coverage of these topics in K–12 school curricula … the need for such a solution was very apparent in the course of this work" (53–54). With the two reports taken together, Macro International highlights the profound lack of understanding that consumers have of these credit card disclosure documents. The Federal Reserve Board, the Office of Thrift Supervision and the National Credit Union Administration voted to prohibit a number of credit card company practices considered anti-consumer on December 18, 2008, but these rules were not to take effect until July 1, 2010. Congress passed and the President signed its own version of needed changes, the Credit Card Act of 2009, to take effect in February of 2010.

Appellate decisions on credit card disclosures disputed in multiple US Circuit Courts of Appeal have held that TILA requires "clear and conspicuous" disclosure of all important elements of credit card agreements. The linguist in this type of case would be examining documents for their being "reasonably understandable" to consumers and in a form "readily noticeable to consumers" (Supplement I to 12 CFR Part 226, Regulation Z). In the future, there will be new requirements and additional disclosures to be made.

Credit card documents are well known to be difficult to understand, despite attempts to make rules that require disclosure. Below, I compare a credit card solicitation (SB-12) modeled by the Macro International study for the Federal Reserve Board with a recent solicitation sent to me for a Barnes and Noble credit card. Both documents have the "Schumer box," a table-like form with two columns, one narrow column on the left announcing the topic of the box and the other wider column on the right providing more detailed information. Both documents have other information that appears outside the Schumer box, but most of this information is different. The model form from the study provides four other sections of information: how the interest will be calculated, state law disclosures (in both forms), a billing rights summary, and how the periodic finance charge is calculated. The Barnes and Noble form has many more sections: a fixed APR section; an introductory rate notice; a default APR section; a credit performance section; and, on the back side, an additional statement with six sections of its own. The model form has information in the Schumer boxes at 11 or 12 point typeface, while the entire Barnes and Noble form is in 8 point typeface, except for the interest rate required to be in 18 point typeface.

There are enhancements to understanding in the model form, such as a section called "Penalty APR and When it Applies." The information on the right for this section puts 31.99% at the top in bold. What follows is a list of conditions when the penalty APR could be applied to the whole balance owed. This is followed by a boldface question,

"How long will the Penalty APR Apply?" and then gives the conditions. The Barnes and Noble solicitation insert shows a typographical dagger in the section "Other APRs" next to "Default APR: Up to 29.99% variable." The dagger refers readers to the bottom of the page and a section labeled "Default APR." Below is the first sentence in that section:

1) If your payment is received late,
2) you fail to pay at least the minimum due,
3) your payment is not honored by your bank,
4) or your balance exceeds your credit card line,
5) the APR on all balances (including any introductory balances) may be increased to the then applicable Default APR.

This forty-nine word sentence is presented in the same 8 point typeface, and it contains a total of five clauses—six counting the to-infinitive clause at 2. Although the "you" pronoun is often offered to make this prose reader-friendly, the type size, the number of clauses and its position at the bottom of the page, away from the Schumer box, makes it challenging for most readers. A number of sentences in the sections outside the Schumer box are similar in difficulty. Clauses one and five are passives, with the credit card company as the invisible actor.

Another issue is that the APR here is called "default." "Default" has a range of meanings, from failure to act to failure to act on legal or financial obligations or even a computer program that assumes a value when no other value is entered. But at least in part because there is a strong legal sense to default and the necessity of going to court to get a judgment of default, default seems to be an inappropriate word to substitute for paying an account late rather than not paying an account at all or to substitute default for incurring more debt than the available credit limit. The model form calls these situations "penalty" APRs, which better characterize the process.

Exophoric references appear throughout the Barnes and Noble form: references to the *Wall Street Journal* for money rates, credit reports and to specific statutes in the state of Wisconsin. There is only one exophoric reference in the model form and that is to the website of the Federal Reserve Board.

What appears above, however, should not be taken to mean that the model form is flawless. As I indicated earlier, the studies completed by Macro International did not take up discourse and syntactic issues with the disclosures. Below is a particularly difficult sentence that appears outside of the Schumer box in the model form, in the "Periodic Finance Charge Calculation."

1) We **compute** the daily balance for each transaction category on each day by the [sic] first **adding** the following to the previous day's daily balance:
2) transactions **made** that day,
3) fees **charged** that day
4) and Periodic Finance Charges **accrued** on the previous day's daily balance,
5) and then by **subtracting** any credits and payments
6) that **are applied** against the balance of the transaction category on that day.

I marked both the finite and non-finite verbs here to show how many different calculations are required for the consumer to total even a single day's daily balance finance charge. Because this material was placed outside the Schumer box, Macro International did not test improvements.

Literacy issues in the US

In discussing literacy with attorneys who are involved in cases where understanding pension plan information or credit card disclosure is involved, I often find that the attorneys operate with some unfounded assumptions about literacy. They proceed as if they think that almost everyone is fully literate. Although common reference works such as almanacs estimate US literacy as 99%, the functional literacy rates are much more nuanced and critical in understanding complex documents. For a linguist assessing the comprehensibility of documents, some understanding of literacy levels is important. Two national assessments of US literacy, one in 1992 and one in 2003, offer some insights into what functional literacy levels are, before assessing the comprehensibility of the particular documents considered here. Both studies measure primarily functional literacy and both studies find a relatively small percentage of the population able to accomplish the more complex tasks.

The 1992 study, *Adult Literacy in America*, interviewed more than 13,000 people, plus an additional 1,000 in each state to produce state-level results (xiv). Reading and subsequent tasks were divided into three categories: prose, document and quantitative. These were tasks where the participants were required to read various passages and documents and then perform an additional task related to the passages or documents. This type of test is in contrast to the more school-centered multiple choice tests, such as the SAT. Results were presented in five levels, based on a 0–500 point scale, with Level 5 representing the most difficult reading and tasks to complete, each level corresponding to a score for each category. Average scores across the entire test population were 276 for the prose tasks, 271 for the document tasks, and 275 for the quantitative literacy tasks. Table 4.1 gives the percentages of proficiencies in each level.

Level 1 was minimal literacy and the category includes some people who could not perform the tasks at all and participants whose first language was not English. The population in Level 1 represents those readers who can perform the most basic of tasks, such as "locat[ing] a single piece of information which is identical or synonymous with the information given in the question or directive" (11). Level 2 was still very basic, but participants in Level 3 were able to complete a range of tasks. Level 4 was more complex, asking participants to "make high level text-based inferences or draw on their background knowledge" (19). Level 5 was most complex and participants could search through information to find specific parts that would allow them to complete very difficult tasks. Level 5 prose tasks "require the reader to search for information in dense text

Table 4.1 Literacy levels percentages and reading types 1992

Task Type	Level 1	Level 2	Level 3	Level 4	Level 5
Prose	21%	27%	32%	17%	3%
Document	23%	28%	31%	15%	3%
Quantitative	22%	25%	31%	17%	4%

Source: Adult Literacy in America 1992.

which contains a number of plausible distracters" (11). Document tasks on Level 5 "require the reader to search through complex displays that contain multiple distracters, to make high-level text-based inferences and to use specialized knowledge" (11). An example of a Level 5 task is "[u]sing a table comparing credit cards, identify the two categories used and write two differences between them" (10). The study indicates that only "[b]etween 6 and 8 million adults nationwide demonstrated success on these types of tasks" (19). Educational levels roughly corresponded to the levels, with Level 1 typically with less than a high school education, high school graduates at the high end of Level 2, college graduates at the high end of Level 3, and those who had some education beyond college were primarily in Level 4 (27).

The 2003 study, *Literacy in Everyday Life: Results from the 2003 National Assessment of Adult Literacy*, presented overall results that were not substantially different from those in 1992, although the survey was given to a larger national sample, 19,000, including 1,200 prisoners (1). The report apparently does not mention a 2003 state-by-state collection of data, so the actual total of the 1992 study was larger. Only in quantitative literacy was there a statistically significant change in overall results, a slight increase. Average results were 275 for prose, 271 for documents, and 283 for quantitative tasks. Seventy of the questions from the 1992 assessment were used in 2003, with new questions added in 2003 but not released. What was different about the 2003 study was their decision to reduce the number of levels from five to four. Level 1 is called Below Basic, Level 2 is Basic, Level 3 is Intermediate, and Level 4 is Proficient. In short, they eliminated Level 5, collapsing the upper Level 4 with Level 5, including the tasks most related to the documents I discuss here. Level 1 in the 1992 study was divided into Levels 1 and 2 in the 2003, presumably also adjusting Levels 2 and 3. Additionally, they added a category called "nonliterate in English," if participants were unable to complete "a minimum number of simple literacy questions" (3). These results were not included in the overall presentation of the data. Table 4.2 gives the percentages of results for all other types of reading and task.

For Level 4, the minimum score required on the reading and the performance was 340. The credit card document comparison, used in both surveys, was rated 387 in 1992 but only 372 in 2003. No detailed information was given in the 2003 report about changes in questions between years. Even with changes, it is important to note that only 13% of the surveyed population was able to achieve Level 4 performance, the level most likely to require interaction with complex texts and documents. Although it is unclear how the study collapsed Levels 4 and 5, it is clear that the overall literacy levels decreased. The Proficient category, used in both reports, dropped 35% in prose literacy, 28% in document literacy, and 38% in quantitative literacy. The Proficient category is the only one in which study participants could carry out the tasks required by reading and acting upon complex documents. The report comments, "Between 1992 and 2003,

Table 4.2 Literacy levels percentages and reading types 2003

Task Type	Level 1	Level 2	Level 3	Level 4
Prose	14%	29%	44%	13%
Document	12%	22%	53%	13%
Quantitative	22%	33%	33%	13%

Source: Literacy in Everyday Life 2003.

there was a decline in the average prose literacy of adults between the ages of 25 and 39 and between the ages of 40 and 49" (v), but this comment does not account for the overall decline in the upper literacy levels. Additional comments clarified the relationship between literacy and income:

> A higher percentage of adults with *Below Basic* prose, document, and quantitative literacy lived in households with income below $10,000 than adults with higher levels of literacy. A higher percentage of adults with *Proficient* prose, document, and quantitative literacy than adults with lower levels of literacy lived in household with incomes above $100,000.
>
> *(Literacy in Everyday Life 2003*: v)

So in addition to the decrease in the Proficient category, there is also a clear association between Proficiency and a household income of more than $100,000 per year. There are, of course, more pension plan participants and credit card holders than just those in households with $100,000 annual income. These results have implications for a forensic linguistic analysis of the comprehensibility of complex documents. The audience for whom these documents are understandable enough to act upon is very small relative to the general population. That is to say, most people cannot understand or act upon these literacy tasks.

Other relevant research

In this section, I examine and review some of the research available to a linguist in determining the likely comprehensibility of a complex document. Because both types of cases I analyze here are civil cases, I recommend a thorough reading of Roger Shuy's (2008b) *Fighting Over Words: Language and Civil Law Cases* as an initial step in conducting a similar analysis. Shuy details an array of linguistic issues he found in these civil cases and many of them are applicable to cases of these types, especially from the sections on business contracts, deceptive trade practices and product liability. In these sections, Shuy outlines findings from his analysis of various documents and his strategies include analyzing topics, conducting semantic analysis, assessing grammatical scope, judging prominence and legibility, and presenting narrative analysis. I also want to suggest in this section that there are some additional aspects for a linguist to consider. First, there are the similarities between the language in the documents that I describe and legal language and discourse. Some of these materials are an especially difficult hybrid of legal and financial languages. Second, the early work on how difficult syntax contributes to slower processing time has been extended and enriched and I briefly review this research. Newer studies find that there are continuing constraints on working memory. Third, the connection between the text world of the attorneys and financial specialists makes it very difficult for them to write for lay understanding. Finally, I suggest that linguists consider the literature of document designers and technical communicators for confirmation of their linguistic analysis.

As the field of legal language and discourse began to emerge in the 1970s and 1980s, there was sustained interest in improving lay understanding of jury instructions (Charrow and Charrow 1979; Elwork *et al.* 1977, 1982). More recently, researchers Bethany Dumas and Peter Tiersma worked with state bar associations and judiciaries to revise state pattern jury instructions, although considerable resistance remains. Although the comprehensibility of product warnings has received attention in the law and language community (Tiersma 2002; Heaps and Henley 1999; Dumas 1990; Shuy 1990b, 2008b), the comprehensibility of other complex documents has received less attention. Frances Rock (2007) has addressed the complexity of the police caution given in England and Wales, a document that functions as both written and spoken text in the legal setting. She examines the multiple communicative purposes of both detainees and police in *Communicating Rights: The Language of Arrest and Detention*. Recently, financial documents, especially those directed at consumers, have proliferated. Although many of these documents are regulated either by federal or state statute or code of regulations, enforcement of consumer-oriented comprehension requirements has remained limited. As many observers suggest, these consumer documents are likely to be contracts of adhesion, that is, a standardized contract in which the consumer is not able to negotiate terms with the other party. Because there is no negotiation, the terms of the contract may be disadvantageous or even harmful to the consumer, yet courts have typically not challenged contracts of adhesion unless they are quite outrageous. Legal scholars Alan White and Cathy Lesser Mansfield suggest that courts are not taking into account the actual literacy levels of most consumers (White and Mansfield 2002).

Peter Tiersma devotes a chapter in *Legal Language* to "What Makes Legal Language Difficult to Understand?" He compiles a list of features that "impede communication" (Tiersma 1999: 203). He includes the following: technical vocabulary; archaic, formal and unusual words; impersonal constructions; overuse of nominalizations and passives; modal verbs; multiple negation; long and complex sentences; and poor organization (Tiersma 1999: 203–10). Some or all of these may appear in legal documents; all detract in various ways from comprehension. To these, I would add several other characteristics including references to inaccessible texts; critical background texts not apparent to lay readers; repetitive use of formal legal names of entities; and common words used with a specialized legal meaning. As Tiersma suggests, the problem isn't that attorneys have a professional vocabulary, language and discourse, but that they must communicate important information to people who are not attorneys.

One study comparing the case law reading strategies of legal professionals (law professors) with novices found significant differences (Lundeberg 1987). When handed an appellate decision to read, legal professionals immediately put the case in context by noticing the headings, the parties, the court, the date, the name of the judge, the decision, the facts of the case, legal terms used, evaluation, and synthesizing the information. Novices were confused about legal terms, ordinary words used with a legal meaning, attempting to define words contextually although unfamiliar with the domain, adding incorrect information, and assigning names to the parties rather than their roles (e.g. plaintiff, defendant). In overall strategy, the professionals spent initial time creating an overview of the case, including looking immediately for the decision. Novices did neither. The result was that the novices did not understand the import of what they were reading. As Lundeberg suggests, the novice would benefit from direct instruction on how to read in this particular domain.

When presented with these types of texts, lay readers are true beginners, relying on the most basic procedures, even if these procedures are those of strong readers. In such a case, the readers are heavily dependent on working memory. The entire knowledge domain is unfamiliar to lay readers and so the transfer between working memory and long-term memory becomes more complicated. Without domain knowledge, readers may not have a means to permanently store or retrieve the new information. Technical vocabulary is often a feature of domain knowledge and is likely to be unfamiliar to those unacquainted with the domain. The key process for lay readers then becomes working memory, previously called short-term memory. The term "short-term" memory dates from the earlier years of psychological study of memory, when short-term memory was seen as a unitary short-term bank of information. Some sixty years ago, George Miller described the limits of "short-term" memory as "the magical number seven plus or minus two," indicating that people seemed capable of managing about seven chunks of information in short-term memory (Miller 1956). Although George Miller's idea has become much elaborated, psychologists, psycholinguists and linguists remain aware of this sort of limit on working memory and still approximate it at around seven. However, the model is no longer unitary and in the US, psychologists have developed a model encompassing three parts: the central executive, a visuospatial sketch pad, and phonological loop (Baddeley 1992). But no matter what the shape of the model is, the limitations on working memory remain.

So lay readers lack access to domain knowledge about specialized areas of information and their working memory presents limitations on easily processing new information. Add to those limitations sentences that are already well known to present processing problems and we have a recipe for comprehension difficulties. Processing problems may include sentence length, complexity, number of embeddings, the presence of negation or passivization, syntactic ambiguity, and the absence of relative pronouns marking clauses. Awareness of these processing issues reaches back as far as the late 1960s and 1970s in the United States, as in Slobin (1966; passives, negatives), Fodor and Garrett (1967; embeddings and presence of relative pronouns), and Larkin and Burns (1977; embeddings and memory) and proceeds forward to the present, as in Lord (2002; subordinate clauses more difficult), Van Dyke and McElree (2006; retrieval interference), Van Dyke (2007; retrieval interference from more than one plausible subject), Reali and Christiansen (2006; pronominal subject clauses more difficult than object clauses), and Ye and Zhou (2008; passives and incompatible sentence alternatives). Although a short sentence may be as difficult to process as a longer sentence if the available slots are filled with technical and unknown terms, very lengthy sentences impose other problems. Embeddings, especially those in the subject NP, slow processing down; ambiguous syntax or scope increases processing difficulties; texts with more of these features impede comprehension more than those sentences with fewer such features. Additional issues may appear when lengthy sentences are presented in a bulleted list of non-parallel items, inconsistently punctuated, as seen in US immigration documents (Stygall 2002).

Discourse level phenomena also may present difficulties to lay comprehension (organization, references to outside texts, cohesion, visual presentations of information, speech acts). As Tiersma (1999) suggests, poor organization may be a feature of legal texts. To the legal professional, a text may appear to be organized sensibly, but this organization may be based on a knowledge of how legal text works that is inaccessible to lay readers. For example, jury instructions often sound disordered to lay jurors. Attorneys, who know that the order of the instructions may roughly follow a pattern book of instructions, find the organization quite sensible, but although it may make sense to the legal professional, it has very few aids to comprehension for lay jurors (Stygall 1991). The lay reader of a particular corporation's financial document may not know that all documents of that type have the same form, perhaps required by statute or regulation. Professional financial readers may unconsciously know the document type, without realizing that lay readers do not have experience of reading many such documents. Thus, the same text may seem sensible to the professional reader but disorganized to the lay reader.

Another feature of professional and academic disciplinary discourse is explicit and visible exophoric referencing; that is, references to other texts completely outside the body of the text. In legal texts, there may be references to judicial decisions, legal journal articles, briefs, regulations or statutes (or all of these). Lay readers are distracted by such references, as they generally lack access to the texts being referenced. As I have suggested elsewhere, these exophoric references mark the text's audience as readers other than laypeople. Professional readers at least would know of the references and how to access the other texts, while lay readers in general would not.

Another set of resources for the linguist working on complex documents are those associated with document designers and technical communicators. As I have reported elsewhere, document designers did work with linguists in the 1970s and early 1980s on projects to improve the overall usefulness of complex documents to readers (Stygall 2002). These projects were often associated with consumer initiatives, such as Roger Shuy's work to make Social Security documents more understandable (Shuy 1998a). With the election of Ronald Reagan as President, emphasis on consumer understanding in the US yielded to an emphasis on the amount of time it took to complete forms for the government. Plain English initiatives were reversed at the federal level and research funding for document design centers was lost. However, during the Reagan administration, a number of colleges and universities began programs in technical communication, sometimes associated with schools of engineering, sometimes associated with English departments. At least two books emerging from this tradition are useful to linguists as reference materials: Paul V. Anderson's *Technical Communication: A Reader-Centered Approach* and Karen A. Schriver's *Dynamics in Document Design*. Another set of resources emerging now in document design of special interest to linguists is the Document Design Companion Series from John Benjamins and *Information Design Journal*, both of which often feature linguists working on documents or collaborations between linguists and document designers.

Conclusion

Many commentators have wondered how legal language and discourse could be improved. Most large companies hire an actuarial/communications or communications consulting firm to work with their staff on developing the notices, plan descriptions or credit card documents of various kinds. To my knowledge, these companies seem not to know of either linguists or technical communicators. A linguist could certainly advise developers on better ways to communicate and on the discourse and syntax to avoid. Some suggest Plain English standards or say that there should be a Plain English law. Although those Plain English standards might help temporarily, it seems likely that the legal language would reappear in a form that meets the Plain English standards but still remains mostly incomprehensible to lay readers. The idea that there would likely be a reformulation back into law—or in this case, legal language—has been discussed by those who theorize law as an autopoietic system, resistant to the aims and principles of other systems (Luhmann 2004; Tuebner 1993; King 1997). Similarly, legislated language change has been remarkably difficult. Together, the two tendencies suggest that while Plain English measures may help understanding in the short term, the prospects for long-term change are problematic. Consequently, I believe that a better strategy would be to combine linguists with document designers to conduct usability testing on a representative sample of the target reading group and then revise the documents as necessary. And the final evaluation of the documents before they go out to lay readers would need to be made by a group including linguists, document designers and attorneys.

In the meantime, linguists working in a forensic setting with these complex documents should examine and analyze them thoroughly, keeping in mind what the literacy levels of varying populations may be. The discourse and linguistic features that may impede reader understanding are prominent in these documents. Although I have described only two types of document here, I could have done the same analysis for real estate Truth in Lending Statements, End User License Agreements (EULAs for computer programs), Medicare forms, asylum requests, military disability forms, lease agreements, rental contracts and a host of others. We live in a world of complex documents that are difficult for almost all readers to understand.

Further reading

Kutner, M., Greenberg, E., Jin, Y., Boyle, B., Hsu, Y. and Dunleavy, E. (2007) *Literacy in Everyday Life: Results from the 2003 National Assessment of Adult Literacy*, Washington, DC: U.S. Department of Education, available online at: http://nces.ed.gov/Pubs2007/2007480.pdf.

Shuy, R. (1998) *Bureaucratic Language in Government and Business*, Washington, DC: Georgetown University Press.

——(2008) *Fighting over Words: Language and Civil Law Cases*, Oxford: Oxford University Press.

Tiersma, P. (1999) *Legal Language*, Chicago: University of Chicago Press.

Legal sources

60 Fed. Reg. 64,320 to 64,324, 1995.

63 Fed. Reg. 68,678, 68,678, 1998.

12 C.F.R. § 226.5 through 226.16.

Amara v. CIGNA, Case No. 3:01CV2361 (MRK), "Memorandum of Decision." United States District Court, District of Connecticut, available online at: www.ctemploymentlawblog.com/erisa.pdf (accessed 30 December 2008).

Consolidated Omnibus Budget Reconciliation Act of 1985, Pub. L. No. 99–272 § 11006, 100 Stat 82, 243 (1986).

Economic Growth and Tax Relief Reconciliation Act of 2001, Pub. L. No. 107–16, § 659, 115 Stat. 38, 140 (2001).

Supplement I to 12 CFR Part 226, Regulation Z.

Truth in Lending Act, 15 U.S.C. § 1601 et seq.

5

Legal writing: attitude and emphasis

Corpus linguistic approaches to 'legal language': adverbial expression of attitude and emphasis in Supreme Court opinions

Edward Finegan

Introduction

The US common law system relies heavily on the written opinions of appellate courts, and it is from such opinions more than statutory law that American jurisprudence is learned. Particularly in the first of the three years required to complete a doctor of laws degree, opinions rendered by appellate court judges are the principal focus of attention in law school classrooms in the United States (Mertz 2007).

Writing about legal decision-making and the presentation of legal opinions, Solan (1993: 1) observes that "Any judge who takes himself and his position seriously struggles with these dual tasks." Having clerked for an associate justice of the Supreme Court of New Jersey, he adds that "judges usually care deeply about making the best decision they can, and about conveying their decision in a manner that makes the decision appear as fair as possible to the parties, and often to the public." Once judges have made a decision about a case, however, they do not typically report the anguish that went into making it. Says Solan: "Any lawyer who has been on the losing side of a close question will recall the shock of reading how easily the judge rejects the losing arguments out of hand, as if they could not have been made by a thinking person" (1993: 2). As we shall see with respect to split decisions made by supreme court justices, "any lawyer" could readily encompass justices on both sides of the decision.

Conley and O'Barr (2005: 129) stress the point that "the details of legal discourse matter because language is the essential mechanism through which the power of the law is realized, exercised, reproduced, and occasionally challenged and subverted." The present chapter focuses on small details of legal language in a legal register that has received relatively little attention from forensic linguists but which is crucially important in the training of attorneys in the United States. In particular, it examines adverbial expressions of attitude and emphasis in decisions rendered by the Supreme Court of the United States and, as a state example, the Supreme Court of California. The opinions rendered by these courts are drafted as written documents intended to be published in

65

written form. Because they are usually not read aloud by the justices, but prepared for publication, they are not drafted as oral documents.

US court systems

By way of background and speaking somewhat generally, the US has two major categories of court systems—a federal system and the various state systems. The federal system comprises 94 judicial districts, whose trial courts are organized into a dozen regional circuits, each with an appellate level. For example, the United States Court of Appeals for the Ninth Circuit handles appellate cases for the district courts in California and in eight neighboring states, including Hawaii and Alaska, as well as in two Pacific Ocean territories. Typically, a panel of three judges hears an appellate case, but occasionally all the judges in a circuit hear a case *en banc*; in the exceptionally large Ninth Circuit, with 28 active circuit judges, an en banc hearing panel comprises a randomly selected 11 judges. Circuit court decisions constitute binding precedent within the district courts of the particular circuit and on subsequent three-judge panels in the circuit but not on other circuits. When different circuits arrive at competing conclusions about a point of federal law, when disagreements arise between individual states, and when it agrees to grant an appeal from a circuit court decision, the US Supreme Court has jurisdiction. The highest court in the land, its decisions, generally speaking, are binding throughout the country. Under the US Constitution, the judicial branch holds equal power with the executive and legislative branches.

As to state courts, there are as many systems as states, and each operates under the constitution and statutes of its state and within the reach of prior appellate decisions of its state. Each state has a highest court and, like federal courts and the US Supreme Court, each typically handles civil and criminal matters. State court systems usually have a website, as with New York's (www.nycourts.gov/) and California's (www.courtinfo.ca.gov/). A wider range of information is available through the website for the National Center for State Courts (www.ncsconline.org/).

Generally, courts of appeal rely principally on written records, notably briefs written by attorneys on each side and *amici* (friend-of-the-court) briefs written by third parties. Given that what most Americans understand about their judicial systems derives principally from experience with trial courts as occasionally broadcast and more commonly dramatized on television, many have only a general understanding of the workings of appellate courts, despite knowing of the existence of their state supreme court and the US Supreme Court. To appreciate how Americans likely perceive their court systems, it may be helpful to think of *LA Law*, *Judge Judy*, and *Law and Order*, the last being the longest-running primetime drama on US television and the most realistic of the court shows. Also popular are the televised hearings in Judge Judy's small claims court, where litigants represent themselves in disputed matters of relatively small financial consequence. Because courtroom dramas of the kind broadcast on television do not produce the *written* opinions that constitute the great bulk of what is studied in US law schools, the opinions that law school students study and practitioners rely on—and which are the focus of this chapter's analysis—deserve more attention than forensic linguists have thus far afforded them.

In mid 2009, to fill a vacancy arising from the retirement of Associate Justice David Souter from the nine-member US Supreme Court, President Barack Obama nominated

Judge Sonia Sotomayor to the post. A member of the federal Second Circuit, Judge Sotomayor was well qualified, and much of the opposition among those who lacked enthusiasm for the nomination focused not on her judicial opinions but on a line in a speech she had delivered eight years earlier. In that speech, she said,

> I would hope that a wise Latina woman with the richness of her experiences would more often than not reach a better conclusion than a white male who hasn't lived that life.

> (Savage 14 May 2009)

Her statement has been contrasted with one credited to Justice Sandra Day O'Connor, the first woman appointed to the US Supreme Court. O'Connor had remarked about judges that, in deciding cases, a wise old man and a wise old woman would reach the same conclusion. Sotomayor's speech is noteworthy, among other reasons, because her nomination prompted widespread discussion about whether and to what degree judges are engines of sheer rationality—pure logicians, even—or are influenced by matters other than knowledge of the law and what might be called legal logic. Thus, the degree to which the language of emotion finds its way into legal opinions is a matter of increasing interest and scrutiny.

Expressing attitude and emphasis

This chapter examines some aspects of the linguistic expression of judicial attitude, taking its examples not from televised courtroom dramas but from written opinions rendered and published in the year 2008 by the United States and California supreme courts. Specifically, it focuses on adverbial expressions of attitude and emphasis. With respect to emphasis, it addresses what appears to be a gap between a prominent feature of supreme court opinions and a near-universal recommendation in legal-drafting textbooks.

As an example of a judge who freely expresses her attitudes, Judge Judy has called one of her books *Beauty Fades, Dumb is Forever* and another *Keep it Simple, Stupid: You're Smarter than You Look*, while a third carries the title, *Don't Pee on My Leg and Tell Me It's Raining*. As in her books, so in her televised courtroom appearances Judge Judy gives voice to strong opinions and unflinching judgments. It is fair to say she wears her sentiments on her sleeve and expresses her attitudes with unmistakable force, and that is doubtless encouraged by her television producers, who have presumably chosen the outspoken judge with successful television ratings in mind. By contrast, appellate court judges, such as the panels mentioned above and the California and US supreme courts examined here, tend to be more circumspect in their precedential decisions. But by no means should a tendency toward circumspection suggest that appellate court judges mute the expression of attitude or the intended emphasis of their written appellate opinions. Not surprisingly, the tagline of Judge Judy's show is "Justice with an attitude," and that tagline tidily captures the thrust of this chapter.

Like other English speakers, judges have a range of grammatical structures through which to convey attitudinal stance in legal opinions. Those forms include:

predicate adjectives

"it is *absurd* to do this"; "It is therefore *unsurprising* that ... ";

attributive adjectives

"It is a *sad* day for the rule of law when such an *important* constitutional precedent is discarded";
"if Delaware could forbid the wharfing out that Article VII allowed New Jersey to permit, Article VII was a *ridiculous* nullity";
"In light of the *fundamental* nature of the *substantive* rights embodied in the right to marry—and their *central* importance to an individual's opportunity to live a *happy, meaningful,* and *satisfying* life as a *full* member of society … ";
"Unable to point to any such evidence, the Court stakes its holding on a *strained* and *unpersuasive* reading of the Amendment's text … ");

verb choice

("the Court *warps* our Constitution"; "the majority *fails* to persuade me"; "The majority *ignores* the fact that plaintiffs already have those rights and privileges").

(All excerpts from court opinions quoted in this chapter come from the corpus of supreme court opinions—COSCO—described below; within the excerpts, internal citations to other court opinions have been silently omitted.) In this chapter, we focus on adverbial expressions of attitudinal stance and emphasis.

As perhaps the most notorious exemplar of an acerbic opinion writer, US Supreme Court Associate Justice Antonin Scalia's attitudes are often palpable. In a case involving "enemy combatants" detained at the United States Naval Station at Guantanamo Bay, a majority of justices ruled that those detainees had certain rights of due process. Scalia dissented and in his dissenting opinion made no attempt to disguise his distaste for the majority opinion. He voiced that distaste by using strong predicate adjectives, as in

In the long term, then, the Court's decision today accomplishes little. … "In the short term, however, the decision is *devastating*" and "It is *nonsensical* to interpret those provisions themselves in light of some general "separation-of-powers principles" dreamed up by the Court.

But a particularly preferred mode in so many examples in his opinions is the deployment of adverbs. If not quite as earthy as Judge Judy, Justice Scalia nonetheless pulls no punches with his attitudes:

Today the Court warps our Constitution in a way that goes beyond the narrow issue of the reach of the Suspension Clause, invoking *judicially* brainstormed separation-of-powers principles to establish a manipulable "functional" test for the extraterritorial reach of habeas corpus. … It *blatantly* misdescribes important precedents. … And, *most tragically*, it sets our military commanders the impossible task of proving to a civilian court … that evidence supports the confinement of each and every enemy prisoner.

In the remainder of this chapter we examine how jurists express attitude and emphasis in their use of adverbials, as in Scalia's "judicially brainstormed," "blatantly misdescribes" and "most tragically" sets an impossible task. Scalia's caustic exploitation of adverbs is by no means a solitary practice. However calm, cool, and collected the logic behind supreme court opinions, the justices' words have teeth—and can bite.

Emphatic adverbials and their prohibition

Some adverbials receive special treatment in legal writing textbooks and handbooks of legal usage. Brian Garner, regarded by many as the dean of American legal usage, notes that from the sense 'as a matter of course' "the phrase *of course* took on the sense 'naturally; obviously; clearly'" and, like them, he says, "is sometimes used to fortify lame propositions. It therefore requires careful, responsible use" (Garner 1995: 614). About *clearly,* another shibboleth among legal drafting experts, Garner quotes a literary scholar talking of judicial style: "when a judge (some other judge) begins a sentence with a term of utter conviction (*Clearly, Undeniably, It is plain that* ...), the sentence that follows is likely to be dubious, unreasonable, and fraught with difficulties" (Garner 1995: 161, citing Gibson 1961: 925). Had that scholar been writing decades later, he could have illustrated his point with examples from Scalia's dissent in a case involving the right of an individual to bear arms: "Story's Commentaries also cite as support Tucker and Rawle, both of whom <u>clearly</u> viewed the right as unconnected to militia service" or "Nothing so <u>clearly</u> demonstrates the weakness of Justice Stevens' case" (underscoring of relevant examples added here and elsewhere throughout the chapter).

Obviously is another adverb that receives unfavorable marks from legal drafting guides. Garner calls it a dogmatic word that "lawyers tend to use when they are dealing with exceptionally obscure matters" (Garner 1995: 161, citing Gilmore 1974: 116, n. 63). He even captions a chapter of *The Winning Brief* with this directive: "Shun *clearly* and its allies" (Garner 2004b: 363), and he justifies the directive on the admittedly paradoxical grounds that words like *clearly* and *obviously* "protest too much. They signal weakness." Elsewhere Garner calls such words "exaggerators," and he notes that "a statement prefaced by one of these words is [often] conclusory, and sometimes even exceedingly dubious" (Garner 2003: 152).

Garner is not alone in objecting to *clearly* and other exaggerators. A drafting textbook used at the University of Southern California's law school directs students to "avoid intensifiers" and offers this curious and provocative explanation:

> Because generations of writers have overused words like "clearly" or "very," these and other common intensifiers have become virtually meaningless. As a matter of fact, they have begun to develop a connotation exactly opposite their original meaning.
>
> (Edwards 2006: 232)

Other legal writing guides make similar comments, and if their assessments are accurate, it is no wonder that authors direct novice legal drafters to "rid your writing" of *clearly, extremely, obviously,* and *very* (Edwards 2006: 233).

The disparagement of such intensifiers, exaggerators, and emphatics in legal language ranges well beyond handbook writers and textbook authors. John G. Roberts, chief justice of the United States Supreme Court, lambasted such adverbials in a discussion session following a speech at Northwestern University law school and lamented their appearance in briefs submitted to the United States Supreme Court.

> We get hundreds and hundreds of briefs, and they're all the same. Somebody says, "My client clearly deserves to win, the cases clearly do this, the language clearly reads this," blah, blah, blah. And you pick up the other side and, lo and behold,

they think they clearly deserve to win. How about a little recognition that it's a tough job? I mean, if it was an easy case, we wouldn't have it.

(Barnes 2007: A15, cited in Long and Christensen 2008)

From the legal writing textbook author to the legal writing usage handbook compiler to the chief justice of the United States Supreme Court, the condemnation of certain kinds of adverbials is loud and consistent.

Adverbs and adverbials

Although not much attended to in scholarship about legal language, adverbs and adverbials are interesting on several grounds. For one thing, they display impressive grammatical flexibility, serving to modify not only verbs, adjectives, and adverbs but entire clauses. They may have within their scope single words, as in (1a), or complicated clauses, as in (1b).

(1)
   a) Defendant contends the challenged condition … is *unconstitutionally* overbroad.
   b) *Certainly* such agreements would require courts to vacate clear errors appearing on the face of an arbitration award that cause substantial prejudice.

Solan (1993) discusses a case (*United States v. Yermian*) at whose heart was the scope of the expression *knowingly and willfully* as it appeared in a section of the United States Criminal Code. The defendant's conviction at trial was overturned on appeal to the Ninth Circuit, which disagreed with the lower court's interpretation of adverbial scope. Then, on appeal to the US Supreme Court, the Ninth Circuit's interpretation of adverbial scope was itself overturned—although the highest court's 5–4 decision underscores how difficult it can be to disambiguate the scope of an adverb unanimously. Schane (2006) discusses wide and narrow adverbial scope in another US Supreme Court case (*Liparota v. United States*), while Tiersma (1999) talks about adverbial scope in statutory law. In legal contexts, then, ambiguities of adverbial scope carry some notoriety.

Besides in scope, adverbials may be ambiguous in other ways (Biber *et al.* 1999: 782ff.; Huddleston and Pullum 2002: 436), and it is possible that this very disposition to ambiguity makes them attractive in legal opinions. Still, despite their playing a prominent role in the expression of attitude and particularly because as emphatics and intensifiers they are the target of proscription and contempt in textbooks on legal drafting, forensic linguists and professional analysts of legal language seldom treat adverbs and adverbials in depth.

Adverbials serve several communicative or grammatical functions, two of which (affect or attitude and emphasis) are examined in this chapter. Not treated here are:

- adverbials marking stylistic stance, such as *briefly, candidly, frankly, honestly, to tell the truth, in truth,* and *in fact,* only the last of which occurs more than sporadically in our corpus of supreme court opinions and seems often an intensifier;
- adverbials marking epistemic stance, such as *logically, psychologically, textually, inevitably* and *naturally,* only the last two occurring more than sporadically in our corpus;

- hedging, as in *about, allegedly, almost, apparently, approximately, arguably, conceivably, generally, hardly, in effect, largely, likely, maybe, nearly, seemingly, virtually, perhaps, possibly, presumably, probably, relatively, reportedly, reputedly*;
- conjoining, as in *accordingly, consequently, however, subsequently, thereby, therefore, thus, nevertheless, nonetheless, in addition, in conclusion, in short, in sum, instead*, and *rather*.

Hedging and conjoining adverbials occur in supreme court opinions but lie beyond the ambit of this chapter. Ditto for adverbials expressing manner or circumstance (*again, then, now, carefully, clearly, deceptively, deliberately, earnestly, erroneously, faithfully, frequently, often, seldom, plainly, quickly, respectfully, swiftly, unreasonably*), which are also frequent but not specifically pertinent to judicial expression of attitude or emphasis.

Noting that both *clearly* and *plainly* are listed among the manner or circumstance adverbials just above highlights the point that adverbials may carry multiple meanings and serve different functions, depending on their context of use. For example, *in fact* may mark stylistic or epistemic stance as well as emphasis, while *clearly* and *plainly* may indicate circumstance, epistemic stance, or emphasis. As another example, consider an adverb that occurs very frequently in COSCO. The adverb *simply*, like so many others, is poly-semous. The *American Heritage Dictionary* lists five senses, including three that are not common in supreme court opinions ('in a plain and unadorned way or an unambiguous way'; 'not wisely or sensibly'; 'frankly, candidly') and two that are common ('merely, only' and 'absolutely, altogether'). Linguists have categorized these senses in different ways, including as manner or circumstance adverbials, markers of stance, and markers of emphasis (see Biber and Finegan 1988, 1989). From the COSCO corpus the sense of 'merely, only' can be seen in examples such as, "'Keep arms' was <u>simply</u> a common way of referring to possessing arms, for militiamen *and everyone else*," while the 'absolutely, altogether' sense appears in "The Court is <u>simply</u> wrong when it intones that *Miller* contained '*not a word*' about the Amendment's history" (underscore here and in other examples added; italics in original).

The corpus of supreme court opinions (COSCO)

To examine adverbial expression of stance and emphatics in supreme court opinions, a corpus can be useful, and constructing one for research or teaching purposes is not dif-ficult. To begin this examination, a corpus comprising cases decided by the US and California supreme courts in the year 2008 was compiled. Cases from a single calendar year encompass decisions rendered roughly in the second half of one term (here, the 2007–8 term) and the first half of another (here, the 2008–9 term). Aiming to avoid strictly procedural decisions, the corpus of supreme court opinions, or COSCO, includes only substantive decisions that were not unanimously decided. Choosing decisions with at least one dissenting opinion proved an expedient way of simultaneously excluding procedural matters (which are otherwise abundant) and including differences of opinion likely to prompt or multiply expressions of attitude and emphasis.

Taken from the Lexis-Nexis database, COSCO includes the majority opinion and all concurring and dissenting opinions for 17 California cases (comprising approximately 259,000 words) and 56 federal cases (comprising about 647,000 words). In all, COSCO contains 905,464 words, including citations. Because a given supreme court opinion usually contains significant internal citation to preceding opinions and occasional internal citation to other parts of the given decision (including concurring and dissenting opinions), frequency counts of linguistic features "per million words" of legal opinions can fairly be viewed as distinctly conservative in that, were the internal citations removed from a judicial opinion as not part and parcel of ordinary language use, the frequency counts of adverbs per million words would increase.

Researchers and students can readily compile corpora of American supreme court opinions, relying on material available through Lexis-Nexis or Westlaw and through websites for individual state courts and the US Supreme Court. In many instances, these resources also make available the briefs that were filed in connection with a case. Further still, at its website (www.supremecourtus.gov/) the US Supreme Court makes available transcripts of oral arguments, which usually last for one hour in all, half an hour for each side, including questions from the bench. Audio recordings of oral arguments before the US Supreme Court have been made since 1955 and are available through the Oyez Project (www.oyez.org), going back several decades, although with somewhat uneven quality. Thus, written texts originating in speech (transcriptions of oral arguments by litigants and questions by justices) and texts originating in writing and not usually intended to be read aloud (briefs, court opinions), as well as audio recordings of the spoken materials, are increasingly available. State supreme court websites often provide archived audio recordings of oral arguments, leaving researchers who need transcripts to produce them on their own. Recordings of oral arguments, which may be highly interactional, are likely to prove invaluable to forensic linguists keen to understand and describe this hitherto largely inaccessible legal register. A corpus of such transcripts, corrected and augmented from audio recordings to any degree of detail a researcher might need, could afford a rich database for study of registers of legal language largely overlooked by linguists. Almost any aspect of the language of oral arguments could be analyzed and in some cases compared with the language of written briefs filed in support of one side or the other or with the written opinions of the court. In contrast to a burgeoning interest in supreme court cases and their attendant written and spoken registers among political scientists and communications specialists, forensic linguists are in the early stages of such analysis (for an application of automated analysis of content in advocacy briefs, see Evans *et al.* 2007; Apitz and Lin 2007). But forensic linguists are beginning to recognize the value of these resources and exploit them (see, e.g. Tracy 2009; Tracy and Craig 2009).

To turn to the principal focus of this chapter, COSCO provides an extraordinary range of adverbials used to express judges' attitudes toward the content of their analysis. The adverbial markers of stance illustrated in examples (2.1–2.7) may be paraphrased as something akin to, "It should not *surprise* us that … "; "I find it *remarkable/inexplicable* that … "; "It is *most important* to note that … "; "It is *significant* that. … "; and "I regard it as *unfortunate* that. … "

(2)
1. <u>Not surprisingly</u>, the parties vigorously disputed the waiver issue, and it sharply divided the Court.
2. <u>Remarkably</u>, this Court does not require petitioners to exhaust their remedies under the statute. …
3. The Court <u>inexplicably</u> concludes, however, that the liquefied natural gas (LNG) unloading wharf at stake in this litigation "goes well beyond the ordinary or usual."

4. <u>Most importantly</u>, the circumstance that the offense is aggravated does not, in every case, provide evidence that the inmate is a current threat to public safety.
5. <u>Significantly</u>, AB 1889 authorizes not only the California Attorney General but also any private taxpayer … to bring a civil action against suspected violators. …
6. <u>Happily</u>, we need not imagine such cases, since they come before our courts every day.
7. <u>Unfortunately</u>, it would likely create, rather than alleviate, confusion to change our terminology at this point.

In COSCO, we may note, *surprisingly* is used almost invariably in the negative, as in (2.1), and *importantly* is almost invariably preceded by *more* or *most*, as in (2.4). As we shall see below, adverbial expression of attitudinal stance is less common than adverbial expression of emphatics.

Also abundant in COSCO are emphatics—adverbs that merely add emphasis to some aspect of content but do not otherwise add content itself. Example (3.1) shows in parenthesis the original utterance but without the emphatic, a contrast intended to highlight the fact that emphatics merely emphasize.

(3)
1. But when discussing these words, the Court <u>simply</u> ignores the preamble. (But when discussing these words, the Court ignores the preamble.)
2. The Navy's alternative course … is <u>surely</u> not what Congress had in mind when it instructed agencies to comply with NEPA "to the fullest extent possible."
3. … an "absolute certainty" standard is <u>plainly</u> inconsistent with <u>Brecht</u>.
4. It is <u>particularly</u> appropriate for us to refrain from employing equal protection doctrine to thwart the will of the voters in this case.
5. A drug purchase was not the only possible explanation for the defendant's conduct, but it was <u>certainly likely</u> enough to give rise to probable cause.
6. But the two readings of the language that Congress chose are not equally plausible: Of the two, Florida's is <u>clearly</u> the more natural.

Frequency of emphatics in COSCO

It would require considerable resources to examine each occurrence of selected adverbs in a corpus of over 900,000 words, and it was not the aim of this chapter to do the kind of exact and detailed study that a research paper would exhibit. Instead, we sought to highlight the availability of a range of linguistic resources for the study of supreme court cases in all their public facets and to illustrate that, contrary to much public belief and considerable legal posturing, both state and federal supreme court opinions are far from lacking in expressions of attitude and emphasis.

For this chapter, COSCO has served principally to identify the character of certain adverbial types in a sample of supreme court opinions. Further, frequency counts of selected adverbs in COSCO, in the *Brown Corpus of Written American English* (Francis and Kučera 1982), and in the *British National Corpus* (http://sara.natcorp.ox.ac.uk/lookup. html) allow tentative comparisons to be made between court opinions and more general ranges of written English. The *Brown Corpus* contains just over 1 million words from 15 genres of American English, while the *BNC* in about 100 million words likewise contains a range of written registers as well as a relatively small portion of speech.

73

Normalizing counts of adverbs in COSCO to frequencies per million words allows rough comparison with frequencies in the *Brown Corpus* as published in Francis and Kučera (1982). Using the Sara simple search of the BNC (http://sara.natcorp.ox.ac.uk/lookup.html) to determine frequencies of specific adverbs and dividing by 100 provided an approximation of frequencies per million words and permits comparisons across the three corpora. No attempt was made to distinguish the different adverbial uses of a given adverbial form (e.g. *plainly*), and in the Tables 5.1 and 5.2 a small limitation to comparing phrasal adverbs is reflected in some blank cells because the published Francis and Kučera (1982) frequencies do not include phrasal adverbs such as *in fact* and *of course*. Still, some rough and ready comparisons can be offered.

Table 5.1 shows frequencies per million words for several attitudinal adverbials across the three corpora. The first five of the seven adverbials are more frequent in COSCO than in *Brown* or *BNC*. The dramatically more frequent occurrences of *properly* and *improperly* in COSCO than in the more general corpora point to judges' special use of these terms to assess earlier court opinions and the decisions of the courts below, which they are considering on appeal. A similar explanation likely applies to the relative frequency of *correctly*. About *unfortunately* (which we have illustrated above) and *fortunately*, it is not surprising that justices seldom use these expressions, given that they so patently express inner emotion.

Table 5.1 Stance adverbials per million words in three corpora

	COSCO	BROWN	BNC
appropriately	15	5	9
correctly	59	13	1
importantly	24	8	13
improperly	23	2	1
properly	207	55	55
fortunately	3	20	16
unfortunately	4	33	46

Table 5.2 Emphatic adverbials per million words in three corpora

	COSCO	BROWN	BNC
simply	375	171	173
indeed	306	146	184
merely	235	135	74
clearly	184	128	150
plainly	88	18	7
precisely	81	48	34
surely	71	47	60
readily	52	43	28
of course	178		297
particularly	163	146	217
actually	163	166	255
in fact	162		163
certainly	84	143	181
fully	71	80	88
especially	71		174
highly	50	94	90

Table 5.2 shows frequencies per million words across the three corpora for selected adverbials commonly used as emphatics. No claim is made here that any listed adverb is an emphatic in all its occurrences; the counts are nevertheless likely to be indicative chiefly of use as an emphatic, particularly in COSCO. Words like *even* and *so*, that are frequent and vary so much in function that comparison across different corpora would certainly be misleading, are not included.

In Table 5.2, the adverbs *simply* (at 375 per million words in COSCO), *indeed* (306 pmw), *merely* (235 pmw), and the notorious *clearly* (184 pmw) occur much more frequently in the supreme court opinions represented in COSCO than in *Brown* and the *BNC*, the more general corpora. Less frequent than those four but still more highly favored in supreme court opinions than in the two general corpora are *plainly*, *precisely*, *surely*, and *readily*. By contrast, *actually*, *certainly*, *fully*, and *highly*—carrying more absolute senses—occur more frequently in the general corpora. *Of course* appears less frequently in COSCO than in *BNC*, and *in fact* appears about equally; as noted earlier published sources provided no usable information for these items in *Brown*. A closer look at actual instances could reveal the reasons, but *of course* seems concessive in a good many supreme court uses, and concession may risk conveying condescension. While most occurrences in COSCO of the Table 5.2 adverbs are probably emphatics, it is necessary to stress that identifying particular functions for these adverbs was not attempted here and therefore, *as emphatics* the cited frequencies are merely indicative and subject to refinement. Besides the emphatic adverbials that we have discussed as occurring in COSCO, several emphatics did not occur even once in our supreme court opinions, including *absolutely*, *totally*, and *wholly* and a set that could be emphatics or represent epistemic stance, namely, *really*, *obviously*, *patently*, and *undoubtedly*.

Efficacy of emphatics in appellate briefs

The frequency of some emphatics in the supreme court opinions in COSCO may be surprising, given the strong criticism of them by drafting experts and members of the judiciary. While *clearly* is not the most frequent emphatic in COSCO, its use in supreme court opinions is notably more frequent than in *Brown* or *BNC*, both of which represent more familiar genres of written English. Others among the condemned emphatics— though not all—are far from uncommon. Given the frequent use of some emphatics— including some of those most explicitly condemned—one must wonder to what end handbook authors like Garner (2004b) and textbook writers like Edwards (2006) are so insistent on legal drafters avoiding such adverbs. In other words, given the nearly universal condemnation of such emphatics, the question that remains is whether attorneys who use those adverbs in their briefs before appellate courts are as disadvantaged by their use as drafting experts would suggest. Given the bad press for intensifiers, one must wonder about their efficacy in legal briefs. Do lawyers and their clients fail more often when a lawyer's brief utilizes the intensifiers condemned by drafting experts and ridiculed by the chief justice of the United States Supreme Court?

Just that question has been addressed in a recent study that exploited the availability of appellate court opinions and the related briefs filed in those cases. Long and Christensen (2008) carried out a statistically sophisticated analysis of correlations between lawyers' use of a dozen adverbial intensifiers (*very*, *obviously*, *clearly*, *patently*, *absolutely*, *really*, *plainly*, *undoubtedly*, *certainly*, *totally*, *simply*, and *wholly*) in their briefs and the outcome of the cases in which the briefs had been filed. They analyzed 400 federal and state appeals cases to determine whether the widespread condemnation of *clearly* and its cousins affected outcomes. They randomly chose federal circuit court cases and state appellate cases from the years 2001–3 roughly in proportion to the number of cases handled by those jurisdictions. They examined only civil cases in which there was "a clearly discernable outcome, usually either 'reversed' or 'affirmed,' and the selected cases had at least one brief for each party—usually the principal and the response brief" (Long and Christensen 2008: 182). They made "every effort … to exclude the selected intensifiers when they were not used as intensifiers" or appeared in quoted materials (2008: 182), a refinement not available to us in the frequency counts of Table 5.1 and Table 5.2. As a measure of intensifier usage rate, Long and Christensen tallied the number of (the twelve) intensifiers per page for each brief.

They found that decisions that were not unanimous prompted high rates of intensifiers in both majority and dissenting opinions and that dissenting judges were "by far the worst offenders." As Long and Christensen put it, "when things are clearly less clear in the judges' chambers, the judges, too, are more likely to use 'clearly' and other intensifiers" (Long and Christensen 2008: 184), precisely as claimed by Garner (2004b) and Edwards (2006). Interestingly, however, no correlation was found generally between intensifier use in lawyers' briefs and the outcome for the clients on whose behalf the briefs had been filed. Still, the analysis did uncover some fascinating correlations; in particular, "the rate of intensifier use is associated with a statistically significant change in the likelihood of success on appeal" (Long and Christensen 2008: 181).

According to Long and Christensen, "the conventional wisdom that intensifiers are associated with losing arguments is validated" for the majority of cases. That means that authors of legal-drafting textbooks should be relieved to learn that "in certain situations, excessive intensifier use in appellate briefs is associated with a statistically significant increase in adverse outcomes for the 'offending' party" (Long and Christensen 2008: 173). Looking closer, however, one may wonder whether it pays not so much to know your judge as to know your judge's writing style! Here's why: for petitioners aiming to get a higher court to reverse a lower-court ruling, the odds of reversal actually improved for appellants with high intensifier usage rates—"but only when the judge writing the opinion is also a prodigious user of intensifiers" (Long and Christensen 2008: 185).

Language and thought

Long and Christensen (2008) cite a study that identified scalar values attributed to the use of the intensifier *very*. Subjects were given sentences to read in which *very* was and was not used in modification of some quality or other—e.g. *very smart*, *very tall*. Cliff (1959) found that intensifiers do indeed intensify and that *very* has a scalar value of 1.25. In other words, readers reading a sentence referring to a *very* tall student judged the student to be about 25 percent taller than a tall one and a *very* smart lecturer about 25 percent smarter than a smart one. Other research, however, has found that when not paired in contrasting sentences (with and without the intensifier) readers did not make a significant difference between adjectives modified and not modified by *very*. Long and Christensen conclude that:

> the best characterization of the literature seems to suggest that intensifiers, if isolated from other forms of powerless speech, or if used in simultaneous comparison

with a phrase omitting the intensifier, actually do what intensifiers seem meant to do—they intensify. On the other hand, when used in connection with other forms of powerless speech, and without reference to a phrase lacking the given intensifier, they may negatively affect the writer's or speaker's perceived credibility or competence—they 'detensify.'

(Long and Christensen 2008: 179–80)

Elsewhere in the psycholinguistic literature, Loftus (1996) has found that the language form used in questioning can affect a witness's reply (see also Eades 2009; Matoesian 1993). Van der Houwen's (2005) discourse analysis of the televised Judge Judy trials also suggests a correlation between the judge's insistence on certain language in litigants' narratives and the way to reaching an acceptable decision among small claims litigants. From various sources, then, it seems fair to say that particular language choices influence a story and presumably the perception of facts behind the story (see Heffer, this volume, for a discussion of narrative in trials).

Eric Kandel, distinguished psychiatrist and winner of the Nobel Prize in Physiology and Medicine in 2000, has marshaled evidence indicating that the physiological healings in the brain that pharmacotherapy accomplishes and that traditional psychotherapy accomplishes are strikingly alike. In other words, as fMRIs and other technologies are beginning to witness, therapeutic drugs and therapeutic talk shows have kindred effects on the brain (Kandel 1998, 2006). It is clear that investigation into the power of discourse to influence the brain is only in its infancy.

Conclusion

Language in use—that is, discourse—doubtless affects perception, albeit in ways that remain unclear and under investigation. Still, we ought not think or let others believe that language form does not matter. Like naïve language judges generally, appellate court judges, including supreme court justices, are not necessarily adept at understanding their own language use, and none of us knows well the effect of reading appellate court opinions on the minds of law students. It is the duty and the responsibility of forensic linguists to be assertive in describing legal language as fully and accurately as possible.

Further reading

Biber, D. and E. Finegan (1988) "Adverbial stance types in English," *Discourse Processes*, 11: 1–34.
——(1989) "Styles of stance in English: Lexical and grammatical marking of evidentiality and affect," *Text*, 9: 93–124.
Biber, D., S. Johansson, G. Leech, S. Conrad and E. Finegan (1999) "Stance adverbials," in *Longman Grammar of Spoken and Written English*, Harlow: Longman, 853–75.
Solan, L. (1993) *The Language of Judges*, Chicago: University of Chicago Press.

6

Legal translation

Translating legal language

Deborah Cao

Introduction

The translation of law has played an important part in the contact between different peoples and different cultures in history, and is playing an even more important role in our increasingly globalised world with the demand for legal translation on the increase. It is commonly acknowledged that legal translation is complex and that it requires special skills, knowledge and experience on the part of the translator to produce such translation. This chapter outlines the key concepts and issues involved in legal translation, in particular the practical aspects of translating law with an analysis of different types of legal texts, including private legal documents, domestic statutes and multilateral legal instruments.

Legal translation defined

Legal translation is a type of specialist or technical translation, a kind of translational activity that involves special language use, that is, language for special purpose (LSP) in the context of law, or language for legal purpose (LLP).

Legal language and legal texts

For our purpose, legal language refers to the language of law and its relation to law and legal process. This includes language of the law, language about law, and language used in legal communicative situations (cf. Kurzon 1997, 1998a, who distinguishes language of the law and legal language which is language about law). Legal language is a variety of language appropriate to different legal occasions and legal situations of use and appropriate to those different legal situations of use. Legal texts refer to the texts produced or used for legal purposes in legal settings.

We may distinguish four major variants or sub-varieties of written legal texts:

(1) legislative texts, for example, domestic statutes and subordinate laws, international treaties and multilingual laws;
(2) judicial texts produced in the judicial process by judicial officers and other legal authorities;
(3) legal scholarly texts produced by academic lawyers or legal scholars in scholarly works and commentaries whose legal status depends on the legal systems in different jurisdictions; and
(4) private legal texts which include texts written by lawyers, for example, contracts, leases, wills and litigation documents, and also texts written by non-lawyers, for example, private agreements, witness statements and other documents, which are used in litigation and other legal situations.

These different sub-text types have their own peculiarities. As noted, legal language is not homogeneous, not just one legal discourse, but 'a set of related legal discourses' (Maley 1994: 13). Legal language does not just cover the language of law alone, but all communications in legal settings.

Legal texts may have various communicative purposes. They can be for normative purposes, as in the case of bilingual and multilingual statutes and other laws and documents that establish legal facts or create rights and obligations. These are mostly prescriptive. Legal texts can also be for informative purposes, as in some legal scholarly works and commentaries, legal advice, correspondence between lawyers, between lawyers and clients, and documents used in court proceedings. These are mostly descriptive. For the translator, then, it is necessary to ascertain the legal status and communicative purpose of the original texts and the target texts, as these may impact on any translation. Also importantly for our purpose, the legal status and communicative purposes of the Source Language (SL) texts are not automatically transferred or carried over to the Target Language (TL) texts. They can be different.

Legal translation and its classifications

In view of the foregoing description of legal language and legal texts, as a generic definition, legal translation refers to the rendering of legal texts from the SL into the TL.

Legal translation can be classified according to different criteria. For instance, legal translation has been categorised according to the **subject matter** of the SL texts into the following categories:

(1) translating domestic statutes and international treaties;
(2) translating private legal documents;
(3) translating legal scholarly works; and
(4) translating case law.

For further discussion, see Cao (2007a).

Legal translation can also be divided according to the **status** of the original texts:

(1) translating enforceable law, for example, statutes; and
(2) translating non-enforceable law, for example, legal scholarly works.

According to Sarcevic (1997), legal translation may be classified according to the **functions** of the legal texts in the SL into the following categories:

(1) primarily prescriptive, for example, laws, regulations, codes, contracts, treaties and conventions. These are regulatory instruments and they are normative texts;

(2) primarily descriptive and also prescriptive, for example, judicial decisions and legal instruments that are used to carry out judicial and administrative proceedings such as actions, pleadings, briefs, appeals, requests, petitions, etc.; and

(3) purely descriptive, for example, scholarly works written by legal scholars such as legal opinions, law textbooks, articles. They belong to legal scholarship, the authority of which varies in different legal systems (Sarcevic 1997: 11).

Sarcevic (1997: 9) defines legal translation as special-purpose communication between specialists, excluding communication between lawyers and non-lawyers.

Legal translation can also be classified in the light of the **purposes** of the TL texts. Firstly, there is legal translation for **normative purposes**. This refers to the production of equally authentic legal texts in bilingual and multilingual jurisdictions of domestic laws and international legal instruments and other laws. These are translations **of** the law. Often such bilingual or multilingual texts are first drafted in one language and then translated into another language or languages. They may also be drafted simultaneously in both or all languages. In either case, the different language texts have equal legal force and one is not superior to another irrespective of their original status. Such legal texts in different languages are regarded as authoritative once they go through the authentication process in the manner prescribed by law. By virtue of this process, such texts are not mere translations of law, but **the law itself** (Sarcevic 1997: 20). Examples of these are the legislation in the bilingual jurisdictions of Canada and Hong Kong, the multilingual legal instruments of the United Nations (UN) and the multilingual laws of the European Union (EU). In the case of the EU, the authentic language versions of EU laws, are equivalent since they have the same legal force and value and can be invoked indiscriminately in appeals to the European Court of Justice by EU citizens or businesses, irrespective of their member state of origin or that country's official language or languages (Correia 2003: 41). They are usually drafted in English or French first to be translated into the other official languages. Nevertheless, they all have equal legal force.

This category of legal translation may also include private documents such as contracts, the bilingual texts of which are equally authentic in a bilingual or monolingual jurisdiction. For instance, in a non-English speaking country, contracts sometimes may stipulate that the versions of the contract in the official language of the country and English are both authentic, even though the language of the court and the country does not include English. In this first category of legal translation, the communicative purposes of the SL and TL texts are identical.

Secondly, there is legal translation for **informative purposes**, with constative or descriptive functions. This includes the translation of statutes, court decisions, scholarly works and other types of legal documents if the purpose of the translation is to provide information to the target readers. This is most often found in monolingual jurisdictions. Such translations are different from the first category where the translation of the law is legally binding. In this second category, the SL is the only legally enforceable language while the TL is not. For instance, a statute written in French from France translated into English for informative purpose for the benefit of foreign lawyers or other English readers is not legally enforceable. This is different from the first category where, for instance, a statute written in French in the bilingual jurisdiction of Canada is translated into English or vice versa and where both the French and English versions are equally authentic. Sometimes, publishers of translations of laws in the second category include a disclaimer to the effect that the translation of such and such a law is for reference only, and that in legal proceedings, the original language text of the law shall prevail. Another example is the translation of the legal instruments of the World Trade Organisation (WTO) which has English and French as its authentic languages. Here only the original texts written in English and French have legal force, while their translations into other languages are not binding, but for information only. In this category, the SL and TL texts may have different communicative purposes.

Thirdly, there is legal translation for **general** legal or **judicial purpose**. Such translations are primarily for information, and are mostly descriptive. This type of translated document may be used in court proceedings as part of documentary evidence. Original SL texts of this type may include legal documents, such as statements of claims or pleadings, contracts and agreements; and ordinary texts such as business or personal correspondence, records, and certificates, witness statements and expert reports, among many others. The translations of such documents are used by clients who do not speak the language of the court, for example, statements of claims, or by lawyers and courts who otherwise may not be able to access the originals such as contracts, correspondence or other records and documents.

Such translated texts have legal consequences attached to them due to their use in the legal process. In practice, for instance, in Australian courts, a sworn affidavit from the translator is normally required as to the quality of the translation and the competency of the translator. Sometimes, the translator is also called upon as a witness in court regarding the translation. For some of these, the otherwise ordinary non-legal documents written by non-lawyers are elevated to legal status because of the special use of the original and the translation. This is similar to court interpreting. Court interpreters in most cases interpret oral evidence of witnesses who may be retelling ordinary events and answering ordinary personal questions. These witnesses could say the same or similar things outside the courtroom in non-legal settings. The main difference is that interpreting a story in a non-legal setting is ordinary interpreting, while interpreting the same in court is legal interpreting, as the interpreted words are used for a legal purpose under special circumstances and conditions. In these situations, the language use or translation use is contingent upon the existence of a legal order which must be considered to be part of the communicative situation. The law's institutional character plays a major part in language use in legal settings (Madsen 1997), thus, should be given prominent consideration in our classifications of legal texts and legal translation. Many parts of the court or litigation documents are the closest to everyday language use in all the sub-types of legal texts.

The third type of translation is different from the second category described above in that it may include ordinary texts that are not written in legal language by legal professionals, but by the layperson. This type of legal translation is often left out in the discussion and classification of legal translation. However, in fact, in the practice of legal translation, it constitutes a major part of the translation work of the legal translator in real life, the 'bread and butter' activities (Harvey 2002: 178).

Thus, we can say that legal translation refers to the translation of texts used in law and legal settings. Legal translation is used as a general term to cover both the translation of law and other communications in legal settings. For the legal translator, it is important to ascertain the status and communicative purposes of both the original text and its translation.

Translating private legal documents

Private legal documents are those that are drafted and used by lawyers in their daily practice on behalf of their clients. They may include deeds, contracts and other agreements, leases, wills and other legal texts such as statutory declaration, power of attorney, statements of claims or pleadings and other court documents and advice from lawyers to clients. The translation of these documents constitutes the bulk of actual translation work for many legal translation practitioners. In this chapter, the linguistic features of major private legal documents in English are examined with regard to translation.

Purpose and status of translated private legal documents

Private legal documents, either original or translated, serve many purposes. Some of the major functions include creating, conferring, varying or negating legal rights and obligations and recording such rights and obligations (Aitkin and Butter 2004). They are also used before courts or legal authorities to protect rights or enforce obligations. Private legal documents are important. It is said that drafting legal documents is like drafting statutes between private parties, setting out the relationships and ground rules in a formal or written form (Dick 1985: 1).

There are different purposes and uses for translated private legal documents. They may be requested by organisations or individuals. For instance, legal documents may be translated for business purpose, such as contracts that are used as part of a business transaction. There are documents that are translated for use by individuals for various purposes, for instance, a will, a statutory declaration, or a marriage certificate. There are documents that are translated for litigation purposes, for instance, statements of claims or pleadings and witness statements. Legal advice of lawyers to their clients may also require translation if they speak different languages. So do instructions of clients to their legal representatives.

The legal status of these translated documents may vary. They may be for informative or for normative purposes. For instance, contracts sometimes stipulate that two language versions are equally authentic, that is, both texts have equal legal force in the court of law. At other times, contracts may stipulate that only one language version, not both, is legally binding. They may nevertheless require translation, and such translations are mainly for informative purposes. Court documents and other litigation documents sometimes may require translations so that all the parties and the court can have linguistic access to documents written in different languages. Today, due to the increased movement of people across national borders for educational, employment, immigration and other purposes, legal certificates such as marriage, divorce, birth and death certificates are often in need of translation.

Key linguistic features of private legal documents

Private legal documents often follow certain established patterns and rules in a particular jurisdiction. The Common Law drafting style has been inherited from the United

Kingdom over the last two to three hundred years and is similar in many ways across the Common Law countries (see Bhatia, this volume). Moreover, the use of standard documents by law firms, called 'precedents', is common, maintaining similar drafting styles. For instance, wills, contracts of sale of land, mortgages and leases of premises are normally in standard forms. Such precedents are often available in law books and now also online. Legal firms usually have their own precedents. For the commonly used legal forms such as marriage, divorce, death, birth certificates and statutory declaration, they are often also in standard form in a particular jurisdiction, issued by the relevant authorities. In these texts, the linguistic form is often as important as the content.

Textual features

Due to the commonalities in private legal drafting in English, certain textual features can be identified. Agreements and contracts, which are among the most commonly translated private legal documents from and into English, are often written in similar styles. Such documents vary in their actual contents, which can be wide-ranging from intellectual property rights transfer to the sale of equipment, depending upon the needs of the clients. They also vary in terms of length and complexity. Some are short and general but most are lengthy and detailed.

In terms of textual components, with respect to general agreements drafted in English, for instance, agreements on business or research collaboration, joint business ventures, or collaborative projects, some common parts and clauses can be identified. They often include the following:

- date of the agreement
- names and addresses of the parties
- recital
- definition clause
- rights, obligations and liabilities of the parties
- *force majeure*
- termination
- breach and remedies
- dispute resolution
- notice
- assignment
- waiver
- warranty and exclusion
- entire agreement clause
- governing law
- language clause, if two or more languages are involved
- signature, date and execution.

Not all agreements have all of these elements, but many cover similar ground.

Key lexical and syntactical features

Lawyers are often criticised for their old or archaic drafting style. In English legal documents, one often finds words such as 'aforementioned', 'hereinafter', 'hereinabove', 'hereunder', 'said', 'such', etc., and these words do not often present enormous problems in translation once the translator gets accustomed to such usage. However, a major linguistic feature of private legal documents written in English that does present a translation challenge is the use of word strings, also known as binomial expressions (Mellinkoff 1963), for instance, 'authorise and direct', 'deemed and considered', 'final and conclusive', 'full and complete', 'observe and perform', 'release and discharge' and 'covenants, conditions and terms'.

Syntactically, in legal documents, a common linguistic feature is that sentences are typically long and complex. This is true in many languages, not just in English. Another one is the extensive use of passive structures. Lawyers like to use passive structures, as these permit the writer to avoid naming or referring to the person or thing that performs the action. For instance, the sentence, 'The contract was breached', simply states the fact. It does not indicate who was the wrongdoer or who breached the contract. There are many instances of the use of passive structures in legal documents with phrases such as 'shall be forthwith terminated', 'may be reinstated and continued', 'to be observed and performed', 'may be rendered', 'written notice be given' and 'indemnity is sought of'. Example (1) is taken from a lease:

> The Lessee covenants with the Lessor to observe and perform the terms, covenants and conditions contained in the said Lease and on the Lessor's part to be observed and performed in the same manner in all respects as if those terms, covenants and conditions, with such modifications only as may be necessary to make them applicable to the said Lease, had been repeated in full in the Lease as terms, covenants and conditions binding on the Lessee in favour of the Lessor.

In this example, we can see that there is the use of word strings or binomials ('observe and perform', 'terms, covenants and conditions'), passive structure ('to be observed and performed') and it consists of one long sentence of 82 words.

English legal language and legal drafting have been undergoing reform and change in the last few decades to make them more accessible and comprehensible to the layperson. In the past twenty or thirty years, in major English speaking countries, there have been efforts by the legal profession to simplify legal drafting and writing style in the Plain English Movement. Nevertheless, legal English and legal drafting are and will remain different from ordinary English (see Bhatia, this volume).

Translating domestic legislation

Essentially, there are two types of situation where municipal statutes are translated. The first type is found in bilingual and multilingual jurisdictions where two or more languages are the official legal languages. Examples include Canada, Switzerland and, more recently, Hong Kong. The second type of translated legislation is found in any monolingual country where its laws are translated into a foreign language or languages for information purposes. We will discuss these two categories in detail next.

Translating laws in bilingual/multilingual jurisdictions

In bilingual and multilingual jurisdictions, the law may be drafted first in one language and then translated into the other language(s). For instance, in Hong Kong, up until

1989, all legislation was enacted in English only, and Hong Kong was a monolingual English Common Law jurisdiction despite the fact that the majority of Hong Kong people have always used Chinese in their daily life. Since the return of Hong Kong to China, both English and Chinese have been made official legal languages in Hong Kong. Before April 1989, Chinese translations of Hong Kong laws were for informative purposes only with no official status. In 1987, the Hong Kong Official Languages Ordinance was amended to give official language status to Chinese in addition to English (Section 3 (1)) and to require that all legislation be enacted and published in both English and Chinese (Section 4(1)). Article 9 of the Basic Law of the Hong Kong Special Administrative Region (1990) also provides that Chinese and English may be used as official languages by the executive authorities, legislature and judiciary. The new law also provided a mechanism for translating and publishing authentic texts, in Chinese, of statutes enacted in English, and the Chinese translated texts went through the formal legislative process of authentication. Since then, Hong Kong statute law has become fully bilingual. Now both the English and Chinese statutory texts are equally authentic, that is, both have equal legal force. The Chinese legislative text is neither subordinate to nor a mere translation of its English counterpart, despite the fact that the laws were first enacted in English, and the Chinese texts were their translation. Today, in Hong Kong, there are two types of bilingual laws: the earlier laws that were enacted first in English and subsequently translated into Chinese and went through the authentication process, and the laws that have been enacted simultaneously in both English and Chinese since 1989.

In other bilingual and multilingual jurisdictions, the law may be drafted in two or more languages with drafters, lawyers, linguists and translators working together producing a working document in the form of a bill that is written in all the relevant languages. Even in such a case, translation is still involved. For instance, in Canada, the practice of bilingual drafting of federal legislation in both English and French, as opposed to translation from one language into another, was standardised in the 1980s, but still translation has been very much part of the process. According to Revell (2004), in Canada, there are three basic models of authoring or drafting bilingual laws: apart from the translation model, there are also the co-drafting and double drafting models. Irrespective of the methods employed, whether it is translation or simultaneous bilingual drafting, in both situations all the language versions are equally authentic, that is, they enjoy equal legal force.

In this type of translation, as the law written in different languages is binding on the citizens concerned with equal legal force, the purpose of such translation is normative. It is related to lawmaking, that is, to establishing new laws and to publishing the law in the official language or languages of the jurisdiction.

Translating laws in monolingual jurisdictions

In contrast, when domestic legislation is translated in monolingual jurisdictions, such translations are used for information purposes, not normative ones. The translated text does not have any legal force, and the original law and the translated text are not equal. Take for example China. The Chinese language is the official language of China. All Chinese laws are enacted in Chinese. However, many people, including legal and other scholars, and the business and legal communities in and outside China, require translation of such laws for information purposes. There are many different translated versions of various Chinese laws, official and non-official. There are private translations by legal publishers and legal academic research bodies as well, but none of these translations enjoys binding legal force in the Chinese or any other jurisdictions.

Possible complexities arising from translated laws

To illustrate the complexity of the translation of statutes and possible legal implications of translation errors of statutes, in a Canadian case, *Gulf Oil Canada Ltd v. Canadien Pacifique Ltée* [1979] C.S. 72 (discussed in Sullivan 2002 and Beaupré 1986), the Supreme Court of Quebec was asked to interpret an Order in Council made pursuant to the federal National Transportation Act of Canada. Under this Order, carriers like the defendant railway were not liable for losses caused by 'acts of God', while the French version provided non-liability for *cas fortuit* or *force majeure*. The court took into account the Civil Law system in interpreting this provision, recognising that in the English and French provisions, the legislature tried to take into account the two legal systems in Canada. It concluded that in Common Law the meaning of 'acts of God' would not include third party negligence, but under Quebec's Civil Code, *cas fortuit* included the negligent act of a third party. The court held that in these circumstances, the Civil Law meaning should prevail. This meant that the civilian understanding of *cas fortuit* or 'acts of God' was applicable in Quebec regardless of which language version was read and relied on by the parties to the case. In particular, the court held that if 'act of God' had been translated by the words 'Acte de Dieu' in the Order, it would not be possible to appeal to the Civil Law concept of *cas fortuit*, consisting of the act of a third party (see Sullivan 2002: 100 and Beaupré 1986). The ambiguity basically arose from the different laws in the two systems.

In a case from Hong Kong, a new bilingual jurisdiction, in *HKSAR v. Lau San Ching and Others* HCMA 98/2002, one of the issues before the court concerned the discrepancy found between the equally authentic English and Chinese laws. One of the main issues was the discrepancy between the English and Chinese versions of an Ordinance, arising from the modal verb 'may', found in the English, and its omission in the Chinese. The relevant section in this case is Section 4(28) of the Summary Offences Ordinance. Its English text reads:

> Any person who without lawful authority or excuse … does any act whereby injury or obstruction whether directly or consequentially, *may* accrue to a public place or to the shore of the sea, or to navigation, mooring or anchorage, transit or traffic. … shall be liable to a fine of $500 or to imprisonment of 3 months [italics added].

The equally authentic Chinese text when back translated into English reads:

> Any person who without lawful authority or excuse … does any act whereby injury or obstruction whether directly or consequentially, *accrues* to a public place or to the shore of the sea, or to navigation, mooring or anchorage, transit or traffic. … shall be liable to a fine of $500 or to imprisonment of 3 months [italics added].

There is a significant discrepancy of meaning between the English and Chinese texts. According to the Chinese text, actual obstruction, be it direct or consequential, must have accrued to a public place for the offence to occur. But according to the English text, obstruction **may** accrue to a public place to create an offence. The Chinese text gives the offence a narrower meaning in that actual obstruction must be caused before an offence can be made out. So, there is a clear conflict between the two authentic texts. We do not know how the variation in the two versions occurred and why an important word 'may' was left out of the Chinese translation. Possibly, it was an oversight or a translation error. As no actual obstruction occurred in this case, the appellant argued that there was no case to answer. The court relied on a number of principles and factors to resolve the discrepancy. The court stated that the word 'may' does not mean 'must', as there is a difference in the use of 'may' and its omission. The appeal was upheld. For bilingual laws in Hong Kong in Chinese and English, see www.legislation.gov.hk which is the Hong Kong bilingual laws information system. It has the English and Chinese legislation and subordinate legislation, constitution and amendments, and bilingual legal terms in Chinese and English.

In short, complexities and difficulties may arise from translated laws, unknown or unforeseen in monolingual laws for the simple fact that the languages and legal traditions may be different giving rise to different implications.

Translating international instruments

The translation of legal instruments in international or supranational bodies such as the UN and the EU forms a special area of legal translation practice. Such translational activities can entail translating multilingual documents such as international instruments of the UN involving several languages, and translating bilateral treaties involving two languages. The translation of legal documents of an international nature, as opposed to domestic laws, has its own idiosyncrasies as well as sharing the characteristics of translating law in general.

Translating multilingual instruments

Today, most multilingual instruments are negotiated under the auspices of international organisations such as the UN, so we will use the UN and the EU as examples in the following discussion. International legal instruments produced under the auspices of the UN are written in its six official languages. In the EU, currently, there are twenty-three official languages.

One important principle in the practice of multilingual law is the principle of equal authenticity. The common practice is that the final clause of a treaty usually specifies the original language(s) in which it was composed and also the fact that all official language texts are equally authentic, that is, have equal legal force. This practice was codified in the 1969 Vienna Convention. Article 33(1) provides that when a treaty has been authenticated in two or more languages, the text is equally authoritative in each language unless the treaty provides or the parties agree that, in case of divergence, a particular text shall prevail. Article 33(3) provides that the terms of the treaty are presumed to have the same meaning in each authentic text. As pointed out, the importance attached to the principle of equal authenticity was intended to confer indisputable authority on each of the authentic texts, *de facto* eliminating the inferior status of authoritative translations (Sarcevic 1997: 199).

As regards the drafting of multilingual instruments relevant to translation, in the EU, as part of the European Community legislative process, a proposal for a particular piece of legislation first comes from the European Commission (EC). As reported by Robinson

(2005), normally, the first step is that the initial draft of a legislative proposal is prepared by the technical department or technical experts for the sector concerned. Drafters must write in either English or French and their choice is determined by the language used in their department. Once the technical department has prepared its preliminary draft, as a second step, the draft is submitted to the other Commission departments as part of the internal consultation procedure. The Commission's Legal Service is consulted on all draft legislation with lawyers specialising in the sector examining the draft for compliance with the law and coherence with other legislation. The legal revisers, who all have dual legal and language qualifications, will examine it for compliance with rules on the form and presentation of legislation, in particularly the *Joint Practical Guide of the European Parliament, the Council and the Commission for Persons Involved in the Drafting of Legislation within the Community Institutions* (available at http://europa.eu.int/eur-lex/lex/en/techleg). As Robinson (2005) points out, at this early stage, the draft exists in only one language. As a third step, the text must then be translated into all the official languages by the Directorate-General for Translation (DGT). At this stage, the legal revisers will have another opportunity to review the text. The legal revisers must also correct formal or terminological errors and ensure that the legal scope is exactly the same in the different language versions. Then, the legislative proposal is submitted to the European Parliament and the Council where it passes through those institutions' internal pre-adoption procedures before their final deliberation and eventual adoption (see also Gordon-Smith 1989).

We can see that translation is an integral part of the legislative process in the EC. Similarly, multilingual drafting was experimented with at the UN, as a means of improving the quality and reliability of parallel texts. (For further discussion of UN multilingual drafting, see Nelson 1987, Tabory 1980 and Rosenne 1983.) Nevertheless, the general practice for international treaties at the UN has been through translation. The draft texts are first produced in English and/or French, and then translated into other languages. Parallel and simultaneous multilingual drafting is rare at the international level. Translation is very much part of the process.

An important factor in the multilateral instrument-making process relevant to translation is the fact that international agreements are negotiated texts which represent the diverse interests of the participating State parties (Tabory 1980; Sarcevic 1997: 204). There are no particular requirements as to the manner of negotiation, the reaching of agreement or the form of a treaty, and as it happens, in international diplomacy, negotiators frequently resort to a compromise that glosses over their differences with vague, obscure or ambiguous wording, sacrificing clarity for the sake of obtaining consensus in treaties and conventions (Tabory 1980; Sarcevic 1997: 204). In the EC, as EU draft legislative texts go through extensive consultation, examination and revision, EU law is often the fruit of difficult compromises (Robinson 2005: 5). As Robinson points out, often changes are made in the draft legislation to achieve policy ends. Sometimes a provision is delicately left vague (known in French as *flou artistique*) to paper over a failure to reach full agreement (Robinson 2005: 7). Consequently, translators should avoid attempts to clarify vague points, obscurities and ambiguities, and as pointed out, those who do run the risk of upsetting the delicately achieved balance and misrepresenting the intent of the parties (Sarcevic 1997: 204; Rosenne 1983: 783). However, there is also the difficult question of how the translator distinguishes the deliberate obscurity that is the expression of a political and often hard-won compromise from inadvertent obscurity produced when those drafting the original text use a language that is not their mother tongue (Correia 2003: 42).

Textual features of international conventions

International conventions normally follow an established format, consisting of the title, preamble, main text, final clauses, an attestation clause and signature block and annex, for instance in (2).

(2)

Convention on International Trade in Endangered Species of Wild Fauna and Flora (1973)

The Contracting States,

Recognising that wild fauna and flora in their many beautiful and varied forms are an irreplaceable part of the natural systems of the earth which must be protected for this and the generations to come;

Conscious of the ever-growing value of wild fauna and flora from aesthetic, scientific, cultural, recreational and economic points of view;

Recognising that peoples and States are and should be the best protectors of their own wild fauna and flora;

Recognising, in addition, that international co-operation is essential for the protection of certain species of wild fauna and flora against over-exploitation through international trade;

Convinced of the urgency of taking appropriate measures to this end;

Have agreed as follows: …

The preamble is normally followed by the substantive provisions set out under such heading as: Part I, Section I or Chapter I, Article 1. The substantive provisions normally start with definitions. For instance, the Convention on International Trade in Endangered Species of Wild Fauna and Flora (1973) starts with (3).

(3)

Article I

Definitions

For the purpose of the present Convention, unless the context otherwise requires:

(a) 'Species' means any species, subspecies, or geographically separate population thereof;

(b) 'Specimen' means:
   (i) any animal or plant, whether alive or dead;
   (ii) in the case of an animal: for species included in Appendices I and II, any readily recognisable part or derivative thereof; and for species included in Appendix III, any readily recognisable part or derivative thereof specified in Appendix III in relation to the species; and
   (iii) in the case of a plant: for species included in Appendix I, any readily recognisable part or derivative thereof; and for species included in Appendices II and III, any readily recognisable part or derivative thereof specified in Appendices II and III in relation to the species;

(c) 'Trade' means export, re-export, import and introduction from the sea;

(d) 'Re-export' means export of any specimen that has previously been imported;. …

Given the practice of translating international conventions into many different languages over the years, much of the legal terminology, format and usage has become established also in different languages. The common usage in different languages for international treaties is most often followed in translation without reinventing the wheel, and importantly, without the risk of creating new problems or miscommunication. Nevertheless, new terminology and new situations constantly appear in human activities requiring new regulations or laws in the international arena. Thus, translation of these instruments with their new terminology into various languages is always a challenge.

Databases and other technological tools accessing international treaties

One of the modern technological developments and innovations that has greatly assisted the work of the translator of international treaties is the information and computer technology related to documentation and translation. International agreements have proliferated since the end of the Second World War. More than 50,000 treaties have been registered with the United Nations since 1945. The UN Treaty Series (UNTS) database (http://treaties.un.org) is an invaluable resource for international lawyers and translators of international law. It contains the treaties and statements of treaties and international agreements registered or filed and recorded with the UN Secretariat in official languages since 1945. It also has the treaties from the League of Nations concluded between 1920–44, among other resources. Apart from the printed volumes of the United Nations Treaty Series, the UNTS database is an online storage and retrieval system for the international instruments published in the UNTS. The site also contains the full text of treaties deposited with the Secretary-General but not yet published in the UNTS. The UNTS database contains the texts of over 50,000 bilateral and multilateral treaties and subsequent treaty actions in their authentic languages, along with a translation into English and French. All treaties and international agreements registered or filed and recorded with the Secretariat since 1946 are published in the UNTS in their original language or languages, together with a translation in English and French as necessary. This is the world's largest database of multilateral treaties deposited with the UN Secretary-General and treaties registered with and published by the UN Secretariat; with over 3 million pages of text in more than 140 languages of various multilateral treaties deposited with the UN Secretary-General, including the major treaties in the areas of human rights, organised crime, terrorism, trade and the environment. It has full text search capability.

Another documentation database is the UN Official Document system (ODS) (http://ods.un.org). This is a multilingual database of UN documents with full text search in six UN official languages. It covers all types of official United Nations documentation, beginning in 1993. Older UN documents are being added to the system. ODS also provides access to the resolutions of the General Assembly, Security Council, Economic and Social Council and the Trusteeship Council from 1946 onwards. This is also accessible by the public via http://documents.un.org.

For the EU, CELEX (http://europa.eu.int/celex) is a source of complete and authoritative information in EU law, and gives access to a broad multilingual range of legal instruments: the founding treaties, binding and non-binding secondary legislation, opinions and resolutions by EU institutions and bodies, and the case law of the ECJ. But it has stopped being updated and has been merged with EUR-Lex.

EUR-Lex (http://eur-lex.europa.eu) is a free public resource tool. It is the result of merging the EUR-Lex site with the CELEX database to provide the biggest documentary holdings existing on EU law. It contains the full texts in EU official languages of the treaties, secondary legislation and preparatory acts in all official EU languages, as well as national implementing measures and case law of the ECJ. It offers extensive search facilities.

The DGT of the EC also has a free on-line CCVista Translation Database (http://ccvista.taiex.be) which contains translations of the legal acts of the EU in all its official languages.

There are various other types of terminology, tools and databases used at the UN and the EC. For the UN, the United Nations Terminology Database – UNTERM (http://unterm.un.org) is a multilingual terminology database which provides UN nomenclature and special terms in all six official UN languages. The database is mainly intended for use by the language and editorial staff of the UN to ensure consistent translation of common terms and phrases used within the Organisation. It has about 70,000 entries in six languages and daily updates. Similarly, in the EC, the main terminology tools include *Eurodicautom* (*Europe dictionnaire automatisé*, http://europa.eu.int/eurodicautom), EC's central terminology database maintained by the DGT. Eurodicautom is a multilingual dictionary which covers all areas of the EC's activities.

Conclusion

Due to the natural differences among languages and cultures, translating from one language into another whatever the subject matter is never easy. It is particularly difficult and complex in the field of law given the additional differences in legal systems and laws. Readers, be they citizens, legislators, lawyers or linguists, should constantly bear in mind that languages and words in different languages are not identical and seemingly identical words may carry very different meanings and connotations (for further discussion, see Cao 2007a, 2007b). Naturally, we cannot and should not expect absolute identity in translation between different languages. Legal language is no exception. Differences are natural and inherent in the diversity of languages as is true with human experiences and human activities in general. It is also what makes life and, for our purpose, translating interesting.

Further reading

Bhatia, Vijay K. (1997) 'Translating legal genres', in Anna Trosborg (ed.), *Text Typology and Translation*, Amsterdam, John Benjamins, 203–16.
Cao, Deborah (2007a) *Translating Law*, Clevedon: Multilingual Matters.
——(2007b) 'Inter-lingual uncertainty in bilingual and multilingual law', *Journal of Pragmatics*, 39: 69–83.
Sarcevic, Susan (1997) *New Approach to Legal Translation*, The Hague: Kluwer Law International.

Legal cases cited

Gulf Oil Canada Ltd v. Canadien Pacifique Ltée [1979] C.S. 72.
HKSAR v. Lau San Ching and Others HCMA 98/2002.

Participants in police investigations, interviews and interrogation

7

Citizens' emergency calls

Requesting assistance in calls to the police

Paul Drew and Traci Walker

Introduction

Whether they are witness to or somehow involved (usually as victims) in incidents of a potentially or manifestly criminal nature, citizens may call the police to seek their assistance. They do so either on the emergency line by dialling 999 (in the UK; 911 in the US, and 118 in much of Europe); or, for incidents which may seem less urgent or serious and which are perhaps more 'local' in nature, by calling their local police station. Either way, citizens call the police about ongoing incidents in order to request police assistance.

The call-takers (who may be serving police officers or civilians) typically question callers about the nature of the incident, often in some detail, in order to determine the appropriate police action. Call-takers enter the information they obtain into a Computer Aided Dispatch (CAD) system, which provides an on-screen data entry form with fixed fields for the type of incident, location, and other relevant details (Whalen 1995). Using a CAD system, call-takers are responsible for dispatching police to the scene of the incident, and therefore need to decide whether urgent police action/attendance is required, in which case police are dispatched for immediate attendance; whether the incident is less urgent, in which case attendance within some hours will be sufficient; or whether any police action is necessary or appropriate – the call-taker may decide that the incident is not a police matter, that it is insufficiently urgent to require police presence (e.g. a caller might instead go to the local police station to report the matter), or even that it is a hoax call. In these respects, call-takers act as gatekeepers, assessing both the genuineness and urgency of the call; they make these (often difficult) judgements on the basis of the information given by callers, in response to questions that they ask about the incident reported, and in relation to which callers have requested assistance.

These questions, and the information that callers provide in their responses, are therefore forensic insofar as they serve as the basis for assessments about the urgency, seriousness and potential criminality of the incident reported. These assessments, in turn, underlie decisions about appropriate police action, and whether and how urgently to dispatch police to the scene. Call-takers' questions, and the interaction between them and callers, are also forensic in another sense; calls to the police are recorded, and these recordings may play a part in crime investigations – and they are frequently used as evidence in criminal hearings. Therefore, calls for police assistance play a significant role both in protecting citizens against crimes, and in criminal investigations and prosecutions.

The structure of emergency calls

Much of the research literature about emergency calls to the police has documented their organisation, and the typical structure that arises from the pattern of stages through which such calls proceed. Researchers, particularly Zimmerman, have shown that emergency calls to the police consist of phases of activity that recurrently unfold in approximately the same order, each phase consisting of a distinctive task or activity (Zimmerman 1984, 1992a; for an overview see Heritage and Clayman 2010). The structure of emergency calls to the police can be summarised as follows:

1. Opening
2. Request
3. Interrogative Series
4. Dispatch Response
5. Closing

This sequence of stages is clearly illustrated in a brief call, example (1) (transcribed according to the conventions widely used in Conversation Analysis).

(1) [Zimmerman 1984: 214] (cited in Heritage and Clayman 2010: ch. 4)

```
 1  911:  Midcity Emergency::,                         Opening
 2        (.)
 3        U::m yeah (.)

- - - - - - - - - - - - - - - - - - - - -

 4        somebody just vandalized my car,              Request

- - - - - - - - - - - - - - - - - - - - -

 5              (0.3)
 6  911:  What's your address.
 7  C:    three oh one six maple
 8  911:  Is this a house or an apartment.
 9  C:    I::t's a house                                Interrogative Series
10  911:  (Uh-) your last name.
11  C:    Minsky
12  911:  How do you spell it?
13  C:    M I N S K Y

- - - - - - - - - - - - - - - - - - - - -

14  911:  We'll send someone out to see you.            Dispatch Response
15  C:    Thank you.=

- - - - - - - - - - - - - - - - - - - - -

16  911:  =Umhm bye.=                                   Closing
17  C:    =Bye.
```

As Heritage and Clayman (2010) note, this five-phase structure is organised around a request for assistance embodied in the caller's report in line 4. That request defines the business of the call (Heritage and Clayman 2010: ch. 4). The research literature focuses on a range of aspects of this structure or sequence of phases, including the significance of how calls are opened (Zimmerman 1992b) and closed (Zimmerman and Wakin 1995); and the 'interrogative series' in which call-takers ask callers a series of questions designed to assess whether the call is genuine, the nature and urgency of the incident, and other necessary details (including descriptions of those involved – information that has become increasingly significant as emergency calls come to be used as evidence in criminal cases). One kind of difficulty that can arise during this interrogative series is callers' resistance to being questioned, often quite closely (Tracey 1997), especially when callers are often quite emotionally disturbed, even hysterical (Whalen *et al.* 1988).

Reporting an incident as 'requesting' police assistance

Although calls to the police are understood as being organised around requests for assistance, callers generally only report an incident, without making a formal or explicit request (Whalen and Zimmerman 1990). For instance, in example (1), the caller reports that 'somebody just vandalized my car' (line 4), without explicitly asking the police to attend; however this is treated by the 911 call-taker as having been a request for assistance, in 'We'll send someone out to see you' (line 14). As Heritage and Clayman (2010) show, callers report incidents through a wide variety of formulations or constructions – reports that are treated, from the outset, as reports of 'actionable problems', for which police assistance is sought.

In a study conducted for the (London) Metropolitan Police Service (Drew 1998), in the majority (a little under 80%) of calls callers only *reported an incident* without overtly requesting police assistance, leaving it to the call-taker/dispatcher to respond to the request that is embedded in that report (Whalen and Zimmerman 1990). This is illustrated in example (2), from the beginning of an emergency call; in this and subsequent examples callers are shown as *Ca* and call-takers as *CT*.

```
(2) [Police Emergency call 29]
 1  CT:    Hello police
 2  Ca:    Yeah hello (becca) uh I live at (address)
 3         (.)
 4  CT:    Y[eah
 5  Ca:    [Right and I'm (not home) my daughter was there (who is
 6         thirteen) and she's home and somebody has broken into the
 7         house
 8         (.)
 9  CT:    ((repeats number)) (.) what's the address you want police
10         to go to.
```

In lines 5–7 Ca gives a brief report of the incident about which she is calling; she does not explicitly ask the police to go round to her home to check on the safety of her daughter. Instead she relies on her report of a potentially dangerous – and therefore urgent – situation to elicit the dispatch of police officers to the scene. Although CT formulates her turn as 'the address you want police to go to', Ca has not used such a construction. She has merely reported that 'somebody has broken into the house'. It is particularly clear from CT's response in lines 9–10 that she understands Ca's report to be an implicit request for police action, simultaneously indicating that she is dispatching police to the scene, just as the CT/dispatcher did in example (1).

So the majority of instances of 'requests' for assistance are of this rather implicit or indirect kind. Callers do not overtly or explicitly formulate a request, but instead report an incident, leaving it to call-takers to find and act on the implied request. The mere act of reporting such an activity (in example (1), vandalising a car, in example (2) breaking in) can function as a request.

Explicitly requesting police assistance

Nevertheless, callers do on occasion explicitly request police assistance, using the kind of request forms with which linguists are familiar. As we have said, explicit request forms are used in perhaps a minority of calls – a little over 20% in the study referred to (Drew 1998), which as far as one can tell is probably consistent with other published studies. However, calls in which callers explicitly request police assistance are of particular interest, partly because of the extensive and influential literature in linguistics on request forms (e.g. Brown and Levinson 1987; Curl and Drew 2008; Wootton 1981, 2005), but especially because when callers have explicitly to ask for (i.e. request) assistance, they may be doing some kind of special 'work' in making the call. They are not relying on a simple report of the problem or incident to do the work of requesting; instead, callers are orienting to the special or 'marked' nature of the call, or rather of the incident about which the call is being made.

We know from previous work that the precise constructions of requests grammatically encode speakers' assessments of the *contingencies* that may be involved in granting (acting on) the request, and of their *entitlement* to whatever is being requested (Curl and Drew 2008). These dimensions of contingency and entitlement are of central importance in calls to the police. One way of thinking about this is to consider why callers generally do not request police assistance by asking 'I wonder if it would be possible for you to … ' – though we will show an instance of just such a form, and what that reveals about something like the 'strength' of the case the caller believes he has for requesting police assistance. At any rate, our focus here is explicit requests for police assistance of the kind illustrated in (3).

(3) [Police emergency call 19]
1 CT: Police eme:rgency can I help you?
2   (0.5)
3 Ca: Yeah hi .hhh e:rm could we have uh police patrol car tuh
4   report to: (0.8) er Old Green House in Grayling.

Although the caller will go on subsequently to describe the incident (to be shown later), his opening turn consists of an explicit request for assistance, using the modal form of the verb 'could we have … '. In all the cases to be considered here, callers make such explicit requests in their opening turns, the grammatical forms of which can have interactional consequences for the ways requests are treated, in light of callers' subsequent descriptions of the circumstances and events for which they are seeking assistance.

Callers sometimes construct explicit requests by first reporting and describing some event, and then subsequently adding an explicit request. Ca does this in example (4). (In all these examples, person and place names, telephone numbers and other potentially identifying details have been omitted. In some examples, where indicated, pseudonyms have been substituted, where that is necessary to follow what is being said.)

```
(4)  [Police emergency call 14]
  1  CT:   Hello ((police identity)).
  2  Ca:   >Hello< un I'm calling from ((house number)) .hhh
  3        ((street name))?=[hhh
  4  CT:                  [(Thank-you).
  5  Ca:   An' the entrance is frum ((street name)) =that's
  6        where my father an' my sister a:re.=.hhh
  7  CT:   Ri:ght.
  8  Ca:   hhh [(N(hh)o(hh))
  9  CT:       [(What can I do for-)
 10  Ca:   >.hh There's a white geezer who's got a kni:fe
 11        ee's tryin to attack my dad<.hhh
 12  CT:   °Mm hm°
 13  Ca:   >Please 'elp him.< hhh .hhh hhh
 14  CT:   Are you near ((names street))?
```

Ca's request in line 13 follows her account of the incident (lines 2–11); her overt request for help is done with an imperative (but an imperative softened by 'please') that might best be described as a kind of *pleading* for assistance (without getting into the prosodic details of how she speaks in line 13, Ca displays extreme distress). In response, CT begins a line of questioning (in line 14) which culminates in his dispatching the police as requested.

Our focus on the lexico-grammatical format of explicit requests in initial position, of the kind illustrated in (3) (rather than the pleadings, in subsequent position, as in (4)), arises from the continuum or cline of request forms to be found in requests in social and 'institutional' interactions (Curl and Drew 2008). We will not review that in detail, but it will be worth giving a broad overview of that finding, as necessary background for considering request forms in calls to the police.

Contingency and entitlement in request forms

A comparison of corpora of mundane, largely social phone calls with out-of-hours calls to a doctor's surgery revealed that modal verbs were the most common form for requests in the former, and 'I wonder if … ' prefaces in the latter. Only about half of the callers to the out-of-hours surgery used grammatically explicit request forms, but those that did favoured 'I wonder if … ' prefacing above any other form. This distribution initially suggested that the form of a request was tied to the sociolinguistic setting – 'intimates' use modal verbs to make requests of each other, while participants in service encounters use 'I wonder if … '. However, closer analysis revealed that, rather than being

Table 7.1 A continuum or cline of request forms

High entitlement/ Low contingency			High contingency/ Low entitlement
Imperatives	*I need you to ...*	*Modals (Could etc.)*	*I wonder if ...*

irrevocably linked to the sociolinguistic setting, request forms instead reflect a speaker's assessment of their entitlement to have a request granted; different forms may be used to display speakers' knowledge of the contingencies surrounding the granting of a request. Modal verbs, especially the construction 'could you', are used to display a high level of entitlement, and/or to claim virtually no obstacles to the granting of a request (low contingency; e.g. a request that a letter be brought along on an already-arranged upcoming visit). Conversely, 'I wonder if ... ' prefaces display an awareness of the contingencies which might militate against the granting of a request, and are used in situations where a speaker's entitlement to what is asked for is low, either by virtue of the situation itself or of the situation as constituted by the sequence-so-far. Rather than functioning as a static reflection of fixed social roles, speakers' deployment of particular request forms is evidence of the grammaticalisation of certain dimensions of social relations – namely, contingency and entitlement. These forms, ranging from imperatives through to conditional forms with 'I wonder if ... ' prefaces, lie along a cline from those which encode high entitlement and low contingency, to those which encode the reverse, that is high contingency and low entitlement (Table 7.1).

Thus, for instance, customers asking for goods or services in shops may use imperative forms, or 'I need ... ', especially if having used that (kind of) shop before they are 'experts' in what that shop can offer, as example (5) in which the customer clearly knows about the service and 'goods' that shop provides (see also Heinemann 2006; Lindström 2005; Vinkhuyzen and Szymanski 2005).

```
(5)  [Shop1]
  1  Ass:    The poster size is eigh[teen by twenty four]
  2  Cus:                      [Well let's do eleven] by seventeen
  3  Cus:    And then I need four of them
  4          (0.5)
  5  Cus:    And I need them coated
```

Since the use of one or another form of request is something speakers can manipulate (i.e. they are not forced to use a particular form in a particular setting), displays of urgency or seriousness can override (or be used to exploit participants' knowledge about) concerns about contingency and entitlement. As mentioned above, the majority of requests in the corpus of calls to the out-of-hours doctor's surgery were constructed as 'I wonder if (you could X)'; what was striking was the skew away from the use of modal verbs. Only in a small minority of cases, such as in example (6), do callers format their requests using modal verbs instead.

```
(6)  [Doctor's out-of-hours calls:1:2:12]
  1  Doc:    Hel:lo:,
  2  Clr:    Hel:lo, is tha' du- doctor
  3  Doc:    Yes, Doctor (name) speaki:ng,
```

```
 4   Clr:    i:i:(Yeah) couldja's (call'd) an' see my wife please,.h[h
 5   Doc:                                                            [Yes:.
 6   Clr:    She's breathless. She can't.hh get 'er breath .hh
 7            ((9 lines omitted))
 8   Doc:    No pain. Does she have a problem with 'er chest, normally?
 9   Clr:    Yeah, she's been sufferin' with this .hhh eh-for the last month or so.[.hh hhh
10   Doc:                                                                          [.hh Right.
11   Doc:    Eh-does she have any: treatment in the house? euh:
12   Clr:    (Wull) she takes (Prumil), .hh a:n:d e:h hh.hh her heart tablet, hh.hhh
13   Doc:    Ri:ght. Okey doke <.h How old is your: wife?
14   Clr:    hh .hhh hhhhh[hh!
15   Doc:                 [Don't worry, I'llb- I'll com[e ( )
16   Clr:                                            [>uh-uh-uh!<Sorry, hh seventy five, .hhh=
17   Doc:    =Right.
18   Clr:    (eh-eh[h!) ((gasping/throat clearing sound))
19   Doc:          [Alright, sir. t.h I'll be round in about ten minutes
```

Formatting their requests for the doctors' out-of-hours assistance with 'I wonder if … '
indexes callers being unsure whether the patient's condition is sufficiently serious to warrant
a home visit by the doctor. By contrast, in example (6) the elderly caller uses the modal
verb when asking the doctor to visit his wife (line 4). The displayed sense of low con-
tingency/high entitlement reflects his portrayal of the seriousness and urgency of the case,
including his descriptions of her condition ('she's breathless. She can't.hh get 'er breath',
line 6), that she's been suffering with this for some time (line 9), that she's being treated for
heart problems (line 12), and of course that she's elderly (line 16). Notice that the doctor's
assessment of the urgency of the case (line 19) matches the caller's (if this doctor agrees or
offers to visit, he more usually says something like 'I'll pop round a little later … ').

Cases such as this, in which callers used a modal verb to request an out-of-hours home
visit by the doctor, were unusual; only four such cases occurred in a corpus of approximately
80 out-of-hours calls. Most explicit requests took the form of being prefaced by 'I wonder
if … '. In calls to the police, by contrast, the reverse was the case; the formats of almost all
of the instances of explicit requests were positioned towards the left 'high entitlement/low
contingency' end of the cline, with the use of modal verbs most frequent; whilst 'I wonder
if … ' was never used in requesting assistance in emergency (999) calls. We now turn,
then, to examining the request formats generally used in calls to the police.

Modal verbs in calls to the police

The emergency call from which the request in example (2) was taken illustrates the most
common format for requests to the emergency number, and a longer extract is
shown in (7).

(7)   [Police emergency call 19]

```
1   CT:    Police eme:rgency can I help you?
2           (0.5)
3   Ca:    Yeah hi .hhh e:rm could we have uh police patrol car tuh report to: (0.8) er Old
4           Green House in Grayling.
```

```
 5  CT:  Old Cream House.
 6  Ca:  Old Green House,
 7       (0.8)
 8  Ca:  In Grayling.
 9       (1.8)
10  Ca:  ((To someone off phone)) (name) get tuh thuh do:or. (1.1)
11  Ca:  Shut this [do:or. [Shut the door don't Shut the door
12  A:             [( ) [Please (name) don't don't don't (.) don't.
13  Ca:  Don't open thuh door (name).
14  A:   Don't op- (.) open thuh door [(name)
15  Ca:                               [Can we have uh
16  CT:  Yeah what wa[s-
17  Ca:              [( )
18  CT:  Yea[h sorry=
19  Ca:     [Thi-
20  Ca:  =There's uh woman here thut's (0.5) claims she's
21       bin raped she's panicked. Thuh bo:yfriend's
22       outside .hh[h
23  CT:             [Right [okay-
24  Ca:             [This is thuh security lodge here.
25  CT:  Right okay hang on a se[con-
26  Ca:                         [The boyfriend's outside un
27       want[s tuh come in.=
28  CT:      [>Yep.<
29  CT:  =Alright so it's Old Green House
```

It is characteristic of such requests that they are in initial position, preceding the report or description of the incident for which assistance is being sought. The caller opens with his request (line 3), made with the modal form of the verb, 'could we have … ' (he uses another modal form of the verb when he 'repeats' his request in line 15, after there's been some audible disturbance in the background, associated with the ongoing incident). Ca only subsequently describes the incident for which assistance is sought (lines 20–27), when asked about it by CT (see the curtailed enquiry in line 16).

Ca's use of the modal form in example (7) displays the presumption of high entitlement and low contingency associated with his request; in other words, the modal verb is a conventionalised request form that presumes the grantability of a request (Watts 2003). There are further features of Ca's account which convey his entitlement to police assistance; particularly that he is a security guard (line 24). Ca's institutional identity is evident earlier, when in line 3 he uses the institutional 'we' (Drew and Sorjonen 1997), and requests that a police car 'report' to the address given. In addition, and as in previous cases, the presumed entitlement encoded in the request form is commensurate with the accountable gravity and urgency of the incident – an alleged rape (lines 20–21), potentially an ongoing assault (lines 21–22) and the disturbance audible in lines 10–14. That match between the degree of entitlement encoded in the modal form of the request, and the 'seriousness' – therefore urgency – of the incident reported, should be kept in mind. We will see how, in some other cases, that match can become compromised.

The way in which modal request forms encode high entitlement, in contrast to more conditional forms, is nicely illustrated in example (8), a call to a local police station (not the emergency number). This example also illustrates the precise congruence between the form in which the request is done, and the 'outcome' of the request (i.e. whether or not it is granted). Calls to local police stations in this city are handled by a call centre, which, if the reason for calling is deemed somehow appropriate, then connects the caller to the relevant department or section within a police station. So in (8) Ca first speaks to the call centre's call-taker (Op), who then connects the caller, as requested, to the Controls Room of the police station (Con).

```
(8)  [Call to police station 27]
  1  Op:               'erator can I help you?
  2  Ca:    →          Yes can I have (Name) Police Station
  3                    please
  4  Op:               Nature of the call?
  5                              (.)
  6  Ca:               Er:m this is (Name) School one of our deputy
  7                    heads has just come in and said we ha:ve (.)
  8                    quite a la:rge group of Asian la:ds who (.)
  9                    wouldn't move o:n (.) from the school and
 10                    he suspects then that it may be drug related
 11  Op:               Right I'm gonna put you through to the control
 12                    room you're not gonna hear a ringing sound
 13                    but stay on the li:ne o[ka:y?
 14  Ca:;                                    [Right okay
 15                             (0.4)
 16  Op:               Thank you.
 17                            (5.0) silence
 18                            (1 min 18 sec) ringing
 19  CALLER IS TRANSFERRED TO CONTROL ROOM
 20  Con:              Hello police station (Name)
 21  Ca:    →          Oh I wonder if you can help me it's (Name)
 22                    School here the deputy head has just come in
 23                    from: (.) lunch time
 24  Con:              Mm hm
 25  Ca:               And he's gone back out again but at-at one
 26                    of our school gates in (Name) Road we had a
 27                    la:rge group of Asian lads that were being
 28                    very persistent and wouldn't move o:n.
 29  Con:              Right.
 30  Ca:               They have moved on now but they may be wandering
 31                    round to another one- nother exit we've got in
 32                    (Name) Road .hh er::m and he seems to think
 33                    they could be drug related or just being a plain
 34                    nuisance
 35                             (0.5)
 36  Ca:               wou[ld somebody like to come and (.) 'ave a
 37  Con:                 [Right.
 38  Ca:               little drive round and see [if they could
 39  Con:                                         [Yeah
```

```
40   Ca:          see and do something about it.
41   Con:         Well there isn't anything they can do if they're
42                not causing any problems
```

Ca's requests in lines 2 and 21 (then in line 36) have been highlighted; it will be plain that the point of interest in (8) is Ca's use of different formats for the requests first to the call centre's operator, and then to the police call-taker in the Control Room. Ca first requests to be put through to a named police station (line 2), rather than questioning whether (or assuming that) he is already there (as most 'inexpert' callers to the non-emergency number do); so he already displays a certain expertise in calling the police. Furthermore, his request form, 'can I have', asserts a high degree of entitlement. In constructing a response to Op's inquiry about the nature of the call, he provides several pieces of evidence that are commensurate with this presumed entitlement. He first identifies himself as a representative of an institution ('this is (Name) School', line 6), thereby having an institutional identity, as did the caller in example (6). Secondly, he uses the present tense 'we *have* quite a large group … ' (lines 7–8), emphasising the ongoing nature and hence urgency of the incident. Finally, he asserts the seriousness of the problem – 'it may be drug related' (line 9). Op's assessment of the 'police-worthiness' of the reported incident is reflected in his immediately agreeing to connect Ca to the police station requested (line 11).

When Ca is connected to the Control Room – to the person who will assess the urgency of the incident and the appropriate police action, if any – Ca abandons his claims of entitlement and employs a different request form. He now selects 'I wonder if … ', a form that, as we have seen, allows for contingencies that might prevent the granting of his ultimate request (to have the potential troublemakers moved away from the school). In the first part of the call, the combination of request form and supporting information about the urgency and seriousness of his request resulted in having his initial request granted; but that request was merely to speak with a particular police station. Now that he has reached that station, he employs an 'I wonder if … ' prefaced request (see line 21). The 'I wonder if … ' request displays a lower level of entitlement and a higher level of awareness of the contingencies surrounding his request. In what follows, the description of the incident that he gives to the police in the Control Room is different, in certain key respects, from the one he gave the call centre operator.

Initially, Ca again identifies himself 'as' an institution. However, this is followed up not with a description of an urgent situation, but rather a situation that has mostly resolved itself: 'we had' (past tense, line 26 – compare 'we have', line 7), 'they have moved on now' (line 30). The problem is also now described as less serious than before: what was previously 'quite a large group' (line 8) is now only 'a large group'; they had congregated at 'one of our school gates' (line 26), a formulation minimising the extent of the disturbance; the purported troublemakers 'may be wandering' (line 30), a verb which avoids attributing any particular goal or direction to its agent. Finally, the deputy head who previously had a suspicion (line 10, 'he suspects it may be drug related') now only 'seems to think' that, but also allows they may only be 'just [being] a plain nuisance' (lines 33–34).

When Ca redoes the request at line 36–40, 'would somebody like to come and have a little drive round and see if they could see and do something about it', the diffidence of his request is consistent with the form he used in line 21. Although he does not re-use the 'I wonder if … ' preface, the request is tentative and vague ('somebody', 'little drive', 'do something') and minimises the amount of work that is needed to be done in spite of using a modal verb – a modal that orients mainly to the contingencies attendant on granting the request and makes little or no claim to entitlement.

Until now, we have seen a kind symmetry, or congruence, between the form in which the request is constructed, and the 'outcome' of the request. In each case when speakers used the modal form in examples (6) (from a call to the doctor), (7) and (8), their requests were granted (the doctor agrees to call immediately, the police are dispatched immediately and the call is put through to the Control Room, respectively); and when in example (8) Ca uses the form conveying greater contingency and lower entitlement, 'I wonder if … ', the police do not agree to attend (lines 41–42, 'there isn't anything they can do if they're not causing any problems'). In other cases this congruence begins to break down, revealing that callers may make stronger claims to entitlement than – in the police call-taker's view, is warranted. In other words, callers may claim a strong sense of being entitled to a service which the police are unwilling – on the 'facts of the case' – to provide.

The first instance to be shown is relatively benign (9). Ca has been put through by the call centre operator to the police station.

(9) [Call to police station 37]

```
 1  Con:      Police ((station name)) good afternoo:n
 2            (2.0)
 3  Con:      ((Station name)) good afternoo:n
 4            (0.4)
 5  Ca:       Oh good afternoon e:r could I speak to
 6            Dick Greaves* please
 7  Con:      Dick:,
 8            (.)
 9  Ca:       Grea:ves (.) G-R-E-A-V-E-S
10            (0.2)
11  Con:      G-R-E-A-V-E-S do you know where he works sir
12            (0.4)
13  Ca:       E:r Oxley I believe in the control room
14            (0.2)
15  Con:      E::r is it Gea:veser or Grea:ves
16  Ca:       Grea:ves (.)-Dick Greaves
17  Con:      Hang on a mi[nute sir]
18  Ca:                   [thank you]
19            (9.0)
20  Con:      Do you know if he's a police officer or a civilian sir
21            (0.4)
22  Ca:       Police officer (.) I believe=
23  Con:      =Do you know his shoulder number
24            (0.4)
25  Ca:       No idea
26  Con:      No idea
27  Ca:       He rung me yesterday at work
```

(*'Dick Greaves' is an entirely fictional pseudonym; we've used these to show the details of the difficulties they have establishing the name of the person to whom Ca wishes to speak and where he works.)

Ca asks to speak to a named police officer, using the form that displays his confidence in his entitlement to speak to him, and the absence of any contingency that might prevent him doing so; that is, he asks 'could I speak to … ' (line 5). Right from the start the control room call-taker evidently has difficulty 'placing' the named police officer. First he does not, apparently, recognise the name (lines 7–11); he then asks Ca where the police officer works, implying that he may not (be recognised) as working at this police station or this department of the station (lines 11–13); when the control room call-taker comes back on the line, he asks for more information about the person requested (lines 20–26). When in line 27 Ca mentions that the person to whom he's requested to speak called him at work yesterday, he reveals that he is returning a call from the named officer; he is not ringing on his own initiative, but complying with a request from the officer, clearly entitling him to have his request granted. In short, Ca has good grounds for supposing that he is entitled to speak to the person requested (he has been asked to call back), and for not expecting any contingencies to intervene. However, there turns out to be a mismatch between that confidence, encoded in his use of the modal 'could I … ', and the ability of the police call-taker to comply, to grant the request. That mismatch, or lack of congruence between the request form, and the 'outcome' – at least up to this point – is benign in the sense that the contingency which prevents granting the request is an inability to do so; the police officer asked for is not recognised as one who works at this police station, in this department.

In other cases, the mismatch between the caller's confidence and the outcome is much less benign. In these cases, it appears that callers make strong claims to entitlement (and, concomitantly, claims to there being a low level of contingency in granting their requests), through request forms that indicate that the incident is serious and urgent. These claims, however, turn out not to be matched by the call-takers' assessments of the 'actual' seriousness or urgency of the incident. So that instead of dispatching police to the scene, the outcome is instead 'no action' – or in the call shown in examples (11) and (12), an (implicit) assessment that the caller is wasting police time.

In example (10), Ca has called the emergency number to report an ongoing incident, preceding which is the explicit request 'could we have … '.

```
(10)  [Police Emergency call 11]
   1  CT:        Hello there this is the police?
   2  Ca:        Hello (0.5) er: could we have somebody to: .hh (street name + apartment
   3             building) er: urgently please. =I'm the porter in uh block uv flats there in
   4             (apartment building name)
   5  CT:        S- Sorry what's the name of the cuh- court.
   6             ((15 lines omitted, checking the address)
   7  CT:        What's the problem?
   8  Ca:        >Well we've got somebody< we got a trespasser
   9             here we're detaining 'im at the moment we need
  10             somebody ((swallow)) quite quickly.
  11  CT:        What's he bin doing?
  12  Ca:        hhh Well he's come on private property with a
  13             bi:cycle we don't know what he's done.
  14                  (0.8)
  15  Ca:        But he shouldn't be o:n here. =He's on private property.
  16                  (0.7)
```

17	CT:	Could you not just tell him to go:?
18		(.)
19	CT:	What do yuh-Why do you need the police tuh
20		go: there.

Having used a modal verb, and stated explicitly that his problem is urgent (line 3), Ca identifies himself as an 'institutional' person, 'I'm the porter in a block of flats'. Once the CT asks for a description of the problem, however, Ca's claims of entitlement begin to unravel. He fails immediately to establish the seriousness of the situation, first stating 'well we've got somebody' (line 8), a vague pronouncement which doesn't ascribe any seriousness to the problem. His self-repair upgrades the transgression to 'trespassing' (line 8), but still falls short of an emergency. Additionally, the caller himself downgrades the urgency of the problem; having initially stated that he needed assistance 'urgently', he now says that he 'needs somebody quite quickly'.

As the control room call-taker did in (9), CT here begins asking a series of 'forensic' questions, which seems to question – that is, be sceptical about – the claimed urgency or seriousness of the incident, about which Ca has made an emergency call. CT first asks 'what's he been doing?' (line 11), to which Ca provides an account which lies behind or 'supports' his claim to have detained a trespasser. His description of the problem is that the 'trespasser' has 'come on private property with a bicycle' (lines 12–13), but that 'we don't know what he's done' (line 13). It is perhaps the evident 'weakness' of that claim to which Ca himself orients, when he adds that, whatever he's done, the trespasser 'shouldn't be o:n here. =He's on private property' (line 15). In his questions in lines 17 and 19–20, 'could you not just tell him to go' and 'why do you need the police to go there', CT treats the incident as not one for which police attendance is appropriate (i.e. not police-able). Indeed, the police are not dispatched to this incident. So there is a mismatch between the confidence of Ca's claims about the urgency of the incident – displayed through the request form, and explicitly by his adding 'urgently' to his request – and CT's treatment of it as not requiring police assistance. It seems as though Ca's use of the modal form of the verb in requesting was strategically designed to contribute to his portrayal of the incident as urgent.

We do not mean to claim that the caller himself does not believe that this event requires or deserves police assistance; there's nothing in the talk to indicate that he is consciously attempting to deceive the police (see his attempt to clarify the problem in line 15 – 'but he shouldn't be on here he's on private property'). So we are not making any cognitive or other psychological attribution by referring to his use of the modal verb form as strategic. Rather, what seems 'strategic' here is the employment of a request form that is used in other situations to successful effect, *when coupled with other descriptive components which portray the seriousness of an incident requiring urgent police assistance*, but which fails here because it is not supported by the provision of such information.

One further instance will have to suffice to illustrate the less benign, more 'strategic' use of verb forms in requests in emergency calls. In this case (11), Ca uses the form 'I need ... ', which displays 'confidence' in the request (see Vinkhuyzen and Szymanski 2005 on the use of 'I need' in American service encounters) – again, high entitlement, low contingency – to an even greater degree than modals, according to the continuum outlined earlier.

(11) [Police Emergency call 70]
```
 1   CT          Police emergency can I help you?
 2                        (0.5)
 3   Ca:         >.hh Yeah I need thuh police right now (police/please)?<
 4   CT:         Yeah what's thuh ^problem?
 5                        (0.8)
 6   Ca:         I-I've bin hh >I've bin hit by a taxi dri:ver?<
 7                        (0.5)
 8   Ca:         .hh Un he's >punched me on thuh face.<
 9                        (0.4)
10   CT:         U:h where a:re you. What's-
11               ((15 lines omitted re caller's location))
12   CT:         Okay are you badly injured. Do you need [un ambulance
13   Ca:                                                 [Yes I am.
14   Ca:         .hh Yes (.) I do.
15   Com:        Okay what's the nature of your injuries sir?
16                        (0.4)
17   Ca:         .hhh >My nose is bleedin,<
18                        (0.7)
19   CT:         You've got a no:se bleed.
20                        (0.5)
21   Ca:         Yeah (he head but[ted me)
22   CT:                          [(With) with a:ll due respect I don't think (.).hh er:m
23               much can actually be done for a no:se bleed but if you=
24   Ca:         =Okay.
25   CT:         D'you wa:nt un ambulance or wha[t.
26   Ca:                                        [>Er no I don't
```

As Ca did in example (10), the caller here too not only uses a request form conveying high entitlement/low contingency, but he 'supports' that – hence warranting his call to the emergency number – with an explicit expression of the urgency of the case, when he adds 'right now' in line 3. Ca then describes the incident in relation to which he's requesting police assistance, 'I've been hit by a taxi driver' (line 6). There might be an ambiguity in this account, since the co-occurrence of 'hit' and 'taxi' might conspire to indicate that the caller is reporting being knocked down, or that his car has been struck by another ('hit' being a term which can refer to being struck by a car, as well as striking someone with one's hand or fist). However, Ca's continuation in line 8 clarifies matters.

Although there is an obvious difference in the potential seriousness of one's injuries when being hit by a car versus being punched by a person, being beaten up is as much a policeable offence as being involved in a motor accident. However, when the caller is asked about the nature of his injuries (in order to inform the ambulance service), he again downplays their seriousness – whether he intends to or not. Although he has claimed to be badly injured (the 'yes I am' response to CT's question, lines 12–13), he describes his injury simply as 'my nose is bleeding'. By this time, it is becoming apparent to CT that the caller's claims about the seriousness of his injuries are, while not necessarily bogus, not entirely accurate – CT's assessment being clearly evident in his response to Ca's continuing account of the attack which caused his injuries (line 21), 'with all due respect I don't think much can actually be done for a nosebleed' (lines 22–23). The upshot is that Ca agrees to not needing an ambulance (lines 25–26).

However, in this instance, CT does dispatch the police to the incident, telling Ca at the end of the call 'Alri:ght we'll get police back down to you as soon as we can sir' (this closing occurs 40 lines after line 26, in data not shown) – thereby complying with Ca's original request for police action. In this respect, then, the (high entitlement) request form and outcome are congruent. In another respect, though, they are not – and that is in relation to CT's assessment of the seriousness and urgency of the incident. In the 40 lines not shown here, CT ascertains that Ca has 'had an accident' with the taxi driver; a traffic accident, with a possible injury, is sufficient to require police presence – and CT acts on the basis of that requirement (it is also evident from his accent that Ca is a member of a racial minority, which the police may regard as an aggravating factor in such an incident). But CT does not dispatch police to the scene on the basis of his assessment of the seriousness of the incident. Example (12) shows the final turns in the call.

(12) [Police Emergency call 70]
```
 1  Ca:  He's ruh-right behind me,=
 2  CT:  =Alri:ght we'll get police back down to you as soon
 3       as we can sir. =Okay?=
 4  Ca:  =Okay.
 5  CT:  Bye bye.
 6  CT:  ((makes a loud snoring sound))
```

After the call has closed, CT displays what he really thinks about the request for police assistance by making a loud, stereotypical snoring sound, which indicates 'boredom' – and thereby, that this is a waste of police time. In other calls, CTs variously display their 'true' assessment of the call, of the seriousness of the incident reported, of the (un) helpfulness of the caller and such like, by adding – after the call has officially closed (but as the receiver is being put down) – sounds or remarks which express, implicitly or explicitly, their disapprobation of the caller's request for assistance. The grounds for their scepticism with callers' requests seem generally to be that they regard the call as a waste of police time, because the incidents are too trivial. At any rate, whilst Ca's use of the (highly) entitled request form is vindicated by the dispatch of police to the scene, there is nevertheless a mismatch between that request form and CT's assessment of the seriousness/ urgency of the incident.

Conclusion

Previous research (Curl and Drew 2008) has shown that in selecting a given lexico-syntactic form of a request, speakers grammaticalise or index their estimation of the degree of entitlement and the likely contingencies involved in granting the request. If speakers regard themselves as entitled to whatever is being requested, and regard the con-tingencies involved as likely to be minimal, they use request forms towards the left hand of the cline described earlier – that is imperatives, *I need ...* , and modal forms of the requesting verb. If, on the other hand, they are uncertain about their entitlement to the service, or are unsure what contingencies might intervene, thereby affecting the possibility of the request being granted, they select forms expressing low entitlement and high contingency, i.e. those to the right hand end of the cline – especially conditional forms such as *I was wondering if* ... .

In this chapter, we have shown how the request forms selected by citizens calling for police assistance, either on the emergency (999) line or to their local police station, similarly encode varying assessments of their entitlement to the service, and the possibility of contingencies influencing or preventing that service being granted. Callers display their confidence in the seriousness and urgency of the incident they are reporting, and for which they would like police assistance, by using the modal verb form; and even, in rare cases, by saying (as Ca does in example 11), *I need* ... . This accounts for callers always using modals (or, more strongly, *I need*, or imperatives, as in example (4)) in calls to the emergency number – at least, when they make explicit requests. Those calling their local police station, by contrast, tend to use conditional forms, as Ca did when he spoke to the police CT in the control room (in example (8)) – displaying that they are less sure of the urgency, and policeability, of what they have to report. In emergency calls, there can be a mismatch between Ca's perception of the seriousness/urgency of the incident, and therefore of their request, and the assessment of CT; callers can seem to claim a great degree of entitlement, and a concomitant lower level of contingency, than may seem to be warranted by 'the facts' – or rather, their account/descriptions of the facts, circumstances, etc., of the incident.

Further reading

Curl, T. and Drew, P. (2008) 'Contingency and action: A comparison of two forms of requesting', *Research on Language and Social Interaction*, 41: 1–25.

Heinemann, T. (2006) '"Will you or can't you?" Displaying entitlement in interrogative requests', *Journal of Pragmatics*, 38: 1081–1104.

Tracey, K. (1997) 'Interactional trouble in emergency service requests: A problem of frame', *Research on Language and Social Interaction*, 30: 315–43.

Whalen, M.R. and Zimmerman, D.H. (1990) 'Describing trouble: Practical epistemology in citizen calls to the police', *Language in Society*, 19: 465–92.

8

Miranda rights

Curtailing coercion in police interrogation: the failed promise of *Miranda v. Arizona*

Janet Ainsworth

Miranda v. Arizona is without a doubt the most famous American criminal law opinion of all time—it is hard to imagine any American who does not recognize its famous warning:

> You have the right to remain silent. Anything you say can be used against you in a court of law. You have the right to the presence of an attorney during any questioning. If you cannot afford an attorney, one will be appointed for you.

In fact, thanks to the worldwide reach of American television and movies, the Miranda warnings are familiar even to citizens of countries in which they have no legal effect. Considered as a vehicle to promote widespread public awareness of law, Miranda is perhaps the most successful educational project of all time. But despite that superficial success, it has failed to achieve its original aim of protecting suspects in police custody from coercive interrogation. As a result, scholars and commentators have called Miranda a "spectacular failure" (Thomas 2004: 1091), a "mistake" (Stuntz 2001: 975), a "farce" (Garcia 1998: 497), an "empty ritual" (Uviller 1996: 124), and a "hoax" (Slobogin 2003: 309). Most scholars agree that Miranda has had little impact on the outcome of police interrogation. Just as before Miranda, the vast majority of arrested persons still make incriminating statements to police under interrogation (Schulhofer 1996: 516–38; Thomas 1996: 957; Donahoe 1998; Leo 2001: 1006–9; cf. Cassell and Hayman 1996; Cassell 1996a). Best estimates put the number of arrestees who answer police questions after receiving Miranda warnings at approximately 80% (Leo 2001: 1009). More to the point, the Miranda-endorsed interrogation regime still permits the police to conduct lengthy incommunicado interrogations in which they are free to lie to the suspect, fabricate "evidence" of his guilt, and alternately browbeat him with exaggerated threats of punishment and cajole him with implied promises of leniency, as long as the Miranda warnings precede the ordeal (White 2001).

Whether or not the Miranda safeguards are effective in constraining coercive practices in police interrogation is a question with serious implications. DNA technology has now conclusively proven that significant numbers of people are convicted for crimes they didn't commit. Although it is impossible to obtain completely reliable statistics on how many innocent people are convicted, best estimates (Thomas 2004: 546; Gilvelber 1997: 1336–46) suggest that at least 6,000 and possibly as many as 40,000 persons are erroneously convicted of serious crimes every year in the United States. Of those that have been ultimately exonerated due to DNA testing, one in four had confessed under police grilling despite being given the Miranda warnings (Drizin and Leo 2004: 905). Psychologists studying the phenomenon of false confessions have identified a number of ways in which police interrogation can sometimes lead innocent people to confess to crimes (Wrightsman and Kassin 1993: 123–39). Once a confession is obtained, conviction is almost inevitable. Even when a coerced confession bears significant indicia of unreliability, a confession is nevertheless powerfully persuasive evidence to juries (Kassin and Sukel 1997). What this means is that, despite the panoply of constitutional constraints on police questioning imposed by Miranda and its legal progeny, problems in police interrogation are still a major contributor to miscarriages of justice in which the innocent are erroneously convicted of crimes.

So, what went wrong? Much of the blame for the failure of Miranda can be laid at the feet of the Supreme Court itself through subsequent cases when it interpreted and fleshed out the mandate of Miranda—cases resting on flawed assumptions about the nature of language and human communication. To understand the failure of Miranda as a public policy initiative, one must first understand why the Supreme Court felt the need to curtail unfettered police interrogation and what they hoped to achieve by implementing the Miranda framework.

Coercion and confessions

The understanding that abusive police interrogation of suspects could result in false confessions is certainly not a new one. In the early twentieth century, the Supreme Court was faced with a series of high-profile cases in which patently abusive, even brutal, police interrogations had led to the conviction of probably entirely innocent defendants based on little more than their extorted confessions (see e.g. *Brown v. Mississippi* 1936). The Court held that the Fourteenth Amendment's due process clause prohibited the introduction into court of any supposed confession that was obtained through coercive police behavior in the course of interrogation. Only voluntary confessions were to be admissible, because confessions that were procured through violence or threats pose an unacceptable risk that they might have been forced from an innocent person. As this voluntariness requirement developed, the Court expanded its reach beyond cases involving physical abuse to include confessions derived from other offensive police practices that might overbear the free will of the suspect. Whenever the conduct of the police interrogation was deemed to be manifestly unfair and overreaching, the resulting confession was held to be inadmissible, even in cases in which there was no serious doubt that it was in fact truthful (see e.g. *Rogers v. Richmond* 1961).

One difficulty with this voluntariness test for the admissibility of confessions was that it required a contextually sensitive assessment of all of the characteristics of the suspect and of the conditions of the interrogation in order to determine whether the suspect's free will had been overborne. Doing this on a case-by-case basis hamstrung police agencies in developing practical regulations and policies to govern interrogations and likewise put immense strain on the courts as a source of judicial oversight. Applying the voluntariness test on a consistent basis proved virtually impossible.

Miranda v. Arizona—an attempt to prevent police over-reaching and to promote reliability of confessions

The Miranda opinion represented an admission by the Court that the due process voluntariness standard was inadequate to prevent abuses in police interrogations that could lead to untrustworthy confessions. In an exhaustive sixty-page opinion, the Miranda Court recounted the long history of abusive interrogation, beginning with the days in which physical abuse and threats of abuse were the order of the day and ending with contemporary law enforcement practices that, while less brutal than earlier interrogations, were in the Court's view equally problematic. Interrogation of suspects behind closed doors, with no witnesses except the interrogators and the suspect, invited coercive tactics that were designed to pressure, trick, intimidate, coax, and cajole arrestees into incriminating themselves. Detailing the many tricks and psychological ploys recommended in police interrogation manuals, the Miranda Court was deeply skeptical that those in police custody could meaningfully resist the psychological pressure inherent in incommunicado interrogation.

The disapproval expressed in Miranda of the current state of police interrogation came close to suggesting that it should not be permitted at all. The Court, for all its jaundiced view of custodial interrogation, did not take that step, however. Instead, it sought, in its words, "to dispel the compulsion inherent in custodial surroundings" (*Miranda v. Arizona* 1966: 458) by giving the suspect information about the legal rights he could interpose to protect himself from police over-reaching. Above all, the arrestee would now need to be explicitly told that he had the right to refuse to answer police questions, and that, if he did choose to do so, he should be conscious that any answers he gave could later be used as evidence against him. Even that advice was in the Court's judgment inadequate as a counterweight to the power of the police who had total domination over the arrestee. After all, the same coercive environment that might compel a person to respond to police questions might also make it difficult for him to make a reasoned decision about whether or not to cooperate, even if he knew that he had a right to remain silent. For that reason, the Court interpolated the requirement that the arrestee be additionally told that he would be permitted to consult with an attorney, if he wished, before deciding whether to answer police questions.

The Miranda majority apparently was convinced that the ability to consult with defense counsel would change the one-sided dynamics of police interrogation from a setting in which the overwhelming power of the state could overbear the will of the arrested person to one in which there was a more level playing field between the suspect and his accusers. Suspects armed with information about their legal rights could then choose whether it was in their best interests to answer police questions. If they were unsure of what their best choice might be, the Miranda warnings informed them that they had the right to consult with an independent agent, an attorney, who was committed to protecting their interests. Understanding their rights and options, arrestees could make rational and informed decisions about how best to respond to police interrogation. At least, that was the world optimistically anticipated by the Supreme Court in its Miranda decision. Reality was, however, to fall far short of this.

Miranda as implemented: no remedy for police coercion after all

The language of warning

The Miranda opinion is predicated on the assumption that, as long as an arrested person understood that he had the right not to respond to police interrogation and that he had the right to have a lawyer assist him in dealing with the situation, the coercion inherent in being in police custody would be dispelled. This could only be true, however, if the language of the Miranda warning were sufficiently clear and comprehensible that the suspect who is given that information actually understood the nature of his rights and the choices that he could make. There is good evidence, however, to suggest that many who are given Miranda warnings do not have that requisite level of understanding.

The language of the warning itself is in places insufficiently clear to adequately inform suspects of their rights. The ordering of the rights within the standard Miranda warning is illogical and confusing, beginning with information about the right not to answer questions, skipping ahead to the implication of deciding to answer questions, and only then going on to inform the suspect about the availability of legal counsel. Syntactically, the warning is couched in a highly embedded structure. For example, note the embedded series of clauses in the warning on the right to have a lawyer:

> You have the right
> > (to have a lawyer present)
> > > (during questioning)
> > > > (to advise you)
> > > > > (prior to questioning)

It is well known that the more highly embedded the language, the more difficult a text is to understand (Shuy 1998b: 56–58).

Sometimes variations on the canonical Miranda warning are given, and in many cases these variations are even less understandable. In a landmark study (Rogers *et al.* 2007), a team of researchers collected 560 variations on Miranda warnings used in state and federal jurisdictions throughout the United States and analyzed them for comprehensibility, using the Flesch Reading Ease test, the Flesch-Kincaid test, and the SMOG readability scale. What they found was that some rights—for example, the right to remain silent—tended to be articulated in language classified as "fairly easy reading material," or language that would be understood adequately by 80% of the general population. Other parts of the warning, however, particularly the warnings involving waiver of rights, were phrased in such complex and convoluted ways that they were classed as "post-graduate reading level." For example, the right of a suspect to have counsel present during questioning and to have counsel appointed in the case of an indigent was presented in such a fashion that only 11% of the general public would likely understand it (Rogers *et al.* 2007: 186).

Consider one version of the warning on the right to counsel that the Rogers team assessed for comprehensibility: "You have the right to consult with, and have present, prior to, and during interrogation, an attorney either retained or appointed" (Rogers *et al.* 2007: 184). Note first that the verbs articulating the nature of the rights in this warning are conjoined, so that the hearer must process each of these rights separately. Further, note that the conjoined verbs "consult with" and "have present" are presented without an immediate direct object, which is not a typical feature of spoken English. In spoken English, hearers expect the direct object to closely follow the verb, whereas in formal written English, the reader can be expected to parse the sentence even when its elements occur in atypical positions. Intervening in this warning between those twinned verbs and the direct object is another doubled element—this time a doubled prepositional phrase, "prior to and during." Even when the direct object "attorney" finally makes an appearance in the warning, it is immediately followed by the doubled adjectives "retained or appointed." English syntax almost always inserts adjectives before modified nouns, but in this case adjectives constructed from verbs are placed in the highly unusual slot after the modified noun "attorney." In addition, the verbal adjectives "retained or appointed" are used in specialized senses rather than in their ordinary meanings. "Retained" generally means "kept" or "held in," not in the meaning used here "hired with one's own funds." Similarly, "appointed" usually means "officially chosen" and not "provided with public funds." Only someone already conversant with the practices of obtaining lawyers would likely understand the specialized meaning of these two verbal adjectives. As a spoken utterance, this sentence violates most of the norms of spoken English and would be challenging to parse even in formal written English and it would be a difficult utterance to understand fully even in the best of circumstances. Needless to say, the context of a high-pressure, anxiety-ridden interrogation room only adds to the difficulty of making sense of such verbiage.

In addition to poorly framed, vague, and circuitous expressions, the Miranda warnings analyzed by the researchers were typically too dense in information for adequate comprehension and recall. Based on their analysis, the researchers concluded that, as used in many jurisdictions, much of the Miranda warning would not be properly understood by a considerable percentage of the general public and would be inadequately understood by an even larger percentage of arrestees, given their statistically lower educational attainment.

As this research shows, it is questionable whether the language of the Miranda warnings suffices to make clear to the average person what their constitutional rights are and what options are open to them in the course of police interrogation. When, however, the suspect is not the average person, the situation is evenly bleaker. Many of those arrested and subjected to custodial interrogation—for example, juveniles, the mentally retarded, and the mentally ill—could well be less capable than the average person of understanding their rights (Solan and Tiersma 2005: 77–82). Empirical research has borne this out. A study looking at the comprehension of the Miranda warnings by mentally retarded individuals concluded that they fail to understand the rights as articulated and that they therefore are not capable of making voluntary and intelligent decisions to exercise or to waive them (Cloud *et al.*: 2002). In fact, that same study demonstrated that even non-retarded individuals with merely slightly lower than average IQs—in the 70s and 80s—have dramatically lower rates of comprehension than do persons of average intelligence (Cloud *et al.* 2002: 571–72). Similar research shows that juveniles, too, have more limited comprehension of the rights than do adults, with markedly lower degrees of understanding by those under the age of fifteen (Grisso 1980). Not surprisingly, perhaps, analysis of cases in which innocent persons were known to have confessed under police interrogation includes disproportionate numbers of those especially vulnerable groups—the young and the cognitively impaired (Drizin and Leo 2004: 963–69, 971–73).

The language of waiver

Assuming that a suspect actually does understand the rights given in the Miranda warning, there is still the question of under what circumstances his responses to subsequent interrogation should be considered legally admissible. The Miranda Court recognized that an arrestee might legitimately want to cooperate with the police and voluntarily respond to questioning, but it maintained a healthy skepticism about the likelihood of any purported waiver of rights, putting what it called "a heavy burden" on the prosecution to demonstrate the validity of any such waiver (*Miranda v. Arizona*, 1966: 475) and cautioning that "a valid waiver will not be presumed simply from the silence of the accused after warnings are given or simply from the fact that a confession was in fact eventually obtained" (*Miranda v. Arizona*, 1966: 475).

Soon enough, however, the Supreme Court retreated from this position. Despite the Miranda Court's presumption against the voluntariness of waiver of rights by arrestees in police custody due to the oppressive atmosphere of incommunicado interrogation, in subsequent cases the Supreme Court has been far more willing to find that suspects have waived their Miranda rights. Even when the police reports of the words by an arrestee purporting to show waiver instead display frank incomprehension of the rights outlined in Miranda, courts have nevertheless counted them as valid waivers. For example, in *North Carolina v. Butler* (1979), the arrestee being questioned while in police custody agreed to answer questions orally but would not put anything in writing or sign the waiver form. The obvious implication of that statement is that the suspect must have erroneously believed that written statements and signed waiver forms would be harmful to him in ways that merely answering oral questions would not be. In short, the only reasonable construction of the suspect's behavior is that he failed to understand that oral statements were every bit as binding on him as written statements and would be fully admissible in court. Yet the Supreme Court allowed the admission of his statements, finding that he had made a knowing and intelligent waiver of Miranda rights on these facts. Wisely, the Court did not even try to attempt to articulate a credible reason why someone would agree to incriminate himself by answering police questions orally but not in writing, despite knowing all along that the oral statements were binding and admissible. Perhaps any such attempt would have strained credulity to the breaking point and beyond (Kamisar 2007: 180–81). Instead of requiring affirmative waiver by the defendant in that case, the Supreme Court noted that his silence in the face of the warnings, coupled with his incriminating responses to police questioning, qualified as "a course of conduct indicating waiver" (*North Carolina v. Butler*, 1979: 373).

After *Butler*, it was no longer necessary for the prosecution to prove that a suspect had articulated either an understanding of his rights or of his desire to waive them and answer questions. Assuming that Miranda rights were read and that the suspect eventually responded to police questions, what the Miranda Court had once called the "heavy burden" on the prosecution to show a knowing, voluntary, and intelligent waiver of rights was satisfied. Having signaled to lower courts that the "heavy burden" on the State to prove waiver was in fact almost no burden at all, the Supreme Court in effect sanctioned lower court inquiry into waiver that was perfunctory at best. Once judges find that the defendant has waived his Miranda rights, moreover, the resulting confession is nearly always then admitted into evidence with no further meaningful examination as to whether it was the product of police over-reaching or coercion (White 2001: 1219–20; Klein 2001: 1070).

Because the making of incriminating statements has come to be treated as itself proof of waiver of Miranda rights, the law fails to protect the most vulnerable arrestees from police coercion and manipulation. A representative example of this occurred in *Miller v. State* (2002). In that case, a defendant, whom the trial judge found to be mentally retarded, was taken into custody and questioned by the police about a homicide. During that interrogation, the police lied to him about his having been seen just outside the victim's office before his death. The police also fabricated a computer printout and fingerprint card purporting to be those of the defendant, and told him falsely that his fingerprints had been found at the death scene. They went on to show him a copy of a report that falsely stated that the victim had died of natural causes, and to suggest to him that the death could have been accidental. Despite the blatant use of lies by the police to a suspect who was arguably particularly vulnerable to such tactics because of his low cognitive capacity, the Indiana Supreme Court had no trouble concluding that his confession was admissible, finding that "beyond a reasonable doubt the defendant had voluntarily waived his rights, and that his incriminatory statements … were voluntarily given" (*Miller v. State*, 2000: 768).

In another case involving an especially vulnerable arrestee, a Vietnamese-speaking suspect with limited English competence was read an error-filled Vietnamese language version of the Miranda warnings. When the police lied to him, telling him that he had been seen at the crime scene, he made incriminating statements. Despite the defective warnings and the fact that he never affirmatively waived his rights in any way, he, too, was held to have validly waived his rights simply by responding to police questioning (*Thai v. Mapes*, 2005). In yet another such case, the reviewing court found a knowing and intelligent valid waiver of Miranda rights, by arguing that the suspect's ability to write his name and answer questions was sufficient proof that he had adequate intelligence to understand the Miranda warnings, and by citing his record of prior convictions as proof that he must have had "at least a rudimentary understanding of his rights" (*U.S. v. Cuevas-Robledos*, 2006). This opinion directly contradicts the Miranda Court's express insistence that evidence of past encounters with the police were inadequate to show appropriate knowledge of one's rights, since what if anything a suspect learned about the constitutional rights in any earlier experience could "never be more than speculation" (*Miranda v. Arizona*, 1966: 471–72).

Not only may the police lie to suspects about the evidence in the case, they may also actively mislead the suspect about the nature of his rights (White 2006). Take, for example, the case of *Soffar v. Cockrell* (2002). In that case, the arrestee asked the interrogating detective how he could get a lawyer. The detective responded by asking Soffar if he could afford to hire a lawyer, knowing that he could not and also knowing full well that the Miranda rules mandate telling arrestees that, if they cannot afford to retain counsel, a lawyer will be appointed for them. The detective's implied assertion that only those with money had the right to counsel was unsuccessful in persuading Soffar to talk, however, because Soffar then asked the detective how he could get a court appointed lawyer and how long it would take to procure one. The detective knew that the law required that suspects must be charged and provided with counsel within 72 hours of arrest, but that is not what he told Soffar. Instead, he lied to him and told him that he didn't know how long it might take, but that he "guessed it could take as little as one day or as long as a month" (*Soffar v. Cockrell*, 2002: 591). Given this discouraging—and untrue—news about the unavailability of legal counsel, Soffar then replied, "So you're telling me I'm on my own." The detective's response, according to his own testimony at two hearings on the issue, was either "Yes, you are," or silence. Either way, the detective succeeded in discouraging Soffar from exercising his right to have a lawyer's assistance by intentionally giving him misleading and false information about his rights. Nevertheless, the 5th Circuit Court of Appeal, in an *en banc* opinion, held that Soffar's waiver of his rights was a knowing, voluntary, and intelligent one, and Soffar's death sentence was affirmed.

Even explicit statements by an arrestee that he is refusing to waive his rights are often of no avail. In one such case, the suspect refused to sign a Miranda waiver form and, in addition, twice explicitly told his interrogators that he was not waiving any rights. When, despite his insistence, the police continued to question him and he made incriminatory responses to police questioning, the reviewing court ignored his explicit assertions that he did not intend to waive his rights and held that the fact that he eventually answered police allegations was enough to prove a valid waiver of his rights (*U.S. v. Acosta*, 2006).

As courts began to treat any response by suspects as evidence of waiver of his rights, police naturally sought to provoke suspect responses. Professor Richard Leo, who has observed hundreds of police interrogations in the course of his research, has detailed various tactics and stratagems adopted by the police in order to get suspects to respond to questioning (Leo and White 1999: 433–35). He notes, for example, that they intentionally undercut Miranda in many ways. Officers minimize the suspect's attention to the significance of the warnings by reciting them in perfunctory, unanimated tones, speaking quickly without making eye contact, and referring to the warnings, often jokingly, as a mere formality to be quickly dispensed with in order to get to more important matters (Leo and White 1999: 433–35). In one such interrogation, the detective began his recitation of the Miranda warnings by saying, "Okay ... let me go ahead and do this here real quick, like I said, so don't let this ruffle your feathers or anything like that, it's just a formality we have to go through, okay" (Leo and White 1999: 434). In another case, the officer joked, "You've probably seen it on TV a thousand times. I know I've said it about ten thousand times." In a similar vein, a detective in another case preceded the warnings with the following:

> In order for me to talk to you specifically about the injury with [victim], I need to advise you of your rights. It's a formality. I'm sure you've watched television with the cop shows, right, and you hear them say their rights and so you can probably recite this better than I can but it's something I need to do and we can get this out of the way before we talk about what's happened.
>
> (Leo and White 1999: 435)

Discourse analyses of the required British cautioning of interrogated suspects show that, like their American counterparts giving Miranda warnings, British police administer cautions in a ritualistic, "hyperfluent" manner, minimizing both their significance and their comprehensibility (Rock 2007: 156–57).

Once the Miranda warning is given, the police often emphasize to the suspect how much they want to hear his side of the story, encouraging him to respond by a variety of framings, such as exaggerating the cruelty or magnitude of the crime as they now understand it without the benefit of the defendant's version, or suggesting that cooperating with the police will result in leniency or even dropping any charges (Leo and White 1999: 437–48). In one interrogation of a juvenile suspect recorded by Leo, the officer framed the Miranda warnings as giving the child the opportunity to confirm that he was not guilty of the crime, saying "Uh, we're gonna give you the opportunity to clear this whole matter up, and that's gonna entail you answering some question to us. Okay? You feel comfortable with that?" (Leo and White 1999: 445). Having framed the interrogation as a positive benefit to the suspect, the perfunctory recitation of the Miranda rights is hardly calculated to effectively warn the suspect about the very real potential of interrogation to provide incriminating rather than exculpatory evidence.

As long as the suspect eventually responds to interrogation, most courts will find an implied waiver of the Miranda rights despite deficiencies in the manner of the warnings and despite lack of any affirmative statement by the accused explicitly waiving his rights. Far from being what the Miranda Court called a "heavy burden" on the prosecution, waiver has become the default presumption whenever the suspect ultimately succumbs to police questioning. Whatever responses a suspect makes to police interrogation are held to constitute conclusive proof that he understood and chose to waive his rights, unless he explicitly takes specific steps to invoke his rights.

The language of invocation

One weakness in the specificity of the Miranda warnings is that they do not provide any guidance to suspects on how to claim their rights if they choose that option rather than waiving them. Given that, it would seem appropriate that courts would liberally construe attempts by suspects to invoke their rights as effective. Instead, the Supreme Court has held that, unless attempted invocations of Miranda rights are made using clear, unequivocal, and unambiguous language, they are legally void (*Davis v. United States*, 1994). Without such a clear and unambiguous invocation, the police can continue their interrogation without restrictions and need not even attempt to clarify whether or not the suspect is trying to assert his rights.

Examination of post-*Davis* case law shows the ways in which courts have bent over backwards construing arrestees' attempts to exercise their Miranda rights as fatally unclear or equivocal, thus denying them the protection of Miranda. Suspects must navigate a veritable linguistic minefield of disqualifying language in trying to exercise their Miranda rights. Some arrestees made the mistake of asking for their right to a lawyer using an interrogative syntactic form instead of an imperative:

- "Could I call my lawyer?" (*Dormire v. Wilkinson*, 2001).
- "May I call a lawyer? Can I call a lawyer?" (*State v. Payne*, 2001).
- "Do you mind if I have my lawyer with me?" (*U.S. v. Whitefeather*, 2006).
- "Can I speak to an attorney before I answer the question to find out what he would have to tell me?" (*Taylor v. Carey*, 2007).

These requests were all rejected as invocations because they were interpreted as merely theoretical questions about the availability of counsel rather than as actual requests for counsel. Reviewing courts here seemed to be under the mistaken impression that interrogative forms can never be meant as imperatives, despite the frequency in ordinary human interaction in which speakers do just that (Solan and Tiersma 2005: 54–62).

Other suspects were unsuccessful in their attempts to assert their rights because they used softened or indirect imperatives or they phrased their assertion of their rights with polite hedges:

- "I think I would like to talk to a lawyer." (*Clark v. Murphy*, 2003).
- "I think I will talk to a lawyer." (*State v. Farrah*, 2006).
- "It seems like what I need is a lawyer … I do want a lawyer." (*Oliver v. Runnels,* 2006).
- "Actually, you know what, I'm gonna call my lawyer. I don't feel comfortable." (*People v. McMahon*, 2005).

Preceding a demand for a lawyer with an initial subjunctive clause doomed the invocation of a suspect who said, "If I'm going to jail on anything, I want to have my attorney present before I start speaking to you about whatever it is you guys are talking about" (*Kibler v. Kirkland*, 2006). Despite that fact that the suspect in this case was indeed going to jail, the mere existence of the initial qualifying clause disqualified this invocation.

Sometimes arrestees need the cooperation of the police in order to get an attorney to be present during questioning. Asking for police assistance in obtaining counsel, however, could render their attempted invocation invalid. For example, the suspect who responded to the Miranda warnings by asking that the police retrieve his lawyer's business card was held not to have invoked his right to counsel (*US v. Tran*, 2006). Similarly unsuccessful was the hospitalized arrestee who asked police, "Could I get a phone in here so I can talk to a lawyer?" (*Jackson v. Commonwealth*, 2006).

Attempts to invoke the constitutional right to remain silent are likewise disqualified if they are deemed to be insufficiently direct and precise. The following responses to the Miranda warnings were all held too ambiguous or equivocal to count as successful invocations of the right to silence:

- "I don't want to talk about it." (*Owen v. State*, 2003).
- "I don't have anything to say." (*State v. Hickles*, 1996).
- "I don't wanna talk no more." (*U.S. v. Stephenson*, 2005).
- "I just don't think I should say anything." (*Burket v. Angelone*, 2000).
- Officer: "Do you want to make a statement to us?" Arrestee: "Nope." (*James v. Marshall*, 2003).

Simply remaining silent during interrogation has also been held to be insufficient as an attempt to claim the Miranda right to remain silent. Apparently, a suspect has to speak up in order to exercise his constitutional right not to speak (*State v. Ross*, 1996).

Even when the suspect tries to claim both the right to remain silent and the right to counsel, lack of sufficient precision often dooms the attempted invocation of Miranda rights:

- "I don't even want to talk unless I have me a lawyer and go through this shit." (*Harper v. State*, 2001).
- "I don't feel like I can talk with you without an attorney sitting right here to give me some legal advice." (*Baker v. State*, 2005).
- "I'll be honest with you. I'm scared to say anything without talking to a lawyer." (*Midkiff v. Commonwealth*, 1995).

- Suspect responded to police questioning with, "Fuck you, talk to my lawyer." (*People v. Varnum*, 2004).
- Arrestee responded to police officer saying, "Having these rights in mind, do you wish to talk to us?" with "Can I put 'no' 'til I get my lawyer?" (*State v. Jackson*, 2001).

These cases are among the most compelling for finding an invocation, in that they exemplify the very concern that led the Supreme Court in Miranda to interpose a right to counsel in the police interrogation context. As the Court saw it, a legally naïve arrestee might well not be in a position to determine how to respond to police questioning, or indeed whether to respond at all, without the assistance of legal counsel to advise him about how best to protect his interests. Those suspects whose attempts at invocation expressly articulate their need for legal advice before answering police questions thus ought to be cases deserving the most generous construal of the adequacy of rights invocations.

A telling indication of the bankruptcy of the Miranda framework as currently implemented is the finding by criminal justice scholars that, once a purported Miranda waiver has been given and questioning begins, almost no suspects ever attempt to end the interrogation by invoking their rights (Stuntz 2001: 998). Yet it must be more the rule than the exception that an interrogation increases both in intensity and focus over time, with more pointed questions, more specific accusations, and a greater adversarial tone as it unfolds. One would expect, then, that suspects who originally waived their Miranda rights under the mistaken impression that they could explain away the case against them would recognize as the heat was turned up that continued participation in the interrogation was no longer in their best interests. The fact that suspects seldom if ever attempt to terminate oppressive interrogations regardless of how onerous they become is strong evidence that they do not think that they have the power to do so.

Questioning "outside" Miranda

Almost immediately after announcing the Miranda framework for police interrogation, the Supreme Court began backpedaling from its underlying logic in a series of cases that permitted the admission of evidence obtained through police interrogation that violated the constraints of Miranda (see e.g. *New York v. Harris* 1971; *Michigan v. Tucker* 1974; *Oregon v. Elstad*, 1985). In permitting expansive use by prosecutors of evidence obtained in violation of Miranda, the Court—wittingly or not—provided a positive incentive for police to ignore the Miranda rule. The primary mechanism for enforcing constitutional constraints on police investigatory practices is, after all, the knowledge by police and prosecutors that illegally procured evidence cannot be admitted in court. Knowledge that intentional violations of the constitution in the course of police investigation will result in no usable evidence thus acts as a positive deterrent to police over-reaching.

It was not long before the police came to appreciate that there were substantial benefits in violating Miranda's strictures. In a process that came to be known as "questioning outside *Miranda*," some agencies actually instructed their officers on the advantages of intentionally violating Miranda, and instructed officers on how to take advantage of circumstances that would allow the evidence into court notwithstanding a purposeful violation of Miranda. For example, some police agencies recommended to officers that they consider violating the constitutional Miranda requirements in order to get a confession, and then, after getting incriminating statements, quickly Mirandizing the suspect and having him repeat the just-procured confession. Even if the suspect refused to repeat the confession, officers were reminded that the illegally obtained confession could still be validly used as impeachment if the defendant testified in his own defense at trial (Leo and White 1999; Weisselberg 2001). In this way, Supreme Court cases permitting the use at trial of evidence acquired through violation of the Miranda framework actually appear in some instances to promote intentional police violations of the law (Leo and White 1999: 448–50).

The Supreme Court reconsiders the Miranda framework

Although the Supreme Court has, in the years since the Miranda opinion, significantly weakened its reach through its subsequent rulings, it has not abandoned it altogether. In 2000, the Court was asked to reconsider the constitutional status of Miranda and overrule it, and to the surprise of many court-watchers, it instead re-affirmed the constitutional validity of the case (*Dickerson v. United States*, 2000). What remains of the Miranda framework, however, is in a real sense an empty shell. Its doctrinal framework has remained in place; however, as a practical matter, Miranda rights are dangerously easy to waive and nearly impossible to invoke successfully. Worse yet, courts have been disinclined to look carefully at whether a confession meets the minimal standards of voluntariness and reliability as long as an initial Miranda waiver can be inferred (White 2001: 1219–20). Far from being a bulwark against coercion in police interrogation, the Miranda requirements, once satisfied, have instead shielded interrogation from the kind of searching judicial inquiry that could expose instances of police over-reaching and undue pressure. To quote Yale Kamisar, widely recognized as the leading legal scholar on Miranda, the Supreme Court is "unwilling to overrule *Miranda* … and also unwilling to take *Miranda* seriously. That is the sad reality" (Kamisar 2007: 230).

The role for linguists in preventing miscarriages of justice

While it is apparent that the Supreme Court has no plans to scrap the Miranda framework in the near future, whatever its deficiencies, within that framework many issues occurring in individual cases present factual questions involving language usage and the appropriate interpretation to be accorded to that language. From a practical perspective, linguists could be extremely helpful in analyzing the discursive structure and linguistic content of interrogations. As Roger Shuy, one of the most experienced American forensic linguists, put it,

> (L)inguists know what to listen for in a conversation. They listen for topic initiations, topic recycling, response strategies, interruption patterns, intonation markers, pause lengths, speech event structure, speech acts, inferencing, ambiguity resolution, transcript accuracy, and many other things. Scientific training enables linguists to categorize structures that are alike and to compare or contrast structures that are not.
>
> (Shuy 1993a: xvii–xviii)

Linguistic evidence could be brought to bear on the question of whether a particular defendant likely had an adequate understanding of his rights from the warnings given to him. Such testimony would be especially pertinent when special reasons exist to be skeptical of whether the defendant had full understanding of the Miranda warnings—for example, when the defendant had diminished cognitive capacity, or was not a proficient English speaker, or was deaf, or was a juvenile, and so forth (see Solan and Tiersma 2005: 77–87). Whether a suspect's language showed that he knowingly and intelligently waived his rights; whether a waiver appeared to be coerced; whether a confession is credible evidence of guilt or instead only acquiescence to overbearing authority; whether the police deceptively promised leniency in return for an admission of involvement; whether a purported confession was of questionable reliability, because all of the pertinent information about the crime was fed to the suspect by the police—all these are issues lending themselves to discursive analysis by linguists, and in a number of instances, linguists have done useful analyses on just such cases (see Shuy 1998b: 17–33, 33–40, 122–39, 174–85). Many different sub-fields of linguistic expertise could be brought to bear on these questions, ranging from interactional discourse analysis (Watson 1990) to Gricean pragmatic analysis (Lakoff 1996) to phonetic analysis of intonation patterns (Shuy 1998b: 70–71) to analysis of topic and response sequences (Shuy 1998b: 33–40).

One factor frequently limiting the ability of linguists to assist in assessing the reliability of confessions in these cases can be the lack of an objective record of the course of the interrogation. The text of the written and signed confession admitted into evidence is the end product of a lengthy process of questions and answers in which multiple, competing, and conflicting narratives of the crime are created. During the interrogation process, details of the facts and attributions of motive and criminal responsibility sometimes originate with the interrogators and other times with the suspect, but by the time the confession is reduced to writing, it can be impossible to determine exactly who was responsible for word choice and narrative sequencing (Heydon 2005). Where there is neither a tape recording nor a transcript of the questioning, the linguist may be forced to reconstruct the interrogation from the memories and notes of the police and of the suspect. This admittedly partial and inaccurate record may stymie the linguist in drawing any valid conclusions (see Shuy 1998b: 58–68, 140–52, 154–73). In addition, written records lack features such as the intonation and phonetic reduction in articulation of the original oral statements, features which provide important clues to the proper interpretation of the meaning of the utterances (Shuy 1998b: 68–72.). Pauses, hesitancy, emotional emphasis, and the like are all key indexes of meaning that are eliminated in the reduction of a purported confession to a written narrative.

If the primary policy concern in regulating police interrogation is in preventing abusive and oppressive interrogations that could result in unreliable confessions, the best remedy to both prevent and detect such practices would be to insist that all custodial police questioning be videotaped. Across the political spectrum, nearly all legal commentators on police practices—both those opposed to Miranda and those who approve of it—agree that videotaping these sessions is highly desirable (Cassell 2001: 486–92; Kamisar 2007: 188–91; Slobogin 2003). In fact, when the Police and Criminal Evidence Act of 1986 made taping of all significant police interrogations mandatory in Great Britain, police administrators themselves found that audio taping their interrogations has been beneficial in promoting effective police investigation (Rock 2007).

Currently American police understand that, when courts come to determine what happened during an interrogation, it is their word against that of the suspect, and in such "swearing contests," the suspect will always be disbelieved (Kamisar 2007: 191). Knowing that the sessions were being taped would likely discourage the police from adopting abusive and unfair tactics in their questioning in the first place. In any event, taping would provide an objective record of what transpired that could later be closely examined to determine exactly what was said, when, and by whom. For example, since the Supreme Court has held that the precise language used by a suspect in attempting to invoke his rights is dispositive in whether he has efficaciously done so, there have been frequent contests over exactly what language was used by the invoking suspect (Shuy 1998b: 58–68). A taped record would eliminate such disputes. The experience of forensic linguists such as Roger Shuy in reconstructing and analyzing police interrogations clearly shows that if taping were required more generally in the United States, linguists could be of inestimable use in preventing miscarriages of justice resulting from unreliable confessions.

Further reading

Leo, Richard A. (2008) *Police Interrogation and American Justice*, Cambridge, MA: Harvard University Press [probably the last word on what goes on behind closed doors in police stations in the US].
Leo, Richard A. and Thomas, George C. (eds) (1998) *The Miranda Debate: Law, Justice, and Policing*, Boston, MA: Northeastern University Press [a very good and eclectic survey].
Rock, Frances (2007) *Communicating Rights: The Language of Arrest and Detention*, Basingstoke: Palgrave Macmillan [a good comparative discourse analysis of the police caution in the UK].
Shuy, Roger W. (1998) *The Language of Confession, Interrogation, and Deception*, Thousand Oaks, CA: Sage [Roger's greatest "hits" regarding police interrogation].
Solan, Lawrence M. and Tiersma, Peter M. (2005) *Speaking of Crime: The Language of Criminal Justice*, Chicago: University of Chicago Press [they include a significant chapter on Miranda].
Weisselberg, Charles D. (2008) "Mourning Miranda," *California Law Review*, 96: 1519–1600 [a more legally focused examination of why Miranda has failed].

Legal cases cited

Baker v. State, 214 S.W. 3d 239 (Ark. S. Ct. 2005).
Brown v. Mississippi, 297 U.S. 278 (1936).
Burket v. Angelone, 208 F.3d 172 (4th cir. 2000).
Clark v. Murphy, 317 F.3d 1038 (9th cir. 2003).
Davis v. United States, 512 U.S. 452 (1994).
Dickerson v. United States, 530 U.S. 428 (2000).
Dormire v. Wilkinson, 249 F.3d 801 (2001).
Harper v. State, Tex. App. LEXIS 7497 (2001).
Jackson v. Commonwealth, 187 S.W.3d 300 (Ky. S. Ct. 2006).
James v. Marshall, 322 F.3d 103 (1st cir. 2003).
Kibler v. Kirkland, U.S. Dist. LEXIS 55719 (D. N.Car. 2006).
Michigan v. Tucker, 417 U.S. 433 (1974).
Midkiff v. Commonwealth, 462 S.E.2d 112 (Va. S. Ct. 1995).
Miller v. State, 770 N.E.2d 763 (Ind. 2002).
Miranda v. Arizona, 384 U.S. 436 (1966).
New York v. Harris, 401 U.S. 222 (1971).
North Carolina v. Butler, 441 U.S. 369 (1979).
Oliver v. Runnels, U.S. Dist. LEXIS 50704 (E. D. Ca. 2006).
Oregon v. Elstad, 470 U.S. 298 (1985).
Owen v. State, 862 So. 2d 687 (Fla. S. Ct. 2003).

People v. McMahon, 31 Cal. Rptr.3d 256 (Cal. App. 2005).

People v. Varnum, 2004 Cal. App. LEXIS 5189.

Rogers v. Richmond, 365 U.S. 534 (1961).

Soffar v. Cockrell, 300 F.3d 588 (5th Cir. 2002).

State v. Farrah, Minn. App. Unpub. LEXIS 984 2006).

State v. Hickles, 929 P.2d 141 (Kan. S. Ct. 1996).

State v. Jackson, 19 P.3d 121 (Kan. S. Ct. 2001).

State v. Payne, 833 So.2d 927 (La. S. Ct. 2001).

State v. Ross, 552 N.W.2d 428 (Wisc. S. Ct. 1996)

Taylor v. Carey, U.S. Dist. LEXIS 12686 (E.D. Ca. 2007).

Thai v. Mapes, 412 F.3d 970 (8th cir. 2005).

U.S. v. Acosta, 363 F.3d 1141 (11th cir. 2006).

U.S. v. Cuevas-Robledos, 2006 U.S. Dist. LEXIS 76300 (D. Oregon 2006).

U.S. v. Stephenson, 152 Fed. App'x. 904 (11th cir. 2005).

U.S. v. Tran, 171 Fed. App'x. 758, U.S. App. LEXIS 5068 (11th cir. 2006.)

U.S. v. Whitefeather, U.S. Dist. LEXIS 17239 (D. Minn. 2006).

9

Witnesses and suspects in interviews

Collecting oral evidence: the police, the public and the written word

Frances Rock

Introduction

Imagine a police interview. What is the main thing going on? Whether your imagined interview was between men, women or was mixed sex; involved adults or a child; a witness, victim or a suspect; a group or only two individuals; whether it was conducted monolingually or through an interpreter; whether it was in a cramped police interview room or a state-of-the-art rape crisis unit, it probably had one key feature: instant, interpersonal interaction between a police officer and lay person. Sure enough, the Code of Practice which regulates detention in England and Wales (Code C) defines *interview* as 'the questioning of a person regarding their involvement or suspected involvement in a criminal offence or offences' (Home Office 2008: 37). So, your imagined police interview probably centred on two main participants, one seeking to elicit information from the other. At the very least, your interview participants, however numerous they are, are probably orienting to talk, even if the interviewee might be trying to avoid doing it. Other chapters of this book have shown the influence of the talk of participants with particular characteristics (Aldridge), the implications of spoken descriptions (Benneworth) and the potential of spoken questions in forming consensus (Holt and Johnson). Talk is obviously crucial to interviews but it is not the only or, I argue, the most important linguistic activity which shapes them. Let's look a little more closely at the interview you had imagined. The other linguistic activities that you might have called to mind are reading and writing. This chapter will focus on the place of reading and writing in police interviews, showing how these activities figure, how they are oriented to and how influential they are on the structures, practices and outcomes of police interviews.

How do reading and writing figure in interviews?

Other chapters of this book have shown the potential for written texts which are created before interviews and 'taken in' to the interview to offer protection, or to fail to do so

(Ainsworth) and the potential for written texts created during interviews to be 'brought out' and influence later parts of the legal system (Ehrlich; Haworth).

These chapters illustrate that reading and writing impinge on interviews as both an input to and an outcome from interviews. The influence of such reading and writing on interviews has increased in those countries which adopt the PEACE method of interviewing. These include England, Wales, Australia and, increasingly, parts of the USA. This model was devised by a British Government Steering Committee (Home Office 1992) and introduced to police personnel in England and Wales through training during the 1990s. The model's influence has been entrenched in Great Britain through its central position in the Association of Chief Police Officers' Investigative Interviewing Strategy which introduced a five-tier interview-training programme designed to classify interviewing skills and train officers across the policing organisational structure. PEACE is also integral to recent moves to professionalise the Police Service through an investigative skills training programme which is being implemented at the time of writing by the National Policing Improvement Agency (2008). The PEACE model, based on techniques from cognitive interviewing and conversational management, proposes that *investigative interviewing*, as opposed to *interrogation*, depends on a very specific set of activities and skills. The concepts denoted by the acronym PEACE are not intended to highlight the importance of reading and writing but as my summary below shows reading and writing are integral to those concepts and thus to contemporary interviewing methods:

Planning and preparation: Takes place before the interview begins and involves both 'legal and logistical issues of interview preparation' (Williamson 2006: 172). This includes activities like making notes about legal topics such as points to prove and identifying practical needs, for example, an appropriate adult to help those interviewees who are unable to read.

Engage and explain: Describes the opening phases of an interview during which the officer will explain the upcoming interview procedure, for example, why someone in the room might be writing during the interview, and the legal issues which relate to the interviewee, such as the right to legal advice.

Account: Denotes the main 'questioning' sequence and therefore has obvious relevance to texts produced during *planning and preparation*. During the account phase, the officer will both use notes written before the interview and make notes for further questioning or subsequent investigation.

Closure: Provides both formal termination of the interview, as the officer explains legally required matters such as what will happen to recordings which might have been made, and informal termination, as the officer explains what might happen next.

Evaluation: Post-interview assessment at this stage provides both a platform for the officer's personal and professional development and, in relation to the investigation itself, the incentive to review the interview records and, if necessary, generate further investigative activities.

PEACE, if followed correctly, requires that officers see the interview not as an isolated activity, clearly delimited from the world outside the interview room, but as part of a chain of activities which are intended to improve interview outcomes in police terms. Inherent in this chain of activities are chains of written and spoken texts; texts created in one setting and used in innovative, and even surprising, ways in another. Inherent too in investigative interviewing and PEACE is the notion that reading and writing are not bounded activities quietly undertaken in solitude then filed away, but part of the tapestry of linguistic activities of everyday life. These notions require further exploration to equip us to move on.

Intertextuality and literacies in police interviews

As Bauman points out, social life is 'discursively constituted, produced and reproduced in situated acts of speaking and other signifying practices that are simultaneously anchored in their situational contexts of use and transcendent of them, linked by interdiscursive ties to other situations, other acts, other utterances' (Bauman 2004: 2). Metaphors have been usefully employed to describe such interdiscursive ties: signifying practices such as texts are seen to become part of a 'web' with other texts (Seebohm 2004), being formed through 'sedimentation' of texts and practices (Pahl 2002; Silverstein and Urban 1996); recycled (Aronsson 1991) and being 'shipped around' creating complex trajectories (Blommaert 2005: 76, see also Maryns 2006: 14–199). This process, frequently, although not exclusively, referred to as recontextualisation, was brought to prominence by Bauman and Briggs. They point out that texts can be decontextualised or treated as 'self-contained, bounded objects, separable from their social and cultural contexts of production and reception' (Bauman and Briggs 1990: 72) having first become extractable through entextualisation (1990: 73). Decontextualisation implies that a text will be recontextualised in a different context (1990: 74) – this recontextualisation, our focus here, will create changes in 'form function and meaning' (1990: 75). Recontextualisation involves both shifting and changing something of a text, discourse, genre or style by slotting it into another text, discourse, genre or style and, crucially, altering its use and environment and creating new meanings (Linell 1998: 145). As this suggests, this process is not 'neutral' but an 'act of control' (Bauman and Briggs 1990: 76). Fairclough points out that specific choices in the way that events are represented and transformed depend 'on the goals, values and priorities of the communication in which they are recontextualised' (Fairclough 1995: 41). Thus research which recognises the way texts develop from, through and into other texts, contexts and discourses gives insight into both the backgrounds or 'secret lives' of texts and, importantly in legal settings, into how particular versions of events, people, places and things get presented and given primacy (Mehan 1996: 253).

Many people tend to think of reading and writing as a set of skills which are taught and tested at school and, if learned well, can be used for a lifetime. This conception has been dislodged by the New Literacy Studies which instead works with a notion of literacy practices – 'the general cultural ways of utilising written language which people draw upon in their lives' (Barton and Hamilton 2000: 7). These practices are taken up in varied ways and for varied purposes under the influence of discursive practices, so that literacy itself is seen as situated in cultures and ideologies (Street 1984). This perspective makes it possible to recognise literacies (multiple realisations of literacy) as 'located in particular times and places' and therefore 'indicative of broader social practices' but also 'positioned in relation to the social institutions and power relations which sustain them' (Barton *et al.* 2000: 1). In turn, this facilitates perspectives on individuals, identities, social processes, social events discourses and broader institutional structures, which are inaccessible through blander, skills-based views of literacy or through the examination of only the traces of literacy events: texts. For example, a skills-based perspective on a police interview with someone who has been categorised as unable to read would assert that that person should be provided with a helper, an appropriate adult, to read written material to them when necessary before and during interview. A more productive alternative would involve investigating issues such as the implications of 'unable to read' here; how texts, reading and writing influence the interview and its socio-legal significance; how the prioritisation of particular forms of knowledge and practice influence the activities and identities of each participant; and through the analysis of both texts and literacy practices, what the presence of the appropriate adult accomplishes.

This chapter uses naturally occurring data from British police investigations to show both how writing which feeds into the interview process influences the content and effect of talk (in the next section), and how writing which comes out of the interview process is created through the interview itself (in the following section).

Writing which is brought into interviews

In the process of the Engage and Explain phase of a PEACE interview with a suspect, one important task for the interviewer is to present the legislation which will apply throughout the interview. In England and Wales, this is accomplished through the statement and, if necessary, explanation of several rights. You might remember that in the first paragraph of this chapter, I noted that the detention rulebook, Code C of the Codes of Practice, defined *interview* as meaning questioning about a criminal offence or offences. The full definition importantly adds that this questioning 'must be carried out under caution' (Home Office 2008: 37). So, in the eyes of the legal institution, for an interview with a suspect to *be* an interview, it must be preceded by a particular form of words, a 'caution'. The caution is thus a constitutive, formal mechanism which frames the interview, marking and delimiting it for the legal institution. The caution is also an important component of the interactional work undertaken by interview participants to accomplish what has been called 'intertextual framing' or framing within an interaction through which text-types are related to one another (MacLachlan and Reid 1994: 13). Officers themselves recognise this framing function describing reciting the caution as being *like putting a flag up and saying 'right now the investigation starts'* and they use the caution along with a range of linguistic and paralinguistic measures to accomplish framing throughout the interview (Rock 2007: 287–92). This form of words will have been read, recited and heard repeatedly by the interviewing officer. Knowing the caution is seen by police officers as an important marker of their professional identity, as one officer put it, *a tool of the trade*. You might like to consider how you would memorise this written formulation:

You do not have to say anything. But it may harm your defence if you do not mention when questioned something which you later rely on in Court. Anything you do say may be given in evidence.

The caution influences interviews most obviously by imbuing words and silences with significances which differ dramatically from those attached to them in other settings (Ainsworth 2008; Shuy 1997). Readers who know something of the legal system in the USA will note that this form of words expresses similar content to the 'Miranda warnings' (see Ainsworth, this volume), which, like the Caution, convey a right not to self-incriminate, but they also state the right to an attorney. This right to legal advice is not missing from the British criminal justice system – suspects should be offered free, independent legal advice repeatedly throughout pre-interview detention (Police and Criminal Evidence Act, 1984: S.58) – but it is not expressed through a formulaic wording. Miranda warnings, along with cautions in most other jurisdictions, are also different from this 'caution' in offering an unqualified right of silence. The qualification provided in England and Wales by the middle sentence above was introduced in the mid 1990s, intended to deter suspects from being silent in interview but then fabricating a story in time for any court attendance. Whether it has been successful is a legal matter, although police officers' reported scepticism about this is unlikely to be insignificant to their speech activities in interview. From a linguistic, sociolinguistic and pragmatic perspective, we can usefully investigate what happens to the caution when it enters police interviews and how it affects those interactions and the participants involved, as I will illustrate below.

As well as the meaning and function of the caution, the form of the wording is also influential (Gibbons 2001b; Cotterill 2000). When the wording was first debated in the House of Lords, one peer remarked, 'I ask the house to consider very carefully whether this is a comprehensible set of words' (Hansard, 23 February 1995, in: Woods 2006: 103). Procedure enshrined in the Codes of Practice acknowledges potential shortcomings of the wording by informing officers that 'If it appears a person does not understand the caution, the person giving it should explain it in their own words' (Home Office 2008: 37). In this way, officers are taken out of the role of animator, i.e. of simply uttering the words authored by the Government, and put into the author role, as they 'take the local environment and the local hearership into consideration' (Goffman 1981a: 255). Police officers' explanations of the caution exemplify literacy practices through which they work on written information in relation to the task at hand. Some always explain it in the same way; others innovate, tailoring their explanations to the suspect in front of them. Thus these explanations also illustrate recontextualisation – officers transfer meaning from the written text into a new context which they come to constitute by establishing expectations, commenting on the source text and confirming or challenging it. Contextualisation cues or 'surface features ... by which speakers signal and listeners interpret what the activity is, how semantic content is to be understood and how each sentence relates to what precedes or follows' (Gumperz 1982: 131) figure here too as we will see.

The police officers in the two extracts below, both speaking at the beginning of separate interviews – one in England, one in Wales – recontextualise the caution in ways which illustrate how the shift in participant roles, from animator to author and the shift from reciting a monologic, written wording to delivering a lesser- or un-scripted dialogue (we cannot be sure which) allow the police officers to accomplish a great deal beyond official cautioning work:

(1) Officer 1

  1 IR: before we go any further (.) I must caution you (.) that is I must tell you
                that you do not have to say anything [states whole caution] do you
                understand that caution (then)

2 IE: yeah

3 IR: I don't wish to be awkward but can you just explain to me what it means to you so that I know you understand it

4 IE: it means (.) if I don't (.) ur open my mouth at court and say something I didn't say (.) previously they'll want to know (.) why (.) I haven't uh given them this new piece of information (.) and why-why it wasn't mentioned before

5 IR: yeah that's (.) that's the majority of it (.) good as- good an explanation as I've heard so far

6 Both: laugh

7 IR: just- just to remind you =

8 IE: = consider I'm coming up for the-

9 Both: ((laugh))

10 IR: just to reiterate and re-emphasise the first bit you do not have to say anything alright (.) so what you said there (.) anything that you later m-(.) mention (.) could go against you if you don't mention it now but bit the first bit-it's a right and entitlement you don't have to say anything I'm going ask you a few questions (.) it's up to you whether you answer them or not the second bit as you say (.) spot on and the third bit is: anything you do say may be given in evidence anything you say it's on this tape (.) we know it's you speaking it can be played in court as evidence

11 IE: yeah

(2) Officer 2

1 IR: before I'm allowed to ask you any questions Darren I've got to caution you and the caution goes like this you do not have to say anything ((states whole caution)) um I'm going to explain what that means to you and that means this (.) the questions that I'm about to ask you during this interview (.) you have Darren a legal right not to answer those if you don't want to I can't make you answer those questions if you wanted to you could sit there and jus-just stare at the walls I don't *personally* advise that you do that *but* that's your right

2 IE: yep

3 IR: okay do you under-you understand that

4 IE: I understand yeah

5 IR: okay the second part of the caution Darren means this *but* it may harm your defence if you do not mention when questioned you're only going to get questioned by me once and that's now okay? something which you later rely on in court and what that means is this if you tell me nowt ((i.e. nothing)) during this interview now which has been indicated by Mr Harris ((solicitor)) and then if this matter went to court you decided to tell the court something *different* the court might be less inclined in certain-certain circumstances to believe you they might think to them-selves well why didn't he say that to the police at the time do you understand that

6 IE: I understand

7	IR:	now anything you do decide to tell *me* (.) is obviously recorded on that interview tape and I can tell the magistrates if it goes to court what you've said alright
8	IE:	yeah

In both officers' talk we can see evidence of a cautioning routine which is typical of this explanation activity. This routine involves stating the official wording, providing an explanation and seeking to assess comprehension at various stages. Both officers begin similarly in that they contextualise the caution as part of police procedure and a felicity condition of interview. In extract (1), this is accomplished through *before we go any further* where pronoun choice and the journey metaphor (Lakoff 1988: 435–40) combine to convey that the officer and interviewee are, to some extent, in things together. Extract (2) on the other hand sees official procedures invoked and problematised as a prelude to cautioning as the officer asserts *before I'm allowed to ask you any questions ... I've got to caution you.* These opening orientations, I suggest, develop throughout each explanation – the explanations are not simply neutral regurgitations of 'facts' presented in the caution, rather through them the officers orient to the upcoming interview and to the suspect and, potentially, establish context and relational positionings for the interview.

Officer 1, whose opening was broadly conciliatory, apparently recognises that asking someone to explain something just said is inherently threatening to both the positive face want to be viewed as competent and thus approved of and the negative face want to be unimpeded by requests for talk (Brown and Levinson 1987). He therefore mitigates his request or plays down its face threat (Fraser 1980). He does this throughout turn 3, explaining that his request is not mischievous, but rather in the suspect's interest. Further mitigation follows in turns 7 and 10 when the officer's own explanation is presented as a reminder (turn 7) and reiteration (turn 9) and minimised, in both cases, through *just*. In turn 5, the officer develops his presentation of self and cooperative orientation to the suspect by delivering an extremely positive graded evaluation (Hunston and Sinclair 2000: 92) of the suspect's words, through a comparative adjective group, *as good ... as* which compares the suspect's explanation to all others that the officer has ever heard. The officer's explanation, though it might be felt to be a little incoherent in places, also attends to the suspect by acknowledging him and anaphorically referring to his contribution (*what you said there*), foregrounding the suspect's autonomy by presenting choices about the exercise of rights as *up to you* and providing further evaluation of the suspect's explanation as *spot on*. The integration of the evaluation into the officer's explanation heightens the sense that the officer is attending to the suspect.

Officer 2, on the other hand, seems to develop the rather confrontational stance he had established through his first turn's orientation to rules and restrictions on interviewing. After stating the caution, he does not query the suspect's comprehension, implying that the suspect is unlikely to understand completely or at all. This implicature is developed by the officer's bald on record (Brown and Levinson 1987: 94–101) statement that he will explain and his failure to seek to establish whether this is required. Maintaining silence during a police interview is extremely difficult due to the pressure of the second part of the question and answer pair that is so central to interviewing. This officer appears to alleviate this difficulty for the suspect by suggesting a way to be silent *sit there and ... stare at the walls.* However the choice of *just* here, along with the personal criticism of this strategy casts perhaps the only viable way to be silent in a police interview (say nothing and look away from the interviewer) extremely negatively. The use of the suspect's first name early in turns 1 and 5 does not appear motivated by a need to establish recipiency as the addressee is clear from the interview context and co-text. *Darren* indeed appears multifunctional indexing power relations through its position and stance through its selection in preference to a *V* form, possibilities usefully discussed in relation to political interviews by Rendle-Short (2007: 1521–22). Through what might be seen as a marked address term (Jaworski and Galasiński 2004) the officer can be said to assert his position in relation to the suspect and his orientation to the information which follows. The details of the explanation are also telling. In turn 5, the officer stresses that questioning is a unique opportunity (*you're only going to get questioned by me once and that's now*) with the implication that this is an opportunity worth taking. This possible encouragement to talk is supported later in the same turn by the officer's placement of reference to the solicitor's advice which implies critique of that advice.

The existence of a right to silence influences police interviews with suspects because it establishes discourse rules about how silence and speech should be interpreted and formalises ways of resisting cooperation with the police, through an explicit rights invocation in the USA or the use of silence in the UK. However, as I have shown, the way that officers deliver the right during the Engage and Explain phase is also influential. In the UK, the opportunity for the interviewing officer to engage in exchanges ostensibly aiming to explain the caution allows space for some innovative and apparently helpful explanation of a crucial right, but, as the extracts above show, also provides for powerful discoursal work. Affiliation in cautioning can be just as potent as disaffiliation. This illustrates Bauman and Briggs's point that examining recontextualisation can reveal 'differential legitimacy in claims to and use of texts, differential competence in use of texts and differential values attached to various types of text' (Bauman and Briggs 1990: 76). Furthermore cautioning sits uncomfortably in the Engage and Explain phase. In turn 8 of extract 1 the suspect says 'consider I'm coming up for', indicating shared knowledge about the suspect's legal situation and the place of this interview in that situation, knowledge which cannot be acknowledged within the cautioning procedure.

Writing which is taken from interviews

Moving from the passage of texts into interview during the Engage and Explain phase of the PEACE structure, the Account phase sees crime narratives elicited and processed so that words can be entextualised and pass out of interview. This places serious cognitive demands on both interviewers and interviewees. Interviewers will undertake a range of activities including listening, devising questions, delivering questions, reacting to answers, writing notes on points for clarification, writing a statement, holding in mind prior utterances, imagining a crime context, reading texts produced by them and others before and during the interview. They will also engage in a range of identity-related activities, such as showing empathy and encouraging disclosure, and in procedural activities, such as ensuring that the interview complies with legal requirements in terms of its duration. Interviewees too will potentially listen and respond to questions, deliver narratives, write or draw (for example mapping a crime location) and undertake a range of strategies for activating short- and long-term memories sometimes with the interviewer's help. In addition, the interviewee may have to work with a range of emotions during the interview such as fear, anger and guilt. Ultimately, both participants share in the reflexive capacity of entextualisation as they 'render stretches of discourse discontinuous with their discursive surround, thus making them into coherent, effective and memorable texts' (Bauman and Briggs 1990: 74). I will now investigate this account phase as it occurs in interviews with a witness. I focus on a witness rather than a suspect interview, as in the previous section, because these involve fewer participants. This makes it easier to maintain the current foci, transformation and literacies. Note that witnesses, unlike suspects, are not cautioned. The caution is a protection against self-incrimination and therefore assumed unnecessary unless demonstrated otherwise.

The extracts below are from an interview with a 'significant' witness. This is a category of witness identified by the police as needing a particularly thorough, highly proceduralised interview. This may be because they have seen a serious crime, such as murder, or experienced one, such as rape, or because they might, in due course, become suspected of the crime under investigation. The significant witness interview has two key characteristics: first, it is likely to be conducted by a police officer with specialist training and, unlike other witness interviews, it will be audio-recorded. In addition to the audio-recording, a written statement will be produced to be signed by the witness as a true record of the event as is routine in Anglo-Welsh witness interviews. Even in relation to significant witnesses, the written statement, rather than recording, may become the main reference text during subsequent investigations, due to its brevity. Thus, written statements have the power to shape investigations, court proceedings and beyond as they are recontextualised through use in those settings. Recontextualisation of the witness's story begins in the witness interview. Through the interview process the witness's experience of a crime event is mediated by such factors as their selective accounting (for whatever reason) (Holmberg 2004), their transformation of their experience into talk, as well as the interviewer's mental representation of the witness's words and entextualisation of the witness's words as they convert talk to text (Komter 2006; Gibbons 2001a). Most of these transformational processes are not observable. We cannot study how objectively the witness encodes their experience, as we did not observe the source event and, even if we had, we could not share their perspective. Likewise, we cannot observe the interviewer's mental processing of the words they hear. We can, however, observe entextualisation. By comparing an audio-recording of a police interview with the resulting written statement we can trace the intertextual processes apparent in spoken negotiation. Comparison can also reveal differences between the spoken interview and the written statement. Police interviews themselves are comprised of multiple recontextualisations because during the interview the officer and witness talk through the narrative several times thereby producing spoken versions which are each different (Johnson 2008b). Officers will typically seek to elicit an initial narrative and will subsequently probe that narrative in order to expand on the initial account, to check and test details and to construct a written version in real time using this talk. In the case of the extracts below, four versions were produced (Rock 2001 elaborates):

Version 1: The witness's account, delivered with minimal intervention by the police officer. The witness narrates the whole event as he sees it and the police officer asks just three questions.

Version 2: The interviewer asks 257 questions which elicit a more detailed but less chronological account. The interviewer makes copious notes throughout this version.

Version 3: The interviewer feeds back information from his notes to the interviewee, seeking confirmation or expansion whilst expanding his notes yet focusing them into a statement.

Version 4:   The interviewer reads the final statement aloud, requesting confirma-
             tion and occasional extra details throughout (Stokoe and Edwards
             2008).

This talk results in a written statement.

Using the notion of literacies as social practices, we can observe that this recontextualisation is constitutive and purposive. The examples below illustrate details of transformational
processes in the police interview by presenting dialogic sections from interviews accompanied by the resulting written text. Line numbers indicate each extract's position in the
original interview. Errors in the written statement are as in the original.

In extracts (3) and (4), below, the officer and witness discuss the layout of a house in
which a murder was committed. Extract (3) is from version 2 during which the officer
pursues details. Extract (4) is from version 4 when the statement is finalised:

(3)   From version 2:

177 IR: describe the man's house and stuff inside
178 IE: ... ((description of objects in the house)) ...
179 IR: he owns the flat
180 IE: he owns the flat yeah
181 IR: okay um is it a house (.) or is it a like a flat =
182 IE: = it's like it's like a it's
             a house but it's like put it like two (.) two houses sort of put it as a flat
183 IR: two floors yeah
184 IE: yeah
185 IR: okay and which floor is his house on =
186 IE: = he's he's on the top

(4)   From version 4:

751 IR: when you get to the top of the stairs where are you
752 IE: urm when you get to the top of the stairs you have to take (.) a right
753 IR: (3.9) yeah
754 IE: and then you have to-when you take a right there's a (.) you got (.) got a
             door-door on your left door on the right (.) and a door in front of you
             but we went (.) in the door on the right
755 IR: and what room was that =
756 IE: = that was the living room

In extract (3), the officer seeks a description and provides prompts around ownership of
the man's home, its status as flat or house and its location within a larger building. The
officer and witness do not return to this until around an hour later in the statement-
making session, when the officer is drafting text during version 4. Then, as illustrated in
extract (4), the officer requests information about the flat's layout and receives not only
that but also an implicit description of the witness's movement through the property.
Extract (5), below, shows how the information from extracts (3) and (4) was incorporated
into the written statement:

(5) From the written statement:

> When we got to the mans [*sic*] house we went in [*sic*] it is a flat on the 1st floor …
> To enter the flat you climb up the stairs turn right into the living room.

The witness's suggestion to *put it like two (.) two houses … put it as a flat* (Extract (3), turn 182) is a spoken answer to a spoken question. Yet the witness orients to the literate dimension of the interaction. He does this by making a direct suggestion about how the officer should formulate his text even though this was not the explicit focus of the question.

As for the officer, his ongoing, attentive writing activities are apparent in the way his written texts relate to the talk as he weaves information from the early and later parts of the interview. Some of that information is introduced by the witness, the notion of *a flat*, a word which is incorporated into the statement, and the location of that flat on the first floor, for which the witness uses the formulation *top floor*. Other information is provided by the officer on the basis of inference. To illustrate, add the two extracts below to extracts (3) to (5), above:

(6) From version 1:

  4 IE: we went to his house anyway and he (.) he invited us in and we was like saw some girls and that and so (.) went up to the house which–(.) the girls (knew) everybody–everybody else there (.) went to the house (.) started having a laugh

(7) From version 2:

175 IR: when you got to the house what happened
176 IE: just talking (.) and laughing and all that and having a little mess about

In both of these extracts, the witness describes his arrival at the murder scene without specifying how he entered the victim's home or to the house's layout, instead noting the invitation to enter and activities inside. Indeed, throughout the interview there is no direct mention of having got to the top of the stairs until the officer introduces this in line 752 (extract (4)) very close to the end of the interview in the final version of the narrative. Thus, the officer has inserted details of location which will no doubt help readers who are downstream in the criminal justice process but does not represent events exactly as the witness did. The officer also shapes the description of the victim's home through the questions he asks (Cederborg 2002: 163). The witness might not have identified the house as a flat without the officer's intervention because elsewhere he recounts having used the word *house* to denote the property whilst at the crime scene on the day of the murder. A final feature of the transformational processes here is that some of the information is lost in the final version. The officer asked about ownership of the flat in line 179 but, despite the witness's confident answer, this information does not materialise in the final statement.

What are the implications of this? Is there a cost, for example, to acting on the witness's voice (Maryns 2006; Trinch and Berk-Seligson 2002: 410–11)? Whilst the transformational processes described above have influenced the formulation of the written statement, it is not clear whether this influence will be adverse and if so for whom (Hill 2003). The degree to which witnesses are represented in their statements is, however, not just a triviality (Jönsson and Linell 1991; Hunt and Borgida 2001). Witnesses' statements can be presented to courts and form the basis of examination, with any discrepancies being highlighted in court, potentially to the great detriment of the witness's testimony (Thornborrow 2002: 56–58). The extracts below illustrate just one way in which this can become a problem. In extract (8), the officer and witness have been discussing an encounter, at some shops, between the witness and the suspects shortly after the alleged murder. The witness explains that he was talking to a local woman when this conversation began:

(8) From version 3:
363 IR: just tell me about the conversation you had at the shop
364 IE: well I was talk-I was talking to ur (.) is this this woman (.) saying ur (.) talking about what was it now urm (.) I can't remember what I was talking about properly (.) just come-was just one of those one-off conversations just (on like that)
365 IR: which woman is this
366 IE: um l-oh well local woman

In version 4 (extract (9)), as the officer is finalising the statement, he refers again to the woman who was introduced by the witness in version 3, linking her to the presence of the suspects:

(9) From version 4:
657 IR: they caught up with you by the shops (.) and said look what he's done to my hand and you could see that Dave had a deep cut in the middle of his right palm and it was bleeding =
658 IE: = yeah =
659 IR: = but it wasn't bleeding that bad you were talking to local woman at the shop you don't know her name

This woman is potentially an important additional source of information and, according to the witness, a feature of the events for him. Her presence in version 4 is therefore not surprising as it indicates that the officer will incorporate mention of her into the final statement. However, in fact she is totally absent from the final statement as extract (10) shows:

(10) From final statement:
As I got down the stairs they were coming down behind me they caught up with us by the shops the offlicence [sic].
David showed us his hand with a cut small but deep to the palm of his right hand, he said look what hes [sic] done to my hand, it was bleeding.

This absence potentially loses an important evidential lead and leaves the witness vulnerable to confusion during cross-examination in any subsequent court appearance. These processes are ubiquitous in witness statements and efforts to understand them will show how recontextualisation can impact on the experiences of victims and witnesses.

Interviewers are aware of and articulate about the influence of transformational processes on police interviews, as Bauman and Briggs have observed 'participants themselves may be directly and strongly concerned with the social management of entextualisation, decontextualisation and recontextualisation' (Bauman and Briggs 1990: 74). Here an officer describes how this affects his work during investigations, when he uses statements from police officers recounting their own experiences:

> all you can go by I mean is what it says in statements obviously when you read a statement it can be different to what's happened out on the street I mean when they write a statement it's detailed but what may have occurred and took maybe 10 15 minutes to sort out you'll have in 2 pages well 2 pages in detail isn't going to cover 15 minutes so you don't always realise exactly what's gone on.
>
> (Author's data)

For him, even the first person transformation of experience implies processes which act on information. Interestingly, he added that his own literacy practices in using these abbreviated texts might involve contacting the police officer to seek an extended verbal account and thus, as an investigator, entering the transformational process himself.

Conclusion

The two ideas of chains of texts and of literacies provide a valuable perspective on police interviews by highlighting their situatedness and their reliance on entextualisation through negotiated talk. Police interviews are influenced by the texts which constitute and define them and which constitute and define the linguistic and paralinguistic activities which they comprise. Police interviews in turn influence legal practices and processes both investigative and judicial yet the mechanisms through which many of those interviews are converted into written format requires much further research.

Further reading

Aronsson, K. (1991) 'Social interaction and the recycling of legal evidence', in N. Coupland, H. Giles and J. Wiemann (eds), *Miscommunication and Problematic Talk*, London: Sage, 215–43.

Gibbons, J. (2001b) 'Revising the language of New South Wales police procedures: Applied linguistics in action', *Applied Linguistics*, 22: 439–69.

Jönsson, L. and Linell, P. (1991) 'Story generations: From dialogical interviews to written reports in police interrogations', *Text*, 11: 419–40.

Shuy, R. (1997) 'Ten unanswered language questions about Miranda', *Forensic Linguistics*, 4: 51–73.

10

Sexual offences

Negotiating paedophilia in the investigative interview: the construction of sexual offences against children

Kelly Benneworth

Introduction

Significant developments in police interviewing practice in the UK have been fuelled by psychological research. Studies have acknowledged the coercive and oppressive features of the traditional adversarial police interrogation (Shepherd 1991; Mortimer 1994; Moston and Stephenson 1993; Williamson 1993) and given rise to the ethical PEACE investigative interview, the rationale for which is outlined in *A Practical Guide to Investigative Interviewing* (National Crime Faculty 2000). In addition to the PEACE protocol of inviting suspects, witnesses and victims of crime to provide uninterrupted accounts of their experiences using open and fair questioning (Clarke and Milne 2001; Griffiths and Milne 2005; Milne and Bull 1999), research has also informed the evolution of the Cognitive Interview, which integrates psychological principles to aid witness accuracy and recall (Fisher and Geiselman 1992; Fisher *et al.* 1989; Geiselman *et al.* 1986).

There is a penchant in psychology for examining investigative interviewing by distilling interview data, cataloguing interview techniques and quantifying responses to questioning. Few studies have adopted detailed, qualitative methods of enquiry to explore how investigative interviewing is put into practice. Methodological approaches such as sociolinguistics, ethnomethodology, conversation analysis and discourse analysis, emerged in opposition to empiricist psychology and sociology and favoured the in-depth, interpretative analysis of naturally occurring interactions. Discourse analysis in particular has examined how competing versions of criminal offences are negotiated and co-constructed in the police interview. Watson (1990) examined the interactional structure of US murder interrogations and noted police interviewers asserting their influence on suspect testimony. Through the use of knowledge claims, such as 'we also *know* about the gun in the Morris homicide' (Watson 1990: 266), officers bolstered facticity and ensured that simple denials were insufficient to counter accusations. Linell and Jönsson (1991) observed a clash between the 'everyday life' perspective of suspects and the 'professional' perspective of the police in Swedish interviews with individuals suspected of

economic offences. Their findings demonstrated how the professional perspective domi-
nated interactions as officers asked closed questions, narrowly defined conditions for
answering, and provided reformulations of the suspects' responses. In a UK police
interview with a suspect accused of violent assault, Auburn *et al.* (1999) explored the
discursive resources used by an officer to manufacture a 'preferred version' of events. The
officer in (1) indicates doubt following an account of a woman accused of seriously
injuring her partner:

(1)   (Extract from Auburn *et al.* 1999: 51)

```
 1   IR:   [suspect's name] you are (.)
 2         I believe first that you're not actually being
 3         honest with your self and with us
 4         in fact I don't believe that you're actually
 5         telling the truth
 6   IE:   I am telling you the truth
 7   IR:   Now [name a] has been stabbed twice
 8         and he's been bitten on the nose
 9   IE:   Yeah
10   IR:   He's in hospital now
11   IE:   mmmh
12   IR:   I believe that you are the person who have
13         actually inflicted those stab wounds to [name a]
14         now think carefully (.) and answer the question
15         honestly
16   IE:   No I didn't do it
```

Auburn *et al.* observed a three-part organisation of disbelief in the talk of the police
officer, first indicated in lines 2–5, as the interviewer discounts the version of events
provided by suspect. The officer accuses the suspect of not only being dishonest with the
institutional 'us' but also engaging in self-deception. The officer then upgrades the
accusation by replacing the indirect 'you're not actually being honest with your self and
with us' with an overt accusation of dishonesty, 'I don't believe that you're actually
telling the truth' (lines 4–5). The officer implies that an objective truth exists into which
the known facts fit and that the accused and the accuser possess this information. Following the suspect's denial in line 6, the officer instructs the suspect to reconsider, 'think
carefully (.) and answer the question honestly' (lines 14–15). The interviewer creates an
expectation that the discrepancy between the accounts of the suspect and police officer
should be resolved through an amendment of the suspect's original account.

In Dutch police interviews with individuals accused of theft, Komter (2003) charts the
progression of an officer's distrust in a suspect's version of events, from questioning the
plausibility of the account with reference to commonsense notions of events and responses, to encouraging the suspect to admit to downgraded versions of the offence. This need
for a detailed, explicit, institutionally preferred version of events has been explained by
Gibbons (2003) as a 'pursuit of precision'. Due to the influential nature of legal formulations, such as whether a killing is described as murder or manslaughter, Gibbons claims that
officers adopt a formal, over-elaborate vocabulary, such as 'I was proceeding down the
highway in a south easterly direction' rather than 'I was walking down the road' (Gibbons
2003: 85), to eliminate misinterpretation in the criminal justice system.

Heydon (2005) claims that the formal communication adopted by officers in Australian police–suspect interviews reflects the negotiation of power relations. The unwillingness of the interviewers to deviate from official language whilst maintaining the conversational floor serves to constrain suspects' responses. These observations are supported by Johnson (2006: 666) who describes police talk as a clash between the legislative and the conversational, with interviewers moving between the two discourses. For example, the conversational 'taken money' is used in conjunction with the legislative 'appropriates property'. Johnson claims that official terminology is necessary to confirm the occurrence of a criminal offence and achieve the goal of the interview. More recently, Edwards (2008) explores the discourse of intentionality (or *mens rea* in legal terms) in UK police–suspect interviews. Establishing intent regarding the consequences of a criminal act is an essential feature of police interviewing and officers are required to confirm whether intent represented premeditation or 'recklessness'. In one interview, a 16-year-old accused of damaging a car admits that he 'smashed the back window' then revises his account by claiming that he 'punched the window'. As 'punch' suggests an action without an effect, the interviewer needs to establish whether there *was* an effect and what degree of intent the suspect had regarding that effect. The interviewer asks 'What was y'r pur:pose when y'punched the window,hhh' and 'Did you inte:nd to cause any damage to the window of the car', to which the suspect replies 'No not really'. Edwards demonstrates that intentionality is a social practice managed and negotiated over the course of an interaction and speakers negotiate how a criminal offence should be described.

In the investigative interview, what is at stake is a *version of events* which is negotiated by a suspect and a police officer. The studies outlined previously have identified discursive devices used by officers to co-construct offences in interviews with individuals suspected of murder, violent assault, criminal damage and theft. Very few studies have examined whether these resources are also evident in cases of child sexual abuse. Allegations of sexual abuse often rely on the testimonies of two individuals, an adult and a child, so obtaining thorough and accurate statements is vital for the progression of the investigation. There is a need for a detailed understanding of how sexual offences against children are constructed in the investigative interview and whether qualitative analysis can be applied to the talk of suspected child sex offenders.

Investigative interviews with suspected sex offenders

The author's research focused on a corpus of tape-recorded and transcribed police interviews with suspected offenders in relation to sexual offences against children. Interviews had been tape-recorded as part of the requirements of the Police and Criminal Evidence Act 1984 (PACE). Analysis of the corpus revealed two distinct approaches to the questioning of individuals suspected of sexual offences against children, which I have termed 'closed' interviewing and 'open' interviewing. These two approaches had implications for how the relationships between the suspects and alleged victims were constructed, how the interaction progressed and how the investigative interview was concluded. To explore these approaches in more detail, the point at which the emotional and/or physical relationship between the suspect and the alleged victim was first mentioned was identified. These descriptions and the surrounding talk were then examined using discourse analysis to explore how the accounts evolved during the interview.

'Closed' interviewing

The police officer's narrative

In a selection of the police interviews there was evidence of questioning characterised by the police interviewer (IR) generating a prolonged account of the offence which involved sexual and legal terminology and minimal suspect intervention, as in (2).

(2)
```
 1  IR:   Okay, what Vicky is saying is that you went
 2        towards her bed and started to push her out of
 3        her bed which she landed on the floor on the
 4        other side, to which then you went round and
 5        she remembers banging her head on the wall, she
 6        landed on her back umm and again she was
 7        wearing knickers. She can't recall what you
 8        were wearing. And that you then proceeded to
 9        take hold of her arms with one of your hands
10        and held them behind her head, before doing
11        that you got hold of her legs and put them over
12        your shoulders? With one hand holding h-her
13        arms behind her head you then took your penis
14        with your other hand and inserted it into her
15        vagina.
```

All of the prolonged police narratives share commonalities. They commence immediately after the interview preliminaries and produce an average of 64 words per turn. The IRs construct 'bodily' accounts using graphic discourse, making the sexual nature of the offences explicit from the onset. For example: 'you then took your penis with your other hand and inserted it into her vagina' ((2), lines 13–15); 'you were masturbating yourself you would be watching pornographic videos'; 'your erect penis was clearly visible'; 'rubbing action from her knee upwards to her towards her thigh area'; and 'started to play with his genitals'. This provides further evidence of the language of precision in police talk, also encouraged in the suspects' versions of events (Benneworth 2009; Gibbons 2003; Heydon 2005; Johnson 2006; Komter 2003).

The narratives include detail relating to the level of sexual development and age of the child, such as 'this is going back to a time when she's not developed properly' and 'Charlotte actually said it's been going on since she was four or five'. The IRs confirm that there has been sexual contact *and* with a child, immediately rendering any account of a relationship as criminal. One narrative also suggests that the alleged victim was a fearful recipient of the suspect's attention, 'she said that she felt scared'. The narratives feature accounts spoken 'on behalf of' the victims in the third person and often in the present (progressive) tense, '*what Vicky is saying* is that you went towards her bed' (1, lines 1–2), '*What Sarah does describe* is that umm she would regularly go into your house', '*Beth describes* umm an incident that she said happened some time last year', '*Matthew is saying* that umm on the first occasion that he went round to your house', and '*Charlotte actually said* it's been going on since she was four or five'. The IRs even attribute explicit and legally precise sexual discourse to the alleged victims. For example, from the 'account' of a 13-year-old, 'what Vicky is saying is ... took your penis ... ' (1), from an 8-year-old, 'she says you were masturbating ... ' and 'she says ... your erect penis ... ' and a 12-year-old, 'he said ... play with his genitals'.

The IR's preference for speaking on behalf of the victim is frequently accompanied by the use of 'direct' quotation, 'he wouldn't stop what he was doing he'd just carry on masturbating', 'in her own words what she saw on the video in case he tried to do that with me', 'he would cuddle me and kiss me on the mouth he would then try and get his tongue into my mouth. I'd hold my mouth tight', 'he would try and undo my trousers and I'd be shaking he'd start kissing me', and 'he's been touching me and feeling me and things'. Direct reported speech, in this case the IRs' use of 'he' to denote the suspect and 'me' to denote the alleged victim, is interactionally salient. Edwards (1997) claims that direct reported speech achieves a sense of perceptual re-experience to bolster the fac-tuality of a claim and Clift and Holt (2007) consider direct reported speech to perform an evidential function, enabling recipients to access utterances they would not normally access. In this case, suspects are presented with the allegations of their victims. In a recent study of a notorious Italian murder case, Galatolo (2007: 207) states that 'the ability to recall the exact proffered words is generally interpreted as being evidence of having directly and effectively heard those words' and this gives the interviewer an advantage over the suspect who is simply presented with these facts.

The suspect's denial

Suspects *do* respond to these elaborate interviewer narratives, however, and when they *do*, they consistently refute the accusations. Given the absence of explicit invitations from the IRs, it is crucial to examine how and where the suspects take the opportunity to deny the allegations and explore how the IRs negotiate the suspects' (IEs) denials. The provision of a prolonged account by the IR eliminates the need for the IE to negotiate blame. However, on a number of occasions, denials materialise *during* the officers' developing narratives, as in (3).

```
(3)
 1  IR:   She said can't really remember it's been going
 2         on for quite a while uh and she talked about
 3         recently the Saturday the most recently the
 4         Saturday before you went into hospital. So what
 5         happened then. She says that you told her to go
 6         go into the front room? You put your hands up
 7         her top and you were messing about with her
 8         boobs.
 9  IE:   No, I'm sorry.
10  IR:   And she indicated actually under the clothing,
11         so you're sort of inside, a vest or t-shirt or
12         whatever she was wearing.
```

The most frequent rebuttals are direct, succinct and lack elaboration, 'No, I'm sorry' ((3), line 9), 'That's false', 'No way', and 'No'. Immediately before each of these denials, all of the IRs had been describing the IEs involvement in sexual activity. In (3) the IE refutes that he put his hands inside the victim's clothing and was 'messing about with her boobs'. In one interview, the IE denies forcing the child to perform a sexual act, 'made her suck your thingy'. In another, the IE disagrees with the allegation that he undressed the alleged victim, 'removed his trousers, and his-and his underwear' and 'started to play with his genitals'. As demonstrated in (3) these denials are often not acknowledged by the IRs, who proceed with their narratives often with the use of 'And' to retain the floor. If we disregard the interjections of the IEs, the IRs' adjacent turns represent continuous utterances, 'You put your hands up her top and you were messing about with her boobs//And she indicated actually under the clothing' ((3), lines 6–10). The IRs do not take the opportunity to pursue the denials with further questioning to establish exactly which allegations the IEs are refuting.

The IEs also provide hypothetical denials, constructing a supposed account of normalised behaviour to avoid explicitly admitting or denying the allegations. The denials utilise three rhetorical devices: 'would', as in, 'the first thing I *would* do is cover up', 'I *wouldn't* know who it was' and 'If I did it *would* have been three or four years ago'; the 'if-then' structure, for example, '*if* I was lying on or sitting in a chair masturbating and I heard my door go *(then)* the first thing I would do is cover up' and '*If* I did *(then)* it would have been three or four years ago'; and 'because', as in, 'No '*cos* Simon was next door with the door wide open?' (4), 'No. [*because*] If I did it would have been three or four years ago' ((5), lines 1–2) and 'the first thing I would do is cover up. *Because* I wouldn't know who it was'. These devices assert the implausibility of the allegations, undermining the logic of the IRs account and subsequently the account of the alleged victim.

(4)

```
10   IE:    ... and held them behind her head, before doing
11          that you got hold of her legs and put them over
12          your shoulders? With one hand holding her arms
13          behind her head you then took your penis with
14          your other hand and inserted it into her
15          vagina.
16   IE:    No 'cos Simon was next door with the door wide
17          open?
18   IR:    She's alleging that you inserted your penis
19          into her vagina and had sex with her.
```

The IRs are not deflected from telling the story by pursuing these explanations. The IR in (4) repeats the previous allegation, 'She's alleging that you inserted your penis into her vagina' ((4), lines 18–19) and the IR in (5) simply continues the account, 'She demonstrates quite clearly the sort of a rubbing action from her knee upwards' ((5), lines 1–2). In another interview, the IR disputes the denial before returning to his narrative, 'but she says you do and that's what the whole that's what she's saying'. The IRs do not permit the hypothetical denials to become the focus of the interview. In each of the IRs' subsequent turns, the logical arguments of the IEs are terminated with an immediate switch from the hypothetical to the observed, tangible actions of the IE, as in (5). 'If' and 'would' ((5), line 1) are replaced by the categorical present tense 'she demonstrates' (line 3).

(5)

```
1   IE:    No. If I did it would have been three or four
2          years ago.
```

```
 3  IR:    She demonstrates quite clearly the sort of a
 4         rubbing action from her knee upwards to her
 5         towards her thigh area and she said when he did
 6         that the skirt, sort of, came up higher toward–
 7         towards her thigh. She said Mum was there and
 8         she said Alice was there as well. And Mum had
 9         shouted at you to stop being so rude. And told
10         you to get off. That you gave you–that you gave
11         her a kiss and it was on the lips she said that
12         she felt scared when you did this when you were
13         were rubbing her leg because of what she'd seen
14         on the videos that she'd watched with you uh in
15         her own words what she saw on the video in case
16         he tried to do that with me.
17  IE:    That's not true.
```

The IRs conclude their narratives with statements addressing incidents of sexual contact precipitated by the IEs, for example, 'you inserted your penis into her vagina and had sex with her', 'she recalled a number of occasions you would try and cover yourself up … but she says soon as you realised it was her then you would carry on', 'you gave her a kiss and it was on the lips … you were rubbing her leg' and 'he'd start kissing me … he'd then undo my trousers in the hallway, he would start doing things, sucking my willy'. The absence of a direct request for a response eliminates the need for the IE to provide an explanation. Consequently, the IEs once again refute the IRs claims with outright denials, 'That's not true' ((5), line 17), 'No. I'm sorry no', 'No it didn't happen' ((6), line 20) and 'No'. The IRs do not challenge the speakers or reintroduce the sexual allegations. Instead, they seek to verify the denials by asking what I call 'closing questions'.

The closing question

The closing questions permit the IRs to summarise the allegations and invite the IEs to confirm the IRs' version of events, 'I thought you were gonna say no hehh heh hehh. So you deny that that took place' ((6), lines 21–22), 'Denying that that took place?' ((7), line 18) and in a further interview 'So you've never masturbated yourself in front … of Sarah?'.

```
(6)
18  IR:    She's alleging that you inserted your penis
19         into her vagina and had sex with her.
20  IE:    No it didn't happen
21  IR:    I thought you were gonna say no hehh heh hehh.
22         So you deny that that took place.


(7)
12  IR:    … she felt scared when you did this when you
13         were rubbing her leg because of what she'd seen
14         on the videos that she'd watched with you uh in
15         her own words what she saw on the video in case
```

16   he tried to do that with me.

17 IE: That's not true.

18 IR: Denying that that took place?

It appears that, for the first time during the closed interviews, IEs are invited to contribute to the interaction. However, the closing questions inhibit any forthcoming response to a 'yes/no' confirmation of the narrative and presuppose negative responses, acknowledged in the responses: 'thought you were *gonna say no* ... so you *deny* ... ' ((6), lines 21–22), '*denying* that took place?' ((7), line 18), and '*So you've never* ... '. Johnson (2006: 666) claims that the practice of 'closing down' an investigative interview highlights the difference between what the suspect considers important and what the police require as evidence for prosecution. Johnson observes that, after questioning the suspect, the officer 'sums up' the evidential facts of the interview by presenting the offence, which in the case of the interviews in (6) and (7) involves the declaratives: 'you inserted your penis into her vagina and had sex with her' and 'you were rubbing her leg' for verification. Although some of these interviews appear 'opened up' to the suspect, the final questions close down the IRs' opportunities to obtain the IEs' version of events. There is no need for the IEs to compromise themselves by telling their side of the story and the IR narratives provide an occasion for the IE to deny the offence. The IEs provide negative responses and deny the IRs' elaborate narratives, leaving them with nothing to 'work with'. The denials to closing questions are accepted by the IRs and the interviews are terminated, as shown in ((6), lines 21–22) and ((7), 17–18), both interviews closing after this point.

'Open' interviewing

The previous section demonstrates how a closed interviewing approach can shape emerging descriptions of an offence. A very different style was also observed in which the police interviewers used euphemistic language and encouraged prolonged accounts from the suspects. This 'opening up' of the interviews to the suspects also had implications for whether and how the offences were described.

The opening question

When the open interviewing style was adopted, the IRs commenced by inviting the IEs to contribute using open-ended preliminary questions (see (8) to (13)). These opening questions occurred early in the interviews and represented the first line of enquiry into the dynamics between the IE and the alleged victim.

(8)
How did you view your relationship with Lucy as it developed?

(9)
Do you wanna tell me about what happened with Sam then?

(10)
Can you tell us about Emily then?

(11)
Do you want to tell us about Danielle?

(12)
Could you tell me what happened with Tom?

(13)
Tell me about Andrew then.

The opening questions share commonalities in terms of how they were asked and what information they conveyed. All of the questions commence immediately after the interview preliminaries and produce an average of nine words per turn, considerably fewer than the closed police narratives, an average of 64 words per turn. Rather than inhibiting any forthcoming response to a 'yes/no' confirmation, the questions employ an open-ended 'tell me about' format, surrendering the floor to the suspect for an unspecified period and resemble the kind of questions recommended in policy for interviewing child witnesses to achieve 'best evidence' (see Aldridge, this volume).

Unlike the previous interviewing style which made the physical nature of the offence explicit from the onset, the opening questions evade the sexual and criminal components of the allegations. There is no mention of bodily contact between the IE and the child although (8), (9) and (12) suggest *something* occurred. The implications of this will be discussed later. The IRs avoid terms which highlight the youthful or maltreated status of the complainant, such as 'the little girl' or 'the victim', opting instead for first names. The IRs ask innocuous questions which could be inviting the IE to describe *any* individual, not necessarily an underage victim of sexual abuse. The non-specific and non-threatening opening turns encourage the IEs to provide equally innocuous accounts of the alleged victims. The utterances 'how did you view your relationship' and 'tell me about Andrew' encourage potentially elongated explanations and do not restrict the subsequent turn to a 'yes/no' response. Other interviews commence with: 'do you wanna', 'can you', 'do you want to' and 'could you', which risk a minimal 'yes/no' response from the IEs, for example: 'no, I don't want to tell you' or 'no, I can't tell you'. However, these opening questions are all treated by the IEs as invitations to tell a story.

The suspect's narrative

The responses to the opening questions also share a range of features, some of which are demonstrated in (14), the response to (9).

(14)
```
1  IE:   Sam was a very good games tester. He used to do
2        a lot of games testing, umm I will admit I was
3        attracted to Sam, I think Sam was attracted to
4        me, we had a very close relationship with each
5        other but I was I tried to keep it as much as
6        possible at arms arms length until it then
7        happened in eighty four I'm not quite sure what
8        date the event was, in the first part of
9        nineteen eighty four my business started to go
```

10	certainly downhill and I started to suffer very
11	badly from depression umm and I became I used
12	to go about every two weeks to get the tablets.
13	During this time it had got to the point where
14	sometimes myself and Sam would be very close,
15	we would often kiss at that point I made it
16	very clear that we weren't going any further.

In all of the interviews characterised by an open style, the opening questions yield elaborate explanations, an average of 145 words per turn, in which the IEs employ 'relationship' discourse and a range of mitigating devices. In addition to first names and informality, emotional, positive and relationship terms are frequently used. For example: 'attracted', 'close', 'relationship', 'kiss', 'friends', 'feel', 'enjoyed', 'rapport', 'encouragement', 'nurture', 'affectionate' and 'cuddle' (see Benneworth 2006).

It is interesting to note that, in response to the three opening questions which imply that something 'happened' ((8), (9) and (12)), the IEs immediately attend to agency. In (14) the suspect and the child are portrayed by the IE as equally responsible and active partners: 'I will admit I was attracted to Sam, I think Sam was attracted to me, we had a very close relationship with each other' (lines 2–5). The use of 'we' generates a sense of mutual accountability which is also evident in other interviews. In response to (8), the IE states 'I mean we could we could we could go on, not bother about anything then other times I said how d'ya feel and she said oh yeah'. One IE shares responsibility with the mother of the alleged victim in response to (13) when a particularly salient incident is portrayed as ordinary and acceptable, 'I gave Tom a bath at my house, I don't deny that. I told his mother that I'd given him a bath'. On the other hand, the opening questions which did not set an agenda ((10), (11) and (13)), were followed by narratives emphasising the accountability of the *victim* as an active agent. For example, in response to (10) the IE states: 'She was a girl who often used to come to me'; for (11): 'she used to come up to me just about every day and stand with me in the playground' and in response to (13): 'he was talking about going into this sort of nightclub he was talking about uh drinking. He was actually talking quite a bit about sex as well. So I actually uh got the impression that he was about the uh late teens'.

All of the IEs use mitigation when describing the relationships between themselves and the alleged victims, specifically involving minimisation, normalisation and victim blame.

Minimisation

The utterance 'it then happened' ((14), lines 6–7) is euphemistic and externalised. The ambiguous pronoun 'it' is without prior referent and is used here to denote the indecent assault of a 12-year-old boy. The suspect distances himself from inciting the physical contact and diminishes his own accountability. The euphemistic and unspecific 'anything' in the expression, 'we could go on, not bother about anything' represents the gross indecency of a 9-year-old girl. The same IE uses the expression 'the little sessions', a playful and child-like description which actually refers to the manufacturing of child pornography. In the claim, 'it took a long while to nurture her' the term 'nurture' suggests a caring, almost parental role for an individual arrested on suspicion of indecently assaulting an 8-year-old. The utterance, 'just for general consoling' once again attends to the notion of support and protection. The use of 'just' has a mitigating function which minimises the significance of the act whilst excluding alternative accounts which cannot be acknowledged. The IE avoids having to include the 'as opposed to' (Lee 1987) leaving the criminal and sexual details of the offence unsaid.

In the utterance 'I simply gave him a bath', the IE assumes responsibility for washing a 13-year-old. However, the incident is minimised with the use of 'simply', which suggests an absence of motive and intent (Lee 1987). In the utterance, 'we used to cuddle up. And everything', the ambiguous 'everything' suggests physical contact located on a continuum from innocuous acts of affection to penetration. The IE also claims 'sort of he was cuddling we was kissing a bit and umm things got a bit further'. The use of 'sort of' and 'a bit' to minimise the offence are coupled with the vague 'things got a bit further' to suggest a progression of bodily contact. This agency-neutralised description ('things' rather than 'we' or 'I') and the use of the delexicalised verb 'go further' (Sinclair and Renouf 1988) contributes to a process of minimising accountability (cf. Wooffitt 1991, who claims that the externalising device 'got' constructs events as unmotivated and lacking individual accountability).

Normalisation

The IE in (14) constructs 'ordinariness' in terms of two individuals embarking on a romantic companionship, 'I was attracted to Sam, I think Sam was attracted to me, we had a very close relationship with each other' (lines 2–5) and 'sometimes myself and Sam would be very close' (line 14). The IE describes the bond between himself and the child as 'very close' and 'a very close relationship', utilising 'we' and 'each other' to enhance the mutuality. The ambiguous use of 'close' avoids physical and emotional discourse. However, the introduction of 'attraction' generates the possibility of desirability and a sexual relationship, despite the fact that the individuals involved are a 49-year-old man and a 12-year-old boy. Another interview employs the seemingly innocuous 'just good friends' to normalise the relationship between a 52-year-old man and a 9-year-old girl, despite them being inappropriate candidates for a sexual relationship or even a good friendship (see Benneworth 2007).

Further attempts to normalise an unconventional bond between a 53-year-old man and an 8-year-old girl include, 'we seemed to develop a sort of rapport, and were on the same wavelength and a sense of humour' and 'we did develop a sort of rapport'. The IEs frequently claim that they and the alleged victims shared emotional connections more typically associated with adult companionships. In the utterance, 'we'd gone up to my room. Andrew laid down on the bed umm I laid down next to him, sort of he was cuddling we was kissing a bit and umm things got a bit further', the 11-year-old is imbued with such maturity and sexual awareness that he becomes a candidate for a sexual partnership.

Victim blame

In response to the opening questions, the IEs also depict the offences as resulting from the victims' actions. The victims are characterised as willing, enthusiastic tutees: 'she quite enjoyed being uh the little sessions'; deceptively mature and sexually aware: 'he was talking about going into this sort of nightclub he was talking about uh drinking. He was actually talking quite a bit about sex as well'; and actively and persistently seeking the company of the IE: 'she used to come up to me just about every day and stand with me', 'she was running up to me so often' and 'he got a bit upset there he wanted to carry on I said we couldn't and umm after that he came round a couple more times and I tried to make a distance between us. Which he didn't seem to like very much'.

The opening questions posed by the IRs permit the IEs to present elaborate self-serving accounts which avoid sexual and criminal discourse and employ mitigating rhetorical devices. These devices help characterise the bodily contact between the IE and the child as either negligible, an acceptable ingredient of an adult relationship or victim-instigated. However, rather than limit the IRs' opportunities to establish accountability, the IEs' self-serving and more importantly, *incomplete* descriptions provide the IRs with an opportunity to challenge the accounts.

The reformulating question

The initial information-gathering opening questions, which encouraged the IEs to construct extended, mitigating narratives, are vital for acquiring potentially incriminating information. However, these testimonies are insufficient without the intervention of the IRs who must move *beyond* these self-serving accounts to confirm the occurrence of sexual contact, as in the question in (15).

(15)
```
 1   IR:     Right. As part of that consoling would you ever
 2           cuddle her and put your arms round her.
```

The IRs' interventions (as in (15)) occur immediately after the IEs' prolonged narratives. Once again, all of the questions are minimal, an average of 13 words per turn, and commence with either 'right' or 'so', 'Right. As part of that consoling … ' (15), 'Right you mean … ', 'Right. How old's Sam … ', 'Right. When you say … ', 'So you both in the bathroom … ' and 'So. You took it in turns … '.

The discursive markers 'right' and 'so' have been the subject of much language research. Raymond (2004) described the stand-alone 'so' as simultaneously managing activities internal to the current turn and that turn's participation within a larger course of action. The markers in the previous extracts perform a reformulating function, indicating acceptance of the prior turn and a transition to a new agenda. In other words, whilst the interventions make reference to the previous narratives, 'Right. As part of *that consoling*' (15), 'Right *you mean* the sexual sessions', 'Right. How old's Sam? When *this*' happening', 'Right. *When you say that* you've touched on the knee' and 'So *you both in the bathroom together*', the markers suggest that specific details require clarification.

Heritage and Watson (1979) claimed that reformulations are designed to project agreement from the original speaker whilst clearing the way for the reformulator's description going on the record. In an analysis of murder interrogations, Watson (1990) described 'so' as an authoritative resource used by the police to reformulate the 'gist' of a suspect's preceding narrative. Indeed, the questions embody a discursive 'switch'; a *transition* from the minimised, normalised accounts of the adult–child relationships. The questions represent a move away from the IRs' 'opening questions', which permit the IEs to construct innocuous explanations, to *direct requests* for information. In an analysis of so-prefaced questions in interviews with child victims of sexual abuse, Johnson (2002) argues that so-prefacing enables the IR to focus questioning on important evidential

detail (see Holt and Johnson, this volume). The questions serve to deconstruct the IEs'
self-serving narratives by exposing sexual activity and criminal accountability obscured by
the prior mitigation. For example, in response to the IE's narrative in (16), the IR's
question seeks an acknowledgment of the IE's criminal liability.

(16)
```
14  IE:   sometimes myself and Sam would be very close
15        we would often kiss at that point I made it
16        very clear that we weren't going any further.
17  IR:   Right. How old's Sam? When this' happening.
```

In (16), the IE constructs a normalised bond between two equal individuals. When the
IR asks, 'How old's Sam? When this' happening' (line 17), he seeks to confirm the
child status of the IE's 'partner' and formulate the relationship as criminal. Other
examples include, 'When you say that you've touched on the knee and on the calf'
((18), lines 1–2) in which the IR switches from the innocuous 'Can you tell us about
Emily then' (10) and a normalised account of 'rapport' with an 8-year-old girl, to a
bodily reference. The IE is then invited to provide a further account of the physical
act, 'can you just expand on *that* a bit for us' ((18), lines 2–3). There is a switch from
the ambiguous, 'Do you want to tell us about Danielle?' (11) and the normalised
'nurturing' and 'consoling' of a young girl by a 53-year-old man, to a specific physical
act, 'would you ever cuddle her and put your arms round her' ((20), lines 1–2).
Another IR switches from an opening question devoid of criminal and sexual discourse, 'Could you tell me what happened with Tom' (12) and the IE's normalised 'I
told his mother … I simply gave him a bath' to a description of physical activity with
sexual connotations, 'So you both in the bathroom together then … Naked?' ((20),
lines 1 and 3). This move towards *specificity* performs the core business of the police
interview: the confirmation of detail specific to the criminal offence for the purpose
of prosecution. To determine whether these reformulations confirm the occurrence
of sexual contact and establish criminal accountability, it is vital to examine the
subsequent turns of the IEs.

The admission

In response to the reformulating questions ((17), line 17; (18), lines 1–3; (19), lines 1–2;
(20), line 1), all of the IEs admit the allegations.

(17)
```
17  IR:   Right. How old's Sam? When this' happening.
18  IE:   Mmm seventy uh seventy four uh he's about
19        twelve.
```

(18)
```
1  IR:   Right. When you say that you've touched on the
2        knee and on the calf, can you just expand on
3        that a bit for us,
4  IE:   Umm just a hand on the knee shake the knee say
5        yes you can do it come on you can do it.
```

(19)

```
1   IR:   Right. As part of that consoling would you ever
2         cuddle her and put your arms round her.
3   IE:   Umm I think probably yes I have.
```

(20)

```
1   IR:   So you both in the bathroom together then?
2   IE:   Yes.
3   IR:   Naked?
4   IE:   Uh at that point he was partially clothed. I
5         was still fully clothed. And I got out of the
6         bath. I put a dressing gown on. Which is pretty
7         well standard procedure cos I keep them behind
8         the bathroom door. And I gave him a dressing
9         gown. Had he of raised any objections I would
10        have left. And he certainly didn't object when
11        he washed my back.
```

However, the admissions are accompanied by discursive devices which mitigate the offending behaviour. In (17) the IE acknowledges the allegations with, 'Mmm seventy uh seventy four uh he's *about* twelve', which attributes uncertainty to the child status of his sexual partner. The disclosure of bodily contact in (18) 'Umm just a hand on the knee shake the knee say yes you can do it' constructs the incident as inconsequential and impersonal. The use of '*a* hand' not '*my* hand', '*the* knee' rather than '*her* knee', '*say* yes you can do it' not '*I said* yes you can do it' and the detached gesture 'shake the knee' reframes the IE's role in the offence as one of support and encouragement. The use of 'just' in 'just a hand on the knee' again minimises both the significance of the contact and the need for an alternative account (Lee 1987). In (19), the admission of physical contact, 'yes I have' is preceded by an attempt to cast doubt on the event in the modalised 'Umm *I think probably*'. One particularly interesting example is the admission in (20). The initial 'Yes' is accompanied by further self-serving discourse which attempts to justify the bathing of a 13-year-old boy. The IE manages the dilemma of confessing to the allegation whilst mitigating his accountability by employing minimising discourse, 'at *that* point he was *partially clothed*. I was still *fully clothed*', normalisation 'which is pretty well *standard procedure*' and victim blame, 'Had *he of raised any objections* I would have left. And *he certainly didn't object* when he washed my back', implying that the child was responsive to the act.

Conclusion

In this chapter I have identified two distinct styles of interviewing with implications for how the relationship between the suspect and the alleged victim is formulated, how police–suspect interactions progress, and how the investigative interview is concluded. There is evidence of a 'closed' interviewing style which is associated with a likelihood of the suspect denying the allegations. In the 'closed' interview, officers assume the role of narrator and formulate an explicitly sexual and criminal narrative, often from the perspective of the victim. By employing discursive devices to hold the floor, the officers restrict the suspects' turns and even in the concluding 'closing' question, which appears to invite a response from the suspect, the next turn limits the suspect to confirming the officers' version of events. By providing no opportunity for the suspect to generate a narrative, the interviewer permits the suspect to refute the allegations with a simple denial. The 'open' approach to interviewing is, however, much more associated with the suspect admitting the allegation. The 'open' interview is characterised by the officer surrendering the floor to the suspect using an 'opening' question which encourages the suspect to tell a story. The suspect is permitted to recount a mitigating narrative, incorporating minimisation, normalisation and victim blame, but the officers then ask a 'reformulating question' which confirms the sexual and criminal aspects of the adult–child relationship and enables the interviewer to elicit an incriminating disclosure from the suspect.

The implications of this approach to analysing police interviews are that we can challenge a number of criticisms directed at discourse analysis. Critics often claim that discourse analysis lacks reliability and rigour, because of its reliance on case study and qualitative analysis. However, the patterns of interactional practice identified in the data offer support for previous interpretations in both pure (Lee 1987; Raymond 2003, 2004; Wooffitt 1991) and applied (Auburn *et al.* 1999; Edwards 2008; Johnson 2006) discourse studies. In addition, rather than representing an abstract methodology lacking contemporary relevance, the findings demonstrate that discourse analysis has a significant practical application and can contribute to our understanding of interactions in forensic settings. If discourse analysis can identify ethical methods of obtaining evidential, unprompted and admissible accounts of sexual offences against children, it has much to offer the study of investigative interviewing.

Although this chapter does not seek to evaluate current investigative interviewing in the UK, it offers a unique qualitative insight into the architecture of police interviews which could inspire new methods of interviewing training and establishing 'best practice'. The 'closed' interview style identified, exhibits features reminiscent of the traditional adversarial police interrogation, whilst the uninterrupted suspect narrative found in the 'open' interview reflects the recent PEACE protocol (National Crime Faculty 2000) and policy on achieving best evidence. These observations emphasise the importance of ethical questioning and of the benefits of discourse analysis for the professional development of police interviewers in the UK and beyond. In terms of practical recommendations for training, the terms 'open' and 'closed' interview, and 'opening', 'reformulating' and 'closing' questions provide a recognisable vocabulary for police officers. This vocabulary can be used by skilled officers to reflect on their own interviewing practices and could be communicated to less experienced officers. A common assertion in police interviewing research is that officers are unable to convince blameworthy individuals to admit their guilt (Milne and Bull 1999). Baldwin (1993: 188) argued that 'the great majority of suspects stick to their starting position – whether admission, denial, or somewhere in between – regardless of how the interview is conducted'. However the research discussed in this chapter suggests that, if an officer can adopt an open interviewing style at the onset of an interview, with the suspect reacting discursively to the style of questioning, this *can* make a difference to the outcome of an interview.

Further reading

Auburn, T., Lea, S. and Drake, S. (1999) '"It's your opportunity to be truthful": Disbelief, mundane reasoning and the investigation of crime', in C. Willig (ed.) *Applied Discourse Analysis: Social and Psychological Interventions*, Buckingham: Open University Press, 44–65.

Benneworth, K. (2006) 'Repertoires of paedophilia: Conflicting descriptions of adult-child sexual relationships in the investigative interview', *The International Journal of Speech, Language and the Law*, 13(2): 190–211.

——(2007) '"Just good friends": Managing the clash of discourses in police interviews with paedophiles', in J. Cotterill (ed.) *The Language of Sexual Crime*, Basingstoke: Palgrave Macmillan, 42–62.

Edwards, D. (2008) 'Intentionality and *mens rea* in police interrogations: The production of actions as crimes', *Intercultural Pragmatics*, 5(2): 177–99.

Griffiths, A. and Milne, R. (2005) 'Will it all end in tiers: Police interviews with suspects in Britain', in T. Williamson (ed.) *Investigative Interviewing: Rights, Research, Regulation*, Willan: Devon, 167–89.

Williamson, T.M. (1993) 'From interrogation to investigative interviewing: Strategic trends in police questioning', *Journal of Community and Applied Social Psychology*, 3: 89–99.

11

Lawyers in interviews

'I advise you not to answer that question': conversation analysis, legal interaction and the analysis of lawyers' turns in police interrogations of suspects

Elizabeth Stokoe and Derek Edwards

Conversation analysis and legal interaction

Conversation analysis (henceforth, CA) emerged in the 1960s in the work of the American sociologist, Harvey Sacks, and his colleagues Emanuel Schegloff and Gail Jefferson. CA's roots are in ethnomethodology (henceforth, EM: literally, 'the study of people's methods'), a programme developed by another sociologist, Harold Garfinkel (1967). His basic idea was that people in society, or *members*, continuously engage in making sense of the world and, in so doing, methodically display their understandings of it: making their activities 'visibly-rational-and-reportable-for-all-practical-purposes' (Garfinkel 1967: vii). Language was central to the EM project of explicating members' methods for producing orderly and accountable social activities. Like Garfinkel, Sacks's aim was to develop an alternative to mainstream sociology: an observational science of society and social action that could be grounded in the 'details of actual events' (Sacks 1984: 26).

CA employs technical transcripts of recordings of everyday and institutional talk of various kinds, and its empirical projects now comprise over forty years of findings about how conversation works. These projects include the analysis of how people take turns in conversation, how turns at talk are designed, what it means to overlap with another speaker or produce a delayed response, how people make reference to one another, how actions (e.g. complaining, questioning, assessing, inviting) are accomplished, how people develop and move through courses of action, how people solve problems in hearing, speaking and understanding, and a range of other conversational phenomena (see Sacks 1992; Schegloff 2007; for introductions see ten Have 2007; Hutchby and Wooffitt 1998).

The various interactional contexts that comprise legal institutions (e.g. courtrooms, police stations, emergency services, prisons, legal documents, lawyers' offices) have provided materials for EM and CA since their beginnings. For example, in his

155

groundbreaking book on EM, Garfinkel (1967: 105) examined jurors' decision-making practices in the allocation of blame and in 'recommending remedies' (see also Manzo 1996 on jury interaction; and see Bittner 1967; Cicourel 1968; Sacks 1972; Sudnow 1965; Wieder 1974, for other classic ethnomethodological studies of legal institutions). A key conversation analytic study was Atkinson and Drew's (1979) investigation of the organisation of cross-examination in courtrooms, focusing on the design of lawyers' questions – particularly those that were designed to allocate blame – and witnesses' responses to such questions (see also Beach 1985; Bogen and Lynch 1989; Burns 2001; Galatolo 2007; Komter 1998; Lynch 2007; Maynard 1984; Pollner 1974; Pomerantz 1987, on courtroom interaction of various kinds). Other sites of investigation include the everyday workings of law firms (e.g. Travers 1997); the production of legal texts and records (e.g. Komter 2006; Meehan 1986; Summerfield and McHoul 2005); and encounters between citizens and the police (e.g. Meehan 1989; Sharrock and Watson 1989; Whalen and Zimmerman 1990). Interaction in places such as courtrooms can constitute some of the most highly consequential moments in people's lives.

This chapter focuses on another potent site of legal interaction: the police interrogation of suspects. More specifically, it focuses on the sorts of things that suspects' lawyers do in police interviews, which is a hitherto unexplored aspect of interrogation settings. In presenting our analysis of lawyers' interventions, we aim also to demonstrate and showcase CA as a method for forensic linguistics.

Police interrogation of suspects

Analysis of 'live' (i.e. recorded) police interviews comprises a minority of work on the topic in general. In contrast to numerous studies of suspects' and police officers' post-hoc *reflections about* their interviewing technique, style and experience (e.g. Dando *et al.* 2008; De Fruyt *et al.* 2006; Holmberg and Christianson 2002; Kassin *et al.* 2007), there are far fewer studies of actual interactions between officers and arrested suspects.

Within the smaller body of work that does analyse real life police interrogations of suspects, in linguistics and discourse analysis as well as CA, much attention has been paid to officers' questioning strategies, issues of power and coercion, and the elicitation and design of suspects' accounts (e.g. Benneworth 2006; Edwards 2006, 2008; Haworth 2006; Heydon 2005; Komter 2003; Johnson 2008b; Linell and Jönsson 1991; Shuy 1998b; Stokoe and Edwards 2008; Watson 1983; Wowk 1984). Some have analysed the physical and embodied aspects of police interviewing, such as how the interview room itself becomes a resource for interaction (LeBaron and Streeck 1997) or how gaze direction between participants can play an important part in the emotionality of an interview (Kidwell 2006).

Missing from both literatures are analyses of the role played by participants *other* than officers and suspects who regularly attend police interviews. These other participants attend in various capacities and include parents (of under-age suspects), lawyers or legal representatives, appropriate adults (for 'vulnerable' suspects who have mental health or learning difficulties) and interpreters. We found two notable exceptions. Nakane (2007) discusses the problems of interpretation – and interpreters – that emerge when police officers interview suspects with a different cultural background (see also Komter 2005; and English; Hale; Kredens and Morris, all this volume). Also Medford *et al.* (2003) examined contributions made by 'appropriate adults', finding that although they say very little, their presence increases the likelihood that a legal representative will also be present (see also Aldridge, this volume). Medford *et al.* (2003: 253) also suggest that the presence of an appropriate adult is associated with 'less interrogative pressure' from police officers and more active involvement from the legal representative. Despite assumptions that lawyers' presence in interviews will benefit suspects, no studies exist of their actual contributions.

Data and method

We drew on a corpus of 109 British police interviews with suspects, recorded by officers as part of standard police procedure and subsequently digitized, anonymized and transcribed. We identified all cases in which lawyers are present, and focused closely on the sequential placement, action orientation and design of their turns to establish the interactional circumstances of lawyers' turns and their trajectory for the subsequent turns of both police officers and suspects. In the data extracts that follow, the title (e.g. 'PN-4') specifies the source of the extract within a larger corpus (e.g. police interview number 4). Abbreviations for participants include P (or P1, P2, etc.) for the interviewing police officer/s; S for the suspect being interviewed; L for the lawyer, usually a solicitor, representing S; and A for an 'appropriate adult', where present, who is usually accompanying a child. Names that could identify persons and places, including police officers, have been altered. Data transcripts use punctuation and other symbols to mark prosody rather than grammar, according to the conventions for conversation analysis (Jefferson 2004).

Descriptive statistical analysis revealed that lawyers were present in 45% of interviews and, of these 44 interviews, they make an intervention of some kind in 64% of cases. The analysis focuses on those lawyers' turns that occur outside the *institutionally provided-for 'slots'* initiated by police officers. These 'slots' are the elicitation of identification from all present parties, under PACE (1984), at the start of each interview, and lawyers' responses to officers' questions at the end of interviews about whether they have anything to add. Extracts (1) and (2) provide examples of each type of 'slot' respectively.

```
(1)  PN-4
 1  P:     I'm pee cee five two oh Inglewood from Packet
 2         Road police station .hh there are no other police
 3         officers present, could you state your (.) >full
 4         name date o'birth< for the [tape] please.
 5  S:                                [Yeh]
 6              (0.3)
 7  S:     ↑Kay Lorna Phelps: (0.3) an' fourteenth of the
 8         sixth nineteen seventy.
 9              (0.5)
10  P:     Okay. =Also present is your solicitor.
11              (0.4)
12  L: →   Jenny Carter ↓Miller Jones.
13              (0.3)
```

```
(2)  PN-104
 1  P:     'S th'anythin' you'd like to add uh (.) mister
 2         Kanjeri:
```

```
3                    (0.4)
4  L: →     No:.
5                    (0.2)
6  L: →     °S' fine.°
```

In each case, the lawyers' turns occur in a responsive 'second' position in an *adjacency pair*. When one speaker takes a turn, they may do a *first action* (a 'first pair part' – e.g. a 'question') such that the recipient is expected to respond with a turn that delivers a *second action* (a 'second pair part' – e.g. an 'answer') paired with the first one. The examples above show the general organization for such turns, although in a small number of cases solicitors use these 'slots' as an opportunity to provide more than a basic self-identification (e.g. to formulate their role in the interview), or to re-open some aspect of the interview.

In the analysis that follows, we investigate 'interjections' by lawyers; that is, turns that are not responsive to police officers' invitations to take an institutionally provided-for turn. These include responses to questions from clients, spontaneous advice not to answer officers' questions, 'repair' operations on officers' questions to, say, seek clarification or make a legal point, and various ways of helping clients to give evidence by eliciting evidence not asked for by officers, or by adding to clients' evidence.

Lawyers' contributions to police interviews with suspects

Outside of the interview's routine beginnings and endings, we found that lawyers respond to questions raised by their clients, or intervene to object to police questioning, raise issues, or offer advice to their client. We start with responses to clients' questions.

Responses to clients' questions

In extract (3), S has been arrested on suspicion of the racially aggravated harassment of her neighbours, and here is claiming that any remarks made to them were provoked by their harassment of her.

```
(3)  PN-114a
1  S:    I'm being provoked by ↑↑the:m.
2               (0.6)
3  P:    Prov[oked in-
4  S:        [Not the [other way round.=
5  P:                 [P-
6  P:    =Provoked into doin' what an' saying wha:t.
7               (0.8)
8  S:    Callin' them:: what they ↑↑are.
9               (0.8)
10  P:   An' what d'you mean by calling them what they a:re.
11              (1.7)
12  S:   Do I 'ave to answer the (p'lice).
13              (0.4)
14  L:   No y'don't 'ave t'[answer ( ).
```

```
15  P:                [( )
16              (0.2)
17  P:     I've already explained ( ).
18              (0.4)
19  S:     ALL I said, (0.5) was about Muslims.=>Is that what
20         he's on about?< Is that what you're on about [ ... ]
```

In response to P's question at line 10, S asks L whether she has to 'answer the (p'lice).' In reply, L tells S that she does not have to answer, and this is followed by a possible reformulation from P at line 17. S then provides an answer of sorts, followed by another question to L, '>Is that what he's on about?<' and one to P, 'Is that what you're on about' (lines 19–20). Her answer here, and these subsequent questions, construct P's questions as somewhat obscure and over-interpretative ('ALL I said ... '). The turns between 11–14 comprise an inserted sequence between S and L, establishing conditions for answering P's question at line 10.

This theme, of not having to answer questions generally, or some questions in particular, is a major preoccupation of lawyer–client talk within the interviews. In extract (3), L tells S that she does not have to answer P's question in response to S's initiating action. Note that despite being told this, S still continues to answer questions. In the next section, we examine cases in which lawyers spontaneously advise suspects not to answer officers' questions.

Spontaneous advice not to answer

Lawyers sometimes spontaneously advise clients not to answer a question; that is, not in response to a question from S, but triggered by some feature of P's questioning. In such cases, lawyers display suspects' 'rights-in-action'; that is, they invoke suspects' rights to 'not say anything' that police officers discuss at the start of the interview, when cautioning them. In extract (4), S has been arrested for the grievous bodily harm of his neighbour. He has admitted assaulting the victim while 'in a rage', rather than in a premeditated way. P has been asking S repeatedly whether he understands the sort of physical injury that might result from S's assault.

```
(4)  PN-61
1   P1:    >Must say< (.) *y-* d'you realise that *it-* it can
2          cause serious harm.
3              (1.0)
4   L:     .pt I advise you not to answer that question.=
5          Mister Brown,
6   S:     hhhhhhhhh
```

In this case, the legal basis of L's intervention is clear; it is addressed at preventing S from admitting to a state of mind, or *mens rea* (Edwards 2008; Stokoe and Edwards 2008), which could amount to recklessness with regard to the consequences of his actions. It can be legally sufficient for such an accusation, that a suspect merely understands an action's likely consequences, rather than requiring premeditation of them (Richardson 2006). Notably in this case, L's intervention is delayed by a full second gap (an interactionally significant amount of time: Jefferson 1989), in which S does not respond; we

will return to that point shortly. Further, L fails to intervene when a second police officer, P2, pursues the point, as in ((4) continued).

```
(4)  PN-61 (continued)
 7                 (0.9)
 8   P1:    (Anything t-)=
 9   P2:                  =What-what do-w'll what d-what do you think.
10                 (0.2)
11   P2:    I mean: (0.3) you've been advi:sed not to answer it
12          but-(0.2) I mean.hh (0.2) it is: (0.2) your chance
13          (0.6) to uh: y'know tell us your side o'the story,
14          if you wish to do so,.hh so: in your opinion, (0.7)
15          if someone gets kicked in the head, (0.5) three times:
16          quite hard, (0.3).hh <what injuries: d'you think that
17          person> is going to get.
18                 (0.4)
19   P2:    As a result.
20                 (2.0)
21   S:     .hhhhhh ↑well hhh I was um: (1.5) I was like- not in
22          me own body. =I was out- [...]
```

Having intervened previously at line 4, L now fails to intervene at lines 18–21, including
the long 2-second gap at line 20 following P2's re-formulation of P1's question. P2 alters
the generic 'do you realise that it can cause serious harm' (lines 1–2) to asking 'in your
opinion' (line 14), given a specific formulation of S's alleged actions (lines 15–16), what
injuries would ensue (lines 16–17). Although S is still not obliged to offer self-damaging
opinion or speculation, L does not repeat the advice not to answer. At line 21, S himself
orients to the question as problematic; his reply is delayed, prefaced by a long in-breath
and the dispreference marker 'well', and other signs of 'perturbation' in the flow of
speech (Schegloff 2007). The sense of L's advice being delayed and then absent, is
enhanced when we compare it to other examples.

In extract (5), S is a juvenile who has been arrested for witness intimidation. Her
mother is also present as 'Appropriate Adult'.

```
(5)  PN-117
 1   P:     ( ... ) Carla's made an allegation (0.3) uh (0.6) kh-y–like
 2          y'said (earlier) that you did have a fi:ght (0.5) on the
 3          tuesday seventh december two thousand and four (1.7) u:h
 4          but y'saying this ws over an argument uh (1.2) you'd
 5          fallen ou:t. (.) The argument was about uh (0.5) Carla
 6          not being a witness for you: for a pending court case.
 7                 (1.3)
 8   S:     Wha:t (0.2) the fi:ght?
 9                 (0.2)
10   P:     Yeh. That was u-(.) the reason for it,=
11   L:                          =Advi:se you not to answer
12          any questions about the fi:ght itself (0.3) u:m my client has made
13          a statement of complai:nt, (0.2) believe it's being investi[gat]ed.
```

```
14  P:                              [Yeh.]
15  P:        O[kay.
16  L:         [Yeh.
17                    .(2.8)
18  P:        Okay. ((P changes topic))
```

At line 11, L provides what we may describe as an effective, 'successful', intervention. It is successful in that P immediately (indeed in slight overlap, line 14) acknowledges and accepts the intervention, and goes on to pursue an alternative topic. There are some key differences between this intervention, and the less successful one in extract (4). First, the intervention is immediate: the 'equals' signs between lines 10 and 11 mark the immediate 'latching' of one turn to the end of another (Jefferson 2004), in contrast to the delay at line 3 in extract (4). Second, in extract (5), L provides P with a legal basis for her advice, that the topic concerns another complaint that is under separate police investigation. So we can begin to specify what 'success' amounts to, and the kind of interactional features that provide for it. The absence in extract (4) of any account by L for why S should not answer, effectively permits P2 to continue with the same troublesome line of questioning, albeit in reformulated terms.

There is another element in the 'success' or effectiveness of lawyers' advice not to answer, that we can show with a further example. Extract (6) comes from an interview prior to that of extract (5), with the same participants.

```
(6)  PN–116
 1  P:        .hhh It's ↑been witnessed by other people.
 2                    (1.2)
 3  P:        who've statemented to say they've actually hav- seen
 4            this happen.
 5                    (0.7)
 6  P:        Now why would they sa:y (.) that happened. If [it hasn't.]
 7  L:                                             [I would ad]vise
 8            you not to answer that question.
 9                    (0.5)
10  S:        No comment,
11                    (0.4)
12  P:        Have you got any: (.) quarrels with Rebecca= is any
13            animosity between you: that would say that she would
14            make these allegations u:p.
15                    (0.6)
16  S:        Yeh,
17                    (0.6)
18  P:        Why would she make them up.
19                    (0.4)
20  S:        Becau:se I might have t'go t'court because her dad
21            assaulted my mate,
```

Again we can understand the basis of L's objection, even though it is not spelled out. P has posed a hypothetical question (line 6), asking S to speculate about other people's motives. Again, L's advice comes without delay (line 7). But also, in this example,

S complies with that advice using the standard verbal format 'no comment' (line 10). This provides a further contrast with extract (4). In extract (6) S's 'no comment' is not responsive to the immediately prior turn (L's advice), but functions as a display of complying with that advice, and as a response to P's question at line 6. If S were to signal no such compliance, as in (4), then P remains at liberty to continue the same line of questioning, because S and not L is the interviewee, and a non-response from S would leave the question still hanging. Notably, in (5) (lines 12–13), L addresses the grounds of her objection directly to P, who then acknowledges the point, which has the effect of cancelling the troublesome question that was put to S. With no further account by L as in (6), and in the absence of overt compliance from S, all that would have happened (as in extract (4)) is that L has given some advice to S. Suspects need to show that they are taking and acting on that advice, and 'No comment' is a standardised way of doing that.

Note again that, in (6), L's advice is successful, in that P does not pursue the question concerning other witnesses. Instead, P starts a similar line of questioning, now inviting S to speculate about why her accuser might invent a false accusation. This time L does not object, across several turn-transition opportunities to do so (notably at lines 15 and 19), and S answers. The absence of intervention by L here is presumably because this line of speculation is helpful rather than damaging to S's position.

We have noted that lawyers may explain to police officers, as in (5), the grounds for their advice to their client not to answer, and that it can lead to the non-pursuance of that line of questioning by P. We have also noted that, despite L's advising S not to answer, trouble may ensue whereby P continues to pursue the question, and S answers it. One way of obviating that trouble is for L to deal directly with P. Rather than advising S not to answer, L may object to P's asking it. In extract (7), L is objecting in this way to the same kind of issue that arose in extract (4). The suspect has been arrested for assault.

(7) PN-100
```
 1  P:    Um:: (.) d'you understand that if you hit him with
 2        the bar (.) that's the kind of injury that you're
 3        gonna: (0.2) cause.
 4  L:    .pt 'e-'e-'e can't answer the question. = it's:
 5        that's a medical issue.
 6  P:    Okay.
 7                    (0.9)
     ((9 lines omitted here))
 8  P:    .pt d'you understand that hitting someone with a bar
 9        may cause injury though.
10                    (0.3)
11  S:    Yeh.
```

As in extract (6), L's intervention targets P's invitation to S to speculate, this time about possible effects of S's actions. Here, *instead* of advising S not to answer a particular question, L objects to P *asking* it. One feature of getting suspects not to answer questions in this way is that L's intervention provides at least minimal grounds for not having to answer: "e can't answer the question. =it's: that's a medical issue' (lines 4–5). Further-more, by directing the objection at P rather than S, such turns may work more directly at closing off P's pursuit of the question. That can be an effective alternative where there is a possibility that S may not heed L's advice, which sometimes happens. However, in the above example the respite is temporary: like P2 in extract (4), P reformulates the question a few turns later. But this time he uses generalized and normative terms rather than details specific to S's alleged action, and L permits S to answer.

The next section considers another type of intervention from lawyers, again targeting police officers' questions, but a different feature of them.

Repair operations on questions and answers

In conversation analysis, 'repair' occurs when a speaker alters something that they or another speaker have just said or started to say (e.g. Drew 1997; Schegloff 1987). The alteration may add something, delete something, or change something, and it may be initiated by either party. Not only is repair a highly organized feature of interaction, falling into systematic types and components, it is also significant in displaying participants' concerns.

In our police–suspect interviews, lawyers deploy repair procedures as a way of doing actions such as objecting to P's questions, seeking clarification, making a legal point, or eliciting helpful evidence from S. In extract (8) at line 9, L uses a targeted repair initiator, requiring P to revise or explain his question before S answers it.

```
(8)   PN-100
  1   P:     U::m (0.3) where did you pick- (1.2) >what was it you
  2          'ad.<
  3                   (0.6)
  4   S:     It'ws'jus' like a piece of alumi:nium.
  5                   (0.5)
  6   P:     Ri:ght what's in tha:t.
  7                   (0.2)
  8   S:     W'll how d'y[(           )-]
  9   L:                 [What d'you mean] what's in that.
 10   P:     How- how heavy is it.
 11   S:     Alumi:n[ium? ( ] )
 12   P:            [Is it-] Is it solid or:
```

S has been describing events leading up to him assaulting a neighbour with a bar. As we will discover in a subsequent extract, P's line of questioning is to do with whether the 'bar' can, in fact, be categorized as a 'weapon', and whether S possesses it for possible violent actions. Here, then, S's answer to P's first question formulates the 'bar' as 'jus' like a piece of alumi:nium', deleting its recognizability as a weapon and instead formulating it as an innocent item anyone might have lying around their property. S displays, maybe disingenuously, trouble with P's follow-up question at line 6 'what's in tha:t' and it is at this point, in overlap, that L initiates repair on P's question: 'What d'you mean what's in that.' We can see that the sequence unfolds around whether or not the bar is heavy or hollow, which is relevant to its being categorized as a dangerous weapon.

Our final section focuses on different ways in which lawyers help clients to formulate their testimony and accounts.

Helping clients formulate testimony

There are various ways in which a lawyer may assist their client to give evidence during police questioning. We illustrate two of those ways here: (1) providing explanations of the 'subtext' of P's questions; and (2) supplementing S's account.

Providing explanations

Lawyers occasionally intervene to explain things, often in ways that alert S to the legal significance of a question, in ways that may forestall S providing a self-incriminating answer. In extract (9), we return to the case of the suspect arrested for assault with a metal bar, also seen in extracts (7) and (8).

```
(9)  PN-100
   1  P:    D'you know why y'went into the garden >or was it
   2        jus' summat you did.<hh
   3              (0.2)
   4  S:    ↑I ↑jus' ↑did ↑it. =I was-(0.5).pff I was ma:d,
   5        (0.2) ↑fri:ghtened or- w'll not frightened I was-
   6        what distressed I'd 'ave to call it?
   7              (0.3)
   8  P:    Righ'.
   9              (0.5)
  10  S:    >I d-< I ↑weren't ↓thinking about° ooh let's-°
  11        let's r- w- (0.2) [↑↑why is it such a ↑pro:blem.
  12  P:                      [(W-)
  13              (0.7)
  14  P:    W'll >what I'm getting at mate is-< I want t-jus'
  15        wanna know why you've put that ba:r in the ga:rden.
  16              (2.1)
  17  P:    Why- why've y'put it in the ga:rden.
  18              (0.2)
  19  S:    >Yeh but-< *u-* (0.6) I don't under-↑↑why is he
  20        asking [that question?
  21  P:           [Cos y'keep it in the-y'keep it in the
  22              (0.3)
  23  S:    In my be:droo[m.
  24  L:                 [The ↑reason 'e's asking the question
  25        is it seems to hi:m, t'the officer: th't you were
  26        trying to <concea:l the ba::r.>
  27  S:    A:h.
  28              (0.2)
  29  S:    Why didn't y'jus' come out an' sa:y that.
  30              (.)
  31  P:    .pt because I want to know why you've put it in the
  32        ga:rden.
  33              (0.4)
  34  S:    Because I jus' ↑di:d. =here's no- (.) no (0.3)
```

```
35        reason, =I jus' came in my hou:se, jus' walked
36        through the hou:se an' jus' walked straight through
37        the house.
```

S has reported that following a fight with his neighbours, he put the bar used to assault them, in his garden, where the police later found it. P starts by asking S why he went into the garden after the assault had taken place. P is pursuing S for an admission that he deliberately tried to conceal the bar, which is articulated explicitly by L in the target lines 24–26. We can see that S struggles to answer P's question in the delivery of his turn at lines 4–6, with repair and reformulation of his reported emotional state '↑fri:ghtened or- w'll not frightened I was- what distressed'. S's orientation to the correct way to describe his emotions, together with the halting of his next turn (lines 10–11) suggests a sense of his difficulty with this line of questioning. He asks '↑↑why is it such a ↑pro:blem' (line 11), to which P reformulates the question with the preface 'w'll >what I'm getting at', and the reformulation asks more directly why S 'put that ba:r in the ga:rden'. A long gap develops, again indicating S's trouble with, and possible recognition of, the legal implications of answering this question. P re-issues the question at line 17, and it is at this point that S addresses L with '↑↑why is he asking that question?'. P provides an account for asking, pointing out a possible inconsistency in S's testimony (why put the bar in the garden when he normally keeps it in his bedroom?).

L's intervention at line 24, starting in overlap with the end of S's prior turn, explains what P is driving at, and does so in terms relevant to the legal implications of S's possible answer. L explains how P's question is oriented to S's possible intent to conceal evidence. At line 27, S displays a new understanding (with 'A:h' – see Heritage 1984) of what L has spelled out for him, and challenges P on not being so direct about it. It is not that S did not necessarily understand the force of P's question. If S had indeed been 'trying to conceal the bar', then he surely did understand it. Rather, it is that accounts, understandings and their legal relevance, are under display here, whether or not naïvely, and L's action is to make those understandings more public. There would indeed be some point for S in behaving disingenuously at lines 4–6 and 10–11, with regard to P's question, as a display of innocence – that so far was he, from having strategically concealed the weapon, that he is having difficulty understanding the point of the question. L's explanation of that point, and S's 'news receipt' of it ('A:h'), essentially co-produce S's innocence on the matter.

Supplementing S's account

There are also occasions when, rather than offering explanations or eliciting evidence from clients, lawyers will add more or less substantial details to S's evidence. In extract (10) we return to the case seen previously in (3), of the suspect arrested for racial harassment of her neighbours. The police officers have been playing audio tapes made by S's neighbours, that allegedly have caught S in the act of racial abuse (for extracts of these recordings see Stokoe and Edwards 2007). Earlier, S denied that it was her voice on the recording. Here, she is challenging the legality of her neighbours' actions.

```
(10)  PN-114c
  1  P1:    [( )
  2  S:     [But <does that give them the ri:ght to do
  3          that>.
```

```
 4                    (0.2)
 5  P1:   What t'ta:pe you.
 6                    (0.2)
 7  S:    T'ta:pe me.
 8                    (1.5)
 9  P1:   [( )-
10  S:    [Is that le:gal f'them t'tape me. =
11  P2:   Y'knew they were ta:pin' you,
12                    (0.5)
13  S:    Not at first I di:dn't?
14                    (0.4)
15  S:    I- (.) I don't even know if 'e's ↑camcordered me.
16                    (0.6)
17  S:    'e come out the other day with a camcorder pointed
18        at me[.
19  L:        [The POint is 'e did it.
20                    (0.3)
21  L:    I mean there does appear t' be a conspiracy against
22        you° but I'm not going to bring that up at this
23        point.
24                    (0.2)
25  L     U:m,
26  S:    I know I don't know if I'm on his camcorder.
27                    (0.9)
28  P1:   There is a camcorder an a' recording of you as well
29        you ↓yes.
30                    (1.0)
31  S:    Ain't that ille:gal.
32                    (0.9)
33  S:    What's he gonna [use ↑that for.
34  P1:                   [( )
35                    (1.3)
36  S:    [What's he going to use ↑me for.]
37  P1:   [(                          )]
38                    (0.2)
39  P1:   If-if it does go to cou:rt there could be obviously
40        big arguments as t'whether that could be played in
41        court or not.
42                    (0.8)
43  P1:   About how you sound and your general beha:viour.
```

Between lines 2–10, S asks whether her neighbours have the 'ri:ght' to tape her, and whether it is 'le:gal'. P's responses throughout are somewhat hedged, and the absence of interventions from L on the legality of such recordings suggests that they may indeed be permissible in court. P's response that 'Y'knew they were ta:pin' you', does not answer S's question and instead takes the form of a proposition for confirmation (with confirmation the strongly 'preferred' answer). S answers that at first she did not know, but then adds that she knew she was being 'camcordered'. It is at this point, in overlap at the end of S's answer, that L intervenes and formulates the upshot of S's previous turns: 'The POint is 'e did it' (line 19). In so doing, L directs attention away from S to the neighbour who made the recording, and introduces a legally relevant implication of it ('conspiracy against you').

Concluding remarks

In this chapter we have used conversation analysis to examine the location, design and action orientation of lawyers' contributions to police interviews with their clients. The aim has been to show the kinds of phenomena that may be revealed by close sequential analysis using technical transcripts of actual interrogations, where lawyers' work is being done. We examined lawyer-initiated actions, responses and interjections including objections to police questioning, advice to clients (both spontaneous and in response to requests), various 'repair' operations on officers' questions, and actions such as questioning clients, and helping them formulate their evidence. Some of those interventions invoked suspects' rights, as explained by police officers at the start of interviews (e.g. that suspects 'do not have to say anything'). One major advantage of lawyers' dealing with such matters within the course of the interrogation, is that not having to answer a question, and the advice not to do so, is tailored to specific questions and their moments, rather than left as generalized principles for clients to have to apply. As we noted, this advantage is all the sharper when lawyers spontaneously interject rather than waiting for clients to ask for advice.

We also considered the 'success' of lawyer interventions – that is, where they halt or deflect the trajectory of an officer's questioning. Success was found to hinge on the intervention's immediacy, as displayed by features of the technical transcript (latching, delays, etc.), and also on whether lawyers provided a rationale for their advice not to answer. Another feature of successful interventions was the manner of suspects' compliance: the standard verbal format 'no comment' by which suspects could not only show that they were acting on the advice not to answer, but also that they were adopting a standard, recognized way of doing that. Another way of obviating an objectionable line of police questioning, and additionally of forestalling suspects not heeding lawyers' advice (we have several cases of frustrated solicitors failing to silence their recalcitrant clients), was for lawyers to bypass suspects and deal directly with officers.

Overall, the benefits of a conversation analysis of legal interactions are only briefly illustrated in this chapter. They include the value of a close examination of the details, often technically revealed, of transcribed talk. They include also a focus on the turn-by-turn sequential actions being done, and the relevance of turn sequences to understanding those actions. Features such as paired actions (e.g. question–answer sequences), and the workings of conversational repair, reveal participants' orientations to the matters they are dealing with, including the relevance of specific verbal formulations to matters of incrimination and intent. By examining the content and sequential organization of lawyers' turns, in recorded settings such as police interrogations, the nature of lawyers' legal work, and its impact on forensic procedures, is revealed in terms of their actual practices.

Further reading

Edwards, D. (2008) 'Intentionality and *mens rea* in police interrogations: The production of actions as crimes', *Intercultural Pragmatics*, 5(2): 177–99.

Heritage, J.C. (1984) 'A change-of-state token and aspects of its sequential placement', in J.M. Atkinson and J. Heritage (eds), *Structures of Social Action: Studies in Conversation Analysis*, Cambridge: Cambridge University Press, 299–346.

Kidwell, M. (2006). '"Calm down!": The role of gaze in the interactional management of hysteria by the police', *Discourse Studies*, 8(6): 771–96.

Stokoe, E., and Edwards, D. (2007). '"Black this, black that": Racial insults and reported speech in neighbour complaints and police interrogations', *Discourse & Society*, 18(3): 355–90.

12

Police interviews in the judicial process

Police interviews as evidence

Kate Haworth

Introduction

Police–suspect interview discourse has a vital function in the England and Wales (E&W) criminal justice process. For the police themselves, the formal interview is a key part of any investigation into a criminal offence. The interview later goes on to have a significant further function as a piece of evidence in itself, exhibited and presented in court as part of the prosecution case. Words spoken during the interview thus have a dual context, being produced in both interview room and courtroom, and a correlating dual function, being both investigative and evidential. Yet these contexts and functions are very different, and perhaps even conflicting, as we shall see.

In addition, interview data undergo several changes in format en route from interview room to courtroom, each of which affects the integrity of the evidence. This 'contamination' of verbal evidence makes a stark contrast with the forensic treatment of physical evidence, which according to long-accepted principle must be preserved as intact as possible.

This chapter will explore the influence of all these factors on police–suspect interviews, and will demonstrate that there are potentially serious implications for their role as evidence. It will also serve to illustrate that linguistics offers a powerful set of tools for unpicking exactly how something as socially significant as criminal evidence can be discursively 'constructed'.

The role of police–suspect interviews

The process begins when the police conduct an interview with someone suspected of committing a criminal offence. The interview is recorded, in the vast majority of cases, onto audiocassette tapes. Some moves are now being made towards digital recording and video recording is occasionally used, but only for the most serious cases. An official transcript known as the 'Record of Taped Interview' (ROTI) is then produced from the audio tape and so from here on the interview interaction is available in two versions; one spoken and one written. In practice, however, the written, rather than the taped version is relied upon.

The interview forms an important part of the initial police investigation. The interviewee may have admitted involvement, or pointed the investigation in a different direction. Witnesses and other suspects will also be interviewed at this stage, and information passed on in any one of these interviews may be crucial in guiding the conduct of the others.

The decision about whether to charge the interviewee, and if so with what offence(s), is generally taken by the Crown Prosecution Service (CPS), and the interview is a key part of the information on which they base their charging decision. This decision can be a delicate one: for example, the distinction between various levels of offence may depend solely on proving the intention, knowledge or awareness of the perpetrator (the *mens rea* element of an offence), but the consequences in terms of sentence length can be enormous. Notable examples are the distinction between murder and manslaughter, and between possession of drugs and possession with intent to supply. It is of course extremely difficult to get 'inside the mind' of the suspect in order to prove this element of an offence, and so their own words at interview can be an extremely important source of evidence.

If the CPS decide to proceed, the interviewee becomes a 'defendant' and the matter will go to trial – unless, of course, a guilty plea is entered. The interview now becomes part of the package of courtroom evidence against the defendant. In some cases, the transcript will be edited further at this stage by agreement between the prosecution and defence, for example to remove inadmissible or prejudicial material which should not be seen by the court.

The manner in which interview data are presented to the court is particularly interesting. Technically, the actual piece of evidence is the audio tape, not the transcript (*R v. Rampling* [1987] Crim LR 823), but transcripts are admissible as 'copies' of the original evidence (s.133 & 134(1) Criminal Justice Act 2003). What happens in practice is that the audio tape is rarely played, and reliance is placed solely on the transcript. The rather bizarre custom is for the transcript to be read out loud or performed. Since the interview forms part of the prosecution case, the normal procedure is for a police witness to act as the interviewer, and the prosecution lawyer to take the part of the defendant interviewee. Although copies of the transcript are also made available to the court, it seems highly likely that the oral performance will become the predominant version in the minds of those present.

Lawyers for both prosecution and defence use the interview material in whatever way they can to support their case. Comparisons are commonly made between what a suspect says at trial and what they said (or at least are *reported* to have said) at interview. The defence will seek to use the earlier interview as evidence of the defendant's consistency; the prosecution will point to any differences as a sign of inconsistency, and therefore dishonesty and potential guilt.

Further, an important legal provision – s.34 Criminal Justice and Public Order Act (CJPOA) 1994 – allows the court to 'draw inferences' if a defendant seeks to rely on something in their defence at trial which they did not bring up during earlier questioning, including their police interview. As Bucke, Street and Brown comment with regard to these 'inferences', '[w]hile the legislation does not specify that these need be adverse to the defendant, the likelihood is that they would be' (Bucke *et al.* 2000: 1). This provision is predominantly aimed at those who invoke their 'right to silence' and make no comment at interview, but it equally affects every suspect who did choose to answer questions but, for whatever reason, 'failed to mention' something which later becomes part of their defence case.

The evidential function of the police–suspect interview is therefore extremely important. It can be observed in action in the following example, taken from the trial of Dr Harold Shipman. Here, Shipman is being cross-examined by prosecution counsel. (The transcription, including the punctuation, is that of the official court transcript.)

(1) Interview evidence in court

Pr: Now I am going to ask you please to look at what you told the police when they interviewed you in relation to Mrs. Mellor's medical history. Could you go please first of all to page 251. Page 251. Do you have it in front of you? We will just wait until everybody has it in front of them. Page 251, a third of the way down. {...} You are aware that this document is an agreed transcript taken from a tape-recorded interview which is admitted to be accurate?

W: It reflects what was said on the day, yes.

Pr: Yes, and can be played if needs be. You don't dispute the content, that this accurately represents the interview do you?

W: No.

[Counsel reads long extracts from the interview]

Pr: {...} you were telling the police that she, page 251, 'She came back 10 days later to tell me about it again.' That's what it says page 251, 'She came back 10 days later to tell me about it again.' That is completely at odds, isn't it, with the evidence you have given this morning?

W: No, I don't think it is.

Pr: {...} Do you agree you gave one version to the police and a different one today?

W: I agree that the version that was taken down in the police station is different from the one I said today, yes.

Pr: Well why did you give a different version to the police to the one that you are giving today?

W: Because today I am more sane.

Pr: Today and in the days preceding today you <u>have</u> had time to conco<u>c</u>t a false story, haven't you?

W: No.

Pr: You had not thought about this line of defence, had you, when you saw the police?

W: I didn't realise I had to have a line of defence when I saw the police.

(Shipman Trial transcript, Day 34, www.the-shipman-inquiry.org.uk/trialtrans.asp)

Aside from the many other fascinating elements of this exchange, this demonstrates the importance of the interview as a piece of evidence in the criminal process. This is, in one sense, the ultimate purpose for the interview – indeed Baldwin (1993) comments that '[i]nstead of a search for truth, it is much more realistic to see interviews as mechanisms directed towards the 'construction of proof'' (327). It can also be seen that the interview's appearance here in a courtroom as a physical exhibit ('page 251, a third of the way down') is completely different functionally and contextually from the site of its original production.

Some problems

The treatment of interview discourse just outlined will ring several alarm bells for anyone who has studied spoken discourse from a linguistic perspective, as it is based on several questionable assumptions.

Firstly, for interviews to be legitimately used as evidence, it is essential to be able to establish exactly what was said during the original interaction. This is entirely dependent on the adequacy of the format in which they are presented. The various different incarnations of the interview are treated by the legal system as if changes in format have no effect on the content, but this is surely not the case.

Secondly, direct comparisons between what was said at interview and at trial assume that an honest person will give exactly the same version of events on two different occasions, even when elicited by a questioner with a very different agenda, in front of a different audience, in a different context and after the passage of some considerable time, with no doubt several re-tellings in between. Again, it is erroneous to assume that these factors will not have any effect.

Thirdly, the current system presupposes an ideal scenario where a police interviewer asks questions about an incident and the interviewee, in replying to those questions, has every opportunity to say whatever they wish. However, given the nature of police–suspect interview interaction, where one participant is prescribed the role of questioner and the other that of respondent, combined with the highly unequal power relations between participants, this ideal scenario surely cannot exist.

In order to challenge some of these assumptions we shall first consider the findings of research into the influence of format, context and audience on interaction, and then illustrate the problems with examples from police–suspect interviews.

Format

The differences between spoken and written modes of language are long established in linguistic research (e.g. Biber 1988; Halliday 1989). This therefore presents a particular set of problems when attempting to convert any text from one format to the other. This difficulty has been fully appreciated by those linguists who need to convert spoken data to a written format to make them accessible to their readers, and hence has become an important methodological consideration in this field (e.g. Ochs 1979).

However, written transcriptions of spoken data are widely used in the criminal justice process without any recognition of these challenges. This has been given some attention by linguists with an interest in the legal system. Walker, an ex-court reporter, has highlighted problems with the process of producing contemporaneous 'verbatim' transcripts of courtroom proceedings (Walker 1986a, 1990), an area also addressed by Eades (1996) and Tiersma (1999: 175–79). Fraser (2003) considers the inherent challenges of transcribing covert recordings such as intercepted telephone calls, while the serious consequences that can ensue when such transcriptions are used as evidence are demonstrated by Shuy (1993a, 1998b), and Coulthard and Johnson (2007: 144–46). Finally, Gibbons (2003: 27–35) describes the difficult representational choices facing those transcribing spoken data for use in legal contexts, highlighting the many inadequacies in current practice.

However, it must be acknowledged that current E&W practice is fairly unusual in even attempting to produce verbatim transcripts of police–suspect interviews from audio recordings. Prior to the introduction of mandatory tape-recording in 1992 (Police and Criminal Evidence Act 1984), formal written records were produced by the interviewers themselves from contemporaneous notes or even memory. Not surprisingly, these have been shown to be poor representations of the interaction which actually took place (Coulthard 1996, 2002). Worryingly, this is still the method used in E&W for obtaining witness statements (see Rock 2001).

This practice is also still used for police–suspect interviews in other jurisdictions. In a Swedish study, Jönsson and Linell (1991) highlight substantial differences between the account produced orally by a suspect and the corresponding written report produced by the interviewer, which they link with differences between spoken and written language. Gibbons makes similar observations of witness interviews in Chilean *audiencias*, and comments: '[t]he question we have to ask is whether the judicial process, and hence justice itself, is threatened by the fact that the judge receives a digested version of the evidence' (Gibbons 2001b: 32). (See also Komter (2002, 2006) on the Dutch system, and Eades (1995) and Gibbons (1995) on Australian cases.) It is significant that the transformations and inaccuracies observed in all these studies nearly always assist the prosecution, not the defence.

Taken together, these studies highlight serious deficiencies in the production of written records of spoken interaction across various legal contexts and jurisdictions over a considerable number of years. The current E&W system of recording and transcribing police–suspect interviews is a significant advance compared with previous practice and with other jurisdictions, but unfortunately this appears to have led to an assumption that problems no longer exist.

Further, in the E&W system the interview data are not only converted from spoken to written format, but also from written back into spoken when the transcript is read out loud in the courtroom. This process has received considerably less academic scrutiny, but it is safe to assume that it is also highly unlikely to be a neutral, problem-free exercise. This is especially true given that the oral presentation is performed only by representatives of the prosecution.

We will now look at an example which demonstrates how the format changes undergone by police interview data affect their evidential integrity (Haworth 2006: 757). It relates to a crucial point in the Harold Shipman trial. It must be acknowledged that the data used here are certainly open to question for exactly the reasons just outlined, given that we must rely on the official trial transcript, but it is nonetheless a striking illustration.

Shipman was a doctor accused of murdering a large number of his patients, often by administering fatal overdoses of diamorphine. In response to a specific question during one of his police interviews, he denied that he kept any dangerous drugs, yet diamorphine was found at his home during a search. Not only did this give him the means to commit the murders, but also this denial at interview proved that he had lied to the police. This significantly undermined his honesty and integrity, an aspect which was relied on heavily by the defence during the trial, tapping into the image of trust and respectability typically accorded to family doctors. This deceitful response at interview was therefore hugely significant, as emphasised repeatedly by the prosecution. However, it appears that errors crept into the version presented in court. According to my own transcription from the audio recording, the relevant exchange is as follows:

(2a) Author's version

IR:er re the drugs, (.) you don't keep drugs in er (.) your surgery, (.) is that correct
IE: I don't keep any drugs (.) if you're talking about <u>controlled</u> drugs

This is a very straightforward – and untrue – denial. Yet the official police transcript puts this differently:

(2b) Police transcript

IE: I've given your drugs. Are you talking about controlled drugs?

There is a crucial difference in meaning here. This version contains a clear implication that Shipman has voluntarily handed over drugs to the police, when in fact he did exactly the opposite: he hid them and lied about it. The official police transcript, which

173

is the version presented to the court as evidence, thus seriously undermines an important prosecution point.

But that is not all. Not surprisingly, during cross-examination the prosecution challenge Shipman about this point, and use exactly this part of the interview to do so. However, the version 'quoted' by prosecution counsel is different again:

(2c) Prosecution version
      IE: I have given you all the drugs. Are you talking about controlled drugs?

(Trial transcript, Day 32)

Compared to the police transcript, this contains the significant addition of 'all'. This version is much more helpful to the prosecution, in that this *would* still amount to a lie: Shipman cannot have given the police *all* the drugs if more were then found at his house. I am certainly not suggesting that this alteration was deliberate, but nevertheless it is certainly helpful to the agenda of the person quoting the 'evidence'.

This example clearly and concisely demonstrates the transformations which interview data can undergo, stage by stage, from interview room to courtroom. It shows that by the time the process reached the crucial stage where the jury were considering the interview as evidence in deciding on their verdict, the content was significantly different from what Shipman actually said in his interview.

Context

As we have seen, a significant feature of police interview discourse is that it does not simply occur in the interview room, but is reproduced and recontextualised from interview room to courtroom (see e.g. Komter 2002). This recontextualisation is not unique to police interviews, however, and has been investigated as a feature of some other institutional, and especially legal, texts.

Walker considers a similar process of taking original data out of context and putting them to a slightly different legal use, namely by judges assessing transcripts of witness evidence when determining appeals. This demonstrates the significance of the chosen representation of certain contextual language features in the transcripts (e.g. pauses, 'ungrammatical speech': Walker 1986a: 418) and their influence on the judges' decision-making process (see also Coulthard 1996). In a rather different take on the same underlying phenomenon, Aronsson (1991) considers the 'recycling' of information in various institutional processes, and highlights the resulting misinterpretation and 'miscommunication' which can result (see also Jönsson and Linell 1991). There is, of course, a strong link between the recontextualisation of the data and the corresponding changes in format just discussed.

This idea of 'messages travel[ling] across sequences of communication situations' (Jönsson and Linell 1991: 422) links with the concept of 'trans-contextuality', as developed in the work of Briggs and Blommaert. Briggs traces elements of a 'confession statement' supposedly made by a young woman in an infanticide case, examining its relation to statements made by others connected with the case and official documents produced in relation to it. He traces what is described as the 'circulation of discourse' (Briggs 1997: 538), in particular the way in which the statement was subsequently used within the judicial process which ultimately convicted the woman. This highlights the strong influence of the wider judicial sequence in which the relevant interaction occurred over the content of the statement produced.

Blommaert addresses similar processes involving narratives of African asylum-seekers in Belgium. He examines how the asylum-seekers' stories, as given in their original interview with immigration officials, are then institutionally processed: '[t]he story of the asylum seeker is remoulded, remodelled and re-narrated time and time again, and so becomes a *text trajectory* with various phases and instances of transformation' (Blommaert 2001: 438). Blommaert shows that these processes go further than simply questions of transcription and format change, emphasising the significant ramifications of the recontextualisations, while also raising important questions of ownership and control over the asylum seekers' stories. It is important to recognise the inequality in access to the transformative processes undergone by such data. Just as with Blommaert's asylum-seekers, police interviewees lose all control over the subsequent 'trajectory' of their words as soon as they have been uttered.

All these studies demonstrate the importance of looking beyond the immediate site of production of institutional discourse, and of seeing such texts as just one part of much wider processes. This is clearly true of police interview discourse and its important role as criminal evidence. The next step is to consider the influence of those wider processes and institutional functions over the interview interaction itself.

Audience

A useful starting point for such an analysis is a consideration of the effect of audience on interaction. It is a well-established principle, from sociolinguistic studies of speaker style (Giles and Powesland 1975b; Bell 1984) to studies of the narrative construction of identity (e.g. Schiffrin 1996), that speakers adapt their talk according to the intended audience. Indeed Sacks, Schegloff and Jefferson describe 'recipient design' as 'perhaps the most general principle which particularizes conversational interactions' (Sacks *et al.* 1974: 727).

But the recontextualisation of police–suspect interview interaction means that it has several different audiences – from those initially present, to lawyers preparing their cases, to the judge and jury of the courtroom – each of which has a slightly different purpose for it. Much depends on how successfully the participants meet the needs of all those audiences during the interview itself. Failure to do so can lead to dire consequences for an interviewee, but is it reasonable to expect them to cater for so many diverse needs? By the same token, how challenging a task is this for police interviewers to manage successfully?

There are some parallels with courtroom discourse, where interaction between questioner and witness is to a large extent a display for the 'overhearing audience' of the jury (Drew 1992). However, although jury members are arguably also the most important audience for police–suspect interview discourse, they are, of course, not present at the original interaction.

It is therefore instructive to consider another context with parallels in this respect. In broadcast news interviews, the presence of an overhearing, non-present and often temporally remote audience is an essential feature, and hence has been the focus of some research (e.g. Heritage 1985; Greatbatch 1988; Clayman and Heritage 2002). This has shown that in that context the overhearing audience is by far the most influential in discursive terms. News interviewers use strategies which position them not as the primary recipients of the interviewee's talk, but as conduits to the overhearing audience who are the real intended target for the interviewee's talk (Heritage 1985: 100).

However, despite the similarities between these contexts, there are some important distinctions. Firstly, Heritage observes of the news interviewer that their 'task is to avoid adopting the position of the primary addressee of interviewee's reports' (Heritage 1985: 115). Yet the police interviewer *is* an intended primary recipient: they are part of the team investigating the offence in question, and may be directly involved in decisions about charging and detaining the interviewee immediately consequent to the interview. The interviewee thus has more than one 'primary' audience to maintain, and they are situated very differently in relation to the talk – physically, temporally and in terms of their purpose. Meanwhile the interviewer has an extremely difficult position to maintain, as both 'conduit' *and* primary recipient of the interviewee's talk – stances which are effectively mutually exclusive. In addition, the role would seem to demand neutrality, yet the interviewer's institutional position as a member of the police force is clearly anything but.

Further, in broadcast interviews the participants are under no illusion regarding the true purpose of the interaction or the primary intended audience. It is less clear whether that can be said of police interviewees. They will be fully aware that they are being recorded and therefore 'overheard', and will probably have a basic grasp of the legal process which may ensue, but this is not the same as knowing the identity and purpose of those who will listen to that recording. On the other hand, the interviewers' relationship with the future audiences is completely different. They belong to the same institutional system, and it is part of their professional role to be aware of the subsequent evidential use of the interview. This is therefore an important distinction between the interviewer's and interviewee's positions.

Data analysis

We will now look at examples from police–suspect interviews to observe the influence of all these aspects in the interaction itself, and how this may affect its future role as evidence. (Transcripts here are the researchers' own.)

(3) Interview 5.11.2/1: Assault PC

IR: so the next question is would you agree that apart from meself and y-
     yers- <u>yourself</u>, there is no-one else present in this [room.]
IE: [mm.] yep.

The interviewer's question here is entirely redundant for the purposes of himself and the interviewee, but is a method of providing information purely for the future audiences for the interview. It is reminiscent of a magician asking a person on stage with him to confirm, for the more distant audience, that there is no rabbit in his hat. It is, of course, an example of exactly the same discursive phenomenon.

Stokoe and Edwards document similar 'silly questions' in police–suspect interviews, especially in connection with 'intentionality' (Stokoe and Edwards 2008: 93), or *mens rea*. For example:

(4) 'Silly question' (Stokoe and Edwards 2008: 90)

IR: Did Melvin give you permission to throw the hammer at his front door?
     (pause)
IE: NO!!

Such questions have a clear evidential function, attempting to establish 'on record' an essential element of the relevant criminal offence. As Stokoe and Edwards comment, '[u]nder the guise of "silly" or "obvious" questions, police officers work to obtain, for the record and for later use in court, something very serious indeed' (Stokoe and Edwards 2008:108).

These examples demonstrate interviewers' clear awareness of, and accommodation to, the future overhearing audiences and the future evidential value of the interview. On the other hand, the following illustrate that interviewees often have no such awareness.

(5) Interview 5.11.2/1: Assault PC

```
 1  IR:   the officer's received injuries that amount to, what we call ABH {...} and I'll
 2        tell you what they are, graze to the left right elbow, graze to the lar- left
 3        right knees, graze to the left right rear shoulder, soreness, at bruising below
 4        right breast and to the nip of his er nobe on his- node on his er on his chest.
 5        (.) okay?
 6  IE:   (there) look there I've got some
 7  IR:   yeah, [(? what you) s-]
 8  IE:         [from falling on] the floor [(?)]
 9  IR:                                     [(I) hear] what you're saying, but the
10        officer's saying, that those (.) those (.) number of bruisings occurred, whilst
11        he was effectively arresting you. (.) and during the struggle that ensued.
```

This interview concerns offences relating to assaulting a police officer while being arrested. But the circumstances surrounding the attempted arrest are confused, with a number of different people involved and the interviewee himself receiving injuries. Yet despite the evidential importance of the information, there is a striking contrast between the amount of detail provided about the officer's injuries and those of the interviewee, who merely invites the interviewer to 'look there' (line 6).

This use of context-dependent deixis displays the interviewee's lack of recognition of the interview's subsequent audio-only format, and his failure to take into account the needs of any non-present audience. It also demonstrates his focus on the interviewer as sole audience for his talk: 'look' can have only one intended recipient here. It is not even clear (to anyone not present) what he means by 'some' – the interviewer's previous turn could provide 'grazes', 'bruising' or even the general 'injuries' as the intended referent. There is thus no evidential value whatsoever to the interviewee's response here.

Yet despite this, the interviewer fails to pursue or provide the missing information for his future audiences. By not establishing evidence of the interviewee's injuries here, the interviewer leaves the defence potentially disadvantaged in any claim of self-defence at a later stage, due to s.34 CJPOA 1994. However, it also leaves a potential gap in the evidence available for future prosecution audiences, particularly in relation to the charging decision.

The following is a further example of what can happen when an interviewee fails to take the future audiences and their purposes into consideration. The interviewee has been shown photographs taken from CCTV footage of the scene of a burglary, showing the perpetrator. The interviewer is alleging that this is the interviewee, yet he fails to make an adequate denial.

(6) Interview 2.26: Burglary

> IR: can you tell me whether or not you were involved in this offence,
>
> IE: like I say I'm not saying anything at this time.
>
> IE: if it goes to court, or whatever the lawyer sees fit, by looking at the evidence that you've showed me, then I will decide on what to do then. in court.
>
> IR: okay.
>
> …
>
> IE: t- to be honest, the photographs don't look that good. er and, (???) show the lawyer them.
>
> IR: right,
>
> …
>
> IE: because to me, all as that shows is, someone who is an average build, looks to me like between brown and black hair, face you cannae make out because it's blurred,
> [there's] (nae) eyes, (nae) nose, [(you can] see)
>
> IR: [okay,]   [cause]   because what we're doing now is arguing whether or not (.) erm whether or not you feel there's enough evidence to get you through a court. but I'm asking you a simple question, which is, have you committed this offence!
>
> IE: well like I say, I'm not saying anything at this time! I'll let the lawyer decide.

What is striking about this example is that it shows an interviewee being explicitly aware of the future court context, while simultaneously failing to consider that those who will be present in that context are also an audience for his current talk. In other words, he has overlooked the multi-purpose, trans-contextual nature of police interview discourse, and is treating the interview as purely investigative, not evidential. His point here is that the photos are not enough on their own to convict him, which may well have been the case. Yet I would argue that for a later court audience attempting to reach a verdict, the photos *combined with these responses at interview* are almost certainly enough, regardless of the quality of the images. He has effectively incriminated himself.

Prosecution v. defence

Thus far we have seen that interviewers do address the future audiences and their purposes during interview interaction. I now wish to refine this observation and suggest that they are not addressing *all* future audiences, but that their professional position will make them focus mainly on collating evidence for the future *prosecution* audiences – by which I mean their fellow investigating officers, the CPS and courtroom prosecutors.

Meanwhile if interviewees focus only on the *interviewer* as their audience, they are likely to take their cue from them in terms of tailoring the content of their utterances. It is also the case that interviewers, with their more powerful institutional and discursive role as questioner, have considerably more control over interview interaction than do interviewees (e.g. Greatbatch 1986). Putting all these factors together, there is a strong likelihood that the account elicited from an interviewee during an interview will end up being tailored much more towards the future *prosecution* audiences, while their own *defence* needs go unmet or even undermined. Indeed, research on police–suspect interview discourse has shown that the prosecution version of events is privileged over the suspect's story (e.g. Auburn *et al.* 1995; Heydon 2005, esp. 116ff.).

This has potentially serious ramifications for the assumption built into s.34 CJPOA that an omission of supporting material for the defence at interview is an indication of guilt. It can have other equally serious consequences in terms of the evidence produced through interview interaction, as shown by the example below. As noted earlier, key elements of a prosecution case often depend on the difficult task of providing evidence of a suspect's knowledge and intentions. In the case already discussed above, relating to assaulting a police officer, a more serious offence is potentially available, namely 'Assault *with intent to resist arrest*' (s.38 OAPA 1861). This has a maximum sentence of two years' custody, compared to six months for a basic 'Assault on a constable' (s.89(1) Police Act 1996). The interviewer's questioning here is clearly designed to elicit – indeed to *create* – evidence regarding this specific offence element, in the form of the interviewee's response.

(7) Interview 5.11.2/1: Assault PC

```
 1  IR:   right when he grabbed hold of yer,
 2  IE:   yep
 3  IR:   why- w- what did you believe he was doing when he grabbed hold of yer.
 4  IE:   what, when he was- I thought he was trying to hurt me at the end of the
 5        day- I was just angry, I didn't know what was going off [(or)]
 6  IR:                                                [no.] when the
 7        officer, grabbed hold of yer,
 8  IE:   yeah
 9  IR:   cos earlier on you actually said at the beginning, that when the
10        off[icer grabbed hold of yer]
11  IE:      [I thought he was just getting me out of the garden.]
12  IR:   you thought that he was going to arrest
13        [yer. and you didn't want to] be arrest[ed.]
14  IE:   [yeah at first yeah.]                    [I didn't] wanna.
15  IR:   [(?)]
16  IE:   [cos] I hadn't done owt wrong at the end of the [day.]
17  IR:                                            [so] am I right making
18        the assumption then, that at the point that he grabbed hold of yer, you
19        thought you were g- being arrested.=
20  IE:   =yeah.
21  IR:   and you didn't want to be ar[rested so-]
22  IE:                               [I'm not gonna lie] yeah.
23  IR:   right. okay th-
24  IE:   I did [r-]
25  IR:         [what] I'm asking you James, is to keep it straight.
26  IE:   yeah I did resist arrest cos I didn't want to get arrested.
```

The sequence begins with the interviewer asking what the interviewee believed was going on at the point that the officer grabbed him. The interviewee's initial response raises two significant points for the defence. Firstly, he states he thought the officer was 'trying to hurt me' (line 4), which supports a potential claim of self-defence. Secondly, he says that he 'didn't know what was going off' (line 5), which indicates that he didn't realise that he was being arrested, which would support a defence to the s.38 offence.

Yet the interviewer does not pick up on either of these aspects, instead interrupting with 'no' (line 6), indicating that this is not the response he wanted. He then suggests an alternative answer, which instead fits a finding of guilt: 'you thought that he was going to arrest yer. and you didn't want to be arrested' (lines 12–13). Significantly, the interviewee does then agree with this proposition, actually echoing the interviewer's words ('you didn't want to', 'I didn't wanna': lines 13–14), despite the fact that this contradicts his immediately prior utterance (line 11), and his original response to the question (lines 4–5). Having received this preferable response, the interviewer moves to a formulation which contains none of the elements of the interviewee's own unprompted utterances, but once again explicitly spells out the elements which would support a prosecution case (lines 17–21). Again, the interviewee agrees with this (line 22).

This sequence is rounded off with a very interesting exchange. The interviewer asks the interviewee to 'keep it straight' (line 25). In response, the interviewee himself provides a form of summary (line 26), but includes only those points repeatedly stressed by the interviewer, and none of those which he raised independently. He also notably uses offence terminology: 'resist arrest'. It is effectively a confession to the more serious offence. In the space of these few exchanges, then, the interviewee has gone from making valid points supporting his defence, to making damaging admissions. What the analysis shows is how this transformation from defence to prosecution evidence is achieved discursively by the interviewer.

Interviews as evidence

This chapter has shown that police–suspect interviews have a significant role as evidence in the criminal justice process. We have also observed the tension created by their dual role as both investigative and evidential. Interviewers are professionally attuned to the subsequent evidential role of the interview, leading to an apparent focus on the needs of the future prosecution audiences, and an inclination not to pursue 'on record' evidence which may support a defence. At the same time, interviewees appear to orientate more to its initial role as part of the preliminary police investigation, and to tailor their account according to cues from the interviewer as sole audience for their talk, often to their cost. Recent research (Haworth 2009) indicates that this can lead to the interview simply confirming whatever version of events the interviewers are currently working on, thus undermining both its investigative and evidential function.

We have also seen that interview data undergo various transformations in format, raising serious questions about evidential consistency. As we move away from the original speech event, the format of the data becomes more corrupted while the uses to which they are put become more important. This is clearly not a desirable correlation.

Overall, linguistic research suggests that, even with the many current safeguards, police–suspect interviews as presented as evidence are still not accurate and faithful representations of the interviewee's words, nor do they present interviewees with a neutral opportunity to put forward their own full version of events. And ultimately, the rather unexpected and self-contradictory result is that the nature of the interview's later role as evidence actually adversely affects its own evidential quality and value.

Further reading

Bell, A. (1984) 'Language style as audience design', *Language in Society*, 13: 145–204. (A useful model for the influence of various audiences on interaction.)

Fraser, H. (2003) 'Issues in transcription: Factors affecting the reliability of transcripts as evidence in legal cases', *Forensic Linguistics*, 10(2): 203–26. (Detailed discussion of the challenges of transcription in legal contexts.)

Heydon, G. (2005) *The Language of Police Interviewing: A Critical Analysis*, Basingstoke: Palgrave. (Extended linguistic analysis of police–suspect interview discourse.)

Komter, M.L. (2002) 'The suspect's own words: The treatment of written statements in Dutch courtrooms', *Forensic Linguistics*, 9(2): 168–92. (Illustration of the evidential use of police–suspect interview records in the Dutch (Roman Law) system.)

Legal cases cited

R v. Rampling [1987] Crim LR 823.

Courtroom genres

Continuam gema

13

The historical courtroom

A diachronic investigation of English courtroom practice

Dawn Archer

Introduction

We can approach the study of legal English of the past in a number of ways. We can trace the development of legal English in general, as Mellinkoff (1963) and Tiersma (2000) do (albeit from different disciplinary perspectives). We can trace the development of linguistic elements that are associated with legal English: for example, Moore (2006) investigates the written discourse marker, 'vidilect', which appears to have developed a genre-specific quotative usage in slander depositions (akin to using 'namely', followed by a direct utterance attributed to the witness/complainant). We can also draw from English extant trial records to investigate the discoursal strategies of the historical courtroom at particular points in time: for example, Kryk-Kastovsky (2000) investigates the turn-taking strategies of what she terms the 'interrogators' and the 'interrogated' in two 1685 trials, *The Trial of Titus Oates* and *The Trial of Lady Alice Lisle*. In this chapter, I will also be outlining the characteristics of courtroom interaction in the English courtroom – but diachronically – so that I can document:

(i.) the way(s) in which courtroom interaction both *shaped* and was *shaped by* legal legislation during this period, and

(ii.) the changing roles of the primary historical courtroom 'players', the judges, the lawyers, the defendants and the witnesses.

The period 1640–1700 will be our initial focus, as defendants and judges seemed to be at their most interactive at this time in English courtrooms (Archer 2005, 2006a). We will then move on to the eighteenth and (to a lesser extent) nineteenth century – the period when a decline in the *inter*activity of defendants and judges is mirrored by an increase in lawyers' *inter*activity. In effect, we begin to witness a move towards adversarialism in its modern form (Cairns 1998). Whether intentionally sought/desired or not, at this early stage, the move towards adversarialism resulted in the increasing restriction of the verbal activities of non-legal participants – so that, by the time of Palmer's infamous murder trial in 1856, courtroom interaction was strikingly similar to the interaction we might hear in Anglo-American courtrooms today: lawyers defined the dispute-in-question between opposing parties, and investigated/advanced that dispute on their behalf, and judges and juries played more of an adjudicative role (Archer 2005).

The English courtroom of the seventeenth century

The trials of 1640–1700 differed from their modern equivalent in a number of ways:

(i) They were usually speedy affairs, not least because several cases tended to be heard at one time, by the same judges and jury, and the verdicts were given at the end.
(ii) When trials were lengthy, judges would often find it difficult to sum up satisfactorily, and jurors would have to retire without 'meat, drink, fire or candle' until they unanimously agreed on a verdict.
(iii) Many seventeenth-century jurists were 'veterans', having been involved in prior jury service. Moreover, extant trial records reveal that jurists could intervene in the courtroom process to make comments or ask questions of the judge and/or of the witnesses as they gave their testimony.
(iv) What lawyers now do remained undone (i.e. there was no opening statement, or assertion of what was going to be advanced against the defendant); instead, the prosecution evidence tended to be presented directly/briefly by the victim (of the crime) and/or witnesses, with the judges keeping them to the narrow track of evidence that related to the issue at hand.
(v) For a substantial part of the Early Modern English (EModE) period, defendants accused of felonies (murder, arson, rape, robbery, burglary) or treason were expected to defend themselves; defence counsel was not granted in treason cases until 1696 and in ordinary criminal cases until the 1730s, after prosecution counsels had become a more regular feature of the court systems.
(vi) The only exception to the rule prohibiting (defence) counsel was on points of law raised by the judge, jurors or defendant. However, anything raised by jurors or defendants had to be certified as constituting points of law by the judges before they could be pleaded.
(vii) The defendants' plight was further complicated as they did not know the precise evidence that would be introduced. In addition, today's presumption of innocence was largely absent in practice. Indeed, the judges' explicit role was to present defendants with evidence that they would have to counter to maintain their innocence. Finally, defendants could not compel the presence of their witnesses.

(See Archer 2006a: 184–85; Beattie 1986: 341, 345; 376–78, 1991: 222; Hostettler 2006: 11, 25–26; Langbein 1978: 274–76, 282; 1999: 315, 325.)

Virtually every jury trial in the second-half of the seventeenth century began with the victim of the crime telling his or her story to the jury (Beattie 1986: 345). In ordinary trials, the judges would then take these 'citizen prosecutors' (Langbein 1999: 325) through their testimony section by section, acting as both examiners and cross-examiners. The citizen prosecutor was usually followed by the witnesses for the Crown, often including a constable who might testify about the circumstances of the defendant's apprehension – what s/he said, what was found, and so on – when this provided strong evidence for the prosecutor. These witnesses gave their evidence under oath, and risked a prosecution for perjury if they were found to have lied. In contrast, defence witnesses and defendants did not testify on oath until 1702 and 1898, respectively (Langbein 1999: 315) – apparently for fear that it would lead to an unacceptable situation whereby opposing parties each swore different 'truths' to God (Hostettler 2006: 29). As a result, defence witnesses' and defendants' testimonies were often regarded as being less credible (Hostettler 2006: 11).

Interactions involving the judge and the defendant (1640–1700)

The prototypical judge was far more (*inter*)active in the seventeenth-century courtroom than judges are today (see, e.g. Culpeper and Kytö 2000; Archer 2005, 2006a). Two factors – the defendants' need to *prove* that the (citizen) prosecutor was mistaken and the lack of defence counsel – meant that seventeenth-century defendants were also more actively involved than their modern equivalents.

The 'no counsel' rule for defendants came about following a ruling at a rape trial in the reign of Edward I, where it was decided that, as the Monarch legally acted against prisoners indicted for felony or treason, lawyers could not 'speak out against the Crown' on the prisoners' behalf (Hostettler 2006: 22). That said, some (near-)contemporaries argued that a defendant's best defence was their own natural and unprepared response to the charges as they were asserted in court. For example, Serjeant William Hawkins (1721: 400) argued that it:

> requires no manner of Skill to make a plain and honest Defence …; the Simplicity and Innocence … having something in it more moving and convincing than the highest Eloquence of Person speaking in a Cause not their own.

For Langbein (2003: 2), however, such attitudes masked a contemporary concern: 'that defence counsel would interfere with the court's ability to have the accused serve as an informational source'.

Officially, seventeenth-century defendants were expected to give their main defence/ explanation of the evidence adduced against them once the prosecution case was completed. But extant trial records reveal that judges would sometimes encourage defendants to intervene during their own questioning of witnesses, so that they might ask pertinent questions whilst the point at issue was in their minds. Thus Col. James Turner was prompted by Lord Bridgman, one of the judges present at his 1663 Old Bailey trial, to 'ask' Sir Thomas Aleyn (Alderman) his 'Questions', in respect to evidence he had given that implicated Turner in a burglary (please note that spellings here and in subsequent quotes reflect the spelling convention(s) of the original trials). According to Sir Thomas de Veil (1748: 81), it was an act of 'benevolence' to allow defendants to ask witnesses questions in this way. In reality, however, a defendant's ability to cross-examine witnesses depended on a number of (inter-related) factors: first, their physical/emotional state, as most defendants were locked up prior to their courtroom appearance (and, as such, were reliant on family/friends for food, clothing and news); second, their intellectual and oratory abilities (i.e. being able to talk effectively in this public setting); third, their having objections of substance to offer, which would be accepted by the Court. These factors may help to explain why Archer (2006a) found that defendants interacted

187

more with judges than with witnesses in the seventeenth century: Archer (2006a) investigated one ordinary (i.e. non-politically motivated) and five State (i.e. politically motivated) trials from the period 1640–79, and discovered defendants' interaction with witnesses was minimal. Yet, those same defendants addressed their judges on 112 occasions. The majority of these turns (i.e. 91) functioned as requests (as opposed to questions), and were made by six men, all of whom faced treason charges. (1)–(5) represent 'typical' requests made by the six:

(1) 'Will you hear me a word Sir?' (*Trial of Charles I 1649*).
(2) 'I desire to have Counsel assigned me' (*Trial of Sir Henry Slingsby 1658*).
(3) 'My Lord, I desire I may hear the Commission read by which you sit' (*Trial of Mordant 1658*).
(4) 'I do humbly move, that I may have time allowed me by this court to send for my Witnesses' (*Trial of Macguire 1644*).
(5) 'I shall crave that there may be nothing taken, in prejudice to my innocency [of the 'niceties in the Law'], from words spoken in simplicity' (*Trial of Dr John Hewet 1658*).

Defendants facing charges of treason were particularly disadvantaged, at this time, as the Crown had enjoyed the representation of counsel in treason trials – usually the Attorney and Solicitor Generals – since the Tudor period (Langbein 1978: 267). As trials like that of Edward Coleman reveal, in all but name, treason trials also tended to be show trials with only one possible outcome – a guilty verdict (and subsequent execution): Edward Coleman (a practicing Catholic) was Secretary to the Duchess of York when Titus Oates claimed he was involved in a 'popish plot' that sought 'the death of the king, and the subversion of the Govt. of England and the protestant religion'. At the commencement of his trial, Coleman expressed concern that 'the violent prejudices that seem to be against everyman in England, that is confess'd to be a Roman Catholick' would mean that 'Justice [would] hardly stand upright' (i.e. prevail). In response, Lord Chief Justice Scroggs informed Coleman: 'we will not do to you as you do to us, blow up at adventure, [and] kill people because they are not of your perswasion'. Unappeased, Coleman requested Counsel. But Scroggs informed Coleman that he would not need Counsel, as 'the [prosecution's] proof' had to 'be [so] plain upon' him that 'the conclusion' became impossible 'to deny'. Scroggs was also careful to inform Oates (the main prosecution witness) that he must tell the 'downright plain truth, and without any arts either to conceal, or … to make things larger then [sic] in truth they are' when giving his evidence, so 'that Mr. Coleman may be satisfied' that he was 'condemned by plain Evidence of Fact' (*Trial of Edward Coleman 1678*). According to Hostettler (2006: 23), Scroggs' 'attempt to justify the denial of counsel' provides 'an early example of the presumption of innocence, with the burden of proof on the prosecution'. Unfortunately, however, the Court was too easily convinced by Oates, and Coleman was found guilty. Some seven years after Coleman's execution, Oates was indicted for perjury, found guilty, flogged and then imprisoned.

The Coleman trial does not reflect the generally held attitudes and behaviour of judges towards defendants of ordinary crime in the seventeenth century, for public records reveal significantly more acquittals in ordinary crime prosecutions than in treason trials (Langbein 1978: 267). The judges' role in ordinary trials involved protecting defendants against illegal procedure, faulty indictments and the like, but what they did not do, in the main, is 'help the accused to formulate a defence or act as their advocates' (Beattie 1991: 223). In fact, extant (felony and treason) trials from the seventeenth century are littered with examples of judges not only commenting upon testimony as it was being given, but also shaping it and, by so doing, influencing how the jurors received/ interpreted it in a way that disadvantaged defendants. Hostettler (2006: 23–24) provides us with an example involving Hyde (one of Turner's judges), this time at the *Trial of John Twyn 1663*: although Hyde informed Twyn at the beginning of his trial that the Court would act as his counsel so 'that [he] suffer[ed] nothing for [his] want of knowledge in matter of law', he went on to inform the jury that he presumed 'no man among [them could] doubt but the witnesses have spoken true; and for answer [they] have nothing but [Twyn's] bare denial'. Mr Justice Kebel acted similarly in the *Trial of John Lilburne 1649*: Kebel informed the jury that he hoped they 'hath seen the Evidence so plain and so fully, that it doth confirm them to do their duty, and to find the Prisoner guilty of what is charged upon him' even before Lilburn had been allowed to make his defence. Fortunately for Lilburn, the jury went against the judge's 'counsel' and found the defendant not guilty (Hostettler 2006: 27).

Unlike today, seventeenth-century judges did not need to be concerned that they might be criticised on appeal for browbeating defendants (or witnesses for that matter), for there were no appeals at this time (Beattie 1986: 345). Yet, historians suggest judges were themselves manipulated (some albeit willingly) so that those in power could 'destroy political opponents', using treason charges (Beattie 1991: 224). Ironically, it was this political manoeuvring that eventually led to better treatment for defendants charged with treason: when those that had suffered the most (i.e. the Whig political class) came to power, they passed an Act – the Treasons Act (1696) – which gave defendants the right to have counsel act for them in all respects, including addressing the jury on the facts as well as on the questions of law (Hostettler 2006: 13). Some five years later, the Act of Settlement (1701) was also passed, and effectively secured the independence of the judiciary (Beattie 1986: 246; Hostettler 2006: 34).

Interactions involving the judges and the witnesses (1640–1700)

As we might expect, seventeenth-century judges frequently interacted with witnesses in felony and treason trials. Moreover, most of the witnesses' turns (i.e. 84.3%–97%) functioned as 'answers' (Archer 2005: 247), the majority of which explicitly provided judges with the information they had requested (and usually no more than what had been requested). Interestingly, Titus Oates provides us with an exception to this pattern (*Trial of Edward Coleman 1678*): Archer (2005: 250) has found that, of fifty witnesses to appear in eight trials representative of the period 1640–80, Oates was one of only two to answer judges' questions using a 'disclaim' (i.e. to answer in a way that indicated he 'could say little to this'). In one of his 'disclaims', Oates also 'supplied' information which had not been explicitly requested: that Coleman had made copies of some important instructions which 'incourage[d]' sympathisers to 'gather ... a Contribution about the Kingdom'. When asked to cite those involved, he made a vague reference to gentry of the Catholic faith:

> Mr. Oates.   I know not any of the Persons, but Mr. Coleman did say he had sent his Suffrages [= instructions] [...] to the Principal Gentry of the Catholicks of the Kingdom of England.

In today's courts, reports of what has been said out of court are kept from the jury on account of the hearsay rule (i.e. the rule forbidding aural testimony or written documents that quote persons not in court). So, too, is evidence of a past conviction (or convictions). But this was not the case during the EModE period.

Although evidence of past convictions usually served to disadvantage seventeenth-century defendants, the *Trial of Elizabeth Cellier 1680* provides us with an example of a defendant using such evidence against a witness: Cellier informed Lord Chief Justice Scroggs that Thomas Dangerfield had 'been Indicted for Burglary' and, as such, should be regarded as an 'unfit witness' (see Archer 2005: 195–96, 251). Although asked to confirm or refute the claim, Dangerfield opted to indirectly challenge Cellier: 'I will take it at [her] Proof'. Scroggs again addressed Dangerfield, asking him 'Have you any more to say? Are there *Waltham Men* here?' Dangerfield's response – 'My Lord, this is enough to discourage a man from ever entring into an honest Principle' – occasioned Scroggs' third and final question to Dangerfield (which was more rhetorical than information-seeking):

> L.C.J.   What? Do you with all the mischief that Hell hath in you think to brave it in a Court of Justice? I wonder at your Impudence, that you dare look a Court of Justice in the Face, after having been made appear so notorious a Villain.

Scroggs went on to release Cellier but committed Dangerfield to the cells.

The infamous Judge Jeffreys

Archer (2005) found Scroggs' treatment of Dangerfield to be an exception in her trial data (taken from the annotated version of the *Corpus of English Dialogues* 1640–1760). However, other linguists (Culpeper and Kytö 2000; Jucker and Taavitsainen 2000; Kryk-Kastovsky 2000, 2006) have documented similar treatment of a witness named Dunne, by the infamous Judge Jeffreys, in the treason trial of Lady Alice Lisle (1685). Although a baker by trade, Dunne was said to have acted as a messenger for Lisle. In the course of his questioning by Jeffreys, Dunne contradicted himself. He also refused to answer eleven of the questions put to him. Moreover, one of his 'silences' lasted 'half a quarter of an Hour', according to a textual comment (Culpeper and Kytö 2000: 60, 62). Such behaviour was extremely unusual in the seventeenth-century courtroom. And an aggravated Jeffreys responded with 'abusive terms, aggressive questioning, irony ... mocking, accusations and strong threats' (Jucker and Taavitsainen 2000: 87). For example, Jeffreys likened Dunne to a 'vile Wretch' and showed disdain for his ability to offer 'horrid Lyes in the presence of God and ... Court of Justice':

> L.C.J.   Why, thou vile Wretch [...] Dost thou take the God of Heaven not to be the God of Truth, and that he is not a witness of all you say'st? Dost thou think because thou precaviratest with the Court here, thou can'st do so with God above, who knows thy Thoughts, and it is infinite Mercy, that for those Falsehoods of thine, he does not immediately strike thee into Hell? Jesus God! there is no sort of conversation nor human Society to be kept with such people as these are, who have no other Religion but only in Pretence, and no way to uphold themselves but by countenancing

Lying and Villainy. Did not you tell me that you opened the Latch your self, and that you saw nobody else but a Girl? How durst you offer to tell such horrid Lyes in the presence of God and of a Court of Justice?

According to Kryk-Kastovsky (2006: 238), this and similar utterances corroborate Jeffreys' 'rhetorical talents' whilst also illustrating his 'predilection for attempting to impress the audience, … by means of verbal cruelty'. Although more explicitly face-threatening than we are used to in a modern courtroom context, the 'intimidation' strategy was effective: Dunne did 'not react in any way to the insults levied at him' or adopt a defensive counter-strategy. Instead, he 'admit[ted] to events and knowledge that he had previously denied' (Jucker and Taavitsainen 2000: 89). Lisle (who firmly adhered to her testimony throughout the trial) was found guilty, and beheaded.

Stephen (1991: 302) is even more scathing of Jeffreys than Kryk-Kastovsky (2006): he describes Jeffreys as 'a kind of demoniacal baboon placed on the Bench in robes and wig, in hideous caricature of justice'. Yet, Jeffreys exhibited a 'controlling' strategy that was not necessarily 'judicially brutal' nor 'manifestly unfair' (cf. Simpson 1984: 275) when acting as Recorder in the *Trial of John Giles 1680*. Like many of his con-temporaries, Jeffreys often resorted to wh-questions when questioning witnesses (see Archer 2005: 185). Although wh-questions (particularly *what*-interrogatives) are regarded as one of the least controlling of question-types in the contemporary courtroom (see, e.g. Woodbury 1984), Jeffreys' wh-questions mostly requested only that information which he deemed to be appropriate to the case. For example, he utilised a string of wh-questions (ten in total) to establish an itinerary of the witness's and Giles's where-abouts/actions on the evening of the alleged attempted murder of the victim, John Arnold. All were restrictive (e.g. 'what time was that?'; 'where did you go at that time?'; 'what did you spend there?'; 'whether did you go from thence?'; 'how long did you stay in *Drury-lane*?'; 'where after that?'; 'who did you meet with all between X and Y … ?'; 'What did you drink there?'; 'How long did you stay there?'; 'What time of Night was it that you went from thence?'). Such a strategy – carefully framing questions so that they appear open-ended but, in reality, allow a tight control over testimony – is similar to that advocated by Koskoff (1983: 11) during the direct examination of witnesses today, so as to 'influence the answers' without falling foul 'of the rule against leading' (cited in Tiersma 2000: 175).

The *Trial of John Giles 1680* also provides us with an example of defence witnesses 'challenging' each other's recall (Archer 2005: 251–52): Elizabeth Crook (a chamber-maid) initially disputed that William Richmond (friend to the defendant) came into his room when she was making his bed but ultimately confirmed that he had. Crook was then asked (by Jeffreys) to state 'What Time of night' it was. She stated 'about Ten a clock'. As the time differed from that given by Richmond, the King's Counsel inter-vened with a comment that implied she and Richmond were engaged in activities that led to their losing track of time:

Kings Coun.	Time passed merrily away with you then.
Rich.	It was Twelve a Clock.
Crook	Why do you say so? Our house was all quiet presently after Eleven.
Rich.	Why will you say so? Were not we Singing and Roaring together?
Record.	Come don't be angry, you were not angry when you were making love together?

The defence witnesses sought to continue to debate the 'time' with one another rather than attend to the face-threatening implicature. However, a seemingly bemused Jeffreys was not as sensitive to their face-needs: he subtly manipulated the implicature so that it became a structural presupposition – that Crook and Richmond had made love. And the structural presupposition, in turn, became a means by which Jeffreys could offer the witnesses some 'advice'.

Viewing witness evidence with bemusement was atypical. Indeed, contemporaries like Henry Fielding tended to be suspicious of evidence given by defence witnesses, in particular: in his *Increase of Robbers*, Fielding (1751: 116) went as far as to claim defendants usually 'procured' their alibis via their 'Newgate Friendship[s]'. Fortunately, some within the legal establishment looked on the defendants' plight more sympathetically. For example, Sir Robert Atkyns (1689) stated that it was:

> a severity in our Law, that a Prisoner for his Life is not allowed the assistance of a grave and prudent Lawyer, or some other friend, to make his defence for him … to matter of fact, as well as to Law.

Atkins also shared Sir John Hawles' (1689: 22–23) view that judges inevitably supported the interests of 'their better client, the king' in treason trials. As noted earlier, the Treason Act (1696) largely came about because of the continued misuse of treason charges by those in power. As we will see in the next section, once introduced, the Act transformed treason trials. However, advocacy practices within ordinary criminal trials changed more slowly.

The English courtroom of the eighteenth century

The first defendant to make use of defence counsel immediately following the implementation of the Treason Act was Charles Cranburne. Although Cranburne was ultimately found guilty at his 1696 treason trial, defence counsel (Shower and Phipps) are said to have set a precedent during the trial that 'was to be followed by other members of the bar' (Hostettler 2006: 36). Indeed, we see a very similar strategy – pointing out 'defects in the Indictment', engaging in 'lengthy legal arguments with the Attorney-General', cross-examining 'prosecution witnesses throughout the trial, questioning the credibility of witnesses and, on occasion, arguing with the judges' (Hostettler 2006: 35) – adopted by Ward and Hungerford in the 1716 trial of Francis Francia. And, on this occasion, the defendant was found not guilty, and discharged. Ward and Hungerford's construction of a counter-crime-narrative that corresponded to the facts as they wanted the jury to perceive them – that is, from Francia's perspective – seems particularly modern (see, e.g. Hale and Gibbons 1999). One aspect of this counter-crime-narrative was achieved via the questioning of two witnesses – the then Secretary of State, Lord Townshend, and his employee, Buckley: Ward initially questioned Buckley – but his question 'suggested' that Francia was not permitted to read through his examination prior to signing it. Buckley's response was to state that he didn't 'remember' the defendant desiring to read it (see Archer 2005: 254–56, for a detailed discussion of this interaction). Later in the trial, Ward questioned Townshend.

Mr. Ward.	I desire to ask your Lordship whether you heard that Declaration read over to him?
Ld. Townshend.	I dare say I did.
Mr. Ward.	Did he not endeavour to excuse himself from signing it, till he had read it himself?
Ld. Townshend.	I don't remember that, I don't know that he made any Difficulty of signing it; but I am sure it could not be because he was refus'd to read it.

Townshend appeared to recognise the implication behind Ward's questioning strategy – the idea that Francia 'was refused to read' his examination – for he immediately refuted the allegation ('I am sure it could not be because he was refus'd to read it').

Francia then addressed some questions to Townshend:

Prisoner.	Was not there any Reluctancy in me to sign it?
Ld. Townshend.	What do you mean? Have not I answer'd that already?
Prisoner.	Did not you offer me some Money to sign it?
Ld. Townshend.	I hope you can't say such a thing of so much Infamy [...]

In spite of the conductivity of his questions – and his 'right' to ask questions of witnesses – Francia obviously lacked the necessary power to achieve his goal: rather than entering into a verbal duel with Francia, Townshend intimated that Francia's accusation (that he had attempted to bribe him) was too scandalous to be taken seriously. He then addressed a 177-word utterance to the whole court – in which he signalled that Francia was the sort who 'begg'd so hard' that *good people* like Townshend felt compelled to give him 'Charity'. In response, Francia framed Townshend as someone who was not generous, but, rather, had ulterior motives for giving Francia the money, by asking (what amounted to) a rhetorical question: 'I desire to know who he ever gave five Guneas to besides me?' His comment prompted one of the judges to 'answer' for Townshend: 'My Lord says it was out of Charity ... he says, he never could refuse his Charity to People that begg'd as you did'. At this point, Hungerford (the second defence lawyer) intervened:

Mr. Hungerford.	I would propose to the Judgment of the Court, whether it is proper to give Evidence of the Substance of a Letter without offering the Letter it self.
Mr. Just. Pratt.	This comes in Answer to Mr. Ward's Question. He ask'd my Ld. Townshend, whether there was not some Promise that this Confession should not be made use of against the Prisoner? His Lordship gives this Account, and justifies himself, how he came to make use of it, and gives this as the Reason.
Mr. Hungerford.	But to give an Account of the Substance of a Letter without producing it, I apprehend, is not according to the Rules of Evidence.

Note that, although Townshend was permitted to address the jury directly, the defence counsel's role was such at this time that his 'interaction' with the jury had to go through the judges. Note, also, that Hungerford waited until Townshend had finished speaking

193

before asking 'the Court whether it [was] proper to give Evidence of the Substance of a Letter without offering the Letter' itself. By asking the question, he effectively implied his own belief (Townshend should not have been permitted to recount anything that had not been previously submitted as evidence). However, a judge once again came to Lord Townshend's aid (for a more detailed discussion, see Archer 2005: 257–59).

Another important component of the defence counsel's strategy was to suggest that Francia was not native to England and, as such, could not be tried for treason. However, Hungerford only managed to elicit one response from the witness, Simon Francia, before the Attorney General intervened:

Mr. Hungerford.	Pray give an Account what you know of the Prisoner, what Country Man he is, and where he was born?
Simon Francia.	He is my Brother, he was born in France at Bourdeaux.
Mr. Att. Gen.	Are you Elder or Younger than he?
Simon Francia.	I am Four Years Elder.
Mr. Att. Gen.	How then can you remember what was done when you was Four Years Old.
Simon Francia.	I can't remember the Day of his Birth, but I was bred up with him at Bourdeaux, we were all born in the same House.

The interruption is extremely significant, of course: the Attorney General was trying to pre-empt the defence counsel's attempt to have Francia acquitted. His (counter-)strategy was to question the accuracy of Simon Francia's recall, given his tender age, using a disjunctive interrogative that asked Francia to state which brother was the eldest, and a wh-interrogative that specifically asked *how* Francia was able to remember. Refuting an argument/appeal before it is even presented is also seen as an effective way of 'inoculating' the audience in today's courts (Lloyd-Bostock 1988: 46, cited in Archer 2005: 162).

The *Trial of Francia 1716* captures the fact that treason trials quickly became direct disputes between defence and prosecution counsel following the implementation of the Treason Act (1696). Yet, it also suggests

(i) examination-in-chief and cross-examination procedures were not as strictly defined at the beginning of the eighteenth century as they are today (see, e.g. the Attorney General's intervention at the beginning of Hungerford's questioning of a friendly witness), and

(ii) defendants and judges were still actively involved in courtroom procedure to some extent.

The emergence of 'advocacy' in criminal trials

Legislation allowing defence counsel in felony cases was not immediately forthcoming following the implementation of the Treason Act, but Old Bailey records indicate judges were beginning to allow defence counsel 'as a favour' (as opposed to a right) from the 1720s (Beattie 1986, 1991; Landsman 1990: 607). As one lawyer lamented in 1751, the involvement of counsel would differ from one trial to the next: a defendant could be 'directed' to 'put his [or her] own questions', for example, or be allowed counsel 'to examine and cross-examine witnesses' on his/her behalf. Alternatively, some counsel were told to 'propose their questions to the Court' as opposed to asking them directly (*State Trials*, Vol. 17: 1022). Even so, the eighteenth-century courtroom witnessed an important move away from the defendant having to prove his innocence and move towards the defence counsel 'probing and seeking to expose the weaknesses of the prosecution case' on their behalf (Hostettler 2006: 40). Put simply, defence (and prosecution) lawyers were increasingly taking centre-stage (especially towards the end of the century) and, by so doing, affecting (the activities of) the other participants. For example, Hostettler (2006: 40–41) cites a defendant who was silenced by his own counsel, William Garrow, after he tried to interrupt him at his 1784 trial so that he might 'put another question' to the alleged victim. The view that defendants should not interrupt/intervene in (defence counsels') arguments is in stark contrast to that exhibited by defence counsel in the *Trial of Francis Francia 1716*. But what appeared to matter some seventy years later was the pursuit of 'professional advocacy' (Cairns 1998: 3).

The 'aggressive' style of William Garrow

In the main, eighteenth-century defence lawyers were careful to attend to any possible challenge implications of the questions they asked of the judges, but tended to be more 'aggressive' when questioning witnesses. Garrow's cross-examination of witnesses was particularly effective, according to Hostettler (2006: 41), for he would use cross-examination as a means of 'comment[ing] on the evidence, refut[ing] or discredit[ing] the prosecution case and aggressively battl[ing] for the accused'. As the latter intimates, Garrow is best known for his work as a defence lawyer: he acted as defence counsel in three-quarters of the 961 cases he undertook at the Old Bailey, according to the *Old Bailey Proceedings Online*. However, in the *Trial of John Elliot 1787*, he acted as prosecuting barrister. His well-documented ability to unnerve witnesses remains evident, nevertheless: one witness questioned by Garrow (over the defendant's apparent 'insanity') complained that he felt 'bullied', adding 'witnesses should be examined with candour, and not put out of temper, and out of their senses, so as not to be able to understand what they say'. In another trial, that of George Stevens and James Day in 1786, Garrow attacked the credibility of a witness (Elizabeth Mason) by repeatedly asking her whether she 'had always told the same story' (Mason had turned King's evidence after being held in custody for several days). It would seem, then, that, during cross-examination, witnesses began to face what defendants had been facing for some time: 'they had to thwart an opposing argument, justify their evidence and, in some cases, defend their character' (Archer 2005: 257). Garrow's behaviour at the *Trial of John Taylor 1800* is also worthy of brief comment, here, for Garrow apparently:

> challenged every witness, prevented prosecution witnesses from answering key questions by introducing points of law, and arrogantly told the court that 'where the law of England does bear me out, I am not afraid of giving offence to any judge'. He also argued that defence counsel's right to cross-examine opened up an opportunity to address the court on all matters. 'I had a right if I could', he maintained, 'indirectly to convey observations to the fact; and whatever other people may say, I shall certainly take the liberty of doing it; for what the law of England will not permit me to do directly, I will do indirectly, where I can.

(Hostettler 2006: 45–46)

Hostettler (2006: 46) believes Garrow provides us with 'a clear example of how far counsel had gone in dominating the courtroom' by the end of the eighteenth century. Hostettler also credits Garrow with 'playing a prominent part in securing rules of evidence for criminal trials' Hostettler (2006: 73). However, the growth of evidential rules was also due to Erskine and other legal contemporaries: together, they helped bring into being the 'best evidence' rule, the rule against hearsay evidence, the inadmissibility of previous convictions, the character rule and the corroboration and confession rules (see Hostettler 2006: 117). Their increasing activity in the courtroom also influenced the roles of the other courtroom participants, such that judges and juries tended to adopt adjudicative roles from the mid-eighteenth century onwards, and defendants became increasingly passive. As we have seen, they also affected the witnesses (especially witnesses for the prosecution), forcing them to become much more defensive (Archer 2005). Yet, the adversarial system as we know it today did not fully come into being until the nineteenth century, after the Prisoners' Counsel Act (1836) removed 'the felony counsel restriction' thus allowing defence counsels to make opening speeches (Cairns 1998: 4; Langbein 2003: 93).

Advocacy post-1836

This final section outlines the advocacy of Cockburn (Attorney-General) and (to a lesser extent) Sargeant Shee (defence counsel) at the *Trial of Palmer 1856*. Fitzjames Stephen, a leading nineteenth-century writer on the criminal law, attended the Palmer trial and described it as exhibiting 'the good side of English Criminal procedure' (1890: 269; see also Cairns' (1998: 163) comment that *Palmer* marks the 'com[ing] of age' of '[t]he adversarial criminal trial').

Stephen was particularly impressed by Cockburn's ability to present 'the jury with a picture of Palmer's guilt in his opening which he [and his team] maintained and reinforced throughout the trial' (Cairns 1998: 163, 176–77). Archer (2006b) has documented the 'key' themes of Cockburn's opening speech and the extent to which those 'key' themes are evident in/appear to have shaped subsequent lawyer–witness interactions, and thus the prosecution's crime narrative (Archer forthcoming: cf. Harris 2001; see also Heffer, this volume), using key word analysis (i.e. the identification of statistically-frequent words/phrases). Archer's (2006b) findings suggest Cockburn's opening speech was similar to the kinds of 'criminal occurrence narrative' (Gergen 1999: 69) commonly utilised by prosecution counsels today: as well as frequently drawing the jury's attention to the victim, *Cook*, and how he suffered before he died, Cockburn was specific about

(i)   the times/places in which the alleged poisoning took place (*Talbot Arms*),
(ii) the people who were involved in the crime itself (i.e. *Palmer*),
(iii) the people whose activities triggered the alleged crime (i.e. *Cheshire*), and
(iv) the people who treated/cared for Cook (i.e. *women, chambermaid, Newton* and *Bamford*) (cf. Snedaker 1991: 134).

Criminal occurrence narratives tend to be interpretative as well as informative. The interpretive element of Cockburn's opening speech was most obvious at the point he established a motive for Palmer's 'actions': statistically-frequent words such as *liabilities, money, bills, forged, betted, debt* and *turf* allowed Cockburn to propose Palmer had initially forged his mother's name to secure a gambling income. However, when that source of funding dried up, and his debts began to mount, he resorted to murder (Archer 2006b). Predictably, the theme of gambling is more evident in the prosecution counsel's interaction with friendly witnesses than it is with non-friendly witnesses (i.e. when the prosecution is constructing/consolidating as opposed to defending their interpretation of events). For example, Cook's *betting book* is mentioned by five friendly witnesses as well as prosecuting counsel: Ishmael Fisher (wine merchant); Elizabeth Mills (chambermaid at the Talbot Arms, where Cook died); Lavinia Barnes (maid); William Henry Jones (surgeon); and William Vernon Stevens (step-father of Cook and executor of Cook's will). Even though witnesses' discussions of the *betting book* were not always occasioned by directly related questions, prosecuting counsel utilised the testimony they gave to establish Cook's *betting book* had been 'in his hand at Shrewsbury' 'on that Thursday' (the day his horse won, 'bringing its owner a considerable sum in prizes and bets' (Cairns 1998: 155)) and 'in his [rented] room on the Monday night before his death'. The five witnesses also confirmed the book/prize money could not be found following Cook's death. Mills and Jones further stated/confirmed they had seen Palmer with Cook's coat 'in his hands' after his death, and Stevens reported a conversation he had had with Palmer on discovering the *betting book* was missing:

William Vernon Stevens	Palmer said, "Oh, it is no [...] use if you find it," [...] I said, "No use, sir! I am the best judge of that [...] I am told it is of use; I understand my son won a great deal of money at Shrewsbury," I am giving the words as nearly as I can, [...] Palmer said, "It is no use, I assure you; when a man dies his bets are done with; [...] besides [...] Cook received the greater part of his money on the course at Shrewsbury" — I said, "Very well, sir, the book must be found [...]" Palmer then, in a much quieter tone, said, "Oh, it will be found, no doubt" [...] calling to the housekeeper [...], I desired that everything in the deceased's room might be locked up, that nothing might be touched [...]

This 'dramatic' re-enactment alluded to Palmer's involvement (cf. Coupland *et al.* 1991: 219) – something that was 'confirmed' when the prosecution later demonstrated 'Palmer had collected the bets and applied the proceeds to his own purposes' (Cairns 1998: 155: see Archer forthcoming for a detailed account).

In today's judicial system, defence counsels can only address the jury once – and most opt to make a closing speech. This was not an issue at the time of Palmer's trial, as defence counsels could not give closing speeches until 1865 (see the Criminal Procedure Act). The Prisoners' Counsel Act did allow defence counsels to give opening speeches, of course. As we might expect, Shee sought to ridicule the idea that Palmer had poisoned Cook for his money in his opening speech for the defence. He also argued that the papers/ correspondence (which had been introduced to 'prove' Palmer's debt) actually proved Palmer's 'innocence', and intimated at additional *letters* that revealed (i) how Palmer had helped Cook, who had helped him in return, and (ii) doctors had admitted to not 'find[ing] strychnia, prussic acid, or any trace of opium' in Cook's remains – thereby alluding to the prosecution counsel's reliance on circumstantial evidence (for a more detailed discussion,

197

see Archer 2006b). Shee's opening speech is best known for one thing, however: his declaration 'that there never was a truer word pronounced than the words which he [Palmer] pronounced when he said "Not guilty" to the charge'. Shee's comment was controversial, even at the time: he was seen to have 'press[ed] … his opinion' rather than 'his argument upon the jury' (Lord Chief Justice's summing up), and challenged 'the division of responsibility between the judge, witnesses and counsel' (Cairns 1998: 155; Watson 1952: 297–98). The Palmer trial therefore demonstrates another important feature of nineteenth-century advocacy: lawyers were seeking to establish the limits of forensic argument by challenging those limits. In so doing, they played a crucial role in the development of the law of criminal evidence, and gave today's (English) criminal system its adversarial shape.

Further reading

The (social/legal) historians Beattie (1986), Cairns (1998), Hostettler (2006) and Langbein (2003) each provide very readable accounts of the development of the English courtroom over time. Mulholland *et al.* (2003), in contrast, detail the development of the English judicial system (between the thirteenth and seventeenth centuries) against the backdrop of the legal systems of European countries.

For (linguistic) accounts of: (i) specific trials, (ii) the development of the historical courtroom, and/or (iii) linguistic features pertaining to the historical courtroom, see Archer (2005), Kryk-Kastovsky (2009) and readings within the 2006 special edition of the *Journal of Historical Pragmatics* edited by Kryk-Kastovsky (in particular, pages 163–263). Those interested in the development of legal English more generally should consult Mellinkoff (1963) and Tiersma (2000). In addition, there are a number of works that have explored the Polish and Russian legal systems – and their diachronic development – from a linguistic perspective (see, e.g. Collins 2001, 2007; Kwarciński 2006) or investigated the linguistic features of the Salem Witchcraft Trials (see, e.g. Archer 2002; Doty and Hiltunen 2002, 2009; Doty 2007; Hiltunen 1996, 2004).

14

Narrative in the trial

Constructing crime stories in court

Chris Heffer

Introduction

Any case brought to court presents a story of wrongdoing (Tiersma 1999). Witnesses expect to tell stories (Conley and O'Barr 1990), lawyers and jurors transform evidence into stories (Pennington and Hastie 1986, 1991), and even judges deliberate with the help of stories (Wagenaar *et al.* 1993). Yet the law as an institution has historically considered the adjudication process as a matter of rigorously testing hypotheses rather than comparing stories and so has introduced numerous anti-narrative checks to trial procedure (Keane 1996). The result is a fascinating tension between narrative and anti-narrative forces that is both played out in the hybrid discourse genres of the trial (Heffer 2005) and is fundamental to the interface between language and law more generally (Brooks and Gewirtz 1996).

Stories are constructed, and have been studied, in a wide variety of different courtroom contexts: in small claims courts (Conley and O'Barr 1990); in plea-bargaining (Maynard 1984); in magistrates' courts (Harris 1984); in traffic courts (Cody and McLaughlin 1988); in Islamic courts (Hirsch 1998); and in historical contexts (Archer 2005 and this volume). This chapter, though, will focus on the most widely studied context, and the one where the tensions between narrative and anti-narrative forces are perhaps at their greatest: contemporary common-law criminal trials before a judge and jury.

I begin with an overview of the relevance of narrative to the trial process in general. I then work in semi-narrative fashion through the linear sequence of trial genres (jury selection → preliminary instruction → opening statements → witness examination → closing arguments → summing-up → deliberation and verdict → sentencing) to show how narrative in a variety of forms manages to emerge in the trial despite the evident institutional anti-narrativity.

Narrative and the trial process

Narrative may be considered more central or more peripheral to the trial process according to one's definition of narrative and one's theory of the trial. A narrow, clause-based definition of narrative (Labov and Waletzky 1967) combined with a truth-testing view of the lawyer's task (Wigmore 1913) and a mathematical model of juror decision-making (Hastie 1993) will lead to the impression that narrative is almost irrelevant to jury trial. On the other hand, a broad approach to narrative based on participants' situated understanding of when 'stories' are involved (Georgakopoulou 2006) combined with a 'storied' view of the lawyer's task (Brooks 1996) and a 'story model' of juror decision-making (Pennington and Hastie 1991) might lead to the impression that the trial is solely about narrative.

While the exceptionally a-chronological and non-linear nature of the trial make it difficult to sustain the claim that it is in the form of a story (Cotterill 2003: 23–25; Gibbons 2003: 157–59), the trial can legitimately be seen as the construction of a story or stories from at least two perspectives. Firstly, the most widely supported and empirically tested theory of jury decision-making, the 'story model' (Hastie *et al.* 1983; Pennington and Hastie 1991), holds that jurors decide cases by constructing their own stories from the evidence and then considering the fit between these stories and the legal charges. Jackson (1988: 65–88) rightly notes that juries will also construct partial stories of the trial they have experienced ('trial stories'), which can affect the plausibility of the putative crime stories. Secondly, prosecutors – though not always defence lawyers (Dershowitz 1996) – see themselves as constructing a story for the jury. In their opening speeches, they often make metadiscursive comment on the tale they are going to tell through their evidence e.g. 'Let's *tell* a different *story*' (Harris 2005: 220). And when they lose a case, they are likely to attribute it to the juries not 'buying' their story: 'I had no idea what was going to be the *hole in the story* that hung him' (Engel 2000: 55).

Given that occurrences of narrative discourse in the trial, as we shall see, are very restricted, the crime story must be conveyed through non-narrative as well as narrative modes of discourse. It is useful to make an operational distinction, then, between the 'crime story', the cognitive template or skeleton structure conceived by lawyer, witness, judge or jury, and instances of narrative discourse in which that story is narrated. Forensic evidence, for example, usually provides support for the crime story but is very rarely conveyed through narrative discourse. The distinction being made here is different from the one made in literary narratology between 'story' and 'discourse' (Chatman 1978), where 'story' is a presumed (and debatable) 'deep structure' in the narrative text (Smith 1980). The crime story is pieced together during the investigatory stages of a case and is not linked to any one telling.

In order to account for the fact that trials intimately involve stories but narrative discourse is comparatively rare, Heffer (2002, 2005) and Harris (2001, 2005) have both turned to Bruner's (1986, 1990, 1996) conception of narrative as a mode of thought. Reasoning in the narrative mode means striving to understand the actions and intentions of humans situated in place and time, while reasoning in the 'paradigmatic' or logico-scientific mode means striving for context-independent logical and scientific descriptions and explanations. The narrative mode is a search for verisimilitude, the paradigmatic mode a search for veracity or verification. While the narrative mode of thought is prototypically realised in narrative discourse and the paradigmatic mode in scientific argument, they can become strategic input to any form of discourse, thus creating the 'hybrid' forms of discourse (neither clearly narrative nor non-narrative) that can be found in the trial.

One way of gaining a very broad initial understanding of the institutional and strategic complexity of 'forensic narrative' (Heffer 2010) in jury trial – its 'fragmentation and contending multiplicities' and its 'special rules of narrative form and shaping' (Gewirtz 1996a: 8) – is to see the trial process as a sequence of genres, each focused primarily on

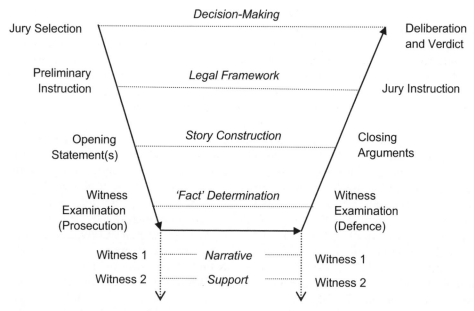

Figure 14.1 A model of jury trial as complex genre (adapted from Heffer 2005: 71)

different evidential goals (Maley and Fahey 1991; Gibbons 2003; Cotterill 2003). Although the genre sequence in a trial is linear, the evidential goals are hierarchical: the 'facts' of the case need to be determined; these are woven into crime stories; the stories are filtered through the legal framework provided by the charges and rules of evidence; and all this takes place within the context of the jury's decision-making process (Heffer 2005: 70–72). In most jurisdictions, the trial genres seem to be paired up in terms of their evidential focus (jury selection with deliberation, preliminary instruction with final jury instruction, opening statements with closing arguments). This creates a neat two-part trial structure indicated in Figure 14.1.[1]

As the trial progresses, the focus moves from the 'higher' goal of decision-making to the 'lower' goal of fact determination and then moves back up to decision-making. However, the discursive work performed in early genres will necessarily influence later ones. For example, both the legal framework and the story constructions will influence the type of facts that counsel will focus on in witness testimony. Similarly, the closing speeches will weave together the facts determined in the evidential phase into convincing narratives but they will also anticipate the legal charge or summing-up by fitting these stories into a clear legal framework.

The following sections attempt to explore how narrative emerges, is implicated in and takes on various distinctive forms through the course of the trial.

Jury selection and narrative scripts

All narratives must have one or more narrators to tell the story and one or more narratees to listen. The primary narrators of the crime story are the lawyers representing the prosecution; the primary narratees are the jurors who will decide the facts of the case. In jurisdictions such as England and Wales where no information about prospective jurors may be obtained and where there are no rights to challenge jurors without cause, lawyers are only able to guess from appearance and body language the narrative inclinations of the audience before them. In many jurisdictions, though, lawyers are allowed to actively de-select jurors via questionnaires and interrogation, or *voir dire* ('to speak the truth'). In this case, lawyers are able to some extent both to pick an audience favourable to their story and to design their narrative presentation to suit that particular audience (Giles and Powesland 1975a; Bell 1984; Cotterill 2003).

One of the main objects of active jury selection, for which specialist 'jury consultants' are employed on many US cases, is to select jurors most likely to share the narrative scripts closest to the party's crime story. Narrative scripts – variously known in the psychological and forensic literature as 'scripts' (Schank and Abelson 1977; Stygall 1994), 'story' or 'narrative schemas' (Mandler 1984; Heffer 2005), 'plots' (Johnstone 2002: 161–63), 'master narratives' (Bamberg 2004; Coulthard and Johnson 2007) and 'narrative typifications' (Jackson 1995; Cotterill 2003) – are cognitive scaffolds for typical narrative action. These scripts are not universal but tend to vary across communities of practice (Lave and Wenger 1991). Scripts of police misconduct and bigotry, for example, are more likely to be held by African-Americans than White Americans (Gates 1995; Hastie and Pennington 1996: 972–73).

In the extreme case of the OJ Simpson criminal trial, which involved almost 1,000 potential jurors and six weeks of *voir dire* interrogation, Cotterill (2003: 17) notes that many of the 293 jointly constructed questions on the jury questionnaire clearly tried to gauge reaction to the parties' proposed storylines. For example, jurors were asked to react to the statement that professional athletes tend to be more aggressive towards women, which linked with the prosecution's story of the testosterone-charged, misogynistic celebrity footballer. They were also asked the following question (with tick-box levels of seriousness): 'How big a problem do you think racial discrimination against African-Americans is in Southern California?'

This was directly linked to the defence story of OJ Simpson being racially targeted by the police, which evokes the narrative script of police bigotry favoured by African-Americans. Since responses to this question were clearly divided on racial lines, when the defence succeeded in empanelling eight out of twelve jurors of African-American origin, Cotterill (2003: 13) notes that they effectively managed to 'design the audience' in their favour as well as being subsequently able to design their story for that audience.

Preliminary instruction and the law of narrative

After being empanelled, the jury receive some form of preliminary instruction on the law. This can range across jurisdictions from, minimally and far from helpfully, the reading of the formal indictment (as in England and Wales) to detailed instructions on the law applying to the case. Preliminary instructions set down in one form or another the 'law of narrative' regulating whether and how stories may be told at trial (Gewirtz 1996b: 136).

The indictment itself sets the confines of forensic narrative in the space delineated by the charges.

On count 1 the defendant stands charged with theft, contrary to section 1, subsection (1) of the Theft Act 1968. The particulars of offence are that the defendant on a day between the 15th day of January 1995 and the 13th day of May 1997 stole cash to the value of £8.58 belonging to a person or persons unknown.

(Author's data)

Far from being a narrative, this is a 'normative syllogism' in which the major premise is the legal rule, the minor premise the crime events and the conclusion is to be determined by the jury (Jackson 1988: 37–45). The legal rule is not actually stated but is referred to intertextually ('section 1, subsection (1) of the Theft Act 1968'), while the crime event ('stole cash') is not narrated but stated as one of the 'particulars of offence'.

The rules of evidence more generally filter out potential narrative elements which are either not considered relevant to the 'facts in issue' (those relating to the legal definition of the offence) or are considered to compromise the fairness of the decision-making process. The exclusion can occur at all levels: from the silencing of entire crime stories because they are not legislated against (as was the case until recently with marital rape stories); through the ruling by the judge that a certain piece of evidence (e.g. an expert report corroborating an element in the crime story) is inadmissible; to the retraction of a witness's answer following an objection that it introduces hearsay.

One form of narrative exclusion is the presumption that jurors come to court as legal blank slates (Lieberman and Sales 1997). Yet lay people have narrative scripts for crime categories and these often do not match those of the law (Smith 1991, 1993). For example, the lay script for kidnap involves a ransom, which is not an ingredient of the legal offence. Smith (1993) notes that such 'lay representations' can be counteracted directly in legal instruction by pointing directly to the mismatching elements between lay and legal conceptions of crime.

Opening statements and the narrative point

The Opening Statement, at least in the US, is the trial lawyer's main opportunity to present their overall story of the crime to the jury. That story, as manifested in the opening statement, has been described variously in the literature as a 'kernel' (Snedaker 1991), 'macro-narrative' (Cotterill 2003), 'master narrative' (Heffer 2005) or 'core narrative' (Gibbons 2003) which, respectively, the 'satellite', 'micro', 'witness' or 'sub' narratives of the witness examination phase then 'fill out, elaborate, and extend' (Snedaker 1991: 134). Harris (2005: 220) describes the opening statement as 'the clearest instance of the narrative mode in a trial'. However, this is narrative strictly at the service of argumentative ends. According to US law, the opening statement is not meant to contain argument (Garner 1999b: 1118), but narrative is a subtle form of argument which slips through the paradigmatic net of the law.

Several researchers (e.g. Harris 2001, 2005; Heffer 2005: 75–77) have noted that the structure of the master narrative text embedded into the opening statement often takes the same form as the central elements of Labov's personal experience narratives (PEN):

Orientation:	who?, when?, what? where?
Complicating Action:	then what happened?
Evaluation:	so what?
Resolution:	what finally happened?

(Labov and Waletzky 1967; Labov 1972, 1997)

203

Harris alters the framework in a number of ways to account for some of the specific features of forensic narrative:

Orientation	as in Labov
Core Narrative	Labov's "Complicating Action", but including acts of saying
Elaboration	a distinctive forensic element providing further details, clarification and explication of the core narrative
Point	Labov's "Evaluation", but specifically related to overall trial aims.

(Harris 2001)

In Labov's model, evaluation occurs both as a structural–functional element that is external to the narrative clauses and interrupts the narrative action to comment on its significance (*E*valuation) and as an ongoing form of appraisal woven into the core narrative clauses and conveyed through a variety of lexical, phonological, grammatical and discoursal means (*e*valuation). Structural evaluation in courtroom narratives makes an explicit evidential Point about the guilt or innocence of the defendant (Harris 2001). Ongoing clause-internal evaluation, on the other hand, functions in a more holistic fashion, gradually building up a certain impression of guilt or innocence (Heffer 2005: 77).

Given the argumentative aim of the opening statement, the Point often frames the Orientation and Core Narrative (Harris 2005), as in the following extract from the prosecution opening of the Marv Albert sexual assault case tried in Virginia in 1997. Ongoing evaluation (including that in non-narrative clauses) is indicated in *italics*; minor Points are in [square brackets]:

Point	May it please the Court, counsel, ladies and gentlemen. On February 12th, *a coarse and crude abuse* of a human being *took place. It took place* at the hands of that man. And *it took place* and was accomplished by his physical *domination* of a 41-year old woman, *a woman who had been his friend; a woman who had been his lover; a woman who* he knew for ten years; *a woman who* had cared for him. *But* it was *a woman whose human dignity* he chose to ignore on this night in his *egocentric quest for sexual gratification.*
Orientation	... At that time, Ms. Perhach was living in Florida, in Miami. She was undergoing the stress and beginnings of the break-up of a marriage. She had two children. And she began to try to get herself back on her feet by seeking employment ...
Core Narrative	... He called her again that day, about 1.30, this time on her cell phone *as she's shopping, again trying to make arrangements for when are we going to meet, got somebody to take the tickets, and, oh, by the way, do you have somebody for the threesome?* ... [H]e grabs her and he throws her on the bed and he jumps on her back. [She is shocked.] He then begins to bite her back. [The first bite is a complete shock.] But *as she realizes what is going on, she says, stop, it hurts.* But he *did not stop.* He *continued* to bite her on the back in a *painful* way. [In fact, he mocked her.] He said, *aw, come on, you know you like this.* ...

Point
It was a crude use of a human being. And the evidence will show that it was done by this man for one purpose. He wanted a scenario that night. And *the dignity of the human being that was with him did not matter.* She was his *property*, and that's a crime.

(Adapted from Harris 2005: 221–23. My analysis.)

In addition to the explicit indications of the probative Point at the beginning and end of the statement ('crude abuse of a human being' points to the technical charge of sodomy), we have other minor Points indicating the complainant's lack of consent ('The first bite was a complete shock') and the defendant's recklessness with regard to her lack of consent ('In fact, he mocked her'). The statement is also replete with Labovian categories of ongoing clause-internal evaluation: intensifying repetition ('a woman who' … 'a woman who'); negative comparators ('he did not stop'); correlatives ('coarse and crude abuse') and explicatives ('again trying to make arrangements … for the threesome'). The switch to the conversational historic present (CHP) at dramatic moments ('He grabs her and he throws her … ') is also, as noted by Schiffrin (1981: 45), an internal evaluation device since it enables the listener to relive the drama as if it were present. So is the sudden switch to direct speech ('make arrangements for when are we going to meet … '). As Harris (2005: 222) notes, the prosecutor makes extensive use of 'those very resources of belief, opinion, intent and subjective evaluation which the rules of evidence prohibit'. It is all these evaluation devices that transform a referential account into an 'evaluated point-laden narrative' (Toolan 2001: 238).

The impression of guilt or innocence built up gradually through ongoing clause-internal evaluation is strengthened through the strategic choice of words. Danet (1980a) found in an illegal abortion case that the prosecution tended to use words such as 'baby' and 'child', emphasising the potential future life, while the defence used detached medical terms such as 'fetus' and 'embryo'. Cotterill (2003: 68–83) shows how the apparently neutral words 'encounter' and 'control', used by prosecutors in the opening statements of the OJ Simpson criminal trial, take on negative semantic associations, or 'semantic prosodies' (Louw 1993), through frequent collocation with negative words such as 'prejudice' and 'problems'. In the Marv Albert opening, the prosecutor appears to be using 'human' and 'human being' in a similarly non-neutral way, perhaps to draw on the double meaning of 'sodomy' as both 'buggery' and 'bestiality'. In all of these ways, then, opening statement narratives may construct a cognitive filter through which jurors will then view the subsequent evidence (Moore 1989).

Witness examination and story construction

Institutionally, the evidential phase of the trial is concerned with the determination, or verification, of the facts, which explains its thesis–antithesis structure:

Prosecution Case → Defence Case

Examination (by friendly counsel) → Cross-examination (by opposing counsel)

Despite the dialectic institutional structure, though, lawyers control the emergence of the crime story during the evidential phase in two ways: by selecting and sequencing their witnesses and by guiding those witnesses through their main examination (called 'direct examination' in the US and 'examination-in-chief' in British and Commonwealth countries).

In most everyday trials, lawyers have little choice in the selection of witnesses but more choice in the sequencing of those witnesses. Advocacy manuals, which should be taken as rough guides to what the profession considers to be good practice, rather than surrogates for empirical observation, recommend following the chronological order of events 'unless other reasons prevail' (Stone 1995: 90). But other reasons, such as the availability of expert witnesses, usually do prevail. While there is some evidence that lawyers in England do make an effort to follow a chronological or at least 'narrative + support' structure, as indicated in Figure 14.1 (Heffer 2005: 80), in the US context both Stygall (1994: 123) and Cotterill (2003: 40) claim that the actual sequence of events is simply ignored. (Clearly, it does not help when a trial involves over 120 witnesses testifying over nine months, as was the case with OJ Simpson.)

Turning to individual witness examinations, at first sight there appears to be very little in the way of narrative discourse. Stygall (1994: 118) comments that the evidential phase of a trial is 'anything but a narrative' and Harris (2005: 220) claims that witness examination follows a paradigmatic mode. Heffer (2005) provides empirical support for these claims. Defining a minimal narrative response, after Labov and Waletzky (1967), as one in which reversing the order of two narrative clauses will lead to a different interpretation (e.g. He fell in the pond so had a whisky v He had a whisky so fell in the pond), he found that in examination-in-chief, where the story is meant to be elicited, only 15% of complainants' turns, 14% of defendants' turns, 12% of other lay witnesses' turns, 6% of police officers' turns and 3% of experts' turns were minimally narrative (Heffer 2005: 116–17). The figures justify a distinction between 'narrative' (complainant, defendant, other lay) and 'support' (police, expert) witnesses, but even so the narrative contributions of 'narrative' witnesses appear few.

These figures, though, do not tell the full story. In the first place, narrative turns tend to be longer than the mean witness turn length in examination-in-chief of approximately 13 words (Heffer 2005: 99), and they tend to be more salient. Extract (1) is from the examination-in-chief of the lead narrative witness in a dangerous driving and assault case.[2]

(1) Examination-in-chief – dangerous driving and assault

23 Q: … whilst you were riding along the road, both you and Miss Walters on your horses, what happened around about noon?

24 A: We heard a car approaching from behind on this road. Because it was a very narrow road, we decided to trot up to get to the corner shown in photograph No.1 to let the vehicle get past. He was impatient. He came up behind us. He started honking his horn and shouting abuse at us.

In this simple exchange, we find the three central elements of narrative discourse in criminal trials as already found in the opening statements: orientation summed up in the barrister's question; a core narrative conveyed through a causally connected series of events relating to the crime – (we) *heard … decided*, (he) *came up … started* (honking); and a set of evaluative clauses (Point) and clausal elements (evaluation) which together allocate blame to the defendant: *it was a very narrow road … he was impatient … honking his horn and shouting abuse.*

This minimal witness story demonstrates another point about the degree of narrativity in witness examinations: while only 12–15% of 'narrative witness' turns provide core narrative, narrative turns, as here, are often followed by a long sequence of turns teasing out the orientation, evaluation and Point in more detail before returning to the core narrative. When considered in this way, Heffer (2005), Harris (2001, 2005) and Gibbons

(2003) have found that almost entire direct examinations can be seen as following a Labovian-style story structure.

A third point which makes these figures deceptive is that at least some of the core narrative is provided by the lawyers themselves in their own turns. Coulthard and Johnson (2007: 102–3) note that of the first 19 questions put to Dr Shipman by his defence counsel, 15 required only confirmation responses. Many of these provide core narrative of Shipman's life (see Extract (2)).

(2)   Examination-in-chief in the Harold Shipman murder trial

  5   Q: Dr Shipman, you were born on the 14th January 1946 in Nottingham?
  6   A: That's correct.
  7   Q: You grew up in the area, went to school in the area and thereafter went to Leeds Medical School?
  8   A: That is also correct.
  9   Q: From there you studied medicine and qualified, obtaining your primary medical qualification in 1970?
 10   A: That's correct.

Similarly, trial lawyers often repeat or reformulate a core narrative element the witness has just related to mark it as salient for the jury and to encourage them to infer the probative Point, as in (3).

(3)
 95   Q: … Did he get past you?
 96   A: … he forced us into the hedge so he could get past.
 97   Q: He forced you into the hedge so he could get past?
 98   A: Yes.

In terms of the turn-by-turn mechanics of narrative construction, early work on lawyers' questions to witnesses (Danet and Kermish 1978; Woodbury 1984) tended to assume a direct relation between question form and degree of control over the answers given. Thus 'wh-' questions were assumed to be open-ended and thus invite narration; polar (yes/no) and either-or questions were considered restricting; and pseudo-declaratives and tag questions were judged to be coercive. Later work (Maley and Fahey 1991: 110–17; Heffer 2005) has shown that question form in itself is not particularly indicative of function. For example, polar questions, as in 'Did he get past you?' above, are often taken as requests for narration while pseudo-declaratives, as in the Shipman examination, are not usually coercive when used in direct examination. Maley and Fahey (1991) distinguish instead between information-seeking and confirmation-seeking questions. Heffer (2005: 110–14) distinguishes two different types of information-seeking 'requests': requests for narration and requests for specification. Requests for narration are linked to a set of grammatical and lexical 'narrative cues', such as wh-questions with the verbs 'happen', 'do' and 'tell' (e.g. 'What happened then?') and polar questions with the verbs 'do' and 'say' and indefinite pronouns like 'anything' (e.g. 'Did he say anything to you?'). However, narrative cues are by no means always taken up since uptake depends considerably on individual witness style.

Running against the tide of narrativity in witness examination are the rules of evidence, the mismatch between the witness and lawyer stories, the testimony style of some witnesses and the dialectic structure of witness examination itself.

The rules of evidence mean that the witness is constrained in terms of telling her own story. In particular, hearsay and speculation, which are staples of everyday narrative, are (in principle at least) excluded from court (O'Barr 1982). The rules are applied, though, at the discretion of the judge, whose primary concern is often to speed up proceedings. This explains why leading questions, which are technically excluded from examination-in-chief, are actually common in the initial phases of examination, as can be seen in the case of Harold Shipman (2) above. There counsel covers the first 24 years of Shipman's life in three narrative turns presented for confirmation. That is possible simply because the events are not in dispute.

The constraints on witness narration are more strategic than regulatory and derive in part from a mismatch between the stories the witness and lawyer want and need to tell. When examining their own witnesses, lawyers face a trade-off between allowing them to narrate 'naturally, spontaneously and conversationally' to enhance trust (Stone 1995: 95) and taking them through their evidence 'by tightly framed questions, in small steps' to ensure that the story that emerges is legally adequate and effective in terms of the overall goal of securing guilt or innocence (Stone 1995: 94). Or, as Jackson (1995: 400) puts it, 'counsel must decide, in effect, who can tell the story better' – witness or counsel. While the question–answer (Q/A) format is generally considered to be the primary anti-narrative element of witness examination (e.g. Stygall 1994; Cotterill 2003; Coulthard and Johnson 2007), it can also be seen as precisely the feature which permits the lawyer to construct their crime story. By assigning fixed questioner/answerer roles, the Q/A format 'constructs a turn-taking organization that gives control of topical organization entirely to the questioner' (Levinson 1992: 86). And topical control means narratorial control.

The testimony style of some witnesses can also run against the narrative tide. The Duke Language and Law Programme in the 1970s identified both 'powerless' v 'powerful' and 'narrative' v 'fragmented' styles of testifying (O'Barr 1982). 'Powerless' witnesses, unlike 'powerful' ones, used such features as hedging, hesitation, intensification, mitigation and honorifics. A witness with a 'narrative' style, like the one from the driving case above, will take non-narrative requests as an opportunity to provide further narrative detail such as an evaluative explanation, as in (4).

(4)
Q: What speed were you going on the horses?
A: We were trotting so we could get to the corner as quickly as we could to let the car come past.

A witness with a 'fragmented' style (5), on the other hand, would offer minimal responses and require several exchanges to convey the same information as that in (4).

(5) [invented example]
Q: What speed were you going on the horses?
A: We were trotting.
Q: Why were you trotting?
A: So we could get to the corner as quickly as we could.
Q: Why did you want to do that?
A: To let the car come past.

O'Barr's team found that mock jurors rated powerless witnesses and those with a fragmented style as very significantly less convincing, truthful, competent, intelligent and trustworthy than 'powerful' and 'narrative' witnesses. Although the powerful/powerless distinction has been challenged (e.g. Kerr-Thompson 2002), it does seem likely that the lawyer's folk perception of powerlessness or enunciative weakness in a witness will influence the degree of control she exercises over that witness. Furthermore, a perceived need to control the witness tightly will, in turn, tend to lead to a 'fragmented' style from the witness, who will tend to adapt to the style of friendly counsel.

Finally, the dialectic structure of witness examination can also disrupt the narrative flow in a number of ways. Objections by opposing counsel (for example for leading the witness or calling for speculation) can interrupt a line of narrative questioning. Such objections are fairly rare in English courts (Heffer 2005: 82–84) but appear common in major US trials (Cotterill 2003: 95–97). More importantly, lawyers need to anticipate cross-examination, as advocacy manuals constantly remind them (Stone 1995). Returning to the lead narrative witness in the dangerous driving case, after making the strong evaluative point about her being forced by the defendant into the hedge, counsel appears to digress into material which clearly does not strengthen the narrative goal (6).

(6)
99 Q: As he went past, did you have anything in your hand?
100 A: Yes, I had my whip. I asked him to back off and, as he drew so close, my whip hit the side of his car.
101 Q: Did you do that deliberately to try to get him to back off or what?
102 A: Yes, as an indication, like a reflex action. If someone is attacking you, you try to defend yourself, don't you?

Clearly, the rider hitting out with her whip detracts from the overall prosecution narrative of blame, and would probably not be a part of the witness's own favoured narrative, but the lawyer is well aware that this will form the mainstay of cross-examination so needs to mitigate the damaging effect before passing the witness over to the opposition. Ehrlich (2007) notes similar anticipatory questions in a Canadian sexual assault case.

Overall, then, trial lawyers do often construct narratives through examination of their own witnesses but they are distinctively forensic narratives displaying considerable discoursal hybridity.

Cross-examination and narratorial credibility

Once the examination of the witness is complete, the opposing side will generally (but by no means always) cross-examine that witness. From a narrative perspective, there are two objects to cross-examination: to dismantle the story co-constructed during examination and to present alternative versions of the facts. Both these aims are achieved primarily through the form, content and management of the lawyer's questions. The witness's answers are, to some extent, irrelevant.

Lawyers are able to argue and narrate against the witness because they wield power in the turn-taking process (Atkinson and Drew 1979; Danet and Bogoch 1980; Dunstan 1980; Harris 1984; Goodrich 1987, 1990; Drew 1990; Matoesian 1993, 1995; Stygall 1994; Eades 2000, 2008b; Cotterill 2003). In the first place, they can control to some extent the nature of the witness's answers through the question form. Although, as we have seen with regard to direct examination, there is no direct correlation between question form and coerciveness, a preponderance of confirmation-seeking questions will clearly convey the message to the witness that this is not an opportunity for free narration. Heffer (2005: 122) found that 44% of 24,000 'questions' from 126 cross-examinations were confirmation-seeking declarative statements ('You went there to have sexual intercourse') or tag-questions ('You raped her that night, did you not?'), compared with 12% in examination-in-chief. A large proportion of the other questions were polar, which, in the general coercive context of cross-examination, would also probably be interpreted as confirmation seeking.

Lawyers can also shape interpretation through the wording of their questions. Loftus (1979, 1992) showed informants a film of a traffic accident and asked 'About how fast were the cars going when they X each other', where X was replaced by 'hit' or 'smashed'. Those asked the 'smashed' question estimated a much higher speed and were far more likely to produce a false memory of broken glass when asked the question 'Did you see any broken glass?' Furthermore, when the question included a presupposition, as in 'Did you see *the* broken glass?', it would also lead to false memories. Presupposition of some sort is almost inevitable in questions, and particularly leading questions. Negatively evaluative presupposition, on the other hand, can be found in 'loaded questions': ones which contain a presupposition the answerer would not want to commit to (Walton 1989: 31). Bülow-Møller (1991) cites the following example:

> Q: It is perfectly understandable that the witnesses were confused as to the origin of fire.

This unfairly presupposes that the witnesses were confused. Hickey (1993: 101) notes that even where the witness rejects the presupposition, the cross-examiner can presuppose the rejected answer in the following question:

> Q: (*suggests that the witness's colleague gave a certain reply to his employer*)
> A: No, he didn't say anything like that.
> Q: And that reply didn't suit you, did it?

Given that cross-examiners control the turn-taking process, they can use silence (see Aldridge, this volume, on the use of silence in cross-examining children) and interruption strategically. Matoesian (1993) notes that a silence following the question, along with an emphatic restatement of the question, can suggest to the jury that the witness is unwilling to answer the question rather than just taking their time to do so.

> Q: Then they're not in substantially the same condition, are they?
> (2.5)
> ARE THEY?
>
> (Matoesian 1993: 144)

On the other hand, the cross-examiner may interrupt where the witness replies in an undesired way, although this strategy appears to alienate jurors (O'Barr 1982: 90).

Clearly, it is in the interest of the witness to resist the line the cross-examiner is taking. Cross-examiners can regain control of the topic under discussion by repeating or reformulating questions that have failed to get the desired answers (Conley and O'Barr 1998: 26–27). Lerm shows how, in one of his own cross-examinations, he manages to turn a witness interruption into a damaging reformulation.

> Q: Good, but I am also …
> A: (interrupts) I did not tell them everything
> Q: Yes, we shall get to that. You did not tell them everything, did you, so you *concealed* certain things, did you not?
>
> Lerm (1997: 172)

Gibbons (2003: 112) describes the above attempts to dismantle the recently constructed witness narrative as 'idea targeted' pragmatic strategies that target the veracity of the tale itself. He also suggests that there are a number of 'person targeted' pragmatic strategies designed to destabilise the witness as reliable narrator. These include: reducing the status of the (particularly expert) witness (Gibbons 2003: 113–14); using forms of address to depersonalise the witness (O'Barr 1982); using personal pronouns to create distance or proximity (Jacquemet 1996); and identifying contradictory statements (Drew 1990). (See also Tkačuková, this volume, for discussion of these pragmatic strategies in a libel trial.)

One person-targeted strategy is the evaluative use of deictic forms. Heffer (2005: 141–50) notes the 'evaluative pointing' that can occur through strategic choices of tense, pronouns and demonstrative forms in counsel's metadiscursive comments on the witness's narration. For example, the form *you are telling the/this jury* is frequently found in the immediate context of words doubting or denying the truth of what the witness has been saying. The act of telling is 'put on stage' through use of the progressive and the marked selection of *the/this jury* 'draws the fact-finders into sharing the cross-examiner's communicative intent' (Heffer 2005: 145).

Another strategy that I would describe as 'person-targeted' (but which Gibbons describes as 'idea targeted') is to subvert the natural order of narration, thereby disrupting the witness's prepared stories and their schemas of how stories should be narrated (O'Barr 1982). The purpose behind such disruption is not so much to attack the ideas (because such disruption will be difficult for the jury to follow too) but to destabilise the witness so that they produce inconsistent answers that impeach their credibility.

In addition to disrupting and destabilising, though, cross-examiners can also narrate alternative stories despite, rather than through, the witness. Wagenaar *et al.* (1993: 58–60) suggest this might be a more effective strategy than attacking the strength of the prosecution evidence even if, logically, all the defence need to do is prove reasonable doubt. In England and Wales, cross-examiners can use the excuse that they need to put their case to the witness if they want to claim that the witness is lying (Keane 1996: 153). Counsel often use the metalinguistic markers *I put to you* and *I suggest* to mark this formally, though this is not strictly necessary (7).

(7)
Q: Let me try again. *I am suggesting* that you knew perfectly well that King in October began to name Jacobs as one of his attackers. Do you follow what *I am putting to you*?

Heffer (2005: 141) suggests that with *put to* counsel are primarily addressing and attempting to intimidate the witness, while with *suggest* they are addressing primarily the jury with the intention of presenting an alternative account of events. Thus, we see the two main functions of cross-examination coming together in these two eminently advocatory metalinguistic markers.

Closing arguments and the trial story

At one level, closing arguments, often considered by trial lawyers as their main performance event in the trial (Walter 1988), provide an opportunity for a reiteration of the crime story in the opening statements. However, the crime story now tends to be viewed through the 'story of the trial' (Jackson 1995). In other words, the crime and investigation stories are viewed through the evidence of the witnesses who gave testimony during the trial. Both parties accept that the plausibility of their stories will depend on the perceived credibility of their witnesses, so paramount to winning their case is persuading the jury of the respective reliability and unreliability of the narrators. Hobbs (2003a) points out that the jury's impression of counsel, the protagonists in the story of the trial, is also crucially important and that managing that impression is a key rhetorical strategy in a US prosecutor's rebuttal argument (one delivered after the defence closing in some US jurisdictions).

No case can present an entirely coherent narrative since there will always be gaps of one sort or another in the evidence. Closing arguments are often, then, about those narrative gaps. Interestingly, lawyers frequently approach these verbal gaps with visual metaphors. They often emphasise through lexical repetition that another version of the crime story is merely a false 'picture' or 'impression' that the opposing party is trying to convey (Heffer 2005: 86). Cotterill (2003: 208–17) shows how the prosecution and defence in the OJ Simpson trial both use the 'jigsaw puzzle' metaphor to argue their respective cases. While the jigsaw is visually effective, it does have the weakness that there are always missing pieces of evidence. Consequently, prosecutor Marcia Clark attempts to persuade the jury, in anticipation of the defence closings, that those pieces are peripheral to the central picture. 'You miss a couple of pieces of the sky sometimes, you do lose those pieces, no big deal. You've got the picture ... you've got all the necessary pieces of the puzzle' (Cotterill 2003: 216–17).

On the other hand, the defence note that 'the prosecution took a photograph or picture of OJ Simpson first, then they took the pieces apart' (Cotterill 2003: 218), essentially accusing the prosecution of finding the evidence to fit the picture.

In many respects, though, the closing arguments are not centrally concerned with the construction and evaluation of narrative but rather attempt to bridge the gap between storytelling and the legal categories to which the jury will soon have to fit the evidence. Indeed, there is some empirical evidence to suggest that 'legal-expository' closing arguments, in which legal elements are outlined along with the evidence that supports or fails to support those elements, might be more effective than narratively organised closings (Spiecker and Worthington 2003). So far, this has only been tested on civil jury trials but it may well also apply to criminal trials.

Jury instruction and narrativisation

In their closing speeches, counsel for the prosecution and defence will show the jury how their evidence is linked with the legal charges, but they will do so in an overtly partisan fashion, giving weight only to those elements which support their own case and employing a full armoury of persuasive rhetoric (Cotterill 2003). The only chance the jury have, then, of receiving non-partisan guidance on how to decide the case is through the judge during his final 'charge' or 'summing-up' to the jury (Figure 14.1).

In most US jurisdictions, the judge is allowed only to guide the jury on the law in a set of, usually prescribed and written, jury instructions (see Tiersma, this volume, on the California jury instructions and their redrafting). Generally, these are written in fairly technical and formal legal language and are poorly understood (Lieberman and Sales 1999). But even if they are understood, no help is given on how to apply these abstract definitions of law to the particular facts of the case (Heffer 2008b). In British Commonwealth jurisdictions, on the other hand, judges tend both to instruct the jury on the law with more discretion over wording and to review the evidence presented in the case in light of that law. This introduces several opportunities for the narrativisation of an otherwise highly paradigmatic genre.

In the first place, given considerable discretion over wording, judges are able to accommodate the language of their instructions to the narrative sensibilities of the jury. In other words, the narrative mode of discourse can become strategic input into this otherwise highly paradigmatic genre, as Heffer (2002, 2005: 17–35, 166–80) showed with regard to 100 English judges' directions on the burden and standard of proof. Secondly, some English judges narrativise their legal instructions by providing narrative examples of legal distinctions (Heffer 2005: 177–80), such as that between knowing and believing that goods are stolen:

> If for example you were standing in Marks and Spencers and you watched a shoplifter steal and then ten minutes later you took the goods from the shoplifter you would receive them knowing that they were stolen. If on the other hand ...

The third, and perhaps principal, way in which narrative can enter into the judge's summing-up is in the review of the evidence, which is included to a greater or lesser extent in most Commonwealth jurisdictions (Wolchover 1989). The review is meant to be as impartial as possible, and judges must present the defence case, however weak. Nevertheless, judges are permitted to comment on both the weight of the evidence and the credibility and plausibility of witnesses.

Henning (1999) analysed the summings-up by different judges of the hung trial and retrial (resulting in conviction) of the same rape and assault case in Tasmania. She argues that the first trial judge's attempt to provide a 'neutral account' simply results in confusion because it fails to flag up the truly salient issues in the case. The second judge provides much more assistance in 'reading' the case, and instead of a bare chronicle of the facts, provides something much more like an evaluated narrative. In Extract (7) the defendant's arrival at the house where the assault took place is, unlike in the first trial, described clearly from the complainant's perspective.

(7)
Well then the next question *you might need* to consider is why did he come down from Y on the 31st July. You *might think*, and I'll read her evidence in detail later, *you might think* that she **obviously** thought that it was to harm her, having regard to the reaction she said (sic, had) when she saw him at the door unannounced, unexpected on a dark and wintry night, raining cats and dogs, holding a rifle and

having shouted through the door before he came in. I'll remind you of that evidence in detail, as I say, later. So she **obviously** thought he was there for no good purpose.

The text has a great deal of internal evaluation, including intensification and emphatic repetition ('she obviously thought'), allusive clichés ('on a dark and wintry night ... ') and colloquialisms ('there for no good purpose'). The judge's comment on the complainant's thought processes is formally attributed to the jurors through the standard judicial formula 'you might think' (Stubbs 1996; Heffer 2005: 200–201; Henning 1999: 209) but use of the comment adjunct *obviously* normalises the comment, bringing it into conformity with a standard of expectation of normal behaviour (i.e. a standard script) (Heffer 2005: 190).

The passage has precisely the sort of 'high rhetorical volume and intensity' which Robertshaw (1998: 182) severely criticises as a source of bias in English summings-up. Henning (1999: 212–13), though, argues that, rather than offering the 'chimera of neutrality', this narrative approach provides a 'balanced' review which reflects the relative strengths and weaknesses of the case and guides jurors towards the legally relevant issues. This might prevent them being swayed by the type of affective evaluation we saw in the prosecutor's opening address in the Marv Albert trial, and which is the stock in trade of the advocate's art in closing speeches. At the same time, there is a very fine line between active assistance and undue influence.

Jury deliberation and narrative decision-making

Once the jury go out to deliberate, we have evidence in various forms that they reason in a narrative fashion. Firstly, experimental psychological evidence suggests that jurors do not weigh up the probability of each individual piece of evidence being true (as mathematical models suggest (Hastie 1993)), but attempt to fit that evidence into narratives which they then judge as plausible or implausible. According to the Story Model (Pennington and Hastie 1986, 1991), jurors integrate the trial evidence with their pre-existing scripts for event sequences similar to those in dispute and their generic expectations about what makes a coherent story. Generally, the adversarial nature of trial cases will ensure that more than one story is constructed and jurors might have different levels of confidence in those variants. The acceptability of a story is determined by its coverage and coherence, while its relative uniqueness contributes to a juror's confidence in that story.

Cotterill (2003: 223) provides an example of how jurors in the OJ Simpson trial integrated the trial evidence with their pre-existing scripts. One of the jurors re-enacts one of the officer's versions of the investigation story.

> you go into the house and you spotted blood prior to going into the house. So you scaled the wall and now you get into the backyard and get Arnelle to let you into the house. No one ever goes upstairs. No one ever searches the house. ... It doesn't make sense.

Cotterill (2003: 223–24) notes how the use of the historic present, reminiscent of the prosecution opening in the Marv Albert trial, both brings the audience closer to the crime events and evaluates the officer's actions as a potential habitual action, thus measuring 'the typicality and by implication the plausibility of the officer's behaviour against a media-created schema of what police officers are meant to do at crime scenes'.

Hastie and Pennington apply their Story Model to jury decision-making in the OJ Simpson trial. They note that while the prosecution, as always, presented a single, linear crime story, the defence presented a number of alternate stories. Two of these stories – the police 'rush to judgment' story and the 'bungling criminal investigators' story (Hastie and Pennington (1996): 966–67) – undermined central elements (and thus the uniqueness) of the prosecution story, thereby reducing confidence. The defence also successfully flagged up inconsistencies in the prosecution evidence, thereby undermining the coherence of the prosecution story. Thus, contrary to the 'popular view' that jurors' judgements in the OJ case were merely 'reflexive reactions evoked by 'prejudice triggers' in the evidence' (e.g. 'Simpson is a black man who beat his white wife', or, 'Simpson overcame a disadvantaged background to become successful in a racist society'), Hastie and Pennington (1996: 969) hypothesise on the basis of the jurors' own remarks that 'most of the jurors' decisions were arrived at primarily through their inferences from the evidence (mediated by the construction of a "story summary")'.

Sentencing and beyond: a moral coda

The verdict, like the original plea, is delivered as a purely paradigmatic choice between 'guilty' and 'not guilty'.[3] However, once the verdict is in and the narrative 'truth' of guilt has been established, the constraints imposed by the 'law of narrative' are loosened. Firstly, counsels' submissions on aggravating and mitigating circumstances broaden the scope of the narrative to include elements previously excluded such as the defendant's criminal record and family circumstances and, in the US as we see in Schweda-Nicholson (this volume), the convicted person may speak himself. Then the judge, in his or her sentencing remarks, broadens the scope of the story further by fitting the defendant's individual conduct within a more general moral sanction against certain behaviour in society. Thus, the behaviour of the defendant in the dangerous driving case cited several times in this chapter is, for the first time, described in lay terms as 'road rage', which in turn is described as a general negative trend in society. Finally, the constraints on the evaluative dimension of narrative are lifted and the verbal intensity of judgment appears to be calibrated with the severity of the crime and the length of the sentence handed down (Heffer 2007). The sentencing of Dr Harold Shipman, for example, is quite unlike any other form of legal text in terms of its evaluative intensity.

> The time has now come for me to pass sentence upon you for these wicked, wicked crimes. Each of your victims was your patient. You murdered each and every one of your victims by a calculated and cold blooded perversion of your medical skills. For your own evil and wicked purposes you took advantage of and grossly abused the trust that each of your victims reposed in you. ... The sheer wickedness of what you have done defies description and is shocking beyond belief.
> (Shipman Trial, Day 58, www.the-shipman-inquiry.org.uk/trialtrans.asp)

In short, the violence of punishment that the words of sentencing represent (Cover 1986) needs to be motivated with more than a purely referential factual account of the crime events.

Conclusion

This chapter has provided a taste of some of the complex issues involved in the construction of stories in court. In particular, it has stressed the multitude of ways in which narrativity of one form or another can emerge in the trial context through its various hybrid genres. I have focused on describing *how* and *why* narrative is constructed in the trial since I believe it is important to understand the ordinary mechanics of trial communication before going on to critique it. Much work in this area has suffered from a merely partial understanding of the trial context, and new readers need to be wary. At the same time, there is now a rich body of socio-critical work on the various forms of narrative inequality that can emerge in the trial. I would point readers, for example, to Ehrlich (2001, 2002) and Matoesian (1993, 2001) on the suppression of rape complainants' narratives, to Eades (1994a, 2008b) on the narrative disadvantage of Aboriginal witnesses, and to Brennan (1994) and Eades (2002) on the narrative vulnerability of child witnesses.

I have no more than hinted here at the major cross-trial and cross-jurisdictional differences in the degree that narrative is allowed to emerge in the various trial genres. I have also ignored for the most part the historical emergence of those genres (see Archer, this volume, for a historical perspective). Both diachronic and diatypic variation, though, can tell us a great deal about the tension between narrativity and anti-narrativity, and this is an area ripe for study. Narrative, in all its manifestations, remains 'in issue' throughout the trial since there is a constant tension between the narrative propensity of the crime events and the legal desire to subject those narratives to scientific verification. Or, as Gewirtz (1996b) simply puts it, 'Law is all about human life, yet struggles to keep life at bay.'

Notes

1 Not all jurisdictions follow this structure. For example, many US jurisdictions have final jury instructions before the closing arguments. I have tried to incorporate many jurisdictional differences by giving my own labels to the genres rather than the extremely diverse legal-professional labels.
2 I number according to turn in the full examination since the position of an extract in the examination is often crucial to understanding its role and significance.
3 Scotland has a third category of 'Not Proven'.

Further reading

Ehrlich, S. (2001) *Representing Rape: Language and Sexual Consent*, London: Routledge.
——(2002) '(Re)contextualizing complainant's accounts of sexual assault', *Forensic Linguistics: The International Journal of Speech, Language and the Law*, 9(2): 193–212.
Matoesian, G. (1993) *Reproducing Rape: Domination through Talk in the Courtroom*, Cambridge: Polity Press.
——(2001) *Law and the Language of Identity: Discourse in the William Kennedy Smith Rape Trial*, Oxford: Oxford University Press.
(The above authors deal with the suppression of rape complainants' narratives.)
Brennan, M. (1994) 'Cross-examining children in criminal courts: Child welfare under attack', in J. Gibbons (ed.) *Language and the Law*, London: Longman: 199–216.
Eades, D. (1994) 'A case of communicative clash: Aboriginal English and the legal system', in J. Gibbons (ed.) *Language and the Law*, London: Longman: 234–64.

——(2002) '"Evidence given in unequivocal terms": Gaining consent of aboriginal young people in court', in J. Cotterill (ed.) *Language in the Legal Process*, Basingstoke: Palgrave: 162–79.
——(2008) *Courtroom Talk and Neocolonial Control*, New York: Mouton de Gruyter.
(These authors deal with the narrative disadvantage of Aboriginal witnesses and the narrative vulnerability of child witnesses.)

15

Prosecution and defense closing speeches

The creation of contrastive closing arguments

Laura Felton Rosulek

Introduction

The closing arguments of trials in adversarial legal systems are important sites of investigation both for discourse analysis in general and for forensic linguistics specifically. During the closing arguments, two speakers take the same people, events, and evidence, and create two opposing representations for the same audience. Understanding how this occurs can reveal how speakers' goals and belief systems affect their use of language. Additionally, these discourses are both persuasive and argumentative, thus providing a prime opportunity to study how such discourses are linguistically created.

In addition to these aspects, closing arguments are especially interesting for forensic discourse analysis for several other reasons. First, the closing arguments are the lawyers' final chances to convince the judge or jurors that theirs is the best account of what really happened; the last chance to put together their most complete and coherent "master narrative" (Gibbons 2003: 155) of the crime, investigation, and the trial. Second, the lawyers produce their argument without having to interact with witnesses. Thus, the arguments are free of outside influences which could affect the lawyers' discourses and language use. Finally, unlike during the examination of witnesses, in the closing arguments lawyers now get to speak directly to the people they are trying to convince.

Research into closing arguments has taken two general focuses: what information or message is included, that is, the ideational content (Halliday 1978) and how lawyers negotiate their interpersonal relationships, that is, the construction of the speaker's role through modality, person, voice (Bakhtin 1981), footings (Goffman 1981b), style, etc. (Halliday 1978). Section two of this chapter presents a discussion of research on the ideational content of closing arguments, specifically the work that has been done on the ways in which lawyers create opposing discourses when starting from the same people and events. The third section in this chapter discusses research that has shown that in the closing arguments lawyers must manage multiple aspects of their identity: both their position of authority and their similarities to the jurors. In section four, I then present an analysis of lawyers' use of quotations to show how a single forensic discourse analysis can explore both the ideational and interpersonal aspects of closing arguments. The final section provides a summary of the results of this analysis and directions for further research.

Ideational content of closing arguments

Several studies have begun to summarize what information is often included in the closing arguments. Walter (1988) finds that lawyers tend to focus on emotional appeals, intellectual issues, legal definitions and refutations. Heffer (2005) argues that trials are about the crime, investigation and trial narratives, but in the closing arguments, the trial narrative becomes the focus with the stories of what happened during the crime and investigation being presented through the descriptions of the witnesses' testimony.

While those studies show how prosecution and defense arguments are similar, others have looked at their differences. They have shown that the two sides tend to focus on different topics. Walter (1988) observes that prosecution lawyers make more references to *good common sense* and to *evidence* or *facts* while defense lawyers place more *onus on jurors* and discuss *reasonable doubt* more frequently. Heffer (2005) describes a case in which the prosecution foregrounds the violent behaviors of the defendant while the defense constructs their narrative as being about the anger of the victim. This analysis is supported by quantitative results which show that the prosecution refers to the defendant more than to the complainants while the defense does the opposite.

Other studies have shown that not only are the two sides focusing on different topics, but they are also often completely ignoring or silencing (Huckin 2002) those discussed by the other side. In a case described in Felton Rosulek (2008), the two sides systematically discuss different topics and ignore those important to the other side. For instance, the prosecution foregrounds the sexual and violent details of the alleged abuse, the length of time the abuse lasted, and the power of the defendant over the victim. The defense, on the other hand, remains silent on those topics, focusing instead on the length of time between the abuse and the victim's report of it and the victim's behaviors, which they did not feel were consistent with those of a victim. In another case, described in Felton Rosulek (forthcoming a), one of the victims is not referenced as an individual by the defense. In this case, there were six victims of various crimes including rape, assault, and robbery. The woman who was kidnapped and raped is the most frequently referenced victim in the prosecution's argument. In the defense argument, this victim was only referenced six times and only as part of the group of victims during the investigation and trial narratives as in (1). The lawyer never refers to her as an individual.

(1)   I submit to you that the photographic lineup was unduly suggestive to the women who were shown the photographic lineup. The in-court identification that you had is this the defendant David Becker sitting in court, you've seen it a bunch of times. The cops did it, the victims did it.

The defense lawyer ignores the crime that was committed against her and the details of her personal identity. This constructs the most violent actions of the defendant against this particular woman as irrelevant to the other charges against him.

Though not as severe as not including a relevant social actor, such as a victim, in an argument, in some cases a side will exclude the defendant or the victim from either the crime, investigation, or trial narratives, while including them in the others. In several cases in Felton Rosulek (2009b), the defense completely omits the defendant from the crime narrative. While they include what the victims were doing at that time, they simply exclude any references to the defendant in this narrative. For example, in the case from which (1) above was taken, the defendant is only referenced once in the defense's crime narrative, though he is referenced relatively frequently in the other narratives included in the argument. In examples like this, the social actors are not completely ignored, only their involvement in one of the narratives is.

While those studies have focused on the differing thematic content of opposing closing arguments, others have centered on the specific lexical choices lawyers make to reference the actors and events that they do choose to include. For example, Cotterill (2003) shows that in the OJ Simpson criminal trial, the lawyers for both sides used metaphors in their closing arguments to emphasize certain people and events and to create different linguistic representations of them. For instance, the prosecution developed the metaphor of OJ Simpson as a time bomb to try to force the jury to see him as powerful, explosive, and volatile. The two sides used metaphors to foreground certain characteristics of the defendant and to silence others.

Felton Rosulek (2008, forthcoming a) shows that it is not just through metaphors that lawyers focus on different characteristics of the victims' and the defendants' identities. Prosecution lawyers will background the unique identity of the person on trial by simply using a functionalization (van Leeuwen 2002) or reference to his role in the local context such as *the defendant* or *the drug dealer*. They will sometimes even refer to him as *this* in the crime story, thus using his role in the here-and-now of the trial to erase his identity during the time of the crime as in example (2) from an aggravated robbery case.

(2)   The defendant approaches her, shoves a gun in her face, points a gun at her, demands her money and jewelry, and robs her.

In some instances, the lawyers even use *the defendant* when recreating direct quotations despite it being impossible in these particular quotations for that to have been the term of reference used. In (3), despite the lawyer representing the victim as referring to her stepfather as *the defendant*, she would not have used this term as he did not yet have this identity in the context in which the quotation took place. Also, due to the participants' relationships, it is unlikely she would have ever used this term when speaking to her mother about him.

(3)   Lizzy would say, "I wish you would divorce the defendant." It wasn't because something he had punished her, sent her to her room, and she was mad. The only time Teri Tand could remember when Lizzy said that statement was when those two were fighting and the defendant was hitting her.

The importance of examples such as (2) and (3) is that the men being referenced were not yet defendants in the context in which the described events took place. However, the prosecution lawyers are applying this identity back in time and further silencing the identities the men had in those contexts.

Additionally, the prosecution will foreground the unique identity of the victim by using his/her name while the defense does the same for the defendant. The pattern found in the sexual abuse case described in Felton Rosulek (2008) is particularly interesting. When the prosecution referred to the victim by name, they used her diminutive nickname, *Lizzy*, though in a few instances they added her surname. The defense, however, only used the victim's full given name, *Eliza*, and more often than not her surname as well. This can be seen in examples (4) and (5), which are the first reference to the victim in each side's argument.

(4) Prosecution: Those were words spoken by the defendant, believed by twelve-year-old Lizzy Smith.

(5) Defense: Your heart goes out to a person on the witness stand like Eliza Smith when she talked a couple days ago about these allegations.

The result was that the prosecution foregrounded her young age and created a sense of familiarity while the defense silenced her youth, foregrounded the appearance that she was the same as any other witness, and created social distance and formality. Overall, through choice of terms of reference for the defendant and the victim, the lawyers create certain identities for them and silence aspects that do not aid the lawyer's case. These results are consistent with other findings in forensic linguistics, regarding terms of reference and lexical choice; though these have not looked specifically at closing arguments (cf. Danet 1980a, 1980b; Luchjenbroers and Aldridge 2007).

Secondly, lawyers will use the semantic properties of the verbs they select to represent processes (Halliday 1994) or events to silence certain aspects of them while foregrounding others. For example, as mentioned above, in the sexual abuse case described in Felton Rosulek (2008), the prosecution includes many explicit details about the abuse. The defense silences them by using generalized terms as in examples (6) and (7).

(6) He did not sexually abuse this young girl.

(7) She testified a few days ago that my client sexually touched her.

By using *sexually abuse* and *sexually touch* even in their denials, the defense silences the potentially more upsetting or off-putting details of the alleged crime. In another sexual abuse case, the prosecution describes the victim's sexual actions as well as his violent behaviors that occurred in the same time frame in detail. The defense, on the other hand, ignores the sexual abuse in their argument, referring to it only as *incidents*. They also silence the specifics of the defendant's violent actions as can be seen in (8).

(8) ... in response to Mr. Wilder's acts of what he did in May of 2001

The lawyer did not deny that the defendant had done these acts. Instead, he ignored the violent nature and the details of what he had done. As these examples show, lawyers use their lexical choices in the closing arguments to control the information they include about events as well as the identities they create for the defendant and the victim. As with terms of reference, studies of other parts of the trial have shown similar results (cf. Danet 1980b; Cotterill 2001; Aldridge and Luchjenbroers 2007).

To summarize, analyses of closing arguments have repeatedly shown that one way in which lawyers in the same case present contrasting ideational content is by focusing on and even silencing different topics, and using lexical items that focus on different characteristics of the social actors and their corresponding processes. This is not to say that lawyers do not try to refute topics raised by the other side. Studies such as Walter (1988) show they do. The point is that an important means of creating opposing arguments is simply presenting narratives with different themes and lexical items. A further demonstration of this will be shown in the data analysis presented below.

Negotiation of interpersonal relationships

In addition to the studies on the ideational content of closing arguments, there has also been a focus on lawyers' interpersonal negotiations, on how they manage their identities and their relationships with the jurors or judge, the context, and the discourse itself.

One set of studies has examined how lawyers create a local identity for themselves. According to Hobbs (2008) lawyers are given a level of respect simply by their role in the proceedings, but they also put on a performance. They adopt a professional identity while trying to create a certain ideal image or character for themselves (Trenholm 1989; Hobbs 2003a). Through this identity, "lawyers must … convey power, authority, and credibility to the opposing sides, to their clients, and where necessary, to juries as well" (Bogoch 1999: 333). However, they also try to build rapport with the jurors or the judge, to seem similar to them, like a friend (Stygall 1994). One linguistic strategy for doing this has been code-switching among a standard code and a dialect that indexes a shared culture or identity. For example, Fuller (1993) and Hobbs (2003a) both examine how an African-American lawyer alternates between African-American English (AAE) and a more standard variety of English, in part so that she can foreground her shared identity with the jurors, many of whom are also African-American.

Other studies have examined the moment-to-moment negotiation of these identities and relationships. One way in which lawyers portray themselves as similar to the jurors is by using first person plural pronouns to construct themselves and the jurors or judge(s) as sharing the same opinions and evaluations. Danet (1980b) shows that an Israeli defense lawyer used *we* to portray himself and the judges as all being in agreement. Felton Rosulek (2009a) shows how lawyers in seventeen closing arguments use *we* to construct the jurors and the lawyers as having had the same experiences during the trial and as believing the same propositions (as in (9) and (10)).

(9)   And what we heard from the doctors is no, that's not – that's not the case

(10)   He is drugged. We know that.

In constructions such as this, lawyers silence any doubts or differences of opinion and experience the jurors may have had.

Another tool for reducing the social distance between lawyers and jurors is to construct jurors as equal participants in the creation of the argument. Pascual (2006) argues that, while on the surface closing arguments appear to be monologues, they are in fact what she calls "fictive trilogues" among the lawyer, the opposing side, and the jurors. Through the argumentative nature of closing arguments, the lawyers address and respond to the points made by the opposing lawyer(s). Additionally, through constructions such as questions, which Walter (1988) finds to be common in closing arguments, lawyers portray the jurors as active interlocutors. Additionally, Felton Rosulek (2009a) shows that lawyers also use first person plural pronouns to construct jurors as co-constructors of the discourse when really they are only the addressees, as in example (11).

(11) The drug addiction, we'll talk about that more later in terms of what happens on this evening.

Through the creation of a fictive trilogue and examples like (11), lawyers ignore the fact that jurors are silent participants and not equal to the lawyer who has all of the control over the information contained in the argument. Thus, active co-participation in the 'talk' is assumed, when it is not a fact.

Through these linguistic strategies, lawyers foreground the similarities among themselves and jurors and ignore or transform the differences. However, lawyers must also appear to be authoritative and competent (Bogoch 1999). Just having the identity of a lawyer, at least in the United States (and in many other countries), grants individuals a position of power and competence within the courtroom that a person who lacks the required education and training cannot achieve (Hobbs 2008). However, that status alone is limited in its benefits. Some of the work of creating a powerful identity is done through first person singular pronouns in which lawyers overtly refer to their role in the context or state their opinions and wants, as in example (12).

(12) I want to go through a couple of things in their statement.

While referring to themselves brings the lawyers' authority and position to the forefront, it does not completely create an authoritative persona. In the following section, I present an analysis of data which shows that in the closing arguments lawyers utilize the authority of others to try to increase their own believability for jurors.

Analysis of lawyers' use of others' authority

Lawyers use the authority of others by presenting their argument through the recreation of discourses originally produced by those with more local authority. The process of reproducing others' discourses has been called direct/indirect reported speech (Holt and Johnson, this volume), character voices (Koven 2002), and constructed dialogue (Tannen 2007 [1989]). In this chapter, the differences between direct and indirect quotations are ignored. Either way, the discourse is still recontextualized when it is recreated (Tannen 2007 [1989]) and that gives it new meaning (Bakhtin 1981; Tannen 1986). Also, while direct quotations may be seen as more accurate representations (Philips 1986), many times they are not (Mayes 1990).

During closing arguments, lawyers spend a significant portion of the time recreating what the witnesses said during the trial (Stygall 1994; Heffer 2005) and the judge's instructions (Stygall 1994). Some of the reasons they do this include supporting or attacking the credibility of the original speaker (Heffer 2005), producing evidence to support their claims (Stygall 1994), and recontextualizing (Bauman and Briggs 1990) or reinterpreting the meaning of what was said (Felton Rosulek forthcoming b). The focus in this section is on when lawyers reproduce others' voices in order to use the source's authority to legitimate (Berger and Luckmann 1966; van Leeuwen 2007) the lawyer's claims.

Table 15.1 Frequency of character voices as sources of legitimation

	Clauses in Legitimating Character Voices	Total Clauses	Percent of Total Clauses
Prosecution's Argument	2514	15286	16.4%
Defence's Argument	1987	14726	13.7%
Rebuttal	307	3432	8.9%

The qualitative and quantitative analyses presented here were carried out by the author on the closing arguments from seventeen felony trials (17 prosecution and 17 defense arguments, 14 rebuttals) that took place in a state district court in the United States. The arguments were first divided into clauses (a clause was defined as having a single verb except for passive, progressive, and perfect markers and modals, as well as any accompanying noun, prepositional, and adverbial phrases). Each clause that was overtly attributed to another speaker (or the lawyer at another time) was marked as a character voice, and when the message the voice was conveying was a tenet in the speaker's argument, it was considered to be legitimation. For instance, when the crime story was presented in the victim's voice or when a medical conclusion that the lawyer was relying on was presented in the doctor's voice, it was legitimation.

As can be seen in Table 15.1, slightly more than one in seven of the 30,012 clauses produced in the prosecution and defense arguments and almost one in eleven of the 3,432 clauses in the rebuttal arguments were character voices that were legitimating the lawyer's argument.

Most of the character voices that served as legitimation were originally produced by lay witnesses who had testified at the trial. In fact, 10.2% of the clauses in the prosecution's arguments, 10.8% of the clauses in the defense arguments, and 5.4% of the clauses in rebuttals were in the voices of lay witnesses whose authority was being used to legitimate the lawyer's argument. The prosecution, on average, quoted 6.6 witnesses, and the defense averaged 6.2. Often, these included the victim(s), the defendant, family members of both, and eyewitnesses. These voices serve as what van Leeuwen (2007) calls "personal authorities." Their knowledge was achieved through personal experiences and their status is only in the local context. They were allowed to testify about their sensory experiences during the crime: what they saw, heard, felt, etc.; and their past interactions with the defendant. However, they were not allowed to offer their opinions. As someone who has first-hand knowledge of the events and people involved in the case and as someone who had pledged to tell the truth, they were considered to be authorities in the courtroom, but only on this specific topic and in this particular context.

In example (13) the words of a lay witness are offered as legitimation of the crime story in an assault trial and are presented as a direct quotation from the victim who had described during her testimony what the defendant had done to her.

(13)   We do have an eyewitness to this assault, however, and we do have direct evidence. We do have direct evidence from the victim herself, from Sharon Kinnison, from her statements. She told Deputy Norland, "I got beat up." She told Deputy May it happened, she said, "Nicky got mad at me." She made a long distance call, international call. "He went off on me and shoved me headfirst into a furnace."

The lawyer refers to the quotations as direct evidence and presents the crime narrative mostly in the voice of the victim, the local authority on what happened, rather than in his own voice as he was not there.

In example (14), when the prosecution lawyer is discussing why the brother of a sexual abuse victim was a credible witness, he indirectly quotes what the young man said about his relationship with the victim and with the defendant, his stepfather. The lawyer, who is not an expert on the relationships between the witness and the victim and the witness and the defendant, uses the witness as an authority on his own relationships.

(14)   He testified that [he and the victim] have a good relationship, but he also testified that he had an okay relationship with the defendant ... Michael Smith has no motive to lie.

In both (13) and (14), the lawyers could have presented the same information in their own voices. However, the lawyer is not a ratified authority on the crime in (13) nor the relationships in (14). The two people quoted, however, are. They have first hand knowledge of these specific situations. Despite the victim in (13) being an alcoholic who had changed her story multiple times and the witness in (14) being a young child, they have more status in this situation to make these particular claims than the lawyer does, and in each case the lawyer uses that to his advantage by quoting them in order to add legitimation to the information he is presenting.

Other than lay witnesses, lawyers also call experts to the witness stand and then quote them in their closing arguments. In this corpus, 2.4% of the prosecution's clauses, 1.3% of the defense's clauses, and 2.0% of the clauses in the rebuttals were in the voices of experts who were legitimating the arguments. In the United States, according to Rule 702 of the Federal Rules of Evidence, expert witnesses are those who are "qualified as an expert by knowledge, skill, experience, training, or education," though the ultimate decision on who qualifies is left to the judge. These are authorities whose status comes from their role outside of the courtroom and their being able to apply their knowledge and skills when analyzing and interpreting evidence inside the courtroom. They are allowed to present their opinions that are specific to the facts of the case or that are generalities they have learned from their work. Lawyers quote both types of opinions to add authority to their claims.

An example of an expert whose opinion on the particular case in question is quoted can be seen in (15). It is an indirect quotation from a doctor who testified for the prosecution against a daycare provider who was charged with shaking one of her clients to death. The defense's argument is that the child had received the injuries by falling from her highchair. The doctor had testified that that could not have been what happened in this case. In the prosecution's argument, the lawyer indirectly quotes her saying:

(15)   And she said it was impossible, that was her word, impossible for these injuries to result from a short fall based on her experience.

An especially interesting part of this particular presentation of a character voice is that the lawyer repeats the word *impossible*, and he foregrounds the fact that the expert witness, a doctor, not the lawyer, had first used the word. The lawyer thus overtly constructs himself as not transforming the quotation for his own purposes. Instead, he, like the jurors, relies on the authority of an expert on this topic, someone who has relevant experience, to make this claim. Regardless of what the jurors think about the lawyer, as long as they believed the doctor, they would accept that the defense's claim could not be true.

An example of an expert's opinion being offered as a generality is in (16), which comes from a child sexual abuse case. The prosecution lawyer recreates what an expert psychologist said about children who have been abused, and then he applies the opinion to the specific case he is discussing:

> (16)   He talked to you it's very rare, first of all, of false allegations. He also told you that the norm is that kids don't report. So what are some things that he looks to? He said consistency of statements is important. The nature of the report. How it comes about. How it fits with other facts that are known to be true. And detail. It's actually much of what we are using to evaluate the testimony of witnesses here. As far as consistency of [the victim's] statement, it's consistent … She testified very consistently with it, in fact, gave even more details than that in 2001.

Here, the lawyer is using the expert to support his claims for how the evidence should be examined. The jurors do not have to believe the lawyer that these parts of the case are important, as an expert thought so as well. In this way, although the expert witness has no personal knowledge of this particular case, the lawyer is still able to use the doctor's authority as an expert to legitimate his own claims that the victim was being honest.

The next set of voices presented as sources of authority are the law and the judge. The judge is the human representative, interpreter, and enforcer of the law in the courtroom. These are what van Leeuwen (2007) calls "impersonal authorities" in that they are the rules that everyone must follow. Clauses in the voice of the law/judge account for 3.2% of the clauses in the prosecution arguments, 1.2% of the clauses in the defense arguments, and 1.4% of the clauses in the rebuttals. There are two main reasons that lawyers call on these voices: to legitimate their claim that something is il/legal and to justify their requests/commands of the jurors.

An example of a lawyer using a legal definition to justify their claim that what occurred is illegal can be seen in (17). In this case, the defendant was charged with second degree murder. The prosecution lawyer is going through the different elements of the crime that need to be present in order for the charge to be met. One is substantial bodily harm; we can see what the prosecution says in (17).

> (17)   Now substantial bodily harm has something of a technical definition. Temporary but substantial disfigurement; temporary but substantial loss or impairment of function of a body member or organ; or a fracture of any body member. In this case you heard substantial medical evidence that Serena Hu suffered massive brain injuries and injuries to her eyes. That is substantial bodily harm.

Example (17) is interesting for two reasons. First, in the first half of the quotation, the lawyer presents the legal definition instead of his own interpretation, to provide authority that this really is the description the jurors have to follow. If he had presented it in his own words, the jurors would have had to trust that his interpretation was correct. Here, they can rely on the ultimate authority. Then, in the second half, he summarizes what the medical evidence said, and then he applies the law to that evidence in his own voice. As a lawyer, he is a legal expert in his own right, and in this instance, he uses his own authority as such to make such a statement without needing to rely on the status of others.

In other instances, lawyers use the voice of the law or judge to mitigate their potentially face-threatening acts. In (18), the lawyer uses the authority of the judge to tell the jurors that they cannot use the defendant's prior bad acts as evidence in this case.

(18) As the Court has instructed you, you should not simply conclude the defendant's a bad person and therefore should be convicted of this.

The judge has more authority to make requests and demands of the jurors. The lawyer making a bald-faced demand or accusation of the jurors might have damaged his relationship with them. Thus, the lawyer uses the authority of the judge to instruct them, instead of using his own voice.

The final set of character voices that lawyers use are from socio-cultural sources outside of the local context of the courtroom. These however, are relatively rare in my corpus, only accounting for 4 clauses in the all of the prosecution arguments (0.02% of clauses), 28 or 0.2% of clauses in the defense arguments, and 2 or 0.06% of the clauses in the rebuttals. When they are used, they often legitimate the lawyer's claims about usual human behavior.

An example of this type of voice occurs in a case in which an assault victim, once she was sober, recanted her story that she had been beaten. The defense had claimed that people are more likely to tell the truth while sober, while the prosecution argues that the opposite is true, legitimating this claim by reproducing a Mexican proverb as in (19).

(19) There's an old Mexican proverb and it says, *solo los niños y los barrachos dicen siempre la verdad*. That means only little children and drunks always tell the truth …
It gave her the courage to tell the truth …

The authority of such sayings comes from their representing a culture's understanding of the way things are (van Leeuwen 2007). The fact that many people have believed this for a long time gives it a special status.

Overall, by using the authority of others, lawyers position their arguments as credible, regardless of whether or not the jurors see the lawyer as personally authoritative. It puts a distance between the lawyer and the claims and gives them a "reduced personal responsibility" (Goffman 1986 [1974]:512) for the information. They do not have to be an expert or even knowledgeable about these subjects. Instead, they can rely on the authority of others who do have reason to know these things. Of course, by choosing to reproduce these particular voices, the lawyers are not neutral participants. They are still responsible for the words they animate. Still, the quoting of authorities, be they lay witnesses, experts, the law/judge, and socio-cultural sources, is one way in which lawyers negotiate interpersonal relationships between the argument they are presenting and the jurors. This resource allows lawyers to use the authority of others, when their own authority may be lacking, or when what they want to say may interfere with the relationship they are building with jurors.

Additionally, this analysis of character voices as sources of legitimation can also be taken a step further to add to our understanding of the ideational content of closing arguments. This is accomplished by determining the response of the other side, when a character voice was used in an argument as legitimation. To accomplish this, for each character voice serving as legitimation, the corpus was analyzed to determine if the other side referred to the same original utterance or even the same information but not in a character voice. This analysis showed that the lawyers took four strategies.

The first strategy was to recontextualize or give new meaning to the utterance so that it no longer supported the other side's claim. For example, this occurred in a case where a father was charged with physically abusing his daughter. His statement that he might have hurt her was used by the prosecution in (20a) to legitimate their claim that he did. If he admitted that he could have done it, then he must have. The defense argued in (20b) that the statement could be explained by the defendant not being aware of what he would have had to have done to injure the child.

(20a)   He said and admitted, "I never ruled myself out as a possibility." ... That reason is because he is the only person who could have, who had an opportunity to, and in fact did commit this crime.

(20b)   And when he had stated, "I never ruled myself out as a possibility," ... What he was saying is that I think – or the reason he's stating that, he was an inexperienced parent at the time that he's being asked these questions he has no idea what kind of force it would have taken to cause these injuries on [the victim].

The defense simply argued that the quotation did not have the meaning the prosecution attributed to it, and therefore, it did not legitimate their argument. Overall, I found that the prosecution recontextualized 8.1% of clauses in the defense arguments that were character voices used for legitimation (often in the rebuttals but also pre-emptively in their main arguments); and the defense recontextualized 5.9% of the clauses in character voices that the prosecution used this way in their main argument and pre-emptively recontextualized 14.0% of those used in the rebuttals.

The second strategy was to falsify the utterance, to claim that it was untrue and therefore did not support the other argument. An example of this occurred in a child abuse story in which the prosecution presented the crime narrative in the voice of the victim. The defense then claimed the story must be false.

(21)   If you're going to believe the story, you have to believe that Jennifer Margosian went for a ride on her bike in a cemetery at one o'clock in the morning in the very heart of [northern US state] winter. I submit to you that that's ludicrous, unbelievable. Common sense dictates that it is not possible.

Their argument was that the victim must not have been telling the truth, so despite the prosecution relying on her authority, their narrative was wrong. In total, the prosecution, in their arguments or rebuttals, falsified 5.3% of the clauses in character voices that the defense used as legitimation. The defense falsified 5.1% of those the prosecution used in their main argument. Interestingly, in three cases, the prosecution reproduced a quotation as legitimation in their rebuttal, despite the defense already having claimed it was false.

The third strategy was to attack the authority of the original speaker. Several studies have shown that expert witness status is constructed and deconstructed in the moment-to-moment interactions of the trial (cf. Renoe 1996; Matoesian 1999). This analysis extends those findings to the closing arguments and to lay witnesses as well. For example, in example (22), the defense claims the victim was not honest and was only telling the jurors what the police had told her to say.

(22) [The victim] gave numerous conflicting statements ... Although she did indicate that she did not remember the incident and those facts were given to her. Those facts were given to her that she related to the police. But who knows what is true and what is false with regard to her.

They claimed that since she did not remember the events and was lying, she could not be considered an authority. Overall, the prosecution attacked the authority of 14.3% of the lay witnesses and 15.8% of the expert witnesses which the defense used as sources of legitimation. The defense claimed that 23.0% of the lay witnesses and 36.4% of the expert witnesses that the prosecution used in their main arguments should not be accepted as authorities. Neither side attacked the status of the law or judge or referenced the socio-cultural sources that the other side used.

The final strategy the lawyers used was to silence (Huckin 2002) the character voice used to legitimate the other side's case. By not referring to the existence of the quotations that supported the other side's argument, they made them irrelevant to their arguments and did not activate them in the jurors' consciousness (though the jurors could have been thinking about them on their own). In total, the defense silenced 89.2% of the clauses in character voices used to authorize the prosecution's claims. The prosecution silenced 87.0% of the defense's utterances used as legitimation. If the character voices were eliminated when the authority of the original speaker was attacked, then 50.4% of clauses in the voices of personal authorities and 38.9% of the clauses in the voices of expert authorities used to legitimate the prosecution's closing arguments were still completely ignored by the defense. The prosecution still silenced 49.8% of the clauses in the voice of a personal authority and 74.2% of the clauses in an expert voice used as sources of legitimation in the defense's arguments. Overall, most of the quotations used to legitimate one side's argument were silenced. Even in the instances where the authority of the original speaker was attacked, what they had specifically said was often ignored.

The findings here pattern much like other studies on the ideational content of closing arguments discussed above. Rather than spending much of their arguments arguing why the other side was wrong, the lawyer simply ignores the character voices or topics that supports the other side's case. In trials, each side will use different quotations, topics, and lexical items as one means of creating opposing arguments.

Conclusion

In this chapter, I have shown how the closing arguments of trials within adversarial legal systems are important sites for forensic discourse analysis. The work that has already been done on the ideational content of arguments shows that prosecution and defense lawyers create different representations of the same events. This is often done, as we have seen, by silencing, ignoring or transforming topics, information, character voices, and lexical terms that support the other side's case and instead focusing on what supports their own argument. Studies of lawyers' negotiations of interpersonal relationships show that they try to balance an authoritative identity with appearing to be similar to the jurors. One way they accomplish this is through using quotations from authorities to legitimate their narratives, claims, and commands.

Despite all that is known, closing arguments are still understudied. Not only does more work need to be done in the areas discussed here, but future work could also try to examine lawyers' linguistic awareness as well as the effects of these linguistic strategies on the jurors.

Further reading

Cotterill, J. (2003) *Language and Power in Court: A Linguistic Analysis of the OJ Simpson Trial*, New York: Palgrave MacMillan.

Felton Rosulek, L. (2008) 'Manipulative silence and social representation in the closing arguments of a child sexual abuse case,' *Text & Talk*, 28(4): 529–50.

Heffer, C. (2005) *The Language of Jury Trial: A Corpus-Aided Analysis of Legal-Lay Discourse*, Basingstoke, Hampshire: Palgrave MacMillan.

Hobbs, P. (2003) '"Is that what we're here about?" A lawyer's use of impression management in a closing argument at trial,' *Discourse & Society*, 14(3): 273–90.

Stygall, G. (1994) *Trial Language: Differential Discourse Processing and Discursive Formation*, Philadelphia, PA: John Benjamins Publishing Company.

Walter, B. (1988) *The Jury Summation as Speech Genre*, Philadelphia, PA: John Benjamins Publishing Company.

16

Sentencing convicted murderers

Convicted murderers' allocutions or leniency pleas at sentencing hearings

Nancy Schweda Nicholson

Introduction

In a detailed analysis of *The People v. Orenthal James Simpson* (State of California (USA)), Cotterill (2003: 3) identifies "styles of testimony and their influence on juries" as an important aspect of trial language. In addition, research has focused on power and features of powerful and powerless language (Conley and O'Barr 2005; Fowler 1985; Fairclough 1989; Gibbons 2003; O'Barr 1982). These two aspects of language can have a significant impact on juries' ongoing perceptions and ultimate decision-making and, as Fairclough (1989: 31) says, "The way in which orders of discourse are structured ... [is] determined by relationships of power in particular social institutions." Power can be found in many aspects of trial language, and studies that have focused on this aspect in the legal discourse analytic literature include treatments of question and answer style (Cotterill 2003); strategies in both direct and cross-examination (Conley and O'Barr 2005); turn-taking protocols (Stygall 1994); interruptions (Heffer 2005); silence (Kurzon 1998b); and jury instructions (Charrow and Charrow 1979; Dumas 2000a). In terms of extended narrative that is not primarily read (like jury instructions), analysis techniques have been primarily applied to lawyers' opening and closing arguments (Cotterill 2003; Felton Rosulek, this volume; Heffer 2005; Stygall 1994). This chapter adds to the list of trial components and characteristics covered by linguistic analysis, as it investigates a monologic discourse event of a different type: the "leniency plea" or "allocution," which may occur during the sentencing phase of a trial in the US judicial system.

Allocution provides the person who has been found guilty as charged with an opportunity to speak. In allocutions, the researcher has access to real, naturally occurring, unedited data, which is preferred over formal interviews (Gubrium and Holstein 2009). The linguistic approach to such data involves applications of elements of discourse analysis and oral narrative (Cameron 2001; Eakin 2008; Halliday 1989; Nunan 1993; Sinclair and Coulthard 1992; van Dijk 1997, 1985) as well as speech act theory (Austin 1962; Searle 1969). In addition, allocutions often contain much autobiographical information, so the literature in this domain is highly relevant (Eakin 2008; Linde 1993; Spence 1997), as is awareness of the role of identity (Eggins 1994; Halliday 1994; Kress 1976). The "social-constructionist" approach to narrative focuses on the ability of the narrator to make sense of his/her experiences and construct "the self" (Wood and Kroger 2000:104). Sabat and Harré (1992: 445) contend that "selfhood is publicly manifested in various discursive practices such as telling autobiographical stories."

The forensic linguistic and legal literature contains many references to the "storytelling" aspect of the courtroom (Cotterill 2003; Heffer 2005 and this volume; Spence 1995). Spence (1995), a noted American lawyer famous for his unconventional approaches to advocacy, provides advice to attorneys with respect to legal strategy options. Many of these are relevant to the current allocution analysis (and to extra-legal situations as well), although the "voice" is not that of an attorney. Spence lists ten elements that constitute the "great power argument". One of these is:

> *Give the argument in the form of a story.* [W]e are genetic storytellers and listeners to stories. ... So, do not forget what you have learned already: jurors ... are conditioned to listen to stories.
>
> (Spence 1995: 203)

He considers the story as the "strongest structure" to be used in the formulation of legal argument (Spence 1995: 113). Moreover, Daley and Daley-Caravella (2004: 164) agree: "The most persuasive evidence used in support of your belief is a human-interest story." Kintsch (1995: 140) describes the role of the listener in discourse comprehension "as constructing a mental representation of the information provided by the text that is integrated with his knowledge, beliefs and goals." Textual coherence is a result of many factors, and plays an important role in autobiography, both from the speaker's and listeners' perspectives (Gernsbacher and Givón 1995; Linde 1993).

Finally, the element of persuasion is evident. Oliver (1957: 7) defines "persuasion" as "any form of discourse that influences thought, feelings or conduct." He emphasizes the "particularity" of every persuasive event: "There is a particular type of speaker addressing a particular type of audience, on a specific occasion, to achieve a goal that is ... special" (Oliver 1957: 62). Phoenix (2008) and van Dijk (2008) examine the important influence of context in constructing a narrative, and Fairclough (1989) discusses the social conditions of production and interpretation. Brazil (1993) also stresses the goal-oriented nature of oral narrative. In the data examined in this chapter, the convicted murderer must attempt to convince the jury that his life is worth sparing or that a lesser sentence is warranted. The elements of persuasive discourse that can sway a jury include telling the truth (Spence 1995; Storey 1997); connecting with the listeners through examples/illustrations to which they can relate (Bedell 2000); making a logical, reasoned argument (Simons 2001); and using "everyday speech" (Minnick 1968:103).

This chapter focuses on the allocutions of two convicted murderers, Rabbi Fred Neulander and Michael Skakel (available at: http://topics.nytimes.com/topics/reference/timestopics/people/n/carol_neulander/index.html and www.trutv.com/library/crime/notorious_murders/famous/moxley/arrested_8.html).

Although their narrative styles are quite distinctive, each convicted person (CP) paints an autobiographical picture of identity and strives to persuade a group of twelve to believe not only his story, but that he is worthy of mercy. Before proceeding to the data analysis, the term "allocution" is discussed, and background information on the cases is presented.

Allocution

In many jurisdictions in the United States, those who have been found guilty of capital crimes have the right to allocute. Each state regulates the opportunity to make an "allocution," defined by *Black's Law Dictionary* as "a mitigating statement made by a defendant in response to the court's inquiry" (Garner 2004a: 83). There are additional meanings of "allocution," however. For example, in the popular television show, "Law and Order," the Prosecutor frequently makes plea deals. When he accepts a plea, he often tells the defense lawyer: "I'll expect your client to allocute." In this context, the Prosecutor often demands that the guilty party provide previously unknown details regarding the crime. If a body and weapon have never been found in a murder case, a condition of the plea agreement may be that the murderer must reveal how the person was killed and the location of the body. Essentially, the individual has an opportunity to speak to the judge and jury during "an allocution." This statement occurs after the person has been found guilty of the crime but prior to sentencing. In fact, allocutions are often a plea for leniency directly before the sentence is pronounced. For example, if the death penalty is a possibility, the guilty party may ask that the sentence be a term of life in prison rather than death.

Judges frequently impose restrictions on the content of allocutions. For example, the individual may not be permitted to dispute the evidence, present an alternative account of the crime or deny guilt (although the latter does not always hold true, as the reader will see in the case of Michael Skakel). The judge's instructions dictate a focus on those persons that have had a positive influence during his/her lifetime, why he/she is a good person, a discussion of past and future good deeds and, of course, remorse for the crime(s) of which he/she has been found guilty. In a 1961 landmark US Supreme Court case (*Green v. United States* 365 U.S. 301), Green claimed that the trial court judge erred when he did not ask him if he would like to speak before sentence was imposed. Green further argued that, because he was not allowed to address the Court, his sentence was illegal. The Supreme Court affirmed the Appellate Court decision that there was no error, and that the sentence was legal because Green's appeal did not clearly demonstrate that he *had* been denied the right to speak. The Court, however, did rule that "trial judges before sentencing should unambiguously address themselves to the defendant, leaving no room for doubt that the defendant had been issued a personal invitation to speak prior to sentencing" (Myers 1997: 799).

Juries look for remorse as they consider the potential sentence. If the individual is, in fact, innocent (or maintains that he/she is innocent), it is inconsistent to show remorse for a crime in which they were not involved. In *Shelton v. State of Delaware* (744 A.2d 465 (Del. 1999)), Shelton argued that the trial court had unreasonably limited the content/scope of his planned allocution. The Delaware Supreme Court rejected Shelton's argument. In a dissenting opinion, Justices Hartnett and Berger wrote: "allocution is so fundamental to a fair trial in a capital case that deprivation of that right violates both State and Federal Constitutional due process" (511 – original opinion; Feldman 2004: 869). However, recently, the Supreme Court of California ruled that a defendant does not have the right to make an unsworn statement in an attempt to lessen punishment (*People v. Blaine Allen Evans* 2008). If the individual wishes to speak before sentence is pronounced, he/she must not only be sworn in, but also be subject to cross-examination (Egelko 2008).

For someone who has not taken the stand to offer testimony during the trial, an allocution is the first (and only) opportunity for the judge and jury to hear the convicted person express himself in his own words, uninterrupted by his own lawyer (during direct examination) or by an aggressive prosecutor shooting rapid-fire questions (during cross-examination). Some allocutions are extremely short, and consist of a simple "I'm sorry" (Gruber 2007). Others, like those discussed here, are lengthy statements that encompass a number of different themes. Such testimony can be sworn (in New Jersey, for example) or unsworn (in the State of Delaware). Defendants may or may not use notes as they speak. They can also read a prepared written statement to the court if they so desire. Moreover, victim impact statements (usually containing aggravating points) as well as pleas for leniency from relatives and friends (characterized by mitigating information) may also be heard at this point. After the CP and others address the court, the jury retires to deliberate on a sentence.

The Rabbi Fred Neulander and Michael Skakel cases

Fred Neulander was a charismatic and beloved rabbi at the M'Kor Shalom Temple in Cherry Hill, New Jersey. Much of the temple's success was directly due to Neulander's popularity. There was a dark side, however, to Rabbi Neulander. At the time of the murder of his wife, Carol, he was carrying on an affair with Philadelphia radio person-ality, Elaine Soncini. She gave Neulander an ultimatum in the late summer of 1994, indicating that she would break off the affair unless he divorced his wife of more than twenty-five years. Neulander proceeded to hire Len Jenoff, a reformed alcoholic whom he was counseling at M'Kor Shalom, to carry out the murder. Jenoff, in turn, recruited Paul Daniels to assist in the killing. Carol was brutally murdered in her home on the evening of November 1, 1994. Although Neulander was a suspect from the start in the murder-for-hire, he eluded prosecution until October of 2001, when Jenoff confessed the entire story to a *Philadelphia Inquirer* reporter. Neulander vehemently denied any involvement (and has never admitted his guilt). At his first trial in 2001, where he testi-fied in his own defense, jurors were unable to agree on a verdict, resulting in a hung jury. The Prosecutor immediately refiled the charges, and Neulander was re-tried in 2002, this time without testifying. In December of 2002, he was found guilty of felony murder and conspiracy to commit murder. After listening to positive and negative statements about the convicted felon (including a 24-minute allocution from Neulander himself), the jury could not reach a decision regarding the death penalty, which was a possibility because of the heinous nature of the crime. As a result, the judge imposed a sentence of life in prison without parole eligibility for 30 years. Neulander's attorneys filed several appeals on his behalf, but their attempts to secure a new trial came to an end in April 2007 (Graham 2007). Neulander is currently serving his term in the New Jersey State Prison in Trenton.

Michael Skakel's story is quite different. Growing up in Belle Haven, one of the most exclusive neighborhoods in extremely wealthy Greenwich, Connecticut, Skakel was a sixteen-year-old child of privilege in 1975. In fact, his father's sister, Ethel, was married to Robert F. Kennedy, US Senator, US Attorney General and 1968 presidential candi-date. Martha Moxley, 15, a popular neighbor of Skakel's, was found murdered close to her home on October 30, 1975. She was beaten and stabbed with a golf club belonging to a set that was found in the Skakel garage. Over the years, many people, including Michael's brother, Tommy, and Michael himself were considered suspects. The crime went unsolved, however, for almost a quarter of a century. Michael Skakel fell under the spell of alcohol and drugs and then spent time in rehabilitation facilities, including the elite Elan School in Poland Springs, Maine. Former Elan "students" would testify at the trial that Skakel had bragged about killing Moxley while there for treatment. The investigation was reopened in 1991, and the prosecution team gathered additional evidence for the next nine years. Skakel was formally charged with Moxley's murder in January of 2000, and his trial finally began in April 2002. Skakel did not take the witness stand, so his August 29 plea for leniency was the first opportunity the court had to hear him speak. In an unfocused and emotional statement, Skakel swore that he did not commit the crime. (In fact, after his arraignment in March 2002, he approached Dorthy Moxley, Martha's mother, and stated: "Dorthy, I feel your pain, but you've got the wrong guy." www.courttv.com/trials/moxley/background.html). Skakel was found guilty, however, in June of 2002 and sentenced to 20 years to life in prison. All appeals were exhausted as of October 2007; however, Skakel's cousin, influential Robert F. Kennedy, Jr., has become involved in an attempt to secure a new trial and prove Skakel's innocence (Brouwer 2007; Cowan 2007; Hewitt 2003).

The interconnectedness of identity and persuasion

Identity

Halliday's (1994: 35) functional theory of linguistics states that the "analysis of lexico-grammatical forms of utterances should be foregrounded as a resource for constructing meaning," and Galasiński (2000) also points out how grammatical and lexical choices have particular functions when used by speakers. Listeners gain information about speaker identity through observing language use, and speakers consciously and unconsciously construct "self" when they speak. Eakin believes that "our practice of self-construction is largely unconscious" (2008: 22) and

> for the most part, we are not left to our own devices when we talk about ourselves, for protocols exist for many of the kinds of self-narration we may need to use—in churches, in courtrooms. ... and so forth.
>
> (Eakin 2008: 28)

Neulander, of course, is a product of the macroculture and microcultures in which he lives (Andrews, Squire and Tamboukou 2008). These cultures exert influence on narrative and identity construction. For example, prior to his arrest, Neulander was an American living in upscale Cherry Hill, New Jersey. The "culture" of the Jewish faith adds another layer to his personal make-up. Respected and popular (perhaps even adored by some of his female congregants), Neulander wielded much power within his temple. Eakin (2008: 22) writes: "we do not invent our identities out of whole cloth. Instead, we draw on the resources of the culture we inhabit to shape them." Neulander's Pharaoh story (2), for example, is replete with religious references in lexical items such as: "If you give me this privilege to *redeem*, to *atone*." Additional examples of Neulander's identity-building include (9): his references to good deeds (such as helping to found a Ronald McDonald house and assisting a young man to obtain his General Educational Development diploma (GED), a high school equivalency credential available to dropouts who complete extra work and pass an exam without returning to a formal educational setting). In sum, Neulander's identity emerges through a largely positive statement illustrated by anecdotes that revolve around religion, family, past good deeds, and a promised future of constructive contributions in prison.

Michael Skakel portrays his identity for the jurors by offering descriptions primarily of a life of pain and sadness, addictions, and a loveless childhood. In developing the argument on the importance of culture, Linde (1993: 163) adds that culture furnishes "'coherence systems' [which are] cultural devices for structuring experience into socially sharable narrative." Example (1) is representative of Skakel's plea.

(1) Michael Skakel allocution (convicted person-Skakel – CP-S)
1 I say that as a man that was condemned by drugs and alcohol, condemned to
2 death from the addiction …
3 [God speaking to him] Michael … you can't use reform school or your Dad
4 or your upbringing as an excuse anymore. …
5 Love was not something in my family. There was a lot of hardship and an
6 enormous amount of pain. …
7 Mr. Fuhrman wrote a book about me filled with lies.

In contrast to the negativity depicted in (1), which is reflected in the use of negation ('can't' plus 'or' and 'or', lines 3–4; 'not', line 5), one positive and bright moment in Skakel's plea is the description of his young son (treated in greater detail under the "Family" theme). His allocution also includes numerous references to God (see "Religion" section), his encounter with Alcoholics Anonymous (AA), and how he traveled to former Eastern Bloc countries with this group. However, when Fuhrman's (1998) book appeared and re-ignited interest in the case, Skakel's job was "taken away" from him. In sum, Skakel's statement constructs an identity of a person who is troubled, fraught with anguish, and reaching out to God for understanding and guidance. As with Neulander, themes of religion and family dominate.

Persuasion

Closely tied to the construction of identity is the resulting persuasive impact (or lack of it) of Neulander's and Skakel's pleas. A key element of an individual's ability to persuade is personal credibility. Oliver (1957: 13–14) discusses the "Good Man" idea, stating "that a … speaker who wishes to convince others exerts influence based on his own reputation and deeds. Moreover, one who is successful in this domain is 'a good man trained in the arts of speech'". Given his dedication to a religious life as a career, it seems quite indisputable that Rabbi Neulander embodied good traits (as delineated in his plea). One cannot help but ask if these remain part of his character, even after the commission of a horrible crime. Michael Skakel also appears to have made positive contributions to society in his life. He emphasizes his struggles with drugs and alcohol, but states that he was reborn and is now free of these negative influences. Whatever their past and current make-up, both men have been convicted of murder. Oliver (1957: 70) notes that "deliberate wrongdoing is the shortest route to loss of public sympathy and esteem." This evaluation suggests that Neulander and Skakel would have minimally persuasive force. Unlike many persuasive speakers who attempt to sell a product or obtain votes in a political election, however, granting leniency requires no financial outlay or ideological commitment on the part of the jurors.

Neulander and Skakel were found guilty of their crimes *before* they made their statements to the court. Inasmuch as allocutions can be powerful tools in an attempt to avoid the death penalty, for example, one must consider the veracity of the statements they contain. Whether under oath or not, convicted murderers are not generally regarded by society as upstanding individuals to be believed and trusted. In other words, there is nothing to stop them from fabricating a story to achieve their goal of a lesser sentence. They really have very little to lose. Galasiński (2000) writes of a "truth bias," a concept related to Grice's (1975) Conversational Maxim of "Quality." In other words, unless otherwise inclined/influenced, most people tend to believe what others tell them. We must question if such a perspective holds true in a specific legal setting such as this one. And Eakin (2008: 34) writes: "Telling the truth – this is surely the most familiar of the rules we associate with autobiographical discourse." In many ways, the content of an allocution is autobiographical, as the judge instructs the guilty person to discuss his/her past as well as prior influences that contributed to shaping identity. Fred Neulander, who was eligible for the death penalty in the murder-for-hire of his wife, was forbidden by the judge to claim innocence for the murder, whereas Skakel denied his guilt twice during his plea.

Payne (2007), Petty and Cacioppo (1986) and Petty and Wegener (1998) discuss the "elaboration likelihood model of persuasion." This model suggests that there are two ways in which to persuade: (1) an individual conscientiously considers the worth of the argument ("central route"); or (2) the presence of a contextual cue (for example, a handsome speaker or a celebrity endorser) results in an attitude change without contemplation of the argument's merits ("peripheral route"). In terms of Neulander, it does not appear that peripheral cues would be at work, as he presents a cohesive and compelling argument. One could suggest, however, that a *negative* peripheral cue could play a role with Skakel. Although his argument is not coherent, his situation is a pathetic one, and this may engender sympathy on the jurors' part.

Without exception, the literature on persuasion focuses on the importance of connecting with the audience (Gardner 2004; Koegel 2007; Luntz 2007; Nowak 2004; Simons 2001; Storey 1997). Among the salient features with respect to influencing and judging the receptiveness of one's listeners (in this case, the jury), Oliver (1957) mentions that a speaker must consider factors like intelligence and educational levels. In the United States, prospective jurors must submit to an information-gathering process, which includes the completion of (often) lengthy questionnaires and in-person interviews (*voir dire*) by both the defense and the prosecution in open court. Consequently, all participants become very familiar with jurors' backgrounds (such as educational level, work history, family situation, and attitudes) before the trial begins.

Oliver also states that a prior relationship with the speaker could influence an audience positively or negatively. Of course, the Neulander jurors had much history with him, as they were present in the courtroom for months, listening to testimony and weighing the evidence. When I interviewed Neulander at the New Jersey State Prison in November 2008 and asked him how he "read" the jury as he pondered what he would say, he stated that he knew they were from an upper middle class area and were likely to be educated and sophisticated. One can, therefore, assume that he built this background knowledge into his speech design. As Gitomer (2007: 195) says, "eloquence is delivering your message in terms of the audience." Issues of identity and persuasion continue to be important in the analysis below.

237

Narrative and thematic analysis of Neulander's and Skakel's allocutions

In terms of allocution organization and structure, Neulander subscribes to a classic piece of rhetorical advice in terms of a beginning, middle and end: "Tell them what you're going to tell them, tell them and tell them what you just told them" Koegel (2007: 32). Altman (2008:18) discusses the concept of "framing," which gives a text a beginning and an end, but does not ensure a particular type of internal structure. Neulander's allocution is fairly well-structured, as one would expect it to be, given his years of experience as a teacher and preacher. He introduces his major theme "days of the years of your life" up front and then references it again many times during his statement, as the reader shall see. Finally, Neulander reprises it in his closing comments. He is clearly a polished public speaker and hoped to use his oratory skills to his advantage. In (2), (which occurs near the beginning of his plea, on page 2 of 12 transcribed pages) we see how he uses rhetorical questions, for example.

Skakel's plea, on the other hand, jumps from topic to topic in a disconnected fashion. It is an emotional series of vignettes that include conversations with God. Skakel does not have a recurrent theme like Neulander, but does repeat specific lexical items. Discussion now proceeds to an examination of several themes that occur in both Neulander's and Skakel's pleas, with an emphasis on religion and family.

Religion

"An essential strategy of human expression and thus a basic aspect of human life, narrative commands our attention" (Altman 2008:1). Rabbi Neulander's allocution *does* command attention. His elegantly articulate statement draws the listener in (see lines 1–2 of (2)). The Rabbi clearly possesses "linguistic intelligence" (Gardner 2004: 31). (In the extracts, bold is used to highlight sections to which I specifically refer in subsequent analysis. These excerpts illustrate repetition, direct address, register, use of synonyms, and his recurring phrase "days of the years of your life.")

(2) Neulander Pharaoh Story (CP-N)
  1 At the end of the Book of Genesis, there's a <u>wonderful</u>, wonderful dialogue between
  2 Pharaoh and the patriarch, Jacob. ... I hope you'll agree with me in a few seconds.
  3 And the Pharaoh asks a question at the outset, the outset of this discussion. ...
  4 if you're not careful, and not careful to read the Hebrew, it seems rather shallow
  5 and ((SHAKES HEAD)) nothing very important
  6 Pharaoh asks Jacob ... he says: I'd like to know how old you are,
  7 but it's said in a very remarkable way.
  8 Usually when there is a **locution**-when there is a **statement**,
  9 the normal pattern in Hebrew ... **let me do it in translation**.
 10 Um-the normal pattern would be to say,
 11 how many are the years of your life?
 12 The question of how old are you, the quantity of your years.
 13 Pharaoh doesn't ask that. Not that way.
 14 He asks ((FIST)) (2.0) **how many ... are the <u>days</u> ... of the years ... of your life**?
 15 That's why you have to be careful.
 16 (4) When he uses that word **the <u>days</u> of the years of your life, our great**

17 **commentators, our great scholars, our great interpreters** tell us ((FIST)) that
18 there is a message. That what's critical is not the quantity,
19 but the question is: <u>what</u> did you do with the days of your life?
20 <u>How</u> did you fill your days? How, how did you make a difference in the world?
21 Were you **selfish or** were you **generous** with your time?
22 Were you (2.5) (TSK) using the **best parts of your brain or** were you **lazy …**
23 **sloppy**? Did you have **a vision for the community or** were you < SLOW
24 **self deceiving** SLOW > and **looking only inwards**?
25 That now is ((FIST)) not an issue of <u>quantity</u> of years.
26 It's an issue of the quality of your experience.
27 And I would like to use that as a **benchmark** (2.0) for that which I speak to you
28 of <u>myself</u> **in the past, in the present**, and **in the future**.
29 The **benchmark** of **a past, <u>my</u> past, my present** and **my future**.
30 Which is in **your** hands and **you** know that.

It is only natural that a rabbi's statement would contain religious references ("Genesis," "Pharaoh," "Jacob," lines 1–2). In fact, one might characterize his allocution as the most important sermon of his life. Just before Neulander shares the story with the jury, he tells them that he is going to "take something from my tradition and see if I can make my request more understandable." Within a minute of beginning his lengthy statement, Neulander makes his pivotal argument to the jury—namely, that he plans to use the days of the years of his [remaining] life to perform good deeds in prison and improve the lives of his fellow inmates. In essence, his approach is embedding—a "story within a story." He also wants the jury to believe that he is someone who *has* lived a good life. Note the parallel structures as Neulander compares a positive attribute with a negative one (lines 21–24). The parallelism is inconsistent, however, in that he mentions a negative trait first in line 21, but the two subsequent comparisons (lines 22–24) position the positive element initially. Perhaps, stating "selfish" first is an unconscious self-reference. It is clear that the parallel positive/negative comparisons have autobiographical connections, ringing true for the disgraced rabbi himself. And, one could suggest that Neulander exemplified *all* of the characteristics (flaws and attributes) he cites. He was "selfish" and "generous" at the same time, for example. Although he did participate in the Ronald McDonald House and other charitable organizations, ultimately Neulander was egotistically focusing on his own needs and desires, predominantly his wish to be with his mistress. He takes on the voice of Pharaoh as he speaks to Jacob in this illustration, but also steps out of his story-teller role to address the jury directly (lines 27 and 28). In line 2, Neulander attempts to connect to the jury, explicitly stating that he wants them to find the story as relevant and interesting as he does. The end of line 7 serves to demonstrate that he has arcane knowledge (the Hebrew language). Although this brief statement may not be perceived negatively by the jury, it has the potential to distance Neulander from them, as they are probably not Hebrew speakers. He may unconsciously be sending the message that he considers himself to be more educated than they are. Possible evidence of a superior attitude is also indicated in his desire to make his "request more understandable." Shortly afterward, Neulander also goes into his "teacher" mode in lines 4 and 5, once again setting himself apart. In this instance, however, "you" is employed as an indirect pronoun. Finally, at the end of the illustration, he ties the entire scenario to himself personally (lines 27–29). In closing this segment of his plea, he also highlights the role of the jury in terms of his fate (line 30). This final line is an explication of something that all in the courtroom already know to be true. Perhaps Neulander says this to show deference—that he is painfully aware of the power they wield.

Throughout the rest of his allocution, Neulander repeats the phrase "the days of the years of your/my/his life" no fewer than 17 times as he speaks for approximately 25 minutes. "Repetition is useful for emphasis, but it should be used with care", says O'Barr (1982: 36). On the other hand, Minnick states: "Repetition ... is effective in stimulating an audience to attend to a speaker's statements" (1968: 63). Do the repetitions become tedious for the jury? Or, do they serve to keep his theme in the forefront (Abbott 2008)? The fact that much of Neulander's plea revolves around religious themes, good works and family, suggests that he attempts to create a non-culpable identity by constantly reminding the jury that he is a rabbi, a religious leader. People listening to such a statement might expect emotion (sadness, grief, tears, sorrow), but there is a clear disconnect between Neulander's demeanor (his "how") and his language use (his "what"). Even though found guilty of the murder-for-hire, Neulander contends that he was not involved in the planning or execution of this crime.

Michael Skakel's largely unstructured and rambling allocution is replete with religious references. In fact, he mentions "God" 20 times over the course of the approximately five transcribed pages, and "Lord," "Jesus" or "Jesus Christ" four times. The following excerpted lines illustrate the relevant contexts in which "God" occurs:

1	I owe everything to the God of my understanding
2	the addiction that, as God is my judge
3	to me, it was God clearly saying
4	the relationship I have with the God of my understanding
5	the God who stands with me today
6	Sometimes I ask, daily, I ask God every day in my cell
7	pain in a lot of people's lives. But, God is ...
8	I turned away from God for a long time
9	for a long time God has come back to my life
10	can't take responsibility for. Only God can take
11	a lie in front of my God who I am going to be in front of
12	place in the whole world was God's child
13	my life in your hands and the Good Lord tells me
14	you impose on me I accept in God's name
15	if you don't believe in God, have a child
16	have a child. God gave me that boy
17	Some people have a lot of God in them
18	to know anything about God so they don't
19	to the prison systems, to the Godless countries
20	because that's what God tells me to do

Skakel even goes so far as to suggest that God is on his side (lines 1 and 5). He talks about "turning away from God" (line 8) and then finding God again (line 9). He contends that God talked to him on several occasions (lines 3, 13, 20).

(3), (4) and (5) are examples of reported speech. In (4), Skakel explicitly tries to distance himself from the crime, portraying himself as a victim.

(3) Conversation with God (CP-S)

1 I actually heard the good Lord say 'Michael, do you want to keep doing it your way?'
2 And I saw blackness and death in an instant.
3 'Or do you want to try it my way?'
4 And I felt the spark of hope.

Note that Skakel's "conversational turns" in (3) are not verbal responses to God, but rather a description of his personal feelings as he surrenders to God's will in terms of getting on the right path.

(4) God addresses Skakel (CP-S)

1 You can no longer have any excuses, Michael …
2 You can't use reform school or your Dad or your upbringing or being kicked out of
3 schools as an excuse any more.

(5) Skakel addresses God (CP-S)

1 Sometimes I ask, daily, I ask God every day in my cell why my life has come to this.
2 I scream to him sometimes and say, "Lord, I have done everything you wanted
3 me to do … why am I here?"

He discusses his connection with Alcoholics Anonymous (overcoming addiction), and refers to Easter (the day that Jesus rose from the dead, which is commonly accepted as a metaphor for personal rebirth). He stresses that he "owe[s] everything to the God of my understanding, my savior Jesus Christ."

At the end of his plea, Skakel repeats the word "pray" five times, stating that he prays for the judge, the Court, the Moxley family, the prosecution, and the press. One could suggest that making an explicit reference to praying for the judge may be a risky undertaking. Skakel probably knows little or nothing about the judge's religious persuasion, and it is certainly possible that he could be offended by the convicted murderer's supplications on his behalf.

Family

Fred Neulander refers frequently to family members during his leniency plea. He speaks about how proud he is of his three children, and what they have become. Most notably, he spends 25% of his statement talking about his deceased wife, Carol. He offers a detailed description of her, in both dispassionate and loving terms. For example, he talks about her skills as a businesswoman, creating and running Classic Cakes, the most popular bakery in Cherry Hill. He praises her business acumen, stressing that she had no training or experience in marketing or the commercial world before she established the company. Neulander says that Carol had "great grit," was "balanced" and had "common sense." Some might suggest that painting this picture of Carol demonstrated a certain detachment. He could have been talking about a mere acquaintance. On the other hand, Neulander also states that Carol had "class," was "remarkable," "bright," "gracious" and "a lady." He becomes emotional when he tells the jury how much he loves and misses her. His depiction of life with Carol culminates in a reported speech dialogue that he relates to the court. Neulander attempts to reach the jury by personalizing what he is

241

about to say. Note the occurrences of repetition, grammatical parallelism ("with your" + noun) and direct address ("your," "each and every one of you"), all characteristic of powerful speech in (6).

(6)   Reported speech dialogue between CP-N and deceased wife

1   We had a little dialogue that I'm sure each and every one of you … might have
2   with your close friend,
3   with your beloved,
4   with your husband,
5   with your wife,
6   with your partner.
7   One of us would say to the other: "I want to grow old with you"
8   and the other would lean over and whisper:
9   "I want to grow old with you, too, but let's do it slowly."

When one reflects on the parts of the allocution that are dedicated to Carol, it reads more like a victim impact statement or a eulogy than a plea for leniency. If one were not aware of the context and the circumstances of the Rabbi's utterance, it would be very easy to assume that Carol had been murdered in some mindless and senseless act of random violence. Neulander's insistence on his undying love is consistent with what an innocent person would say, and the sheer volume of the statement dedicated to Carol makes the listener think about the persuasive impact as well as the credibility of his story. Does he spend so much time deifying her because it is an indirect way of demonstrating innocence to the jury? Vinnie Politan, a longtime Court TV reporter who covered the Neulander trial, was in the courtroom that day. After the plea, he described the jury's reaction when Neulander was speaking so glowingly about his wife. Politan said some of the jurors were shaking their heads and looking down, and others had expressions of disdain and disgust on their faces. "They weren't buying it [his story]" (Court TV Coverage 2003).

Family plays an important role in Skakel's statement as well. Early on, Skakel describes his life as a child in completely negative terms: "It's true that I didn't have love—love was not something in my family. There was a lot of hardship [emotional, not monetary] and an enormous amount of pain." Springer (2008) faults Skakel's famous defense attorney, Micky Sherman, for not "humanizing" Michael enough. When we reviewed the allocution together, Springer told me that none of the information about Alcoholics Anonymous, his horrible family life as a child, or his wife's hatred of him and his son came out at trial. Since Skakel did not take the stand in his own defense, this was the first time the jury heard any of these details about his personal life. Of course, at this point, Skakel had already been found guilty, so the only possible mitigation was a less-than-maximum sentence. Skakel appears to love his three-year-old son, George, very much, and it seems that he has played a major role in his upbringing. He often recounts anecdotal conversations with his son during the allocution. An extremely negative characterization, however, is reserved for Skakel's ex-wife, Margot, from whom he was divorced in 2001. The convicted murderer quotes his son: "Mom says that you are going to prison and only bad men go to prison." His son compares his mother to Skakel's scratchy beard by saying she is "rough." Overall, the reader has the impression that, in addition to pleading for a lesser sentence, he is also begging the court to have mercy on his son, who will be raised by the mother when Skakel is sent to prison. As evidenced in (15), line 10, Skakel does not, however, express strong negative feelings about his ex-wife to his son. Notable are the deification of Carol Neulander and the demonization of Margot Skakel. In terms of the victims, Michael Skakel never mentions Martha Moxley by name, although he refers to her family. Neulander, however, dedicates a large portion of his statement to a description of his murdered wife, Carol.

Linguistic and rhetorical patterns

Register

Whereas Skakel uses simple, ordinary lexical items in his allocution, Neulander some-times includes words that are uncommon, even archaic. McDonald posits "Eight Rules for Good Writing." Many of these apply to speaking as well. One of the Rules is to avoid "inflated language – pedantic and high-sounding phrases" (McDonald 1986: 73). Neulander breaks or, one could say, exploits this rule numerous times during his allo-cution and at some risk, as O'Barr warns when he says: "[u]sing unfamiliar words to make an impression may be seen as ... insincerity" (1982: 32). Spence concurs: "Words that are directed to the sterile intellectual head-place should be abandoned" (1995: 104).

(7) Neulander addresses the jury at the outset (CP-N)

1 It was very **fortuitous** that yesterday I did not have the opportunity to address you.
2 and I'm definitely sure that ... I could not have spoken **cogently** ...
3 (4) Mr. Riley and Mr. Lynch yesterday spoke to you of requesting your **cogency**,
4 your wisdom, your thought, your analytic gifts ... in making this ... *very* difficult decision.

In lines 3 and 4 of (7), Neulander begins by attributing desirable qualities to the jurors and flattering them, in essence, by telling them how smart he believes they are. Additional examples include the following: "She [Carol] used it with skill ... she used it **adroitly**"; "I have acknowledged for the longest time my behavior that was **reprehensible**"; and "the best congregation in the world. And that's not just **hyperbole**".

(8) Teaching plea (CP-N)

1 ((HANDS)) < PLEADING That's all I want PLEADING > ..((HANDS)) is that opportunity
2 to teach. And that's why I'm here,
3 I **beseech** you,
4 I **importune** you..
5 I beg of you for that privilege.

What are the jurors' possible reactions to words like those highlighted in (8)? Austin (1962) and Searle's (1969) discussion of "speech acts" is taken up by numerous scholars (e.g. Wood and Kroger 2000). Within "locutions" (statements, utterances), speaker intention ("illocutionary force") definitely plays a role. Neulander's goal in generating the locution is to persuade the jury not to sentence him to death. However, the effect of a statement on its audience ("perlocutionary force") may be different from that which was intended by the speaker. In this way, there may be a disconnect between the illo-cutionary and perlocutionary. In Neulander's case, as McDonald (1986) and O'Barr

(1982) suggest, the jury members could be alienated by his choice of words. Oliver (1957: 111) writes: "When you come to the point of asking for a decision, don't let an active ego spoil what you have accomplished by insisting upon a triumphant display of your own superior smartness." On the other hand, they could also be impressed with his command of English and view him as an intelligent person who could make some real contributions in prison. Neulander's choice of hyperformal lexical items (like "hyper-bole" instead of "exaggeration," for example) may also interfere with conveying the intended message (Axelrod 2007). In other words, when jurors stop to focus on a word that they do not understand, they may miss something important. The use of "language that draws attention to itself" can distract the listener from one's argument or message (McDonald 1986: 220).

In terms of lexical choice and phrasing, none of Skakel's words is representative of a high register. He is very conversational and easily accessible. His focus on religion is very different from that of Rabbi Neulander, however. Neulander "comes by his religious stories honestly," whereas Skakel goes on and on about God and Jesus in a largely dis-jointed manner. Skakel, I believe, attempted to elicit more sympathy from jurors than did Neulander. The many references to his young son were heart-wrenching to hear. On the other hand, much was made of the fact that Skakel had been living his life as a free man for almost 30 years, while Martha Moxley went to an early grave.

Murder-for-hire, the crime of which Neulander was convicted, is a calculated and premeditated offence, one that is often associated with a cold and unfeeling heart. It was alleged throughout both trials that Neulander intentionally had Jenoff and Daniels commit the murder on a night when his son, Benjamin (a medical student), would be on duty as an Emergency Medical Technician (EMT) in order to deflect any suspicion from him. A juror might well believe it cruel and callous for a father not to care about how his son would feel when, summoned to his own home on an emergency call, he found his mother beaten to death on the living room floor. The contrast between this vision of Neulander and how he presented himself in his leniency plea could not be stronger.

Grammatical parallelism, lexical patterns, tense shifts, repetition and synonymy

The Neulander allocution includes a variety of rhetorical and linguistic strategies designed to hold his audience's interest. For example, "[p]arallelism helps satisfy … [the] … ..innate craving for order and rhythm" (Garner 1999b: 184). In Neulander's case, (8) exhibits grammatical parallelism, repetition and tense shift. In (9), Neulander talks about how he plans to help other inmates learn to read.

(9) Neulander as teacher (CP-N)

1 I'm a good **teacher**,
2 I was a good **teacher**,
3 I can be a good **teacher**, and I want to help

The tense shift reverts to his "past, present and future" comments in (2) lines 27–29, although they do not occur in the same order.

In (10), Neulander talks about Carol's accomplishments.

(10) Carol Neulander as businesswoman (CP-N)

1 Carol Neulander, my wife, started a business with no **background** in **business** and no
2 **training** in **business**.
3 She started a bakery with no **background** in **baking** and no **training** in **baking**.

The grammatical parallelism in (10) foregrounds his point.

(11) Neulander closing (CP-N)
1 Ladies and Gentlemen, ... (3) If you give me this privilege ... to redeem, ... to atone,
2 (1.5) what will happen is ... **the days of the years of your life** will indirectly ...
3 be made more rich because you've given me the privilege in **the days of the**
4 **years of my life**
5 to reach out and change for the better ... (2.5) **the days ... of the years ... of the life**
6 of so many men I have yet to meet.
7 (5) Thank you, ladies. Thank you, gentlemen.

Within a persuasion framework, "personal relevance" appears to be significant when individuals believe that the issue will exert an important influence on their own lives (Petty and Cacioppo 1986: 144). In (11), Neulander tries to persuade the jury that they will feel good if they spare his life. In addition to repetition and direct address, Neulander follows a classic piece of rhetorical advice—a strong ending: "Your job is to tell a compelling story and make the audience think and react favorably *by making your point at the end*" (author italics) (Gitomer 2007: 86).

In (12), Neulander cleverly places his declarations of undying love for Carol just before and after a reference to his adulterous behavior. He buttresses the bad with the good. This is his only reference to personal wrongdoing within the allocution. Also, note the repetition, tense shift, and alliteration in (12).

(12) Neulander's love for his murdered wife (CP-N)
1 That was her **wonderful warm** ability.
2 (9) ((LOOKS DOWN)) <(TREM) And-(TREM)> <(SOLEMN) And I miss her
3 and I **loved** her ...
4 and I **love** her. Now there are those who I'm sure behind their hands who
5 would ... (3.0) would
6 snicker. (TSK) I have acknowledged for the longest time **my behavior** that was
7 reprehensible,
8 and **my behaviour** that was (1) **disgraceful** (SOLEMN)> and note that that's a
9 theological
10 word <(SLOW) **disgraceful** (SLOW)> <(SOLEMN) and yet (CLEAR THROAT)
11 you must believe *I* loved her-(TSK) and love her (SOLEMN)> .
12 (2) ((FIST)) and I wanted to spend the **days of the years of my life**,
13 (6) **long days of long years of my life** with her.

A cursory reading of (12) might leave the reader with the wrong impression about Neulander's reference to his "reprehensible" and "disgraceful" behavior. In this statement, he refers to unfaithfulness in his marriage, not to the fact that he arranged to have his wife killed. He has maintained his innocence all along, and continues to do so (Schweda Nicholson 2008). And note, even as he pleads for his life, he cannot step out of the religious instructional mode, as he highlights the "theological" meaning of the word "disgraceful."

His usage of "love" in both the past and present tense reflects an attempt to persuade the jury that he continues to love Carol even though she is no longer part of this world.

Skakel also uses the lexical item "love," but in a very different way in (13).

(13) Declaration of innocence (CP-S)
    1 I have been accused of a crime that I would **love** to be able to tell them that I did so
    2 they can sleep. I would **love** to be able to say I did this so the Moxley family could
    3 have rest and peace, but I can't, your Honor. To do that would be a lie in front of
    4 my God.

From a linguistic point of view, Skakel's repeated use of "love" in (13) seems incongruous. Someone might "love" to go on an exotic trip, to be able to afford a luxurious car, or to meet a famous person, but "love" to say that you murdered someone? The use of the word in this context is simply off-putting and bizarre. Shortly after this statement, he reaffirms: "I am innocent as charged."

Within reiteration, synonymy is a familiar rhetorical tool, generally used to make a point stronger and direct audience focus (Nunan 1993). Neulander has a habit of providing multiple synonyms for verbs, nouns and adjectives when he talks, and especially likes triplets, as in the case of (2), lines 16–17; (7), lines 3–4; and (8), lines 3–5. He further states, "I have heard men sing with **great power**, with **great beauty** and with a **gusto**." He describes the days of his life between November 1, 1994 (Carol's death) and January 16, 2003 (the day he was sentenced) as "dark, unproductive, diminished." In (6), he provides no fewer than five terms from the same semantic domain. Neulander also employs a classic persuasive strategy in (6) in which he attempts to focus on "common ground" between himself and the jurors. "Identification" portrays commonality and overlap, engaging listeners through shared experience and perspectives (Oliver 1957: 168). At times, he also provides a more accessible equivalent for a word that his audience may not know, as in "when there is a **locution** … when there is a **statement**," and "[t]he **portals** of a library are **gateways**." However, he also does this in the reverse, by providing the more common lexical item first, followed by the more sophisticated term, as in "she used it with **skill**, she used it **adroitly**."

Finally, as Neulander discusses the diverse opportunities that reading provides, he makes a request of the jury, extending it through use of near-synonyms (14).

(14) Teaching reading (CP-N)
    1 and I would like very much the privilege,
    2 if you will give it to me,
    3 of helping people find … (< 1) those worlds that **enthuse**, that **excite**,
    4 that that that **lift the spirit** … (< 1) and **lift the mind**.

Reported speech

Reported speech is a common narrative rhetorical device in which the speaker takes on the voice/role of another, often prefaced or followed by a third person statement such as "she said" (Holt and Johnson, this volume; Tannen 1993; Wood and Kroger 2000). In (7), Neulander describes what the attorneys said. Within (2)—his Pharaoh story—there are numerous instances of reported speech. In an early example, Skakel has an assertion–

denial sequence: "The prosecution says ... the fact of the matter is ... ." Notable in Skakel's statement is reported speech of several conversations with his young son. Skakel's strategy is to depict himself as a loving father, who has participated in raising a good and caring boy. It may also be suggested that Skakel singles out interchanges with his son as a persuasive technique, hoping that the jury will be swayed by these portrayals of loving interactions, that is, "How can Skakel be such a bad guy if he is a devoted father and his son loves him deeply?" Perhaps the most compelling is (15), which illustrates a double level of reported speech (an embedding), as Skakel recounts what his son said to him as well as what the mother said to the son.

(15) Reported conversation between CP-S and son, son and mother)

1 A week before he said, "Daddy", he said, "Mommy says she hates me, Dad."
2 And I [Skakel] said, "What did she say?"
3 She says she hates me ... "
4 And I said, "Does that make you sad?"
5 And he said: "And a little mad, too."
6 He said "she said she hates you too."
7 I said, "Well, that's okay."
8 Then he said: "Do you hate Mom? Do you hate Mom?"
9 I said, "No, kiddo, I don't hate anybody ... " [lots of intervening text here]
10 I said, "I care about your Mom, I love your Mom, but I don't like the things she does."

Conclusion

This chapter has analyzed two convicted murderers' pleas for leniency by employing techniques taken from the linguistics, narrative, autobiography, identity, and persuasion literature.

Who is served by these persuasive allocutions? Conger (1998: 43) points out that, if it is the speaker that primarily benefits, then he considers the statement to be "manipulative persuasion." Of course, in this particular setting and given this type of discourse, all present understand the implications of the statement and the goals of the speakers. But, does the jury itself gain from the plea for leniency? In (11), lines 2–3, Neulander explicitly suggests to the jury that *they* will indirectly benefit by showing him leniency. One could suggest that, by sparing Neulander's life and by reducing the potential sentence for Skakel, the juries show mercy and, in turn, experience positive feelings for being less harsh than they might have been.

Returning to the notion of power in the courtroom, it can be said that, by providing a forum for the CPs to speak uninterruptedly, the court cedes power to them. Neulander and Skakel have been found guilty and face long prison terms, so these men are essentially powerless in many ways (Fairclough 1989). *What* they say and *how* they say it are crucial: the allocutions may result in a shorter, less severe sentence. As a result, the pressure is on them to *seize* that power and to assert some influence over their fate. Neulander's description of his wife is "powerful" in the picture that it paints "because of the vividness of the impression" (Minnick 1968: 103). On the other hand, one could also suggest that it is simultaneously "powerless" as it further cements the idea in the minds of the jurors that the victim was a wonderful person. In reality, the jury could not reach a unanimous decision on the death penalty issue, so the judge herself pronounced sentence: life imprisonment without the possibility of parole until 30 years have passed.

The literature on forensic linguistics would benefit from additional studies of leniency pleas, as this subject has been largely ignored by the research community. In order to shed further light on this very specific discourse type, it would be worthwhile, for example, to examine whether allocutions vary significantly depending on the nature and severity of the crime. Moreover, research could investigate where leniency pleas are permitted worldwide, as well as linguistic variations and their bases in differences among cultures and legal systems.

Eakin (2008: x) says: "[L]ife stories are not merely *about* us but in an inescapable and profound way they *are* us." Inasmuch as allocutions provide an opportunity for the CP to make a relatively brief statement (usually extemporaneously), the pressures to say just the right thing and persuade the jury are enormous, particularly when the accused does not testify during the trial. The leniency plea, then, may be the first time the jury hears from the individual that they have observed in the courtroom for many weeks or months. For the CPs, choosing from many decades of formative experiences when deciding what to say is a truly daunting task. Their lives pass before the jury, and the stories they choose to tell frequently have life and death consequences. There is, perhaps, no more potentially powerful use of language than one that has self-preservation as its goal.

Further reading

Conley, J. and O'Barr, W. (2005) *Just Words: Law, Language and Power*, Chicago: University of Chicago Press.

Cotterill, J. (2003) *Language and Power in Court: A Linguistic Analysis of the O.J. Simpson Trial*, New York: Palgrave MacMillan.

Coulthard, M. and Johnson, A. (2007) *An Introduction to Forensic Linguistics: Language in Evidence*, New York: Routledge.

Eakin, J.P. (2008) *Living Autobiographically: How We Create Identity in Narrative*, Ithaca, NY: Cornell University Press.

Heffer, C. (2005) *The Language of Jury Trial*, New York: Palgrave Macmillan.

Storey, R. (1997) *The Art of Persuasive Communication*, Hampshire, England: Gower Publishing Limited.

Legal cases cited

Green v. United States 365 U.S. 301.

Lay participants in the judicial process

17

Instructions to jurors

Redrafting California's jury instructions

Peter Tiersma

Background

The function of a trial is to resolve disputes. Although some conflicts can be resolved purely by the application of legal principles, most trials involve disputes about a state of affairs or occurrence that took place in the past. Thus, a court must typically decide factual issues. Once it has done so, it can apply legal principles to the facts in order to arrive at a judgment.

During the middle ages there were differing methods of ascertaining the facts, or determining which party was telling the truth. Sometimes the parties were allowed to decide the matter by swearing an oath. Knights might decide a case by engaging in trial by battle. Perhaps the most interesting procedure was trial by ordeal. The ordeal by water, for instance, involved being thrown into a pond or other body of water. If the party sank, she had told the truth and was quickly rescued. If she floated, the water (being pure) had rejected her, exposing her claims as lies. All these methods of proof relied on divine intervention and hence required the cooperation of the church. Ordeals ended when a church council in 1215 declared that priests could no longer participate and because God no longer spoke through these rituals, they became meaningless (Baker 1990: 5–6).

Without divine intervention, how can courts know which party is telling the truth? Medieval English judges began to call twelve *juratores* ("persons who have been sworn") to court. They were summoned from the place where the dispute had taken place. The jurors were expected to have personal knowledge of the truth. Eventually, jurors began to decide what happened based upon evidence presented to them in court. In fact, today jurors are required to determine the facts *solely* on the basis of admissible evidence; they are generally disqualified if they have any prior knowledge of the facts or conduct an independent investigation (Baker 1990: 88–89; Levy 1999).

For many centuries, judges would give no instructions to jurors, although they might answer questions. Because the jurors were expected to reach a verdict, they would have to decide whether a party was guilty or liable based largely on their own sense of justice. This was true also in the English colonies of North America, which later became the United States. The American revolutionaries trusted the common sense of citizens and held that jurors should be able to decide not only the facts of a case, but also the rules of law that ought to be applied to reach a verdict (Levy 1999: 69–76).

This state of affairs began to change as the United States industrialized. Predictable legal principles were important for the growth of commerce and industry. By the end of the nineteenth century, the Supreme Court held that "it is the duty of juries in criminal cases to take the law from the court and apply that law to the facts" (*Sparf v. United States*, p. 102). This principle, which was later extended to civil cases, meant that judges had to instruct jurors on the relevant legal principles.

Creating a set of instructions for every case took a great deal of time and effort. Moreover, each judge's instructions would necessarily be somewhat different from those used by other judges. Soon cases began to be reversed because of errors in wording. Such problems led to the establishment of a committee of judges and lawyers in California, who in the 1930s and 1940s began to draft *standard* (also called *pattern*) instructions. The idea spread. Most American state and federal courts currently use standardized jury instructions (Nieland 1979).

Pattern instructions have indeed saved judges and lawyers time and money. Because they are usually drafted by committees of judges and lawyers, rather than a single judge, they tend to be accurate statements of the law, which has reduced the number of appeals for instructional error (Schwarzer 1981). Yet for the most part, they have not proven to be particularly comprehensible for the ordinary citizens who comprise the jury.

Developments in California

As mentioned, the state of California was a pioneer in the development of standardized instructions. The initiative was carried out by committees of the Superior Court of Los Angeles County, who created two sets of instructions. The civil version was originally called the *Book of Approved Jury Instructions* (or *BAJI*) (Committee on Standard Jury Instructions, Civil, 2004). The criminal instructions were known as *California Jury Instructions: Criminal* (or *CALJIC*) (Committee on Standard Jury Instructions, Criminal, 2003). Although not drafted by an official statewide body, they were commonly used throughout the state and generally regarded as accurate statements of the law. They were sometimes criticized as not being easy for jurors to understand, but the BAJI and CALJIC committees stoutly resisted any efforts to make them more comprehensible, fearing that use of ordinary English would make them legally less accurate:

> It has been bruited that our instructions are written in English that is "too good", "too highbrow"; that they ought to be written in the "language of the street" …
> In respect of this criticism, we ourselves have run into two difficulties: (1) the law has not been written in "the language of the street", and the one thing an instruction must do above all else is to correctly state the law. This is true regardless of who is capable of understanding it. (2) Jurors do not appreciate condescension … They want to look up to the judge, respect him as a learned man, and hear him speak in refined English.
>
> (Committee on Standard Jury Instructions, Civil, 1956: 44)

The problem of comprehension was addressed in a study undertaken by Robert and Veda Charrow in the late 1970s. The Charrows recorded a set of 14 BAJI instructions on audio tape (instructions, especially at that time, were often delivered orally by the judge). They played the tape twice to 35 subjects, who consisted of people called to jury duty but who had not yet served. Participants were then asked to paraphrase the instructions; these paraphrases were recorded and analyzed. Roughly speaking, only about one-third of the information contained in the instructions found its way into the paraphrases. Even when the Charrows conducted a further analysis that concentrated on the legally most important information, only about half of that information appeared in the participants' paraphrases.

Next, the Charrows tried to isolate some of the linguistic features of the BAJI instructions that appeared to make them more difficult to process. They identified a number of such features, including the use of technical terminology, convoluted word order, excessive embedding, multiple negation, and the use of passive verbs in subordinate clauses. They then rewrote the instructions to eliminate some of these troublesome linguistic features and repeated their experiment.

For example, the Charrows replaced difficult lexical items with more ordinary English. Where BAJI told jurors that the actions of an agent "would be imputed" to the employer or principal, the Charrows' revision stated that actions of the agent "would transfer" to the employer or principal. Cumulatively, this type of revision led to a 47% increase in comprehension. Another illustration is that several passive constructions were converted to their active equivalents. This produced an increased comprehension rate of over 48%. Overall, redrafting the instructions increased comprehension by around 35–40% (Charrow and Charrow 1979).

Several studies since then have confirmed the Charrows' findings. The most recent substantial research was conducted by Bradley Saxton (1998). Saxton gave questionnaires to Wyoming jurors immediately after they were discharged from service in actual trials. Ninety-seven percent of these former jurors believed that they understood the instructions either very well or completely. In reality, when participants were asked true/false questions about specific legal rules on which they had been instructed, only about 70% of their responses were correct. For example, around 40% of the participants who had served in criminal cases believed that the fact that the state brought a charge against the defendant was evidence that he or she had committed the crime, which is directly contrary to their instructions. And approximately 31% wrongly believed that once the state produced evidence that the defendant had committed the crime, the burden shifted to the defendant to prove his innocence.

The committee that drafted and updated the BAJI instructions ignored the Charrows' research, even though it appeared in a prominent legal journal. This was true even after the California Supreme Court cited the Charrows' study approvingly and suggested that the committee use its conclusions to improve the language of an "admittedly confusing instruction" on causation (Tiersma 1993: 54).

The situation changed only after the state lost a famous murder case against former football player OJ Simpson. Many people came to the conclusion that California's criminal justice system, and the jury in particular, was not working properly. The Judicial Council asked a special commission to study the matter. One of its recommendations was that the Council should appoint a task force to draft new instructions "that accurately state the law using language that will be understandable to jurors." They should be submitted to the Judicial Council and the California Supreme Court for approval (Kelso 1996).

The task force was divided into two subcommittees, one civil and the other criminal. They started their work in 1997. The committees consisted of judges and lawyers, two members of the public, and a law professor (the author of this chapter) whom they sometimes called their "linguistic consultant." Each committee had the services of a staff attorney, who conducted research and did much of the preliminary drafting. Members met in person several times a year to discuss proposed instructions. Typically, the proposed instructions would be projected onto a screen from a laptop computer and would be edited on the computer during the course of the meeting. Some were quickly approved, while others led to extensive debate until satisfactory language was hammered out.

All of the new instructions were circulated to the state's legal institutions (mostly courts and bar groups) for public comment. The committees received a large amount of feedback, which often led to improvements. In 2003, a full set of new civil instructions (given the name *CACI*) was approved by the California Judicial Council for use in the courts (Judicial Council 2003). The new criminal instructions (known as *CALCRIM*) were approved a few years later (Judicial Council 2006).

Old v. new: some civil instructions

To better understand the linguistic difficulties posed by the old instructions, and to see to what extent the new ones have improved the situation, it is useful to compare the two. We will first examine some civil instructions, beginning with the old (BAJI) instruction and then comparing it to the closest equivalent in CACI.

As printed, the instructions typically have a great deal of material in square brackets, indicating that certain language is optional or that the judge must choose between two or more alternatives. When they are read to jurors, who these days generally receive a written copy, the judge will have decided which language to include and the brackets will have been eliminated. In the following, I have chosen what appears to be the most common formulation and have deleted the brackets. Also, in some cases I have provided only part of the instruction in order to facilitate comparison between old and new.

A final preliminary comment is that in speaking of the "old" instructions I do not wish to suggest that they are no longer used. Some judges, mostly in Los Angeles, continue to read them to juries, either because they have been using those instructions for many years, or because they are philosophically opposed to explaining the language of statutes and judicial opinions in ordinary English.

BAJI 1.00. Respective Duties of Judge and Jury
Ladies and Gentlemen of the Jury:

It is now my duty to instruct you on the law that applies to this case. It is your duty to follow that law.

As jurors it is your duty to determine the effect and value of the evidence and to decide all questions of fact.

You must not be influenced by sympathy, prejudice or passion.

BAJI 1.00 is obviously an introductory instruction and is not bad in terms of language. It is, however, phrased in relatively formal terms, which was typical of the BAJI committee's approach. Informing jurors to "determine the effect and value of the evidence" is hardly ordinary English, although jurors probably know what it means.

There is no new instruction that parallels BAJI 1.00 exactly, but there is one which is given at the end of trial and which covers the same ground:

CACI 5000. Duties of the Judge and Jury

Members of the jury, you have now heard all the evidence. It is my duty to instruct you on the law that applies to this case. You will have a copy of my instructions with you when you go to the jury room to deliberate.

You, and only you, must decide what the facts are. You must consider all the evidence and then decide what you think really happened. You must decide the facts based on the evidence admitted in this trial. You must not let bias, sympathy, prejudice, or public opinion influence your decision.

Notice that instead of telling jurors to "determine the effect" of the evidence, CACI 5000 advises them to "decide what you think really happened," which is a far more fluent way of saying it.

The following old instruction is more problematic:

BAJI 1.01. Instructions to Be Considered as a Whole

If any matter is repeated or stated in different ways in my instructions, no emphasis is intended. Do not draw any inference because of a repetition.

Do not single out any individual rule or instruction and ignore the others. Consider all the instructions as a whole and each in the light of the others.

The order in which the instructions are given has no significance as to their relative importance.

Although it is the judge who repeats an instruction and does not thereby intend to emphasize it over the other instructions, BAJI has a strong aversion to the use of the first person. Instead, it prefers impersonal (often passive) constructions, such as "is repeated" and "is intended." Overuse of passives is a common feature of legalese (Tiersma 1999). In the first paragraph, the statement that jurors should not "draw any inference because of a repetition" is a very awkward way of saying that just because the judge repeats something, jurors should not assume that it's more important than the other things the judge may have said only once. The second paragraph is not too bad, but the third is again horribly stilted.

The equivalent language in the new instruction (also part of CACI 5000) is much more ordinary and understandable:

Pay careful attention to all the instructions that I give you. All the instructions are important because together they state the law that you will use in this case. You must consider all of the instructions together. …

If I repeat any ideas or rules of law during my instructions, that does not mean that these ideas or rules are more important than the others are. In addition, the order of the instructions does not make any difference.

American jury instructions typically address the question of what is, or is not, evidence that jurors can consider in reaching a verdict, as in the following:

255

BAJI 1.02. Statements of Counsel—Stipulation to a Fact—Evidence Stricken Out—Insinuations of Questions

Statements of counsel are not evidence; however, if counsel have stipulated to a fact, accept that fact as having been conclusively proved.

Do not speculate as to the answers to questions to which objections were sustained or the reasons for the objections.

Do not consider any evidence that was stricken; stricken evidence must be treated as though you had never known of it.

A suggestion in a question is not evidence unless it is adopted by the answer. A question by itself is not evidence. Consider it only to the extent it is adopted by the answer.

One of the problems that legal language can pose for members of the public is its use of technical vocabulary. The word "stipulate" in the first paragraph has a specific legal meaning (to conclusively admit or agree that something is the case), which BAJI does not explain to jurors. The second paragraph not only contains several levels of embedding, but also adds another legal phrase (to "sustain an objection") that may not be familiar to many jurors. The word "stricken" is also odd—usually it means that someone got an awful disease (as in "he was stricken by malaria"). Finally, the notion that answers "adopt" questions must seem very strange to most people. Below is the equivalent language from the new instructions:

CACI 106. Evidence

The attorneys' questions are not evidence. Only the witnesses' answers are evidence.

You should not think that something is true just because an attorney's question suggests that it is true. However, the attorneys for both sides can agree that certain facts are true. This agreement is called a stipulation. No other proof is needed and you must accept those facts as true in this trial.

Each side has the right to object to evidence offered by the other side. If I do not agree with the objection, I will say it is overruled. If I overrule an objection, the witness will answer and you may consider that evidence. If I agree with the objection, I will say it is sustained. If I sustain an objection, you must ignore the question. If the witness did not answer, you must not guess what he or she might have said or why I sustained the objection. If the witness has already answered, you must ignore the answer.

Sometimes an attorney may make a motion to strike testimony that you have heard. If I grant the motion, you must totally disregard that testimony. You must treat it as though it did not exist.

CACI 106 contains almost exactly twice as many words as the BAJI instruction. Often the old instructions were simply too terse and cryptic. Plain language need not necessarily be longer than traditional legalese, but in some cases a clear explanation inevitably requires more words. I daresay that jurors who hear or read CACI 106 have a far better understanding of what is happening during trial than would those who are confronted with the BAJI equivalent.

One of the most important issues in any trial is the burden of proof. The standard required in California civil cases was formerly expressed in BAJI 2.60:

BAJI 2.60. Burden of Proof and Preponderance of Evidence

"Preponderance of the evidence" means evidence that has more convincing force than that opposed to it. If the evidence is so evenly balanced that you are unable to say that the evidence on either side of an issue preponderates, your finding on that issue must be against the party who had the burden of proving it.

You should consider all of the evidence bearing upon every issue regardless of who produced it.

After explaining that the plaintiff has the burden of proving their case by a "preponderance of the evidence" (which was omitted in the above), the instruction proceeds to define the term. It begins well enough when it states that the plaintiff's evidence must have more convincing force than the opposing evidence. But the next sentence is very problematic, especially the use of the arcane verb "preponderate." The new instruction defines the burden of proof more clearly:

CACI 200. Obligation to Prove—More Likely True Than Not True

When I tell you that a party must prove something, I mean that the party must persuade you, by the evidence presented in court, that what he or she is trying to prove is more likely to be true than not true. This is sometimes referred to as "the burden of proof."

After weighing all of the evidence, if you cannot decide whether a party has satisfied the burden of proof, you must conclude that the party did not prove that fact. You should consider all the evidence that applies to that fact, no matter which party produced the evidence.

In criminal trials, the prosecution must prove facts showing that the defendant is guilty beyond a reasonable doubt. But in civil trials, such as this one, the party who is required to prove a fact need only prove that the fact is more likely to be true than not true.

The new instruction avoids "preponderate" and instead explains the burden in very ordinary terms: whether something is more likely to be true than not true. The instruction also confronts a possible area of confusion head-on by distinguishing the civil standard from the criminal burden of proof. This is particularly important in modern times, when criminal trials—and the reasonable doubt burden of proof—are commonly depicted on television and in film.

Many civil disputes involve vehicle accidents. This may produce a claim by the injured party for negligence, a type of tort or delict. To win a negligence claim, the plaintiff must prove that the defendant violated a duty that he or she owed to the plaintiff. This duty is the subject of BAJI 5.50:

BAJI 5.50. Duty of Motorists and Pedestrians Using Public Highway

Every person using a public street or highway, whether as a pedestrian or as a driver of a vehicle, has a duty to exercise ordinary care at all times to avoid placing himself or others in danger and to use like care to avoid an accident from which an injury might result.

A "vehicle" is a device by which any person or property may be propelled, moved, or drawn upon a highway.

A "pedestrian" is any person who is afoot or who is using a means of conveyance propelled by human power other than a bicycle. The word "pedestrian"

257

also includes any person who is operating a self-propelled wheelchair, invalid tricycle, or motorized quadrangle and, by reason of physical disability, is otherwise unable to move about as a pedestrian, as earlier defined.

The first two paragraphs are not too bad, although the phrase "to use like care" is quite formal. The definition of "pedestrian" in the third paragraph is a good idea, since it is an ordinary word that is used here in an unusual way to include people in wheelchairs and "motorized quadrangles" (whatever that might be!). The CACI equivalent is far more straightforward:

CACI 700. Basic Standard of Care
A person must use reasonable care in driving a vehicle. Drivers must keep a lookout for pedestrians, obstacles, and other vehicles. They must also control the speed and movement of their vehicles. The failure to use reasonable care in driving a vehicle is negligence.

A closely related instruction lays out in more detail the duties of both drivers and pedestrians:

BAJI 5.51. Amount of Caution Required in Ordinary Care—Driver and Pedestrian
While it is the duty of both the driver of a motor vehicle and a pedestrian, using a public roadway, to exercise ordinary care, that duty does not necessarily require the same amount of caution from each. The driver of a motor vehicle, when ordinarily careful, will be alert to and conscious of the fact that in the driver's charge is a machine capable of causing serious consequences if the driver is negligent. Thus the driver's caution must be adequate to that responsibility as related to all the surrounding circumstances. A pedestrian, on the other hand, has only his or her own physical body to manage to set in motion a cause of injury. Usually that fact limits the capacity of a pedestrian to cause injury, as compared with that of a vehicle driver. However, in exercising ordinary care, the pedestrian, too, will be alert to and conscious of the mechanical power acting on the public roadway, and of the possible serious consequences from any conflict between a pedestrian and such forces. The caution required of the pedestrian is measured by the danger or safety apparent to the pedestrian in the conditions at hand, or that would be apparent to a person of ordinary prudence in the same position.

This instruction is an elaboration on, or explanation of, the general standard of care relating to motor vehicles. The style is again formal and almost pedantic. It sounds like a university physics lecture delivered in the days when professors read their notes to the students.

It is usually a good idea for instructions to tell jurors why a particular rule applies. People are more likely to comply with an order if they understand its purpose, as opposed to obeying what seem to be arbitrary commands. Yet here the explanation for the rule does not seem all that important. It's perfectly obvious to anyone who has ever ridden in one that a car is a far greater potential danger than a pedestrian.

The new instruction assumes that the jurors have a certain amount of experience and common sense. It is therefore much shorter than the BAJI equivalent:

CACI 710. Duties of Care for Pedestrians and Drivers

The duty to use reasonable care does not require the same amount of caution from drivers and pedestrians. While both drivers and pedestrians must be aware that motor vehicles can cause serious injuries, drivers must use more care than pedestrians.

Criminal instructions

As noted above, the original California instructions had a separate set devoted to criminal law, called *CALJIC*, or *California Jury Instructions: Criminal*. The project to create new instructions therefore also created a separate criminal set, which is referred to as *CAL-CRIM*. The introductory instructions for both sets of criminal instructions (dealing with evidence and trial procedure) are similar to the corresponding civil instructions, so we will turn to what is often considered the most critical issue in a criminal trial, the burden of proof. We once again compare the old instruction with the new one.

CALJIC 2.90. Presumption of Innocence—Reasonable Doubt—Burden of Proof

A defendant in a criminal action is presumed to be innocent until the contrary is proved, and in case of a reasonable doubt whether his guilt is satisfactorily shown, he is entitled to a verdict of not guilty. This presumption places upon the People the burden of proving him guilty beyond a reasonable doubt.

Reasonable doubt is defined as follows: It is not a mere possible doubt; because everything relating to human affairs is open to some possible or imaginary doubt. It is that state of the case which, after the entire comparison and consideration of all the evidence, leaves the minds of the jurors in that condition that they cannot say they feel an abiding conviction of the truth of the charge.

There are numerous problems with the old instruction. The language was copied verbatim from an 1850 Massachusetts case. Note that it never defines what a reasonable doubt *is*; it merely defines what it *is not*. It addresses the jurors in the third person. And "abiding conviction" is not very ordinary language (Tiersma 1999: 194–96).

As a member of the CALCRIM committee, I advocated that we adopt language used by many jurisdictions, simply telling jurors that their decision must be based on the evidence and that they must be "firmly convinced" of the truth of the charge. It is elegant in its simplicity and, in my view, says it all. California, however, long ago adopted a statutory definition of reasonable doubt in Penal Code section 1096, which formed the basis for the old instruction. The CALCRIM committee likewise felt compelled to use the statutory language, although it did rearrange the wording to make it more comprehensible:

CALCRIM 220. Reasonable Doubt

The fact that a criminal charge has been filed against the defendant is not evidence that the charge is true. You must not be biased against the defendant just because he has been arrested, charged with a crime, or brought to trial.

A defendant in a criminal case is presumed to be innocent. This presumption requires that the People prove each element of a crime beyond a reasonable doubt.

259

Whenever I tell you the People must prove something, I mean they must prove it beyond a reasonable doubt.

Proof beyond a reasonable doubt is proof that leaves you with an abiding conviction that the charge is true. The evidence need not eliminate all possible doubt because everything in life is open to some possible or imaginary doubt.

In deciding whether the People have proved their case beyond a reasonable doubt, you must impartially compare and consider all the evidence that was received throughout the entire trial. Unless the evidence proves the defendant guilty beyond a reasonable doubt, he is entitled to an acquittal and you must find him not guilty.

Besides some improvements in organization, the main change was to rephrase the standard into a positive statement. Recall that the old instruction defines "reasonable doubt," which is almost inherently a negative concept. Instead, the new instruction defines "proof beyond a reasonable doubt," a seemingly minor change, but one that allows the standard to be stated positively: "proof that leaves you with an abiding conviction that the charge is true."

The definitions of crimes are also critical in a criminal case. The following is the previous instruction on murder. Alternatives relating to felony murder and killing of a fetus have been omitted for clarity of presentation. The instruction begins by laying out the basic elements of the crime:

CALJIC 8.10. Murder—Defined
Defendant is accused of having committed the crime of murder, a violation of Penal Code section 187.

Every person who unlawfully kills a human being with malice aforethought is guilty of the crime of murder in violation of section 187 of the Penal Code.

A killing is unlawful, if it is neither justifiable nor excusable.

In order to prove this crime, each of the following elements must be proved:

1. A human being was killed;
2. The killing was unlawful; and
3. The killing was done with malice aforethought.

The organization of this instruction is bizarre. First it lays out the basic requirements for murder, then it explains what "unlawful" means in the context of murder, then it repeats the requirements of murder in virtually the same words, but arranged as elements in a numbered list. There is no reason to repeat the requirements for the crime, and doing so in slightly different words has the potential to lead to confusion.

Jury instructions are traditionally highly impersonal and abstract statements of the law that avoid naming the parties, referring instead to "a person" or "a human being." Yet if prosecutors accuse someone of murder, surely they must know in almost all cases who the victim was. And the state is accusing a specific person or group of persons of having committed the murder, so why set forth the elements in the passive voice? Perhaps the reason is that the instruction was also intended for use with felony murder, where the defendant did not himself kill the victim. It would be more sensible to have a separate instruction in such cases.

On the positive side, the CALJIC committee did realize that "malice aforethought" is not a phrase that jurors are likely to understand, so they defined it:

CALJIC 8.11. "Malice Aforethought"—Defined

"Malice" may be either express or implied.

Malice is express when there is manifested an intention unlawfully to kill a human being.

Malice is implied when:

1. The killing resulted from an intentional act,
2. The natural consequences of the act are dangerous to human life, and
3. The act was deliberately performed with knowledge of the danger to, and with conscious disregard for, human life.

The mental state constituting malice aforethought does not necessarily require any ill will or hatred of the person killed.

The word "aforethought" does not imply deliberation or the lapse of considerable time. It only means that the required mental state must precede rather than follow the act.

It's not evident why the jury needs to master the distinction between express and implied malice. Notice also that express malice in particular is defined in abstract and impersonal terms. Adding the last two paragraphs was a good idea, because both "malice" and "aforethought" are used here in unusual ways. Misunderstanding is especially likely when instructions contain words which seem to be ordinary, but which have a meaning that deviates from normal usage. The CALJIC committee was apparently aware of this problem, but its definitions are not exactly paragons of clarity.

The new language on murder incorporates the concept of malice aforethought, resulting in a single instruction:

CALCRIM 520. Murder With Malice Aforethought

The defendant is charged with murder.

To prove that the defendant is guilty of this crime, the People must prove that:

1. The defendant committed an act that caused the death of another person; AND
2. When the defendant acted, she had a state of mind called malice aforethought; AND
3. She killed without lawful excuse or justification.

There are two kinds of malice aforethought, express malice and implied malice. Proof of either is sufficient to establish the state of mind required for murder.

The defendant acted with express malice if she unlawfully intended to kill.

The defendant acted with implied malice if:

1. She intentionally committed an act;
2. The natural consequences of the act were dangerous to human life;
3. At the time she acted, she knew her act was dangerous to human life; AND
4. She deliberately acted with conscious disregard for human life.

Malice aforethought does not require hatred or ill will toward the victim. It is a mental state that must be formed before the act that causes death is committed. It does not require deliberation or the passage of any particular period of time.

The new instruction is an improvement in several ways. It is less abstract in that it states that the People (i.e. the prosecution) must prove the elements. The CALJIC version simply stated that the elements "must be proved." And CALCRIM also makes it clear that the *defendant* (not some unnamed person) must have committed the acts in question. The same is true of the victim, who is referred to as "another person." I would have preferred inserting the defendant's and victim's names, but admittedly it should be obvious to the jury who the defendant is and who the victim was. Finally, the new instruction, like CALJIC, continues to refer to express and implied malice.

The instruction is much improved, but there clearly are limits to what can be achieved, even by a committee of lawyers and judges committed to explaining the law in ordinary English. Sometimes lawyers and judges are so accustomed to using a term that it is unthinkable to use a plainer substitute (as was the case with "malice aforethought"). On other occasions a word or phrase is in the penal code. In such cases, retaining and then defining the technical word or phrase may be the only option.

The problem of death penalty instructions

California, like the majority of American states, still has the death penalty, although it has seldom been carried out during the past two or three decades. Nonetheless, dozens of people are sentenced to death each year in California. It is a jury's responsibility to decide whether there are "special circumstances" that make a person convicted of first-degree murder "eligible" for the death penalty. If the jury finds that at least one special circumstance is true, it must then decide whether the defendant should be put to death, or should instead be sentenced to life in prison. The jury is told that it must make this decision by balancing the aggravating factors against any mitigating factors. If aggravation outweighs mitigation, it should return a verdict of death.

As I have shown elsewhere, jurors do not seem to understand the concept of mitigation very well (Tiersma 1995). It is therefore critical to explain the legal meaning of aggravation and mitigation in the clearest possible terms. Unfortunately, CALJIC did a poor job in this regard. Its definitions of the terms "aggravating factor" and "mitigating factor" are presented below:

> **CALJIC 8.88. Penalty Trial—Concluding Instruction**
> An aggravating factor is any fact, condition or event attending the commission of a crime which increases its guilt or enormity, or adds to the injurious consequences which is above and beyond the elements of the crime itself. A mitigating circumstance is any fact, condition or event which does not constitute a justification or excuse for the crime in question, but may be considered as an extenuating circumstance in determining the appropriateness of the death penalty.

The definition of "aggravating factor" is turgid and borders on the ungrammatical. Do facts really "attend" the commission of a crime? Moreover, does a crime have guilt? Perhaps most importantly, the definition does not tell jurors that an "aggravating factor" is not merely something that aggravates them.

The definition of "mitigating factor" is even worse. Amazingly, it begins in the negative, solemnly intoning that a justification or excuse is not mitigation. This is an absurd statement. Obviously, a justification or excuse, even if the jurors believed that it did not forestall a conviction, could nonetheless function as a mitigating factor on the penalty. How the statement found its way into California's capital jury instructions is a long story, but the language was copied virtually verbatim from a legal dictionary, which was concerned with distinguishing mitigation from similar concepts (Tiersma 2005: 388–92). If this weren't bad enough, the instruction proceeds to define a "mitigating factor" as an "extenuating circumstance." This violates the basic lexicographic principle that a word should be defined using words that are more—not less—common than the item being defined.

Although not perfect, the new instruction is substantially more understandable:

CALCRIM 763. Death Penalty: Factors to Consider

An aggravating circumstance or factor is any fact, condition, or event relating to the commission of a crime, above and beyond the elements of crime itself, that increases the wrongfulness of the defendant's conduct, the enormity of the offense, or the harmful impact of the crime. An aggravating circumstance may support a decision to impose the death penalty.

A mitigating circumstance or factor is any fact, condition, or event that makes the death penalty less appropriate as a punishment, even though it does not legally justify or excuse the crime. A mitigating circumstance is something that reduces the defendant's blameworthiness or otherwise supports a less severe punishment. A mitigating circumstance may support a decision not to impose the death penalty.

Because of the highly politicized nature of the death penalty, the CALCRIM committee was extremely reluctant to make changes to these definitions. Thus, the word "enormity" remains. The same is true for the statement about justification and excuse, although it has been reworded to avoid the false impression that just because something might be a justification or excuse, it cannot constitute mitigation. In addition, language has been inserted in the definitions of both words to clarify their meaning. The average citizen may not know what an "extenuating circumstance" is, but should have little trouble understanding that mitigation "is something that reduces the defendant's blameworthiness or otherwise supports a less severe punishment."

Conclusion

The reason for instructing jurors is to promote the rule of law. All parties to a lawsuit, particularly criminal defendants, have a right to have their cases decided by consistent legal principles that are accessible to the public. With respect to jury instructions, the rule of law has often been an empty promise. California's revision of its instructions has brought the promise closer to reality. One hopes that its experience will inspire other jurisdictions to do the same.

Further reading

Heffer, Chris (2005) *The Language of Jury Trial: A Corpus-Aided Analysis of Legal-Lay Discourse*, Basingstoke: Palgrave.

Marder, Nancy S. (2006) 'Bringing jury instructions into the twenty-first century,' *Notre Dame L. Rev.*, 81: 449.

Tiersma, Peter M. (2006) *Communicating with Juries: How to Draft More Understandable Jury Instructions*, Williamsburg, VA: National Center for State Courts.

Vidmar, Neil and Valerie P. Hans (2007) *American Juries: The Verdict*, Amherst, NY: Prometheus Books.

18

Rape victims

The discourse of rape trials

Susan Ehrlich

Introduction

Feminist critiques of the law have often cited the rape trial as exemplifying much of
what is problematic about the legal system for women. Smart (1989: 161), for example,
argues that the rape trial is illustrative of the law's *juridogenic* potential: that is, frequently the harms produced by the so-called remedy are as negative as the original
abuse. Other legal theorists have created terms for the rape trial —"judicial rape" (Lees
1996: 36) and "rape of the second kind" (Matoesian 1995: 676)—in order to make
visible the *re*-victimization that women can undergo once their complaints of rape
enter the legal system. What is perhaps surprising about these kinds of claims is the fact
that sexual assault and rape statutes in Canada and the United States have undergone
widespread reform over the last four decades. For example, legislation in the 1970s
through the 1990s in Canada and the United States abolished, among other things,
marital exemption rules, which had made it impossible for husbands to be charged with
raping their wives; corroboration rules, which required that complainants' testimony be
supported by independent evidence; resistance rules, which required that complainants
show evidence that they physically resisted their attackers; and recent complaint rules,
which obligated complainants to make prompt complaints in order that their testimony
be deemed credible. In addition, rape shield provisions were introduced, restricting the
conditions under which complainants' sexual history could be admissible as evidence.
So, given this kind of reform, why do rape trials continue to defy the law's statutory
objectives? Following Conley and O'Barr (1998: 3), I suggest that the rape trial's failure
to deliver justice to rape victims lies *not* in the details of rape and sexual assault statutes
but rather "in the details of everyday legal practices." And, because *language* has been
shown to play a crucial role in everyday legal practices, this chapter demonstrates how
linguistic analysis can reveal some of the discriminatory qualities of rape trials as well as ways
that such qualities have been contested.

The adjudication of rape cases

In her book-length study of well-known American acquaintance rape trials, Sanday (1996) comments on the discrepancy that often exists between "law-as-legislation" and "law-as-practice" (Smart 1986). On the one hand, Sanday praises recent rape statutes in the states of New Jersey, Illinois, Washington and Wisconsin that deem sexual aggression as illegal in the absence of what she terms the "affirmative consent" of complainants. On the other hand, Sanday (1996: 285) points to the failure of such statutory reform in the context of sexist and androcentric cultural stereotypes: "although our rape laws define the line [between sex and rape] ... , these laws are useless if juror attitudes are affected by ancient sexual stereotypes." Within the Canadian context, Comack makes similar observations about judges' attitudes: despite the widespread reform to Canadian sexual assault law in the 1980s and 1990s, Comack (1999: 234) argues that "judicial decisions continue to reflect traditional cultural mythologies about rape." Comack's claims are supported by research on the language of sexual assault trial judgments (e.g. Coates et al. 1994; Coates and Wade 2004). For example, in investigating judges' decisions in Canadian sexual assault trial cases between the years of 1986 and 1992, Coates et al. (1994) found judges to have extremely limited "interpretive repertoires" in the language they deployed in describing sexual assault. In describing "stranger rapes," judges employed a language of assault and violence; however, in describing cases where perpetrators were familiar to their victims and often trusted by their victims, the language judges used was often that of consensual sex. For example, the unwanted touching of a young girl's vagina was described as "fondling" in one trial judgment; in another, a judge described a defendant as "offering" his penis to his victim's mouth. Thus, in spite of the fact that 1983 statutory reforms in Canada explicitly reconceptualized sexual assault as a crime of violence, many of the judges adopted a language of erotic, affectionate and consensual sex when describing non-stranger rape.

These kinds of results give empirical substance to Sanday's and Comack's claims about the "ancient sexual stereotypes" and "traditional cultural mythologies" that inform the adjudication of rape cases. They are also illustrative of the legal system's differential treatment of stranger rape vs. acquaintance rape—a phenomenon also documented within the American legal system by legal scholar, Susan Estrich. Estrich (1987), in her book *Real Rape*, makes the argument that the legal system takes the crime of rape seriously in cases where the perpetrator is a stranger, and in particular, an armed stranger "jumping from the bushes" and attacking an unsuspecting woman. By contrast, when a woman is forced to engage in sex with a date or an acquaintance, when no weapon is involved and when there is no overt evidence of physical injury, the legal system is much less likely to arrest, prosecute and convict the perpetrator. One could argue that in these latter kinds of cases, when there is no physical evidence and/or corroboration that rape has occurred, it is much easier for judges and juries to invoke their own (potentially problematic) ideas about male and female sexuality. As Tiersma (2007) points out, consent can be communicated indirectly (e.g. through silence), with the result that, in situations where a man has not physically hurt or overtly threatened a woman, judges and juries must *infer* whether a woman has consented to sex or not. And, in line with Sanday's and Comack's comments above, Tiersma (2007: 93) acknowledges that "these inferences may rest on questionable or offensive ... assumptions." For instance, Tiersma cites a recent case "in which a Texas judge determined that a woman's request that a man use a condom was evidence of consent, despite the fact that he had threatened her with violence." In the words of da Luz and Weckerly (1993: 95), "caution [was] construed as consent" by this particular judge.

The remainder of this chapter has two goals. First, I consider research that has investigated the discourse of acquaintance rape trials and demonstrated that the kinds of questionable cultural assumptions discussed by Sanday, Comack and Tiersma (among others) are not only evident in the attitudes of some juries and judges, they also circulate within trials. In particular, defense lawyers in criminal rape trials have been shown to strategically draw upon cultural mythologies surrounding rape as a way of impeaching the credibility of complainants. Second, I consider research that explores the possibility that the kinds of cultural mythologies drawn upon by judges, juries and defense lawyers in rape trials can be contested. In fact, I suggest that, because of its *adversarial* nature, the rape trial provides a unique forum for investigating ways that dominant notions of sexual violence are reproduced discursively *as well as* ways they might be resisted and challenged.

Questions in trial discourse

Adversarial dispute resolution, of which trials are a notable example, requires that two parties come together formally, usually with representation (e.g. lawyers), to present their (probably different) versions of the dispute to a third party (e.g. judge, jury, tribunal) who hears the evidence, applies the appropriate laws or regulations, and determines the guilt or innocence of the parties. Lawyers have as their task, then, convincing the adjudicating body that their (i.e. their client's) version of events is the most credible. Apart from making opening and closing arguments, however, lawyers do not themselves testify. Rather, it is through the posing of questions that lawyers must elicit testimony from witnesses that will build a credible version of events in support of their own clients' interests, in addition to testimony that will challenge, weaken and/or cast doubt on the opposing parties' version of events. Atkinson and Drew (1979: 70) note that while trial discourse is conducted predominantly through a series of question–answer sequences, other actions are accomplished in the form of such questions and answers. For example, questions may be designed to accuse witnesses, to challenge or undermine the truth of what they are saying, or in direct examination, to presuppose the truth and adequacy of what they are saying. To the extent that witnesses recognize these actions are being performed in questions, they may design their answers as rebuttals, denials, justifications, etc.

Atkinson and Drew (1979) have called the question–answer turn-taking system characteristic of the courtroom, *turn-type pre-allocation*, to indicate that the types of turns participants can take are pre-determined by their institutional roles. In courtrooms, for example, lawyers have the right to initiate and allocate turns by asking questions of witnesses but the reverse is not generally true; witnesses are obligated to answer questions or run the risk of being sanctioned by the court. An important dimension of this type of asymmetrical turn-taking, according to Drew and Heritage (1992a: 49), is the fact that it provides little opportunity for the answerer (typically a lay person) to initiate talk and thus allows the institutional representative "to gain a measure of control over the introduction of topics and hence of the 'agenda' for the occasion." Within the context of the courtroom, researchers (e.g. Conley and O'Barr 1998) have argued that the interactional control of questioners (i.e. lawyers) is most pronounced during cross-examination when the use of leading questions allows cross-examining lawyers to impose their (i.e. their clients') version of events on evidence. As Gibbons (2003: 98) points out, one way that cross-examining lawyers manage to construct a version of events during questioning that serves the interests of their own clients is by "includ[ing] elements of this desired version ... in the questions."

While a number of researchers have developed taxonomies of questions used in the courtroom (e.g. Danet *et al.* 1980; Harris 1984; Walker 1987), for the purposes of this chapter I elaborate on Woodbury's (1984) taxonomy of question "control," because it categorizes questions according to questioners' ability to "control" information, or in Gibbons' words above, according to questioners' ability to include "elements of the[ir] desired version of events" in questions. Indeed, for Woodbury (1984: 199), control refers "to the degree to which the questioner can impose his [sic] own interpretations on the evidence." Thus, within Woodbury's continuum of control, broad wh-questions, such as *And then what happened?*, display little control because they do not impose the questioner's interpretation on the testimony: there is no proposition communicated to a judge and/or jury other than the notion that "something happened." By contrast, yes–no questions display more control than wh-questions within Woodbury's taxonomy. For example, the yes–no question with a tag, *You had intercourse with her, didn't you?*, contains a substantive proposition—i.e. "the addressee had intercourse with some woman"—that is made available to a judge and/or jury, irrespective of the addressee's (i.e. witness's) answer. Indeed, for Conley and O'Barr (1998: 26), controlling questions, in Woodbury's sense, have the effect of transforming cross-examination "from dialogue into self-serving monologue." That is, even if a controlling question with damaging content is answered in the negative, Conley and O'Barr argue that "the denial may be lost in the flow of the lawyer's polemic."

In my own work (Ehrlich 2001), I have expanded Woodbury's taxonomy of "control" to include questions with presuppositions—questions that I argue are even more controlling than the kinds of yes–no questions exemplified above. That is, on one analysis, a question always contains a variable or unknown quantity, which the addressee of a question is being asked to supply (Lyons 1977). For example, the addressee of the yes–no question with a tag exemplified above, *You had intercourse with her, didn't you?*, has the ability to disconfirm the proposition (i.e. "the addressee had intercourse with some woman") contained within the declarative part of the question. By contrast, presuppositions cannot be denied with the same effectiveness or success. Consider, for example, the question in (1), adapted from Atkinson and Drew (1979: 211).

(1) Lawyer: When you were having *in*tercourse with her the first time (3.5) did you say anything to her then?

In uttering this question, the lawyer takes for granted (i.e. assumes) that the witness has had intercourse with some woman and is asking about speech events that might have taken place during the intercourse. What is important for my purposes is that this presupposition continues to be taken for granted (i.e. remains in evidence) even if the addressee answers the question in the negative. Thus, in contexts where cross-examining lawyers attempt to include elements of their own client's version of events in their questions, presuppositions are even more powerful then the declaratives of yes–no questions in controlling evidence. The contrast among the kinds of propositions made available and/or presupposed by the question-types discussed here can be seen in (2) and (3). The question-types are ordered from less "controlling" to more "controlling."

(2) Yes-No Questions without Presuppositions, e.g. *You had intercourse with her, didn't you?*
Proposition made available (but denied if question answered in the negative): The addressee had intercourse with some woman.

(3) Yes-No Questions with Presuppositions, e.g. *When you had intercourse with her, you said something to her, didn't you?*
Proposition made available (but denied if question answered in the negative): The addressee said something to some woman when having intercourse with her.
Proposition presupposed: The addressee had intercourse with some woman.

The power of questions to control information in acquaintance rape trials

A central argument of this chapter is that the problematic cultural assumptions typically brought to bear on the adjudication of rape trials are also evident within the discourse of rape trials; in particular, cross-examining lawyers have been shown to invoke cultural mythologies surrounding rape as a way of undermining the credibility of complainants. In this section, I demonstrate how these kinds of cultural myths are encoded within the "controlling" questions of defense lawyers when cross-examining complainants, in particular, within the presuppositions and declaratives of the lawyers' yes-no questions.

The specific kinds of cultural assumptions discussed in this section (Ehrlich 2001; 2003) involve what Sanday might call "an ancient sexual stereotype"—an outdated statutory rule within sexual assault and rape law called the utmost resistance standard. Until the 1950s and the 1960s in the United States, the statutory requirement of utmost resistance was a necessary criterion for the crime of rape (Estrich 1987); that is, if a woman did not resist a man's sexual advances to the utmost, then rape did not occur. While, as noted above, this standard is no longer encoded in rape statutes in the United States and Canada, it does circulate within the discourse of rape trials. The following examples come from a Canadian acquaintance rape trial in which the accused, Matt (a pseudonym), was charged with sexually assaulting two different women, Connie and Marg (pseudonyms), in their university residences three nights apart. (Matt was convicted of sexual assault in the case involving Marg, on the basis of corroboration from witnesses, and acquitted in the case involving Connie.) Although both complainants described their experiences as sexual assault, in the examples that follow the defense lawyer represents the women's behavior as lacking in forceful and direct resistance. Because the complainants' actions do not seem to meet the standard of resistance deemed appropriate by the defense lawyers, I suggest that these types of representations have the effect of calling into question the complainants' allegations of sexual assault.

Many of the questions (shown in italics below) asked by the defense lawyer identified options that the complainants could have pursued in their attempts to resist the accused; moreover, these options were consistently presented as reasonable options for the complainants to pursue. Examples (4) and (5), for instance, show the cross-examiner suggesting that "seeking help" was a reasonable option for Connie.

(4) L: And I take it part of your involvement then on the evening of January 27th and having Mr. A. come back to your residence that you felt that you were

in this comfort zone because you were going to a place that you were, very familiar; correct?

CD: It was my home, yes.

L: *And you knew you had a way out if there was any difficulty?*

CD: I didn't really take into account any difficulty. I never expected there to be any.

L: I appreciate that. *Nonetheless, you knew that there were other people around who knew you and obviously would come to your assistance, I take it, if you had some problems, or do you know?* Maybe you can't answer that.

CD: No, I can't answer that. I can't answer that. I was inviting him to my home, not my home that I share with other people, not, you know, a communal area. I was taking him to my home and I really didn't take into account anybody else around, anybody that I lived near. It was like inviting somebody to your home.

L: Fair enough. And I take it from what you told us in your evidence this morning that it never ever crossed your mind when this whole situation reached the point where you couldn't handle it, or were no longer in control, to *merely* go outside your door to summon someone?

CD: No.

(5) L: What I am suggesting to you, ma'am, is that as a result of that situation with someone other than Mr. A., you knew what to do in the sense that if you were in a compromising position or you were being, I won't use the word harass, but being pressured by someone you knew what to do, didn't you?

CD: No, I didn't. Somebody had suggested that, I mean, I could get this man who wasn't a student not be permitted on campus and that's what I did.

L: What—*but I am suggesting that you knew that there was someone or a source or a facility within the university that might be able to assist you if you were involved in a difficult situation, isn't that correct, because you went to the student security already about this other person?*

CD: Yeah, okay. If you are asking if I knew about the existence of student security, yes, I did.

The italicized sentences in examples (4) and (5) are "controlling" questions in Woodbury's (1984) sense. That is, in producing such questions the defense attorney communicates certain propositions to the judge and jury in the declarative portion of the yes-no questions, specifically, that Connie knew there were university resources available to women who found themselves in difficult situations. The italicized questions in (4) and (5) also contain presuppositions. The predicate, *know*, is a factive predicate, which means that it presupposes the truth of its complement. Thus, in uttering the three italicized questions above, the defense lawyer presupposes that "there was a way out," "there were other people around who knew Connie" and "there were resources at the university to help those in difficult situations." Indeed, due to the presupposed nature of these propositions, even if Connie had denied her knowledge of the availability of help, what is communicated by lawyer's questions is the fact that help *was* available within the university. Note that the final question of example (4) not only identifies an option that Connie could have pursued, it also represents this option as an unproblematic one, given the presence of the word, *merely – It never ever crossed your mind ... to merely go outside your door to summon someone?*

So, what are the inferences that a judge and jury might draw from the information communicated by the defense lawyer's questions? If help was available, and if Connie admits at certain points in the questioning that she was aware of its availability, as we see in the last turn of example (5), then her failure to seek help suggests that she was *not* in "a difficult situation" and that she did not require assistance. Put somewhat differently, Connie's failure to seek help casts doubt on her credibility, specifically, it calls into question her allegations of sexual assault.

Examples (6) and (7) show both the judge and the cross-examining lawyer asking Connie and Marg, respectively, why they didn't utter other words in their various attempts to resist Matt's sexual aggression. Again, we see an emphasis on the seemingly reasonable options that were not pursued by the complainants.

(6) L: And in fact just raising another issue that I would like you to help us with if you can, this business of you realizing when the line was getting blurred when you said "Look, I don't want to sleep with you," or words to that effect, yes, you remember that?

CD: Yes.

L: Well, when you said that, what did that mean or what did you want that to mean, not to have intercourse with him?

CD: Yeah, I mean, ultimately, that's what it meant. It also, I mean –

The Court: *You didn't want to sleep with him but why not, "Don't undue [sic] my bra" and "Why don't you knock it off"?*

CD: Actually, "I don't want" – "I don't want to sleep with you" is very cryptic, and certainly as he got his hands under my shirt, as he took off my shirt, as he undid my bra, as he opened my belt and my pants and pulled them down and I said, "Please don't, please stop. Don't do that. I don't want you to do that, please don't", that's pretty direct as well.

(7) MB: And then we got back into bed and Matt immediately started again and then I said to Bob, "Bob where do you get these persistent friends?"

L: Why did you even say that? You wanted to get Bob's attention?

MB: I assumed that Bob talked to Matt in the hallway and told him to knock it off.

L: You assumed?

MB: He was talking to him and came back in and said everything was all right.

L: Bob said that?

MB: Yes.

L: But when you made that comment, you wanted someone to know, you wanted Bob to know that this was a signal that Matt was doing it again?

MB: Yes.

L: A mixed signal, ma'am, I suggest?

MB: To whom?

L: What would you have meant by, "Where do you get these persistent friends?"

MB: Meaning Bob he's doing it again, please help me.

L: *Why didn't you say, "Bob, he was doing it again, please help me?"*

MB: Because I was afraid Matt would get mad.

L: You weren't so afraid because you told Bob, "Where do you get these persistent friends?" Did you think Matt would be pleased with that comment because it was so general?

MB: I didn't think about it but I thought that was my way of letting Bob know what was going on.

271

Connie reports saying *Look, I don't want to sleep with you* at a certain point in the evening and Marg recounts one of several incidents when she attempts to elicit Bob's help (Bob is the pseudonym for a friend of the accused) by saying *Bob where do you get these persistent friends*. Yet, in the italicized questions above, these expressions of resistance are problematized by the judge and the defense lawyer, respectively. In example (6) the judge asks Connie why she hasn't said *Don't undue [sic] my bra* and *Why don't you knock it off* and in example (7) the defense lawyer asks Marg why she didn't say *Bob, he was doing it again, please help me*. It is significant that both of the questions that preface the words not produced by the complainants are negative interrogatives (i.e. *why not* and *why didn't you say*)—interrogatives that Heritage (2002: 1432) argues are often used to "frame negative or critical propositions." This means that when the judge and the defense lawyer produce questions of the form "Why didn't you say X," not only are they calling attention to utterances that were *not* produced by the complainants, they are also communicating a negative and/or critical attitude towards the fact that such utterances were not produced. Once again, then, the inferences generated by these questions serve to call into question the complainants' allegations of sexual assault: because they did not express their resistance directly and forcefully, the judge and/or jury might wonder whether they had really been threatened by the accused.

The examples above are illustrative of the way cross-examining lawyers (and, in one case, a judge) use "controlling" questions to create a version of events that supports their own clients' case and undermines the credibility of the opposing side's case. My argument is that the information contained within the declarative portions and the presuppositions of the defense lawyer's questions created a powerful ideological lens through which the events in question came to be understood. More specifically, by repeatedly posing questions that represented the complainants as *not* pursuing "obvious" and "easily-executed" strategies of resistance, the defense lawyer suggested that the complainants' behavior did not meet the "utmost resistance" standard, thereby undermining the complainants' allegations of sexual assault. From my point of view, what is problematic about the resistance standard invoked by the defense lawyer is the fact that it downplays and obscures the unequal power dynamics that often characterize male/female sexual relations. In excerpt (6), for example, Marg reports enlisting Bob's help in order to end Matt's sexual aggression because she feared that a more direct approach would provoke Matt's anger. The defense lawyer, however, suggests that Marg should have employed more direct words in resisting Matt's violence and characterizes her strategic act of resistance as nothing more than a *mixed signal*. Thus, Marg's act of resistance, which could have been framed as an intelligent and thoughtful response to a man's escalating sexual violence, was instead characterized by the defense lawyer as an inadequate act of resistance.

Syntactic repetition: intensifying the control of questions in acquaintance rape trials

Like Ehrlich's (2001) work described above, Matoesian's (2001) analysis of the William Kennedy Smith rape trial also focuses on the role of defense lawyers' "controlling" questions in undermining the credibility of complainants. Matoesian, however, not only demonstrates how the referential content of "controlling" questions is involved in this task, he also shows how such referential content is intensified and exaggerated through "creative and improvisational poetic structures" (Matoesian 2001: 33) such as structural repetition and parallelism.

The interactional means by which inconsistency is created in witness testimony is a major theme of Matoesian's (2001) analysis of the William Kennedy Smith rape trial. William Kennedy Smith (the nephew of the late President John Kennedy and the late Senators Robert and Edward Kennedy) was charged with, and subsequently acquitted of, simple battery (unwanted touching) and second-degree sexual battery (rape without the use of a weapon) in the state of Florida in 1991. In Part I of his book, Matoesian focuses on some of the inconsistencies in "logic" imputed to the testimonies of the complainant, Patricia Bowman, and her primary witness, Ann Mercer, during their cross-examination by the defense attorney, Roy Black. While Matoesian notes that the exposing of inconsistencies in witness testimony is a *generic* trial practice designed to undermine the credibility of witnesses, in this particular case he argues that the "logical" standard against which the two women's testimonies were measured—and rendered inconsistent—was not a gender-neutral standard, but rather a male standard of sexuality, what he terms "the patriarchal logic of sexual rationality." In Matoesian's words, "there is an inconsistency between the victim's version of events and the *expectations of patriarchal ideology* governing victim identity" (2001: 40; emphasis in original).

In example (8) below, Matoesian (2001: 46) argues that Roy Black's (RB) questions to Patricia Bowman (PB) functioned to create an inconsistency "between the victim's claim of having been raped and her actions with the defendant *before* the alleged incident" (emphasis mine).

(8)
1   RB: And you were interested in *him* as a person.
          (0.9)
2   PB: He seemed like a nice *person*.
          (0.5)
3   RB: Interested enough that tuh-(0.5) to give him a ride home.
          (0.9)
4   PB: I saw no-(.) no *problem* with giving him a ride *home* as I stated because it was
5   up the street it wasn't out of my *way* (.) he hadn't *tou:ched* me (.) I felt no
6   *threats* from him and I assumed that there would be *security* at the *home*.
          (0.5)
7   RB: You were interested *enough* (.) that you were *ho:ping* that he would ask for
8   your pho:ne *number*.
          (0.7)
9   PB: That was *later*.
          (0.7)
10 RB: Interested enough (.) tha:t when he said to come into the *hou:se* you went into
11   the *hou:se* with him.
          (1.6)
12 PB: I (woul-) it wasn't necessarily an interest with *William* (.) it was an interest in
13   the *house*.
          (0.6)
14 RB: Interested enough that uh: at sometime during that period of time *you took*
15   *off your panty hose?*

(1.2)

16 PB: I still don't *know* how my panty hose came off.

In this excerpt, Roy Black's "controlling" questions (in Woodbury's sense) make available to third-party recipients (i.e. the jury in this case) a number of propositions that are confirmed by Patricia Bowman: that she gave the defendant a ride home, that she went into the house with him, and that she hoped he would ask for her telephone number. (Note that while Bowman acknowledges that her panty hose came off, she doesn't confirm the proposition that she was the one to take them off.) And, as Matoesian (2001: 47) points out, when these propositions are brought together, Patricia Bowman's actions begin to look more like precursors to a consensual sexual interaction than to the crime of rape. For Matoesian, then, it was not just the propositional content of a series of questions like the ones above that functioned to construct Patricia Bowman's testimony as inconsistent; it was also the coherence created by their juxtaposition. The defense attorney, Roy Black, had impressive oratorical skills and, according to Matoesian, employed these skills to amplify and intensify the "inconsistencies" in the complainant's testimony. More specifically, Black foregrounded the referential content of his questions (and his talk, more generally) by using "creative and improvisational poetic structures" (Matoesian 2001: 33), such as structural repetition and parallelism. In excerpt (8), for example, an element of the main clause of line 1—*interested*—is incorporated into the syntactic frame, *interested enough* plus complementizer, and then this syntactic frame is repeated four times (in lines 3, 7–8, 10–11 and 14–15), each time with a different complement clause. In this way, a semantic link is created between the referential content of the complement clauses that are embedded within the syntactic frame, *interested enough* plus complementizer. As Matoesian says, "incremental repetition ... unifies and organizes otherwise disparate particulars of evidence into a coherent, gestalt-like pattern of persuasive parallelism" (Matoesian 2001: 57). That is, the syntactic repetition in example (8) functions to create a link among a series of events that might not otherwise appear connected; and, the fact that these events are more compatible with consensual sex than with the crime of rape intensifies the inconsistency in Patricia Bowman's testimony.

Resisting the cultural mythologies surrounding rape

The power of answers to control information

A defining characteristic of institutional discourse is the differential speaking rights assigned to participants based on their institutional role. In legal contexts, as we have seen, lawyers (and judges) have the right to initiate and allocate turns by asking questions of witnesses but the reverse is not generally true; witnesses do not typically ask questions of lawyers and, if they do, they risk being sanctioned by the court. While the claim that "asking questions amounts to interactional control" (Eades 2008b: 37) is a pervasive one in the literature on courtroom discourse, it is not a claim that has gone unchallenged. Based on a study of Aboriginal witnesses in Australian courts, for example, Eades (2000) argues that the syntactic form of questions has no predictable effect on the form of witness responses. In a similar way, Matoesian (2005b: 621) has questioned the assumption that "questions … are more powerful than answers," suggesting that such an assumption "risks the problem of reifying structure."

> Just as we assume questions do more than merely question (for instance in court they may work as accusations, etc), why presume any less of answers (which may recalibrate the question, produce a new question and so on)? A more detailed consideration of answers and how they function in detail may demonstrate just how powerful they are.
>
> (Matoesian 2005b: 621)

Drew (1992) provides precisely this kind of "detailed consideration of answers" in his analysis of a rape victim's cross-examination. In particular, Drew shows how the complainant (i.e. the rape victim) in this particular trial often produced "alternative descriptions" in her answers—descriptions that contested the cross-examining lawyer's version of events. That is, rather than providing "yes" or "no" answers to the cross-examining lawyer's yes-no questions (what Raymond (2003) calls type-conforming answers to questions), the complainant provided competing descriptions that transformed the lawyer's damaging characterizations into more benign ones. In (9) below, for example, (taken from Drew 1992: 486) the cross-examining lawyer, through the use of "controlling" questions, attempts to represent the events that preceded the alleged rape as precursors to a consensual sexual interaction. (This is similar to the strategy adopted by Roy Black in example (8).)

(9)   16 A: Well yuh had some uh (p) (.) uh fairly lengthy
      17   conversations with the defendant uh: did'n you?
      18   (0.7)
      19 A: On that evening uv February fourteenth?
      20   (1.0)
      21 W: We:ll we were all talkin.
      22   (0.8)
      23 A: Well *you* kne:w, at that ti:me. that the
      24   defendant was. *in*:terested (.) in *you* (.)
      25   did'n you?
      26   (1.3)
      27 W: *He:* asked me how I'(d) bi*n*: en
      28   (1.1)
      29 W: J-just stuff like that

While the lawyer's questions in lines 16–17 and 23–25 suggest that there was a closeness or intimacy developing between the defendant and the complainant, Drew argues that the complainant's answers, although not containing any "overt correction markers" (Drew 1992: 487), do not support this version of events. Rather, the complainant provides answers that depict a lack of intimacy between the complainant and the defendant, that is, a scene in which there were a number of people who *were all talkin* and in which the defendant issued a greeting that was more friendly than intimate. What is significant about Drew's analysis for the present discussion is the fact that the answerer is shown to "control" evidence (in Woodbury's sense) by resisting and transforming the propositions contained in the declarative portions of the lawyer's yes-

275

no questions. In fact, Drew comments explicitly on the need to be attentive to the way that competing descriptions from witnesses may influence juries: "the complainant's attempts to counter the lawyer's descriptive strategies, and hence herself control the information which is available to the jury, should not be overlooked" (Drew 1992: 517).

Direct examination

Given the adversarial nature of the English common law system, there are always (at least) two competing versions of events put forward in the courtroom. Thus, in the same way that answers may contest the version of events put forward by the questions of cross-examining lawyers, it should also be possible for the question–answer sequences of *direct* examination to convey an alternative narrative to the one provided by cross-examining lawyers. Indeed, in what follows, I provide examples from a Canadian rape trial (Ehrlich 2006, 2007) where, I suggest, the prosecuting lawyer anticipated and attempted to challenge another kind of defense strategy in acquaintance rape trials (and one exemplified above): that the complainant did not resist her perpetrator sufficiently and therefore engaged in consensual sex. This particular case involved a sexual assault that took place during a job interview; the accused interviewed the complainant for a job and subsequently invited her to see his work in the trailer attached to his van. According to the complainant's testimony, the accused sexually assaulted her in the trailer for a period of approximately two hours. The accused was acquitted by the trial judge and by the Alberta Court of Appeal (a provincial court). Upon appeal to the Supreme Court of Canada, the acquittal was overturned and a conviction was entered for the accused.

Atkinson and Drew (1979: 136), in their investigation of courtroom discourse, have noted that witnesses often display their recognition that a series of questions is leading to a "blame allocation" by producing "justification/excuse components in answers." In other words, witnesses will provide defenses and justifications in their answers even though the questions asked of them "do not actually contain any blame-relevant assessments of witnesses' actions" (Atkinson and Drew 1979: 138). Such defenses and justifications will thus appear *prematurely* within the course of a trial, that is, before they are actually elicited by a cross-examining lawyer. In the same way that witnesses may provide justifications for their actions prematurely, I am suggesting that examples (10) to (15) show that lawyers may also anticipate critical assessments of their witnesses' actions from opposing lawyers and will thus design their questions to elicit premature or preemptive defenses and justifications for such actions.

In contrast to the adversarial, combative nature of cross-examination, direct examination, has been characterized by both legal practitioners and by scholars as supportive and cooperative. In particular, open-ended questions, or questions that display little "control" in Woodbury's sense, tend to be more frequent in direct examination than in cross-examination. This can be seen in the excerpts (10–14). In each of the examples, the prosecuting attorney begins her turn by asking a broad wh-question, such as *What happened then?*, to which the complainant responds by describing an event or a series of events. Immediately following such an answer, the lawyer asks a narrower wh- question—a why-question that attempts to elicit the complainant's motivation for performing a particular action that she has described. What is significant about these why-questions, for the purposes of this paper, is that they allow the complainant to represent herself as having actively pursued strategies of resistance, either strategies meant to discourage the defendant's sexual advances or strategies meant to avoid more intense and/or prolonged instances of violence from the defendant.

(10)   L: Was he inside the van or trailer when you first got there?

       A: I believe he was inside the van, but – he might have stepped out to meet me.

       L: What happened once you got there?

       A: I asked him if we could go inside the mall, have a cup of coffee and talk about whatever

→   L: Why did you want to go inside the mall to talk?

       A: *Because it was – it was a public place. I mean, we could go in and sit down somewhere and talk.*

(11)   L: What happened then?

       A: He said, Why don't we just talk inside the van here. And he sat into his driver's seat, and I opened the door, and I left the door open of the passenger seat and I sat down there.

—> L: And why did you leave the door open?

       A: *Because I was still very hesitant about talking to him.*

(12)   L: What happened after you agreed to see some of his work?

       A: He went around to – no, first, he said, Okay, I'd like to pull the van into the shade. It was a hot day, and there was cars that were parked under the shade … of a tree, I believe, and he got out, and he went and he stepped inside, and he said, Come on up and look. So I stepped up inside, took about two steps in, I didn't, like, walk around in it. And then he went to the door, closed it, and locked it. (some intervening turns)

       L: Had you expected him to lock the door?

       A: Not at all. I left the door completely wide open when I walked in there for a reason.

→   L: And what was that reason?

       A: *Because I felt that this was a situation that I shouldn't be in, that I – with anybody to be alone in a trailer with any guy with the door closed.*

(13)   L: Did he say anything when he locked the door?

       A: He didn't say anything about the door being locked, but he asked me to sit down. And he sat down cross-legged.

       L: What did you sit on?

       A: Just the floor of the trailer.

→   L: Now, why did you sit down when he asked you to sit down?

       A: *Because I figured I was in this trailer, the door was locked, he was not much more than this stand is away from me here, probably only a couple of feet away from me. I felt that I was in a situation now where I just better do what I was told.*

(14)   L: And what happened then?

       A: He told me that he felt very tense and that he would like to have a massage, and he then leaned up against me with his back towards me and told me to rub his shoulders and I did that.

       L: And up to the time he told you he was tense and wanted a massage, had the two of you talked about you giving him a massage?

> A: I believe all he had said right before that is that he liked to have them, and he was tense feeling and that was all.
> L: Had you ever offered to give him a massage?
> A: No.
> L: Did you want to give him a massage?
> A: No.
> (some intervening turns)
→ L: If you didn't want to give him a massage at that point in time, why did you touch his shoulders?
> A: *I was afraid that if I put up any more of a struggle that it would only egg him on even more, and his touching would be more forced.*

(15) L: And what happened then?
> A: Then he asked me to turn around the other way to face him, and he said he would like to touch my feet or he would like to massage my feet, so I did (sic). And he was just touching my feet.
> L: Did you want him to massage your feet?
> A: No.
→ L: Why did you turn around?
> A: *Because I guess I was afraid. I was frozen. I just did what he told me to do.*

In the italicized portions of (10) to (12), the complainant represents herself as attempting to create circumstances that will discourage that accused's sexual aggression: she suggests going inside the mall to talk because it is a *public* place and she leaves the doors open to the van and the trailer, respectively, because she is hesitant about talking to the accused alone in a confined space. In the italicized portions of (13) to (15), the complainant represents herself as attempting to prevent more extreme acts of violence from the accused: she complies with all of his requests (e.g. that she sit down, that she massage him, that she turn around so he can massage her feet) out of fear that not complying will *egg him on even more.* Indeed, such responses reflect strategies that many victims of sexual violence employ to prevent more prolonged and extreme instances of violence. As researchers on violence against women have asserted, submitting to coerced sex or physical abuse can be "a strategic mode of action undertaken in pre-servation of self" (Lempert 1996: 281). That is, if physical resistance on the part of victims can escalate and intensify violence, as some research shows (e.g. Dobash and Dobash 1992) and many women (are instructed to) believe, then submission to coerced sex is undoubtedly the best strategy for survival. In a general way, then, what is important about the prosecuting attorney's questioning in examples (10) to (15) is the fact that her why-questions served to elicit responses that highlighted and emphasized the complainant's active deployment of strategies meant to resist the accused's escalat-ing sexual violence. In this way, the lawyer can be viewed as anticipating, and attempting to preempt, a certain kind of "blame allocation" from the defense—that the complainant did not resist the accused "to the utmost" and thus engaged in consensual sex. The preceding discussion is significant because it shows that the cultural rape mythologies often invoked by defense lawyers can be challenged in courtrooms by alternative kinds of narratives. More specifically, in the direct examination of the sexual assault trial just described, the complainant's actions were contextualized within a sense-making framework that acknowledged the structural inequalities that can characterize male–female sexual relations and the effects of such inequalities in shaping women's strategies of resistance.

Conclusion

According to Gibbons (2003: 98), the primary way that cross-examining lawyers construct a version of events that supports their own clients' interests is by including "elements of this desired version" of events in their questions. Drawing upon Woodbury's notion of question "control," I have shown how cross-examining lawyers in acquaintance rape trials can incorporate "elements" into their "controlling" questions that are strategically designed to undermine the credibility of complainants. More specifically, by encoding damaging cultural mythologies (e.g. the utmost resistance standard; the patriarchal logic of sexual rationality) into the declarative portions and presuppositions of questions—and by repeating elements of these questions over extended sequences of talk—I have argued that defense lawyers can cast doubt on complainants' allegations of sexual assault and rape.

I began this chapter by pointing to the cultural mythologies that often inform the adjudication of sexual assault and rape cases in Canada and the United States in spite of four decades of progressive statutory reform. What this chapter has demonstrated is the way that these same cultural mythologies can make their way into rape trial discourse, potentially reinforcing the problematic cultural assumptions held by judges and juries. As Shulhofer says about the failure of rape law reform in the United States,

> social attitudes are tenacious, and they can easily nullify the theories and doctrines found in the law books. The story of failed reforms is in part a story about the overriding importance of culture, about the seeming irrelevance of law.
>
> Shulhofer (1998: 17)

If it is true that culture is of paramount importance in the legal system's treatment of rape and sexual assault, then the rape trial becomes an important site for viewing this culture "in action." Cross-examining lawyers exploit damaging cultural narratives about rape as a way of undermining the credibility of complainants; and, given the *adversarial and dynamic* nature of the trial, witnesses, in their answers and prosecuting lawyers, in their questions, have the potential to produce competing cultural narratives about rape, as I have demonstrated. Put somewhat differently, if the rape trial provides a window onto culture "in action," then it not only provides a forum for viewing discriminatory narratives about rape but also for viewing the potential for these narratives to be changed.

Further reading

Cotterill, J. (ed.) (2007) *The Language of Sexual Crime*, Basingstoke, Hampshire: Palgrave Macmillan.

Conley, J. and O'Barr, W. (2005) *Just Words: Law, Language and Power* (second edition), Chicago: University of Chicago Press.

Ehrlich, S. (2001) *Representing Rape: Language and Sexual Consent*, London: Routledge.

Matoesian, G. (1993) *Reproducing Rape: Domination through Talk in the Courtroom*, Chicago: University of Chicago Press.

——(2001) *Law and the Language of Identity: Discourse in the William Kennedy Smith Rape Trial*, New York: Oxford University Press.

19

Youth and gangs

Sociolinguistic issues in gang-related prosecutions: homies, hearsay and expert standards

Mel Greenlee

Introduction

A decade ago Solan (1999) addressed the following question regarding the role of linguists as expert witnesses: can the legal system use experts on meaning? His article examined linguists' expertise with regard to various types of legal texts (for example, contracts, patents, jury instructions, interrogations) and reviewed the possible role of linguists according to standards for expert scientific evidence in court. He concluded that linguists can help the justice system in many instances where language is complex and/or ambiguous, serving as "tour guides" to the analysis of language and to how the range of possible meanings is determined. Ultimately, the judge or jury decides which meaning fits.

This chapter considers a potential role for linguists in legal proceedings related to gangs, an arena in which the current "tour guides" are rarely specialists in sociolinguistics or pragmatics, although criminal liability in these cases (and in the civil realm, injunctive restrictions on basic civil liberties) may turn on the interpretation of language evidence in context. The chapter takes a critical justice perspective, noting from the outset that public rhetoric urging a "war on crime" in California may distort the perception of youth and their behavior. Just as sociologists have shown that fear of youth gang crime may be more driven by notions of moral panic than actual crime statistics (Greene and Pranis 2007: 8–9; Nichols and Good 2004: 55–57), the characterization of language in defining a crime and youth involvement in it may also contradict the facts about youth behavior and mask significant sociolinguistic variation. In both instances, the work of sociolinguists and ethnographers suggests that youth behavior is viewed as more uniform (and more sinister) than it actually is. Teens who perform rap lyrics, use graffiti on their possessions, or adopt particular nicknames may do so to establish and maintain social identity. Their use may make their elders nervous, but it does not define youngsters as criminals, or make these fixed characteristics of their users.

This chapter will first address over-determination of meaning in characterizing certain types of language behavior as gang-related, giving examples from California civil and criminal case trial transcripts, court opinions, and other documents. Next, it will critique current experts and examine the legal rules governing their testimony in gang prosecutions. It concludes with suggestions, not for substituting linguists for current experts, but for using information from sociolinguistic and ethnographic studies to provide a more informed and nuanced view, avoiding inappropriate application of criminal stigmata.

Legal issues related to gangs

The legal issues that arise in California criminal trials involving gang activity generally concern whether: 1) the defendant is a member of a gang, 2) the offense charged is gang-related, or somehow motivated by the accused's connection to the group, and 3) the offense was carried out with the specific intent to benefit or promote a gang's alleged criminal agenda (California Penal Code 186.22). These questions are complicated by long-standing definitional debates (Bursik and Grasmick 2006: 3; Sullivan 2005: 171). Esbensen *et al.* (2001: 122) note the definition of "gang" has been disputed for three decades. In theory, the three questions are independent: a crime might be committed by a gang member, but, for an individual everyday purpose completely unrelated to the gang's alleged criminal activities. For example, a young gang member might be arrested for driving under the influence, unrelated to gang activities. However, in many California cases, the three questions are linked, at least in prosecutors' arguments, so if the first question is answered "yes," the rest may follow. Affirmative answers, especially to all three questions (concerning membership, offense, and intent) may result in a significantly enhanced sentence. If a defendant is found guilty of a homicide where these three conditions are met, that defendant could face life in prison or even eligibility for the death penalty (Caldwell and Fisher-Ogden 2004: 647).

What is a gang?

The definition of Criminal Street Gang (CSG), under the California Penal Code section 186.22, the STEP Act, passed in 1988 and subsequently amended (de Vries 2002: 204–205), is:

1. An ongoing association of three or more persons, with a
2. Common name, sign or symbol
3. One of the group's "primary activities" is criminal (based on a long list of offenses)
4. Individually or collectively, members have engaged in a "pattern of criminal gang activity".

The definition above, like those used in other states, has been criticized for circularity; a *gang* is made up of persons who engage in a pattern of criminal *gang* activity (Gomez 2004: 622). For linguists, it is worth noting the second defining criterion refers to language, and the list of offences in the third criterion includes language-related crimes, such as high-value graffiti, and threats (California Penal Code §186.22(e)). In gang prosecutions, language evidence may include nicknames, slang, tattoos, gang signs, graffiti, and certain speech acts (among them "hit-ups", often interpreted as a challenge or threat) (Jackson 2004). The relationship between a criminal act and alleged motive to benefit a gang may also be established by what the defendant (or others) said. (See, e.g. *People v.*

Margarejo (2008) 162 Cal. App.4th 102: fleeing from police while making gang hand signs interpreted as intent to benefit gang agenda.)

Nicknames

For gang membership, identifying information may come from field interview cards, police street contacts, and/or a statewide gang database. Along with descriptive information about the person, the database contains the youth's nickname or "moniker" (Espiritu 2005: 190; *People v. Castro* (2006) WL459890, noting moniker of "Crow"). Woe to the defence attorney whose client's nickname is Bam-bam, Diablo (devil), or Trigger. Although the client may have carried the nickname from childhood (Diablo was a name given to one child because of the shape of his forehead, and another was called Trigger because he ate like a horse), the state will likely use these nicknames to argue that the defendant in a gang trial is violent by nature.

Argot and slang

Linguists and ethnographers have historically examined speech varieties of gangs and marginalized communities, providing a wealth of information on vocabulary, etymology and style-shifting (see, e.g. Ornstein-Galicia (1987) on Caló; Galindo (1993) on conversational interchange and style-shifting between Chicanas). The lexical and grammatical innovations in Caló, a popular variety of speech long used in Southwest Latino communities, are heard not only on the street, but even in theatre productions. (Sanchez 1983: 134). Yet police officers may characterize Caló as a mish-mash of English and Spanish associated with prison inmates. (See *People v. Zepeda*, transcript at 592: "It's just it's an adopted language that the traditional Sureños gangs and Norte gangs adopted … It's kind of a conglomeration of Spanish and English. … You hear it in the prison gangs a lot too.") Popular expressions given this interpretation might include: "letra" (letter), "calmontes" (a variant of "cálmate" (relax)), and even the word "varrio" itself, a variant spelling of standard "barrio" (neighborhood). Although Caló may have begun as an underworld argot, the present-day connection between this form of speech and criminal motivation or membership is dubious (Sanchez 1983: 128). Like an allegedly sinister nickname, use of Caló is likely to be brought out when its speaker is accused of being a gang member or having committed an offense for a gang's benefit.

Table 19.1 is a glossary of "gang-slang" terms distributed to parents by a local police department (Redwood City Police Department 2007). Many parents of American teenagers know their children are familiar with these words and may use them, whether or not they are involved in gangs. This is true in my area, where "Nut up" usually means "to go crazy", not "angry". In living communities, speech styles and vocabulary described as slang are highly variable (Bucholtz 2006); relying on them as gang indicators tends to over-identify gang participation.

Tattoos

The images and writings in tattoos may also be over-interpreted. Police sweeping urban neighborhoods may ask young men to raise their shirts to see if they have what police consider to be gang-related tattoos. These marks are then prominently listed in official

Table 19.1 Glossary of 'gang slang' terms distributed to parents in Redwood City, California

Safeguarding your child from gangs	
Some common slang words gangs use	
Gangbanger:	Active gang member
Home boy or home girl:	Gang member
Jump in:	Gang initiation
Nut up:	Angry
OG:	Original gang member
Packing:	Carrying a gun
Rag:	Color of a gang
Shooter:	Gang member who is carrying a gun
Tagger:	Someone who uses graffiti
Wannabe:	Youngster who wants to be a gang member

documents, such as field identification cards, police reports, and probation records (Espiritu 2005: 190; Wright 2005: 121).

Like the unfortunate young man whose sweetheart is now Louise, but whose chest still says "Rosie," the tattoo may outlast the relationship (McGreevy and Banks 2006; Curiel 2008). Community workers find young men who are working fathers may keep their tattoos, even though no longer active in street groups. Similarly, tattooed images of ethnic or religious symbols (the Virgin of Guadalupe, praying hands, or the "laugh-now, cry-later" of drama masks) may be over-identified with gang participation (López 2002: 48, 52–53). For this reason, urban groups who work with marginalized young people (such as CARECEN in San Francisco or Homies Unidos in Los Angeles) offer a service of removing tattoos.

Gang hand signs

Hand signs such as Margarejo's "HP" (meaning Highland Park), the "14" of the Norteño group, or the "C" of Crips are so ubiquitous in the media that YouTube has spawned countless spoofs and satirical take-offs; on the internet one may view a baby allegedly making gang signs, fraternity brothers imitating hand signs, and even geek-blogger signs. Ethnographers have shown that among youth street gangs, hand signs are used in greetings, to tell whether a newcomer is friend or foe, and to show solidarity, among other purposes (Conquergood 1994). Police take signs made in the home neighborhood very seriously, even when they find them confusing or ambiguous – so seriously that when civil injunctions are issued against gangs in a neighborhood, the ban generally includes the gang's hand signs. (See, e.g. *People v. Norteño* 2007: persons subject to the injunction prohibited from "flashing, meaning using one's … hands or … fingers, to form the number[-] 14.")

In Margarejo's case, one officer testified that in making hand signs while driving away from the police, Margarejo intended to "terrorize" the neighborhood, even though he appeared to be laughing and there was no evidence of what, if anything, the bystanders on the street understood from his gestures. The officer observed most bystanders "looked like they did not belong to gangs." Defense counsel at trial elicited the following (transcript at 917) in extract (1).

(1) (D is Defense Counsel and W is Witness)

D: How can you be joking around and terrorizing people at the same time? You agree that doesn't make sense, does it?

W: Very few things about gang activity seem to make sense, sir.

Despite this concession, Margarejo received an enhanced sentence based on a gang-related motive.

Prohibitions on signing may continue even after sentencing and release. A paroled gang member most likely will be prohibited from associating with gang members or using gang signs. In the movie *Mi Vida Loca*, a young woman recently released from prison is doing her best to "go straight" when she sees friends who are active gang members. Seated in a local café, they sign to her through the window with their neighborhood letters "EP" and are puzzled when she only waves back.

Graffiti

Figure 19.1 shows a piece of graffiti indicative of gang presence in a neighborhood. The writers are recognizably associated with a Norte-oriented local group, by the incorporation of the number 14 (X4) and by the cross-outs of the letter S, a symbolic representation of rivalry with the Sureño group. The graffiti also includes the gang nicknames of its authors, Misterio and Sniper. Susan Phillips's well-documented book, *Wallbangin'* (1999), includes a history, colorful examples, and explanation of much of the gang graffiti in Los Angeles neighbourhoods.

Karen Adams and Anne Winter's survey of over 1,000 pieces of graffiti (Adams and Winter 1997) demonstrates that graffiti has many functions, not only the ones frequently mentioned in law enforcement testimony. Graffiti may indeed delineate boundaries, but it also honours the dead, sets out a roll call of group members, shows social networks, and addresses emotional concerns. Matthew Hunt (1996: 88–89) considered graffiti from a structural point of view, examining the distinctive morphology in different types of

Figure 19.1 Graffiti photo 1

Table 19.2 Common functions and examples of graffiti

Boasts:	"Rifamos" (we rule)
Challenges:	"¿Y qué?" (so what?)
Insults:	"Bitch"
Expressions of emotion:	"Mr. Solo y La Josie – BH"

(couple's name was written above the initials of their gang name)

Memorials:	"Tank – RIP"

(nickname of member (Tank) written above his gang initials (BH))

graffiti in Los Angeles. He observed, "Gang members regularly cross out the graffiti of other gangs, but such practices are certainly not always death threats." (Hunt 1996: 144). Table 19.2 shows representative examples of graffiti messages.

Similar graffiti syntax (with cross-outs) and roll-call lists have been observed in many locales. Some of the writing conventions have also been observed in other media. In *People v. Miller* (2007) 2007 WL 1229401, the prosecution argued that a letter containing crossed-out names allegedly written by the defendant signified death threats against the named individuals, one of whom was referred to as "That bitch Diablita".

The broader meaning of cross-outs is simple enmity or rivalry. A good example comes from high school data collected by Mendoza-Denton (2008: 52); in a girls' bathroom, she observed a graffiti cross-out of the word NORTE with an inscription above, "Puro Sur Mexico 100%" and an arrow below noting: "Putaaas" (whores). The southern group's cross-out of the northern one's name (and the insulting comments) were an expression of contempt, not death threats.

Speech acts

Language rituals are discussed in many California cases, and often mentioned in injunctions against street gangs. Among the most complex is one called "the hit-up" (Docuyanan 2000: 114). In form, it is a question, such as "Where are you from?" Police officers consider it a challenge to fight, a provocation, and/or a threat of immediate harm (Valentine 1995: 17). One officer testified a shooting "always" follows these words (*People v. Gutierrez* 2007 WL 3138384). Yet in the proper context this question is innocuous; moreover, the hit-up ritual is subject to spoofing and playful use, like other seemingly sinister utterances such as mock-threats and insults (Mendoza-Denton 2008: 67–73).

Thus, interpretation of any of these language features relies heavily on context. There is a danger of overbreadth in associating them too exclusively with gang membership. With the possible exception of the hit-up at its most sinister, these features and practices can be observed in wider use among young speakers and as part of the language repertoire of particular communities (like Caló). In determining meaning in context, the language analyst would seek to gather more information about the common understanding of these conventions not only by the speakers or writers but also of others in the speech community.

Was the offense gang-related?

The relationship between alleged gang membership and the offense is an important component of gang prosecutions; here again, the connection is often language-based.

A court may consider as signs of gang relationship, the fact that a gang name was shouted when the crime was committed or a hit-up made, or that later a gang member bragged about the crime in some medium. See *People v. Albarran* (2007) 149 Cal. App.4th 214, reversing gang-related charge for lack of these indicia. The prosecution argued that a shooting after a birthday party must have been gang-related because Albarran was a gang member, and members of another group were present at the party, although not targeted. An officer's testimony about criminal activity committed by other persons affiliated with Albarran's gang took seventy pages of trial transcript, but no connection of this evidence to the shooting at issue, or to Albarran himself, was established. The officer's far-ranging testimony even interpreted graffiti by others as a threat to murder police officers.

People v. Chapman (2003) WL 1958893, an unpublished California case, also illustrates how far liability for such crimes, based on aiding and abetting a gang member with intent to advance a gang's criminal agenda, may extend. Both sides acknowledged there was little evidence Chapman was a gang member. Accused of aiding a necklace snatching with an armed gang member co-perpetrator, Chapman was new to the neighborhood and city, had no gang tattoos or initiation, and was of different ethnicity from most members of the gang. Because he allegedly made a hit-up to the victim in Spanish, "¿Qué barrio?" (what neighborhood?), before his co-defendant snatched the chain, an officer was allowed to give extensive testimony associating the co-defendant's group with a notorious, violent Latino prison gang, suggesting Chapman had assisted the gang's agenda by uttering those words as a challenge to an intruder, a challenge which would only have been made by an actual gang member. Chapman's 14-year sentence, with enhancement under the STEP Act, was upheld on appeal.

Who is the gang expert? Two gang syllogisms

In California gang prosecutions, the usual witnesses concerning these issues are police officers. Their testimony is admitted based on their perceived experience with gang members. The evidentiary rules for such experts are discussed below. One basis for their role may be syllogistic reasoning by the trial judge: "Gangs do crime; cops know crime and gangs; therefore, gang cops are the experts" (Klein 1997: 521). Although most academics have less day-to-day familiarity with youth on the street than do police officers, the nature of the experience may affect the testimony's quality and reliability, particularly when the case turns on interpreting subtle questions of language and intent and the witness is a member of the prosecution team.

Faigman *et al.* (2007) observed similar police roles (and voiced similar concerns about reliability) in cases involving drug-trafficking: "We ... believe ... courts ought to provide a more discriminating analysis of the methods underlying" experience-based testimony provided by police officers (see also Moreno 2004: 7–9, 54; Solan and Tiersma 2005: 193).

Federal courts have sounded a cautionary note where the "analytical gap" between the officer's testimony and the conclusion drawn is too great. Where an expert "testifies as to the meaning of seemingly innocuous activities", the court must be alert to the possibility that the expert's opinion is based on impermissible speculation (*U.S. v. Freeman* (9th Cir. 2007) 498 F.3d 893, 903–4; *U.S. v. Hermanek* (9th Cir. 2002) 289 F.3d 1076). (See also Gray, this volume, on the differential evaluation of expertise.)

A second syllogism commonly operative in these prosecutions relies on profiling: gangs are criminals; defendant is a gang member; therefore, defendant is a criminal (i.e. guilty) (Shoop 1994; see also *People v. Robbie* (2001) 92 Cal. App.4th 1075, 1084–85, critiquing profiling in a different context). Most large urban police departments have gang units, who inventory groups on the street and testify as experts in gang trials (Webb and Katz 2006). To establish the first premise, the officers may provide information on crimes by other persons or groups with whom the defendant is allegedly associated via gang ties. Since the gang statute implies broad conspiracy liability (Mayer 1993: 972; Klein 1996: 865; De Vries 2002: 200), the evidence such experts introduce, as in the Chapman and Albarran cases above, may be quite far-ranging, including actions even of persons unknown to the accused. The description of gang behaviour in such testimony has been criticized as over-inclusive ("if it walks like a duck") as to who is a member, the relationship of the offence to gang membership, and the alleged perpetrator's subjective intent (Burrell, 1990; Istratescu, 2007; *People v. Robbie* (2001) 92 Cal. App.4th 1075, 1084–85).

This may also be true regarding language behavior. Unless care is taken in evaluating testimony regarding language behavior in context, "guilt by linguistic association" may result (Solan and Tiersma 2005: 194). Sinister meanings may be inferred due to an expert's preconception that the speakers are engaged in illegal activity. Recent psychological research has shown that perception may also be unconsciously influenced by pervasive and long-standing social prejudice (Eberhardt *et al.* 2004).

One might compare the usual "gang expert" (in Solan's tour guide analogy) to the tour guide who delights in sending a frisson of fear through his charges by graphically describing events at notorious crime scenes. In establishing the alleged connection between offence, group and intent, the officer may view ambiguous or even innocuous behavior as sinister, and youth groups as more organized and predictable than they really are (Klein 1996: 866). Yet because judges usually accept that law enforcement officers are the most knowledge experts and capable of predicting behavior, their testimony is routinely admitted on all three elements. (See Groscup and Penrod 2003: 1151: empirical study of expert evidence in over 1,000 trials shows police officer testimony admitted over 80% of the time).

Standards for expert testimony

How well does such expert testimony fit within the legal standards for expert evidence? California's threshold criteria for admitting such evidence refer to proper qualification of the expert, relevance vs. prejudice, and assistance to the decision maker, usually a jury. Most important, they also refer to reliability of the methods used to arrive at expert conclusions (California Evidence Code § 801; *People v. Gamez* (1991) 235 Cal. App.3d 957, 965–66; *U.S. v. Hermanek* (9th Cir. 2002) 289 F.3d 1076).

For scientific evidence, California uses the Kelly test, which requires that the reliability of the method of analysis be established via an expert who is properly qualified, and that correct scientific procedures were used in the particular case. In addition, the theory to which the expert will testify must be one which has general acceptance in the scientific field (*People v. Kelly* (1976) 17 Cal. 3d 24).

Rule 702 of the Federal Rules of Evidence, requires that to be admissible, expert evidence must be:

(a) relevant,
(b) based on materials generally relied on by experts in the field, and
(c) less prejudicial than probative.

(*Garcia v. Carey* (9th Cir. 2005) 395 F.3d 1099, 1103)

For scientific evidence, the federal Daubert test has four threshold requirements (*Daubert v. Merell-Dow Pharmaceuticals, Inc.* (1993) 509 U.S. 579):

(1) The theory or technique can be and has been tested;
(2) it has been subjected to peer review and publication;
(3) it has a known rate of error; and
(4) it is widely accepted in the scientific community.

In addition, where expertise is technical or experiential, a trial court must ensure the expert is qualified, employs reliable principles and methods and has applied these reliably to sufficient data (*Kumho Tire v. Carmichael* (1999) 536 U.S. 137, 152–53).

Whether the testimony of law enforcement gang experts is subject to the standards – federal or state – for admitting scientific evidence is a subject of debate (Agrimonti 1995; Moreno 2004). California courts and case law on gang experts appear to focus most heavily on the witness's experience and assistance to jurors (see, e.g. *People v. Gamez* (1991) 235 Cal. App.3d 957, 966), while permitting police officer expert testimony to "slip[-] in under the gatekeeper's door" (Hansen 2002: 34). This practice is in line with Groscup and Penrod's survey data: courts readily accept experience-based "expertise" of police officers, but rarely consider the methods of the witness with respect to a scientific reliability test (Moreno 2004: 4–6).

Gang experts arguably should be subject to a rigorous scientific evidentiary standard, such as the Daubert or Kelly test, particularly regarding the specific intent element of statutes such as the STEP Act (Gomez 2004: 604). If officers claim to use scientific methods to predict behaviour and decipher intent (even for the "hypothetical person"), the error rate of those predictions or analytic methods must be established (Burrell 1990: 771; Istratescu 2007). The methods of analysis for "Dr. Cop on the Stand" should be subject to more exacting scrutiny. Hansen (2002: 34) and Moreno (2004: 54) have questioned the over-willingness of trial courts to accept law enforcement experts' testimony on behavior, habits, and language codes of drug trafficking.

Hearsay

Experts, unlike lay witnesses, are allowed to rely on hearsay, even though the United States Constitution entitles defendants to confront the evidence against them and a witness generally may not report in testimony a statement (or writing) as proof of the matter stated if the statement was made outside of court by a "declarant" not subject to cross-examination (*Crawford v. Washington* (2004) 541 U.S. 36; Yermish 2006: 16). Thus, a statement by A that B is a gang member, overheard by C (who later testifies) would ordinarily not be admissible against B to prove that B is in fact a gang member.

These rules, however, are relaxed for expert witnesses. An expert witness may rely on hearsay in forming his or her opinion, but the jury is instructed to consider that hearsay only is the basis for the expert's opinion, not for its truth (Yermish 2006). Let's say that A tells C that B shot at someone in a rival gang. At B's trial, only C is available. A's statement to C is not admissible to prove B shot at someone. However, A's statement could be used as the basis for a gang expert's testimony that, hypothetically, a person in B's circumstances would commit such a crime for the benefit of a gang (see e.g. *People v. Gamez* (1991) 235 Cal. App.3d 957, 968–69).

How hearsay works in a gang trial

The gang expert may bring in extensive information about other people, events, and times, to establish the "CSG" has a primary activity of committing crimes and that the defendant's actions are consistent with an intent to benefit the gang (see Albarran case above). Often, the officer who testifies as an expert is also involved directly in the case investigation. In *People v. Zepeda* (2008) 167 Cal. App.4th 25, three officers testified, including one who seized incriminating material in a search, and another who gave a PowerPoint presentation covering seventy pages of transcript; the testimony encompassed hearsay concerning numerous acts of other alleged gang members. As one prosecutor noted, the expert may bring in the "juicy stuff" by basing an opinion on "almost anything" (Jackson 2004: 25–27).

The expert's testimony may be based on information from confidential informants, a local or statewide database (with information entered years before), or other sources not subject to review or cross-examination (*People v. Gardeley* (1997) 14 Cal. 4th 605; Mahoney 2004: 398–99; Gomez 2004: 618; Wright 2005: 123). Experts may rely on out-of-court statements by gang rivals, or other persons who never testify. For example, a police officer might testify that he spoke with members of a rival group, who claimed that the defendant's gang had committed the crime in question out of revenge for a prior assault. Jurors at trial would be instructed, when the expert testified, that the rivals' accusation could not be considered as evidence of defendant's guilt. Instead, jurors would be told to consider such evidence only as a foundation for the expert's opinion (Jackson 2004: 26; *People v. Gamez* (1991) 235 Cal. App. 4th 957).

However, empirical studies have shown that such "limiting instructions" may have precisely the opposite effect on jurors' consideration of hearsay evidence. Jurors may actually pay greater attention to inadmissible hearsay highlighted by the limiting instruction (Eichhorn 1989: 345; Fischoff 2005: 805).

> It is the essence of sophistry and lack of realism to think that an instruction or admonition to a jury to limit its consideration of highly prejudicial evidence to its limited relevant purpose can have any realistic effect. It is time that we face the realism of jury trials and recognize that jurors are mere mortals.
> (*People v. Gibson* 1976, 56 Cal. App.3d 119, 130, acknowledged)

When gang evidence forming the basis for the expert's opinion is sensational and remote, the defendant's inability to subject it to reliability testing may amount to a denial of fundamental fairness at trial.

Gang experts as language experts

Thus far, it is clear that gang experts may present hearsay evidence, (extensive and sometimes remote) evidence about other gang members and acts to establish gang membership, gang connectedness of offences, and "hypothetical" intent of the actors. One might well ask: how good are law enforcement gang "experts" at deciphering language puzzles?

Consider a California case, tried several years ago and still on appeal, that turns on "the writing on the wall". The prosecutor argued that the 18-year-old defendant, "Victor", was one of a group who robbed and killed a marijuana dealer. A major piece of evidence was, literally, the "writing on the wall" near a crime scene. The prosecutor's theory was that the Raymond Avenue Crips had taken credit for the deed and Victor was a Crips member. The connection between the gang, the crime, and the defendant was established by graffiti on an arcade wall across the street from the victim's house; Victor's "moniker" ("Trecherous") and other names were written on the wall, along with another phrase. The trial evidence photograph of the graffiti in Figure 19.2, taken nearly two years after the crime, shows the key phrase. The writing was "translated" by a sheriff's deputy testifying as a gang expert. Based on his experience, he both deciphered the writing and addressed its significance or illocutionary force, stating that the wall said "Do-re-me $" and the function of these words was a boast, meaning "to obtain money in a robbery or a burglary". Although he did not explain how he arrived at his interpretation, he apparently took "do-re-me" and "$" to refer to money, and the nearby roll-call list of names of the Raymond Avenue Crips (including Victor's nickname) to be part of the same utterance. Since the unknown graffiti author did not testify, cross-examination of the writer was not possible, and the graffiti was hearsay. Moreover, the timing of the writing (in whole or part) was entirely unclear. The jury saw only the

Figure 19.2 Graffiti photo 2

photograph and heard the expert's interpretation, that it was an admission confirming Victor's guilt.

Both parts of the officer's opinion are open to serious unresolved questions. The deputy's method of analysing the phrase was opaque at best. Victor's defence counsel could have put up more resistance to this evidence than shown in the trial record. Moreover, a close look at the lower right of the photograph reveals that, contrary to evidentiary requirements, the expert's testimony was not helpful to the jury, but quite misleading. In accepting his "translation", jurors ignored what was in front of their own eyes, like parade viewers observing a naked emperor pass by. Although the expert asserted that the wall says, "Do-re-me $", it actually says "Do or Die". After Victor was convicted and sentenced, his defence team found the author of the graffiti who confirmed his authorship, as well as his name (Lil Drac) and those of others on the wall. Lil Drac said he had not written the $, and he confirmed that the real phrase was "Do or Die", an expression of group loyalty. Victor's new attorneys contend that without the deputy's testimony regarding this erroneous and unfounded admission of guilt, Victor would not have been convicted of capital murder or sentenced to death.

Critiques

Testimony by law enforcement experts in gang trials has been criticized on several grounds. One concerns officers' dual role as investigators and experts, which may create bias (Solan and Tiersma 2005: 193). Nevertheless, because jurors are told the officer is "an expert", they may be inclined to accept the testimony and ignore or discount contrary evidence before their eyes. Groscup and Penrod (2003, note 32) cite juror surveys in which police witnesses are rated very favourably and as more honest than other witnesses. Their favoured status and dual role is all the more reason a rigorous scientific evidence test should apply to admissibility of their testimony. Expert testimony founded on unreliable hearsay is "a house built on sand" – as unreliable as the hearsay on which it is predicated (Mahoney 2004).

At least in Victor's case, both the hearsay evidence and its interpretation were available at trial. However, in other cases where the hearsay comes in via confidential investigation reports or statements of informants in field interviews, the jury has substantially less ability to judge the reliability of the basis for the expert's testimony.

A second critique, and perhaps more relevant for linguistic purposes, is that law enforcement witnesses hold and present an overly monolithic view of youth groups and their behavior, including their language behavior. Yet because of the witnesses' status, jurors may accord more credence to them as language experts than they really deserve. Crime statistics and surveys estimate that many of those accused under the gang statutes are under 24, with a large number in the 16–24 range. Teenagers, regardless of alleged gang status, are notoriously inventive, inclined to use language creatively and to follow language fashion. Moje (2000: 669) found that many teenagers take on what adults perceived as "gangsta dress" styles in an effort "simply ... not to stand out." Language rituals, including those literacy practices identified with gangs, serve these students as a way to take a social position in the world (Moje 2000: 679).

A similar social indexing function for what law enforcement may regard as "gang slang" has been observed among youth in other communities (Bucholtz 2006) and even among recent English learners (Ibrahim 1999: 367). Sociolinguists have discussed the phenomenon

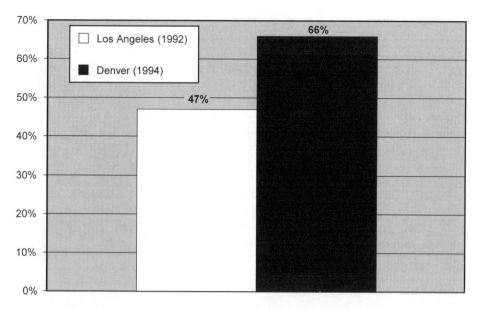

Figure 19.3 Over-representation of African American youth in gang databases

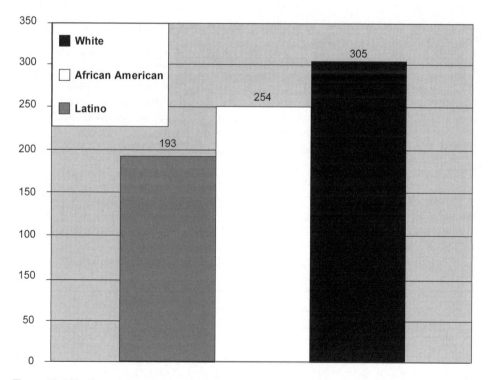

Figure 19.4 Youth sentence averages in days as a function of race

of "crossing" – where youth may adopt features of speech varieties they consider cool, seeking to get the 'pluses' of sounding tough or trendy, without the minuses of that speech variety and group (Reyes 2005). Just as everyone who wears baggy pants is not a gang member, not everyone who says "Cuz" or "Nut-Up" is a gang participant, much less a criminal. In fact, peer evaluations of such poseurs or "wannabes" can be scathing (Cutler 1999: 438): "You know they like practice in front of the mirror, pull their pants down to their knees, I don't know."

Finally, statistics indicate gang charges, and gang prohibitions such as civil injunctions in urban areas, are overly applied to minority youth (Beres and Griffith 2004; Espiritu 2005). In two representative cities, minority youth representation in these databases in the early 1990s was clearly disproportionate to their percentage of the population (see Figure 19.3: Information from Wright 2005). Furthermore, demographic studies of youth have shown that for the same offense, minority youth are more likely to enter the criminal justice system and to receive lengthier sentences than their white peers (Figure 19.4: Information summarized by Building Blocks for Youth).

Conclusions and suggestions

Studies of youth speech varieties have shown that styles and boundaries are more fluid and changing over time than recognized by the profiling of gang syllogism (Bucholtz 2006; Cutler 1999). Ethnographic and linguistic studies have the further advantage that academics who are collecting the data in the community do not arrest their language informants, and thus may be more likely to accurately separate the broader issue of language behavior from the blanket notion that certain dress and language equate to criminality (Mendoza-Denton 2008: 79–82).

Linguists and ethnographers have clearly demonstrated that when it comes to language, youth is the vanguard of change (Trudgill 1988; Eckert 1997). Many phenomena identified as gang-related today are part of the fluid communicative styles adopted for particular purposes and times. They will probably someday become as quaint as the expressions "Daddy-O" or "Groovy", and as classic as a zoot suit (see Madden 2007).

It would help defense lawyers challenging gang prosecutions to have access to information about language practices, to refute the most common tenets of gang expert testimony. For example, is "¿Qué Barrio?" used only by gang members? Do cross-outs always or usually mean death threats? What are the additional functions of rituals like "the hit-up" and graffiti lists? To what extent, if any, is Caló criminally connected? As Klein points out, in cases where gang membership is ambiguous, social science testimony may provide accuracy and challenge errors in broad claims about youth behavior (Klein 1997).

Sociolinguistic studies of youth groups who are and are not affiliated, in the context of natural interactions, and as changing over time, could be useful counterexamples to the law enforcement readiness to classify even random and innocent behavior of minority community members as having criminal intent, and to brand membership (and allegedly associated linguistic features) as a long-term fixed trait. Officers are less likely than communication experts or linguists to appreciate youth's creative use of language, which displays an "efflorescence of semiosis" (Conquergood 1994: 27). To keep up with changes in what youth are doing and saying is a challenge (Towner 2008: 39; Cotter and Walking Turtle 2001: 127). The equation between language and gang membership also fails because for the majority of youth who do join gangs, membership is short-lived (Beres and Griffith 2004: 949–50). However, for the most part, law enforcement databases do not recognize such changes in status (see Curiel 2008 and Winton 2008, acknowledging the need to revise such databases).

As Tiersma and Solan (2002) have shown, the real difficulty may be not in getting the linguistic work done – ethnographic and sociolinguistic research has so far provided a rich background for analyzing contextual meaning – but in overcoming a general judicial hostility toward social science testimony (Groscup and Penrod 2003: 1145–46), convincing the gatekeeper that such testimony is relevant and reliable, and permitting juries to hear alternative theories of meaning where language forms such a core of the group practices and intent figures so strongly in liability. At present, the tour guides to meaning offer only a limited range of options. Appropriate research and collaboration between the legal and linguistic communities will make possible a knowledge base that more accurately reflects community practices and the vibrant, innovative contribution of its youth.

Further reading

Adams, K. and A. Winter (1997) 'Gang graffiti as a discourse genre', *Journal of Sociolinguistics* 1/3: 337–60.

Bucholtz, M. (2006) 'Word up: Social meanings of slang in California youth culture', in J. Goodman and L. Monaghan (eds) *Interpersonal Communication: An Ethnographic Approach*, London: Blackwell, 243–67.

Docuyanan, F. (2000) 'Governing graffiti in contested urban spaces', *Political and Legal Anthropology Review*, 23: 103–21.

Moreno, J. (2004) 'What happens when Dirty Harry becomes an (expert) witness for the prosecution?' *Tulane Law Review*, 79: 1–54.

Phillips, S.A. (1999) *Wallbangin': Graffiti & Gangs in L.A.*, Chicago: University of Chicago Press.

Legal cases cited

Crawford v. Washington (2004) 541 U.S. 36.

Daubert v. Merell-Dow Pharmaceuticals, Inc. (1993) 509 U.S. 579.

Garcia v. Carey (9th Cir. 2005) 395 F.3d 1099.

Kumho Tire Co. v. Carmichael (1999) 526 U.S. 137.

People v. Albarran (2007) 149 Cal. App.4th 214.

People v. Castro (2006) 2006 WL 459890 (unpublished).

People v. Chapman (2003) WL 1958893 (unpublished).

People v. Gamez (1991) 235 Cal. App.3d 957.

People v. Gardeley (1997) 14 Cal. 4th 605.

People v. Gibson (1976) 56 Cal. App.3d 119.

People v. Gutierrez (2007) 2007 WL 3138384 (unpublished).

People v. Kelly (1976) 17 Cal. 3d 24.

People v. Margarejo (2008) 162 Cal. App.4th 102.

People v. Miller (2007) 2007 WL 1229401 (unpublished).

People v. Norteño, San Francisco Superior Court Case No. 464492, Permanent Injunction, June 17, 2008.

People v. Robbie (2001) 92 Cal. App.4th 1075.

People v. Zepeda (2008) 167 Cal. App.4th 25.

People v. Freeman (9th Cir. 2007) 498 F.3d 893.

People v. Hermanek (9th Cir. 2002) 289 F.3d 1076 .

20

Vulnerable witnesses

Vulnerable witnesses in the Criminal Justice System

Michelle Aldridge

Introduction

The aim of this chapter is to review the linguistic experiences of vulnerable witnesses within the Criminal Justice System. We focus on children and people with communication disabilities and examine how such witnesses cope linguistically with investigative police interviews and court appearances. By looking at the way police officers interview vulnerable witnesses and by analysing witnesses' understanding of concepts and their ability to develop a narrative and answer questions, we will evaluate whether or not they are prejudiced linguistically. Focusing on court procedures – video-recorded interviews and special measures such as intermediaries and communication aids for the witness – we will assess whether enough is being done to enable these witnesses to tell their story. While we will concentrate on the system currently in operation in England and Wales, where appropriate we will compare this with how witnesses are interviewed and examined in other countries, in an attempt to determine what still needs to be done to achieve justice for all.

In the first section, we identify what is meant by *vulnerable witnesses* in England and Wales and describe the legislation that has been passed to support them through the legal process. The second section reviews the experiences of children and disabled people in the initial police interview. Section three describes their experiences in court and considers the impact of special measures. All the data used in this chapter are taken from real video-recorded police interviews with child witnesses. All identities have been removed.

Vulnerable witnesses in the legal system

Historically, children were considered to be the 'most dangerous of all witnesses' (Whipple 1911: 308). According to Goodman (1984: 2) they were viewed as 'highly

296

suggestible, unable to differentiate fantasy from reality' and possessing what today we would call very 'malleable memories'. Fortunately, over time, society's attitudes have changed and those concerned have begun to appreciate that 'children's apparent lack of credibility may have as much to do with the competence of adults to communicate with them as it does with their (in)ability to remember and relate their experiences accurately' (Saywitz 1995: 115).

In the 1980s and 1990s, several inquiries into child protection occurred (e.g. The Cleveland Report 1988; Pigot Report 1989; Clyde Report 1992) and it became clear that children were not receiving a fair hearing. It was apparent that no allowance was being made for their developing cognitive and linguistic abilities and that they simply could not cope with interviewing procedures. In brief, their stories were going untold. Changes to procedures were made through the Criminal Justice Acts of (1991) and police interviews with child witnesses were encouraged to be video-recorded and used as the child's evidence-in-chief in court. At the same time, the Home Office introduced *The Memorandum of Good Practice on Video Recorded Interviews for Child Witnesses for Criminal Proceeding* (MOGP 1992) which was a set of guidelines designed to assist interviewing professionals in the conduct of initial video interviews. This encouraged a phased approach with four phases: *rapport, free narrative, questioning* and *close*, which are compatible with and underpin the PEACE interview framework advocated by the Association of Chief Police Officers (ACPO) (ABE 2007: 21). The MOGP also made a number of recommendations about the planning and length of the interview and offered guidelines on talking with children, such as using age appropriate language, listening to the child rather than directly questioning him or her; never stopping a child who is freely recalling significant events (MOGP 1992: 6) and encouraging the child to provide an account in his or her own words and at his or her own pace (MOGP 1992: 17). The introduction of the video interview brought about substantial change and was accompanied by training days for police officers specialising in child interviewing. For the first time, police officers were trained in how to talk with, rather than just to, child witnesses, and were encouraged to ask children open narrative eliciting questions such as 'please tell me what happened' and 'please tell me more about' rather than more constrained agenda-focused questions.

It soon became obvious, however, that children were not the only group to struggle through the legal process and in 1999 the *Youth Justice and Criminal Evidence Bill* was passed. Part 2 of this Bill embodied the legislative provision of *Speaking Up for Justice* (1998) which included a number of special measures intended to address the problems of vulnerable and intimidated witnesses within the court process (Burton *et al.* 2007: 1). To support these changes the MOGP was replaced by *Achieving Best Evidence in Criminal Proceedings: Guidance for Vulnerable and Intimidated Witnesses, Including Children* (ABE 2002). In 2007, ABE was up-dated, in part, to take account of the *Code of Practice for Victims of Crime* (2005).

Since 2002, vulnerable witnesses in England and Wales have been defined as:

> Young people under 17 years of age and any witness whose quality of evidence is likely to be diminished because they suffer from a mental disorder; or have a significant impairment of intelligence and social functioning; or have a physical disability or disorder.
>
> (ABE, Home Office 2007: 2)

Intimidated witnesses are those 'whose quality of testimony is likely to be diminished by reason of fear or distress at the prospect of giving evidence' (ABE, Home Office 2007: 2). Witnesses (not suspects) who fall into these categories are entitled to apply for conditions within the legal procedure known as 'Special Measures'. These include:

- Screening the witness from the accused
- Giving evidence by live link
- The removal of wigs and gowns
- Giving evidence in private
- Video recording of evidence-in-chief
- Video recording of cross-examination and re-examination
- Examination through intermediary
- Provision of aids to communicate.

An intermediary is someone who the court approves to communicate to the witness the questions that the court, the defence and the prosecution teams ask, and to communicate the answers that the witness gives in response. (For further information, see the *Intermediary Procedural Guidance Manual* (Office for Criminal Justice Reform 2005)). Children are also protected from cross-examination by the accused in person and there should be no mention of their sexual history in court. Normally, children aside, 'special measures' are not automatic but have to be requested. The police and prosecutors must identify vulnerability and apply to the Crown Prosecution Service (CPS) on a case basis. Eligibility is determined at the pre-trial hearing. The CPS will be rigorous in its selection of these special measures and may suggest any, all or none of the above. The measures are designed to preserve the essentials of a proper challenge to a witness's evidence and should not alter the defendant's position, but only those deemed necessary will be used. The Judge will explain to the jury which measures are being used and why. The witness can, of course, choose to opt out of the special measures.

Vulnerable witnesses in the police interview

Children

Since 1992, child witnesses have been interviewed under the recommendations of MOGP and more recently ABE. For many children this means that they attend a purpose-built interview suite and give their evidence to a specially trained police officer. The witness can request a male or female interviewer but for ease, in this text, unless otherwise stated, we will refer to the interviewer as 'she' and to the witness as 'he'. (We acknowledge fully, of course, that females can be child witnesses and interviewing officers can be male.)

The interview is video-recorded in order to be used as the child's evidence-in-chief and, once recorded, is submitted to the CPS to determine whether it is adequate and whether it is in the public interest to proceed with the case. If so, a copy is made available to the defence. We will now reflect on each of the phases of the interview to consider the child's linguistic competence and the interviewer's linguistic performance through these phases.

The phased interview – building rapport

Here the interviewer has a number of objectives including:

(a) describing, out loud, the environment, the layout of the room, including the recording equipment, the persons present and the purpose of the interview for the child;

(b) assessing the child's cognitive abilities by getting him talking on neutral topics through the use of a range of open questions, such as 'I don't know you very well yet, so please tell me something about what you do after school' or 'What are your favourite hobbies or television programmes?'

(c) exploring his understanding of truth and lie; and

(d) explaining the ground rules in order to shift social distance and empower the child to interact.

The child is told that he may request a break if necessary and that to say that he doesn't remember is better than guessing an answer. It is important that, during this phase, the interviewee gains some control of the process and content of his disclosure (Shepherd and Milne 2006: 132). The interviewer should demonstrate that she is interested in what the witness has to say and doesn't know everything, so interviewer turns such as 'Shall we talk a bit about the things you like and your house cos I don't know you very well yet do I?' are encouraged, along with turns that signal that she might have to repeat questions: 'Sometimes, I may say a question more than once, that may be because I didn't hear you very well.' Failure to explain such repetition often leads to a breakdown in the interview as we see in (1).

(1) Police interview with a child witness aged 3

IE: I've got a poorly bum
IR:Have you? Why?
IE: I have
IR:Why is your bum poorly?
IE: It is
IR:What do you mean by poorly? What's it like?
IE: It's poorly
IR:Does it hurt?
IE: No
IR:Why's it poorly then?
IE: It isn't poorly
IR:It isn't poorly?
IE: Let's do some jigsaws

Here, a talkative child gives up trying to explain his problem, as the interviewer seems to be challenging what he is saying; he subsequently loses confidence to talk through the rest of the interview. This demonstrates the importance of the ABE guidance; listening to the child and resisting questioning is crucial.

Although seemingly straightforward, getting a conversation going in this phase can be a significant challenge, if we consider that the child has probably been socialised not to talk to strangers and certainly not about sex and, furthermore, has a fear of telling anyone 'their secret'. Interviewers also have to overcome differences in shared understanding and use of vocabulary. Our lexical understanding changes all the time. The author had a stark reminder of this while listening to the radio and hearing: 'The Ospreys have had triplets'. This produced a mental picture of local rugby players holding up babies for a photo call. The next line 'And their nesting behaviour' completely shattered this image and generated a bird frame. (For further reading on how the author uses terms such as 'frame' and 'script' see Luchjenbroers and Aldridge 2007; Aldridge and Luchjenbroers 2007.) The importance of this example is: an interviewer cannot assume that her interlocutor's understanding of words is the same as her own. 'Ospreys' is the name of a rugby team in South Wales and I regularly watched them play. Potential misunderstanding and miscommunication can occur at any time in the interview, as we see in (2a) and (2b).

(2a) Police interview with a child witness aged 6

IR:What do you do after school?
IE: I like milkshake
IR:Do you! So do I! What's your favourite flavour?
IE: It's on the telly

(2b) Police interview with a child witness aged 5 years

IE: My brother's horrible to me
IR:Is he? What does he do?
IE: He don't let me play on the Playstation
IR:Ooh, isn't he wicked!
IE: (in distressed state) No! he's not, he's horrible

In (2a) the interviewer is unaware that 'milkshake' is a popular television programme and in (2b) the interviewer uses 'wicked' without allowing for its more recent sense, widely used among young people: meaning 'very good', 'accomplished' and having positive connotations. The potential outcome of clashes of understanding is that children are less likely to communicate, so interviewers must be trained to think as a child, to negotiate understanding, to be sensitive to misunderstanding and attentive to repair.

Miscommunication can also occur when children do not understand the institutional talk they may encounter during the investigation and where interviewers fail to take account of the difficulties of using a professional register. Aldridge et al. (1997) asked presumed non-abused children to describe roles and labels that they would hear in the legal setting. (3) lists typical explanations by children of institutional vocabulary with respondents' ages in brackets.

(3)
A police lady gets people in prison (aged 6).
When you're arrested, a policeman will come along and put you in chains (aged 8).
A court is a sort of jail (aged 5).
Witnesses whip people when they're naughty (aged 7).
Witnesses are people who have done something naughty (aged 7).
Prosecution is when you die, you get hanged or something like that (aged 7).
Judges get money at pet shows (aged 7).
A judge judges people like when you go to jail and have to tell the judge what you've done (aged 7).

Holding concepts such as these, we can only imagine a child's potential fright when told a police lady wants to talk with him, or he has to go to court. It is crucial, then, that the rapport phase facilitates meaningful and reassuring understanding of institutional roles and terms. A police officer might say: 'my job means that I talk to lots of children, so there's nothing to worry about', to ensure that the child doesn't believe that being interviewed by the police is an indication of wrongdoing. The child must also be given the opportunity for a court visit before he has to attend for his own case so that he can familiarise himself with the setting, procedures and court personnel.

A final place where the interviewer has to listen to the child's vocabulary is when the accused has deliberately given the witness what we might label 'false friend vocabulary'. For example, a four-year-old witness talked about 'boxing with his grandfather'. Only after substantial questioning did it become apparent that 'boxing' was being used to describe anal intercourse. All these examples show us that the interviewer cannot assume she shares knowledge and usage of vocabulary with her interviewee.

One final area of important talk in the rapport phase is establishing the importance of telling the truth, though there is no legal requirement to administer the oath. Interviewers are ill advised if they ask a child for a definition as (4) illustrates.

(4) Police interview with a child witness aged 5

> IR: Do you know what a lie is?
> IE: Yes
> IR: What is a lie?
> IE: Tigers

Here, the child didn't understand the question and or replied elliptically, perhaps, as if the interviewer was asking about lions? (This suggestion was made by Professor John Gibbons (pc).) Such exchanges show the child to be vulnerable in the courtroom process. If the child can answer this way to a relatively straightforward question then the defence lawyer could make the judge and jury wonder how credible a witness the child is. It is now recommended (cf. ABE, Home Office 2007: 24) that rather than seeking a definition, the child should be asked to judge from examples like in (5).

(5) Exploring the difference between truth and lies: example for younger children

> IR: Let me tell you a story about John. John was playing with his ball in the kitchen and he kicked the ball against the window. The window broke and John ran upstairs into his bedroom. John's mummy saw the broken window and asked John if he had broken the window. John said 'no mummy'.
> IR: Did John tell a lie or the truth, or don't you know?
> IR: What should he have said?

Following the rapport phase and once the interviewer is confident that the child is as settled as possible, she will move the interview on to the free narrative stage and then on to questioning.

Free narrative phase

In the free narrative phase, the child should be encouraged to provide in his own words an account of the relevant events. Here, the interviewer is a facilitator not an interrogator and she should use open questions such as 'please tell me what happened?' and 'please describe what happened next?' Davies and Westcott (1999) claim that this phase is crucial to the outcome of the case, since juries find free narratives persuasive, as they present the child's rather than the interviewer's account and, in providing a monologue, children are free from any suggestions that adult questions may offer. The interviewer should provide a framework for the child to build his own account around with lines such as 'I want you to start at the beginning, take your time and tell me what happened.'

This phase, though, is not without difficulty because young children can find account giving difficult. We know, for example (e.g. Goodman and Melinder 2007: 12), that 'open-ended questions typically elicit the most accurate, albeit often the most skeletal, reports from children'. (6) is a typical account.

(6)   Police interview with a child witness aged 10

IR: It's ok to tell me.

IE: He said lie down for a minute and I said no and then I lied down and he got it in and he put it in here and he turned me over and licked my bum and that's all of it.

An adult witness would be most unlikely to answer in this way; a lot of information is missing and the interviewer will need to ask questions to supplement the very short account given. Quality and detail relating to the alleged offence are lacking (see also Walker and Warren 1995: 159), as we can also see in extract (7).

(7)   Police interview with child witness aged 6

IR: Can you tell me what happened? Can you do that?

IE: I came home, my dad sent me up to go in the bath. I got out the bath my dad gave me the towel and said 'go downstairs and get dry'. I dried underneath and there was all blood on the towel.

How did the blood get there? A more mature witness would not give his narrative this way. Thus, while the accuracy of what is reported does not vary with age, the omission of detail does. However, it remains a fact that in most interviews the narrative phase will have to be supplemented by questions and reassurance from the interviewer, which will help elicit a full account, as in (8).

(8)   Police interview with a child witness aged 9

IR: Please tell us as much as you can remember

IE: Well, I was in the bath. I was getting out of the bath. No, I had a quick bath, I was getting out then my dad come up and he had a sweet wrapper and, em, I dried myself and then no, he squeezed, no sorry.

IR: Take your time.

IE: I stayed in the bath for half an hour, I came out, had a quick bath, dried myself, he squeezed my willy very tight and he smacked me for no reason.

In brief, the younger the child, the more the interviewer is likely to have to prompt. As shown in (9a), a young child might offer a single piece of information while an older child (9b) can link events together.

(9a) Police interview with a child witness aged 5

IR:Tell me what happened?

IE: Jimmy put mummy's tights on.

(9b) Police interview with a child witness aged 9

IR:Tell me what happened?

IE: I was sitting on the van and what he done, he touched my bum and then after that he put his hand under my shirt, this shirt.

More 'scaffolding' (Bruner 1978) of the child's narrative will be needed with young children.

Problems with vocabulary occur in this phase too, simply because a young child will not have the rich vocabulary necessary to re-count what has happened. Compare (10a) with (10b).

(10a) Police interview with a child witness aged 4

IE: He touched my leg.

IE: Phil put his fingers in my private.

(10b) Police interview with a child witness aged 9

IE: He rubbed my leg.

IE: He pushed his fingers into my private parts.

Bell and Loftus (1985) report (amongst others) that juries are more influenced by vivid and powerful language than by powerless language, so we might anticipate (10b) having a greater impact on a listener than (10a), even though they are describing similar events. The interviewer will therefore have to work harder to elicit the first witness's story.

Questioning

When planning questions to elicit details of the alleged offence, the interviewer should follow a step-wise approach, beginning with open questions and reserving direct/ leading questions until last. Interviewers are advised to ask wh-questions in the order they are acquired by children, namely: *what, where, who, when, how. Why* should be avoided as it tends to attribute blame. While the wh-form is important, the interviewer must continue to think as a child. The correct wh-word in itself is not sufficient. Consider (11).

(11) Police interview with a child witness aged 9

IR:You said he was kneeling down and one hand was doing what you described, what was his other hand doing?

IE: Don't know.

Syntactically, the interviewer's style is appropriate (it is a straightforward initial *what* question), but we assume she is basing her question on the adult script of masturbation. The child, who is most likely unaware of this, cannot understand the relevance of the hand not touching her. The interviewer's lack of account of the child's likely perspective and world knowledge leads to trouble in the talk. Example (12), from a rapport phase, also exemplifies the danger of assuming that straightforward syntactic form equals trouble-free answering.

(12)   Police interview with a child witness aged 6

IR: What did you do in the summer holiday?
IE: I played for Arsenal,
IR: Are you sure? Where?
IE: I did for two weeks.

This case failed because it was argued that the child was fantasising and therefore, his account could not be reliable; at the age of 6 he could not have played for Arsenal. More patient listening to and questioning about the child's world would have revealed that he had indeed been to an Arsenal football school over the vacation and had 'played the Arsenal way'.

With each new topic, an interviewer will ideally work through wh-questions from *what* to *how*, but with consideration of whether all wh-forms should be used. *How* questions are very difficult for young children. Interviewers often ask how something felt, as in (13).

(13)   Police interview with child witness aged 14 years

IR: How did you feel when he did that? [penetration]
IE: I felt, em, hurt and er terrible.
IR: How did you feel inside?
IE: Em, I don't know, it's sort of hard to say.

It is known (e.g. Aldridge and Wood 1997) that children find it hard to articulate their feelings. Indeed, the above question is ambiguous, even to an adult, as to whether the child is being asked a physical or mental question. The problem children have in understanding *how*-questions was illustrated in the following experimental setting (Javan 2009). Children had watched a cartoon and were then asked a series of questions; one of them was (14).

(14)   How did the duck come out of the closet?

The expected answer was 'on a skateboard'. Although the questioner used 'how' to refer to a physical action, nearly all the 20 children (aged 10) provided an answer that referred to what the duck was wearing, indicating that they interpreted 'how' as referring to his physical appearance. Likewise, very few children can express coercion or conflicting emotions, so it is not surprising that in a real interview, when asked 'do you like Daddy?' (the accused), the child responds 'yes', because he doesn't have the vocabulary to say that he loves Daddy but hates what Daddy does. Saarni and Harris's (1989: 85) data demonstrate this conflict: "I couldn't feel happy and scared at the same time; I would have to be two people at once!" Our data also show how a young child's emotional vocabulary is semantically limited (15).

(15) Mother waiting with a 4-year-old child before an investigative interview (Child kisses her support worker on the cheek.)

Mother: Hey stop that, you're embarrassing him.
Child: I'm not embarrassing him, I'm kissing him.

Measurements are another difficult area. Interviewers are often keen to establish detail of time, manner and place, and yet such descriptions are often outside the linguistic competence of a young child as in (16).

(16)   Police interview with a child witness aged 4

IR:How long have you been staying at Mary's house?
IE: Don't know.
IR:How far away is it?
IE: Three miles or maybe thirty miles.

Interviewers are well advised to avoid such detail for as long as possible. The interviewer should, however, avoid over-hasty transition from the free narrative phase into a specific questioning phase as (17) illustrates.

(17)   Police interview with a child witness aged 8

IR:Do you think you can tell me what happened?
IE: Silence.
IR:It's ok to tell me about the things that happened.
IE: Yesterday night.
IR:Yesterday night?
IE: Nods.
IR:Where were you?

Here the child is rushed into answering a *where*-question, after a silent response to the initial *what*-question, rather than being prompted again with a 'what happened next?' question. It is important that the interviewer divides the witness's account up into manageable topics and that they are systematically dealt with (to completion) before moving on to something else (ABE, Home Office 2007: 29).

As well as planning the order of her questions from *what* through to *how*, the interviewer must also be encouraged to listen to the type of responses the child is giving. For example, apparently in order to please, children will often answer questions pragmatically in order to maintain turn-taking, without either listening to the question or understanding it. The interviewer should, therefore, be encouraged to listen for the strategies that children adopt in answering wh-questions. In (18a) and (18b), for example, the young children do not appear to understand *when* and *why*, so they reply as if the questions are *where* forms.

(18a) If you don't understand a particular question, respond as if it's in a form you do understand (Ervin Tripp 1970).

IR:When did this happen?
IE: In my bedroom (child aged 4).

(18b) Interview with a child aged 3

IR:Why does Grandad smack you?
IE: [points] here.

In (19) he adopts another of Ervin Tripp's (1970) strategies: If you don't understand the question, give a stereotypical response.

(19) Interview with a child aged 3

    IR:Have you seen these before? Any of these people? (showing picture).
    IE: Yeah.
    IR:Where's that?
    IE: In Sainsbury's.
    IR:Is there anywhere else you play apart from at home?
    IE: Yeah
    IR:Where else do you play?
    IE: In Sainsbury's.

The inappropriate responses created through these coping strategies potentially weaken the child's account (see Haworth, this volume, on the interview as evidence) and create doubt as to whether the child can give a reliable testimony. The interviewer needs to be ready to re-phrase questions once these coping mechanisms kick in. Similarly, interviewers need to be wary of using *yes/no* questions and tag questions, as young children (particularly under the age of seven) are vulnerable to answering 'yes' to these question forms. This is particularly true in the rapport phase where establishing ground rules (as in 20) can encourage the child to say 'no' and resist answering from thereon.

(20)
    IR:Is it ok to sit here and have a chat with you?

Likewise, alternative questions need to be asked with care as, adopting a recency strategy, many young children will respond with the last option heard. Other question types to avoid include passives (were you hurt by him?); negative questions (Did you not see him in the room?) and multiple questions (Was it yesterday you went to the house and was he there?) (see Walker 1999 for more on these aspects of questioning children). Once detailed information has been gathered, the interviewer will move into closure.

Closure

Here the interviewer should take time to ask whether the child has any questions and to answer them honestly and as accurately as possible. The child should also be thanked for his contribution and will be told about what will happen next (see ABE, Home Office 2007: 30 for more detail). The video-interview then becomes the child's evidence-in-chief. It will be submitted to the Crown Prosecution Service who will decide whether to take the case forward. A copy of the video is given to the defence. The child may now receive therapy, but any counselling received must be disclosed to the defence.

People with disabilities

Much of what we have said above about children will apply to people with learning disabilities, but we are reminded by Westcott and Cross (1996) and Marchant and Page

(1997) that both children and adults with disabilities are particularly vulnerable to abuse.

> Children who cannot communicate easily with others may be 'ideal' for abusers to target, since they will face extreme difficulties in trying to tell someone – by whatever means – of their experiences. Further, they may not even have been given the necessary vocabulary (and by implication, permission) to describe abusive activities or private body parts.
>
> (Westcott and Cross 1996: 84)

> The scales of justice are tipped against all child victims when the main evidence is their oral testimony and they are undoubtedly tipped even further for children whose impairments affect their communication.
>
> (Marchant and Page 1997: 78)

When planning to interview a witness with a disability, a range of issues need to be considered, including:

(a) access: can the witness, for example, independently enter the interview room, have a drink and use the toilet facilities? and
(b) communication needs: does the witness speak or does he use a non-verbal communication system such as sign language or an augmentative communication system? Is an intermediary needed?

Let us consider first, the disabled witness who uses verbal communication but may have some difficulties in speech understanding and production. It is assumed that the initial interview will follow the same four stages as with non-disabled children, and that similar issues may arise, as discussed above, but it may well be the case that even greater planning is needed. Firstly, for example, the interviewer must know the mental age of the witness. A forty-year-old man with Down Syndrome may present for interview, but he may have the mental age of a six-year-old. It is also likely that someone with a disability will have a shorter attention span than someone who is not disabled, so greater consideration must be given to using props such as dolls, dolls' houses, paper and crayons, and an intermediary. Their speech may be less clear, so attention must be paid to make sure that the best quality audio equipment is used. The interviewer must be trained, because the witness's language production and comprehension may be different from that of a non-disabled person. These differences include phonological, lexical, syntactic and pragmatic difficulties.

Phonological disabilities

Non-disabled children pass through a typical path in their acquisition of phonemes with some, such as fricatives and affricates, being acquired later than phonemes such as plosives and nasals (cf. Vihman 1996 for detail). One in ten children in the pre-school years experience speech difficulties (cf. Edelman 2009) and thus many witnesses may not have particularly clear articulation. The interviewer, therefore, will need training about which sounds to expect to be difficult, about which substitution errors are likely to occur and how to interview in a way that lip readers will follow. The interviewer will need to use the rapport phase wisely in order to tune into possible substitution patterns and to try to 'crack the code' of the speech they are listening to. Witnesses with a hearing impairment may have phonological differences and a 'flatter' intonation. Witnesses with Down Syndrome will have impaired phonological abilities as will some people with cerebral palsy. Alternatively, some witnesses may have clear articulation but a different delivery because of a stutter. Witnesses with autism may have an idiosyncratic intonation pattern and make use of 'non-speech' noises. Again, training will be needed to advise the interviewer on how to deal with the stutter, when to wait and when to intervene.

Vocabulary

Witnesses with communication disorders may have different vocabulary usage. For example, people with Down Syndrome, will have a slower word retrieval, and so more time will be needed for them to tell their story. Their vocabulary may be less rich, they may make greater use of general purpose words such as *do* and *put* and so their account may be less graphic and have less impact. Some conditions such as Williams Syndrome may result in witnesses having an unusual vocabulary, rich in some areas, but pro-foundly lacking in others. Other people, like those who have had a stroke and have Broca's aphasia, for example, will understand almost all that is said to them, but will struggle to produce a sentence. Such behaviour could be misunderstood, interpreted as if the witness doesn't wish to cooperate and so those involved will need training. Similarly, the interviewer can't assume that she shares the same understanding of word meaning as the witness so she must consider ways of understanding the witness's worldview.

Grammar and syntax

People with communicative difficulties are likely to have greater difficulty with grammatical words (determiners, prepositions, etc.) rather than lexical or content words (nouns, verbs, adjectives and adverbs). There are people with little productive grammatical ability – especially witnesses with Down Syndrome, Broca's aphasia and Specific Language Impairment – but many people with communicative disorders find grammar difficult to use and understand (cf. Fletcher and Ingram 1995). Children with autism may have pro-blems with grammar and questions (Kremer-Sadlik 2004) and because of their tendency to echo, they will make great use of pronoun reversals. Many witnesses will have problems in dealing with location (prepositions), describing manner (adverbs) and time of events. Small grammatical words such as determiners (*a/the*); modal verbs (e.g. *will, can*), complementisers (e.g. *that, whether*) are also problematic for many, causing great productive difficulties and comprehension issues when it comes to reporting past events. The interviewer will need to keep the questions as straightforward as possible, avoiding past, negative and passive constructions. In brief, sentences should be kept simple and in the present tense.

Pragmatic difficulties

Some people have an intact language structure, but still have problems with pragmatics, which means that they use social language inappropriately. People with autism may have difficulty with aspects of language use such as turn-taking, listener perspective and choice of speech act. The impact of these pragmatic problems is that these witnesses may mistakenly be taken to be anti-establishment, arrogant and potentially deceitful, so the interviewer needs to know what to expect and how to deal with it.

To summarise, people with a communication disorder can have one or several of the following general characteristics:

- limited cognitive skills;
- problems with understanding the nature of the events which constituted the alleged offence;
- problems with understanding the ensuing procedures, increased stress, diminished performance;
- poor adaptation;
- poor memory;
- limited language production (phonological, lexical, semantic, syntactic and pragmatic);
- limited language comprehension (Sanders *et al.* 1997).

This means that to successfully complete an investigative interview with a witness with a communicative disability, the interviewer must:

- ensure full understanding of the witness's needs and abilities;
- have realistic expectations based on training and information;
- consider room access, comfort while there, scope of the video camera, etc.;
- consider the use of props;
- involve an intermediary and perhaps an expert witness;
- use top quality recording equipment.

Many witnesses with communication disorders are going to struggle to communicate within the legal system. Many will benefit greatly from the assistance of special measures, especially the involvement of an intermediary, but, as we acknowledge below, such support has its own difficulties.

Witnesses whose first language isn't speech – the deaf and those with alternative communication systems – will also need considerable assistance to cope with the legal system. In Britain, the deaf communicate using British Sign Language (BSL). This is a language in its own right and gives its users the same opportunities to express creatively their message in a way that is equivalent to speech. The BSL user then does not have a communication disorder, but he is likely to need an interpreter to go through the legal system. In order to make the legal process equal for all, a matter to which we return in the final section, a great deal of training needs to take place for interpreters, interviewing officers and lawyers, judges and indeed the members of the public who will serve on the jury in these cases. An even greater challenge to the system is presented by those witnesses who use an alternative communication system, perhaps a recognised system such as Makaton or a symbol or light system that may be unique to one witness. These systems, while giving the individual communicative opportunities, are limited and will call for new thinking within the Criminal Justice System. For example, witnesses may have only a limited number of signs and/or symbols, so the investigation will need to be carried out within those boundaries and an intermediary who is familiar with the system will need to be involved. It is clear that there needs to be a great deal of public awareness raising, if such cases are ever going to succeed in court. The following quote, from Mencap, illuminates the picture: 'If we are on our own we're not listened to, we should be listened to, we should be heard, it's not fair, people do things to us and we're not heard ... action should be taken' (Mencap 1999: 24).

Vulnerable witnesses in the court room

When a case goes to court, the police interview is shown in the courtroom as the witness's evidence-in-chief. Unfortunately, however, the vulnerable witness still has to go to court for cross-examination, although this will typically happen in a link room or behind a screen. It has been suggested that this experience may, in fact, be worse for witnesses than giving their entire evidence live because under this system 'witnesses are plunged directly into hostile cross-examination at trial without the "warm up" that examination-in-chief arguably provides' (Ellison 2001: 57) and Brennan (1994: 216) describe children's experiences in the court system as being 'abused again'. In court, the witness is subjected to the well-known linguistic strategies used by defence lawyers: coercive questioning and intimidation tactics (Brennan 1994; Conley and O'Barr 2005; Ehrlich and Matoesian, this volume) which distress the witness and potentially distort the evidence by discrediting the prosecution case and diverting the focus of the jurors away from the central issues (Ellison 2001: 111).

The work of Eades and Brennan is particularly notable in an Australian context in relation to children and cross-examination. Eades' research focuses particularly on Aboriginal children and disadvantage in the legal system (see, for example, Eades 1992, 1995, 2000). In Eades (2002, 2003b, 2004) she discusses linguistic cross-examination practices in the Pinkenba case, which involved three Aboriginal boys aged 12, 13 and 14 who alleged that six police officers had taken them against their will in three police cars and abandoned them on wasteland, from where they had to find their way home. In Eades (2004: 499) she argues that, in addition to 'unrestrained' and 'haranguing behaviour', which included shouting at the witness, 'the manipulation of Aboriginal ways of using English was central to this defence strategy' and she highlights the particular use of 'silence and gratuitous concurrence'. An illustration of the strategies, particularly of the use of silence and 'gratuitous concurrence' is given and is reproduced in (20).

(20) Gratuitous concurrence in cross-examination of Barry (B, pseudonym) in the Pinkenba case (DC is Defence Counsel).

```
1  DC:  And you knew (1.4) when you spoke to these six police in
2        the Valley that you didn't have to go anywhere with them if
3        you didn't want to, didn't you?
4  B:   (1.3) No.
5  DC:  You knew that, Mr (1.2) Coley I'd suggest to you, PLEASE DO
6        NOT LIE. YOU KNEW THAT YOU DIDN'T HAVE TO GO
7        ANYWHERE if you didn't want to, didn't you (2.2) DIDN'T YOU?
8        (2.2) DIDN'T YOU, MR COLEY?
9  B:   (1.3) Yeh.
```
(Eades 2004: 500)

Using a critical (socio)linguistic approach Eades (2004: 500) explains that these tactics contributed to the success of the defence case (on behalf of the police officers) which led to

the magistrate accepting defence counsels' construction of these victim-witnesses as criminals with 'no regard for the community', and the reinterpretation of the alleged abduction as the boys voluntarily giving up their liberty while the police took them for a ride. As a result, the charges against the police officers were dropped.

(Eades 2004: 500)

Brennan's (1994) and Brennan and Brennan's (1988) work also focuses on children in the Australian courts. He says:

Questions asked in cross-examination are aimed at not admitting the experience of the child and attempt to influence the child's response quite deliberately. Whatever the rationalisation for the court procedures they are generally not recognising the needs of the child, or the admissibility of evidence gathered and cross-referenced outside the combative, interrogating context of the courtroom.

(Brennan 1994: 206)

Brennan focuses on some of the general characteristics of questions which are capitalised on in cross-examination: complexity, which makes the listener work hard; connected and unconnected utterances, which require 'constant reorientation'; volume or number of questions, which might 'make a witness acquiescent'; and making material significant for the hearer in terms of 'display[ing] evidence' (Brennan 1994: 208–10). He also exemplifies a huge array of linguistically tactical questions, which can constitute powerful tools of cross-examination: use of negatives; juxtaposition of topics that are not overtly related; nominalisations; multifaceted questions; unclear questions; embedding; and many more (Brennan 1994: 212–16). The final one, embedding, is illustrated in example (21), which is certainly complex and also contains negation ('*in*correct') and nominalisation ('a tripping').

(21) Complexity, embedding, negation and nominalisation in a cross-examination question to a 15-year-old

Q: Would it be incorrect to suggest that it was not so much a tripping but because of the state of inebriation of yourself, that you fell over?

(Brennan 1994: 216)

One might imagine that in the current English and Welsh system, where special measures have been introduced in an attempt to ameliorate the experience of vulnerable witnesses, including children, they might fare better. But, despite being supported by the special measures, vulnerable witness still struggle to cope. Conviction rates are typically low. 6.5% is the 2007–8 conviction rate for domestic violence and rape victims in England and Wales, compared with 34% for criminal cases in general (Afua Hirsch, *Guardian* 13 March 2009. Last accessed 6 May 2009). We will now reflect on the success or otherwise of the special measures.

Evaluation of the special measures

The MOGP and then ABE heralded real developments in investigative interviews and raised awareness of the interviewing difficulties that witnesses and interviewers can experience. The new procedures, of course, had a number of teething problems:

311

interviewers were initially nervous of being on camera and there were a number of technical difficulties with the equipment. But, on the whole, the recommendations were welcomed and have certainly improved witness confidence in the criminal justice system. For example, a report by Hamlyn *et al.* (2004) suggested that 76% of the child witnesses were satisfied with special measures; indeed, 44% of these felt that they would not have been able to give evidence without them. Another report (Plotnikoff and Woolfson 2004) highlighted the importance of the live link opportunity for child witnesses. Our own survey (Aldridge and Williams 2006) confirms these findings:

- Witnesses previously too frightened to come forward may now do so.
- Some of the special measures (such as the removal of wigs and gowns and the introduction of an intermediary) may well reduce stress for vulnerable witnesses.
- The fact that the evidence-in-chief can be recorded before the court case begins means that it can occur earlier, so the witness's memory may be sharper.

South Wales was a pilot area for the introduction of an intermediary for children and people with disabilities and the officers involved spoke highly of this measure. The following quotes taken from Aldridge and Williams (2006) are examples:

- An intermediary gave opportunities to those who previously would not have had a hearing in court.
- I got the information I needed but I had to use an intermediary.
- The intermediary explained to me what the witness said, understood her personal and social issues needs and helped me get the interview suite ready.
- The intermediary certainly made the witness more relaxed.

But, as with all progress, there are reported disadvantages including:

- Planning and resources: Officers reported that much more time was needed in planning a case and they felt that there were not sufficient intermediaries available. They requested more training in how to perceive and interpret the measures; they were particularly anxious about being able to identify people as vulnerable and they were not confident about putting their training into use, requesting more guidance and monitoring of interview performance in the workplace.
- Public awareness: Officers felt that they, the lawyers, the judges and the public needed awareness raising exercises to understand how special measures worked and to dispel common myths and prejudices that all children and people with disabilities will be unreliable witnesses. Many felt that calling these witnesses 'vulnerable' just added to the stereotype of limitations rather than empowering them.
- Impact: Some officers expressed doubts that giving evidence via video and/or link room was as effective as giving live evidence in the courtroom, though research in England and Wales and in Australia does not support this concern (Taylor and Joudo 2005).
- Quality of evidence: Some officers feared that the quality of the video-evidence was poor and this does seem to be a real concern as illustrated in the following report.

A Crown Court Judge (Keen 30th January 2009) 'criticised police after he was forced to dismiss a case because of the poor standard of video evidence'. He was 'critical of the way the interview room was set up, with the camera positioned to show the female child witness from the side' and the fact that she was being interviewed by a male officer using repetitious and unhelpful questions. It was reported that the prosecution had been forced to withdraw other cases in the area because the jury could not hear what the vulnerable witnesses were saying.

Implementation of these special measures is a phased one, with no pre-recording of cross-examination as yet. Thus, while the special measures are a change in procedure, they are limited in scope, and we wonder whether in practice there has been a great deal of change. Davies *et al.* (1995) found no difference between the guilty verdicts delivered for cases involving videotaped evidence as opposed to live cases. Indeed, at the time of writing, in British courts, acquittals have increased and we must wonder whether the introduction of special measures has encouraged the CPS to proceed with cases once thought impossible but yet, once in cross-examination the witnesses still do not present as credible.

Conclusion

Examples of special measures can be found in Australia, Canada, Hong Kong, Ireland, Israel, New Zealand, Scotland, South Africa and the USA as well as in England and Wales. But all reports suggest that the adversarial system is problematic for vulnerable witnesses. A quote from one of our officers summarises the current position:

> The criminal justice system struggles to provide an adequate stage on which vulnerable witnesses can perform. The court doesn't accept [that] the young child or the disabled witness can be reliable. I've no confidence in barristers – they're not trained in the needs of vulnerable witnesses. CJS cannot cater for everyone. Special measures do not provide an equal footing for such witnesses. The burden of proof is beyond most witnesses.
>
> (Aldridge and Williams 2006)

We agree with Ellison (2001: 12) that 'there is a clear and seemingly irreconcilable conflict between the needs and interests of vulnerable witnesses and the basic assumptions and resultant evidentiary safeguards of the adversarial trial process'. While, the changes in the initial interview are to be welcomed, there remains a problem with the dual function of the video interview (Aldridge and Luchjenbroers 2008), since it has both to gather evidence for use in criminal proceedings and act as the prosecution case. These tasks may be incompatible. Combining this with the fact that cross-examination still goes on linguistically unchecked, we wonder whether tinkering with the system can ever work. As Ellison (2001: 7) states 'the approach currently in operation can be described as one of accommodation, in that solutions have been primarily sought and crafted within the constraints of the established trial framework' and 'the above discussions show the significant limitations of the accommodation approach'. It seems that the adversarial system cannot easily offer justice for vulnerable witnesses and we must now turn our attention to research the popular contention that inquisitorial style criminal proceedings hold inherent advantages for vulnerable witnesses.

Further reading

Bottom, B., Najdowski, C. and Godman, G. (2009) *Child Victims, Child Offenders: Psychology and the Law*, Guilford: The Guilford Press.

Lamb, M., Hershkowitz, I., Orbach, Y. and Esplin, P. (2008) *Tell Me What Happened*, New York: Wiley.

Pipe, M., Lamb, M., Orbach, Y. and Cederborg, A. (2007) *Child Sexual Abuse: Disclosure, Delay, and Denial*, Mahwah, NJ.: Erlbaum.

Walker, A.G. (1999) *Handbook on Questioning Children: A Linguistic Perspective*, (2nd edition) Washington, DC: ABA Center on Children and the Law.

Westcott, H., Davies, G. and Bull, R. (2002) *Children's Testimony: A Handbook of Psychological Research and Forensic Practice*, Chichester: Wiley.

21

False confessors

A jihadi heart and mind? Strategic repackaging of a possibly false confession in an anti-terrorism trial in California

Gillian Grebler

Introduction

In April 2006, after a nine-week trial and nine days' deliberation by a jury, a young Californian man was found guilty of providing material support to terrorists. The conviction could carry up to 39 years in prison. The government had a videotaped confession from 22-year-old Hamid Hayat, as well as hours of surreptitiously recorded conversation between him and Nassim Khan, an FBI "cooperating witness." In addition to "material support," Hayat was convicted of three counts of making false statements to the FBI, denying on three occasions that he had been to a militant training camp in Pakistan, been trained there, and returned to the United States with the intent to commit violent jihad. But we have cause to wonder whether in fact those three alleged denials actually told the true story of Hayat's time in Pakistan, and whether the confession upon which the case was built told a story that was false.

False confessions

A false confession is a narrative which tells a tale of something that did not happen, or of a place that might never have existed. It can happen spontaneously, as a "voluntary" false confession, or be induced through interrogation. When police interrogate suspects in an accusatory, "guilt-presumptive" manner, a suspect may make a false confession. When suspects come to doubt the validity of their own memory and to believe, usually temporarily, that they are guilty of a crime, their confession can be referred to as a "coerced-internalized" false confession (see Wrightsman and Kassin, 1993 for this typology). When they comply with interrogators while retaining knowledge of their innocence, their confession is called "coerced-compliant."

There is now a large and growing literature by psychologists and linguists on police-induced false confessions. Much is known about how they arise from the use of tactics and ploys used by interrogators (see for example, Ofshe and Leo 1997a; Shuy 1998b), about the psychological vulnerabilities of the suspects who make them (Gudjonsson 1992; Kassin and Gudjonsson 2004). We know in particular that children and juveniles are especially vulnerable to accusatory, guilt-presumptive interrogation (Redlich and Goodman 2003; Drizin and Colgan 2004; Redlich et al. 2004). We know something about the difficulties that can arise when non-native or non-English speakers are interrogated (Berk-Seligson 2002).

We know also that "actual innocence" does not protect suspects, but may put them at risk (Kassin 2005) in a number of ways: after initial encounters, investigators conclude that innocent suspects are guilty, suspects waive their rights "naively believing in the transparency of their innocence", they may "elicit" confrontational interrogations and be led to confess through the use of tactics and strategies. Police and others cannot differentiate between uncorroborated true and false confessions.

Public awareness and legal safeguards against the dangers of false confession developed much earlier in the UK than the US. In the UK, high profile wrongful convictions came to public attention during the 1970s. Advocacy organizations such as Liberty and Justice were active. Ludovic Kennedy's *10 Rillington Place*, about the wrongful hanging of Timothy Evans, brought false confessions to a large audience as early as 1961 and had an effect on Evans's eventual posthumous pardon. The 1977 Fisher Report into the Murder of Maxwell Confait, led to the Royal Commission of Criminal Procedure (1979–1981). BBC Television's program *Rough Justice* reinvestigated important cases, which were then referred back to the Home Office and Court of Appeal. Research into police inter-rogation was directed by the Police Foundation. MENCAP and MIND supported research into police interrogation of mentally disabled and mentally ill suspects and wit-nesses (Tully and Cahill 1984; Cahill et al. 1988). This activity led to the Police and Criminal Evidence Act PACE (1984) which mandated tape recording in cases of serious crime. Gisli Gudjonsson's landmark study of Police Interrogation and False Confessions, cataloguing the psychological and institutional factors that go into false confessions was published in 1992. The Criminal Cases Review Commission, an independent body responsible for investigating suspected miscarriages of criminal justice in England, Wales and Northern Ireland was established in 1995. Forensic linguistic expertise (e.g. Coulthard 2005) was used in the reinvestigation of cases in which disputed confessions were central. The PEACE method of police interrogation was put into effect during the mid-1990s. US research started during the late 1980s with the research of psychologists Kassin and Wrightsman, Richard Ofshe and later his student, Richard Leo, and by linguist Roger Shuy. This expertise began to be recognized and used by attorneys. There has been a huge increase in attention in the last ten years with the establishment of Innocence Projects across the country, the proliferation of DNA exonerations and a great deal of media attention.

Confession evidence is gathered in an interactional setting, one of asymmetric power, in which police interrogators are trained (Inbau et al. 1986; Reid and Associates online; Walkley 1987) to get a confession and an account of the crime with sufficient informa-tion to establish the intent or mental state of the suspect. Unfortunately, innocent people are as susceptible to its pressures as guilty suspects and can be made to provide false confessions.

This problematic and complex evidence is then de- and recontextualized in various ways and at various points during the course of trial, a process shown in recent forensic linguistic work that takes an "intertextual" approach to trial data (see for example,

Cotterill 2002; Johnson 2008c; Matoesian 2001; Rosulek 2008 and this volume). This "repackaging" is done strategically and emotively to create coherent, compelling and persuasive accounts.

Confessions come laden with social and moral meaning. In *Troubling Confessions*, Peter Brooks (2000) considers the role of confessions in religion, literature and law, leaving us in no doubt that they take on a performative reality as they are spoken and are framed as true, sincere and serious.

Once entered into evidence, confessions are highly probative. In two large studies of proven false confessions, false confessors who pleaded not guilty and took their cases to trial were convicted by juries between 73 and 81% of the time. As social psychologist Saul Kassin wrote in the *New York Times* in 2002,

> Juries so readily convict innocent defendants in false confession cases because false confessions are counterintuitive – most jurors simply cannot imagine that they would ever confess to a crime they did not commit.
>
> (Kassin 2002)

A false confession raises a challenging question: what does it take to get an innocent suspect to put his or her own reality on hold, to move into the "frame" of guilt insisted upon by the interrogator, and then to produce a fictional account in apparent cooperation with this powerful co-teller? As Ochs and Capps (2001: 259) put it, "conversational partners may drown out one or another version of what happened by reformulating or contradicting the casting of past events." When Hamid Hayat's father, a US citizen since 1997, was asked why he told FBI agents that Hamid had been to a training camp, he explained that he was telling a story because "they were not believing when I was telling the truth" (Frontline 2006).

> Whatever they tell, say yes, yes, yes, either wrong or right. I was trying to go home. ... they was calling me liar. So then I make a story, that's all, because I want to go home. ... I never went to camp. There is no camp in Pakistan. Never. No camp.

When a confession is the primary evidence in a case, both its voluntariness and reliability have to be considered. Questions of voluntariness can be considered by judges in pre-trial "suppression" hearings. What brought the suspect to admit; what were the conditions of arrest and detention, the length of interrogation, the tactics and strategies used by interrogators? Was the defendant given and did he understand his Miranda Rights, did he grasp the implications of waiving them? (See Ainsworth, this volume, for some of the problems associated with this.)

Once a confession is allowed into testimony, jurors must decide how reliable it is. Does it "fit" what else is known about the alleged crime (Ofshe and Leo 1997b)? Are there inconsistencies in it (Shuy 1998b)? They have to be guided in this analysis by the defense attorney and sometimes by expert witnesses.

Laurence Rosen (2006) describes the process of collective decision-making that juries undertake as they strive for a verdict. They do not, he says, simply "sort through all the data to reach a collective decision" but

> put together a narrative as they individually listen to the trial, matching each new piece of information to the story they've been telling themselves along the way. As

they view the entire body of evidence and begin to discuss the case among themselves jurors work towards a collective narrative, one that necessarily depends on
the ways in which narratives are generally created in their culture.

(Rosen 2006: 148)

As Heffer (2002 and this volume) points out, a jury trial is a complex genre whose
opening address and closing arguments are in the mode of story construction and jurors
make decisions to a large extent through story-making (Bennett and Feldman 1981;
Pennington and Hastie 1993; Amsterdam and Bruner 2002).

Jurors may be influenced by the believability, lifelikeness and compellingness of the
stories told, on what clinical psychologist Donald Spence (in Ochs and Capps 2001) calls
narrative truth. In contrast to historical truth, which aims to come as close as possible to
what "really" happened (and which surely should be the goal of a jury decision), narrative truth depends on "continuity and closure and the extent to which the fit of the
pieces takes on aesthetic finality" (Spence in Ochs and Capps, 2001: 285).

Confessions are given inordinate weight at every stage of a criminal case (Wrightsman
and Kassin 1993). Recent academic studies of wrongful conviction cases show that
15–20% contained confessions in evidence (Drizin and Leo 2004; Gross et al. 2005). In a
recent article, Leo and Davis (2009) consider the relationship between false confessions
and wrongful convictions in the United States, pointing to an important gap in
knowledge. Too little is known, they say, about what leads so inexorably from a police-
induced confession to a conviction, in other words what makes confessions so compelling
for judges and jurors.

In this chapter, I explore the question of compellingness by looking at the life of a
problematic confession: its "production" at FBI headquarters and the multiple ways it
was "used" during the trial, during examination and cross-examination, as well as in
opening and closing arguments, and at the comments the judge made concerning it.
I describe the process by which the defendant's story is rejected by his interrogators and
replaced by the government story, the repackaging of this story into a probatively
powerful confession, and the strategic retelling of the confession in rebuttal argument.
I consider the narrative devices used by the government in rebuttal and the extent to
which these may have influenced the decision-making of the jury.

The case

Surveillance, arrest and interrogation

After September 11, 2001 the United States government began to identify and investigate Pakistani American youths who had been to Pakistan to study at religious schools,
madrasas, affiliated with banned militant groups; 22-year-old Hamid Hayat, born in
Stockton, California, in 1983, was the first to be arrested.

Hayat is part of a small, largely working-class Pakistani community whose families
began to arrive during the early 1900s to work on the railroads and in the fields. The
FBI's Joint Terrorism Task Force, set up in Sacramento after September 11, had been
investigating the Lodi Moslem community since 2003. Cooperating witness, Nassim
Khan, had infiltrated the community in 2002, befriended Hamid Hayat and began
secretly tape-recording their conversations in March 2003. In February 2006, the

Director of National Intelligence, John Negroponte, delivered the Annual Threat Assessment in Washington, DC. He told the Senate Intelligence Committee that federal authorities had uncovered a network of Islamic extremists in the San Joaquin County farming town of Lodi.

Hamid Hayat's first knowing contact with the investigation was on May 30, 2005 when his flight from Pakistan was rerouted to Japan, he was interviewed by an FBI agent and deemed safe to return to the US. When Hayat was eventually charged with three counts of lying to the FBI, the interview in Japan was the basis of the first count.

The second count was based on an interview on June 3, 2005 at his home. The two FBI agents took various publications, Hamid's scrapbook and a tawiz or traveler's prayer from his wallet. The local media called it a "raid." The agents asked Hamid and Umer Hayat to come to FBI headquarters the next day to help with the investigation. When they arrived, they were separated and Hamid was taken into an interview room to be questioned by Agent Harry Sweeney. Sweeney read Hayat his rights at 12:30 p.m.

The third count was based on the first three and a half hours of a four-hour interrogation during which Hamid again answered questions about his time in Pakistan telling the agents that he played cricket, helped his mom, and spent time with his cousins. But at 4 p.m., Hamid Hayat stopped denying that he had been at a training camp and made what Agent Sweeney considered his first "admission," saying that he had been to a training camp in 2000. Forty-five minutes later, he made his second admission: that he had been to a training camp in 2003.

Hayat's confession has all the risk factors that are by now well known from the analysis of proven false confessions: the defendant was young, with a compliant personality, his language abilities in English were weak, and at the time of interrogation he was exhausted because of the time difference between Pakistan and California, and from working the night shift. We do not know whether he understood his rights and he certainly did not understand the implications of waiving them. Although he was interrogated for over thirteen hours, he never seemed to grasp the fact that he was a suspect; he thought and was allowed to think, that he was helping the agents with their investigation.

This crucial first three and a half hours of the thirteen hour interrogation of June 4 and 5 was not videotaped so our only way to evaluate the voluntariness of the confession is through Agent Sweeney's notes and the things he said during cross-examination. In fact, the defense attorney's questioning allows us to learn enough about it to cause concern about both its voluntariness and its truthfulness.

Hayat's initial admission came after repeated denials and the use of several well-known interrogation tactics. Sweeney told Hayat—falsely—that there were satellite photos of him at a training camp, and later, that he had failed his polygraph test. He then used what interrogators call a minimization tactic (Inbau et al. 1986), suggesting to Hayat that perhaps he had been to a religious rather than a military training camp, mitigating the seriousness of the accusation. Because the first interrogation was not recorded we cannot know whether the "admissions" Hayat gave Sweeney were hypothetical or real. When Sweeney asked Hayat whether it was *possible* that he had gone to a training camp in 2000 under the mistaken impression that it was a religious camp, Hayat may have answered, that yes, it was possible. And Hayat could have been operating within this frame of the possible throughout the remainder of his interrogations.

The post-admission narrative

Once FBI Agent Sweeney considered that Hayat had made admissions, he set in motion an order to videotape and handed Hayat on to Agent Schaaf, whose job it was to seek details to verify and bring to life the sparse admissions. Two further interrogations were conducted that same evening, and both were videotaped. During these nine hours, agents and suspect worked together until the early hours of the morning to shape "the unfolding tale" (Ochs and Capps, 2001), the joint production of an admission narrative.

What began as two opposing stories was transformed into one: the FBI version, which became the key evidence in the trial.

In a coerced-compliant false confession, the interrogator sometimes leads a suspect to his first admission by asking him for a hypothetical description. We cannot know whether this happened during the first interrogation since it was not recorded, but during the second interrogation, the agent invites Hayat to imagine a scenario and tell what he sees (1).

(1) (GS is Agent Schaaf and HH is Hayat)
1 GS: So, all right. And uh, so tell me, what put, put me in the front seat
2   of the bus. What am I seeing as you're coming into the camp? Uh
3   here I am, I mean through your eyes tell me what you're seeing as you
4   come out
5 HH: Um just go inside and you're not gonna go try to take bus inside.

When the agent tries the same approach again a little later Hayat does not seem to understand and fails to come up with anything (2).

(2)
1 GS: So that's, do you go up the main route into the camp?
2 HH: I mean, on walk we go?
3 GS: Yes.
4 HH: Yeah, we walk.
5 GS: Ok.
6 HH: We walk.
7 GS: Ok. And so tell me, alright, take me on the walk. What happens on
8   the walk?
9 HH: Nothing happens.

When dominant co-tellers such as police interrogators insist that the truth is a lie and "contend that certain unremembered events transpired" (Ochs and Capps 2001), the story that emerges often has signs of what linguists call the language of uncertainty—it is full of vagueness, hedging, pauses and self-correction (or what conversational analysts call self-repair). It will contain the subjunctive and conditional formulations indicative of what Ofshe and Leo (1997b) call the "grammar of confabulation."

In (3) and throughout this interrogation we hear the interrogating officer, who is trying to ask questions about something he knows nothing about, and the defendant, trying to cooperate by answering his questions, both using this language of uncertainty (note 'I assume' in line 3). Agent Schaaf is trying to help Hayat describe a place where Hayat may never have been and which in fact may not even exist. In line 2, Agent

Schaaf uses "these camps" and in line 8, Hamid uses "there," but this doesn't mean that each is referring to the same place and the mass of people described is also very different: "hundreds" (line 2) versus "not over 50" (line 7).

(3) Interview with Hamid Hayat, p.10
```
 1  GS:  So, um during the course of the time that you're there um how many
 2        people did you ob-I mean, usually these camps have, you know, hundreds
 3        of people coming and going so that I assume that this is, the way you're
 4        describing it, would sound similar in that regard. Is that, is that right?
 5  HH:  Like hundreds of people.
 6  GS:  Yeah, yeah, you know.
 7  HH:  I didn't see that much like uh over 50 people I'll say. I didn't see
 8        over 50 people there, Sir.
 9  GS:  At any one time?
10  HH:  One time you know I see, I see like you know all together all the
11        time I like you know, about like 70.
```

In the early hours of the morning, when Hayat was asked again about possible targets of terrorist action, he is still vague (4).

(4) Interview with Hamid Hayat (p. 175 transcript)
```
 1  HH:  Like buildings and I'll say buildings.
 2  TH:  What kind of buildings?
 3  HH:  Bigger building, you know, buildings.
 4  TH:  Buildings? Commercial buildings?
 5  HH:  You know commercial, projects and like those kind of buildings.
 6        I'll say
 7  TH:  Umm, alright you're not
 8  HH:  Yeah, but I am not sure about the buildings you guys are talking about.
 9        The big ones, I'll say, you know finance, I'll say finance and things like that.
```

And a little later, asked yet again in (5)

(5)
```
 1  TH:  But I need you to tell me details about targets, what they said you
 2        know. And, this is where I need your memory to come back.
 3  HH:  Like I said sir, you know, big buildings and you know
 4        hospitalities and you know, finance buildings, banks and what's it called
 5        ah, hmmm maybe like you know uh stores, stores
 6  TH:  What kind of stores?
 7  HH:  Stores, like food stores, anything like that.
```

This exchange was cited in the first affidavit for Hayat's arrest, which read, "Hamid advised that he specifically requested to come to the United States to carry out his jihadi mission. Potential targets for attack would include hospitals and large food stores" (Affidavit, June 2005).

Like people who have made what we know to be false confessions, Hayat did not seem to understand the implications of his admissions. Like others (like his father Umer) he may have been aiming simply for a short-term result, an end to the interrogation. Hamid repeatedly asked to see his father, he offered to return another day, he offered to take the agents' numbers and report anything suspicious to them. At about 6 p.m., after two hours of interrogation by Agent Gary Schaaf, Hayat seems to think the interview is over. He asks Schaaf

(6)
1 HH: Do you have a card sir?
2 GS: I will. I don't have one on me.
3 HH: I contact you (UI).
4 GS: Yeah.
5 HH: How bout beeper to (UI) remember anything to contact you.

Later, after nearly thirteen hours of interrogation, Hamid still did not seem to understand that he was a suspect. He offered to return the next day. He is surprised that he is about to be arrested and that he is going to jail. He has stopped asking for his father. Now all he wants is sleep.

(7)
1 HH: So I come back here tomorrow? Again.
2 TH: No, no. You're not leaving here tonight, no.
3 HH: No, I mean ah, tomorrow. I'm going to be here tonight. Staying
4   here? In the building?
5 TH: No. no you're going to go, you're going to go to jail.
6 PA: Hamid you're going to jail.
7 HH: Yeah, so am I going to get a place to sleep over there like that?
8 PA: It's jail Hamid you understand that?
9 HH: Yeah, I know, I know it's a jail, but can I lay down because my
10   head (HH points to his head) is hurting, I want to sleep.

Closing arguments: adversarial storytelling

In closing argument, government prosecutor Robert Tice-Raskin repackaged this problematic and possibly false confession to paint a picture of a young man with a jihadi heart and a jihadi mind, who admitted "in his own words" attending a military training camp. The surreptitiously tape recorded conversations made by cooperating witness Nassim Khan were also drawn upon in the prosecution's closing argument to characterize Hayat as having a "jihadi heart and mind." The prosecutor quoted in full a disturbing conversation in which Hayat speaks approvingly about the murder of Daniel Pearl. Although the defense successfully attacked Khan's credibility at trial, Hayat's jury were not given the benefit of a linguistic analysis of the tapes (Shuy 1993a, 2005 and this volume). This kind of analysis would have revealed to the jury the conversational strategies Khan used to elicit and encourage Hayat's anti-American talk, letting them understand why the tapes are "troublesome, seductive and ultimately unfair" (Shuy 2005) as evidence. Khan played on a relationship of apparent friendship, misplaced trust and hidden power, in which he tried to persuade Hamid to go to a training camp, in Shuy's words, to "seduce" him, using the stock of "conversational strategies" that cooperating witnesses typically use. Hayat's jury hears his apparently damning words doubly removed from their interactional context because they are translated from the Pashto (and occasional Urdu).

The defense attorney on the other hand, was certain that the prosecution had not proved that Hayat had been to a training camp. In discussing Hayat's confession during her closing argument (8) she reminded the jury that the police had intimidated Hamid, the police used questionable tactics, he was exhausted, and he was asked many leading questions. He didn't "know what was happening to him" (8).

(8) (Transcript of closing arguments, page 4319)

1 He didn't realize that by telling the FBI what they wanted to hear, that he
2 attended a camp in Pakistan, that he had just gotten himself into a whole lot of
3 trouble. It's really quite sad to watch that video and watch [Hayat] say things
4 that make no sense. They don't even make sense to the agents who are
5 listening to them. And you really see him trying to cooperate and provide the
6 answers the best that he can.

Agent Timothy Harrison offers to help Hayat in exchange for his cooperation. One example of several is in excerpt (9) from his interview at 2 a.m.

(9) Interview

1 TH: Okay I'll meet you, I'll meet you half way, alright.
2 HH: What's that mean half way? You want me to cooperate.
3 TH: Cooperate.
4 HH: Cooperate, yeah I get that sir.
5 TH: Yeah you gotta give me something, in order for me to go help you.
6 HH: Okay.
7 TH: You know, to tell my bosses that you're cooperating, that
8   you're working with us. You know you're in a bad situation, you know,
9   but it could be a lot worse, and there's a lot we can do to help you.
10   But you got to help us, you gotta work with us. (HH nodding) All right.

More basic even than the fact that Hayat is trying to cooperate and appears to be operating within a different "frame" to that of his interrogators, we do not know how much Hayat understands of the interrogator's language, as in the exchange in (10).

(10)
     TH: Which way was north?
     HH: What do you mean north?

The rebuttal argument

If the confession is not valid, if the apparently remembered experience of being at a training camp is not reliable, then there is no evidence with which to charge Hamid Hayat. As the defense attorney said at trial (11):

(11) (Transcript of defense closing argument, page 4319–20)

And so that's what you have, Ladies and Gentlemen, you have a meaningless confession. You have Hamid Hayat being intimidated into saying things that the FBI wanted him to say ... The entire interview was meaningless, and it does not prove that Hayat went to a camp. And because [Hayat's] statements come from a meaningless confession and they are completely unreliable, the government ladies and gentlemen, is left with nothing.

But it is essential to the prosecution case that the jury begins its deliberations with the confession intact. Because the government has the burden of proof, the prosecution gets the last word with a "rebuttal" argument. David Deitch uses this "extremely powerful tool for the plaintiff" (Read 2007: 279–80) to great effect.

In rebuttal, Deitch discredits the defense closing argument. He "relegitimizes" (Rosulek 2008 and this volume) the confession which the defense attorney had carefully presented as "meaningless" and "unreliable." He retells the story of the interrogation, erases apparent gaps, uncertainties and contradictions in the confession and characterizes the defendant as a youth capable of committing great violence for ideological reasons. He plays on the fears and uncertainty jurors may feel in a post-9/11 United States, and leaves them with a sense that it is their responsibility to protect the public by upholding the government case.

The first weakness that Deitch set out to relegitimize is the point where Hamid Hayat stopped denying and began to admit, a pivotal moment upon which the voluntariness of the admission and the reliability of the narrative details hinges. The defense attorney had brought this crucial moment into question during the trial in her careful cross-examination of Agent Sweeney (12).

(12) Defense cross-examination

  1 Q: And your recollection is during that first three and a half hour
  2   period in all of his responses he denied any connection to jihadi training?
  3 A: That is correct.
  4 Q: Okay. Now let's move into that second portion, when he makes his
  5   initial – did you call it an admission.
  6 A: Admission. Confession. Yes.
  7 Q: Do you recall the question that you asked when he ultimately said
  8   that at about 3:30? …
  9 A: My question to him was, Is it possible, Hamid, that you didn't
10   know that you were going to a jihadi training camp? Is it possible that
11   you may have thought it was something else, like a religious education
12   camp?
13 Q: Okay. Did he give you any inclination that that may have been a
14   possibility?
15 A: No, he did not.
16 Q: And when you asked that question, what was his response?
17 A: His response was that, yes, that, in fact, was the case.
18 Q: What were the words he uttered; do you recall?
19 A: I don't recall the exact words.
20 Q: … Do you recall, was it a yes, or was it a yes with detail?
21 A: I recall that it was a yes with detail.
22 Q: The first time you asked? …
23 A: No. Actually, the first time I brought up that topic and asked that
24   direct question, or that direct issue, it wasn't necessarily an automatic yes,
25   that's it. There may have been several times that I raised that particular
26   issue.

In the rebuttal Deitch characterized that crucial turning point as a "breakthrough," to overcome juror's concerns about its elicitation (13, line 9).

(13)

1 Hamid Hayat told Harry Sweeney, in response to questions, that he had
2 gone to Pakistan to help out his mom, that he had gone to get married, that
3 he played cricket, that he hung out with friends, and that he'd sometime go
4 and travel to eat in American style restaurants. Hamid Hayat specifically
5 denied to Special Agent Sweeney that he had ever received any weapons
6 training at a jihadist training camp, and that he had ever received any
7 training at a jihadist camp to fight against the United States. He denied
8 that more than once. After doing that though, there was a moment in
9 which there was a breakthrough. Harry Sweeney asked Hamid Hayat, Is it
10 possible that you didn't know that you were going to a jihadi training
11 camp? Is it possible that you may have thought it was something else, like
12 a religious education camp? After Harry Sweeney posed that
13 question, Hamid Hayat confessed for the first time.

The government had to prove that Hayat was at a militant training camp. The agents tried to establish its location but got vague and contradictory information from Hayat. The rebuttal repackages this problematic gap to produce what prosecutor David Deitch calls the "consistent thread" of Balakot, making it sound as if Hayat told Agent Sweeney three times that he was there ((14), lines 1–4). Deitch continues, suggesting that Hayat himself repeated the name out loud six times in a row ((14), lines 5–6).

(14)

1 So when Hamid Hayat goes on video, he's already given away a lot of
2 information. And perhaps the most important piece of information he's
3 given away, I'll say it in one word, Balakot. Balakot. He told Harry
4 Sweeney the camp was in the area of Balakot. …
5 And he repeated, at least six times during the videotaped interview,
6 Balakot, Balakot, Balakot, Balakot, Balakot. Balakot.

In the rebuttal argument details that emerged at length and which were often later contradicted in the interrogation are presented as if they are undisputed facts. Vague images, invariably suggested first by the interrogator and then integrated into the account (15), become vivid in rebuttal.

(15)

1 GS: Ok. Now tell me about rifle training. There's …
2 HH: Oh, rifle training is very hard sir, you know, they make me stand
3   over here in I say I barely could pick it up it's very heavy, you know, I'm
4   skinny you know
5 GS: Was it a big so, tell me what kind of rifle it is, do you remember?
6 HH: It was a shotgun, I think sir.

In the rebuttal the material in (15) was transformed into "Hamid Hayat recalled that he trained with what he described as being a rifle or shotgun." And an interview exchange about Kalashnikovs became, in the prosecutor's words: "He also stated that he was aware that they had Kalashnikovs and indicated that he, in fact, had seen one." Information about possible explosive training proposed by Schaaf became amplified in rebuttal: "Hamid Hayat also admitted that he consistently heard a lot of explosions while he was at camp." Deitch uses subjective verbs which cannot be contradicted: Hayat, he says, "admitted," "indicated," "remembered," and "recalled" details of the training camp. This way of casting narrative "events as what they or another 'remember'" (Ochs and Capps (2001: 284), is strategic in that it presupposes "that the events truly occurred" gaining an "authenticating power."

In her closing argument, the defense attorney demonstrated that every detail about the training camp was introduced by the agents. This seems like a serious indictment. But research has shown that human memory does not always distinguish amongst sources of information (Shuy 1993a; Schachter 2001) and the rebuttal argument (16) plays on this weakness.

(16)
1 Hamid Hayat didn't just make up these details about this camp. Why
2 was he able to describe a camp in the outskirts of Balakot, with this trail
3 through the woods, over the mountains, opening into a field and so forth?
4 He may have gotten a lot of the details wrong either because of lack of
5 recollection or because of the kind of lying and gauging that I've talked
6 about but he sure got a lot of the details right. Someone who had not been
7 to that camp, it would be an awful coincidence to get all of those right and
8 for it to match.

In the rebuttal argument events are "materialized" ((16), lines 2–3) and arranged in a temporal and causal order to achieve an appearance of reality. Disparate physical details that came into the narrative through a series of alternative, either/or, questions ((17), lines 2 and 6) are pulled together (18) to portray a journey with a beginning and an arrival: Hayat's movement from home to camp entails a bus journey and then a trail that goes through woods, over mountains, into a field.

(17)
1 GS: Um and uh and then you're uh what time do you, do you leave at
2   night or in the daytime or
3 HH: From where to the camp?
4 GS: From from Pindi yeah.
5 HH: Uh daytime, sir.
6 GS: So you left in daytime. Did you arrive in dark or was it,
7 HH: Yeah it was dark when we arrived, yes, sir.

(18)
1 He recounted to the agents that he arrived by bus at nighttime, that
2 he followed an unidentified male who had a flashlight, and then they went
3 up a zigzag road up a mountain. And you will recall, when you see him on
4 videotape, the way Hamid Hayat would describe with his hands how he would
5 go up the various zigzag portions of that road. Hamid Hayat indicated that at
6 the end of that hike he reached a field, and that there were trees all around
7 him.

To make the description even more concrete, Deitch reminds jurors that they saw Hayat gesturing on videotape when "describing" the road ((18), lines 4–7). He creates a sense of heightened reality by highlighting Hayat's "live" appearance on videotape ((19), lines 1–2), calling upon the jurors' sense of televisual reality to give them confidence in the existence of the road Hayat described. Richard Sherwin (in Scelfo 2001) warns us that "visual persuasion" can be used to "short-circuit the ideal of rational deliberation and supplant it by a more emotional form of judgment." In ((19), line 3) Deitch compounds the emotional impact by repeating the word "repeatedly."

(19)

   1 During the course of the videotaped interviews, again, where you
   2 had chance, folks, to see Hamid Hayat live, he gave a fairly
   3 detailed confession in which he repeatedly, repeatedly confirmed
   4 that he had attended a jihadi camp both in 2003–4 as well as
   5 earlier in 2000.

In fact, Hayat's interrogators never heard him "repeatedly, repeatedly confirm" that he had attended a jihadi camp. On the contrary, they struggled with him to produce a coherent, convincing and legally sound confession narrative and although Hamid Hayat wanted very much to cooperate, they did not succeed. Towards the end of the third interrogation, after 3 a.m. Agent Aguilar, sitting in with Agent Harrison, says:

(20)

   1 PA: Hamid, we keep asking you these questions and, and you're
   2   giving us the answers you are taking I mean why, why aren't you
   3   being truthful here?
   4 HH: I don't get that, like the questions you guys are asking again,
   5   you know. What question, you ask me again, I try my best you know.

Deitch ends his argument (21) with a highly emotive, imagined scene in which he discredits the defense portrayal of Hayat as harmless by projecting him as the possible future agent of horrific violence.

(21)   End of prosecution rebuttal
   1 But there is a more important point here. Let's say that Hamid Hayat came
   2 back, how thin or not thin do you think you need to be to spray a crowd
   3 with an AK-47? How thin or not thin do you think you have to be to
   4 wear a backpack full of explosives into a crowded shopping mall? How
   5 thin or not thin do you think you need to be to drive a Ryder truck full of
   6 explosives into a public building?

Then, in a bold rhetorical move ((22), lines 2–5) he "animates" Hamid Hayat, by creating a fictionalized confession as if actually spoken by him in an uninterrupted monologue. The attributed words imply clear intention on Hayat's part to carry out the charged actions.

(22)

   1 There is lots of evidence here, ladies and gentlemen. Lots of evidence
   2 to show that a man, Hamid Hayat, said, I'm going for training, I'm going

3   to be trained to commit jihad, and that he returned and said, Yes, I did go,
4   and I was trained to commit jihad, and I came back here with the intent to
5   do just that, consistent with his conversations and consistent with the
6   physical evidence that you've seen in this trial.

Hayat is made to tell a very simple story with a clear chronology and Deitch's "breakthrough into performance" (Hymes 1981), his use of direct discourse, carries an inordinate power. As Tannen (1989:133) writes, "By giving voice to characters, dialogue makes story into drama and listeners into an interpreting audience to the drama ... Thus understanding [of this type of] discourse is in part emotional." In the case of Hayat, the dramatic dialogue conveyed by using direct reported speech is one of the features that make both the prosecution and rebuttal arguments compelling. Shonna Trinch (2005b and forthcoming), in her study of direct reported speech in Latina domestic abuse affidavits, suggests that the role of direct reported speech varies by setting but is always contextual, always meaningful.[1] Kandel (2002) points to the persuasive force of reported speech in legal settings where it can give a strong appearance of veracity, specificity, and accuracy of memory, involve the hearer emotionally, and make what is narrated in this form especially salient, memorable and significant to the hearer.

The verdict

We do not know whether Hayat was ever at a military training camp or whether he admitted only to the *possibility* of having been at one and then cooperated with the interrogators to describe a camp he had never been to and which may never have existed. If the latter is the case, if Hayat was induced through interrogation to confess falsely, the jury should have been told about the frequency and causes of false confession in order to evaluate his confession. They should have been told that Hayat was similar to suspects known to have confessed falsely, and that he was questioned in a manner known to have generated false confessions.

Perhaps the defense could also have softened the emotional force of the rebuttal with an attempt to convey Hayat's experience: how confused he might have been about his role, surprised when the police did not believe him, isolated without his father, exhausted by the repeated questioning, puzzled at his continued failure to satisfy his interrogators when he was trying so hard to help. The defense did not give the jurors this crucial information. Without it, they were unable to counter the compelling re-legitimation of the confession put forth in the rebuttal argument.

After nine days of deliberation, the jury found Hayat guilty on four counts: one count of providing material support or resources to terrorism, and three counts of lying about it to the police. In October 2006, Hayat's defense attorneys submitted a motion for a new trial.

According to the jury foreman Joe Cote, in an interview just after the trial (Waldman 2006), the outcome was uncertain when they began deliberations. According to Cote, it was reviewing the videotaped interrogation for a second time that made the difference.

The first time the jurors saw the videotape he says, they were bothered by the leading questions and "pressure tactics" used by the FBI interrogators. But they had got an instruction from US District Judge Garland E. Burrell stating that "the government may utilize a broad range of schemes and ploys to ferret out criminal activity." Also crucial according to Cote, by the time they viewed the videotape for the second time, the jurors had absorbed all the other evidence, and by this time, they had heard the closing arguments.

Cote said that judging from Hayat's mild demeanor in court and his recent marriage, he did not seem to pose much danger. But then, said Cote, he thought of the faces of the terrorists caught on videotape before last summer's bombings in London and said he thought they looked just as non-threatening. "Can we, on the basis of what we know, put this kid on the street? … On the basis of what we know of how people of his background have acted in the past? The answer is no." There are "So-called new rules of engagement and I don't want to see the government lose its case."

Future directions

Much research has been done on false confessions. We know who tends to make them, how they get made, what their makers feel like at the time of interrogation and afterwards. We know the ways Miranda is given so as to encourage suspects to waive their rights (Leo 1998; Ainsworth, this volume). We know what happens when the right to an attorney is invoked with the "wrong" words (Ainsworth 1993 and this volume; Solan and Tiersma 2005). We understand the effects of different kinds of questions. We know that police officers can alight on the wrong suspect, assume his or her guilt and in an accusatory, guilt-presumptive interrogation drive for an admission, and supply critical details of the narrative (Hill 2003). We know that interrogators are trained to get the kinds of details that confirm an admission with information only the perpetrator could know, and that fill out a story, providing sensory and interactional details of the crime scene. We know that, armed with a confession, police investigators often proceed with "tunnel vision," excluding other lines of investigation and other possible suspects (Findley and Scott 2006; see also Solan, this volume, on biases).

Overwhelmingly academics, lawyers and advocates call for mandatory videotaping of police interrogations. In order for these recordings to be useful we need to develop ways to analyze the tapes using multimodal methods that consider prosody, gaze, gesture and other nonverbal aspects of the interrogation (Goodwin 1994, 2000; 2007; Mateosian, this volume) attending to the effect of camera angle (Lassiter 2004; Lassiter et al. 2006), intentional "audience manipulation" by interrogators doing the recording (Coulthard 2002) and remembering (Sherwin 2002) that visual evidence has persuasive power of its own.

In 1996, Phillip Meyer wrote that:

> the nature of lawyering practice and storytelling at trial is changing rapidly. Many of these changes are the result of new technologies, especially the use of aural and visual "paratexts" at trial … The impact of this new storytelling technology at trial is profound.
>
> (Meyer 1996)

We should continue to apply the findings of cognitive and social science to understand the making of false confessions and the decision-making of judges and juries when considering them. Conversational analysis can help make a case for the fact that sociality, cooperativeness, politeness, and "preference for agreement" constrain confession-makers as they do ordinary conversationalists. It can shed light on the "interlocutory relationship" of suspect and interrogator, a relationship which as Brooks (2000: 6) says "urges towards speech," and it can illuminate the workings of "linguistic coercion."

Linguistic anthropologists interested in the role of narrative in creating and maintaining collective memory and in the functioning of social memory in specific institutions

(Mendoza-Denton 2008), can help explain how the human proclivity to story-making and particular narrative devices such as reported speech influence individual and collective decision-making.

Conclusion

> Storytelling has a pragmatic efficacy. In pretending to recount the real, it manufactures it. It renders believable what it says, and it generates appropriate action ... The voices of narration transform, reorient and regulate the space of social interaction.
>
> (De Certeau 1986: 200)

Narrative strategies make a story compelling, seem to give it an anchor in reality, generate emotion and enhance involvement. They can also be used to manipulate listeners and obscure reality. As Jerome Bruner (2004: 15) says, "We seem to have no other way of describing 'lived time' save in the form of narrative" and that makes us very susceptible to the effect of story.

Legal decision-makers should be guided to see the intentionality in the gathering and presentation of legal evidence, to "understand their subtle strong persuasive effect" (Kandel 2002). As Kandel (2002: 8) says, "Rhetorical devices are like the brushstrokes of a master painter."

There are instances of true stories supplanted by false stories which are then so compellingly told that they convince decision-makers of their reliability. Hayat's trial may be one of them. In the closing arguments, the original interaction on which the evidence was co-produced (both between the cooperating witness Khan and the defendant Hayat, and between the police officers and the suspect) are erased while other, imagined relationships are created and new meanings assigned. By using as evidence talk that was spoken by the defendant these closing arguments gain a superficial air of authenticity—especially with regard to the so-called confession—a speech act which always seems to generate an expectation of sincerity.

The prosecution's closing arguments portray a young man with a jihadi heart and a jihadi mind. And they accomplish this portrayal, they claim, through his own words captured forever on tape. By focusing on his own words, they gain the authenticating power that reported speech can bring. However, the jury isn't reminded that these "own words" emerged from the constraining and coercive context of interrogation.

In October 2006, Hayat's attorneys submitted a motion for retrial. The motion was denied by Judge Burrell. While the jury seems to have struggled with the evidence, according to Cote reaching its decision "with a heavy heart," Burrell shows no sign of such struggle. On 10 September 2007, at the Federal District Court in Sacramento, he sentenced Hayat to 24 years in prison. According to an article in the NY Times (11 September 2007), Hayat was solemn and attentive as the words of Judge Burrell were translated into Urdu.

> Hamid Hayat attended a terrorist training camp and returned to the United States, ready and willing to wage violent jihad when directed to do so, regardless of the havoc such acts could wreak on persons and property in the United States, and then lied to the FBI on three separate occasions.
>
> (NY Times, 11 September 2007)

Burrell added that the evidence suggested a likelihood of recidivism and an unlikelihood of rehabilitation.

An appeal was heard in June 2009 (available online at: www.ca9.uscourts.gov [Accessed 3 August 2009]) and awaits decision. Meanwhile Hamid Hayat has been transferred to a prison in Indiana, far from his family and community in Lodi.

The Hayat case, like other anti-terrorism cases in the United States after September 11, 2001, is one which the prosecution characterized as preemptive: no crime had been committed. In fact it may have been wholly fabricated, a case where actual truth may have been trumped by narrative truth. And yet the repercussions for the defendant, his family and the Moslem community in Lodi are pervasive.[2]

Charles Briggs (1996: 30) reminds us that "Close study of who controls the processes by which stories are told and retold, as well as how they are interpreted, challenged and co-opted, is … of central importance to social scientific and humanistic inquiry."

Continuing research and education about false confessions is essential in order to prevent wrongful convictions. The reliability and trustworthiness of every confession should be considered before it is entered into evidence. Leo and Ofshe (1998) recommend a mandatory "reliability hearing" before a confession is allowed into evidence. If, as in the Hayat case, a judge does allow a problematic confession into evidence the jurors should be fully informed about the dangers of false confessions.

Notes

1 Diez (2005) looks at reported speech in asylum interviews and Johnson and Holt (this volume) in police interviews. Galatolo and Mizzau (2005) describe yet another specific function of direct reported speech they say has emerged from the analysis of their testimony data from an Italian court—"in the context of lay witness' testimony, direct reported speech can be a tool for covertly expressing one's point of view about events, bypassing the rule that prevents one from expressing individual opinions and evaluations while testifying."

2 The Hayat case may be an example of the "collateral damage" that can result from the so-called war on terror. Kent Roach and Gary Trotter (2005) warn that the "temptation of departing from normal legal standards and engaging in prejudgment, prejudice, and stereotyping may be particularly high in emotive and devastating cases involving allegations of terrorism and fears of continued acts of terrorism … In addition, the risk of wrongful convictions in terrorism cases, both before and after 9/11, are likely to fall disproportionately on particular groups, such as racial and religious minorities, or those with radical political views."

Further reading

Gudjonsson, G. (2003) *The Psychology of Interrogations and Confessions: A Handbook*, London: Wiley.

Hepworth, M. and Turner, B.S. (1982) *Confession: Studies in Deviance and Religion*, London: Routledge and Kegan Paul.

Leo, R. (2008) *Police Interrogation and American Justice*, Cambridge, MA: Harvard University Press.

Leo, R.A. and Thomas G.C. III (eds) (1998) *The Miranda Debate: Law, Justice and Policing*, Chicago: Northeastern University Press.

Reid, J. and Associates, www.reid.com for a frequently updated compendium of trial and appeal court decisions regarding Miranda, police interrogation and confession evidence.

Shuy, R.W. (1993) *Language Crimes*, Oxford: Blackwell.

White, W.S. (2003) *Miranda's Waning Protections*, Ann Arbor, MI: University of Michigan Press.

Case documents

Affidavit, June 6, 2005 Eastern District of California. Available online at: www.washingtoninstitute.org/documents/42b18c1d93623.pdf.

U.S.A. Plaintiff v. Hamid Hayat and Umer Hayat No. CR.S – 05 – 240 Reporter's Transcript, Jury Trial, February 16 – April 12.

FBI Interrogations with Hamid Hayat – Transcript and Video.

Translated transcriptions of Khan tapes (Pashto to English, some Urdu).

www.milnet.com for many of the case documents and articles regarding the Hayat case.

Recorded Interview of Hamid Hayat, June 4 and 5, 2005.

Appeal heard – June 10th 2009 *USA v. Hayat*, 10457, San Francisco, CA. Available online at: www.ca9.uscourts.gov/media/view_subpage.php?pk_id = 0000003604 (accessed 3 August 2009).

22

Representing oneself

Cross-examination questioning: lay people as cross-examiners

Tatiana Tkačuková

Introduction

Witness examination is an essential principle of the adversarial legal system. Through examining witnesses, the prosecution and the defence present their versions of events to the judge and jury. While it is expected that witnesses are prepared for examination-in-chief, cross-examination proceeds in a hostile atmosphere and is feared by witnesses, as it is an intimidating experience. It is also feared by novice barristers, as the success of the case can depend on their cross-examination skills. What is more important, though, is that the principle of cross-examination can easily turn into a tool for distorting the truth instead of revealing it (Riding 1999: 415–18). Facts speak for themselves: the main aim of a cross-examiner is to discredit the testimonies of witnesses by casting doubt on their credibility or their presentation of events (Gibbons 2003: 112). This is achieved by controlling witnesses through coercive questioning.

Linguistic research on witness examination and particularly cross-examination aims to minimize the injustices and alert legal professionals to problematic practices. Forensic linguists, together with psychologists, anthropologists and legal professionals, have gradually contributed to several changes in legitimate cross-examination tactics and examination proceedings in general. Studies on rape trials, for instance, have contributed to the fact that lawyers cannot any longer subject rape witnesses to questioning on their sexual history without a serious reason, as this was found to be an unfair pragmatic cross-examination strategy (Brereton 1997: 251; Gibbons 2003: 231; Ehrlich, this volume). Gibbons (2003: 202–5, 231) reports on how judges change the proceedings (e.g. by using video links to create a better environment for the child, eliminating structurally complex questions, making sure there is no misunderstanding) as they become more aware of problems that children experience in the witness box and Aldridge (this volume) reports recent changes that have taken place for vulnerable witnesses in England and Wales.

The first aim of this chapter is to look in detail at the research on cross-examination questions and strategies. The author then draws on this research in order to bring to light a topic that has so far been neglected: lay people as cross-examiners. Self-represented litigants (also *pro se* litigants) have previously been the subject of research just in small claims cases and divorce cases where such litigants present their case before a judge, usually without calling witnesses (Conley and O'Barr 1998; O'Barr and Conley 1990). This chapter focuses on the high-profile libel case *McDonald's Corporation v. Helen Steel and David Morris* tried in the Royal Courts of Justice in London from June 1994 until December 1996.

Steel and Morris (the defendants) were accused in a writ by McDonalds UK and US (the plaintiffs) of publishing a leaflet which accused McDonalds of poor practice in relation to six major areas: the link between food and disease (heart disease and cancer); advertising; animal treatment; food poisoning; employment practices; starvation in the Third World; and destruction of the rainforest. In the media, the case became widely referred to as the 'David and Goliath case', since the two litigants-in-person, without any previous experience of legal proceedings (Steel and Morris), were facing a top libel lawyer representing McDonald's (Mr. Rampton QC). In defiance of all the obstacles, the self-represented litigants managed to prepare a strong case against McDonald's. The outcome of the trial shows that they won several important issues (e.g. they managed to prove that McDonald's exploits children in their advertisements; offers bad working conditions; advertises deceptive information on the nutritional value of their food) and lost in less important issues (e.g. according to Mr. Justice Bell, Steel and Morris did not bring sufficient evidence that McDonald's is responsible for the destruction of rainforests; discarding of litter on the streets; firing pro-union workers).

This chapter exemplifies in what ways cross-examination performed by the professional counsel is different from cross-examination performed by the two litigants in person.

Overview of research on cross-examination questioning

Linguistic research on cross-examination questioning falls into several categories. Studies dating back to the 1980s (Woodbury 1984; Danet *et al* 1980; Philips 1987; Harris 1984) tend to adopt a quantitative approach towards different question types, since at that time the growing popularity of computer-aided data processing allowed the processing of more extensive samples. Typically, such studies concern themselves with the coerciveness reflected in the syntactic structure of different question types (Woodbury 1984; Danet *et al*. 1980) and the effect of questions on the length or type of responses from witnesses (Danet *et al*. 1980; Harris 1984). Though the function of different question types in context is not a major concern in most quantitative studies, pragmatic aspects are sometimes also included in the analysis (Woodbury 1984; Philips 1987; Harris 1984). From the more recent quantitative studies, Luchjenbroers (1997) and Heffer (2005) are of particular importance. Luchjenbroers (1997) takes a complex look at statistics on question distribution and answer types, whereas Heffer (2005, ch. 4) relates his statistics to the way different questions and responses contribute to narratives constructed by the prosecution and, on some occasions, also by the defence (see also Heffer, this volume).

Linguistic research starting from the 1990s reflects the development of such linguistic sub-disciplines as pragmatics, CA and CDA, as scholars turn their focus towards pragmatic aspects of cross-examination questioning. New approaches to data allowed researchers to consider power relations during witness examination from a variety of aspects. The research on cross-examination strategies shows how lawyers coerce witnesses into preferred replies (Conley and O'Barr 1998; Aldridge and Luchjenbroers 2007; Drew 1990; Matoesian 2005a; Cotterill 2003; Gibbons 2003: 112–127; Ehrlich, this volume). An inseparable part of the struggle for control is the witnesses' attempts to put forward their own versions and minimize the lawyers' influence (Drew 1992; Drew 1990; Atkinson and Drew 1979; Janney 2002). There are other fascinating directions the research can take. Researchers have, for instance, emphasized such issues as manipulation of cultural stereotypes and ideologies through questioning (Aldridge and Luchjenbroers 2007; Matoesian 1997) or the struggle over lexical choices (Eades 2006; Cotterill 2004). A valuable source of additional research on questioning comes from the related area of police interrogations (Newbury and Johnson 2006; Heydon 2005; Johnson 2002; Benneworth, this volume).

Research challenges – Data

Studies on courtroom discourse face a serious methodological complication: the access to data. Heffer (2005: 53) describes the difficulties of acquiring data – it is prohibited to make any notes during trials and official audio recordings of hearings are virtually impossible to obtain (see also Drew 1985). Court transcripts are easier to obtain, but even so not all parts are transcribed (parts that are not important for possible appeals are usually not transcribed) and the cost for transcripts may be very high (Heffer 2005: 53). One of the options is to draw the data from court transcripts available on the internet (e.g. OJ Simpson trial, the Shipman trial) or search the databases of widely publicized trials (e.g. CourtTVNews, Famous Trials).

Outside common law countries, it is not very common to transcribe courtroom proceedings verbatim. In the Czech Republic, for instance, key witnesses' testimonies are transcribed verbatim only in criminal cases. In civil cases, witnesses' testimonies are just summarized (the contents of a summary are usually dictated by the judge) but the participants have the right to demand a particular part of the testimony to be transcribed verbatim.

In general, court transcripts are made to preserve a verbatim record of everything said in court. Their complete accuracy is, of course, unachievable due to the nature of spoken language (Fraser 2003; Eades 1996; Walker 1986b). Just one example of the limitations of transcription is that the mere necessity of including punctuation in the written text makes the transcription dependant on the stenographers' interpretation of an utterance (Fraser 2003; Eades 1996; Walker 1986b; Haworth, this volume). Other potential perils that researchers need to be aware of derive from the fact that the transcripts are produced purely for legal purposes and stenographers can't be expected to record features that are not of immediate interest to linguists or legal professionals (e.g. simultaneous speech, interruptions, third turns). Interruptions are, for instance, usually indicated with dashes, but such a simplified system does not make it clear when exactly interruptions begin and for how long simultaneous speech lasts (Walker 1986b: 211–13).

The data for the current chapter are drawn from the court transcripts available from the McSpotlight web page (www.mcspotlight.org/case/trial/transcripts/index.html, accessed 30 June 2009). Performing a linguistic analysis of oral discourse which is based on written transcripts is certainly disadvantageous – had the author been in the position of Slembrouck (1992) having access to both written and spoken versions, the study would have benefited significantly. However, the seriousness of this drawback is diminished by the fact that the current study concentrates on the formal features of cross-examination questions and the function of questions in the context of cross-examination strategies.

Research challenges – Question types

A researcher conducting a study on cross-examination question types faces an important decision in selecting an adequate typology of questions. An obvious option is to follow the widely accepted categorization of questions into open and closed questions (Huddleston and Pullum 2002: 867). Open questions are wh-questions (e.g. 'What is it?'), whereas closed questions are alternative questions ('Is it black or white?'), yes/no questions ('Is it black?'), declarative questions ('This is it?') and tag questions (e.g. 'It's nice, isn't it?'). Such classification of questions rests on the formal features of questions (i.e. their syntactic structure) and the type of answers expected.

The type of answers expected is related to the degree of coerciveness of different question types. Out of the most frequent types of closed questions, yes/no questions, are generally regarded as the least coercive type as they offer at least a limited possibility for witnesses to digress. In comparison to yes/no questions, tag questions and declarative questions are strongly biased towards a confirmative answer and so they are more coercive (Huddleston and Pullum 2002: 881, 894). Apart from coercing witnesses into type-conforming replies, these types of questions offer one more obvious advantage to counsels: they are perceived as statements and as such help to change the questions into evidence (Hobbs 2003b: 486–87). Tag questions and declarative questions thus become a powerful tool which enables counsels to give evidence on behalf of witnesses and reduce witnesses to the role of minimal responders. But it is tag questions that are considered by some scholars (Woodbury 1984: 205; Berk-Seligson 1999: 36) to be the most coercive type of questions as they have an additional pragmatic meaning: they imply that the person knows that the questioner is right. Gibbons (2003: 101), however, warns of relying heavily on the form of questions since intonation, or tone of voice, is equally important for defining the degree of coerciveness.

It is also necessary to keep in mind that the semantic and pragmatic properties of questions go beyond the strictly formal categories outlined above. Modality is a resource, which, as Gibbons (2003: 100) points out, can be understood either in terms of direct-ness/indirectness or in terms of embedding information within a modal verb frame. For example, an indirect request or statement, 'I wonder whether he was there', is less constraining than a direct question 'Was he there?' and in terms of embedding information within a modal verb frame, 'Could you tell us what the colour of the car was?' is more polite than: 'What was the colour of the car?' In courtroom questioning modality is used to establish pre-conditions for more specific questions (Rigney 1999: 87). Another pragmatic category important for courtroom questions is factuality, for example, 'Is it true that you lied to the police?' or 'As a matter of fact, did you lie to the police?' Rigney (1999: 91) argues that factuality maximizes the level of coerciveness in questions because the information embedded in the question is presented as a truthful fact. Depending on the nature of data and the aim of the study, it may thus be important to consider incorporating semantic or pragmatic properties into the typology of questions.

An ideal typology of cross-examination questions would reflect cross-examiners' control over witnesses and over the message to be heard by the intended audience, the judge and the jury. It is, however, almost impossible to combine all the aspects into one typology. Gibbons (2003: 102–7) thus suggests several typologies of questions. One of them sorts questions according to the deniability of the information from the perspective of a defendant or witness whereas a different one lists questions according to their coerciveness.

The detailed typology of questions used for this study can be found on the web pages that accompany the *Handbook*, available at: http://www.forensiclinguistic.net/. The present chapter deals with the most important formal question types: wh-questions, yes/no questions, declarative questions and tag questions. Alternative questions were omitted due to their rare occurrence in the data.

Quantitative analysis of cross-examination questions

The corpus was prepared with the help of Jan Pomikálek from the Faculty of Informatics, Masaryk University in the Czech Republic. The sample for analysis comprises 21 days of cross-examination of key expert witnesses (7 cross-examination days by Rampton and 14 cross-examination days by Steel and Morris). The sample of cross-examination questions asked by Steel and Morris was extracted from three periods of the trial: their very first cross-examination conducted in July 1994, their later cross-examinations in July and September 1994, and cross-examinations they conducted towards the final stages of the case in May 1996. Figures 22.1 and 22.2 contrast the occurrence of different question types used by the professional lawyer and the two litigants-in-person (Figure 22.1 concentrates on Steel, Figure 22.2 concentrates on Morris).

As it could be expected, we can see from Figures 22.1 and 22.2 that wh-questions occur more often in the *pro se* litigants' cross-examination. Rampton uses wh-questions very rarely, as they do not restrict the response boundaries as effectively as closed questions. Towards the end of the trial the occurrence of wh-questions in Morris's usage decreases significantly, which is related to his increased use of closed questions (especially declarative questions and tag questions). Steel, however, does not show any variance. Her frequent use of wh-questions can be explained by her occasional hesitance to use more coercive closed questions ('This dietary advice that you think is a – well, what do you think of it?' – 22 July 1994).

Out of closed questions, the most striking difference is in the occurrence of tag questions. While tag questions are the most frequent type of questions used by the counsel,

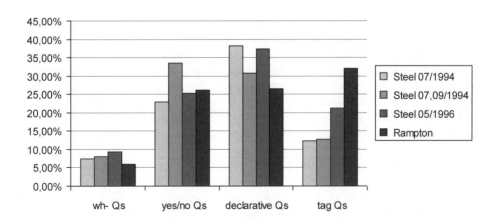

Figure 22.1 The ratio of cross-examination questions used by Mr. Rampton QC and Steel during the three periods

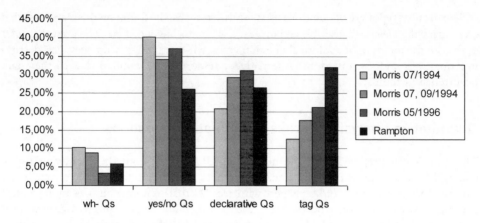

Figure 22.2 The ratio of cross-examination questions used by Mr. Rampton QC and Morris during the three periods

Table 22.1 The comparison of the self-represented litigants' declarative questions and tag questions in two different periods

	tag questions
Steel – July 1, 1994	Steel – May 22, 1996
(1) This leaflet was available in stores, was it not?	(3) It is fair to say, is it not, that (…) since you last gave your evidence [against the existence of causal links] there have been a considerable number also pointing to the suggestion that there are such causal links?
	declarative questions
Morris – July 21, 1994	Morris – May 22, 1996
(2) So the fruit pies up to 1989 used to include beef tallow?	(4) But presumably the reason that the fat consumption has been causally linked to heart disease is precisely because the body is unable to cope with the high levels of fat in the bloodstream?

neither of the defendants makes use of tag questions to such an extent. Nonetheless, towards the final stages of the case both Steel and Morris increase the occurrence of tag questions (from approximately 12% to 21%), which means that they become more coercive. With declarative questions, the situation is opposite. Both litigants-in-person use them slightly more often than the counsel does. What is more important, though, is the use of tag questions and declarative questions. Table 22.1 contrasts example questions asked by the litigants in person at the beginning of the trial and towards the final stages.

As the first column in the table shows, at the beginning of the trial Steel and Morris used declarative questions and tag questions mostly to check for facts (questions 1–2). Closed questions, however, have much more potential; they are used by lawyers to lead witnesses into the preferred answer and persuade the audience into accepting the message embedded in questions (see example (1) for closed questions asked by the counsel). As can be seen from the second column (questions 3–4), Steel and Morris's questions become more coercive. Even the length of questions suggests that they put more effort into influencing witnesses. Steel's question (question 3) bears an implication that her arguments are well founded and that there is conflicting evidence to the witness's view. Morris's declarative question (question 4) is likewise more coercive than the earlier one. Thus, the defendants' move towards coerciveness is reflected both in the occurrence and also the use of tag questions and declarative questions.

While *pro se* litigants experience problems with the use of tag questions and declarative questions, there are no striking differences between the counsel and the lay people in the use of yes/no questions. It is not surprising since yes/no questions are more common in everyday conversation than declarative questions or tag questions.

Question types in the service of pragmatic cross-examination strategies

Cross-examiners face a multiple task: discredit the witness, propose an alternative approach to the events, and persuade the audience. This is achieved purely by means of questioning, until they come to closing speeches. The syntactic form of questions helps to define the response boundaries and elicit type-conforming replies. There is, however, a more complex phenomenon behind the art of cross-examining. It is a strong under-standing of the interaction between meaning, context, and communication that helps counsels to corner witnesses effectively. This section aims to link the two inseparable parts of cross-examination and relate question forms to pragmatic strategies.

Cross-examination strategies used by barristers cover a wide range of tactics including lexical means (particular choices of words used in questions – see Cotterill 2004) or prosodic means (ironic tone or prolonged pauses after significant replies can be used strategically to convey additional meanings – see Gibbons 2003: 117–26). Gibbons (2003: 112) differentiates between idea-targeted and person-targeted pragmatic strategies. Idea-targeted pragmatic strategies challenge the testimony, whereas person-targeted pragmatic strategies cast doubt on the personal characteristics of witnesses. The latter type is of particular importance for cross-examination of expert witnesses because it is always possible to challenge scientific expertise. It is, nonetheless, important to realize that it is impossible to draw a strict borderline between the two types of pragmatic strategies as the same means can be used for both (e.g. vocabulary choice is listed in Gibbons under the idea-targeted strategies, but it is shown to be used for discrediting the professional status of the witness, as in example (1)).

The following sections illustrate the differences between the counsel and the lay litigants-in-person in the use of pragmatic tactics (see also, Matoesian, this volume, on use of gesture and multimodality in cross-examination).

Person-targeted pragmatic strategies by Mr. Rampton QC

Among the most widely used person-targeted pragmatic strategies is the 'status manip-ulation tactic' (Gibbons 2003: 113). Example (1) illustrates the counsel's persistent undermining of the professionalism of an expert witness.

(1) Cross-examination of Barnard (W) by Rampton (Pr) – 11 September 1994

  1 Pr: How much of your time is spent looking after your medical patients, your
  2   psychiatric patients?
  3 W: Currently?

 4 Pr: Yes.
 5 W: One morning per week.
 6 Pr: What do you do the rest of the time?
 7 W: I write books, I conduct research and I work at the Physicians Committee for
 8   Responsible Medicine with the other physicians and staff we have there.
 9 Pr: You see, I am willing to concede that somebody who has a preliminary
10   qualification of general medicine, may in one sense have an advantage over a
11   judge sitting in court in England or a barrister standing on his feet in that he
12   will more readily understand the biological or physiological mechanisms of
13   terminology. The other qualification which I imagine – you correct me if I
14   am wrong – you propose for your presence in this case is that you have spent
15   a lot of time reading the literature; is that right?
16 W: I have spent a great deal of time reviewing literature and talking with experts
17   about its meaning.
18 Pr: That is a task which can as easily be performed by an intelligent layman, or
19   very nearly, as it can be by you?
20 W: Certainly have always encouraged lay persons to learn as much as they can
21   about the links between diet and disease. If they care to spend their time
22   dusting off the medical literature in the library, I would encourage that.
23   (…)
24 Pr: You said you talk to experts in the field; we can do the same; you would
25   encourage us to do so, would you not?
26 W: Certainly.
27 Pr: Much of your time if you are only doing psychiatry one day a week or one
28   morning a week, whatever it is, you tell us is spent writing. It must have been
29   quite a labour to produce this book. Was it a labour, hard work?
30 W: I devoted a considerable amount of time reading the literature, talking with the
31   researchers, trying to put their words into a useful way that might be of benefit
32   to the reader.

Rampton's initiating turns present specific information about the proportion of the witness's practical experience and theoretical expertise. His open question in line 6 elicits only a short response that fits the boundaries set by the question. Starting with line 9, prosecuting counsel pursues the chosen line of argument and suggests that with some training lay people can do the same things as Dr. Barnard does. To elicit a positive reaction from the witness, Rampton chooses to make use of a special strategy that is described as a 'false friend' strategy by Aldridge and Luchjenbroers (2007: 102). The counsel overtly admits that the witness's qualification is of an advantage ('I'm willing to concede'; 'more readily understand the biological or physiological mechanisms of terminology'). On the other hand, the use of the modal verb 'may' (line 10) for a weak degree of possibility covertly suggests that medical qualification is only a minor advantage. The adjective 'preliminary' (line 9) further demeans the witness's qualification. The discourse marker 'you see' (line 9) is also loaded with strong pragmatic meaning; it was found by Hale to signal 'proclaimed knowledge' when used in cross-examination questions (Hale 1999: 69). By using it, Rampton covertly suggests that it is clear that lay people can read medical literature.

There is one more tactic that the counsel employs in lines 9–13. He breaks the expected distribution of adjacency pairs and instead of asking a question, Rampton makes use of a third turn. The following question (lines 13–15) changes the seemingly supportive third turn into an evaluative turn. Evaluative third turns were recorded in other sources (Gibbons 2003: 124; Matoesian 2005a: 746) as an effective means for rebuffing the veracity of witnesses. Here the third turn works well together with the following agreement tag question (lines 13–15) for casting doubt on the professionalism of the witness. The counsel, in fact, implies that the witness is only reporting the work of others and accuses him of committing an expert equivalent of 'hearsay'. The subsequent closed questions are framed into the same narrative (lines 18–19, 24–25). The counsel corners the witness by gradually 'nailing down' (Matoesian 2005a) his series of questions to the response he wanted to obtain (line 26). In his next third turn (lines 27–28), counsel re-establishes the fact that the witness spends most of his time doing theoretical research. Through presupposing the answer (lines 28–29) to his following question and using a strong modal verb 'must', counsel diminishes the work of the expert witness. The tactic of answering one's own questions is noted by Chang (2004: 717) to be a very coercive strategy. There is yet another way that counsel challenges the witness. By using the noun 'labour' (line 29) to refer to the process of writing, he stresses the fact that it must have been extremely difficult and maybe even below the level of the witness's expertise.

As is evident from the sample, counsel's questions are mostly coercive closed questions that covertly 'smuggle' the intended message (Aldridge and Luchjenbroers 2007: 93). His lexical choices ('a preliminary qualification of general medicine' in lines 9–10, 'quite a labour' in line 29, 'produce this book' in line 29) create lexical landscaping (Cotterill 2004: 527) that questions the witness's expertise, presupposing that the same task can be done by lay people.

Person-targeted pragmatic strategies by Steel and Morris

This section offers two examples of person-targeted pragmatic strategies used by the lay litigants-in-person, one at an early stage of the proceedings (2) and the second in the final stages of the proceedings (3). Both examples were chosen in such a way as to reflect similar situations as in (1), that is, status reduction tactics.

(2) Cross-examination of Arnott (W) by Steel (D1) and Morris (D2) – 12 September 1994

1 D1: Is it fair to say, by and large, that you have concentrated on treatment rather
2   than research into causes, prevention?
3 W: That is only partly true. I am very much concerned with treatment, that is
4   absolutely right. But in order to treat patients, one has to have some
5   understanding about the possible causation and the mechanisms by which
6   causative agents may give rise to cancer because treatment, part of treatment is
7   prevention, if one can, and part of treatment is also removing various factors
8   which may be responsible for causing the cancer; it is not just the
9   administration of anti-cancer type treatment. In fact, for example, some of the
10   chapters of books I have written are concerned with all aspects of cancer; for
11   example, the geographical distribution, possible aetiology as well as treatment.
12 D1: Right. What sorts of things have you studied in relation to prevention?
13 W: Well, large studies, for example, on cigarette smoking and lung cancer. I have
14   been very much involved with studies on diet, their possible implications in

341

15   cancer. Radiation exposure, and the possibility that that may have an influence
16   in the development of cancer, particularly childhood cancer; a lot of studies in
17   that aspect of things; genetic aspects and, you know, there are a variety of
18   studies that I have been involved with which have looked at possible causation
19   of cancer in terms of trying to prevent the development of the cancer.
20   D1:   What exactly have you studied in relation to diet as you know in terms of
21   preventing cancer?
22   W: Well, I have obviously done a very extensive literature search. I worked, when
23   I was in Scotland, I worked in conjunction with the gastroenterological unit at
24   the Western General hospital there, where some of our patients actually
25   participated in some of the studies they were carrying out, looking at various
26   aspects of diet and possible causation of cancer. These are the main ones.
27   D1:   Right.
28   (...)
29   D2:   Can you give some examples of the recognition you have in the field of
30   treatment in your academic field, recognition you have by that field in terms of
31   maybe chairing bodies or conferences or participation?
32   W: Well, I am, I have been Secretary of the British Stomach Cancer Group. I have
33   been a member of the working party of the Medical Research Council looking
34   at colorectal cancer and also involved with the Medical Research Council
35   looking at new forms of treatment (...).
36   (...)
37   D1:   What percentage of all those things was involved in, was, kind of, looking up
38   the causes of cancer as opposed to treatment?
39   W: I would say about a third.
40   D1:   Right.

Example (2) shows that in comparison to the counsel, the lay litigants-in-person are not as successful with their status reduction tactics. At the very beginning, in an attempt to emphasize that the witness does not have much experience with the research, Steel asks a closed question (lines 1–2). Her question, however, elicits an evasive reply. Neither do her next routinized wh-questions (Philips 1987) lead towards the desired aim (lines 13, 22–23). What is more, when Morris asks a yes/no question (lines 29–31), he basically invites the witness to comment on his achievements, which is expected in examination-in-chief, but not the cross-examination. It is only in lines 37–8 that Steel manages to make her point that the witness is more concerned with the treatment rather than the research.

It would be a mistake to view the fixed distribution of turns during examination in terms of adjacency pair question–answer sequences only. As examples (1) and (2) demonstrate this is not the case in courtroom interaction any more than it is in conversation. Counsel and the *pro se* litigants do use third turns (see lines 12, 27, 40 in example (2)), but their function is different. Rampton's third parts are evaluative and challenging, whereas Steel's third turns consist of the discourse marker 'right' which seems to be accepting the witness's contribution. According to Hale (1999), such discourse markers are common in everyday conversation where they function as cohesive devices. In cross-examination, they usually signal control, coerciveness or contradiction (Hale 1999: 59). However, the way novice cross-examiner Steel uses 'right' as a third turn corresponds to its everyday use of signalling comprehension or acknowledgement.

Example (3), from the final stage of the proceedings, illustrates a similar situation when the *pro se* litigants attempt to challenge the veracity of the witness.

(3)   Cross-examination of Preston (W) by Steel (D) – 7 May 1996

 1   D: (…) I am asking you before you made this statement, did you actually research
 2   what the situation was or did you just put down any old rubbish?
 3   W: I took advice.
 4   D: You took advice from who?
 5   W: From my solicitors, lawyers.
 6   D: So your solicitors told you what to put in the statement?
 7   W: No. I took advice from them.
 8   D: What do you mean? I am asking you whether, when you made this statement,
 9   which is supposed to be about things within your own knowledge, whether you
10   researched it before you wrote the statement or whether you just put down any
11   old rubbish?
12   W: I discussed it with the people who were involved and my counsel.

Example (3) leads us into the question of politeness strategies during cross-examination. Several researchers (e.g. Cashion 1985; Harris 2003) have focused on the connection between politeness and power and have come to the same conclusion. Surprisingly, those participants who hold the most powerful roles tend to use politeness strategies abundantly to redress the face-threatening acts that they have to perform. But these participants can also choose not to use politeness strategies in case they need to explicitly show their power. According to Harris (2003: 33), it is negative politeness features that are especially relevant to institutional settings (i.e. those strategies that prevent imposing on the speaker or impeding them). The counsels in Cashion's study (1985: 13) were found to exhibit mostly negative politeness features whereas positive politeness strategies (strategies that attend to the speaker's needs to be liked) occurred only rarely. In his cross-examination, Rampton employs a negative politeness strategy 'correct me if I'm wrong' to avoid imposing his knowledge on the witness (see lines 13–15 in example (1)).

In order to make the witness admit his mistake, Steel nails down his answers with a series of closed questions (lines 1–2, 4, 6). In lines 1–2 and 8–11, Steel performs a face-threatening act without any attempt to redress it. Instead of catching the witness in an intricately designed web of closed questions, she explicitly confronts him without the desired result. In a way, the contest with the witness puts her in a less powerful position while the witness insists on his vague answers (lines 3, 7, 12) and manages to avoid self-incrimination (c.f. Janney 2002: 460).

Thus, in comparison to Steel's performance at the early stage of the hearing (see example (2)), there is some improvement in the use of questions, but the use of cross-examination strategies is still not expert.

Idea-targeted pragmatic strategies

Examples (4) and (5) below illustrate the differences between counsel and the litigants-in-person in their use of pragmatic strategies when cross-examining expert witnesses on the nutritional value of McDonald's meals. Steel and Morris had to prove that a McDonald's diet causes cancer and other diseases. Rampton chose to show that research linking diet to health problems has been inconsistent and that there may be other more serious causes. Example (4) shows how Rampton evokes Galileo's struggle for the truth in order to bring to light the idea that even widely accepted facts may be erroneous.

(4) Cross-examination of Cannon (W) by Rampton (Pr) – 3 October 1994

  1 Pr: It was widely held at one time, we can agree perhaps, that the world was flat,
  2   was it not?
  3 W: Yes.
  4 Pr: Certain people were persecuted for holding that maybe that view was wrong?
  5 W: Yes.
  6 Pr: It turned out that the people who were persecuted were right, did it not?
  7 W: You mean Gallileo, for example, was right?
  8 Pr: Yes.
  9 W: Indeed so.
10 Pr: The world is not flat, is it?
11 W: It is generally agreed that the world is round, indeed so, yes.
12   (…)
13 Pr: Virtually every respectable medical man would now accept, perhaps you
14   would agree, that there is a causal relationship – I stress the word 'causal' –
15   of between a diet high in fat and, particularly, saturated fat and the incidence
16   of cardiovascular disease, would they not
17 W: Yes.

By asking short closed questions (lines 1–2, 4, 6, 10), Rampton narrows down a complicated narrative to short phrases, which are easy to comprehend and remember. The counsel uses 'natural narrative structure' (Gibbons 2003: 123) in order to bring to light the topic of widely known misconceptions. After developing a strong narrative, the counsel asks a question on the existence of causal links (lines 13–16) and elicits a positive reply. But the question is perceived in the context of the preceding exchanges and the witness appears to be holding yet another erroneous opinion. Counsel continues in the chosen line of argument when cross-examining other expert witnesses, highlighting the notion that modern science cannot prove the connection between diet and heart disease and cancer.

Example (5) shows one of the most celebrated moments in the trial when the litigants-in-person managed to elicit a damaging reply from a McDonald's expert witness.

(5) Cross-examination of Arnott (W) by Morris (D) – 12 September 1994

  1 D I want to ask you about another document about advice to the public. 'A diet
  2   high in fat, sugar, animal products and salt and low in fibre, vitamins and
  3   minerals is linked with cancer of the breast and bowel and heart disease.'
  4   Is that a reasonable statement?
  5 W It has been linked, yes.
  6 D So would that be a reasonable statement?
  7 W Well, it depends to whom it is being directed.
  8 D The public.
  9 W If it is being directed to the public, then I would say it is a very reasonable
10   thing to say, but if it is directed towards the scientific community, then I think
11   one would be a bit more careful in the language which one is using.
12 D That is actually a quote from the London Greenpeace fact sheet which is the
13   subject of the libel action.

Morris chose not to identify the document he is reading the quotation from (lines 1–3) offering a reasonable explanation to the judge: 'I just wanted to not colour any possible professional response'. In line 6, Morris repeats his question to elicit a more definite reply. He then uses a third turn (line 12–13) to reveal the source of the document, that is, the fact sheet that contained criticism of McDonald's business practices. Although Morris's strategy is much simpler than Rampton's, he managed to elicit a crucially damaging reply from the McDonald's witness, who agreed that the most important statement against McDonald's diet was very reasonable. Often the litigants-in-person, however, did not manage to make witnesses agree.

Contrary to example (5), example (6) illustrates a situation where Morris did not manage to show that the witness was providing a misleading answer. Prior to the exchange in the example, Morris and the witness were talking about an allegation of a large amount of sugar added to McDonald's drinks.

(6) Cross-examination of Wheelock (W) by Morris (D) – 22 July 1994

1 D: How do you define the word 'nutritious'?
2 W: Well, it is something which pertains to nutrition.
3   (...)
4 D: So sugar is nutritious?
5 W: Oh, yes, sugar is a source of calories.
6 D: But it has not a range of nutrients?
7 W: No, it has not.
8 D: It is just the sugar?
9 W: It has calories. Again it depends what you actually want at the time.

In line 1, Morris asks a wh-question to find out how the expert witness defines the word 'nutritious'. According to the witness's definition, any type of food can be nutritious. In his following closed questions (lines 4, 6), Morris tries to resist such an approach, but the witness still insists on his standpoint that sugar is nutritious because it has calories. The declarative question in line 4 is so-prefaced (Johnson 2002). Cotterill (2003: 152) describes 'so' summarizers occurring in her data during cross-examination as very powerful follow-ups that are widely used by lawyers to 'oblige the witness to concede and reiterate in an explicit form something damaging'. Cotterill's example (2003: 153) is: 'So that after nine months of investigation, you discovered on Saturday that this important piece of evidence was perfectly innocuous; is that right?' (Cotterill 2003: 153). Morris's use of 'so' is much more simple. Though his question summarizes what was said before, there is only implied criticism and no other embedded message. He has to follow it up with additional information in lines 6 and 8. Line 8 has a question mark at the end of the sentence, indicating that this is a declarative question for agreement. In this turn, Morris provides an argument rather than asking an information-seeking question. We see how asking an initial wh-question leads to an answer from which additional ideas are generated for confirmation. Though successful, the lay cross-examiner fails to fully exploit the pragmatic resources of so-prefaced questions in the ways that professional counsel does.

Conclusion

Noticeable changes in the frequency and use of closed questions over time, for example the increase in the occurrence and restrictive use of tag questions, indicate the *pro se* litigants' awareness of the necessity to gain control over the witness replies. But at the same time some aspects are left underestimated; their closed questions often lack discrediting embedded messages and thus allow witnesses to formulate replies without major restrictions. Even the *pro se* litigants' third turns are supportive instead of being challenging. They also appear powerless when they compete with a witness, since the witness manages to avoid self-incrimination (see example (3)). All in all, formal aspects of cross-examination like restrictive questions are easier to observe and adopt, but pragmatic strategies and the art of narrating through questioning are more difficult to acquire without a solid understanding of the basic principles of the adversarial system and without professional practice.

The self-represented litigants' mixed progress over the course of the trial can be accounted for by the hypothesis that they developed an interlanguage and additional competence as the hearings progressed, comparable to second language learners who develop an interlanguage as they learn a new language. In the case of Steel and Morris, a more exact term would be an *inter-genre* instead of an interlanguage, as previously suggested by Trinch (2005a). Her study focuses on lay Latina women who come for protective order interviews as victims of domestic violence and have to adapt their language to the genre of report when interacting with legal professionals. The author's conclusion is that the laywomen do develop an inter-genre, but only to a very limited extent. In the current study, the situation is slightly different. The two self-represented litigants do learn from the counsel but since they do not receive any assistance on cross-examination questioning and its purpose, their development remains unstable as they have other matters to concentrate on during cross-examination.

This study shows that lay litigants-in-person do need help: an informative brochure on courtroom discourse, cross-examination questions and strategies would be very helpful to *pro se* litigants as it is only fair to show them what legal professionals do with language.

Further reading

A detailed typology of questions used for this study can be found on the web pages that accompany the *Handbook*, available at: http://www.forensiclinguistics.net/

Aldridge, M. and Luchjenbroers, J. (2007) 'Linguistic manipulation in legal discourse: Framing questions and "smuggling" information', *International Journal of Speech, Language and the Law*, 14(1): 85–107. (The paper concentrates on the influence of the wording of questions on the perception of rape witnesses' testimonies.)

Bülow-Møller, A.M. (1992) 'The notion of coercion in courtroom questioning'. (Eric Document Reproduction Service No. ED 359752.) (The paper relates question forms to their function in courtroom examination; special attention is paid to the effect of questions on the audience.)

Cotterill, J. (2004) 'Collocation, connotation, and courtroom semantics: Lawyers' control of witness testimony through lexical negation', *Applied Linguistics*, 25(4): 513–37. (The paper emphasizes the role of lexical choices in the contest between lawyers and witnesses.)

Section II

The linguist as expert in legal processes

Expert and process

23

Trademark linguistics

Trademarks: Language that one owns

Ronald R. Butters

Historical and theoretical perspectives

The rise of linguistic testimony about trademarks

Trademark linguistics is an established area of forensic linguistic theory and practice: "One type of case in which linguists routinely testify [in the United States] is trademark litigation, often with both sides offering linguistic testimony" (Ainsworth 2006: 262). Testimony is also reported in Canada (Chambers 2008: 35), Australia (Eades 1994b: 119), Chile (Oyandel and Samaniego 2004), South Africa (Sanderson 2007), and, recently, Great Britain (Heffer 2008a; Olsson 2008a).

In the United States, the earliest known linguistic consulting about a trademark was undertaken by the dialectologist Raven I. McDavid, Jr. (see McDavid 1977: 126) and the lexicographer and dialectologist Frederic Cassidy (*WSM, Incorporated, Appellant, v. Dennis E. Hilton and Country Shindig Opry, Inc., Appellees*, 1984 U.S. App.724 F.2d 1320). They were joined at about the same time by two eminent American lexicographers, Allen Walker Read and Jess Stein, who testified for opposing sides in the same case (reported in detail in Bailey 1984). Thirty years later, one eminent linguist had testified in so many cases that they formed the backbone of an entire book (Shuy 2002), and at least a dozen American linguists had been active trademark consultants. There is a growing body of scholarly literature (e.g. Adams 2005; Adams and Westerhaus Adams 2005; Baron 1989; Butters 2007a, 2007b, 2008a, 2008c; Butters and Westerhaus 2004; Clankie 2002; Creech 2005, 2007; Dinwoodie 2008; Durant 2008; Lentine and Shuy 1990; Nunberg 2001; Shuy 2008; Tamony 1986). Japanese scholars have written about trademark linguistic theory (Okawara 2006; Hotta 2007a, 2007b; Hotta and Fujita 2007), and there is passing mention in the German context (Kniffka 2007: 29, 139–40), but the scholars of neither country instance actual courtroom testimony.

Definitions and terminology

Trademarks (or just MARKS), like copyrights, are proprietary language—bits of linguistic or semiotic material that people, corporations, and institutions in a very real but limited sense own. Paraphrasing Landau (2001: 405–6),

> A trademark is a symbol, phrase, or name used by a maker of a product or provider of a service to distinguish the product or service from others of its kind. It is a name for or symbol or phrase associated with a brand of a kind of thing, rather than with the kind of thing itself.

MARKS may be words or phrases (e.g. BRAND NAMES such as *Apple, Mac, Applecare Protection Plan*); symbols, logos, and designs (e.g. the profile of an apple with a bite taken out of it); slogans or taglines (e.g. "Think different," "It Does What a PC Does, Only Better"); and, in the past decade, internet domain names (apple.com, imac.com, imacapple.com, imac-apple.com, podmart.com). Ownership of all the marks just mentioned is claimed by the computer company, Apple Inc.

In the United States, the symbol "®" is often attached to a mark (e.g. *Mac*®) to indicate that the mark has been properly registered with the federal government's United States Patent and Trademark Office (USPTO); the symbol "TM" indicates a claim for common-law viability of a mark that has not been registered with the USPTO. Technically, TRADEMARKS identify goods, while SERVICE MARKS identify services.

Trademark and copyright are distinct concepts. Trademark laws have a narrow focus: they grant control over the linguistic and semiotic entities (MARKS) by means of which providers of goods and services identify what they market to the public. Copyright laws, however, protect broader linguistic and semiotic entities that are in themselves products, granting rights to individuals to control the results of their creative enterprises (novels, poems, plays, essays, letters, musical compositions, paintings, etc.). Copyright issues arise for forensic linguists who pursue questions of plagiarism, authorship identification, and forensic stylistics.

Trademark litigation and the forensic linguist

Shuy writes (2002: 182–83), "issues of phonology, morphology, syntax, lexicography, semantics, pragmatics, and discourse … are likely to be relevant in a trademark case," and he notes that semiotic analysis may be employed as well (134–35). Especially important are (1) experience in applied linguistics such as one finds in lexicography and (2) the sort of interest in empirical data that dialectologists and sociolinguists deal with centrally in their professional enterprises.

Most trademark disputes occur when a party attempts to protect its established linguistic property (called the SENIOR MARK) from encroachment by a party that uses or plans to use a new, similar or identical mark (the JUNIOR MARK). In the US there are two principal venues for action, (1) the USPTO and (2) the federal courts.

The USPTO receives trademark renewal applications and new applications. If the USPTO denies an application, attorneys for the applicant may appeal the decision to a subdivision called the Trademark Trial and Appeal Board (TTAB). Applications are sometimes denied for reasons having to do only with features of the mark itself (if, for example, the USPTO finds it to be obscene); denial may also arise if the owner of a registered mark has filed an objection to the applicant's mark on the grounds that the new mark infringes upon the established one, in which case both sides will present their cases to the TTAB.

Federal courts are where a trademark owner brings suit against an alleged infringer; decisions of the TTAB are also sometimes appealed to the courts.

Generally, forensic experts in trademark cases are involved in three or four stages. Typically, the first duty of a forensic expert will be the preparation of an EXPERT REPORT, which is often submitted under oath. If opposing counsel has already commissioned an expert report, the first expert may be asked for a REBUTTAL REPORT. Even COUNTER-REBUTTAL reports happen occasionally.

Next, opposing counsel usually requires the experts to appear for a DEPOSITION in which the expert will be questioned, under oath, about the report. Depositions are usually taken in face-to-face confrontation (sometimes videotaped) in a law office and recorded by a trained court reporter; telephone depositions are also possible. Theoretically, depositions can go on indefinitely, though in practice they generally last between three and eight hours.

Many trademark cases are SETTLED between the parties by agreements entered into without going to court. If not, the linguistic trademark expert may actually TESTIFY AT TRIAL. Courtroom cases often are not decided by juries but by a judge acting alone in a procedure known as a BENCH TRIAL—or in preliminary proceedings in which the judge decides if the outcome of the case is so apparent that having an actual trial would be a waste of time (SUMMARY JUDGMENT).

Forensic linguists confront four issues in trademark litigation. Only occasionally do linguists give expert advice on what is termed (1) the PROPRIETY OF THE MARK; these are cases in which the USPTO rejects a proposed mark as "immoral, deceptive, or scandalous … disparaging" (a provision found in a federal statute, 15 USC 1052, "Trademarks Registrable on the Principal Register; Concurrent Registration", www.bitlaw.com/source/15usc/1052.html). Forensic linguists have analyzed *Fat Bastard Wine*, *Redskins*, and *Dykes on Bikes*—all initially rejected on propriety grounds (for further discussion, see Butters 2008c: 243–44; Butters 2007b: 336). Even rarer for forensic linguistic consultation is (2) DILUTION—though it is one of potential increasing interest (Butters 2008a: 507–20). In these cases, owners of a famous mark allege that the use of the mark by a lesser-known enterprise weakens the public's perception of the uniqueness of the famous mark—or sullies the mark through disreputable association. For example, in *Starbucks Corp. c. Wolfe's Borough Coffee, Inc.* (477 F.3d 765, 81 U.S.P.Q.2d 1927 [2d Cir. 2007]), the plaintiff alleged dilution of its famous mark in an attempt to prevent the defendant's use of *Mister Charbucks* for its coffee.

The two most frequent areas in consulting and testimony will be analyzed in this chapter: (3) LIKELIHOOD OF CONFUSION and (4) STRENGTH OF THE MARK. The chapter concludes with a discussion of the forensic linguist's ethical responsibilities with respect to the role of trademarks in society.

The two main consulting areas (case studies)

Likelihood of confusion

If consumers seem likely to confuse one mark with a similar one, then the senior mark's owner may attempt to block use of the junior mark. SIMILARITY is categorized as likeness in SIGHT, SOUND, and MEANING; in addition, SIMILARITY OF USE is also pragmatically relevant.

Likelihood of confusion was an issue in *Circuit City Stores, Inc. v. Speedy Car-X, Inc.*, 35 U.S.P.Q.2d 1703 (E.D. Va. 1995), wherein I was consulted by Circuit City's attorneys. Circuit City, having opened several of what it planned as a national chain of used-car stores, began using *CarMax* as the chain's trademark; soon, a long-established automotive repair service named *CAR-X* opposed them in federal court, arguing that *CarMax* and *CAR-X* are so similar that customers would be confused about the ownership of the two enterprises. My goal as consulting linguist was to explain the marks' linguistic similarities and differences in a way that would help the bench-trial judge decide if the likelihood of confusion was so great that *CarMax* should not be allowed to use its mark.

The category of SIGHT

SIGHT takes in the totality of the appearance of a trademark, including also such semiotic features as color, typeface, and design, but most particularly orthography and spelling. SIGHT is especially important when the public's exposure to trademarks is from signage, print-media advertising, television ads, and, of course, on packages.

One complication in *Circuit City* was that *CAR-X* is not always spelled the same way: one also finds *Car-X*, as well as two spellings without a hyphen, one in the firm's website (www.carx.com), the other in a stylized logo (itself a registered trademark which the reader can view on the website) in which the "c" and "a" are lower-case italic letters, in what appears to be a typeface known as *IMPACT*, and the "r" is represented by the well-known symbol for medical prescriptions, an upper-case "R" with the slant leg extended to make an "x" ( ); the words "AUTO SERVICE" fit neatly under the "ca" and the first half of the R, on a line with the "x"; the letters are in black ink against a yellow background, and the entire logo is surrounded by a thick black line that forms a rectangle with rounded edges.

Even so, regardless of which spelling is selected, the beginnings and endings of the two marks are in some sense identical: *Car-X* can be said to be just *CarMax* with the internal hyphen replaced by *-Ma-*. And it is a well-accepted principle of psycholinguistics that the beginnings and endings of words are the most important to recognition and memory:

> There is abundant evidence that the initial portions of words are of crucial importance to word identification. ... [M]emory storage of words assigns greater weight to the two ends of the words than to the middle, and probably particular weight to the initial positions.
>
> (Cutler 1982: 19)

Moreover, *CarMax* and *CAR-X* share four of the six graphemes found in *CarMax* and four of the five found in *CAR-X*. Thus 73% (8/11) are identical—and they are arranged in the same order.

On the other hand, there are major sight differences that serve to distinguish the two marks one from another semiotically. (1) In typeface, CAR_x uses italic Impact and the noticeably eccentric hybrid character, while CarMax uses a heavy roman typeface, perhaps Gill Sans Ultra Bold. (2) The yellow background of the CAR_x logo contrasts with the rich blue of the *CarMax* logo. (3) The CarMax logo has no border, whereas the CAR_x logo has a thick black border. (4) The black letters of the CAR_x logo contrast with yellow letters in the *Car* of CarMax and the white letters of the *Max* portion, which is (5) underlined in a gold broken line. (The reader can view the CarMax logo on the CarMax website www.carmax.com/.)

With respect to SIGHT, then, the two marks display considerable differences as well as similarities. All of the data is important for the consideration of the judge or jury.

The category of SOUND

Each word has two syllables, with a primary stress on the first syllable. Seven phonemes comprise *CarMax*: [kar•mæks]; *CAR-X* has six: [kar•eks] or [kar•ɨks] (depending on style and dialect). The [r] may be deleted in some dialects. Thus, quantificationally, the two marks share 10 phonemes out of 13, or 77% (8 of 12, or 67%, for those dialects with post-vocalic /r/ deletion). Again, the marks phonologically share their beginnings—and endings—and the phonemes are arranged in the same order. Such features could to some degree inhibit speakers' ability to remember which word refers to which business—and hearers might sometimes be unsure which referent was intended in a context where either might be uttered (e.g. *Did you pick up your car at that CarMax/ CAR-X place?*).

However, the pronunciation of *CarMax* also differs from the pronunciation of *CAR-X* in significant ways:

1. *CarMax* always has one more phoneme, [m], than does *CAR-X*.
2. Distinctive features of which [m] is acoustically composed are sharply different from all of the other phonemes in the two words: [m] is the only nasal and the only labial.
3. Physiologically, speakers must close their lips in the middle of uttering *CarMax*, whereas *CAR-X* must be pronounced with the lips open.
4. The second syllable of *CarMax* is pronounced much more loudly and forcefully than the second syllable of *CAR-X*, especially in normal or allegro style.
5. The vowel of the second syllable of *CarMax* differs from the second syllable of *CAR-X* by three distinctive features: [æ] is a low non-tense front vowel, whereas [ɨ] is a high lax central vowel.
6. In many dialects of American English, the [r] will be deleted in *CarMax* but not in *CAR-X*.

These significant, noticeable "sound" differences will act as psycholinguistic agents for distinguishing the trademark and preventing confusion.

Quantificational comparisons and distinctive feature analysis must be reported with prudence. Shuy (2002: 75) speaks in praise of "another linguist, [who] ... very successfully used distinctive feature analysis to show that the sound of 'Little Dolly' were only 13 percent different from those used in the name of his client, 'Little Debby'." However, it is not clear how such figures are related to psychological reality:

- Are some distinctive features more important than others?
- How do feature similarities interact with the location of phonemes in words?
- Are acoustic effects on the hearer's memory different from the effects that differences in the physiological work of uttering has on speakers?

355

Various American court decisions have found all of the following pairs of marks to be confusingly similar, yet the raw percentage of phonemic overlap between them varies considerably:

SMIRNOFF/SARNOFF [smIrnaf]/[sarnaf]	10/13 = 77%
DYPRIN/DIAPARENE [dayprIn]/[dayæpłrin]	12/16 = 75%
SMIRNOFF/SERRANOV [smIrnaf]/[sErłnaf]	10/14 = 71%
SMIRNOFF/SMARKOFF [smIrnaf]/[smarkaf]	10/14 = 71%
AVENT/AVANCE: [łvent]/[łvæns]	6/10 = 60%
PROZAC/HERBROZAC [prozæk]/[hrbrłzæk]	8/14 = 57%
BONAMINE/DRAMAMINE [bonłmin]/[dramłmin]	8/15 = 53%

Also, it may well be that quantifications, especially counts of distinctive features rather than phonemes, may be so complex that juries and judges will be more confused than enlightened. For this reason, Shuy cautions particularly about distinctive-feature counts (2002: 12, 75, 112).

The category of MEANING

Courts generally rely on dictionary definitions for words as important evidence in trademark disputes. However, dictionaries give relatively little information about trademarks per se: even unabridged dictionaries have entries for no more than a small percentage of marks, and dictionaries generally disclaim any explicit authority with respect to the trademark status of the words that they list as entries (Landau 2001: 407–8). It is thus not surprising that neither *CarMax* nor *CAR-X* are found in standard dictionaries. Indeed, they are COINED words—they have no ordinary dictionary meanings in and of themselves.

Courts seek to base likelihood of confusion on the MEANING marks will have to the ordinary persons who are likely to purchase the product or service (hereafter, p/s) to which the mark refers. The meaning of MEANING in the legal context of trademarks includes (1) denotations and connotations and (2) any specific referential association that may have developed between the p/s and a source (i.e. the company offering the p/s for sale). The technical term for the latter association is SECONDARY MEANING, and it is affected by such various factors as the general reliability of the p/s, the market share of the p/s, and the effectiveness of the advertising of the p/s—factors at best only indirectly amenable to linguistic analysis. If secondary meaning is strong enough, the marks are given the technical appellation FAMOUS MARKS.

Apart from secondary meaning, trademarks generally have no ordinary denotations at all (except in the case of exceptionally famous marks, which may acquire a type of denotative meaning by metaphorical extension). However, many marks may have homonyms that are ordinary words (e.g. *Apple/apple*, but not *Exxon*). Thus, a trademark's connotations will depend largely on the denotations and connotations of the words or word-like elements of which it is composed. For some coined words (e.g. *Kodak, Exxon*) there may be only the vaguest of connotations. *CarMax* and *CAR-X*, however, have component parts that themselves are ordinary words (*Car*), morphemes (*Max, -X*) and sememes (R_x), which themselves have denotations and connotations. Thus, the meanings of the composing units adhere to the marks themselves.

A meaning analysis of a trademark thus begins with the dictionary definitions of the component words and morphemes, even if they are only arbitrarily related to the enterprise that the trademark refers to. In the case at hand, *car* has only one clearly relevant meaning, "automobile," and it is found at the beginning of both marks. Thus, it is clear that the two marks have some meaning similarity.

That, however, is where the obvious meaning overlap ends. The linguist must also compare the meanings of *Max* and R_x as used in the respective marks. As is often the case with trademarks, *Max* is not explicitly defined as an ordinary word in standard dictionaries, though they do sometimes list the slang or informal usages *max* and *to the max*, a clipped form of *maximum* (see, for example, the *New Oxford American Dictionary*, s. v. *max*: "*informal* a maximum amount or setting ... at the most"). Thus, the consulting linguist will do well to analyze the term's meaning through independent lexicographical research. This consists of inductively examining the empirical data that a lexicographer would normally consider if a trademark-sense entry were contemplated for a dictionary:

- *CINEMAX* is the second element in the trademark of an American national pay-television channel.
- *D-MAX Imaging Co.* was the name of a desktop publishing firm in Durham, North Carolina.
- *OfficeMax* is the name of an office supply store chain.
- *RE/MAX* is the name of a chain of real estate agencies.
- *T.J.Maxx* is the name of a chain of clothing stores.
- *UMAX* is a name of a computer-equipment manufacturer.

These uses parallel and surely give rise to the connotations that consumers will infer for a mark such as *CarMax*.

As a part of a trade name, then, *MAX* conveys a strong sense that the product or service being offered to the public is au courant and superlative: *CINEMAX* is "the maximum in modern cinema"; *OfficeMax* offers "the best possible up-to-date office furniture and supplies," etc. Similarly, *CarMax* suggests "the best and most state-of-the-art place for cars."

The meaning of the second syllable of *CAR-X* is far less clear, in part because the meaning of *-X* is diffuse, and partly because the CAR-X firm displays the **ca** sememe prominently in its advertising, suggesting that the "X" of *CAR-X* is related to the established symbol for medical prescriptions. In confirmation, an internet search revealed that other businesses use R_x it this way as well, e.g. R_x *Gallery and Wine Bar* (San Francisco) and *ScoreR$_x$* a company that helps people increase their credit scores. The inductive conclusion is clear: speakers of current American English will infer that CAR_x is intended to convey the meaning "car prescriptions"—a place where one would take an automobile for repairs with the same confidence and certainty that one would feel about a pharmacy. Such a meaning accords precisely with the nature of the CAR-X business, which is automobile repairs and service.

Otherwise, the *-X* of *CAR-X* contributes little to the connotative meaning because *X* has many semiotic functions ("ten," "the unknown," a position on a map," "a kiss," "the signature of an illiterate person," "something crossed out"), none of which seems particularly related to cars. This, in itself, separates the final element *Max* of *CarMax* (which has specific meaning) from the final element *-X* of *CAR-X* (which has no specific meaning).

The assignable connotative meaning of *CAR-X* then, is demonstrably distinct from that of *CarMax*, despite the identity of the first element.

Ethics and outcomes

How far a linguist can go in testifying to the ultimate issue is a thorny question, much debated by linguists and not easily resolved (Shuy 2006; Butters 2008b; see also Coulthard 2007). As is generally true in experts' consulting, it is not the job of the linguist to determine whether the scientific facts are legally compelling enough to sustain or deny the lawsuit. That is a decision that only a judge or jury can make; the linguistic evidence is only part of the evidence that is relevant to the outcome of a case. The linguistic expert's goal must be to provide the court with all of the relevant linguistic evidence upon which to base legal decisions.

In *Circuit City*, I testified with a good deal of professional confidence that ordinary consumers would not be very likely to confuse *CarMax* and *CAR-X* if one considered only the linguistic grounds. The trier of fact agreed that, in sight, sound, and especially meaning, the factors that could create substantial confusion among CAR-X's customers were less significant than the factors that made the two marks distinct; furthermore, a pragmatic factor further served to distinguish the two: CarMax sells automobiles; CAR-X services them. Circuit City was allowed to keep using its *CarMax* mark.

Strength of mark

Definitions

Whether a trademark is deemed WEAK or STRONG depends on where it is deemed to fall along a continuum of categories, (1) GENERIC, (2) DESCRIPTIVE, (3) SUGGESTIVE, (4) FANCIFUL, and (5) ARBITRARY, where (1) is the weakest and (4) and (5) are the strongest.

Marks that fall into categories (3)–(5) generally are absolutely protected from use by competitors. FANCIFUL MARKS are coined words made up from morpheme-like material—*Kodak*, for example. ARBITRARY MARKS are genuine words that have no meaning relationship to the enterprises they name (*Apple*, for example, denotes a kind of fruit but as a trademark for a brand of computers and a music-recording company has nothing to do with fruit). Thus, neither FANCIFUL nor ARBITRARY marks have either a denotative or strongly connotative relationship to the products or services they refer to.

SUGGESTIVE marks do not literally denote the products or services offered to the public, but they nonetheless strongly connote the enterprises they refer to. For example, the trademark *Beanie Baby*, a soft, plush, pellet-filled doll, may bring to mind "doll" (from *Baby*), "small" (from the-*y* diminutive ending), and "pellet-filled" *(Beanie)*. Such associations are thought to be a help to the memory of consumers in mentally keeping the brand apart from others. Suggestive marks also frequently create positive associations, as in the names of many sports teams: the Minnesota professional football team is not literally composed of Vikings, but Vikings are legendary for fierceness in battle, and Minnesota is popularly thought to be the home of the descendants of many Scandinavians. *CarMax* contains the suggestive element *Max* and the descriptive element *Car*; the-*X* of *CAR-X* is presumably arbitrary (or perhaps fanciful), whereas the R_x in the *CAR$_x$* logo is suggestive.

DESCRIPTIVE marks merely denote some major aspect of the product or service being offered to the public, as in the *Car* of *CarMax* and *CAR-X*; generally, laudatory terms such as *pure* and *tasty* are also considered descriptive.

Landau (2001: 406) defines GENERIC, as it applies both to lexicography and the law, as: "an ordinary ... term, not for the brand of a thing but for the kind of thing itself." A putative trademark is *generic* if the term is like *aspirin, automobile, theme park,* even (as applied to fruit) *apple*—one that denotes the product or service itself and not the brand name (e.g. *CVS, Chevrolet, Universal Studios, Harry&David's Fruit Gifts*).

Generic marks are so weak that they cannot be trademarks at all for the entities that they denote. The rationale for this is simple: if merchandisers were allowed to own generic terms, then there would be no straightforward way for their competitors to refer to their own products. This would not only be confusing to the purchasing public, but it would also give the owners of the generic mark an unfair advantage in the marketplace. Descriptive marks are also inherently weak, and they can only be legitimate trademarks if it can be demonstrated that they have acquired significant SECONDARY MEANING, that is, that the mark is in no little measure FAMOUS (see SUGGESTIVE marks, below).

Challenging putatively weak marks

Which category a mark falls into is often the subject of litigation, and linguists are frequently engaged to write reports and give testimony in such cases. Solan and Tiersma note,

> morphology can be a helpful tool in trademark disputes. ... [Strength of mark] issues are obviously linguistic questions, and courts deciding trademark cases usually allow linguistic expertise to be taken into consideration.
>
> (Solan and Tiersma 2005: 248n42)

However, the type of linguistic expertise required is much more a matter of practical applied linguistics than theoretical morphology. The forensic linguist is not reanalyzing medieval Celtic verb structure according to the latest redaction of theoretical syntax. Rather, the forensic linguist considers objective, empirical data to focus intensely and in depth upon one or two morphemes using the essential methodology of lexicography:

1. access a relevant and representative body of data;
2. examine the data inductively so as to form conclusions about the meanings of the words in the minds of the persons who created the data.

In strength-of-mark cases, the owner of the senior mark trademark challenges the use or projected use of the competitor's junior mark as INFRINGEMENT. The junior's owner generally claims that the senior mark is either generic or descriptive without secondary meaning.

I wrote a report (in *Steak n Shake Co. v. Burger King Corp.,* 323 F. Supp 2d 983, 985 [E.D. Mo. 2004]) in which the plaintiffs, a chain of fast-food restaurants, had long marketed a type of sandwich that they called a *Steakburger*. Steak n Shake apparently never attempted to register the trademark, but they were able to claim de facto (COMMON LAW) trademark rights because of their long and allegedly exclusive use of *Steakburger* as a trademark. When Burger King began also using *Steakburger* in advertising a new sandwich that they marketed in their fast-food chain, they were almost surely aware of Steak n Shake's use. However, when Steak n Shake brought the suit, Burger King's attorneys successfully defended their junior use of the term by asserting that *steakburger* is a generic term for "burger sandwich made from steak." Therefore, *steakburger* could not be a valid trademark for a sandwich made from beef. Attorneys for Steak n Shake countered that their *Steakburger* is suggestive, or at worst a famous descriptive mark (having significant secondary meaning).

In analyzing *steakburger*, I again made use of dictionaries and lexicographical methodology. In addition, I surveyed the scholarly literature concerning the word hamburger— literature that itself makes use of, and influences, the lexicographical methodology.

The earliest dictionary record of the word *steakburger* that I found was that of the 1961 publication of the second edition of *Webster's New Twentieth Century Dictionary of the English Language, Unabridged,* 2d edn (Publisher's Guild, Inc./World):

> **burger** [from *hamburger*] a combining form meaning *sandwich of ground meat (and),* as in steak*burger,* cheese*burger,* etc. [Slang.]

A similar definition is found in the *Shorter Oxford Dictionary on Historical Principles,* 5th edn, 2002:

> **steak** … Comb. & phrases: **steakburger** a beefburger made of minced steak

These are important because both the definitions describe exactly the sandwich that Steak n Shake calls its *Steakburger,* but without any reference to source: it is a kind of thing, rather than the name of a kind of thing. Moreover, the definitions span a forty-year period, demonstrating a continuity of usage that indicates that the generic status of steakburger has been firmly established for some time. Finally, the 1961 definition treats *steakburger* as not only generic, but exemplary of an entire class of ground meat sandwiches using the suffix-*burger,* of which *steakburger* is but one of many.

The lexicographical record is amplified if one looks at specialized lexicographical literature. Thus, Pound (1938: 157) wrote, "The ending of 'hamburger' is having good success irradiating itself. *Cheeseburgers,* made of ham and cheese, and *chickenburgers* may now be had in many dining places as well as at highway stands." A year later, Arnold Williams (1939: 154) cited, the following *burger* words that he had recorded in "a notebook kept on travels about the country": *chickenburger, cheeseburger, clamburger, lamburger, rabbitburger, nutburger, porkburger, Wimpyburger, goonburger,* and *demonburger.*

A multitude of other examples can be cited from scholarly literature and from more specialized dictionaries in which the morpheme-*burger* appears and is always used in a totally generic way. The meaning of the compounds is assumed to be transparent from the denotative component parts. Source is never identified.

Another source of evidence that the courts find persuasive in genericness cases is that of third-party use—cases in which the senior mark is clearly used generically by competitors and the public at large. A search of newspapers, magazines, and the internet from the 1930s on, found an abundance of examples in which *steakburger* was used to denote a kind of sandwich, without any indication that the users intended to use it in reference to their own particular brand. Such evidence overwhelmingly indicates that *steakburger* is generic, and, even if it did not, there could scarcely be secondary meaning if the only source of identification of *steakburger* and Steak n Shake is Steak n Shake's own advertising. Moreover, Steak n Shake's claims of historic exclusive (and original coinage) disappeared in the face of the linguistic record.

In the trial in which I participated, Burger King prevailed. The judge declared *steakburger* to be generic as a name for sandwiches and indicated agreement that the linguistic history demonstrated that it was generic from the beginning. Interestingly, Burger King seems to use *steakburger* sparingly in its recent advertisements, and only as a generic term that characterize their "Steak House Burger" sandwiches (www.restaurantnewsresource.com/article31839.html). And Steak n Shake continues to advertise "Our famous Steakburger" and to indicate that they claim common-law trademark rights to the term ("STEAKBURGER™": www.steaknshake.com/menu/burger.asp), even if they are unable to register the brand because of its apparent genericness.

Genericide

Steakburger has always been generic; if no litigation had taken place before *Burger King,* it was because nobody ever chose to use the term in a way that Steak n Shake found threatening enough to pursue in court. In a different kind of genericness case, the junior mark claimants assert that, while the senior mark may have at one time been strong, it has been a victim of its own success, becoming generic over a period of time. Many trademarks have gone this route (sometimes referred to as GENERICIDE): *aspirin, escalator,* and *trampoline,* for example (at least in the United States). When speakers sometimes use *Xerox* to refer in general to photocopies, photocopying machines, and the general process of photocopying, without regard to whether they are actually referring to products manufactured by the Xerox firm, they are using the brand name as if it were generic. If the general population of photocopy product users ever comes to believe that *Xerox* is not a brand name, then Xerox will likewise lose its right to its own brand. Similarly, *Hoover* as a term associated with vacuum cleaners is recognized primarily as a brand name in the United States, but in the UK it has become genericized to the extent that, in common speech, it is often used as a verb for the process of using a vacuum cleaner.

The law makes a distinction between the commercial meanings that typical consumers actually attach to a trademark and the shorthand (or, to use the technical linguistic term, SYNECDOCHICAL) uses that a consumer may make of that trademark. A trademark linguist may need to tease out from the data whether a trademark has truly undergone legal genericide or is merely exhibiting symptoms of synecdochical use.

The function of trademarks in modern society: uses and abuses of linguistics

Although the ideal of "freedom of speech" is thought of as a fundamental right, all societies impose penalties for a variety of verbal civil and criminal acts: defamation, obscenity, sexual harassment, perjury, forgery, extortion, illegal solicitation, inciting a riot, offering or accepting a bribe, treasonously repeating state secrets, threatening another with harm to life or property.

Even so, some people view the existence of proprietary interest in language as an insult to free speech rights and take exception to laws that allow persons to "own" words, phrases, and logos—even for the limited purpose of brand identification. For example, the media were amusedly sardonic when reporting that a Canadian teenager, Michael Rowe, had received warnings that he must stop using the web address www.MikeRoweSoft.com, which he had registered as a domain name, because it infringed upon the proprietary rights of the Microsoft Corporation (Sieberg 20 January 2004). Not wishing to seem like greedy bullies, Microsoft reportedly tempered its initial demands after Rowe's situation was widely publicized, offering Rowe "an Xbox with some games," which he reportedly accepted (Kotadia 2004; see also Wikipedia 2008). Clankie summarizes this highly negative concept of trademarks:

> That a common language expression can be withdrawn from use for no other purpose than financial profit is, in my opinion, a far more criminal action than is another company actually using it in violation of the law.
>
> Clankie (2002: 160)

Clankie's extreme condemnation too easily reduces trademark ownership to naked capitalist greed, failing to consider that a trademark worth fighting over is probably as much a focus of "financial profit" for the infringer as it is for the infringed-upon. The simplistic view that trademarks are a "criminal" insult to free speech ignores positive and important values of brand identification in modern society. Historically, trademarks originally became the object of legal protection in large part to shield honest businesses from unfair competition. If an upstart competitor were allowed to use an established respected brand name, the upstarts would appropriate for free the valuable reputation of the senior mark's owners. The senior owner would have no control over the quality of the upstart's product; inferior items sold by an upstart under the senior name would harm the reputation of the senior name owner and even facilitate an infringer's lower pricing. Moreover, reliable brand names are useful to consumers, who employ the reputation of established marks when making choices between competing products and services.

Misgivings about proprietary language are voiced as well by forensic linguists and legal scholars in more sophisticated critiques of potential free-speech implications of trademark law. Referring to a famous case (*McDonald's Corporation v. Quality Inns, International, Inc.* 695 F. Supp. 198, 215–16 (D. Md. 1988.) in which he testified for the defendants (wherein a world-famous restaurant chain prevented another large company from using *McSleep* as a hotel trademark), an eminent forensic linguist writes, "one can still wonder why it is that the expenditure of money can determine who can have ownership of a word, much less a prefix [*Mc*]" (Shuy 2002: 109); "expenditure of money" refers to advertising outlays used to create in the public mind a linguistically arbitrary association between a single bound morpheme, *Mc-*, and the goods offered for sale in fast-food restaurants.

One answer to Shuy's rhetorical question may simply be that there seems little social benefit in creating a system that would make it easier for one megacompany (Quality Inns) to use a morpheme that another megacompany (McDonald's) has long used as a product identifier. Moreover, altering the rules that currently govern trademarks and advertising would surely have disruptive effects that Shuy does not consider.

But Shuy (2002: 2) also has in mind a more profound, related, challenge, one that is not totally unrelated to Mike Rowe's encounter with Microsoft. Elsewhere, Shuy points out the danger to free speech that arises when trademark litigation (or even the threat of it) is used as a means of asserting "authority over what can be said or written, and [what can] not"—a form of censorship. For example, dictionary writers have long struggled with trademark lawyers' threats of lawsuits:

> Some trademark owners are hostile to any inclusion of trademarks in a dictionary, [demanding that trademarks be] ... entered in capitalized form and identified as

trademarks. ... Almost all trademark owners are concerned to have their trade-marks identified [in dictionaries] as trademarks, and lawyers often try to specify to lexicographers the exact form which they find acceptable. ... Trademark owners or their lawyers [make] ... importunate demands, even threats [of legal action]. ... The dictionary editor must do battle to include any [registered] trademarks, and he is under great pressure to distort the facts of usage.

(Landau 2001: 406–8)

The lawyers are merely trying to protect their clients' trademarks, but in so doing they may inadvertently be agents of censorship of the honest, professional work of lexico-graphers (or journalists, who may also sometimes be the recipients of similar warnings from attorneys). Of course, it is unlikely that dictionary makers could actually be sued for freely using a word in a way that a trademark owner might dislike (Richardson 2004: online 12). For example, as early as 2003 the McDonald's Corporation announced their objection to the *Merriam-Webster Dictionary*'s new entry, *McJob*, which was defined—on the basis of actual usage—as "a low-paying job that requires little skill and provides little opportunity for advancement" (*BBC News* 2003; *Merriam-Webster Online Dictionary* 2009). Similar pressure was brought to bear in the UK in 2007, when the *Oxford English Dictionary* added a similar definition (BBC News 2007). *McJob* is not actually a trademark of McDonald's Corporation, but, as we have seen above, McDonald's were victorious in asserting proprietary trademark rights in the USA to the *Mc* morpheme. Even so, despite McDonald's effort to change the lexicographer's conclusions about the public's percep-tion of the connotations of *McJob* (but no actual lawsuits for trademark infringement or dilution), the dictionary definitions remain today exactly as they were in 2003 and 2007 (see *Oxford English Dictionary* Online 2009).

Still, legal pressure has without question functioned as a kind of de facto censorship based on trademark law, as Landau attests. Citing Shuy's censorship warnings, Richardson, notes cases where trademark owners brought suit merely because, they

[were] unready to allow uses of their trade marks that they believe could reflect badly on them, or are controversial, or lie too far outside the scope of their activ-ities, no matter their overall social value (and including cases where those who wish to use will pay).

(Richardson 2004: online 11, 27)

For example, the *Star Wars* mark owners sued to prevent its use in a critique of government military policies, claiming "trademark infringement, unfair competition, misappropriation, [and] disparagement" (*Lucasfilm, Ltd v. High Frontier* 622 F Supp 931 [1985]). The case was dismissed, but, as Richardson notes, even if "plaintiffs generally fail in legal terms, the worry is [that] their ability to threaten will be enough to stop the practice"—the expense of defending one's linguistic usage in court "raises the spectra of unfree speech in a society that generally values free speech and may even provide for it in its Constitution," a point that Shuy makes as well (2002: 13–14).

Moreover, such legal pressures do not always fail. Pullum (2004a, 2004b, 2004c) comments on how dilution litigation can restrain the use of trademarks for small businesses (a threat from the giant Lexus-Nexus caused a small linguistics start-up to drop the use of their chosen brand name, *Lexeme*). Richardson also reports on *MGM-Pathe Communications Co v. The Pink Panther Patrol* 774 F Supp 869 (1991), wherein a public safety campaign mounted by a gay community organization was forced to changed its name (identical to that of a famous MGM-owned movie) because the court

> held [it] too likely confuse the public about possible sponsorship (which the First Amendment would not exempt) irrespective of the defendant's political motives and the absence of evidence of actual confusion.

The problem of the rich using their wealth to manipulate the legal system to censor or otherwise bully the poor is characteristic of a wide variety of types of civil cases, not just trademark litigation. Even so, the forensic linguist has a citizen's right to be concerned about such issues and even propose changes in the law (though Landau, Pullum, Shuy, and Richardson do not), and the discussion of these and other ethical issues is certainly a proper subject for trademark linguistic theory. As for individual cases, as Shuy points out in a different book (2006: 123), "working on a case does not mean that you have to agree with or support the accusations or positions of the clients on either side"—and, furthermore, forensic linguists are free to "avoid such cases" as their "own moral reasons" may dictate, on the rare occasions where one is asked to use one's forensic linguistic expertise on behalf of a cause that one may disapprove of.

Further reading

The foundational work on trademark forensic linguistics remains R. Shuy's 2002 book, *Linguistic Battles in Trademark Disputes* (see also the "Trademarks" chapter in his 2008 *Fighting Over Words: Language and Civil Law Cases*). The portions of S. Landau's 2001 book *Dictionaries: The Art and Craft of Lexicography* (2nd edn) offer invaluable insights into lexicographical methodology and practice. Clankie's book presents the best list of genericized (and pseudogenericized) brand names in print. For specific discussion of genericness issues, see R. Butters and J. Westerhaus, "Linguistic change in words one owns: how trademarks become 'generic'" (2004). Concerning dilution, see R. Butters, "A Linguistic Look at Trademark Dilution" (2008).

Legal cases cited

Circuit City Stores, Inc. v. Speedy Car-X, Inc., 35 U.S.P.Q.2d 1703 [E.D. Va. 1995].
Lucasfilm, Ltd v. High Frontier 622 F Supp 931 [1985].
McDonald's Corporation v. Quality Inns, International, Inc. 695 F. Supp. 198, 215–16 [D. Md. 1988].
MGM-Pathe Communications Co v. The Pink Panther Patrol 774 F Supp 869 [1991].
Starbucks Corp. v. Wolfe's Borough Coffee, Inc. (477 F.3d 765, 81 U.S.P.Q.2d 1927 [2d Cir. 2007]).
Steak n Shake Co. v. Burger King Corp., 323 F. Supp 2d 983, 985 [E.D. Mo. 2004].
WSM, Incorporated, Appellant, v. Dennis E. Hilton and Country Shindig Opry, Inc., Appellees, 1984 U.S. App.724 F.[2d 1320].

24

Consumer product warnings

Composition, identification, and assessment of adequacy

Bethany K. Dumas

Introduction

Definitions

Warnings, whether labeled as such or not, are generally considered to be

> statements about future events or states that are not in the hearer's best interest, and which are uttered in situations in which it is not obvious to both the hearer and the speaker that the event will occur or that the state will transpire.
>
> (Searle 1969: 67)

Warnings are thus like *promises* and *threats* in that they refer to possible future actions (Fraser 1975, 1998). They are different from *promises* in that the future action is not in the hearer's best interest; they are different from *threats*, a special type of warning (Fraser 1975, 1998), in that the future action will be the result of the hearer's actions, not the action of the one doing the threatening. I have suggested that evidence of the close similarity between *warnings* and *promises*, if we categorize a *threat* as a special type of *warning*, is illustrated by the frequent occurrence in informal conversation of the joking rejoinder, "Is that a threat or a promise?" (Dumas 1992: 268).

Warnings may be either direct or indirect and either literal or nonliteral. That is, many warnings are highly context-dependent, and their interpretation may depend upon lesser or greater amounts of inferencing. They can also be categorized as categorical warnings or hypothetical warnings. Searle suggests that categorical warnings fulfill the function of advising, not requesting. Such warnings inform hearers or readers that certain results will follow certain modes of behavior, but the warnings do not attempt to get a given individual to modify his or her behavior. An example, tongue-in-cheek, is a statement on a menu that says, "Eating Any Selection From The Enclosed MENU Can Be Dangerously Habit Forming!"

Hypothetical warnings are phrased in such a way that they fulfill the function of requesting. The basic logical structure for a hypothetical warning is "If X, then Y," though the *if* and *then* elements may be implicit, rather than explicit. Thus an example might be "Give me your money or I'll shoot," a statement that is generally regarded as a demand that the individual spoken to turn over money. (It is also a special type of warning, a threat.) Warnings can also be categorized as *imperative* or *informational* (Tiersma 2002 and see below). Categorical warnings are generally informative, while hypothetical warnings are at least partly imperative.

It has long been recognized that all these categories are fuzzy. Further, there is overlapping among the sets of categories. Vanderveken (1990: 174) points out and Tiersma (2002: 363) affirms that the speech act of warning is "systematically ambiguous between an assertive and directive use" and shares features of both the informative/categorical and imperative/hypothetical styles. Below are examples of real-life warnings used in my earlier research (Dumas 1992: 277–78); I include them here with new category labels in order to illustrate the complexity and ambiguity of the classification schemes.

Example 1. *Take heed, sweet soul.*
—nonliteral, indirect, hypothetical, imperative

Example 2. *Let me tell you something straight. When you go and snitch to anyone that we had anything to do with this, you'll find a snitch tattoo on your forehead.*
—literal, direct, categorical, informative

Example 3. *Komsing Causes Lung Cancer, Heart Disease, Emphysema, and May Complicate Pregnancy*
—literal, indirect, hypothetical, informative

Example 4. *Warning: The Surgeon General Has Determined That Komsing Is Hazardous to Your Health*
—literal, direct, categorical, informative

Example 5. *This is the final warning. I have acted as a gentleman should, have given you ample time to consider my demands before an unfortunate incident occurs. You have twenty-four hours to introduce a bill in the Congress of the United States of America to return to me, as the rightful heir to James Smithson, the Smithsonian Institution and its belongings. Time has run out, sirs.*
—literal, direct, hypothetical, imperative/informational

Legal requirements

When used on consumer products, warning labels are often designed to meet specific legal requirements. Warnings on US tobacco products, for instance, must comply with specific wording requirements; further, manufacturers of tobacco products such as cigarettes sold in the US must use six rotating warnings. As Tiersma (2002) points out, the kinds of consumer products generally involved in litigation about warnings and other safety information are those that serve a useful function, but also have "potential risks or dangers associated with their use" (p. 54). Such cases thus fall within the legal standards for product liability law, a fairly new development in law (Tiersma 2002: 54; Shuy 2008).

As Tiersma (2002) documents, the legal standards for warnings are more difficult to apply when products are intended for use by non-native speakers of English with limited proficiency. Symbols, pictograms, and color can be used to assist in achieving adequacy, but symbols can be misunderstood by members of different cultures, so they must be used with care. More research is needed with respect to the issue of warnings addressed to non-native speakers of English (or any local language).

Warnings have been used and known by speakers of the English language since at least the fourteenth century. We thus have a situation in which a common, ordinary term and concept, *warning*, is put to a special use where legal requirements in product liability law are concerned. This chapter will explore the nature and function of warnings in product liability law, describe and evaluate techniques for assessing and increasing adequacy of such warnings, and suggest strategies for continuing to improve warning and other safety information adequacy.

Nature and function of warnings and warning labels

Nature of warnings and warning labels

In order to assess warning adequacy and effectiveness, it is necessary to recognize the difference between a *warning* and a *warning label*. Government agencies often prescribe the wording of some product warnings, and the prescriptions often specify that consumer products must carry specific warning labels such as *Danger!*, WARNING, or *Caution*. However, for various reasons, including the fact that industries often lobby successfully to have their preferred wording used in legislation about warning labels, statements labeled as warnings may actually be other kinds of speech acts. For instance, one of the rotating warnings required on cigarette packages reads thus: "SURGEON GENERAL'S WARNING: Quitting Smoking Now Greatly Reduces Serious Risks to Your Health."

On its surface, the text suggests that it is a promise, not a warning. In spite of the label **WARNING**, the text of the message suggests that good will result if the one being warned quits smoking. The text does, of course, imply a warning, a warning that might be worded thus: "SURGEON GENERAL'S WARNING: Continuing to Smoke Greatly Increases Serious Risks to Your Health." However, a strong argument can be made that if we are serious about advising consumers about health risks we should reduce reliance on such inferencing.

It is also necessary to recognize the difference between *imperative* and *informational* warnings, between warnings like *Do Not Climb Beyond This Point* and *Climbing Beyond This Point May Result in Injury and Death*. As Tiersma (2002) points out (citing Fraser 1998 and Vanderveken 1990), all warnings contain both a bit of a directive (even if it is indirect, as above) and some information. One question needing further research is whether one style is more effective than the other. There is probably not a single answer, and Tiersma is probably right when he suggests that some consumer products, including cigarettes, probably need warnings that are both imperative and informational, perhaps something like "*do not smoke cigarettes; smoking can kill you.*" He is also probably right when he suggests that "Many governments will balk at the imperative element, however, given the tax revenues that derive from smoking" (Tiersma 2002: 64).

And certainly private interest groups sometimes lobby against what are perceived to be effective consumer product warnings. Such lobbying is frequent where Congressional action is involved. The interests of private interest groups, as I have previously pointed out (Dumas 1992), are often at odds with those of the average consumer, and such groups often have enormous sums of money at their disposal. One such group is the

Tobacco Institute, the lobbying arm of the tobacco industry. The wording of cigarette package warnings in the USA has always been the result of a compromise between Congressional proposals and successful lobbying efforts of the Tobacco Institute and other private groups.

The very existence of lobbying efforts by private interest groups suggests that there is some general knowledge about what constitutes an adequate warning—or at least that many individuals assume that they know what constitutes an adequate, i.e. effective warning. And linguists are in general agreement about what constitutes an adequate warning, even though there may not be complete agreement about the effectiveness of warnings that are more informative than imperative. My own position is that hypothetical warnings are more effective than categorical warnings and that, as Tiersma suggests, the best warnings should be both informational and imperative. I also agree with Tiersma that imperative warnings are better when it is not possible to provide both informational and imperative language.

Functions of warnings and warning labels

In general, warnings and warning labels have a variety of functions. They sometimes seem to serve primarily merely to call attention to items, often for comic effect. For instance, a few years ago, cartoons showed warning labels on raw eggs, stating that they contain cholesterol. And in a cartoon strip, a child was questioned about why she was eating only French fries for lunch. She replied that if they were dangerous there would be a warning on the side of each one. Equally revealing are the annual results of the Wacky Warning Label Contest (conducted by Michigan Lawsuit Abuse Watch, M-LAW, and designed to reveal how lawsuits, and concern about lawsuits seem to have created a need for common sense warnings on products). The first-place winner in 2005 was a toilet brush, an item for cleaning the inside of a toilet, which warned: "Do not use for personal hygiene"; another winner that year was a popular scooter for children that warned, "This product moves when used" (www.mlaw.org/wwl/pastwinners.html). The 2007 Grand Prize went to a label on a small tractor that warns, "Danger! Avoid Death" (www.mlaw.org/wwl/).

But the primary function of warnings and warning labels in the legal context is to inform of and reduce risk. For a warning on a product to be adequate, it must get the attention of the intended user and must convey to the product user comprehensible information about potential risks and methods of avoiding then. My earlier analyses of consumer product warnings were conducted on the basis of three general guidelines for consumer product warnings that insure that they come to the attention of the user and provide information about both risks and how to avoid them. They need to be displayed on products which would be unreasonably dangerous without such warnings. They need to be directed to the ultimate users of the product and to any individuals who might be expected to come into contact with it. And they need to be able to (1) catch the attention of a reasonably prudent person in the circumstances of use, (2) be understandable, and (3) convey a fair indication of the nature and extent of the potential danger to the individual.

These functions of warnings were suggested by Shuy:

1. Name the hazard or risk.
2. Explain how to avoid the hazard or risk.
3. Explain what to do if injury occurs.

(Shuy 1998b: 171)

In quoting Shuy 1998b, Tiersma (2002: 64) points out that both Shuy and the American National Standards Institute (ANSI) recognize implicitly the dual function of warnings in that they require language about both the risk and methods of avoiding risk.

More recently, Shuy has provided this statement of the function of consumer product warnings and warning labels:

> Warnings ... should identify and describe the nature and danger of the risk. Then they should tell the reader how to avoid it. Finally they should communicate those things in clear and understandable language.
>
> (Shuy 2008: 72)

There is this general agreement that warnings have a dual function, but it is less clear how those dual functions can best be accomplished; the topic is addressed in the following section.

Warning adequacy

Warnings on cigarette packages

My initial research on consumer product warnings began in 1985 with the specific goals of identifying (1) the legal issues involved in cigarette warning litigation, and (2) the issues of warning adequacy from the point of view of both linguistic and human factors analysis. My research began after I received a telephone request from a local attorney to research the adequacy of cigarette warnings. I replied that I would have to do some preliminary work before I could tell him whether I thought I would be useful to him in a case against R. J. Reynolds Tobacco Company (*Roysdon v. R. J. Reynolds Tobacco Co.*, 623 F. Supp. 1189 [E. D. Tn. 1986]).

In my initial literature search, I discovered that there were two lines of research, one by linguists (e.g. Searle 1969; Fraser 1975) and one by human factors analysts (e.g. Lehto and Miller 1986; Miller and Lehto 1987). The linguists had focused on discourse analysis and speech act identification, while the human factors analysts had focused on such issues as type size, placement, and the general visibility of warning labels, as well as the usefulness of graphic images. I drew on both in planning my own empirical research.

I also familiarized myself with the legislative history of warning label requirements on cigarette packages and with the role of the Federal Trade Commission (FTC) in that history. I also examined some federally mandated warning labels used on prescription drugs. Finally, I analyzed the six cigarette warnings in order to identify potential problems with content and readability and to formulate hypotheses for research. I studied the legislative history of the warning label requirements in order to discover the factors which had been identified as important by the drafters. As I studied, I learned that required warnings have usually been significantly weaker than those initially proposed. Legislation mandating use of the original (1965) cigarette package warning "Caution: Cigarette Smoking May Be Hazardous to Your Health" had the effect of preempting a proposed FTC Trade Regulation Rule that would have required all cigarette packages and advertisements to warn that "Cigarette Smoking is dangerous to health and may cause death from cancer and other diseases" (The Trade Regulation Rule for the Prevention of Unfair or Deceptive Advertising and Labeling of Cigarettes in Relation to the

Health Hazards of Smoking). Had Congress not preempted that requirement, the very first federally mandated warning would have mentioned specific negative consequences of smoking cigarettes (specific diseases) and would have specified that smoking is dangerous, not merely hazardous.

Later the FTC proposed a modified version of the warning, which, had it been adopted, would have required all cigarette packages and advertisements to carry this message: "Warning: Cigarette Smoking Is Dangerous to Health and May Cause Death From Cancer, Coronary Heart Disease, Chronic Bronchitis, Pulmonary Emphysema, and Other Diseases" (34 Fed. Reg. § 7919 [1969]). Sadly, Congress amended the text to read: "Warning: The Surgeon General Has Determined That Cigarette Smoking Is Dangerous To Your Health" (15 U.S.C. §§ 1331 et seq., 1970).

Since then four rotational warnings, still in current use, were adopted. Again, the impetus for change seems to have come from the FTC. A May 1981 FTC Staff Report on the Cigarette Advertising Investigation (Staff Report) sets out the reasons why that agency thought the 1970 warning was ineffective. The first factors, identified on the basis of common sense, were (1) overexposure (the warning was "worn out"), (2) lack of novelty (it contained no new information), (3) the abstract and general nature of the wording, and (4) the lack of personal relevance of the warning. Also, the unchanging size and shape of the 1970 warning were felt to contribute to its ineffectiveness. Later market research surveys reported by the FTC suggested additionally that (1) if warnings were to be effective, they should be short (one idea per warning), simple, and direct; and (2) disease-specific warnings, that is, those listing specific diseases as possible consequences of smoking, are far more effective than non–disease-specific warnings.

The proposal to use a rotational warning system evolved partly as a way to address the four problems already cited. The FTC recommended that the rotational warnings should be selected in accord with four criteria: (1) medical accuracy, (2) demonstrable filling of a gap in consumer knowledge about health hazards, (3) intelligibility, and (4) ability to "prompt consumers to think about the health hazards of smoking" (Staff Report pp. 5–33). Sample warnings prepared by the FTC meet all those criteria. Representative ones include the following:

1. WARNING: Smoking causes death from cancer, heart attacks and lung disease.
2. CARBON MONOXIDE: Cigarette smoke contains carbon monoxide and other poison gases.
3. WARNING: Smoking may be addictive.
4. LIGHT SMOKING: Even a few cigarettes a day are dangerous.

Again, we find the same pattern of FTC-proposed warnings mentioning specific negative consequences of smoking, followed by Congressionally promulgated warnings which mention fewer or weaker specific negative consequences of smoking. The four rotating warnings currently required are a good deal weaker and certainly less comprehensive than the first ones proposed by the FTC.

I also examined some federally mandated warning labels used on prescription drugs. Most of the warnings were brief, appear to be medically accurate and certainly filled gaps in my own knowledge about health hazards. They were generally intelligible and, as a consumer, I felt that they would prompt me to think about health hazards. Most striking was the use of graphic symbols (e.g. automobiles, outlines of faces) and color contrast. It seemed obvious that warning label designers could comply with the FTC-proposed criteria and that the resulting warnings could be medically accurate, fill gaps in consumer knowledge about health hazards, be intelligible and "prompt consumers to think about the health hazards of smoking."

My empirical research was carried out by means of written categorization, rank-ordering, and paraphrase experiments, as well as rapid and in-depth anonymous interviews. On the basis of the pilot study, I concluded that there was

> strong evidence for the existence of objective criteria by means of which the relative adequacy of warnings on cigarette packages [could] be assessed and that those objective criteria [were] for the most part not characteristic of present or past cigarette package warnings.
>
> (Dumas 1992: 262–63)

I further suggested that warnings differ by degree and that consumers show some uniformity in classifying warnings as strong or weak and that strong warnings generally have at least some of the following characteristics, while weak ones lack one or more of these characteristics.

1. They are often formulated as hypothetical warnings or contain strong warning words like *POISON*.
2. They mention specific possible negative consequences and lack such modal qualifiers as *may* and *could*.
3. They are easy to see.
4. They are written in simple syntax and in ordinary, everyday language.

Federally mandated cigarette package warnings display characteristics of weak warnings: (a) qualifying language (e.g. the modal auxiliaries *may* and *can*), (b) unusual syntax (e.g. the double-*ing* construction as in *Quitting smoking now*, and (c) technical and semi-technical vocabulary (e.g. *fetal injury*, *carbon monoxide*). The warnings lack significant information (What are the precise dangers? Who will be affected? To what extent?). The warning labels are hard to read because of their position on the side of the package, their small type size and the fact that they often appear in hard-to-read color combinations (e.g. gold on red).

Space limitations constitute another problem. Later research by graduate students reported that some pregnant women thought that Low Birth Weight was a desirable result of smoking. It was unclear whether that was because they interpreted the statement to mean that their weight would be lower at birth or that having a baby weighing less would be desirable. Attempting to propose alternative wordings makes it clear that some problems inherent in the warning would take more words to clear up than there is room for on the package. The usual need for brevity is a serious obstacle to the formulation of adequate warnings. An informationally adequate warning might read thus: "Smoking by pregnant women may cause injury to the baby before birth, as well as dangerous health problems resulting from the baby's being born prematurely or underweight." Also, there is some evidence that two of the present rotating warnings have the effect of weakening the effectiveness of the one disease-specific warning in current use.

These were my recommendations:

1. Either formulate the warnings as hypothetical or use strong conventional warning labels like POISON.
2. Avoid unnecessary qualifying language, e.g. the modal auxiliaries *may* and *can*.

371

3. List specific undesirable consequences of unsafe behavior.
4. Make the warnings conspicuous in all ways, e.g. color contrast, type size, and position on product.
5. Write the warnings in simple syntax and in ordinary vocabulary.
6. Include specific information about negative consequences on each label in a rotational series.
7. Do not narrow the target population by addressing specific labels to different portions of that population (e.g. pregnant women).
8. When considering the use of rotating warnings, consider that differences in the strength of individual warnings may have the effect of weakening stronger warnings.
9. Field-test all proposed warnings. (This step would appear to go without saying, but, given the history of proposed federally mandated warnings, it is clear that it does not.)

(Dumas 1992: 300–301)

Shortly before the trial, I was able to obtain a copy of the Confidential Version of the 1981 Federal Trade Commission Staff Report on the Cigarette Advertising Investigation, a document that revealed that the Tobacco Institute had conducted research similar to that I had just conducted and had used the results to lobby for changes in proposed new cigarette warnings.

I testified at trial in the *Roysdon v. R. J. Reynolds* case, but I was not allowed to testify as to the ultimate issue, i.e. whether the warnings on cigarette packages are or have in the past been adequate to inform consumers about the health risks of smoking. That is because shortly before trial Judge Thomas G. Hull of the Eastern District of Tennessee, the presiding judge, ruled that the federally mandated warnings on cigarette packages are adequate as a matter of law. This ruling had the effect of removing the issue from consideration. In my testimony, I described my research methods, summarized my conclusions about how warning labels are perceived by consumers, and summarized published information about how the Tobacco Institute had conducted research into how warning labels are perceived, prior to lobbying Congress about the wording of current cigarette package warnings.

Further, at the end of the plaintiff's presentation (including my testimony), Judge Hull dismissed the suit, ruling that the plaintiff had made no case. He gave two reasons for doing so: (1) the federal statute on cigarette package labeling had preempted state common-law actions based on alleged inadequacies, and (2) common knowledge about tobacco was such that cigarettes are not unreasonably dangerous. The plaintiff appealed, but the Sixth Circuit upheld the ruling of the trial court, stating that the smoker's claim under state law, based on the tobacco company's failure to provide adequate warnings, was preempted where the warnings required by the Cigarette Labeling and Advertising Act, 15 U.S.C.S. §§ 1331–41, were given. The district court directed a verdict for the tobacco company because the smoker failed to establish a prima facie case that the cigarettes were defective or unreasonably dangerous. The court held that a "defective condition" was one that that rendered a product unsafe for normal or anticipatable handling and consumption, Tenn. Code Ann. § 29-28-102(2). Since, there was no evidence that the use of the cigarettes presented risks greater than those known to be associated with smoking, the court held that no reasonable jury could find that they were defective in the sense that they were improperly manufactured or contained dangerous impurities. Extensive public information regarding the risks of smoking precluded a jury question as to whether the cigarettes were unreasonably dangerous (*Roysdon v. R.J. Reynolds Tobacco Co.*, 623 F.Supp. 1189 [E.D. Tn. 1986]).

The ultimate outcome of this case was that the Sixth Circuit Court affirmed the dismissal of the smoker's claim, holding that the failure to warn claim was preempted, and affirmed the order directing a verdict for the tobacco company. The appellate court held that the cigarettes presented no greater risks than risks associated with smoking, and so were not defective. The court also held that the availability of extensive public information about the risks of smoking precluded asking a jury whether the cigarettes were unreasonably dangerous (*Roysdon v. R.J. Reynolds Tobacco Company*, 849 F.2d 230 [6th Cir. 1988], rehearing denied 1988). The plaintiff did not appeal to the Supreme Court.

Warnings on a manufacturing product

A few years later, I was asked to evaluate the adequacy of both warnings and safety information contained in Material Safety Data Sheets (MSDS), safety information statements that often accompany industrial products. Such statements have the potential to convey much more safety information than can be printed on a product label. In two 1990 cases, *Whitis v. Loctite Corporation* and *Davis v. Loctite Corporation*, plaintiffs were workers who developed disabling contact dermatitis; they alleged that the cause was a glue product, Loctite RC/609, used on the assembly line, that was manufactured by the defendant corporation Loctite and furnished to the manufacturing company.

I began my research with photocopies of warning labels on the glue containers and of the MSDS, the *American National Standard Guide for Classifying and Labeling Epoxy Products According to Their Hazardous Potentialities* (1978) (ANSI Standard) and medical reports on the effects of Loctite RC/609 on the human body and also of the medical conditions of the plaintiffs. Although medical causality was, of course, not within my area of expertise, I was asked to assess whether the warnings were adequate to warn potential users of severe and possibly disabling dermatitis: whether the MSDS adequately warned employers that use of the glue could result in disabling contact dermatitis; to take precautions with employees; and to give additional warnings to employees, including the information that using vinyl gloves and rubber finger cots might not be adequate protection.

The following labels appeared on various sizes of glue containers:

CAUTION: MAY IRRITATE SENSITIVE SKIN. Contains methacrylic ester. Wash after skin contact. KEEP AWAY FROM CHILDREN. [found on the back of one container]

CAUTION: MAY IRRITATE SENSITIVE SKIN. READ CAUTION ON BACK LABEL. [found on the front of one container]

CAUTION: Contains methacrylic ester. Wash after skin contact. KEEP AWAY FROM CHILDREN. [found on the back of the container which directed the user to the back of the container]

The language on the latter two labels contains a total of seven sequenced information chunks (Shuy 1990b) or idea units (Chafe 1985). They read thus:

CAUTION: MAY IRRITATE SENSITIVE SKIN. READ CAUTION ON BACK LABEL.

CAUTION: Contains methacrylic ester.
Wash after skin contact.
KEEP AWAY FROM CHILDREN.

The warning label on the front of the container functions primarily for reference value. It mentions the possibility of a harmful effect following its use, then directs the reader to a second label. Unfortunately, the second label, on the back of the container, is not much more informative. It again mentions the possibility of skin irritation, but says nothing about severe, even disabling dermatitis. I suggested that a highly informative warning might read something like this:

> WARNING! IF you handle this product without wearing gloves, you risk DISFIGUREMENT and DISABILITY. ALWAYS WEAR GLOVES WHEN HANDLING THIS PRODUCT.

Further, one of the statements, including the technical term *methacrylic ester*, is probably meaningless to the average consumer or worker, probably meaning less even than *carbon monoxide*, prominent in one of the rotating cigarette warnings.

There is a great deal of highly technical information in the MSDS as well as information about possible health risks and recommended precautions. That information is not prominently displayed and there is no evidence that the employer is expected to convey any of the information to an employee. Two precautions suggest that gloves (rubber or plastic) be worn and that "prolonged skin contact" be avoided, but in the cases at issue, employees were wearing vinyl gloves at all times they were in contact with Loctite RC/609. Clearly, the safety information provided by the manufacturer was inadequate to warn of the dangers inherent in exposure to the glue.

I testified for parts of two days at trial. Aside from plaintiffs, the only other witness was the medical doctor who testified about the severity of the disabling dermatitis caused by exposure to Loctite RC/609. It was so severe that one plaintiff, who was pregnant, was told that she would be have to wear gloves in order to change her baby's diapers. The jury found for the plaintiffs and awarded the largest amount of damages ever in a civil case in Anderson County, Tennessee. However, as I soon learned, while the jury was deliberating, the plaintiffs, worried about the outcome, reached a "high–low" agreement with the defense. A high–low agreement is a settlement that is contingent on a jury's award of damages and that sets a minimum amount that the defendant will pay the plaintiff if the award is below that amount and a maximum amount that the defendant will pay if the award is above that amount, regardless of the amount of the jury award.

The jury verdict was for far more than the "high" amount agreed on. However, the plaintiffs felt that the defense had a good chance of winning on appeal, so both sides agreed to live with the "high–low" figures and also to retain all trial exhibits, including charts and other materials used by witnesses. Those materials would thus be unavailable for future litigation. After trial, I learned that the jury had been strongly pro-defense prior to hearing my testimony. The verdict and jury award amount were based on linguistic evidence of a failure to warn (Dumas 2000b).

Cleaning product risk, carbon monoxide poisoning, toxic shock syndrome, and toxic gas poisoning

In his recent discussion of four product liability cases in which he testified as an expert witness, Shuy (2008) provided rich data from cases involving carbon monoxide poisoning, toxic shock syndrome, and toxic gas poisoning (Ch. 8–11 of *Fighting Over Words:*

Language and Civil Law Cases). In a case involving carbon monoxide poisoning in a recreational vehicle, he compared ANSI requirements with three owner's manuals, concluding that two manuals failed to meet ANSI standards in a number of ways. He made use of topic, topic sequencing, speech act, and semantic analysis to reach his conclusions (*Fighting Over Words*, p. 106). In a case involving use of a cleaning product on a ship, Shuy compared regulatory standards with the label on the tin of cleaning compound, concluding that the label was not consumer-friendly and that it minimized the danger. In a case involving tampon-induced toxic shock syndrome, Shuy analyzed tampon box warnings and package inserts in order to assess the adequacy of the warnings. He also made some suggestions for warning label revision, suggesting reordering, reduced syntactic complexity and redesign, both to increase the likelihood that a consumer would pay attention to the text and to enhance readability. In the fourth case, the question of whether a pilot's speech changed over the course of a four-hour period was at issue. It was assumed that if the pilot's cognitive abilities were diminished over a period of time (due to the possible presence of a toxic substance), that would be reflected in his speech. But the pilot showed no meaningful change in syntax, speech acts, pause fillers, pronunciation, or conversational cooperativeness (Shuy 2008: 128–29).

Conclusion

I suggested at the outset of this chapter that I would summarize research about the nature and functions of warnings, describe and evaluate techniques for assessing and increasing adequacy of warnings, and then suggest strategies for continuing to improve warning and other safety information adequacy. Summaries of past research reveal clearly, I think, both the complexity of assessing the adequacy of consumer product warnings and other safety information and the reasons for the difficulties of applying reasonable standards—and also the real difficulties of composing effective warning labels, especially in contexts where space is quite limited.

The role of context, both in our society as a whole and in particular personal or commercial contexts, is important. In our society, we face, for instance, the fact that effective warning information on tobacco products might have the effect of reducing tax revenues (Tiersma 2002). In industry, some warnings appear to be constructed with more attention to their anti-litigation function than their effectiveness, and as noted above, product warnings often have to compete for consumers' attention with package construction designed to attract consumers. However, as linguists we have the tools to improve the quality of warnings if others empower us to do so. One example of package construction designed to attract consumers comes from 2007, when R.J. Reynolds introduced Camel No. 9 cigarettes, clearly designed to attract female smokers. The cigarettes were described as "light and luscious," and their packages feature what the *New York Times* called "hot-pink fuchsia" and "minty-green teal" colors; flowers surrounded the packs in magazine ads ("City Room; Female Smokers And a P.R. Coup").

The packaging strategy is not new. A 2008 exhibit of historic cigarette ads at the New York Public Library's Science, Industry and Business branch, "Not a Cough in a Carload," displayed historic cigarette ads that were designed to override medical information and conventional notions of appropriate behavior, especially for women:

[I]n 1928, Edward Bernays, often considered the father of modern public relations, was retained by American Tobacco Company to help get women to smoke.

Recognizing that women were still riding high on the suffrage movement, Mr. Bernays used the equality angle as the basis for his new campaign. He convinced a number of genteel women, including his own secretary, to march in the 1929 Easter Day parade down Fifth Avenue and light up cigarettes in a defiant show of their liberation.

.... [T]he media ate it up:

Ten young women turned out, marching down Fifth Avenue with their lighted "torches of freedom," and the newspapers loved it. Two-column pictures showed elegant ladies, with floppy hats and fur-trimmed coats, cigarettes held self-consciously by their sides, as they paraded down the wide boulevard. Dispatches ran the next day, on page one, in papers from Fremont, Nebraska, to Portland, Oregon, to Albuquerque, New Mexico.

The Times published an article the next day on the Easter Parade, with headline saying in part, "Group of Girls Puff at Cigarettes as a Gesture of 'Freedom'"

....

The cigarettes became known as "torches of freedom."

Cigarette companies then started tailoring their messages to women. One of the most resonant themes was that smoking would keep women slim (even then, women thought thinner was better).

("Female Smokers And a P. R. Coup")

Recently, Philip Morris USA began marketing cigarettes labeled "Virginia Slims Superslims Lights" that also appear to be directed primarily to female smokers. The cigarettes themselves are much thinner than most cigarettes; twenty of them fit into a package called a "Purse Pack" that is much thinner than most cigarette packages. The packages are lavender and silver and green and silver. I first saw them when I purchased packs of Camel No. 9 cigarettes. The packages are so tiny that I did not believe that one could hold twenty cigarettes. I purchased and opened a package to verify the contents. Both the sales clerk and I were astonished to find twenty cigarettes inside the package.

Clearly, the contest continues. The contest is sometimes portrayed as one between conscience and profits or between comprehensibility and profits, but the contest also involves the full role of context in communication scenarios, including the psychology of risk assessment as noted above. Linguists cannot address the issues of profit versus conscience, but we can address the issues of comprehensibility and also the full role of context. My earlier suggestions about improving written and graphic warning labels and Material Safety Data Sheets were restricted primarily to comprehensibility issues. I now suggest that linguists can further contribute to increasing the effectiveness of safety information statements, including warnings and such documents as Material Safety Data Sheets, by focusing attention on the likelihood that even strong, effectively worded warning information may appear in contexts in which glamour and style compete with health concerns. How do we counter that? One possibility is to incorporate the lure into some warnings, possibly by stating something like this: "Lose weight by smoking? Yes! All of it! You die!" or "Smoking: A Sure Slow Death" or even "Look Good While You Die – Smoke!" Additional research into the relationship between locutionary and illocutionary acts and perlocutionary effects is still needed if we want to improve on the persuasiveness of warnings—but then, on the other hand, such research may simply enable advertisers to be even more successful in selling cigarettes and other tobacco products.

Further reading

Cotterill, J. (ed.) (2002) *Language in the Legal Process*, Houndmills, Basingstoke, Hampshire and New York: Palgrave Macmillan: 54–71. (Contains chapter by Tiersma on "The Language and Law of Product Warnings.")

Dumas, B.K. (1992) "Adequacy of cigarette package warnings: An analysis of the adequacy of federally mandated cigarette package warnings," *Tennessee Law Review*, 59: 261–304. (Contains details of warning label analysis.)

——(2000) "Warning labels and industry safety information standards: The case of Loctite RC/609," in J. Peyton and P. Griffin (eds) *Language in Action: New Studies of Language in Society*, Cresskill, NJ: Hampton Press, 302–17.

——(2001) "Warnings," in J. Mitchie (ed.) *Reader's Guide to the Social Sciences*, London and Chicago: Fitzroy Dearborn. Vol. 2, 1747–48. (Overview with bibliography.)

Shuy, R.W. (2008) *Fighting Over Words: Language and Civil Law Cases*, Oxford: Oxford University Press. (Contains data from four product liability cases.)

Legal cases cited

Bogle v. McDonald's Restaurants Ltd., Neutral Citation [2002] EWHC 490 (QB), Case No: HQ0005713.).

Liebeck v. McDonald's Restaurants, P.T.S., Inc., No. D-202 CV-93-02419, 1995 WL 360309 (Bernalillo County, N.M. Dist. Ct. Aug. 18, 1994).

Roysdon v. R. J. Reynolds Tobacco Co., 623 F.Supp. 1189 [E.D. Tn. 1986].

Roysdon v. R. J. Reynolds Tobacco Company, 849 F.2d 230 [6th Cir. 1988].

25

The forensic phonetician

Forensic speaker identification by experts

Michael Jessen

Introduction

Forensic speaker identification is the most important task within the field that is known as *Forensic Phonetics and Acoustics* or *Forensic Speech and Audio Analysis*. The former term corresponds to the name of the organisation *International Association for Forensic Phonetics and Acoustics* (IAFPA; see their website www.iafpa.net), which hosts an annual international meeting and is represented in the journal *International Journal of Speech, Language and the Law*. Although it has been made very clear by the IAFPA that phoneticians are not privileged among its membership over, for example, speech engineers, in fact phoneticians and linguists are traditionally most strongly represented in the organisation. The second term, Forensic Speech and Audio Analysis, is entirely neutral with respect to any underlying academic field (phonetics) and this is the term used for the name of a working group within ENFSI (European Network of Forensic Science Institutes; see www.enfsi.eu). In that group, engineers and computer scientists are at least as strongly represented as phoneticians and linguists. This is partially due to the fact that forensic speech and audio analysis comprise many activities other than speaker identification, which can benefit from a speech and audio engineering perspective. Such activities include both audio enhancement, i.e. the attempt to increase the intelligibility of poor-quality speech through advanced filtering and other signal processing procedures, and audio authentication, i.e. detecting indications that an audio recording has been manipulated. Since these activities outside of speaker identification are not excluded from the scope of the IAFPA, it makes little sense to see a difference in meaning between the two terms Forensic Phonetics and Acoustics and Forensic Speech and Audio Analysis, so they will be treated as synonymous. A third term, which should also be seen as synonymous is *Forensic Speech Science*. This is the name of the first academic programme that was established in that field at the University of York, UK in 2007 (see www.york.ac.uk/depts/lang/postgrad/forensic.htm).

Forensic speaker identification can be divided into several sub-tasks. A classification that has proven useful in forensic practice is shown in Table 25.1.

If audio recordings exist of both the unknown speaker (i.e. the offender in situations such as kidnapping, stalking or drug dealing) and a suspect, it is possible to conduct a

Table 25.1 Different tasks of forensic speaker identification

	Audio recording of unknown speaker available	No audio recording available, but witness available
Suspect exists	Speaker comparison [if suspect is cooperative or prior recordings of the suspect exist and can be used]	Suspect previously known to the witness: regular witness statement Suspect not previously known to the witness: voice line-up
No suspect exists	Speaker profiling and/or presentation of unknown speaker voice in the media	Rare expert involvement; possible future: acoustic phantom picture using speech synthesis

speaker comparison and use it as evidence in court. An alternative term for speaker comparison is *voice comparison*, which means the same. If the suspect is cooperative, a recording can be made of his speech and the forensic expert can have a large amount of control over this recording. For example, it is possible to make a transcript of the unknown speaker's utterances and then ask the suspect to read them or repeat them in appropriate chunks of speech. Such a procedure results in text identity, which can be useful for some subsequent activities such as the measurement of vowel formants. (Formants are resonance frequencies that result from the shape of the vocal tract and they are measured in Hertz (Hz); the lowest resonance frequency is called the first formant – commonly abbreviated as F1 – and the highest resonance frequency used for most forensic applications is the third formant, F3.) However, text identity is not a requirement in forensic speaker identification, and reading or (less so) repeating can result in unnatural prosody, which creates its own problems. Therefore, the recording of a suspect should also contain speech that is uttered as spontaneously as possible. If, however, the suspect is not cooperative and does not agree to have his voice recorded, it will depend on the legal system of the country and the circumstance of the case whether prior recordings of the suspect, perhaps taken from police interviews or from telephone surveillance, can be used. Another form of uncooperative behaviour occurs when a suspect agrees to a recording, but then tries to disguise his voice in an apparent or subtle way. In such a case, the expert has to decide from a forensic-phonetic perspective whether this evidence can still be used. The methodology used in speaker comparisons involves a wide variety of both auditory and acoustic parameters and will be addressed in Section 3.

If an audio recording exists of the unknown speaker, but no suspect has been found, it is still possible to create a *speaker profile* based on the recording. Synonymous terms for such activity are *voice analysis* and *voice profiling*. Speaker profiles are usually requested by the police in an ongoing investigation for the purpose of finding a suspect. Information useful for that purpose includes age, sex, region, social status and foreign language background. Speaker profiling is addressed in more detail in Section 2. In the same situation in which a speaker profile is requested, it is also possible to present audio samples of the unknown speaker to the general public, using mass media such as TV, radio or the internet. This is usually only implemented in high-profile cases, partially because the subsequent expert work required in evaluating all the responses from the public (including conducting many subsequent speaker comparisons) can be substantial.

Some forensic cases begin with a speaker profiling stage and end with a speaker comparison stage. Perhaps the most remarkable example is the Yorkshire Ripper case, where these two stages lay 30 years apart. In the early stages, a speaker profile was provided of a caller claiming to be the Yorkshire Ripper, who between 1975 and 1980 had murdered 13 women in Leeds, Bradford, Huddersfield and Manchester. Later it was discovered that the calls had been made by a hoaxer. A suspect hoaxer was eventually found through DNA analysis in 2005. A speaker comparison between the voice of the suspect and the voice from the calls in the 1970s revealed strong indications that these two voices belonged to the same individual. The Yorkshire Ripper case is described in detail in Ellis (1994) and French *et al.* (2006).

In some situations, no recording of the unknown speaker is available, but a witness has heard the person speaking. In some cases, such as robbery or rape, the witness may also be the victim. In these situations, it makes a difference, both scientifically and legally, whether or not the witness knew the offender from before the crime. In the former situation, the task required of the witness is called *familiar-speaker identification* and in the latter *unfamiliar-speaker identification*. Familiar-speaker identification enters the evidential process in the form of a regular witness statement. Here the challenge might be to ascertain – based on scientific knowledge about human speaker perception in general – whether such a witness statement is reliable or whether adverse conditions occurred that cast doubt on its reliability. Such adverse conditions include short utterances, distance, additive noise and unusual utterance modes such as shouting (see Blatchford and Foulkes 2006 for a recent case study and further references). Cases with unfamiliar-speaker identification require a different methodology and can be addressed in terms of a *voice line-up*, also referred to as *voice parade* (see Nolan 2003).

In the fourth possibility shown in Table 25.1, somebody has witnessed the crime but no suspect and no recording exists. Although this scenario occurs frequently in reality, experts are only rarely asked for their involvement (at least this holds for Germany). Perhaps this is because there is no established forensic methodology for such a scenario. What would be very useful here is some way of creating what in the visual domain are known as phantom pictures or photofit pictures (Nolan 1983: 208 for that suggestion). Current technologies in speech synthesis developed under the terms 'voice transformation' and 'voice conversion' are very promising (Stylianou 2008 for overview).

Speaker comparison and speaker profiling, which were shown on the left side of Table 25.1, fall into the province mentioned in the title of this chapter, i.e. speaker identification by experts (see Künzel 1995; Broeders 2001 for the term). The term *speaker identification by experts* is opposed to *naïve speaker identification* which denotes the situations shown on the right-hand side of Table 25.1. To be more precise, although the identification process in naïve speaker identification is performed by individuals who are not trained with respect to speech analysis, the framework in which these perceptions by naïve listeners are elicited is a professional one, in which experts are involved in the planning and execution of procedures such as voice line-ups. An alternative term for speaker identification by experts is *technical speaker identification* (Nolan 1983, 1997). As Nolan (1997) points out, the adjective *technical* has to be understood in a broad sense – as not only covering the use of instruments such as spectral analysers, but also as referring to non-instrumental methods such as auditory-based phonetic transcription. In this chapter the former term will be kept, which presents an opportunity to think more closely about the kind of qualifications that are needed by an expert in forensic speaker identification. Since this issue depends on the different methods that are used, this task will be postponed towards the end of this chapter.

Speaker profiling

Within the domain of speaker profiling it is useful to make a distinction between the task of speaker classification and the task of identifying salient speaker characteristics that can be understood in lay terms. Speaker classification (see Müller 2007 for the full range of that term) can be understood as the task of inferring from speech evidence the "class" or "category" to which a speaker belongs. As mentioned above, this includes region, age, sex, and social background. One reason why speaker classification is useful in an ongoing police investigation is because the information that is derived about the unknown speaker can be used by the police directly, without any further need to listen to the voice. For example, if a speech sample is found to contain indications of both a Russian foreign accent and a local dialect from the southwest of Germany close to Stuttgart, Germany (as occurred in a case of organised drug smuggling in 2005), the police can focus their attention on the population with these characteristics.

But a speech sample might also contain other features that are striking and noteworthy speaker characteristics in the perception and categorisation of a layperson, although these features might have nothing to do with speaker classification. For example, a voice might be very high- or low-pitched, the speaker might speak in a very fast or slow manner or in a very careful or sloppy manner; there might be creaky, breathy, harsh or nasal voice quality and so forth. When descriptions like these are given to the police and perhaps made available to a wider public (along with speaker classification information, such as the presence of a particular accent), it is possible that investigating police officers or someone from the public will have a candidate who fits this description. Therefore, the voice profiling task should not be limited to speaker classification, but should also be performed with a view to eliciting speech features that might be striking speaker characteristics from a layperson's perspective.

Another task that can become relevant in speaker profiling, but also in speaker comparisons, is to draw conclusions about transitory speaker states, such as stress and emotion or the intake of drugs or alcohol.

An important terminological point that emerges from this discussion and that will recur in the section on speaker comparison is the distinction between *speaker classification* and *speaker-specific characteristics*. The features that are used for speaker classification are by definition not speaker-specific but rather characteristics of sets of speakers. Features such as a high-pitched voice or a fast speech rate, on the other hand, are individual features. That does not mean that speakers are *uniquely* characterised by these individual features; there is still a long way to go until we know whether, and if so, how speakers can be completely individualised by speech evidence alone (Nolan 1997 for discussion). But it means that information about pitch and speech rate is important in the forensic task of distinguishing individual speakers.

Figure 25.1 shows the speaker classification domains that have been used in casework or might be used more intensively in the future (body size). The different domains have

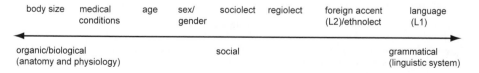

| body size | medical conditions | age | sex/ gender | sociolect | regiolect | foreign accent (L2)/ethnolect | language (L1) |

organic/biological (anatomy and physiology)   social   grammatical (linguistic system)

Figure 25.1 Domains in forensic speaker classification

381

been roughly organised according to whether their motivation lies primarily in organic/ biological factors, or social factors or whether the main influence is that of a linguistic system.

There is a certain correlation between **body size** (i.e. the height of a speaker, and to a more limited extent the weight) and the length of the vocal tract (distance from larynx to lips). Vocal tract length, in turn, can be estimated from the measurement of vowel formants. The correlation is not high, which is why no accurate estimate of body size from formant frequencies is so far possible. More research in this area is necessary (see Rendall *et al.* 2005 for a recent study). However, what can be said is that a speaker with very low formant frequencies is likely not to be a short person and someone with very high formants is likely not to be tall (Greisbach 1999). Based on laboratory data (Jessen *et al.* 2005) compiled by the *Bundeskriminalamt* (BKA), this statement by Greisbach can be confirmed (Figure 25.2). Figure 25.2 shows that a negative correlation occurs between body size and the average frequency of the third formant (according to the LTF-method shown in Figure 25.5). Although the correlation is very weak in the mid-range of formant frequencies and body height measures, there are clear patterns at the extremes. Speakers with formants in the high range above 2500 Hz have small or medium body size, whereas speakers with formants in the low range below 2200 Hz have above-average body size. In addition, the results for the average second formant (not shown) are similar to those of the third formant.

As a practical example, in a case of organised drug dealing in a German town close to the Polish border, the unknown speaker was called *der Kurze* by his accomplices (collo-quial form of 'the short one'). His formant frequencies were above average in the male adult population. The suspect, who had similar formant values and who later turned out to be identical with the unknown speaker, was in fact below average in stature.

Indices of **medical conditions** in speech are found, first of all, in the domain of language, speech and voice pathology. In particular, those disorders that are of forensic use have long-term effects, and exclude, for, example, laryngitis, which comes and goes rapidly. Examples of medical conditions that have been used in casework are stuttering as

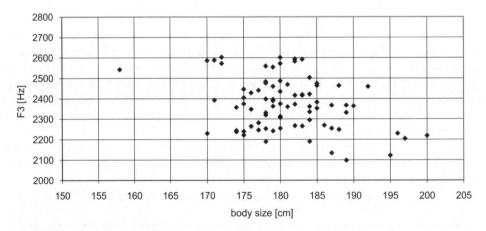

Figure 25.2 Negative correlation between body size [cm] and average frequency of third formant [Hz] among 81 adult male speakers of German

well as malformations of sibilant fricatives – also known as sigmatism – although telephone bandpass limitations impose a strong challenge to the analysis of sigmatisms. Künzel (1987: 65, 71) mentions a case of left-wing terrorism where a spectrographically detectible whistle sound occurred as a rare characteristic of the production of the postalveolar voiceless sibilant fricative by the offender. Medical conditions outside speech-language pathology that have been applied forensically include obstruction in the breathing pathways, which sometimes co-occurs with obesity. Another relevant domain is the effect of psychiatric disorders on speech (Darby 1981). In the speech evaluation of medical conditions, collaboration with qualified physicians and speech-language pathologists is advisable.

Turning to the domain of **age**, most of the criminal offenders in our casework are male and between 20 and 40 years old, sometimes up to 50 but rarely beyond. However, most of the changes in speech patterns occur below and above that age range, i.e. in childhood and puberty as well as in the transition into old age. These are also the age ranges for which most of the research has been done, whereas very little information is available for the forensically most relevant range. Most information is available on the influence of age on the fundamental frequency level (f0). For male adults there is a decrease in f0 up to about the age of 40, then from about 50 an increasing pattern that continues into old age. For female adults there is a gradual decrease from young adulthood on, sometimes accelerated during menopause; there might be a slight increase again at old or very old age (Baken and Orlikoff 2000: 173–76; Schötz 2006: 83). In a recent large-scale study, Schötz confirmed this pattern and also found that speech rate is a good age correlate, because it decreases gradually for both males and females (Schötz 2006: 110). She found another salient correlate – increasing intensity range – which requires further research. In forensic casework, the age domain of speaker classification is most commonly approached by performing an age estimation that is based on overall perceptual impression. Research has shown that the average differences between perceived age and chronological age are around six years, and that forensic experts are slightly better at this task than laypersons (Braun 1996). Age correlates, especially those at young and old age, are primarily based on biological factors. There can also be age correlates that are motivated by social factors and that usually interact with gender and social status (Foulkes and Docherty 2006). Finally, age can be motivated by the linguistic system when it occurs as a reflection of sound change. Wells (1999), for example, shows that overt pronunciation of [h] in words like *white* declined from speakers born in 1933 to speakers born in 1973 and later. Good reviews on age in speech production and perception are provided by Linville (2001) and Schötz (2006, 2007).

The next domain to be discussed is **sex/gender** (the term *sex* is usually used for the biological aspects and the term *gender* for the socio-cultural aspects of the male–female distinction). Deciding whether the unknown speaker in a recording is a man or a woman is usually not an issue because laypersons and phoneticians alike are, under most circumstances, able to perceptually identify the sex of the speaker among the adult population (before the onset of old age). This success of perceptual sex classification is largely based on the fact that most women have a much higher average pitch level than most men. The importance of pitch for sex identification has also been shown in perception experiments (Coleman 1976). This difference can be explained by male–female differences in vocal fold length, which is about 60% longer in men than women (Titze 1994: 173). The forensic-phonetic expert is able to quantify and objectify the pitch level

383

of a speaker by applying fundamental frequency (f0) analysis. According to a study of read speech based on 100 male and 50 female adult speakers of German, men on average have a pitch level of about 115 Hz and women of about 210 Hz (Künzel 1989). More important than the average across many speakers is the *distribution* of the f0 values of men and women in an estimate of the population. The range of mean f0 from the lowest-pitched to the highest-pitched voices is from about 80 to 170 Hz in men (Künzel 1989; Jessen *et al.* 2005) and from about 165 to 260 Hz in women (Künzel 1989; Simpson and Ericsdotter 2007). This information about f0 distribution can prove useful in situations where perceptual sex classification is difficult because the pitch of the unknown voice is too low for a typical female and too high for the typical male voice. In such a case, the expert can state whether and to what degree the given f0 evidence is more consistent with male or with female speech. The f0 distributions mentioned here were obtained from laboratory recordings under neutral speech conditions. When loud and emotional speech is taken into account, there can be more overlap between the two distributions (see also Figure 25.4).

There are situations, however, where pitch is not available as a cue to speaker sex. This could be because the pitch level is unreliable due to voice disguise (e.g. when a creaky voice is used), or because the speech is voiceless, as in a whisper (which can be another voice disguise strategy). In such cases – or in addition to the pitch evidence – other phonetic cues to speaker sex can be used. One important source of sex differences lies in the acoustic effects of differences in the length of the vocal tract, which is about 12% longer in men than women (Fitch and Giedd 1999). The vocal tract length effect can be captured by measuring the formant frequencies F1 to F3 (formants higher than F3 are usually not accessible in telephone speech). Women tend to have higher formant frequencies than men (Hillenbrand *et al.* 1995). Formant frequencies have similar importance for perceptual sex identification as f0 (Lehiste and Meltzer 1973; Mullennix *et al.* 1995). But, because the perceptual effects that are due to vocal tract length are difficult to transcribe phonetically and difficult to distinguish from perceived pitch, sex/gender determination is a case where acoustic-phonetic methods are very important in speaker classification (Jessen 2007b for further discussion of this point).

Although the characteristics of sex/gender that have been discussed so far have an organic/biological motivation, this motivation is not sufficient to account for all male–female differences in speech. One important point is that biologically determined differences can be exaggerated or minimised due to socio-cultural factors. For example, Johnson (2006) shows that male–female formant differences can be larger among speakers of Russian than among speakers of Danish. This is more likely to be due to socio-cultural differences in these speech communities than to differences between the linguistic systems. Other sources of evidence indicating that sex/gender characteristics go beyond anatomy and physiology are male–female differences in childhood, where organic differences are too small to account for all the observable speech differences (Whiteside 2001), or influences of sexual orientation, where some speakers adopt characteristics of the opposite sex/gender (Munson and Babel 2007).

As much as the *facts* show ambiguous status between biological and social factors, so do the *explanations*. It has been shown that women have a wider vowel space than men – meaning that the different vowels of a language are more distant from each other acoustically in female than male speech (Diehl *et al.* 1996). Women also tend to show fewer instances of word-final stop deletion and other forms of reduction in the production of consonants (Byrd 1994). Both increased vowel space and decreased consonant reduction can be interpreted as forms of increased articulatory precision. Biological explanations state that increased articulatory precision among women is a compensation for the loss of intelligibility that occurs because formant structure is less-well defined in high-pitched voices (Diehl *et al.* 1996). Furthermore, because women have a smaller cross-section of the vocal tract, it is easier for them to reach articulatory targets than it is for men (Simpson 2001). Social explanations state that increased articulatory precision is a special case of the tendency among women to speak more standard-like ("correct" in a prescriptive sense) and to approach levels of higher prestige, which has been observed in sociolinguistics (Cheshire 2002 for discussion). These and other sex/gender characteristics reported in the literature can be drawn upon in cases where determination of sex/gender is difficult.

A practical example of sex/gender determination is a case from 2003 where the airport in Düsseldorf, Germany, received several telephone calls in which it was claimed that a bomb would detonate unless all take-off and landing actions were terminated for a day. The case was taken seriously because affiliation to a terrorist organisation was claimed by the caller and all aircraft movements were indeed stopped for the day. It was difficult to determine the sex of the speaker, because the person spoke very loudly (both male and female speakers have a high average f0 in loud speech and can be difficult to distinguish). The effect of vocal tract resonances was ambiguous as well. There were a few short passages, however, where enough evidence could be found to conclude that the speaker was likely to be female, but had lowered resonances due to lip rounding, which was used as a voice disguise. This conclusion turned out to be correct. There was no terrorist background, but what had happened was that a woman created the entire scenario because she had had a fight with her boyfriend and did not want to join him for a vacation on a flight that would depart that day.

The speaker profiling domains of **sociolect, regiolect (dialect)** and **foreign accent/ ethnolect** will not be discussed here for reasons of space and because the reader can become familiar with them through a wide range of text- and handbooks (e.g. Chambers *et al.* 2002; Doughty and Long 2003). Furthermore, the specifics of these three speaker-profiling domains depend strongly on the language and the country. For example, the specifics of regional, social and ethnic differentiation are different in Germany to those in the UK. Experts who want to do casework in a specific language and in a specific country need to become familiar with the local situation, so a general overview across languages and countries is of little help. In contrast, sex and the other speaker-profiling domains that have been discussed here are more universal, which is mainly due to their biological aspects. Further information about forensic speaker classification can be found in Künzel (2004), French and Harrison (2006) and Jessen (2007b).

The rightmost term **'language'** in Figure 25.1 accounts for situations where the language classification of the relevant speakers that was provided by other parties is not correct or not sufficiently accurate. This has occurred in cases from language areas with a dense distribution of different languages (e.g. Caucasus) or with a complicated pattern of multilingualism (e.g. Berber vs. Arabic in North Africa).

Speaker comparison

In the discussion of speaker profiling a distinction was made between speaker classification on the one hand and speaker characteristics that can be understood in lay terms on the other hand. In speaker comparisons, a similar distinction can be made. Firstly, speaker classification is part of speaker comparison, as it is part of speaker profiling. Secondly, speaker comparisons report speaker-specific characteristics, but in contrast to speaker profiling these are analysed not from the layperson's, but from the expert's perspective. This situation is summarised in Figure 25.3.

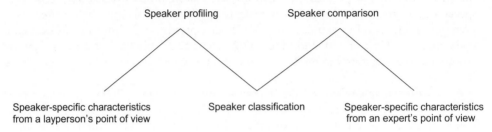

Speaker profiling   Speaker comparison

Speaker-specific characteristics from a layperson's point of view   Speaker classification   Speaker-specific characteristics from an expert's point of view

Figure 25.3 Tasks in speaker profiling and speaker comparison

There can be overlap between the two strategies of reporting speaker-specific characteristics. For example, in both speaker profiling and speaker comparisons an unusually high speech rate would be reported. But it is clear that the range of speaker characteristics that are analysed is wider and the accuracy of the results higher in speaker comparisons than in speaker profiles. For example, speaker-specific characteristics that require acoustic measurements are only reported in speaker comparisons.

There are two main ways in which speaker classification becomes important in speaker comparisons. Firstly, speaker classification can lead to very strong evidence *against* the identity of two speakers. This situation occurs if two speakers show categorically different values in one or more speaker classification domains. For example, if one speaker is identified as being young, say around 20 years, and another is probably over 50 (and the recordings are contemporary), this is a strong indication that the speakers are not identical. An analogous situation occurs with dialect mismatch, although here the possibility of bidialectal competence has to be taken into account. Secondly, if a speaker classification feature is very rare in the population, this can lead to very strong evidence *in favour of* the identity of two speakers. The best examples are various medical conditions, the rarity of which is demonstrated in the medical literature. Also, dialects, sociolects and foreign accents can be rare but usually this depends on the context of the case. For example, it makes a huge difference in terms of the percentage of the local population that produces a Bavarian dialect, whether the case took place in a Bavarian town (with many speakers of Bavarian around) or close to the Danish border (with few speakers of Bavarian around). This, however, is contextual information that is not always made known to the expert, and even if it is known, it is not clear to what extent this 'a-priori' information (Rose 2002) should be included in the analysis.

Turning now to the speaker-specific characteristics from an expert's point of view, a compilation of features that are frequently used in speaker comparison cases is shown in Table 25.2. The classification proposed in Table 25.2 is a slight deviation from the classification *Stimme, Sprache, Sprechweise* 'voice, language, manner of speaking' that has been used in the BKA (Künzel 1987, 1995; Gfroerer 2006). The most important difference lies in the category 'idiolectal' vs. 'language', where in the previous BKA approach the categories dialect, sociolect and foreign accent are included in the language category, whereas according to

Table 25.2 Important speaker-specific characteristics in speaker comparisons

Organic	Idiolectal	Habitual
1. average fundamental frequency (f0)	4. individual aspects of sociolect, regiolect and foreign accent	7. articulation rate
2. (long-term) formant frequencies	5. linguistic-phonetic details	8. f0-variability
3. voice quality	6. forensic-linguistic features	9. dysfluent behaviour

the present proposal these categories are assumed to be part of speaker classification. The advantage of the present approach is that the two concepts speaker classification and speaker-specific characteristics (Figure 25.3) are distinguished more clearly.

The pitch level and its acoustic correlate, the **average fundamental frequency (f0)**, have already been mentioned as an important correlate of sex/gender, which is anatomically motivated primarily by the length of the vocal folds. The same motivation also holds within the sexes, where large differences between speakers occur. A classical study of inter-speaker differences in f0 that has been mentioned above is the one by Künzel (1987, 1989). A more recent study, again on German, was performed by Jessen et al. (2005) with consistent results, but a wider range of speech styles. The results on mean fundamental frequency for spontaneous speech (in a laboratory situation) and spontaneous speech in Lombard condition (exposure to 80 dB white noise over headphones, causing an increase in vocal loudness) is shown in Figure 25.4 (see Jessen et al. 2005 for a survey of other Lombard studies).

Figure 25.4 shows, for example, that for normal vocal loudness a mean f0 of 115 Hz is something that occurs very frequently among men, i.e. it is typical, but that a value of 85 or one at 165 Hz is something that is very rare (nontypical). Due to these differences in

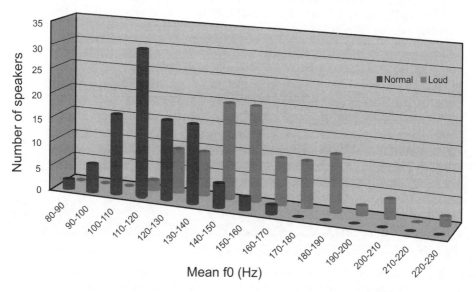

Figure 25.4 Histogram of mean f0 in spontaneous speech among 100 male adult speakers of German. Results are presented for Lombard speech (light columns, back row) and speech at normal vocal loudness (dark columns, front row)

typicality, the strength of the evidence in favour of identity is stronger if unknown and suspect fall into the same nontypical interval than if they fall into the same typical interval (Jessen 2008b for explanation of this example in terms of Bayesian statistics; see Rose 2002 for other Bayesian examples). The figure also shows that the distribution shifts towards higher f0 values when speech is produced more loudly than normal. Loud speech occurs frequently in forensic casework. The upward shift of f0 under this condition is a case of 'intra-speaker variation', which is a phenomenon that is frequently found in forensic speech analysis. In order to deal with intra-speaker variation it is important that the expert has knowledge from the literature and from casework experience about its sources and magnitudes.

Average f0 has also been investigated on 100 male adult speakers of British English (Hudson *et al.* 2007). The mean f0 across speakers was 106 Hz for spontaneous lab speech, whereas it was 120 Hz for essentially the same speech style in Jessen *et al.* (2005) on German. One explanation for this discrepancy is that average f0 differs slightly between different linguistic communities (cf. the discussion in Section 2 about sociocultural influences on acoustic correlates of sex/gender). Similar language dependencies of average f0 are reported by Braun and Wagner (2002).

Formant frequencies have been mentioned above as important male/female correlates which are due to differences in vocal tract length. As with f0, the same holds within the sexes. There are different ways to capture speaker-specific aspects of formant structure. The method that has been used frequently in our laboratory is the Long-Term Formant Distribution (LTF), which was first proposed by Nolan and Grigoras (2005). According to the method that we use, a speech signal is edited in a way that only vocalic portions remain in which formant structure is clearly visible. Subsequently, automatic formant tracking is applied and any remaining errors of formant tracking are corrected manually. The resulting formant tracks are exported and further statistics, most importantly averaging, are applied. The stage prior to exporting is illustrated in Figure 25.5. The quality and quantity of forensic material can differ, so that in some cases no long-term formant analysis is possible.

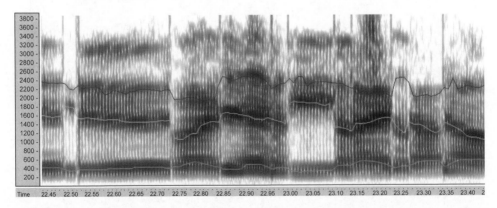

Figure 25.5 Illustration of LTF-method: spectrogram (time in seconds on x-axis; frequency in Hz on y-axis) together with formant tracks for F1, F2 and F3 (from bottom to top) on vocalic portions of a speech signal. Example taken from a case of blackmail to the owner of a discotheque

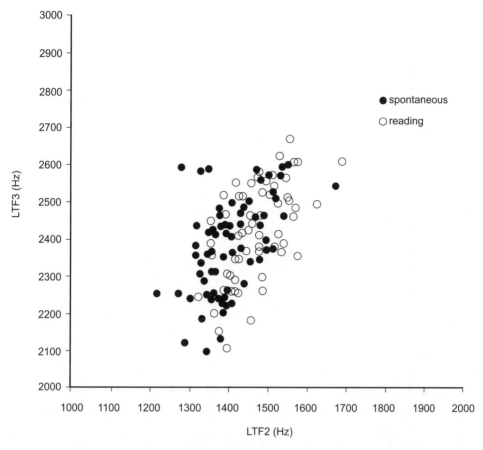

Figure 25.6 Reference data for average LTF values [Hz] in spontaneous speech (closed circles) and read speech (open circles) for 71 male adult speakers of German. Long-term second formant on x-axis, long-term third formant on y-axis (after Moos 2008a)

Figure 25.6 shows the average LTF of 71 of the 100 male adult speakers of German in the corpus on which the f0-parameters in Jessen *et al.* (2005) were investigated (Moos 2008a, 2008b). The LTF measurements were based on a version of the corpus that was transmitted by mobile phone. Figure 25.6 gives a good impression of the amount of inter-speaker variation that can be found with the LTF method. According to this figure, a speaker in a case with, for example, an LTF2 of 1300 Hz and LTF3 of 2200 Hz would be quite rare in the population. The figure also shows that LTF2 and LTF3 are to a certain extent correlated, which is predicted by a simple tube model of the vocal tract (Reetz and Jongman 2009 for introduction). Furthermore, the values for reading and spontaneous speech differ slightly (higher in reading). Although probably no such multi-speaker LTF study has been performed on other languages, casework experience so far has shown that essentially the same formant space is used by speakers of other languages as well.

It will now be illustrated how LTF evidence can be used in casework. In December 2007, a young man made an anonymous call to the police emergency centre in a town close to Kassel in Germany. In the call he warned about a planned school shooting in a centre for occupational studies that was located in the neighbourhood. The police

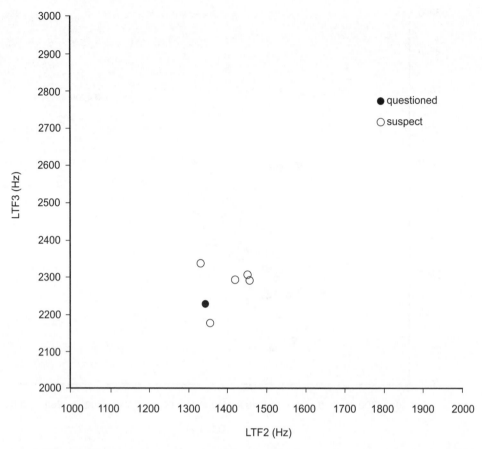

Figure 25.7 Average LTF values [Hz] in a forensic case, with one value for the questioned (= unknown) speaker (closed circle) and one separate value for each of the five readings of the transcribed text by the suspect (open circles)

identified a suspect and he agreed to make a recording. The police transcribed the text that was spoken in the anonymous call, and it was read by the suspect five times. It would have been beneficial to have had samples of spontaneous speech as well, but the police did not consult with an expert before the suspect recordings were made. LTF measurements were made along with other phonetic parameters. Figure 25.7 shows that the location of the LTF2/F3 value of the questioned speaker is within the range of the five values obtained from the suspect recording. There was a certain tendency for higher values in the suspect material. This is consistent with the result of Moos (2008a, 2008b) that LTF values in read speech are on average slightly higher than in spontaneous speech. Along with the overlap between the values of the questioned and the suspect speaker, Figure 25.7 also shows that the values found in this case were somewhat below average relative to the distribution shown in Figure 25.6. The overlapping pattern (high similarity) and the below-average pattern (relatively low typicality) provide evidence for the identity of questioned speaker and suspect.

Other ways of capturing speaker-specific formant information besides LTF are the measurement of vowel centre formant frequencies (see Rose 2002) or the measurement of formant dynamics (see McDougall 2006; Morrison 2008). Formant information is among the most important evidence in speaker comparisons, but there is also more research that needs to be done in this area in order to understand the full potential of this information (Rose 2006).

Turning to **voice quality** in Table 25.2, it is understood by us in the broad sense proposed by Laver (1980) of including both laryngeal characteristics such as creaky, breathy, harsh, and pressed voice and supralaryngeal settings such as (open and closed) nasality, lip rounding and jaw lowering. Due to the frequency limitations of telephone speech that occur regularly in forensic material and due to quality limitations such as the presence of noise or signal distortions, voice quality is difficult to measure acoustically in casework. Therefore, our primary approach to voice quality assessment is auditory. Further information and discussion on voice quality in forensic speaker identification is provided by Köster and Köster (2004) and Nolan (2005).

Fundamental frequency, formant frequency and voice quality have been classified as 'organic' in Table 25.2. This classification was made because there is an organic basis for speaker differences, such as length of vocal tract and vocal folds. This is not to imply that the features classified under that label are entirely determined by organic factors. We have seen, for example, that socio-cultural factors can influence average f0 and formant structure. Especially the classification of voice quality under the label organic is preliminary; further research might show that the third category 'habitual' is more appropriate. This issue also depends on the particular voice qualities involved. For example, harsh/rough voice quality has a strong organic foundation, whereas lip rounding is to be found in the habitual domain. There are also some overall voice quality differences with speakers of different languages and dialects (Braun and Wagner 2002 for data and overview).

Although a classic notion in linguistics, the concept of **'idiolect'** (see second column of Table 25.2) is still open for discussion as far as its implications for forensic speaker identification are concerned (Nolan 1997; Jessen 2008b; Grant (this volume) for some aspects). Here three types of phenomena are included under this concept. Firstly, idiolect includes situations where a speaker *combines* aspects of several regional, social and multilingual varieties. The idea behind this concept of idiolect is that a speaker might change location and social setting in the course of their lifetime, carrying certain features of each of them along the way. Such a biography leaves room for many idiosyncrasies (thanks to Francis Nolan for making this reading of idiolect clear to me). Second language acquisition can be a related source of speaker idiosyncrasies (Oksaar 1987), for example, because an individual has acquired a second language to a certain level and in a certain pattern – based on factors such as aptitude, motivation, duration of exposure, or the age of first exposure. A related aspect of idiolect is the possibility that a speaker uses a certain combination of characteristics of a dialect while excluding other characteristics of the same dialect. A special case of this possibility is the notion of *degree* of dialect, i.e. whether a speaker displays stronger or weaker signs of a dialect (or other variety). Degree of dialect can also be evident from the consistency of occurrence or the strength of a phonetic/phonological (or other) characteristic of a dialect.

The second reading of idiolect is in terms of linguistic-phonetic details that are not, or not only characteristics of dialects and other language varieties. An example is stop epenthesis (insertion of a stop consonant) in words like *hen'ce* or *el'se*. Although stop epenthesis has been shown to be subject to dialectal variation (Fourakis and Port 1986), it is also subject to speaker variation within the same dialect (Yoo and Blankenship 2003;

Jessen 2008b). Other examples of potential idiolectal phonetic details mentioned in the forensic literature include glottalisation of word-final /p,t,k/ or velarisation of postvocalic /l/ in English (Nolan 1983) as well as spirantisation (change from stop to fricative) of intervocalic /b/ or the phonetic manifestation of the glottal stop in German (Künzel 1987). Moosmüller (1997) mentions further examples of speaker-specific segmental phenomena that are free of dialectal and sociolectal variation. She points out that prosodically weak positions and casual speaking styles are a good place to look for these idiosyncratic patterns.

The third reading of idiolect is the one that has been worked out more comprehensively in forensic linguistics than in forensic phonetics and that includes idiosyncratic aspects of syntax and the lexicon (Coulthard 2004). One type of idiosyncratic feature that occurs in spoken language is the use of stereotypical expressions, such as the frequent use of *you know*. Stereotypical expressions are not completely speaker-specific, of course, but the selections of stereotypical expressions and the frequency with which they are used are only found in a limited number of speakers.

The third category used in Table 25.2 is called **habitual**. In a sense, this category is defined negatively: speaker characteristics that are subsumed under this category do not have any obvious organic foundation nor are they related to the linguistic conventions that are required or expected by the language system or the social community. The examples of habitual features that are given in the table and often used in casework, are articulation rate (Jessen 2007b for introduction and population statistics) and f0-variability (Jessen *et al.* 2005 for further explanation). Dysfluent behaviour, especially the use of fillers (also called filled pauses) of the type *uh* and *um*, is another type of habitual feature that according to a study on the BKA corpus mentioned above carries much speaker-specific information (Tschäpe *et al.* 2005). This is consistent with evidence that fillers are not intentionally used by the speaker (Corley and Steward 2008). Speaker variation in the use of fillers was also found by de Leeuw (2007).

Whereas the term 'idiolectal' is used here for speaker idiosyncrasies that are more closely associated to linguistic systems ('grammars'), the term 'habitual' is used for idiosyncrasies that are extra-grammatical (e.g. grammars do not specify a certain speech tempo). Furthermore, idiolectal features are also often segmental whereas habitual features are commonly prosodic, but there are exceptions. There are also uncertainties about where to locate certain phenomena. For example, coarticulation (neighbouring sounds influencing each other in phonetic detail) has been shown to be an important source of speaker variation (Nolan 1983). Is coarticulation idiolectal because it deals with (segmental) phonetic details that are associated with the linguistic system (e.g. coarticulation patterns can differ between languages), or is it habitual because it is about the freedom of how to get from one phonological target to the next and because it changes on the axis between a habitually careful or a 'slurred' manner of speaking? This example shows that the three-way classification in Table 25.2 is only a rough guideline on how to distinguish different kinds of speaker-specific characteristics (see Nolan 1983 and Rose 2002 for further classifications).

Conclusion

In this chapter an overview of speaker profiling and speaker comparison – two tasks within forensic speaker identification – has been presented. It should have become clear during the presentation that these tasks require experts that have an academic back-ground in phonetics and linguistics. As for the phonetic part, both auditory phonetic transcription and acoustic phonetic measurements are necessary, including in many 'extra-grammatical' domains such as speaker-specific voice quality and articulation rate. Linguistic knowledge is required for the identification of dialects and other linguistic varieties and is very important if casework is required in a foreign language, where cooperation with informants or other linguists is necessary. When any lack of knowledge becomes apparent in a particular case, the expert needs to know where to look for fur-ther literature in linguistics and phonetics and must be able to understand it. The BKA is sometimes approached by forensic institutes from other countries asking whether it can provide training in forensic speaker identification and certify that the attendees are competent in carrying out casework independently. On these occasions, we point out that training of this sort is only possible if there is a previous academic background in phonetics, linguistics or a closely related discipline, but that such training is not possible from scratch. It is true that certain aspects of speaker identification methodology can be taught quite easily, such as how to measure average f0 or long-term formants. However, this trained knowledge is only sufficient as long as the case is easy. However if, for example, the quality is low and it not clear where the third formant is located or whether a certain acoustic pattern is part of speech or of non-speech noise, more in-depth knowledge about speech production and its acoustic consequences is necessary. Or, for example, if formant patterns do not match despite other ample evidence of identity, it is important to have a good knowledge of different potential sources of intra-speaker var-iation. There are many different ways in which a case can be difficult and where in-depth knowledge about speech and language is necessary. It is the opinion of the author that academic phonetic and linguistic training is necessary in order to carry out casework in speaker identification, but this position does not go undisputed in the forensic speech and audio analysis community. Although explicit statements are rare, there is a strong impression that in some countries forensic speaker identification is seen as a technical problem that can be solved by purchasing particular speech analysis equipment and/or applying automatic speaker recognition. Automatic speaker recognition is an important development, but it should be seen as an addition to phonetic/linguistic methods, not as a replacement. Automatic speaker recognition could not be addressed in this chapter, but introductory information and further references are provided in Jessen (2008a).

Further reading

Hollien, H. (1990) *The Acoustics of Crime: The New Science of Forensic Phonetics*, New York: Plenum. (A textbook that gives a good impression of the full range of forensic phonetics and acoustics – including topics outside of speaker identification – and that contains many references to previous literature in the historical development of the field.)

Jessen, M. (2008) 'Forensic phonetics', *Language and Linguistics Compass*, 2: 671–711. (A recent review of forensic speaker identification with an emphasis on speaker comparison theory and methodology, including automatic speaker recognition.)

Nolan, F. (1983) *The Phonetic Bases of Speaker Recognition*, Cambridge: Cambridge University Press. (A classical monograph that lays many terminological and conceptual foundations in forensic speaker identification and that contains relevant phonetic experiments.)

——(1997) 'Speaker recognition and forensic phonetics', in W.J. Hardcastle and J. Laver (eds) *The Handbook of Phonetic Sciences*, Oxford: Blackwell. (An important review which makes it clear that forensic work is an important application of phonetics and that forensic phonetics is an established field within phonetics.)

Rose, P. (2002) *Forensic Speaker Identification*, London: Taylor and Francis. (A modern textbook in forensic speaker identification that emphasises acoustic phonetics and Bayesian reasoning and that provides interesting perspectives for the future of the field.)

Website Appendices

The following references are supported by accompanying conference Powerpoint presentations, which can be viewed on the *Handbook*'s accompanying website available at: http://www.forensiclinguistics.net/.

Jessen, M. (2008b) 'Categorical v. Continuous Variations Between Speakers', paper presented at the 17th Annual Conference of the International Association for Forensic Phonetics and Acoustics, Lausanne. Supported by: *IAFPA 2008 Jessen.ppt*

Moos, A. (2008b) 'Long-Term Formant Distribution (LTF) Based on German Spontaneous and Read Speech', paper presented at the 17th Annual Conference of the International Association for Forensic Phonetics and Acoustics, Lausanne. Supported by: *IAFPA 2008 Moos.ppt*

Tschäpe, N., Trouvain, J., Bauer, D. and Jessen, M. (2005) 'Idiosyncratic Patterns of Filled Pauses', paper presented at the 14th Annual Conference of the International Association for Forensic Phonetics and Acoustics, Marrakesh. Supported by: *IAFPA 2005 Tschaepe et al.ppt*

26

The forensic linguist

The expert linguist meets the adversarial system

Lawrence M. Solan

Science in the adversarial system

The academic world and the world of litigation produce an awkward mix. Lawyers are in the business of winning their cases. Academics are in the business of engaging in disinterested research in an effort to uncover truths. Academics, including those who work in the "hard sciences," are accustomed to such tasks as evaluating competing theories, each of which has its own strengths and weaknesses. Criteria of evaluation generally include both descriptive and explanatory adequacy and sometimes such things as Occam's Razor and other measures of parsimony and elegance. In linguistic theory, for example, competing syntactic accounts are frequently judged on the breadth of the phenomena they are able to explain without resort to *ad hoc* solutions. The more elegant solution that covers more ground wins. In this realm, uncertainty is the norm. Those engaged in scientific inquiry do not close up shop once they have achieved some progress. Rather, they continue their explorations, often revising (and sometimes even discarding) earlier hypotheses as new data and new explanations come to light.

The legal system is also designed to uncover truths. But, in places that employ an adversarial system, it does not do so by conducting disinterested research, but rather through the vigorous presentation of evidence slanted toward different positions. The assumption—more a matter of faith—is that the better sets of facts, arguments and theories presented in the court room will rise to the top, and that thereby the quest for truth will be served (see Landsman 1984). For this reason, during the litigation process, lawyers are likely to exploit the uncertainty of opposing experts. This can lead to serious discomfort when an expert accustomed to living with a level of uncertainty as a professional matter finds himself the subject of ridicule in the courtroom (see, e.g. Shuy 2006; Coulthard and Johnson 2007 for discussion).

Philosopher/legal scholar Susan Haack, drawing on the work of Peirce, comments on the difference between scientific and legal inquiry:

> Distinguishing genuine inquiry, the real thing, from pseudo-inquiry or "sham reasoning," C.S. Peirce – a working scientist as well as the greatest of American

philosophers – wrote that "the spirit … is the most essential thing – the motive"; that genuine inquiry consists in "actually drawing the bow upon truth with intentness in the eye, with energy in the arm." For the same reason, I am tempted to write of advocacy "research" (in scare quotes); for it is something of a stretch to call advocacy research "research" at all. Advocacy "research" is like inquiry insofar as it involves seeking out evidence. But it is part of an advocacy project insofar as it involves seeking out evidence favoring a predetermined conclusion; and it is undertaken in the spirit, from the motive, of an advocate. In short, it is a kind of pseudo-inquiry.

(Haack 2008: 1071)

Making matters worse, lawyers are not required to be sincere in their attacks (Post 1987; Solan 2008). They are not permitted to lie outright. Nonetheless, the lawyer who believes the opposing expert's position to be valid remains obliged to find holes in the analysis and to exploit them vigorously. If a coroner makes a computational error in computing the time of death, the lawyer will—in fact, must—take maximum advantage of the mistake even if the lawyer believes the time of death in the report to be correct. At least that is so in the United States.

It is somewhat ironic that scientific investigation accepts more uncertainty than does the legal process, since it is the legal system's assumption that scientific knowledge is crisp and factual that makes it attractive to the legal system in the first place (see Berger and Solan 2008 for discussion). Nonetheless, that is often the case. The imperfect match between scientific inquiry and the structure of the adversarial system presents a challenge for the expert witness. One lawyer wants the witness to act as a good team player, while the other attempts to rip him or her to shreds. In this article, I bring to the attention of the forensic linguistic community a number of issues that have been raised more generally about expert evidence in the adversarial system that might be important to the field as it develops.

A large body of literature demonstrates that in interpreting facts, people (including experts) tend to be biased toward confirming the result that they have already reached. People are aware of such tendencies in others, but deny it in themselves. This means that even experts with high moral integrity will tend to cast their conclusions in a way that is helpful to the position they have espoused. Moreover, people tend to view positive results without regard to underlying base rates. This has led to the acceptance of forensic identification techniques that are not adequately grounded in science. The proliferation of DNA analysis in legal settings makes the absence of such analysis in other forensic sciences particularly salient, but the problem has been there all along.

The legal system has reacted to these problems in different ways. In the United States, there has been a growing emphasis on the importance of valid and replicable methodology in court, as evidenced by the United States Supreme Court's 1993 *Daubert* decision and it progeny. The UK, while also considering a move in that direction (see Law Commission 2009), has required experts to certify that they understand their first obligation is to be straightforward and disinterested. Both are positive developments.

I begin by discussing some of the cognitive biases that have been discussed in the recent psychological and legal literature. Awareness of them can both help the expert linguist to understand some of the pitfalls of entering the all-or-nothing fray of litigation, and further help to understand the intensity of the current push toward developing reliable methodologies on which experts can base their testimony. I then turn to developments in the legal system directed at addressing some of these problems. Finally, this chapter turns to forensic linguistics in particular, and discusses various standards that the field may adopt on its own behalf.

The challenge facing forensic identification sciences

The need to make forensic science more scientific

Forensic identification techniques have been under serious scrutiny and attack in the United States during the past decade. To take a dramatic example, until recently bullet lead analysis had been a staple of law enforcement agencies in criminal cases. For more than thirty years, analysts, in particular from the FBI, would testify that the lead from a questioned bullet and that from a reference box of ammunition associated with the defendant, "were analytically indistinguishable," "came from the same batch," "were consistent with their having come from the same box of ammunition," and so on. (Giannelli 2007: 200). Disturbingly, difficulty in determining how to couch conclusions about the firmness of an identification shows itself in forensic linguistic identification as well. But more disturbingly, bullet lead analysis has now been shown to be without scientific basis. In 2004, the National Research Council (NRC), which is the research arm of the National Academies (formerly the National Academy of Science) issued a devastating report (NRC 2004). Among its conclusions was that the output from a single "melt" of lead "can range from the equivalent of as few as 12,000 to as many as 35 million 40-grain, .22 caliber longrifle bullets" (NRC 2004: 6). Courts began jumping ship and, in 2005, the FBI abandoned the procedure.[1] Prior to that, the analysis was used in many criminal trials involving firearms, including death penalty cases. The recognition that this forensic procedure is not provably reliable has had its consequences. Based on the discredited technology, in 2008, a Florida court overturned the conviction of a man who had spent ten years in prison for killing his wife based on the discredited technology. The legitimacy of many other convictions has been brought into question.[2]

Lead bullet analysis is not alone. Even fingerprint identification, long considered an airtight method, has been questioned in recent years. Significantly, the history of fingerprint identification reveals that it developed in the absence of studies demonstrating their uniqueness. That has always been taken as a matter of faith (Mnookin 2001a). This is not to say that fingerprinting has been unsuccessful as a tool for law enforcement. The Innocence Project announces on its web page that there have been 240 post-conviction DNA exonerations in the US courts of people who had been convicted of crimes, but of those, only two involved incorrect testimony about fingerprints. In one case, an analyst testified that the comparison was inconclusive when in fact, it had excluded the defendant; in the other, the crime lab compared two sets of the defendants' known prints to each other, rather than comparing the prints at the crime scene to the defendant's known prints.[3] Moreover, while few disagree that fingerprint comparison can be very accurate in most cases (but see Cole 2004), fingerprints in forensic settings are often both partial and degraded and we do not know the rate at which accuracy and consensus diminish as the amount of information is decreased. A case in point is the FBI's incorrect fingerprint identification of an American Muslim as the Madrid bomber (see Dror *et al.* 2005).

The same holds true for handwriting analysis, which has received particularly brutal treatment in the literature on the admissibility of expert testimony (see Risinger and Saks

1996; Mnookin 2001b, but see Moenssens' 1997 defense of the field). Here, again, the issue is not whether document examiners ever get it right. Of course they do. Rather, the issue is that handwriting analysis was not put to the test to determine its limits. Even when a document examiner has been well-trained and is a person of integrity, without the implementation of techniques that have been validated, we do not know where an expert's expertise begins and ends, other than as a matter of trust.

More broadly, in 2009, the National Research Council of the National Academies came out with a report on the status of forensic identification. Entitled *Strengthening Forensic Science in the United States: A Path Forward* (NRC 2009), among its findings were the following:

> Two very important questions should underlie the law's admission of and reliance upon forensic evidence in criminal trials: (1) the extent to which a particular forensic discipline is founded on a reliable scientific methodology that gives it the capacity to accurately analyze evidence and report findings and (2) the extent to which practitioners in a particular forensic discipline rely on human interpretation that could be tainted by error, the threat of bias, or the absence of sound operational procedures and robust performance standards. ... Unfortunately, these important questions do not always produce satisfactory answers in judicial decisions pertaining to the admissibility of forensic science evidence proffered in criminal trials.
>
> (NRC 2009: S-7)

The report, thus, criticizes both the various forensic disciplines for not policing themselves adequately, and the courts for falling asleep at the job and not performing their gatekeeping function with adequate standards. What should be done? The report suggests:

> A body of research is required to establish the limits and measures of performance and to address the impact of sources of variability and potential bias. Such research is sorely needed, but it seems to be lacking in most of the forensic disciplines that rely on subjective assessments of matching characteristics. These disciplines need to develop rigorous protocols to guide these subjective interpretations and pursue equally rigorous research and evaluation programs.
>
> (NRC 2009: S-6)

Cognitive biases in forensic science

What are the biases to which forensic scientists are so susceptible? They are the same biases to which scientists of all sorts may succumb. First among them are *observer effects*, in particular *confirmation bias*. Observer effects refer to the long-recognized fact that "context and expectations influence an individual's perceptions and interpretations of what he observes." (Risinger *et al.* 2002: 12). Recognition of this potential drives a great deal of methodology in science, especially in areas of medical research where double-blind studies are the norm. Even when patients are randomly selected for participation, it is only when both the doctor administering the treatment and the patient receiving it are unaware of whether the patient is receiving the experimental treatment or is a member of the control group receiving a placebo that the results of clinical trials are deemed reliable. The concern is that otherwise subtle, even unconscious cues may lead to distortions in the results.

In the case of forensic experts, one of the most important cues is prior knowledge of the result that the party engaging the expert would like them to reach. This leads to confirmation bias, the "unwitting selectivity in the acquisition and use of evidence" in which people are likely to engage (Nickerson 1998: 175). In fact, even when we have no stake in the outcome, we tend to look at data selectively to confirm tentative conclusions we have reached. In a famous study using a card game, Wason and Johnson-Laird (1972) found that people quickly see the significance of information that may prove them right or wrong. In contrast, most people ignore evidence that can disconfirm a working hypothesis but cannot otherwise serve to strengthen the hypothesis.

Once we have taken a position on a matter, information that supports that position becomes more salient, and information that tends to disconfirm it becomes less so (Nickerson 1998; Simon 2004). To take a classic example from the psychological literature, Darley and Gross (1983) showed two groups of subjects a videotape of a child taking an academic test. One group of subjects was told that the child came from a high socioeconomic background, the other group told that the child came from a low socioeconomic background. They were then asked to evaluate the child's academic ability based on what they observed of the child's behavior while she took the test. The results were dramatic. Those who were told that the child came from a wealthy background rated her ability as greater than did those who were told she was economically disadvantaged. Both groups supported their ratings by referring extensively to evidence from the videotape.

Real-life experiences abound. It happens, for example, when the police, certain that they have apprehended the guilty party and acting in good faith, ignore evidence of another's guilt and of their suspect's innocence as they build their case. Malcolm Coulthard discusses a number of such cases in his writings (see, e.g. Coulthard 2004). In one, convinced that they had apprehended four men who killed a 13-year old newspaper delivery boy, the police extracted a confession from one of them—Patrick Molloy. However, the police denied that the language contained in the confession was language that they had suggested to him and that he had accepted under duress, as he alleged. The four were convicted, and Coulthard was consulted on appeal, at which time he found the transcript of a police interview to be unrealistically identical to that of a statement attributed to him. The Crown conceded error during the appeal process, based on other evidence of the defendants' innocence. Such things happen when the police are so convinced that they have the right person that they feel justified in cutting corners. The doctoring of an interview record is misconduct, but the motivation to do so comes largely from confirmation bias.

Confirmation bias also occurs when an expert witness focuses in a report on the information that bolsters the position taken, and understates or ignores information that would tend to lead to a contrary position. Dror *et al.* (2005) presented five experienced fingerprint analysts with separate pairs of fingerprints for comparison. In each case, the pair was one that the analyst had himself identified as a match sometime earlier in the ordinary course of business. The experimenters also showed each of these five pairs of prints to independent examiners, who agreed that each pair of prints constituted a matched set. However, a confederate told each of these experts that the questioned prints were the ones erroneously identified by the FBI as a match in the Madrid bombing case.

The experts were then told to ignore this contextual information in conducting their analysis. The result was that three of the five experts found no match, one said he could not decide, and only one came to the same conclusion he had reached earlier: that there was a match.

Making things worse, not only are we subject to this bias, but we each have a "bias blind spot" (Pronin et al. 2002). That is, we have a propensity to think that our own beliefs are objective, while the beliefs of others are colored by various biases that influence them. Even when such biases are brought to our attention, we tend to recognize them as applying to others—not to ourselves. In other words, we see bias in others, analytical crispness in ourselves. Pronin and Kugler attribute this asymmetry to the fact that "people over-value thoughts, feelings, and other mental contents, relative to behavior, when assessing their own actions, motives, and preferences, but not when assessing others'" (Pronin and Kugler: 2007: 566). They call this the "Introspection Illusion." Their studies first confirmed the bias blind spot. When, for example, Harvard students were told that some people tend to be biased toward self-serving views of their academic or job performance, they attributed this bias more to other, similarly situated students than to themselves. They further said that they judged themselves more by evaluating their own thoughts and motives, and judged others based more on their actual behavior. Whether judging themselves or others, the more they relied on thoughts and motives, the less bias they found. The more they relied on behavior, the more bias they found. Significantly, when participants were told in advance that relying on introspection instead of evaluating their own behavior can lead them to a biased assessment, they took heed and were no longer subject to the bias blind spot (Pronin and Kugler 2007: 575). This finding may have significant ramifications in the forensic arena.

Judicial reactions to expert evidence in the US and the UK

We have now identified two problems facing the expert linguist: the brutality of the adversarial system, including snide and personal attacks on individuals working within standard scientific paradigms, and a broad concern that the forensic identification sciences lack adequate scientific foundation. This section deals with how the courts have grappled with the second of these issues. The next section will deal with the tension between the two problems, and how forensic linguistics might develop to jointly address them.

Linguistic expert testimony is widely accepted in both English and American courts. However, the courts in the US and the UK have engaged different strategies to deal with the need for ensuring reliable expert testimony. While American courts have focused more on the need for valid and reliable methodology, British courts have concentrated on requiring experts to certify that they have conducted their analysis in a neutral, disinterested manner. Both approaches have something to offer in response to the issues raised above.

The Daubert standard in American courts: the judge as gatekeeper

For most of the twentieth century, American courts admitted scientific evidence if it had "gained general acceptance in the particular field in which it belongs." The standard was derived from a 1923 court of appeals case, Frye v. United States, a case that involved a lie detector test that measured systolic blood pressure. The problem with the Frye test, however, is that it is subject to manipulation by changing the definition of "the particular field in which it belongs." Among lie detector analysts, the device in question in *Frye* might be perfectly acceptable. Among social scientists and medical experts, waiting for the results of validation testing, it might be unacceptable. Moreover, as noted at the beginning of this article, science is often not about certainty, but rather about controversy. The "right" theory may have been articulated, but is not yet generally accepted, whether because of the sociology of the scientific community, or because the theory is in development and has not yet been shown to be able to handle crucial cases and to explain apparent counterexamples.

These problems with the Frye standard were recognized in 1975, when the Federal Rules of Evidence were first adopted. The standard under Rule 702 as originally enacted was that expert evidence should be admitted, "if it will assist the trier of fact to understand the evidence or to determine a fact in issue." It was not clear from the rule's language, however, whether this standard was intended to replace Frye, or merely to explain the goal of the Frye standard.

The Supreme Court of the United States answered that question in three cases decided in the 1990s, which have come to be called the Daubert trilogy. The first case, *Daubert v. Merrell Dow Pharmaceuticals, Inc.*, was decided in 1993. The issue there was whether Bendectin, an anti-nausea drug taken during pregnancy, caused birth defects in the plaintiff's children. Most of the scientific literature said that it did not, but the plaintiff wished to have an expert testify to challenge the scientific literature and to discuss animal studies which suggested that Bendectin might indeed cause birth defects in children.

Ultimately, the case was sent back to the lower appellate court, which ruled that the expert testimony was not admissible because it lacked the indicia of scientific validity. In determining whether proffered testimony is scientifically valid, the standard would no longer be whether it was generally accepted by the scientific community. Rather, the testimony must have a "grounding in the methods and procedures of science" (p. 590). This grounding may be evidenced by four nonexclusive criteria: whether the theory offered has been tested; whether it has been subjected to peer review and publication; the known rate of error; and whether the theory is generally accepted in the scientific community (p. 593). Note that the fourth criterion is the Frye standard, which has now become one of a number of nonexclusive factors that a court will consider.

The second case in the Daubert trilogy, *General Electric Company v. Joiner*, concerned the standard of review for appellate courts of Daubert decisions made at trial. The Court held that rulings about the admissibility of expert testimony should be overturned only if the trial court abused its discretion. This is a very lax standard, and it means in essence that the decisions of trial judges to admit or reject expert evidence will rarely be reviewed seriously, and even more rarely reversed.

Finally, in *Kumho Tire Company v. Carmichael*, the Supreme Court held that the Daubert approach applies not only to scientific testimony, but also to experts who testify based on their experience. The expert in that case was called to testify on the cause of tire damage based on his experience in the tire industry. The Court held that his opinion based upon experience that cannot be tested did not meet evidentiary standards. The determining fact is whether the expert "employs in the courtroom the same level of intellectual rigor that characterizes the practice of an expert in the relevant field" (p. 152).

As a result of these three cases, the Federal Rules of Evidence were amended to permit expert testimony if it will "assist the trier of fact to understand the evidence or to determine a fact in issue," and if:

(1) The testimony is based upon sufficient facts or data,
(2) The testimony is the product of reliable principles and methods, and
(3) The witness has applied the principles and methods reliably to the facts of the case.

(Rule 702, Fed R. Evid.)

It should be noted that all three cases in the Daubert trilogy were civil cases in which an individual was suing a corporation, and in all three, the courts held that the expert's proffered testimony did not pass muster. It was the legal academic community, and to some extent criminal defense lawyers, who subsequently argued that the Daubert approach should apply to the forensic identification sciences, which were inadequately validated notwithstanding their claims (see, e.g. Risinger and Saks 1996). It is still not at all clear that American courts apply these principles evenhandedly in civil and criminal cases alike (Risinger 2000), or for that matter, that the actual rulings of courts differ significantly depending upon whether a jurisdiction applies the Frye standard or the Daubert standard (Cheng and Yoon 2005). Nonetheless, Daubert has colored the debate about forensic testimony, which often is offered as scientific even though validations studies have not been conducted in a scientific manner.

Expert certification of neutrality in the UK

The UK has taken a somewhat different approach (see Law Commission 2009), although, at the time of writing, Daubert-like standards are under consideration there as well. Rather than focusing on the methodology, the UK has traditionally focused on the credentials and integrity of the expert. Aware of the temptation for experts to present biased evidence, Civil Procedure Rules have been enacted requiring experts to affirm that they are acting in a neutral manner. The rules state explicitly that

1. It is the duty of an expert to help the Court on matters within his expertise.
2. This duty overrides any obligation to the person from whom he has received instructions or by whom he is paid.

(Civil Procedure Rule 35.3)

Expert reports must contain a statement that the expert understands his duty to the court and that he has complied with that duty (Civil Procedure Rules 35.10).

Similarly, Appendix 11 to the Admiralty and Commercial Courts Guide (2002) imposes neutrality on experts. Because the material may not be familiar to those who do not work within the British courts, it is worth quoting in full:

1. It is the duty of an expert to help the court on the matters within his expertise: rule 35.3(1). This duty is paramount and overrides any obligation to the person from whom the expert has received instructions or by whom he is paid: rule 35.3(2).
2. Expert evidence presented to the court should be, and should be seen to be, the independent product of the expert uninfluenced by the pressures of litigation.
3. An expert witness should provide independent assistance to the court by way of objective unbiased opinion in relation to matters within his expertise. An expert witness should never assume the role of an advocate.

4. An expert witness should not omit to consider material facts which could detract from his concluded opinion.
5. An expert witness should make it clear when a particular question or issue falls outside his expertise.
6. If an expert's opinion is not properly researched because he considers that insufficient data is available, this must be stated in his report with an indication that the opinion is no more than a provisional one.
7. In a case where an expert witness who has prepared a report is unable to confirm that the report contains the truth, the whole truth and nothing but the truth without some qualification, that qualification must be stated in the report.
8. If, after exchange of reports, an expert witness changes his view on a material matter having read another expert's report or for any other reason, such change of view should be communicated in writing (through the party's legal representatives) to the other side without delay, and when appropriate to the court.

(*Admiralty and Commercial Courts Guide*, 2002: 151)

Admirably, the goal is to reduce the adversarial nature of scientific debate in the litigation context. No doubt these standards accomplish that goal to some extent. However, given both the pressure placed on experts and the bias blind spot discussed earlier, it is not likely to accomplish that goal up to the level of purely disinterested scientific standards. Experts will continue to be tempted to write short, uninformative reports in order to keep the opposing party from preparing a rebuttal adequately; present few if any counterexamples to their analysis in their main reports; or to be as helpful to opposing parties during cross-examination as they would be if they believed themselves to be entirely neutral; or to raise issues on their own that might compromise their party's position, even if they would have done so in an academic climate. As Sanders notes:

> [W]hen [experts] do fail to present adequate justification for a belief, often it is not because they fail to present the best case for a position but that they fail to tell the "whole truth" about their belief and present with equal force the evidence for and against it.

(Sanders 2007: 1558)

Thus, it should not be surprising that the UK is considering a move toward focusing on valid methods.

The direction of forensic linguistics

I have identified two problems facing the linguist who ventures into the world of litigation: One is a problem that experts have with the legal system—its intolerance of uncertainty in scientific inquiry, notwithstanding that scientists accept that the current best account may not ultimately survive further the test of time. This, combined with the aggressive advocacy of the adversarial system, can lead lawyers to ridicule even experts who are prominent researchers in their fields. The result of this hostility is a reluctance on the part of many top scholars to participate in the system at all (see Coulthard and Johnson 2007 for discussion and also Gray, this volume). The second problem that the legal system has with experts is that the experts themselves provide inadequate protection against bias by failing to develop methods that have been independently validated. This is the main thrust of the National Research Council (2009) report on forensic science in the United States.

I would like to argue here that in fact these are the same problem, at least in large part. Fixing the second will reduce the severity of the first in that the best way for an expert to avoid bias and to reduce the stress associated with defending one's professional opinion in court is to employ reliable methods that have been proven valid. A second, somewhat less effective, approach is for experts to submit to proficiency testing. This is not as good as the first method, because even proficient experts can succumb to bias in a forensic setting. Nonetheless, I explore the benefits of proficiency testing below.

Developing valid methodology

The basic concern in developing methods that will be acceptable in court and meet the standards of normal science is to develop and test those methods outside the litigation context. Not only is litigation-driven research more prone to bias, but it is less highly valued by the courts for that reason. In fact, as Haack (2008) points out, once Mrs. Daubert's case was sent back to the lower court for additional proceedings, the judge there commented on the reduced reliability of scientific evidence gathered for the purpose of the litigation itself. Judge Kozinski commented there: "[I]n determining whether proposed expert testimony amounts to good science, we may not ignore the fact that a scientist's normal workplace is the lab or the field, not the courtroom or the lawyer's office." (*Daubert 2*, 1316–17 n.3) He further contrasted the increased likelihood of bias when the result is tied to remuneration, with independent research conducted as normal science, which carries its own indicia of reliability.

The development of valid methodology has produced positive results in other forensic fields. For example, as mentioned above, handwriting analysis has been in ill repute in the United States because of its inability to describe a valid method with provable rates of accuracy. In part because of that criticism, the government has funded research in that area, resulting in improved technology that has been accepted under Daubert analysis. In a 2002 case, *United States v. Prime*, the trial court summarizes some of that progress— including a greater understanding of the rate of error—in admitting the testimony of a handwriting expert who had been involved in these improvements to that field. Academic critics have also begun to recognize this progress (see, e.g. Giannelli 2003: 8–9).

How such research is to be conducted in the linguistic arena differs from one subfield to another. The forensic phonetic literature, for example, is replete with studies of what circumstances make it easier or harder to recognize a speaker by his or her voice (see Yarmey forthcoming for a good summary). Moreover, some researchers are developing automated systems that are being tested for rates of error in terms of both misses (failure to identify) and false alarms (false identification; see Solan and Tiersma 2005 for discussion of some of these developments.). At the same time, there has been some movement toward the proficiency testing of those phoneticians who use both aural and acoustical information to form judgments, a trend to which I return below.

When it comes to authorship identification, some researchers have attempted to identify criteria which, taken in combination, can diagnose both authorship and non-authorship. Chaski (2005), for example, uses aspects of punctuation, marked syntactic structures and word length in combination. Her results are impressive, and she has been permitted to testify in cases after Daubert scrutiny, although the process has still not been tested for validity and reliability through independent means. My point here is a basic one: the research upon which expert testimony is based is best conducted in the lab, outside the context of a particular dispute, as Judge Kozinski prescribes. Other researchers have employed similar research methods, using criteria for identification that differ from Chaski's, sometimes using sophisticated mathematical modeling (see, e.g. Stamatatos 2006).

Recent research into the conventions of text messaging shows promise for research along these lines. Grant (this volume) discusses cases in which two possible authors of a questioned text message use in general quite different styles of abbreviation and ellipsis in their texting. Once pointed out, one's intuition is that such differences will predict authorship, although research confirming this has not yet been published. Grant himself suggests some ways in which such research could be structured. Olsson (2003) observes that while some texters are entirely consistent in their use of stylistic conventions, some are not, and the amount of inconsistency varies from person to person. This diversity should be taken into account in determining—based on research from corpora that are already available or which are gathered for research purposes—how predictive of co-authorship and non-authorship these conventions are.

In other subfields of forensic linguistics, the methodology may require only that the types of materials examined and the arguments made be standardized to the extent that a consensus develops about what might be useful to the legal community. Linguists frequently testify in trademark disputes, for example. Those who conduct frequent analyses, for the purpose of determining the confusability or the strength of a mark, might publish their approaches in order to set best practices for the field. This, at least to some extent, is occurring (see Shuy 2002; Butters 2008a and this volume).

Proficiency as a substitute for methodology

Those who have practiced in the area of forensic linguistics, especially in the area of authorship identification, might respond to the call for methodology as follows: "I have been doing this for a long time, and I am very good at it. I cannot tell in advance exactly which features in a particular case will be diagnostic of authorship, so requiring that I develop a methodology that is tightly defined will require me to ignore data that might be important in an individual case." In discussing some prominent cases involving authorship identification, Peter Tiersma and I (Solan and Tiersma 2005) note that the absence of established methods might lead some insightful analysis to remain unacceptable in the courtroom. We therefore suggest that research projects be initiated to discover and validate reliable methods that will stand up to evidentiary scrutiny.

Perhaps, however, proficiency testing, if done properly could serve as an intermediate level of validation while a field conducts research into replicable methods. In a recent lecture, Professor Jennifer Mnookin has referred to this as the "black box" approach to forensic identification, and argues that it might be useful in some instances. The concern is that in some instances, Daubert may be causing us to throw the baby out with the bathwater, rejecting skilled diagnosis based on experience (see Sanders 2001 for discussion). Medical diagnosis is in part an art in which the most skilled diagnosticians are unable to articulate what separates them from the rest of the pack (see Groopman 2007). It would not be surprising if practitioners of forensic linguistic identification also developed skills that more than meet the standard of being helpful to the trier of fact.

Valid proficiency testing is difficult to accomplish. The biggest problem is developing materials that are relevant to real-life forensic problems. For example, when a document has only two possible authors, rejecting one of them is sufficient to establish the other as the author (assuming only one person wrote the document). In other cases, however, the question is whether a particular suspect wrote a document, and there is no information about who else might have written it otherwise. How many other potential authors should the expert be able to reject before reaching an opinion that the suspect is the likely author? These are difficult questions that must be resolved before proficiency testing can be designed in a meaningful way.

Notwithstanding these difficulties, information about a practitioner's proficiency might be useful to the legal system, especially during the development of validated methodologies. In fact, the success rate of proficient practitioners might be compared with that of other methods, particularly automated ones. Cambier-Langeveld (2007a) conducted a study in which she pitted phoneticians using the auditory-acoustic method against semi-automatic and automatic speaker recognition systems. The result was that the machines produced fewer false alarms than the phoneticians, but at the same time failed to make some correct identifications that the phoneticians were able to make. Some phoneticians were extremely good and outperformed the machines, but disturbingly, the phoneticians varied in their level of skill, highlighting the importance of proficiency testing at the minimum. Without that testing, the individual who goes before the jury with confidence and charisma may be the one who prevails, regardless of actual skill.

Even experts who are proven to be good at what they do through proficiency testing will be subject to bias when they conduct their analysis in a litigation context. Thus, I do not advocate this approach as a long-term goal in the development of forensic linguistics. Nonetheless, it might play a role in preserving insight while the field moves ahead.

Conclusion

I have explored here two related, but seemingly distinct problems that arise when the expert linguist enters the world of litigation: the legal system is unrealistic about what science can do, and the forensic community has not adequately developed valid and reliable methods. I have attempted here to show how these problems can be solved together, through a single approach to methodology, and have suggested that proficiency testing might bridge the gap in the short term.

It will be up to both the academic and the forensic linguistics communities to move the field ahead in these directions. To do so is particularly difficult given the dual role that many play as both academics and consultants. Yet some thirty years ago, it was the academic linguists and phoneticians who demanded that forensic use of spectrograms (voice prints) be used judiciously since they had not been proven accurate in forensic settings. The field of forensic linguistics remains capable of moving itself forward in the early part of the twenty-first century.

Notes

The author wishes to express his gratitude to Susan Haack and Michael Risinger for valuable comments on an earlier draft of this article.
1 Eric Lichtblau, 'F.B.I. Abandons Disputed Test for Bullets from Crime Scene', *New York Times*, Sept. 2, 2005, p. A2.

2 Judge Overturns Jimmy Ates' Conviction: Use of Junk Science Leads to Release, press release of the Florida Innocence Project, available online at: www.oranous.com/innocence/JimmyAtes/Ates%20Press%20Release%2012%2017%202008%20FINAL.pdf (accessed 16 July 2009).
3 www.innocenceproject.org/docs/DNA_Exonerations_Forensic_Science.pdf, visited June 21, 2009.

Further reading

Darley, John M. and Paget H. Gross (1983) 'A hypothesis-confirming bias in labeling effects,' *Journal of Personality and Social Psychology*, 44: 20–33.
Giannelli, Paul C. (2007) 'Wrongful convictions and forensic science: the need to regulate crime labs,' *North Carolina Law Review*, 86: 163–235.
National Research Council of the National Academies (2009) *Strengthening Forensic Science in the United States: A Path Forward*, Washington, DC: The National Academy Press.
Pronin, Emily and Matthew Kugler (2007) 'Valuing thoughts, ignoring behavior: The introspection illusion as a source of the bias blind spot,' *Journal of Experimental Social Psychology*, 43: 565–78.
Sanders, Joseph (2007) 'Expert witness ethics,' *Fordham Law Review*, 76: 1539–84.
Shuy, Roger (2006) *Linguistics in the Courtroom: A Practical Guide*, Oxford: Oxford University Press.

Laws and cases cited

Daubert v. Merrell Dow Pharmaceuticals, Inc., 509 U.S. 579 (1993).
Daubert v. Merrell Dow Pharmaceuticals, Inc., 43 F.3d 1311, (9th Cir. 1993)("*Daubert 2*").
Frye v. United States, 293 F. 213 (D.C. Cir. 1923).
General Electric Company v. Joiner, 522 U.S. 136 (1997).
Kumho Tire Company v. Carmichael, 526 U.S. 137 (1999).
United States v. Prime, 220 F. Supp. 2d 1203 (W.D. Wash. 2002).
Admiralty and Commercial Courts Guide, Appendix 11 (UK) (2002) available online at: www.hmcourts-service.gov.uk/docs/guide.pdf.
Civil Procedure Rule 35.3 (UK).
Federal Rules of Evidence, Rule 702 (US).

Multilingualism in legal contexts

27

Nationality claims

Language analysis and asylum cases

Diana Eades

Introduction

In the first two decades of the development of forensic linguistics, most expert linguistic evidence was in criminal and civil law. However, the most recent legal area in which linguists are becoming involved concerns immigration, specifically in relation to the use of 'language analysis' in the investigation of the nationality claims of asylum seekers who do not have any official documents from their country of origin. This is most commonly referred to as Language Analysis in the Determination of Origin, or LADO (although it has also been referred to as *linguistic identification*, as in Eades and Arends 2004; and LingID, as in Eades *et al.* 2003). Language analysis is often sought by immigration departments for use in their administrative processing of claims to asylum, but, given that appeals against decisions of administrators can end up in the legal process, where linguists can be called on as experts to give counter-analyses, then this work comes within forensic linguistics.

According to the United Nations High Commission for Refugees (UNHCR 2008), at the end of 2007, there were 11.5 million refugees worldwide and 647,000 new applications for asylum or refugee status. Contrary to the widespread myth that refugees are flooding industrialised countries, the UNHCR estimates that only about 14% of the world's refugees are living outside their region of origin. That is, most refugees flee to neighbouring countries. Nevertheless, the fear of being 'swamped' by asylum seekers is commonly voiced in industrialised countries (UNHCR 2007: 16) and it is in this climate of fear, serious human rights abuses and unprecedented global movement that LADO work is situated.

This chapter aims to provide an overview of how LADO work is carried out, and some of the specific linguistic issues involved. The first section below outlines the way in which LADO works. There follows an introduction to some concerns of linguists about problematic assumptions and practices. A sample report is then presented and discussed in order to exemplify some of the issues involved in language variation, multilingualism and language contact. Of particular concern are the problems which arise from LADO judgements and reports being produced by 'native speakers' who have not been trained in linguistics. The chapter concludes with a discussion about the challenges for linguists who move beyond expertise in individual cases and/or in scholarly research to engage in 'expert awareness raising'. This chapter draws in part on my earlier work on this topic, namely in Eades and Arends (2004), Eades (2005), Eades (2008a) and Eades (2009).

How LADO work is done

Asylum seekers are people who have left their home country and who claim refugee status in one of the approximately 150 countries which are signatories to the 1951 United Nations Refugees Convention. In assessing claims for asylum, the main issue for the determining authority (typically the immigration department) is to ascertain whether the applicant has a 'well-founded fear of being persecuted' in their home country. Thus, in immigration interviews, applicants recount their experiences in their home country, which have often involved the persecution of themselves or of family members. Applicants also explain why they are currently unable to return to their home country because of fear of future persecution. The immigration department typically refers to current information about the human rights situation in that country, such as reports by the US State Department or the online factbook of the US Central Intelligence Agency. In this way, the department assesses such factors as the plausibility of the applicant's story, and the recent and current situation in the country from which the applicant has fled. But, a second major concern arises in cases where applicants have no official documentation which can prove their national origin or citizenship. For example, in Australia during the years when many asylum seekers said they were fleeing persecution in Afghanistan (1999–2002), there was a widespread view that many of these people were actually from Pakistan and were not genuine refugees. It is relevant to note that there are many reasons why asylum seekers arrive in a new country without travel documents. For example, Hazaras in Afghanistan were not eligible for Afghan travel documents during Taliban rule (Brennan 2003: 51).

When an immigration officer suspects that an asylum seeker's claims about their origin are not truthful, a tape-recorded interview is conducted for the purposes of language analysis. Such interviews are sometimes carried out in the asylum seeker's first language by an interpreter, and sometimes by an immigration official with the help of an interpreter. But frequently in some countries, the interview is carried out by an immigration officer using an international lingua franca such as English, which is not the first language of either the interviewer or interviewee. The tape-recorded interview is usually analysed either within the department or by one of the small number of private companies in Europe who do this work. However, the practice of the Swiss government is different in that the interviews are carried out by phone by the linguist who will carry out the analysis (Baltisberger and Favaro 2007).

Generally, the aim of the analysis is to make a judgement on the basis of the recorded speech about the speaker's claims about origin, whether this is national, regional or ethnic. Sometimes the analysis comments on the applicant's claims about the countries in which they (say they) have lived. The analysis can also include making a judgement about whether the speech on the recording is 'authentic' in the sense of being the way that the person 'really speaks', or whether, on the contrary, the speaker is trying to sound like someone from a particular background. For example, in several of the Australian cases studied by Eades *et al.* (2003), the language analysis concluded that the speaker was a Hazara from Pakistan who was trying to speak as if he was from Afghanistan, because of alleged pronunciation or word choice, as we will see in the example below.

The analyst's judgement is communicated in a written report to the immigration department, where it can form the basis of a decision about the granting of asylum, or where it can be one of many factors involved in making such a decision. To give an example which appears to typify the use of LADO in a number of countries, an asylum seeker in Australia who claimed to be from Afghanistan was denied refugee status by the immigration department, largely on the basis of a report by a European language analysis company (see RRT 2000 for details of this case). This company analysed a short tape-recording of the asylum seeker speaking to an interpreter in the immigration detention centre in Australia, and found that the man was speaking the Hazaragi dialect of Dari, which is 'mainly spoken in central Afghanistan but also in Pakistan and Iran'. On the basis of the interviewee's use of one Urdu word, and his pronunciation of 'some words with a slight Urdu accent', the conclusion of the analyst was that the dialect used by the asylum seeker 'may, with considerable certainty, be said to originate from the Quetta region' of Pakistan. In coming to this conclusion on the basis of some Urdu influence in the applicant's speech, the analyst ignored the fact that Urdu is also spoken in some parts of Afghanistan (Grimes 1992). The analysis also ignored the fact that the border between Afghanistan and Pakistan is porous, and that people escaping Afghanistan have to travel through Pakistan. The LADO report played an important role in the decision of the immigration department that this applicant was from Pakistan, and not from Afghanistan, as he claimed. The government decision was later overturned by an appeal to the Refugee Review Tribunal, which raised a number of doubts over the assumptions in the language analysis. It is also worth pointing out that in this case the applicant had reported that he 'had had difficulty understanding the interpreter because the interpreter had not been Hazara' (but presumably a speaker of a different variety of the language).

Linguists' concerns

Several linguists have raised concerns about some of the LADO reports they have seen (usually, but not always, when asked to provide a counter-expertise report). In 2003, a group of Australian linguists including the author (Eades *et al.* 2003) examined decisions of 58 Australian appeals in the Refugee Review Tribunal in cases in which LADO reports had been used. This report concluded (p. 179) that the 'language analysis' being used in Australian asylum seeker cases at that time appeared 'to be based on "folk views" about the relationship between language and nationality and ethnicity, rather than sound linguistic principles'. Concerns over cases in the Netherlands and Belgium have been raised by Arends (in Eades and Arends 2004); Corcoran (2004); Maryns (2004, 2006). Readers are directed to these publications for examples of LADO, and linguistic discussion of them. Eades and Arends (2004) also raised concerns about the confidence with which Simo Bobda *et al.* (1999: 303) claim that 'the regional and national origin of [sub-Saharan] African speakers of English can very reliably be identified' on the basis of linguistic 'clues' in their use of English as a second language. Among the issues raised is that Simo Bobda *et al.*'s discussion 'makes insufficient allowance for variation within a language variety, as well as for bilingual speech, assuming that each speaker will consistently use a variety of English which is bounded by geographical and/or political borders' (Eades and Arends 2004: 184).

A major concern addressed in all of these publications by linguists is the reliance in many of the LADO reports on folk linguistic views about language use and the relationships between language varieties. (Folk linguistics refers to 'popular beliefs about language, many of which differ from professional linguistic understandings' Swann *et al.* 2004: 112.) For example one such LADO report stated that on one occasion in his 15-minute interview, an applicant 'uses a typical Pakistani word *patata* (= potatoes), which indicates that he has lived in Pakistan for a period of time' (cited by the New Zealand Refugee Status Appeals Authority RSAA 2002). Such an 'analysis' appears to be based on an unsubstantiated popular belief about the use of a particular word. A linguist who had lived and worked in Pakistan for more than 12 years gave contra-analysis in this New Zealand case. She pointed out that even 'if *patata* is used in Pakistan the use of a single vocabulary item is not proof of residence in Pakistan. Vocabulary from non-indigenous food stuffs is typically borrowed'.

Linguists' concerns over LADO reports being written by analysts who base their 'language analysis' on folk linguistics have not been restricted to Australia, New Zealand, the Netherlands and Belgium. In 2004, an international group of linguists (Language and National Origin Group) released a 2,000-word document titled *Guidelines for the Use of Language Analysis in Relation to Questions of National Origin in Refugee Cases* (http://www. forensiclinguistics.net/). These Guidelines (as I will now refer to them), were intended to provide some elementary understanding for governments, lawyers and refugee advocates of linguistic issues relevant to LADO, particularly 'in deciding whether and to what degree language analysis is reliable in particular cases'. The authors took 10 months to produce the Guidelines, engaging in lengthy email deliberations about how best to explain relevant linguistic issues to non-linguists. The 19 signatories came from six countries. About half of them had direct LADO experience, either in producing reports for immigration departments, or in responding to such reports as experts providing counter-analysis.

The Guidelines document comprises seven general guidelines and four more specific ones. The general guidelines address the general limitations of linguistic expertise, for example explaining that linguists should not be asked to make determinations about national origin, nationality or citizenship (Guidelines 1 and 2). Rather, linguistic analysis can sometimes be used to draw reasonable conclusions about the country of socialisation of a speaker, that is where the speaker has learned, implicitly and/or explicitly, how to be a member of a local society, or of local societies. And there is no necessary connection between a person's region of socialisation on the one hand and the political or bureaucratic categories of national origin, nationality or citizenship, on the other hand. However, sometimes the indications about a person's region of socialisation which are revealed in the linguistic analysis of that person's speech may assist immigration departments in their determination of the political or bureaucratic dimensions. Another issue addressed by the general guidelines concerns the qualifications and expertise required to carry out LADO. Guideline 3 states that 'language analysis must be done by qualified linguists', and Guideline 7 explains that 'the expertise of native speakers in not the same as the expertise of linguists'.

Readers are referred to the full Guidelines (http://www.forensiclinguistics.net/) and also to discussion of them in Eades (2005, 2008a, 2009). The more specific guidelines (numbers 8–11) provide basic linguistic guidance on these four topics:

(#8)   the relationships between linguistic borders and national borders
(#9)   language mixing
(#10)   where the language of the interview is not the speaker's first language
(#11)   where the dialect of the interviewer or interpreter is different from the dialect of the interviewee.

Sample LADO report

In order to exemplify some of the concerns of linguists about the assumptions and practices which are often involved in LADO, I present an example below. This is the full 'language analysis' report prepared in 2001 by a European company for the Australian government (and cited in the Federal Court decision in the appeal in this case, FCA 2003). Eades *et al.* (2003) found evidence that indicates this report was typical of the reports being prepared for the Australian and other governments by two large European companies. Although the Australian government is understood to be currently using LADO much less than it did a few years ago (Eades 2009), its use continues in many European countries.

My purpose in citing this example is not to enter into a discussion of whether the applicant had a well-founded fear of persecution. While this is the ultimate issue to be decided in asylum seeker cases, it is not an issue for linguistic expertise. Nor is it my purpose to make any judgement about this applicant's claim to be a citizen of Afghanistan, an issue on which I can have no opinion, having no relevant expertise. But this report exemplifies a number of issues that concern linguists. Readers who are interested in the counter-analysis presented by a linguist, or in tracing the long legal history of this complex case from the immigration department to the Refugee Review Tribunal and then to the Federal Court of Australia, should read FCA (2003).

Full report (section numbers added)
[Report heading]: LINGUISTIC AND TEXTUAL ANALYSIS
Date: 3.12.2001 File no: CONARA 089
Language: Dari

[preamble]: The criteria used for linguistic and/or textual analysis of this type include local or regional language characteristics of a phonological, morphological, syntactic and lexical nature (i.e. elements of sound, patterns of word formation, the formation of grammatical sentences, and vocabulary); for some languages, stylistic traits; and, in textual analysis, handwriting.

The following observations were made in conjunction with a study of the tape/ document submitted for analysis. As many linguistic aspects as possible were taken into consideration.

[1] The applicant speaks Dari. His Dari dialect is called Hazaragi. Hazaragi is mainly spoken in central Afghanistan, but there are also Hazaragi speaking minority populations in for example Pakistan and Iran. The applicant speaks colloquial language. His accent is Pakistani.

[2] He speaks ungrammatically and says for example: "SAIS. MO KE ASTA AZ QARIE HAIDER BUDE. QARIE HAIDER KE ASTA DA SE QOL TAQSIM SHODA BUD. YAK BA NAME SAWSANGE HAIDER, YAK BA NAME QANTAR GHOE HAIDER WA YAK BANAME LAKHCHAGE HAIDER, INA KE BUD DAR BAINE WOLESWALI JAGHORI BUD WA DAR BAINE WOLAYATE GHAZNI BUD. I MONTEQE AZ MO KE ASTA I ANGORI YAGAN SE SAD RAH PAIPIYADA DUR BUT WA YAGAN YAK SAT."

[3] The applicant uses the Hazaragi verb prefix "MO", for example "MOKAD", "MONA", "MOSHA" and "MOGA".

[4] He uses common Hazaragi words such as "GALA", "LATA PERO", "PORTA", "GOLKHO" and "SHIGHAI".

[5] He pronounces final "T" as "D" in the word "SAT" and final "D" as "T" in the word "BUD". These are also Hazaragi traits.

[6] He pronounces many words with a Pakistani pronunciation, for example "ONJAGA", "BAZI", "NERGAW", "MEDGAW", "KHATOM", "NOMAZ" and "TOBGANTAI".

[7] He uses the Urdu words "PAN", "BAD", and "TASOWA". Urdu is not spoken in Afghanistan.

[8] The applicant's Hazaragi dialect is Pakistani. His mother tongue is Dari.

[9] Observations made in conjunction with a study of the dialect/language variant occurring in the text/tape recording submitted for analysis suggest that:
The dialect/language variant occurring in the text/tape recording may with considerable certainty be said to originate from: PAKISTAN, BALUCHISTAN.

Discussion of sample report

Apart from the general preamble about the criteria used for analysis and the general preamble to the closing statement, this analysis comprises 230 words.

Preamble

The general introduction to the report suggests that it will comprise phonological, morphological, syntactic and lexical analysis, but what is actually to be presented is then more aptly referred to as 'observations'.

[1] The applicant speaks Dari

The opening of the substantive part of the report presents the analyst's conclusion about the applicant's language (Dari), dialect (Hazaragi), language style (colloquial) and accent (Pakistani). The analyst's claim about the dialect and accent are taken up in the report. The opening paragraph also explains that Hazaragi Dari is spoken in Afghanistan, Pakistan and Iran.

[2] He speaks ungrammatically and says for example: 'SAIS. MO KE ASTA AZ QARIE'

The first matter of concern for linguists is in the diagnosis that the applicant 'speaks ungrammatically' and the supporting evidence given. As no analysis of the 67-word extract is provided as evidence for ungrammatical speech, it is impossible to be sure how this term is being used. Does it mean for example that the applicant is using ungrammatical expressions which typify a language learner? Or is the analyst using the term in the folk linguistic sense to mean that the applicant is speaking a non-standard variety? We note that this 67-word extract is presented with unconventional full capitalisation and conventional punctuation. It does not indicate pauses, false starts, repairs or other features of language learners' speech. This would tend to suggest that the analyst's assertion that the applicant 'speaks ungrammatically' refers to the use of some non-standard features. If so, what features? Further, there is nothing in the rest of the report which could support the view that the applicant is a learner of Hazaragi Dari. There is no indication of which features are ungrammatical or non-standard, and no indication of what speaking grammatically would be. This raises the concern that the analyst has no awareness of the realities of language variation.

Central to sociolinguistics, studies of language variation have established some basic findings about language use which are at odds with much folk linguistic belief and prescriptivism about how a language should be spoken. Thus, for example, sociolinguists have found that the varieties of English spoken by both African-Americans in the US and by Australian Aborigines have their own grammatical rules, which differ from the Standard English of these countries in systematic ways (e.g. Labov 1972; Kaldor and Malcolm 1991). Even so, many non-linguists still describe the way in which African-Americans speak English as ungrammatical (for example when they hear an African-American say *He be walking* instead of *He usually walks*).

[3] The applicant uses the Hazaragi verb prefix 'MO', for example 'MOKAD'

[4] He uses common Hazaragi words such as 'GALA'

[5] He pronounces final 'T' as 'D' in the word 'SAT' and final 'D' as 'T' in the word 'BUD'. These are also Hazaragi traits

These next three paragraphs of the report provide examples of Hazaragi grammatical, lexical and phonological features observed by the analyst in the applicant's speech. From the point of view of the applicant's claim, these observations of Hazaragi features are not contradictory, as the applicant claims to be a speaker of the Hazaragi dialect of the Dari language. But, like paragraph [2], these paragraphs are also confusing: if the applicant has these listed features of Hazaragi in some of his speech, what language variety does he speak in the rest of the interview? Presumably, it is Dari, but not Hazaragi Dari? To what extent is Hazaragi Dari distinctive from other varieties of Dari?

It is notable that these three paragraphs of the report, like the preceding ones, use capital letters, rather than any form of phonetic or phonemic transcription. This is particularly problematic for paragraph [5], as well as for [6] below, as they deal with phonology.

[6] He pronounces many words with a Pakistani pronunciation, for example 'ONJAGA'

This is a confusing statement, as there are many languages spoken in Pakistan. What particular 'Pakistani pronunciation' does the applicant have? And what exactly are the cited forms? Are these the conventional spellings of Dari words for which the applicant does not have an Afghan Hazaragi pronunciation? If so, how does his pronunciation differ from that of Afghan Hazaragi for these words? Or are these forms the analyst's representation of the applicant's 'Pakistani pronunciation'? Whatever these forms represent, the fact that no phonetic indications of the alleged pronunciations are given adds to the vagueness of this statement.

[7] He uses the Urdu words 'PAN', 'BAD', and 'TASOWA'. Urdu is not spoken in Afghanistan

This paragraph reveals an idealised view of language usage, in which each individual speaker is supposed to speak only one language at a time, and never use words borrowed from one language while speaking another. This folk linguistic view is at odds with the findings of linguistic research that show that multilingualism is the norm in many societies throughout the world, and that many bilingual speakers use more than one language variety in a single interaction, an issue addressed in Guideline 9 (see for example Edwards 2004: 5; Auer and Wei 2007; Wei 2000). It also wrongly claims that Urdu in not spoken in Afghanistan, an error found in other LADO reports, as indicated above. However, even while Urdu is not spoken as much in Afghanistan as it is in Pakistan, it appears that the applicant had quite a bit of contact with people from Pakistan. He claimed to have spent time while living in Afghanistan helping at his uncle's shop, which was situated in a market town on the main road to Pakistan (FCA 2003: #3). In addition to contact there with people travelling to and from Pakistan, he also reported spending time in Pakistan after his escape from Afghanistan (#5). In contact situations such as these, people often acquire features from other language varieties.

This paragraph also reveals a homogeneistic view about the relationship between language and social group, which is based on the erroneous assumption that each social group uses just one discrete language variety (see Eades 2005, 2008a).

[8] The applicant's Hazaragi dialect is Pakistani. His mother tongue is Dari.

The report concludes that the applicant speaks Dari as his mother tongue, and that the particular dialect of Dari that he speaks is the Hazaragi dialect of Pakistan.

[9] ... The dialect/language variant occurring in the text/tape recording may with considerable certainty be said to originate from: PAKISTAN, BALUCHISTAN

No evidence is given to support the analyst's decision that the language variety spoken by the applicant on the tape originates from the Baluchistan region of Pakistan. We have seen that the complete evidence given in the report to support this finding comprises the allegation of a 'Pakistani pronunciation' of 'many words', of which seven were cited. The other negative comment about the applicant's speech is that he speaks 'ungrammatically'.

No connection is made in the report between the analyst's assertion that the applicant speaks 'ungrammatically', and the assertion that he is a speaker of the Pakistani Hazaragi dialect of Dari. We have seen above that the analyst gives no indication of how he is using the term 'ungrammatically'. As mentioned above, it most likely reflects a folk view about deviation from a standard variety. If this is the case, do Pakistani Hazaragi speakers typically speak 'ungrammatically'? Do they speak 'ungrammatically' more often than speakers of Afghanistan Hazaragi? There is no *analysis* of the allegedly ungrammatical features in the applicant's speech, and there is also no reference to the ways in which Hazaragi dialects differ between speakers in Pakistan and speakers in Afghanistan.

Without such analysis and comparison, there are many unanswered questions. For example, is it possible that the applicant speaks a variety of Hazaragi Dari from an area of Afghanistan with which the analyst is not familiar? How long is it since the analyst was in Afghanistan, and what regions of the country did the analyst travel to? How much regional variation is there in Hazaragi Dari? How much ethnic and social variation? These are all issues which need to be considered in evaluating the claim in this report that the applicant speaks 'ungrammatically'.

But information concerning the qualifications and expertise of the analyst in this case was not provided to the applicant. This is typical of LADO cases and contrasts with other situations where the opinion of experts is considered in the context of their training and publications. In much LADO work, analysts remain anonymous, and no information about the nature of their expertise is provided, although in Switzerland the applicant has to be provided with 'complete information concerning the origin, training and qualifications' of the LADO analyst (Singler 2004: 236).

In this sample Australian case, the European company provided general information about the 'minimum requirement for an analyst', namely (FCA 2003: #14):

1. that the analyst has the language in question as his mother tongue
2. that he/she has proved capable of listening, making and formulating observations on a linguistic level
3. that he/she is able to give logical and credible answers to questions put by [the company's] linguist in conjunction with the assessment writing
4. that his/her assessment fits in with other assessments in the same case (cross checking)
5. that he/she has passed a thorough test where he/she shall identify languages and dialects
6. that he/she has passed our security control.

As the Federal Court judge in this case pointed out, this company did not require 'an academic education with the language in question as a specialty' (#14).

The analyst must have been a native speaker of the Dari language, and also s/he must have received formal education in order to fulfil the assessment-writing requirement. The applicant, on the other hand, told interviewers that he never went to school and was illiterate, mostly doing farm work, when not helping in his uncle's shop (FCA 2003: #3). In many countries, educated people regard the speech of uneducated and/or rural speakers as ungrammatical. Thus, the assertion that the applicant 'speaks ungrammatically' may simply be the analyst's folk linguistic way of observing that the applicant does not speak the standard variety, or that he does not speak the same regional, ethnic or social variety as the analyst.

Regardless of what is meant by asserting that the applicant 'speaks ungrammatically', the report gives no indication of how this 'observation' relates to the conclusion that his speech is colloquial Hazaragi Dari with a Pakistani accent. It is possible that speaking 'ungrammatically' is merely intended as synonymous with speaking colloquially. But perhaps it implies something 'inauthentic' about the applicant's speech? For example, could it imply that the applicant is trying to speak Hazaragi Dari as if he is from Afghanistan, and being unable to do this, instead speaks 'ungrammatically'?

We have seen that there is no detailed analysis provided in this report to support the observations, nor any indication of what variant forms would have been expected if the applicant was a speaker of Afghanistan Hazaragi Dari as he claimed, rather than of

Pakistani Hazaragi Dari, as the analyst claimed. From conference discussions about LADO in the last few years, it has become clear that reports are kept deliberately short and vague in such ways, because of concerns that specific analysis would provide assistance for any future dishonest asylum seekers who wish to 'cheat' in their LADO interviews. Thus, representatives of immigration departments have expressed the view that people might be able to use specific details in LADO reports to learn 'inauthentic' ways of speaking, in order to 'masquerade' as a speaker of a variety which is not their own. The issue of 'inauthentic' speech in LADO interviews will be taken up below.

Similar concerns appear to be involved in some cases of preventing applicants and their advisors from having access to the interview tape and the full LADO report. In some cases, all that is provided is a letter which quotes extracts from the report. In the sample case discussed here, the Federal Court judge remarked that 'there appears to be some concern that the provision of such reports to applicants will enable them to coach others so they can anticipate the things looked for by language analysts in future'. The judge found this reason 'questionable' (FCA 2003: #12).

Linguistics, folk linguistics and native speakers

Not all LADO reports are based on folk linguistics (although it is difficult to access reports written by linguists). Singler (2004) argues that there can be a valid place for linguistic analysis, that is, analysis carried out by linguists following linguistic principles and methods. As Baltisberger and Favaro (2007: 86) point out, analysts used for LADO work by the Swiss government have university training in linguistics and have specialised in one or more of the languages spoken by the applicant. Singler explains that several factors have enabled him to provide linguistic analysis in Swiss cases where applicants claim Liberian origin. In addition to his own expertise on Liberian varieties of English, Liberia is an unusual country linguistically, owing to its colonial and related linguistic history. Being the only country in West Africa which was colonised by people from the United States, the English varieties spoken in Liberia show regular differences from neighbouring Anglophone countries, which were colonised by the British. Thus, the widely spoken Liberian Vernacular English shows influences from African–American Vernacular English, while both School English and International English in Liberia are modelled on American English. In this way, these Liberian varieties are distinctive and the Liberian situation contrasts with that in the rest of Anglophone West Africa. Further, unlike many other areas of the world, the linguistic border is aligned with the national border. These factors lead Singler to conclude that 'even in the face of an interviewing situation that greatly inhibits the use of the vernacular, linguistic analyses in asylum cases *can* – in some circumstances – be done right' (2004: 235, emphases in original). He details these circumstances as: '*if* the linguistic situation is straightforward, *if* the analyst is truly a specialist in linguistics, and *if* the analyst has detailed local linguistic and cultural knowledge'.

However, as we have seen, not all countries that use LADO reports in their immigration processing rely on trained linguists. For some regions of the world from which people are fleeing persecution, there has been no linguistic research and there are no trained linguists. In such situations, countries such as the Netherlands (Cambier-Langeveld 2007b) rely on the judgement of native speakers who work in conjunction with, or under the supervision of trained linguists who do not necessarily know the languages in question. However, unless these linguists have expertise in the languages in question, how can they assess the soundness of the judgements of the native speakers? The supervision by a linguist without expertise in the language(s) in question would arguably not be sufficient to ensure that the native speaker's judgement is linguistically valid. It is true that native speakers can play a valuable role in assisting linguists in any kind of linguistic analysis, but this is not the same as asking native speakers for their *judgements* about where someone grew up, or whether someone speaks the same dialect as they do. The sample report discussed above shows some of the problems which can arise when such a judgement is made by a native speaker relying on folk views about language.

In the debate over the role of native speakers in making LADO judgements, the main point of contention seems to revolve around the need for native speakers to detect 'non-authenticity'. For example, Cambier-Langeveld (2007b: 17) claims that 'Linguists who are not native speakers are not in the best position to judge the authenticity [of the speech of the asylum seeker]'. It appears that a major concern of governments is that an asylum seeker may speak a certain language variety with a degree of fluency that can persuade a linguist that their origin claims are genuine, but that only a native speaker can really tell if they are 'faking it'. Such a belief appears to ignore sociophonetic research about the distinction between variations which speakers are highly aware of and those which only a linguistically trained observer is aware of, but which may in fact characterise a particular accent (Labov 1994: 78; Mesthrie *et al.* 2000: 91). Thus, if careful analysis of a person's accent is carried out by a linguistically trained analyst, the question of whether or not a person is faking their accent can be considered in a measured and theoretically sound way.

Further, without even considering problems with the notion of 'native speaker' (see e.g. Rampton 1995; Pennycook 2001), research in perceptual dialectology raises doubt over the reliability of native speaker judgements, even where the native speakers are educated. Clopper and Pisoni (2006) provide a good summary of some of this research, which indicates that the recognition of the region of origin of a speaker of one's own language is not straightforward (e.g. Preston 1993). For example, in a study of the recognition of the regional origin of Welsh speakers of English, Williams *et al.* (1999) found that schoolteachers were accurate in only 52% of cases. And in their own study in the US, Clopper and Pisoni (2004) found that only 31% of 'naïve listeners' (i.e. those without linguistic training) were accurate in categorising unfamiliar talkers by dialect (see also Fraser 2009). While these studies show that relying on the judgements of educated native speakers can be problematic, we could expect that doing this in LADO cases can be even more problematic, given the possible ethnic rivalries and political tensions involved.

From expertise to awareness raising

LADO in asylum seeker cases is an area where forensic linguistic work takes one or more of three approaches. For some linguists, their work in this area is in preparing linguistic expert reports and sometimes giving related evidence in court. At other times, their work is in scholarly research and writing (e.g. Singler 2004; Maryns 2004). Finally, following the release of the Guidelines, the 19 linguists comprising the Language and National Origin Group have engaged in a third kind of linguistic work, which we can call expert awareness raising. The LNOG group believes that as experts we have a responsibility to draw attention to the ways in which serious injustice can be perpetrated by the misuse of language analysis.

But it is important to remember that the issue of asylum seekers is highly political, and this is an area where linguistic expertise cannot exist in an a-political vacuum. Despite this, it is important for linguists (and other scholars) to separate political *argument* from scholarly argument. Thus, it should not matter from a linguistic point of view whether a language analysis makes a conclusion which supports or contradicts the claims of an asylum seeker (although this political position is untenable for some linguists, I have found). If it is made on the basis of flawed assumptions and linguistically inadequate analysis, then it is up to linguists to point this out.

This separation of political argument from scholarly argument has some similarities with the position in which experts find themselves in the adversarial Anglo-American legal system (in countries such as Australia, the UK and the US). As experts in this legal system, linguists must continually be on the alert for attempts in court to draw them into adversarial rather than scholarly argument on their expertise, because once this happens, the linguist is considered to have over-stepped their expertise, and their evidence is in danger of being disallowed. Similarly, in matters of linguistic awareness raising, it is important to distinguish between what we can say on the basis of our linguistic expertise, and what we might want to say as part of a political debate (and thus, not as 'experts'). This distinction can be particularly difficult and not all linguists are willing to make it. But I have found that some influential people, such as government officials and politicians, are unwilling to hear from linguists if we cannot make this distinction.

So, while linguists may be driven by questions of social justice for some of the world's most powerless and oppressed people, our awareness raising must be restricted to the areas in which we have recognised expertise, namely those involving the ways in which language analysis contributes to understandings about a speaker's origins. Hopefully, our scholarly awareness raising can be taken up by those involved in bureaucratic and legal decision-making.

And we must always remember that the ultimate problem being addressed by LADO work is not a linguistic one. Linguists are not responsible for, or qualified to provide a solution to problems relating to asylum seekers' claims about origin, whether national, ethnic or regional. But we might be able to do something to address the errors and injustices brought about by problematic language analysis, by using our expertise in reports to governments, evidence in courts, academic publications, and expert awareness raising.

Further reading

Eades, D. and Arends, J. (2004) 'Using language analysis in the determination of national origin of asylum seekers: An introduction', *International Journal of Speech, Language and the Law*, 11(2): 179–99.

Eades, D., Fraser, H., Siegel, J., McNamara, T., and Baker, B. (2003) 'Linguistic identification in the determination of nationality: A preliminary report', *Language Policy*, 2(2): 179–99.

Fraser, H. (2009) 'The role of "educated native speakers" in providing language analysis for the determination of the origin of asylum seekers', *International Journal of Speech Language and the Law*, 16(1): 113–38.

Maryns, K. (2004) 'Identifying the asylum speaker: Reflections on the pitfalls of language analysis in the determination of national origin', *International Journal of Speech, Language and the Law*, 11(2): 240–60.

28

Non-native speakers in detention

Assessing non-native speaking detainees' English language proficiency

Fiona English

Introduction

I first became involved in this area of work in 1994 as the result of a speculative enquiry from a London law firm to the university department in which I worked. The case concerned a nightclub confrontation which had resulted in a fatal stabbing and the detainee, an eighteen-year-old Turkish Cypriot man with English as an additional language, was on remand in prison. The acting solicitors wanted 'an opinion', as they put it, 'on the defendant's level of comprehension and his ability to articulate accurately in English in each of the interviews'. They were particularly concerned about the initial interview, where there had been neither a solicitor nor an interpreter present and where their detainee had, essentially, incriminated himself. They were convinced that, as a result of poor English language skills, he had failed to understand not only his rights under the law but also much of the line of questioning that followed.

This chapter draws on my work as an expert witness in relation to the English language proficiency of non-native detainees and, using examples from actual cases, it describes the approach I use in assessing a detainee's proficiency in order to fulfil the request to 'give an opinion'.

Evidence of English language ability is a normal pre-requisite for non-native speakers of English seeking entry to communicatively demanding contexts such as university study or certain work environments. However, for those lay people involved in legal encounters such as through arrest, interrogation and court interaction, the checks are far less rigorous even though the stakes are arguably much higher. As Eades (2006: 524) points out when referring to cases relating to asylum claims 'an interviewee with limited proficiency in the language of the interview may – simply because of language difficulties – appear to be incoherent or inconsistent, thereby leading the interviewer to a mistaken conclusion concerning the truthfulness of the interviewee' (see Eades, this volume, on testing in asylum claims cases). Of course, the circumstances of an arrest and interrogation do not allow for formal pre-testing but, given that language proficiency is fundamental to the reliability of evidence gained through police interviews, its relevance needs to be taken more fully into account.

This is not to say that no account is taken of English language proficiency in these situations, as can be seen in the following clause from the UK Police and Criminal Evidence Act (PACE).

> If the detainee appears deaf or there is doubt about their hearing or speaking ability or ability to understand English, and the custody officer cannot establish effective communication, the custody officer must, as soon as practicable, call an interpreter for assistance in the action under paragraphs 3.1–3.5.
>
> (Home Office, *PACE code C Section 3.12*, 2008)

There are two main points of interest here. The first is that the assessment and subsequent decision is left to the discretion of the police officers, who are unlikely to have expertise in this area. Secondly, what constitutes 'effective communication' is open to wide inter-pretation even amongst professionals. Under such circumstances, errors of judgement are inevitable, leading to decisions based on mistaken assumptions about language proficiency as in 'he understands English perfectly', stated by one police officer about a Lithuanian detainee, or 'you've spoken perfect English' referring to the Cypriot man above.

Such errors are often further compounded by detainees' own misconceptions of their English language ability, a phenomenon identified by Ross (1998), who points out that learners have difficulty in giving accurate estimations of their own second language skills tending to either underestimate or overestimate their ability. Added to this is a kind of lin-guistic bravado, perhaps relating to the context, that can make detainees reluctant to admit any kind of weakness, let alone linguistic disadvantage. The exchanges in (1), taken from the case involving the Turkish speaker mentioned above, illustrate this and should, in fact, have given much greater cause for concern about his English language ability than it actually did.

(1) Interview with detainee Mr O (IE) by police interviewer (IR) at police station

1 IR: My friend, my friend, this interview we've spoke now for an hour and a half.
2 IE: Yeah.
3 IR: And you've spoken perfect English.
4 IE: Yeah.

This was despite the detainee's obvious difficulties in expressing himself adequately as can be seen in (2), which is an extract taken from shortly before the exchange in (1) and which typifies the several hours of video-taped interview.

(2) Interview with detainee Mr O (IE) by police interviewer (IR) at police station

1 IR: Which man, which man had this shining thing?
2 IE: Who wear white thing.
3 IR: The white thing?
4 IE: White, white shirt.
5 IR: Is he the man you stabbed in the backside?
6 IE: Yeah
7 IR: Yeah?
8 IE: Yeah

9 IR: And how long was this shining thing?
10 IE: Fifteen second it's
11 IR: How, how, how?
12 IE: Five seconds. How long? Ah yeah [responding to IR's gesture], I can't remember.
13 IR: You can't remember
14 IE: I see something shining but I can't remember.

The consequences of such faulty English under circumstances like these can be very serious as was indeed the case here. In fact, although an interpreter had finally been called in at the behest of the solicitor, the detainee only sought help from him towards the end of the series of interviews, when he finally began to realise that he was struggling.

Similar concerns are documented by Cotterill (2000), Rock (2007) and Pavlenko (2008) who focus particularly on issues concerning rights. Cotterill investigates how the 'caution' is delivered orally, particularly in relation to paraphrasing, and the impact this can have in shaping interviews and Rock's comprehensive study of rights communication in the UK demonstrates the difficulties in articulating this crucial information effectively. Pavlenko's discussion offers a study involving a Russian student in the USA who was a murder suspect. In that case, although the she had a high level of English language proficiency, the suspect's failure to adequately understand the significance of the Miranda warnings and their legal implications led her to completely misjudge the seriousness of the situation she was in. Whilst neither Cotterill nor Rock focus on non-native speakers, their work provides valuable insights into the problem of communicating complex information and Pavlenko's discussion, with its focus on a non-native speaker, illustrates the misconceptions that can arise as the result of the interview's sociolinguistic complexity.

However, it is not only interactions around rights that can be problematic. As extracts (1) and (2) indicate, all interactions between police, lawyers and lay people, particularly non-native lay people, have the potential for miscommunication.

In the next section, I provide a brief discussion of language testing and sampling as used in applied linguistics and language education research in order to provide a theoretical context for my assessments for forensic purposes. I then consider how testing for forensic purposes differs, before moving on to discussing the tests themselves.

Language testing

Language testing in applied linguistics and language education research

Language testing is most usually associated with language learning and teaching and has developed to serve three main purposes. The first concerns achievement, usually in relation to a course of study and entails testing what has been learned and is not relevant to the current discussion. The other two purposes, however, are fundamental to my work. One concerns proficiency and entails evaluating a person's level in order to predict how they might handle a given situation. The other relates to research where assessment is used to provide data for specific types of analysis.

There is a substantial literature on language testing offering useful overviews of the field (e.g. Bachman and Palmer 1996; McNamara 2000). Bachman's (2000) review of language testing at the turn of the century offers a concise and highly informative account which highlights important theories that have been particularly significant. Of particular relevance to the current discussion is assessment based on performance. This offers the opportunity to analyse *production*, which concerns the linguistic resources used (vocabulary, grammar and pronunciation) and *proficiency*, which concerns communicative effectiveness in oracy and literacy. This approach to language assessment owes much to Canale and Swain's (1980) influential work on the assessment of communicative competence, following on from Hymes (1974). More specifically, Weir (1990), Skehan (1998) and Ellis (2003) focus particularly on communicative language testing, including testing with tasks, and the implications of such approaches.

Task-based activity is an important methodology in relation to learning and teaching, and tasks are used widely in language assessment and research. Essentially, a task is an activity which provides a meaningful context in which communication can take place. 'A task is an activity which requires learners to use language, with the emphasis on meaning, to attain an objective' (Bygate *et al.* 2001:11). Examples of tasks are simulations of 'real world' activity such as planning and designing a weekend trip to the seaside or more focused activities such as the construction of a story based on a set of pictures. Tasks are used in many public language tests such as the International English Language Testing Services (IELTS) in which tasks associated with academic work are used to assess the language proficiency of non-native speaking university applicants (see Shaw and Weir 2007). They are also used extensively in research, particularly in collecting samples of performance. Of particular relevance to the current discussion is the suggestion by Bachman and Palmer (1996) that task-based tests allow inferences to be made about a person's abilities to use language in specific situations.

My approach owes much to the work of Gorman *et al.* (1990) which analysed and evaluated language performance across the school curriculum drawing on recorded face-to-face assessments of task performance, followed by analysis of the samples obtained during the tests. This methodological combination enables me not only to provide information on a detainee's proficiency but also to exemplify features of production which might influence overall performance. I discuss this in more detail later when describing the tests and tasks I have used in this work.

Unlike most testing of this type, which is used to comment on current or potential performance, my assessments are used to make inferences about past performance during police interviews. This can be seen as problematic since the circumstances in which the assessment samples are obtained are very different from those that applied during the police interviews. For one thing, the experience of a language assessment is unlikely to be as challenging as that associated with arrest and detention. Another factor is that a detainee may have participated in English language classes whilst on remand and hence is likely to have improved since the time of arrest. However, despite these reservations, a linguistic profile of the detainee based on performance during face-to-face assessments can provide useful and sometimes important insights into his earlier performance during the interviews. My discussion of different cases below shows how this works in practice.

Language testing for forensic purposes

The main purpose for the kind of language assessments I am concerned with in this chapter is the provision of information about a particular person's use of English, in other words, a linguistic profile. In the case referred to above, although my assessment was based only on an evaluation of the videotapes and transcripts of police interviews, I was able to provide a description of the detainee's production of English on the one hand and use it to comment on areas of concern during the interviews. However, relying on police interview tapes alone may provide only a partial view of a detainee's English language ability. These interviews are, as already mentioned, extremely complex communicative events involving communicative strategies unique to such contexts, for example, avoidance strategies on the part of the detainee and coercion strategies on the part of the interrogators. As Coulthard and Johnson (2007: 201) suggest while referring to courtroom cross-examination, Gricean 'rules' of communication are subverted if not completely flouted. Pavlenko (2008) also refers to the strategic manipulation of the flow of the interviews and the strategies employed to disguise, for example, the saliency of certain questions. Moreover, my experience of working only with tapes, as in the case above, led me to the conclusion that face-to-face assessments would enable me to *test* proficiency through differently focused tasks as well as *describe* features of production through the collection of performance samples. As Ellis and Barkhuizen (2005:21) point out, 'what learners know is best reflected in their comprehension of input and in the language they produce'.

A key difference between language testing for 'normal' purposes and language testing for forensic purposes concerns the reporting process, particularly in relation to an audience consisting of legal professionals, the judiciary and the police. This makes it a tricky document to produce, as it has to 'speak' to people who draw on different frames of knowledge compared to language and linguistics professionals. The 'expert' has to balance disciplinary knowledge in undertaking the assessments and analysing the samples with the task of presenting it in a way that is accessible and meaningful for a non-professional audience, each of whom, as Coulthard (2005: 1) explains, 'is in some senses an expert on language' by dint of their being language 'users'.

A further consideration regarding audience is the adversarial nature of courtroom interaction whereby, no matter how strong the linguistic evidence might be, it will never 'convince' the opposing barrister whose job it is to refute the arguments. As Coulthard and Johnson (2007: 201) point out 'Novice academic experts may be deceived into thinking that they are still in an academic environment and that, if they are sufficiently coherent and persuasive, they can convince the cross-examiner of the correctness of their opinion' (see also Solan, this volume). In the light of my experience, I have learned that evidence, both in the written report and in case of a court appearance, needs to be highly explicit with illustrative examples. It must not be overly disciplinary in its discourse, though sufficiently so to be considered professionally valid. It must provide enough background to the assessment materials and analytical criteria without becoming too technical and it must provide readily accessible information about performance and its implications. I give examples from some of my reports later in the chapter.

Another area that needs to be considered concerns the circumstances in which the language data are obtained. I am not referring to the police interview samples which are outside the control of the assessor, but the face-to-face tests in which the assessor has direct involvement. It is important to consider the possible effects of the environment in which the test is conducted, how the tests are perceived by the testee and how familiar the testee is with language testing as a procedure. These factors may influence the willingness or ability to participate and ultimately the quality of performance data that can be collected. Willingness, for example, may depend on the detainee's attitude toward the test, how convinced he is of its usefulness or his attitude towards anything connected with the legal process in the first place. He may also be unfamiliar with the kinds of activity associated with the assessment, such as describing pictures, spotting the differences, doing listening comprehension activities and may have no idea of how to do them, or consider them childish.

A good example of how easy it is for an assessor to take task knowledge for granted comes from a recent case where I introduced a 'spot the differences' task, assuming that the testee would recognise it. In this case, there was no issue of 'childishness' but rather a conceptual problem. He had simply never 'played' this game and had no understanding either of what to do or of its relevance in the assessment. This resulted in a somewhat laboured performance as, despite my willingness to forgo the task, having started he did not want to give up. Of course, for the purposes of the forensic assessment, task completion is not necessarily important as it is a means to obtain speech data. From the detainee's perspective, however, completion can be experienced as achievement and inability to complete can be experienced as 'failure' which can be very demotivating.

There are a number of strategies for dealing with these issues. One is to create a context of mutuality whereby both parties, the tester and the testee, acknowledge the situation and agree to suspend 'belief'. Another is to ensure that the materials used, particularly images and other texts, have some kind of relevance to the detainee's context. For instance, as part of a reading comprehension test, I used the detainee's local newspaper as a resource. Finally, it is important to ensure that the detainee understands what he is supposed to be doing and, as far as the task completion aims are concerned, why. This requires the assessor to be responsive and flexible, to balance the forensic needs to obtain data and the detainee's need to complete the task.

With regard to the last point, there have been a number of discussions examining the issue of whether a detainee might under-perform in an attempt to strengthen his case. For example, Coulthard and Johnson (2007: 137) have suggested that face-to-face language assessments might be open to challenges of underperformance and my court experience confirms this. They point out that 'although applied linguists have a great deal of experience in assessing the linguistic performance of non-natives, most of their tests are predicated on the assumption that the testee is trying to do their best', whereas, they argue, language assessment for forensic purposes might result in a defendant doing his worst because he thinks it might help his defence.

However, in my experience, it is rare for a detainee to underperform, as it is quite a difficult thing to maintain throughout an extended face-to-face interview. The simplest way would be to contribute nothing or almost nothing, but, as I explain to both the detainee and to the acting solicitors, silence will not help the case, unless, of course, his English really is that weak. The more a detainee produces the more informative a report can be. What tends to happen is that a test effect comes into play and the detainee, caught up in the assessment process, strives to do well. Evidence of this might include expressions of irritation at not 'getting' something during a listening comprehension task, requests for an extract to be played again or attempts to seek the appropriate word during a discussion task. In such cases, it is important for the assessor to take the initial performance as evidence of general comprehension and use the repeat occasions as a source of evidence of specific problems to include in the linguistic profile.

Conducting an assessment

An assessment involves three main phases: obtaining a linguistic profile of the detainee based on face-to-face testing data; juxtaposing the linguistic profile against the police interviews; and producing a report. The report includes information about the assessment procedures, the linguistic profile itself and, drawing on the profile, an opinion of whether poor language proficiency might have played any part in the interviews.

Methodology

Testing is usually carried out in one of two places, depending on the circumstances, and usually lasts up to an hour. If the detainee is on bail, it usually takes place on the premises of the acting solicitors but if he is on remand it takes place in the prison. It may be assumed that testing in a prison might lead to a somewhat constrained interaction, but my experience is otherwise. In fact, because the language assessment breaks the routine of prison life, the detainee tends to be extremely willing to talk, particularly with someone from outside the prison or legal community and about topics other than matters of their legal case. This can be highly motivating and productive and often results in spontaneous authentic conversation.

The assessments themselves involve conversational strategies in that I participate in the performance as a co-respondent. To enable later analysis, the entire process is voice recorded including whilst the detainee is engaged in listening or reading comprehension tasks. This aspect of performance provides very useful information about task processing in relation to these less obviously 'productive' activities where requests for clarification and help, expressions of frustration or satisfaction can provide further evidence of the detainee's language performance. What is more, it can be referred to as evidence of willingness and effort in response to potential claims of underperformance.

Test materials

The main aims in undertaking these tests are to obtain performance samples for later analysis and to evaluate the detainee's communicative proficiency. For this, I draw on both conversational discussion, which facilitates the assessment process, and task-based assessment materials, which enable focus on particular genres, communicative strategies as well as specific lexical and grammatical features.

Conversational discussion serves several purposes. In the first instance, it helps create an informal and relaxed environment through talking about familiar topics such as personal information and family, although it is necessary to be cautious here to avoid any discomfort on the part of the detainee. It provides the opportunity to clarify the purposes of the assessment and the procedures involved, including why the whole process is being recorded, an important point to clarify as this too could worry the detainee. It also enables the assessor to gauge the detainee's general level of English language before deciding on which tasks to use and how to use them. Further opportunities for discussion may arise naturally during the process of task completion, thereby increasing the sample size and expanding its repertoire of genres and topics. These discussions can also offer the chance to learn more about the detainee's sociolinguistic background, such as length of residence in the UK, language preferences in different domains, attitudes to English and opportunities for using it, which can be helpful in producing the linguistic profile.

429

The task materials are generally based around visual resources such as photographs or diagrams and task instructions are given orally, thereby avoiding potential problems relating to English literacy. I choose a range of images to cater for different interests and to elicit information about the detainee's ability to talk about particular topics which may have a bearing on the case itself, such as clothing or explanation of particular types of activity. This enables me to explore lexical range or familiarity with certain grammatical forms (e.g. elaborated questions, sequencing adverbs) that typify the genres involved in police interviews. Tasks include images of everyday scenarios such as the workplace or the home, images of people and places, sequences of images for 'story' telling and puzzle images for speculation.

An Example

Photographs such as those in Figures 28.1 and 28.2 provide a context for discussion and the opportunity to explore the detainee's ability to deal with questions about a scene and describe what is going on.

Figure 28.1 Street scene photo 1

Figure 28.2 Street scene photo 2

Tasks might include the following:

1. The assessor asks for a description of one of the pictures to see if she can match the description to the picture being described. This provides samples of speech associated with descriptions including use of prepositions, present tenses and vocabulary range.
2. The assessor takes one picture and asks speculative questions about it, including questions about where it is, where the people might be going, what they are doing and what might happen next. The assessor can use a mixture of direct and embedded questions to explore how easily these are handled and can encourage the use of speculative grammatical forms such as modal verbs or conditional clauses.

This approach offers flexibility in how the assessor wishes to use the materials and enables her to link task choice to the circumstances. Pictures of scenes like these can also provide the chance for further discussion, particularly if there is some kind of connection between the image and the experience of the detainee. In a recent case with a Vietnamese detainee, I used the photograph in Figure 28.1 which he recognised as a Hong Kong street scene. This led him to talk about the time he spent in Hong Kong, friends

431

he had still living there and then onto his experiences leaving Vietnam back in the 1980s as can be seen from extract (3) from the recorded sample.

(3) Assessment of detainee Mr. C (AE) by the author as assessor (AR)
1   AE: Mayb::e (.) Hong Kong?
2   AR: Yeah it is
3   AE: In Hong Kong? (.) Yes beca:use I (.) I been Hong Kong (.) before
4   AR: [Mmm]
5   AE: [Many times]
        [...]
6   AE: Did you go to the er what you call the (.) the mountain?
7   AR: Oh the er Victoria Peak?
8   AE: Yeah yeah (.) look at at night (.) it's nice
9   AR: [It's beautiful yeah]
10 AE: You can see the street (.) You can see the (.) what the sea?
11 AR: The harbour
12 AE: Yeah yeah harbour
        [...]
13 AE: I wa:::s um in Hong Kong 19:79
14 AR: [Mmm]
15 AE: When I came t::o England
16 AR: [Mmm]
17 AE: And I came back for two two time

From the moment he recognised the photograph of being from Hong Kong (line 1), Mr. C's position changed from being a 'testee' to a mutual participant in a conversation. His own knowledge enabled him to ask his own questions (line 6), provide his own information (line 8) and then go on to volunteer information about how he had come to be in Hong Kong (line 13). This shift from a task to a conversation enabled me to explore his personal association with the UK and English language as well as obtain background information about his former life in Vietnam in a natural and unforced way. It produced a rich source of linguistic and sociolinguistic data, not to mention a substantially more relaxed and enthusiastic atmosphere throughout the rest of the assessment. Of course, such informality, which is so helpful in obtaining authentic performance data, could lead to criticisms of partiality due to overfamiliarity with the detainee, as suggested by Peter Gray (this volume). However, as he also goes on to say, professionalism, both as a practitioner and a researcher, offers an effective defence against such claims.

I also use audio texts for specific focus on listening comprehension. In this case, I choose published language teaching audio texts which are generally better produced than those I might record myself. They offer a variety of genres such as anecdotes or explanations and involve different speakers and different regional accents which allows for comment on whether the detainee's comprehension might have been hindered by a speaker's accent. Published recordings also tend to be graded and as such offer a point of reference that is accessible to non-linguists. In most cases, I modify the activities that accompany these texts to ensure that they are appropriate for the needs of the assessment in hand.

Occasionally, as in cases such as fraud where there is dispute relating to specific documents, I develop reading tasks. These include texts that discuss topics which are relevant to the case and comprehension tasks that test different reading skills from basic information location to drawing inferences.

Analysing the performance samples

The analysis involves examining two sample sets; one obtained during the face-to-face assessment and the second being the recordings and transcripts of the police interviews. I have developed the practice of always analysing and describing the assessment samples before moving onto the police interview data. This, I believe, ensures greater impartiality in conducting the assessments, although it is fair to say that the way in which I have developed the assessment tasks has been greatly informed by my growing familiarity with the discourse of police interviews.

Assessment samples

The assessment samples are analysed from the perspectives of production (pronunciation, grammar and vocabulary) and proficiency (communicative effectiveness and task outcomes). The focus on proficiency allows me to comment on a detainee's ability to deal with certain communicative situations, including the handling of certain types of questions, whilst the focus on production enables me to identify linguistic features which typify his use of English and draw inferences on how this may affect successful communication. Sometimes it is helpful to link these to issues related to mother tongue transfer (Faerk and Kasper 1987) as problems associated with this are often misunderstood and hence underestimated by non-professionals. Observation comments (e.g. 'he seems to be struggling with this one', 'he raced through that reading text') made during the assessments can add useful contextual information regarding the detainee's handling of the tasks. This information comprises the main content of the linguistic profile to be juxtaposed with the police interview data.

Police interview samples

This is a fundamental aspect of the work in that it is the reason why my advice has been sought in the first place. It is a lengthy process involving careful analysis of the video or audio tapes and transcripts of the interviews. The aim is to gain an overall impression of the interactions between the participants, compare the detainee's performance in the interviews with that during the face-to-face assessment, identify examples of communication breakdown or miscommunication and match these with performance features from the assessment. It is also necessary to discover any resolved or unresolved miscommunications as these are what have most bearing on the case.

It is also important to consider whether and how the police themselves deal with the detainee's language. In some cases, there is a tendency to overestimate proficiency, though as Pavlenko (2008) points out, this may be a deliberate strategy. In other cases, the police are more conscientious in acknowledging difficulties associated with English and work harder to check comprehension. Although these interviews provide a very rich source of data, particularly for a linguistic ethnographer (Rock 2006), it is difficult to decide where to draw the line. However, the kind of report that is helpful in the context of a language assessment needs to offer concrete and accessible evidence usable in court. Therefore, it is necessary to limit the analysis to those aspects which can be compared with the linguistic profile; that is, examples of faulty grammar, imprecise vocabulary and difficult pronunciation which lead to misunderstandings or misrepresentation of the events being discussed during the interviews.

Producing the report

The report is the most salient aspect of the expert's work as it is this which is used as evidence. In this discussion, I am using three examples from actual cases. For purposes of anonymity I have replaced all names of detainees, referring to them by letters, Mr. 'A', Mr. 'B' and Mr. 'C'. All other names are represented by initials.

My reports usually contain the following sections: assessment procedures and rationale; linguistic profile derived from the assessments; implications in relation to the police interviews; additional information; and concluding remarks. The intention is to provide a systematic and explicit account of the process as well as both a summary and detailed explanation of the findings.

Assessment procedures and rationale

Under the first heading I include a general overview of the circumstances of the assessment as (4) demonstrates.

(4) Report on Mr. A
I met Mr. A at the offices of W. & Co on Tuesday 13th September 20XX in order to carry out an assessment of his standard of spoken English. According to the police charge record, Mr. A 'speaks very good English' (MG/DD/A: p. 2) 'understands English perfectly' (p. 17) and 'spoke to the doctor in fluent English' (p. 17). In the light of these comments, the purpose of my assessment was to explore the extent of Mr. A's proficiency through a more formal evaluation procedure.

This kind of framing provides a justification for the report and establishes a backdrop against which to present the assessment. Not all cases offer such strongly articulated expressions of police confidence in the detainee's language proficiency, though in most police interviews that I have examined there is some reference to good language ability. In the case of Mr. C, a different framing was relevant (5).

(5) Report on Mr. C
It is important to note that Mr. C has been in prison for eight months, fully immersed in an English speaking environment and taking regular classes in English language. In such a context his level of English is likely to have improved substantially, so my assessment must be understood with this in mind.

The report then goes on to explain the purposes of the assessment in general and provide detail of each of the assessment tasks and the rationale behind them. This ensures that readers of the report understand the scope of the assessment, the relevance of the tasks and the kind of information that is provided. Extract (6), from the case of Mr. B, exemplifies this.

(6) Report on Mr. B – Picture Story

I showed Mr. B a set of three pictures concerning a road incident involving a vehicle and its passengers. The pictures were designed to be arranged to produce a short narrative. I told Mr. B that he could put them in whatever order he liked so as to make a story which he could then tell me. This involved describing the incident and explaining why it had happened and what the consequences might be. I also asked Mr. B a number of questions, using different question forms, about certain aspects of the story he had told.

Rationale

Narrative is a familiar activity for everyone but it has a particular relevance in police interviews. I wanted to see how well Mr. B could sequence events and how effectively he could elaborate on them. I also wanted to test how well he dealt with different questioning strategies, such as embedded or elaborated questions, common in police interviews.

The linguistic profile

As explained above, the linguistic profile is used to comment on the detainee's proficiency in English indicating areas of concern. As a key component of the report, it is necessary to exemplify features that typify his production and performance and demonstrate how these might affect communication. In one trial, the judge dismissed the case, which revolved around whether the detainee had understood what a police officer had said. This was in direct response to the profile I had produced, which indicated that the detainee might have difficulty in understanding unfamiliar regional accents. It turned out that the chief witness, namely the arresting police officer, had a strong Glaswegian accent.

The summary of findings in extract (7) comes from Mr. B's report and is an example of a linguistic profile.

(7) Report on Mr. B
Summary of Findings

Mr. B was very co-operative and forthcoming throughout the whole assessment. He spoke freely, which gave me a good opportunity to evaluate his use of English and his comprehension ability.

1. Mr. B can speak freely, though inaccurately, about familiar topics.
2. He has a confident manner when speaking and perseveres to get his meaning across.
3. His English is heavily marked by a strong Turkish accent and he has difficulty in producing certain sounds (e.g. /w/ instead of /v/, /e/ (as in men) instead of /a/ (as in man), /d/ instead of /ð/ (as in *they*)
4. He frequently misses hearing certain key sounds, such as *un-* as in **un**important.
5. His grammar is seriously flawed, particularly his use of the following:
    auxiliaries (is, be, have, etc.) (e.g. I living …)
    verb tenses (simple past, etc.) (e.g. I go last week)
    prepositions (to, for, at, etc.) (e.g. I get to home)
    phrasal verbs (look *after*, get *over*, etc.) (e.g. She look to the children)
    articles (the, a, etc.) (e.g. I go to pub)

435

6. He does not recognise embedded questions (e.g. I wonder what they're doing?)
7. He does not understand elaborated requests or questions (e.g. Do you think you could tell me what's going on in this picture?)
8. He appears reluctant to admit his failure to understand which can result in a communication breakdown.
9. He sometimes responds to questions he mistakenly thinks have been asked rather than what has *actually* been asked. In other words, he sometimes does not know that he has not understood.

This summary of findings (7) is followed by more detailed discussion of performance on each of the tasks (8) in order to demonstrate the evidence with which the linguistic profile was produced.

(8) Discussion of performance tasks – Mr. B

Picture Story

Mr. B was able only to tell a very scant story based on the pictures, despite the explicitness of the plot, the additional prompts I gave and the familiarity that might be expected of the situation.

He was unable to respond to the embedded or elaborated questions that I asked and could only answer when I simplified them as direct questions with extra non-verbal indications such as pointing to the relevant details in the pictures.

e.g. Elaborated Question: 'What **do you think** is going on here?'
rephrased as 'What's going on here?'
Embedded Question: '**Can you tell me** what's happening here?
rephrased as 'What's happening here?

The kind of information in (7) and (8) can then be juxtaposed with the police interviews as in (9).

(9) Interview with detainee Mr. B (IE) by police interviewer (IR) at police station

1 IR: Do you accept that that was you making that contact?
2   Mr. K does not respond, so DC. R makes a second attempt, this time presenting the question as an assertion
3 IR: The phone calls made by your phone were made by you?
4 IE: Maybe I phone him, maybe he phone me...

It is impossible in such a case for the expert to say whether the detainee did or did not understand the line of questioning in this case and the lack of response in line 2 may be attributed to momentary consideration before deciding on how to answer. However, the evidence from the test outlined above indicates that there may be some element of doubt about the level of comprehension displayed.

In Mr. C's case, although there were few examples of communication failure, there were incidences where his faulty grammar led to misinterpretations as illustrated by the exchange in (10).

(10) Interview with detainee Mr. C (IE) by police interviewer (IR) at police station

1 IE: I don't want to get involved with him in this matter.

2 IR: So if you don't want anyone involved you lie do you?
3 IE: Yeah

The implication of the interviewer's construction of Mr. C's statement is that it is Mr. C who doesn't want to get involved with the other person rather than, as is later clarified, that Mr. C doesn't want to get that person involved in his problems. Hence, Mr. C's desire to protect the other person is construed quite differently as a result of Mr. C's faulty phrasing. This might lead to a more negative impression of Mr. C than might otherwise be the case.

Additional information

For the purposes of these assessments the analysis rarely includes socio-pragmatic aspects as in Maley (2000) nor does it consider cultural and ideological experience as in Blommaert (2005). This is not to say that such a focus would be irrelevant. In fact, as Eades (2005) or Blommaert (2005) argue, socio-cultural factors play a fundamental role in interactions with the law, particularly in relation to understanding contextual features connected to practices and power relations. However, I have so far refrained from explicitly reporting on these aspects, partly because they are not easily demonstrated to a lay audience and partly because the evidence they might offer would be more speculative than that afforded by a linguistic focus. Nevertheless, there is one sociolinguistic issue that needs to be addressed as it is often raised in cross-examination. I am referring to the issue of low-level English proficiency despite several years' residence in the country. This is a phenomenon that is widely experienced by members of the public, but little understood, and it is for this reason that I make reference to it, where relevant, in my report, as in the example (11).

(11) Report on Mr. C
A further point to note concerns the length of time Mr. C has been living in the UK. It is reasonable to assume that after 30 years residence, someone would have fully mastered the language and that no problems would be encountered in using English across a wide range of contexts. However, it is often the case that people who remain within their own ethnic and linguistic community have a level of English language proficiency that is lower than might be assumed given their length of time in the country. This phenomenon has been well documented both in the media (e.g. Mansur, 2007) and in scholarly literature (e.g. Wei, 1994, Carr-Hill et al. 1996). … In other words, language proficiency depends as much on the contexts in which one uses it as on the length of time one lives in a given country. In the case of Mr. C, most of his interactions, until his arrival in prison, have taken place within the Sino-Vietnamese community.

Such additional information can make a difference to how the rest of the report is received. However, as with all the evidence provided, its effectiveness depends largely on the use that is made of it in the proceedings.

Giving an opinion

This part of the report is where an opinion is given. It draws inferences from the findings of the assessment and comments on their implications in the interviews. Extract (12) from Mr. A's report exemplifies this. In this case, the issue concerned an oral rendition of an official document relating to drink driving.

(12) Report on Mr. A

Mr. A's English language proficiency is far from 'perfect', as suggested in the police report cited earlier. His use of English is full of grammatical inaccuracies and his vocabulary limited. His understanding of spoken English is problematic in that it fluctuates between comprehension, apparent comprehension and clear lack of comprehension as demonstrated in my detailed findings above.

Having examined the proforma texts used in the police procedures I can confidently state that it is highly unlikely that Mr. A would have understood much of the language used.

The texts contain items of vocabulary which are far beyond the level of his comprehension let alone his own production (e.g. *alleged, consumed, offence, specimens, device, proportion, disregarded, render, liable, prosecution*).

The grammatical structures involved are complex for someone with Mr. A's level of English. For instance, consider the following:

I require you to provide two specimens of breath for analysis by means of an approved device. (A14)

This sentence contains:
- the *subjunctive* (I require you to provide)
- *participial phrasing/reduced relative clause* (for analysis – instead of ... which is for analysis),
- *idiomatic phrasing* (by means of)
- *participial phrasing/reduced relative clause + passive structure* (*an approved device* – instead of a device which is approved by ...).

Taking these two aspects (vocabulary and grammar) together, and Mr. A's standard of English as discussed above, it can be said with a high degree of confidence that such discourse was beyond his comprehension.

It is the opinion part of the report which is referred to by both defence and prosecution lawyers, which is why it needs to be explicit, comprehensible and as unambiguous as possible. The rest of the report, including description of the test materials and the linguistic profile, serves as evidence to support the 'opinion'.

Conclusion

The process of assessing English language proficiency for forensic purposes is, as has been seen, more complex than may be understood in the judicial process. Work of this type is relatively unusual, at least in the British context, and for the most part law firms rely on psychologists' reports, based largely on psychometric tests, to evaluate language competence. In relation to non-native speakers, these are unlikely to be reliable. It might be argued that a simple standardised proficiency test could be devised to check a detainee's ability prior to an interview. Although this might be better than the somewhat arbitrary method currently applied, it would be difficult to monitor and such a test would necessarily be a rather blunt instrument which might result in further complications. The advantage of the approach I have described here is that it provides detailed information which can shed light on actual incidences of performance. Furthermore, by providing examples of performance, the report can raise issues that tend to go unrecognised but which may have important implications for all concerned. For instance, evidence of how non-native detainees struggle with certain grammatical structures such as embeddedness or idiomatic expressions such as phrasal verbs, often mistakenly thought to be 'easy', can help police interviewers adjust their own language choices accordingly.

The difficulty in embarking on one of these assessments is in finding a balance between what to report on and considering how the different audiences will make use of the report. However, my experience has shown that the introduction of professional applied linguistic input in this context offers a new dimension to the legal process. Regardless of whether the evidence produced succeeds in influencing the outcome, and it is worth saying that it sometimes does, the inclusion of this kind of information ensures that language and intercultural communication is foregrounded as an issue to be more seriously taken into account.

It is clear that there is great scope for academic research in this field. In my experience, the process of providing an assessment has become increasingly difficult the deeper I go into the analysis and the more I learn about the process. It is not possible for a report, with its very particular function, to double up as a piece of research. However, it is certainly possible for researchers to use the data that is collected during an assessment to investigate further, outside the context of the 'expert' report itself. Such work could provide precisely the kind of evidence that is needed to support the arguments being made with regard to the problems faced by non-native speakers embroiled in the legal process.

Further reading

Blommaert, J. (2005) *Discourse*, Cambridge: Cambridge University Press.

Coulthard, M. and Johnson, A. (2007) *An Introduction to Forensic Linguistics: Language in Evidence*, London: Routledge.

Ellis, R. and Barkhuizen, G. (2005) *Analysing Learner Language*, Oxford: Oxford University Press.

McNamara, T. (2000) *Language Testing*, Oxford: Oxford University Press.

29

Court interpreting

The need to raise the bar:
Court interpreters as specialized experts

Sandra Hale

> I am concerned that so many people who put their trust in the administration of justice … have suffered from incompetent interpretation. If you do not understand the proceedings through competent interpretation, you are denied justice.
>
> (Moustacalis, in Todd 2008)

Introduction

Much has been said and written about incompetent interpreting in the courtrooms. Yet, little seems to have been done to achieve systematic improvements that will lead to a better administration of justice. Multiple factors contribute to this impasse, but its underlying cause seems to be the general lack of recognition of the complex nature of court interpreting as a highly specialized activity (Christensen 2008). Many are quick to criticize the interpreter's performance, but few are willing to advocate rigorous pre-service university training, to provide adequate working conditions and to pay professional rates that are commensurate with the difficulty of the task (Morris 2008). On the one hand, courts are happy to employ untrained bilinguals to act as interpreters at very little expense; on the other, they wonder why these poorly paid, untrained individuals are not performing satisfactorily (Berk-Seligson 2008). The answer should be obvious, yet little is being done at the systemic level to rectify this anomaly. Either the legal professionals do not see the connection, or they do not consider the issue important enough to take any action. What should indeed be surprising is that, given the current employment conditions, poor remuneration and lack of recognition, there are still many highly trained, competent and professional interpreters in the market whose work is undervalued, unrecognized and unacknowledged.

There also seems to be an underlying misconception, as implied by the introductory quotation, that it is only the accused who does not understand the language of the courtroom who needs interpretation in order to ensure a fair trial. The fact is that when one participant cannot understand or be understood, it is the legal process itself that suffers and justice cannot be done. A lawyer's best efforts to ask the most strategic questions in order to elicit the answers that will benefit his/her case can be thwarted by inadequate interpretation. A jury's attempts to evaluate the credibility of a witness can be frustrated by inadequate interpretation. A magistrate's evaluation of the evidence presented in another language will be flawed if based on inadequate interpretation. I use the word *inadequate* deliberately. *Inadequate* does not refer only to the interpreter's level of competence, but also to the interpreter's specialist training in court interpreting and prior preparation. In addition, the interpreter's opportunity to render an adequate interpretation depends heavily on the physical working conditions and the behavior of all the participants involved in the interaction.

The 2007 Critical Link 5 Congress[1] highlighted the necessity for all participants of interpreted interactions to assume some of the responsibility for the quality of the interpretation and the success of the communication. The misconception that interpreters perform "a purely mechanical function, much like a hearing aid, microphone, or typewriter" (NSWLRC 2004: 62), portrays interpreting as an activity devoid of thought, judgment or effort and removes from the main speakers any responsibility to help the interpreter understand and render the message accurately. Interpreted proceedings cannot be expected to be the same as monolingual proceedings, no matter how competent the interpreter. Allowances must be made in order to accommodate the interpreter. Before the event, interpreters need to be briefed with as much background information as possible in order to adequately prepare. During the event, speakers' turns at talk must be clear and of manageable length, and the interpreter should be given permission to interrupt the proceedings if and when clarification is required or a reasonable request warranted. The physical working conditions are also important, including proper acoustics so the interpreters can hear the speakers clearly, comfortable seating to allow for note taking and reference material, access to drinking water and permission to take regular breaks. Ideally, for long trials, interpreters should work in pairs, which is the current practice in conference interpreting. This creates a quality assurance mechanism, because the interpreters can monitor each other's performance, as well as take regular breaks. However, even if such conditions were granted, only competent interpreters with the correct specialist training would be able to offer a quality service.

Lack of awareness about the complexity of interpreting and the need for high standards

Although some countries have accreditation or certification systems that provide some type of benchmark for competence, in no country is any type of training compulsory before interpreters are allowed to practice. It is still not uncommon in some countries for the police or the courts to use bilingual volunteers, including children or police officers, as interpreters (Berk-Seligson 2000; Roberts-Smith 2009; Allimant and Anne 2008). Ahmad comments on the inconsistency that exists in the United States, where:

> lawyers rarely subject interpreters to the level of scrutiny regarding qualifications and reliability to which they would subject other types of expert. Indeed, it is nearly inconceivable that untrained, untested, unpaid volunteers would be used as

expert witnesses with the frequency with which such volunteers are used for legal interpretation.

(Ahmad 2007: 1059)

In a review article, Len Roberts-Smith, a former Australian Chief Justice, comments that "monocultural or Anglophone lawyers and judges" lack an understanding of interpreting issues, resulting in forensic error. He reviews a number of cases where poor interpretation created legal problems and attributes these to one of the following causes:

1. The absence of anyone to interpret due to either a misconception from some judges and lawyers that interpreters are an obstacle to communication or to the unavailability of interpreters;
2. The provision of unqualified bilinguals or interpreters qualified in the wrong language; and
3. The use of the services of "professional accredited" interpreters who are not trained and who do not possess the high level skills necessary to perform at the required level (Roberts-Smith 2009).

Such lack of recognition for trained interpreters and lack of awareness of the complexity of court interpreting is not unique to English-speaking countries. A study of court interpreting in Ecuador revealed a similar attitude (Berk-Seligson 2008). When asked about who interprets for indigenous populations who do not speak Spanish, a judge said: "We call in a person who understands the Quichua language and who translates it into Spanish. There are two or three people who live nearby. They are called. They collaborate. They aren't paid. They are collaborators" (Berk-Seligson 2008: 20). Berk-Seligson comments that, ironically, although these judicial officers are happy to call on non-professionals, there are always vehement criticisms of their work (2008: 27). Studies from other countries such as Malaysia (Ibrahim 2007); Spain (Ortega Herráez and Foulquié Rubio 2008; Giambruno 2008); Austria (Kadric 2000) and Denmark (Christensen 2008) have produced similar findings.

Hertog et al. comment on the fear that surrounds the establishment and enforcement of adequate standards for legal interpreters (Hertog et al. 2007). They speculate that not only may governments fear having to pay adequate fees to qualified interpreters, but also unqualified practitioners may fear losing their work and educational institutions may fear not attracting sufficient numbers of students or students with the high level of bilingual competence required to become interpreters. They conclude that "this unholy trinity of, often unnecessary, fear has hindered and still hinders progress" (Hertog et al. 2007: 164). It is ironic that the fear is based on issues other than the potential for misinterpretation and for the grave consequences it can have on the administration of justice.

Court interpreters as highly trained professionals

[C]ourt interpreters must be properly trained, the difficulty and importance of their work fully recognized, their pivotal role in the judicial process acknowledged and accepted by judicial authorities, and their compensation established in accordance with their responsibilities.

(Giambruno 2008: 48)

Compulsory pre-service training will not guarantee error-free interpretation, just as legal training does not guarantee error-free lawyering. However, it will guarantee both a minimum standard and professional status for interpreters. The different skills that interpreters need as their everyday tools are acquired through rigorous training and consistent practice. The main ones include the acquisition of pre-assignment preparation skills, specialized note taking and memory aide skills, and competence in the different interpreting modes: short consecutive, long consecutive and simultaneous interpreting and sight translation. Knowing when to use each of these modes, how accuracy is constrained by each of them and the consequences of the interpreter's choices on the interaction are competencies that can only be acquired through adequate training based on sound theories and on the results of practical applied research. See (Hale 2007) for more details.

Added to these generic skills, court interpreters need to acquire specialized knowledge of the legal system, of different legal settings, of bilingual legal terminology and of the discourse practices and strategies particular to the courtroom. Qualified interpreters will also be familiar with a code of ethical conduct that will guide them on issues of impartiality, confidentiality, and their role in providing a true reflection of the voice of the original speakers, as far as the situation and the participants will permit. Another crucial area of competence is the interpreter's ability to manage the interaction, to know when and how to intervene to highlight a translation ambiguity or difficulty or explain a translation choice that may impact on the case at hand. The next section will review each of these areas of competence with illustrative examples.

Court interpreting competence

Prerequisite to becoming an interpreter: high level bilingual competence

Interpreting is a highly complex activity that requires as a base, a native or native-like level of competence in at least two languages in a variety of genres and registers. This in itself is a rare ability that should be valued as such, as normally only those who have received formal bilingual education and have lived in at least two different language communities throughout their lives can acquire such high levels of bilingualism. Very few professions require such a demanding prerequisite to train in their field.

The pool of competent bilinguals in all of the language combinations which require interpreters is undoubtedly very limited. This fact alone makes it crucial for such people to be provided with the necessary incentives to pursue a career as highly specialized interpreters. It is an unfortunate reality that many of the best interpreting graduates in Australia (Ozolins and Hale forthcoming) do not practice as interpreters for very long, choosing to retrain for other more profitable and less demanding professions. On the other hand, examples of people who act as interpreters, but who lack basic linguistic competence, abound. These people are, of course, not necessarily trained, accredited or even paid for their services. Even if they have every intention of interpreting accurately, their lack of basic skills does not allow it. For example, Ahmad (2007: 1061) comments

443

on an affidavit taken through an interpreter, which was replete with grammatical errors, basic vocabulary and very short sentences, giving the impression that the speaker was an uneducated person, when in fact he was a university academic. Berk-Seligson (2000) gives examples of police officers in the United States who, despite their inadequate Spanish language skills, insist on asking questions in Spanish, making it very difficult for the suspects to understand.

Examples of inadequate English competence can also be found in Australia, with different implications on the outcome of the case. Example (1) below shows an instance of a Korean interpreter's grammatical inadequacy in English.

(1)
Interpreter: Ben Kim said someone is going to Central Coast.
Counsel: to the Central Coast?

(Lee 2009a:106)

The interpreter's omission of the definite article is highlighted by counsel's need to clarify the utterance, adding unnecessarily to the length of the case and possibly creating confusion for the witness, who does not understand why his/her answer is being repeated by counsel. Another example of inadequate interpreting leading to an obvious consequence can be found in a recent Refugee Review Tribunal hearing, where the Arabic interpreter continually misinterpreted "persecution" as "prosecution" and "witness" as "martyr," confusing the witness and leading to an appeal on the grounds of poor interpretation (*Szldy & Ors v. Minister for Immigration & Anor* [2008] Fmca 1684).

However, even if a person is a balanced, competent bilingual, this does not guarantee their ability to interpret. The misconception that any bilingual, including children, can automatically be called upon to interpret is unfortunately still prevalent. Roberts-Smith (2009) provides an example of police asking a fifteen-year-old girl, who was visiting the inmate they needed to interview, to interpret. When she left, the interview continued without her, and on the record it was written "interpreter quit here", automatically attributing to the girl the title of "interpreter." A similar situation can be seen in example (2), where the police prosecutor implies that a child was sufficiently competent to act as the interpreter for her mother. Interestingly, the mother qualifies the daughter's "interpreting" performance in an insightful manner, proposing that the child was not interpreting, but providing her own version of the facts and supplying her with some words when needed.

(2) (*The interpreter's version was removed from the example*) (PP is police prosecutor; W is witness.)

PP: Your daughter Karen was there, wasn't she?
W: *Sí, estaba conmigo* (Yes, she was with me)
PP: And she speaks English?
W: *Sí* (Yes)
PP: And she speaks good English?
W: *Sí* (Yes)
PP: And she speaks Spanish as well?
W: *Sí* (Yes)
PP: And she assisted you in giving your version of events to the police, didn't she?

W: *Bueno, mi hija dio la..la versión de ella, de lo que vio y me ayudó a mí las cosas que yo no ... que ella me preguntaba que yo no sabía cómo contestarla' porque no sé el inglés po'* (Well, my daughter gave her ... her own version of what she saw and she helped me with the things that I didn't ... that she asked that I didn't know how to answer because I don't speak English, you know).

(*Police v. X. Assault case*, Fairfield Local Court, NSW, 1996)

Bilingual helpers will normally do what the witness above stated; they will give their own summary of what they heard. Qualified interpreters are taught to aim at achieving faithful and complete renditions of what the speaker said, attempting to maintain the appropriate register and style. Faithful interpreting, however, is a complex and at times controversial concept. Although widely discredited, the idea that faithful interpreting equates to word-for-word translations is still common among some legal practitioners (Hale 2007; Lee 2009b). A number of scholars have based their theories of accurate interpreting on communicative theories of discourse and pragmatics, which also extend to translation theories (House 1977; Nord 1997; Mason and Stewart 2001; Berk-Seligson 1990, 2002; Hale 1996, 2004, 2007). These theories argue against the concept of literal, word-for-word translations, as such translations generally fail to achieve an accurate representation of the communicative point and effect of the original utterances. While, it is beyond the scope of this chapter to explain these theories in detail, the underlying concepts will be reviewed below, with accompanying examples.

Understanding the interpreting process

Untrained interpreters generally base their choices on personal intuition. Formal training attempts to systematize those choices by providing theories to guide and inform interpreters in the process. From a discourse/pragmatic perspective, the interpreter's goal is to interpret from the source to the target language in such a way that the listeners in the target language understand and react to the message in the same way that listeners in the source language would; this has been referred to as "pragmatic equivalence" (see House 1977; Hale 2007). Within a Speech Act theory framework (Austin 1962), the interpreting process can be roughly explained in the following way: when listening to the source speech, the interpreter analyses it in terms of its locutionary act (the words uttered), illocutionary act (what is performed by those words), and perlocutionary act (what is achieved through them). In other words, the interpreter needs to fully understand the communicative function of the utterance and the likely effect on the listeners. Such understanding of the utterance will largely depend on the speech event itself, on its participants, and on the knowledge shared by those participants. To interpret faithfully, the interpreter needs to bridge the gap that exists between the two languages and cultures by aiming to render the illocutionary act and at the same time aspiring to achieve the intended perlocutionary act. This is often done at the expense of the locutionary act. The examples below will illustrate some of the differences that exist across languages at the various levels of the language hierarchy: lexical, grammatical, semantic and pragmatic.

(3)
Spanish sentence: A la niña la mordió el perro.
Lexical translation (literal, word-for-word):   To the girl it (feminine) bit the dog.

Semantic translation: The dog bit the girl.
Pragmatic translation: It was the girl that was bitten by the dog.

One difference between languages is word order, as exemplified in (3), which clearly demonstrates that a literal, word-for-word translation would be inadequate in English. Hale (2007) proposes that interpreting competence can be matched with the approach the interpreter adopts when rendering his/her translation. For example, a person whose bilingualism is rudimentary will approach translation at the lexical level and produce a literal translation; untrained interpreters will tend to approach translation at the sentence level, concentrating only on the propositional content and produce semantic translations; and the most competent, trained interpreters, will approach translation at the discourse level and attempt to produce pragmatic translations. In (3), we can see that the semantic translation produces the correct propositional content: the dog bit the girl. The Spanish utterance, however, uses a marked structure leading to the presumption that in context, a possible distinction needs to be made between what animal bit which child, hence the marked theme position of the girl/object, even though the clause is in the active voice. The same effect can be achieved in English by resorting to a cleft construction. In order to achieve a pragmatic translation, the interpreter needs to choose from a different grammatical resource in English in order to match the original intention rather than the original words, or structure. This process can be further complicated when context, participants and culture are added to the equation.

This complex process is not widely understood let alone applied by untrained interpreters. Research has found that many tend to translate semantically, not pragmatically, thus inadvertently changing the illocutionary and perlocutionary acts of the original utterances (Hale 1996; Berk-Seligson 1999; Fraser and Freedgood 1999).

Overcoming challenges caused by cross linguistic differences

Trained interpreters will face as many challenges as untrained interpreters. However, trained interpreters will ideally have received the tools to deal with such challenges. They will also have the resources to not only make informed choices, but also to explain those choices to the court when necessary.

Languages differ at all levels of the linguistic hierarchy. Interpreters need to be competent at all levels in each language, and be able to make judgments about what aspects of the original utterance to sacrifice in order to achieve a pragmatic rendition when interpreting. This is particularly difficult in court interpreting, where subtle changes to utterances can lead to changes in the evidence and to the evaluation of witness credibility. This section will present a number of examples to illustrate cross linguistic differences that require high level expertise to produce adequate, accurate interpretations.

At the grammatical level, a number of challenges can arise. One such challenge is interpreting tense and aspect accurately between English and Chinese. In English, tense and aspect are manifested mostly through verbal morphology, whereas in Chinese the use of adverbial markers and context carry these same meanings, thus making it difficult for interpreters to choose the most accurate renditions (Lin 2006). In the case of Arabic and Spanish, Hale and Campbell (2002) present the results of an empirical study which demonstrates the number of choices translators are confronted with. The study found that the categories that produced the highest number of alternatives, and therefore created the greatest difficulty in finding translation equivalents, were official terms, metaphors and complex noun phrases (Hale and Campbell 2002). One example was the seemingly unproblematic English noun phrase "case management," which caused difficulty at both semantic and the grammatical levels because in neither Arabic nor Spanish can a noun modify another noun.

Another very subtle difference between Spanish and English is the way speakers verbalize motion. For example, Slobin (1996) found that English speakers tend to express the manner of the motion by using manner verbs such as "*staggered* into the room," whereas Spanish speakers rarely describe the motion at all and when they do, do so by adding an adjunct of manner *"entró tambaleándose"* (entered staggering). In a study of the way interpreters interpreted manner verbs in witness testimonies, Filipovic found that

> as a result of the habitual need to express manner in English, different lexical choices are made in the English translation that add information about the manner of motion, not present in the Spanish original due to the use of manner-neutral lexical items, which could result in different interpretations of the situation described.
>
> (Filipovic 2007)

One such example is (4).

(4)

Witness:	pero … salió por la seven
Literal translation:	*But … (he/she/you formal) exited via the seven*
Interpreter:	the suspect ran up 7th street.

(Filipovic 2007: 253)

Filipovic explains that the English questioning persistently insists on more detail about the manner in which an action took place, while such information tends to be absent from Spanish descriptions. This may lead interpreters to believe that they need to add descriptions of manner, as in (4), where *salió* (went out) is translated as "ran up." Such translation demonstrates the interpreter's own perception of the event, which may not necessarily match the reality, as the details were not specified in the original. The interpreter is possibly also attempting to make the English version sound more natural and pragmatically appropriate, but such an addition may impact on the propositional content of the utterance. In a legal case, a witness's detailed description of what they saw is crucial and any subtle changes produced by the interpreter, as in example (4), can impact on the consistency of the accounts by different witnesses. The interpreter is therefore presented with the difficult task of deciding how to achieve the illocutionary and perlocutionary acts without interfering with the propositional content. Filipovic goes on to explain that the interpreter's assumption that everyone was running in the chase scene turned out to be incorrect, as it was later made clear that some people were on bicycles.

Another example provided by Filipovic is the difficulty in translating the non-agentive reflexive pseudo-passive from Spanish into English, as in (5).

(5)

Witness:	Se me cayó en las escaleras
Literal translation:	To-me-it-happened that (she/he/it) fell on the stairs.

(Filipovic 2007: 262)

447

The Spanish utterance in (5) poses a translation challenge that is difficult to overcome without an explicit explanation to the court. As (5) clearly shows, a literal word-for-word translation would not produce an accurate rendition. The interpreter in this case interpreted the utterance as either "I dropped her" or "she fell," both of which are accurate translations but neither conveys the same subtle meaning of the original. In this case, both translations caused confusion, leading to the same question about the dropping of the victim being asked nine times. The difficulty was caused by the different expressions of intentionality in Spanish and English. The Spanish utterance "*se cayó*," could be translated as "s/he/it fell," as the gender is unspecified and the interpreter needs to clarify it, unless it is understood from previous information. The addition of "*me*," as in the example "*se me cayó*" indicates that the speaker was involved in holding or carrying the person who accidentally fell out of the speaker's grasp. The English "I dropped her" could indicate that the speaker deliberately let go, whereas the Spanish clearly indicates that the dropping was unintentional and intentionality is crucial in legal cases. This is a clear example of a situation where the interpreter would be justified in intervening to explain the translation difficulty, as a subtle misunderstanding of this utterance could have major legal implications.

At the discourse level, interpreting challenges occur when utterances can be translated easily at the lexical or semantic levels, but due to pragmatic differences, they do not portray the same illocutionary and perlocutionary acts. Interpreting speech acts such as polite requests in courtroom questions, can cause difficulties in some languages. In English polite requests are normally performed indirectly, by the use of a modal interrogative, such as "Could you tell the court what happened?" When interpreters hear this utterance, they firstly need to understand that it is an indirect speech act which functions as a polite request, and not as a genuine question about the listener's ability to speak. The illocutionary act, therefore, is a polite request for specific information regarding an event. Languages such as Russian or Czech, for example, formulate such requests directly by the use of the imperative followed by a politeness marker (Searle 1975; Mir 1993). A Russian interpreter, for instance, would need to change the indirect speech act into a direct speech act in order to match the illocutionary and perlocutionary acts in the target language.

Understanding the discourse strategies of the courtroom

Another layer of complexity is added to the interpreter's task when interpreting in the courtroom, due to the constraints placed upon the interpreting process by the setting and by the strategic use of language itself. Studies of the discourse of the adversarial courtroom in particular, have shown the significance of language as a metaphorical tool (Danet and Bogoch 1980; Drew and Heritage 1992b; Gibbons 2003). Different types of questions are used by lawyers to achieve specific goals depending on the type of examination. The form and the words used in questions can influence the answers they elicit, and even the recollections they trigger in eye witnesses (Harris 1984; Loftus 1979; Maley and Fahey 1991). Similarly, the language and style used by witnesses when giving evidence can impact significantly on how convincing or credible they are (O'Barr 1982).

A number of studies of court interpreting found that even competent, accredited interpreters who had not received specialized legal interpreting training, were not aware of the significance of certain linguistic features of courtroom discourse, and consequently tended to unjustifiably omit or disregard them. Examples include arbitrary changes of question type (Hale 2004; Pérez González 2006); the omission of discourse markers to preface lawyers' questions (Hale 1999); the omission of coercive tag questions during cross-examination (Hale 2001; Rigney 1999) and changes to levels of politeness and changes of style and register in witness testimonies, all of which led to different evaluations of character (Krouglov 1999; Berk-Seligson 1990/2002; Hale 2004).

The changes found in these studies were generally not explainable by cross linguistic pragmatic differences; rather they were usually the result of interpreters disregarding what they seemed to consider superfluous features of speech. Example (6) shows an unjustified change of question type, from an open question to a polar interrogative eliciting a very different answer.

(6)
Question: Yeah, can you tell the court to the best ... to the best of your recollection, to the best of your memory?
Interpreter: *¿Pero algo recuerda usted?*
              (But you remember something?)

(Hale 2004: 58)

The English question is an indirect request to the witness to tell the court what s/he remembers. The interpreted question changes the expected answer to a yes/no response, which would then require a further question to get the witness to describe the events. The interpreted version not only omits the reference to the court but also changes the register and level of politeness. The interpreter deviated completely from the question's original intention.

Example (7) shows the omission of the discourse marker *well*.

(7)
Question: And uh you tell the court that you have no prior convictions?
Interpreter: *¿Dice usted a la corte de que no ha tenido antes ninguna condena?*
              (Are you saying to the court that you have not had any convictions before?)
Answer: *No.*
Interpreter: No.
Question: Well, is it correct that you have no prior convictions?
Interpreter: *¿Es correcto decir que usted no ha tenido condenas anteriores?*
              (Is it correct to say that you have not had convictions before?)

(Hale 2004: 64)

The use of *well* in this case indicates that the lawyer was dissatisfied with the answer because it was ambiguous; an ambiguity that was caused by the original question. It is not clear whether the answer "no" refers to "no I don't tell the court" or "no, I have no prior convictions." In order to clarify the answer, the lawyer asks another question, which he links with the discourse marker *well*. Pragmatically, *well* implies "let me put it another way," which maintains coherence in the discourse, however, the interpreter omits the initial discourse marker altogether and simply translates the rest of the question, but this omission changes its pragmatic effect. *Well* in this case could have been translated as "*Bueno, pero*" (well, but) or by the conditional "*Entonces, sería correcto decir ...*" (Then, would it be correct to say ...).

One common complaint from judicial officers has been that:

> evidence given through an interpreter loses much of its impact ... The jury does not really hear the witness, nor are they fully able to appreciate, for instance, the degree of conviction or uncertainty with which his evidence is given; they cannot wholly follow the nuances, inflections, quickness or hesitancy of the witness; all they have is the dispassionate and unexpressive tone of the interpreter.
>
> *(Filios v. Morland* [1963] S.R. (NSW) 331, *per* Bereton J
> at 332–33, in Roberts-Smith 2009)

The fear expressed above has been confirmed by the results of experimental studies. However, it has also been found, that interpreters can be trained to maintain certain features of discourse that will minimize the impact of the interpreter on the evaluation of witness credibility (Berk–Seligson 1990; Hale 2004). Based on authentic transcripts, Hale (2004) conducted a number of experiments to ascertain whether the stylistic characteristics classified by O'Barr (1982) as powerless and powerful speech styles, determined the way jurors evaluated the credibility, trustworthiness and competence of witnesses. The results showed that Spanish jurors rated the Spanish speaking witnesses who spoke in the powerful style as more credible, more competent and more trustworthy. The same results were obtained from English speaking jurors, thus corroborating O'Barr's study, both for English and Spanish speaking jurors. When the ratings of the original Spanish witnesses were compared with the interpreters' renditions, it was found that the interpreters who interpreted accurately at the propositional level but changed the style of the original from powerless to powerful, obtained a better evaluation on all three points. When interpreters maintained the propositional content, but changed the style from powerful to powerless, they received a less positive evaluation than did the original witness on all three points. However, when the interpreters maintained as much as possible of both the propositional content and the style of speech, the impact of the interpreter was minimal and the juror evaluations showed no statistically significant differences. The results of the above study show that with adequate training, competent interpreters can produce renditions that are stylistically, propositionally and pragmatically accurate, which will counteract the negative effects of the interpreter's intervention mentioned by Judge Brereton above.

Understanding the role of the court interpreter

Misunderstanding of the interpreter's role is common among non-professionals hired as interpreters. Instead of seeing themselves as impartial interpreters, they see themselves as advocates or gatekeepers. Such attitudes may be manifested overtly, in their comments or advice to their "client" or to the legal practitioner (as in (8)); or covertly, either through the omission of utterances they deem irrelevant or through the addition of information (as in (9)). At the one extreme, we find examples like example (8) provided by Ahmad (2007), where a Burmese priest acts as a volunteer interpreter.

(8)
Lawyer to client: Is there someone there that we could speak to?
Reverend Sen: Why is it necessary for you to speak with them?
(*volunteer interpreter addresses lawyer, without interpreting into Burmese*)

| Lawyer: | Reverend, would it be possible for you to just translate what we said? If Mae has questions about why we would like to speak with them, we can answer then. |
| Reverend Sen: | I have helped many Burmese to apply for asylum, and I don't see why this information is important. Please explain it to me before I translate for Mae. |

(Ahmad 2007: 1005)

Reverend Sen cannot be blamed for acting in this way. He is not a professional interpreter and is not bound by any professional ethical code, nor has he received any training. The responsibility here lies with the lawyers who did not hire the services of a professional interpreter and expect a volunteer to act as one.

Ibrahim (2007) gives another example of an interpreter in Malaysia, who unbeknown to the Bench, persuaded an unrepresented accused to change his plea from not guilty to guilty based on what the interpreter himself considered to be evidence against the accused which would most certainly lead to a conviction. Ibrahim explains that the interpreter is considered by the Malaysian legal system to be "a bilingual intermediary, clerk of the court, and advocate of unrepresented accused, [who] receives little or no training and is not paid appropriately for the responsibilities (s)he carries" (Ibrahim 2007: 209).

In Austria, studies of paid interpreters in asylum interview settings also found examples of role confusion, where some interpreters interwove their own comments into their renditions and covertly took on the role of pseudo immigration officials (Pöllabauer 2004; Kolb and Pöchhacker 2008) This can be seen in example (9).

(9)

Adjudicator: (→App)	Und haben Sie Ihre Religion ausgeübt?
	(And did you practice your religion?)
Interpreter:	Did you practice that religion?
Applicant:	Yeah, I was a Christian! *And I go to church.*
Interpreter:	*Yes, but but*-look, there are many Christians who never go to ch-You went to church?
Applicant:	Yes.
Interpreter:	Ich bin in die Kirche gegangen.
	(I went to church).

(Kolb and Pöchhacker 2008)

In (9) the answer "Yeah, I was a Christian!" was not interpreted into German, presumably because the interpreter did not agree with the implication that Christians practice their religion, a personal opinion the interpreter makes explicit to the applicant but not to the rest of the tribunal. Here the interpreter holds a private conversation in English for no reason other than his/her disagreement with the applicant's proposed inference. It is impossible to say whether this interpreter had received any specialist training and whether s/he understood the consequences of his/her choices.

In example (10), we see the interpreter being confronted with a claimant who does not understand his role. The interpreter is interpreting to the claimant simultaneously in whispering mode, while others are giving evidence. This is standard practice in court interpreting, but while the interpreter interprets, the claimant must not make any comments, as that would interfere with the interpreter's rendition. In (10) we see that the claimant intervenes by commenting to the interpreter that s/he did not have a contract. The interpreter then tries to explain his/her role in the subsequent turn.

(10) Interpreting simultaneously while others are giving evidence

Arbitrator: [addressing the defendant]
               Do you have a lease with this lady?
Interpreter: [for the benefit of the Polish-speaking claimant—in Polish]
               Do you, Ma'am, have a contract with this lady?
Claimant: (in Polish) But I don't have a contract
Interpreter: (to claimant, in Polish)
               No, no no, Ma'am. I'm only translating what the lady is asking.
                                                    (Angermeyer 2005: 215)

Unrealistic expectations of the role of the interpreter added to poor working conditions and inadequate pay have led to interpreters refusing to take on court assignments or leaving the profession altogether. Ibrahim speaks of the "perpetual shortage of interpreters in Malaysian courts, as senior ones retire and new ones either resign after a short period or do not come forward at all" (Ibrahim 2007: 213).

A parallel can found with Australian Aboriginal interpreters, as expressed in the quotation below:

I stopped doing court interpreting years ago. … They just didn't really understand what the interpreter's role was, and I just got sick of sort of being blamed, you know, for allowing people to go free or putting people in.

                                                    (Cooke 2009)

Acquiring the expertise to know when and how to intervene to offer expert opinion

Interpreters are constantly faced with difficult choices about how best to interpret each utterance, and need to continually make judgments about the likely impact of any changes on the legal process, so as to alert the court to potential misunderstandings. A well-trained competent court interpreter will have the expertise to intervene to explain situations where potential misunderstandings arise, where direct equivalents are not possible, or where a linguistic strategy does not have the same effect in the target language. Such interpreter expertise should be valued and welcomed by the court. Lee (2009a) speaks of difficulties encountered by Korean interpreters due to ambiguity and inexplicitness found in Korean utterances. In an interview with Korean court interpreters, she found that most were reluctant to interrupt the court proceedings to seek clarification when utterances were ambiguous. Lee (2009a) argues that the interpreters' reluctance to intervene is mainly due to the intimidating atmosphere of the court, which tends to ignore the presence of the interpreter or not to view them as experts.

On the other hand, Berk-Seligson (1990) and Hale (2003) found that untrained Spanish interpreters interrupted the proceedings for a number of unjustified reasons, for example, in order to point out to counsel that a question just asked had been asked previously, or to attempt to help the witness answer a question. Attempts to make clarifications were also found to create more confusion. These untrained interpreters demonstrated a lack of understanding of the discourse strategies of the courtroom and of the role of the interpreter as well as inadequate linguistic and interpreting expertise.

Conclusion

Despite the law's claim to "precision," language is imprecise (Gibbons 2003), misunderstandings are common in monolingual situations and the potential for misunderstanding in bilingual situations is even greater. Legal systems have failed to recognize the complexities of court interpreting, and have been content to "make do" with less than adequate interpreting services provided by unqualified bilinguals. Such bilinguals, however, are often subject to unrealistic expectations, criticized for their failings, overworked and underpaid or even unpaid. The inadequate performance of these bilingual helpers has at best led to appeals on the grounds of poor interpretation and at worst to no action at all, with unknown consequences.

If justice is to be served, things need to change. The system must firstly acknowledge that highly competent court interpreters are crucial for the successful conduct of bilingual proceedings and secondly, the system must be prepared to pay for a quality service. On the one hand, the demand for trained, competent interpreters will lead to the creation of high quality university programs. On the other, incentives such as adequate remuneration, decent working conditions and due recognition will lead to high level bilinguals choosing to complete the relevant training to enter the profession.

Interpreters who receive adequate training will be educated not only on linguistic, cultural and interpreting issues, but also on the discourse practices of the courtroom and the requirements of the setting and its participants. Similarly, legal professionals are to be educated about the requirements of interpreters in order to perform adequately, with all participants assuming some of the responsibility for the success of the interaction. Ultimately, legal professionals need to work together with interpreters to achieve their goals and recognize them as expert participants, rather than "mere" translation machines. Only when the bar is raised on court interpreting, will quality services be guaranteed and justice served.

Notes

1 The Critical Link international conference series is dedicated to interpreting in legal, medical and welfare settings. CL5, was held in Sydney, Australia, from 11 to 15 April 2007. Its theme was "Quality in interpreting: A shared responsibility".

Further reading

Berk-Seligson, S. (1990/2002) *The Bilingual Courtroom: Court Interpreters in the Judicial Process*, Chicago: Chicago University Press. (This book reports the first and one of the largest data-based studies into court interpreting in the USA.)

Cook, M., Eades, D. and Hale, S. (eds) (1999) "Special issue on Legal Interpreting," *Forensic Linguistics*, 6(1). (This special issue of *Forensic Linguistics* provides a compilation of research papers on different aspects of legal interpreting covering a wide range of topics from different perspectives.)

Hale, S. (2004) *The Discourse of Court Interpreting*, Amsterdam and Philadelphia, PA: John Benjamins. (This book reports the results of one of the largest data-based studies into court interpreting in Australia looking at the discourse practices of interpreters, lawyers and witnesses in fine detail.)

——(2006) "Themes and methodological issues in court interpreting research," in Hertog, E. and B. van der Veer (eds), *Linguistica Antverpiensa. Taking Stock: Research and Methodology in Community Interpreting* (5/2006), Antwerp: Hoger Instituut voor Vertalers &Tolken (205–28).

(This chapter provides a review of the main research into court interpreting.)

Mikkelson, H. (2000) *Introduction to Court Interpreting*, Manchester: St Jerome. (This is a useful introduction to court interpreting for those wanting to know more about the discipline or wanting to become court interpreters.)

Russell, D. and S. Hale (eds) (2008) *Interpreting in Legal Settings*, Washington, DC: Gallaudet University Press. (This is an edited volume of articles on spoken and signed language court interpreting from around the world.)

30

Interpreting outside the courtroom

'A shattered mirror?' Interpreting in legal contexts outside the courtroom

Krzysztof Kredens and Ruth Morris

Introduction

Globalization has brought ever larger numbers of people to places where the local legal systems were not used to dealing with speakers of other languages, or if they were, with only a small linguistic range. Inevitably, non-proficient or 'second-language' speakers become involved in law enforcement practices, whether as victims, witnesses or suspects. In order to ensure equal access to justice, decision-makers in a rapidly growing number of countries must nowadays find ways of coping with the resulting increased linguistic diversity at all stages of the judicial process.

Given the nature of courtroom language, with its highly structured discourse, competing narratives and speech styles, court interpreting is often regarded as the most important sub-domain of legal interpreting (see Hale, this volume). However, in the context of forensic linguistics, no less relevant are issues of interpreter-mediated communication in other legal and forensic contexts; this chapter is devoted to just such issues.

In the law enforcement chain that begins with a crime, interpreters for second-language speakers, whether they be suspects, victims or witnesses, can be an all-important link. Unless the highest standards are maintained at all stages, failure may result further down the line, at trial or at a subsequent appeal. In what follows we discuss interpreting at five stages of the judicial process: initial contact, police interviews, client–lawyer interactions, probation meetings and prison visits. These different stages do not necessarily pose different kinds of linguistic problem. Rather, they can each be associated with certain consequences (1) for the interpreter, who may be subjected to different kinds of pressure and often forced to take on unexpected roles, (2) for the second-language speaker, who will be variously disadvantaged depending on the context, and, finally, (3) for the administration of justice.

Emergency interpreting

A second-language speaker's experience of law enforcement may begin with an emergency call to the police. In the UK, when a caller is deemed to have limited proficiency in English, the police service operator uses a telephone interpreting service, such as Language Line, which claims on its website to be able to provide 24-hour access to interpreters working in over 170 languages (www.languageline.co.uk). Language Line operates worldwide – in New York, for example, all police precincts have had direct, instant access to the service since July 2005. The programme was originally piloted in 2004 in some of the city's most ethnically diverse communities. Police officers were equipped with cellular and dual-handset speaker-phones which had direct, instant access to interpreters of over 150 different languages, in order to better assist immigrant victims of domestic violence. In its first month, the line was used three dozen times for nine languages: Bengali, Korean, Cantonese, Mandarin, Russian, Sinhalese, Farsi, Spanish and Hindi (Worth 2004).

Telephone-based remote interpreting, while a most welcome development, is not without its problems, most of which have to do with the absence of the non-verbal cues that normally facilitate turn-taking and also enable the interpreter to make decisions about pragmatic aspects of the message. The interpreter is disadvantaged also because, as Moser-Mercer (2003) writes, 'the coordination of image and sound, the piecing together of a reality far away and the concomitant feeling of lack of control, all draw on mental resources already overcommitted in this highly complex skill' (http://aiic.net/ViewPage. cfm/article879). Additionally, it often happens that individuals requiring police assistance are emotionally distressed. In such cases, the interpreter may actually have to intervene by taking over, whether explicitly or implicitly, the task of assuaging the caller's agitation in order to be able to obtain relevant information.[1]

The need for what can be termed 'emergency interpreting' may arise in situations where the police respond to an emergency call by arriving at the location only to find that they are unable to communicate with the individuals concerned. This problem is well illustrated by the case of Robert Dziekański, a Polish man who died after being tasered by officers of the Royal Canadian Mounted Police at Vancouver Airport in October 2007. Although his death seems to have been triggered by a combination of factors – including a delayed flight; failure by airport staff to locate Dziekański following a request from his mother, who was waiting for him in the arrivals hall; and his disorientation following a prolonged period in a confusing environment (he had never flown before) – the most important factor was probably his inability to communicate in English. After he left the immigration waiting area, some nine hours after his arrival, he became agitated and, apparently in an attempt to attract attention, threw a computer monitor onto the floor and overturned a table. When the police officers arrived, they were unable to establish communication and, finding his behaviour threatening, tasered him five times, following which he died on the scene. The police officers were also erroneously advised by bystanders that Dziekański spoke Russian, which – though ultimately of no consequence to what followed – illustrates a further problem integral to emergency situations. A crucial, often overlooked element is the proper identification of the specific language spoken by an individual with whom the police need to communicate, and/or even the need to provide an interpreter or other effective means of communication with witness, victim, or suspect. Widespread assumptions – such as that most people from Eastern Europe can speak Russian, or that people from India or

Pakistan can all understand each other through a common language, be it Urdu or Hindi, or that everyone from South America speaks Spanish – can result in miscarriages of justice (see the Florida case of *Petrona Tomás* and England's *Iqbal Begum* below). As made all too clear by the Dziekański case, unless the appropriate method is chosen in a specific instance, communication may be defective at best or non-existent at worst.

Failing access to a reliable telephone interpreting service, a partial solution may be the use of modern technology such as portable voice translators, which use speech recognition systems and small electronic libraries of set phrases encoded as audio files. This, accompanied by the arguably universal semiotics of the police uniform, may be effective in at least telling those involved that they are being taken to the police station, where an interpreter will join them. However, the increasing availability of mobile telephony may make possible remote but on-the-spot interpreting at the moment of arrest; conceivably, even for the users of sign language by means of a 3G cellphone.

If used appropriately, telephone interpreting can be beneficial but, as noted above, it is not a satisfactory substitute for an on-the-spot interpreter in most situations. In addition, cultural issues may further complicate situations involving individuals not familiar with local rules. In the 1979 English appeal of *Beck v. Sager*, a drink-driving case, it was held that the second-language-speaking defendant's failure to understand what was being required of him (to give a sample of either blood or urine), as well as to understand the penal consequences of a failure to comply with this demand, was due to him being 'mentally unable' to provide a specimen. Sager, a Libyan air force cadet training near Carlisle, had very little idea about the entire legal and cultural notion of driving under the influence of drink or being tested for the presence of alcohol in the body. The second-language speaker's quandary is clear from Sager's own comments at the appeal, shown in extract (1).

(1)
I think he mean what I understand. I did not feel it was necessary to get someone to explain for me. I think I understand. I did not ask for a friend to come and explain the language at any time. I do not know why he want blood, my reason for not giving blood – there was no reason. I understand at the time the sergeant wanted blood. My flying instruction is carried out in English. I would not have given blood if allowed to take my car.

(*Beck v. Sager* [1979] RTR at 479)

Tellingly, in those pre-telephone interpreting days the appellate court in the shape of Lord Justice Bridge commented wryly (2):

(2)
It is found that, during this procedure, the defendant at no time asked for an interpreter. I dare say it would have been no good if he had, because Arabic interpreters are probably fairly scarce at Carlisle; but at all events he neither asked for an interpreter nor indicated any misunderstanding, and the police, perfectly reasonably no doubt on their part, honestly believed that he had understood all that was said to him. But the justices came to the conclusion that he did not in fact understand much of what was said to him.

(*Beck v. Sager* [1979] RTR at 480–81)

Clearly, if none of the parties involved realize that there is a misunderstanding, the ready availability of interpreting services will not solve the problem.

The police interview

Article 6 of the European Convention on Human Rights, which addresses the right to a fair trial, stipulates in its section 3(1) that everyone charged with a criminal offence has the right to be informed promptly, 'in a language which he understands and in detail', of the nature and cause of the accusation against him. Article 14.3(a) of the International Covenant on Civil and Political Rights uses almost identical language.

The problem of the administration of rights in a form that makes sense to the person to whom they are administered is particularly acute in the United States, and serves as grounds for many appeals. There have been numerous cases where the so-called Miranda rights, communicated to suspects either during arrest or when in police custody, have been ostensibly administered in a language of which they have no or only a poor understanding (particularly when Spanish is used in the case of individuals from Central or South America whose mother tongue is not Spanish and who may not even have any knowledge of the language), or by individuals working on behalf of the police (often police officers or police administrative personnel) who have an inadequate command of the language into which they are supposedly interpreting. One notable case is that of Petrona Tomás, a 15-year-old girl from Guatemala, charged in Florida with the first-degree murder of her newborn child. In November 2002, police in Palm Beach County twice questioned the girl, whose mother tongue was an indigenous language called Kanjobal. However, the police questioned her in Spanish, a language that all involved in the case agree she could not speak with any fluency. The police did not try to find a Kanjobal interpreter and her father, who four years before had sold her, waived her Miranda rights. The transcript of the police interview contains mostly one-word answers to often disjointed and leading questions, yet it was the basis for a first-degree murder indictment (Moffett 2003).

In her first statement, Tomás repeatedly told the police the baby had been stillborn. However, Pacenti (2002) reports that in the second of two statements, made from her hospital bed just hours after she gave birth, Tomás appeared to have trouble understanding the questions from Sergeant Enrique Ponce (3).

(3)
Ponce: Did you see when the baby was breathing?
Tomás: Huh?
Ponce: When … when … when the baby was born you saw him breathe, no, for 10 minutes?
Tomás: No.
Ponce: No?
Tomás: No, no.
Ponce: Did you tell us … She is saying no now. … Did you see the baby breathe when he was born?
Tomás: Yes.

Police practice when dealing with second-language speakers varies greatly worldwide. For example, in Britain and Australia, on the whole, police forces work with outside interpreters from the interview stage onwards. In the United States, standard practice is for the police to try to manage with the linguistic skills of their own officers, with one officer conducting the interrogation and another acting as 'interpreter'. Often problems abound, as Berk-Seligson (2000) shows on the basis of a review of appellate cases from 1965 to 1999 drawn from three states – California, Florida and New York. In particular, she identifies the absence of clear-cut demarcations between certain sorts of legal actors and others, such as court interpreters, community interpreters and police interpreters. Where the police employ an incompetent interpreter, there will inevitably be major pitfalls, as illustrated by the 1999 Ohio case of Alejandro Ramirez (*State of Ohio v. Alejandro Ramirez*, 135 Ohio App. 3d 89; 732 N.E.2d 1065). The defendant, who had arrived in the United States from Mexico four months earlier, did not speak a word of English. Due to a complicated set of circumstances, he was initially persuaded by his housemates to confess to the police that he had shot an intruder, even though he had been drunk and asleep at the time of the shooting. He had erroneously been informed by his fellow Mexicans that he would simply be deported. However, after it emerged that the intruder had died, Ramirez was charged with and subsequently found guilty of murder. Certain police failings emerged when he appealed his conviction, among other things that during his questioning, his Miranda rights were not properly explained to him, the interpreter made many errors and gave her own opinions without clearing her answers with the defendant and the police did not contact the Mexican consulate.

Since the defendant spoke no English, the police had used a local administrative assistant, Jennifer Rodriguez, as interpreter. She had been used as a Spanish/English interpreter by the police several times before, but had no formal training. Her knowledge of Spanish came from taking several Spanish classes in college almost 20 years earlier and from living for several months in Mexico. She was not familiar with legal terms in either language. On the basis of the material submitted to it, the appellate court found that the interpreter provided Ramirez with an unintelligible version of his Miranda rights, something that back-translated as: 'you have the right that something ... that you ... ah ... can use against yourself in a court of law'. In addition, she made many grammatical and semantic errors in her translation: for example, she translated the word 'rights' using the word for 'right-hand side' or 'right hand' (*derecha*), instead of the term used in legal contexts (*derecho*) and translated Ramirez's 'hmm' as 'yes'. She also omitted parts of the Miranda rights. In particular, she did not advise the defendant of his right to have an attorney present during questioning nor did she stop her translation of the Miranda rights when the defendant indicated he was not following what was being said.

During Ramirez's trial, defence attorneys had argued that his confession should be suppressed because he did not understand its ramifications when he made it. An expert witness (a college professor unversed in forensic linguistics) engaged by the prosecution to analyse the administration of Ramirez's rights failed to accurately convey the actual shortcomings of the interpreter's poor performance. Nevertheless, the outcome of the appeal stated: 'Miranda warnings given to appellant were insufficient to adequately apprise him of his rights. The translated Miranda warnings were confusing, and certain aspects of the warnings were simply not given' (*State of Ohio v. Alejandro Ramirez* 732 N.E.2d 1065 at 1067). The court overturned the murder conviction and Ramirez eventually pleaded guilty to involuntary manslaughter.

Writing specifically about cautions delivered through interpreting, with special reference to Japanese native-speaker suspects in the Australian criminal investigation system,

Nakane (2007) identifies a number of factors which may lead to difficulties in communicating the suspect's rights in police interviews:

(1) rendering an originally written legal text in a face-to-face speech mode;
(2) the degree to which the illocutionary force and the legal implications of the caution can be maintained in the translation;
(3) the interpreter's understanding of the meaning and legal implications of the cautions;
(4) the dynamics of interpreter-mediated interaction;
(5) the degree to which cultural or institutional gaps are to be bridged by the interpreter; and
(6) the interpreter's professional competence.

Nakane reports that both Shuy (1997) and Gibbons (2001a) argue that in some cases they had worked on, there was some evidence that the suspects tend to say 'Yes' to the comprehension check question when they actually have little understanding of the cautions, what Eades (2002) has called 'gratuitous compliance'. Nakane quotes a passage which illustrates this point to perfection. Taken from Coldrey (1987: 84–85, cited in Gibbons 2003: 209), the material graphically illustrates the problems involved with cautioning an Aboriginal man, who is ostensibly an English speaker and hence no interpreter is involved in the exchange (4).

(4)
IR: Right. Now I want to ask you some questions about the trouble out there but I want you to understand that you don't have to answer any questions at all. Do you understand that?
IE: Yes.
IR: Do you have to tell me that story?
IE: Yes.
IR: Do you have to though?
IE: Yes.
IR: Do you, am I making you tell me the story?
IE: Yes.
IR: Or are you telling me because you want to?
IE: Yes.

The exchange in (4) makes it clear that the problem lies with the suspect's inability to understand the questions he is being asked by the police officer, who is trying hard to convey the intent of the cautions. The question is to what extent a competent, trained, experienced interpreter would have been able to overcome these problems, which fall in part under Nakane's category (5), the degree to which cultural or institutional gaps are to be bridged by the interpreter.

As is clear from Nakane's paper, and as Hale also makes clear in her chapter on court interpreting in this volume, even high-level proficiency in the languages concerned combined with two-way interpreting skills, do not necessarily guarantee the provision of high-calibre communication in the legal system. Many aspects, some of them not directly related to the interpreting itself, play a role in determining the quality, and hence effectiveness or otherwise, of interpreting. Thus, Gibbons (2001a: 443) reports that in

New South Wales, the police were found to be reluctant to use interpreters, for a number of reasons, including delays, financial aspects, and the perceived negative effects of interpreter mediation (impeding police officers' reading of non-verbal signals and the suspect's gaining of extra time to answer questions). Gibbons identifies past 'gross under-use' of interpreters by NSW Police. A new version of the force's *Code of Practice* was subsequently produced on the basis of input from a range of people, including Gibbons. It reads: 'Use an interpreter when someone cannot understand and speak the English language well enough to enable them to *fully* understand and *fully* reply to questions. *If in doubt, get an interpreter* (Gibbons 2001a: 444, though the italicization has been added for this chapter). Gibbons further makes the point that even apparently clear-cut instructions, for example on how to question suspects, often fail because they lack explicitness. Clearly this was the case in *Beck v. Sager*, discussed above, where even the defendant failed to realize that he did not understand the whole purpose of the police procedure. The point is that communication is a continuum from unattainable perfection to total non-communication. As the final NSW Police *Code of Practice* cautions: 'Do not presume that people understand even the most simple [sic] questions'. This means that even the most competent interpreter cannot necessarily overcome a lack of comprehension on the part of the suspect. Gibbons makes the point that yes/no questions are not a good way of checking comprehension (as can be seen in extract (4)). In fact, he argues that encouraging narrative accounts of a sequence of events when interviewing (rather than 'interrogating') suspects is more likely to prove effective (Gibbons 2001a: 446).

Gibbons also suggested to the New South Wales Police that the new Code of Practice include a reference to the new NSW *Procedures for Evidence Act*, which are far more extensive and considerably more explicit. With regard to criteria for using an interpreter, the latter read:

> Use an interpreter if the person (suspect or witness) you are interviewing: is unable to communicate in English; has a limited understanding of English; is more comfortable communicating in their own language. NB: Just because someone can speak English to do everyday tasks does not mean they can cope with the added stress of a police interview.
>
> (Gibbons 2001a: 445)

As Russell (2000) shows, when the caution is being administered by English police officers, they are supposed to check that the second-language speaker has understood its implications, by paraphrasing the caution and *lowering the register*. However, as she points out, the catch is that the police, being untrained in linguistics, are often unable to make the switch from the 'legal' caution to the 'in your own words' version. As a result, as Russell says, 'the burden for lowering the register falls squarely, if not fairly, upon the interpreter.' The drawback, of course, is that interpreters manage this with varying degrees of success, depending, of course, upon their competence and experience, but also upon their own understanding of the caution, particularly as many interpreters are simply native speakers of the language and are as untrained as the officers themselves (Russell 2000: 42–43). The whole process is therefore fraught with dangers, as testified to by the number of cases in which defence claims are advanced that the defendant failed to understand the administration of the caution or Miranda rights and expert witnesses testify on the issue (see Berk-Seligson 2000). Even when, as Rock points out, the police have made other language versions of the caution available in written and sometimes spoken versions (Rock

2007: 145), firstly not all languages are covered, and, secondly, without the presence of an interpreter there is nobody to act as intermediary between the second-language speaker and the duty officer in order to clarify implications and ask for rights to be enforced.

Sourcing interpreters

Police forces have three main ways to source interpreters, if they do not have within-force individuals able to act as interpreters. There may be a professional association of police interpreters, a register of qualified interpreters, either public or held by the police, or they may outsource the provision of interpreters to an agency. In the Republic of Ireland, for example, the latter arrangement applies to the entire police force, the *Garda*. An April 2009 article in the *Irish Times* reported a highly negative assessment of the interpreting services provided to the Irish police, which since January 2009 have been outsourced to agencies on the basis of tender. The resultant selection of interpreters is so poor that not only have their overseas criminal records not been checked, but some reportedly lack basic accreditation and language proficiency. Thus, a Chinese interpreter hired to assist in interviewing a suspect was found to be an illegal immigrant. The *Irish Times* report indicated that the Irish police representative association (GRA) wants out-sourcing to be abolished. Furthermore, according to Detective Tom O'Sullivan, who is attached to the Interpol National Central Bureau at *Garda* HQ and is also a qualified interpreter and translator, feedback within the police force indicates that individual interpreters are frequently of poor quality. In addition, while the agencies are earning considerable profits, the individual interpreters are being paid extremely low rates. O'Sullivan made the point that by removing agencies from the equation, interpreters could be paid decent wages and the police force could make significant savings. Instead of the agency system, the GRA would, reportedly, prefer police officers to be provided with a list of interpreters in their areas whose academic qualifications, language skills and criminal records have been verified. O'Sullivan also claimed that a system of using vetted individuals is in place in the UK and Australia and works well (Lally 2009).

Sadly, the glowing picture painted by O'Sullivan of the situation on the other side of the Irish Sea is not entirely accurate. Of the 43 police forces in England and Wales, a number use outsourcing to agencies. As in Ireland, the result of these arrangements is that the rates paid to interpreters drop, agencies preferentially use unqualified individuals and, concomitantly, qualified competent interpreters are less likely to want to work for agencies, so the upshot is a deterioration in the quality of interpreting. In a British parliamentary debate (11 March 2009), the government representative stated:

> Police forces are outsourcing their requirement for interpreters as a pragmatic approach because they need to progress investigations. They have to get the balance right, to make sure that investigations are carried out fairly, with a high level of proof, and to make sure that people are not spending time in custody unnecessarily. We must all recognize that those issues are difficult to balance, while ensuring that we maintain the quality of interpreting.
>
> (*Hansard*, 11 March 2009: Column 136WH, online)

No speaker made the point that administrative staff, possibly civilian, could handle the sourcing of properly qualified interpreters, thereby avoiding or at least minimizing the need to outsource engagements.

Transcript issues

So far this chapter has focused on common-law systems encountering second-language speakers outside the courtroom. Komter (2002) explains how in Dutch trials, suspects are confronted with the written statements they made to the police and the investigating judge, earlier in the criminal law process. These statements are supposed to be written down as far as possible in the suspect's own words, but they are in fact the police officers' written versions of what was said in the interrogating room. They are simultaneously reports of previous talks held in the police interrogating room and part of the interaction in the courtroom, both of which are conducted for a different purpose. Thus, suspects are held accountable for what they supposedly told the police, and if they argue with this, judges can rebut their protests by pointing out that they themselves have told this to the police. The implications where a third party, the interpreter, has been present in the police interview room and where either the same or another interpreter subsequently mediates the courtroom interaction can be imagined. Since police interrogations are not usually audio- or video-taped in the Netherlands, and because the records are made by the police themselves, Komter indicates, it is impossible to prove what the suspect actually said to the police.

A related problem exists in England, where – although interviews with suspects are routinely tape-recorded – only monolingual (English) transcripts of interpreter-mediated interviews are prepared by the police and may have to be subsequently (back-)translated into the second language for the benefit of the non-English speaking suspect. This kind of document, normally sourced by the suspect's lawyers, poses interesting strategic questions *per se* but is fraught with problems when, as is commonly the case, the translator has no access to the original recordings and relies solely on the police transcript, which may in turn be inaccurate or incomplete.

In such cases, due to the almost infinite number of linguistic permutations available, the back-translated version in the suspect's language is highly likely to differ, perhaps significantly, from the actual words they uttered. If a second-language speaker is confronted with what he supposedly said at a police interview, in a variation on 'Chinese whispers', it is highly likely that anything the interpreter in the second language produces will differ from what was actually said at the police interview. The only way to avoid such issues is to insist on obtaining an acoustically clear tape recording of everything said in both languages, without any overlapping material, accompanied by an accurate transcript.

In the following transcribed and translated excerpt (5) from a videotape of police questioning of a mother in a baby abuse case, the interpreter (a police officer):

- uses the third person (*she*) instead of the first (*I*);
- completes an incomplete statement;
- changes intensity (from 'grab' to 'yank');
- changes a possibility into a certainty ('could' to 'going to');
- does not reproduce repetitions (*agarrar* is once rendered as 'pick up', once as 'yank');
- fails to render a diminutive (*bracito* is rendered as arm, not 'little arm');
- omits material ('it wasn't on purpose');
- renders a pronoun (*ella*) as a noun ('this lady');
- renders something less specific ('you could do something') with a more specific formulation ('you're going to hurt the baby');

- changes the order of phrases and modifies the wording (starts with 'Don't pick him up like that', when this is in fact material towards the end of the suspect's version).

In sum, this is an unprofessional performance which in fact led to no charges being brought.

(5)

Suspect:	Que no lo, que no lo agarrara así, porque yo luego lo agarré por el bracito. No fue a propósito, pero, lo agarré por el bracito, y ella me dijo, 'No lo agarres así que eso, esto, a lo mejor, tú agarrándolo así, tú le pudiste hacer eso, las ... los ... '
Translation:	That I shouldn't, that I shouldn't grab him up like that, because then I did grab him up by his little arm. It wasn't on purpose, but I picked him up by his little arm, and she said to me, 'Don't pick him up like that, since that, this, maybe you picking him up like that, you could do something to the, the ... '
Interpreter:	(Over suspect's words) Don't pick him up like that. So she yanked him by one arm. And she ... Okay ... This lady told her, saw her picking her up the baby up, and told her don't, don't pick the baby up like that. You're going to hurt the baby like that.

Lawyer–client interaction

The lawyer–client consultation meeting is likely to pose fewer problems for the interpreter. The context is not as formal as that of the police interview and certainly more relaxed than emergency situations, prisons or probation offices, with the goals of the parties common rather than divergent. Most problematic seem to be the usual pitfalls of legal–lay communication; as Gibbons (2003:172) notes, 'much lawyer–client interaction is spent negotiating ways round this lack of shared [legal] knowledge'. If this is the case, even more effort has to be expended where second-language speakers are involved, because of the need to explain legal concepts that do not necessarily exist in their culture.

Most second-language speakers are unable to pay for legal representation themselves and have to rely on state-provided solutions. This has obvious consequences for power issues in lawyer–client interactions. Additionally, because providing state-sponsored legal aid is not as well remunerated as representing individuals of independent means, solicitors working with second-language speakers may have limited financial resources, which in turn could have a negative impact on the quality of the interpreting. In England, there is no requirement for solicitors to use accredited interpreters and, as a result, law firms may choose cost, as a primary consideration when sourcing interpreters, even at the expense of quality,

When it comes to the interaction between lawyers and interpreters, a revealing study is that by Foley (2006), who investigated perceptions of duty and partiality among the two professions, and found that they 'have markedly different cultural notions as to who their client is (and whether duties are owed and to whom)' (Foley 2006: 99). While the lawyers spoke of 'a delicate balancing act' between their duties to the person they represent, to the court and to the profession, some of the interpreters rejected the notion of a 'client', and others said that even if they did have a client – be it the second-language speaker, the court, the police or the lawyer – they owed no duty to them in the sense that lawyers did. Ahmad (2007: 1002), a lawyer, sees the interpreter's presence as 'inject[ing] the subjectivity of a third person – her thoughts and feelings, attitudes and opinions, personality and perception – into what previously had been the exclusive province of the lawyer and client' and addresses his colleagues thus:

> Once we acknowledge the subjectivity that inheres in interpretation, we can move in one of two directions: either to squelch that subjectivity and attempt to force the interpreter back into the fictive box of technology; or to embrace the subjectivity, draw it out further, scrutinize it rigorously, and engage it dialogically. Most lawyers, and the legal system as a whole, attempt the former. I argue unambiguously for the latter.
>
> (Ahmad 2007: 1003)

Finally, the difficulties faced by defendants working with lawyers are exemplified by the English case of Iqbal Begum. After Mrs. Begum had been sentenced to life imprisonment for murdering her husband and served some five years in prison, her conviction was appealed, on the grounds that she had pleaded guilty without understanding with what she was charged. In point of fact, it turned out that there had been no effective communication between her and her legal representatives from the very beginning, since she did not understand the individual engaged to interpret at the pre-trial and trial stages. She had remained silent throughout the entire time that she was in custody, even in sessions with her legal representatives. In its ruling that the trial had been a nullity, since no proper plea had been made, the appellate court observed that

> unless a person fully comprehends the charge which that person faces, the full implications of it and the ways in which a defence may be raised to it, and further is able to give full instructions to solicitor and counsel so that the court can be sure that that person has pleaded with a free and understanding mind, a proper plea has not been tendered to the court.
>
> (*Iqbal Begum* (1991) 93 Cr.App.R. 96 at 100)

Probation offices

In many jurisdictions around the world, individuals convicted of a relatively minor crime may be placed under probation supervision and thereby avoid incarceration, provided that they complete a course of action intended as punishment and designed to prevent them from re-offending. This may involve community service work, completion of a drug rehabilitation programme, finding a job, or staying away from known criminals. Imposed by the court, such measures are enforced by probation officers, who meet their supervisees on a regular basis throughout the probation period. Particularly important is the first of such meetings, where the conditions of the court order are explained and provisions made for them to be adhered to. At this early stage, effective communication plays a particularly important role because, if the offender misunderstands the probation conditions and breaches the order, he or she may have to return to court and end up in prison after all. This is illustrated by the case of Alex Ramirez, a Mexican immigrant to the USA. On 13 April 2006 in the Superior Court of New Jersey, Ramirez, having pleaded guilty to violating probation, said in his defence that an important reason for the violation was his inability to communicate with his probation officer. It is sobering to read the judge's response to Ramirez:

> Now, so let me understand this. Not only do we have to let him come into the country illegally and stay here, not only do we have to provide him with public assistance, not only do we have to provide him with free health care, not only do we have to provide him with a free attorney when he gets in trouble, now he wants a bilingual probation officer, because otherwise it's inconvenient for him.
>
> (http://pdfserver.amlaw.com/nj/citta-complaint040109.pdf)

Probation supervision meetings are interesting from a linguistic point of view as they seem to occupy middle ground between legal and 'lay' language. The probation officer's primary aim is determined by legal requirements, but to achieve it certain communicative goals have to be pursued with only limited use of specialized discourse. The institutional is thus combined with the interpersonal, a situation with potentially adverse effects for the judicially unversed offender: what seems like a friendly chat can in fact have serious legal repercussions. All this means that the interpreter must be sensitive to even the slightest changes in register and respond accordingly, because, when used in a legal context, certain lexical items take on new meanings. In England, when a police officer uses the verb 'caution' at the beginning of an interview with a suspect ('I'm going to caution you now'), the most frequently encountered definition ('warn or advise') has little to do with the legal meaning of 'formally inform one of one's legal rights and consequences of one's decision to withhold information from the interviewing police officers'.

Another interesting aspect is the seemingly limitless semantic scope of the supervision interview. While interpreters can expect some legal terminology, the fairly unstructured nature of the interaction is conducive to the emergence of unexpected topics with their domain-specific vocabulary. Fairly frequent are for example medical terms, whose accurate rendition is essential if the probation officer is to make a fully informed decision about the offender's ability to perform certain actions. This can be illustrated with an example from a recent supervision meeting interpreted by one of the present authors. When the offender was asked a routine question about health issues preventing him from undertaking community work at a building site, he answered with the story, complete with specialized medical vocabulary, of a meniscus cartilage tear he had suffered several years before.

Another surprise afforded by probation supervision meetings may be the necessity to switch modes of interpreting. In many probation offices in the UK for example, prior to starting community service, offenders are asked to watch health-and-safety videos. Given the related temporal and technical constraints, simultaneous interpreting may then be the best option. Finally, sight translation, that is delivery of a spoken version of a written text, provided on the spot, is routinely used when the content of a form filled in by probation officers with input from supervisees needs to be relayed back to them.

Prisons

Interpreting in prison settings is arguably the most under-explored topic in the literature. There appear to be no systematic studies dealing with the nature and/or problems of interpreter-mediated communication in correctional institutions.[2] The considerations that follow are thus based on the experience of one of the authors working in the UK.

On the face of it, by this stage of the law enforcement chain, second-language speakers, already familiar with the role of the interpreter, should create few problems. Yet, prolonged isolation in a linguistically alien environment often means that inmates treat interpreter-mediated visits not only as a welcome change in the daily routine, but also as an opportunity to interact with someone of the same or similar cultural background (see also English, this volume). Viewed as an ally or confidant, the interpreter is then erroneously expected to take on roles outside of the professional remit (Morris 1999). An inmate may address him or her directly with questions regarding the latest news, or ask for a message to be passed on to someone outside. Linguistically the problems are similar to those characteristic of probation supervision meetings, with the notable difference that inmates with long sentences gradually learn the language of the jurisdiction, including prison argot, which they may use when code-switching. Not infrequently, they also attempt to ask or answer some of the questions themselves, still relying on the interpreter for more complex meanings and legal jargon.

A rarely mentioned aspect of prison interpreting is the influence of the culturally conditioned stigma of imprisonment. Inmates from some cultures when confronted with an interpreter, who they assume shares the same values, may try and exculpate themselves in front of the interpreter for fear of losing face. In such situations, the inmate's visitors are mere hearers and the interpreter becomes the addressee for the message, to use Hymes's (1977) terms. Needless to say, in such cases the presence of the interpreter affects not only the dynamics of the conversation, as is normally true of any interpreter-mediated exchange anyway, but also its content.

Finally, it needs to be said that extralinguistic factors play a significantly greater role in the prison setting than elsewhere. The negative impact of the physical environment, the discomfort of the entry procedure, and contact with potentially dangerous individuals can all contribute to the interpreters' increased stress levels (as can some aspects of the interaction itself) and, consequently, can affect the quality of the job.

Conclusions

There is nothing basically new about the issues of interpreting in non-court settings in the early twenty-first century. Technology can sometimes offer solutions which, although not necessarily perfect, nevertheless enable interpreters to assist in communication where otherwise nothing could have been done. However, the need for competent interpretation remains as vital as ever. Having an incompetent telephone interpreter mediate between prisoner and counsel is potentially worse than having no interpreter at all. In today's cash-strapped situation, the efficient use of resources is vital. Bowing to the pressure to outsource and award a contract for the provision of interpreters in the legal system to the cheapest bidder is often the opposite of a wise allocation of resources. Employing correctly trained civilian staff to source quality interpreters for police forces would be a time- and money-efficient use of resources. Interpreters should be viewed as a quality resource which must be sourced appropriately for the particular task to be dealt with, not as faceless voices to be bought in bulk through for-profit companies who treat interpreters as commodities to be exploited in order to maximize their revenues, not to serve the ends of justice. The equal access principle, which has increasingly come to underpin the modern criminal justice system, requires legal systems to expand their framework of reference beyond the narrow view, so that linguistic equality must also include such matters as pre-sentencing reports and correctional programmes. To expect interpreters to undertake costly training and then not be appropriately compensated is unrealistic.

The future, if not exactly bright, seems quite promising. In England and Wales for example, thanks in no small measure to the rapid growth of forensic linguistics and its more and more visible social presence, some police forces are beginning to recognize and respond to at least some of the problems discussed here, although the outsourcing phenomenon, with its negative ramifications, is a worrying trend in various jurisdictions. The perspective of the legal profession, however, is still one of impractical expectations, with the interpreter viewed as a passive, machine-like entity.[3] This kind of perception is not new. In 1979 in *United States v. AnguloaI*, the Court instructed the jury following the replacement of an incompetent interpreter that '[a]n Interpreter really only acts as a transmission belt or telephone'; a former Australian Supreme Court judge, in turn, stated that '[t]he interpreter should look upon himself rather as an electric transformer, whatever is fed into him is to be fed out again, duly transformed' (Wells 1991, in Hale and Gibbons 1999: 207). As a result, the tacit assumption in the legal system has been that the interpreter's version is always a faithful reflection of the original. Meanwhile, a more fitting metaphor of the interpreting process in legal and forensic contexts is possibly that of a shattered mirror: the contours, shapes and colours can still be discerned in the fragmented reflection but some fine, but potentially crucial, details may be missing because of the cracks. Some of the damage is inevitable: typological differences between languages and the presence of language-specific pragmatic assumptions mean that it may be simply impossible to reproduce some meanings successfully. There is then an unavoidable tension between the law needing absolutes and meaning being inexact. However, as demonstrated in this chapter, there are a number of extralinguistic factors that result from work-related pressures, disparate expectations, ignorance and inadequate professional practice, which, unlike the linguistic issues, could be addressed by institutional, or possibly even legislative, solutions for all stages of the judicial process, minimizing the distortion in the semantic mirror.

A more detailed account of the case *State of Ohio v. Alejandro Ramirex* can be found on the *Handbook*'s accompanying website available at: http://www.forensiclinguistics.net/

Notes

1 A 2009 position paper of the US-based National Association of Judiciary Interpreters and Translators discusses numerous issues to do with appropriate use of telephone interpreting in the legal system. See http://tinyurl.com/najit-paper.
2 But see Milton and de Sena França (2001), writing about the situation in Brazil.
3 This is the picture that emerges following the authors' own professional experience as well as discussions with members of the Aston Interpreter Network, a group of practising interpreters and academics meeting regularly at Aston University to exchange ideas and best practice.

Further reading

Berk-Seligson, S. (2000) 'Issues in pre-trial phases of the judicial process', *Forensic Linguistics: The International Journal of Speech, Language and the Law*, 7(1): 213–38.
Colin, J. and Morris, R. (1996) *Interpreters and the Legal Process*, Winchester: Waterside Press.

Cooke, M., Eades, D. and Hale, S. (eds) (1999) *Forensic Linguistics*, 6(1) (special issue devoted to interpreting in legal contexts).

Morris, R. (1995) 'The moral dilemmas of court interpreting', *The Translator*, 1(1): 25–46.

Cases cited

Beck v. Sager [1979] RTR 475.

Chief Constable of Avon and Somerset Constabulary v. Singh [1988] RTR 107.

Commonwealth v. Vose (1892) 157 Mass. 393, 32 N.E.355.

Iqbal Begum (1991) 93 Cr.App.R. 96.

R. v. Attard (1958) 43 Cr.App.R. 90.

State of Kansas v. Van Pham 675 P.2d 848 (Kan. 1984).

State of New Jersey v. Alex Ramirez 04-06-1127(2006).

State of Ohio v. Alejandro Ramirez 135 Ohio App. 3d 89; 732 N.E.2d 1065 (1999).

State of Florida v. Eulalia Miguel a/k/a/ Petrona Tomas Case No. 02–11821 CF A02.

State of New Jersey v. German Marquez, A-5044-07T4, July 1 2009.

State of Ohio v. Speer, 180 Ohio App.3d 230, 2008-Ohio-6947 (2008).

United States v. Anguloa 598 F2d 1182 No. 78–1183 (1979).

United States v. Santana 503 F.2d 710 (1974).

Ulibarri et al. v. City & County of Denver et al., Civil Action No. 07-CV-01814-WDM-MJW (D. Colo. 2007) (Second Amended Complaint filed February 4, 2008).

www.ccdconline.org/files/2008.02.04amendedcomplaint – final.pdf, accessed 13 July 2009.

Authorship and opinion

31

Experts and opinions

In my opinion

Malcolm Coulthard

Prof Meadow wrongly stated in Mrs Clark's trial in 1999 that there was just a 'one in 73 million' chance that two babies from an affluent family like hers could suffer cot death. The actual odds were only one in 77.

(*The Guardian*, 15 July 2005)

Introduction

The vast majority of witnesses who give evidence in court have some personal involvement in the case and are there to recount relevant facts and experiences. However, there is a second category of witness, the *expert witness*, who has no personal involvement and who is there to help the court by giving their opinion, based on professional expertise, about some aspect(s) of the forensic evidence – be it the time and manner of death, footprints, DNA traces, recorded conversations or text messages. Few experts are engaged full time with court work. They are professionals across a wide range of disciplines – archaeologists, doctors, dentists, engineers, research scientists and of course linguists and phoneticians. I know of only one forensic linguist and a very small number of forensic phoneticians who work full-time on casework. The majority of expert linguists are academics who do occasional casework and rarely go to court: most of them average fewer than ten cases a year and one court appearance every two years. For this reason, giving evidence in person in court can be a stressful experience. As Shuy observes: For those who have never experienced cross-examination, there is no way to emphasise how emotionally draining it can be. ... Testifying is not for the weak at heart' (Shuy 2002: 3–4).

Nor indeed for the weak at stomach – one of my former colleagues eventually gave up acting as an expert document analyst after some 25 years, because he could no longer cope with the vomiting which preceded most of his appearances in the witness box.

Giving evidence can also be profoundly frustrating for the academic expert. As Maley observes, in an excellent paper examining linguistic aspects of expert testimony,

473

expert witnesses, particularly if they are new and inexperienced, tend to be quite unaware of the extent to which shaping and construction of evidence goes on. … All too often they emerge frustrated from the courtroom, believing that they have not been able to give their evidence in the way they would like and that their evidence has been twisted and/or disbelieved.

(Maley 2000: 250)

And this despite the fact that experts are generally allowed speaking turns that are, on average, some three times longer than those of ordinary witnesses (Heffer 2005).

In the past twenty years, there has been a rapid growth in the frequency with which courts in a number of countries have called upon the expertise of linguists. The cases range from determining whether a Greek doctor said 'can' or 'can't' (Baldwin and French 1990), through disputes about the meaning and ownership of individual morphemes in a trademark case (Shuy 2002), the degree of similarity in pronunciation and therefore the confusability of two trademarks (Gibbons 2003) and the opacity of individual words in jury instructions (Levi 1993), to the 'ownership' of particular words and phrases in a plagiarism case (Turell 2004) and accusations of the fabrication of whole texts in two murder cases (Coulthard 2002). Many more examples of expert linguistic evidence can be found in Section 2 of this *Handbook*, particularly the chapters by Butters, Dumas, Eades, English and Jessen and also in Coulthard and Johnson (2007), particularly chapter 6.

Usually the linguist uses standard analytic tools to reach an opinion, although very few cases require exactly the same selection from the linguist's toolkit. However, occasionally, cases raise new and exciting questions for descriptive linguistics, which require basic research, such as how can one measure the 'rarity' and therefore the evidential value, of short sequences of words (see Coulthard 2004), or of shared *hapaxes*, that is words which only occur once (Woolls and Coulthard 1998) or the reliability of verbal memory (Coulthard and Johnson 2007, 132–35) or how can one calculate the probability of two different authors having produced a set of disputed texts messages (Grant this volume).

Once the analysis has been done and an opinion reached, the expert is faced with two communicative problems: firstly, how can s/he best explain the analysis and express the derived opinions in a report written for an audience of legal professionals; and, secondly, if later called on to give oral evidence in court, how can s/he cope with the unusual interactional rules?

All experts face these challenges, but expert linguists have two additional and unique problems: lawyers and judges are also professionally and centrally concerned with detailed analysis of language and thus regard themselves as experts too, and also all native speakers are in some sense experts on the structure and meaning of their own language. So, for instance, it is very difficult to call a linguist to give evidence on word meaning, because courts are mainly interested in two kinds: *technical* and *commonsense meaning*. Technical meaning is specialised legal meaning, which can be significantly different from denotative meaning in non-legal settings. Thus, the British *Road Traffic Act* (1972 c.20 ss.82) requires the use of specified lights on vehicles during the 'hours of darkness'. The meaning of the phrase 'hours of darkness' is not negotiable, that is, it is not something that someone accused of an offence can try to define to his advantage by using a dictionary or even a corpus, with or without the help of a linguist. The Act itself gives the definition '"hours of darkness" means the time half-an-hour after sunset and half-an-hour before sunrise'. Whether the accused considered it to be dark or not at the time of the offence is irrelevant. Then there is *commonsense* meaning, which is what a jury, being representatives of the common man, collectively think a word means – so much so that juries have traditionally been denied dictionaries inside the jury room. Again no need for a linguistics expert.

Solan (1998) argues that even so, there is a role for the linguist, which is to explain and elucidate facts about language and usage as a result of which judge and jury will then be in the same position as the linguist and so can make linguistically informed decisions. In Solan's words:

> my linguistic training has made me more sensitive to possible interpretations that others might not notice and I can bring these to the attention of a judge or jury. But once I point these out and illustrate them clearly, we should start on an equal footing.
>
> (Solan 1998: 92)

Thus, for instance, linguists have been allowed to give evidence about textual ambiguity, for example Kaplan *et al.* (1995) and Prince (1981). To rephrase Solan's observation, linguists are experts not only in the nature of interpretation, but also in the nature of linguistic encoding. One British example of an expert sensitising the lay audience comes from my own evidence in the Appeal of Robert Brown. Brown claimed that a monologue confession attributed to him had in fact been elicited by question and answer and then transformed by the interviewing officers into monologue form. As one part of my evidence in support of Brown's claim, I focused on the two clauses:

> 'I was covered in blood, my jeans and a blue Parka coat and a shirt were full of blood'.

To a linguist it is clear that the phrasing of the subject of the second clause, 'my jeans and a blue Parka coat and a shirt' is most unnatural; no one would refer to an item of their own clothing with the indefinite article 'a' once they had begun a list with the possessive determiner, 'my'. The most likely use of 'a' in this context would be to distinguish between 'mine' and 'not-mine'. For example, the utterance "I looked round the room and I saw my jeans and a blue Parka coat and a shirt, they were full of blood", would be perfectly natural in a context where some of the clothes belonged to someone else, but this, of course, was not the meaning intended in this narrative, where all the clothes belonged to the narrator. The phrase "a blue Parka coat and a shirt" could occur, again quite naturally, as a result of the careless conversion of a sequence of short questions and answers into monologue form. One could see how this might indeed have happened in this case by looking at the following actual sequence taken from the record of a preceding police interview with Brown:

> What were you wearing?
> I had **a** blue shirt and **a** blue parka.

In this context the use of the indefinite article is normal – as noted above, when items are introduced for the first time, the indefinite article is the natural choice. Once the oddity of the phrase and the occurrence of a similar phrase in the interview had been pointed out to the Appeal Court judges, they were as competent as any linguist to draw inferences from the linguistic oddity.

Another of Solan's points is that, although juries and judges may well be able to analyse individual words, phrases and even sentences as well as any professional linguist, they may have problems analysing longer documents:

> Of course a jury can read the document[s]. … But not all jurors, without help, can focus on a phrase in paragraph 24 of a contract that may have an impact on how another word should be interpreted in paragraph 55.
>
> (Solan 1998: 94)

In the Brown Appeal it was important to draw the attention of the judges to two pairs of phrases occurring in two different documents, one a record of a dictated statement, the other a record of an interview:

i) Statement: I asked her if I could carry her bags she said "Yes".
    Interview: I asked her if I could carry her bags and she said "yes".

ii) Statement: I picked something up like an ornament.
    Interview: I picked something up like an ornament.

Linguists of most persuasions are in agreement that the likelihood of two speakers independently producing exactly the same phrasing reduces dramatically with the length of the expression, as does the likelihood of one speaker choosing two identical phrasings on different occasions. However, this linguist's 'knowledge' does not coincide with lay belief – there is a common mis-conception, for instance, that people can remember word-for-word stretches of conversations and report them verbatim later. When faced with the problem of convincing the Appeal Court judges of the evidential significance of the identical expressions occurring in supposedly independent verbatim records of separate interactions, I chose the following procedure.

Firstly, by looking at the occurrences of the words 'I asked her if I could carry her bags' in a series of Google searches of some 6 billion documents, I demonstrated that even short sequences of words can be unique encodings. The results at the time were as follows:

Table 31.1 Word sequence length and frequency

Sequence	No. of Occurrences
I asked	2,170,000
I asked her	284,000
I asked her if	86,000
I asked her if I	10,400
I asked her if I could	7,770
I asked her if I could carry	7
I asked her if I could carry her	4
I asked her if I could carry her bags	0

Using these examples, I argued that, if there was not a single instance of anyone having ever produced this nine-word sequence, the chances of even longer sequences occurring twice in different documents was infinitesimal, unless, of course, one sequence was derived or copied from the other. When writing this chapter, I re-checked the Google figures above for 'I asked her if I could carry her bags', I found, to my horror, six instances of the phrase. However, as the adage goes, 'it is the exception that proves the rule'. There is now a website devoted to Robert Brown's case, which carries the disputed statement (www.eamonnoneill.net/c&p.htm [accessed 28 August 2009]), so one of the instances is the original saying; three of the others are web-versions of Coulthard (2004), an article which I wrote about the case; one is from Coulthard and Johnson (2007) where I also mention the case; and the final instance is in a Dutch university PowerPoint presentation which quotes the example from my article. In other words, all six instances are quotings of the same single saying.

On becoming a linguistic expert

For linguists wanting to move into expert witness work the criteria vary from country to country. Up to now, Australia and Britain have shared essentially the same position, which is that it is the expert rather than the method that is recognised and so courts can allow opinion evidence from anyone considered to have 'specialised knowledge based on ... training, study or experience [provided that the opinion is] wholly or substantially based on that knowledge' (Australian Evidence Act 1995 Sec 79).

Usually, once an expert has been accepted by one court, s/he will be accepted by other courts at the same level and rarely challenged. The expert is retained and paid by one side, but, even so, is legally appointed by the court. Indeed, since 2007, experts in Britain have been required to state explicitly in their written reports that they are aware of their duty to the court and of the necessity to make the court aware of any counter-evidence in the data they have analysed (see also Solan in this volume).

So far, there have been no explicit requirements, as there are in the USA following the Daubert ruling (see below), about the nature of the expert's theoretical position nor about the particular methodology and evidence on which the expert bases his/her opinion. So, once an expert has been retained, it is up to the court to determine, *'ad hoc*, the sufficiency of [his/her] expertise and the relevance of that expertise' (Bromby 2002: 9). As part of this process both the competence of the expert and the reliability of the method(s) s/he has used can be subjected to detailed examination in court and this can last for many hours, as I know from recent experience. In the most recent case in which I was called to give evidence, the judge sent the jury home before lunch and took the whole afternoon to hear legal argument about the admissibility of my evidence and then had me examined and cross-examined for over an hour, before he eventually decided to allow me to give my evidence in open court the following day. For details of the case, see *Northern Echo*, 21 Feb 2008, available at: www.thenorthernecho.co.uk/news/indepth/jennynicholl/2061834.Snared_by_texts_meant_to_throw_police_off_scent/ (accessed 21 August 2009). Following the conviction of the accused, the defence lodged an appeal, solely on the grounds of the admissibility of the linguistic evidence, but the appeal was not allowed.

Even after an expert has been allowed to give evidence, the judge(s) and/or the jury may decide that the evidence was not helpful, persuasive or even relevant and choose to ignore it. Indeed, occasionally, at the end of a trial, experts are censured by the court – 'in our judgment, although Professor Canter is clearly an expert in his field, the evidence tendered from him was not expert evidence of a kind properly to be placed before the court', (*Gilfoyle (No 2)* [2001] 2 Cr App R 5 (57), para 25). At other times, particular methodologies, like CUSUM (Hardcastle 1997), have been deemed to be unacceptable, while Professor Meadow, whose statistical error is referred to in the quotation at the head of the chapter, was subsequently disciplined by his professional body and struck off the medical register.

As I write, the situation in Britain is changing rapidly and radically. In 2008, the British Government appointed a former Police Detective Chief Superintendent as the first Forensic Science Regulator. His brief is to 'operate independently to ensure that quality standards apply across all forensic science services' (http://police.homeoffice.gov.uk/operational-policing/forensic-science-regulator/about-the-regulator/ [accessed 1 August 2000]). In 2009, the Regulator published a consultation paper on forensic practitioner registration, which recommended that an accreditation system be set up based on internationally recognised ISO standards and assessed by the UK Accreditation Service (UKAS).

At the same time the UK Law Commission also published a consultation paper on the admissibility of expert evidence in which they observed 'We believe the current approach to the admissibility of expert evidence in criminal trials is in need of reform' (Law Commission 2009: iii). In their opinion

> The criminal courts have … adopted a policy of *laissez-faire*. In effect [they] permit the adduction of any expert evidence, so long as it is not patently unreliable, [as a consequence] juries are not denied access to evidence which might be helpful.
> (Law Commission 2009: 22)

They attributed this problem, at least in part, to a basic flaw in the system: 'there is little if any guidance for trial judges … faced with the task of having to screen expert evidence to determine the question of admissibility' (Law Commission 2009: 16). The solution the Law Commission went on to propose was the creation of a new statutory test for determining the admissibility of expert evidence in criminal proceedings, which is likely to be modelled on the system currently in force in the United States, embodied in Rule 702 of the Federal Rules of Evidence, referred to informally as the Daubert test. British forensic linguists await the outcome with great interest and in some quarters some trepidation, after reading Tiersma and Solan (2002). If a Daubert-type system is introduced, some currently accepted methodologies may be disallowed and others may need to be modified to meet the Daubert criteria (though see McMenamin, this volume, for some pragmatic discussion).

The American legal system, unlike the current Anglo-Australian, approves the technique(s) that a witness uses rather than the witness him/herself. Rule 702 allows any expert to testify as a witness if and only if:

> the testimony is based upon sufficient facts or data, [and]
> the testimony is the product of reliable principles and methods, and
> the witness has applied the principles and methods reliably to the facts of the case.

Rule 702 is designed to take account of the 1993 Supreme Court ruling in the appeal case *Daubert v. Merrell Dow Pharmaceuticals*, which dramatically changed the nature of admissible evidence. The main argument in the appeal was whether expert evidence could be rejected on the grounds that the expert(s) involved had not published their work. In their ruling the Supreme Court observed that 'the adjective "scientific" implies a grounding in the methods and procedures of science' and then went on to propose four criteria with which to evaluate 'scientific'-ness:

1. whether the theory ... has been tested;
2. whether it has been subjected to peer review and publication;
3. the known rate of error; and
4. whether the theory is generally accepted in the scientific community.

(509 U.S. at 593 as quoted in Tiersma and Solan 2002: 224)

This ruling left open the question of whether it covered evidence which was descriptive rather than theoretical, but a ruling in 1999, in the case of *Kumho Tire Co. v. Carmichael*, confirmed that it did: 'the general principles of Daubert apply not only to experts offering scientific evidence, but also to experts basing their testimony on experience' (119 S.Ct. 1173 as quoted in Tiersma and Solan, 2002: 224).

So, where does that leave the American forensic linguist and, at some point in the future, the British forensic linguist? On the positive side, Tiersma and Solan note that, 'courts have allowed linguists to testify on issues such as the probable origin of a speaker, the comprehensibility of a text, whether a particular defendant understood the Miranda warning, and the phonetic similarity of two competing trademarks' (Tiersma and Solan 2002: 221).

However, in other areas the situation is more problematic, partly, perhaps, because non-linguists have claimed ownership of the labels for linguistic concepts. The Van Wyk case in 2000 seemed to set a precedent for excluding *stylistic analysis*, as the court refused to allow the expert to give evidence about the authorship of disputed documents; however, as McMenamin (2002) points out, the expert in the case had at the time no qualifications in linguistics. McMenamin (2004 and this volume) argues a strong case for the scientific nature of his own brand of forensic stylistics and therefore for its acceptability under Daubert. Indeed, he shows how to express opinions statistically in terms of mathematically calculated probabilities, in a case study of the significant documents in the JonBenét Ramsey case (McMenamin 2004: 193–205).

Even so, it must be conceded that, in cases where conclusions depend on observations about the frequency or rarity of particular linguistic features in the texts under examination, many linguists would have considerable difficulty in stating a 'known rate of error' for their results, even if this phrase is interpreted as a likelihood ratio. It is for this reason that some British linguists will be forced to change their way of reaching and presenting their opinions (see French and Harrison 2007). Other forensic linguists, who previously would have given an opinion, may choose to restrict their role to that of educator/teacher/'tour guide' (Solan 1998). For instance, they might provide the jury with linguistic facts like those in Table 31.2, which the jury could not possibly have

Table 31.2 Comparison of suspect and candidate author choices

Intended	Suspect	Candidate Author
Item	*Choices*	*Choices/occurrences*
be	be	b (7)
come	come	com (14)
I will +verb	I will	ill (10)
they	they	dey (3)
Yes (as one-word response)	Yes	Ya (14)

assembled for themselves. A set of suspect text messages which had been sent from a known phone at around the time its owner was murdered did not use abbreviations for the five items in the table, but an analysis of some 300 text messages sent by the phone's owner over the previous three days showed that she abbreviated all of them consistently – there were 48 occasions when one of the five items was texted in abbreviated from and no counter-examples of full forms being used. With this information and some tutorial input from the expert about linguistic behaviour being rule-governed, the jury could reach an informed conclusion.

Expressing expert opinions

The majority of forensic linguists and phoneticians have traditionally felt that they were unable to express their findings statistically in terms of mathematically calculated probabilities and so have expressed them as a semantically encoded opinion. Indeed, some experts simply expressed their opinion without giving any indication to the court of how to evaluate its strength, or of how their opinion fitted with the two legally significant categories of 'on the balance of probabilities' and 'beyond reasonable doubt'. However, a growing number of experts now use a fixed semantic scale and attach that scale as an Appendix to their report to enable the reader to assess their degree of confidence in their opinion.

Until fairly recently I used the eleven-point scale of opinions detailed below, which I had adapted from a scale used by many members of the International Association of Forensic Phonetics:

> **Most positive**
> 5 'I personally feel *quite satisfied* that X is the author'.
> 4 'It is in my view *very likely* that X is the author'.
> 3 'It is in my view *likely* that X is the author'.
> 2 'It is in my view *fairly likely* that X is the author'.
> 1 'It is in my view *rather more likely than not* that X is the author'.
> 0 'It is not possible to express an opinion'.
> -1 'It is in my view *rather more likely than not* that X is *not* the author'.
> -2 'It is in my view *fairly likely* that X is *not* the author'.
> -3 'It is in my view *likely* that X is *not* the author'.
> -4 'It is in my view *very likely* that X is *not* the author'.
> -5 'I personally feel *quite satisfied* that X is the *not* author'.
> **Most negative**

If I had set out to use this particular scale to express an opinion in the text messaging case outlined above, I would have given my opinion as point -3, i.e. that it was *likely* that the phone owner had *not* written the particular text messages, but I would have agonised long and hard over whether *likely* or *very likely* was a better semantic label to convey my assessment of the strength of the evidence on which I was basing my opinion. Broeders suggested that what is happening in such cases is that:

> experts, in using degrees of probability, are actually making categorical judgements,
> i.e. are really saying yes or no. Even if they use a term like *probably (not)*, I think

they are subjectively convinced that the suspect did or did not produce the sample material.

(Broeders 1999: 237)

That observation would certainly be true for me; in other words I am subjectively convinced that the phone owner did not send the messages, but at the same time I feel the evidence is not strong enough to allow an opinion of 'I personally feel *quite satisfied* that'. Broeders went on to observe that the choice of a given degree of likelihood on a scale like this is irremediably subjective and experience-based, which is why two experts might reach opinions of differing strengths based on exactly the same data. Even so, he stressed that a subjective judgement should not be condemned simply because it is subjective: 'The crucial question is not whether [it] is subjective or objective, but whether it can be relied on to be correct' (Broeders 1999: 238).

Nevertheless, a growing body of opinion is opposed to the use of semantic scales, especially because, even when they *are* accepted by a court, an unsolvable problem remains – how can one be sure that judges and juries will attach the same meanings to the labels as did the experts who chose and applied them? This point was brought home to me at a court martial where I expressed my opinion as 'very likely' using the above 11-point scale while another expert expressed her opinion as 'very strong support' using a different 9-point scale. Neither of us was allowed to tell the jury how many points there were on our respective scales, let alone show the full scale. We could not even gloss the particular category we had chosen, even though at the same time the defence lawyer did his best to persuade the other expert to lower her opinion from 'very strong' to 'strong'.

An added semantic complication is that, at the end of a trial, the triers of fact themselves are not allowed the luxury of degrees of confidence; they have to work with a binary choice of Guilty or Not Guilty. So, however hedged an expert's opinion is when s/he presents it, the judge(s) and jury have ultimately to make a categorical judgement. (See also Gray, this volume on a judge's viewpoint.)

There is an even more serious problem. Broeders (1999) and later Rose (2002), writing about the reaching and encoding of opinions, noted that an expert can offer an opinion on two things: either on the probability of a *Hypothesis* – so in linguistic cases, for example, on the hypothesis that the accused is the speaker/author – given the strength of the *Evidence* which s/he has analysed, which is what I did above. Or, the expert can offer an opinion on the probability that the *Evidence* would occur in the form and quantity in which it does occur, given the **two** *Hypotheses* that the accused **is** and also, crucially, **is not** the speaker/author.

Both authors recommend the second approach. Indeed Rose quotes Aitken (1995: 4) in arguing that the former type of opinion, which, he says, is tantamount to the expert deciding on the likelihood of the accused being guilty, is actually the exclusive role of the judges of fact and for this reason all responsible scientists must confine themselves to talking only about the likelihood of the evidence. Rose supports his argument by pointing out that no expert can make an estimate of the likelihood of guilt or innocence on the basis of the linguistic evidence alone; only those with access to all of the available evidence can assess the value of each piece of it. And even then, there may be another piece of evidence that is missing which would have shown it could not have been the accused and then a miscarriage of justice may occur.

So, for example, a forensic handwriting colleague of mine once concluded, after exhaustive comparisons, that it was *very likely* on the basis of the evidence he had analysed, that a disputed signature on an Irish will, which had been written with a ballpoint pen, was genuine. But then, fortunately before committing his opinion to paper, he realised that the will was dated before the invention of ballpoint technology! Similarly, Hollien (2002) reports a case where he was fully convinced, after a detailed comparison of the phonetic evidence, that a voice tape-recorded making a threatening phone call was that of the accused. The similarities between the samples were so marked that he felt able to discount one dissimilarity, that is until the twin brother of the accused appeared in the witness box and Hollien realised that the threatening voice was actually the brother's.

Broeders and Rose both go on to argue that not only does the approach which focuses on the probability of the evidence have logic on its side, it also has the added advantage that it enables probability to be expressed mathematically rather than semantically. Essentially the method involves calculating the *likelihood* that for instance a text message would be in a particular form if an accused had and crucially also had not sent it. For example, imagine a text message which includes the abbreviation 'ill' for 'I will'. We discover after analysing a sample of attested texts sent by the accused over the previous three days that in 100% of the possible messages where 'I will' could have occurred the accused had used 'ill'. In other words, if the accused had written the text and followed her normal practice she would almost certainly have chosen to use 'ill'. (Whatever previous statistics tell us a language user always has the freedom to make a different choice – sometimes deliberately for the forensically important purpose of disguise.) Imagine that at the same time we also discover that in a representative sample of text messages produced by the general population the abbreviation 'ill' also occurs, although only 10% of the time. So, if this particular text had not in fact been sent by the accused there is still a 10% chance that it would include the *ill* abbreviation. So, how do we assess the evidential strength of this finding? Simply by dividing one percentage likelihood by the other, i.e. 100/10 to get a *ratio* of *likelihoods* of 10.

Interpretation of a likelihood ratio, however, is not quite so simple for the jury. It is certainly true that, as Broeders (1999: 230) expresses it, 'to the extent that the likelihood ratio exceeds 1 the evidence lends greater support to the [prosecution] hypothesis, [while] if it is smaller than 1 it supports the alternative hypothesis'. So in this case, it is 10 times more likely that the item 'I will' would occur as 'ill' if it was produced by the accused than if it were produced by a member of the general population. But how does a likelihood ratio of 10 or 100 or even 1000 help the jury as they work towards a verdict encoded semantically? We will return to this question later.

Coulthard (2004) and Grant (this volume) suggest that language users can be distinguished one from another in terms of characteristic but differing preferred linguistic selections and co-selections. In other words, candidate author A may not simply use the abbreviation 'ill' on all occasions, but may use 'com' for 'come' and 'b' for 'be' exclusively as well and is thus distinguishable from candidate author B who uses 'I will', and 'come' exclusively and 'be' and 'b' apparently interchangeably. A major advantage of the method of expressing the weight of evidence statistically by means of likelihood ratios is that it allows the expert to take account of co-selections by combining several independent ratios together to produce a composite likelihood ratio. Independent likelihood ratios can be combined to make this composite ratio by simple multiplication and thus all extra ratios which are greater than 1.0 will increase the overall likelihood ratio, while any ratio of less than 1.0 will reduce it.

So, let us continue our invented example by focusing on the single text message 'ill com. b ther n n owa' (I'll come. Be there in an hour). We may find that 'com' and 'b' are quite common abbreviations in the general population and thus produce low likelihood ratios of 2.0 and 3.5, but when these are combined with the likelihood ratio of 10 already calculated for *ill*, they produce, by multiplication, the much higher ratio of 70. So, now after including all three features, we can say that this text message is 70 times more likely to include these three abbreviations if the accused had sent it than if a member of the general population had.

However, let us not forget Hollien's dissimilar feature, which he chose to ignore. One strong argument in favour of the likelihood ratio approach is that it also allows the easy incorporation of counter indications. Experts using the 'evidence-to-evaluate-the-hypothesis' approach, have to decide *ad hoc* what weight to give to any evidence which does not support the indication of the majority of the features analysed – should they, for example, allow such evidence to reduce their opinion by one or two degrees of certainty or perhaps by none at all. By contrast, with a likelihood ratio approach, any measurement which shows that it is less likely that the accused wrote the text than that a member of the general population did, will simply reduce the cumulative ratio.

So let us now also consider the features 'ther', 'n', 'n', 'owa' each of which, we now discover, the accused does not abbreviate, although some of the general population do. So we now have to add in four negative likelihood ratios of 0.75, 0.80, 0.95 and 0.66, respectively. The overall likelihood ratio will now be reduced to 26.33. In other words, a consideration of all the linguistic evidence in this single text message shows that it is some 26 times more likely that the message would be in this form if the accused had sent it than if she had not.

While such a mathematical approach has obvious attractions, it does present very real problems for both phoneticians and linguists. Firstly, how does one establish what is a relevant population of speakers or of language samples for comparison purposes and how does one access and then analyse the data from that population, particularly in a world where lawyers and courts are not willing to pay for what might be thought to be basic research.[1] At least in the area of forensic phonetics, there are already agreed reference tables for a small number of features like pitch of voice and stammering and solid evidence about the effects of telephone transmission on the pitch of the first formants of vowels (Künzel 2001). In the area of linguistics, however, there is much less reference data, although specialist corpora are now beginning to be created: McMenamin (2002: 154), for instance, ahead of his time, reported using a corpus of 742 envelope addresses for comparison purposes. More recently, specialist text message corpora have been created, (see for instance Grant this volume and Tagg 2009), but these corpora are still quite small at around 10,000 messages. Of course, for some purposes, (see Coulthard 1994a) evidence can be drawn from general corpora like the *Australian National Corpus*, the *British National Corpus*, the Collins *Bank of English* and the *American National Corpus*. Even search engines like Google and Yahoo, with access to literally billions of texts can, if used properly, provide useful information about usage. Nevertheless, for much of the work they have traditionally undertaken, forensic linguists do not have access to population statistics.

And then, even if we were able to calculate likelihood ratios, we would still need to know how to evaluate their significance. As we have said there is the added worry about whether a lay jury can actually cope with likelihood ratios, or whether they simply introduce even more confusion – to date there is no research into whether individual jury members can cope with large likelihood or probability numbers. But although the expert may well have accurate figures in his report, the jury do not see the report and most lawyers are not happy with probabilities and, at the end of the day, the jury has to reach a semantically encoded decision.

Rose (2002: 62) notes, although he does not recommend it, that some experts have attempted to solve the interpretation problem by collapsing likelihood ratios into five semantically labelled groupings:

Table 31.3 Suggested semantic labels for likelihood ratios

Likelihood ratio	Semantic gloss
10,000+	Very strong
1,000–100,000	Strong
100–1,000	Moderately strong
10–100	Moderate
1–10	Limited

But criminal courts work with the concept of 'beyond reasonable doubt' which does not have a defined likelihood ratio, although a lay juror, along with statistician A. P. Dawid (2001: 4), might be happy to equate the phrase with 'one chance in a hundred'. However, in the absence of agreed semantic labels, some experts may 'translate' their figures into everyday situations for the jury, so Professor Meadow on one occasion characterised the rareness of an event by comparing it to the chances of backing long odds winners in a major horse race year after year. On the other hand, one area of forensic investigation, DNA analysis, presents its evidence using highly persuasive enormous numbers which most lay people have difficulty dealing with: 'His counsel, Rebecca Poulet QC, reminded him of DNA evidence which showed his profile matched that of the attacker, with the chances of it being anyone else being one in a billion' (http://news.bbc.co.uk/1/hi/england/3496207.stm [accessed 1 August 2009]).

Conclusion

So what can and should the linguistics community do? In 2007 a group of UK forensic phoneticians, produced a position statement on expressing opinions (French and Harrison 2007), in which they noted that while in principle they accepted

> the desirability of considering the task of speaker comparison in a likelihood ratio (including Bayesian) conceptual framework ... the lack of demographic data, along with the problems of defining relevant reference populations [were] grounds for precluding the quantitative application of this type of approach in the present context.
>
> (French and Harrison 2007:142)

For this reason they set the goal as that of assessing whether a particular questioned voice fitted the description of the suspect voice. Such an assessment is a two-stage process. First, the analyst assesses the voice in terms of the compatibility of its features with those of the suspect voice. At this stage there are three possible outcomes, a negative decision that the two voices are 'not compatible', in which case the voice is excluded from further consideration, or 'insufficient evidence to proceed', or 'compatible'. A compatible decision essentially means that it is impossible to exclude the voice as a potential match. There now follows a second stage, in which the degree of compatibility is assessed in terms of the distinctiveness of the shared items. This is measured on a five-point scale ranging from 'not distinctive' to 'exceptionally distinctive'. As Rose and Morrison observe 'it is implied that the likelihood that the samples have been produced by [the] same speaker will be greater if their shared cluster of features is distinctive or unusual' (Rose and Morrison 2009: 142).

So we have a situation where many UK phoneticians and linguists are aspiring to use likelihood ratios but are actually using a method which does not provide the statistical evaluation which Daubert sees as essential for a scientific approach. There are three ways forward for the linguistic community. Firstly, as it is already acknowledged that some experts are more experienced and more skilful than others, it would be possible to introduce a system of blind testing of individual experts and publish known error rates for experts rather than for methods. Secondly, the creation of more and larger databases will enable linguists to derive more reliable population statistics and be able, in some areas at least, to start to produce likelihood ratios. Thirdly, more research into other statistical methods for evaluating the significance of candidate author data, of the kind reported by Grant (this volume), will provide a securer foundation for opinions.

The Law Commission's consultation document referred to above proposed dividing expert evidence into two types: *scientific* and *experience-based*. One of the proposed criteria for determining whether scientific evidence is sufficiently reliable to be admitted, is the production of 'margin of error data' (Law Commission 2009: 53). The category of *experience-based* evidence seems to allow for the continuing recognition of individual successful experts, using, among several criteria:

i) the expert's qualifications, practical experience, training and publications and his or her standing in the professional or other expert community; and
ii) whether the expert's methodology or reasoning has previously resulted in a demonstrably valid or erroneous opinion.

(Law Commission 2009: 56–57)

The UK forensic phonetics community responded collectively to the consultation document and one of their observations was on the proposed expert dichotomy:

We consider there to be a continuum between experience based evidence and narrowly scientific evidence. … For example, in our own field certain methods for analysing speech samples derive from the physics of sound and are clearly very much at the narrowly scientific end of the continuum. However, the conclusion one arrives at does not arise algorithmically or automatically from applying these methods. Rather, it relies on experience and bringing to bear knowledge of the likely effects of factors such as the speaking situation (in terms physical and social parameters), the range of variation encountered in a particular dialect, the speaking style used, the state of the speaker and the recording characteristics (e.g. direct conversation or telephone). In view of this, it must be recognised that evidence arising from the analysis of speech samples will, inevitably, involve both narrow scientific and experience-based elements.

(undated IAFPA response to Consultation document: 1)

The interesting question now is how the final recommendations of the Law Commission will influence British forensic linguists and phoneticians. Provided it is accepted that some of their work is high quality experience-based evidence the major positive change will be the introduction of rigorous assessment for experts. If, however, linguists and phoneticians are grouped with those who provide purely scientific expertise the consequences could be very serious indeed.

Note

1 Morrison, in a letter in which he also corrects some inaccuracies in my characterisation of the likelihood ratio analysis in Coulthard and Johnson (2007), observes: "I do not share [Coulthard's] pessimism about the potential for obtaining funds for the collection of databases for forensic application, in fact I believe that given the current concerns about crime and terrorism in many parts of the world this is a research activity for which it should be relatively easy to obtain funding from national governments and law-enforcement agencies. For example, the Australian Research Council (ARC) has specifically identified safeguarding Australia from terrorism, crime, and other threats as a priority area for research funding (my colleagues and I are currently preparing a major grant application in which we are seeking funding from the ARC and Australian law-enforcement agencies for forensic-voice-comparison research including the compilation of a database of 1000+ Australian English voices). Over the last quarter of a century, a great deal of time and money has been expended worldwide on collecting DNA databases for forensic use, and presentation of evidence from DNA comparison is now a ubiquitous component of criminal trials. ... Similar support must be given to all credible forensic science disciplines if they are to achieve the degrees of reliability needed to serve the goals of justice ... Over the last decade, the Guardia Civil in Spain has spent hundreds of thousands of Euros on forensic-voice-comparison research, including the collection of large databases of Spanish voices, making presentation of likelihood-ratio forensic-voice-comparison evidence commonplace in Spanish courts (in 2008 the Guardia Civil submitted 98 forensic-voice-comparison reports to the courts)" (Morrison 2009: 8).

Further reading

Aitken, C. (1995) *Statistics and the Evaluation of Evidence for Forensic Scientists*, Chichester: John Wiley.

French, P and Harrison, P (2007) 'Position statement concerning use of impressionistic likelihood terms in forensic speaker comparison cases', *International Journal of Speech, Language and the Law*, 14(1): 137–44.

Redmayne, M. (2001) *Expert Evidence and Criminal Justice*, Oxford: OUP.

Rose, P. and Morrison, G.S. (2009) 'A response to the UK Position statement on forensic speaker comparison', *International Journal of Speech, Language and the Law*, 16(1): 139–163.

Tiersma, P. and Solan, L. (2002) 'The linguist on the witness stand: forensic linguistics in American courts', *Language*, 78: 221–39.

32

Forensic stylistics

Theory and practice of forensic stylistics

Gerald R. McMenamin

Introduction

The purpose of this chapter is to outline the theory and practice of forensic stylistics as a technique that utilizes the linguistic analysis of writing style for the purpose of authorship identification. For a longer, more detailed treatment of the same subject matter, I refer the reader to McMenamin (2002). As in most of my previous work on forensic stylistics, I write for readers of varying backgrounds, so linguists may simply want to skip over sections whose purpose they recognize to be foundational.

Language and linguistic stylistics

Language is the internal system human speakers and writers develop and use to communicate. A *dialect* is a variety of language that appears when a particular group of speakers develops consistent patterns of language use, called "class characteristics" in forensic science. An *idiolect* (Bloch 1948: 7) is a variety of language developed by the individual speaker as a uniquely patterned aggregate of linguistic characteristics observed in his or her language use, often called "individual characteristics" in forensic science.

Linguistics is the study of the nature and development of the internal system of language as well as of the ways language is used in all its communicative contexts. One area of linguistics that is necessary for the understanding of stylistic analysis is the study of *linguistic variation*. William Labov was the first of many researchers who have succeeded in many ways throughout the last half century in identifying the forces that lead to linguistic diversity and relating them to the basic system of language as it is affected by non-linguistic events or forces (Labov 2002).

With respect to group diversity, the individual creates his systems of verbal behavior to resemble those of the groups he identifies with, what Labov (2002: 19) refers to as "the general tendency towards accommodation and the pressure of community norms." One can then examine factors that may cause group (and I would add, individual) divergence from the norm, that is, change away from the community norm. Labov (2002: 19) indicates that language diversity can be the result of the need for distinctiveness, breaks in communication networks, and the individual's process of language acquisition and learning.

Style is seen as that part of human behavior that reflects individual variation in activities that are otherwise invariant. Fashion is a good example of style because, while most elements of dress are common to a group, structured as they are by social convention (e.g. "What not to wear!"), individual variation is tolerated, accepted, and even encouraged. In much the same way, the elements of language that are common to all members of a speech community are what enable communication, while linguistic style is the result of what an individual selects to use from the array of linguistic tools available to his or her own group or, for that matter, to other groups of speakers. Interestingly, by the way, the clothes-language analogy is also used in the other direction, that is, language as a basis for understanding personal style. Recall the *sartorial eloquence* metaphor in Elton John's lyrics:

> You've a certain sartorial eloquence
> And a style that's almost of your own

William Labov (2002: 8) distinguishes between customs (stable forms) and fashions, "forms that change rapidly within and across generations." Citing Katz and Lazarsfeld (1955), Labov (2008: 2) says, "Change and diffusion of fashions – in clothing and cosmetics – appears to be closer to linguistic change and diffusion than any other form of linguistic behavior." A professional American work environment requires business attire for men, with its conventional invariants of shirt, tie, suit, shoes, etc. All these elements of dress will nonetheless demonstrate endless variation in their cut, size, shape, color, quality, cleanliness, and condition in the resultingly unique sartorial ensemble of every given man in that work place. The development of such style in children and adults is related to the ongoing acquisition of personal criteria for making individual choices, a lifelong process of learning and development. Style in all realms of human activity is acquired early by children, and once acquired has significant staying power.

Style in language is not always unambiguously defined. Style in spoken language is linguistic variation that is directly related to the social context of conversation. Style in written language reflects both a writer's conscious response to the requirements of genre and context as well as the result of his or her unconscious and habituated choices of the grammatical elements acquired through the long-term experiential process of writing. Style is in part, then, the sum of the recurrent choices the writer makes in the process of writing. *Recurrent* refers to those choices that become subconscious habits of choice, that is, repeated selection of one form over other available forms. And *choices* can be described as variations within a norm (*favor/favour*), or deviations from a norm (*They know it./They knows it.*).

Stylistics is the study of style in language. Traditionally, the focus of literary stylistics was the aesthetic quality of expression or the prescriptive conformity of language to the rules of grammatical correctness and social propriety. *Linguistic stylistics*, in contrast, is the scientific interpretation of style-markers as observed, described and analyzed in the language of groups and individuals.

Style markers are the observable result of the habitual and usually unconscious choices an author makes in the process of writing. There are two general types:

1. Choice of optional forms:
   I give you my heart. / I give my heart to you. / I give to you my heart.
2. Deviation from a norm:
   I am working today. / *I'm working today.* vs. *I be working today.*

For further discussion of the nature and occurrence of style markers, see McMenamin (1993: Appendices 1 and 2), and McMenamin (2001).

Stylistic variation is reflected as class characteristics observed in the writing of distinct social and geographical groups, and also as individual features observed in the idiolect of single writers who share a language or dialect. Class features in writing are the graphic analog of dialect characteristics in spoken language. A class feature of adolescent girls, for example, would be the use of an iconic heart replacing the word *love* in a text. Among the most common class features are those that appear as deviations from the norm which are common to careless or under-educated writers, like mixing homonyms such as *its/it's*, *effect/affect*, or *their/there* as in (1), a questioned letter and (2), known writing from a possible writer of (1).

(1) Questioned letter

    Q1:10   ... submitting **there** full Application ...
    Q1:12   ... as part of **there** D/A ...
    Q1:15   ... as part of **there** paperwork ...
    Q13:24   ... bells on **there** cats ...

(2) Known writings

    K12:11   ... I am answering **there** question ...
    K26:11   ... to seek **their** approval ...
    K32:12   ... forwarded **there** letter to you ...
    K54:16   ... on **there** Companies involvement ...

Interestingly, the group characteristics of a spoken dialect may also appear in the writing of speakers of a particular linguistic variety. For example, different words may be homonymous in certain social or regional dialects, therefore appearing as homonyms in the written language, as may be seen in the absence of contrast between *then/than* in (3).

(3) Questioned

    1:15   ...more valuable **then** the Santa Cruz property

Known Geraldine
    16:14   ...keep her there any more **than** a couple of days.

Known Marguerite
    10:11   ...and took more **then** what was distributed to her.
    10:19   ..."the San Leandro property is more valuable" **then** the Santa Cruz property.
    12:24   ...in any one other **then** her the statements...
    12:40   ...he would be more **then** happy to discuss the matter...
    13:19   ...took care of her mother more **then** what she did.

On the other hand, individuating features, while not necessarily unique to a writer, are not commonly observed. For example, in a corpus study of over 1,100 American letter writers, 514 writers recorded a phone number. Table 32.1 shows the frequency distribution of their phone-number forms, demonstrating the relative occurrence of each form, which will constitute the basis for a quantitative determination of where to draw the line between individual and group.

Table 32.1 Phone number formats (USA)

No.	Format	n	%
1	000, 000-0000	1	0.20
2	0000000000	3	0.58
3	Misc. Forms	3	0.58
4	1+000+0000000	7	1.36
5	000 0000000	7	1.36
6	000.000.0000	11	2.14
7	000/000-0000	15	2.92
8	000 000-0000	29	5.64
9	000 000 0000	29	5.64
10	000-000-0000	159	30.93
11	(000) 000-0000	250	48.64
	TOTAL	514	99.99

The analysis of style is carried out using one or a combination of three models outlined by Wachal (1966: 4): resemblance, consistency, and population. The so-called *resemblance model* is used when external factors so narrow candidate authors that the authorship task is to exclude or identify just one or a few suspect writers. For example, an ex-husband trying to gain custody of his children writes letters defaming his former wife, and he is the only person other than her who has knowledge of the events related in the letters. The *consistency model* is used to determine if various writings were written by the same author. This can be the principal task in cases involving a group of writings, one or more of known authorship but others of questioned authorship. Establishing the consistency of a group of writings is frequently the first step in a resemblance case when external circumstances do not demonstrate common authorship of a body of questioned writings. The *population model* is occasionally used in forensic contexts when the pool of candidate authors is large, that is, not limited to just one or two suspect writers. In this instance, the resemblance model is used repeatedly on one possible author after another until all are excluded. For example, a California governor once received a letter describing the in-office sexual escapades of the director of a large state agency. (The letter even contained an elaborate drawing of the red-velvet covered Victorian style couch in his office!) The writings of all employees in the office were analyzed to systematically exclude all but one as the letter writer.

In the above discussion of models of analysis for questions of authorship, I have used the terms *Questioned* and *Known*. In the forensic sciences, there is a bullet, fingerprint, blood stain, fiber, email, etc., whose origin is questioned. The case only becomes viable if and when a possible reference source is found for the questioned item, that is, a gun, fingerprint, DNA sample, piece of clothing, computer, etc., from a possible suspect. The same requirements must be met in the linguistic analysis of style: a Questioned writing, one whose authorship is in doubt or unknown vis-à-vis Known exemplars, writings attested to have been produced by one or more possible authors.

The description of style

The description of style, often referred to as *qualitative* analysis, is the first step in the analysis of style. Subsequent measurement of style is based on the description and categorization of linguistic elements. Qualitative evidence is also generally more "demonstrable" than quantitative results, and it is the belief of many forensic analysts that qualitative findings appeal to the nonmathematical but structured sense of probability held by judges and juries (Cohen 1977).

Qualitative inquiry can be rigorous if conditioned by careful framing of research questions, systematic observation, data that are the direct outcome of observation, reliable methods of description and analysis, valid interpretation of results, and a statement of the basis for every conclusion (Johnstone 2000).

The most important step for systematic observation in both the description (and subsequent measurement) of linguistic variation is the identification of the *linguistic variable*, that is, the isolation of structural linguistic units that carry significance with respect to group or individual writing style. Preferred variables, as first articulated by Labov (1966b: 6) are those that are high in frequency, immune from total suppression (and I would add, conscious suggestion), codable, and widely distributed throughout a particular population (and I would add, individual). The variable is a class of variants ordered along a continuous dimension as determined by extralinguistic variables, such as particular individual authors. The linguistic variant of a given variable is a particular instance of the variable, and a shift in the distribution of variants reflects a change in extralinguistic factors affecting the variable (Labov 1966b: 15), for example, different authors if applied to stylistic analysis. Labov indicates further:

> The variable is of course an abstraction. In actual texts, we meet with variants only. However, the move from variant to variable is the basic step which must be taken here. It implies that the speech performance of the individual or group is best explained through the assumption of an underlying linguistic continuum, in which categories form, reform and dissolve.
>
> (Labov 1966b: 21)

The measurement of style

While qualitative and quantitative factors influence stylistic analysis, it is my view (already expressed above) that linguistic assessments of style precede their expression as numerical values and are often a more realistic representation of the facts. If description is not viewed as the input to measurement, the analyst risks considering the occurrence of any one variant of a variable to be a random event, when he or she knows that it is or could be in fact systematically conditioned. Labov (2008:2) articulates this simply as, "the assumption is that the distribution of its variants is of linguistic interest."

This being said, the measurement of variation in written language is an important complement to description and is necessary when using the occurrence of linguistic units to draw conclusions relative to authorship. Quantification of data makes decision-making related to hypothesis testing easier and more precise, and it meets linguistic and judicial criteria for scientific findings and evidence.

Various researchers (e.g. Grant and Baker 2001) have been working on aspects of quantification of textual elements, especially those related to the selection and significance of style markers. I outline basic tests that lend themselves to evaluating the significance of the relationship of variables across comparison writings: frequency distributions, standard error of difference, t-Test, analysis of variance, proportion test, chi square, coefficient of correlation, and probability of occurrence calculations (McMenamin 2008: 138). An example of more significant advances in quantification comes from the recent work of Grant (2007), who carefully examines the issues which have complicated attempts to quantify results in authorship studies and suggests quantitative strategies for identifying potential style markers (see also Grant, this volume).

Forensic stylistics

Forensic linguistics encompasses applications of linguistic analysis to forensic contexts, for example, voice analysis, translation and interpretation, dialect identification, discourse analysis, and authorship identification, to name a few. Linguists study the habitual variation represented by any given speaker/writer by observing samples of their spoken and written language. The constellation of the patterned uses of language of an individual can be described as a unique set and thereby used to identify the language of that writer. When applied to items of written language in dispute, the analysis of linguistic variation is often referred to as *forensic stylistics*.

At this point, it is important to distinguish between linguistic stylistics and document examination. The focus of forensic stylistics is on the consistent, variable, idiosyncratic use of language as such. The focus of forensic document examination is on handwriting, typewriting, computer-generated documents, paper, ink, etc. While there is some overlap between these two fields of inquiry (e.g. typing habits that reflect underlying language patterns), their practitioners find little practical difficulty keeping them separate.

Cases of questioned authorship typically present the linguist with a questioned writing to be first contrasted (for possible exclusion of the author) then compared (for possible identification of the author) to a set of exemplar writings known to have been written by a writer suspected of authoring the questioned material. The author's style is exhibited in a writing sample large enough to demonstrate the individual variation present in the underlying linguistic patterns internal to the habitual language used by the author. Individual differences in writing style are related to individual choices of alternative forms made available to the writer by the large stock of linguistic alternatives held in common by all the speaker/writers of the author's group, that is, speech community. Thus, individuality in writing style results from a given writer's unique position within the group, as represented by his or her individual aggregate set of habitual linguistic choices.

Case examples of variables may help to make the concept of style marker *clear:*

Case 1:

This is a spelling example (Figure 32.1) resulting from work done for the recent movie, *Zodiac*, produced and directed by David Fincher. This is not an issue of misspelling, but instead one of separation of the diagraph -gh in words like *right* and *night*. Fincher suspected a man named Arthur L. Allen as the writer of the threatening letters sent by the serial killer calling himself the Zodiac. Although this and other features were suggestive of authorship, no conclusion was possible due to the paucity of Known writings from the now-deceased Allen. Other examples can be seen at http://www.zodiacmovie.com/.

QUESTIONED Zodiac

Q Zodiac 4:16 "right"

KNOWN Arthur L. Allen

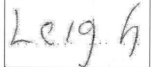

K Allen 2:5 "Leigh"

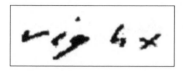

Q Zodiac 7:12 "right"

Q Zodiac 8:6 "night"

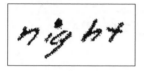

Q Zodiac 12:5 "night"

Figure 32.1 Spelling: separation of graphemic units in digraph -gh-

Case 2:

This punctuation example (Figure 32.2) comes from a criminal matter related to a "peeping tom" who wrote letters to his victim in addition to spying on her through her bedroom window. In the Questioned as well as Known writings, numerous unmotivated parentheses appear around underlined words. These words, however, are not parenthetical to their respective sentences. The writer appears to be using parenthesis in conjunction with underlining as a means of placing emphasis on these words. (Fewer examples are presented than appeared in both sets of writings due to the excision of the most offensive expressions.)

Case 3:

This was a case of adult siblings in dispute among themselves over their mother's Will. The son who lived closest to his mother was suspected by his siblings of having created a new Will with added provisions favoring only him. Known typed writings of the deceased mother demonstrated an invariable pattern in the use of end-quotes: quote marks enclosing stated words and phrases appear with punctuation *before* (inside) the quotes, but

493

KNOWN Writings of Suspect

disrespectfull little (Bitch)

KS 1-9

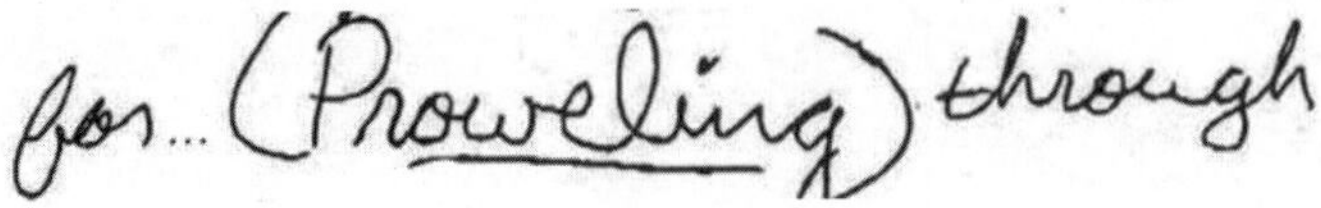

for... (Proweling) through

KS 1-11

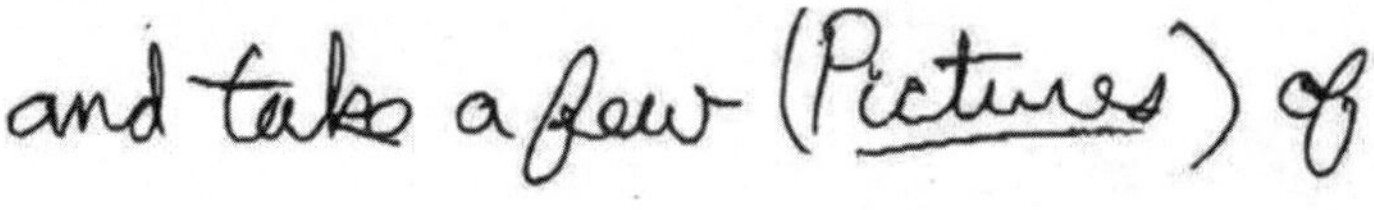

and take a few (Pictures) of

KS 2-4

then (Put Then On The aInternet)

KS 2-8

QUESTIONED Writings

(Please) Keep it

Q 2-4

wondering why You (Shave)

Q 7-2

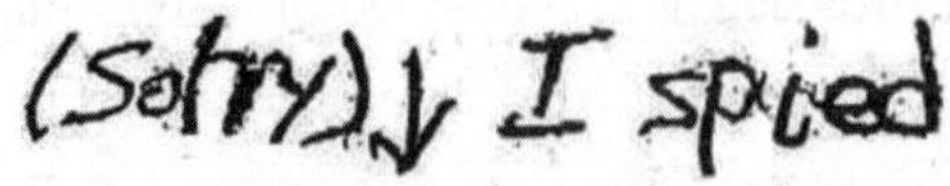

(Sorry) I spied

Q 7-9

Figure 32.2 Punctuation: unmotivated parentheses

KNOWN WRITINGS of Deceased Mother

End-quotes used for statements

232	, wrote a terse/"Is this yours?" and sent it to her chagrin
479	off the line, get off the/line." The electricity was develop
511	for some tools from the house!" He was a new hired man, no
531	and put some more peas on it." My father did not smoke, an

End-quotes used for emphasis

520	ing B E E R. (Idaho was "dry", Wyoming "wet) I was so su
569	ather always went "first-class". Even on a short train trip
715	er she ran so did the "Indian". He at last caught up with
742	Idaho was "dry", Wyoming "wet". My mother worked for Presby

KNOWN WRITINGS of Suspect Son

End-quotes used for statements

65	88 you repeatedly cried "Wolf!" to/your family and friends,
71	the/former love of your life," James D. Flinner, of various
545	Instead of saying, "How nice!" Marie deftly inserted her/fi

End-quotes used for emphasis

15	s for his "final arrangements." Previously, Ernest/had writt
67	Linford. Your "other brother," Floyd Whiting, as usual, did
90	t, and the "love of your life," James D. Flinner,/suffered at
94	Avenue, the Winterland "cabin," the house at 1940 Juniper St.

QUESTIONED WILL

End-quotes used for statements

50	mind, but I can make YOU mind!" Starting I 1984 I had orgina
66	man said,"The buck stops here." I also have to/cite the old
168	might as well have the game." From what I am able to piece

End-quotes used for emphasis

124	and/a Ph.D. from this "school," evidently without having tak
245	pregnant with her "love child." We were living in Laramie in
309	Floyd for this absurd "advice," and he gently reminded Lloyd
326	and me about her "situation." Larry himself told me next to

Figure 32.3 Punctuation: end-quote marks

quote marks used for emphasis appear with punctuation after (outside) the quotes. In contrast, the punctuation in the Questioned writings as well as in the Known writings of the suspect son occurs only *before* (inside) the quote marks in all cases. (Only a few illustrative examples are provided in Figure 32.3 of the many that occurred for each pattern.)

In the same case, the spelling of *already* vis-à-vis *all ready* also varied between the suspect son, his mother, and her purported Will, as can be seen in the data of Figure 32.4.

KNOWN WRITINGS of Deceased Mother

47   get to work. Since Erne was all ready fit to be tied
47   to be tied because we hadn't all ready left for Laramie, I
84   were Dorothy/Sayres I would all ready have the solution to

KNOWN WRITINGS of Suspect Son

209   by 1997 she estimated he had already extracted his "1/3"
295   two required meetings have already been held. All of the
312   since Tom Long's law firm was already engaged with the legal
565   /stopped. It also makes the already unpleasant job for the

QUESTIONED WILL

06   seems to be over. We had already been thoroughly soaked
18   be stopped. It also makes the already unpleasant job for the
36   at 22 months of age, Judy was already bossy. Our second/

Figure 32.4 Spelling: *already*

Case 4:

This was a matter involving an estranged married couple, each saying the other wrote certain damaging letters. These data represent variable use of the relative pronoun in the letter-salutation, "To whom it may concern." The Questioned writings (Figure 32.5) contained the subject form *who*, but the writings of the wife demonstrated a patterned use of the object pronoun *whom*.

Case 5:

This case involved two employees who were both suspected of defrauding their company. Writings (Figure 32.6) related to the fraud demonstrated similarities (use of *which* for *who*) to the writing of one employee and differences from that of the other (use of *who* for *who*).

QUESTIONED

KNOWN

To Who it May Concern:
Q1:2

To Whom It May Concern
KMP6:7

To Who It May Concern:
Q2:2

To Whom It May Concern:
KMP8:2

To Whom It May Concern:
KMP16:6

To Whom It May Concern:
KMP23:7

To whom it may concern,
KMP26:5

Figure 32.5 Word formation: to *who* it may concern vs. to *whom* it may concern

QUESTIONED Letter

0391	another guy from outside the company which left because of fra
0535	he accused of my service director which had recruited me for
0797	by some one from outside the company which was fired after two mon
1010	that involved a closer (Marvin Finch) which he was accused of steal

KNOWN Writing of Suspect #1

3335	general manager with other associates who have the willingness to
3390	deals, however, there are those who you haven't talked to th
3645	and bring a qualified individual who has no interest but to p

KNOWN Writing of Suspect #2

3804	find out from an outsider (customer) which has no relationship with
4161	Steven Bernthal ... June 29th 2005 which leased a car on June
4278	an application of Mr.. Mario Ponce which purchased a 2001 model

Figure 32.6 Syntax: Impersonal relative "which" for personal "who" or "whom"

Case 6:

In this matter, it was claimed that certain speakers who shared a first language other than English had together concocted a Will for a decedent whose native language was English. The writer(s) of the Questioned Will shared the same variation in sequencing tenses as the suspect authors of the Known writings (Figure 32.7).

KNOWN Writings

1:8	I told him that I am a very good cook and
1:17	James kept ... asking me when am I coming back.
1:18	He was saying that he is very attracted to me
1:23	he promised that he will help me look for a job
2:17	He told me that he will make a Will which
2:18	He added that all I had to do is love him.

QUESTIONED Writings

1:16	I made sure that she will be taken care of just in case if I died.
1:18	Frank told me they got engaged and their church wedding will be next year
1:25	He also said that he has a Will that says
2:8	he called Cela his wife, because that's what she is to him
2:28	He said she is the only one that is worth of it.
2:34	he said that his Will is perfectly good

Figure 32.7 Syntax: sequence of tenses: main clause (past) followed by subordinate clause (present)

Case 7:

A woman's existing Will directed her estate to her daughter. After the death of the testatrix, a more recent Will appeared, naming her husband as beneficiary. The data presented differences in the positioning of objects within a sentence. Three possibilities for sequencing the indirect object (IO) and direct object (DO) in English are shown in (4).

(4)

Variation #1	I	give	John	my estate.
	S	V	IO	DO

```
Variation #2   I   give   my estate   to John.
               S   V      DO           to + IO
Variation #3   I   give   to John     my estate.
               S   V      to + IO     DO
```

Corpus analysis would probably prove the third variation to be the most marked, and possibly a more formal form appropriate to the writing-context of a Will. In this case (Figure 32.8), the Questioned Will demonstrates the marked Variation 3 (with one occurrence of the less formal Variation 2), the Known existing Will contains only Variations 1 and 2, and the Known writings of the suspect author (the husband) contain scores of instances of Variation 3 (and some of Variation 1).

QUESTIONED Will

QW1:3	I ... give and bequeath all personal property ... to my husband Will Smith ....
QW1:9	I ... give and bequeath to my daughter Clarice Smith, nothing.
QW1:13	I give to my nephew Marvin Lipp one hundred thousand dollars.

KNOWN Existing Will

EW1:7	I give and bequeath all tangible property ... to my daughter.
EW2:2	All the rest ... I give to my daughter.
EW2:7	It is my wish that she provide my husband a monthly allowance.
EW2:16	I specifically give all of the powers enumerated to my Executrix.
EW3:4	I hereby give my fiduciaries the power to allocate the expenses ....

KNOWN Suspect Writer

KS389:24	Please send to me, a copy of any letter you send.
KS39:6	... she will return to the front office, the telephone and the fax machine.
KS297:10	I ... give to my accountant freedom to ....
KS302: 11	I ... give to my beloved husband authority to ....
KS348:12	The management company will send to you the money for ....

Figure 32.8 Syntax: order of indirect and direct objects within the sentence

Further case examples of linguistic style-markers

The following (Figures 32.9 to 32.21) are linguistic examples from various cases, presented here to demonstrate some of the potential for stylistic variation of punctuation, morphology, lexis, syntax and discourse in written language.

Punctuation

Questioned Letters

QW1:3	Nina,s [Nina's]

Known Writings

K98:12	Kerri,s
K140:21	Harrison,s
K140:25	Rose,s
K158:7	Harrison,s
K165:25	Rex,s

Figure 32.9 Comma for apostrophe

Questioned Letters

> Q1:16   ... to Town Council .
> Q1:18   ... in the very near future .
> Q3:23   ... approval from Council .
> Q7:23   ... and vehicle access .

Known Writings

> K6:10   ... can enter amicably .
> K6:11   ... favorable decision .
> K7:21   ... work reference only .
> K8:21   ... of Forest Property .
> K9:17   ... Company seal with date .

Figure 32.10 Sentence-final punctuation spaced away from last word

Morphology

Questioned Letters

> Q1:11   as anticipate [anticipated].
> Q1:23   the undersign [undersigned].

Known Writings

> K65:27   ... paddocks that will be remediate .... [remediated]
> K138:28   This is the guarantee schedule .... [guaranteed].
> K149:15   Your recommend buffer .... [recommended].

Figure 32.11 Absent *–ed* inflections

Questioned Letters

> Q2:13   ... your several council meeting with council .... [meetings]
> Q4:5   ... all six structure [structures]
> Q9:7   ... the various meeting [meetings]

Known Writings

> K35:20   ... need time and dates [times]
> K96:1   ... both project [projects]
> K97:7   ... to discuss the different way stage one .... [ways]
> K101:10   ... all the six land owner will pay [owners]
> K156:22   ... all your invoice to works .... [invoices]

Figure 32.12 Absent plural inflection

Questioned Letters		Known Writings	
Q7:27	sub divisional	K125:21	de stump
Q7:28	sub divisional	K147:15	sub catchment
Q8:15	sub division	K149:9	sub divide

Figure 32.13 Prefix separation

Questioned   Known Writings

3:43   Meyer fax'es his letter dated 3/3/00   16:6   the financials that were FAX'd to
4:22   You FAX'd everything   18:7   We FEDEX'd you
                                                    23:19   he FAX*d me his version.
                                                    23:21   Sean FEDEX'd samples
                                                    34:7   I am FAX'ing you a copy

Figure 32.14 Apostrophe inserted before inflectional suffix

Questioned Letters
Possessive for plural:

    Q1:32   our wife's will attend [wives]
    Q1:33   the lady's on the council will [ladies]

Plural for possessive:

    Q2:19   your friends land [friend's]

Known Writings
Possessive for plural:

    K12:18   Malcolm Edward's [Edwards]
    K55:1   boundaries of zoning's for wetlands [zonings]
    K151:9   your good self's [selves]
    K153:1   some area's [areas]
    K153:2   the tree's near the road [trees]

Plural for possessive:

    K1:19   companies [company's]
    K7:15   companies [company's]
    K48:23   other tenants houses [tenants']
    K160:17   their banks permission [bank's]

Figure 32.15 Plural/possessive confusion

Questioned Letters

    Q2:25   ... do you real want .... [really]
    Q3:8   ... he was a complete negative person due to .... [completely]
    Q43:5   ... encroachment of environmental sensitive areas. [environmentally]
    Q46:15   ... the regrettably situation .... [regrettable]

Known Writings

    K2:5   ... worked out in a similarly arrangement if the .... [similar]
    K51:20   This is a very financial and economically sound decision .... [financially]
    K69:20   ... the environmental sensitive areas .... [environmentally]
    K70:34   ... the environmental sensitive issues .... [environmentally]
    K125:1   was total unfair. [totally]
    K125:16   ... employ part time workers temporary until [temporarily]
    K140:26   ... will be full resolved [fully]

Figure 32.16 Adverb/adjective substitution

Lexicon

	Phrasal Form	No. in Questioned	No. in Known
1	development application	1	4
2	Development Application	3	19
3	D/A application	10	6
4	D/A	9	56
5	DA	11	65

Figure 32.17 Five variations of form on the same lexical phrase

Syntax

Questioned Letter

Q1:9   This letter certify that ....

Q1:22   ... and should any organization wishes to discuss this matter ....

Q3:14   ... with alterations that was necessary in approving ....

Known Writings

K1:9   ... and we does not have the army to fight ....

K1:18   If the company sign a agreement with ....

K69:20   ... the environmental sensitive areas .... [environmentally]

K5:2   ... at present our company still use the project house ....

K13:23   ... all his works is finished.

K17:3   If the owner wish to sell the Sherwood Forest property ....

K18:2   Environmental runoffs ... is the full responsibility of the project ....

Figure 32.18 Subject/verb agreement

Questioned Writings [one example; embedding structure not shown]

Q3:17   "We would like to make recommendation for approval on the 31st May 2000 for Council to approve the Coastal Stage 1 after it has been on public exhibition for two weeks this is different to what we told you before but legally council has to, before approving your DA and then the remaining total stages would be approved after Council adopts the full LES and LEP and this will not be until mid September 2000 as we had no difficulties in approving the company's Development Application, however, we feel it is important that we address all legal and government authority issues prior to releasing your DA approval from council."

Known Writings [one example; embedding structure not shown]

K1:26   "I have been asked to step aside from all day to day operations within the Forest property, there is lots of items to be completed regarding the property and even just last week end, your house and equipment was damaged in a freak hail storm no one from Smith Lawyers came out to inspect the property, but I helped out and looked after tenancy and covered all the broken windows to your premise and other tenants houses, this is even that I have not been paid this month and even your staff member was not paid until last week and other creditor have not been paid and lots of cheques have bounced and you can just think of all the bad rumors going around."

Figure 32.19 Long periodic sentences with multiple levels of embedding

Questioned Letters

Q1A1:15   ... your professionalism in submitting a lengthy detailed submission ....

Q1A1:20   ... working closely with ... Mr Le Fay in resolving all obstacles ....

Q1A1:21   ... resolving all obstacles in providing the company a DA approval ....

Q1A2:4   ... resolve all problems in allowing our company full approval this ....

Q1:17   I look forward in working closely with the company ....

Example from Known Writings

162:21   We look forward to an good out come
        in assuring the company
            that Sherwood Forest property has priority
          in working closely with council
           in making sure
              it will be successful
                  in meeting to the satisfaction of the owner
                  in producing a township for all
                      to enjoy in years to come.

Figure 32.20 *VERB + in + V-ing*

Discourse

Questioned Letters (3)

Q1A2:6   Should you have any queries pertaining to the enclosed please do not hesitate to contact the undersigned.

Q2:21   Should you have any quires regarding this enclosed letter please don't hesitate to contact the writer ....

Q5:6;   Should you have any queries pertaining to the enclosed please do not hesitate to contact the undersigned.

Known Letters [10 of 30 instances]

K5:13   Should you have any queries pertaining to the enclosed please do not hesitate to contact the undersigned ....

K6:13   Should you have any queries pertaining to the enclosed please do not hesitate to contact the undersigned.

K9:14   Should you have any queries pertaining to the enclosed please do not hesitate to contact the undersigned.

K14:11   Should you have any queries pertaining to the enclosed please do not hesitate to contact the undersigned ....

K17:12   Should you have any queries pertaining to the enclosed please do not hesitate to contact the undersigned.

K25:14   Should you have any queries pertaining to the enclosed please do not hesitate to contact the undersigned.

K27:19   Should you have any queries pertaining to the enclosed please do not hesitate to contact the undersigned.

K30:28   Should you have any queries pertaining to the above please do not hesitate to contact the undersigned.

K31:20   Should you have any queries pertaining to the enclosed please do not hesitate to contact the undersigned.

Figure 32.21 Identical content of letter-closings

Limitations of forensic stylistics

Linguistic limitations to the theory and practice of forensic stylistics have been identified in recent years and have long been studied in authorship attribution research (McMenamin 1993, 2002). Directly confronting such limitations provides direction to the ongoing development of stylistic analysis and of forensic authorship analysis. Specific concerns presently center around four principal observations, each of which will be considered here in turn.

Observation 1: The selection of stylistic variables used for comparison and contrast has been said to be arbitrary and subjective. The criteria for selection of style markers do not appear to be specified or justified.

The selection of stylistic variables is taken from the theory of variation analysis developed by William Labov and others, and proposed as far back as 1966. I refer the reader to the discussion of the linguistic variable in *The Description of Style* section of this chapter. To be yet more specific, Labov (2008: 3) outlines the process for defining the linguistic (dependent) variable:

Step 1. Notice variation: alternative ways of saying the same thing.
Step 2. Define the envelope of variation: the largest environment in which the variation occurs.
   a. Accompany reports of occurrences of a variant with reports of all non-occurrences.
   b. Set aside neutral cases: environments where it is not possible to distinguish variants.
   c. Note exclusions: individual items that behave in idiosyncratic fashion.
Step 3. Define the (independent) constraints on the variable (e.g. writing context or author).

Observation 2: The frequency of occurrence of stylistic variables is not well defined, resulting in analytical methods that do not include rigorous statistical analysis of written texts.

Frequency of occurrence is, in fact, well defined if one follows the steps just outlined for coding variants of style variables. Successful statistical approaches to the general and forensic analysis of style go back decades (see McMenamin 1993). More recently, Grant and Baker (2001) describe the statistical and linguistic bases of Principal Component Analysis, a method for measuring the collective range of variation needed for authorship identification. In addition, I outlined some basic measures in McMenamin 2002. Among the many researchers now working to develop more reliable measures of style, the work of Tim Grant (2007) is the most promising, wherein he proposes a text-sampling strategy to identify potentially useful, reliable, and valid style markers.

Observation 3: Given that reference to a linguistic norm is needed for the analysis of linguistic variation, a norm that is inaccessible for any reason weakens the analysis.

Recall that style variables can be of two types: deviations from a norm and variations within a norm. The clear cases, often those not requiring reference to a corpus, are variables that are prescriptive errors, that is, deviations from the conventions of an established norm. However, many useful style markers represent variation within a norm, that is, multiple error-free ways of saying the same thing. It is here that corpus-based determination of style-marker significance is important.

Another seldom mentioned linguistic limitation of current practice in authorship attribution is the inability to clearly differentiate between group vs. individual variation, commonly referred to in the forensic sciences as class vs. individual features. A corpus-based approach to style-markers that will first identify group variables makes it then possible to assign remaining variables to the set of individuating style markers (i.e. those associated with individual identification) based on relative frequencies of occurrences of identified linguistic variables.

With respect to the need to refer to a community norm in order to establish individual variation, it has long been clear that such work is indispensable to successful stylistic analysis. Labov (1966b), for one, clearly makes this case: "The central finding of sociolinguistics is that the community is the stable and systematic unit, and that the behavior of individuals cannot be interpreted without prior knowledge of the community pattern."

Other more detailed outlines of the need to use tools from corpus linguistics to describe and establish group norms in particular cases are found in Coulthard (1994a), McMenamin (2004), and Solan and Tiersma (2004).

Recognition of the need for a reference corpus does not mean that establishing a norm for any given analysis is in any way easy. The corpus for a given case should match as much as possible the context of writing of the text(s) under scrutiny, meaning that an *ad hoc* corpus may have to be assembled in the event that one enabling a *pares cum paribus* analysis does not already exist.

Observation 4: The relative significance of stylistic variables cannot be determined because it is not yet possible to determine levels of conscious intervention as stylistic choices are made in the writing process, assuming that the most telltale markers are those least consciously used.

It would, of course, be very useful to find a method to test a writer's level of consciousness at any given point in the writing process. However, a performance approach to the observation and analysis of writing behavior appears to be as adequate as it is for the description of spoken language. Labov's research related to levels of style (casual to formal) has demonstrated that variation is more consistent in casual speech, so this may be a place to begin research on writing, that is, attempting to study an individual's writings that are grouped by level of attention paid to the process of writing itself or to other aspects of the writing context that would result in text that is formal (more conscious) or casual (less conscious).

Legal limitations to forensic stylistics relate to the standards for the admissibility of scientific evidence. Forensic stylistics presents no real limitations in countries or venues that rely on a "general acceptance" test like that first laid out in the US by the District of Columbia Court of Appeals in *Frye v. United States* (1923), wherein expert opinion based on a scientific technique was admissible if the technique was generally acceptable in the relevant scientific community. However, starting with the US Supreme Court's decision in *Daubert v. Merrell Dow Pharmaceuticals* (1993), the reliability of scientific evidence in federal and many state venues is now to be judged on five specific factors:

1. whether the theory or technique can be tested;
2. whether the theory or technique has been subjected to peer review and publication;
3. the known or potential rate of error;
4. the existence of standards controlling the operation of the technique; and
5. general acceptance in the relevant scientific community.

Stylistic analysis stands up to the Daubert criteria (Coulthard 2004; McMenamin 2004), although the research area of immediate need is the establishment of error rates for stylistic analysis. However, the fact that forensic stylistics meets to a greater or lesser extent all but one Daubert criterion makes the technique reliable even while error-rate research is being done. In fact, in the later decision of *Kumho Tire v. Carmichael* (1999), the US Supreme Court emphasized flexible application of the Daubert criteria as opposed to rigidly applying any particular Daubert factor in a given case.

However, this does not mean that judicial criteria external to the academic discipline of forensic linguistics, such as those set out in Daubert, cannot provide impetus for improvement in the methodology of forensic stylistics. On the contrary, Grant (2009: 3), for example, correctly observes, "Because of the American pressure [from Daubert] it is likely that the number and variety of quantified approaches will increase in forensic authorship analysis." However, I see the increased rigor of quantification as second in importance to the resolution of another thorny problem: the reconciliation of two distinct approaches to the identification of style markers. If the judicial requirements are to be fully realized, that is, (1) having standards controlling the analysis of style and (2) achieving general acceptance of forensic stylistics in the scientific community (linguistics), it will be necessary to find a middle ground between those who pre-select style markers for analysis, based on whatever criteria, versus those who hold that the style markers used for analysis of a particular set of writings must be first observed as linguistic variables in those very writings. I have previously referred to these respective approaches as *top-down* vis-à-vis *bottom-up*.

My position is known: the basic data for linguistic analysis is language as it is used by speakers and writers as they communicate with each other. Therefore, objective stylistic analysis of language structures is to be based directly on the language being observed and analyzed. Such a data-driven approach precludes the introduction of predefined language features (variables). Some consequent advantages to this approach are that the analyst can take full advantage of all variation presented, it may be easier to separate variation related to authorship vs. that resulting from context of writing, and high levels of variation may make it possible to work with shorter samples.

Another position is one taken by a number of analysts (e.g. most recently Grant 2009) that as long as the variables are demonstrably discriminating and applied in the same fashion to all writings under study, they can be used as reliable style markers. The obvious value of such an approach is that, if and when the ultimate list of diagnostic variables is discovered for a particular context of writing within a given speech community, it can be universally and reliably applied by any analyst.

It is my view that the identification of a context-free set of style markers is not presently a realistic goal for forensic stylistics. Consider forensic sciences such as DNA profiling, ballistics, fingerprints, footwear or tyre track impressions, forensic anthropology, archaeology, geology, entomology, odontology, pathology, toxicology, or psychology. DNA profiling, used to identify individuals on the basis of varying sequences of DNA, is the only forensic science that I am aware of that is able to pre-specify those polymorphic loci on the genome that will apply in every laboratory case. DNA is a lot like language: compared to what all individuals share, very little of DNA or language varies from person to person. However, it is not possible to determine what linguistic elements (what on the genome of linguistic competence—just allow me the metaphor!) will present variation without first observing the language in question. While I do not expect that a functional short-list of reliable style markers for any given language will be found soon, I am certain that further research will identify a middle ground between these two positions.

Putative limitations are imagined limitations articulated by linguists who write or speak with an agenda toward something other than that of usual scientific inquiry. For example, a linguist who once testified that the generally accepted methods of stylistics are not based on well established theoretical principles, proposing instead a theoretical position viewing linguistic variation as a feature of linguistic performance, simply overlooked the inherent variability of language (McMenamin 2001). Such a position cannot be taken seriously because it reflects woefully inadequate knowledge of variation theory and analysis, that is, seeing language as an object inherently possessing ordered heterogeneity. This approach to variation was articulated early on by Weinreich, Labov and Herzog:

> The key to a rational conception of language change – indeed of language itself – is the possibility of describing orderly differentiation in a language serving a community. ... nativelike command of heterogeneous structures is not a matter of ... "mere" performance, but is part of unilingual linguistic competence.
>
> (Weinreich, Labov and Herzog 1968: 101)

It has also happened that the expert linguist simply asserted her position in a case rather than empirically proving it, even simultaneously resorting to arbitrary *ad hominem* arguments in the often strained context of the courtroom. Such behavior threatens the admissibility of any and all linguistic evidence more than the method being argued for or against ever could.

Other cases of imagined limitations are associated with linguists who are distracted by irrelevant issues, for example the strongly stated objection by Crystal (1995: 382) that if he were dead he would be turning over in his grave because his published theory of style was being applied to written language, to the momentary exclusion of spoken language.

A more serious artificial limitation is the occasional arrogance of the expert who simply does not allow for an approach other than the one he or she proposes. See, for example, a discussion related to this problem in McMenamin 2001, wherein I examine a proposed approach to authorship analysis that rejects as unscientific and irrelevant to current theory and practice hundreds of studies over a century of previous work in stylistics. Science by nature allows for simultaneous study and testing of multiple hypotheses, without regard to the burning desire of one researcher to be right or to the external (e.g. legal) need for immediate methodological agreement and procedural standards.

It is also my belief that objections to stylistic analysis have at times been occasioned by analysts' inability to separate science from business. For example, a researcher may develop what appears to be an interesting method of authorship identification. However, if he or she neglects to present the work to the "relevant scientific community" in such a way that it can be peer reviewed, and even goes so far as to seek a patent on the method, such actions speak to a reversal of expected priorities, by putting personal pecuniary interests before one's commitment to scientific inquiry.

Conclusion

Neither the more important challenges for forensic stylistics, like quantification and style-marker identification, nor the mere pesky problems related to the occasional misguided analyst, have to stand in the way of progress. The research needed to strengthen the science is clearly specified here and elsewhere for anyone who takes it up. However, the condition for doing the research necessary to meet any of these challenges is cooperation, and as Gawande observes, when there is a mixture of views within communities of researchers and professional practitioners, it is the collaborative leaders of the particular scientific community who set the norms and thereby define the character of the community:

> [Those] that set norms encouraging the free flow of ideas and collaboration, even with competitors, produced enduringly successful communities, while those that mainly sought to dominate did not.
>
> (Gawande 2009: 42)

Further reading

Coulthard, Malcolm (2004) "Author identification, idiolect and linguistic uniqueness," *Applied Linguistics*, 25(4): 431–47.

——(1994) "On the use of corpora in the study of forensic texts," *Forensic Linguistics: The International Journal of Speech Language and the Law*, 1(1): 27–41.

Grant, Tim D. (2005) *Authorship Attribution in a Forensic Context*, Unpublished PhD Dissertation, University of Birmingham, Birmingham.

Kniffka, Hannes (2007) *Working in Language and Law: A German Perspective*, New York: Palgrave Macmillan.

33

Text messaging forensics

Txt 4n6: Idiolect free authorship analysis?

Tim Grant

Introduction

Danielle Jones disappeared on 18 June 2001; she has not been seen since and her body has never been found. Within hours of her disappearance two text messages were sent from her phone which, the police suspected, might have be written by her Uncle, Stuart Campbell. In the first case of its type to reach the UK courts, Malcolm Coulthard offered a linguistic analysis which showed that the messages were unlikely to have been written by Danielle. Stuart Campbell was convicted of Danielle's murder on the 19 December 2002 at least in part because of the linguistic evidence. In a parallel case, Jenny Nicholl disappeared on 30 June 2005. Once more Malcolm Coulthard was able to offer a linguistic analysis suggesting that she was unlikely to have texted the final messages sent from her phone and that her lover, David Hodgson, was one of a small group of possible authors. Hodgson was convicted of Jenny's murder on 19 February 2008.

Further evidence of the potential utility of forensic linguistics in the examination of text messages was provided in 2007 when I was given permission to carry out a survey of mobile telephone seizures by the Northamptonshire Police, a medium-sized semi-rural force, located in the East Midlands of the UK and covering about 900 square miles and a population of 640,000. The police in the UK have powers to seize mobile phones and the information they obtain ranges from the location of the phone at any particular time, to the call record and details of the SMS text messages sent and received. I was given access to all 186 phones seized during a three-month period, from which a total of some 10,000 text messages were recovered. Further analysis of the case files showed that for only twelve of these phones was there any suspicion that the owner had not sent all of the messages. Perhaps unsurprisingly in none of the cases was a forensic linguist employed to resolve these potential disputes. However, the degree of actual and potential investigative interest in the authorship of text messages appears to be growing and this raises some very real theoretical and methodological problems, not least whether such short and fragmentary texts are amenable to any form of authorship analysis.

Coulthard makes the strong claim that

> The linguist approaches the problem of questioned authorship from the theoretical
> position that every native speaker has their own distinct and individual version of
> the language they speak and write, their own idiolect, and … this idiolect will
> manifest itself through distinctive and idiosyncratic choices in texts.
>
> (Coulthard 2004: 432)

Even if the first claim here, that every speaker has their own idiolect, can be sustained,
there is no necessary implication from it that an individual's idiolect will be measurable in
every text produced by that person, whatever its length. It would be perfectly rational to
hold Coulthard's view and to also hold that a substantial and varied body of text would be
required before manifest idiolectal features became noticeable or measurable. Coulthard's
working definition of the idiolect as a 'distinct and individual version of language' only
becomes useful to the authorship analyst if an idiolectal feature repeats itself, either within
one text or across several texts by the same author. In the context of text messaging it may
be that individual messages are considered too short to allow the possibility of idiolectal
analysis, but conversely it may be possible to analyse idiolect in text messages by examining
many messages written by the same individual. Further to this, although Coulthard claims
his definition to be a 'theoretical position', a distinction must be made between observation and theory. On the one hand, there is the observation of features which might
comprise an idiolect, that is to say idiolectal analysis requires an empirical study which
produces evidence of consistency and distinctiveness. On the other hand, a linguistic
theory of idiolect is required, which would provide explanation of any empirical evidence.
The analysis of authorship may depend conceptually on theories of idiolect as distinctive
versions of language but practically and methodologically authorship analysis depends on
the facility to detect consistent patterns of language use. If consistent patterns can be
detected, then the next step will be to determine how distinctive any such patterns are.
Practical authorship analysis may depend less on a strong theory of idiolect than on the
simple detection of consistency and the determination of distinctiveness.

The principal theoretical question this chapter addresses is whether authorship analysis
can be valid as the mere detection of degrees of consistency and the determination of
degrees of distinctiveness, or whether in its practical application it must rest implicitly or
explicitly on a particular and strong theory of idiolect. Consistency and distinctiveness may,
of themselves, be evidence that an idiolect exists, but they do not constitute an explanatory
theory of idiolect. In this theoretical sense, authorship analysis based only on consistency and
distinctiveness can be considered idiolect free, or at least idiolect light. Below, following a
theoretical discussion of different theories of idiolect and their explanatory usefulness, a
method will be demonstrated that measures consistency and distinctiveness in text messaging authorship analysis. The chapter then concludes with a discussion of whether such an
analysis in fact depends upon or requires the practitioner to subscribe to a theory of idiolect,
and whether one particular theory of idiolect has advantages over any other.

Authorship analysis and theories of the linguistic individual

Current work in forensic authorship analysis has tended to polarise between those who
argue that work on authorship requires a strong understanding of the cognitive

mechanisms of textual production on the one hand (Chaski 2001; Howald 2009), and on the other those who believe a stylistic understanding of language production is sufficient to explain authorial consistency and distinctiveness (McMenamin 2001). This debate has proved important in the United States Court system. Howald (2009) supporting Chaski's (2001) position, argues that stylistic approaches to authorship analysis are theoretically weak and therefore should fail the legal admissibility tests applied by the American courts. Some of this debate seems to rest on alternative conceptions of the idea of the linguistic individual and indeed on different theories of idiolect.

Cognitivist theories of idiolect

A set of theories of idiolect (which I shall refer to as cognitivist theories) suggest that individual language production is largely determined by linguistic competence. Competence is conceptualised here as the cognitive capacity of an individual to produce language and as such is reflected in linguistic performance. If one holds a cognitivist view of the linguistic individual then one good approach for authorship analysis involves trying to measure their cognitive capacity. Such approaches analyse particular aspects of language which are well explained by cognitive models of language production; aspects such as syntactic complexity or measures of the mental lexicon. It is possible in a general sense to measure such features and demonstrate variation between authors and groups. For example, quantitative and computational linguists can, at least with longer texts, describe mathematically, features of individuals' language production in terms of word frequency distributions (Baayen 2001; Holmes 1998; Grant 2007) syntactic structures (Chaski 2001; Spassova and Grant 2008) and other observable markers of authorship. The successful employment of these approaches in the resolution of authorship attribution problems does in fact depend upon, and thus demonstrate, degrees of consistency and distinctiveness. However, the cognitivist theories of language production upon which these approaches rest do not of themselves explain consistency within an author's textual production, nor distinctiveness between any two authors. To have a well worked out theory of language production is different in this sense from having an explanatorily strong theory of idiolect. A theory of idiolect must provide an explanation as to why one individual's production is consistent across texts, and must also explain why that individual's language is distinctive as compared with that of other individuals. Cognitivist theories may be better at explaining consistency within an individual's textual production but it is more difficult to elaborate cognitive explanations of distinctiveness between individuals. In describing language production systems cognitivist theorists tend to assume minimal individual differences or assume that differences between individuals are relatively uninteresting.

A good example of this cognitivist reduction in interest in individual linguistic variation is Chomsky's move from his earlier interest in the dichotomy between competence and performance to his later, allied but distinct theoretical dichotomy between internal and external language; *L-I* and *L-E*, respectively (Chomsky 1985). Theories of language competence can incorporate the possibility of variation between individuals, however, the more recent dichotomy between *L-I* and *L-E* holds less explanatory power in this respect. In these theories, theoretical primacy is given to understanding individual internal language capacity, *L-I*, rather than the less essential *L-E*, where distinctions between natural languages and their variants are seen as rather uninteresting. The research focus is not on differences between different individuals' *L-I* (arguably there are none) but rather on what is common to all individuals in *L-I*. This theoretical work is one of the foundations for the development of cognitive science in the late 1980s and early 1990s and cognitive science has in turn informed the more recent biologically focused project of cognitive neuroscience. Where cognitive linguists proposed information processing models or architectures for language production the neuroscientists looked to realise these models in terms of particular brain locations and processes.

In order to understand the implications of this to forensic work, we need to trace a brief history of an area where cognitive psychologists and neuroscientists have made some progress in explaining just one small part of language production. One such area is child language acquisition and a small part of this literature focuses on the way children learn irregular past tense verbs which is sometimes said to demonstrate a U-shaped learning curve. Initially children produce these irregular forms accurately, for example, English 'went' as a past tense for 'go' and 'was' for 'is'. In the next stage of learning, however, children appear to unlearn these verb forms now creating errors such as 'goed' or 'wented'. This stage represents the 'dip' in the U-shaped learning curve. In the final stage of learning, representing a rise out of the learning curve dip, children's performance improves again and they begin to use the correct forms for irregular past tense verbs again.

Beretta *et al.* (2003) examined alternative cognitive models attempting to explain this U-shaped learning curve. Some cognitive models propose a rule-based system whereby the first language learner produces regular verbs using a *stem+ed* production model and there is also an entirely separate part of the model devoted to simply memorising the small number of irregular verbs (e.g. Pinker and Ullman 2002). This type of model is referred to as a '*rules plus memory model*' and it is argued that the developmental interaction between these two elements can explain the U-shaped learning curve. A less recent and entirely different model, based on neural networks, is provided by Rumelhart and McClelland (1986) who argue that associative learning alone can account for the U-shaped learning curve. Their model contains only a single processing network and is unified in the sense that regular and irregular forms are learnt in a single system.

These two models both appear to accurately explain the observable data but at this stage in the historical development of the field, they both faced the same reasonable criticism; this is that although each model was conceived to be consistent with experimental results, there is no strong sense in which they could have claimed to be real. That is to say, neither model could claim to be related either to the biological foundations of language production, or to the social reality of language use. Choosing between two models which are both consistent with the available experimental data is entirely arbitrary. The solution to this problem came with the development of brain imaging techniques over the last ten years. This has made real the understanding that there are very specific brain locations through which different aspects of language are produced. In the case of learning past tense verbs, Beretta *et al.* (2003) report the discovery that the production of regular and irregular verbs actually occurs at two separate brain locations. This new evidence can provide a reason for choosing Pinker's rules plus memory model over Rumelhart and McClelland's associative model with its implication of a single structure.

Developments such as these in cognitive neuroscience have important implications for discussions of idiolect which in turn, are important for work in authorship analysis. With regard to idiolect, the main implication is that, just as we as a species share biological structures, so too we share brain structures in language production. The general focus of cognitive neuroscience is not on variation between individuals, but on shared commonalities. If I as a speaker of English have two neurological structures for the production of past tense verbs then so too will you. Adopting a cognitive view of language production tends to make the explanation of idiolectal variation more difficult rather than easier. Of course, it is not impossible to develop a cognitive neuroscience of idiolectal variation. Just as we recognise minor biological differences between individuals, so we may argue for similar individual differences in cognitive structures. To ignore cognitive neuroscience in discussions of idiolect would be reckless, but it is extremely difficult to use this body of work to explain actual individual differences between texts written by the same or different authors. By contrast stylistic theories of idiolect can and indeed do explain individual differences between authors.

Stylistic theories of idiolect

Forensic stylistics is sometimes seen as being in opposition to more cognitivist approaches to idiolect. From the cognitivist perspective, it has been suggested that those who take a more stylistic approach to authorship analysis have a weaker theory of idiolect and that the variables used are not on as solid a foundation in terms of linguistic theory (Howald 2009). Proponents of the more stylistic approaches naturally take issue with such an evaluation arguing that theories of stylistic variation are essential to understanding differences which occur between individuals (McMenamin 2002). My argument is that understanding language variation stylistically, as the interaction between habit and context, does not imply a lack of linguistic theory so much as an alternative linguistic theory. Stylistic and variationist theories of language are less focused on providing species-wide explanations of language production than on developing explanations as to how and why language varies and/or remains constant across sociolinguistic contexts. Such an approach may in fact be able to provide a better explanation of variation between individuals than cognitivist approaches. Individuals will have different linguistic experiences and these will be revealed in their language production. This is not idiolect free authorship analysis, but rather authorship analysis which has a different conception of the nature of idiolect.

Johnstone (1996, 2009) studying the language of Barbara Jordan, and Kredens (2002, 2003) studying the language of Morrissey, separately describe the consistency of individual linguistic stance across texts, contexts and indeed across a lifetime of textual production. In these detailed descriptions, it is possible to draw some individual historical and social explanations for consistent features of language use. For example, Johnstone (1996: 155) concludes of some low-level aspects of Barbara Jordan's style that her language reflects 'her disregard for appearances, and her lifelong refusal to adapt to social expectations about how a southern black woman should live and behave'. In other words, Johnstone is arguing that, Jordon's language draws upon her individual social history and upon a construction of herself as a participant in that history. Such case studies are invaluable in demonstrating the development and persistence of a linguistic individual across a variety of sociolinguistic contexts. Perhaps even more important for theories of idiolect and for forensic authorship analysis such insights allow us to develop explanations for the specifics in an individual's style. In this respect, one possible criticism of these studies might be their choice of interesting individuals; Johnstone's case study of Barbara Jordan, a United States political figure famous for her oratory, and Kredens' case study of singer songwriter, Morrissey, known for his imaginatively gloomy lyrics, are together somewhat elitist choices, perhaps unrepresentative of the average language user. Both individuals may in different ways be aiming to project a particular persona through their public language and have the talent and linguistic skill to achieve this. These concerns aside, the approach taken by both Johnstone and Kredens suggests that individuals taking a constant or repeated linguistic stance can create stylistic traits which in turn can be construed as the creation of a linguistic individual.

In so far as these stylistic approaches only identify consistent and distinctive features of linguistic output for an individual, they fare no better than cognitivist approaches in suggesting a strong theory of idiolect. There is, however, rather more of an attempt at explanation for the creation of a linguistic individual amongst these theorists and in particular a live debate as to whether the intersection of sociolinguistic factors *determine* a linguistic individual (as discussed by Kredens 2002) or whether an individual's history and context are *resources* which can be drawn upon, a position preferred by Johnstone (1996, 2009). One advantage of this idea that we might draw upon our individual sociolinguistic resources in the creation of a linguistic persona is that it allows for the additional possibility that we might also draw upon other language resources. In particular, it is possible to speculate that a linguistic individual might draw upon a combination of sociolinguistic resources and cognitive resources. Accepting that an idiolect may not be determined by either cognitive capacities or sociolinguistic history, but that each may provide resources and constraints in the creation of a linguistic individual suggests the possibility of a more unified theory of idiolect.

A unified approach to the linguistic individual

Coulthard (2004) demonstrated just how individual an apparently everyday utterance can be. Using a series of Google searches he shows how the apparently everyday phrase 'I asked her if I could carry her bags', is probably a unique utterance. He points out that at each stage in the construction of the phrase from a one-word utterance, to a two-, three-, four- and eventually nine-word utterance it increases in rarity to become apparently unique. He suggests 'I asked her' may be a pre-formed idiom, and so too, 'if I could' but where these appear together to form, 'I asked her if I could … ', this showed only 7,740 Google hits in 2004. There is apparently a fairly open choice as to the verb which might follow this construction. In Coulthard's example, the word 'carry' is used and shows its rarity by scoring only seven Google hits. A range of alternative words might have replaced it. These include, 'take', 'hold', 'bring', etc. One idiolectal question is why one individual would use 'carry', whilst another individual might use 'bring'. Work on lexical priming offers one answer to such a question.

Hoey's (2005) work on lexical priming is situated firmly in a corpus-based tradition and yet aspects of lexical priming have long been researched by cognitive psychologists interested in the mental lexicon. Hoey's work concentrates on collocation, and details how one word *primes* the occurrence of its collocates. Although Hoey is not, in this work, interested in theories of idiolect he does discuss how such collocates emerge and from this one can infer how priming and collocation can spread from one individual to another and how an individual's own language can be affected by these collocational pressures. In contrast, cognitive psychologists' interest in priming has been experimental, and has described systematic patterns in reaction time as to how a word's frequency, rarity and semantic relation affects our ability to recognise or recall it (e.g. Sloboda 1986). These two perspectives on lexical priming might be seen as coming together in the developing interest of the cognitivist neuroscientists in the malleability or plasticity of the brain.

Recent work in cognitive neuroscience considers not only the cognitive structures common between individuals but also how the brain is altered by environmental stimuli.

Greenfield (2008) describes the plasticity of the brain to external stimuli. At a gross level this can be illustrated by the example of how London taxi drivers, who have to memorise 'the Knowledge' of the driving geography of London before obtaining a license, develop an expanded area of the hippocampus. A more linguistic example might include evidence that bilinguals develop different parts of their brain to speak their different languages (e.g Ibrahim 2008). Using evidence such as this Greenfield elaborates a description of the mind as the 'personalisation of the brain' by individual external stimuli each making tiny incremental changes to neuronal activity and structure. Extrapolating from such a model it is possible to conceive the beginnings of a theory of idiolect as the personalisation of the language systems by exposure to differing linguistic stimuli. One potent force of such personalisation would be the statistical weight of collocation. My exposure to a certain variety of language containing one set of collocates would be different from my neighbour's and this personalisation would gradually cause individual differences in our language production. Idiolectal consistency and variation would draw on the resource of my cognitive capacity for language production and also draw on the complexity of my personal sociolinguistic history. According to this potential theory of idiolect, the cognitive capacity is itself structured but malleable and the sociolinguistic history is realised in incremental changes to that neuro-cognitive capacity.

In conclusion, theories of idiolect cannot merely notice consistent and distinctive features of the language of an individual. They should also attempt to provide explanations for these facts. We have seen that although cognitivist theories can provide convincing explanations for some aspects of language production these theories hold less power in and of themselves in explaining individual variation. Conversely, while stylistic approaches to the linguistic individual do concentrate on providing explanations for language variation between individuals they are perhaps less interested in explaining how these might be realised psychologically. I have speculatively indicated a possible future path which might help these different and sometimes competing theories of idiolect to provide complementary explanations for the construction of an individual. The question that remains is how far these theoretical discussions of idiolect can or should impact on forensic authorship analysis.

Text messaging authorship analysis

In the two text messaging cases referred to at the beginning of the chapter, the problem brought to the linguist by the police was to determine which of two authors was more likely to have written a series of messages. In forensic casework, this is perhaps the most common type of problem, at least when the linguist is commissioned by the police. Typically, by the time the police approach a linguist they will have identified a suspect and are trying to build an evidential case to put to the suspect in interview. In the Danielle Jones and the Jenny Nicholl cases, the question put was whether it was more likely that the queried messages were written by the suspect or by the supposed victim. The police investigators may have, or believe they have, other non-linguistic evidence which makes the possibility of a third unknown person, already very unlikely or even impossible. It is of course possible to write a conditional opinion of the sort that, if it is known that one of the two candidate writers did write the disputed text message, then of these two X is a more likely author than Y. Clearly, however, such a conditional opinion is not ideal. In the UK system the expert works for the Court even if instructed by the police and it would be better practice ethically and methodologically to step back from the expectations of the police and truly account for the possibility of other potential authors. This raises the question of how rare one person's text messaging style might be, or even whether it could be unique.

The issue of linguistic distinctiveness between individuals has two levels which may be independent. If it can be demonstrated that the suspect exhibits a consistent style in text messaging and also that the victim has a consistent but different style then the first level of distinctiveness will have been proved. I shall refer to this as pair-wise distinctiveness and I will argue that answering this question does not depend upon a strong theory of idiolect, but only upon the degree of consistency of style within each author and the difference which is demonstrable between them. To this extent, any such analysis might be characterised as idiolect-free authorship analysis. The second possible level of distinctiveness, however, may have more profound implications for theoretical discussions of idiolect. This would occur if one person's text messaging style can be said to be distinctive, unusual or even unique against a reference population of text messages. This I shall refer to as population-level distinctiveness. As we shall see, it is possible to explore questions of consistency of style and both pair-wise and population distinctiveness using statistical methods. These methods were in fact developed in forensic psychology for the investigation of serial crime (e.g. Bennell and Canter 2002; Woodhams and Toye 2007).

The issue of consistency is also one of degree and has to be judged in the context of pair-wise as well as population-level distinctiveness. In a recent text messaging case in which I was involved, the linguistic issue involved determining which of two people was the more likely writer of a sequence of 20 text messages. For each writer I was provided with about 200 messages of known authorship. Within this known set, some features appeared to be absolutely consistent and absolutely discriminating. For example, every time Author A used the word 'don't' they spelt it 'dont', i.e. without the apostrophe. In contrast, every time Author B used the word 'don't' they used the abbreviation, 'dnt'. Other features demonstrated only degrees of consistency; Author A for example, always used the standard spelling, 'just', while Author B used 'just' about one third of the time, 'jst' two thirds of the time. The spelling 'jst' in a particular message obviously contains some authorship information but, it can be argued that, in the context of pair-wise distinctiveness, so too does the spelling 'just'. This spelling is more consistent with author A than B. Calculating the degree to which this can be used in determining an opinion, however, requires statistical sophistication (see Lucy 2005 for a good introduction on the application of Bayesian inferencing to resolving this sort of problem).

In the Jenny Nicholl murder case, Coulthard took a more traditional descriptive linguistic approach. He initially analysed a series of messages known to have been written by Nicholl and later also a series of messages known to have been written by Hodgson. From this examination, he identified nine low-level stylistic features which were seen to discriminate between the text messaging styles of the two possible authors. Some of these messages are now in the public domain and these include eleven messages known to have been written by Nicholl (reproduced in Table 33.1) and seven known to have been written by Hodgson (reproduced in Table 33.2). A further complication with Hodgson's messages was that two of the messages were produced on request in a police interview thereby giving Hodgson the opportunity to deliberately disguise his style. Finally, there were four disputed messages (reproduced in Table 33.3).

Example features used by Coulthard in this case include the abbreviation 'im' for 'I am', a lack of a space after using '2' for 'to' (both used by Nicholl and not Hodgson)

Table 33.1 Messages from the trial of David Hodgson for the murder of Jenny Nicholl: Known messages of Jenny Nicholl

---

Sum black+pink k swiss shoes and all the other shit like socks.We r goin2the Indian.Only16quid.What u doin x

Yeah shud b gud.i just have2get my finga out and do anotha tape.wil do it on sun.will seems keen2x

Shit is it.fuck icant2day ive already booked2go bowling.cant realy pull out.wil go2shop and get her sumet soon.thanx4tdlin me x

No reason just seing what ur up2.want2go shopping on fri and2will's on sun if ur up2it

Sorry im not out2nite havnt seen u 4a while aswel.ru free2moro at all x

No im out wiv jak sorry it took me so long ive had fone off coz havnt got much battery

Only just turned my fone.havnt lied bout anything.no it doesnt look good but ur obviously jst as judgmental than the rest.cu wen I cu&I hope its not soon

I havnt lied2u.anyway im off back2sleep

I know I waved at her we wer suppose2go at4but was a buffet on later on so waited.anyway he had a threesome it was great cu around

Im tierd of defending myself theres no point.bye

Happy bday!will b round wiv ur pressent2moz sorry i cant make it2day.cu2moz xxx

---

.

Table 33.2 Messages from the trial of David Hodgson for the murder of Jenny Nicholl: Known messages of David Hodgson

---

has he got his phone on him

ave dun he aint got it he will b in witherspoons she in
got puddings and tissues in me pnckets.ave2 hope he rings b4 he goes up back in 30

put it on at 3.30 at 150 ok and top on at 4.45 but dont put glass lid on just the suet ok and the spuds separate

put them on at ten 2 ok thats 4.50 ok

Messages produced in police interview

HI JENN TELL JACKY I Am KEEPING My PhONE of because I am living in Scotland with my boyfriend I mite be in trouble with my dad myself. DaDs going to kill me I told him I was leaving Keswick why Does he hate me everyone hates me in RICHMOND you are the only mate I have got Have to go see you.

Hi jenn tell jacky i am keeping my phone of because i am living in Scotland with my boyfriend i might be in trouble with dad myself dads going to kill me i told him i was leaving Keswick why does he hate me everyone hates me in Richmond you are the only mate i have got have to go see you

---

and the use of 'me' and 'meself' rather than 'my' and 'myself' (used by Hodgson and not Nicholl). He judged these to be consistently used by each of the two candidate authors.

Coulthard was the only linguist to give evidence at trial and his opinion was careful and correct. He was able to say that the suspect messages were inconsistent with the described style of Jenny Nicholl. A slide demonstrating this point and used by Coulthard in presenting his analysis can be seen at http://news.bbc.co.uk/1/hi/sci/tech/7600769. stm. His conclusion with regard to Hodgson was measured. He gave the opinion that '*Linguistic features identified in Mr Hodgson's and the suspect texts are compatible with their*

Table 33.3 Messages from the trial of David Hodgson for the murder of Jenny Nicholl: Disputed messages

---

Thought u wer grassing me up.mite b in trub wiv me dad told mum i was lving didnt giv a shit.been2 kessick camping was great.ave2 go cya

Hi jen tell jak i am ok know ever 1s gona b mad tell them i am sorry.living in Scotland wiv my boyfriend. shitting meself dads gona kill me mum dont give a shite.hope nik didnt grass me up.keeping phone of.tell dad car jumps out of gear and stalls put it back in auction.tell him i am sorry

Y do u h8 me i know mum does.told her i was goin.i aint cumin back and the pigs wont find me.i am happy living up here.every1 h8s me in rich only m8 i got is jak.txt u couple wks tell pigs i am nearly 20 aint cumin back they can shite off

She got me in this shit its her fault not mine get blame 4evrything.i am sorry ok just had 2 lve shes a bitch no food in and always searching me room eating me sweets.ave2 go ok i am very sorry x

---

having been produced by the same person' and when pressed at trial he emphasised that Hodgson was one of a group of possible authors, and that the linguistic evidence could not go further than that (personal communication). The description of the consistencies in style and this pair-wise distinctiveness contributed to the case which convinced the jury to convict David Hodgson of Jenny Nicholl's murder and an appeal on the grounds that the linguistic evidence was unsound failed.

One challenge for forensic authorship analysts when considering text messages is to adopt something like the approach demonstrated in Coulthard's method and expression of opinion and to develop this approach further. In particular, comparisons between authors could be enhanced if the descriptive methods used by Coulthard can be developed to enable the quantified comparison of degrees of consistency and distinctiveness. Fortunately, forensic linguistics can borrow from its sister discipline of forensic psychology to achieve this aim.

Forensic psychology and case linkage work

Forensic psychologists have been involved in developing methods to determine whether a particular crime is an independent event, or alternatively, whether it is in fact part of a series of linked crimes committed by the same offender. This work, known as case linkage, typically relies on the statistical or computational analysis of offenders' behaviours in databases of offences and depends upon the twin principles of behavioural consistency and behavioural distinctiveness. The parallels with authorship analysis as described are clear. These case linkage principles have been investigated and demonstrated across a series of types of crime including car crime (Tonkin *et al.* 2008), commercial burglary (e.g. Bennell and Canter 2002; Woodhams and Toye 2007), sexual crime (e.g. Santtila *et al.*, 2005b; Woodhams, Grant and Price 2007), arson (Santtila *et al.* 2005a) and murder (Salfati and Bateman 2005) and a theoretical discussion exploring the nature of behavioural consistency in forensic work is beginning to be well developed (Woodhams and Toye 2007; Woodhams, Hollin and Bull 2007). Methods taken from this body of work can be adapted and applied to text messaging authorship analysis. Instead of scoring the presence and absence of crime scene behaviours, we can score the presence and absence of stylistic features.

Statistical consistency and distinctiveness

Returning to the Nicholl case, these methods can be exemplified even with the relatively small number of publicly available text messages. Because of the small number of messages, it is a simple matter to code each text as having or lacking each of the features noticed by Coulthard. The presence of each feature in each text message is scored as a one and its absence is scored as a zero. This creates an array of zeros and ones for every message sent. An example is shown as Table 33.4.

Using these representations, pairs of messages can then be compared for similarity or dissimilarity using a binary correlation analysis called Jaccard's coefficient. Jaccard is a statistical tool for measuring the degree of similarity. It produces results ranging from zero to one, with zero indicating total dissimilarity and one indicating identity. For the purposes of this worked example, I wish to follow Coulthard's analysis and this produces a slight peculiarity in results. Coulthard's method is to use reciprocal coding to create a series of contrasts, for example, Nicholl's use of 'im' with the suspect's 'I am' and this produces two coding columns which indicate the presence of 'im' in some of Nicholl's messages but none of Hodgson's whereas for 'I am' the reverse pattern is true. This choice of features, along with the small number of messages, together produces the mathematical effect of reducing some of the Jaccard scores to zero and this in turn requires the use of one-sample t-tests (with a test score of zero) to make some of the comparisons. This, however, does not affect the theoretical or practical implications of the method more generally. Calculations for both t-tests and Jaccard coefficient will be performed by most statistics programme (such as SPSS) and described in their manuals and help files and also in most introductory text books on statistics (e.g. Dancey and Reidy 1999).

One feature of Jaccard which is crucial for both the analysis of text messages and for its parallel use in criminal case linkage is the fact that the occurrence of two absence scores, two zeros, has no effect on the overall similarity metric. A writer may be consistent in their preference of 'im' over 'I am' but this consistency will not be revealed in every message. In a similar vein in crime analysis, the absence of evidence of the carrying of a weapon at a scene is not evidence of its absence from that scene and Jaccard allows for this.

Having calculated Jaccard's coefficient between pairs of messages it is very straightforward to statistically demonstrate consistency of style and pair-wise distinctiveness between authors. To demonstrate the degree of consistency in Nicholl's messages using this coding system it is possible to take all of Nicholl's eleven messages and pair each message with every other. This produces 110 pairs and subsequently 110 Jaccard scores (mean = 0.23, SD = 0.20). A similar process can be carried out with Hodgson's seven messages creating 42 Jaccard scores (mean = 0.11; SD = 0.19). Removing the messages which Hodgson produced at interview leaves 20 Jaccard scores and raises the mean Jaccard score slightly and reduces the standard deviation (mean = 0.15; SD = 0.12).

If we move to examine all the pairs of messages where each pair contains a Nicholl text and a Hodgson text the Jaccard scores fall to zero for each and every one of these possible between-author pairs. (Included in this analysis are those text messages elicited from Hodgson during police interview.) This zero score is a representation of the difference in style between Hodgson and Nicholl. It is atypical to score zero, rather than a low decimal close to zero, but as commented above this is at least in part an artefact of using Coulthard's features which result in reciprocal coding. The zero result perhaps argues for a broader description of the messages than the nine features chosen by Coulthard for

Table 33.4 Example coding of text message

Text message	im	I am	am not / I'm not/	aint/	ive/	ave/	my/ myself/	me/ meself/	of/	off/	to=2 - space/	to=2 + space/	cu/	cya/	fone/	phone	shit/	shite/
got puddings and tissues in me pnckets.ave2 hope he rings b4 he goes up back in 30	0	0	0	0	0	1	0	1	0	0	0	1	0	0	0	0	0	0

their absolute discriminatory power. Nevertheless, the zero score makes the point statistically that Coulthard was making descriptively; Nicholl's and Hodgson's texts are demonstrably stylistically distinct from one another. We have demonstrated that pair-wise distinctiveness exists in this case. It is possible to reinforce this assertion by statistical testing. The appropriate test is a one-sample t-test and this shows a significant reduction in similarity when messages paired between the two authors are compared with Nicholl's within-author pairs ($t_{(109)}$ = 12.02, p < 0.01, Cohen's d = 1.55). There is also a significant reduction in similarity when the between-author pairs are compared with Hodgson's within-author pairs ($t_{(41)}$ = 3.79, p < 0.01, Cohen's d = 0.81). Collectively these results demonstrate statistically consistency of style within the text messages of Nicholl and consistency in the style within the text messages of Hodgson and also distinctiveness between the two styles.

Thus far, only texts of known authorship have been examined. The forensic questions require consideration of the disputed messages. When these disputed messages are paired with Nicholl's messages these mixed pairs are shown to be significantly less similar than the Nicholl-only pairs of messages ($t_{(145)}$ = 9.38, p < 0.01, Cohen's d = 1.41). In contrast to this result there is no significant reduction in similarity when pairs of texts known to have been written by Hodgson are compared with pairs with one Hodgson text and one disputed message ($t_{(62)}$ = 8.36, p = 0.41, Cohen's d = 0.14). In summary, Nicholl's and Hodgson's styles each demonstrate a degree of internal consistency and distinctiveness from one another. Nicholl's texts can also be shown to be distinctively different from the disputed texts but Hodgson's texts cannot.

This statistical demonstration of pair-wise distinctiveness and its post hoc application to Coulthard's case supports but adds little evidential weight to Coulthard's own descriptive analysis. Being able to measure consistency and distinctiveness is a methodological advance in that it allows some quantification of stylistic distance between groups of texts and thus some quantification of probabilities that one group of texts is inconsistent with another. The method however is intended to address only pair-wise distinctiveness. This distinctiveness can be shown to exist irrespective of whether there is any strong explanation for it and in this sense the method might be said to be idiolect free.

The pair-wise approach, does, however, suggest a further method for demonstrating population-level distinctiveness. The forensic psychology studies investigate which sets of features are most discriminating at a population level (e.g. Woodhams and Toye 2007) and a similar analysis can be carried out on text messaging features. Such an analysis would help determine empirically which sorts of features are most useful in idiolectal discrimination. Such an empirical finding might then have theoretical implications. For example, it might be shown that in text messaging a tendency for abbreviation is more generally discriminating between authors than the use of grammatical ellipsis. If such a finding arose, it would provoke questions as to why one type of feature might show more between–author variation than another.

This is just one aspect of the considerable further work to be carried out on these techniques and some of it is already underway. A general description of texting language is already developing outside of the forensic field (e.g. Crystal 2008) and this is already proving useful in exploring the population-level questions. In addition the statistical techniques used in case linkage are also under rapid development not least with the creation of a taxonomic similarity measure (Woodhams *et al.* 2007a) developed in relation to sexual crime. The application of this taxonomic similarity to text messaging forensics is also being explored. In spite of the speed of development, it is already possible to reflect on the implications of methods such as these for understandings of idiolect and of the role of idiolectal theories in forensic casework.

Implications for theories of idiolect

As we have seen, it is possible to construct a method for authorship analysis based on stylistic variation. The steps which comprise this method can be clearly described and followed to produce replicable results on the same data set and can also be applied to different data sets. The method primarily demonstrates that different authors can be consistent and distinctive in their style of textual production. This does not mean that individuals are absolutely consistent; language is naturally variable. Neither does it mean that every author will be consistent in the same way. This method allows for and detects the fact that one author may be consistent in, for example, a form of abbreviation, whilst another author may tend to punctuate in an idiosyncratic manner. This is a strength of this method and it is a contrast with more traditional stylometric approaches. The stylometric approaches tend to carry with them the assumption that a 'good' marker or feature of authorship is one which will show between-author variation and within-author consistency across a sample of authors (e.g. Chaski 2001; Grant 2007). Examples of such stylometric markers might include measures involving word frequency distributions, frequency of use of functional words, or measures of syntactic structures. Many stylo-metric approaches are very successful in dealing with longer texts written in standard language variants but they do tend to struggle with the short and fragmentary language of text messaging.

Using the technique described here, it is possible to demonstrate not only consistency but also to show pair-wise distinctiveness between text messages by two authors. Observation of stylistic consistency and distinctiveness in this way is good evidence that idiolect exists. Observation that the writings of some, many or most authors can be dis-criminated using stylometric markers of authorship is also good evidence that idiolect exists. As I have argued above, however, mere observation and description of consistency and distinctiveness is not a theory of idiolect. Theories have to have explanatory power. Any investigation limiting itself to observation and description of consistency and dis-tinctiveness in authorship style might fairly be considered idiolect free authorship analysis.

It is possible to draw separate parallel conclusions outlining the possible contribution to a theory of idiolect of both the stylistic and the cognitivist stylometric approaches to authorship analysis.

Using a more stylistic, sociolinguistic or variationist approach in observing specific features of a particular author's language we may be able to explain some of those fea-tures by appealing to that author's social and linguistic background. The use of 'me' for 'my' in a text message might, for example, be explained in terms of the dialect back-ground and pronunciation of that writer. Such specific explanations, however, may not always be available to us. Why a second individual with a similar social and geographic background, and perhaps with a similar pronunciation, chooses to follow the more standard spelling may well seem inexplicable. At a general level, however, we can provide some explanation of stylistic variation between individuals. This explanation rests on the fact that individuals vary in their social and linguistic history, and in their lexical priming, and this produces variation in the sociolinguistic resources upon which they draw for language production.

521

Using a more stylometric approach in observing specific features in an individual's language may not commit one to an interest in cognitivist theories of language production but many stylometric measures will be based on insights derived from such theories. To claim that a measure is based on a cognitive or neuropsychological understanding of language production does not of itself explain between-author variation in that measure. Without relying on sociolinguistic explanations, why two individuals with similar cognitive and neurological structures vary in such a measure may well seem inexplicable. At a general level, however, we can provide some explanation of cognitive variation between individuals. This explanation rests on the fact that individuals may show some variation in their biology, but there will also be variation in sociolinguistic history and thus in lexical priming, and this produces personalisation of the neurological and cognitive resources upon which they draw for language production.

With regard to theories of idiolect, I would argue that consistency and pair-wise distinctiveness are matters of empirical observation upon which forensic authorship analysis can rely. Any such comparison must be based in sound methods which can convincingly demonstrate the degrees of consistency and distinctiveness found in a particular comparison of texts known to have been written by the authors but the results of such comparison have little to contribute to theoretical discussions of idiolect. Such matters of fact do not of themselves explain idiolect. The possibility of pair-wise distinctiveness, wider distinctiveness or even population-level distinctiveness, however, does seem to demand some explanation. To the extent that it can be shown that one individual's language is measurably unique in the population of all language users, this is, or would be, an astounding fact. Even less extreme individual linguistic distinctiveness demands a combination of cognitive and social investigation and demands a combination of cognitive and social explanations. Observable individual linguistic uniqueness demands a theory of idiolect.

Further reading

Crystal, D. (2008) *Txtng: The Gr8 Db8*, Oxford: OUP.

Grant, T. (2007) 'Quantifying evidence for forensic authorship analysis', *International Journal of Speech, Language and the Law*, 14: 1–25.

Greenfield, S. (2008) *ID: The Quest for Identity in the 21st Century*, London: Sceptre.

Howald, B.S. (2009) 'Authorship attribution under the rules of evidence: Empirical approaches in the layperson legal system', *International Journal of Speech, Language and the Law*, 15: 219–47.

Johnstone, B. (2009) 'Stance, style, and the linguistic individual', in Jaffe, A. (ed.) *Sociolinguistic Perspectives on Stance*, Oxford: Oxford University Press.

34

Plagiarism

Four forensic linguists' responses to suspected plagiarism

Malcolm Coulthard, Alison Johnson,
Krzysztof Kredens and David Woolls

Introduction

Although according to Angélil-Carter (2002: 2) 'plagiarism is a modern Western concept which arose with the introduction of copyright laws in the Eighteenth century', its avoidance is now a basic plank of respectable academic scholarship. Student plagiarism is currently a hot topic, at least for those who teach and study in British and American universities. There are companies selling both off-the-shelf and written-to-order term papers and others, like *Turnitin.com*, offering electronic detection services in an attempt to prevent the use of such essays. In 2002, the Vice Chancellor of Monash University was forced to resign when examples of frequent plagiarism were discovered in his earlier academic work (www.abc.net.au/news/newsitems/200207/s604549.htm [last accessed 18 August 2009]) and most Anglo-American universities have warnings against and definitions of plagiarism on their websites. Indeed, Pennycook (1996: 213) notes that in the mid-1990s Stanford University's documents about plagiarism were reproduced by the University of Oregon, apparently without attribution, and suggests, whimsically, that there is 'one set of standards for the guardians of truth and knowledge and another for those seeking entry'.

At its simplest, plagiarism, or more accurately the type of plagiarism linguists are competent to deal with, is the theft, or unacknowledged use, of text created by another. Part of the definition on the University of Birmingham website when Coulthard and Johnson worked there in the late 1990s was as follows – the highlighting in bold is ours as we wish to focus on those phrases.

PLAGIARISM AND CHEATING IN EXAMINATIONS
Plagiarism is a form of cheating in which the student **tries to pass off someone else's work as his or her own**. ... **Typically, substantial passages are 'lifted' verbatim** from a particular source **without proper attribution** having been

made. To avoid suspicion of plagiarism, students should make appropriate use of references and footnotes.

(University of Birmingham http://artsweb.bham.ac.uk/arthistory/
declaration_of_aship.htm [accessed 1 August 2009])

A first problem is that, in the University of Birmingham definition, plagiarism is presented as a conscious attempt to deceive – 'tries to pass off' – however, teachers and markers cannot evaluate intentions, but only whether a text actually *does* pass off – in other words many students may indeed be guilty of 'passing off' without being guilty of intending or 'trying to pass off'. For this reason the responsibility of knowing how to attribute properly and checking that one has done so, must be passed over to the student, so that no teacher has to decide if the unacknowledged borrowing was deliberate or not. University departments now tend to insist that students sign a cover which they attach to all work submitted for assessment which says something like the following:

I know what plagiarism is and I confirm that none of this work is plagiarised.

Semantically, the most difficult part of the Birmingham definition of plagiarism is: 'typically, substantial passages are lifted verbatim'. What in fact do 'substantial' and 'verbatim' mean? Certainly, the detection program *Turnitin* works by searching for longish identical strings, but much deliberate plagiarism is not of this kind at all. In the two short passages (examples 1a and 1b), taken from published biographies of the American philanthropist Andrew Carnegie (one by J. F. Wall 1970 and one by J. Mackay 1997), we can see substantial similarities, which we have highlighted with **bold** for identical words and *italic* for close paraphrases, but Mackay strenuously denied plagiarism and would certainly not be considered guilty under the University of Birmingham characterisation.

(1) Two biographies of Andrew Carnegie
(1a) With all of these problems it was little short of a miracle that the "stichting" board *was ready to lay* the corner**stone** for the building *in* **the summer of 1907** at **the opening of the Second Hague International Conference**. It then **took six** *more* **years** before **the Palace** *was completed* during which time there *continued to be squabbles* **over details**, *modifications of architectural plans and lengthy discussions about furnishings* … *For ten years the Temple of* **Peace** was *a storm of* **controversy**, **but** *at last,* **on 28 August 1913, the** Grand **Opening ceremon***ies were held.*

(Wall 1970, *Andrew Carnegie*)

(1b) The *foundation* **stone** *was not laid until* **the summer of 1907**, *in nice time for* **the opening of the Second Hague International Conference**. Actual construction of **the palace took** *a further* **six years**, delayed and exacerbated by constant *bickering* **over details**, *specifications and materials*. *For an entire decade* the **Peace** *Palace* was *bedevilled by* **controversy, but** *finally*, **on 28 August 1913, the opening ceremon**y *was performed.*

(Mackay 1997, *Little Boss: A Life of Andrew Carnegie*)

Nevertheless, many academics would want to classify the Mackay text as plagiarism on the grounds that it presents very similar content, in the same sequence, using many of the same words. Over the last decade, linguistic studies have focused on manual and computationally assisted detection of plagiarism with particular reference to lexical similarities in authorship in student writing (Coulthard 2004; Johnson 1997; Woolls 2003, 2006). As we will see below, we now have a computer program which will enable plagiarism of the similar but not always identical type to be detected.

Academic and non-academic plagiarism is widely discussed in the media and is a constant cause for concern at exam boards in the compulsory and post-compulsory education sectors and, despite widespread use of plagiarism detection services and implementation of plagiarism guidelines, policies and learning contracts across universities, plagiarism continues to exist there and in the wider world too. Most notorious in recent times was the *Da Vinci Code* case, which Coulthard and Johnson (2007: 3) discuss briefly. In this chapter we examine what the practice actually entails, focusing on lexical, grammatical and textual features that contribute to making texts linguistically similar enough to be considered plagiarised. We ask similar questions to the two posed by Johnson (1997): how different are separately authored texts on the same topic and how similar must two texts be before one can assert with confidence that one was derived from the other or both from a third text? And we examine plagiarism in both pedagogic and non-pedagogic contexts in student writing and in writing in the wider world and in publishing. We detail some of the practical issues that arise when we examine what writers actually do with material they share between each other or take from electronic sources. After our linguistic analysis of what plagiarism is, we include a number of case studies from the work of each of the authors. These exemplify some of the differing strategies used when writers take and adapt material from web sources: cut-and-paste, re-arrangement, insertion, omission, rewriting and 'patchwriting' (Howard 1999; Pecorari 2002). One case looks at student responses to an essay task and a second case considers the rewriting of extended unacknowledged passages from a published book, identifying the problematic adaptive strategies used by the student. Two more come from the area of translation studies and another two from court cases.

The implications of these case studies are considered, and we suggest that the lessons learned have preventative potential. By examining what happens when writers fail to acknowledge their borrowings properly, it is possible to equip future learner-writers for the challenging task of writing successfully. But first, we offer a brief example of some casework in student plagiarism, which illustrates the kinds of claims that suspected plagiarists make and the kinds of responses that forensic linguists can give.

Writer claims and forensic linguists' responses

At one point in fairly quick succession two of us, Coulthard and Woolls, worked on three similar cases of student plagiarism. In all three, the student had been found guilty by their university and penalised severely. All three protested their innocence and asked for our help; two had already hired solicitors and indeed paid us for our work. One, a law student, having sent us copies of the claimed plagiarised texts, made the mistake of going on holiday and leaving us with the phone number of her mother. We asked these mother for more comparative data and she obligingly sent a set of floppies containing not only most of her daughter's assessments for the year, but also other documents authored, according to the Properties file, by 'A satisfied Microsoft User' a year earlier. Two of these documents were obviously sources for two of the submitted assessments.

A second, a student nurse, accused of plagiarising from a fellow student, admitted that she had plagiarised from the same student the previous year and indeed sent us two pairs of essays, so that we could see what she did when she really was plagiarising! In this case, there was no doubt that the two students had produced texts that were too similar to be independent. The only question was the direction of the borrowing, as both claimed the other was the guilty one. On the face of it, our client was the less likely – her text had fewer spelling mistakes and more cited references with dates and page numbers. However, an hour in the Medical library (how much time Google would have saved) showed that the nurse had simply taken attributed, but not cited, reports from the other essay and turned them into quotations with invented page numbers. So the opening of this paragraph could have been rewritten with a false attribution as:

> A second, a student nurse, accused of plagiarising from a fellow student, admitted that she 'had plagiarised from the same student the previous year'.
>
> (Coulthard 2001: 79)

A third student provided perhaps the case with the most unexpected resolution. Plagiarism from a published source had been identified and the student acknowledged that the work was plagiarised but claimed that he had not written the essays in question. This case required stylometric analysis and from both the analytical and computational perspectives, we found that the disputed work looked very similar to the undisputed work provided to us. When we reported this to our client's lawyers and explained that we could not offer any support to him, they said their client was unhappy with this opinion and enclosed further undisputed material for our analysis to reinforce his claims.

Both the original and additional material was in hard copy rather than electronic format and, during the preparation process of the second batch for electronic entry, Woolls noted a peculiarity of this printed material. While the text lines were absolutely straight against the top and bottom edges of the paper, the left and right margins were not vertically parallel but gradually moved from left to right, forming a slight but measurable rhomboid shape rather than the perfect rectangle justified text should produce. Checking back against the disputed texts, the same pattern was found in them. Although we obviously could not definitively say that the same printer had been used, the presence of the same printing idiosyncrasy in both disputed and undisputed material led us to return all the material to the client's lawyers, as the presence of a consistent mechanical fault simply reinforced our opinion that there was common authorship.

The linguistic analysis of textual similarity and plagiarism

Johnson (1997) established that a quantitative statistical comparison of the vocabulary used in two or more texts can support a qualitative textual analysis, in order to establish whether a case of plagiarism has occurred. Using software available to her (*Vocalyse* and *File Comparison*, both early programs written by Woolls which developed into *Copycatch Gold* 2002), she showed that comparing the use of particular vocabularies between writers was helpful in deciding whether texts were uniquely produced. The most significant finding of her research was that measures of the following lexical features provided useful confirmatory results:

i) a high percentage of shared vocabulary;
ii) a high number of shared *hapax legomena* (words that occur only once in a text);
iii) a low number of unique *hapax legomena*.

In Case Study (1) of Bill, Bob and Barry discussed below, the three student writers main-tained that they had written their texts independently and no plagiarism or collusion had occurred, but the lexical and structural similarities between the texts suggested the oppo-site. The question in this, as in all cases of suspected plagiarism and disputed authorship, is: what linguistic evidence is there that leads to an opinion about the significance of the similarity of the texts and therefore suspected plagiarism and what counter-evidence is there that the texts are different and therefore uniquely authored? Next, we outline the ways in which a computer can be programmed to look for plagiarism, by examining lexis.

Looking for plagiarism electronically

Coulthard and Johnson's (2007, Chapter 9) discussion of plagiarism draws attention to the need for electronic assistance to handle the task of identifying and verifying textual authorship because of the massive amount of relevant material that is available electro-nically. They explicitly mention one program, *Copycatch Gold* (Woolls 2002), which implements the principles for identifying suspicious matching across texts. Woolls (in this volume) explores the underlying concept of similarity which underlies all automated efforts in this field.

Identity

If anyone takes the immediately preceding paragraph in its entirety and inserts it into another text, human readers who have already read it will normally recognise it when reading the other text. They might also detect a style shift between the transported para-graph and its new surrounding co-text. They might then be sufficiently intrigued to track down the source text to confirm their suspicions. But there is another way of approaching the task and here a computer program can come into play. Several things will be true:

1. the number of characters will be identical (576, including spaces)
2. the frequency count of each character will be identical (i.e. $< a > = 34, \ldots < x > = 4$)
3. the number of words will be identical (83)
4. the number of sentences will be identical (3)
5. the sentence lengths will be identical
6. all sequences of characters will be identical
7. all sequences of words will be identical
8. all sequences of sentences will be identical

Notice that all the above require no comprehension or knowledge of the prior existence of the text and are features which would not be used by a human at all, as they are not readily accessible, nor required for the task. For a computer programmer, on the other hand, these features all have the property of being countable and readily identifiable, and using any one of them provides a means of recognising that the two paragraphs are related. In the field of information retrieval, this aspect of texts is frequently called a fingerprint. Using mathematical techniques, it is possible to produce a single number for a document which will uniquely identify it. Producing such a fingerprint and looking in other locations which store each document by its fingerprint code, a computer system can identify or retrieve duplicates. By extending the principle to paragraphs, to sentences or to short sequences of words, individual sections of texts can be located in the same way.

Handling change

As we have pointed out above, wholesale copying is the exception rather than the rule in plagiarism cases. The reason for this becomes obvious if we consider an example. In the paragraph above we have a sentence starting 'Woolls (in this volume) ... '. The opening of this sentence is going to need changing by anyone borrowing the paragraph. The simplest option might be to omit the sentence altogether, which would change the paragraph and document level fingerprint. Another option would be to re-write the sentence as, for example: 'Underlying all automated efforts in this field is the concept of similarity, as discussed in Woolls (forthcoming).' This has produced some re-ordering, the omission of some words and the insertion of others. The sentence count for the paragraph remains the same as in the original, but all the other identical features are lost. However, it can be seen from the items highlighted in bold in example (2) below, that two sequences, one six words long and the other three words long, are present in both sentences; in addition the word 'underlying' has been retained but moved.

(2) Similarity and change
2a Original sentence:　　Woolls (in this volume) explores the underlying **concept of similarity** which lies behind **all automated efforts in this field.**
2b Changed sentence:　　Underlying **all automated efforts in this field** is the **concept of similarity**, as discussed in Woolls (2010).

The retention of some word sequences is typically necessary for anyone attempting to conceal copying, because their primary need is that the sentences they modify are still coherent and it is difficult to borrow even just two successive sentences from a source text and to do so without reproducing at least some of the phrases in their entirety. And it is this fact that underlies the success of most of the web plagiarism detection tools, which generally operate by looking, using fingerprinting or simple word sequences of between six and eight identical words. As can be seen, only one such sequence exists in (2b) (the other sequence is of only three words), but that would be sufficient to identify the sentence as a candidate for plagiarism, as we will see below.

Web plagiarism

Web plagiarism detection provides a particular challenge because of the sheer amount of data available on the internet. Although it is obvious that only a small subset of the billions of pages of electronic material held in both public and private sites is likely to be appropriate for any particular academic or commercial assignment, finding related material is extremely challenging. A human reader finding a suspect passage has recourse to search engines which, at the time of writing (2009), allow searching on the basis of a single word, an unordered set of words, or a running sequence of words, which are identified by enclosing the sequence in inverted commas, and these words are indexed at the full document level. Staying with example (2), while we were writing a draft of this chapter on 1st August 2009, we performed a web search, using Google™, for "all automated efforts in this field" as a complete phrase. No exact matches were returned. This contrasts with 64,700 results for a search on "concept of similarity", which reduced to 41,200 when expanded to "the concept of similarity". When we searched for "underlying concept of similarity" only five matches were found, four from the field of information retrieval and one from the field of secondary education. With this search information, we have ascertained that the original sentence (2a) doesn't have a recorded source outside this chapter.

But this doesn't help us with the problem of the re-written sentence (2b), a problem facing both human analysts and computer programs. We were only able to refine our search to include "underlying" because we had access to the source text. Knowing that we have at least 41,200 potential sources for our suspect text doesn't help us much at all, nor does the complete absence of a match for the second phrase, since we cannot even work on the assumption that both phrases occur in the same document, let alone in the same sentence in both documents. Yet that is what we need for accurate identification of plagiarism. Humans and computer programs alike have to be able to identify suitable sequences, perform searches and assess the results. Humans will tend to home in on particularly interesting or significant passages, but will not know whether or to what extent they have been changed. Computer programs are capable of looking for any or all sequences in a whole document, given sufficient computational time and resources, but they can only determine significance based on rules provided by the programmer.

However, this does not mean that web plagiarism detection is impossible. Rather the contrary. The usefulness of sequence identification in programmatic terms is that it doesn't have to occur more than once in a given document for that document to be identified as a candidate source. Given the need we mentioned above for writers who borrow (and plagiarise) to retain phrases in order, we have an explanation for why such computer programs have been successful in identifying web sources. But to control the computational load it is necessary for such systems to impose some minimum word sequence level on the task, as our example indicates, and a minimum length of between six and eight words is currently the most likely mechanism used, although the actual details of commercial detection engines are clearly not generally available. But, as example (2) also shows, it does not take too much alteration of the basic text to make the task of the detection program extremely difficult. One way of tackling this problem is to build a corpus of the most likely sources for any given field, be it academia, journalism or law, and then use that as the primary area of search with specialist detection methodologies. This approach was pioneered by iParadigms Inc., a company with its origins in Berkeley, California. It requires all data submitted for comparison to be made permanently available for future comparisons, so providing a growing and broad base for future source identification, and this has the advantage that it greatly reduces reliance on the indexing and search methodologies of general search engines. When all the data is available, it is possible to build indexes which are specifically geared around the nature of the problem, which in this case is generally the identification in two or more supposedly independently produced texts of identical word sequences. Woolls (this volume) explores what can be done when this type of data is available.

Case studies

Case study 1 – Bill, Bob and Barry

Johnson's (1997) study investigated a case of suspected plagiarism among three student texts and three further control texts (students who answered the same question but

Table 34.1 Lexical similarities between Bill, Bob and Barry

Bill	Bob	Barry
It is essential for all teachers **to understand the history of Britain as a multi-racial, multi-cultural nation.**	In order for teachers to competently acknowledge the ethnic minority, **it is essential to understand the history of Britain as a multi-racial, multi-cultural nation.**	It is very important for us as educators to realise that **Britain as a** nation has become both multiracial and multicultural.

where no plagiarism was suspected). Her labelling of the six texts as T1, 2 and 3 for the suspect *Texts* and C1, 2 and 3 for the *Control* texts has since been replaced in plagiarism talks given by Johnson and Woolls, the suspect texts becoming Bill, Bob and Barry and the control texts Gill, Gerry and George (it is easier to remember them as Baddies and Goodies). In a 500-word sample from the beginning of each essay, Johnson found identical words and sequences of words. Table 34.1 shows the identical sequences in bold that were easily observed. However, we can also see that there is much more similarity between the texts than just identical sequences, because some of the alterations discussed above have been made. Bill and Bob share 'it is essential' and 'to understand the history of Britain as a multi-racial, multi-cultural nation', though one of them, Bob, uses the 14 words in a continuous sequence, whereas the other, Bill, has a sequence of three and then shortly afterwards a sequence of eleven lexical items. Barry has only one shared identical string a mere three words long, 'Britain as a' but has made major changes to the lexis which means that his text paraphrases, rather than directly repeats, those of Bill and Bob. Nevertheless, it is clearly the same sentence. 'Essential' is semantically equivalent to 'important', 'multiracial and multicultural' are not hyphenated, their order is reversed and they are linked by 'and'. Any measure of identity therefore will under-report the degree of similarity between the texts and a more subtle measure of similarity has to be devised, as Woolls (this volume), demonstrates.

This kind of qualitative analysis gives the reader a general impression of the scale of similarity, but a quantitative analysis of vocabulary is more accurate and is essential for any serious allegation of plagiarism outside teaching and learning. Johnson's (1997) quantitative analysis of the first 500 words of each of the six essays allowed some evaluation of different measures of identity between texts and also provided an opportunity for comparison. Some of her results are shown in Table 34.2.

Table 34.2 Similarity and uniqueness of voice in six student essays as percentages

	Bill	Bob	Barry	Gill	Gerry	George
Lexical hapaxes as % of total lexical items	79.7%	76.4%	81.9%	82.1%	77.9%	75.0%
Unique lexical tokens as a % of tokens in file	16.6%	15.3%	39.1%	61.1%	54.3%	54.4%
Shared lexical types/tokens as % of total tokens		12.5%/49.3%			2.6%/17.9%	

The percentage of lexical hapaxes in the essays (the nouns, verb, adjectives and adverbs that are used only once by each writer, in row 1) did not vary a great deal between the writers, but Johnson compared the wordlists for these hapaxes and found that while Bill, Bob and Barry shared a large number of once-only items, Gill, Gerry and George had overwhelmingly individual once-only vocabularies. The uniqueness of Gill, Gerry and George's voices was highlighted when the lexical tokens unique to each writer were calculated as a percentage of the total tokens in each file (Table 34.2, row 2) and the similarity between the suspect texts was seen to be high when compared with the lexical words in common between the 'Goodies'. Even writing on the same topic, these writers shared only 17.9% of lexical tokens, compared with the 'Baddies' who shared very nearly half.

Case study 2 – plagiarising a translation

There is a long tradition of people translating texts into other languages without acknowledgement, which started well before there was a concept of the ownership of ideas and their textualisations and before plagiarism came to be seen as an academic sin. It is obviously more difficult to demonstrate plagiarism through translation than same-language plagiarism, although one looks first for the evidence of shared content and the very similar sequencing of the content typical of same-language plagiarism that we noticed in the Carnegie example (1).

Of more linguistic interest are cases where we have not one but two or more translations of the same text for comparison purposes. One would naturally expect more similarity between two translated texts that between two original texts written on the same topic, because the translations are necessarily constrained by the wording of the original. Thus, for example, one would expect translations of the same text to have more shared hapaxes and even more shared phrases and consequently for it to be more difficult to demonstrate plagiarism.

Turell (2004) discusses the case of one Spanish translator of Shakespeare's *Julius Caesar* accusing the author of a later translation of plagiarism and outlines the linguistic strategies she used to demonstrate it. She was fortunate in that there were also two earlier published translations in addition to the supposed plagiarised text itself and the one from which it was claimed to have been plagiarised. She could thus compare all four translations (using *Copycatch Gold*, Woolls 2002), each with every other one, a total of six comparisons, and then work out an expected baseline for shared vocabulary, for shared hapax words and for shared hapax phrases. Table 34.3 is a summary of her findings.

Table 34.3 Comparisons between four translated texts

Criterion	Non-suspect comparisons	Suspect comparison
% of shared vocabulary	64.3; 67.3; 67.7; 73.5; 75.3	83.9; i.e. 11.4% greater than next largest.
No. of shared hapaxes	393; 432; 445; 668; 698	1049; i.e. 50.3% greater than next largest.
No. of shared hapax phrases	31, 46, 46, 47, 48	164; i.e. 242% greater than next largest

Case study 3 – plagiarising a dictionary

If plagiarism in student writing or in translations of literary texts raises interesting questions, matters get even more complicated in the case of lexicography. Surprisingly, plagiarism in dictionary making is rarely discussed in the literature (though see Williams 1992). Single words, with the exception of trademarked ones, are not protected by copyright. Also, crucially, defining the same lexical items for different dictionaries is bound to involve similar word choices and all lexicographers consult previous dictionaries, so the essential question that arises is the degree of creativity possible within the editorial conventions and typographical constraints characteristic of dictionary entries. In the case of bilingual dictionaries, plagiarism of a significant proportion of entries cannot be detected let alone demonstrated – for example, the majority of the names for plants, animals, and geographical locations have only one equivalent in the target language.

All this is inevitably exploited by some dictionary-makers. Burchfield (1992) discusses the case of the Australian *Macquarie Dictionary* (1981), which he found to be based on the *Hamlyn Encyclopedic World Dictionary* (1971), which in turn he traced back to *The American College Dictionary* (1947). He evaluated the amount of material shared by all three dictionaries at about 93 per cent and commented that 'the exact wording and ordering of senses has been carried over, and deemed appropriate, from an American dictionary of 1947 to a British one of 1971 and then to an Australian one of 1981' (Burchfield 1992: 153).

One notable case with a judicial finale involved a nine-year legal battle in Polish courts between PWN (Polish Scientific Publishers) and Kurpisz Publishing House. PWN claimed that a significant proportion of the entries in the *Practical Dictionary of Contemporary Polish* (1994) published by Kurpisz were identical to those found in PWN's *Dictionary of the Polish Language* (1978). Kurpisz contended that all dictionaries are alike by their very nature and hence cannot be original creations, and that in any case the Polish language belonged to the whole nation. The court of the first instance rejected PWN's claim, a verdict upheld by the Court of Appeal. The case then went to Poland's Supreme Court, which in November 2002 opined that

> The choice of headwords, the way of defining, and the composition of difficult entries are instances of creative activity of authors of Polish language dictionaries, as defined in Chapter 1 of the Copyright Act of 4th February 1994.
>
> (Supreme Court of the Republic of Poland, PWN
> v. Kurpisz, II CKN 1289/00)

The relevant section of Chapter 1 of the Polish Copyright Act, which is Article 3 reads:

> Collections, anthologies, selections and data bases are subject to copyright, even if they contain unprotected material, if the selection made, arrangement or composition are creative in character.
>
> (Polish Copyright Act 1994 (1.3))

The Supreme Court's opinion was binding on the Court of Appeal, which then reviewed the case in 2004 and returned a verdict ordering Kurpisz to pay substantial damages to PWN.

In November 2002, one of the present authors, Kredens, was approached by the creator of a software package consisting of both a Polish–English and an English–Polish translation tool and a Polish–English and English–Polish dictionary. He claimed that an overwhelming part of his two dictionaries had found their way into a competitor's translation program, which also included two dictionaries, and was published after the said software package. What follows is a brief description of the analysis undertaken on the English–Polish parts of the competing sets.

A simple qualitative analysis revealed obvious similarities, but, even if the two dictionaries had been produced independently, one would expect, from what was said above, significant similarity. However, in this case, most of the entries examined were identical and the dictionaries shared a number of other significant attributes. One of them was the overrepresentation in both dictionaries of medical terms starting with the morpheme *hyper* (e.g. hyperthermaesthesia, hyperthermalgesia, hyperthermia, etc.). The client's dictionary had 336 of those, the competitor's 326, and two English–Polish dictionaries chosen as reference material (see below) contained only two. Also overrepresented were biblical terms and Scottish dialect forms. These impressionistic observations obviously had to be backed up by substantive findings, in essence by obtaining quantitative data.

The two English–Polish dictionaries both contained some 110,000 entries. A statistically representative sample of 1,200 randomly generated entries was first examined, revealing that 70 per cent of the entries were translated identically. To ensure that figure was not the result of chance and could be safely extrapolated onto the dictionaries in their entirety, four more analytical categories were chosen, which included:

- most frequent words; these normally have many senses, which are difficult to categorise and order, and the relevant entries are thus unlikely to be identical across any two dictionaries;
- verbs of movement (walk, run, swim, etc.); motion events are lexicalised differently in English and Polish, with the latter making extensive use of reflexive verbs. A thesaurus was used to identify such entries, which were then cross-checked;
- evaluative adjectives (ugly, beautiful, great, etc.); these were also identified with the help of a thesaurus and then cross-checked;
- culture-bound terms (e.g. cider, quango, tabloid, Oxbridge), which often do not exist or have no direct equivalent in the target language and so have to be explained.

Subsequently, the figures obtained were compared with those derived from two other dictionaries – *Practical English–Polish Dictionary* (Stanisławski *et al.* 1986) and *English–Polish Dictionary* (Fisiak 1996) – and are presented in Table 34.4 below (where A is the

Table 34.4 Comparisons between the two competing dictionaries and two reference dictionaries (figures show percentages of shared definitions between pairs of dictionaries)

	A–B	C–D	A–C	A–D	B–C	B–D
Sample	70	16	11	12	12	12
Most frequent	65	14	8	8	7	6
Verbs	55	15	9	11	8	10
Adjectives	60	12	7	11	7	9
Culture-bound terms	95	4	4	6	4	6

client's dictionary, B – the allegedly offending dictionary, C – Stanisławski *et al.* 1986 and D – Fisiak 1996).

Following this simple statistical analysis, an error analysis was carried out and identical spelling mistakes as well as instances of shared inadequate lexicographic practice were identified, as exemplified in the following:

a) Spelling mistakes common to both dictionaries[1] – these were identified following close reading of randomly chosen entries.
   - desintegration [disintegration]
   - gairish [garish]
   - metting-pot [melting-pot]
   - oi-quenching [oil-quenching]

b) Inadequate lexicographic practice:
   - *off-licence* – koncesja alkoholowa, koncesja na wynos (A and B)
     (the most obvious translation of *sklep monopolowy* [a shop where alcohol is sold] is missing; it is absent also from Stanisławski *et al.* 1986 but present in Fisiak 1996)
   - *convertible* – samochód otwarty (A); kabriolet, samochód otwarty (B)
     (*samochód otwarty* [open car], though grammatically and semantically correct, is a made-up phrase with no evidence of usage in the sense of 'a convertible'" in the two most popular corpora of Polish (NKJP and PELCRA[2]); that sense is missing from Stanisławski *et al.* 1986 and present in Fisiak 1996 as *kabriolet* only).

The totality of these findings allowed the forensic linguist to produce the following conclusions:

Either:	The author(s) of dictionary A used lexicographic substance most of which had been created by the author(s) of dictionary B;
Or:	the author(s) of dictionary B used lexicographic substance most of which had been created by the author(s) of dictionary A;
Or:	the author(s) of dictionary A and the author(s) of dictionary B used lexicographic substance most of which had been created by the author(s) of a third, unknown source.

After eight years, the case is still ongoing, although for reasons better suited to a volume on civil law procedure.

Case study 4 – a plagiarised police statement

There are many examples in the UK from pre-PACE (1994) times of the police creating confession statements or interview records by copying and adapting text from other documents – a process parallel to plagiarism and detectable in the same way. One of the most famous is the police interview with Molloy which was a crucial part of the Carl Bridgewater murder investigation; for details see Coulthard (2004) or Coulthard and Johnson (2007: 191–96). Example (3) is another example, this time road rage incident statements written by two police officers with, it was claimed, no collaboration, consultation or even underlying notes. It is evident that while there is some information that is not shared between the statements, much of the wording is identical (note these statements have been anonymised, but the crucial linguistic features are authentic).

In the extracts from Statements F and M in example (3), which have been inter-lineated to facilitate comparison, **bold** is used to mark those morphemes, words and phrases which are shared by the two statements and *italic* is used to indicate text which is a simple substitution caused by the change of narrator, e.g. I/we, my/our.

(3)   Statement F and Statement M interlineated

F: **The** driver **did not indicate and did not leave a safe distance between our** two
M: **The** vehicle **didn't indicate and** the driver **didn't leave a safe distance between our**
F: **vehicles,** which meant *I* had **to brake hard** in order **to avoid colli**ding with the rear of
M: **vehicles,** causing *Miss Ford* **to break hard to avoid** a **colli**sion. I felt the front of
M: our car lower and the seat belt tighten across my chest, as I physically moved forward in
F: this vehicle. *I* **sounded** *my* **car horn alert**ing **the driver of** this vehicle to *my* **presence**
M: my seat. *Miss Ford* **sounded** *our* **car horn** to **alert the driver of** the Peugeot of *our* **presence**.

Of course, in justifying one's opinion that one text was derived from the other, it is good to have other supportive observations. In this case

a)   both officers made the same spelling mistake 'quite' for 'quiet' in the same context
     F: became suddenly quite
     M: became very quite.
b)   at the same point in the narrative they both used the same non-standard past tense 'broke' for 'braked'.
     F: the driver of the white saloon broke hard
     M: Miss Ford broke hard
c)   they chose on four separate occasions to make the same decision about the need or otherwise for an area code, for example:
     M: travelling south on Brighton Hill, NW4.
     F: travelling South bound on BRIGHTON HILL NW4.
     M: I continued south along Brighton Hill.
     F: We continued along Brighton Hill

Case study 5 – suspect witness statements

A similar example comes from an asylum case where Coulthard was requested by the Refugee Legal Centre to undertake a linguistic examination of a series of 49 witness statements concerning the alleged participation of Celestin Ugirashebuja, the former *bourgmestre* of Kigoma in Rwanda, in the killings of Tutsi civilians in 1994 (see www.trial-ch.org/en/trial-watch/profile/db/facts/celestin_ugirashebuja_610.html [accessed 17 August 2009]). Coulthard was asked to comment on any linguistic oddities in the statements and to evaluate their significance. Surprisingly, he was originally asked to work on English translations of the statements, even though the originals were written in French, though some of them may have been taken through an interpreter. The court insisted on working with translations, but Coulthard's evidence was based on the French originals of which selections are presented in (4a and b). As in (3) **bold** is used to indicate identity across several statements, *italic* to indicate paraphrases and/or identity across two state-ments and statements have been interlineated to aid comparison.

(4a) **... ordonné la mise en place des barrières ...**
  38 M UGIRASHEBUJA **a ordonné la mise en place des barrières** *afin que* les *personnes persécutées* ailleurs ne viennent pas *s'y réfugier*
  47 *Il a aussi* **ordonné la mise en place des barrières**, *afin qu'*aucun *Tutsi ne puisse s'échapper*
  45 *Il a aussi* **ordonné la mise en place des barrières**, *pour empêcher la fuite de l'ennemi.*
  46 *Il a* **ordonné la mise en place des barrières** *pour empêcher la fuite des traîtres*

(4b) **Hilux/couleur**
  19 le **véhicule commun***al, un véhicule* **de marque Hilux de couleur blanche**
  20 du **véhicule commun***ale, une voiture*   **de couleur blanche**
  23   *Il s'agissait d'* **une camionnette de marque Hilux de couleur blanche**
  22 du **véhicule** *de la* **commun***e,* **une camionnette de marque hilux de couleur** *rouge.*
  12   *Il s'agissait d'* **une camionnette Toyota Hilux de couleur** *rouge*
  16 j'ai pu remarquer la **camionnette de marque Toyota Hilux de couleur** *rouge,*
  8   une camionnette de marque hilux
  18.   *un véhicule* **de marque Toyota**   **de couleur** *rouge*

On the basis of these and similar examples Coulthard argues that the statements could not have been produced independently, which did not of course mean that they were untrue, nor even that they were created like the police statement above by one being based on a pre-existing written text. One could for instance imagine a lawyer who went to interview with a set of common detailed questions to many of which he elicited confirmatory answers producing statements with significant numbers of shared phrases. What the court needed to know in this case was that, whatever else these statements were, they were not produced by witnesses freely recounting events to someone who simply noted down what they said.

Case study 6 – handling complex documents electronically

Special consideration needs to be given to some documents, either because of issues arising during conversion between word processed format and the plain text frequently required between comparison programs, or because of the requirement to compare only individual parts of answer papers with their equivalent parts in other answer papers. In regard to the first problem, Woolls has found that embedded tables, charts and spreadsheets offer particularly difficult challenges when using formatted document to text converters, because most such converters tend to output each cell of a table or spreadsheet as a separate line. For programs based either on paragraph breaks or full sentence identification, this produces a very large number of one word paragraphs or sentences, and most comparison methods require more than one word to provide meaningful results. Users of comparison programs need to be clearly advised as to what particular programs will and will not be able to compare.

As an example of the second problem, in professional examinations done online students are frequently tested on their knowledge of the complexities of a business decision by use of a scenario, setting out the full fictitious but realistic history of a particular business or medical issue. They are required to read this scenario, and then answer a series of questions dealing with legal or financial aspects of a business scenario, or the diagnostic or ethical aspects raised in a medical scenario. In such cases, the comparison requirement is not document with document, but question with question. This is partly because the underlying level of repetition will obviously rise if several answers refer back to the same base scenario, so many answers will accidentally look more like several of the answers in comparison documents if not treated separately, and partly because the questions frequently cover discrete areas of the problem and some might lend themselves to plagiarism from source data more than others.

While human assessors can normally identify which answers relate to which questions, however unclear or inconsistent the signals provided by the candidates, it is by no means easy for a computer program designed to handle large quantities of electronic data to do the same. For example, here are some possibilities for referring to the first question in such a paper. 'Question 1', 'quest 1', 'Q 1', 'Q1', 'Question One', 'One', 'Answer 1', '1.'. None of these is incorrect, all are capable of interpretation by a human reader, but all offer different problems to a computer system: space or no space between words and numbers, words for numbers, different forms of reference to the answer, upper and lower case use, punctuation and many other variants. Then, assuming a program can identify the first question, a programmer has to devise a way of finding out where questions 2, 3, etc. start and finish and indeed whether all the questions have been answered and if they have been answered in sequence.

So, it is vital that any plagiarism detection solution for multiple online examination answers to a common scenario is as accurate as possible and contains a reporting mechanism detailing where disruption to the identification process might have happened (for example, if the student didn't identify the question they were answering). If this is not done, then an answer to question five, which might be on finance, might well end up being compared with an answer to question three, which might cover legal issues. Comparison of this false pair would produce a low level of similarity, and once the error has been made, the imbalanced comparison would continue throughout the answer paper, missing any direct copying between the true answers to questions three and five in a pair of answer papers.

The lesson from this is that any set of documents where direct comparison of the full text is unsuitable needs to be closely examined for internal reference consistency and completeness, and it must be expected that not all such documents will be capable of reliable comparison by electronic methods.

Conclusion

The case studies have demonstrated just a few of the ways in which writers plagiarise and have shown some of the forensic linguistic responses and solutions to suspected plagiarism. We have also demonstrated a range of methodologies that are innovatively generated in the course of investigating problematic and suspect texts. These include increasingly more ingenious and accurate software solutions, or more precisely software that produces sentence level and lexical outputs for forensic linguists to interpret and which enables us to make decisions and provide opinions in allegations of plagiarism. The reader will have recognised that responses to plagiarism are necessarily both quantitative and qualitative and involve manual and computational generation of results and careful analysis and interpretation in order to provide an opinion. What the reader will also have recognised is that techniques are rigorous and increasingly sophisticated and this alone ensures that plagiarism prevention is possible, if writers are aware of the power of forensic linguistics and linguists to analyse their writing. Woolls (this volume) provides concrete evidence of the power of detection to be preventative in the case of his Universities and Colleges Admissions Service (UCAS) work. After running a pilot project and then implementing a detection program for two full years of admissions, the number of applicants who plagiarised their personal statements fell between January 2008 and January 2009 by 26%. Prevention and detection of plagiarism therefore work hand-in-hand and an ultimate goal is to reduce levels of plagiarism even further, by ensuring the continuation of sophisticated detection programs, warning users of their existence and effectiveness and educating writers to have confidence in their own powers of expression.

Notes

1 Cf. Williams' discussion of 'bugwords', i.e. 'non-existent word[s] deliberately included in a dictionary, so that it can be used to support allegations of copying if it reappears in the dictionaries of other publishers'.
2 See http://nkjp.pl and http://korpus.ia.uni.lodz.pl, respectively.

Further reading

Buranen, L. and Roy, A.M. (eds) (1999) *Perspectives on Plagiarism and Intellectual Property in a Postmodern World*, Albany, NY: State University of New York Press.
Howard, Rebecca Moore (1999) *Standing in the Shadow of Giants: Plagiarists, Authors, Collaborators*, Stamford, CT: Ablex.
Love, H. (2002) *Attributing Authorship: An Introduction*, Cambridge: Cambridge University Press.
Pecorari, D. (2008) *Academic Writing and Plagiarism: A Linguistic Analysis*, London: Continuum.

Section III

New debates and new directions

35

Multimodality and forensic linguistics

Multimodal aspects of victim's narrative in direct examination

Gregory M. Matoesian

Introduction

Despite the recent spate of excellent textbooks, monographs and review essays on language and law or what is often referred to as forensic linguistics (Conley and O'Barr 2005; Gibbons 2003; Coulthard and Johnson 2007; Travers 2006; Conley 2006; Maynard 2006; Ehrlich 2001; Eades 2008b; Solan and Tiersma 2005), researchers rarely mention the role of bodily conduct and how it relates to language use in legal settings. In fact, the first major textbook in the field, *Just Words* (now in its second edition) is quite revealing in its title, representative of prevailing sentiments that legal discourse consists solely of verbal conduct.

In this chapter I demonstrate that legal discourse involves much more than *just words* and that language and embodied conduct work together as co-expressive semiotic partners – as multimodal resources – in utterance construction and the production of meaning in courtroom talk. Although multimodality encompasses written texts, material artefacts, technical devices, gesture and other semiotic forms, I limit my focus in this chapter to gesture, gaze and postural orientation and how these are interwoven into the stream of verbal activity in a rape victim's narrative during direct examination. Incorporating a broader contextual focus, I also display how multimodal resources function in the ascription of blame, constitution of identity, and the emergence of multiparty participation frameworks in her narrative performance. Focusing on just words neglects the role of multimodal activities in legal proceedings – how both language and embodied conduct mutually contextualize one another in a reciprocal dialectic – and leaves the study of forensic linguistics with an incomplete understanding of legal discourse. To borrow a line from Doug Maynard's recent work (2006: 477), studying courtroom language without the visual component "loses the phenomena" and erases relevant activities that participants orient to in legal performance. In a similar vein, Jones and LeBaron (2002: 512) note: "To systematically ignore either vocal or visible behaviors in a study of face-to-face interaction is to stunt understanding of the phenomena under investigation."

And, in his study of legal gestures, Hibbitts (1995: 51) mentions that "a fully-accurate and nuanced understanding of how the law actually works requires an appreciation of other texts in law's semiotic field."

To provide a more detailed understanding of its significance, I analyze an instance of multimodal activity from a victim in a rape trial as she addresses motivational issues during redirect examination. As Ehrlich (2001: 108–9) notes, direct examination permits the victim to construct a narrative in her own voice, making the narrative come "alive" and captivate the jury's attention, in contrast to cross-examination which involves deconstruction by the defence attorney. Re-direct (also called re-examination) examination, in particular, is of crucial significance because it allows the prosecution and victim to rebut the defence attorney's impeachment from the immediately prior cross-examination. Considered by some as the penultimate moment in the prosecution's case, the victim's narrative in this instance creates an emotionally charged moment of high drama as she discusses ulterior motives for going forward with charges against the defendant. But her narrative consists of quite a lot more than just speech. She synchronizes talk, gesture and gaze as co-expressive resources to shape a rhythmically integrated and affective form of persuasive discourse. In the process, she grounds victim resistance in a sophisticated multimodal constellation of multiple participation frames to forge identity, orchestrate epistemic stance and distribute responsibility in the sociolegal organization of sexual assault.[1] More generally, we will see how multimodal conduct is brought to bear on the local contingencies confronting the victim's motivational narrative and the incremental alignments and realignments she deploys to shape a coherent accusation against the defendant, rebutting the defence attorney's impeachment attempt in the process.

The chapter begins with a selective overview of the literature on multimodal resources (limited to gesture, gaze and postural orientation) and a discussion of the dynamic interplay between speech and bodily conduct in the production of utterances, participation and identity. I discuss theoretical advances in the study of gesture and other forms of bodily conduct to show their relevance and significance for analysing legal discourse, as well as their limitations. The next section provides background information on the rape trial and the motivational issues surrounding the case. The ensuing analysis of motivational data demonstrates not only how multimodal conduct is relevant to the study of the victim's narrative in direct examination, but also how institutional forms of speech synchronized gestures may reveal novel directions for the study of gesture, gaze and talk as situated forms of activity.

The role of gesture, gaze and posture in courtroom talk

Gesture in courtroom talk

A fleeting glimpse into any courtroom will reveal participants talking – and much more. Attorneys gaze at witnesses when addressing them, beat out the rhythm of their talk with distinct hand movements, and extend an open palm facing upward when posing a contrastive question to reveal an inconsistency in testimony. By the same token, witnesses raise their right hands when taking the oath, spread both palms upward and horizontally as if pleading to "give me a break", and curl their fingers under the thumb while extending an arm and index finger to point out the accused among co-present participants. And judges may raise a spread, outward facing palm while admonishing a witness to stop talking while they rule on a pending objection.

The orthodox way of referring to these gestural and embodied activities is to call them "nonverbal", but that implies that they, first, occur isolated from speech and, second, play a subordinate role relative to speech, little more than affective ornamentation to the more central verbal modality (Norris 2004; Jones and LeBaron 2002). Let me address both issues in turn.

According to Kendon (2004) and McNeill (1992: 37) gestures or gesticulations refer to *ad hoc* hand motions that generally, though not invariably, co-occur with speech; that is to say, gestures lack the specific form-meaning or arbitrary signifier-signified conventions of language. This omits from the category "gesticulation" language like systems that rely on form-meaning conventions such as emblems or quotable gestures (for example the "OK" sign or sign languages of the deaf, which convey meaning independently). Whereas speech is sequential, segmental, arbitrary and combinatory (that is, lower-level constituents combine to form higher-level constituents), speech synchronized gestures convey meaning instantaneously – "on the spot" as it were – and synthetically; they convey visuospatial images in co-temporal, spontaneous movements with speech, movements in which the parts derive their meaning "globally" from the whole (McNeill 2005: 10). In Figure 35.1, for example, when the victim states: "What he did to me was wro:::ng" and points to the defendant on "he", the meaning of such visual action is "co-expressive" with her words, obtaining its gestalt-like sense and significance only when combined with speech. Moreover, the deictic vector of the point begins prior to production of its lexical counterpart to synchronize their co-temporal interplay; that is, the gesture stroke (or meaning conveying phrase of the gesture) accompanies its speech counterpart so that both arrive simultaneously at the climactic moment of meaning-making (McNeill 1992). As Kendon (2004) has shown in some detail, and as we will see in the analysis later, speakers continually adjust and readjust "speech-gesture ensembles" so that one coordinates with the other to achieve discursive balance and semantic coherence – coherent courses of improvisational action.

Thus, rather than being separate or isolated sign systems, gesture and speech constitute dynamically fused multimodal signal streams that feed into utterance construction and the production of discourse coherence. If this is true, then nonverbal and verbal are inaccurate and misleading terms to conceptualize what is more accurately referred to as multimodal discourse, of which speech and gesture function as equal partners in the embodied materialization of meaning (Kendon 2004; McNeill 1992,

Figure 35.1 What he *did* to *me* was wro:::ng

2005; Goldin-Meadow 2003). Jones and LeBaron (2002: 499) capture this point forcefully when they state: "verbal and nonverbal messages have been studied separately, as though they were independent rather than co-occurring and interrelated phenomena."

We can see why gesture and speech play a reciprocal role in co-present interaction if we address the second item above: the misconception that gesture plays a subordinate role to speech. If gestures were minor embellishments of verbal action then we could perhaps dispense with a description of their contribution to discourse on the grounds that they are mere redundant supplements to speech. However, gestures may be subordinate to speech on some occasions, superordinate on others, and may work equally on still others (Norris 2004). Whatever the degree of interplay, speech synchronized gestures rarely convey the same information as their lexical counterparts, often producing information not captured adequately or as vividly in speech. Because they *perform* meaning visually, gestures add another dimension to speech: complementing or clarifying verbal messages, performing distinct speech acts, intensifying commitment to an assertion (functioning as stance markers), foregrounding information, coordinating the rhythm of speech – parsing it into significant segments – and pointing out objects of attention in the extralinguistic world via spatial–temporal proximity (Kendon 2004: 281–82). According to Cassell and McNeill (1991: 376): "certain aspects of events may be conveyed in gesture and not in speech, or vice versa, or different aspects may be conveyed in each medium, giving us a more complete view of the speaker's conception of the event." For example, we will observe (see Figure 35.1) when the victim states, "what he did to me was wrong", she simultaneously

1. points towards the defendant to create a focus of joint attention,
2. beats out the rhythm of her words using the same pointing gesture to foreground points of significance, and
3. in so doing bestows an emotionally charged epistemic stance to her words: performs an accusatory speech act.

Focusing on the verbal component of her message alone would exclude the dramatic features of this interactional episode and the affective lesson it imparts (to the jury) in the motivational dialogue. Indeed, as Goldin-Meadow (2003: 3) notes: "To ignore gesture is to ignore part of the conversation."

In the semiotic division of labor, gestures do not merely encode or represent spatio-visual information; they constitute embodied actions that elaborate or even transform the content of verbal conduct, creating a dynamic fusion of disparate yet complementary modes of expression to yield a more vivid, coherent and integrated *performance* of meaning in social interaction.

Gaze and postural orientation in courtroom talk

Along with gesture, gaze and postural orientation (the direction in which people position their bodies) often accompany speech (but not as the same necessary accompaniments as gestures) to create multimodal laminations of meaning construction in discourse (Goodwin 1981). Although the study of gesture has received the most theoretical development in recent scholarship, gaze and postural orientation often coordinate with both speech and gesture in interaction to:

(1) select the recipient of an utterance,
(2) create a focus of joint attention,
(3) display engagement with or disengagement from select participants, and
(4) most important for the chapter, contextualize emergent forms of participation in the temporally unfolding rhythms of situated activity, distributing multiple layers of multiparty involvement simultaneously based on institutional roles and responsibilities.

As we will see shortly, the victim deploys gaze and postural orientation – in concert with talk and gesture – to distribute differential legal obligations to specific participants and assign their emergent relevance in the ongoing narration, revealing an improvisational density and flexibility in the interpenetration of multiple sign systems.

As I demonstrate in the ensuing analyses, a more adequate conceptualization of legal language requires a detailed appreciation and understanding of the role of multimodal channels of interaction and their meaning making potential in context. If courtroom discourse is multimodal and if multimodal conduct conveys meanings not necessarily transmitted by verbal means alone, then it follows that omitting such information may obscure a more comprehensive and robust description of what people are actually doing in legal proceedings – and thus "lose" the phenomenon.

Limitations and methodological implications of multimodal analysis

Before turning to the data and analysis, two methodological issues – perhaps specific to courtroom discourse – need to be broached.

(1) There are practical and logistical considerations that figure in the use of multi-modal forms of data. In their informative overview, Jones and LeBaron (2002) recommend that 'future studies of face-to-face interaction be grounded in audio-visual records'. While this would be an optimal scenario for studying courtroom interaction, it is often not feasible. Frequently, video recordings of the proceedings are not permitted (at least not in the US nor in the UK) and even in those cases where they are, it is quite different from videotaping everyday conversations where researchers can position camera angle (or even deploy multiple cameras) to include the entire set of participants. Instead, researchers have to rely on third parties (like Court TV), which means that the available visual record will be selective in what is recorded, and rarely will all engaged participants and relevant interactive contours of bodily conduct be captured on video. And such limitations apply to the current data also.

(2) Except for doctor–patient encounters (see Heath 1986), most studies of gesture and multimodal conduct have been carried out on everyday conversations on the one hand or in experimental settings on the other (see Matoesian 2008a, 2008b for exceptions in trial talk). Neither institutional interaction in general nor multimodal interaction in the adversary context in particular has been the topic of systematic description and analysis, leaving researchers with a host of empirical questions to contemplate. Does multimodal conduct operate in distinct ways in the courtroom, specifically tailored to the local contingencies and combative logic of trial talk?

Similarly, most studies of speech synchronized gesture have analysed how they figure as integrated meaning-making resources in utterance construction and in the production of coherent courses of action. But in the highly adversarial setting of the rape trial does multimodal conduct organize more substantive strategies, such as the production of accusations, blame and motivation? Does it circulate in the articulation of moral stance and social identity, indexing broader forms of sociolegal organization? In the conflict laden exchanges in the courtroom, do hybrid and multifunctional forms emerge, often simultaneously? These are just a few of the issues relevant to both the study of legal discourse and gesture.

I turn now to the main analysis of the chapter. In the ensuing case, we will see in concrete detail how the victim's ulterior motives during re-direct materialize in the synchronization of speech, gaze and gesture and how incorporating the integration of these semiotic resources into the analysis of legal discourse offers a new direction for future studies in forensic linguistics in general and for direct examination in particular.

Direct examination of the victim in the William Kennedy Smith rape trial

Background to data extract (1)

The William Kennedy Smith rape trial was one of the most infamous and widely publicized trials of the last century, involving a member of the famous Kennedy family and the daughter of a wealthy industrialist in West Palm Beach, Florida. Patricia Bowman met Smith at the trendy Au Bar nightclub in the early morning hours of March 30, 1991. After the club closed around 3 a.m., she gave Smith a ride home to the Kennedy estate, where (a short time later) she claimed he raped her while the two were on the lawn.

A crucial part of the rape case, like most date and acquaintance cases, involved the issue of motivation for making the charges. The defence (represented by Roy Black) proposed that Bowman had ulterior or extra-legal motives for making the charges: that she disliked men, that she was interested in fame or money, that she was mentally unbalanced, and that she felt rejected or betrayed by the defendant, who had "led her on" regarding his true intentions during the course of the evening (to mention but a few). On the other hand, the prosecution claimed that the victim was motivated solely by legal factors relevant to the sexual assault. After a lengthy cross-examination, in which the defence attributed a host of unsavoury ulterior motives to the victim (see Matoesian 2001), the prosecuting attorney (in re-direct) posed the following question, in extract (1), to the victim. (There is an accompanying DVD clip of the entire data set on the website accompanying this book available at: http://www.forensiclinguistics.net/.)

(1) Victim re-direct examination
(PA = Prosecuting Attorney; DA = Defence Attorney; J = Judge; V = Victim; D = Defendant; p = point; b = beat; pb = pointing beat; IFT = index finger touching thumb.)

001   PA: Do you have any ulterior motive for going through this Ms Bowman?
002   (1.7)

```
003  V:    Yes.
004                          (.6)
005  PA:   What is that?
006                          (.4)
007  DA:   Objection yer honor (.6) motivation
                          [
008  V:                      ((gaze moves toward DA))
009                          (2.3)
010  J:    Overruled.
                    [
011  V:              ((gaze returns to PA))
012                      (1.7)
013  V:    ((V moves from home position to gaze and point at D)) =
           (p)        (pb)    (pb)       (pb+hold)
014  V:    = What he did to me was wro:::ng (1.3)
           [((gaze and left hand pointing toward D at turn-initial position))
           ((short beats on did and was))
           ((post stroke hold on wro:::ng into the 1.3 pause))
           ((on did gaze moves to PA))

           (p)          (pb pb pb)
015        I have a child
           [((points to herself on I then downward bunched fingers point
           with index finger extended on child))
016                   (0.8)
           ((point and gaze moves toward D during pause))
                       (p)        (pb)      (pb) (pb+hold)
017        ((in-breath)) What he did to me was wro:::ng
           ((gaze shifts to PA on was, to jury on post-stroke hold))
018                   (1.0)
           ((during pause slight head shift to the right toward jury))
                       (b)
019        n' it's not right (.)
           [((gesture shifts to PA))
           ((gaze to PA on n' it's, shifts to jury on not right))
           ((first head shift increment to right towards jury))

           ((IFT)) (b)      (b)        (b)
020        n' I don't want to live the rest of my life
           [((gesture shifts to PA))
           ((gaze to PA, shifts to jury on the rest))
           ((second head shift increment to right))
021        ((arm and finger shifts to point to D))

                   (p) (pb) (pb+hold)
022        in fear of that man
           [((gaze at PA, then shifts to jury on post-stroke hold))
           ((third head shift increment to right))
023                   (0.5)
```

	(b)	(b)
024	n' I don't wanna be responsible for him doin it	
	[[((gaze to PA))	((jury)) (PA)

	(b)
025	to somebody else.
026	DA: I object yer honor.
027	V: [(((return to home position+gaze+head direction to DA))

Embodied accusations

In rape trials – like other criminal trials – defence attorneys routinely raise questions about the victim's extra-legal motives for making the accusation, and the case under scrutiny here represents a poignant instance. During cross-examination, the defence questioned the victim at length about ulterior motives for fabricating the charge against the defendant, some conscious, others unconscious: that she disliked men, that she was hurt because the defendant would not let her spend the night, that she was mentally disturbed, that she was looking for publicity, that she was upset about being "used" sexually and being "misled" by the defendant's true intentions. By ascribing ulterior motives, the defence assembles an interpretive template for framing and assessing the credibility of the victim's account, an account based not on legally relevant criteria but on malicious factors irrelevant to ultimate issue in the case.

By the same token, the prosecution and victim must convince the jury otherwise: that the victim's accusation consists solely of legally relevant facts. In line 1, the prosecuting attorney begins her re-direct examination of the victim with a question about ulterior motives "for going through with this", and after the victim's avowal ("Yes") she poses the further question: "What is that?" That the victim admits possessing ulterior motives seems, on the face of it, a rather unorthodox response because the defence rather than prosecution typically ascribes such motives to impeach the victim's credibility in rape trials. Given the defence attorney's vigorous imputation of ulterior motives in the prior stage of questioning, however, more than a simple denial appears warranted in response.

After the objection sequence, we see the victim steer the logic of motive ascription and avowal in a quite unanticipated yet favourable direction, elaborating her 'ulterior' motive with the fused relative in line 14: "What he did to me was wro:::ng." And there is more than a verbal component to the answer, for if we consider the victim's actions in line 13, notice that she begins with an embodied response well before the start of the fused relative. Following the judge's overrule on the objection, she turns from DA to PA, moves out of home or rest position (Sacks and Schegloff 2002), and raises her left arm/wrist and finger to point at the defendant: an elevation and extension of the arm in a bent elbow position with the index finger extended and other fingers tightly curled under the thumb. As she switches on the deictic vector of the point, she also shifts postural alignment and projects gaze toward the defendant, creating him as the focus of joint attention. As her utterance proceeds in line 14, the pointing gesture coincides with onset of the verbal component ("What he") – a delicately laced synchronization of verbal and visual modalities so that both arrive simultaneously in a semantically coherent course of action. Just as important, while the victim realigns gaze from the defendant to the prosecuting attorney on "did" she maintains the pointing gesture at the defendant – a noticeably marked post-stroke hold (where the gesture is suspended in position for a period of time after the gesture stroke) – not only over the entire verbal component, but also into the 1.3 second utterance final pause (in line 14, Figure 35.1).

But the victim does more than orchestrate a semantically coherent and temporally synchronized course of gesture-speech action; her pointing gesture does more than indicate the defendant's bearing from a deictic centre. In fact, the pointing gesture involves quite a lot more than just pointing – more than indicating the defendant's location in space.

According to Kendon (2003), McNeill (2005) and Kita (2003), index finger pointing refers to those actions whose primary or sole function is to indicate direction, and in lines 13–14 we indeed see how ostensive gestural deixis is directionally anchored, projecting a vector from the finger to the defendant. As she switches on the spatial vector, we see gesture, gaze and speech align perfectly in the production of her utterance (each arriving simultaneously on the pronoun "he"), and that reflects our prior discussion of the joint interplay between speech and gesture: that speakers adjust and readjust gesture–speech modalities to achieve intricately interwoven structures of discursive action.

When we dissect this in more microscopic detail, however, notice that her pointing gesture evolves into short beats on the stressed syllables "*did*" and "*me*", and a series of unaccented "shaking" beats on "wro:::ng". As mentioned previously, beats refer to the rhythmic function of gestures – how gestures visualize or (perhaps more accurately) orchestrate aspects of discursive structure through horizontal and/or vertical movements. According to Streeck (2008), they enact the musical and informational flow of an utterance, highlighting points of emphasis, parsing significant segments into discretely organized units of relevance. In this case, the victim resets the pointing gesture as a multifunctional – double duty – narrative resource for not only switching on the deictic vector but also mapping out significant segments of her utterance, fusing the deictic on the one hand with the pragmatic function on the other to create a hybrid gesture of considerable complexity. When these two functions collide and fuse, they yield an accusatory moral stance that ascribes blame and allocates responsibility for the sexual assault. Put another way, gestural deixis mutates into accusatory beats. Indeed, upon closer inspection, the pointing beat recalibrates into an accusatory gesture during vowel lengthening (on "wro:::ng") and further into the 1.3 second ensuing pause, where it not only stands alone as a post-stroke hold but simultaneously displays an unmarked finger shake (three micro beats while pointing at the defendant) – intensifying blame by foregrounding the defendant as a joint focus of attention.

In a recent work, Goodwin (2003) has demonstrated how the ostensibly simple deictic gesture of pointing derives its meaning from the broader stream of semiotic activities in which it is embedded, and in line 14 (Figure 35.1) we can witness such meaning construction in the victim's narrative-in-progress. First, she maintains index finger extension in a post-stroke hold toward the defendant while simultaneously withholding speech, and second shifts participation structure via gaze realignment toward the prosecuting attorney to map an accusatory moral stance onto the deictic vector of the point: a highly affective and emphatic stance toward the information imparted. That is, once the deictic vector rotates into directional alignment she retools and redeploys it as a beat to hammer out points of emphasis. Just as germane, pointing and shaking an accusatory finger at the defendant while directing talk to a different recipient packs an additional modal punch, transforming her "ulterior" motives into an accusatory account. And that imagistic meaning would be lost without detailed consideration of the embodied component.

Thus far we have seen how gestures and other bodily actions possess a type of emergent flexibility and multifunctionality that, in concert with speech, are specifically tailored and adapted to the contingencies of direct examination: assembling accusations and blame (and, as we will see, in a more or less "ulterior" strategy in legal terms). Moreover, although the victim's words convey very little stress, her utterance is still laden with affective evaluation – with intense modal meaning – in the temporal coordination of bodily stance and speech, forms of meaning that would be lost to description and analysis by focusing only on the latter. As we will see below, she is just getting warmed up.

Gesture and the emergent organization of maternal identity

In line 14, the victim realigns gaze from the defendant to the prosecuting attorney on the *do*-verb, and in line 15 (Figures 35.2 and 35.3), she continues this gaze pattern in the ensuing comment: "I have a child". On the first person pronoun, Bowman points to herself with the left hand but then immediately, in a fluid improvisation, aborts the point and produces a downward gesture consisting of several bunched finger beats (with the fingers facing down and palm inwards) that reach the stroke phase on "child". In this supple movement, she transforms personal reference deixis with the extended index finger to a bunched three or four-finger display to make an emphatic point; her self-reflexive finger point transforms into the bunched gesture on the downward motion, a type of discontinuous gliding gesture that begins as a self point but one displaced and merged immediately into a different form that synchronizes with her production of the noun phrase "child". Put another way, she accelerates tempo of the self point and then

Figure 35.2 |

Figure 35.3 have a *child*

implements a cut-off to reconfigure a new gesture that coordinates with the emphatic finger points on "child".

Mobilizing an ingenious demonstration of displaced rhythm to preserve the integrity of talk–gesture synchronicity, she produces a parenthetical afterthought or aside – but not an unimportant one. While the defence attributed an array of unseemly motives – that she was a woman scorned or revengeful – the victim reframes ulterior motives as an issue of moral authority, a discourse of maternal responsibility. She contextualizes gender identity not as sexual relation (a woman picked up in a bar) but as a family relation, where the downward gesture on child may be metaphoric in the sense that the child is lower in age and smaller than herself. The defendant did not merely sexually assault a woman but a mother with a child, and the bunched finger beats, by visualizing both pragmatic and propositional structure in an emphatic display of bodily stance, intensify the immorality of such a crime. Thus we see the role of gesture not only to coordinate interaction, adjusting and readjusting its form and trajectory to keep pace with the emergent contingencies of utterance construction, but also in concert with speech, to contextualize maternal identity, activate epistemic stance, and build creative accusatory accounts in legal performance. We see how identity and stance are not only realized through grammatical resources but also contextually situated and multimodally emergent.

Repeating and recycling the accusation

Where is the victim's ulterior motive in all this? What is becoming transparent at this stage is that the victim's avowal of ulterior motive represents less a rebuttal of the defence attorney's impeachment strategy than a symbolic vehicle for assembling a litany of accusations against the defendant. Doubtless, the only thing "ulterior" is not the victim's motive but her deployment of motive as an interactional resource for attacking the defendant's moral character. Still, and with much greater precision, the victim and the prosecuting attorney mobilize ulterior motive as an explicit metapragmatic resource for shaping a sonorous recitation of moral condemnation against the defendant, steering the topic toward his unscrupulous behaviour rather than the victim's state of mind. Although legal research often notes that rape victims in particular and witnesses in general are powerless on the stand, less research has shown how witnesses compose a persuasive voice in court, and the victim's accusatory narrative here constitutes, *mutatis mutandis*, a mirror image of defence strategy: a powerful form of multimodal resistance.

Figure 35.4 What he did to me was wro:::ng

In line 17 (Figure 35.4), the narrative develops further as the victim repeats and recycles her accusation ("What he did to me was wro:::ng"), repeating not only verbal but visual conduct as well, returning her pointing gesture to the defendant during the pause in line 16 and gazing in his direction on "was". Although the victim repeats the fused relative, she alters gestural configuration in terms of tempo and elevation: slower tempo and steep upward/downward motions for more pronounced emphasis. That is to say, the second recycled and repeated fused relative is accompanied by marked pointing beats – heightened elevation on the upswing and increased acceleration on the down-swing – though still incorporating the autonomous post-stroke gestural hold toward the defendant during vowel lengthening (on "wro:::ng") and after utterance completion. By withholding speech on the post-stroke hold, the victim bestows a powerful sense of modal intensity to her verbal conduct: a pronounced shift in the fused relative, now the first component in an emerging multimodal parallel structure.

Just as crucial, she not only shifts gaze to the prosecuting attorney after her initial gaze at the defendant but also, while still maintaining a pointing gesture in his direction, rea-ligns her gaze and postural orientation to the jury during the post-stroke hold (albeit briefly), adding an emergent dimension of subordinate participation into the unfolding narration. In a supple display of multimodal dexterity, she intimates a high degree of contempt toward the defendant – perhaps inviting the jury to agree with that assess-ment – by pointing at him while simultaneously moving into a state of gaze with other participants, participants responsible for prosecuting and evaluating his actions. To "rearrange" (Goffman 1959), she directs a form of "uncivil" inattention toward the defendant by discussing his blame relevant actions and immoral traits while directing that talk to other co-present recipients.

The sequence progresses through a multimodal parallel structure consisting of the contracted coordinating conjunction (explicitly marking the parallel structure in pro-gress), general ascription concerning the defendant's actions built as a contrast off the prior blame component ("n' it's not right") and elevated pointing beat to the prosecuting attorney: a steeply marked elevation on the contracted conjunction and acceleration on the downswing stroke "right" in line 19 (Figure 35.5).

From the pointing beat's downswing position (at the bottom of the motion) in Figure 35.5, she retracts her hand shape to execute an index finger touching thumb or precision gesture (in which the tip of the thumb touches the tip of the index finger to form, as Kendon (2004: 225) notes, a "ring" shape that "makes prominent some fact or

Figure 35.5 n' it's not right

Figure 35.6 n'I don't want to live the rest of my life

idea"), directs this new gesture (still with the left hand) via a low vertical arc movement to the jurors and aligns gaze to the jury box in the middle of the utterance (on "rest" in line 20) to shape a new – and main – participation structure. Next, she redeploys the precision gesture to map beats onto stressed syllables and, in the process, mobilizes postural adjustments in the form of three distinct incremental shifts to the right (on lines 19, 20 and 22), a progression of short head shifts imposed on each intonation unit that culminate in perfect visual alignment with the jury and that accentuate their institutional relevance. Finally, the third verbal component in the emerging parallel structure repeats the contracted coordinating conjunction to link the accusatory litany in Figure 35.6 ("n'I don't want to live the rest of my life in fear of that man").

Thus far, we have seen how the victim's visual activity moves laterally/horizontally from defendant to prosecutor to jury (inter turn participation), and up/down vertically on the first two pointing beat gestures (intra turn). At the same time, her verbal activity consists of parallel blame imputations regarding the defendant's behaviour coordinated through the contracted conjunctions. The first two parts of the litany refer to general blame attributes ("wrong" and "not right"). The third and fourth segments, however, shift to more specific, first person mental attributes ("n' I don't want to live the rest of my life in fear of that man" and "n' I don't want to be responsible for him doin it to somebody else") that repeat the verb of cognition, contracted negative and infinitive.

Consider the relation between grammar, legal identity and the body as this unfolds. The first general attribution is in the past tense ("was wro:::ng"), in which gaze and pointing beat are directed at the defendant, indicating past behaviour. The second intonation unit ("it's") is in the present tense and directed to the prosecuting attorney, who is institutionally responsible for prosecuting the case in the here and now. On the other hand, the jury, who would be responsible for evaluating the crime in the future deliberation, is the primary (not sole) recipient of the specific components in the parallel structure ("I don't want to live" and "I don't want to be responsible"), each referring to grammatically marked future projections. Specifically, the want-type (mental desire verb "want" to the infinitival complement) infinitives encode future projections, and it is the jury's institutionally endowed obligation to evaluate these; that is to say, the jury is institutionally responsible for the future outcome of the case. Just as crucial, the shift from general moral evaluations ("not right", "wrong") to specific cognitive verbs ("wanna") corresponds metaphorically to gestural shape. The victim deploys pointing beats for the former, but shifts to the gesture of precision or specificity in the latter, and this alternation in gestural form activates not only a change in participant alignment, but

553

also a new relation to her utterance (from past and present to future projection): an embodied shift in footing (Goffman 1981a). In so doing, she contextualizes a delicate or vulnerable identity (perhaps a delicate gesture for a delicate woman) and that her fate (and the fate of other potential victims) will soon be in the jury's hands. As Morris (1977: 58) observes: the ring or precision gesture is used when the speaker wants to "express himself delicately and with great exactness. This hand emphasizes the fineness of the points he is stressing." As the reader will also notice in the video clip, ring gesture onset is prominently marked – almost as if she is "winding up" for a delivery – to convey precisely this point.

Here we can see in vivid detail how grammar, gesture, and participation merge into a multimodal constellation of institutional relevance. We see how stylistic features of visual and verbal conduct are not only rhythmically integrated – how verbal and embodied parallelism intersect in polyrhythmic modalities – but institutionally anchored as well. When her gesture moves from the prosecutor to the jury, she shifts from a steeply elevated vertical pointing motion to a horizontal index finger tip touching thumb gesture movement with a very low arc trajectory en route. Once at its participation destination the gesture is recalibrated and redeployed to beat out her main points of emphasis, still using the precision gesture shape. In a strikingly nimble multimodal performance, both gestural form and trajectory are significantly altered to recontextualize the new participation structure and new activity being transacted: a different participation structure in play with a different texture of legal relevance. In more theoretical terms, gesture shapes the infrastructural context in which such poetic improvisation can take place.

Multimodal and multiparty forms of participation

At the end of the intonation unit ("in *fear* of *that man*" in line 22 and Figure 35.7), the victim reactivates the deictic vector – retracting the precision gesture and restoring the index finger extension – but not until gesture onset begins, early enough to co-occur with its verbal complement, the noticeably stressed demonstrative "*that man*". As this occurs, she realigns her point back to the defendant while simultaneously adjusting her gaze and postural orientation to both jury and prosecuting attorney (indeed, the stressed demonstrative imparts a marked pragmatic sense in addition to reference). In so doing, she maps an emphatic moral stance onto the deictic vector of the point, while maintaining multimodal frames of participation encompassing multiple strands of relevance. That is, she not only switches to the deictic vector to coincide with the demonstrative but, once synchronized, resets it to beat out the rhythm of her accusation, engaging the

Figure 35.7 in *fear* of *that man*

Figure 35.8 n' I don't want to be responsible...

defendant without disengaging from either the jury or the prosecuting attorney by maintaining gaze and postural orientation. Following this, she, first, adds the final element to the parallel structure by repeating the contracted coordinating conjunction, cognitive verb, and infinitive; and, second, maintains the pointing beat into the indefinite pronoun ("n' I don't wanna be responsible for him doin it to somebody else" in lines 24–25 and Figure 35.8) to complete the dense rhythmic structure: a gestural hybrid of deixis, beat, and bodily stance.

More substantively, the victim reframes ulterior motives as an issue of moral order, of moral authority. By downplaying the sexual and foregrounding a protective mother identity, she demonstrates how she is responsible not only for protecting a child but for protecting others against future crimes by this sexual predator, engaging the jury's sense of responsibility for the future well being of other vulnerable women in the process. It is her responsibility to keep him from doing "it" again. Still more symbolically, this demonstrates how the cultural voice of maternal authority emerges not only from denotational text but in the intricate polyrhythmic texture of multimodal form itself; that is to say, the victim not only conveys her sentiments to the jury and PA but also, in and through the accusatory beats, fosters the impression of reprimanding an obstinate and impenitent child – the defendant. Just as germane to the above point, by pointing at the defendant while directing her gaze and postural orientation to other participants she projects her legal identity as a rape victim: a victim unable or too afraid to gaze at her assailant. In the process, we can see how, in Michael Silverstein's (1998: 226) words, "what was said maps onto what was done" or how "denotational text maps onto interacting text". The victim not only constructs forms of participation but also enacts culture in the iconic form of multimodal performance.

Back to ulterior motives

If we consider the re-direct narrative in technical legal terms, the victim's ulterior motives neither resurrect her credibility nor broach her motivational state after a sharp defence impeachment. In a furtive turn of events, she reinforces and repeats the criminal charges against the defendant through an emotionally riveting spate of accusatory accounts. Still more accurately, she goes beyond the charge of rape to portray the defendant as a dangerous individual, shifting from the criminal act *per se* to criminal character ("in *fear* of *that man*") and moral identity ("wrong", "not right" as an entire course of conduct): an indirect attack on the defendant's moral character. That the defendant has not even taken the stand at this juncture in the case bestows a further measure of distinction to her narrative; since he has not yet taken the stand it is legally improper to attack his character unless he opens himself up to impeachment (notice the defence attorney's objection in line 26). The points I wish to make are these. First, rather than consider rape victims in the courtroom as passive recipients for defence imputations of motive, for fabricating the assault charges (often with a psychoanalytic twist), we can see how Bowman not only resists defence impeachment of motive but also assembles rather ingenious – multimodal and social organizational – resources for directing her own character attacks against the defendant. This is not to say that ulterior motives are absent in her narrative. Rather, her multimodal stance, especially her deictic beats, bequeaths a strong accusatory sense to the talk – meaning that would be lost to analytic description without considering the role of the body in and as cultural-legal action. And, second, rather than consider bodily conduct as some type of nonverbal leakage that reveals an objective inner truth (often with a psychoanalytic twist) we can see how it functions as a discursive resource in the constitution of legal realities and organization of direct examination.

Conclusion

In this chapter I have demonstrated – indeed the participant has demonstrated – how a dense constellation of multimodal resources – gaze, gesture and talk – is brought to bear on the emergent and contingent social projects confronting the victim in direct exam-ination, including accusations, identity and stance. As her narrative unfolds, we have seen how accusatory accounts are differentially distributed to institutionally anchored recipients in temporally synchronized gesture-speech units – how verbal and visual laminations of participation, legal identity and epistemic stance are generated through multimodal patterns and off-kilter rhythms. Such multimodal actions display how the law is not only *talked* but *embodied* into being as well.

In the semiotic division of labour, each multimodal increment contextualizes distinct accusatory activities and fragments legal recipiency into institutionally emergent forms of relevant participation. Speech specifies the moral grounds of the accusatory litany; pointing gestures pick out the defendant's vector in the deictic field; rhythmic beats ground affective and epistemic stance by hammering out points of significance; and gaze movements draw multiple participants into the motivational account and keep shifting institutional alignments in play simultaneously. More theoretically, bringing multimodal analysis into the realm of forensic linguistics opens up a microcosmic direction for a more discriminating exploration of how the victim can dramatize her story – construct her own voice sponta-neously – in a rhythmically intricate, highly interactive and emotionally compelling narrative, a narrative that is fluidly improvised yet uncannily synchronized. That she manages to foster such a persuasive impression reveals the value of multimodal analysis not only for direct examination in rape trials but also for legal discourse more generally.

Note

1 Participation refers to the interactive and embodied positioning of speaker and recipient roles in the micro social organization of discourse (Goodwin 2007: 53; Goodwin and Goodwin 2004). Stance possesses an array of meanings and here I use it quite generally as the *multimodal* marking of the speaker's degree of certainty of or commitment to their statement (epistemic stance) and to evaluation, attitude and affect conveyed in propositional content.

Further reading

Goodwin, C. (2003) 'Pointing as situated practice', in S. Kita (ed.) *Pointing: Where Language, Culture, and Cognition Meet*, Mahwah, NJ: Lawrence Erlbaum, 217–41.

Kendon, A. (2004) *Gesture*, New York: Cambridge University Press.

Kita, S. (2003) 'Pointing: A foundational building block of human communication', in S. Kita (ed.) *Pointing: Where Language, Culture, and Cognition Meet*, Mahwah, NJ: Lawrence Erlbaum, 1–8.

Matoesian, G. (2008) 'You might win the battle but lose the war: Multimodal, interactive, and extra-linguistic aspects of witness resistance', *Journal of English Linguistics*, 36(3): 195–219.

Norris, S. (2004) *Analyzing Multimodal Interaction*, New York: Routledge.

Sacks, H. and Schegloff, E. (2002) 'Home position', *Gesture*, 2: 133–46.

36

Terrorism and forensic linguistics

Linguistics and terrorism cases

Roger W. Shuy

Introduction

Of the ten priorities listed by the FBI on its website, the **first three** say that it will protect the US from terrorist attack, from foreign intelligence efforts at espionage, and from cyber-based, high technology crimes. The bureau's remaining priorities include combating public corruption, criminal organizations, white-collar crime and crimes of violence, protecting citizens' civil rights, supporting other crime-fighting organizations and upgrading the bureau's current technology. Note that protecting against terrorist attack is the top priority.

Successful investigations of terrorism throughout the world share the same criteria:

(1) An operation needs to have good reason to suspect that some kind of terrorist activity is happening or likely to happen. Simply trolling for possible suspects is not an acceptable procedure in any kind of law enforcement activity.

(2) Once there is good evidence to suspect terrorism, a plan for catching the suspects is conceived, which often involves undercover work, including tape-recording conversations that may lead to a conviction. This process can be tricky, because often there are suspects who interact with others who have no intention of committing a terrorist act, so the operation needs to take special care in sorting out the potentially guilty from the innocent.

(3) Next, the agent doing the tape-recording needs to elicit irrefutable evidence on tape that the target(s) are actually guilty of planning or having carried out specific acts of terrorism. This task is even trickier, because such evidence depends on the skills of the undercover agent to both avoid creating a crime and putting words into the targets' mouths while eliciting inculpatory language that will stand up at trial.

(4) Finally, the prosecutor must assess the evidence carefully and with integrity, and use it only when it satisfies the legal requirements for prosecution.

When law enforcement agencies follow these four criteria, they can produce effective and beneficial results that keep a nation's citizens safe from terrorist activities. But when they fail to do so, the results can be disastrous, in terms of the ruined lives of innocent people, depleted budget resources, misuse of personnel and the waste of huge amounts of taxpayer's money.

Without doubt, law enforcement agencies often follow the above criteria and bring terrorists to justice, but there is reason to believe that sometimes there are serious problems in the way federal law enforcement agencies go about their business. These problems include failing to locate the right suspects in the first place, failing to correctly identify what terrorist activities were planned and who actually planned or committed them and carrying out an ineffective intelligence analysis of the evidence actually collected.

A recent month-long conference on Terrorism and Security Studies was held at the George C. Marshall Center in Germany for government representatives and terrorism experts from 40 countries. The major topics included defining terrorism, the international tools and laws that had been found useful in combating it, global financing and the use of diplomacy and cooperation (Airy 2009). Unfortunately, nothing was reported about the linguistic issues discussed in this chapter.

Linguistic analysis of conversations in terrorism cases is essentially the same as that used in any other case, bribery, drug dealing or solicitation to murder, in which audio recordings constitute major evidence. This chapter highlights some of the problems that law enforcement (including anti-terrorism units) have had with language as evidence, and then illustrates these problems with a recent terrorism case in Toledo, Ohio.

Four problems

Problem 1: Finding the right suspects

A recent representative example is a 15-month undercover Homeland Security surveillance project in Maryland between March 2005 and May 2006 (*Washington Post*, 17 February 2009). The Maryland targets were peace activists and death penalty opponents, who were suspected of being terrorists. Agents spent 288 hours investigating them. Results? Nothing, even though the agency's reports revealed that among the "threats to public safety" they investigated was a poetry reading ceremony held on the anniversary of the bombing of Nagasaki.

The first problem with some terrorism investigations, then, is that government agencies can be overly suspicious of the wrong people, apparently including some 40% of the US population who oppose the death penalty and an even larger number who think the Iraq war should be ended. It would also appear that undercover agents sometimes focus their efforts on uneducated, gullible, less than perceptive, preoccupied suspects, who are likely to be easier to catch and convict. In many cases, they are newcomers to the country, often with limited English and, as a result, less sensitive to the nuances of the language used around them.

Problem 2: Determining who created the alleged crime

Sometimes an alleged crime scenario is created and encouraged by the undercover agents themselves. When this has happened in recent years, juries have sometimes acquitted the defendants, most of whom are Middle Eastern males, some already US citizens. For

559

example in the Dallas "Holy Land" case, the jurors at the first trial (which in fact ended in a mistrial), reported that they felt the undercover FBI agent had encouraged the defendants to perform acts that they would otherwise have been unlikely to carry out; in other words that the idea of committing the alleged crime was created by the investigators and not the defendants (*New York Sun*, 16 July 2007).

A similar example was the "Liberty City" case in Miami, where the criminal conspiracy was also generated by the government's own informant (*Miami Herald*, 16 May 2009), who created what he termed an "al-Qaeda oath" and then led the relatively uneducated defendants in reading it aloud on tape. They were subsequently arrested and charged with terrorism against the US. They counter-claimed that they read the oath aloud only to endear themselves to the agent in order to eventually bilk him into giving them money. Some jurors evidently believed, perhaps with considerable justification, that this was at least two steps away from any intent to plan or carry out terrorist activities.

Problem 3: Accurately determining the agendas of the targets

The FBI and Homeland Security express pride that no successful terrorist attacks have taken place in the US since 9–11, but from these and other on-going US terrorist cases, a pattern emerges that begs for linguistic analysis. Some of the accused may well be guilty of planning or attempting terrorist acts, but others may only seem to be. Careful analysis of the tape-recorded evidence can often demonstrate that they had very different agendas. By agendas here, I mean the topics that are uppermost in their minds.

Topic analysis should be carried out on all evidentiary conversations, to derive clues to intentions and agendas. No science can get inside the minds of speakers, but the topics they introduce, recycle and omit give the clearest available clues to their intentions (Shuy 1982, 1990a, 1993a, 1998b, 2001, 2005). Ignoring such data is clearly failing to carry out an adequate intelligence analysis.

Problem 4: Lack of careful intelligence analysis before suspects are indicted

In many terrorism cases, undercover agents covertly record hundreds of hours of conversations. Unfortunately, law enforcement agents and subsequent listeners, like jurors, are tempted, even inclined, to assume guilt simply because the suspects were present during the taping (Shuy 1993a). In analyses of such conversations, linguists can contribute by:

(1) using their skills in phonetics, morphology and syntax to correct the government's transcripts;
(2) using their discourse analysis, semantics and pragmatics skills to identify and keep track of the speakers' topics, themes, schemas and agendas;
(3) using their speech act skills to identify and accurately distinguish between various crucial speakers who request, promise, agree, deny, etc.; and,
(4) using their presentational skills to put all this together in a form that jurors can easily understand and remember—usually as charts and visual aids.

Such linguistic analyses are parallel to what law enforcement specialists call intelligence analysis (Godfrey and Harris 1971: 30), the primary goal of which is first to obtain accurate records of what was said by whom; then to put it all together in context;

identify and distinguish between such speech acts as agreements and denials; and determine when the targets have either not heard or not attended to what was said to them (Harris 1976: 30–34). The latter is often clarified in videotaped evidence, where it is clear that a particular target was either not present or not within hearing range of inculpatory statements made by others. The intelligence analyst should then formulate multiple hypotheses, not just the hypothesis of guilt. If s/he does not do so, the prosecution can easily go awry, as was evidenced in the famous case of *U.S. v. John DeLorean* (Shuy 1993a: 68–85).

Terrorist case example

All four of these prosecutorial problems were manifested in the 2008 Toledo, Ohio terrorism case of *US v. Mohammad Amawi, Marwan El-Hindi, and Wassim Masloum*, all convicted of terrorism in June 2008. The case provides examples of several different aspects of typical US terrorist prosecutions.

I spent seven months consulting with the attorneys for one of the defendants, Marwan El-Hindi. Linguistic analysis clearly demonstrated that El-Hindi's agenda was very different from that for which he was accused. It also showed that the undercover agent created the evidence of El-Hindi's alleged illegal intent and capitalized on El-Hindi's inability to listen carefully and interpret the agent's ambiguity, indirectness and hints. Finally, it showed that when the agent became discouraged by El-Hindi's failure to follow his encouragement to set up a terrorist training cell, he abandoned that scenario and created a new one which involved El-Hindi downloading videotapes and internet transmissions from the Middle East and emailing them to him. It was this act that led to all three men being convicted of the terrorist activity of abetting the enemy.

Background

Although all three defendants were Muslims living in Toledo, they had not even met until they were brought together briefly by the agent. Amawi, 28, was a dual citizen of the US and Jordan. El-Hindi, 44, was a naturalized US citizen from Jordan and Masloum, 26, an immigrant from Lebanon, was a legal permanent US resident. Amawi worked in a travel agency, El-Hindi was a self-employed businessman, and Masloum was a college student.

The FBI had recruited Darren Griffin, an ex-Army Special Forces member and a former drug user with unspecified money problems, who had previously worked very briefly for the FBI as a federal drug agent on a three-year contract to try to discover unspecified terrorist activities in the Toledo community. For this work, Griffin testified at trial that he was paid some $350,000.

Claiming to have his own private security business, Griffin's technique was to hang around Toledo mosques, claiming he was a recent convert to Islam and pretending to be disenchanted with US foreign policy. He grew a beard, wore Arab clothing and took on the role of what he thought to be an Islamic extremist. He told various people at the mosque that he hated the president, wanted to do violence to the US government and to train Muslims for violent jihad. He made little or no progress and, ironically, several American Muslims at the mosque actually reported him to the FBI.

Eventually, he met the three defendants, brought them together and tape-recorded their conversations. They had no previous criminal records and their alleged conspiracy was orchestrated and implemented by the agent himself. In February 2006, the defendants were charged with conspiring to kill or injure people in the Middle East, including US troops serving in Iraq and with providing the support and resources to do so. Amawi was also charged with threatening President Bush, a charge based on his severe verbal criticisms, and with distributing bomb-making information, by downloading and emailing the very videotapes that Griffin had requested. El-Hindi was accused of sharing information (the videotapes) about terrorist training activities, including plastic explosives, rockets, and bombs (the videotapes were downloaded onto his home computer). Masloum, who was present on only a couple of the tapes, was charged with requesting the agent to train him to carry out violent jihad in the Middle East. He was very overweight and wanted physical training as he was about to be drafted in the Lebanese army.

Alleged motivations of the targets

In terrorism cases the agents try to determine motivation, develop scenarios in which they can record criminal action or intent and use conversational strategies that will encourage the targets to inculpate themselves. In this case, Griffin worked hard to show that the defendants were primarily concerned with training that would lead to violent jihad, but this was not easy.

Amawi, the Toledo travel agent and devout Muslim, had recently visited his native Jordan, where he learned much about the views of friends and relatives about the Iraq war. Clearly the brightest of the three, he was technologically competent enough to access television programs and internet resources from the Middle East. The prosecution claimed that Amawi's motive was his desire to return to the Middle East and personally engage in extremist jihad.

El-Hindi, also a devout Muslim, was a bumbling business entrepreneur, whose only income at that time came from commission earned by recruiting medical students for European medical schools. A father of five, he was involved in a bitter and complicated divorce, probably an important reason for his lack of attention to what the agent was saying (or hinting) to him. On tape, over and over again El-Hindi shows his deep concerns about the educational problems of poor Muslims in the Middle East and of Muslim children in US schools. Among other half-baked projects, he wanted to buy or rent a property and open a religiously oriented school. At trial, Griffin called El-Hindi the "money man" in the alleged conspiracy, although none of El-Hindi's schemes to obtain grants had ever got even to the proposal stage.

Masloum's interest was simply to prepare for this future military service; the prosecution claimed that he wanted military training in order to commit violent jihad.

The agent's two scenarios

As is common in covert operations like this, the government had to create a believable scenario in which a possible terrorist crime might be committed. After agent Griffin began trolling for prospects at the mosque and was rebuffed by several members, he turned his attention first to Amawi, who was vocal against the Iraq war. In fact, most of the 300 hours of taped conversations were with Amawi. After Griffin ran into El-Hindi at the mosque, he was intrigued by his puffing about his business capabilities. Any potential terrorist act would need to be financed somehow and El-Hindi appeared to be a promising participant. Masloum was more an accidental afterthought, participating in very few of the conversations.

Griffin's first scenario was to get El-Hindi to recruit other Muslims to form a terrorist cell, although he never said this explicitly to El-Hindi. He talked about training people, but was very vague about what kind of training he would provide and the ambiguous word, "training" was key in the prosecution case.

Both El-Hindi and Masloum were overweight and out of shape and there is considerable evidence from the taped conversations that whenever they agreed with Griffin's offer of training, they were thinking of physical training—he was a former Special Ops soldier who claimed to be an expert in physical fitness. El-Hindi mentioned some names of friends and colleagues as possible recruits for such training, but no matter how many times Griffin reminded him, El-Hindi never got around to inviting anyone and the alleged terrorist cell never developed.

After a year or so, it became clear that the initial scenario of starting a terrorist cell was going nowhere, so Griffin and his handlers changed their scenario to what the prosecution referred to as "electronic jihad." Griffin arranged for the three men to meet for the first time for dinner at El-Hindi's home, to talk and to watch videotapes from the war in Afghanistan. Since the targets knew that Griffin was a new convert to Islam, they spent a large portion of the time talking about religious matters. The videotape of this meeting shows clearly that El-Hindi, the host, cook and meal-server, spent a great deal of his time in the kitchen, thus missing much of the ongoing conversations in the living room.

Like most immigrants, the defendants were anxious to hear news about "home," so they often watched Middle East television news programs and scoured the internet. Much of the evidence used by the government at trial was collected when Griffin asked the men to download specific programs and internet information for him. Some of it included scenes that allegedly depicted military tactics used by US and foreign armies in the Afghan and Iraqi war zones, evidence that the government said had provided Griffin with his "training" materials. It was on the basis of such evidence that the prosecutor claimed the suspects had participated in "electronic jihad." The terrorist charge against the cook, El-Hindi, came from the videos Griffin had him email to him.

Agent's conversational strategies used to implement his two scenarios

Undercover agents are encouraged to follow a three-step process in their efforts to elicit and record evidence of criminal activity or intentions (Shuy 2006: 7–9):

1. Let the suspects talk freely, thereby self-generating their own evidence of guilt. If this fails then:
2. Drop hints that the suspects might pick up on and expose their own culpability. If this fails then:
3. Represent the illegality of the enterprise clearly and unambiguously. This is a requirement of the FBI's own guidelines for agents during undercover operations (Heymann 1984).

Griffin's undercover strategy never got beyond step 2 in his conversations with El-Hindi, who talked freely on a multitude of topics (step 1), but none related to the subject of the investigation. Over half of the topics El-Hindi introduced concerned his personal problems with his divorce, his attempt to remarry and the welfare, health and education of his five young children (see also Grebler, this volume, for similar talk in another alleged terrorism case). Less frequent topics were about his various efforts at starting business ventures; his desire to establish a school for Muslim children and to help poor Muslims in the US and Middle East; his many complaints about people he thought had cheated him in past business ventures; discourses on religion; and his concern that local Muslims should be protected from home intrusions and harassment. In the tape-recorded evidence, there is no indication of him recognizing or even being aware of Griffin's many hints of illegality. To El-Hindi, at least, Griffin never made a single clear and unambiguous representation of the illegality of his enterprise.

Agent's strategy in scenario one: using "training" ambiguously

As I mentioned earlier, the prosecution claimed that when Griffin talked about "training" he conveyed the meaning of training for violent jihad. In the 13 taped conversations in which El-Hindi was a participant, Griffin brought up "training" 122 times, but of these, 111 are vague, ambiguous or unspecific. The 11 other references were defined as: training in security protection; training neighborhood kids to shoot air rifles; handgun training for home self-protection; and training for physical fitness. He was never specific or explicit to El-Hindi that his "training" meant training for violent jihad.

In these same 13 conversations, El-Hindi himself mentions "training" 42 times, only five of which are contextually vague or ambiguous. If a target with less than competent use of English could be clear in his meaning about training, it is curious that the agent was not equally clear. El-Hindi's 37 specific references to "training" were: training in the Koran; training in physical fitness for himself and others; training American Muslims for self-protection; training in recreation; training horses; training for getting grants; and training to be a certified Arabic/English translator. El-Hindi never talked about training for extremist jihad. In fact, he argued against violent jihad several times.

It is important to remember that Griffin never once told El-Hindi explicitly that the training program was to prepare him and others for extremist jihad. Instead, he took advantage of his vague and unspecified mentions of "training" to allow later listeners to the tapes to think that that was what he meant.

The English system of referencing requires a first defined reference to which later vague or potentially ambiguous items refer back. Thus, unless pronouns such as "he" or "it" have previously defined references, their meaning remains unclear. Based on El-Hindi's responses to Griffin's vague and ambiguous references to "training" and on his own uses of the word "training," it is clear that El-Hindi never understood Griffin's general hints.

In contrast, in a tape-recorded conversation with two other men who were not indicted in this case, Griffin was very clear that his "training" was for handguns and other weapons which would be used in violent jihad. If Griffin could be that clear to *others* when El-Hindi was not present, it is curious that his grammatical referencing was never clear and unambiguous to El-Hindi himself.

In *Creating Language Crimes* (Shuy 2005) I described eleven conversational strategies commonly used by undercover agents. The most frequent of these strategies is to employ ambiguity to make the taped conversation appear to be about something that, in fact, the target does not comprehend. Griffin used this strategy very commonly in his conversations with El-Hindi. Since my role in this case was only to analyze the conversations involving El-Hindi, I cannot vouch for the way agent Griffin used "training" to Amawi and Masloum in conversations when El-Hindi was not present. However, it is clear that to El-Hindi he was always ambiguous, except for the few occasions when he related training to benign topics. And, since there was no other reported contact between the three defendants, there is no evidence that El-Hindi could have discovered Griffin's intended meaning of "training" from them.

The ambiguity strategy works well even on native English speakers, especially on those who, like El-Hindi, tend to be so absorbed in their own agendas that they pay little attention to what others are saying. Although the prosecution claimed that Griffin had been clear and unambiguous about meaning training for terrorist purposes, his actual strategy was to suggest at least six quite different meanings: training Muslims in techniques of personal security; physical fitness training; training in life skills; training in education and religion; training horses; and training to be a certified translator. There follow examples of each.

Training for personal security

Griffin talked about security throughout these conversations, allegedly to indicate that Muslims must be careful to avoid being caught training for extremist jihad. But El-Hindi's own very different definition of "security" was evident from several descriptions of him and other Muslim Americans being detained at airports and being attacked on the streets. After El-Hindi described his own experience of being mugged, Griffin continues:

Griffin:	The biggest thing is security, you know.
El-Hindi:	That's what I'm saying.
Griffin:	We have to be extra careful because … they're after Muslims.

Although it would appear here that El-Hindi and Griffin are agreeing on a definition of security, the overall context of their conversations shows that they had very different schemas. Even when Griffin bravely dips his toe in the water and tries to be a bit clearer about his goal for weapons training, El-Hindi still doesn't get it:

Griffin:	There's definitely stuff to teach kids. You know, it's basic stuff, as far as weapons training. Weapons training is basic.
El-Hindi:	I was in good relation with Ji'atan Academy and he trained in …

The on-going topic here is the possibility that they could rent or buy the private school building. The Ji'atan Academy teaches karate to children. El-Hindi appears to interpret Griffin's use of "weapons" as karate instruction.

Up to this point in their conversations, Griffin's use of the words, "train" and "training" without exemplification, continues to mean military-type training to him while El-Hindi continues to consider it training for the purpose of self-protection. Next, Griffin adds "VIP" to the equation:

Griffin:	I'm gonna train some other guys … so we'll, and uh, basically how we're gonna do it, uh, I found out too is they could be my VIP protection team.
El-Hindi:	This is something I want to get into too.

565

It flatters El-Hindi to be considered a VIP, because he is vain enough to consider himself one of the important businessmen who would participate in the physical training Griffin would offer.

Training for physical fitness

Next, Griffin takes the meaning of "training" in another direction.

El-Hindi: I lost about twenty pounds since I came back.
Griffin: It's like you're gonna be in training too.
El-Hindi: I am. I am. I have to. I have to.

El-Hindi is very aware that his middle-aged body is terribly out of shape, but Griffin doesn't miss the opportunity to sneak in "training."

Training for life skills

Even when Griffin gets a bit bolder with his hints about "training," El-Hindi's responses show that he still doesn't get it. A few months earlier El-Hindi had flown to Egypt specifically to find and bring home two sons of a friend, who had squandered their college tuition money to fly to Cairo. Their parents feared that the boys were going to get involved politically, possibly even to join in jihad. Griffin disbelieved his reasons for the trip and reported to his handlers that El-Hindi had gone to Egypt to organize a jihadist cell.

Shortly after their return, the two young men met Griffin at an Arab convention held in a Chicago hotel. Griffin talked with the two young men about weapons training and pro-Arab topics, recording the conversation with a miniature microphone hidden in his watch. El-Hindi was at the same convention, to promote his business of recruiting medical students but was not a participant in this conversation. Later the same day, Griffin talked to El-Hindi about the boys and they agreed that they were headstrong and stupid, much in need of instruction about many things, including ways to protect themselves. This was captured on tape as well:

El-Hindi: Listen, before we do anything, brother, you give them like a small thing and see if they hang onto it.
Griffin: They can't because we're talkin' security here. We're talkin' my livelihood and everything ... I'm puttin' together a training program and I've already started training some of these brothers that are going, that, that need it. And they gotta protect theirself. We have to stay in communication though because this is serious, you know.
El-Hindi: Help the needy. Help the needy.

The prosecution used this exchange to try to show that El-Hindi wanted the boys to join the still unformed cell for training in violent jihad. In contrast, El-Hindi was warning Griffin to take whatever life-skill training he might provide them slowly, one step at a time. From what Griffin had previously said about training for security, El-Hindi could easily understand this to mean that they were in need of self-protection training.

566

Training for education and religion

Throughout the 13 conversations, El-Hindi often spoke about finding a suitable location to build a school for Muslim children to learn the Koran, to have suitable recreation, and possibly also to serve as a Muslim mosque. Griffin volunteers to do the physical education part, but he is impatient with El-Hindi's slow pace in bringing it all about. El-Hindi is not a careful listener, here or anywhere else in the tapes. On two separate occasions, a month apart, Griffin raised the ante a bit by indicating that they could *mask* his training by making it look like something else.

Griffin's first reference was on November 23, very near the end of his conversations with El-Hindi:

El-Hindi (talking about the school): The first floor make it like a prayer area,
          mosque and—
Griffin: And everything else training.
El-Hindi: Oh yeah.
Griffin: 'Cause that's how we could **mask** it.
El-Hindi: You will fall in love with that place. Two floors.
Griffin: You know, like you were sayin' before, we'll do the daycare and use
          the rest of the money for, you know, the training and everything.
El-Hindi: I got to get in shape quick.

It is difficult to know what El-Hindi understood by Griffin's "mask it," but if Griffin had wanted to be more explicit, he certainly could have used a word that might be more clearly understood by a non-native English speaker, such as "disguise" or "hide," "conceal," "cover up," or even the more commonly used military word, "camouflage." El-Hindi's lack of reaction to Griffin's effort to indicate illegality is shown by the fact that he continues his on-going excitement about finding a building that will contain a school with a recreational facility for Muslim children with a mosque attached. His "oh yeah" in response to Griffin's use of "training" is consistent with his desire to have a school that trains children in the Koran, regular education curriculum, recreation, and physical education.

Griffin's second use of "mask" came almost a month later:

Griffin: My training and everything, it's in the millions of dollars. You know
          who I work for, so I'm getting in shape and getting ready and
          everything too.
El-Hindi: I need to get in shape too. Are we gonna have something for kids and
          adults or—
Griffin: If we **mask** it with uh, you know, the training.
El-Hindi: For the kids?
Griffin: We can automatically do it for the adults too. We'll cater it toward the
          kids and then, you know, we can always bring the uh, the adults along.

Here Griffin recycles his use of "training" to indicate physical training and El-Hindi immediately understands it that way, saying once again that he himself needs to get in shape. Then Griffin repeats his "mask it," with his proposed training program. El-Hindi clearly doesn't get Griffin's meaning, asking if the training would be for the kids. It goes

567

without saying that weapons-training for children was not a reasonable idea. Griffin's use of "it" is vague, as usual.

Training horses

One of El-Hindi's futile and unwise business ideas was to bid on a tender from an Egyptian police department to build a camp where their officers could train. Part of the tender was to supply horses, horse-trailers, trucks, and other items. El-Hindi subsequently called several Michigan vehicle manufacturers about the price for trucks and various breeders about the cost of horses.

> El-Hindi: They will establish a whole program training for shooting, training for horses … a whole camp. Training for everything, even for swimming … It's going to be a huge camp to train for horses, you know, horses, camels, martial arts and weapons.

This, of course, was taken by the government's intelligence analysts as El-Hindi's willingness to agree with Griffin's weapons training ideas. Despite the fact that this was an Egyptian police-training project, El-Hindi's reference to it as a "camp" where the police would practice shooting furthered the government's highly doubtful claim that he really wanted to set up a camp in Egypt for violent jihad.

Training to become a certified translator

Another of El-Hindi's many never-completed business ideas was to become a certified translator of English and Arabic. He saw an advertisement, liked the idea, and reported it to Griffin:

> El-Hindi: They are offering six weeks training here … They want you to represent them in the United States for unlimited access, uh, translation from English to Arabic and from Arabic to English. They want to make contracts for Arab people.

There are many more examples of the way "training" was used by both Griffin and El-Hindi, but these are representative and typical.

(2) The agent's conversational strategy of fishing fails

I mentioned earlier that undercover agents follow three steps in their operations (let the target talk himself into guilt, then drop hints of illegality, and finally, be specific about the illegality).With El-Hindi, Griffin certainly dropped hints of illegality, but El-Hindi gave no evidence of understanding and Griffin never reached the important step (required by FBI Guidelines: Heymann 1984) of being explicit, clear, and unambiguous about that illegality. The above discussion of his ambiguity strategy provides some examples of Griffin's hinting style and for the defense attorneys I produced a chart citing 47 such hints, which I referred to as "fishing." Notably, all of Griffin's fishing hints failed to achieve his goal, largely because the two men had very different schemas throughout their conversations. The following are representative examples.

Griffin wants El-Hindi to find a location where he could "train."

> Griffin: I'm actually looking for like a farm to buy because then you could have goats, train, do everything there.
> El-Hindi: That's what you need. Farming.

El-Hindi was always thinking about his own schema, ways to make money, in this case by farming. Griffin tries to get El-Hindi to let him "train" the two young men he had brought back to from Egypt.

> Griffin: They don't have any training so what we gotta get across to them is you just goin' over there to commit suicide. That's not jihad. So we have to reel those guys in.
> El-Hindi: I told them, "listen, you have some money. You really wanna benefit the people here?" They said, "yes." I said, "let's slaughter some animals and give to the poor people. And then you are helping a lot of people." So he gave me money, probably a thousand. And I want to slaughter a lot of, thanks be to God, amen, I wanna give to the poor people. They get the reward. We are going on a mission of change.

Here El-Hindi interprets Griffin's "jihad" in his own schema of feeding local poor people, part of his "mission for change." In any case, the agent used "jihad" in the context of what the boys and not what he and El-Hindi might do.

On one of the occasions when they are watching videos from the Middle East, Griffin fishes again:

> Griffin: What else are they taking applications for? For actual fighters?
> El-Hindi: No, no. I didn't see that … The way I understand it, they don't need fighters. All they need is some push from the outside to educate people.

This passage shows that El-Hindi's focus on the videotapes reflected his own education schema, something very different from Griffin's schema about violent jihad.

El-Hindi stayed firmly on his own legal agendas

Analysis of conversations includes not only the linguistic analysis of the targets' responses to agents' topics illustrated above (a defensive strategy), but also the benign and legal topics generated by the targets themselves (an offensive strategy). El-Hindi's contributions were notable in that he self-generated no inculpatory evidence and stayed firmly with his own agendas of raising money for charitable work and building a school for local Arab children.

El-Hindi self-generated no inculpatory statements

In most undercover operations investigators hit the jackpot when the targets say something indicating their illegal intentions. In all of the tapes in this case, El-Hindi never introduced a topic that could be interpreted as favoring violent jihad. The only other way that El-Hindi could have implicated himself would have been through voluntary statements about his own ideas and plans. Griffin tried to modify three of El-Hindi's own agendas toward this end:

1. setting up a corporation that would get grants to be used to support training,
2. using the school he wanted to buy or rent to house his training, and
3. watching videos and internet programs from the Middle East.

Throughout the tapes, Griffin pushed El-Hindi very hard to get busy on these plans (see also Grebler, this volume, on this strategy). Although there are many instances of each, space permits only a representative sample.

El-Hindi planned to set up an official non-profit organization to get grant money

As we have seen, Griffin considered El-Hindi the "money man" and kept trying to get him to set up a corporation to provide resources for training programs. The prosecution made much of this "organization," attempting to make it look like a syndicate or cell operation. So when El-Hindi reported that he had gone to a lawyer to set up a perfectly legal non-profit organization, Griffin was shocked:

El-Hindi: Before I check on the grants, we have to establish the, uh, non-profit organization. I will call it in, God willing, and see what they, I will tell the lawyer what exactly we need for the non-profit organization that we planning.
Griffin: What lawyer?
El-Hindi: There's a lawyer, the one who does my corporation.
Griffin: (changes the subject)

Two months passed before they talked about this again:

El-Hindi: You have to submit all tax papers then. Before, it was only you submit the federal ID number and that's it.
Griffin: You have to submit your taxes?
El-Hindi: You have to submit the actual paper, the certificate and everything.

Despite Griffin's attempts to divert the idea, El-Hindi's plan is to apply for a legal non-profit organization to do legal charity work.

El-Hindi planned to set up a school and mosque

Another of El-Hindi's recurring topics was to build a school for Muslim children which Griffin kept trying to convert into a place where he could also conduct weapons training. El-Hindi, however, seemed oblivious. This was his agenda from the very beginning of his conversations with Griffin:

El-Hindi (talking about a Maumee school that was closing and soon to be for sale):
I took Ameer with me to see if, if we can uh, close a deal on buying the building and convert it into a mosque over there … We could get

grants to teach the children how to swim, right? …

Griffin: If we had a building, it'd be perfect because we could do it at night. There's no prying eyes and all that good stuff, so we'll see.

El-Hindi: It's a private building, I mean. They're going to come and search?

Griffin: No, no. That's not it.

El-Hindi: And we're not gonna be doing something illegal anyway.

Griffin: No, no. We can't shoot or any of that other good stuff.

El-Hindi: Well, it's just training.

Despite Griffin's many efforts to the contrary, El-Hindi said he believed what they are planning was perfectly legal and Griffin's notion of training would be physical education. A month later, in their next recorded conversation, El-Hindi recycled the school topic:

El-Hindi: I would like to set up a salafi school over here, for the kids, Koran memorization and Hadith memorization. You can bring your kids to it. It's going to be one of the best in the United States. I wanna get a school, God willing, we need a place.

El-Hindi's stayed with his plan to build a school for children to learn the Koran along with the regular school subjects. He remained deaf to whatever Griffin hinted about using it for other purposes. One of the important contributions a linguist can make in a case like this is to mark, organize, and keep track of the agendas of the speakers.

El-Hindi agreed to the agent's request to send him videos from the Middle East

As noted earlier, the agent devised the "electronic jihad" scenario after it had become obvious that El-Hindi was never going to bring together a group of men to form a terrorist cell. Griffin videotaped the meeting; the quality was terrible but, along with the much better audio, it was usually possible to tell who was present during the evening's conversation. Some allegedly damaging statements were made when El-Hindi was out of earshot, but when he was present the conversation was mostly about Islamic religious practices and his own marriage and divorce problems.

After dinner, they moved to an adjoining room where they watched videotapes from the Middle East. It was here that the charges against El-Hindi were framed. At trial, the jury saw the videos, including some that showed very violent scenes of tanks being blown up and a US marine being killed at a checkpoint in Iraq. These might be considered news films in some parts of the world, but for the jurors in this case, they were gruesome reminders of enemies of the US.

The fact that it was Griffin who arranged this showing and who specifically asked the men to locate examples of military scenes, did not seem to matter to the prosecution or, in fact, to the jury. The men dutifully located such examples, played them, and then as requested, downloaded them for Griffin. The act of downloading and then sending the files to Griffin became the cornerstone of the charge that they had engaged in "electronic jihad." And this was the specific charge for which El-Hindi was convicted.

Evidence that the agent realizes his efforts are failing

The issue of intelligence analysis, noted earlier, plays an important role in determining whether or not the data gathered is sufficient to indict the target. The direct evidence for indictment usually comes either from the target's own explicit, inculpatory statements or from the target's inculpatory responses to the agent's hints or fishing efforts. Neither of these gave the government much to work with in El-Hindi's case. But the agent's words can also provide clues as to whether or not the undercover operation is working well. In other unrelated cases on which I've worked in the past, such evidence appeared after the agent completed the conversation, but let the recorder keep running as he returned to his base. On more than one occasion, I've heard the agent vent his disappointment to his fellow agents with words like, "I'm sorry but I just couldn't get him to admit anything."

The tapes in this case are not as dramatic, but there are still some strong clues to indicate that Griffin felt his efforts were not working with El-Hindi. I prepared a chart of these for defense use when they cross-examined Griffin, including the following representative sample that occurred during the last month of his substantive conversations with El-Hindi:

Griffin: 'Cause we really gotta get things going 'cause we can easily tie them together.

Griffin: But I mean like it's like everything we have before, you know, we always say something, you know, we're gonna do it but we don't follow through. We got to stay focused. We have to move together.

Griffin: Just whatever grant stuff you got, if you say we gotta establish a organization, then fine, let's do it. We gotta start marching with that, you know. So let's do it, you know, 'cause the time for talking is over. We, we, I have to move forward, so I want you with me, you know, when we do our projects.

Griffin: We all have to play our part. We can't sit and talk any more 'cause that's what too many Muslim brothers are doing right now. They're sitting and talking about it but they're not helping the nation at all.

After this recorded conversation, Griffin stopped pushing El-Hindi to get focused and move forward setting up a training program. That tactic clearly hadn't worked because El-Hindi's schema and agenda of helping the poor and establishing a school for Muslim children continued to put him on a very different wave-length. From that point on, Griffin's conversations with El-Hindi contained no more mentions of training and no more fishing. It was clear that his scenario of "electronic jihad" then became the government's only avenue to net El-Hindi as a terrorist.

What can we learn from the El-Hindi prosecution?

This story does not have a happy ending for the defendants. The jury was unmoved by the defense's effort to point out the issues described here and they found El-Hindi guilty of terrorism. We can speculate about the effectiveness of the prosecution's attack or the ineffectiveness of El-Hindi's defense, but there seems to be much more to it than this. To this day, the US and much of the world remain in a state of fear, engendered originally from the tragic events of 9–11, and fed daily by politicians who thrive on such fear. Some are convinced that terrorist activity surrounds them daily, and in many countries, including the US, citizens of Middle Eastern descent remain the prime suspects. Unfortunately for El-Hindi, he fit that broad profile. Reviewing this case, we now ask whether the agent focused on the right suspects, whether the prosecutor examined the targets' agendas and whether an effective intelligence analysis was made.

Did the government find the right suspects?

Regardless of the outcome, this case illustrates many of the problems law enforcement officers face when they charge suspects with terrorism. Rather than seeking out situations where terrorism was happening or likely to happen, agent Griffin trolled for possible suspects in a place where American Muslims congregated, failed for a while and then focused on a suspect who seemed to fit his profile. From the language in evidence, however, El-Hindi was not the right suspect, but that seemed not to matter.

This case had three targets who were recorded conversing together only a few times, but who were recorded individually many times. The lawyers with whom I worked instructed me not to analyze the tapes in which Amari and Masloum appeared together or separately without El-Hindi, so I couldn't judge whether they produced genuinely incriminating utterances (but from all appearances, Masloum was considerably less likely). If Amawi was indeed guilty, there is a very good chance that his guilt contaminated the case against El-Hindi, since it is not unusual for all indicted defendants to be found guilty, even if only one of them was. When this happens, the problem lies at least partially in the legal system's own intelligence gathering, intelligence analysis, and trial procedures. So it is not possible to say for sure that the government located any, some, or all of the right suspects in this case, but, based on the undercover recordings, it is clear that El-Hindi provided no evidence of being guilty of anything with which he was charged. It is highly likely that the prosecution pursued only one hypothesis—that of guilt. This would suggest that the prosecutor's intelligence analysis was inadequate.

Did the government investigate the agendas of the speakers?

There is no evidence in the prosecutor's trial presentation that he had any concern for (or knowledge of) the conversational agendas of either El-Hindi or agent Griffin. To discourse analysts this seems very strange, since conversational agendas and schemas are the very foundation of what is being discussed.

In criminal court cases it is common for both the prosecution and the defense lawyers to focus only on small pieces of talk (words and sentences) and pay little or no attention to the significance of the holistic information that could be provided if they would make the effort (or get linguistic help) to examine the speakers' topics, agendas, schemas, and the significance of their responses. People do not commonly recognize the fact that words and sentences extracted from their original conversational context are capable thereby of having a different meaning.

One first step for prosecutions of any type, is to analyze the speakers' agendas and schemas, as revealed through the topics they introduce and recycle (Shuy 1993a, 2005). Prosecutors and police make much of the notion of "motive," but they usually look for this motive *outside* of the language evidence. The language clues found *within* the recorded conversations are fruitful evidence of motives, however, and this information is readily available, if lawyers would only look for it. This is a crucial contribution that linguists can provide.

Was a proper and effective intelligence analysis made?

There are four essential steps in the process of intelligence analysis (Harris 1976: 30):

(1) collecting data
(2) evaluating the data for usefulness
(3) analyzing the data for meaning
(4) reporting findings

Undercover agent Griffin was responsible for collecting the data. No doubt his handlers reviewed his tapes throughout this two-year investigation and it is proper to give them credit for adequately evaluating, analyzing and then deciding that their first scenario, that of trying to get El-Hindi to form a cell that Griffin could train for violent jihad, was a failure. The replacement scenario, however, was another matter. The prosecution's final analysis was that El-Hindi's *intent* was to select videotapes and internet programs that would help Griffin in his alleged, but non-existent, efforts to train people to commit violence against the US. A more careful evaluation of these conversations shows a distracted, naïve and gullible El-Hindi meekly complying with Griffin's request to forward these materials. It is difficult to see how this shows his overall illegal intent. Perhaps if this meeting had taken place in Amawi's or Masloum's home, El-Hindi would be less likely to have been charged. Accurate intelligence analysis would also have shown that throughout Griffin's two scenarios, El-Hindi said nothing inculpatory about a violent jihad. In fact, El-Hindi's own words and actions evidenced that he was opposed to such actions.

There is every indication in the tapes that the prosecution's intelligence analysis was faulty. The alleged offensive materials were found in El-Hindi's home when he hosted a dinner meeting that was orchestrated by the agent. Griffin also orchestrated El-Hindi's emailing the materials to his home computer. That's all the prosecution could factually claim about El-Hindi's involvement and apparently that's all they thought was needed.

Spoken language is more difficult to process than written language, which may be one reason that the government's intelligence analysis erred. Speech goes by the listener very quickly, making it necessary to review to it many times. The commonly used technique is to produce a written transcript of the speech, but a transcript can't reveal important information such as head nodding, non-verbal communication signals or indeed, whether the listeners were even present or responding with language that evidences attention to or understanding of the agent's allegedly inculpatory hints.

Because of the speed of speech, people who participate in conversations are often less able to determine all the inferences and nuances of what is being said than are later privileged listeners who can listen at their leisure and replay as many times as they want. Jurors also assume that the defendants are guilty, not only because they were indicted and brought to trial, but also because the evidence was recorded. However, later listeners are also highly disadvantaged when they listen to a tape that had a specific meaningful context at the time it was made, but which is much less clear in the courtroom. Add to this the fact that the prosecution focuses on individual words and sentences rather than entire contextual indicators of meaning and intent and the case against El-Hindi is made much easier for jurors.

Conclusions

Many people in western nations still fear that anyone with Arabic appearance and an Arabic name is likely to be a terrorist, making prosecutions like El-Hindi's appear to be reasonable and necessary. In some cases, these fears are supported by irrefutable evidence—but not always. The clear danger remains that this strong fear can lead law enforcement officers to select the wrong suspects, to focus on the wrong person in a group under investigation, to neglect analyzing the discourse context in which the alleged criminality takes place, and to produce an inadequate intelligence analysis.

Such prosecutions can go astray by basing their claims of guilt on ambiguous representations made by undercover agents and by failing to understand when the agent's efforts to hint at or fish for inculpatory responses have actually netted nothing. And sometimes, the prosecution distorts by omitting relevant facts like the target's statements of intention to act legally. The case against El-Hindi illustrated all of these weaknesses.

If the prosecutors had called on linguists to analyze these conversations before the case went to trial, El-Hindi might never have been indicted. When the prosecutors leave it to the defense alone to make use of linguistic analysis, there is always a very good possibility that the judge will not permit the linguist to offer such testimony at trial, which is exactly what happened in this case. El-Hindi is now serving a prison sentence of 14 years.

Further reading

Shuy, R.W. (1990) 'The analysis of tape recorded conversations,' in P.P. Andrews and M.B. Peterson (eds) *Criminal Intelligence Analysis*, Loomis, CA: Palmer Press, 117–48.

——(1993) *Language Crimes: The Use and Abuse of Language Evidence in the Courtroom*, Malden, MA and Oxford: Blackwell.

——(1998) *The Language of Confession, Interrogation, and Deception*, Thousand Oaks, CA and London: Sage Publishing.

——(2005) *Creating Language Crimes*, New York: Oxford University Press.

37

Computational forensic linguistics

Searching for similarity in large specialised corpora

David Woolls

Introduction

This chapter addresses the ways in which computers can be used to assist the work of the forensic linguist. The emphasis is on computational document comparison and in particular on the identification of high levels of similarity between the whole or parts of two documents, which the forensic linguist can use to decide questions of shared or suspicious authorship. One of the central problems discussed is how to handle very large quantities of data efficiently and reliably. The need for computer assistance has grown rapidly in the twenty-first century, with most companies and educational institutions holding their data in electronic form and often making it openly available on the Internet. There is both the need to monitor for misuse of such electronic material and for the existence of prior work or duplicated material in databases. Another major area examined is the need for flexibility in any computer program which has the objective of identifying similarity. Identifying consecutive sequences of words only finds unmodified copying (cut and paste), whereas more sophisticated modifications involve insertion, deletion, re-ordering or thesaural changes and all these require word-level searching. Arising from this, the power of using simple lists of particular words or parts of words, rather than undertaking full grammatical parsing, is explored and explained.

Computational forensic linguistics

Computational forensic linguistics, as the name implies, is a branch of computational linguistics, a discipline which has its roots in the 1950s, when computers first entered the commercial and academic world. Computational linguistics embraces a wide range of subjects, of which perhaps the best known are information retrieval, lexicography and machine translation, but it also covers automated parsing, categorisation of texts and summarisation. The discipline generally works with large corpora, which it uses to derive statistics to assist in these tasks. The use of computers for collusion detection was reported by Johnson (1997) closely followed by Woolls and Coulthard (1998). Woolls (2003) explores the development and expansion of such tools, and Woolls (2006) addresses the work along with wider aspects of plagiarism and its detection.

In the area of computational forensic linguistics discussed in this chapter, while the number of documents can be extremely large, the comparison requirement is generally between two documents and in particular between the sentences of two documents. That is, it is not sufficient to report that two documents are similar to each other, because the user often already knows or suspects this to be the case. What s/he needs to know is where exactly in the document the similarities appear and how to evaluate them as unremarkable or significant. The preliminary and theoretical discussion in this chapter is based on just five sentences. This is partly because the work undertaken is almost always highly confidential and so real examples are not readily available and, even if they were, it would necessarily take up a lot of space to illustrate their workings. But working with single sentences also highlights the complexity of language, and what has to be taken into account in designing computer programs that will provide accurate and comprehensible results for the human reader. The discussion then moves on to two case studies to illustrate the computational linguistic principles.

Sentences

In order to compare any two items, there need to be elements that are potentially present in both. As far as sentences are concerned, these elements are primarily words and punctuation. The single, very famous sentence that I focus on is taken from the opening to *Pride and Prejudice* by Jane Austen. I use it to demonstrate the elements that can be used by a computer program for the purposes of similarity searching. In doing so, it might at times appear that I am stating the obvious but, as nothing is obvious to a computer program, it is important to start at this very basic level. What will become evident is that the computational treatment of texts is a matter of deciding what best to include to approximate what we as humans generally do intuitively when we read a text. Here is the sentence:

'It is a truth universally acknowledged, that a single man in possession of a good fortune, must be in want of a wife.'

Identification of words

What can a computer program do with this sentence? A number of things. First, it can divide it up into its component words by identifying items that have spaces on either side. This, however, isolates some 'words' that look like non-words to a human reader, because of the punctuation that is attached to them: for example <'It> <acknowledged,> and <wife.'> . We now see that there is a need to give the computer a list of punctuation items plus an instruction to remove them from the front and back of the 'words' it has found. However, it is usually not desirable to simply ignore the punctuation, because the use of punctuation is a structural decision made by a writer and as such can be distinctive. Indeed, some programs treat individual items of punctuation as 'words' in their own right. And of course the punctuation placed around the word **words** in the preceding sentence, was used to indicate that it was not being employed in its normal meaning, so perhaps '*words*' in this case should be considered to be a separate wordform from *words*.

577

Once we have isolated the words they can be organised into alphabetical order. In computer terms this would actually mean that, of the words in our illustrative sentence, <It> would come first in the list, because capital I and lower case i have different numerical values. So, if we want a true alphabetical list we need case-insensitive ordering, which means treating both <I> and <i> as the same letter, either by making all words uppercase or all words lowercase.

Indexing

Another extremely useful thing we can use the computer for is to produce an index of exactly where all these words occur. Primarily we can record for each word which document or documents it occurs in. It is common to add details of the location of each word within each document, so that any word and also the words close to it can readily be recovered. This is similar to the index at the back of this book. This technique lies behind the operation of web search engines. The results are located by finding all the documents which contain the word or words of the search term and the search result 'snippets' are built from the words close to the search terms in the selected documents. The present author's method also records which sentence the words occur in, which is clearly necessary to perform the sort of sentence comparison described later in the chapter.

Measurements and patterns

We can do other things with our list of words – we can measure the lengths of the words in characters and we can count the number of times each word occurs. For example, the shortest word in our sentence is <a> with just one character and it occurs four times. A computer can easily sort the words in any combination of alphabetical, length and frequency order. Or again, we can get the computer to look for patterns. In this sentence there is one obvious pattern – the sequence <of a> appears twice – and one perhaps less obvious pattern <in x of a> also appears twice, where the **x** represents the word **possession** in the first case and **want** in the second. Winter (1994) describes such a pattern as a matching contrast relation realised by *repetition by replacement*, which indicates that **possession** and **want** are in an antonymic relationship in this particular sentence.

There is another pattern which humans are able to observe, but which cannot be directly identified by a computer without some knowledge of word classes. It is possible to attempt to replicate the human observation of patterns in a computer program. The primary pattern here is <a> followed by a noun – which is itself followed by another short word or other more complex patterns. One frequent modification to the base pattern is the presence of one or more adjectives before the noun, and another is an adverb preceding the adjectives. Humans learn this and other patterns either from reading or from formal lessons in grammar. We cannot readily give computers this *knowledge* but we can provide lists of common endings for all four main word classes and indicate which patterns are equivalents. Examples of the components of such lists are included in Table 37.1. A pattern rule for a noun phrase might therefore be: **a [adverb] [adjective] noun** (where the square brackets indicate optional inclusion).

Table 37.1 Word ending lists for all four main lexical classes

Some Noun endings	–s, –es, –ure, –ry,–ance, –ment
Some Verb endings	–ed, –es, –s, –en, –ing, –ise, –ize
Some Adjective endings	–ish, –al,–ous, –ic, –ary,–ful
Some Adverb endings	–ly, –ward, –where

Classification

A computer can only simulate learning at best, but it is possible to identify, for almost any language, those whole words that perform functions and to identify those beginnings and endings of words which act as markers of word classes. Using such lists, combined with fundamental rules, computer programs have been written that can fully parse sentences with a very high degree of accuracy (see for example the free *CLAWS* parser at http://ucrel.lancs.ac.uk/claws/). In the programs written by the present author a simpler approach is taken using an extended list of *function words* (commonly called a Stop List) and treating all other words as *content words*, that is words whose meaning is being organised by the function words and which can frequently be classified by their endings, using the word-endings list.

Computers can also learn the probability of the ordering of such words and parts of words, to deduce what sort of word might fill the gap, if the program cannot find it within the dictionary it is using. Given such lists of function words and word endings computers can also split sentences or complete documents into their broad compositions. The 450-strong function word list used by the author frequently accounts for over 50% of a full text. Our illustrative 23-word sentence has 13 function words and 10 content words, that is, 57% function words.

Comparing sentences

Now we have illustrated the complexity of what is going on in a single sentence and how computers can be programmed to recognise this, we need to address how we go about comparing two sentences. This requires the introduction of two concepts used throughout the comparison methodology described below.

The first concept is called **fuzzy matching**. If we want to identify similarity rather than identity, we need to be able to specify that the two sentences under consideration form some sort of match, even if not all their words are identical. This facility is present in the Advanced Search features of web search engines, where the searcher can explicitly include or exclude certain words from the search. This is called Boolean searching, because Boolean logic always produces a true or false result for a condition; either a word is there or it isn't. This works well when the user knows, or thinks they know, what words might be of assistance in obtaining better search results, but, when one is comparing large numbers of sentences, it is not possible to specify particular words for each of them, so the comparison has to be performed in a fuzzy way. That is, as long as a certain number or percentage of words are present in both sentences we will consider the pair to be a potential match.

The second concept is that of a **chunk**. We can, of course, use all the words in a sentence and find out how many of them are present in both, but some sentences are quite long and complex and other comparison cases include examples where there is a long stream of words containing no punctuation or capitalisation. The classic case of very long sentences is the Claims Section of a patent application. By law, each claim has to be a single sentence. As claims are central to the future effectiveness of a granted patent, patent attorneys attempt to squeeze as much detail as possible into each claim, so a 'sentence' can often run to several lines. This is achieved by the use of the semi-colon, which is not seen as a sentence boundary by patent law, nor indeed in linguistics by many descriptions of what constitutes a sentence. This is not too difficult to handle, of course, as long as the users of the software program have no objection to breaking a string of words before reaching a 'normal' sentence boundary, that is, when it encounters a semi-colon.

Rather more problematic are those texts where there is an absence of both punctuation and upper case letters, as this example illustrates:

> this is a good song i like it i think that it has some potential for the radio the singer is great i like the singer alot and the vocals are great too this is a hot song that can actually make it somewhere but u would have to push this song 4real
>
> (author's data)

This is a review written online as an immediate response to music the writer has just listened to, and it looks more like transcribed speech than normal written text. To handle regular orthographical marking, extended sentences as well as the review example above, we need a common system of demarcation that can be applied to both orthodox and non-orthodox texts, so that comparison is possible at a similar level between segments so demarcated. This is what is meant by a chunk. To handle this we have made use of the work of linguists and psycholinguists.

A chunk might be a traditional clause or phrase, or it might be a stretch of a sentence that has a minimum number of words and a recognisable lexical boundary marker. The term has its roots in psycholinguistics. Miller (1956) reported that we could hold around seven items in short term memory. Spoken 'sentences', connected sections of speech all of which are required for the listener to make sense of what the speaker is referring to, are frequently much longer than this in terms of words, of course. Because of the short recall length, each of these smaller chunks must make sense in themselves so they can be encapsulated and fed into the next chunk, and in this way we can make sense of an extended spoken argument with no need for explicit punctuation. In speech we are, of course, assisted by rhythm, intonation and frequently, though not always, visual clues. Where we have just a transcript, or simply written data, we can use the words that identify the conceptual boundaries to break up any stream of words into shorter segments.

From the linguistic perspective, we employ the work of Fries (1952) who was interested in describing the structure of English in order to provide non–native speakers with a description and a highly organised sequence of exercises to teach how the language worked. He had decided that teaching traditional formal grammar was not helpful to the rapid acquisition of conversational language skills. He covertly recorded telephone conversations and set himself the task of identifying what he called the *minimum free utterances* that resulted in a response and then describing their components and extensions, not in the terms of traditional grammar, but into what he called classes. The classes were numbered based on their relative frequency of occurrence and their position in the resultant utterances, which were not called sentences. Although it goes against the spirit of his exercise, Class 1 words loosely approximate to nouns, Class 2 to verbs, Class 3 to adjectives and Class 4 to adverbs. As all the recordings were of conversations, which don't include punctuation, no boundary markers are included in his examples, other than initial capitalisation of the utterances.

It will be seen that this corresponds with what we have with the music review sentence above. The interest for computational sub-sentence analysis is that Fries also identified a relatively small number of words, which clearly did something to introduce, organise or link the free utterances. These he named function words as a consequence. He further subdivided this list into their different functions. The ones that interest us are those that signal boundaries to the listener, since we can make yet another list of such words and use them to segment the text. If we do that with the review sentence, we get this:

1. this is a good song
2. i like it
3. i think that it has some potential for the radio
4. the singer is great
5. i like the singer alot and the vocals are great too
6. this is a hot song that can actually make it somewhere
7. but u would have to push this song 4real

Notice that there are seven chunks, the two longest of which contain eleven words, and the boundary words are in initial position: **this**, **I**, **the**, **but**. The artist reading this review will be in no doubt that the writer likes the song, and will be able to separate the various comments quite readily by the signals of the boundary words. Chunks 5 and 6 both comprise more than one clause but can be argued to act as a single unit in this stream of words. This illustrates both the utility of Fries' function words and the three concepts – positive evaluation, identification of potential and a need to promote the song – which can act as a memorable summary to fulfil Miller's criterion.

Sentence similarity

Now we can illustrate how this helps us with comparison. Here is another review by the same person, already broken into chunks.

1. i like the guitar
2. i think that this song is really good
3. i think that it has some potential
4. i think that it has alot of potential
5. but u have to really push this song
6. that may make this song get somewhere

We need to rearrange the chunks to show the matching as in Table 37.2. In a commercial system, the order of the originals would be preserved and a system of cross-referencing similar to that shown in the table would be used to identify which chunks the system had recognised as matching. Identity of word is shown in regular font, differences in italics, and underlining has been used to identify related concepts.

Table 37.2 Similarity, difference and identity in two reviews

Chunk	Review 1	Chunk	Review 2
1.1	this is *a* good song	2.2	*i think that* this song is *really* good
1.2	*i like it*		
1.3	i think that it has some potential *for*	2.3	i think that it has some potential
	the radio	2.4	i think that it has *alot of* potential
1.4	*the singer is great*		
1.5	i like the *singer alot and the vocals are*	2.1	i like the *guitar*
	great too		
1.6	this *is a hot* song that *can actually make it*	2.6	that *may* make this song *get* somewhere
	somewhere		
1.7	but u *would* have to push this song *4real*	2.5	but u have to *really* push this song

This example shows the complexity involved in comparing a single stream of words.

1. The repetition in 2.3 and 2.4 shows the need for some decision about whether to show matches once or twice. Chunk 2.3 matches the first part of 1.3 exactly, so might be considered to have priority over chunk 4, but this requires there being a rule for the program to employ.
2. We need to consider the direction of comparison. From shorter to longer would give 2.3 a score of 100%, from longer to shorter 70% (7 out of 10 words matched in 1.3).
3. We need to consider whether we are going to include function words or not in the measurement. If we decide not to, from shorter to longer would give 2.3 a score of 100%, (think, has, potential) from longer to shorter 75% (3 out of 4 words matched in 1.3).
4. If we include function words, we need a way of excluding the second **the** in 1.5 (the vocals), since this is not part of a match.
5. Matching on particular functions may be helpful. There is match of modal use in 1.6 and 2.6, with **can** in the former being replaced by **may** in the latter.

There are other layers of complexity. If we encounter this sentence: '*A man who possesses a fortune needs a wife.*' we need to decide whether this is similar to our original sentence. The new sentence falls into two chunks and in Table 37.3 we can see that it is certainly not completely different, in terms of the words themselves at least, after the first six words of the original.

We might have started from the premise that the relation between any two sentences is going to be scalar. Identity means 100% similarity; completely different means 0% similarity. But when we consider actual sentences it is more complicated than simply looking for the presence or absence of identical words. Table 37.4 takes the matched components of Table 37.3, recording the running total of matches, from identical upwards, in column 2 and calculates the similarity percentages at each stage. Column 3

Table 37.3 Comparison of original sentence with new sentence

Austen	that	a	man	in	possession	of	a	good	fortune
Exact match		A	man				a		fortune
Lemma match					who possesses				
Austen	must	be	in	want	of	a	wife		
Exact match						a	wife		
Synonym match				needs					

Table 37.4 Measuring similarity

		New sentence		Austen		Austen Content only
Total words in sentence		9		23		10
Match type (from table 37.3)	Running total of words matched	% match		% match	Running total of content words matched	% match
Exact repetition (**a, man, fortune, wife**)	4	44%		17%	3	30%
Exact repetition including all 3 instances of **a**	6	67%		26%		
Lemma (**possess★**)	7	78%		30%	4	40%
Synonym (**in want of/needs**)	8	89%		35%	5	50%
Composite (**who possess★**)	9	100%		39%		

calculates from the perspective of the new nine-word sentence, and column 4 from the perspective of the Austen 23-word original. Columns 5 and 6 show the word counts and percentage calculations from the perspective of the Austen sentence when only the ten content words it contains are used for comparative purposes. As can be seen, there are thirteen different possible measurements for this sentence alone, ranging from just 17% if we only include exact matches with all the words that Jane Austen used in her sentence, to 100% if we measure from the perspective of the new sentence and include all partial similarity and repeated matching.

Table 37.4 shows that variation in what might be classed as similar is the crux of the issue for any measurement of similarity at sentence level. A decision mechanism needs to be built into a computer program to allow it to perform reliable and consistent comparison. The author uses the principles of

1. excluding around 450 function words from the initial comparison because their structural function makes them a requirement in sentences, so co–occurrence of the function words themselves is frequently not an indicator of similarity;
2. assuming that any sentence with more than 50% of the content words matched in some way warrants being considered a candidate for similarity;
3. including the function words in the final presentation, as shown in the review example, Table 37.3 above, because the structural similarity is part of what makes the sentences similar;
4. performing all comparisons from the shorter sentence to the longer.

We are still left with the linguistic fact that it is evident that the two sentences are far from equivalent semantically, as the list below shows.

1. there is no evaluation of the truth of the bare statement,
2. *a single man* and *a man* are not necessarily equivalent, and certainly not here, because a *married* man is clearly not in need of a wife,
3. there is no stated requirement for the fortune to be a *good* one
4. and the modality of *must be* is omitted.

So in this sense, they might be considered to be completely different despite all the words in common. But it **is** possible to get from the long version to the short one, and with a little imagination from the short to the long, so the sentences might well be considered similar. Whether it makes any sense to have a percentage attached to the similarity is also questionable, as you will have seen by now.

Re-ordering

The above discussion has so far looked only at direct matching at the lexical level while retaining the word order. The actual situation is more complex, since changing from the active to the passive, at least in English, always changes the word order and introduces at least one additional word, with the reverse obviously being true. Consider the simple proposition 'Dogs chase cats'. This is generally true. 'Cats chase dogs' may or may not be true, but it certainly doesn't mean the same thing, whereas 'Cats are chased by dogs' does, even though there are more words and **chase** and **chased** are not identical. Most sentences are not as short as this, of course, but most sentences *are* composed of phrases and clauses which can be this short and so the combination effect of identity/difference and word order can result in quite a few problems for a computer program. This is especially the case where **are** and **by** in the above example appear on a function word list, so would not immediately be taken into account at the comparison stage, leaving the different word order as a puzzle for the program with no functional assistance to resolve it.

As humans, we have a different way of identifying these relationships, and attempts have been made using neural networks to get computers to do the same, with some success, particularly in the recognition of similarity of authorship. For this, computers are given a base set of known texts and a set of rules for learning the patterns of individual usage. Comparing the features of a text of unknown origin with the features extracted allows the derivation of a degree of similarity. Usually the unknown text is believed to be by one of two or three authors, so the author with the best match on features is considered the most likely author.

Even without using such techniques, which are not possible where there is only one pair of texts available, there is another feature of written language that is helpful to the computational cause. The recognition of lexical similarity between what one is reading and what one has read before is so surprising that we frequently go back and check, and in the majority of cases are correct in our recognition and can identify a prior source for that sentence. Quite how we as humans do that over time and with much other reading in between is outside the scope of this chapter. But computers can be given a large number of texts and the task of exhaustively comparing them, and simply highlighting where similarity exists, for humans to subsequently make a decision about.

Document similarity

We have concentrated on sentence similarity partly because that is the central component of the work described below and partly because complete documents are clearly composed of sentences. But documents can be compared directly. Documents that share a lot of sentences will also share a lot of words, and various measures are available to allow the vocabulary similarity of two documents to be established, all of which are intended to return higher scores for related documents. Such scoring methods sit behind most information retrieval methodologies where a set of documents needs to be identified as a potential source for answers to queries.

In addition, when comparing documents on occurrence and word frequency, it becomes apparent that words that are shared but occur infrequently, particularly only once (also called *hapax legomena*), are prime indicators of a relationship between the two documents, and especially so if the two documents are of similar lengths (see Johnson 1997, for example, on *hapax legomena* and plagiarism). This feature is the result of the way we write. In a document like an essay even as long as 4,000 words, a word frequency count normally shows that between 60% and 70% of the content vocabulary items used occur only once and a further 15% occur only twice. And comparing the word lists of two independently produced documents on the same subject will normally show a great deal of difference in the words which occur only once or twice. These are quite straightforward measures, but there are clearly more complex ways of achieving such comparisons. The problems arise when only parts of documents are being used and, in particular, single or short sets of sentences.

Paraphrase

Finally, we need to point out what is very difficult for computers to handle, even with a thesaurus. Here is another version of our sentence. '*Everyone agrees on one thing about rich bachelors. They really should get married.*' Now, this is not as beautiful or well constructed as the original, but it might be considered to say much the same thing. It preserves some element of the evaluation of the statement and the modality of the suggested answer to the implied problem. However, it also has no words in common with the original and uses two sentences rather than one. The complete absence of lexical matching and the use of a very compact expression *rich bachelor* in place of eight words, *a single man in possession of a good fortune*, which has the effect of switching the effective word order as well, sets a very difficult task for computational comparison. And of course, paraphrase is encouraged by teachers and is often not considered to be plagiarism. The missing element for a computer program, when compared to a human reader, is that the human reader would undoubtedly recognise the dependence if they knew the original or had the words in front of them. Any computer program based on word similarity would completely miss the semantic match.

Case study 1 – UCAS

The Universities and Colleges Admissions Service (UCAS) handles admissions to almost all the universities in the United Kingdom. Each applicant has to submit a personal statement including their background and their motivation for studying their chosen subject. During the monitoring process which UCAS routinely performed, it became evident that some of the applicants' personal statements were very similar, and some were traced back to advice sites on the Internet. UCAS decided that they needed a fully automated system that would check all incoming personal statements against not only all others in the current year but also all those submitted in at least the two previous years, as well as with material collected from known openly available websites.

The scale of the requirement was very large, with approaching 600,000 applications each year, most of them received in a four-month period. Nearly 40,000 applications were submitted on the 2009 final deadline day alone. Comparing each document with every other requires a very very large number of comparisons, for instance a mere five documents requires ten comparisons and 100 need 4,950.

The UCAS requirements were extremely challenging. They requested that the computer program be able to identify similarity at sentence level, because they believed that wholesale use of internet material was rare, and that merging and modifying sentences from a number of sites was more likely. In addition, they needed the results of each batch of 125 applications in under 10 minutes, so that their Verification Unit could make decisions without appreciably changing the target time for handling applications in the existing system.

Procedure

In any such task, it is important to identify the nature of the input data and the requirements of the end user. The first determines how the task can be done and the second determines what has to happen to the results of any analysis. In this case, there were several elements that influenced program design and implementation.

Data

First, all the data to be monitored had been submitted in electronic form over the previous three years and were held solely on UCAS's computers and were available as plain text. This removed three of the major difficulties that can impair computational forensic linguistics: data conversion from written or typed to electronic form, data dispersed over the Internet and data in a variety of electronic formats.

Secondly, all the data was of roughly the same length, with the majority of applicants making use of all the available 4,000 characters. This meant that document comparison at word level would show comparable word distribution patterns, allowing flexibility in deciding what should be indexed.

Thirdly, the data would be fed from an existing system, designed to process the full applications in batches of around 125, so there was a natural rhythm to the flow of data which could be built into the system.

End user requirements

The requirement here was threefold.

1. the UCAS Verification Unit needed a very simple but clear summary of the applications received at any given time;
2. they needed to be able to see the nature of the similarities between the incoming material and the matched personal statements in a single document; and
3. they needed this to keep up with the flow from the existing system, so to be as near to real-time as possible.

In all computational forensic linguistics, the presentation of the output needs to be built into the program, as distinct from a manually prepared report which can be built from spreadsheets, graphs and charts as well as a word processor.

Analysis

We have mentioned in the Document comparison section that all English texts share the property that around 50% of the words will be function words and 50% lexical. So, in an average length sentence (20 words), this means that approximately ten words in each sentence will be lexical. Secondly, as also mentioned already, texts of under 1,000 words each share the property that most of the lexical items will only occur once (*hapax legomena*) or twice (*dis legomena*). This is particularly the case where the 650 words in the personal statement have to cover a number of different aspects, leaving little room for repetition, so the *hapax* words can be as much as 70% of the lexical vocabulary. And in personal statements, we can expect that the words used will differ from statement to statement, as they should represent the writer's personal opinions, assessment or description of the common topic, and all of these factors will determine the word choice, along with the background vocabulary of the individuals concerned.

This is helpful because it allows efficient indexing and comparison. *Hapax* words can clearly occur in only one sentence each, so it becomes much simpler to identify whether they occur in the same sentence in any two texts simply by recording the file and sentence number for each such word and counting how many words are shared by sentences from different documents. Using *hapax* words is also useful because they provide a limit on the size of any index system used. If indexing is by *hapaxes*, not only is the list shorter than if all words are taken into account, but the number of documents recorded where those words occur will be much lower, making the amount of checking for co-occurrence when using such an index a much less complex and time-saving process.

Indexing

As has been noted above, a computer program can be designed to find all the *hapax* words in each document and build an index of which documents and which sentences they occur in. Then it can read any document, identify the *hapax* words in each sentence of that document and check whether that word exists in the index. With careful comparison techniques, it can then find out how many of the words in the current sentence are found in another sentence in the set of all the other documents. A highly optimised version of this useful feature lies at the heart of the eventual solution.

Accuracy

Central to all computational forensic linguistics is the need for accurate reporting. This might seem obvious, but there are unusual considerations in this particular area. All other forensic linguistics is based on experts in the field forming an opinion. By contrast, in computational forensic linguistics, it is far more likely that a non-linguist will be asked to form an opinion based on the linguistics output. This would be a subject specialist where essays are being compared, or an administrator with specialised skills in human resource management or similar in a commercial organisation. At UCAS, the verification unit had expertise in the detection of fraudulent applications, but none in linguistics. So the users needed to be able to rely totally on the data they saw and be assured that it was complete. Presenting data which doesn't appear to be copying and proves not to be, known as a false positive, both creates more work, as any report requires examination, and also reduces confidence in the efficacy of the program. At the same time, the users need to be confident that nothing has been missed by the program operation, known as a false negatives. This is much more problematic. With the vast number of comparisons needed for a UCAS size data set, this cannot be checked by hand, so it has to be founded on logically demonstrable principles, which can then be verified by planting known cases in the dataset and making sure that all such cases are discovered.

In standard plagiarism detection there is a need to find the source(s) in order for a successful case to be built. In UCAS's case, it was only necessary to demonstrate that one or more examples of the incoming statement could be found in whole or in part in their existing database or in a web source. But they did need to be able to see the matching and to make it available to both the applicant and the university admissions tutors. To do this, a maximum of three identified sources was set, with each source being shown in a different colour, so all users of the data could see the location and extent of the borrowing. Inexact matches, such as variations in spelling or tense, were also highlighted, to show where attempts at disguise had occurred. This presentation assists decision-making and evidence provision in a single document. An example of a multiple sourced personal statement is available on the website accompanying this handbook, available at: http://www.forensiclinguistics.net/.

Effectiveness

The program has been running for two years' at the time of writing, and has identified over 26,000 cases for the Verification Unit to assess, which is a little under 3% of the applications in each year. However, behind this apparent stability, the number of serious cases requiring UCAS notification of applicant and admissions tutors dropped by 26% between January 2008 and January 2009.

Case study 2 – Online music reviews: Slicethepie

Comparisons are not always done between different authors. The case studied here is that of Slicethepie, a web–based financing platform for the music industry. This is the case that provided the two reviews analysed in Table 37.2 above. Slicethepie employs site users, called scouts, to review and rate music tracks collected from unrecorded artists, and pay the scouts a small sum of money for each review. The scouts have to listen to at least one minute of each track without knowing either the name of the artist or the title and then provide a review. After submitting their review, they learn both who and what they have been listening to. Some scouts, to maximise their revenue, were discovered to be writing a single review and then copying it into the submission box for other tracks as soon as the track had finished, while others were using a template and making minor modifications. As the purpose of the review was to provide genuine, useful feedback to the artists, Slicethepie needed to intercept such practices at the earliest possible stage.

Analysis

As with all forensic casework, each computational case has to be analysed, in particular to ensure that the correct data are being fed to the program. The company initially believed they required a similar system to that of UCAS, but volumes of around 6,000 reviews per day would quickly have generated a huge comparison task and analysis quickly revealed something else. The true requirement was for comparing the incoming reviews from individual scouts with their own prior submissions, rather than with the submissions of other scouts, as they didn't see the reviews written by other scouts. This reduced the size of the task considerably, but it also revealed the linguistic problem mentioned above, that many of the reviews were lacking in punctuation, capitalisation and sometimes even spaces. The reviews could also vary considerably in length; a minimum of 15 words was required, but there was no upper limit.

Procedure

As with all cut and paste methods, if the scouts were simply using that methodology a straightforward comparison of the content of two of a single scout's reviews would have been sufficient. But the tendency to minor modification and the omission or insertion of segments meant that sentence-by-sentence comparison was still required, in order to prevent false matching of musical terminology across sentences in reviews where no copying was taking place. So the chunking principle described above was used. A small number of boundary markers combined with commas and the normal sentence period marker (where present) were used to subdivide complete reviews into such chunks. In this case, no prior identification of true sentence boundaries was used. This is another important difference between this computational method and normal reading practice. As already noted, the important factor here is that all comparisons should be on the same basis, so that a punctuated version and an unpunctuated version of the same writing are treated identically by the comparison program.

User requirement

In another change from UCAS, Slicethepie required two elements: firstly side-by-side presentation of the reviews, with a simple system identifying similarity and difference, and secondly, an ordering of the matched reviews according to the extent of similarity, so that they could identify the main offenders readily and deal with the others in order of severity. There is an illustration of the presentational style on the website (available at: http://www.forensiclinguis tics.net/).

Going live

The system as initially built greatly assisted the retrospective identification of the scouts using copying, but couldn't prevent the duplicate reviews from getting into the database and being seen by the artists. So the company requested a live system. The music is delivered to the scout using the Adobe Flash player. While this is primarily aimed at delivering pictures, video and music to web users, it has a programming language behind it. By providing a modified version of the program in this language, it was possible to monitor what the scouts were doing while they were logged into the Slicethepie site. In this case, the base system described above was enhanced to include monitoring for minimum and maximum review length in words, for appropriate musical content, for attempts to circumvent length restrictions by internal repetition of chunks of text or holding keys down and other possibilities that deeper analysis of the practices of the scouts revealed.

In addition to enhanced detection, an immediate feedback system was devised that gave appropriate commentary on the nature of the problem identified by the program. The feedback was designed to allow multiple messages for each problem to be created by the Slicethepie administrators, so that users didn't always see the same message. For example, an overly short contribution might trigger a 'Would you mind writing a little more please?' one time and 'You have only written 12 words. The artist would benefit from a bit more feedback.' the next time. An example of the feedback is also available on the website accompanying this *Handbook* (available at: http://www.forensiclinguistics.net/).

Such a system requires that the underlying program only reports to scouts who are abusing the system and produces comments that are appropriate to what has been found, so great care needs to be taken in the construction of the logic behind the diagnostics and response.

Effectiveness

The desired effect of reducing the amount of unhelpful and repetitious material getting into the database was achieved immediately, with a corresponding reduction in the amount of administration time required to deal with the problem. An unanticipated side effect was that the Slicethepie team noted a considerable improvement in the quality of the reviews getting through the submission process, presumably as there was an awareness in all scouts that their work was being closely monitored.

Conclusion

We have shown that for both creators and users of computational forensic linguistic tools it is necessary to have a very clear understanding of the limitations which inevitably surround attempting to use a machine to provide the equivalent of a human reader's capabilities. The strengths are clearly the size of data and the speed of processing of the texts, without mental fatigue and with consistent application of the rules. The weaknesses come from the complexity of the concept of similarity and the fact that any computer program can only be an approximation of what human readers can recognise and handle with ease. We believe that strong visual presentation allows the end users of the output to recognise true similarity and gain insight into why the program has selected and marked sentences as showing similarity when it is sometimes less obvious at first reading. We have also shown that active use of an appropriate response can have a positive effect on user behaviour, which was an unexpected consequence.

Further reading

Journal of Literary and Linguistic Computing (a general source of computational applications to literature and linguistics).
Abney, S.P. (1994) *Parsing by Chunks*. Available online at: www.vinartus.net/spa/90e.pdf (accessed 31 March 2009) (an implementation of chunks for grammatical parsing).
Brazil, D. (1995) *A Grammar of Speech*, Oxford: Oxford University Press.
Sinclair, J. McH. and Mauranen, A. (2006) *Linear Unit Grammar: Integrating Speech and Writing*. Studies in Corpus Linguistics 25, Amsterdam: John Benjamins (detailed illustrations of chunks being used in grammars).
See also Computational Forensic Linguistics.ppt on the accompanying website (http://www.forensiclin guistics.net/).

38

The future for forensic linguists in the courtroom

Cross-cultural communication

Peter R. A. Gray[1]

As its title suggests, this book is intended to function as a handbook of forensic linguistics. I have been asked to provide a final chapter, expressing the point of view of a judge about some aspects of forensic linguistics. The two aspects I have chosen are related to the lack of communication between those engaged in the practice of the law and those in the field of forensic linguistics. The first is the fundamental ignorance on the part of most lawyers that there even is another profession concerned with the study of the language used in the functioning of the legal system. The second is the problems that forensic linguists can encounter when asked to give evidence as experts in court.

To put my remarks in context, I think it advisable that I tell the reader something of my experience. Between 1972 and 1984, I practised as a barrister in Melbourne. In my early days, I was involved in a wide variety of cases, including minor criminal proceedings before magistrates, claims for damages for personal injuries, and minor commercial disputes. The mid-1970s were a time of great opportunities for those at the Victorian Bar. My practice expanded quite quickly into one dealing principally with matters of commercial law, equity and property. In 1978, I began to receive briefs in labour law matters. This aspect of my work developed rapidly into a specialisation which required me to travel all over Australia. In 1984, I had the very good fortune to be appointed as a judge of the Federal Court of Australia, a position I still hold. Initially, my judicial work was principally in the field of labour law, although it has since expanded into areas of public and commercial law.

The court of which I am a judge deals with almost no criminal law; the work is spread across a range of aspects of federal law and is interesting and challenging. The criminal cases that it does hear involve regulatory offences with relatively small maximum penalties, so that there have been no criminal trials involving juries. It is therefore a very long time since I have been in a courtroom with a jury.

During the 1990s, I was also appointed as Aboriginal Land Commissioner, pursuant to the *Aboriginal Land Rights (Northern Territory) Act 1976* (Cth). This Act operates only in the Northern Territory of Australia and enables groups of Aboriginal people to seek from the Commissioner findings that they were the traditional Aboriginal owners of specific areas of Crown land, as a result of which the Commissioner would recommend that the land concerned become Aboriginal land under the Act. As a result of the operation of this Act, approximately half of the land in the Northern Territory is now Aboriginal; the freehold titles, along with traditional entitlements of various kinds, are held by various land trusts for the benefit of Aboriginal people. The hearings conducted under this Act were administrative investigations, rather than trials resembling court proceedings. Hearings were conducted routinely on the land in question and travelled from site to site by four-wheel drive vehicle or helicopter. It was very common for the Aboriginal claimants to supplement their oral evidence of traditional attachments to land by demonstration of those attachments through ceremonial performances, involving dancing and singing, with appropriate designs painted on their bodies and the use of sacred objects.

In the course of dealing with Aboriginal land claims, I had many dealings with anthropologists and linguists, people whom I had not previously encountered. For each claim, I was entitled to engage a consulting anthropologist. There were two such persons, each of whom gave me different and very valuable perspectives on a number of issues. In addition, it was typical for the claimants to have the assistance of one or more anthropologists or linguists in the preparation and presentation of their claims and their reports were vital in providing a framework to enable me to understand the oral evidence of the claimants themselves. In a number of claims, linguists functioned as anthropologists. They had become associated with the claimants over a number of years for the purpose of studying the claimants' language or languages and, as language and culture are inseparable, the linguists had become the leading experts on the kinship systems of the claimant groups and their relationships with land tenure.

My involvement in Aboriginal land claims prompted an interest in cross-cultural communication. I continue to be an active member of committees at the national and state levels, aiming to educate judges, magistrates and tribunal members in Aboriginal cultural awareness, to minimise the injustice that arises from misunderstandings in legal proceedings. It was this interest in cross-cultural communication that led me to my first biennial conference of the International Association of Forensic Linguists (IAFL), held in Sydney in 2003. I applied to become a member of the IAFL and, although I do not have any qualifications in linguistics, I was permitted to join and have enjoyed attending subsequent biennial conferences.

Legal profession ignorance of forensic linguists

In the late 1970s, I was briefed to act for a defendant in a defamation suit. My client was the former wife of the plaintiff. The divorce had been acrimonious. The plaintiff claimed that my client had been involved in the preparation of a letter in which defamatory statements about him appeared. The letter was addressed to the plaintiff's sister, but to the address at which the plaintiff lived and at which his sister did not live. It purported to have been written by someone who had been a friend of the sister many years before, but had married and gone to live in the United States. The letter had been posted from the United States, but the plaintiff alleged that its posting had been contrived by the defendants. My client denied any involvement in the preparation or posting of the letter. One issue arose from the allegation that the letter had been typed on a typewriter owned by my client. By a subterfuge, the plaintiff had managed to obtain a sample of the typeface of my client's typewriter. This sample consisted of each letter of the alphabet typed once in upper case and once in lower case. I had no difficulty obtaining the services of a professional forensic document examiner. Forensic document examination had existed as a professional discipline for many years and there were several eminent textbooks on the subject. The expert was prepared to give evidence that such a sample provided no proper basis for the conclusion that the letter was typed on the particular typewriter as the font concerned was used by several European typewriter manufacturers. He argued that a much larger sample was necessary to determine whether minor imperfections in the imprint of particular letters were repeated consistently, so that they could be demonstrated to be the result of imperfections in the faces of the particular keys, rather than imperfections in the ribbon or the paper.

Another issue also intrigued me. The text of the letter included a considerable number of expressions that I conceived to be idiomatic, specifically American-English idiom. Having regard to the level of my client's education, and to the fact that she had spent her entire life in a particular locality on the eastern fringes of Melbourne, without ever travelling overseas, I wondered whether she could have written a letter that appeared to be so authentically American-English. At the same time, I was aware that exposure to American television programmes, which constituted the bulk of programmes shown on Australian television, was very likely to have educated a regular viewer in the American vernacular. I wondered whether it would be possible to obtain the services of an expert witness, who could conduct some sort of testing of my client's facility with American-English, and give evidence as to the improbability of her having written the letter. Neither I, nor the solicitor who had briefed me in the case, knew of any such expert.

What I needed, of course, was a forensic linguist, with expertise in author identification. It is hardly surprising that I did not know that such a person existed in the late 1970s, because unlike forensic document examination, forensic linguistics had hardly surfaced in Australia at that time (see Eades 1994b and 1995 on early work). Such expertise in dialects of English as existed in Australia at that time was more likely to have been focused on dialects spoken by Aboriginal people than on dialects spoken in other English-speaking countries. No doubt I, like many other people at that time, would have assumed that a linguist was a person with knowledge or command of several languages, rather than someone who was interested in the structure and function of languages in general.

As it turned out, the defamation case never came to trial. My account of the case is included here only to illustrate my ignorance at that time, as well as the obviousness of the need for expertise of a kind now relatively common among forensic linguists.

In associating with forensic linguists at conferences, and in reading the literature of forensic linguistics, I have been struck by one overwhelming fact. There appears to be virtually no communication between forensic linguists and lawyers. It is true that there are eminent forensic linguists who have qualified as lawyers and practised law, before deciding to specialise in forensic linguistics. For the most part, however, there is a massive lack of cross-cultural communication. I have had many conversations with lawyers in which I have revealed my interest in forensic linguistics, only to be asked what forensic linguistics is. My response is that forensic linguists study the legal system and legal processes for their language, rather than for their legal content. It appears that the state of ignorance I possessed in the late 1970s persists in the vast majority of lawyers at the present time. A couple of recent illustrations will suffice.

The National Judicial College of Australia is the primary body responsible for the continuing education of judges. Each year, it conducts a course for recently appointed judges as well as a number of courses about specific issues of interest to judges whatever their length of experience. I was quite excited to receive notification of a course devoted to the language of the courtroom, but my excitement turned to dismay when I read that every presenter on the course was a judge. There were sessions dealing with the composition of judges' directions to juries in criminal trials, and of sentencing remarks. I contacted the administration of the college, to suggest that it might be helpful to involve forensic linguists in the preparation and presentation of such a course. The response I received was that many judges had already been exposed to the expertise of Sandra Hale in the introductory courses. My mistake had been to assume that the administration of the college would have been aware that the interests of forensic linguists include analysis of the language of such things as directions to juries in criminal trials and sentencing remarks. The assumption underlying the college's response appears to be that forensic linguistics is about interpreters. There is no doubt that forensic linguists are interested in courtroom communication from one language to another and indeed this is a vital part of many court proceedings, particularly in a multicultural society such as Australia. In her chapter in this volume, Sandra Hale does an excellent job of drawing attention to the need for high quality interpretation from one language to another, and to the disadvantages of seeing the task of interpreters as being to translate mechanically and literally. However, a focus on interpretation is not the sole concern of forensic linguists. I should have drawn the attention of the college to work done by forensic linguists about directions to juries in criminal trials, as exemplified in the chapter by Peter Tiersma in this book (although such work has not yet been done in Australia).

My second experience of judicial ignorance is more recent. Ron Butters, the author of a chapter in this book on the use of expert forensic linguists in trademark disputes, sought my assistance in ascertaining whether there have been any cases in Australia concerning trademarks, in which forensic linguists have given expert evidence about the way in which particular expressions in trademarks are likely to be perceived. As I do not claim to have any expertise in trademark litigation, I emailed those of my colleagues in Sydney and Melbourne who constituted panels hearing such cases. None of them was aware of any trademark cases in which forensic linguists have given evidence in Australia.[2] Several of the judges of whom I made enquiries drew my attention to a case that turned out to be concerned with copyright and where the relevant expert gave evidence about the translation of a particular expression from one language to another. Once again, interpretation appears to have been regarded as the limit. The response from one judge was interesting. He had not heard of a trademark case involving a forensic linguist giving evidence and went on to volunteer the opinion that he hoped that this would never happen, because it might lead to post-modernism.

What can be done to redress the lack of communication between lawyers and forensic linguists? Lawyers have a greater obligation to be aware of developments that affect the legal system than does anyone else. One of the problems of ignorance is that it invariably includes ignorance of ignorance: we do not know what it is that we do not know. Even if lawyers have heard of forensic linguistics, the innate conservatism of lawyers remains a problem. The response to the question, 'how many judges does it take to change a light bulb?' is the puzzled and anxious repetition of the word 'change?' It is often said that the genius of the common law is that it has changed over the centuries to adapt itself to changes in society. Changes have been slow, however, and have often been forced on lawyers by reforming legislation. The historical account of changes in English courtroom practice between the seventeenth and nineteenth centuries in Dawn Archer's chapter in this volume contains many examples of changes being imposed by Parliament. Even when new opportunities emerge in the law, lawyers usually manage to change them into something that looks very like the old and familiar. Consequently, I see little hope of lawyers volunteering to be influenced by forensic linguists in Australia. Attributing to lawyers the sole responsibility to overcome the communication gap is not likely to result in the elimination of the gap.

On the other hand, forensic linguists are not ignorant of lawyers. The solution to the communication failure might well involve forensic linguists reaching out towards lawyers more than they do at present. Collaborative research between linguists and lawyers in academic institutions would be valuable. Forensic linguists could submit papers for publication in legal journals, instead of restricting them to journals circulating among linguists. Similarly, the submission of papers for presentation to legal conferences would be a way in which many lawyers could be introduced to the notion that there are people who study a wide variety of aspects of language use in the legal system.

One area in which linguists have been valuable to the legal system has been the plain English movement. To some extent, the use of plain English has been forced on lawyers by legislation or government action, requiring that documents such as insurance policies be written in ways that can be understood more readily by both those who sell their services to the public and by their clients. We are also said to live in an era of plain English in legislation, although there is material for any number of papers about the obscurities of the language used in Australian legislation in recent years. There is no reason why the plain English movement could not extend to courtroom language in judges' directions to juries or sentencing remarks. Judges would benefit from the sorts of analyses of courtroom discourse exemplified by the chapters in the present volume by Gregory Matoesian and Laura Felton Rosulek.

Forensic linguists as expert witnesses

Traditionally, there have been tensions involving the evidence of expert witnesses in common law courts. On the one hand, lawyers, including judges, recognise that there is a need to have expert evidence about subjects that are beyond the realm of general knowledge. On the other hand, lawyers, including judges, distrust experts in fields other than law. There is a deep-seated fear of being led to wrong conclusions by experts with vested interests or pet theories. There is an inability, or unwillingness, to grasp unfamiliar methods of reasoning. There is even an element of what I call God complex. Lawyers spend so much of their time acting for clients who are totally dependent on their services in the lawyers' areas of specialisation that they become used to being authoritative. In the course of legal practice, it is normal to acquire some familiarity with a wide range of other specialist areas. I have known, for example, many lawyers who practised for many years in claims for damages for personal injuries, and acquired enormous amounts of medical knowledge. Similarly, lawyers who have practised in cases involving allegations of defective construction work acquire considerable amounts of engineering and architectural knowledge. The list could be extended. A lawyer whose experience covers a number of areas of legal practice will have some acquaintance with a variety of areas of specialist knowledge. The combination of a belief in the lawyer's own authority and the possession of a little knowledge about a number of specialist areas can easily lead to the view that the lawyer knows all that is necessary to be known about everything. Acting under such a misapprehension, a lawyer can easily treat with contempt an expert giving evidence unfavourable to the lawyer's client.

The negative attitude towards experts has been reflected in the traditional rule that an expert witness cannot give an opinion as to an ultimate question: only the judge or the jury can determine the ultimate question. This rule has now been abolished by statute in Australia (Section 80 of the *Evidence Act 1995* (Cth)), removing one area of objection to the evidence of expert witnesses. Legislation in the same or similar terms has been adopted by some States of Australia and its adoption is being considered by others. The distrust of experts is also reflected in the free rein that has been given traditionally to opposing counsel to cross-examine expert witnesses. Obviously, a way to win a case is to discredit the other side's expert. In some areas, people with the necessary expert knowledge have declined to undertake forensic work, because they dislike having to defend their methods, and their professional reputations, against vigorous cross-examination in a public process. As a consequence of the way in which anthropologists have been cross-examined in native title cases in Australia, there are very able anthropologists who refuse to perform investigations and provide reports in such cases.

Another cause of tension is that some expert disciplines are perceived to be more exact than others. The opinions of an engineer, a physicist, a chemist or even a medical practitioner are somehow perceived to have more weight than those of a sociologist, a psychologist or an anthropologist. The negative attitude towards interpretive sciences probably extends to linguists who give evidence about matters such as the capacity of a particular person to have understood an interview process or to have given answers in the terms alleged, or about the identification of a person's origins from analysis of the language he or she uses.

One further area of tension has arisen in relation to the identification of the expert with the interests of the clients on whose behalf he or she gives evidence. Practising in the field of claims for damages for personal injuries, I learned very quickly that certain forensic medical experts were always engaged to provide opinions on behalf of injured plaintiffs, while others were always retained by defendants' insurers. Not surprisingly, there tended to be an observable gap between the evidence of representatives of the two groups about the severity of a particular plaintiff's injuries, the likely future effect of those injuries, and their impact on the plaintiff's life and capacity. The lawyers, including the judge, in a particular case would know whether a particular forensic medical expert had the reputation of being a 'plaintiff's doctor' or a 'defendant's doctor'. To some extent, this same concern about identification with the client's interests pervades attitudes towards other forensic experts. Similarly, in defective construction cases, some experts were believed to favour aggrieved building owners, while others were thought to be giving evidence designed to minimise the damages their builder clients would have to pay.

The problem of identification with the client's interests has been a particularly severe one in cases in my court concerning native title. Some judges have expressed distrust of the evidence of anthropologists (and other experts, including linguists functioning as anthropologists), given on behalf of Aboriginal people claiming to hold title to tracts of land by reason of traditional Aboriginal laws and customs.[3] There are many reasons for the distrust. They may include the fact that the anthropologist concerned has spent many years gathering the data on which his or her opinion is based and that this data-gathering has been by means of interviews with the very people who have become the applicants in native title cases. Inevitably, close and warm relationships develop. Anthropologists are perceived to have lost their objectivity and to have become advocates for those whose societies they have studied. Compounding this problem is an ethical principle, commonly accepted by anthropologists, that forbids them from using information divulged to them against the interests of persons from whom they have acquired the information in the course of their research. In other words, an anthropologist who has worked closely with a group of people who become involved in a native title case will not agree to give evidence on behalf of a party resisting the native title claim (usually a government or a proposed developer of the land concerned). Thus, the only anthropologists who will give evidence on behalf of parties opposing native title claims will be those who have done no field research among the people claiming native title. For this reason, they can only provide opinions based on the available literature, and opinions about the validity of the research methods and reasoning of the researcher anthropologists who give evidence for those claiming native title. (Lawyers too have ethical principles that prevent them from using information acquired in acting for a client against the interests of that client in another case. So, it is a little surprising that the adoption of the equivalent ethical principle by anthropologists should have attracted the criticism from lawyers that it sometimes has.)

Thus, it has been possible to criticise some anthropologists for being too close to the parties on whose behalf they are giving evidence and to criticise others for not being close enough to those parties.[4] On the other hand, there have been judges who have recognised that the fact that an expert witness is not truly independent of the party calling him or her to give evidence is not a disqualification.[5] One judge has also said that evidence given by an anthropologist of his or her observations over a long period (i.e. the gathering of data) may be direct evidence and not evidence of opinion.[6] In a criminal trial, it will be common for the prosecution's forensic experts to be engaged wholly in the preparation of evidence on behalf of the police or the relevant prosecutorial authority. Their lack of independence should not disqualify them from giving evidence.

A further difficulty that seems to confront anthropologists as witnesses in native title cases may arise simply because those who speak with authority about the cultures and societies of particular groups of indigenous people do so because they themselves have gathered the data on which their opinions are based. To many lawyers, including judges, the concept of an expert witness is someone who is presented with certain facts and invited to give a relevant opinion about the consequences of those facts. It is true that, in many cases, experts will be called to give opinions on given sets of facts, without having had any prior involvement in ascertaining what those facts are. Such cases seem to have given rise to the expectation that the expert will always be independent of the facts on which he or she comments. In fact, in many cases, the expert will have been a participant in the process of gathering data. For instance, a medical practitioner who has treated an injured plaintiff is not regarded as incapable of giving evidence of a diagnosis and a prognosis for that person simply because he or she has gathered the information on which his or her opinion is based from the history provided by the injured plaintiff and his or her own observations of the injuries.

The forensic linguist who has read what I have written so far about expert witnesses is likely to be dismayed. How can any witness overcome the judicial and legal distrust of someone who operates in a field of interpretive science, who gathers the data from the subject directly and uses the data so gathered to form an opinion, and who may have developed a relationship with the subject in the course of that process, causing him or her to identify with the subject's interests? Add to this the problem that lawyers may perceive the forensic linguist's field as not being one involving a sufficient level of expertise, but one that the lawyer could just as easily command. (I suspect that the expressed fear of a forensic linguist giving evidence in a trademark case, because it might lead to post-modernism, is a consequence of regarding all such cases as involving nothing more than ordinary usage of language.)

The only answer I have, and it is in no way a complete answer, is thorough professionalism. The forensic linguist's qualifications, experience, research, methods and reasoning will all come under scrutiny, and must withstand such scrutiny for the opinion to be accepted. There is little doubt that acceptance has come to a much greater extent in the United States and in England, than it has in Australia. Acceptance can be achieved only by demonstrating that opinions given by forensic linguists are professional opinions, acceptable, even if not actually accepted in the particular case. Guides such as that set out in Fiona English's chapter will no doubt be of great importance and assistance to any forensic linguist who is starting out. Papers and textbooks of that kind are obviously very important. They do have a double edge, however. As lawyers become more familiar with the process, the well-prepared cross-examiner will consult the published literature in order to undermine the methodology of the forensic linguist expert. The professionalism of the expert therefore requires that he or she be fully conversant with the literature, and omit no step recommended in the literature unless well able to justify the omission.

One of the great difficulties any expert has in expressing an opinion is quantification. As Malcolm Coulthard pointed out in his excellent address to the dinner at the 2007 biennial conference of the International Association of Forensic Linguists in Seattle, expressions of likelihood in terms of statistical probabilities or percentages have their difficulties. So also does the use of standard phrases. In the course of my judicial career, I have declined to make findings in accordance with the evidence of two former police forensic document examiners. In one case,[7] the issue was whether certain minutes of a trade union committee had been falsified. It was the practice of the president to sign the minutes of each previous meeting, once they had been approved, as a true and correct record of that meeting. The president was alleging that signatures purporting to be hers on a number of sets of minutes were forgeries. The forensic document examiner was called to give evidence that, on his comparison of the president's admittedly genuine signatures and the questioned signatures, he was satisfied that there was a 'strong probability of common authorship'. In the other case,[8] the question was whether one or more persons had filled out multiple ballot papers in the course of a trade union election. Another forensic document examiner gave evidence that crosses appearing in squares on a number of ballot papers demonstrated a 'strong probability of common authorship'. It struck me as odd that the same phrase should be used by two different experts, but there were other reasons in both cases for me to disbelieve the evidence of the experts. I do take the view, however, that the use of a standard phrase to encapsulate an assessment could well lead to the devaluation of the impact of that phrase. This may not matter in front of juries, but judges may come to achieve familiarity with the phrase and to discount it accordingly.

All is not necessarily grim in the world of expert witnesses. Significant steps have been taken by my court to ameliorate the plight of experts, and to ensure that their evidence is given more weight. In this respect, my court has been something of a pioneer, in Australia, if not in the world.

In the first place, the court has issued a practice direction, containing guidelines for expert witnesses,[9] designed to remind expert witnesses that they must approach the giving of evidence on a truly independent basis and not on the basis that they are there to serve the interests of the party who calls and pays them. The practice direction contains the following admonitions:

1   General duty to the court

1.1   An expert witness has an overriding duty to assist the Court on matters relevant to the expert's area of expertise.

1.2   An expert witness is not an advocate for a party even when giving testimony that is necessarily evaluative rather than inferential.

1.3   An expert witness's paramount duty is to the Court and not to the person retaining the expert.

The practice direction contains some helpful advice as to what should appear in an expert report. This includes such things as: details of the expert's qualifications and of the literature or other material used in making the report; assumptions of fact made by the expert; a summary of each opinion provided in the report; reasons for each opinion; a statement of the questions or issues that the expert was asked to address; any qualification about incompleteness or inaccuracy of the conclusion; and any question or issue that falls outside the expert's area of expertise. In the report of an expert witness, filed with the court prior to the trial, it is usual for the expert to say that he or she has read the practice direction and heeded it.

The other relevant changes are in the procedures for dealing with experts when each side proposes to call an expert, one to refute the opinion of the other.[10] Routinely, the court will order that the two experts confer prior to the trial and produce for the court a joint document, setting out the matters on which they are agreed, the matters on which they are not agreed, and the reasons for their disagreement. The practice note referred to above states that, at such a conference, 'it would be improper for an expert to be given, or to accept, instructions not to reach agreement'. At the trial, the expert witnesses are not called in the course of each party's case, to be examined in chief, cross-examined and re-examined, as is usual current practice. Rather, the opposing expert witnesses are called at the conclusion of all of the other evidence led by both parties. Having been duly affirmed or sworn, they are then required to debate directly between themselves the matters on which they are not agreed, so that the judge and the lawyers can observe the debate. Only when this debate has been exhausted will the lawyers be permitted to question the witnesses. The judge will also ask any questions that he or she considers will help to clarify the issues.

The process of dealing with the expert witnesses at a trial in this manner is known as the 'hot tub'. It has proved very successful. One judge has said:

In my experience, the Hot Tub procedure brings a number of benefits which include the following. First, the experts give evidence at a time when the critical issues have been refined and the area of real dispute narrowed to the bare minimum. Secondly, the judge sees the opposing experts together and does not have to compare a witness giving evidence now with the halfremembered [sic] evidence of another expert given perhaps some weeks previously and based on assumptions which may have been destroyed or substantially qualified in the meantime. Thirdly, the physical removal of the witness from his [sic] party's camp into the proximity of a (usually) respected professional colleague tends to reduce the level of partisanship. Fourthly, the procedure can save a lot of hearing time ... [in one case] the lay evidence took some four weeks but the expert evidence of two distinguished economists was disposed of in a day ... [in another case] the evidence of two experts as to bank interchange payments took a day, and that of five economists another day.

Peter Heerey, Recent Australian Developments,
CJQ 2004, 23(Oct), 386–95 at 391

The procedure has thus helped to ameliorate any tendency for expert witnesses to regard themselves as hired guns for the parties calling them to give evidence. The very fact that the opposing experts have to deal with each other has led to much more common ground than was found in expert conflicts in trials of the old style. The fact that the experts have been able to argue their points of view directly with each other in the courtroom, without the interference of lawyers, promotes an atmosphere in which personal and professional standing can remain intact, so that experts are more inclined to be prepared to give evidence. Concessions that are made are not seen to have been extracted by skilful or overbearing cross-examination, but to be made genuinely. The judge's task of deciding between the opinions of conflicting experts is made easier by an understanding of the way in which conflict arises and by observing how that conflict is expressed on both sides.

I cannot promise that the realm of expert evidence will ever become a paradise, either for the expert witnesses, or for the lawyers. Whatever system is adopted, experts will always need to be rigorous in their approach to giving opinions about matters in dispute in court proceedings. All that can be said is that lawyers, including judges, are becoming increasingly aware of the problems that face expert witnesses, and are beginning to take steps that will minimise those problems.

Conclusion

I have attempted to present some aspects of what I see as a lack of cross-cultural communication between lawyers and forensic linguists, particularly in Australia. Whilst that lack of communication is very largely to be laid at the feet of lawyers, it seems to me that forensic linguists can do more than lawyers are likely to do to open up dialogue between the two professions. I have endeavoured to suggest ways in which such dialogue might be opened. It is my hope that, in the future, lawyers will allow themselves to accept the benefit that some understanding of the work of forensic linguists can offer to them. There is no doubt that the legal system would be improved if the work of forensic linguists were to be heeded by lawyers to a greater extent than it has been.

I also express the hope that courts will continue to devise procedures and methods that will facilitate the giving of expert evidence, including the evidence of forensic linguists. Recognition that we have much to learn from forensic linguists would be a good start, but would not be a complete answer in individual cases, in which one side will always be wishing to discredit the expert who gives evidence against that side's case. By removing at least some of the process from the responsibility of the lawyers, and transferring it to the responsibility of the experts, I am encouraged to believe that the giving of expert evidence will be facilitated. The hot tub may not be altogether enjoyable for experts, but it is likely to be more so than vigorous cross-examination, as well as being beneficial to the interests of justice.

Notes

1 I am greatly indebted to Diana Eades for her helpful comments and suggestions. Responsibility for any errors and omissions in this chapter remains with me.

2 Diana Eades has since drawn to my attention *Mobil Oil Corporation v. Registrar of Trade Marks* [1984] VR 25, a judgment of King J of the Supreme Court of Victoria. The case concerned an attempt to register the word 'Mobil' as a trademark, in respect of a class of goods including sporting articles, games and playthings. There was controversy as to whether the word 'mobile' would be pronounced as it would be by many speakers of American English, so as to sound like 'Mobil', and would therefore be incapable of registration. Two linguists gave evidence: Professor Hammarström of Monash University and David Blair of Macquarie University. The summary of the evidence appears in the judgment at pp 32–33 of the report.

3 For example, Sackville J in *Jango and Others v. Northern Territory and Others* [2006] FCA 318 (2006) 152 FCR 150 at [304]-[342] available at www.austlii.edu.au/cgi-bin/sinodisp/au/cases/cth/FCA/2006/318.html?query=title(Jango) and Lindgren J in *Harrington-Smith and Others on behalf of the Wongatha People v. State of Western Australia and Others (No 2)* [2003] FCA 893 (2003) 130 FCR 424 available at www.austlii.edu.au/cgi-bin/sinodisp/au/cases/cth/FCA/2003/893.html?query=title (Harrington-Smith).

4 For example, *The Members of the Yorta Yorta Aboriginal Community v. The State of Victoria & Ors* [1998] FCA 1606 at [55] and [61] available at: www.austlii.edu.au/cgi-bin/sinodisp/au/cases/cth/FCA/1998/1606.html?query=title(Yorta%20Yorta).

5 For example, Selway J in *Gumana and Others v. Northern Territory of Australia and Others* [2005] FCA 50 (2005) 141 FCR 457 at [163] available at: www.austlii.edu.au/cgi-bin/sinodisp/au/cases/cth/FCA/2005/50.html?query=title(Gumana).

6 Selway J in *Gumana and Others v. Northern Territory of Australia and Others* [2005] FCA 50 (2005) 141 FCR 457 at [160].

7 *Geneff v. Peterson & Ors* (1986) 19 IR 40 at 58–60 available at: www.austlii.edu.au/cgi-bin/sinodisp/au/cases/cth/FCA/1986/432.html?query=title(Geneff).

8 *Re Carter; Re Federated Clerks Union of Australia, Victorian Branch (No 1)* (1989) 32 IR 1 at 4–14 available at: www.austlii.edu.au/cgi-bin/sinodisp/au/cases/cth/FCA/1989/192.html?query=title (Carter). The expert in that case used a number of different descriptions to indicate various levels of certainty on his part. Only one of those descriptions was 'a strong probability of common authorship'.

9 Guidelines for expert witnesses in proceedings in the Federal Court of Australia – Practice direction, 5 May 2008 available at: www.fedcourt.gov.au/how/prac_direction.html.

10 Order 34A Federal Court Rules available at: www.comlaw.gov.au/ComLaw/Legislation/Legislative InstrumentCompilation1.nsf/0/E98CF094B28FA4CDCA25752800179995/$file/FederalCourtRules V1.doc.

39

Concluding remarks

Future directions in forensic linguistics

Malcolm Coulthard and Alison Johnson

'If we could first know where we are and whither we are tending, we could better judge what to do and how to do it.'

From Abraham Lincoln's 16 June 1858,
'House Divided' Speech (Online at www.ushistory.org)

Introduction

As our discipline comes of age, with two whole decades of specialised research and writing behind us, we have been able to bring together a comprehensive volume of chapters written by both established and up-and-coming forensic linguists. Many of them have suggested directions for future work and map out a rich and promising territory for the next generation of researchers to explore.

In Section I, the Language of the Law and the Legal Process, we see two common issues emerging. First, the complexity of legal language and the challenges this presents for lay people involved in the legal process. This is treated in chapters by Bhatia, Stygall, Drew and Walker, Tiersma and Aldridge and the theme also runs into Section II, where authors consider how the expert linguist negotiates this comprehensibility gap when acting as interpreter and assessor (Hale, Kredens and Morris and English).

The second issue is one of legal rights; how are these rights asked for, given, negotiated and denied? Our authors present different and sometimes conflicting accounts of the current global picture. The chapters about Britain written by Stokoe and Edwards and Rock present a very different picture from the one painted by Ainsworth for the United States. This suggests that the US has something to learn from the UK in terms of access to and intervention by lawyers in the interrogation process. Both of these issues have a linking theme – that of power – and there are, not surprisingly, many chapters concerned with this topic. Felton Rosulek shows us the power of lawyers' closing speeches and Tkačuková the disadvantaged position of lay people when they represent themselves in court. The relationship between power and advantage and disadvantage is seen starkly in the chapters by Ainsworth, Eades, Ehrlich, Grebler, Greenlee, Shuy and Stygall and this critical forensic linguistics focus is one which will certainly be taken forward into the next two decades of research and writing. As Wodak (2007: 209) says the aim of critical linguistics is to 'demystify discourses by deciphering ideologies' and a critical approach in forensic linguistics means that we unpack the ways that power and dominance are done in legal contexts and how disadvantage and control are produced. We know that 'language is not powerful on its own – it gains power by the use powerful people make of it' (see Bhatia, this volume), and we have seen how this is exploited in a number of the chapters. It is only by scrutinising and exposing powerful ideologies in action (such as those discussed by Shuy, this volume) that forensic linguists can make a difference in terms of acting in the social world and effecting change. CDA looks outside the text 'to get a sense of its social context' as it sees that meanings in texts are created through having 'a broad perspective on the social order' (Fairclough 2001: 129). Problems in legal texts are social problems and a critical forensic linguistic approach enables us to provide analyses that suggest change and make an impact in the socio-legal world.

Section II focuses on the linguist as an expert in legal processes and all of the authors show us that a solid descriptive methodology is at the heart of this work, though many of these methods are pioneering and emergent. Justice Gray, in his chapter in Section III, speaks about some of the dangers for experts if they make their methods public – lawyers will consult the literature and be more prepared for cross-examination – but he also offers a fascinating glimpse into his own courtroom and possibly a new way of treating expert witnesses and their evidence: the 'hot tub'. Greenlee sees the advantage of a developing forensic literature as a resource for defence lawyers.

The final section, entitled New Debates and New Directions is the most forward looking. Here, we offer only a brief glimpse of four new directions for forensic linguistics: multimodal analysis (Matoesian), computational approaches (Woolls) and the future role of experts in the courtroom from both the perspective of a linguist (Shuy) and from a judge (Gray). And in this, the closing chapter, we continue that discussion, highlighting some other important directions in which we think the discipline will develop during the next decade and some of the issues it might pursue.

The written language of the law

Communication through written text is difficult at the best of times (Coulthard 1994b) and texts written by lawyers to communicate information unambiguously to lay readers are in the main particularly problematic – typically much more emphasis has been placed by the writer on unambiguousness than on communicativeness. In addition to the huge array of statutes and laws that govern our behaviour, and texts like temporary restraining orders, jury instructions, the UK police caution and the US Miranda warnings, forensic linguists have usefully focused on tenancy agreements, house purchase contracts, insurance proposals, credit card terms and product packet warnings, on the relatively long texts we find inside medicine packets and on very short texts such as road signs or automated messages on websites. What is interesting for forensic linguists about all these texts is that the lay readers who are their supposed target audience often have difficulty understanding them fully (see Stygall, for example, in this volume). Of course, there are occasions when obfuscation is deliberate, as Dumas (this volume), argues is the case with some cigarette package warnings. Describing and suggesting solutions for the problematic nature of legal–lay communication is a theme running through many of the chapters and this will continue to concern forensic linguists for the foreseeable future.

For example, Jury Instructions have been the focus of a significant amount of research over the years. Dumas (2000a) reports work extending back several years on communicative problems associated with the Tennessee pattern jury instructions and in particular with the instruction for 'reasonable doubt', which at the time she wrote was in the form of the fixed written text reproduced below, which judges would read out to the jury. Jury instructions in general are a good example of the difficulty of categorising legal language as spoken or written. They are written texts intended to be read aloud, but, as we can see clearly from a reading of this particular instruction, presented immediately below, they are certainly not designed to sound like speech.

> Reasonable doubt is that doubt engendered by an investigation of all the proof in the case and an inability, after such investigation, to let the mind rest easily as to the certainty of guilt. Reasonable doubt does not mean a captious, possible or imaginary doubt. Absolute certainty of guilt is not demanded by the law to convict of any criminal charge, but moral certainty is required, and this certainty is required as to every proposition of proof requisite to constitute the offense.
>
> (Tennessee Pattern Jury Instructions – Criminal, 4th ed. 1995, 7:14)

We wonder how many times you, our reader, would need to reread this definition before you thought you knew what the phrase 'reasonable doubt' signified and how little you would have understood if you, like the Tennessee jurors, had only heard it read aloud and only once. If, as a member of the jury, you had asked for clarification, the judge would have merely read the text aloud for a second time. The laudable explanation for this refusal to explain or gloss is that the judge thereby avoids the possibility of a subsequent appeal against conviction on the grounds that s/he had misdirected the jury. This solution does not, of course, avoid a subsequent appeal on the grounds that the jury did not understand the judge's instruction.

As Dumas points out, the three sentences of this instruction contain eleven clauses, two of the sentences have subordinate clauses embedded within other subordinate clauses and all three sentences contain complicated nominal groups and difficult lexis. Dumas offers a suggested more comprehensible revision, but it is four times as long as the original. What we see here is a definition which may be legally watertight, but which is communicatively flawed and worse, such semantic obscurity could cause a miscarriage of justice. Dumas, acting as expert witness, did indeed argue in another case that there was serious doubt as to whether the members of a jury which had sentenced a man to death, had actually understood the meaning of 'reasonable doubt' 'as the court intended' (Dumas 2002: 246–47).

One of the key critical and reformist projects of the late twentieth and early twenty-first century has been the Plain Language movement and this campaign has at times successfully ventured into the legal world, but this has usually been when initiated by lawyers – in most professional fields, but particularly in medicine and law, it is extremely difficult to change anything from the outside. However Tiersma (this volume), a trained linguist as well as a law professor, was fortunate enough to be invited to act, over a period of six years, as 'linguistic consultant' to two committees made up of judges and lawyers which were set up in 1997, following the perceived debacle of the first O J Simpson murder trial, in order to redraft the California Pattern Jury Instructions so that they would 'accurately state the law using language ... understandable to jurors' (Kelso

1996). The resulting, much more comprehensible, Instructions became effective in 2006. The California definition of 'reasonable doubt', which can usefully be compared with the Tennessee instruction above, was rewritten as:

> Proof beyond a reasonable doubt is proof that leaves you with an abiding conviction that the charge is true. The evidence need not eliminate all possible doubt because everything in life is open to some possible or imaginary doubt.
>
> (California Plain Language Rewrite, 2005)

One hopes that, following the lead of California, more States will decide not only to redraft their instructions but also to involve linguists in the process. Even so, as linguists we are fully aware of the communicative differences between spoken and written language and we should still campaign for a move towards the adoption of a system like that currently used in the English courts where the jury instructions are not lexically and grammatically dense written-to-be-read texts, but rather encoded in spoken language which is composed in real time. In addition to the use of the lexis and grammar of speech, an added help to the jury would be lexical simplification, for instance the use of 'sure' instead of 'beyond reasonable doubt'. Heffer (2006) analysing English criminal trials from the 1990s found that in 93 out of the 100 summings-up he examined, the judges used 'sure' in the grammatical Complement slot, predicated of 'the jury' acting as grammatical Subject, as an ordinary language substitute for 'reasonable doubt': 'so that you are sure'; 'make/making you sure'; 'feel sure'; 'must be sure'. Of the remaining seven judges, five combined 'sure' with 'reasonable doubt' – 'sure beyond (a/any/all) reasonable doubt'; the remaining two used 'reasonable doubt' with no gloss.

In addition, the inclusion of everyday examples, if possible framed in colloquial language, as an integral part of instructing the jury, should be encouraged. For example, Heffer (2002: 241) provides an extract where a judge is illustrating the concept of 'handling goods knowing or believing them to be stolen':

> If for example you were standing in Marks and Spencers and you watched a shoplifter steal and then ten minutes later you took the goods from the shoplifter you would receive them knowing that they were stolen. If on the other hand you were not in Marks and Spencers when the shoplifter stole that elegant hat and you were outside in The Crown and Robe and somebody came up to you and said 'Look what I have just nicked from Marks and Spencers' you do not have direct knowledge of it, but you have the belief based on what you have been told. So that is the distinction.

The English Caution is another written-to-be-spoken legal text that has come in for a great deal of scrutiny. When, in England and Wales in 1994, the law was changed in order to place conditions on the right to silence, a new 60-word version was produced. This was quickly found to be too wordy for police officers to remember and, in 1995, it was reduced to the following 37 words:

> You do not have to say anything. But it may harm your defence if you do not mention when questioned something which you later rely on in court. Anything you do say may be given in evidence.

A government spokeswoman, Baroness Blatch, said in the House of Lords that she believed this version would be both 'easy for the police to remember and easy for suspects to understand'. Her confidence would appear to have been unfounded, and several forensic linguists (Cotterill 2000; Russell 2000 and Rock 2007) have found major problems with the second sentence, particularly, but not exclusively, with the words and phrases presented in bold below.

> But it may **harm** your defence if you do not **mention when questioned** something which you later **rely** on in court.

Among the many linguistic problems are:

i)   that 'harm' is usually used with animate objects and so the meaning of 'harm your defence' is at best obscure;
ii) that the suspect cannot know how important something needs to be in order to be classified as 'something which you later rely on' in a future defence;
iii) nor indeed, until there is a specific accusation, what defence may be needed;
iv) that 'mention' usually collocates with unimportant facts, certainly not facts one might 'rely on';
v)   that the phrase 'when questioned' is crucially ambiguous – does it mean 'in response to questions' put by the interviewer or 'during the whole period when you are being questioned';
vi) to put this problem more explicitly, is an omission during the interview of something later relied on supposed to be the fault of the interviewing officer, who didn't ask the right questions or of the interviewee, who should have volunteered the information?

So far attempts to have the English and Welsh Caution redrafted have failed, despite quite general dissatisfaction, unlike in the state of NSW in Australia, where Gibbons (2001a) worked with the Police to improve their Caution.

In the absence of a change in wording, both police and suspects in the UK have to rely on the individual police officer who is enjoined to ensure that the interviewee understands the caution. The problem is, as Rock (2007) clearly illustrates, that some officers are very much better at ensuring understanding than others. This therefore raises other questions for the police to confront, hopefully through research undertaken jointly with linguists; for instance, should it be left to the individual linguistically untrained police officer to assess a given suspect's understanding and to encode the necessary explanations as s/he thinks best or should there be a standardised pre-formulated explanation of the caution to be used with all suspects? And as Stokoe and Edwards (this volume) show, any amount of confirmation of understanding at the beginning of an interview does not guarantee that the suspect will take up their rights or feel able to assert them in the interview.

The language of interaction in the legal process

Police interviews

Both the US Miranda Warnings and the UK police caution explicitly advise the suspect of their right to remain silent. The Miranda warning is superficially much more positive:

'you have the right to remain silent' as compared with the UK caution 'you do not have to say anything. But it may harm your defence … '. However, Janet Ainsworth's analysis of the Miranda warning in her chapter in this volume demonstrates how successive Supreme Court judgments have produced a situation in which it is very difficult for the suspect to actually claim his or her right to silence. This is an area where all the necessary descriptive groundwork has been done to provide a solid basis for a campaign to restore the constitutional right to silence; what is now needed is a pro-active stance.

As we noted above, the most recent UK police caution strongly recommends suspects not to exercise their right to silence on the grounds that doing so might harm their defence. However, detailed analysis of interviews by Haworth (2009 and this volume) shows how difficult it can be for the average interviewee to contribute what s/he considers to be relevant information. Indeed she makes a strong case for rethinking what is currently the main purpose of the interview – to provide evidence for prosecution – on the grounds that not only is it unfair to the suspect in that he is not allowed to provide defence evidence but it can also be prejudicial to the police as well, in that they may proceed with a fatally flawed prosecution case. If her preliminary findings are confirmed, they will provide the basis for joint police/linguist research which could lead to changes in the nature and organisation of investigative interviews.

At the same time, it will be necessary to consider the implications of the fact that, despite the strength of the warning of the potential dangers of remaining silent embodied in the Caution, there is little evidence in research so far of UK juries being explicitly reminded of the inferences they can legitimately draw. Stokoe and Edwards' chapter, which looks at the so far unresearched area of lawyers' turns in police interviews, invites a re-consideration of existing procedures. Ainsworth, in her chapter on the non-invocation of rights by suspects and the very small number who actually have lawyers present, highlights the difficulties and injustices faced by defendants in the American system. Stokoe and Edwards' chapter shows us some of the beneficial effects of what lawyers can do in their interventions, when present. Though they interact for relatively few turns in interviews (and there are rules on when and how they can intervene), lawyer interventions work positively to invoke suspects' rights (i.e. the fact that they 'do not have to say anything'). Stokoe and Edwards show that one of the major benefits of this is that the lawyers' interventions are tailored to a specific moment, meaning that suspects do not have to answer that specific question. This moment-by-moment intervention means that rights are dealt with in situ rather than left as generalised principles for the suspects themselves to have to choose when to apply, as is the case with the general warning issued at the start of interviews. (The danger of course, for the suspect, is that they may never do.) Spontaneous interjections by lawyers are more much effective than if the unrepresented suspect has to wait and ask for advice later. Successful lawyer interventions may also halt or deflect the trajectory of an officer's questioning, although Stokoe and Edwards also show that suspects often fail to heed their lawyer's advice and answer anyway. Lawyers who bypass suspects and deal directly with officers are most effective, though this has potential costs, both to the relationship with the client (in terms of possibly alienating and/or disenfranchising them) and with the interviewer (in terms of being obstructive). There is much future work to be done investigating the effects of the presence and absence of a lawyer, and, given the generally beneficial effects for the defendant, there should be more research into the circumstances in which and reasons why lawyers are not requested (see Ainsworth, this volume and Rock 2007).

On performing interview records

We mentioned above that in the UK it is normal not only to transcribe investigative interviews, but also to perform them in court. Paradoxically, rather than play the original recordings of the police interviews in court, the preference is to reconvert the transcribed version into a performed dialogue, for which the police witness usually plays him/herself and the prosecuting lawyer plays the accused. Even stranger things can occur. In a case in Bermuda, involving text messages sent between a 14-year-old girl, Rhiana, and her 32-year-old lover, Selassie, 'Police officer Peter Stableford and Crown counsel Larissa Burgess played the roles of Selassie and Rhiana as they read the prolific texts to the jury yesterday' (*The Royal Gazette*, August 15 2009, available at: www.royalgazette.com/siftology. royalgazette/Article/article.jsp?articleId=7d987ab3003000f&sectionId=60 [accessed 15 August 2009]). And Coulthard and Johnson (2007) show how a similar technique was used in the Harold Shipman trial in the UK where police officer and prosecuting counsel 'played' interviewing officer and Shipman, respectively.

What all playwrights and actors know only too well is that performance involves interpretation; lawyers are either blissfully unaware of this or choose to exploit its significance. In addition, as Haworth (2009) demonstrates, performance can include both accidental and deliberate misinterpretations and mistakes, all of which can be prejudicial to the accused. Finally, Holt and Johnson, Felton Rosulek and Matoesian in their chapters in this volume show how both lawyers and witnesses use the theatricality of the courtroom and the pragmatic and multimodal resources of language, to powerfully present their opinions and their testimonies. It is incumbent on the forensic linguistic community to increase awareness of the non-neutrality of performance and work towards a better solution. This is a critical forensic linguistic endeavour arising out of close analysis of data.

Working with an interpreter

There has already been a great deal of valuable research into the problems of interpreted interaction in courtrooms (Berk–Seligson 2002; Hale this volume), though outside the courtroom there has been much less work (see Kredens and Morris this volume). The major finding seems to be that problems derive mainly from the lack of sufficiently well-trained interpreters. These problems are compounded not infrequently by the lack of training for police and legal professionals on how to work successfully with an interpreter (see Gray this volume).

The problems of professionalising interpreting are only partly academic – poor remuneration works against attracting the best into the field – but so far as they are academic, forensic linguists need to involve themselves more actively in training both interpreters and legal professionals, with the latter group being the more difficult to gain access to. Sandra Hale in NSW, Australia, contributes one lecture on court interpreting to a regular course for trainee judges and the Aston Centre for Forensic Linguistics runs hands-on courses teaching police officers how to work with an interpreter, but this is only a drop in the ocean. In an ideal world all police and legal professionals who work in countries with a large proportion of non-native speakers, should have a short course on working with an interpreter as an integral part of their training.

Another research area which has just emerged is the nature and successfulness of video-link-mediated interpreted interaction. Recently, in order to save time and money, courts have introduced video links which enable prisoners to participate in committal and bail hearings without leaving the prison to attend court. Even prisoners who need the help of interpreters are now participating in such hearings and research is just beginning into how satisfactory this process actually is and will if necessary, suggest improvements or even its abandonment.

Finally, Aldridge (this volume) reports how earlier research into the difficulties experienced by vulnerable witnesses in general and by children in particular brought about changes in the ways in which evidence was elicited in court. Innovations included the provision of screens for certain witnesses and allowing children's evidence-in-chief to be video-recorded in advance. However, Aldridge reports that sadly, in the main, the changes have not substantially improved the situation and concludes that radical measures are needed:

> It seems that the adversarial system cannot easily offer justice for vulnerable witnesses and we must now turn our attention to research the popular contention that inquisitorial style criminal proceedings hold inherent advantages for vulnerable witnesses.
>
> (Aldridge, this volume: 313)

One theme that ties much of the above discussion together is the lack of communication and genuine collaboration between institutions and researchers. Gray (this volume) talks of the need for cross-professional communication between linguists and lawyers. What is also needed is more general communication: between linguists and interpreters; lawyers and judges; and police, prison and probation officers. Gray urges linguists to start the ball rolling, so that is a major challenge for the next decade.

The linguist as expert witness

The role of the expert witness

The role and position of the expert witness is rarely simple. In countries with an investigative legal system, the expert is usually appointed by the court; in those operating an adversarial system, experts are typically briefed and paid by one of the disputing parties. Not unnaturally, experts in the latter system are likely to feel some kind of loyalty, consciously or unconsciously to 'their' side, as Solan (this volume) eloquently points out. At the time of writing, there is a move in the UK both to clarify the role of the expert and to ensure the relevance and reliability of the evidence provided.

As far as clarifying their role goes, all UK experts must now acknowledge that their 'overriding duty is to the court and not the party calling [them] to testify'. In addition, experts contracted by the Crown Prosecution Service are obliged to append a Declaration of Understanding similar to the following:

> I am an expert in forensic linguistics. I confirm that I have read the guidance contained in the booklet known as Disclosure: Expert's evidence and unused material which details my role and documents my responsibilities, in relation to revelation as an expert witness. I have followed the guidance and recognise the continuing nature of my responsibilities of revelation. In accordance with my duties of revelation, as documented in the guidance booklet, I confirm that:

a. I have complied with my duties to record, retain and reveal material in accordance with the Criminal Procedure and Investigations Act 1996, as amended;

b. I have compiled an Index of all material. I will ensure that the Index is updated in the event I am provided with or generate additional material;

c. in the event my opinion changes on any material issue, I will inform the investigating officer, as soon as reasonably practicable and give reasons.

In 1997, with support from the Home Office, a small group of bona fide members of the profession – including Angela Gallop of Forensic Access – got together to discuss what to do about the lack of regulation. The upshot was the establishment of the Council for the Registration of Forensic Practitioners (CRFP) – an independent regulatory body to promote public confidence in forensic practice in the UK (www. forensic-access.co.uk/ forensic-access-publications/benchmark-newsletter/crfp.htm [acce- ssed 1 August 2009]). CRFP accreditation was based on rigorous peer review of forensic practitioners and the intention was that in the long term it would be difficult for an unregistered practitioner to continue to give evidence. Mainly through the efforts of Tim Grant, forensic linguistics was accepted as a CRFP discipline in 2008, but, at roughly the same time, a government subsidy was withdrawn and, in early 2009, the Council was forced to close.

Paradoxically, at almost the same time the UK Forensic Science Regulator proposed that forensic providers, including expert witnesses, should be accredited to accepted standards by a recognised independent body. So far there are no details, but yet another change is afoot. As a rough generalisation, up to the time of writing in 2009, courts in the UK have approved the expert witness, whereas courts in the States have approved the method. In other words, in the UK an individual judge could approve an expert who was felt to have useful expertise to offer and the expert could within reason use whatever method s/he considered appropriate, while in the States, no matter how distinguished the expert, s/he would have to demonstrate that the method used satisfied first the Frye and latterly the Daubert test (Tiersma and Solan 2002). The consequence has been that whereas expertise in the areas of handwriting and voice analysis has long been accepted in the UK, it was typically not accepted in the United States.

However, in 2009, the UK Law Commission proposed that there should be a new statutory test for determining the admissibility of expert evidence in criminal proceedings, which is likely to be very similar to the Daubert test. Forensic linguists and phoneticians are awaiting developments with interest and wondering which of their methods will be approved without dispute, which will need to be modified and which will be disallowed.

There has been interesting descriptive work on the expert witness in court. Heffer (2005) has documented how experts are allowed longer turns, Maley (2000) and Maley and Fahey (1991) have shown how the expert's evidence can be (mis)used for their own purposes by the courtroom lawyers and Shuy (2006) has produced a 'nuts and bolts guide'. What we have not yet seen is a personal account written by an inexperienced academic about giving expert evidence in court. For an academic used to both presenting information in well-structured ways and to engaging in clarificatory debate, the courtroom might seem to hold few surprises. However, it does.

First of all the academic may take a while to realise that there is no point in engaging in debate with the cross-examining lawyer as s/he is paid not to be convinced. Worse, the responses should not even be directed to the questioner who is purportedly asking questions on behalf of the court, but rather to the jury, or perhaps, at least in an English court, it is even better to address their responses directly to the judge who will summarise the evidence for the jury at the end of the trial. But what is most difficult for the expert, is the fact that what s/he considered to be a well organised, well argued written report may be at worst mangled, at best presented less than successfully, through the typical lawyer–witness elicitation process. The expert may very well feel disempowered.

Two interesting questions for future research are firstly, whether the growing availability of courts with PowerPoint facilities will change the nature of the expert/lawyer power relationship, by returning control over content and sequencing to the expert; and secondly, whether a competent lecturer with (audio)visual resources can indeed present evidence more successfully than the traditional elicitation method allows, or whether the lawyer with his case overview is still better placed to select and sequence items from the expert's report.

As we noted above, in the adversarial system, expert witnesses are contracted by prosecution or defence. A consequence of this is that, typically, they give their evidence as part of the case for the side that contracted them and consequently, if there are experts on both sides, their evidence may be heard several days apart, further complicating the situation for the jury. To rectify this, some courts now ask the experts to produce a joint report in advance of appearing, which specifies where they agree and disagree, while Judge Gray (this volume) reports, as a further modification, a 'hot tub' system he has introduced into his own court.

> The opposing expert witnesses are called at the conclusion of all of the other evidence led by both parties. Having been duly affirmed or sworn, they are then required to debate directly between themselves the matters on which they are not agreed, so that the judge and the lawyers can observe the debate. Only when this debate has been exhausted will the lawyers be permitted to question the witnesses. The judge will also ask any questions that he or she considers will help to clarify the issues.
>
> (Gray, this volume: 599)

New forensic tools

The work on student collusion which began with Johnson (1997) and led to the development of the plagiarism detection program *Copycatch* (Woolls and Coulthard 1998; Woolls 2002) has now been significantly developed to work on large collections of texts. A more recent version of the *Copycatch* program is in regular use in universities worldwide, particularly in the British Open University where batches of 3,000 essays on a single topic are not uncommon. *Copycatch* was customised for UCAS (the Universities and Colleges Admissions Service) to process applications for admission to UK universities. All applicants must submit a personal statement of up to 4,000 characters (around 600 words) as part of their application, but there were growing suspicions that some of the statements were not sufficiently personal. In 2006–7, a study by Woolls of a sample corpus of 50,000 such statements found that 234 of them related a dramatic incident involving 'burning a hole in pyjamas at age eight'. A further 175 contained a statement which involved 'an elderly or infirm grandfather' and 370 statements contained a sentence which included 'a fascination for how the human body works'. The hole in

611

the pyjamas accident was found to originate in a model personal statement placed on an Internet website devoted to advice to applicants.

Model Personal Statement

Ever since I accidentally burnt holes in my pyjamas after experimenting with a chemistry set on my 8th Birthday, I have always had a passion for science. Following several hospital visits during my teenage years to explore my interest, the idea of a career that would exploit my humanity and problem-solving abilities always made medicine a natural choice.

(UCAS 7/03/07 www.ucas.ac.uk/website/news/media_releases/2007/ [accessed 1 July 2009])

Below is an extract from one of the suspect applications with the borrowed items in bold.

Ever since I burnt holes in my dress **after experimenting with** my brother's **chemistry set** when I was 10, **I have always** been **passion**ate about the **sciences. Following several visits** to the local **hospital during my teenage years** as a result of minor accidents, **the idea of a career that would** help people **always made** physiotherapy **a natural choice**.

A version of *Copycatch* is now used to compare all the 500,000 personal statements submitted annually both with each other and with a growing database of statements from previous years. As one might hope, knowledge of the existence of the program seems to have reduced significantly the incidence of the plagiarism it was designed to detect. Here we can see how a program, which was a gleam in the eye in 1995, became, in little over a decade, a highly reliable tool. We expect the next decade to see some of the tools currently under development have a similar impact. We will mention only two.

Firstly, there is still a need for an internet-searching equivalent to the *Copycatch* suite of programs. Most universities worldwide use *Turnitin* to detect internet plagiarism, but it works with chunks of language which are too large and, given the way more sophisticated plagiarists adapt the texts they have borrowed, only a *Copycatch* type of program will be adequate, particularly if one wants to find chunks of as little as seven or eight running words, which Coulthard (2004) suggests can be indicative of borrowing (see also Coulthard, Johnson, Kredens and Woolls, this volume).

Secondly there is a growing interest in trying to determine the age, gender and first language of authors – the forensic applications for such programs obviously range from the investigative use by police and security services in order to narrow the range of suspects to manageable proportions, to the confirmatory in authorship attribution cases – it is easy to think of past cases where candidate authors differed in terms of age, gender and/or first language and where a reliable program would have saved many hours of work. Unsurprisingly, most of the development work is being done on texts written in English, but early results are promising, (Koppel *et al.* 2009; Grant *et al.* 2009), and once these methodologies have been refined, there is no reason why they should not also be adapted for use with other languages.

One recent development – the creation of reference corpora – will help to make some approaches to authorship attribution more acceptable to a Daubert test. Whereas forensic phoneticians have long had population statistics for the distribution of certain features like, for instance, pitch of voice and certain speech defects, which could allow them to say that for example a particular suspect voice had a particularly high average pitch that was only found in one male in a hundred in the general population, until recently, forensic linguists have had no such data, with the exception of McMenamin (2002) who reported a collection of some 700 envelopes with California addresses. On the basis of this collection, he could observe in one reported case that two particular features that co-occurred in the suspect addresses were co-selected on only 1% of the envelopes in his reference corpus.

Now significant corpora of appellant decisions (see Finegan, this volume), suicide notes, police statements and particularly of text messages, are being compiled (see Tagg 2009 and Grant this volume). What this means is that whereas, for instance, analysis in early text messaging cases had to rely on simply comparing past messages sent by the candidate authors with the suspect messages, it is now possible to refer to population statistics for crucial features and to begin to move towards calculating error rates. And Finegan challenges new researchers and students to compile corpora from readily available material from Lexis-Nexis or Westlaw and through websites such as the US Supreme Court (www.supremecourtus.gov/) and through the Oyez Project (www.oyez.org) for oral arguments before the US Supreme Court (which have been made since 1955 and are available, going back several decades). These are amazing and unexplored resources for forensic linguists researching legal register.

Asylum seekers

As Eades (this volume) describes, many governments use language analysis as an aid in the determination of the origin and therefore the genuineness of asylum seekers. Concerned forensic linguists in several countries at the turn of the century tried to alert governments to problems in the methodology and to the unreliability of some of the companies involved. In 2004, nineteen linguists and phoneticians produced a set of 'Guidelines for the Use of Language Analysis in Relation to Questions of National Origin in Refugee Cases' (www.lagb.org.uk/language-origin-refugees.pdf). The guidelines were endorsed by a dozen professional organisations including the IAFL and the IAFPA. However, problems continue. Some companies are not following the guidelines and Fraser, looking from a purely phonetic standpoint, suggests that what is needed is

(a) a proper research programme which would investigate people's actual abilities in recognising, discriminating and identifying accents under various sociolinguistic conditions; (b) collaboration between LADO [Language Analysis for Determining Origin] agencies and linguists to develop analysis and testing procedures; and (c) a system of accreditation by an independent, international authority for the agencies that carry out LADO.

(Fraser 2009: 113)

Obviously such a programme could easily be expanded to include linguistic issues as well and innovative work reported above on detecting first languages would be very relevant.

Concluding observations

As a profession we are working towards a utopian future where anyone who is arrested both understands and is able to claim their rights; where anyone who needs the help of an interpreter is able to have one and where the prejudicial effect of interpreting on the legal process is reduced to an absolute minimum; where all legally significant interactions are audio- or video-recorded; and where all expert opinions, whether on the origin of an asylum speaker, the authorship of a disputed text, the comprehensibility of a text or the confusability or two trademarks, are reliable and reproducible. This *Handbook* is a guide to progress so far; we hope to be able to report significant improvements by the time of the second edition but in the meantime, there is a lot of corpus linguistic, computational and inter-cultural work to be done.

References

15 U.S.C. §§ 1331 et seq., [1970] Federal Cigarette Labeling and Advertising Act, (1970).

34 Fed. Reg. § 7919 [1969], An Amendment of the Federal Cigarette Labeling and Advertising Act, 15 U.S.C. §§1331 et seq. (1965).

Abbott, H.P. (2008) *The Cambridge Introduction to Narrative*, Cambridge: Cambridge University Press.

Adams, K. and Winter, A. (1997) 'Gang graffiti as a discourse genre', *Journal of Sociolinguistics*, 1(3): 337–60.

Adams, M. (2005) 'Lexical property rights: trademarks and American dictionaries', *Verbatim: The Language Quarterly*, 30: 1–8.

Adams, M. and Westerhaus, J. (2005) 'Surnames and American trademark law', *Names: A Journal of Onomastics*, 53: 259–73. Available online at: www.adobe.com/products/flashplayer/ (accessed 8 June 2009).

Agrimonti, L. (1995) 'Note: the limitations of Daubert and its misapplication to quasi-scientific experts: a two year case review of Daubert v. Merrell-Dow Pharmaceuticals, Inc., 113 S. Ct. 2786 (1993)', *Washburn Law Journal*, 35: 134–56.

Ahmad, M.I. (2007) 'Interpreting communities: lawyering across language difference', *UCLA Law Review*, 54(5): 999–1086.

Ainsworth, J. (1993): 'In a different register: the pragmatics of powerlessness in. police interrogation', *The Yale Law Journal*, 103(2): 259–322.

——(2006) 'Linguistics as a knowledge domain in the law', *Drake Law Review*, 54: 651–69.

——(2008) '"You have the right to remain silent … " but only if you ask for it just so: the role of linguistic ideology in American police interrogation law', *International Journal of Speech, Language and The Law*, 15: 1–21.

Airy, J.T. (2009) 'Valuable lessons learned at an international counterterrorism forum', *The FBI Law Enforcement Bulletin*, August (1–9).

Aitken, C. (1995) *Statistics and the Evaluation of Evidence for Forensic Scientists*, Chichester: John Wiley.

Aitken, J.K. and Butter, P. (2004) *Piesse – The Elements of Drafting*, 10th edn, Sydney: Lawbook Co.

Aldridge, M. and Luchjenbroers, J. (2007) 'Linguistic manipulations in legal discourse: framing questions and "smuggling" information', *International Journal of Speech, Language and the Law*, 14(1): 85–107.

——(2008) 'Vulnerable witnesses and problems of portrayal: a consideration of videotaped interviews in child rape case', *Journal of English Linguistics*, 36(3): 266–84.

Aldridge, M. and Williams, C. (2006) 'A survey of police officers' attitudes of interviewing with special measures', unpublished ms.

Aldridge, M. and Wood, J. (1997) 'Talking about feelings: young children's ability to express emotions', *Child Abuse and Neglect*, 21: 1221–33.

Aldridge, M., Timmins, K. and Wood, J. (1997) 'Children's understanding of legal terminology: judges get money at pet shows, don't they?', *Child Abuse Review*, 6: 141–46.

Allen, L.E. (1957) 'Symbolic logic: a razor-edged tool for drafting and interpreting legal documents', *Yale Law Journal*, 66(6): 833–879.

Allimant, A. and Anne, S. (2008) 'No room … homelessness and the experiences of women of non-English speaking backgrounds', paper presented at *5th National Homelessness Conference*, Adelaide, Australia.

Altman, R. (2008) *A Theory of Narrative*, New York: Columbia University Press.

American National Standards Institute (1978) *American national standard guide for classifying and labeling epoxy products according to their hazardous potentialities*, New York: ANSI.

Amsterdam, A.G. and Bruner, J. (2002) *Minding the Law*, Cambridge, MA: Harvard University Press.

Anderson, P. (2007) *Technical Communication: A Reader-Centered Approach*, 6th edn, Boston, MA: Thomson/Wadsworth.

Andrews, M., Squire, C. and Tamboukou, M. (eds) (2008) *Doing Narrative Research*, Thousand Oaks, CA: Sage Publications, Inc.

Angélil-Carter, S (2002) *Stolen Language? Plagiarism in Writing*, London: Longman.

Angermeyer, P.S. (2005) 'Who is "you"? Polite forms of address and ambiguous participant roles in court interpreting', *Target*, 17: 203–26.

Apitz, G. and Lin, J. (2007) 'Interfaces to support the scholarly exploration of text collections', in *Proceedings of the CHI 2007 Workshop for Exploratory Search and HCI*, San Jose, CA. Available online at: www.umiacs.umd.edu/~digidock/publications.html.

Archer, D. (2002) '"Can innocent people be guilty?" A sociopragmatic analysis of examination transcripts from the Salem witchcraft trials', *Journal of Historical Pragmatics*, 3(1): 1–30.

——(2005) *Questions and Answers in the English Courtroom (1640–1760)*, Amsterdam and Philadelphia, PA: John Benjamins.

——(2006a) '(Re)initiating strategies: judges and defendants in Early Modern English courtrooms', *Journal of Historical Pragmatics*, 7(2): 181–211.

——(2006b) 'Tracing the development of advocacy in two nineteenth-century English trials', in M. Dossena and I. Taavitsainen (eds) *Diachronic Perspectives on Domain-Specific English*, Bern: Peter Lang, 43–67.

——(forthcoming) 'Tracing the crime narratives within the Palmer trial (1856): from the lawyer's opening speeches to the judge's summing up', in C. Heffer, F. Rock and J. Conley (eds) *Textual Travels in Legal-Lay Interaction*, Oxford: Oxford University Press.

Aronsson, K. (1991) 'Social interaction and the recycling of legal evidence', in N. Coupland, H. Giles and J. Wiemann (eds) *Miscommunication and Problematic Talk*, Newbury Park and London: Sage.

Atkinson, J. and Drew, P. (1979) *Order in Court: The Organisation of Verbal Interaction in Judicial Settings*, London: Macmillan.

Auburn, T., Drake, S. and Willig, C. (1995) '"You punched him, didn't you?": versions of violence in accusatory interviews', *Discourse & Society*, 6(3): 353–86.

Auburn, T., Lea, S. and Drake, S. (1999) '"It's your opportunity to be truthful": disbelief, mundane reasoning and the investigation of crime', in C. Willig (ed.) *Applied Discourse Analysis: Social and Psychological Interventions*, Buckingham: Open University Press, 44–65.

Auer, P. and Wei, L. (2007) 'Introduction: multilingualism as a problem? Monolingualism as a problem?', in P. Auer and L. Wei (eds) *Handbook of Multilingualism and Multilingual Communication*, Berlin: Mouton de Gruyter, 1–14.

Austin, A.D. (1984) *Complex Litigation Confronts the Jury System: A Case Study*, Frederick, MD: University Publications of America.

Austin, J.L. (1962) *How to Do Things with Words*, Oxford and New York: Oxford University Press.

Australian Evidence Act 1995. Available online at: www.comlaw.gov.au/ComLaw/Legislation/ActCompilation1.nsf/0/0A3CF7EBACDD51B0CA25719A00060BE6/$file/EvidenceAct1995_WD02.pdf (accessed 10 January 2008).

Axelrod, A. (2007) *Getting Your Way Every Day*, New York: American Management Association (AMACON).

Baayen, R.H. (2001) *Word Frequency Distributions*, Dordrecht: Kluwer Academic Publishers.

Bachman, L. (2000) 'Modern language testing at the turn of the century: assuring that what we count counts', *Language Testing*, 17: 1–42.

Bachman, L. and Palmer, A. (1996) *Language Testing in Practice*, Oxford: Oxford University Press.

Baddeley, A. (1992) 'Working memory', *Science*, 255(5044): 556–59.

Bailey, R. (1984) 'Dictionaries and proprietary names: the air-shuttle case', *Dictionaries*, 53–65.

Baken, R.J. and Orlikoff, R.F. (2000) *Clinical Measurement of Speech and Voice*, San Diego, CA: Singular.

Baker, J.H. (1990) *An Introduction to English Legal History*, 3rd edn, London: Butterworths.

Bakhtin, M. (1981) 'Discourse in the novel', in M. Holquist (ed.) *The Dialogic Imagination: Four Essays by M. M. Bakhtin*, Austin: University of Texas Press, 259–422.

Baldwin, J. (1993) 'Police interview techniques: establishing truth or proof?', *British Journal of Criminology*, 33: 325–52.

Baldwin, J. and French, P. (1990) *Forensic Phonetics*, London: Pinter.

Baltisberger, E. and Favaro, S. (2007) 'When informants don't want to inform: how to get relevant data in the particular context of linguistic analyses for the determination of origin (LADO)', in M.T. Turell, M. Spassova and J. Cicres (eds) *Proceedings of the 2nd European IAFL Conference on Forensic Linguistics/Language and the Law*, Barcelona: Universitat Pompeu Fabra, 85–90.

Bamberg, M. (2004) 'Considering counter narratives', in M. Bamberg and M. Andrews (eds) *Considering Counter Narratives: Narrating, Resisting, Making Sense*, Amsterdam: John Benjamins, 351–71.

Barnes, R. (2007) 'Chief Justice counsels humility: Roberts says lawyers must put themselves in Judges' shoes', *The Washington Post*, February 6, A15.

Barnhart, C.L. (ed.) (1947) *American College Dictionary*, New York: Random House.

Baron, D. (1989) 'Word law', *Verbatim*, 16: 1–4.

Barton, D. and Hamilton, M. (2000) 'Literacy practices', in D. Barton, M. Hamilton and R. Ivanič (eds) *Situated Literacies: Reading and Writing in Context*, London: Routledge, 7–15.

Barton, D., Hamilton, M. and Ivanič, R. (2000) 'Introduction: exploring situated literacies', in D. Barton, M. Hamilton and R. Ivanič (eds) *Situated Literacies: Reading and Writing in Context*, London: Routledge, 1–6.

Bauman, R. (2004) *A World Of Others' Words: Cross-Cultural Perspectives on Intertextuality*, Oxford: Blackwell Publishing.

Bauman, R. and Briggs, C. (1990) 'Poetics and performance as critical perspectives on language and social life', *Annual Review of Anthropology*, 19: 59–88.

BBC News (2003) 'McDonald's Anger over McJob Entry', 9 November, BBC News Online, accessed 23 March 2009, http://news.bbc.co.uk/2/hi/americas/3255883.stm.

——(2007) 'McDonald's Seeks "McJob" Rewrite', *BBC News Online*, 20 March 2007, accessed 23 March 2009, http://news.bbc.co.uk/2/hi/business/6469707.stm.

Beach, W.A. (1985) 'Temporal density in courtroom interaction: constraints on the recovery of past events in legal discourse', *Communication Monographs*, 52: 1–18.

Beattie, J.M. (1986) *Crime and the Courts in England 1660–1800*, Oxford: Clarendon Press.

——(1991) 'Scales of justice: defence counsel and the English criminal trial in the eighteenth and nineteenth centuries', *Law and History Review*, 9(2): 221–67.

Beaupré, M. (1986) *Interpreting Bilingual Legislation*, Toronto: Carswell.

Bedell, G. (2000) *3 Steps to Yes*, New York: Crown Business.

Bell, A. (1984) 'Language style as audience design', *Language in Society*, 13: 145–204.

Bell, B. and Loftus, A. (1985) 'Vivid persuasion in the courtroom', *Journal of Personality Assessment*, 49: 659–64.

Bennell, C. and Canter, D. (2002) 'Linking commercial burglaries by modus operandi: tests using regression and ROC analysis', *Science and Justice*, 42: 153–64.

Bennett, W.L. and Feldman, M.S. (1981) *Reconstructing Reality in the Courtroom*, London: Tavistock Publications.

Benneworth, K. (2006) 'Repertoires of paedophilia: conflicting descriptions of adult–child sexual relationships in the investigative interview', *International Journal of Speech, Language and the Law*, 13(2): 190–211.

——(2007) '"Just good friends": managing the clash of discourses in police interviews with paedophiles', in J. Cotterill (ed.) *The Language of Sexual Crime*, Basingstoke: Palgrave Macmillan, 42–62.

——(2009) 'Police interviews with suspected paedophiles: a discourse analysis', *Discourse and Society*, 20 (5): 555–569.

Beres, L. and Griffith, T. (2004) 'Gangs, schools and stereotypes', *Loyola Los Angeles Law Review*, 37: 935–78.

Beretta, A., Campbell, C., Carr, T.H., Huang, J., Schmitt, L.M., Christianson, K. and Cao, Y. (2003) 'An Er-Fmri investigation of morphological inflection in German reveals that the brain makes a distinction between regular and irregular forms', *Brain and Language*, 85: 67–92.

Berger, M.A. and Solan, L.M. (2008) 'The uneasy relationship between science and law: an essay and introduction', *Brooklyn Law Review*, 73: 847–54.

Berger, P. and Luckmann, T. (1966) *The Social Construction of Reality*, Harmondsworth: Penguin Books.

Berk-Seligson, S. (1990/2002) *The Bilingual Courtroom: Court Interpreters in the Judicial Process*, Chicago: The University of Chicago Press.

——(1999) 'The impact of court interpreting on the coerciveness of leading questions', *Forensic Linguistics*, 6(1): 30–56.

——(2000) 'Interpreting for the police: issues in pre-trial phases of the judicial process', *Forensic Linguistics*, 7(2): 212–37.

——(2002) 'The Miranda warnings and linguistic coercion: the role of footing in the interrogation of a limited-English speaking murder suspect', in J. Cotterill (ed.) *Language in the Legal Process*, London: Palgrave Macmillan, 127–46.

——(2008) 'Judicial systems in contact. Access to justice and the right to interpreting/translating services among the Quichua of Ecuador', *Interpreting*, 10: 9–33.

Bhatia, V.K. (1982) *An Investigation into Formal and Functional Characteristics of Qualifications in Legislative Writing and its Application to English for Academic Legal Purposes*, PhD thesis, University of Aston in Birmingham.

——(1983) 'Simplification v. easification: the case of legal texts', *Applied Linguistics*, 4(1): 42–54.

——(1987a) 'Language of the law', *Language Teaching*, 20(3): 227–34.

——(1987b) 'Textual-mapping in British legislative writing', *World Englishes*, 6(1): 1–10.

——(1993) *Analysing Genre: Language Use in Professional Settings*, London: Longman.

——(1994) 'Cognitive structuring in legislative provisions', in J. Gibbons (ed.) *Language and the Law*, London: Longman, 136–55.

——(1997) 'Translating legal genres', in A. Trosborg (ed.) *Text Typology and Translation*, Amsterdam: John Benjamins, 203–16.

——(2004) *Worlds of Written Discourse: A genre-based view*, London and New York: Continuum.

——(2005) 'Specificity and generality in legislative expression: two sides of the coin', in Bhatia, V.K., Engberg, J., Gotti, M. and Heller, D. (eds) *Vagueness in Normative Texts*, Bern: Peter Lang, 337–356.

Bhatia, V.K. and Candlin, C.N. (2004) 'Analysing arbitration laws across legal systems', *Hermes*, 32: 13–43.

Bhatia, V.K., Candlin, C.N. and Engberg, J. (eds) (2008) *Legal Discourse across Cultures and Systems*, Hong Kong: Hong Kong University Press.

Bhatia, V.K., Engberg, J., Gotti, M. and Heller, D. (2005) *Vagueness in Normative Texts*, Bern: Peter Lang.

Biber, D. (1988) *Variation across Speech and Writing*, Cambridge: Cambridge University Press.

Biber, D. and Finegan, E. (1988) 'Adverbial stance types in English', *Discourse Processes*, 11: 1–34.

——(1989) 'Styles of stance in English: lexical and grammatical marking of evidentiality and affect', *Text*, 9: 93–124.

Biber, D., Johansson, S., Leech, G., Conrad, S. and Finegan, E. (1999) 'Stance adverbials', in *Longman Grammar of Spoken and Written English*, Harlow: Longman, 853–75.

Bittner, E. (1967) 'The police on skid row: a study of peace keeping', *American Sociological Review*, 32: 699–715.

Blatchford, H. and Foulkes, P. (2006) 'Identification of voices in shouting', *International Journal of Speech, Language and the Law*, 13: 241–54.

Bloch, B. (1948) 'A set of postulates for phonemic analysis', *Language*, 24(1): 3–46.

Blommaert, J. (2001) 'Investigating narrative inequality: African asylum seekers' stories in Belgium', *Discourse & Society*, 12(4): 413–49.

——(2005) *Discourse*, Cambridge: Cambridge University Press.

Bogen, D. and Lynch, M. (1989) 'Taking account of the hostile native: plausible deniability and the production of conventional history in the IranContra Hearings', *Social Problems*, 36: 197–224.

Bogoch, B. (1999) 'Courtroom discourse and the gendered construction of professional identity', *Law and Society Inquiry*, 24(2): 329–75.

Braun, A. (1996) 'Age estimation by different listener groups', *Forensic Linguistics*, 3: 65–73.

Braun, A. and Wagner, A. (2002) 'Is voice quality language-dependent?', in A. Braun and H.R. Masthoff (eds) *Phonetics and its Applications: Festschrift for Jens-Peter Köster on the Occasion of his 60th Birthday*, Stuttgart: Steiner.

Brazil, D. (1993) 'Telling tales', in M. Coulthard (ed.) *Advances in Spoken Discourse Analysis*, London: Routledge, 154–69.

Brennan, F. (2003) *Tampering with Asylum*, Brisbane: University of Queensland Press.

Brennan, M. (1994) 'Cross-examining children in criminal courts: child welfare under attack', in J. Gibbons (ed.) *Language and the Law*, London: Longman, 199–216.

Brennan, M. and Brennan, R.E. (1988) *Strange Language – Child Victims under Cross-Examination*, Wagga Wagga, NSW: Charles Sturt University.

Brereton, D. (1997) 'How different are rape trials? A comparison of the cross-examination of complainants in rape and assault trials', *British Journal of Criminology*, 37(2): 242–261.

Brière, E. (1978) 'Limited English speakers and the Miranda rights', *TESOL Quarterly*, 12(3): 235–45.

Briggs, C. (ed.) (1996) *Disorderly Discourse: Narrative, Conflict and Inequality*, New York: Oxford University Press.

——(1997) 'Notes on a "confession": on the construction of gender, sexuality and violence in an infanticide case', *Pragmatics*, 7(4): 519–46.

Broeders, A.P.A. (1999) 'Some observations on the use of probability scales in forensic identification', *Forensic Linguistics: International Journal of Speech, Language and the Law*, 6, ii: 228–41.

——(2001) 'Forensic speech and audio analysis, forensic linguistics 1998 to 2001: a review', 13th *INTERPOL Forensic Science Symposium*, 16–19 October 2001, Lyon, France. Available online at: www.interpol.int/Public/Forensic/IFSS/meeting13/Reviews/ForensicLinguistics.pdf.

Bromby, M.C. (2002) *The Role and Responsibilities of the Expert Witness within the UK Judicial System*, dissertation presented for the Diploma in Forensic Medical Science. Available online at: www.caledonian.ac.uk/lss/global/contactmaps/staff/bromby/DipFMSDissertation.pdf. (accessed 9 January 2008).

Brooks, P. (1996) 'The law as narrative and rhetoric', in P. Brooks and P. Gewirtz (eds) *Law's Stories: Narrative and Rhetoric in the Law*, New Haven, CT: Yale University Press, 14–22.

——(2000) *Troubling Confessions: Speaking Guilt in Law and Literature*, Chicago: University of Chicago Press.

Brooks, P. and Gewirtz, P. (eds) (1996) *Law's Stories: Narrative and Rhetoric in the Law*, New Haven: Yale University Press.

Brouwer, J. (2007) 'Kennedy cousin will stay in jail', *Sunday Mirror*, 28 October 2007, p. 28.

Brown, P. and Levinson, S. (1987) *Politeness: Some Universals in Language Usage*, Cambridge: Cambridge University Press.

Bruner, J. (1978) 'The role of dialogue in language', in A. Sinclair, R. Jarvella and W.J.M. Levelt (eds) *The Child's Conception of Language*, New York: Springer-Verlag, 241–56.

——(1986) *Actual Minds, Possible Worlds*, Cambridge, MA: Harvard University Press.

——(1990) *Acts of Meaning*, Cambridge, MA: Harvard University Press.

——(1996) *The Culture of Education*, Cambridge, MA: Harvard University Press.

——(2004) 'Life as narrative', *Social Research*, 71(3) 691–710. (Originally published in *Social Research* 54 (1), Spring 1987).

Bucholtz, M. (2006) 'Word up: social meanings of slang in California youth culture', in J. Goodman and L. Monaghan (eds) *Interpersonal Communication: An Ethnographic Approach*, London: Blackwell, 243–67.

Bucke, T., Street, R. and Brown, D. (2000) 'The right of silence: the impact of the Criminal Justice and Public Order Act 1994', *Home Office Research Study 199*, London: Home Office.

Bülow-Møller, A.M. (1991) 'Trial evidence: overt and covert communication in court', *International Journal of Applied Linguistics*, 1(1): 38–60.

Burchfield, R. (1992) *Unlocking the English Language*, New York: Hill and Wand.

Burns, B. (2001*) A Theory of the Trial*, Princeton, NJ: Princeton University Press.

Burns, S. (2001) '"Think your blackest thoughts and darken them": judicial mediation of large money damage disputes', *Human Studies*, 24(3): 227–49.

Burrell, S. (1990) 'Gang evidence: issues for criminal defence', *Santa Clara Law Review*, 30: 739–84.

Bursik, R. and Grasmick, H. (2006) 'Defining and researching gangs', in Egley, A., Maxson, C.L., Miller, J. and Klein, M.W. (eds) *The Modern Gang Reader*, 3rd edn, Los Angeles, CA: Roxbury Publ. Co., 2–13.

Burton, M., Evans, R. and Saunders, A. (2007) 'Vulnerable and intimidated witnesses and the adversarial process in England and Wales', *International Journal of Evidence and Proof*, 11(1): 1–23.

Butters, R. (2007a) 'Changing linguistic issues in US trademark litigation', in M. Turell, M. Spassova and J. Cicres (eds) *Proceedings of the Second European IAFL Conference on Forensic Linguistics/Language and the Law*, Barcelona: Universitat Pompeu Fabra, 29–42.

——(2007b) 'Sociolinguistic variation and the law', in R. Bayley and C. Lucas (eds) *Sociolinguistic Variation: Theories, Methods and Applications*, Cambridge: Cambridge University Press, 318–37.

——(2008a) 'A linguistic look at trademark dilution', *Santa Clara Computer and High Technology Law Journal*, 24: 507–19.

——(2008b) 'Review of Shuy (2006)', *Language in Society*, 37(2): 300–4.

——(2008c) 'Trademarks and other proprietary terms', in J. Gibbons and M. Turell (eds) *Dimensions of Forensic Linguistics*, Amsterdam: Benjamins, 231–47.

Butters, R. and Westerhaus, J. (2004) 'Linguistic change in words one owns: how trademarks become "generic"', in A. Curzan and K. Emmons (eds) *Studies in the History of the English Language II*, Berlin/New York: Mouton de Gruyter, 111–23.

Buttny, R. and Cohen, J.R. (2007) 'Drawing on the words of others at public hearings: Zoning, Wal-Mart, and the threat to the aquifer', *Language in Society*, 36: 735–56.

Bygate, M., Skehan, P. and Swain, M. (2001) *Research Pedagogic Tasks: Second Language Learning, Teaching and Testing*, London: Longman.

Byrd, D. (1994) 'Relation of sex and dialect to reduction', *Speech Communication*, 15: 39–54.

Cahill, D., Grebler, G., Baker, A. and Tully, B. (1988) *Vulnerable Testimony: Police Interviewing of Mentally Handicapped and Mentally Disordered People in Connection with Serious Crime,* unpublished monograph, London: Royal Society for Mentally Handicapped Children and Adults.

Cairns, D.J.A. (1998) *Advocacy and the Making of the Adversarial Criminal Trial 1800–1865*, Oxford: Clarendon Press.

Caldas-Coulthard, C.R. and Coulthard, M. (1996) *Texts and Practices. Readings in Critical Discourse Analysis*, London: Routledge.

Caldwell, H. and Fisher-Ogden, D. (2004) 'Stalking the jets and the sharks: exploring the constitutionality of the gang death penalty enhancer', *George Mason Law Review*, 12: 601–50.

Caldwell, R. (1982) 'Specialist informant interviews', reported in Bhatia, 1982.

Cambier-Langeveld, T. (2007a) 'Current methods in forensic speaker identification: results of a collaborative exercise', *International Journal of Speech, Language and the Law*, 14: 223–43.

——(2007b) 'Hot issues in the field of "language analysis"', paper presented at the IAFPA 16th annual conference of the International Association of Forensic Phonetics and Acoustics, 2007. Available online at: www.iafpa.net/confprog07.htm (accessed 26 November 2008).

Cameron, D. (2001) *Working with Spoken Discourse*, Thousand Oaks, CA: Sage Publications, Inc.

Canale, M. and Swain, M. (1980) 'Theoretical bases of communicative approaches to second language teaching and testing', *Applied Linguistics*, 1: 1–47.

Cao, D. (2007a) *Translating Law*, Clevedon: Multilingual Matters.

——(2007b) 'Inter-lingual uncertainty in bilingual and multilingual law', *Journal of Pragmatics*, 39: 69–83.

Carr-Hill, R., Passingham, S., Wolf, A. and Kent, N. (1996) *Lost Opportunities: The Language Skills of Linguistic Minorities in England and Wales*, London: The Basic Skills Agency.

Cashion, J.L. (1985) 'Politeness in courtroom language', conference paper available as Eric Document Reproduction Service, No. ED 254 882.

Cassell, J. and McNeill, D. (1991) 'Gesture and the poetics of prose', *Poetics Today*, 12(3): 375–404.

Cassell, P.G. (1996a) '*Miranda*'s social cost: an empirical reassessment', *Northwestern University Law Review*, 90: 387–499.

——(1996b) 'All benefits, no costs: the grand illusion of *Miranda*'s defenders', *Northwestern Law Review*, 90: 1084–1124.

——(2001) '*Miranda*'s social cost: An empirical reassessment', *Northwestern University Law Review*, 90: 387–499.

Cassell, P.G. and Hayman, B.S. (1996) 'Police interrogation in the 1990's: an empirical study of the effects of *Miranda*', *UCLA Law Review*, 43: 839–931.

Cederborg, A. (2002) 'The discourse of police interviews: the case of sexually abused children', in H. Giles (ed.) *Law Enforcement, Communication and Community*, Amsterdam: John Benjamins.

de Certeau, M. (1986) *Heterologies: Discourse on the Other*, trans. B. Massumi, Minneapolis, MN: University of Minnesota Press.

Chafe, W.L. (1985) 'Linguistic differences produced by differences between speaking and writing', in D.R. Olson, N. Torrance and A. Hildyard (eds) *Literacy, Language and Learning: The Nature and Consequences of Reading and Writing*, London: Cambridge University Press, 105–23.

Chambers, J.K. (2008) 'Curriculum Vitae'. Available online at: www.chass.utoronto.ca/~chambers/ (accessed December 2008).

Chambers, J.K., Trudgill, P. and Schilling-Estes, N. (eds) (2002) *The Handbook of Language Variation and Change*, Oxford: Blackwell.

Chang, Y. (2004) 'Courtroom questioning as a culturally situated persuasive genre of talk', *Discourse and Society*, 15(6): 705–22.

Channell, J. (1994) *Vague Language*, Oxford: Oxford University Press.

Charrow, R. and Charrow, V. (1979) 'Making legal language understandable: a psycholinguistic study of jury instructions', *Columbia Law Review*, 79: 1306–74.

Chaski, C. (2001) 'Empirical evaluations of language-based author identification techniques', *International Journal of Speech, Language and the Law*, 8(1): 1–65.

——(2005) 'Who's at the keyboard? Authorship attribution in digital evidence investigations', *International Journal of Digital Evidence*, 4: 1–13.

Chatman, S. (1978) *Story and Discourse*, London: Cornell University Press.

Cheng, E.K. and Yoon, A.H. (2005) 'Does Frye or Daubert matter? A study of scientific admissibility standards', *Virginia Law Review*, 91: 471–512.

Cheshire, J. (2002) 'Sex and gender in variationist research', in J.K. Chambers, P. Trudgill and N. Schilling-Estes (eds) *The Handbook of Language Variation and Change*, Oxford: Blackwell.

Chomsky, N. (1985) *The Logical Structure of Linguistic Theory*, Chicago: University of Chicago Press.

Christensen, T.P. (2008) 'Judges' deviations from norm-based direct speech in court', *Interpreting*, 10: 99–127.

Cicourel, A.V. (1968) *The Social Organization of Juvenile Justice*, New York: Wiley.

Clankie, S. (2002) 'Theory of genericization on brand name change', *Studies in Onomastics*, 6, Lewiston, New York: Edwin Mellen.

Clarke, C. and Milne, R. (2001) *National Evaluation of the PEACE Investigative Interviewing Course*, London: Home Office.

Clayman, S. and Heritage, J. (2002) *The News Interview: Journalists and Public Figures on the Air*, Cambridge: Cambridge University Press.

Cliff, N. (1959) 'Adverbs as multipliers', *Psychological Review*, 66(1): 27–44.

Clift, R. and Holt, E. (2007) 'Introduction', in E. Holt and R. Clift (eds) *Reporting Talk: Reported Speech in Interaction*, Cambridge: Cambridge University Press, 1–15.

Clopper, C.G. and Pisoni, D.B. (2004) 'Some acoustic cues for the perceptual categorization of American English regional dialects', *Journal of Phonetics*, 32: 111–40.

——(2006) 'Effects of region of origin and geographic mobility on perceptual dialect categorization', *Language Variation and Change*, 18: 193–221.

Cloud, M., Shepherd, G.B., Barkoff, A.N., Shur, J.V., Chi, U. and Rev, L. (2002) 'Words without meaning: the constitution, confessions, and mentally retarded suspects', *University of Chicago Law Review*, 69: 495–624.

Coates, L. and Wade, A. (2004) 'Telling it like it isn't: obscuring perpetrator responsibility for violent crime', *Discourse and Society*, 5: 189–206.

Coates, L., Bavelas, J. and Gibson, J. (1994) 'Anomalous language in sexual assault trial judgements', *Discourse and Society*, 5: 189–206.

Cody, M.J. and McLaughlin, M.L. (1988) 'Accounts on trial: oral arguments in traffic court', in C. Antaki (ed.) *Analysing Everyday Explanation: A Casebook of Methods*, London: Sage, 113–26.

Cohen, L. (1977) *The Probable and the Provable*, Oxford: Clarendon Press.

Coldrey, J. (1987) 'Aboriginals and the criminal courts', in K.M. Hazlehurst (ed.) *Ivory Scales: Black Australia and the Law*, Sydney: University of New South Wales Press.

Cole, S.A. (2004) 'Grandfathering evidence: fingerprint admissibility rulings from Jennings to Llera Plaza and back again', *American Criminal Law Review*, 41: 1189–1276.

Coleman, R.O. (1976) 'A comparison of the contributions of two voice quality characteristics to the perception of maleness and femaleness in the voice', *Journal of Speech and Hearing Research*, 19: 168–80.

Collins, D. (2001) *Reanimated Voices: Speech Reporting in a Historical Pragmatic Perspective*, Amsterdam: John Benjamins.

——(2007) 'Speech reporting and the suppression of orality in seventeenth-century Russian trial dossiers', *Journal of Historical Pragmatics*, 1: 175–99.

Comack, E. (1999) 'Theoretical excursions', in E. Comack (ed.) *Locating Law: Race/Class/Gender Connections*, Halifax, Nova Scotia: Fernwood Publishing, 19–68.

Committee on Standard Jury Instructions, Civil, of the Superior Court of Los Angeles County, California (1956) *California Jury Instructions: Civil*, St. Paul, MN: West Publishing Co.

——(2004) *California Jury Instructions: Civil*, St. Paul, MN: West Group.

Committee on Standard Jury Instructions, Criminal, of the Superior Court of Los Angeles County, California (2003) *California Jury Instructions: Criminal*, St. Paul, MN: West Group.

Conger, J. (1998) *Winning 'Em Over*, New York: Simon & Shuster.

Conley, J.M. (2006) 'Comment – power is as power does', *Law and Social Inquiry*, 31(2): 467–75.

Conley, J.M. and O'Barr, W.M. (1990) *Rules versus Relationships: The Ethnography of Legal Discourse*, Chicago: University of Chicago Press.

——(1998/2005) *Just Words: Law, Language and Power*, Chicago: University of Chicago Press.

Conquergood, D. (1994) 'Homeboys and hoods: gang communication and cultural space', in L. Frey (ed.) *Group Communication in Context: Studies of Natural Groups*, Hillsdale, NJ: Lawrence Erlbaum, 23–55.

Coode, G. (1845) *On Legislative Expression, or, the Language of the Written Law*, Oxford: Oxford University Press.

Cooke, M. (2009) 'Interpreter ethics versus customary law: quality and compromise in aboriginal languages interpreting', in S. Hale and U. Ozolins (eds) *Critical Link 5. Quality in Interpreting: A Shared Responsibility*, Amsterdam and Philadelphia, PA: John Benjamins Publishing Company, 85–98.

Corcoran, C. (2004) 'A critical examination of the use of language analysis interviews in asylum proceedings: a case study of a West African seeking asylum in the Netherlands', *International Journal of Speech, Language and the Law*, 11(2): 200–21.

Corley, M. and Steward, O.W. (2008) 'Hesitation dysfluencies in spontaneous speech: the meaning of um', *Language and Linguistics Compass*, 2: 589–602.

Correia, R.D.C. (2003) 'Translation of EU legal texts', in A. Tosi (ed.) *Crossing Barriers and Bridging Cultures: The Challenges of Multilingual Translation for the European Union*, Clevedon: Multilingual Matters, 21–37.

Cotter, C. and Walking Turtle, E. (2001) *USA Phrasebook: Understanding Americans and Their Culture*, 2nd edn, Victoria, Australia: Lonely Planet.

Cotterill, J. (2000) 'Reading the rights: a cautionary tale of comprehension and comprehensibility', *Forensic Linguistics*, 7: 4–25.

——(2001) 'Domestic discord, rocky relationships: semantic prosodies in representation of marital violence in the O.J. Simpson trial', *Discourse & Society*, 12(3): 291–312.

——(2002) 'Intertextuality in the trials of O.J. Simpson', in J. Cotterill (ed.) *Language in the Legal Process*, Hampshire/New York: Palgrave Macmillan.

——(2003) *Language and Power in Court: A Linguistic Analysis of the OJ Simpson Trial*, Basingstoke and New York: Palgrave Macmillan.

——(2004) 'Collocation, connotation, and courtroom semantics: lawyers' control of witness testimony through lexical negation', *Applied Linguistics*, 25(4): 513–37.

Coulthard, M. (1994a) 'On the use of corpora in the analysis of forensic texts', *Forensic Linguistics*, 1(1): 27–43.

——(1994b) 'Evaluating texts', in R.M. Coulthard (ed), *Advances in Written Text Analysis*, London: Routledge, 1–11.

——(1996) 'The official version: audience manipulation in police records of interviews with suspects', in C.R. Caldas-Coulthard and M. Coulthard (eds) *Texts and Practices: Readings in Critical Discourse Analysis*, London: Routledge, 166–78.

——(2002) 'Whose voice is it? Invented and concealed dialogue in written records of verbal evidence produced by the police', in J. Cotterill (ed.) *Language in the Legal Process*, New York and Basingstoke: Palgrave, 19–34:

——(2004) 'Author identification, idiolect and linguistic uniqueness', *Applied Linguistics*, 25(4): 431–47.

——(2005) 'The linguist as expert witness', *Linguistics and the Human Sciences*, 1(1) 39–58.

——(2007) 'In my opinion', in M. Turell, M. Spassova and J. Cicres (eds) *Proceedings of the Second European IAFL Conference on Forensic Linguistics/Language and the Law*, Barcelona: Universitat Pompeu Fabra, 43–56.

Coulthard, M. and Johnson, A. (2007) *An Introduction to Forensic Linguistics: Language in Evidence*, London/New York: Routledge.

Coulthard, M. and Montgomery, M. (1981) *Studies in Discourse Analysis*, London: Routledge.

Coupland, N., Giles, H. and Wiemann, J.M. (1991) *'Miscommunication' and Problematic Talk*, Thousand Oaks, CA: Sage Publications.

Cover, R.M. (1986) 'Violence and the word', *Yale Law Journal*, 95: 1601–29.

Cowan, A.L. (2007) 'Skakel loses in effort to gain a new trial', *The New York Times*, 26 October 2007, p. B4.

Creech, R. (2005) *Law and Language in the European Community: The Paradox of a Babel 'United in Diversity'*, Groningen: Europa Law Publishing.

——(2007) 'Missing the mark: assessing trademarks for distinctiveness and descriptiveness in Europe's multilingual environment', in K. Kredens and S. Gozdz-Roszkowski (eds) *Language and the Law: International Outlooks*, Frankfurt: Peter Lang, 371–78.

Crystal, D. (1995) 'Review of *Forensic Stylistics*', *Language*, 71(2): 381–84.

——(2008) *Txtng: The Gr8 Db8*, Oxford: Oxford University Press.

Crystal, D. and Davy, D. (1969) *Investigating English Style*, London: Longman.

Culpeper, J. and Kytö, M. (2000) 'Gender voices in the spoken interaction of the past: a pilot study based on Early Modern English trial proceedings', in D. Kastovsky and A. Mettinger (eds) *The History of English in a Social Context*, Berlin: Mouton de Gruyter, 53–89.

Curiel, J. (25 March 2008) 'S.F. gives ex-gang members way to get off list', *San Francisco Chronicle*.

Curl, T. and Drew, P. (2008) 'Contingency and action: a comparison of two forms of requesting', *Research on Language and Social Interaction*, 41: 1–25.

Cutler, A. (1982) 'Guest editorial: the reliability of speech error data', in A. Cutler (ed.) *Slips of the Tongue and Language Production*, The Hague: Mouton, 7–28.

Cutler, C. (1999) 'Yorkville crossing: white teens, hiphop, and African American English', *Journal of Sociolinguistics*, 3: 428–42.

Daley, K. and Daley-Caravella, L. (2004) *Talk Your Way to the Top*, New York: McGraw-Hill.

Dancey, C.P. and Reidy, J. (1999) *Statistics without Maths for Psychologists*, London: Prentice Hall.

Dando, C., Wilcock, R. and Milne, R. (2008) 'The cognitive interview: inexperienced police officers' perceptions of their witness/victim interviewing practices', *Legal and Criminological Psychology*, 13: 59–70.

Danet, B. (1980a) '"Baby" or "fetus": language and the construction of reality in a manslaughter trial', *Semiotica*, 32: 187–219.

——(1980b) 'Language in the legal process', *Law and Society Review*, 14(3): 445–564.

Danet, B. and Bogoch, B. (1980) 'Fixed fight or free for all? An empirical study of combativeness in the adversary system of justice', *British Journal of Law and Society*, 7: 36–60.

——(1994) 'Orality, literacy, and performativity in Anglo-Saxon wills', in J. Gibbons (ed.) *Language and the Law*, London: Longman, 100–35.

Danet, B. and Kermish, N.C. (1978) 'Courtroom questioning: a sociolinguistic perspective', in L.N. Massery (ed.) *Psychology and Persuasion in Advocacy*, Washington, DC: Association of Trial Lawyers of America, National College of Advocacy, 413–41.

Danet, B., Hoffman, K.B., Kermish, N.C., Rafn, H.J. and Stayman, D (1980) 'An ethnography of questioning in the courtroom', in R.W. Shuy and A. Shnukal (eds) *Language Use and the Uses of Language*, Washington, DC: Georgetown University Press: 222–34.

Darby, J.K. (ed.) (1981) *Speech Evaluation in Psychiatry*, New York: Grune and Statton.

Darley, J.M. and Gross, P.H. (1983) 'A hypothesis-confirming bias in labeling effects', *Journal of Personality and Social Psychology*, 44: 20–33.

Davies, G. and Westcott, H. (1999) 'Interviewing child witnesses under the memorandum of good practice: a research review', *Police Research Series Paper*, 115.

Davies, G., Wilson, C., Mitchell, R. and Milsom, J. (1995) *Videotaping Children's Evidence: An Evaluation*, London: Home Office.

Dawid, A.P. (2002) 'Bayes's theorem and weighing evidence by juries', in R. Swinburne (ed) *Bayes's Theorem, Proc. Brit. Acad. 113*, 71–90.

Deak, M. (2009) 'Despite contention over lack of translation, court upholds Plainfield man's conviction'. Available online at: www.mycentraljersey.com/article/20090701/NEWS/907010365 (accessed 9 July 2009).

Delbridge, A. (ed.) (1981) *The Macquarie Dictionary*, Sydney: Macquarie Library Pty, Ltd.

Dershowitz, A.M. (1996) 'Life is not a dramatic narrative', in P. Brooks and P. Gewirtz (eds) *Law's Stories: Narrative and Rhetoric in the Law*, New Haven, CT: Yale University Press, 99–105.

Dick, R.C. (1985) *Legal Drafting*, Toronto: Carswell.

Diehl, R.L., Lindblom, B., Hoemeke, K.A. and Fahey, R.P. (1996) 'On explaining certain male–female differences in the phonetic realization of vowel categories', *Journal of Phonetics*, 24: 187–208.

Diez, I.G. (2005) 'The transformation of asylum seekers' narratives through the asylum procedure', paper presented at the *International Association of Forensic Linguists 7th Biennial Conference on Forensic Linguistics/Language and Law*, Cardiff University, UK, July 2005.

van Dijk, T. (ed.) (1985) *Handbook of Discourse Analysis, Vol. 4*, London: Academic Press.

——(1991) *Racism and the Press*, London: Routledge.

——(1997) *Discourse Studies: A Multidisciplinary Introduction*, London: Sage Publications, Inc.

——(2008) *Discourse and Context: A Sociocognitive Approach*, Cambridge: Cambridge University Press.

Dinwoodie, G.B. (2008) 'What linguistics can do for trademark law', in L. Bently, J. Davis and J. Ginsburg (eds) *Trade Marks and Brands: An Interdisciplinary Critique*, Cambridge Intellectual Property and Information Law, 10, Cambridge: Cambridge University Press, 140–58.

Dobash, R.E. and Dobash, R.P. (1992) *Women, Violence and Social Change*, London: Routledge.

Docuyanan, F. (2000) 'Governing graffiti in contested urban spaces', *Political and Legal Anthropology Review*, 23: 103–21.

Donahoe, J.J. (1998) 'Did *Miranda* diminish police effectiveness?', *Stanford Law Review*, 50: 1147–80.

Doty, K.L. (2007) 'Telling tales: the role of scribes in constructing the discourse of the Salem witchcraft trials', *Journal of Historical Pragmatics*, 8(1): 25–41.

Doty, K.L. and Hiltunen, R. (2002) '"I will tell, I will tell": confessional patterns in the Salem witchcraft trials, 1692', *Journal of Historical Pragmatics*, 3(2): 299–335.

——(2009) 'Formulaic discourse and speech acts in the witchcraft trial records of Salem, 1692', *Journal of Pragmatics*, 4(1): 458–69.

Doughty, C.J. and Long, M.H. (eds) (2003) *The Handbook of Second Language Acquisition*, Oxford: Blackwell.

Drew, P. (1985) 'Analysing the use of language in courtroom interaction', in T.A. van Dijk (ed.) *Handbook of Discourse Analysis, Vol. 3*, London: Academic Press, 133–47.

624

——(1990) 'Strategies in the contest between lawyer and witness in cross-examination', in J.N. Levi and A.G. Walker (eds) *Language in the Judicial Process*, New York: Plenum Press, 39–64.

——(1992) 'Contested evidence in courtroom cross-examination: the case of a trial for rape', in P. Drew and J.C. Heritage (eds) *Talk at Work: Interaction in Institutional Settings*, Cambridge: Cambridge University Press, 470–520.

——(1997) '"Open" class repair initiators in response to sequential sources of trouble in conversation', *Journal of Pragmatics*, 28: 69–101.

——(1998) 'Metropolitan police service emergency and non-emergency telephone call handling: a study of the handling of enquiries and incident reports made over the telephone by members of the public to MPS operator centres, control rooms and the new Scotland Yard information room', *Report to the Metropolitan Police Service*, London.

——(2003) 'Comparative analysis of talk-in-interaction in different institutional settings: a sketch', in P. J. Glenn, C.D. leBaron, J. Mandelbaum and R. Hopper (eds.) *Studies on Language in Social Interaction*, Mahwah, NJ: Lawrence Erlbaum Associates, 293–308.

——(2004) 'Conversation analysis', in K. Fitch and R. Sanders (eds) *Handbook of Language and Social Interaction*, Mahwah, NJ: Lawrence Erlbaum, 71–102.

Drew, P. and Heritage, J. (1992a) 'Analyzing talk at work: an introduction', in P. Drew and J. Heritage (eds) *Talk at Work: Interaction in Institutional Settings*, Cambridge: Cambridge University Press, 3–65.

——(eds) (1992b) *Talk at Work: Interaction in Institutional Settings*, Cambridge: University of Cambridge Press.

Drew, P. and Sorjonen, M.J. (1997) 'Institutional discourse', in T. van Dijk (ed.) *Discourse Analysis: A Multidisciplinary Introduction*, London: Sage, 92–118.

Drizin, S.A. and Colgan, B.A. (2004) 'Tales from the juvenile confession front: a guide to how standard police interrogation tactics can produce coerced and false confessions from juvenile suspects', in G.D. Lassiter (ed.) *Interrogations, Confessions and Entrapment*, New York: Kluwer/Plenum.

Drizin, S.A. and Leo, R.A. (2004) 'The problem of false confession in the post-DNA world', *North Carolina Law Review*, 82: 891–1007. Available online at: www.ssrn.com/abstract=1134094.

Dror, I.E., Charlton, D. and Péron, E. (2005) 'Contextual information renders experts vulnerable to making erroneous identifications', *Forensic Science International*, 156: 74–78.

Dumas, B.K. (1990) 'An analysis of the adequacy of federally mandated cigarette package warnings' in J. N. Levi and A.G. Walker (eds) *Language in the Judicial Process*, NY: Plenum Press Corp., 309–52.

——(1992) 'An analysis of the adequacy of cigarette package warnings: an analysis of the adequacy of federally mandated cigarette package warnings', *Tennessee Law Review*, 59: 261–304.

——(2000a) 'US pattern jury instructions: problems and proposals', *Forensic Linguistics*, 7(1): 49–71.

——(2000b) 'Warning labels and industry safety information standards: the case of Loctite RC/609', in J. Peyton and P. Griffin (eds) *Language in Action: New Studies of Language in Society*, Cresskill, New Jersey: Hampton Press, 302–17.

——(2002) 'Reasonable doubt about reasonable doubt: assessing jury instruction adequacy in a capital case', in J. Cotterill (ed.) *Language in the Legal Process*, Basingstoke: Palgrave, 246–59.

Dunstan, R. (1980) 'Contexts for coercion: analyzing properties of courtroom "questions"', *British Journal of Law and Society*, 7: 61–77.

Durant, A. (2008) '"How can I tell the trade mark on a piece of gingerbread from all the other marks on it?", naming and meaning in verbal trade mark signs', in L. Bently, J. Davis and J. Ginsburg (eds) *Trade Marks and Brands: An Interdisciplinary Critique*, Cambridge: Cambridge University Press, 107–39.

van Dyke, J. (2007) 'Interference effects from grammatically unavailable constituents during sentence processing', *Journal of Experimental Psychology*, 33(2): 407–30.

van Dyke, J. and McElree, B. (2006) 'Retrieval interference in sentence comprehension', *Journal of Memory and Language*, 55(2): 157–66.

Eades, D. (1992) *Aboriginal English and the Law: Communicating with Aboriginal English Speaking Clients: A Handbook for Legal Practitioners*, Brisbane: Queensland Law Society.

——(1994a) 'A case of communicative clash: aboriginal English and the legal system', in J. Gibbons (ed.) *Language and the Law*, London: Longman, 234–64.

——(1994b) 'Forensic linguistics in Australia: an overview', *Forensic Linguistics*, 1(2): 113–32.

——(1995) 'Aboriginal English on trial: the case for Stuart and Condren', in D. Eades (ed.) *Language in Evidence: Linguistic and Legal Perspectives in Multicultural Australia*, Sydney: University of New South Wales Press, 147–74.

——(1996) 'Verbatim courtroom transcripts and discourse analysis', in H. Kniffka, S. Blackwell and M. Coulthard (eds) *Recent Developments in Forensic Linguistics*, Frankfurt am Main: Peter Lang GmbH, 241–54.

——(2000) '"I don't think it's an answer to the question": Silencing aboriginal witnesses in court', *Language in Society*, 29: 161–95.

——(2002) '"Evidence given in unequivocal terms": gaining consent of aboriginal kids in court', in J. Cotterill (ed.) *Language in the Legal Process*, Basingstoke: Palgrave, 162–79.

——(2003a) 'Participation of second language and second dialect speakers in the legal system', *Annual Review of Applied Linguistics*, 23: 113–33.

——(2003b) 'The politics of misunderstanding in the legal process: aboriginal English in Queensland', in J. House, G. Kasper and S. Ross (eds) *Misunderstanding in Spoken Discourse*, London: Longman, 199–226.

——(2004) 'Understanding Aboriginal English in the legal system: a critical sociolinguistics approach', *Applied Linguistics*, 25(4): 491–512.

——(2005) 'Applied linguistics and language analysis in asylum seeker cases', *Applied Linguistics*, 26(4): 503–26.

——(2006) 'Lexical struggle in court: aboriginal Australians versus the State', *Journal of Sociolinguistics*, 10 (2): 153–80.

——(2008a) 'From expertise to advocacy: forensic linguistics and advocacy in asylum seeker cases', in F. Olsen, A. Lorz and D. Stein (eds) *Law and Language: Theory and Society*, Düsseldorf: Düsseldorf University Press, 87–118.

——(2008b) *Courtroom Talk and Neocolonial Control*, Berlin and New York: Mouton de Gruyter.

——(2009) 'Testing the claims of asylum seekers: the role of language analysis', *Language Assessment Quarterly*, 6(1): 30–40.

Eades, D. and Arends, J. (2004) 'Using language analysis in the determination of national origin of asylum seekers: an introduction', *International Journal of Speech, Language and the Law*, 11(2): 179–99.

Eades, D., Fraser, H., Siegel, J., McNamara, T. and Baker, B. (2003) 'Linguistic identification in the determination of nationality: a preliminary report', *Language Policy*, 2(2): 179–99.

Eakin, J.P. (2008) *Living Autobiographically: How we Create Identity in Narrative*, Ithaca, NY: Cornell University Press.

Eberhardt, J.L., Goff, P.A., Purdie, V.J. and Davies, P. (2004) 'Seeing black: race, crime, and visual processing', *Journal of Personality and Social Psychology*, 87: 876–93.

Eckert, P. (1997) 'Why ethnography?', in U.B. Kotsinas, A.-B. Stenström and A.-M. Karlsson (eds) *Ungdomsspråk i Norden*, Stockholm: MINS 43, 52–62.

Eclavea, R. (1982) 'Annotation: admissibility of testimony concerning extrajudicial statements made to, or in presence of, witness through an interpreter', *American Law Reports* 4th series, 12: 1016.

Edelman, G. (2009) 'Improving provision for children with speech, language and communication difficulties: the role of the voluntary sector', *Current Paediatrics*, 14(3): 223–28.

Edwards, D. (1997) *Discourse and Cognition*, London: Sage.

——(2006) 'Facts, norms and dispositions: practical uses of the modal *would* in police interrogations', *Discourse Studies*, 8(4): 475–501.

——(2008) 'Intentionality and *mens rea* in police interrogations: the production of actions as crimes', *Intercultural Pragmatics*, 5(2): 177–99.

Edwards, L.H. (2006) *Legal Writing: Process, Analysis, and Organization*, 4th edn, New York: Aspen.

Edwards, V. (2004) *Multilingualism in the English-speaking World*, Oxford: Blackwell.

Egelko, R. (2008) 'Court limits defendant's right to seek mercy', *The San Francisco Chronicle*, 25 July 2008. Available online at: www.sfgate.com/cgi-bin/article/comments/view?f=/c/a/2008/07/25/BA5511V00L.DTL (accessed 6 August 2009).

Eggins, S. (1994) *An Introduction to Systemic Functional Linguistics*, London: Pinter Publishers Ltd.

Ehrlich, S. (2001) *Representing Rape: Language and Sexual Consent*, London and New York: Routledge.

——(2002) '(Re)contextualizing complainant's accounts of sexual assault', *The International Journal of Speech, Language and the Law*, 9(2): 193–212.

——(2003) 'Coercing gender: language in sexual assault adjudication processes', in J. Holmes and M. Meyerhoff (eds) *The Handbook of Language and Gender*, Oxford: Blackwell Publishers, 645–70.

——(2006) 'Constraining the boundaries of gendered identities: trial discourse and judicial decision-making', in J. Baxter (ed.) *Speaking Out: The Female Voice in Public Contexts*, Basingstoke: Palgrave Macmillan, 139–58.

——(2007) 'Legal discourse and the cultural intelligibility of gendered meanings', *Journal of Socio-linguistics*, 11(4): 452–77.

Eichhorn, L. (1989) 'Social science findings and the jury's ability to disregard evidence under the federal rules of evidence', *Law & Contemporary Problems*, 42: 341–53.

Ellis, R. (2003) *Task-based Language Learning and Teaching*, Oxford: Oxford University Press.

Ellis, R. and Barkhuizen, G. (2005) *Analysing Learner Language*, Oxford: Oxford University Press.

Ellis, S. (1994) 'The Yorkshire ripper enquiry: part I', *Forensic Linguistics*, 1: 197–206.

Ellison, L. (2001) *The Adversarial Process and the Vulnerable Witness*, Oxford: Oxford University Press.

Elwork, A., Sales, B. and Alfini, J. (1977) 'Juridic decisions: in ignorance of law or in the light of it?', *Law and Human Behavior*, 1: 123–41.

——(1982) *Making Jury Instructions Understandable*, Charlottesville, VA: Michie.

Engberg, J. and Heller, D. (2008) 'Vagueness and indeterminacy in law', in V.K. Bhatia, C.N. Candlin and J. Engberg (eds) *Legal Discourse across Cultures and Systems*, Hong Kong: Hong Kong University Press.

Engel, S. (2000) *Context is Everything: The Nature of Memory*, New York: W.H. Freeman and Company.

Ervin Tripp, S. (1970) 'Discourse agreement: how children answer questions', in J. Hayes (ed.) *Cognition and the Development of Language*, New York: Wiley, 79–109.

Esbensen, F.L., Winfree, T., He, N. and Taylor, T.J. (2001) 'Youth gangs and definitional issues: when is a gang a gang and why does it matter?', *Crime & Delinquency*, 47: 105–30.

Espiritu, N. (2005) '(E)racing youth: the racialized construction of California's Proposition 21 and the development of alternative contestations', *Cleveland State Law Review*, 52: 189–208.

Estrich, S. (1987) *Real Rape*, Cambridge, MA: Harvard University Press.

European Commission (2003) 'Joint practical guide of the European Parliament, the Council and the Commission for persons involved in the drafting of legislation within the community institutions'.

Evans, M., McIntosh, W., Lin, J. and Cates, C. (2007) 'Recounting the courts: applying automated content analysis to enhance empirical legal research', *Journal of Empirical Legal Studies*, 4(4):1007–39.

Faerk, C. and Kasper, G. (1987) 'Perspectives on language transfer', *Applied Linguistics*, 8(2): 111–36.

Faigman, D., Kaye, D., Saks, M. and Cheng, E. (2007) *Modern Scientific Evidence: The Law and Science of Expert Testimony*, Minneapolis: West Pub. Co.

Fairclough, N. (1989) *Language and Power*, London: Longman.

——(1995) *Media Discourse*, London: Arnold.

——(2001) 'Critical discourse analysis as a method in social scientific research', in R. Wodak and M. Meyer (eds) *Methods of Critical Discourse Analysis*, London: Sage, 212–28.

FCA (Federal Court of Australia) (2003) Applicant WAFV of 2002 v. Refugee Review Tribunal [2003] (17 January 2003). Available online at: www.austlii.edu.au/au/cases/cth/FCA/2003/16.html (accessed 26 November 2008).

Feldman, A.D. (2004) 'High court study: a divided court in more ways than one: the supreme court of Delaware and its distinctive model for judicial efficacy, 1997–2003', *Albany Law Review*, 67: 849–92.

Felton Rosulek, L. (2008) 'Manipulative silence and social representation in the closing arguments of a child sexual abuse case', *Text & Talk*, 28(4): 529–50.

——(2009a) 'First person plural pronouns as persuasive devices in the closing arguments of criminal trials', poster at the American Association of Applied Linguistics (AAAL) Conference.

——(2009b) *The Sociolinguistic Construction of Reality in the Closing Arguments of Criminal Trials*, unpublished doctoral dissertation, University of Illinois, Urbana, IL.

627

——(forthcoming a) 'The sociolinguistic creation of opposing representations of defendants and victims', *International Journal of Speech, Language, and Law*.

——(forthcoming b) 'Legitimation and the heteroglossic nature of closing arguments', *GURT 2008: Proceedings of the Georgetown University Roundtable in Linguistics*, Washington DC: Georgetown University Press.

Filipovic, L. (2007) 'Language as a witness: insights from cognitive linguistics', *International Journal of Speech, Language and the Law*, 14: 245–67.

Findley, K.A. and Scott, M.S. (2006) 'The multiple dimensions of tunnel vision in criminal cases', *Wisconsin Law Review*, 2: 291–397.

Fischoff, S. (2005) 'Gangsta' rap and a murder in Bakersfield', *Journal of Applied Social Psychology*, 29: 795–805.

Fisher, R.P. and Geiselman, R.E. (1992) *Memory-Enhancing Techniques for Investigative Interviewing: The Cognitive Interview*, Springfield, IL: Charles C. Thomas.

Fisher, R.P., Geiselman, R.E. and Amador, M. (1989) 'Field test of the cognitive interview: enhancing the recollection of actual victims and witnesses of crime', *Journal of Applied Psychology*, 74: 722–27.

Fisiak, J. (ed.) (1996) *Collins English–Polish Dictionary*, Warsaw: Polska Oficyna Wydawnicza.

Fitch, W.T. and Giedd, J. (1999) 'Morphology and development of the human vocal tract: a study using magnetic resonance imaging', *Journal of the Acoustical Society of America*, 106: 1511–22.

Fletcher, P. and Ingram, R. (1995) 'Grammatical impairment', in P. Fletcher and B. MacWhinney (eds) *The Handbook of Child Language*, Oxford: Blackwell, 603–22.

Flückiger, A. (2008) 'The ambiguous principle of clarity of the law', in A. Wagner and S. Cacciaguidi-Fahy (eds) *Obscurity and Clarity in the Law: Prospects and Challenges*, Burlington, VT: Ashgate, 9–24.

Fodor, J. and Garrett, M. (1967) 'Some syntactic determinants of sentential complexity', *Perceptions and Psychophysics*, 2(7): 289–96.

Foley, T. (2006) 'Lawyers and legal interpreters: different clients, different culture', *Interpreting*, 8(1): 97–104.

Foulkes, P. and Docherty, G. (2006) 'The social life of phonetics and phonology', *Journal of Phonetics*, 34: 409–38.

Fourakis, M. and Port, R. (1986) 'Stop epenthesis in English', *Journal of Phonetics*, 14: 197–221.

Fowler, R. (1985) 'Power', in T. van Dijk (ed.) *Handbook of Discourse Analysis, Vol 4*, London: Academic Press, 61–82.

Foyle, R. (2002) 'Legislative language in the EU: the crucible', *International Journal for the Semiotics of Law*, 15: 361–74.

Framer, I. (2001) 'Interpreters and their impact on the criminal justice system: the Alejandro Ramírez Case', *Proteus*, IX(1–2, 1–6). Available online at: http://languageaccess.us/uploads/Interpreters%20and%20Their%20Impact%20PDF.pdf (accessed 5 August 2009).

Francis, G. (1994) 'Labelling discourse: an aspect of nominal-group lexical cohesion', in Coulthard, R. M. (ed.) *Advances in Written Text Analysis*, London: Routledge, 83–101.

Francis, W.N. and Kučera, H. (1982) *Frequency Analysis of English Usage: Lexicon and Grammar*, Boston: Houghton Mifflin.

Fraser, B. (1975) 'Warning and threatening', *Centrum*, 3: 169–80.

——(1980) 'Conversational mitigation', *Journal of Pragmatics*, 4: 341–50.

——(1998) 'Threatening revisited', *Forensic Linguistics: International Journal of Speech, Language and Law*, 5(2): 159–73.

Fraser, B. and Freedgood, L. (1999) 'Interpreter alterations to pragmatic features in trial testimony', paper presented at the annual meeting of the American Association for Applied Linguistics (21, Stanford, CT, 6–9 March, 1999).

Fraser, H. (2003) 'Issues in transcription: factors affecting the reliability of transcripts as evidence in legal cases', *Forensic Linguistics*, 10(2): 203–26.

——(2009) 'The role of "educated native speakers" in providing language analysis for the determination of the origin of asylum seekers', *International Journal of Speech, Language and the Law*, 16(1): 113–38.

French, P. and Harrison, P. (2006) 'Investigative and evidential applications of forensic speech science', in A. Heaton-Armstrong, E. Shepherd, G. Gudjonsson and D. Wolchover (eds) *Witness Testimony, Psychological, Investigative and Evidential Perspectives*, Oxford: Oxford University Press.

——(2007) 'Position statement concerning use of impressionistic likelihood terms in forensic speaker comparison cases', *International Journal of Speech, Language and the Law*, 14(1): 137–44.

French, P., Harrison, P. and Windsor Lewis, J. (2006) 'R v. John Samuel Humble: the Yorkshire ripper hoaxer trial', *International Journal of Speech, Language and the Law*, 13: 255–73.

Friedman, L.M. (1993) 'How I write', *4 SCRIBES Journal of Legal Writing*, 3: 5.

Fries, C.C. (1952) *The Structure of English*, New York: Harcourt, Brace and Company Inc.

Frontline, (2006) 'The Enemy Within', item on Public Broadcasting Station PBS, July 24, 2006

Fuhrman, M. (1998) *Murder in Greenwich: Who Killed Martha Moxley?* New York: HarperCollins Publishers.

Fuller, J. (1993) 'Hearing between the lines: style switching in a courtroom setting', *Pragmatics*, 3: 29–43.

de Fruyt, F., Bockstaele, M., Taris, R. and van Hiel, A. (2006) 'Police interview competencies: assessment and associated traits', *European Journal of Personality*, 20(7): 567–84.

Galasiński, D. (2000) *The Language of Deception: A Discourse Analytical Study*, Thousand Oaks, CA: Sage Publications, Inc.

Galatolo, R. (2007) 'Active voicing in court', in E. Holt and R. Clift (eds) *Reporting Talk: Reported Speech in Interaction*, Cambridge: Cambridge University Press, 195–220.

Galatolo, R. and Mizzau, M. (2005) 'Quoting dialogues and the construction of the narrative point of view in legal testimony: the role of prosody and gesture', *Studies in Communication Science*, Special Issue 'Argumentation in Dialogic Interaction', June 2005: 217–31.

Galindo, L. (1993) 'The language of gangs, drugs and prison life among Chicanas', *Latino Studies Journal*, 4: 23–43.

Garcia, A. (1998) 'Is *Miranda* dead, was it overruled, or is it irrelevant?', *St. Thomas Law Review*, 10: 461–98.

Gardner, H. (2004) *Changing Minds*, Boston: Harvard Business School Press.

Garfinkel, H. (1967) *Studies in Ethnomethodology*, Englewood Cliffs, NJ: Prentice-Hall.

Garfinkel, H. and Sacks, H. (1970) 'On formal structures of practical actions', in J.C. McKinney and E. A. Tiryakian (eds) *Theoretical Sociology*, New York: Appleton Century Crofts, 338–66.

Garner, B. (1995) *A Dictionary of Modern Legal Usage,* 2nd edn, Oxford and New York: Oxford University Press.

——(1999a) *The Winning Brief*, New York: Oxford University Press.

——(ed.) (1999b) *Black's Law Dictionary*, 7th edn, St. Paul, MN: West Publishing Co.

——(2003) *Garner's Modern American Usage*, Oxford and New York: Oxford University Press.

——(ed.) (2004a) *Black's Law Dictionary*, 8th edn, Eagan, MN: West Publishers.

——(2004b) *The Winning Brief,* 2nd edn., Oxford and New York: Oxford University Press.

Gates, H.L. (1995) 'Thirteen ways of looking at a black man', *New Yorker*, 23 October 1995.

Gawande, A. (2009) 'The cost conundrum', *The New Yorker*, Annals of Medicine section, 1 June 2009, 36–44.

Geiselman, R.E., Fisher, R.P., MacKinnon, D.P. and Holland, H.L. (1986) 'Enhancement of eyewitness memory with the cognitive interview', *American Journal of Psychology*, 99: 385–401.

Georgakopoulou, A. (2006) 'Thinking big with small stories in narrative and identity analysis', *Narrative Inquiry*, 16(1): 122–30.

Gergen, K. (1999) *An Invitation to Social Construction*, Thousand Oaks, CA: Sage Publications.

Gernsbacher, M. and Givón, T. (eds) (1995) *Coherence in Spontaneous Text*, Philadelphia, PA and Amsterdam: John Benjamins.

Gewirtz, P. (1996a) 'Victims and voyeurs: two narrative problems at the criminal trial', in P. Brooks and P. Gewirtz (eds) *Law's Stories: Narrative and Rhetoric in the Law*, New Haven, CT: Yale University Press, 135–61.

——(1996b) 'Narrative and rhetoric in the law', in P. Brooks and P. Gewirtz (eds) *Law's Stories: Narrative and Rhetoric in the Law*, New Haven, CT: Yale University Press, 2–13.

Gfroerer, S. (2006) 'Sprechererkennung und Tonträgerauswertung', in G. Widmaier (ed.) *Münchener Anwaltshandbuch Strafverteidigung*, München: Beck, 2505–26.

Ghai, Y. (1997) *Hong Kong's New Constitutional Order: The Resumption of Chinese Sovereignty and the Basic Law*, Hong Kong: Hong Kong University Press.

Giambruno, C. (2008) 'The role of the interpreter in the governance of sixteenth- and seventeenth-century Spanish colonies in the "New World"', in C. Valero Garcés and A. Martin (eds) *Crossing Borders in Community Interpreting: Definitions and Dilemmas*, Amsterdam and Philadelphia, PA: John Benjamins Publishing Company.

Giannelli, P.C. (2003) 'Admissibility of scientific evidence', *Oklahoma City University Law Review*, 28: 1–15.

——(2007) 'Wrongful convictions and forensic science: the need to regulate crime labs', *North Carolina Law Review*, 86: 163–235.

Gibbons, J. (ed.) (1994) *Language and the Law*, London: Longman.

——(1995) 'What got lost? The place of electronic recording and interpreters in police interviews', in D. Eades (ed.) *Language in Evidence: Linguistic and Legal Perspectives in Multicultural Australia*, Sydney: University of New South Wales Press, 175–86.

——(2001a) 'Revising the language of New South Wales police procedures: applied linguistics in action', *Applied Linguistics*, 22(4): 439–69.

——(2001b) 'Legal transformations in Spanish: an "audiencia" in Chile', *Forensic Linguistics*, 8(1): 24–43.

——(2003) *Forensic Linguistics: An Introduction to Language in the Justice System*, Oxford: Blackwell.

Gibson, W. (1961) 'Literary minds and judicial style', *New York University Law Review*, 36: 915–30.

Giles, H. and Powesland, P.F. (1975a) 'A social psychological model of speech diversity', in H. Giles and P. Powesland (eds) *Speech Style and Social Evaluation*, New York: Harcourt, Brace, 154–70.

——(1975b) *Speech Style and Social Evaluation*, London: Academic Press.

Gilmore, G. (1974) *The Death of Contract*, Columbus, OH: The Ohio State University Press.

Gilvelber, D. (1997) 'Meaningless acquittals, meaningful convictions: do we reliably acquit the innocent?', *Rutgers Law Review*, 49: 1317–96.

Gitomer, J. (2007) *Little Green Book of Getting Your Way*, Upper Saddle River, NJ: Financial Times Press.

Godfrey, D and Harris, D. (1971) *Basic Elements of Intelligence*, Washington, DC: US Government Printing Office.

Goffman, E. (1959) *Presentation of Self in Everyday Life*, New York: Doubleday.

——(1981a) *Forms of Talk*, Philadelphia, PA: University of Pennsylvania Press.

——(1981b) 'Footing', in *Forms of Talk*, Philadelphia, PA: University of Pennsylvania Press, 124–57.

——(1986) *Frame Analysis,* Boston, MA: Northeastern University Press.

Goldin-Meadow, S. (2003) *Hearing Gesture*, Cambridge, MA: Harvard University Press.

Gomez, P. (2004) 'It is not so simply because an expert says it is so: the reliability of gang expert testimony regarding membership in criminal street gangs: pushing the limits of Texas Rule of Evidence 702', *St. Mary's Law Review*, 34: 581–622.

Goodman, G. (1984) 'The child witness: an introduction', *Journal of Social Issues*, 40(2): 1–7.

Goodman, G. and Melinder, A. (2007) 'Child witness research and forensic interviews with young children: a review', *Legal and Criminal Psychology*, 12: 1–19.

Goodrich, P. (1987) *Legal Discourse: Studies in Linguistics, Rhetoric and Legal Analysis*, Basingstoke: Macmillan.

——(1990) *Languages of Law: From Logics of Memory to Nomadic Masks*, London: Weidenfeld and Nicholson.

Goodwin, C. (1981) *Conversational Organization*, New York: Academic Press.

——(1994) 'Professional vision', *American Anthropologist*, 96(3): 606–33. Available online at: www.sscnet.ucla.edu/clic/cgoodwin/94prof_vis.pdf (accessed 6 August 2009).

——(2000) 'Practices of seeing: visual analysis: an ethnomethodological approach', in T. van Leeuwen and C. Jewitt (eds) *Handbook of Visual Analysis*, London: Sage Publications. Available online at: www.sscnet.ucla.edu/clic/cgoodwin/publish.htm (accessed 6 August 2009).

——(2003) 'Pointing as situated practice', in S. Kita (ed.) *Pointing: Where Language, Culture, and Cognition Meet*, Mahwah: Lawrence Erlbaum, 217–41.

——(2007) 'Participation, stance, and affect in the organization of activities', *Discourse and Society*, 18(1): 53–73.

Goodwin, C. and Goodwin, M. (2004) 'Participation', in A. Duranti (ed.) *A Companion to Linguistic Anthropology*, Oxford: Blackwell, 222–44.

Gordon-Smith, D. (1989) 'The drafting process in the European Community', *Statute Law Review*, 10: 56–68.

Gorman, T.P., White, J., Brooks, G. and English, F. (1990) *Language for Learning*, London: Department for Education and Science.

Gotti, M. (2005) 'Vagueness in the model law on international commercial arbitration', in V.K. Bhatia, J. Engberg, M. Gotti and D. Heller (eds) *Vagueness in Normative Texts*, Bern: Peter Lang, 227–53.

Government of Hong Kong, (1984) *Sino-British Joint Declaration 1984*.

——(1990) *The Basic Law of the Hong Kong Special Administrative Region of the People's Republic of China*.

Government of Hong Kong, Court of Final Appeal, (1999) 'Chan Kam Nga', Hong Kong Law Report Digest 1 at 310, HKSAR.

Graham, T. (2007) 'Neulander appeals come to an end', *Philadelphia Inquirer*, 18 April 2007, p. B01.

Grant, T. (2005) *Authorship Attribution in a Forensic Context*, unpublished PhD Dissertation, University of Birmingham, Birmingham.

——(2007) 'Quantifying evidence for forensic authorship analysis', *International Journal of Speech, Language and the Law*, 14(1): 1–25.

Grant, T. and Baker, K. (2001) 'Identifying reliable, valid markers of authorship: a response to Chaski', *Forensic Linguistics*, 8(1): 66–79.

Grant, T., Smith, D. J., Kredens, K. and Spencer, S. (2009) 'Identifying an author's native language', unpublished research report produced for Qinetiq (Intelligence and Digital Security Division).

Greatbatch, D. (1986) 'Aspects of topical organization in news interviews: the use of agenda-shifting procedures by interviewees', *Media, Culture and Society*, 8: 441–55.

——(1988) 'A turn-taking system for British news interviews', *Language in Society*, 17: 401–30.

Grebler, G. (2005a) '"And then what did she say?" Making confession statements believable and compelling (even when they are false)', paper presented at the *International Association of Forensic Linguists 7th Biennial Conference on Forensic Linguistics/Language and Law*, Cardiff University, UK, July 2005.

——(2005b) 'Language issues in (false) confession evidence', paper presented at *International Linguistic Association 50th Anniversary Conference on Language and Law*, New York City, April 2005.

Greene, J. and Pranis, K. (2007) *GangWars: The Failure of Enforcement Tactics and the Need for Effective Public Safety Strategies*, Washington, DC: Justice Policy Institute.

Greene, S. (2009) 'A sign of apathy for deaf', *The Denver Post*, 7 July 2009. Available online at: www.denverpost.com/news/ci_12818667 (accessed 13 July 2009).

Greenfield, S. (2008) *ID: The Quest for Identity in the 21st Century*, London: Sceptre.

Greisbach, R. (1999) 'Estimation of speaker height from formant frequencies', *Forensic Linguistics*, 6: 265–77.

Grice, H.P. (1975) 'Logic and conversation', in P. Cole and J. Morgan (eds) *Syntax and Semantics 3: Speech Acts*, New York: Academic Press, 41–58.

Griffiths, A. and Milne, R. (2005) 'Will it all end in tiers: police interviews with suspects in Britain', in T. Williamson (ed.) *Investigative Interviewing: Rights, Research, Regulation*, Willan: Devon, 167–89.

Grimes, B. (1992) *Ethnologue: Languages of the World*, 12th edn, Dallas, TX: Summer Institute of Linguistics.

Grisso, T. (1980) 'Juveniles' capacity to waive *Miranda* rights: an empirical analysis', *California Law Review*, 68: 1134–66.

Groopman, J. (2007) *How Doctors Think*, New York: Houghton Mifflin.

Groscup, J. and Penrod, S. (2003) 'Battle of the standards for experts in criminal cases: police vs. psychologists', *Seton Hall Law Review*, 33: 1141–65.

Gross, S.R., Jacoby, K., Matheson, D.J., Montgomery, N. and Patil, S. (2005) 'Exonerations in the United States, 1989 through 2003', *Journal of Criminal Law and Criminology*, 95(2). Available online at: www.ssrn.com/abstract=753084 (accessed 6 August 2009).

Gruber, K. (2007) *A Linguistic and Ethnographic Analysis of Apology Narratives Performed in the Context of Federal Sentencing Hearings*, unpublished PhD dissertation, University of Chicago.

Gubrium, J. and Holstein, J. (2009) *Analyzing Narrative Reality*, Thousand Oaks, CA: Sage Publications, Inc.

Gudjonsson, G. (1992) *The Psychology of Interrogations, Confessions and Testimony*, Chichester: John Wiley and Sons, Ltd.

Gumperz, J. (1982) *Discourse Strategies*, Cambridge: Cambridge University Press.

Gumperz, J., Aulakh, G. and Kaltman, H. (1982) 'Thematic structure and progression in discourse', in J. Gumperz (ed.) *Language and Social Identity*, New York: Cambridge University Press, 22–56.

Gunnarsson, B.-L (1984) 'Functional comprehensibility of legislative texts: Experiments with a Swedish Act of Parliament', *Text* 4(1–3): 71–105.

Gusfield, J. (1980) *Illusions of Authority*, Chicago: Chicago University Press.

Gustafsson, M. (1975) *Some Syntactic Properties of English Law Language, Publication No. 4,* Department of English, Turku: University of Turku.

——(1984), 'The syntactic features of binomial expressions in legal English', *Text*, 4(1/3): 123–41.

Haack, S. (2008) 'What's wrong with litigation-driven science? An essay in legal epistemology', *Seton Hall Law Review*, 38: 1053–83.

Hager, J. (1959) 'Let's simplify legal language', *Rocky Mountain Law Review*, 32: 74–86.

Hale, S. (1996) 'Pragmatic considerations in court interpreting', *Australian Review of Applied Linguistics*, 19: 61–72.

——(1999) 'Interpreters' treatment of discourse markers in courtroom questions', *Forensic Linguistics*, 6 (1): 57–82.

——(2001) 'How are courtroom questions interpreted? An analysis of Spanish interpreters' practices', in I. Mason (ed.) *Triadic Exchanges. Studies in Dialogue Interpreting*, Manchester: St. Jerome.

——(2003). '"Excuse me, the interpreter wants to speak" – Interpreter interruptions in the courtroom: why do interpreters interrupt and what are the consequences?', *Proceedings of the Third Critical Link Conference*, Montreal, May 2001. Available online at: www.criticallink.org/proceedings/5.pdf (accessed 6 August 2009).

——(2004) *The Discourse of Court Interpreting: Discourse Practices of the Law, the Witness and the Interpreter*, Amsterdam and Philadelphia, PA: John Benjamins.

——(2007) *Community Interpreting*, Hampshire: Palgrave Macmillan.

Hale, S. and Campbell, S. (2002) 'The interaction between text difficulty and translation accuracy', *Babel*, 48: 14–33.

Hale, S. and Gibbons, J. (1999) 'Varying realities: patterned changes in the interpreter's representation of courtroom and external realities', *Applied Linguistics*, 20(2): 203–20.

Halliday, M.A K. (1973) *Language in a Social Perspective: Explorations in the Functions of Language*, London: Edward Arnold.

——(1978) *Language as Social Semiotic: The Social Interpretation of Language and Meaning*, London: Edward Arnold.

——(1989) *Spoken and Written Language*, Oxford: Oxford University Press.

——(1994) *An Introduction to Functional Grammar*, 2nd edn, London: Edward Arnold.

Hamlyn, B., Phelps, A., Turtel, J. and Sattar, G. (2004) 'Are special measures working? Evidence from surveys of vulnerable and intimidated witnesses', *Home Office Research Study*, No. 283, London: HMSO.

Hammersley, M. (2006) 'Ethnography: problems and prospects', *Ethnography and Education*, 1(1): 3–14.

Hanks, P. (1971) *Hamlyn Encyclopedic World Dictionary*, Feltham: Hamlyn.

Hansen, M. (2002) 'Dr. Cop on the stand: judges accept police officers as experts too quickly, critics say', *American Bar Association Journal*, 31–4.

Hardcastle, R.A. (1997) 'Cusum; a credible method for the determination of authorship?', *Science and Justice*, 37(2), 129–38.

Harris, D. (1976) *Basic Elements of Intelligence*, Washington, DC: US Law Enforcement Assistance Administration.

Harris, S. (1984) 'Questions as a mode of control in magistrates' courts', *International Journal of the Sociology of Language*, 49: 5–28.

——(2001) 'Fragmented narratives and multiple tellers: witness and defendant accounts in trials', *Discourse Studies*, 3(1): 53–74.

——(2003) 'Politeness and power: making and responding to "requests" in institutional settings', *Text*, 23(1): 27–52.

——(2005) 'Telling stories and giving evidence: the hybridisation of narrative and non-narrative modes of discourse in a sexual assault trial', in J. Thornborrow and J. Coates (eds) *The Sociolinguistics of Narrative*, Amsterdam: Benjamins, 215–37.

Harvey, M. (2000) 'A beginner's course in legal translation: the case of culture-bound terms', *ASTTI/ ETII*: 357–69.

——(2002) 'What's so special about legal translation?', *Meta*, 47(2): 177–85.

Hastie, R. (1993) 'Algebraic models of juror decision processes', in R. Hastie (ed.) *Inside the Juror*, Cambridge: Cambridge University Press, 84–115.

Hastie, R. and Pennington, N. (1996) 'The O.J. Simpson stories: behavioral scientists' reflections on "The People of the State of California v. Orenthal James Simpson"', *University of Colorado Law Review*, 67: 957–76.

Hastie, R., Penrod, S. and Pennington, N. (1983) *Inside the Jury*, Cambridge, MA: Harvard University Press.

ten Have, P. (2007) *Doing Conversation Analysis* (2nd edn), London: Sage.

Haworth, K. (2006) 'The dynamics of power and resistance in police interview discourse', *Discourse & Society*, 17(6): 739–59.

——(2009) 'Police interview discourse and its role(s) in the judicial process', unpublished thesis, University of Nottingham.

Heaps, C. and Henley, T. (1999) 'Language matters: wording considerations in hazard perception and warning comprehension', *Journal of Psychology*, 133: 341–42.

Heath, C. (1986) *Body Movement and Speech in Medical Interaction*, New York: Cambridge University Press.

Heffer, C. (2002) '"If you were standing in Marks and Spencers": narrativisation and comprehension in the English summing-up', in J. Cotterill (ed.) *Language in the Legal Process*, Basingstoke: Palgrave, 228–45.

——(2005) *The Language of Jury Trial: A Corpus-Aided Analysis of Legal–Lay Discourse*, Basingstoke/New York: Palgrave Macmillan.

——(2006) 'Beyond "reasonable doubt": The criminal standard of proof instruction as communicative act', *International Journal of Speech, Language and the Law*, 13(2): 159–188.

——(2007) 'Judgement in court: evaluating participants in courtroom discourse', in K. Kredens and S. Gozdz-Roszkowski (eds) *Language and the Law: International Outlooks*, Frankfurt am Mein: Peter Lang, 145–79.

——(2008a) 'Report of Dr. Christopher Heffer dated 28 August 2008. re Bambino Mio Limited, Claimant and Cazitex N.V., Defendant', unpublished manuscript.

——(2008b) 'The language and communication of jury instruction', in J. Gibbons and M.T. Turell (eds) *Dimensions of Forensic Linguistics*, Amsterdam: John Benjamins, 47–65.

——(2010) *Forensic Discourse*, London and New York: Continuum.

Heinemann, T. (2006) '"Will you or can't you?" Displaying entitlement in interrogative requests', *Journal of Pragmatics*, 38: 1081–1104.

Henning, T. (1999) 'Judicial summation: the trial judge's version of the facts or the chimera of neutrality', *International Journal for the Semiotics of Law*, 12: 171–213.

Heritage, J. (1984) 'A change-of-state token and aspects of its sequential placement', in J.M. Atkinson and J. Heritage (eds) *Structures of Social Action: Studies in Conversation Analysis*, Cambridge: Cambridge University Press, 299–346.

——(1985) 'Analysing news interviews: aspects of the production of talk for an overhearing audience', in T.A. van Dijk (ed.) *Handbook of Discourse Analysis*, Vol. 3, London: Academic Press, 95–119.

——(2002) 'Ad hoc inquiries: two preferences in the design of routine questions in an open context', in D.W. Maynard, H. Houtkoop-Steenstra, N.C. Schaeffer and J. van der Zouwen (eds) *Standardization and Tacit Knowledge: Interaction and Practice in the Survey Interview*, Chichester: Wiley, 313–34.

——(2003) 'Designing questions and setting agendas in the news interview', in P. Glenn, C.D. LeBaron, J. Mandelbaum (eds) *Studies in Language and Social Interaction*, Mahwah, NJ: Lawrence Erlbaum Associates Inc, 151–77.

Heritage, J. and Clayman, S. (2010) *Talk in Action: Interactions, Identities, and Institutions*, New York: Blackwell.

Heritage, J. and Sorjonen, M. (1994) 'Constituting and maintaining activities across sequences: *And*-prefacing as a feature of question design', *Language in Society*, 23: 1–29.

Heritage, J. and Watson, D. (1977) 'Recent developments in the sociology of language in Britain', *Sociolinguistics Newsletter*, 8: 2–6.

——(1980) 'Aspects of the properties of formulations in natural conversations: Some instances analysed', *Semiotica* 30–33/4: 245–62.

Heritage, J. and Watson, R. (1979) 'Formulations as conversational objects', in G. Psathas (ed.) *Everyday Language: Studies in Ethnomethodology*, New York: Irvington Press, 123–62.

Hertog, E., Corsellis, A., Rasmussen, K.W., van den Bosch, Y., van der Vlis, E. and Keijzer-Lambooy, H. (2007) 'From Aequitas to Aequalitas: Establishing standards in legal interpreting and translation in the European Union', in C. Wadensjö, B. Englund Dimitrova and A.L. Nilsson (eds) *The Critical Link 4*, Amsterdam and Philadelphia, PA: John Benjamins Publishing Company, 151–66.

Hewitt, B. (2003) 'A plea for mercy: as his family fights to free him, convicted murderer Michael Skakel finally speaks', *People Weekly*, 59.18, 12 May 2003.

Heydon, G. (2005) *The Language of Police Interviewing: A Critical Analysis*, Basingstoke: Palgrave Macmillan.

Heymann, P. (1984) Testimony before the Subcommittee on Civil and Constitutional Rights of the House Committee on the Judiciary 96th Congress, March 4, 36–39.

Hibbitts, B. (1995) 'Making motions: the embodiment of law in gesture', *The Journal of Contemporary Legal Issues*, 6: 51–82.

Hickey, L. (1993) 'Presupposition under cross-examination', *International Journal for the Semiotics of Law*, 6 (16): 89–109.

Hill, C.A. and King, C. (2004) 'How do German contracts do as much with fewer words?' *Chicago-Kent Law Review*, 79: 889–926.

Hill, M. (2003) 'Identifying the source of critical details in confessions', *Forensic Linguistics*, 10(1): 23–61.

Hillenbrand, J., Getty, L.A., Clark, M.J. and Wheeler, K. (1995) 'Acoustic characteristics of American English vowels', *Journal of the Acoustical Society of America*, 97: 3099–3111.

Hiltunen, R. (1984) 'The type and structure of clausal embedding in legal English', *Studies of Legal Discourse*, 4(1/3): 107–21.

——(1996) '"Tell me, be you a witch?": questions in the Salem witchcraft trials of 1692', *International Journal for the Semiotics of Law*, 9(25): 17–37.

——(2004) 'Salem 1692: a case of courtroom discourse in a historical perspective', in R. Hiltunen and S. Watanabe (eds) *Approaches to Style and Discourse in English*, Osaka: Osaka University Press, 3–21.

Hirsch, S. (1998) *Pronouncing and Persevering: Gender and the Discourses of Disputing in an African Islamic Court*, Chicago: University of Chicago Press.

Hobbs, P. (2003a) '"Is that what we're here about?" A lawyer's use of impression management in a closing argument at trial', *Discourse and Society*, 14(3): 273–90.

——(2003b) '"You must say it for him": reformulating a witness' testimony on cross-examination at trial', *Text*, 23(4): 477–511.

——(2008) 'It's not what you say, but how you say it: the role of personality and identity in trial success', *Critical Discourse Studies*, 5(3): 231–48.

Hoey, M. (2005) *Lexical Priming. A New Theory of Words and Language*, London: Routledge.

Hollien, H. (1990) *The Acoustics of Crime*, New York: Plenum.

——(2002) *Forensic Voice Identification*, London: Academic Press.

Holmberg, U. (2004) 'Crime victims' experiences of police interviews and their inclination to provide or omit information', *International Journal of Police Science and Management*, 6: 155–70.

Holmberg, U. and Christianson, S.A. (2002) 'Murderers' and sexual offenders' experiences of police interviews and their inclination to admit or deny crimes', *Behavioural Sciences and the Law*, 20(1–2): 31–45.

Holmes, D.I. (1998) 'The evolution of stylometry in the humanities', *Literary and Linguistic Computing*, 13(3): 111–17.

Holt, E. (2009) 'Reported speech', in S. D'Hondt, J.O. Östman and J. Verschueren (eds) *The Pragmatics of Interaction: Handbook of Pragmatics Highlights 4*, Amsterdam: John Benjamins, 190–205.

Holt, E and Clift, R. (eds) (2007) *Reporting Talk: Reported Speech in Interaction (Studies in Interactional Sociolinguistics 24)*. Cambridge: Cambridge University Press.

Holt, E.J. and Johnson, A.J. (2006) 'Formulating the facts: Questions and repeats in police/suspect interviews', Paper at *International Conference on Conversation Analysis*, Helsinki, May 2006.

Home Office (1989) *Pigot Committee: Report of the Advisory Group on Video Evidence*, London: HMSO.

——(1992) *Circular 22*, HMSO: London.

——(1998) *Speaking up for Justice: Report of the Interdepartmental Working Group on the Treatment of Vulnerable or Intimidated Witnesses in the Criminal Justice System*, London: HMSO.

——(2002/2007) *Achieving the Best Evidence in Criminal Proceedings: Guidance for Vulnerable and Intimidated Witnesses, including Children*, London: Home Office.

——(2007) *Achieving the Best Evidence in Criminal Proceedings: Guidance on Interviewing Victims and Witnesses, and Using Special Measures*, London: Home Office.

——(2008) *PACE Code C: Code of Practice for the Detention, Treatment and Questioning of Persons by Police Officers*, London: HMSO.

Home Office and the Department of Health (1992) *Memorandum of Good Practice on Video-recorded Interviews with Child Witnesses for Criminal Proceedings*, London: HMSO.

Home Office, Crown Prosecution Service and Department for Constitutional Affairs (2005) *Code of Practice for Victims of Crime*, London: Office for Criminal Justice Reform.

Hostettler, J. (2006) *Fighting for Justice: The History and Origins of Adversary Trial*, Hook: Waterside Press.

Hotta, S. (2007a) 'A linguistic exploration of trademark dilution', in M. Turell, M. Spassova and J. Cicres (eds) *Proceedings of the Second European IAFL Conference on Forensic Linguistics/Language and the Law*, Barcelona: Universitat Pompeu Fabra, 179–86.

——(2007b) 'Morphosyntactic structure of Japanese trademarks and their distinctiveness: a new model for linguistic analysis of trademarks', in K. Kredens and S. Gozdz-Roszkowski (eds) *Language and the Law: International Outlooks*, Frankfurt am Mein: Peter Lang, 379–92.

Hotta, S. and Fujita, M. (2007) 'The psycholinguistic foundation of trademarks: an experimental study', in M. Turell, M. Spassova and J. Cicres (eds) *Proceedings of the Second European IAFL Conference on Forensic Linguistics/Language and the Law*, Barcelona: Universitat Pompeu Fabra, 173–78.

House, J. (1977) *A Model of Translation Quality Assessment*, Tubingen: Gunter Narr Verlag.

van der Houwen, F. (2005) *Negotiating Disputes and Achieving Judgments on Judge Judy*, unpublished PhD dissertation, University of Southern California.

Howald, B.S. (2009) 'Authorship attribution under the rules of evidence: empirical approaches in the layperson legal system', *International Journal of Speech, Language and the Law*, 15: 219–47.

Howard, R.M. (1995) 'Plagiarisms, authorships, and the academic death penalty', *College English*, 57, 788–805.

——(1999) 'The new abolitionism comes to plagiarism', in L. Buranen and A.M. Roy (eds). *Perspectives on Plagiarism and Intellectual Property in a Postmodern World*, Albany, NY: State University of New York Press, 87–95.

Huckin, T. (2002) 'Textual silence and the discourse of homelessness', *Discourse and Society*, 13: 347–72.

Huddleston, R. and Pullum, G.K. (2002) *The Cambridge Grammar of the English Language*, Cambridge: Cambridge University Press.

Hudson, T., de Jong, G., McDougall, K., Harrison, P. and Nolan, F. (2007) 'F0 statistics for 100 young male speakers of standard southern British English', *Proceedings of the 16th International Congress of Phonetic Sciences*, Saarbrücken, Germany, 1809–12. Available online at: www.icphs2007.de/conference/papers/1570/1570.pdf.

Hunston, S. and Sinclair, J. (2000) 'A local grammar of evaluation', in S. Hunston and G. Thompson (eds) *Evaluation in Text: Authorial Stance and the Construction of Discourse*, Oxford: Oxford University Press.

Hunt, J. and Borgida, E. (2001) '"Is that what I said?": witnesses' responses to interviewer modifications', *Law and Human Behaviour*, 25: 583–603.

Hunt, M. (1996) 'The sociolinguistics of tagging and Chicano gang graffiti', unpublished PhD dissertation, U. Southern California.

Huntington, R. (1991) 'European unity and the tower of Babel', *Boston University International Law Journal*, 9: 321–46.

Hutchby, I. and Wooffitt, R. (1998) *Conversation Analysis*, Oxford: Polity Press.

635

Hymes, D. (1977) *Foundations in Sociolinguistics: An Ethnographic Approach*, London: Tavistock Publications.

——(1981) *"In Vain I Tried to Tell You"*: Essays in Native American Ethnopoetics, Philadelphia: University of Pennsylvania Press.

Ibrahim, A. (1999) 'Becoming black: rap and hip-hop, race, gender, identity and the politics of ESL learning', *TESOL Quarterly*, 33: 349–69.

Ibrahim, R. (2008) 'Performance in L1 and L2 observed in an Arabic–Hebrew bilingual aphasic following brain tumor: A case constitutes double dissociation', *Psychology Research and Behaviour Management*, 1: 11–9.

Ibrahim, Z. (2007) 'The interpreter as advocate. Malaysian court interpreting as a case in point', in C. Wadensjö, B. Englund Dimitrova and A.L. Nilsson (eds) *The Critical Link 4. Professionalisation of Interpreting in the Community*, Amsterdam and Philadelphia, PA: John Benjamins Publishing Company.

Ikane, J. (2007) 'Problems in communicating the suspect's rights in interpreted police interviews', *Applied Linguistics*, 28(1): 87–112.

Inbau, F.E., Reid, J.E. and Buckley, J.P. (1986) *Criminal Interrogation and Confessions*, Baltimore, MN: Williams and Wilkins.

Istratescu, C. (2007) *Fighting Gang Allegations: A Conceptual and Methodological Approach*, CPDA: Advanced Trial Skills Institute.

Jackson, A. (2004) *Prosecuting Gang Cases: What Local Prosecutors Need to Know*, Los Angeles, CA: American Prosecutors Research Institute.

Jackson, B.S. (1988) *Law, Fact and Narrative Coherence*, Liverpool: Deborah Charles Publications.

——(1995) *Making Sense in Law*, Liverpool: Deborah Charles Publications.

Jacquemet, M. (1996) *Credibility in Court: Communicative Practices in the Camorra Trials*, Cambridge: Cambridge University Press.

Janney, R.W. (2002) 'Cotext as context: vague answers in court', *Language and Communication*, 22: 457–75.

Javan, S. (2009) *Little Bodies don't mean Little Minds: An Investigation into Children's Facilitation of Audience Design when Constructing Referring Expressions in the Context of an Investigative Police Interview*. Unpublished dissertation.

Jaworski, A. and Galasiński, D. (2004) 'Vocative address forms and ideological legitimization in political debates', *Discourse Studies*, 2: 35–53.

Jefferson, G. (1989) 'Preliminary notes on a possible metric which provides for a "standard maximum" silence of approximately one second in conversation', in D. Roger and P. Bull (eds) *Conversation: An Interdisciplinary Perspective*, Clevedon: Multilingual Matters, 166–96.

——(2004) 'Glossary of transcript symbols with an introduction', in G. Lerner (ed.) *Conversation Analysis: Studies from the First Generation*, Amsterdam: John Benjamins, 13–31.

Jessen, M. (2007a) 'Forensic reference data on articulation rate in German', *Science and Justice*, 47: 50–67.

——(2007b) 'Speaker Classification in forensic phonetics and acoustics', in C. Müller (ed.) *Speaker classification I: Fundamentals, Features, and Methods*, Berlin: Springer.

——(2008a) 'Forensic phonetics', *Language and Linguistics Compass* 2: 671–711.

——(2008b) 'Continuous v. categorical variations between speakers', paper presented at the *17th Annual Conference of the International Association for Forensic Phonetics and Acoustics*, Lausanne.

Jessen, M., Köster, O. and Gfroerer, S. (2005) 'Influence of vocal effort on average and variability of fundamental frequency', *International Journal of Speech, Language and the Law*, 12: 174–213.

Johnson, A. (1997) 'Textual kidnapping: a case of plagiarism among three student texts', *International Journal of Speech, Language and the Law*, 4(ii): 210–25.

——(2002) 'So … ? pragmatic implications of so-prefaced questions in formal police interviews', in J. Cotterill (ed.) *Language in the Legal Process*, Basingstoke: Palgrave Macmillan, 91–110.

——(2006) 'Police questioning', in K. Brown (ed.) *The Encyclopedia of Language and Linguistics*, Vol. 9, Oxford: Elsevier, 661–72.

——(2008a) 'Changing stories: Achieving a change of state in suspect and witness knowledge through evaluation in police interviews with suspects and witnesses', *Functions of Language*, 15(1): 84–114.

——(2008b) '"From where we're sat … ": negotiating narrative transformation through interaction in police interviews with suspects', *Text & Talk*, 28(3): 327–49.

——(2008c) 'From interview to courtroom – the evidential narrative as courtroom object', paper presented at Georgetown University Roundtable, Georgetown University, Washington, DC.

Johnson, K. (2006) 'Speaker normalization in speech perception', in D.B. Pisoni and R.E. Remez (eds) *The Handbook of Speech Perception*, Oxford: Blackwell.

Johnstone, B. (1996) *The Linguistic Individual*, Oxford: Oxford University Press.

——(2000) *Qualitative Methods in Sociolinguistics*, New York: Oxford University Press.

——(2002) *Discourse Analysis*, Oxford: Blackwell.

——(2009) 'Stance, style, and the linguistic individual', in A. Jaffe (ed.) *Sociolinguistic Perspectives on Stance*, Oxford: Oxford University Press.

Jones, S. and LeBaron, C. (2002) 'Research on the relationship between verbal and nonverbal communication: emerging integrations', *Journal of Communication*, 52(3): 499–521.

Jönsson, L. and Linell, P. (1991) 'Story generations: from dialogical interviews to written reports in police interrogations', *Text*, 11(3): 419–40.

Jucker, A.H. and I. Taavitsainen (2000) 'Diachronic speech act analysis: insults from flyting to flaming', *Journal of Historical Pragmatics*, 1(1): 67–95.

Judicial Council of California (2003) *Civil Jury Instructions*, Newark, NJ: LexisNexis Matthew Bender.

——(2006) *Criminal Jury Instruction*, Newark, NJ: LexisNexis Matthew Bender.

Kadric, M. (2000) 'Interpreting in the Austrian courtroom', in R. Roberts, S. Carr, D. Abraham and A. Dufour (eds) *The Critical Link 2: Interpreters in the Community*, Amsterdam and Philadelphia: John Benjamins.

Kaldor, S. and Malcolm, I. (1991) 'Aboriginal English – an overview', in S. Romaine (ed.) *Language in Australia*, Cambridge: Cambridge University Press, 67–83.

Kamisar, Y. (2007) 'On the fortieth anniversary of the *Miranda* case: why we needed it, how we got it – and what happened to it', *Ohio State Journal of Criminal Law*, 5, 163–203.

Kandel, E. (1998) 'A new intellectual framework for psychology', *American Journal of Psychiatry*, 155: 457–69.

——(2006) *In Search of Memory: The Emergence of a New Science of Mind*, New York: W. W. Norton.

Kandel, R.F. (2002) 'Why evidence scholars should study conversation', *International Commentary on Evidence*, 1(2): article no. 7. Available online at: www.bepress.com/ice/vol1/iss2/art7.

Kaplan, J.P., Green, G.M., Cunningham, C.D. and Levi, J.N. (1995) 'Bringing linguistics into judicial decision making: semantic analysis submitted to the US Supreme Court', *Forensic Linguistics: International Journal of Speech, Language and the Law*, 2(1): 81–98.

Karton, J. (2008) 'Lost in translation: international criminal tribunals and the legal implications of interpreted testimony', *Vanderbilt Journal of Transnational Law*, 41(1): 1–54. Available online at: www.translationsdecoder.com/lostintranslationvanderbiltschooloflaw.htm (accessed 12 July 2009).

Kassin, S. (2002) 'False confessions and the jogger case', *The New York Times OP-ED*, 1 November 2002, p. A31.

——(2005) 'On the psychology of confessions: does innocence put innocents at risk?', *American Psychologist*, 60: 215–28.

Kassin, S. and Gudjonsson, G.H. (2004) 'The psychology of confession evidence: a review of the literature and issues', *Psychological Science in the Public Interest*, 5(2), 33–67. Available online at: www.williams.edu/Psychology/Faculty/Kassin/research/confessions.htm.

Kassin, S., Leo, R.A., Meissner, C.A., Richman, K.D., Colwell, L.H., Leach, A. and La Fon, D. (2007) 'Police interviewing and interrogation: a self-report survey of police practices and beliefs', *Law and Human Behaviour*, 31(4): 381–400.

Kassin, S. and Sukel, H. (1997) 'Coerced confessions and the jury: an experimental test of the "harmless error" rule', *Law and Human Behavior*, 21: 27–47.

Katz, E. and Lazarsfeld, P. (1955) *Personal Influence*, Glencoe, IL: Free Press.

Katz, J. (2009) 'When cops speak Spanglish to a non-English speaker', *Simple Justice Blog*. Available online at: www.katzjustice.com/underdog/permalink/LanguageIssues.html (accessed 1 May 2009).

Keane, A. (1996) *The Modern Law of Evidence*, 4th edn, London: Butterworths.

Kearns, J. (2006) 'Lodi Muslims: under the "eye of suspicion"', Public Broadcasting Station PBS, 24 July 2006.

Keen, L. (2009) 'Judge is horrified by quality of video evidence', *South Wales Echo*, 30 January 2009. Available online at: www.walesonline.co.uk/news/cardiff-news/2009/01/30/ (accessed 16 June 2009).

Kelso, J.C. (1996) 'Final report of the blue ribbon commission on jury system improvement', *Hastings L.J.*, 47: 1433.

Kendon, A. (2003) *Gesture*, New York: Cambridge University Press.

Kendon, A. and Versante, L. (2003) 'Pointing by hand in "Neopolitan"', in S. Kita (ed.) *Pointing: Where Language, Culture, and Cognition Meet*, Mahwah: Lawrence Erlbaum, 109–37.

Kennedy, L. (1961) *10 Rillington Place*, London: Victor Gollancz.

Kerr-Thompson, J. (2002) '"Powerful/powerless" language in court: a critical re-evaluation of the Duke Language and Law Programme', *International Journal of Speech, Language and the Law*, 9(2): 153–67.

Kidwell, M. (2006) '"Calm down!": the role of gaze in the interactional management of hysteria by the police', *Discourse Studies*, 8(6): 771–96.

King, M. (1997) *A Better World for Children? Explorations in Morality and Authority*, London: Routledge.

Kintsch, W. (1995) 'How readers construct situation models for stories: the role of syntactic cues and causal inferences', in M. Gernsbacher and T. Givón (eds) *Coherence in Spontaneous Text*, Amsterdam and Philadelphia: John Benjamins, 139–60.

Kirsch, I., Jungeblut, A., Jenkins, L. and Kolstad, A. (2002) *Adult Literacy in America*, 3rd edn, Washington DC: US Department of Education. Available online at: http://nces.ed.gov/pubs93/93275.pdf (accessed 10 December 2008).

Kita, S. (2003) 'Pointing: a foundational building block of human communication', in S. Kita (ed.) *Pointing: Where Language, Culture, and Cognition Meet*, Mahwah: Lawrence Erlbaum, 1–8.

Klein, M. (1996) 'Framing the juvenile justice problem: the reality behind the problem', *Pepperdine Law Review*, 23: 860–67.

——(1997) 'What are street gangs when they get to court?', *Valparaiso University Law Review*, 31: 515–21.

Klein, S.R. (2001) 'Identifying and (re)formulating prophylactic rules, safe harbors, and incidental rights in constitutional criminal procedure', *Michigan Law Review*, 99: 1030–80.

Kniffka, H. (2007) *Working in Language and Law: A German Perspective*, Basingstoke: Palgrave Macmillan.

Koegel, T. (2007) *The Exceptional Presenter*, Austin, TX: Greenleaf Book Group Press.

Kolb, W. and Pöchhacker, F. (2008) 'Stories retold: interpreting in asylum appeal hearings', in D. Russell and S. Hale (eds) *Interpreting in Legal Settings*, Washington, DC: Gallaudet University Press.

Komter, M.L. (1998) *Dilemmas in the Court Room. A Study of Trials of Violent Crime in the Netherlands*, Mahwah, NJ: Lawrence Erlbaum.

——(2002) 'The suspect's own words: the treatment of written statements in Dutch courtrooms', *Forensic Linguistics*, 9(2): 168–92.

——(2003) 'The interactional dynamics of eliciting a confession in a Dutch police interrogation', *Research on Language and Social Interaction*, 36(4): 433–70.

——(2005) 'Understanding problems in an interpreter-mediated police interrogation', in S. Burns (ed.) *Ethnographies of Law and Social Control: Sociology of Crime, Law & Deviance*, Vol. 6, Amsterdam: Elsevier, 203–24.

——(2006) 'From talk to text: the interactional construction of a police record', *Research on Language and Social Interaction*, 39(3): 201–28.

Koppel, M., Schler, J., and Argamon, S. (2009). 'Computational methods in authorship attribution', *Journal of the American Society for Information Science and Technology*, 60(1), 9–26.

Koskoff, T.I. (1983) 'The language of persuasion', in *The Litigation Manual: A Primer for Trial Lawyers*, Chicago: Section of Litigation, American Bar Association, 110–111.

Köster, O. and Köster, J-P. (2004) 'The auditory-perceptual evaluation of voice quality in forensic speaker recognition', *The Phonetician*, 89: 9–37.

Kotadia, M. (2004) 'MikeRoweSoft settles for an Xbox', c|netNews.Com, January 26. Available online at: http://news.com.com/2100–1014_3–5147374.html (accessed 20 December 2008).

Koven, M. (2002) 'An analysis of speaker role inhabitance in narratives of personal experience', *Journal of Pragmatics*, 34: 167–217.

Kozin, A.V. (2008) 'Unsettled facts: on the transformational dynamism of evidence in legal discourse', *Text & Talk*, 28(2): 219–38.

Kredens, K. (2002) 'Idiolect in authorship attribution', in P. Stalmaszczyk (ed.), *Folia Linguistica Anglica* 4, Lodz: Lodz University Press.

——(2003) 'Towards a corpus-based methodology of forensic authorship attribution: a comparative study of two idiolects', in B. Lewandowska-Tomaszczyk (ed.) *PALC'01: Practical Applications in Language Corpora*, Frankfurt am Mein: Peter Lang.

Kremer-Sadlik, T. (2004) 'How children with autism and Asperger Syndrome respond to questions: a "naturalistic" theory of mind task', *Discourse Studies*, 6(2): 185–206.

Kress, G. (ed.) (1976) *Halliday: System and Function in Language*, London: Oxford University Press.

Krouglov, A. (1999) 'Police interpreting: Politeness and sociocultural context', *The Translator*, 5: 285–302.

Kryk-Kastovsky, B. (2000) 'Representations of orality in Early Modern English trial records', *Journal of Historical Pragmatics*, 1(2): 201–30.

——(2006) 'Impoliteness in Early Modern English courtroom discourse', *Journal of Historical Pragmatics*, 7(2): 213–44.

——(2009) 'Speech acts in Early Modern English court trials', *Journal of Pragmatics*, 41(3): 440–57.

Künzel, H.J. (1987) *Sprechererkennung: Grundzüge forensischer Sprachverarbeitung*, Heidelberg: Kriminalistik Verlag.

——(1989) 'How well does average fundamental frequency correlate with speaker height and weight?', *Phonetica*, 46: 117–25.

——(1995) 'Field procedures in forensic speaker recognition', in J. Windsor Lewis (ed.) *Studies in General and English Phonetics. Essays in Honour of Professor J. D. O'Connor*, London: Routledge.

——(2001) 'Beware of the "telephone effect": The influence of telephone transmission on the measurement of formant frequencies', *International Journal of Speech, Language and the Law*, 8(1) 80–99.

——(2004) 'Tasks in forensic speech and audio analysis: a tutorial', *The Phonetician*, 90: 9–22.

Kurzon, D. (1997) 'Legal languages: varieties, genres, registers and discourses', *International Journal of Applied Linguistics*, 7(2): 119–39.

——(1998a) 'Language of the law and legal language', in L. Christer and M. Nordman (eds) *Special Language: From Humans Thinking to Thinking Machines*, Clevedon: Multilingual Matters, 283–90.

——(1998b) *Discourse of Silence*, Amsterdam and Philadelphia, PA: John Benjamins.

Kutner, M., Greenberg, E., Jin, Y., Boyle, B., Hsu, Y. and Dunleavy, E. (2007) *Literacy in Everyday Life: Results from the 2003 National Assessment of Adult Literacy*, Washington, DC: US Department of Education. Available online at: http://nces.ed.gov/Pubs2007/2007480.pdf (accessed 11 December 2008).

Kwarciński, W. (2006) 'A diachronic speech act analysis of sworn testimonies in Polish criminal trials', *Journal of Historical Pragmatics*, 7(2): 293–314.

Kytö, M. and Culpeper, J. (2006) *A Corpus of English Dialogues 1560–1760*, Oxford Text Archive. Available online at: http://ota.ahds.ac.uk/ (accessed 24 August 2009).

Labov, W. (1966a) 'The linguistic variable as a structural unit', *Washington Linguistics Review*, 3: 4–22.

——(1966b) *The Social Stratification of English in New York City*, Washington, DC: Center for Applied Linguistics.

——(1972) *Language in the Inner City: Studies in the Black English Vernacular*, Philadelphia, PA: University of Pennsylvania Press.

——(1994) *Principles of Linguistic Change, vol. 1: Internal Factors*, Oxford: Blackwell.

——(1996) 'When intuitions fail', in L. McNair, K. Singer, L. Dolbrin and M. Aucon (eds) *Papers from the Parasession on Theory and Data in Linguistics*, Chicago Linguistic Society, 32: 77–106.

——(1997) 'Some further steps in narrative analysis', *Journal of Narrative and Life History*, 7(1–4): 395–415.

——(2002) 'Driving forces in linguistic change', *International Conference on Korean Linguistics*, Seoul National University, 2 August 2002. Available online at: www.ling.upenn.edu/~wlabov/Papers/DLFC.htm.

——(2004) 'Quantitative reasoning in linguistics', in Ulrich Ammon, Norbert Dittmar, Klaus J. Mattheier, and Peter Trudgill (eds) *Sociolinguistics/Soziolinguistik: An international handbook of the science of language and society/Ein internationales Handbuch zur Wissenschaft von Sprache und Gesellschaft*, Vol 1. 2nd edition, New York and Berlin: Walter de Gruyter, 6–22.

Labov, W. and Waletzky, J. (1967) 'Narrative analysis: oral versions of personal experience', in J. Helms (ed.) *Essays on the Verbal and Visual Arts: Proceedings of the 1996 Annual Spring Meeting of the American Ethnological Society*, Seattle, WA: University of Washington Press, 12–44.

Lakoff, G. (1988) 'Cognitive semantics', in U. Eco (ed.) *Meaning and Mental Representation*, Bloomington: Indiana University Press.

Lakoff, R.T. (1996) 'True confessions? pragmatic competence and criminal confession', in Gerhardt, J., Guo, J., Kyratzis, A. and Slobin D.I. (eds) *Social Interaction. Social Context, and Language: Essays in Honor of Susan Ervin-Tripp*, Hillsdale, NJ: Lawrence Erlbaum.

Lally, C. (2009) 'Interpreters for gardaí are not vetted abroad', *Irish Times*, 30 April 2009. Available online at: www.irishtimes.com/newspaper/ireland/2009/0430/1224245683458_pf.html (accessed 12 July 2009).

Landau, S. (2001) *Dictionaries: The Art and Craft of Lexicography*, 2nd edn, Cambridge: Cambridge University Press.

Landsman, S. (1984) *The Adversary System: A Description and Defense*, Washington, DC: American Enterprise Institute.

——(1990) 'The rise of the contentious spirit: adversary procedure in eighteenth century England', *Cornell Law Review*, 50: 498–609.

Langbein, J.H. (1978) 'The criminal trial before the lawyers', *University of Chicago Law Review*, 45: 263–316.

——(1999) 'The prosecutorial origins of defence counsel in the eighteenth century: the appearance of solicitors', *Cambridge Law Journal*, 58(2): 314–65.

——(2003) *The Origins of the Adversary Criminal Trial*, Oxford: Oxford University Press.

Lantigua, J. (2002) 'Unraveling the mystery of Petrona', *Palm Beach Post*, 24 November 2002. Available online at: www.racematters.org/petronatomas.htm (accessed 9 July 2009).

Larkin, W. and Burns, D. (1977) 'Sentence comprehension and memory for embedded structure', *Memory and Cognition*, 5(1): 17–22.

Lassiter, G.D. (ed.) (2004) *Interrogations, Confessions and Entrapment*, New York: Kluwer/Plenum.

Lassiter, G.D. and Geers, A.L. (2004) 'Bias and accuracy in the evaluation of confession evidence', in G.D. Lassiter (ed.) *Interrogations, Confessions and Entrapment*, New York: Kluwer/Plenum, 197–265.

Lassiter, G.D., Ratcliff, J., Ware, J., Lezlee, J. and Irvin, C.R. (2006) 'Videotaped confessions: panacea or pandora's box?', *Law & Policy*, 28(2): 192–210. Available online at: www.ssrn.com/abstract=889148.

Lave, J. and Wenger, E. (1991) *Situated Learning: Legitimate Peripheral Participation*, Cambridge: Cambridge University Press.

Laver, J. (1980) *The Phonetic Description of Voice Quality*, Cambridge: Cambridge University Press.

Law Commission (2009) *The Admissibility of Expert Evidence in Criminal Proceedings in England and Wales. Consultation Paper 190.* Available online at: www.lawcom.gov.uk/docs/cp190.pdf.

LeBaron, C.D. and Streeck, J. (1997) 'Built space and the interactional framing of experience during a murder interrogation', *Human Studies*, 20: 1–25.

Lee, D. (1987) 'The semantics of *just*', *Journal of Pragmatics*, 11: 377–98.

Lee, J. (2008) 'City room; female smokers, and a P.R. coup', *The New York Times*, 11 October 2008 (A16).

——(2009a) 'Interpreting inexplicit language during courtroom examination', *Applied Linguistics*, 30: 93–114.

——(2009b) 'Conflicting views on court interpreting examined through surveys of legal professionals and court interpreters', *Interpreting*, 11(1): 35–56.

Lees, S. (1996) *Carnal Knowledge: Rape on Trial*, London: H. Hamilton.

de Leeuw, E. (2007) 'Hesitation markers in English, German, and Dutch', *Journal of Germanic Linguistics*, 19: 85–114.

van Leeuwen, T. (2002) 'The representation of social actors', in M. Toolan (ed.) *Critical Discourse Analysis*, London: Routledge, 302–39.

——(2007) 'Legitimation in discourse and communication', *Discourse and Communication*, 1(1): 91–112.

Lehiste, I. and Meltzer, D. (1973) 'Vowel and speaker identification in natural and synthetic speech', *Language and Speech*, 16: 356–64.

Lehto, M.R. and Miller, J.M. (1986) *Warnings, Vol. 1: Fundamental, Design, and Evaluation Methodologies*, Ann Arbor, MI: Fuller.

Lempert, L. (1996) 'Women's strategies for survival: developing agency in abusive relationships', *Journal of Family Violence*, 11: 269–89.

Lentine, G. and Shuy, R. (1990) '*Mc-*: meaning in the marketplace', *American Speech*, 65: 349–66.

Leo, R.A. (1998) '*Miranda* and the problem of false confessions', in R. A. Leo and G. C. Thomas (eds) *The Miranda Debate: Law, Justice and Policing*, Boston: Northeastern University Press, 271–82.

——(2001) 'Questioning the relevance of *Miranda* in the twenty-first century', *The Michigan Law Review*, 99(5): 1000–1029.

——(2009) 'False confessions: causes, consequences and implications', *The Journal of the American Academy of Psychiatry and the Law*, University of San Francisco Law Research Paper No. 2009–11. Available online at: www.ssrn.com/abstract=1328623.

Leo, R.A. and Davis, D. (2009) 'From false confession to wrongful conviction: seven psychological processes', *Journal of Psychiatry and Law*. Available online at: www.ssrn.com/abstract=1328622.

Leo, R.A., Drizin, S.A., Neufeld, P.J., Hall, B.R. and Vatner, A. (2006) 'Bringing reliability back in: false confessions and legal safeguards in the twenty-first century', *Wisconsin Law Review*, 2006(2): 479–538 University of San Francisco Law Research Paper No. 2009–04. Available online at: www.ssrn.com/abstract=1134948.

Leo, R.A. and Liu, B.L. (2009) 'What do potential jurors know about police interrogation techniques and false confessions?', *Behavioral Sciences and the Law*, 27(3): 381–99. Available online at: www.ssrn.com/abstract=1404078.

Leo, R.A. and Ofshe, R.J. (1998) 'The consequences of false confessions: deprivations of liberty and miscarriages of justice in the age of psychological interrogation', *Journal of Criminal Law and Criminology*, 88(2): 429–96.

Leo, R.A. and Richman, K.D. (2008) 'Mandate the electronic recording of police interrogations', *Crime and Public Policy*, 6(4): 791–98. Available online at: http://ssrn.com/abstract=1141335.

Leo, R.A. and White, W.S. (1999) 'Adapting to *Miranda*: modern interrogators' strategies for dealing with the obstacles posed by *Miranda*', *Minnesota Law Review*, 84: 397–472.

Lerm, H. (1997) 'Language manipulation in court cross-examination: "how powerful is the sword"', in K. Müller and S. Newman (eds) *Language in Court*, Port Elizabeth: Vista University.

Lerner, G.H. (1991) 'On the syntax of sentences-in-progress', *Language in Society*, 20: 441–58.

Levi, J (1993) 'Evaluating jury comprehension of the Illinois capital sentencing instructions', *American Speech*, 68, i: 20–49

Levinson, S. (1992) 'Activity types and language', in P. Drew and J. Heritage (eds) *Talk at Work: Interaction in Institutional Settings*, Cambridge: Cambridge University Press, 66–100.

Levy, L.W. (1999) *The Palladium of Justice: Origins of Trial by Jury*, Chicago: Ivan R. Dee.

Lieberman, J. and Sales, B. (1997) 'What social science teaches us about the jury instruction process', *Psychology, Public Policy and Law*, 3(4): 589–644.

——(1999) 'The effectiveness of jury instructions', in W.F. Abbott and J. Batt (eds) *A Handbook of Jury Research*, Philadelphia, PA: American Law Institute, 18–73.

Lin, J.W. (2006) 'Time in a language without tense: the case of Chinese', *Journal of Semantics*, 23: 1–53.

Linde, C. (1993) *Life Stories: The Creation of Coherence*, New York: Oxford University Press.

Lindsey, J.M. (1990) 'The legal writing malady: causes and cures', *New York Law Journal*, 12 December 1990.

Lindström, A. (2005) 'Language as social action: a study of how senior citizens request assistance with practical tasks in the Swedish home help service', in A. Hakulinen and M. Selting (eds) *Syntax and Lexis in Conversation*, Amsterdam: John Benjamins, 209–33.

Linell, P. (1998) 'Discourse across boundaries: on recontextualisation and the blending of voices in professional discourse', *Text*, 18: 143–57.

Linell, P. and Jönsson, L. (1991) 'Suspect stories: perspective-setting in an asymmetrical situation', in Marková, I. and Foppa, K. (eds) *Asymmetries in Dialogue*, Hemel Hempstead: Harvester Wheatsheaf, 75–100.

Linell, P. and Luckmann, T. (1991) 'Asymmetries in dialogue: some conceptual preliminaries', in Marková, I. and Foppa, K. (eds) *Asymmetries in Dialogue*, Hemel Hempstead: Harvester Wheatsheaf, 1–20.

Linell, P., Alemyr, L. and Jönsson, L. (1993) 'Admission of guilt as a communicative project in judicial settings' *Journal of Pragmatics*, 19: 153–76.

Linville, S.E. (2001) *Vocal Aging*, San Diego, CA: Singular.

Loftus, E. (1979) *Eyewitness Testimony*, Cambridge, MA and London: Harvard University Press.

——(1992) *Witness for the Defence*, New York: St. Martin's Press.

——(1996) *Eyewitness Testimony: With a New Preface*, Cambridge, MA: Harvard University Press.

Long, L.N. and Christensen, W.F. (2008) 'Clearly, using intensifiers is very bad – or is it?', *Idaho Law Review*, 45:171–89.

López, J. (2002) *Gangs: Casualties in an Undeclared War*, Dubuque, IA: Kendall Hunt Pub. Co.

Lord, C. (2002) 'Are subordinate clauses more difficult?', in J. Bybee and M. Noonan (eds) *Complex Sentences in Grammar and Discourse: Essays in Honor of Sandra A. Thompson*, Amsterdam and Philadelphia, PA: John Benjamins, 223–34.

Louw, B. (1993) 'Irony in the text or insincerity in the writer? The diagnostic potential of semantic prosodies', in M. Baker, G. Francis and E. Tognini-Bonelli (eds) *Text and Technology*, Amsterdam: Benjamins, 157–76.

Luchjenbroers, J. (1997) '"In your own words ... " Questions and answers in a supreme court trial', *Journal of Pragmatics*, 27: 477–503.

Luchjenbroers, J. and Aldridge, M. (2007) 'Conceptual manipulation with metaphors and frames: dealing with rape victims in legal discourse', *Text & Talk*, 27(3): 339–59.

Lucy, D. (2005) *Introduction to Statistics for Forensic Scientists*, London: Wiley.

Luhmann, N. (2004) *Law as a Social System*, trans. Klaus Ziegert, Oxford: Oxford University Press.

Lundeberg, M. (1987) 'Metacognitive aspects of reading comprehension: studying understanding in legal case analysis', *Reading Research Quarterly*, 22(4): 407–32.

Lundquist, L. (1995) 'Indefinite noun phrases in legal texts: use, function and construction of mental spaces', *Journal of Pragmatics*, 23(1): 7–29.

Luntz, F. (2007) *Words That Work: It's Not What You Say – It's What People Hear*, New York: Hyperion.

da Luz, C.M. and Weckerly, P.C. (1993) 'The Texas "condom-rape" case: caution construed as consent', *UCLA Women's Law Journal*, 3: 95–104.

Lynch, M. (2007) 'Law courts as perspicuous sites for ethnomethodological investigations', in S. Hester and D. Francis (eds) *Orders of Ordinary Action: Respecifying Sociological Knowledge*, Aldershot: Ashgate, 107–19.

Lyons, J. (1977) *Semantics*, Cambridge: Cambridge University Press.

McDavid, R. (1977) 'Evidence', in D. Shore and C. Hines (eds) *Papers in Language Variation: SAMLA-ADS Collection*, Alabama: University of Alabama Press, 125–32.

McDonald, D. (1986) *The Language of Argument*, New York: Harper & Rowe Publishers, Inc.

McDougall, K. (2006) 'Dynamic features of speech and the characterization of speakers: towards a new approach using formant frequencies', *International Journal of Speech, Language and the Law*, 13: 89–126.

McGreevy, P. and Banks, S. (2006) 'On paper, leaving a gang is difficult; L.A. uses injunctions to fight thugs, but those who go straight find it's hard to get off the list', *Los Angeles Times*, 23 March 2006.

Mackay, J. 1997 *Little Boss: A Life of Andrew Carnegie*, Edinburgh, Mainstream.

MacLachlan, G. and Reid, I. (1994) *Framing and Interpretation*, Melbourne: Melbourne University Press.

The McLibel Trial: Court Transcripts, 1 June 2006. Available online at: www.mcspotlight.org/case/trial/transcripts/index.html.

McMenamin, G.R. (1993) *Forensic Stylistics*, Amsterdam: Elsevier.

——(2001) 'Style markers in authorship studies', *International Journal of Speech, Language and the Law*, 8: 93–97.

——(2002) *Forensic Linguistics – Advances in Forensic Stylistics*, Boca Raton, Florida: CRC Press.

——(2004) 'Disputed authorship in U.S. law', *International Journal of Speech, Language and the Law*, 11(1): 73–82.

McNamara, T. (2000) *Language Testing*, Oxford: Oxford University Press.

McNeill, D. (1992) *Hand and Mind*, Chicago: University of Chicago Press.

——(2005) *Gesture and Thought*, Chicago: University of Chicago Press.

Macro International (16 March 2007) *Design and Testing of Effective Truth in Lending Disclosures,* submitted to the Board of Governors of the Federal Reserve System, Washington, DC. Available online at: www.federalreserve.gov/dcca/regulationz/20070523/execsummary.pdf (accessed 5 January 2009).

——(15 December 2008) *Design and Testing of Effective Truth in Lending Disclosures: Qualitative Study,* submitted to the Board of Governors of the Federal Reserve System, Washington, DC. Available online at: www.federalreserve.gov/newsevents/press/bcreg/bcreg20081218a7.pdf (accessed 5 January 2009).

Madden, H. (2007) 'Zooting up/brighten prom night with flash, dash – and panache', *San Francisco Chronicle,* 29 April 2007.

Madsen, D. (1997) 'Towards a description of communication in the legal universe: translation of legal texts and the Skopos theory', *Fachsprache – International Journal of LSP,* 19(3): 17–27.

Mahoney, P. (2004) 'Houses built on sand: police expert testimony in California gang prosecutions: did Gardeley go too far?', *Hastings Constitutional Law Quarterly,* 31: 385–410.

Maira, S. (2007) 'Deporting radicals, deporting La Migra: the Hayat case in Lodi', *Cultural Dynamics,* 19 (1): 39–66.

Maley, Y. (1985) 'Judicial discourse: the case of legal judgment', in J. E. Clark (ed.) *The Cultivated Australian,* Hamburg: Buske, 159–75.

——(1987) 'The language of legislation', *Language and Society,* 16: 25–48.

——(1994) 'The language of the law', in J. Gibbons (ed.) *Language and the Law,* London: Longman, 11–50.

——(2000) 'The case of the long-nosed Potoroo: the framing and construction of witness testimony', in S. Sarangi and M. Coulthard (eds) *Discourse and Social Life,* London: Longman, 246–69.

Maley, Y. and Fahey, R. (1991) 'Presenting the evidence: constructions of reality in court', *International Journal for the Semiotics of Law,* 4(10): 3–17.

Mandler, J.M. (1984) *Stories, Scripts and Scenes: Aspects of Schema Theory,* Hillsdale, NJ: Lawrence Erlbaum.

Manzo, J. (1996) 'Taking turns and taking sides: opening scenes from two jury deliberations', *Social Psychology Quarterly,* 59: 107–25.

Manzoor, S. (2007) 'The language of loneliness', *The Guardian,* 12 September 2007.

Marchant, R. and Page, M. (1997) 'The memorandum and disabled children', in H. Westcott and J. Jones (eds) *Perspectives on the Memorandum: Policy, Practice and Research in Investigative Interviewing,* Aldershot: Arena.

Marshall, C. (2007) '24-year term for Californian in terrorism training case', *New York Times,* 11 September 2007.

Maryns, K. (2004) **'**Identifying the asylum speaker: reflections on the pitfalls of language analysis in the determination of national origin', *International Journal of Speech, Language and the Law,* 11(2): 240–60.

——(2006) *The Asylum Speaker: Language in the Belgian Asylum Procedure,* London/Manchester: St. Jerome Publishing.

Mason, I. and Stewart, M. (2001) 'Interactional pragmatics, face and the dialogue interpreter', in I. Mason (ed.) *Triadic Exchanges: Studies in Dialogue Interpreting,* Manchester: St Jerome.

Matoesian, G. (1993) *Reproducing Rape: Domination through Talk in the Courtroom,* Cambridge: Polity Press.

——(1995) 'Language, law and society: policy implications of the Kennedy Smith rape trial', *Law and Society Review,* 29: 669–701.

——(1997) '"You were interested in him as a person": Rhythms of domination in the Kennedy Smith Rape Trial', *Law & Social Inquiry,* 22(1): 55-93.

——(1999) 'The grammaticalization of participant roles in the constitution of expert identity', *Language in Society,* 28(4): 491–521.

——(2000) 'Intertextual authority in reported speech: Production media in the Kennedy Smith rape trial', *Journal of Pragmatics,* 32: 879–914.

——(2001) *Law and the Language of Identity: Discourse in the William Kennedy Smith Rape Trial,* Oxford/New York: Oxford University Press.

——(2005a) 'Nailing down an answer: participations of power in trial talk', *Discourse Studies,* 7(6): 733–59.

——(2005b) Review of J. Cotterill, "Language and power in court: a linguistic analysis of the O.J. Simpson trial"', *Journal of Sociolinguistics,* 9: 619–22.

——(2008a) 'You might win the battle but lose the war: multimodal, interactive, and extralinguistic aspects of witness resistance', *Journal of English Linguistics*, 36(3): 195–219.

——(2008b) 'Role conflict as an interactional resource in the multimodal emergence of expert identity', *Semiotica*, 171(1/4): 15–49.

Matsumoto, K. (1999) '*And*-prefaced questions in institutional discourse', *Linguistics*, 37(2): 251–74.

Mayer, J. (1993) 'Individual moral responsibility and the criminalization of youth gangs', *Wake Forest Law Review*, 28: 943–86.

Mayes, P. (1990) 'Quotation in spoken English', *Studies in Language*, 14(2): 325–63.

Maynard, D.W. (1984) *Inside Plea Bargaining: The Language of Negotiation*, New York: Plenum Press.

——(2006) 'Comment – bad news and good news: losing vs. finding the phenomenon in legal settings', *Law and Social Inquiry*, 31(2): 477–97.

Medford, S., Gudjonsson, G.H. and Pearse, J. (2003) 'The efficacy of the appropriate adult safeguard during police interviewing', *Legal and Criminological Psychology*, 8: 253–66.

Meehan, A.J. (1986) 'Record-keeping practices in the policing of juveniles', *Urban Life*, 15(1): 70–102.

——(1989) 'Assessing the "police-worthiness" of citizen's complaints to the police: accountability and the negotiation of "facts"', in D.T. Helm, W.T. Anderson, A.J. Meehan and A.W. Rawls (eds) *The Interactional Order: New Directions in the Study of Social Order*, New York: Irvington, 116–40.

Mehan, H. (1996) 'The construction of an LD student: a case study in the politics of representation', in M. Silverstein and G. Urban (eds) *Natural Histories of Discourse*, Chicago: The University of Chicago Press.

Mellinkoff, D. (1963) *The Language of the Law*, Boston, MA: Little Brown and Co.

Mencap (1999) *Bullying Wrecks Lives: The Experience of Children and Young People with a Learning Disability*. Available online at: www.mencap.org.uk/document (accessed 16 July 2009).

Mendoza-Denton, N. (2008) *Homegirls: Language and Cultural Practice among Latina Youth Gangs*, New York/Malden, MA: Blackwell Publishing.

Merriam-Webster Online Dictionary (2009) 'McJob', Merriam-Webster Online: www.merriam-webster.com/dictionary/McJob (accessed 23 March 2009).

Mertz, E. (2007) *The Language of Law School: Learning to Think Like a Lawyer*, New York: Oxford University Press.

Mesthrie, R., Swann, J., Deumert, A. and Leap, W. (2000) *Introducing Sociolinguistics*, Philadelphia, PA: John Benjamins.

Mey, J.L. (2001) *Pragmatics: An Introduction,* 2nd edn, Oxford: Blackwell.

Meyer, P.N. (1996) 'Desperate for love II: further reflections on the interpenetration of legal and popular storytelling in closing arguments to a jury in a complex criminal case'. Available online at: http://tarlton.law.utexas.edu/lpop/etext/usf/meyer30.htm.

Mildren, D. (1999) 'Redressing the imbalance: aboriginal people in the criminal justice system', *Forensic Linguistics*, 6(1): 137–60.

Miller, G.A. (1956) 'The magical number seven, plus or minus two: some limits on our capacity for processing information', *The Psychological Review*, 63: 81–97.

Miller, J.M. and Lehto, M.R. (1987) *Warnings, Vol. 2: The Annotated Bibliography with Topical Index*, Ann Arbor, MI: Fuller.

Milne, R. and Bull, R. (1999) *Investigative Interviewing: Psychology and Practice*, Chichester: Wiley.

Milne, R., Savage, S. and Williamson, T. (eds) (2006) *Investigative Interviewing*, Uffcolme, Devon: Willan Publishing.

Milton, J. and de Sena França, L.H. (2001) 'The selection and training of interpreters in the community at the Catholic University, São Paulo (PUC-SP)', paper presented at the *Critical Link 3* conference. Available online at: www.criticallink.org/files/CL3_Milton_deSenaFranca.pdf (accessed 12 July 2009).

Minnick, W. (1968) *The Art of Persuasion*, Boston, MA: Houghton Mifflin.

Mir, M. (1993) 'Direct requests can also be polite', paper presented at the *7th Annual International Pragmatics Conference*, University of Illinois.

Mnookin, J.L. (2001a) 'Fingerprint evidence in an age of DNA profiling', *Brooklyn Law Review*, 67: 13–70.

——(2001b) 'Scripting expertise: the history of handwriting identification evidence and the judicial construction of reliability', *Virginia Law Review*, 87: 1723–1845.

Moenssens, A.A. (1997) 'Handwriting identification evidence in the post-Daubert world', *UMKC Law Review*, 66: 251–343.

Moffett, D. (2003) 'Petrona's story', *Palm Beach Post*, 28 September 2003. Available online at: www. petronatomas.com/article.shtml (accessed 9 July 2009).

Moje, E. (2000) '"To be part of the story": the literacy practices of gangsta adolescents', *Teachers College Record*, 102(3): 651–90.

Mojediddi, W. (2006) 'How politics influenced the case of US v. Hamid Hayat', Chance Lecture, Boalt Law School, UC Berkeley, 5 September 2006.

Moore, A. (1989) 'Trial by schema: cognitive filters in the courtroom', *UCLA Law Review*, 37: 273–340.

Moore, C. (2006) 'The use of videlicet in Early Modern slander depositions: A case of genre-specific grammaticalization', *Journal of Historical Pragmatics*, 7(2): 245–263.

Moos, A. (2008a) 'Forensische Sprechererkennung mit der Messmethode LTF (long-term formant distribution)', unpublished MA thesis, Universität des Saarlandes, Department of Phonetics and Phonology. Available online at: www.psy.gla.ac.uk/docs/download.php?type=PUBLS&id=1286

——(2008b) 'Long-term formant distribution (LTF) based on German spontaneous and read speech', paper presented at the *17th Annual Conference of the International Association for Forensic Phonetics and Acoustics*, Lausanne.

Moosmüller, S. (1997) 'Phonological variation in speaker identification', *Forensic Linguistics*, 4: 29–47.

Moreno, J. (2004) 'What happens when Dirty Harry becomes an (expert) witness for the prosecution?', *Tulane Law Review*, 79: 1–54.

Morris, D. (1977) *Manwatching*, New York: Abrams.

Morris, R. (1999) 'The gum syndrome: predicaments in court interpreting', *Forensic Linguistics*, 6(1): 6–29.

——(2008) 'Missing stitches: An overview of judicial attitudes to interlingual interpreting in the criminal justice systems of Canada and Israel', *Interpreting*, 10: 34–64.

Morrison, G.S. (2008) 'Forensic voice comparison using likelihood ratios based on polynomial curves fitted to the formant trajectories of Australian English /ai/', *International Journal of Speech, Language and the Law*, 15: 249–66.

——(2009) 'Comments on Coulthard & Johnson's (2007) portrayal of the likelihood-ratio framework', *Australian Journal of Forensic Sciences*, in press.

Mortimer, A. (1994) 'Asking the right questions', *Policing*, 9: 111–24.

Moser-Mercer, B. (2003) 'Remote interpreting: assessment of human factors and performance parameters'. Available online at: http://aiic.net/ViewPage.cfm/article879 (accessed 23 May 2009).

Moston, S. and Stephenson, G. (1993) 'The changing face of police interrogation', *Journal of Community and Social Psychology*, 3: 101–15.

Mulholland, M., Pullan, B.S., Melikan, R.A. and Pullan, A. (2003) *The Trial in History*, Manchester: Manchester University Press.

Mullennix, J.W., Johnson, K.A., Topcu-Durgun, M. and Farnsworth, L.M. (1995) 'The perceptual representation of voice gender', *Journal of the Acoustical Society of America*, 98: 3080–95.

Müller, C. (ed.) (2007) *Speaker Classification*, Vols. 1 and 2, Berlin: Springer.

Munson, B. and Babel, M. (2007) 'Loose lips and silver tongues, or, projecting sexual orientation through speech', *Language and Linguistics Compass*, 1: 416–49.

Myers, C. (1997) 'Note: encouraging allocution at capital sentencing: a proposal for use immunity', *Columbia Law Review*, 97: 787–818.

Myers, M.L., Iscoe, C., Jennings, C., Lenox, W., Minsky, E. and Sacks, A. (1981) *Federal Trade Commission Staff Report on the Cigarette Advertising Investigation*, Washington, DC: Federal Trade Commission.

Nakane, I. (2007) 'Problems in communicating the suspect's rights in interpreted police interviews', *Applied Linguistics*, 28(1): 87–112.

National Association of Judiciary Interpreters & Translators Position Paper (February 2009) 'Telephone interpreting in legal settings'. Available online at: www.najit.org/Publications/Position Papers/Telephone Interpreting.pdf (accessed 9 July 2009).

National Crime Faculty (2000) *A Practical Guide to Investigative Interviewing*, National Crime Faculty, Bramshill: National Crime Faculty and National Police Training.

National Research Council of the National Academies (NRC) (2004) *Forensic Analysis: Weighing Bullet Lead Evidence*, Washington, DC: The National Academy Press.

——(2009) *Strengthening Forensic Science in the United States: A Path Forward*, Washington, DC: The National Academy Press.

Nelson, L.D.M. (1987) 'The drafting committee of the third United Nations conference on the law of the sea: the implications of multilingual texts', *British Yearbook of International Law*, 57: 169–99.

New Oxford American Dictionary (2001) Oxford: Oxford University Press.

New South Wales Law Reform Commission (NSWLRC) (2004) *Blind or Deaf Jurors* (Discussion paper No 46). Sydney: New South Wales Law Reform Commission.

Newbury, P. and Johnson, A. (2006) 'Suspects' resistance to constraining and coercive questioning strategies in the police interview', *International Journal of Speech, Language and the Law*, 13(2): 213–40.

Nichols, S. and Good, T. (2004) *America's Teenagers – Myths and Realities: Media Images, Schooling and the Social Costs of Careless Indifference*, Mahwah, NJ: Lawrence Erlbaum.

Nickerson, R.S. (1998) 'Confirmation bias: an ubiquitous phenomenon in many guises', *Review of General Psychology*, 2: 175–220.

Nieland, R.G. (1979) *Pattern Jury Instructions: A Critical Look at a Modern Movement to Improve the Jury System*, Chicago: American Judicature Society.

Nolan, F. (1983) *The Phonetic Bases of Speaker Recognition*, Cambridge: Cambridge University Press.

——(1997) 'Speaker recognition and forensic phonetics', in W.J. Hardcastle and J. Laver (eds) *The Handbook of Phonetic Sciences*, Oxford: Blackwell, 744–67.

——(2003) 'A recent voice parade', *International Journal of Speech, Language and the Law*, 10: 277–91.

——(2005) 'Forensic speaker identification and the phonetic description of voice quality', in W.J. Hardcastle and J. Mackenzie Beck (eds) *A Figure of Speech: A Festschrift for John Laver*, Mahwah: Lawrence Erlbaum Associates.

Nolan, F. and Grigoras, C. (2005) 'A case for formant analysis in forensic speaker identification', *International Journal of Speech, Language and the Law*, 12: 143–73.

Nord, C. (1997) *Translating as a Purposeful Activity: Functionalist Approaches Explained*, Manchester: St Jerome.

Norris, S. (2004) *Analyzing Multimodal Interaction*, New York: Routledge.

Nowak, A. (2004) *Power Speaking*, New York: Allworth Press.

Nunan, D. (1993) *Introducing Discourse Analysis*, London: Penguin.

Nunberg, G. (2001) 'That's correct', *California Lawyer*. July, Available online at: www-csli.stanford.edu/~nunberg/CLRedskins.pdf.

O'Barr, W.M. (1982) *Linguistic Evidence: Language, Power and Strategy in the Courtroom*, New York: Academic Press.

O'Barr, W.M. and Conley, J.M. (1990) 'Litigant satisfaction versus legal adequacy in small claims court narratives', in J.N. Levi and A.G. Walker (eds), *Language in the Judicial Process*, New York and London: Plenum.

Ochs, E. (1979) 'Transcription as theory', in E. Ochs and B.B. Schiefflen (eds) *Developmental Pragmatics*, New York: Academic Press, 43–72.

Ochs, E. and Capps, L. (2001) *Living Narrative: Creating Lives in Everyday Storytelling*, Cambridge, MA: Harvard University Press.

Ofshe, R. and Leo, R. (1997a) 'The decision to confess falsely', *Denver Law Review*, 74(4): 979–1122.

——(1997b) 'The social psychology of police interrogation: the theory and classification of true and false confessions', *Studies in Law, Politics and Society*, 16: 189–251.

Okawara, M. (2006) 'Linguistic analysis of some Japanese trademark cases', unpublished doctoral thesis, University of Sydney.

Oksaar, E. (1987) 'Idiolekt', in U. Ammon, N. Dittmar and K.J. Mattheier (eds) *Soziolinguistik: Ein internationales Handbuch*, Vol.1, Berlin: de Gruyter.

Old Bailey Proceedings Online (www.oldbaileyonline.org), May 1856, trial of William Palmer (t18560514–490).

Oliver, R. (1957) *The Psychology of Persuasive Speech*, New York: David McKay Company, Inc.

Olsson, J. (2003) 'Preliminary observations on author variation in mobile phone texting', unpublished ms. Available online at: http://www.thetext.co.uk (accessed 29 August 2009).

——(2008a) *Forensic Linguistics*, 2nd edn, New York: Continuum.

——(2008b) 'Statement of witness: report into allegations of intellectual property infringement with respect to the Internet domain name *www.oraclecontractors.com*', unpublished manuscript.

Oppel, R. (1999) 'No small change as pension plans are converted', *New York Times*, 24 October 1999: 3, 12.

OPSI (2008) *The Criminal Justice and Immigration Act*. Available online at: www.opsi.gov.uk/acts.htm (accessed 1 July 2009).

Ornstein-Galicia, J. (1987) 'Chicano Caló: description and review of a border variety', *Hispanic Journal of Behavioural Sciences*, 9(4): 359–73.

Ortega Herráez, J.M. and Foulquié Rubio, A.I. (2008) 'Interpreting in police settings in Spain. Service providers and interpreters perspectives', in C. Valero Garcés and A. Martin (eds) *Crossing Borders in Community Interpreting: Definitions and Dilemmas*, Amsterdam and Philadelphia, PA: John Benjamins Publishing Company.

Oxford English Dictionary Online (2009) 'McJob'. http://dictionary.oed.com/cgi/entry/00303924?query_type=wordandqueryword = McJobandfirst = 1andmax_to_show = 10andsingle = 1andsort_type = alphaandcase_id = SWfP-3czyuD-15006andp = 1andd = 1andsp = 1andqt = 1andct = 0andad = 1andprint = 1. [entry dated March 2001] (accessed 23 March 2009).

Oyandel, M. and Samaniego, J. (2004) 'Report written for the court's consideration in a likelihood-of-confusion case in 2005 involving rival trademarks *Paltomiel* and *Palto con Miel*', Tribunal de Defensa de la Libre Competencia, Sentencia N 24/2005, Republica de Chile, 4. Available online at: http://mail.fne.cl/db/tabla.nsf/f34cb3b7c2bb5deb8425733e005faa18/4a2b5134307725af0425705a0052ecfe/$FILE/Sentencia-24-2005.pdf (accessed December 2008).

Ozolins, U. and Hale, S. (2009) 'Introduction: Quality in interpreting: a shared responsibility', in S. Hale and U. Ozolins (eds) *Critical Link 5. Quality in Interpreting. A Shared Responsibility*, Amsterdam and Philadelphia, PA: John Benjamins.

Pacenti, J. (2002) 'Secret safe place for newborn: teen's statement on dead baby contradictory', *Palm Beach Post*, 4 December 2002. Available online at: www.mobile-da.org/secretsafeplacefornewborns/newslistdetail.php?storyID=258 (accessed 10 July 2009).

Pahl, K. (2002) 'Ephemera, mess and miscellaneous piles: texts and practices in families', *Journal of Early Childhood Literacy*, 2: 145–65.

Pascual, E. (2006) 'Questions in legal monologues: fictive interaction as argumentative strategy in a murder trial', *Text & Talk*, 26(3): 383–402.

Pavlenko, A. (2008) '"I'm very not about the law part": non-native speakers of English and the Miranda Warnings', *TESOL Quarterly*, 42: 1–30.

Payne, C. (2007) 'The elaboration likelihood model of persuasion: implications for trial advocacy', *International Journal of Speech, Language and the Law*, 14(2): 309–12.

Pecorari, D.E. (2002) *Original Reproductions: An Investigation of the Source Use of Postgraduate Second Language Writers*, unpublished PhD thesis, University of Birmingham.

——(2008) *Academic Writing and Plagiarism: A Linguistic Analysis*, London: Continuum.

Pennington, N. and Hastie, R. (1986) 'Evidence evaluation in complex decision making', *Journal of Personality and Social Psychology*, 51(2): 242–58.

——(1991) 'A cognitive theory of juror decision making: the story model', *Cardozo Law Review*, 13: 519–57.

——(1993) 'The story model for juror decision making', in R. Hastie (ed.) *Inside the Juror: The Psychology of Juror Decision Making*, New York: Cambridge University Press.

Pennycook, A. (1996) 'Borrowing others' words: text, ownership, memory and plagiarism', *TESOL Quarterly*, 30, 201–30.

——(2001) *Critical Applied Linguistics: A Critical Introduction*, Mahwah, NJ: Lawrence Erlbaum.

Pérez González, L. (2006) 'Interpreting strategic recontextualization cues in the courtroom: corpus-based insights into the pragmatic force of non-restrictive relative clauses', *Journal of Pragmatics*, 38: 390–417.

Petty, R. and Cacioppo, J. (1986) 'The elaboration likelihood model of persuasion', *Advances in Experimental Social Psychology*, 19: 123–205.

Petty, R. and Wegener, D. (1998) 'Attitude change: multiple roles for persuasion variables', in D. Gilbert and S. Fiske (eds), *The Handbook of Social Psychology*, New York: McGraw-Hill, 323–90.

Philips, S.U. (1986) 'Reported speech as evidence in an American trial', in D. Tannen and J. Alatis. (eds) *Language and Linguistics: The Interdependence of Theory, Data, and Application. Georgetown University Round Table on Languages and Linguistics (GURT) 1985*, Washington, DC: Georgetown University, 154–79.

——(1987) 'On the use of WH Questions in American courtroom discourse: a study of the relation between language form and language function', in L. Kedar (ed) *Power through Discourse*, Norwood: Ablex.

——(1992) 'Evidentiary standards for American trials: just the facts' in J.H. Hill and J.T. Irvine (eds) *Responsibility and Evidence in Oral Discourse*, Cambridge: Cambridge University Press, 248–59.

Phillips, S.A. (1999) *Wallbangin': Graffiti & Gangs in L.A.*, Chicago: University of Chicago Press.

Phoenix, A. (2008) 'Analysing narrative contexts', in M. Andrews, C. Squire and M. Tamboukou (eds) *Doing Narrative Research*, London: Sage Publications Ltd, 64–77.

Pinker, S. and Ullman, M.T. (2002) 'The past-tense debate: the past and future of past tense', *Trends in Cognitive Sciences*, 6: 456–63.

Plotnikoff, J. and Woolfson, R. (2004) 'In their own words; the experience of 50 young witnesses in criminal proceedings', *NSPCC Policy Practice Research Studies*, London: HMSO.

Poe-Yamagata, E. and Jones, M.A. (2000) *And Justice for Some*, Washington, DC: National Council on Crime & Delinquency.

Polack, K. and Corsellis, A. (1990a) 'Non-English speakers and the criminal justice system part 1', *New Law Journal*, 1634–36.

——(1990b) 'Non-English speakers and the criminal justice system, part 2', *New Law Journal*, 1676–77.

Pöllabauer, S. (2004) 'Interpreting in asylum hearings: issues of role, responsibility and power', *Interpreting*, 6: 143–80.

Pollner, M. (1974) 'Mundane reasoning', *Philosophy of the Social Sciences*, 4: 35–54.

Pomerantz, A.M. (1987) 'Descriptions in legal settings', in G. Button and J.R.E. Lee (eds) *Talk and Social Organization*, Clevedon: Multilingual Matters, 226–43.

Post, R. (1987) 'On the popular image of the lawyer: reflections in a dark glass', *California Law Review*, 75: 379–89.

Pound, L. (1938) 'Jottings', *American Speech*, 13: 157–58.

Preston, D.R. (1993) 'Folk dialectology', in D. Preston (ed.) *American Dialect Research*, Philadelphia: John Benjamins, 333–78.

Prince, E. (1981), 'Language and the law: a case for linguistic pragmatics', *Working papers in Sociolinguistics*, Austin: Southwest Educational Development Laboratory, 112–60.

——(1984) 'Language and the law: reference stress and context', in D. Schiffrin (ed.) *Meaning, Form and Use in Context*, Washington DC: Georgetown University, 240–52.

Pronin, E. and Kugler, M. (2007) 'Valuing thoughts, ignoring behavior: the introspection illusion as a source of the bias blind spot', *Journal of Experimental Social Psychology*, 43: 565–78.

Pronin, E., Lin, D.Y. and Ross, L. (2002) 'The bias blind spot: perception of bias in self and others', *Personality and Social Psychology Bulletin*, 28: 369–81.

Pullum, G. (2004a) 'Don't say "lexeme" or we'll break your legs', *Language Log*. Available online at: http://158.130.17.5/~myl/languagelog/archives/000618.html (accessed January 2008).

——(2004b) 'It wasn't Lexus, it was Lexis!', *Language Log*. Available online at: http://158.130.17.5/~myl/languagelog/archives/000632.html (accessed January 2008).

——(2004c) 'Database company to Toyota: rename that automobile!', *Language Log*. Available online at: http://itre.cis.upenn.edu/~myl/languagelog/archives/000728.html (accessed January 2008).

Radelet, M., Bedau, H.A. and Putnam, C.E. (1992) *In Spite of Innocence*, Boston: Northeastern Press.

Rampton, B. (1995) *Crossing: Language and Ethnicity among Adolescents*, London: Longman.

Raymond, G. (2003) 'Grammar and social organization: Yes/No interrogatives and the structure of responding', *American Sociological Review*, 68: 939–67.

——(2004) 'Prompting action: the stand-alone "so" in ordinary conversation', *Research on Language and Social Interaction*, 37(2): 185–218.

Read, D.S. (2007) *Winning at Trial*, Louisville, CO: National Institute for Trial Advocacy.

Reali, F. and Christiansen, M. (2006) 'Processing of relative clauses is made easier by frequency of occurrence', *Journal of Memory and Language*, 57(1): 1–23.

Redlich, A.D and Goodman, G.S. (2003) 'Taking responsibility for an act not committed: the influence of age and suggestibility', *Law and Human Behavior*, 27: 141–56.

Redlich, A.D., Silverman, M., Chen, J. and Steiner, H. (2004) 'The police interrogation of children and adolescents', in Lassiter, G.D. (ed.) *Interrogations, Confessions and Entrapment*, New York: Kluwer/ Plenum, 107–25.

Redmayne, M. (2001) *Expert Evidence and Criminal Justice*, Oxford: OUP.

Reetz, H. and Jongman, A. (2009) *Phonetics: Transcription, Production, Acoustics, and Perception*, Chichester: Wiley-Blackwell.

Reid, J. and Associates (online) www.reid.com for a frequently updated compendium of trial and appeal court decisions regarding Miranda, police interrogation and confession evidence.

Rendall, D., Kollias, S. and Ney, C. (2005) 'Pitch (F0) and formant profiles of human vowels and vowel-like baboon grunts: the role of vocalizer body size and voice-acoustic allometry', *Journal of the Acoustical Society of America*, 117: 944–55.

Rendle-Short, J. (2007) '"Catherine, you're wasting your time": address terms within the Australian political interview', *Journal of Pragmatics*, 35: 1503–25.

Renoe, C. (1996) 'Seeing is believing? Expert testimony and the construction of interpretive authority in an American trial', *International Journal for the Semiotics of Law*, IX(26): 115–37.

Renton, D. (1975) *The Preparation of Legislation*, London: HMSO.

Revell, D.L. (2004) 'Authoring bilingual laws: the importance of process', *Brooklyn Journal of International Law*, 29(3): 1085–1105.

Reyes, A. (2005) 'Appropriation of African American slang by Asian American youth', *Journal of Sociolinguistics*, 9(4): 509–32.

Richardson, M. (2004) 'Trade marks and language', *Sydney Law Review*, 9: 193. Available online at: www.austlii.edu.au/cgi-bin/sinodisp/au/journals/SydLRev/2004/9.html?query=%22Trade%20Mark %22%20AND%20linguist (accessed December 2008).

Richardson, P.J. (ed.) (2006) *Archbold 2006: Criminal Pleading, Evidence and Practice*, London: Sweet & Maxwell.

Riding, A. (1999) 'The crown court witness service: little help in the witness box', *The Howard Journal*, 38(4): 411–20.

Rigney, A. (1999) 'Questioning in interpreted testimony', *Forensic Linguistics*, 6(1): 83–108.

Risinger, D.M. (2000) 'Navigating expert reliability: are criminal standards of certainty being left on the dock?', *Albany Law Review*, 64: 99–152.

Risinger, D.M. and Saks, M.J. (1996) 'Science and nonscience in the courts: Daubert meets handwriting identification expertise', *Iowa Law Review*, 82: 21–74.

Risinger, D.M., Saks, M.J., Thompson, W.C. and Rosenthal, R. (2002) 'The Daubert/Kumho implications of observer effects in forensic science: hidden problems of expectation and suggestion', *California Law Review*, 90: 1–56.

Roach, K. and Trotter, G. (2005) 'Miscarriages of justice in the war against terrorism', *Pennsylvania State Law Review*, 109: 4. 967–1041. Available online at: http://ssrn.com/abstract=742628.

Robertshaw, P. (1998) *Summary Justice*, London: Cassell.

Roberts-Smith, L. (2009) 'Forensic interpreting – trial and error', in S. Hale and U. Ozolins (eds) *Critical Link 5. Quality in Interpreting: A Shared Responsibility*, Amsterdam and Philadelphia: John Benjamins Publishing Company, 13–36.

Robinson, W. (2005) 'How the European commission drafts legislation in 20 languages', *Clarity*, 53: 4–10.

Rock, F. (2001) 'The genesis of a witness statement', *Forensic Linguistics*, 8(2): 44–72.

——(2006) 'Looking the other way: linguistic ethnography and forensic linguistics', *UK Linguistic Ethnography Forum Papers*. Available online at: www.ling-ethnog.org.uk/documents/papers/rock2006. pdf (accessed 12 July 2009).

——(2007) *Communicating Rights: The Language of Arrest and Detention*, Basingstoke, London: Palgrave Macmillan.

Rogers, R., Harrison, K.S., Shuman, D.W., Sewell, K.W. and Hazelwood, L.L. (2007) 'An analysis of *Miranda* warnings and waivers: comprehension and coverage', *Law and Human Behavior*, 31: 177–92.

Romero, B.G. (2008) 'Here are your right hands: exploring interpreter qualifications', *University of Dayton Law Review*, 34(1): 15–33.

Rose, P. (2002) *Forensic Speaker Identification*, London: Taylor and Francis.

——(2006) 'Technical forensic speaker recognition: evaluation, types and testing of evidence', *Computer Speech and Language*, 20: 159–91.

Rose, P. and Morrison, G.S. (2009) 'A response to the UK position statement on forensic speaker comparison' *International Journal of Speech, Language and the Law*, 16(1): 139–63.

Rosen, L. (2006) *Law as Culture: An Invitation*, Princeton, NJ: Princeton University Press.

Rosenne, S. (1983) 'The meaning of "authentic text" in modern treaty law', in R. Bernhardt, W.K. Geck, G. Jaenicke and H. Steinberger (eds), *Festschrift für Hermann Mosler*, Berlin and New York: Springer, 759–84.

Ross, S. (1998) 'Self-assessment in second language testing: a meta-analysis and analysis of experiential factors', *Language Testing*, 15: 1–20.

Rosulek, L.F. (2008) 'Legitimation and the heteroglossic nature of closing argument in criminal trials', paper presented at Georgetown University Roundtable 2008, Georgetown University, Washington, DC.

RRT (Refugee Review Tribunal, Australia). (28 August 2000). N00/34478. Decision and reasons for decision. Available online at: www.austlii.edu.au/au/cases/cth/rrt/2000/835.html (accessed 19 March 2008).

RSAA (Refugee Status Appeals Authority, New Zealand) (2002) Refugee Appeal No. 73545/02. Aviailable online at: www.refugee.org.nz/Fulltext/73545–02.htm (accessed 29 October 2004).

Rumelhart, D.E. and McClelland, J. (1986) 'On learning the past tenses of English verbs', in D.E. Rumelhart and J. McClelland (eds) *Parallel Distributed Processing*, Boston, MA: MIT Press, 216–71.

Russell, S. (2000) '"Let me put it simply … ": the case for a standard translation of the police caution and its explanation', *Forensic Linguistics*, 7(1): 26–48.

Saarni, C. and Harris, P.L. (eds) (1989) *Children's Understanding of Emotion*, Cambridge: Cambridge University Press.

Sabat, S. and Harré, R. (1992) 'The construction and deconstruction of self in Alzheimer's disease', *Ageing and Society*, 12: 443–61.

Sacks, H. (1972) 'Notes on police assessment of moral character', in D. Sudnow (ed.) *Studies in Social Interaction*, Glencoe, IL: Free Press, 280–93.

——(1984) 'Notes on methodology' (edited by Gail Jefferson). in J.M. Atkinson and J. Heritage (eds), *Structures of Social Action: Studies in Conversation Analysis*, Cambridge: Cambridge University Press, 21–27.

——(1992) *Lectures on Conversation*, vols. I and II, (edited by G. Jefferson), Oxford: Blackwell.

Sacks, H. and Schegloff, E. (2002) 'Home position', *Gesture*, 2: 133–46.

Sacks, H., Schegloff, E. and Jefferson, G. (1974) 'A simplest systematics for the organization of turn-taking for conversation', *Language*, 50(4): 696–735.

Salfati, C.G. and Bateman, A.L. (2005) 'Serial homicide: an investigation of behavioural consistency', *Journal of Investigative Psychology and Offender Profiling*, 2: 121–44.

Sanchez, R. (1983) *Chicano Discourse: Sociohistoric Perspectives*, Rowley, MA: Newbury House.

Sanday, P.R. (1996) *A Woman Scorned: Acquaintance Rape on Trial*, New York: Doubleday.

Sanders, A., Creaton, J., Bird, S. and Weber, L. (1997) *Victims with Learning Disabilities: Negotiating the Criminal Justice System*, Oxford: University of Oxford Occasional Papers.

Sanders, J. (2001) 'Complex litigation at the millenium: Kumho and how we know', *Law and Contemporary Problems*, 64: 373–415.

——(2007) 'Expert witness ethics', *Fordham Law Review*, 76: 1539–84.

Sanderson, P. (2007) 'Linguistic analysis of competing trademarks', *Language Matters*, 38: 132–49.

Santtila, P., Fritzon, K. and Tamelander, A.L. (2005a) 'Linking arson incidents on the basis of crime scene behaviour', *Journal of Police and Criminal Psychology*, 19: 1–16.

Santtila, P., Junkkila, J. and Sandnabba, N.K. (2005b) 'Behavioural linking of stranger rapes', *Journal of Investigative Psychology and Offender Profiling*, 2: 87–103.

Sarcevic, S. (1997) *New Approach to Legal Translation*, The Hague: Kluwer Law International.

Savage, C. (14 May 2009) 'A judge's view of judging is on the record', *The New York Times*. Available online at: www.nytimes.com/2009/05/15/us/15judge.html (accessed 31 August 2009).

Saxton, B. (1998) 'How well do jurors understand jury instructions? A field test using real juries and real trials in Wyoming', *Land and Water Literary Review*, 33: 59.

Saywitz, K. (1995) 'Improving children's testimony: the question, the answer and the environment', in M.S. Zaragoza, J. Graham, G.C.N. Hall, R. Hirschman, and S. Yossef (eds) *Memory and Testimony in the Child Witness*, London: Sage, Vol 1: 109–40.

Scelfo, J. (2001) 'When law goes pop', An Interview with Richard Sherwin, *Stayfree Magazine*, Issue 18. Available online at: www.stayfreemagazine.org/archives/18/sherwin.html.

Schachter, D. (2001) *The Seven Sins of Memory: How the Mind Forgets and Remembers*, Boston, MA and New York: Houghton Mifflin Company.

Schane, S. (2006) *Language and the Law*, London: Continuum.

Schank, R.C. and Abelson, R.P. (1977) *Scripts, Plans, Goals and Understanding: An Inquiry into Human Knowledge Structures*, Hillsdale, NJ: Erlbaum.

Scheck, B., Neufeld, P. and Dwyer, J. (2000) *Actual Innocence*, New York: Doubleday.

Schegloff, E.A. (1987) 'Some sources of misunderstanding in talk-in-interaction', *Linguistics*, 25: 201–18.

——(1988) 'Presequences and indirection: applying speech act theory to ordinary conversation', *Journal of Pragmatics*, 12: 55–62.

——(2007) *Sequence Organization: A Primer in Conversation Analysis*, Vol. 1, Cambridge: Cambridge University Press.

Schiffrin, D. (1981) 'Tense variation in narrative', *Language*, 57(1): 45–62.

——(1994) *Approaches to Discourse*, Oxford: Blackwell.

——(1996) 'Narrative as self-portrait: sociolinguistic constructions of identity', *Language in Society*, 25: 167–203.

Schötz, S. (2006) 'Perception, analysis and synthesis of speaker age', unpublished PhD. dissertation, Lund University, Sweden. Available online at: http://person2.sol.lu.se/SusanneSchotz/downloads/Thesis_S_Schoetz_2006.pdf

——(2007) 'Acoustic analysis of adult speaker age', in C. Müller (ed.) *Speaker Classification I: Fundamentals, Features, and Methods*, Berlin: Springer.

Schriver, K. (1997) *Dynamics in Document Design*, New York: Wiley.

Schulhofer, S. (1996) '*Miranda*'s practical effects: substantial benefits and vanishingly small social costs', *Northwestern Law Review*, 90: 500–563.

——(1998) *Unwanted Sex: The Culture of Intimidation and the Failure of Law*, Cambridge, MA: Harvard University Press.

Schwarzer, W.W. (1981) 'Communicating with juries: problems and remedies', *California Law Review*, 69: 731.

Schweda Nicholson, N. (22 November 2008) Unpublished interview with Rabbi Fred Neulander', New Jersey State Prison, Trenton.

Scollon, R. (1998) *Mediated Discourse as Social Interaction: A Study of News Discourse*, London: Longman.

Scollon, R. and Scollon, S. W. (2003) *Discourses in Place: Language in the Material World,* London: Routledge.

Searle, J. (1969) *Speech Acts: An Essay in the Philosophy of Language*, London: Cambridge University Press.

——(1975) 'Indirect speech acts', in J. Cole and J. Morgan (eds) *Syntax and Semantics Vol. 3, Speech Acts*, New York: Academic Press: 59–82.

Seebohm, T. (2004) *Hermeneutics: Method and Methodology*, London: Kluwer Academic Publishers.

Seidman, A.W., Seidman, R.B. and Abeyesekere, N. (2001) *Legislative Drafting for Democratic Social Change: A Manual for Drafters*, London: Kluwer Law International.

Sharrock, W.W. and Watson, D.R. (1989) 'Talk and police work: notes on the traffic in information', in H. Coleman (ed.) *Working with Language*, New York: Norton, 431–49.

Shaw, S and Weir, C.J. (2007) *Examining Writing in a Second Language, Studies in Language Testing 26*, Cambridge: Cambridge University Press and Cambridge ESOL.

Shepherd, E. (1991) 'Ethical interviewing', *Policing*, 7: 42–60.

Shepherd, E. and Milne, R. (2006) '"Have you told management about this?" Bringing witness interviewing into the 21st century', in A. Heaton-Armstrong, E. Shepherd, G. Gudjonsson and D. Wolchover (eds) *Witness Testimony: Psychological, Investigative and Evidential Perspectives*, Oxford: Oxford University Press, 131–52.

Sherwin, R.K. (2002) *When Law Goes Pop*, Chicago: University of Chicago Press.

Shipman interviews audio files. Available online at : http://news.bbc.co.uk/1/hi/in_depth/uk/2000/the_shipman_murders/the_shipman_files/613627.stm (accessed 31 March 2009).

Shipman trial transcript. Available online at: www.the-shipman-inquiry.org.uk/trialtrans.asp (accessed 12 August 2009).

Shoop, J. (1994) 'Image of fear: minority teens allege bias in gang profiling', *Trial*, 30(3): 12–16.

Shuy, R.W. (1982) 'Topic as the unit of analysis in a criminal law case', in D. Tannen (ed.) *Analyzing Discourse: Text and Talk*, Washington, DC: Georgetown University Press, 113–26.

——(1990a) 'The analysis of tape recorded conversations', in P.P. Andrews and M.B. Peterson (eds) *Criminal Intelligence Analysis*, Loomis, CA: Palmer Press, 117–48.

——(1990b) 'Warning labels: language, law, and comprehensibility', *American Speech*, 65(4): 291–303.

——(1993a) *Language Crimes: The Use and Abuse of Language Evidence in the Courtroom*, Malden, MA and Oxford: Blackwell.

——(1993b) 'Using language evidence in money laundering trials', *American Speech*, 68(1):3–19.

——(1997) 'Ten unanswered language questions about Miranda', *Forensic Linguistics*, 4(2): 175–95.

——(1998a) *Bureaucratic Language in Government and Business*, Washington, DC: Georgetown University Press.

——(1998b) *The Language of Confession, Interrogation, and Deception*, Thousand Oaks, CA and London: Sage Publishing.

——(2001) 'Discourse analysis in the legal context', in D. Schiffrin, D. Tannen and H. Hamilton (eds) *The Handbook of Discourse Analysis*, Oxford: Blackwell, 437–52.

——(2002) *Linguistic Battles in Trademark Disputes*, Basingstoke/New York: Palgrave Macmillan.

——(2005) *Creating Language Crimes*, New York: Oxford University Press.

——(2006) *Linguistics in the Courtroom: A Practical Guide*, Oxford: Oxford University Press.

——(2008) *Fighting over Words: Language and Civil Law Cases*, Oxford: Oxford University Press.

Shuy, R.W. and Staton, J.J. (2000) 'Review of Grisso, Thomas "Instruments for assessing understanding and appreciation of Miranda Rights"', *Forensic Linguistics*, 7(1): 131–36.

Sieberg, D. (20 January 2004) 'Microsoft takes on teen's site MikeRoweSoft.com.' *CNN News*. Available online at: http://edition.cnn.com/2004/TECH/internet/01/20/rowe.fight/index.html (accessed 25 August 2009).

Silverstein, M. (1998) 'The improvisational performance of culture in realtime discursive practice', in R. K. Sawyer (ed.), *Creativity in Performance*, London: Ablex, 266–312.

Silverstein, M. and Urban, G. (1996) 'The natural history of discourse', in M. Silverstein and G. Urban (eds), *Natural Histories of Discourse*, Chicago: The University of Chicago Press, 1–17.

Simo Bobda, A.S., Wolf, H.G. and Lothar, P. (1999) 'Identifying regional and national origin of English-speaking Africans seeking asylum in Germany', *Forensic Linguistics*, 6(2): 300–319.

Simon, D. (2004) 'A third view of the black box: cognitive coherence in legal decision making', *University of Chicago Law Review*, 71: 511–84.

Simons, H. (2001) *Persuasion in Society*, Thousand Oaks, CA: Sage Publications.

Simpson, A.P. (2001) 'Dynamic consequences of differences in male and female vocal tract dimensions', *Journal of the Acoustical Society of America*, 109: 2153–64.

Simpson, A.P. and Ericsdotter, C. (2007) 'Sex-specific differences in f0 and vowel space', *Proceedings of the 16th International Congress of Phonetic Sciences*, Saarbrücken, Germany, 933–36. Available online at: www.icphs2007.de/conference/Papers/1333/1333.pdf.

Simpson, A.W. (ed.) (1984) *Biographical Dictionary of the Common Law*, London: Butterworths.

Sinclair, J.M. and Coulthard, M. (1992) 'Towards an analysis of discourse', in M. Coulthard (ed.), *Advances in Spoken Discourse Analysis*, London and New York: Routledge, 1–34.

Sinclair, J.M. and Renouf, A. (1988) 'A lexical syllabus for language learning', in R. Carter and M. McCarthy (eds) *Vocabulary and Language Teaching*, Harlow: Longman, 140–58.

Singler, J. (2004) 'The "linguistic" asylum interview and the linguist's evaluation of it, with special reference to applicants for Liberian political asylum in Switzerland', *International Journal of Speech, Language and the Law*, 11(2): 222–39.

Skehan, P. (1998) *A Cognitive Approach to Learning Language*, Oxford: Oxford University Press.

Slater, S. and Valente, C. (2009) 'Barclays to end final salary pensions'. Available online at: http://uk.reuters.com/article/idUKTRE5522Y620090603 (accessed 3 June 2009).

Slembrouck, S. (1992) 'The parliamentary Hansard "Verbatim" Report: the written construction of spoken discourse', *Language and Literature*, 1(2): 101–19.

Slobin, D.I. (1966) 'Grammatical transformations and sentence comprehension in childhood and adulthood', *Journal of Verbal Learning and Verbal Behavior*, 5(3): 219–27.

——(1996) 'Two ways to travel: verbs of motion in English and Spanish', in M. Shibatani and A. Thompson (eds), *Grammatical Constructions. Their Form and Meaning*, Oxford: Clarendon Press.

——(2001) 'Discourse analysis in the legal context', in D. Schiffrin, D. Tannen and H. Hamilton (eds) *The Handbook of Discourse Analysis*, Oxford: Blackwell, 437–52.

Sloboda, J. (1986) 'Reading a case study of cognitive skills', in A. Gellatly (ed.) *The Skillful Mind*, Oxford: Oxford University Press.

Slobogin, C. (2003) 'Toward taping', *Ohio State Journal of Criminal Law*, 1: 309–22.

Smart, C. (1986) 'Feminism and the law: some problems of analysis and strategy', *International Journal of the Sociology of Law*, 14: 109–23.

——(1989) *Feminism and the Power of Law*, London: Routledge.

Smith, B.H. (1980) 'Narrative versions, narrative theories', *Critical Inquiry*, 7: 209–18.

Smith, V.L. (1991) 'Prototypes in the courtroom: lay representations of legal concepts', *Journal of Personality and Social Psychology*, 61: 857–72.

——(1993) 'When prior knowledge and law collide: helping jurors use the law', *Law and Human Behavior*, 17(5): 507–36.

Snedaker, K. (1991) 'Storytelling in opening statements: framing the argumentation of the trial', in D. Papke (ed.) *Narrative and the Legal Discourse: A Reader in Storytelling and the Law*, Liverpool: Deborah Charles Publications, 132–57.

Solan, L. (1993) *The Language of Judges*, Chicago: The University of Chicago Press.

——(1998) 'Linguistic experts as semantic tour guides', *Forensic Linguistics*, 5 (ii): 87–106.

——(1999) 'Can the legal system use experts on meaning?', *Tennessee Law Review*, 66: 1167–99.

——(2008) 'Talking like a person, thinking like a lawyer (and vice versa)', in M. Solly, M. Conoscenti and S. Campagna (eds) *Verbal/Visual Narrative Texts in Higher Education*, Bern: Peter Lang.

Solan, L.P. and Tiersma, P. (2004) 'Author identification in American courts', *Applied Linguistics*, 25(4): 448–65.

——(2005) *Speaking of Crime: The Language of Criminal Justice*, Chicago: University of Chicago Press.

Solomon, N. (1996) 'Plain English: From a perspective of language in society', in R. Hasan and G. Williams (eds) *Literacy in Society*, London: Longman, 279–307.

Spassova, M.S. and Grant, T. (2008) 'Categorizing Spanish written texts by author gender and origin by means of morpho-syntactic trigrams', paper presented at the Conference, *Curriculum, Language and the Law*, Dubrovnik, 18–21 September.

Spence, G. (1995) *How to Argue and Win Every Time*, New York: St. Martin's Griffin.

Spence, L. (1997) *Legacy*, Athens, OH: Swallow Press/Ohio University Press.

Spencer-Wendel, S. (10 July 2004) 'Teen suspect gets probation in baby's death', *Palm Beach Post*. Available online at: www.palmbeachpost.com/news/content/auto/epaper/editions/saturday/news_0 4fe26f6f445312f003f.html (accessed 9 July 2009).

Spiecker, S. and Worthington, D. (2003) 'The influence of opening statement/closing argument organizational strategy on juror verdict and damage awards', *Law and Human Behavior*, 27(4): 437–56.

Springer, J. (16 April 2008) Unpublished interview, Port Jefferson, NY.

Stamatatos, E. (2006) 'Authorship attribution based on feature set subspacing ensembles', *International Journal of Artificial Intelligence Tools*, 20: 1–16.

Stanisławski, J., Billip, K. and Chociłowska, Z. (1986) *Podręczny słownik angielsko-polski* [A Practical English–Polish dictionary], 7th edn, Warsaw: Wiedza Powszechna.

Stayfree Magazine, Issue 18. Available online at: www.stayfreemagazine.org/archives/18/sherwin.html.

Stephen, F. ([1863] 1890) *A General View of the Criminal Law*, 2nd edn, London: Macmillan.

Stephen, L. (1991) *Hours in a Library*, London: The Folio Society.

Stokoe, E. (2009) '"For the benefit of the tape": formulating embodied conduct in designedly uni-modal recorded police-suspect interrogations', *Journal of Pragmatics*, 41 (10): 1887–1904.

Stokoe, E. and Edwards, D. (2007) '"Black this, black that": racial insults and reported speech in neighbour complaints and police interrogations', *Discourse & Society*, 18(3): 355–90.

——(2008) '"Did you have permission to smash your neighbour's door?" Silly questions and their answers in police-suspect interrogations', *Discourse Studies*, 10(1): 89–111.

Stone, M. (1995) *Cross-examination in Criminal Trials*, 2nd edn, London: Butterworths.

Storey, R. (1997) *The Art of Persuasive Communication*, Farnham: Gower Publishing Limited.

Stratman, J.F. and Dahl, P. (1996) 'Readers' comprehension of temporary restraining orders in domestic violence cases: a missing link in abuse prevention?' *Forensic Linguistics*, 3 (ii): 211–31.

Streeck, J. (2008) 'Gesture in political communication: a case study of the democratic presidential candidates during the 2004 primary campaign', *Research in Language and Social Interaction*, 41(2): 154–86.

Street, B. (1984) *Literacy in Theory and Practice*, Cambridge: Cambridge University Press.

Stubbs, M. (1996) *Text and Corpus Analysis: Computer-assisted Studies of Language and Culture*, Oxford: Blackwell.

Stuntz, W.J. (2001) '*Miranda*'s mistake', *Michigan Law Review*, 99: 975–99.

Stygall, G. (1991) 'Texts in oral contexts: the "transmission" of jury instructions in an Indiana trial', in C. Bazerman and J. Paradis (eds) *Textual Dynamics of the Professions*, Madison, WI: University of Wisconsin Press.

——(1994) *Trial Language: Differential Discourse Processing and Discursive Formation*, Amsterdam and Philadelphia, PA: John Benjamins.

——(2002) 'Textual barriers to United States immigration', in J. Cotterill (ed.) *Language in the Legal Process*, Houndmills: Palgrave.

Stylianou, Y. (2008) 'Voice transformation', in J. Benesty, M.M. Sondhi and Y. Huang (eds) *Springer Handbook of Speech Processing*, Berlin: Springer-Verlag.

Sudnow, D. (1965) 'Normal crimes: sociological features of a penal code in a public defender's office', *Social Problems*, 12: 255–76.

Sullivan, M. (2005) 'Maybe we shouldn't study "gangs": does reification obscure youth violence?', *Journal of Contemporary Criminal Justice*, 21: 170–90.

Sullivan, R. (2002) *Sullivan and Driedger on the Construction of Statutes*, 4th edn, Toronto: Butterworths.

Summerfield, T. and McHoul, A. (2005) 'Family as a commonsensical device and its place in law', *International Journal for the Semiotics of Law*, 18(3): 242–61.

Svartvik, J. (1968) *The Evans Statements: A Case for Forensic Linguistics*, Göteborg: University of Gothenburg Press.

Swales, J.M. and Bhatia, V.K. (1983) 'An approach to the linguistic study of legal documents', *Fachsprache,* 5(3): 98–108.

Swann, J., Deumert, A., Lillis, T. and Mesthrie, R. (2004) *A Dictionary of Sociolinguistics*, Edinburgh: Edinburgh University Press.

Szymczak, M. (ed.) (1978) *Słownik języka polskiego* [Dictionary of the Polish Language], Warsaw: PWN.

Tabory, M. (1980) *Multilingualism in International Law and Institutions*, New York: Sijthoff & Noordhoff.

Tagg, C. (2009) *A Corpus Linguistics Study of SMS Text Messaging*, unpublished PhD thesis, University of Birmingham.

Tamony, P. (1986) 'Coca-Cola: the most-lawed name', in K. Harder (ed.) *Names and Their Varieties: A Collection of Essays on Onamastics*, Lanham, MD: American Name Society/University Press of America, 197–202.

Tannen, D. (1986) 'Introducing constructed dialogue in Greek and American conversational and literary narrative', in F. Coulmas (ed.) *Direct and Indirect Speech*, Berlin: Mouton de Gruyter, 311–32.

——(1989) *Talking Voices*, New York: Cambridge University Press.

——(1993) *Framing in Discourse*, New York/Oxford: Oxford University Press.

——(2004) *Conversational Style*, New York: Oxford University Press.

——(2007) *Talking Voices: Repetition, Dialogue and Imagery in Conversational Discourse*, 2nd edn, Cambridge: Cambridge University Press.

Taylor, N. and Joudo, J. (2005) *The Impact of Pre-Recorded Video and Closed Circuit Television Testimony by Adult Sexual Assault Complainants on Jury Decision Making: An Experimental Study*, Canberra: Australian Institute of Criminology. Available online at: www.aic.gov.au/publications/rpp/68/index.html (accessed 16 June 2009).

Tennessee Pattern Jury Instructions – Criminal, 4th edn (1995) New York: West.

Thomas, G.C. (1996) 'Plain talk about the *Miranda* empirical debate: a "steady-state" theory of confessions', *UCLA Law Review*, 43: 933–59.

——(2004) 'History's lesson for the right to counsel', *University of Illinois Law Review*, 545–97.

Thornborrow, J. (2002) *Power Talk: Language and Interaction in Institutional Discourse*, London: Longman.

Thornton, G.C. (1996) *Legislative Drafting*, London: Butterworth.

Tiersma, P. (1993) 'Reforming the language of jury instructions', *Hofstra Law Review*, 22: 37.

——(1995) 'Dictionaries and death: do jurors understand mitigation?', *Utah Law Review*, 1.

——(1999) *Legal Language* (hbk), Chicago: University of Chicago Press.

——(2000) *Legal Language* (pbk), Chicago: University of Chicago Press.

——(2002) 'The language and law of product warnings', in J. Cotterill (ed.) *Language in the Legal Process*, Basingstoke, Hampshire and New York: Palgrave Macmillan, 54–71.

——(2005) 'The new Black's', *Journal of Legal Education*, 55: 386.

——(2007) 'The language of consent in rape law', in J. Cotterill (ed.) *The Language of Sexual Crime*, Basingstoke, UK: Palgrave Macmillan, 83–103.

Tiersma, P. and Solan, L. (2002) 'The linguist on the witness stand: forensic linguistics in American courts', *Language*, 78: 221–39.

Titze, I. (1994) *Principles of Voice Production*, Englewood Cliffs, NJ: Prentice Hall.

Todd, R. (2008) 'Court interpreters inadequate?', *Law Times*, 21 April.

Tonkin, M., Grant, T. and Bond, J.W. (2008) 'To link or not to link: a test of the case linkage principles using serial car theft data', *Journal of Investigative Psychology and Offender Profiling*, 5: 58–77.

Toolan, M. (2001) *Narrative: A Critical Linguistic Introduction*, 2nd edn, London: Routledge.

Towner, B. (2008) 'What are they talking about? 50 words that kids think you don't know', *AARP Bulletin*, 39.

Tracy, K. (1997) 'Interactional trouble in emergency service requests: a problem of frame', *Research on Language and Social Interaction*, 30: 315–43.

——(2009) 'How questioning constructs judge identities: oral argument about same-sex marriage', *Discourse Studies*, 11(2):199–221.

Tracy, K. and Craig, R.T. (2009) 'Membership category terms in court discourse about same-sex marriage', paper presented at *9th Biennial Conference on Forensic Linguistics/Language and Law*, Amsterdam.

Travers, M. (1997) *The Reality of Law: Work and Talk in a Firm of Criminal Lawyers*, Aldershot: Ashgate.

——(2006) 'Understanding talk in legal settings: what law and society studies can learn from a conversation analyst', *Law and Social Inquiry*, 31(2): 447–65.

Trenholm, S. (1989) *Persuasion and Social Influence*, Englewood Cliffs, NJ: Prentice-Hall.

Trinch, S. (2005a) 'Acquiring authority through the acquisition of genre: latinas, intertextuality and violence', *Speech, Language, and the Law*, 12(1): 19–47.

——(2005b) 'Disappearing discourse: performative texts and identity in legal contexts', paper presented at the International Linguistic Association, *50th Anniversary Conference on Language and Law*, New York City, April 2005.

——(forthcoming) 'Disappearing discourse: performative texts and identity in legal contexts', *Critical Inquiry in Language Studies*, 7(1–2).

655

Trinch, S. and Berk-Seligson, S. (2002) 'Narrating in protective order interviews: a source of interactional trouble', *Language in Society*, 31: 383–418.

Trosborg, A. (1995) 'Statutes and contracts: an analysis of legal speech acts in the English language of the law', *Journal of Pragmatics*, 23: 31–53.

——(1997) *Rhetorical Structures in Legal Language: Discourse Analysis of Statutes and Contracts*, Tübingen: Gunter Narr Verlag.

Trudgill, P. (1988) 'Norwich revisited: recent linguistic changes in an English urban dialect', *English World-Wide*, 9: 33–49.

Tschäpe, N., Trouvain, J., Bauer, D. and Jessen, M. (2005) 'Idiosyncratic patterns of filled pauses', paper presented at the *14th Annual Conference of the International Association for Forensic Phonetics and Acoustics*, Marrakesh.

Tuebner, G. (1993) *Law as an Autopoietic System*, Oxford: Blackwell.

Tully, B. and Cahill, D. (1984) *Police interviewing of the mentally handicapped: an experimental study*, The Police Foundation, UK.

Turell, T. (2004) 'Textual kidnapping revisited: the case of plagiarism in literary translation', in *Speech, Language and the Law*, 11(i): 1–26.

UNHCR (United Nations High Commissioner for Refugees) (2007) *The 1951 Refugee Convention: Questions and Answers*, Geneva: United Nations High Commissioner for Refugees.

——(2008) *2007 Global Trends: Refugees, Asylum-seekers, Returnees, Internally Displaced and Stateless Persons*, Geneva: United Nations High Commissioner for Refugees.

Uviller, R.H. (1988) *Tempered Zeal*, Chicago: Contemporary Books.

——(1996) *Virtual Justice: The Flawed Prosecution of Crime in America*, New Haven CT: Yale University Press.

Valentine, B. (1995) *The Gang Intelligence Manual*, Boulder, CO: Paladin Press.

Vanderveken, D. (1990) *Meaning and Speech Acts, Volume I: Principles of Language Use*, Cambridge: Cambridge University Press.

Vernon, M. and Coley, J. (1978) 'Violation of constitutional rights: the language impaired person and the Miranda Warnings', *Journal of Rehabilitation of the Deaf*, 11(4): 1–8.

Vihman, M. (1996) *Phonological Development: The Origins of Language in the Child*, Oxford: Blackwell Publishers.

Vinkhuyzen, E. and Szymanski, M.H. (2005) 'Would you like to do it yourself? Service requests and their non-granting responses', in K. Richards and P. Seedhouse (eds) *Applying Conversation Analysis*, New York: Palgrave Macmillan, 91–106.

de Vries, L. (2002) 'Guilt by association: proposition 21's gang conspiracy law will increase youth violence in California', *University of San Francisco Law Review*, 37: 191–225.

Wachal, R.S. (1966) 'Linguistic evidence, statistical inference and disputed authorship', unpublished PhD dissertation, University of Wisconsin.

Wadensjö, C. (1998) *Interpreting as Interaction*, London and New York: Longman.

Wagenaar, W.A., van Koppen, P.J. and Crombag, H.F.M. (1993) *Anchored Narratives: The Psychology of Criminal Evidence*, Hemel Hempstead: Harvester Wheatsheaf.

Wagner, A. (2002) 'The legal discourse of the Common Law: a game of chess', *International Journal for the Semiotics of Law*, 15: 345–60.

Waldman, A. (2006) 'Prophetic justice', *The Atlantic*, October issue.

Walker, A.G. (1986a) 'Context, transcripts, and appellate readers', *Justice Quarterly*, 3(4): 409–27.

——(1986b) 'The Verbatim Record: the myth and the reality', in S. Fisher and A.D. Todd (eds), *Discourse and Institutional Authority*, Norwood, NJ: Erlbaum, 205–22.

——(1987) 'Linguistic manipulation, power and the legal setting', in L. Kedar (ed.), *Power through Discourse*, Norwood, NJ: Ablex, 57–80.

——(1990) 'Language at work in the law: the customs, conventions, and appellate consequences of court reporting', in J.N. Levi and A.G. Walker (eds), *Language in the Judicial Process*, New York: Plenum Press, 203–44.

——(1999) *Handbook on Questioning Children: A Linguistic Perspective*, 2nd edn, Washington, DC: ABA Center on Children and the Law.

Walker, A.G. and Warren, A. (1995) 'The language of the child abuse interview: Asking the questions, understanding the answers', in T. Ney (ed.) *True and False Allegations of Child Sex Abuse: Assessment and Case Management*, New York: Bruner-Mazel, 153–62.

Walkley, J. (1987) *Police Interrogation: A Handbook for Investigators*, London: Police Review Publications.

Wall, J.F. (1970) *Andrew Carnegie*, New York: Oxford University Press.

Walter, B. (1988) *The Jury Summation as Speech Genre*, Amsterdam and Philadelphia, PA: John Benjamins Publishing Company.

Walton, D. (1989) *Informal Logic: A Handbook for Critical Argumentation*, Cambridge: Cambridge University Press.

Wang, W.S-Y. (1980) 'Assessing language incompetence', *The Linguistic Reporter*, 22(8): 2.

Wardhaugh, R. (1985) *How Conversation Works*, Oxford: Blackwell.

Wason, P.C. and Johnson-Laird, P.N. (1972) *Psychology of Reasoning: Structure and Content*, Cambridge, MA: Harvard University Press.

Watson, D.R. (1983) 'The presentation of victim and motive discourse: the case of police interrogations and interviews', *Victimology*, 8: 31–52.

——(1990) 'Some features of the elicitation of confession in murder interrogations', in G. Psathas (ed.) *Interaction Competence: Studies in Ethnomethodology and Conversation Analysis*, Washington, DC: University Press of America, 263–95.

Watson, E.R. (1952) *Trial of William Palmer*, revised edition, London and Edinburgh: William Hodge.

Watts, R.J. (2003) *Politeness*, Cambridge: CUP.

Webb, V. and Katz, C. (2006) 'A study of police gang units in six cities', in A. Egley. C.L. Maxson, J. Miller, M.W. Klein. (eds) *The Modern Gang Reader*, 3rd edn, Los Angeles CA: Roxbury, 349–60.

Wei, L. (1994) *Three Generations, Two Languages, One Family*, Clevedon: Multilingual Matters.

——(2000) 'Dimensions of bilingualism', in L. Wei (ed.) *The Bilingualism Reader*, London: Routledge, 3–25.

Weinreich, U., Labov, W. and Herzog, M.I. (1968) 'Empirical foundations for a theory of language change', in W. Lehmann and Y. Malkiel (eds) *Directions for Historical Linguistics*, Austin, TX: University of Texas Press, 95–195.

Weir, C. (1990) *Understanding and Developing Language Tests*, London: Prentice Hall.

Weisflog, W.E. (1987) 'Problems of legal translation', *Swiss Reports presented at the XIIth International Congress of Comparative Law*, Zürich: Schulthess, 179–218.

Weisselberg, C.D. (2001) 'In the stationhouse after *Dickerson*', *Michigan Law Review*, 99: 1121–67.

Wells, J.C. (1999) 'British English pronunciation preferences: a changing scene', *Journal of the International Phonetic Association*, 29: 33–50.

Wells, W.A.N. (1991) *An Introduction to the Law of Evidence*, S. Australia: A. B. Caudell.

Westcott, H. and Cross, M. (1996) *This Far and No Further: Towards Ending the Abuse of Disabled Children*, Birmingham: Venture Press.

Whalen, J. (1995) 'A technology of order production: computer-aided dispatch in public safety communications', in P. ten Have and G. Psathas (eds) *Situated Order: Studies in the Social Organization of Talk and Embodied Activities*, Washington, DC: University Press of America, 187–230.

Whalen, J., Zimmerman, D.H. and Whalen, M.R. (1988) 'When words fail: a single case analysis', *Social Problems*, 35: 335–62.

Whalen, M.R. and Zimmerman, D.H. (1990) 'Describing trouble: practical epistemology in citizen calls to the police', *Language in Society*, 19: 465–92.

Whipple, G. (1911) 'The psychology of testimony', *Psychological Bulletin*, 8: 307–9.

White, A. and Mansfield, C. (2002) 'Literacy and contract', *Stanford Law and Policy Review*, 13: 233–66.

White, J.B. (1982) 'The invisible discourse of the law: reflections on legal literacy and general education', *Michigan Quarterly Review*, 420–38.

White, W.S. (2001) '*Miranda*'s failure to restrain pernicious interrogation practices', *Michigan Law Review*, 99: 1211–47.

——(2006) 'Deflecting a suspect from requesting an attorney', *University of Pittsburgh Law Review*, 68: 29–75.

Whiteside, S. (2001) 'Sex-specific fundamental and formant frequency patterns in a cross-sectional study', *Journal of the Acoustical Society of America*, 110: 464–78.

Wieder, D.L. (1974) 'Telling the code', in R. Turner (ed.) *Ethnomethodology: Selected Readings*, Harmondsworth: Penguin, 144–72.

Wigmore, J.H. (1913) *The Principles of Judicial Proof*, Boston, MA: Little, Brown and Company.

Wikipedia (2008) 'Microsoft vs. MikeRoweSoft'. Available online at: http://en.wikipedia.org/wiki/Mike_Rowe_(student) (accessed December 2008).

Williams, A. (1939) 'Hamburger progeny', *American Speech*, 14(2): 154.

Williams, A., Garrett, P. and Coupland, N. (1999) 'Dialect recognition', in D. Preston (ed.) *Handbook of Perceptual Dialectology*, Philadelphia: Benjamins, 345–58.

Williams, J. (1992) 'The question of plagiarism and breach of copyright in the dictionary-making process (with particular reference to the UK)', in H. Tommola, K. Varantola, T. Salmi-Tolonen and J. Schopp (eds.), *Euralex '92 Proceedings. Papers submitted to the 5th EURALEX International Congress on Lexicography in Tampere, Finland, 4–9 August 1992*, Department of Translation Studies, University of Tampere: Tampere, 561–70.

Williamson, T.M. (1993) 'From interrogation to investigative interviewing: strategic trends in police questioning', *Journal of Community and Applied Social Psychology*, 3: 89–99.

——(2006) *Investigative Interviewing*, Uffcolme, Devon: Willan Publishing.

Winter, E. (1994) 'Clause relations as information structure: two basic structures in English', in M. Coulthard (ed.) *Advances in Written Text Analysis*, London: Routledge, 46–68.

Winton, R. (10 October 2008) 'Gang member is first to be lifted from city's court-imposed limits', *San Francisco Chronicle*, p. B4.

Wodak, R. (2007) 'Pragmatics and critical discourse analysis: a cross-disciplinary inquiry', *Pragmatics and Cognition*, 15(1): 203–25.

Wolchover, D. (1989) 'Should judges sum up on the facts?', *Criminal Law Review*, 781–92.

Wood, L. and Kroger, R. (2000) *Doing Discourse Analysis: Methods for Studying Action in Talk and Text*, Thousand Oaks, CA: Sage Publications, Inc.

Woodbury, H. (1984) 'The strategic use of questions in court', *Semiotica*, 48(3/4): 197–228.

Woodhams, J. and Hollin, C. (2008) 'Incorporating context in linking crimes: an exploratory study of situational similarity and if-then contingencies', *Journal of Investigative Psychology and Offender Profiling*, 5: 1–23.

Woodhams, J. and Toye, K. (2007) 'An empirical test of the assumptions of case linkage and offender profiling with serial commercial robberies', *Psychology, Public Policy, Law*, 13: 59–85.

Woodhams, J., Grant, T.D. and Price, A.R.G. (2007) 'From marine ecology to crime analysis: improving the detection of serial sexual offences using a taxonomic similarity measure', *Journal of Investigative Psychology and Offender Profiling*, 4: 17–27.

Woodhams, J., Hollin, C. and Bull, R. (2007) 'The psychology of linking crimes: review of the evidence', *Legal and Criminological Psychology*, 12.: 233–49.

——(2008) 'Incorporating context in linking crimes: an exploratory study of situational similarity and if-then contingencies', *Journal of Investigative Psychology and Offender Profiling*, 5: 1–23.

Woods, N. (2006) *Describing Discourse: A Practical Guide to Discourse Analysis*, London: Hodder Arnold.

Wooffitt, R. (1991) '"I was just doing X ... when Y": some inferential properties of a device in accounts of paranormal experiences', *Text*, 11(2): 267–88.

Woolls, D. (2003) 'Better tools for the trade and how to use them', *International Journal of Speech, Language and the Law*, 10(i): 102–12.

——(2006) 'Plagiarism', in K. Brown (ed.) *The Encyclopedia of Language and Linguistics*, 2nd edn, Vol. 9, Oxford: Elsevier.

——(forthcoming) 'Detecting plagiarism', in L. Solan and P. Tiersma (eds), *The Oxford Handbook of Language and Law*, Oxford: Oxford University Press.

Woolls, D. and Coulthard, R.M. (1998) 'Tools for the trade', *International Journal of Speech, Language and the Law*, 5(i): 33–57.

Wootton, A.J. (1981) 'Two request forms of four year olds', *Journal of Pragmatics*, 5: 511–23.

——(2005) 'Interactional and sequential features informing request format selection in children's speech', in A. Hakulinen and M. Selting (eds) *Syntax and Lexis in Conversation*, Amsterdam: John Benjamins, 185–207.

Worth, R. (2004) 'Translating crime reports by cellphone', *New York Times*, 22 April. Available online at: www.nytimes.com/2004/04/22/nyregion/translating-crime-reports-by-using-a-cellphone.html (accessed 8 August 2009).

Wowk, M.T. (1984) 'Blame allocation, sex and gender in a murder interrogation', *Women's Studies International Forum*, 7: 75–82.

Wright, J. (2005) 'The constitutional failure of gang databases', *Stanford Journal of Civil Rights & Civil Liberties*, 2: 115–42.

Wrightsman, L.S. and Kassin, S.M. (1993) *Confessions in the Courtroom*, Newbury Park: Sage.

Yarmey, D. (forthcoming) 'Factors affecting lay persons' identification of speakers', in L.M. Solan and P.M. Tiersma (eds) *The Oxford Handbook of Language and Law*, Oxford: Oxford University Press.

Ye, Z. and Zhou, X. (2008) 'Involvement of cognitive control in sentence comprehension: evidence from ERPs', *Brain Research*, 1203(8): 103–15.

Yermish, S. (2006) 'Crawford v. Washington and expert testimony: limiting the use of testimonial hearsay', *Champion Magazine*, 30 November: 12–16.

Yoo, I.W. and Blankenship, B. (2003) 'Duration of epenthetic [t] in polysyllabic American English words', *Journal of the International Phonetic Association*, 33: 153–64.

Zgółkowa, H. (ed.) (1994) *Praktyczny słownik współczesnej polszczyzny* [Practical Dictionary of Contemporary Polish], Poznań: Kurpisz.

Zimmerman, D. (1984) 'Talk and its occasion: the case of calling the police', in D. Schiffrin (ed.) *Meaning, Form and Use in Context: Linguistic Applications*, Washington, DC: Georgetown University Press, 210–28.

——(1992a) 'The interactional organization of calls for emergency assistance', in P. Drew and J. Heritage (eds) *Talk at Work: Social Interaction in Institutional Settings*, Cambridge: Cambridge University Press, 418–69.

——(1992b) 'Achieving context: openings in emergency calls', in G. Watson and R.M. Seiler (eds) *Text in Context: Contributions to Ethnomethodology*, Newbury Park, CA: Sage, 35–51.

Zimmerman, D. and Wakin, M. (1995) 'Thank You's and the management of closings in emergency calls', paper given at the *90th Annual Meetings of the American Sociological Association*, Washington, DC.

Index